THE GREAT
ROMANTICS

Byron P. B. Shelley John Keats

THE GREAT ROMANTICS

SELECTED POEMS

LORD BYRON

PERCY BYSSHE SHELLEY

JOHN KEATS

QUALITY PAPERBACK BOOK CLUB
NEW YORK

Lord Byron selection by Katharine Washburn

Percy Bysshe Shelley selection by David Rosen

Printed in the United States of America

THE GREAT ROMANTICS

TABLE OF CONTENTS

CONTENTS

CONTENTS

JOHN KEATS

CONTENTS

CONTENTS

THE GREAT
ROMANTICS

SELECTED POEMS

LORD BYRON

GEORGE GORDON, LORD BYRON was born in 1788 to Captain John Byron and Catherine Gordon of Gight. Afflicted with a club foot, Byron acquired the title of Baron when his father died in 1798. He attended the Harrow School and later went on to Cambridge. His first published poetry, an 1807 collection titled *Hours of Idleness*, was badly received by the *Edinburgh Review*, a slight Byron addressed two years later by penning the vicious satire "English Bards and Scotch Reviewers." In 1809, Byron voyaged to Portugal, Spain, Greece, and the Levant; he returned to England two years later with a sharp interest in Greece's struggle for liberation from Turkey. Back in England, Byron published the first two cantos of *Childe Harold's Pilgrimage* to great acclaim. In 1815, he married Annabella Milbanke, with whom he had a daughter. One year later, Byron's wife had left him, his finances were in disarray, and he was plagued by charges of incest brought after his half-sister Augusta gave birth to a baby believed to be his. That April, Byron left his native country for the last time.

After moving to Geneva, Byron wrote "The Prisoner of Chillon" and Canto III of *Childe Harold*. For the next several years, he travelled from town to town in Italy, writing steadily. In 1821, he moved with the 17-year-old countess Theresa Guiccioli to Pisa, where they lived in lodgings provided by Shelley.

In 1823, Byron sailed for Greece, determined to join the fight for that country's independence. Before he had the chance to display his commitment in battle, he was struck by fever and died.

CHILDE HAROLD'S PILGRIMAGE

A ROMAUNT

[In reading *Childe Harold* one should remember that it is really two, or even three, poems written at quite different periods in Byron's poetical development. The first and second cantos represent the time of his early travels, when he was comparatively unskilled as a poet and unversed in the world. The stanzas begin with an awkward attempt to imitate the archaic language of Spenser, and there is an equally awkward confusion of the poet himself and his hero, who are neither wholly merged together nor yet fully distinguished. Nevertheless it is of these two cantos that Byron uttered the famous remark : ' I awoke one morning and found myself famous.' Canto I. was begun at Joannina in Albania, October 31, 1809, and Canto II. was finished at Smyrna, March 28, 1810. They were published in March, 1812. Between that date and the writing of the third canto came Byron's life in London, and the composition of the Oriental Tales ; there came also his marriage and the fatal rupture. It was, indeed, during the first months of his melancholy exile that he returned to *Childe Harold.* Canto III. was completed at Diodati, on Lake Geneva, in July, 1816, and was published the same year. To compare these stanzas with those of the earlier cantos is to see how much Byron had grown in depth of feeling and in technical skill. The poem gains in force by the frankness with which the poet now speaks in his own person. With the first line, 'Is thy face like thy mother's, my fair child,' we feel that we have come to the true Byron. The fourth canto, though published separately, is in the same tone as the third. It was written at Venice between June of 1817 and January of 1818, and was published immediately. As with most of his works the poem suffered manifold changes while going through the press, and later editions brought other alterations. The stanzas to ' Ianthe ' (Lady Charlotte Harley) had been written in 1812, but were first printed in 1814 as a dedication to the seventh edition of Cantos I. and II.]

L'univers est une espèce de livre, dont on n'a lu que la première page quand on n'a vu que son pays. J'en ai feuilleté un assez grand nombre, que j'ai trouvé également mauvaises. Cet examen ne m'a point été infructueux. Je haïssais ma patrie. Toutes les impertinences des peuples divers, parmi lesquels j'ai vécu, m'ont réconcilié avec elle. Quand je n'aurais tiré d'autre bénéfice de mes voyages que celui-là, je n'en regretterais ni les frais ni les fatigues. — *Le Cosmopolite.*

PREFACE

[TO THE FIRST AND SECOND CANTOS]

The following poem was written, for the most part, amidst the scenes which it attempts to describe. It was begun in Albania ; and the parts relative to Spain and Portugal were composed from the author's observations in those countries. Thus much it may be necessary to state for the correctness of the descriptions. The scenes attempted to be sketched are in Spain, Portugal, Epirus, Acarnania, and Greece. There, for the present, the poem stops : its reception will determine whether the author may venture to conduct his readers to the capital of the East, through Ionia and Phrygia : these two cantos are merely experimental.

A fictitious character is introduced for the sake of giving some connection to the piece ; which, however, makes no pretension to regularity. It has been suggested to me by friends, on whose opinions I set a high value, that in this fictitious character, Childe Harold, I may incur the suspicion of having intended some real personage : this I beg leave, once for all, to disclaim — Harold is the child of imagination, for the purpose I have stated. In some very trivial particulars, and those merely local, there might be grounds for such a notion ; but in the main points, I should hope, none whatever.

It is almost superfluous to mention that the appellation ' Childe,' as ' Childe Waters,' ' Childe Childers,' etc., is used as more consonant with the old structure of versification which I have adopted. The ' Good Night,'

in the beginning of the first canto, was suggested by *Lord Maxwell's Good Night*, in the *Border Minstrelsy*, edited by Mr. Scott.

With the different poems which have been published on Spanish subjects, there may be found some slight coincidence in the first part, which treats of the Peninsula, but it can only be casual ; as, with the exception of a few concluding stanzas, the whole of this poem was written in the Levant.

The stanza of Spenser, according to one of our most successful poets, admits of every variety. Dr. Beattie makes the following observation : ' Not long ago I began a poem in the style and stanza of Spenser, in which I propose to give full scope to my inclination, and be either droll or pathetic, descriptive or sentimental, tender or satirical, as the humour strikes me ; for, if I mistake not, the measure which I have adopted admits equally of all these kinds of composition.' Strengthened in my opinion by such authority, and by the example of some in the highest order of Italian poets, I shall make no apology for attempts at similar variations in the following composition ; satisfied that, if they are unsuccessful, their failure must be in the execution, rather than in the design sanctioned by the practice of Ariosto, Thomson, and Beattie.

LONDON, *February*, 1812.

ADDITION TO THE PREFACE

I have now waited till almost all our periodical journals have distributed their usual portion of criticism. To the justice of the generality of their criticisms I have nothing to object : it would ill become me to quarrel with their very slight degree of censure, when, perhaps, if they had been less kind they had been more candid. Returning, therefore, to all and each my best thanks for their liberality, on one point alone shall I venture an observation. Amongst the many objections justly urged to the very indifferent character of the ' vagrant Childe ' (whom, notwithstanding many hints to the contrary, I still maintain to be a fictitious personage), it has been stated, that, besides the anachronism, he is very *unknightly*, as the times of the knights were times of love, honour, and so forth. Now, it so happens that the good old times, when ' l'amour du bon vieux tems, l'amour antique ' flourished, were the most profligate of all possible centuries. Those who have any doubts on this subject may consult Sainte-Palaye, *passim*, and more particularly vol. ii. p. 69. The vows of chivalry were no better kept than any other vows whatsoever ; and the songs of the Troubadours were not more decent, and certainly were much less refined, than those of Ovid. The ' cours d'amour, parlemens d'amour, ou de courtoisie et de gentillesse ' had much more of love than of courtesy or gentleness. See Roland on the same subject with Sainte-Palaye. Whatever other objection may be urged to that most unamiable personage Childe Harold, he was so far perfectly knightly in his attributes — ' No waiter, but a knight templar.' By the by, I fear that Sir Tristrem and Sir Lancelot were no better than they should be, although very poetical personages and true knights ' sans peur,' though not ' sans reproche.' If the story of the institution of the ' Garter ' be not a fable, the knights of that order have for several centuries borne the badge of a Countess of Salisbury, of indifferent memory. So much for chivalry. Burke need not have regretted that its days are over, though Marie-Antoinette was quite as chaste as most of those in whose honours lances were shivered, and knights unhorsed.

Before the days of Bayard, and down to those of Sir Joseph Banks (the most chaste and celebrated of ancient and modern times), few exceptions will be found to this statement ; and I fear a little investigation will teach us not to regret these monstrous mummeries of the middle ages.

I now leave Childe Harold to live his day, such as he is ; it had been more agreeable, and certainly more easy, to have drawn an amiable character. It had been easy to varnish over his faults, to. make him do more and express less, but he never was intended as an example, further than to show that early perversion of mind and morals leads to satiety of past pleasures and disappointment in new ones, and that even the beauties of nature and the stimulus of travel (except ambition, the most powerful of all excitements) are lost on a soul so constituted, or rather misdirected. Had I proceeded with the poem, this character would have deepened as he drew to the close ; for the outline which I once meant to fill up for him was, with some exceptions, the sketch of a modern Timon, perhaps a poetical Zeluco.

LONDON, 1813.

TO IANTHE

NOT in those climes where I have late
 been straying,
Though Beauty long hath there been
 matchless deem'd;
Not in those visions to the heart display-
 ing
Forms which it sighs but to have only
 dream'd,

Hath aught like thee in truth or fancy
seem'd.

Nor, having seen thee, shall I vainly
seek

To paint those charms which varied as
they beam'd:

To such as see thee not my words were
weak;

To those who gaze on thee what language
could they speak ?

Ah ! may'st thou ever be what now thou
art, 10

Nor unbeseem the promise of thy spring,

As fair in form, as warm yet pure in
heart,

Love's image upon earth without his
wing,

And guileless beyond Hope's imagining !

And surely she who now so fondly rears

Thy youth, in thee, thus hourly brighten-
ing,

Beholds the rainbow of her future years,

Before whose heavenly hues all sorrow dis-
appears.

Young Peri of the West ! — 't is well for
me

My years already doubly number thine;

My loveless eye unmoved may gaze on
thee, 21

And safely view thy ripening beauties
shine;

Happy, I ne'er shall see them in decline;

Happier, that while all younger hearts
shall bleed,

Mine shall escape the doom thine eyes
assign

To those whose admiration shall suc-
ceed,

But mix'd with pangs to Love's even love-
liest hours decreed.

Oh ! let that eye, which, wild as the
Gazelle's,

Now brightly bold or beautifully shy,

Wins as it wanders, dazzles where it
dwells, 30

Glance o'er this page, nor to my verse
deny

That smile for which my breast might
vainly sigh

Could I to thee be ever more than friend.

This much, dear maid, accord; nor ques-
tion why

To one so young my strain I would com-
mend,

But bid me with my wreath one matchless
lily blend.

Such is thy name with this my verse
entwined;

And long as kinder eyes a look shall
cast

On Harold's page, Ianthe's here en-
shrined

Shall thus be first beheld, forgotten
last: 40

My days once number'd, should this
homage past

Attract thy fairy fingers near the lyre

Of him who hail'd thee, loveliest as thou
wast,

Such is the most my memory may de-
sire; —

Though more than Hope can claim, could
Friendship less require ?

CANTO THE FIRST

I

OH, thou ! in Hellas deem'd of heavenly
birth,

Muse ! form'd or fabled at the minstrel's
will !

Since shamed full oft by later lyres on
earth,

Mine dares not call thee from thy sacred
hill:

Yet there I 've wander'd by thy vaunted
rill;

Yes ! sigh'd o'er Delphi's long-deserted
shrine,

Where, save that feeble fountain, all is
still;

Nor mote my shell awake the weary Nine

To grace so plain a tale, this lowly lay of
mine.

II

Whilome in Albion's isle there dwelt a
youth, 10

Who ne in virtue's ways did take delight;

But spent his days in riot most uncouth,

And vex'd with mirth the drowsy ear of
Night.

Ah me ! in sooth he was a shameless
wight,

Sore given to revel and ungodly glee;

Few earthly things found favour in his
 sight
Save concubines and carnal companie,
And flaunting wassailers of high and low
 degree.

III

Childe Harold was he hight:—but whence
 his name
And lineage long, it suits me not to
 say; 20
Suffice it, that perchance they were of
 fame,
And had been glorious in another day:
But one sad losel soils a name for aye,
However mighty in the olden time;
Nor all that heralds rake from coffin'd
 clay,
Nor florid prose, nor honey'd lies of
 rhyme,
Can blazon evil deeds or consecrate a crime.

IV

Childe Harold basked him in the noon-
 tide sun,
Disporting there like any other fly,
Nor deem'd before his little day was
 done 30
One blast might chill him into misery.
But long ere scarce a third of his pass'd
 by,
Worse than adversity the Childe befell,—
He felt the fulness of satiety;
Then loathed he in his native land to
 dwell,
Which seem'd to him more lone than Ere-
 mite's sad cell.

V

For he through Sin's long labyrinth had
 run,
Nor made atonement when he did amiss;
Had sigh'd to many though he loved but
 one,
And that loved one, alas! could ne'er be
 his. 40
Ah, happy she! to 'scape from him whose
 kiss
Had been pollution unto aught so chaste;
Who soon had left her charms for vulgar
 bliss,
And spoil'd her goodly lands to gild his
 waste,
Nor calm domestic peace had ever deign'd
 to taste.

VI

And now Childe Harold was sore sick at
 heart,
And from his fellow bacchanals would
 flee;
'T is said, at times the sullen tear would
 start,
But Pride congeal'd the drop within his
 ee.
Apart he stalk'd in joyless reverie, 50
And from his native land resolved to go,
And visit scorching climes beyond the
 sea;
With pleasure drugg'd, he almost long'd
 for woe,
And e'en for change of scene would seek
 the shades below.

VII

The Childe departed from his father's
 hall:
It was a vast and venerable pile;
So old, it seemèd only not to fall,
Yet strength was pillar'd in each massy
 aisle.
Monastic dome! condemn'd to uses vile!
Where Superstition once had made her
 den, 60
Now Paphian girls were known to sing
 and smile;
And monks might deem their time was
 come agen,
If ancient tales say true nor wrong these
 holy men.

VIII

Yet oft-times in his maddest mirthful
 mood
Strange pangs would flash along Childe
 Harold's brow,
As if the memory of some daily feud
Or disappointed passion lurk'd below:
But this none knew, nor haply cared to
 know;
For his was not that open, artless soul
That feels relief by bidding sorrow flow,
Nor sought he friend to counsel or con-
 dole, 71
Whate'er this grief mote be which he could
 not control.

IX

And none did love him; though to hall
 and bower
He gather'd revellers from far and near,

He knew them flatt'rers of the festal hour,
The heartless parasites of present cheer.
Yea ! none did love him — not his lemans dear —
But pomp and power alone are woman's care,
And where these are light Eros finds a feere;
Maidens, like moths, are ever caught by glare, 80
And Mammon wins his way where Seraphs might despair.

X

Childe Harold had a mother, not forgot
Though parting from that mother he did shun;
A sister whom he loved, but saw her not
Before his weary pilgrimage begun:
If friends he had, he bade adieu to none.
Yet deem not thence his breast a breast of steel:
Ye, who have known what 't is to dote upon
A few dear objects, will in sadness feel
Such partings break the heart they fondly hope to heal. 90

XI

His house, his home, his heritage, his lands,
The laughing dames in whom he did delight,
Whose large blue eyes, fair locks, and snowy hands,
Might shake the saintship of an anchorite,
And long had fed his youthful appetite;
His goblets brimm'd with every costly wine,
And all that mote to luxury invite,
Without a sigh he left, to cross the brine
And traverse Paynim shores and pass Earth's central line.

XII

The sails were fill'd, and fair the light winds blew, 100
As glad to waft him from his native home;
And fast the white rocks faded from his view,
And soon were lost in circumambient foam.
And then, it may be, of his wish to roam

Repented he, but in his bosom slept
The silent thought, nor from his lips did come
One word of wail, whilst others sate and wept
And to the reckless gales unmanly moaning kept.

XIII

But when the sun was sinking in the sea
He seized his harp, which he at times could string 110
And strike, albeit with untaught melody,
When deem'd he no strange ear was listening.
And now his fingers o'er it he did fling,
And tuned his farewell in the dim twilight; —
While flew the vessel on her snowy wing,
And fleeting shores receded from his sight,
Thus to the elements he pour'd his last 'Good Night.'

1

' ADIEU, adieu ! my native shore
Fades o'er the waters blue ;
The Night-winds sigh, the breakers roar,
And shrieks the wild sea-mew. 121
Yon Sun that sets upon the sea
We follow in his flight ;
Farewell awhile to him and thee,
My native Land — Good Night !

2

' A few short hours and He will rise
To give the Morrow birth ;
And I shall hail the main and skies,
But not my mother Earth.
Deserted is my own good hall, 130
Its hearth is desolate ;
Wild weeds are gathering on the wall ;
My dog howls at the gate.

3

' Come hither, hither, my little page !
Why dost thou weep and wail ?
Or dost thou dread the billows' rage,
Or tremble at the gale ?
But dash the tear-drop from thine eye ;
Our ship is swift and strong,
Our fleetest falcon scarce can fly 140
More merrily along.' —

4

' Let winds be shrill, let waves roll high,
I fear not wave nor wind ;
Yet marvel not, Sir Childe, that I
Am sorrowful in mind ;

For I have from my father gone,
 A mother whom I love,
And have no friend, save these alone,
 But thee — and one above.

5

'My father bless'd me fervently, 150
 Yet did not much complain;
But sorely will my mother sigh
 Till I come back again.' —
'Enough, enough, my little lad!
 Such tears become thine eye;
If I thy guileless bosom had,
 Mine own would not be dry. —

6

'Come hither, hither, my staunch yeoman,
 Why dost thou look so pale?
Or dost thou dread a French foeman? 160
 Or shiver at the gale?' —
'Deem'st thou I tremble for my life?
 Sir Childe, I'm not so weak;
But thinking on an absent wife
 Will blanch a faithful cheek.

7

'My spouse and boys dwell near thy hall,
 Along the bordering lake,
And when they on their father call,
 What answer shall she make?' —
'Enough, enough, my yeoman good, 170
 Thy grief let none gainsay;
But I, who am of lighter mood,
 Will laugh to flee away.

8

'For who would trust the seeming sighs
 Of wife or paramour?
Fresh feres will dry the bright blue eyes
 We late saw streaming o'er.
For pleasures past I do not grieve,
 Nor perils gathering near;
My greatest grief is that I leave 180
 No thing that claims a tear.

9

'And now I'm in the world alone,
 Upon the wide, wide sea;
But why should I for others groan,
 When none will sigh for me?
Perchance my dog will whine in vain,
 Till fed by stranger hands;
But long ere I come back again
 He'd tear me where he stands.

10

'With thee, my bark, I'll swiftly go 190
 Athwart the foaming brine;
Nor care what land thou bear'st me to,
 So not again to mine.
Welcome, welcome, ye dark blue waves!
 And when you fail my sight,
Welcome, ye deserts, and ye caves!
 My native land — Good Night!'

XIV

On, on the vessel flies, the land is gone,
And winds are rude in Biscay's sleepless
 bay.
Four days are sped, but with the fifth,
 anon, 200
New shores descried make every bosom
 gay;
And Cintra's mountain greets them on
 their way,
And Tagus dashing onward to the deep,
His fabled golden tribute bent to pay;
And soon on board the Lusian pilots leap,
And steer 'twixt fertile shores where yet
 few rustics reap.

XV

Oh, Christ! it is a goodly sight to see
What Heaven hath done for this delicious
 land,
What fruits of fragrance blush on every
 tree,
What goodly prospects o'er the hills ex-
 pand! 210
But man would mar them with an im-
 pious hand!
And when the Almighty lifts his fiercest
 scourge
'Gainst those who most transgress his high
 command,
With treble vengeance will his hot shafts
 urge
Gaul's locust host, and earth from fellest
 foemen purge.

XVI

What beauties doth Lisboa first unfold!
Her image floating on that noble tide,
Which poets vainly pave with sands of
 gold,
But now whereon a thousand keels did
 ride
Of mighty strength, since Albion was
 allied 220
And to the Lusians did her aid afford, —
A nation swoln with ignorance and pride,
Who lick yet loathe the hand that waves
 the sword
To save them from the wrath of Gaul's
 unsparing lord.

XVII

But whoso entereth within this town,
That, sheening far, celestial seems to
 be,

Disconsolate will wander up and down
'Mid many things unsightly to strange ee:
For hut and palace show like filthily;
The dingy denizens are rear'd in dirt; ₂₃₀
Ne personage of high or mean degree
Doth care for cleanness of surtout or
　　shirt,
Though shent with Egypt's plague, un-
　　kempt, unwash'd, unhurt.

XVIII

Poor, paltry slaves! yet born 'midst
　　noblest scenes —
Why, Nature, waste thy wonders on such
　　men?
Lo! Cintra's glorious Eden intervenes
In variegated maze of mount and glen.
Ah me! what hand can pencil guide, or
　　pen,
To follow half on which the eye dilates
Through views more dazzling unto mortal
　　ken　　　　　　　　　₂₄₀
Than those whereof such things the bard
　　relates,
Who to the awe-struck world unlock'd
　　Elysium's gates?

XIX

The horrid crags by toppling convent
　　crown'd,
The cork-trees hoar that clothe the shaggy
　　steep,
The mountain-moss by scorching skies im-
　　brown'd,
The sunken glen whose sunless shrubs
　　must weep,
The tender azure of the unruffled deep,
The orange tints that gild the greenest
　　bough,
The torrents that from cliff to valley leap,
The vine on high, the willow branch below,
Mix'd in one mighty scene, with varied
　　beauty glow.　　　　　₂₅₁

XX

Then slowly climb the many - winding
　　way,
And frequent turn to linger as you go,
From loftier rocks new loveliness sur-
　　vey,
And rest ye at 'Our Lady's house of
　　woe;'
Where frugal monks their little relics
　　show,
And sundry legends to the stranger tell:

Here impious men have punish'd been,
　　and lo!
Deep in yon cave Honorius long did dwell,
In hope to merit Heaven by making earth
　　a Hell.　　　　　　₂₆₀

XXI

And here and there, as up the crags you
　　spring,
Mark many rude-carved crosses near the
　　path;
Yet deem not these devotion's offering —
These are memorials frail of murderous
　　wrath:
For wheresoe'er the shrieking victim hath
Pour'd forth his blood beneath the assas-
　　sin's knife,
Some hand erects a cross of mouldering
　　lath;
And grove and glen with thousand such
　　are rife
Throughout this purple land where law
　　secures not life.

XXII

On sloping mounds, or in the vale beneath,
Are domes where whilome kings did make
　　repair;　　　　　　₂₇₁
But now the wild flowers round them only
　　breathe;
Yet ruin'd splendour still is lingering
　　there.
And yonder towers the Prince's palace fair:
There thou too, Vathek! England's
　　wealthiest son,
Once form'd thy Paradise, as not aware
When wanton Wealth her mightiest
　　deeds hath done,
Meek Peace voluptuous lures was ever
　　wont to shun.

XXIII

Here didst thou dwell, here schemes of
　　pleasure plan,
Beneath yon mountain's ever beauteous
　　brow;　　　　　　₂₈₀
But now, as if a thing unblest by Man,
Thy fairy dwelling is as lone as thou!
Here giant weeds a passage scarce allow
To halls deserted, portals gaping wide —
Fresh lessons to the thinking bosom, how
Vain are the pleasaunces on earth sup-
　　plied,
Swept into wrecks anon by Time's ungentle
　　tide!

XXIV

Behold the hall where chiefs were late convened !
Oh, dome displeasing unto British eye !
With diadem hight foolscap, lo ! a fiend,
A little fiend that scoffs incessantly, 291
There sits in parchment robe array'd, and by
His side is hung a seal and sable scroll,
Where blazon'd glare names known to chivalry,
And sundry signatures adorn the roll,
Whereat the Urchin points, and laughs with all his soul.

XXV

Convention is the dwarfish demon styled
That foil'd the knights in Marialva's dome.
Of brains (if brains they had) he them beguiled,
And turn'd a nation's shallow joy to gloom. 300
Here Folly dash'd to earth the victor's plume,
And Policy regain'd what arms had lost:
For chiefs like ours in vain may laurels bloom !
Woe to the conqu'ring, not the conquer'd host,
Since baffled Triumph droops on Lusitania's coast !

XXVI

And ever since that martial synod met,
Britannia sickens, Cintra ! at thy name;
And folks in office at the mention fret,
And fain would blush, if blush they could, for shame.
How will posterity the deed proclaim ! 310
Will not our own and fellow-nations sneer,
To view these champions cheated of their fame,
By foes in fight o'erthrown, yet victors here,
Where Scorn her finger points through many a coming year ?

XXVII

So deem'd the Childe, as o'er the mountains he
Did take his way in solitary guise.
Sweet was the scene, yet soon he thought to flee,
More restless than the swallow in the skies;
Though here awhile he learn'd to moralize,
For Meditation fix'd at times on him; 320
And conscious Reason whisper'd to despise
His early youth misspent in maddest whim;
But as he gazed on truth his aching eyes grew dim.

XXVIII

To horse ! to horse ! he quits, for ever quits
A scene of peace, though soothing to his soul;
Again he rouses from his moping fits,
But seeks not now the harlot and the bowl.
Onward he flies, nor fix'd as yet the goal
Where he shall rest him on his pilgrimage;
And o'er him many changing scenes must roll, 330
Ere toil his thirst for travel can assuage,
Or he shall calm his breast, or learn experience sage.

XXIX

Yet Mafra shall one moment claim delay,
Where dwelt of yore the Lusians' luckless queen;
And church and court did mingle their array,
And mass and revel were alternate seen, —
Lordlings and freres, ill-sorted fry I ween !
But here the Babylonian whore hath built
A dome, where flaunts she in such glorious sheen,
That men forget the blood which she hath spilt, 340
And bow the knee to Pomp that loves to varnish guilt.

XXX

O'er vales that teem with fruits, romantic hills
(Oh, that such hills upheld a freeborn race !),
Whereon to gaze the eye with joyaunce fills,

Childe Harold wends through many a
pleasant place.
Though sluggards deem it but a foolish
chase,
And marvel men should quit their easy
chair,
The toilsome way, and long, long league
to trace,
Oh ! there is sweetness in the mountain
air,
And life that bloated Ease can never hope
to share. 350

XXXI

More bleak to view the hills at length
recede,
And, less luxuriant, smoother vales ex-
tend;
Immense horizon-bounded plains suc-
ceed !
Far as the eye discerns, withouten end,
Spain's realms appear whereon her shep-
herds tend
Flocks whose rich fleece right well the
trader knows —
Now must the pastor's arm his lambs
defend,
For Spain is compass'd by unyielding
foes,
And all must shield their all, or share Sub-
jection's woes.

XXXII

Where Lusitania and her Sister meet, 360
Deem ye what bounds the rival realms
divide ?
Or ere the jealous Queens of Nations
greet,
Doth Tayo interpose his mighty tide ?
Or dark Sierras rise in craggy pride ?
Or fence of art, like China's vasty
wall ? —
Ne barrier wall, ne river deep and wide,
Ne horrid crags, nor mountains dark and
tall,
Rise like the rocks that part Hispania's land
from Gaul:

XXXIII

But these between a silver streamlet
glides,
And scarce a name distinguisheth the
brook, 370
Though rival kingdoms press its verdant
sides.

Here leans the idle shepherd on his
crook,
And vacant on the rippling waves doth
look,
That peaceful still 'twixt bitterest foe-
men flow;
For proud each peasant as the noblest
duke:
Well doth the Spanish hind the difference
know
'Twixt him and Lusian slave, the lowest of
the low.

XXXIV

But ere the mingling bounds have far
been pass'd,
Dark Guadiana rolls his power along
In sullen billows, murmuring and vast,
So noted ancient roundelays among. 381
Whilome upon his banks did legions
throng
Of Moor and Knight, in mailèd splendour
drest:
Here ceased the swift their race, here
sunk the strong;
The Paynim turban and the Christian
crest
Mix'd on the bleeding stream, by floating
hosts oppress'd.

XXXV

Oh, lovely Spain ! renown'd, romantic
land !
Where is that standard which Pelagio
bore,
When Cava's traitor-sire first call'd the
band
That dyed thy mountain streams with
gothic gore ? 390
Where are those bloody banners which of
yore
Waved o'er thy sons, victorious to the
gale,
And drove at last the spoilers to their
shore ?
Red gleam'd the cross, and waned the
crescent pale,
While Afric's echoes thrill'd with Moorish
matrons' wail.

XXXVI

Teems not each ditty with the glorious
tale ?
Ah ! such, alas, the hero's amplest
fate !

When granite moulders and when records fail,
A peasant's plaint prolongs his dubious date.
Pride ! bend thine eye from heaven to thine estate, 400
See how the Mighty shrink into a song !
Can Volume, Pillar, Pile, preserve thee great ?
Or must thou trust Tradition's simple tongue,
When Flattery sleeps with thee and History does thee wrong ?

XXXVII

Awake, ye sons of Spain ! awake ! advance !
Lo, Chivalry, your ancient goddess, cries;
But wields not, as of old, her thirsty lance,
Nor shakes her crimson plumage in the skies:
Now on the smoke of blazing bolts she flies,
And speaks in thunder through yon engine's roar ! 410
In every peal she calls, 'Awake ! arise !'
Say, is her voice more feeble than of yore,
When her war-song was heard on Andalusia's shore ?

XXXVIII

Hark ! heard you not those hoofs of dreadful note ?
Sounds not the clang of conflict on the heath ?
Saw ye not whom the reeking sabre smote;
Nor saved your brethren ere they sank beneath
Tyrants and Tyrants' slaves ? — the fires of Death,
The bale-fires flash on high; from rock to rock
Each volley tells that thousands cease to breathe; 420
Death rides upon the sulphury Siroc,
Red Battle stamps his foot, and Nations feel the shock.

XXXIX

Lo ! where the Giant on the mountain stands,
His blood-red tresses deep'ning in the sun,
With death-shot glowing in his fiery hands,
And eye that scorcheth all it glares upon, —
Restless it rolls, now fix'd, and now anon
Flashing afar, — and at his iron feet
Destruction cowers to mark what deeds are done;
For on this morn three potent Nations meet, 430
To shed before his Shrine the blood he deems most sweet.

XL

By Heaven ! it is a splendid sight to see
(For one who hath no friend, no brother there)
Their rival scarfs of mix'd embroidery,
Their various arms that glitter in the air !
What gallant War-hounds rouse them from their lair,
And gnash their fangs, loud yelling for the prey !
All join the chase, but few the triumph share;
The Grave shall bear the chiefest prize away,
And Havoc scarce for joy can number their array. 440

XLI

Three hosts combine to offer sacrifice;
Three tongues prefer strange orisons on high;
Three gaudy standards flout the pale blue skies;
The shouts are France, Spain, Albion, Victory !
The foe, the victim, and the fond ally
That fights for all, but ever fights in vain,
Are met — as if at home they could not die —
To feed the crow, on Talavera's plain,
And fertilize the field that each pretends to gain.

XLII

There shall they rot, Ambition's honour'd fools ! 450
Yes, Honour decks the turf that wraps their clay !
Vain Sophistry ! in these behold the tools,

The broken tools, that tyrants cast away
By myriads, when they dare to pave their
way
With human hearts — to what ? — a
dream alone.
Can despots compass aught that hails
their sway ?
Or call with truth one span of earth their
own,
Save that wherein at last they crumble
bone by bone ?

XLIII

Oh, Albuera, glorious field of grief !
As o'er thy plain the Pilgrim prick'd his
steed, 460
Who could foresee thee, in a space so
brief,
A scene where mingling foes should boast
and bleed !
Peace to the perish'd ! may the warrior's
meed
And tears of triumph their reward pro-
long !
Till others fall where other chieftains
lead,
Thy name shall circle round the gaping
throng,
And shine in worthless lays, the theme of
transient song.

XLIV

Enough of Battle's minions ! let them
play
Their game of lives, and barter breath
for fame, —
Fame that will scarce re-animate their
clay, 470
Though thousands fall to deck some sin-
gle name.
In sooth 't were sad to thwart their noble
aim
Who strike, blest hirelings ! for their
country's good,
And die, that living might have proved
her shame;
Perish'd, perchance, in some domestic
feud,
Or in a narrower sphere wild Rapine's path
pursued.

XLV

Full swiftly Harold wends his lonely way
Where proud Sevilla triumphs unsub-
dued;

Yet is she free — the spoiler's wished-for
prey !
Soon, soon shall Conquest's fiery foot in-
trude, 480
Blackening her lovely domes with traces
rude.
Inevitable hour ! 'Gainst fate to strive
Where Desolation plants her famish'd
brood
Is vain, or Ilion, Tyre might yet survive,
And Virtue vanquish all, and Murder cease
to thrive.

XLVI

But all unconscious of the coming doom,
The feast, the song, the revel here
abounds;
Strange modes of merriment the hours
consume,
Nor bleed these patriots with their coun-
try's wounds;
Nor here War's clarion, but Love's re-
beck sounds; 490
Here Folly still his votaries inthralls;
And young-eyed Lewdness walks her
midnight rounds:
Girt with the silent crimes of Capitals,
Still to the last kind Vice clings to the
tott'ring walls.

XLVII

Not so the rustic; with his trembling
mate
He lurks, nor casts his heavy eye afar,
Lest he should view his vineyard deso-
late,
Blasted below the dun hot breath of war.
No more beneath soft Eve's consenting
star
Fandango twirls his jocund castanet: 500
Ah, monarchs ! could ye taste the mirth
ye mar,
Not in the toils of Glory would ye fret;
The hoarse dull drum would sleep, and
Man be happy yet !

XLVIII

How carols now the lusty muleteer ?
Of love, romance, devotion is his lay,
As whilome he was wont the leagues to
cheer,
His quick bells wildly jingling on the
way ?
No ! as he speeds, he chants ' Vivā el
Rey ! '

And checks his song to execrate Godoy,
The royal wittol Charles, and curse the
 day 510
When first Spain's queen beheld the
 black-eyed boy,
And gore-faced Treason sprung from her
 adulterate joy.

XLIX

On yon long, level plain, at distance
 crown'd
With crags, whereon those Moorish tur-
 rets rest,
Wide-scatter'd hoof-marks dint the
 wounded ground;
And, scathed by fire, the greensward's
 darken'd vest
Tells that the foe was Andalusia's guest:
Here was the camp, the watch-flame, and
 the host,
Here the bold peasant storm'd the
 dragon's nest;
Still does he mark it with triumphant
 boast, 520
And points to yonder cliffs which oft were
 won and lost.

L

And whomsoe'er along the path you meet
Bears in his cap the badge of crimson
 hue,
Which tells you whom to shun and whom
 to greet.
Woe to the man that walks in public
 view
Without of loyalty this token true !
Sharp is the knife, and sudden is the
 stroke;
And sorely would the Gallic foeman rue,
If subtle poniards, wrapt beneath the
 cloke,
Could blunt the sabre's edge or clear the
 cannon's smoke. 530

LI

At every turn Morena's dusky height
Sustains aloft the battery's iron load;
And, far as mortal eye can compass
 sight,
The mountain-howitzer, the broken road,
The bristling palisade, the fosse o'er-
 flow'd,
The station'd bands, the never-vacant
 watch,
The magazine in rocky durance stow'd,
The holster'd steed beneath the shed of
 thatch,
The ball-piled pyramid, the ever-blazing
 match,

LII

Portend the deeds to come: — but he
 whose nod 540
Has tumbled feebler despots from their
 sway,
A moment pauseth ere he lifts the rod;
A little moment deigneth to delay:
Soon will his legions sweep through these
 their way;
The West must own the Scourger of the
 world.
Ah Spain ! how sad will be thy reckon-
 ing-day,
When soars Gaul's Vulture, with his
 wings unfurl'd,
And thou shalt view thy sons in crowds to
 Hades hurl'd.

LIII

And must they fall ? the young, the
 proud, the brave,
To swell one bloated Chief's unwhole-
 some reign ? 550
No step between submission and a grave ?
The rise of rapine and the fall of Spain ?
And doth the Power that man adores or-
 dain
Their doom, nor heed the suppliant's ap-
 peal ?
Is all that desperate Valour acts in vain ?
And Counsel sage, and patriotic Zeal,
The Veteran's skill, Youth's fire, and Man-
 hood's heart of steel ?

LIV

Is it for this the Spanish maid, aroused,
Hangs on the willow her unstrung guitar,
And, all unsex'd, the anlace hath es-
 poused, 560
Sung the loud song, and dared the deed
 of war ?
And she, whom once the semblance of a
 scar
Appall'd, an owlet's larum chill'd with
 dread,
Now views the column-scattering bay'net
 jar,
The falchion flash, and o'er the yet warm
 dead
Stalks with Minerva's step where Mars
 might quake to tread.

LV

Ye who shall marvel when you hear her
tale,
Oh! had you known her in her softer
hour,
Mark'd her black eye that mocks her
coal-black veil,
Heard her light, lively tones in Lady's
bower, 570
Seen her long locks that foil the painter's
power,
Her fairy form, with more than female
grace,
Scarce would you deem that Saragoza's
tower
Beheld her smile in Danger's Gorgon
face,
Thin the closed ranks, and lead in Glory's
fearful chase.

LVI

Her lover sinks — she sheds no ill-timed
tear;
Her chief is slain — she fills his fatal
post;
Her fellows flee — she checks their base
career;
The foe retires — she heads the sallying
host.
Who can appease like her a lover's
ghost? 580
Who can avenge so well a leader's fall?
What maid retrieve when man's flush'd
hope is lost?
Who hang so fiercely on the flying Gaul,
Foil'd by a woman's hand, before a bat-
ter'd wall?

LVII

Yet are Spain's maids no race of Ama-
zons,
But form'd for all the witching arts of
love.
Though thus in arms they emulate her
sons,
And in the horrid phalanx dare to move,
'T is but the tender fierceness of the
dove,
Pecking the hand that hovers o'er her
mate: 590
In softness as in firmness far above
Remoter females, famed for sickening
prate;
Her mind is nobler sure, her charms per-
chance as great.

LVIII

The seal Love's dimpling finger hath im-
press'd
Denotes how soft that chin which bears
his touch;
Her lips, whose kisses pout to leave their
nest,
Bid man be valiant ere he merit such:
Her glance how wildly beautiful! how
much
Hath Phœbus woo'd in vain to spoil her
cheek,
Which glows yet smoother from his
amorous clutch! 600
Who round the North for paler dames
would seek?
How poor their forms appear! how lan-
guid, wan, and weak!

LIX

Match me, ye climes which poets love to
laud;
Match me, ye harams of the land where
now
I strike my strain, far distant, to applaud
Beauties that ev'n a cynic must avow —
Match me those Houries, whom ye scarce
allow
To taste the gale lest Love should ride
the wind,
With Spain's dark-glancing daughters —
deign to know,
There your wise Prophet's paradise we
find, 610
His black-eyed maids of Heaven, angeli-
cally kind.

LX

Oh, thou Parnassus whom I now survey!
Not in the phrensy of a dreamer's eye,
Not in the fabled landscape of a lay,
But soaring snow-clad through thy na-
tive sky,
In the wild pomp of mountain majesty!
What marvel if I thus essay to sing?
The humblest of thy pilgrims passing by
Would gladly woo thine Echoes with his
string,
Though from thy heights no more one
Muse will wave her wing. 620

LXI

Oft have I dream'd of Thee, whose glo-
rious name
Who knows not, knows not man's divinest
lore;

And now I view thee, 't is, alas ! with
 shame
That I in feeblest accents must adore.
When I recount thy worshippers of yore
I tremble, and can only bend the knee;
Nor raise my voice, nor vainly dare to
 soar,
But gaze beneath thy cloudy canopy
In silent joy to think at last I look on Thee !

LXII

Happier in this than mightiest bards have
 been, 630
Whose fate to distant homes confined
 their lot,
Shall I unmoved behold the Hallow'd
 scene,
Which others rave of though they know
 it not ?
Though here no more Apollo haunts his
 grot,
And thou, the Muses' seat, art now their
 grave,
Some gentle spirit still pervades the spot,
Sighs in the gale, keeps silence in the cave,
And glides with glassy foot o'er yon melo-
 dious wave.

LXIII

Of thee hereafter. — Ev'n amidst my
 strain
I turn'd aside to pay my homage here; 640
Forgot the land, the sons, the maids of
 Spain,
Her fate, to every freeborn bosom dear;
And hail'd thee, not perchance without a
 tear.
Now to my theme — but from thy holy
 haunt
Let me some remnant, some memorial
 bear;
Yield me one leaf of Daphne's deathless
 plant,
Nor let thy votary's hope be deem'd an idle
 vaunt.

LXIV

But ne'er didst thou, fair Mount, when
 Greece was young,
See round thy giant base a brighter choir;
Nor e'er did Delphi, when her priestess
 sung 650
The Pythian hymn with more than mortal
 fire,
Behold a train more fitting to inspire

The song of love than Andalusia's maids,
Nurst in the glowing lap of soft desire:
Ah ! that to these were given such peace-
 ful shades
As Greece can still bestow, though Glory
 fly her glades.

LXV

Fair is proud Seville; let her country
 boast
Her strength, her wealth, her site of an-
 cient days;
But Cadiz, rising on the distant coast,
Calls forth a sweeter though ignoble
 praise. 660
Ah, Vice, how soft are thy voluptuous
 ways !
While boyish blood is mantling, who can
 'scape
The fascination of thy magic gaze ?
A Cherub-hydra round us dost thou gape,
And mould to every taste thy dear delusive
 shape.

LXVI

When Paphos fell by time — accursèd
 Time !
The Queen who conquers all must yield
 to thee —
The Pleasures fled, but sought as warm
 a clime;
And Venus, constant to her native sea,
To nought else constant, hither deign'd
 to flee; 670
And fix'd her shrine within these walls of
 white;
Though not to one dome circumscribeth
 she
Her worship, but, devoted to her rite,
A thousand altars rise, for ever blazing
 bright.

LXVII

From morn till night, from night till
 startled Morn
Peeps blushing on the revel's laughing
 crew,
The song is heard, the rosy garland worn;
Devices quaint and frolics ever new
Tread on each other's kibes. A long adieu
He bids to sober joy that here sojourns: 680
Nought interrupts the riot, though in lieu
Of true devotion monkish incense burns,
And love and prayer unite, or rule the hour
 by turns.

LXVIII

The Sabbath comes, a day of blessed rest;
What hallows it upon this Christian shore?
Lo ! it is sacred to a solemn feast;
Hark ! heard you not the forest-monarch's roar ?
Crashing the lance, he snuffs the spouting gore
Of man and steed, o'erthrown beneath his horn;
The throng'd arena shakes with shouts for more; 690
Yells the mad crowd o'er entrails freshly torn,
Nor shrinks the female eye, nor ev'n affects to mourn.

LXIX

The seventh day this, the jubilee of man.
London, right well thou know'st the day of prayer:
Then thy spruce citizen, wash'd artisan,
And smug apprentice gulp their weekly air;
Thy coach of hackney, whiskey, one-horse chair,
And humblest gig through sundry suburbs whirl;
To Hampstead, Brentford, Harrow make repair;
Till the tired jade the wheel forgets to hurl, 700
Provoking envious gibe from each pedestrian churl.

LXX

Some o'er thy Thamis row the ribbon'd fair,
Others along the safer turnpike fly;
Some Richmond-hill ascend, some scud to Ware,
And many to the steep of Highgate hie.
Ask ye, Bœotian shades, the reason why ?
'T is to the worship of the solemn Horn,
Grasp'd in the holy hand of Mystery,
In whose dread name both men and maids are sworn,
And consecrate the oath with draught, and dance till morn. 710

LXXI

All have their fooleries; not alike are thine,
Fair Cadiz, rising o'er the dark blue sea !
Soon as the matin bell proclaimeth nine,
Thy saint adorers count the rosary.
Much is the VIRGIN teased to shrive them free
(Well do I ween the only virgin there)
From crimes as numerous as her beadsmen be;
Then to the crowded circus forth they fare;
Young, old, high, low, at once the same diversion share.

LXXII

The lists are oped, the spacious area clear'd, 720
Thousands on thousands piled are seated round;
Long ere the first loud trumpet's note is heard,
Ne vacant space for lated wight is found.
Here dons, grandees, but chiefly dames abound,
Skill'd in the ogle of a roguish eye,
Yet ever well inclined to heal the wound;
None through their cold disdain are doom'd to die,
As moon-struck bards complain, by Love's sad archery.

LXXIII

Hush'd is the din of tongues; on gallant steeds,
With milk-white crest, gold spur, and light poised lance, 730
Four cavaliers prepare for venturous deeds,
And lowly bending to the lists advance;
Rich are their scarfs, their chargers featly prance:
If in the dangerous game they shine today,
The crowd's loud shout and ladies' lovely glance,
Best prize of better acts, they bear away,
And all that kings or chiefs e'er gain their toils repay.

LXXIV

In costly sheen and gaudy cloak array'd,
But all afoot, the light-limb'd Matadore
Stands in the centre, eager to invade 740
The lord of lowing herds; but not before
The ground with cautious tread is traversed o'er,
Lest aught unseen should lurk to thwart his speed:

His arms a dart, he fights aloof, nor more
Can man achieve without the friendly
 steed —
Alas ! too oft condemn'd for him to bear
 and bleed.

LXXV

Thrice sounds the clarion; lo ! the signal
 falls,
The den expands, and Expectation mute
Gapes round the silent circle's peopled
 walls.
Bounds with one lashing spring the mighty
 brute, 750
And, wildly staring, spurns with sounding
 foot
The sand, nor blindly rushes on his
 foe:
Here, there, he points his threatening
 front, to suit
His first attack, wide waving to and fro
His angry tail; red rolls his eye's dilated
 glow.

LXXVI

Sudden he stops; his eye is fix'd: away,
Away, thou heedless boy ! prepare the
 spear:
Now is thy time, to perish, or display
The skill that yet may check his mad
 career.
With well-timed croupe the nimble
 coursers veer; 760
On foams the bull, but not unscathed he
 goes;
Streams from his flank the crimson tor-
 rent clear:
He flies, he wheels, distracted with his
 throes;
Dart follows dart; lance, lance; loud bel-
 lowings speak his woes.

LXXVII

Again he comes; nor dart nor lance avail,
Nor the wild plunging of the tortured
 horse;
Though man and man's avenging arms
 assail,
Vain are his weapons, vainer is his force.
One gallant steed is stretch'd a mangled
 corse;
Another, hideous sight ! unseam'd ap-
 pears, 770
His gory chest unveils life's panting
 source;

Though death-struck, still his feeble
 frame he rears;
Staggering, but stemming all, his lord un-
 harm'd he bears.

LXXVIII

Foil'd, bleeding, breathless, furious to the
 last,
Full in the centre stands the bull at
 bay,
Mid wounds, and clinging darts, and
 lances brast,
And foes disabled in the brutal fray:
And now the Matadores around him play,
Shake the red cloak, and poise the ready
 brand:
Once more through all he bursts his thun-
 dering way — 780
Vain rage ! the mantle quits the conynge
 hand,
Wraps his fierce eye— 'tis past — he sinks
 upon the sand !

LXXIX

Where his vast neck just mingles with
 the spine,
Sheathed in his form the deadly weapon
 lies.
He stops, he starts, disdaining to decline;
Slowly he falls amidst triumphant cries,
Without a groan, without a struggle dies.
The decorated car appears, on high
The corse is piled — sweet sight for
 vulgar eyes;
Four steeds that spurn the rein, as swift
 as shy, 790
Hurl the dark bulk along, scarce seen in
 dashing by.

LXXX

Such the ungentle sport that oft invites
The Spanish maid, and cheers the Spanish
 swain;
Nurtured in blood betimes, his heart de-
 lights
In vengeance, gloating on another's pain.
What private feuds the troubled village
 stain !
Though now one phalanx'd host should
 meet the foe,
Enough, alas, in humble homes remain
To meditate 'gainst friends the secret
 blow,
For some slight cause of wrath, whence
 life's warm stream must flow. 800

LXXXI

But Jealousy has fled : his bars, his
 bolts,
His wither'd centinel, Duenna sage !
And all whereat the generous soul re-
 volts,
Which the stern dotard deem'd he could
 encage,
Have pass'd to darkness with the vanish'd
 age.
Who late so free as Spanish girls were
 seen
(Ere War uprose in his volcanic rage),
With braided tresses bounding o'er the
 green,
While on the gay dance shone Night's lover-
 loving Queen ?

LXXXII

Oh ! many a time and oft had Harold
 loved, 810
Or dream'd he loved, since Rapture is a
 dream;
But now his wayward bosom was un-
 moved,
For not yet had he drunk of Lethe's
 stream;
And lately had he learn'd with truth to
 deem
Love has no gift so grateful as his
 wings:'
How fair, how young, how soft soe'er he
 seem
Full from the fount of Joy's delicious
 springs
Some bitter o'er the flowers its bubbling
 venom flings.

LXXXIII

Yet to the beauteous form he was not
 blind,
Though now it moved him as it moves the
 wise: 820
Not that Philosophy on such a mind
E'er deign'd to bend her chastely-awful
 eyes:
But Passion raves itself to rest, or flies;
And Vice, that digs her own voluptuous
 tomb,
Had buried long his hopes, no more to
 rise:
Pleasure's pall'd victim ! life-abhorring
 gloom
Wrote on his faded brow curst Cain's un-
 resting doom.

LXXXIV

Still he beheld, nor mingled with the
 throng;
But view'd them not with misanthropic
 hate:
Fain would he now have join'd the dance,
 the song; 830
But who may smile that sinks beneath his
 fate ?
Nought that he saw his sadness could
 abate:
Yet once he struggled 'gainst the demon's
 sway,
And as in Beauty's bower he pensive
 sate,
Pour'd forth this unpremeditated lay,
To charms as fair as those that soothed his
 happier day.

TO INEZ

1

Nay, smile not at my sullen brow;
 Alas ! I cannot smile again:
Yet Heaven avert that ever thou
 Shouldst weep, and haply weep in vain. 840

2

And dost thou ask what secret woe
 I bear, corroding joy and youth ?
And wilt thou vainly seek to know
 A pang, ev'n thou must fail to soothe ?

3

It is not love, it is not hate,
 Nor low Ambition's honours lost,
That bids me loathe my present state,
 And fly from all I prized the most:

4

It is that weariness which springs
 From all I meet, or hear, or see ; 850
To me no pleasure Beauty brings,
 Thine eyes have scarce a charm for me.

5

It is that settled, ceaseless gloom
 The fabled Hebrew wanderer bore ;
That will not look beyond the tomb,
 But cannot hope for rest before.

6

What Exile from himself can flee ?
 To zones, though more and more remote,
Still, still pursues, where-e'er I be,
 The blight of life — the demon Thought.

7

Yet others rapt in pleasure seem, 861
 And taste of all that I forsake;

Oh, may they still of transport dream,
 And ne'er, at least like me, awake!

8

Through many a clime 't is mine to go,
 With many a retrospection curst;
And all my solace is to know,
 Whate'er betides, I've known the worst.

9

What is that worst? Nay do not ask —
 In pity from the search forbear: 870
Smile on, nor venture to unmask
 Man's heart, and view the Hell that's there.

LXXXV

Adieu, fair Cadiz! yea, a long adieu!
Who may forget how well thy walls have
 stood?
When all were changing thou alone wert
 true,
First to be free and last to be subdued.
And if amidst a scene, a shock so rude,
Some native blood was seen thy streets to
 dye,
A traitor only fell beneath the feud:
Here all were noble, save Nobility; 880
None hugg'd a conqueror's chain, save fallen
 Chivalry!

LXXXVI

Such be the sons of Spain, and strange
 her fate!
They fight for freedom who were never
 free,
A Kingless people for a nerveless state;
Her vassals combat when their chieftains
 flee,
True to the veriest slaves of Treachery;
Fond of a land which gave them nought
 but life,
Pride points the path that leads to
 Liberty;
Back to the struggle, baffled in the strife,
War, war is still the cry, 'War even to the
 knife!' 890

LXXXVII

Ye who would more of Spain and Span-
 iards know,
Go, read whate'er is writ of bloodiest
 strife;
Whate'er keen Vengeance urged on for-
 eign foe
Can act, is acting there against man's
 life:
From flashing scimitar to secret knife,

War mouldeth there each weapon to his
 need —
So may he guard the sister and the
 wife,
So may he make each curst oppressor
 bleed,
So may such foes deserve the most remorse-
 less deed! 899

LXXXVIII

Flows there a tear of pity for the dead?
Look o'er the ravage of the reeking plain;
Look on the hands with female slaughter
 red;
Then to the dogs resign the unburied
 slain,
Then to the vulture let each corse re-
 main;
Albeit unworthy of the prey-bird's maw,
Let their bleach'd bones and blood's un-
 bleaching stain
Long mark the battle-field with hideous
 awe:
Thus only may our sons conceive the scenes
 we saw!

LXXXIX

Nor yet, alas, the dreadful work is done;
Fresh legions pour adown the Pyrenees;
It deepens still, the work is scarce be-
 gun, 911
Nor mortal eye the distant end foresees.
Fall'n nations gaze on Spain; if freed,
 she frees
More than her fell Pizarros once en-
 chain'd:
Strange retribution! now Columbia's
 ease
Repairs the wrongs that Quito's sons sus-
 tain'd,
While o'er the parent clime prowls Murder
 unrestrain'd.

XC

Not all the blood at Talavera shed,
Not all the marvels of Barossa's fight,
Not Albuera lavish of the dead, 920
Have won for Spain her well-asserted
 right.
When shall her Olive-Branch be free
 from blight?
When shall she breathe her from the
 blushing toil?
How many a doubtful day shall sink in
 night,

Ere the Frank robber turn him from his
spoil,
And Freedom's stranger-tree grow native
of the soil !

XCI

And thou, my friend, since unavailing
woe
Bursts from my heart and mingles with
the strain —
Had the sword laid thee with the mighty
low,
Pride might forbid e'en Friendship to
complain; 930
But thus unlaurel'd to descend in vain,
By all forgotten, save the lonely breast,
And mix unbleeding with the boasted
slain,
While Glory crowns so many a meaner
crest !
What hadst thou done to sink so peacefully
to rest ?

XCII

Oh, known the earliest, and esteem'd the
most !
Dear to a heart where nought was left so
dear !
Though to my hopeless days forever
lost,
In dreams deny me not to see thee here !
And Morn in secret shall renew the
tear 940
Of Consciousness awaking to her woes,
And Fancy hover o'er thy bloodless bier,
Till my frail frame return to whence it
rose,
And mourn'd and mourner lie united in re-
pose.

XCIII

Here is one fytte of Harold's pilgrimage:
Ye who of him may further seek to know,
Shall find some tidings in a future page,
If he that rhymeth now may scribble moe.
Is this too much ? stern Critic, say not
so:
Patience ! and ye shall hear what he be-
held 950
In other lands, where he was doom'd to
go:
Lands that contain the monuments of
Eld,
Ere Greece and Grecian arts by barbarous
hands were quell'd.

CANTO THE SECOND

I

COME, blue-eyed maid of heaven ! — but
thou, alas,
Didst never yet one mortal song in-
spire —
Goddess of Wisdom ! here thy temple
was,
And is, despite of war and wasting fire,
And years, that bade thy worship to ex-
pire:
But worse than steel, and flame, and ages
slow,
Is the dread sceptre and dominion dire
Of men who never felt the sacred
glow
That thoughts of thee and thine on polish'd
breasts bestow.

II

Ancient of days ! august Athena !
where, 10
Where are thy men of might ? thy
grand in soul ?
Gone — glimmering through the dream
of things that were:
First in the race that led to Glory's
goal,
They won, and pass'd away — is this the
whole ?
A schoolboy's tale, the wonder of an
hour !
The warrior's weapon and the sophist's
stole
Are sought in vain, and o'er each mould-
ering tower,
Dim with the mist of years, gray flits the
shade of power.

III

Son of the morning, rise ! approach you
here !
Come — but molest not yon defenceless
urn. 20
Look on this spot — a nation's sepul-
chre !
Abode of gods, whose shrines no longer
burn.
Even gods must yield, religions take
their turn;
'T was Jove's, 't is Mahomet's, and other
creeds
Will rise with other years, till man shall
learn

Vainly his incense soars, his victim
 bleeds, —
Poor child of Doubt and Death, whose
 hope is built on reeds.

IV

Bound to the earth, he lifts his eye to
 heaven —
Is 't not enough, unhappy thing, to know
Thou art? Is this a boon so kindly
 given, 30
That, being, thou wouldst be again, and
 go,
Thou know'st not, reck'st not to what
 region, so
On earth no more, but mingled with the
 skies ?
Still wilt thou dream on future joy and
 woe ?
Regard and weigh yon dust before it
 flies,
That little urn saith more than thousand
 homilies.

V

Or burst the vanish'd Hero's lofty
 mound;
Far on the solitary shore he sleeps:
He fell, and falling nations mourn'd
 around;
But now not one of saddening thousands
 weeps, 40
Nor warlike worshipper his vigil keeps
Where demi-gods appear'd, as records
 tell.
Remove yon skull from out the scatter'd
 heaps:
Is that a temple where a God may dwell ?
Why ev'n the worm at last disdains her
 shatter'd cell !

VI

Look on its broken arch, its ruin'd wall,
Its chambers desolate, and portals foul:
Yes, this was once Ambition's airy hall,
The dome of Thought, the palace of the
 Soul.
Behold through each lack-lustre, eyeless
 hole, 50
The gay recess of Wisdom and of Wit
And Passion's host, that never brook'd
 control:
Can all saint, sage, or sophist ever writ,
People this lonely tower, this tenement
 refit ?

VII

Well didst thou speak, Athena's wisest
 son !
' All that we know is, nothing can be
 known.'
Why should we shrink from what we
 cannot shun ?
Each hath his pang, but feeble sufferers
 groan
With brain-born dreams of evil all their
 own.
Pursue what Chance or Fate proclaimeth
 best; 60
Peace waits us on the shores of Acheron:
There no forced banquet claims the sated
 guest,
But Silence spreads the couch of ever wel-
 come rest.

VIII

Yet if, as holiest men have deem'd, there
 be
A land of souls beyond that sable shore,
To shame the doctrine of the Sadducee
And sophists, madly vain of dubious lore;
How sweet it were in concert to adore
With those who made our mortal labours
 light !
To hear each voice we fear'd to hear no
 more ! 70
Behold each mighty shade reveal'd to
 sight,
The Bactrian, Samian sage, and all who
 taught the right !

IX

There, thou ! — whose love and life, to-
 gether fled,
Have left me here to love and live in
 vain —
Twined with my heart, and can I deem
 thee dead,
When busy Memory flashes on my brain?
Well — I will dream that we may meet
 again,
And woo the vision to my vacant breast:
If aught of young Remembrance then
 remain,
Be as it may Futurity's behest, 80
For me 't were bliss enough to know thy
 spirit blest !

X

Here let me sit upon this massy stone,
The marble column's yet unshaken base;

Here, son of Saturn, was thy fav'rite
 throne,
Mightiest of many such! Hence let me
 trace
The latent grandeur of thy dwelling-
 place.
It may not be: nor ev'n can Fancy's eye
Restore what Time hath labour'd to de-
 face.
Yet these proud pillars claim no passing
 sigh;
Unmoved the Moslem sits, the light Greek
 carols by. 90

XI

But who, of all the plunderers of yon fane
On high, where Pallas linger'd, loath to
 flee
The latest relic of her ancient reign, —
The last, the worst, dull spoiler, who was
 he?
Blush, Caledonia, such thy son could be!
England, I joy no child he was of thine:
Thy free-born men should spare what
 once was free;
Yet they could violate each saddening
 shrine,
And bear these altars o'er the long-reluctant
 brine.

XII

But most the modern Pict's ignoble
 boast, 100
To rive what Goth, and Turk, and Time
 hath spared:
Cold as the crags upon his native coast,
His mind as barren and his heart as hard,
Is he whose head conceived, whose hand
 prepared,
Aught to displace Athena's poor remains:
Her sons too weak the sacred shrine to
 guard,
Yet felt some portion of their mother's
 pains,
And never knew, till then, the weight of
 Despots' chains.

XIII

What! shall it e'er be said by British
 tongue,
Albion was happy in Athena's tears? 110
Though in thy name the slaves her bosom
 wrung,
Tell not the deed to blushing Europe's
 ears;

The ocean queen, the free Britannia, bears
The last poor plunder from a bleeding
 land:
Yes, she, whose gen'rous aid her name
 endears,
Tore down those remnants with a harpy's
 hand,
Which envious Eld forbore, and tyrants left
 to stand.

XIV

Where was thine Ægis, Pallas, that ap-
 pall'd
Stern Alaric and Havoc on their way?
Where Peleus' son? whom Hell in vain
 enthrall'd, 120
His shade from Hades upon that dread
 day
Bursting to light in terrible array!
What! could not Pluto spare the chief
 once more,
To scare a second robber from his prey?
Idly he wander'd on the Stygian shore,
Nor now preserved the walls he loved to
 shield before.

XV

Cold is the heart, fair Greece, that looks
 on thee,
Nor feels as lovers o'er the dust they
 loved;
Dull is the eye that will not weep to see
Thy walls defaced, thy mouldering shrines
 removed 130
By British hands, which it had best be-
 hoved
To guard those relics ne'er to be restored.
Curst be the hour when from their isle
 they roved,
And once again thy hapless bosom gored,
And snatch'd thy shrinking Gods to north-
 ern climes abhorr'd!

XVI

But where is Harold? shall I then for-
 get
To urge the gloomy wanderer o'er the
 wave?
Little reck'd he of all that men regret;
No loved-one now in feign'd lament could
 rave;
No friend the parting hand extended
 gave, 140
Ere the cold stranger pass'd to other
 climes:

Hard is his heart whom charms may not
enslave;
But Harold felt not as in other times,
And left without a sigh the land of war and
crimes.

XVII

He that has sail'd upon the dark blue sea
Has view'd at times, I ween, a full fair
sight;
When the fresh breeze is fair as breeze
may be,
The white sail set, the gallant frigate
tight;
Masts, spires, and strand retiring to the
right,
The glorious main expanding o'er the
bow, 150
The convoy spread like wild swans in
their flight,
The dullest sailer wearing bravely now,
So gaily curl the waves before each dash-
ing prow.

XVIII

And oh, the little warlike world within !
The well-reeved guns, the netted canopy,
The hoarse command, the busy humming
din,
When, at a word, the tops are mann'd on
high:
Hark, to the Boatswain's call, the cheer-
ing cry !
While through the seaman's hand the
tackle glides;
Or schoolboy Midshipman that, standing
by, 160
Strains his shrill pipe as good or ill betides,
And well the docile crew that skilful urchin
guides.

XIX

White is the glassy deck, without a stain,
Where on the watch the staid Lieutenant
walks:
Look on that part which sacred doth re-
main
For the lone chieftain, who majestic
stalks,
Silent and fear'd by all — not oft he
talks
With aught beneath him, if he would
preserve
That strict restraint, which, broken, ever
balks

Conquest and Fame: but Britons rarely
swerve 170
From law, however stern, which tends their
strength to nerve.

XX

Blow ! swiftly blow, thou keel-compel-
ling gale !
Till the broad sun withdraws his lessening
ray;
Then must the pennant-bearer slacken
sail,
That lagging barks may make their lazy
way.
Ah, grievance sore and listless dull
delay,
To waste on sluggish hulks the sweetest
breeze !
What leagues are lost before the dawn of
day,
Thus loitering pensive on the willing seas,
The flapping sail haul'd down to halt for
logs like these ! 180

XXI

The moon is up; by Heaven, a lovely
eve !
Long streams of light o'er dancing waves
expand;
Now lads on shore may sigh, and maids
believe —
Such be our fate when we return to
land !
Meantime some rude Arion's restless
hand
Wakes the brisk harmony that sailors
love;
A circle there of merry listeners stand,
Or to some well-known measure featly
move,
Thoughtless, as if on shore they still were
free to rove.

XXII

Through Calpe's straits survey the steepy
shore; 190
Europe and Afric on each other gaze,
Lands of the dark-eyed Maid and dusky
Moor
Alike beheld beneath pale Hecate's blaze:
How softly on the Spanish shore she plays,
Disclosing rock and slope and forest
brown,
Distinct, though darkening with her wan-
ing phase;

But Mauritania's giant-shadows frown,
From mountain-cliff to coast descending
 sombre down.

XXIII

'T is night, when Meditation bids us feel
We once have loved, though love is at an
 end; 200
The heart, lone mourner of its baffled
 zeal,
Though friendless now, will dream it had
 a friend.
Who with the weight of years would wish
 to bend,
When Youth itself survives young Love
 and Joy ?
Alas, when mingling souls forget to blend,
Death hath but little left him to destroy !
Ah, happy years ! once more who would not
 be a boy ?

XXIV

Thus bending o'er the vessel's laving
 side,
To gaze on Dian's wave-reflected sphere,
The soul forgets her schemes of Hope and
 Pride, 210
And flies unconscious o'er each backward
 year.
None are so desolate but something dear,
Dearer than self, possesses or possess'd
A thought, and claims the homage of a
 tear;
A flashing pang ! of which the weary
 breast
Would still, albeit in vain, the heavy heart
 divest.

XXV

To sit on rocks, to muse o'er flood and
 fell,
To slowly trace the forest's shady scene,
Where things that own not man's domin-
 ion dwell,
And mortal foot hath ne'er or rarely
 been; 220
To climb the trackless mountain all un-
 seen,
With the wild flock that never needs a
 fold;
Alone o'er steeps and foaming falls to
 lean;
This is not solitude, 't is but to hold
Converse with Nature's charms and view
 her stores unroll'd.

XXVI

But 'midst the crowd, the hum, the shock
 of men,
To hear, to see, to feel, and to possess,
And roam along, the world's tired deni-
 zen,
With none who bless us, none whom we
 can bless;
Minions of splendour shrinking from dis-
 tress ! 230
None that, with kindred consciousness
 endued,
If we were not would seem to smile the
 less,
Of all that flatter'd, follow'd, sought, and
 sued;
This is to be alone; this, this is solitude !

XXVII

More blest the life of godly eremite,
Such as on lonely Athos may be seen,
Watching at eve upon the giant height,
Which looks o'er waves so blue, skies so
 serene,
That he who there at such an hour hath
 been
Will wistful linger on that hallow'd spot;
Then slowly tear him from the witching
 scene, 241
Sigh forth one wish that such had been
 his lot,
Then turn to hate a world he had almost
 forgot.

XXVIII

Pass we the long, unvarying course, the
 track
Oft trod, that never leaves a trace behind;
Pass we the calm, the gale, the change,
 the tack,
And each well known caprice of wave and
 wind;
Pass we the joys and sorrows sailors find,
Coop'd in their wingèd sea-girt citadel;
The foul, the fair, the contrary, the kind,
As breezes rise and fall and billows swell,
Till on some jocund morn — lo, land ! and
 all is well. 252

XXIX

But not in silence pass Calypso's isles,
The sister tenants of the middle deep;
There for the weary still a haven smiles,
Though the fair goddess long hath ceased
 to weep

And o'er her cliffs a fruitless watch to
 keep
For him who dared prefer a mortal bride:
Here, too, his boy essay'd the dreadful
 leap
Stern Mentor urged from high to yonder
 tide; 260
While thus of both bereft, the nymph-queen
 doubly sigh'd.

XXX

Her reign is past, her gentle glories gone:
But trust not this; too easy youth, be-
 ware !
A mortal sovereign holds her dangerous
 throne,
And thou may'st find a new Calypso there.
Sweet Florence, could another ever share
This wayward, loveless heart, it would be
 thine:
But, check'd by every tie, I may not dare
To cast a worthless offering at thy shrine,
Nor ask so dear a breast to feel one pang
 for mine. 270

XXXI

Thus Harold deem'd, as on that lady's
 eye
He look'd and met its beam without a
 thought,
Save Admiration glancing harmless by:
Love kept aloof, albeit not far remote,
Who knew his votary often lost and
 caught,
But knew him as his worshipper no more;
And ne'er again the boy his bosom sought:
Since now he vainly urged him to adore,
Well deem'd the little God his ancient sway
 was o'er.

XXXII

Fair Florence found, in sooth with some
 amaze, 280
One who, 't was said, still sigh'd to all he
 saw,
Withstand, unmoved, the lustre of her
 gaze,
Which others hail'd with real or mimic
 awe,
Their hope, their doom, their punishment,
 their law,
All that gay Beauty from her bondsmen
 claims:
And much she marvell'd that a youth so
 raw

Nor felt, nor feign'd at least, the oft-told
 flames,
Which, though sometimes they frown, yet
 rarely anger dames.

XXXIII

Little knew she that seeming marble
 heart,
Now mask'd in silence or withheld by
 pride, 290
Was not unskilful in the spoiler's art,
And spread its snares licentious far and
 wide;
Nor from the base pursuit had turn'd
 aside,
As long as aught was worthy to pursue:
But Harold on such arts no more re-
 lied;
And had he doted on those eyes so blue,
Yet never would he join the lovers' whin-
 ing crew.

XXXIV

Not much he kens, I ween, of woman's
 breast,
Who thinks that wanton thing is won by
 sighs;
What careth she for hearts when once
 possess'd ? 300
Do proper homage to thine idol's eyes,
But not too humbly or she will despise
Thee and thy suit, though told in moving
 tropes:
Disguise ev'n tenderness if thou art wise;
Brisk Confidence still best with woman
 copes;
Pique her and soothe in turn, soon Passion
 crowns thy hopes.

XXXV

'T is an old lesson; Time approves it
 true,
And those who know it best, deplore it
 most;
When all is won that all desire to woo,
The paltry prize is hardly worth the
 cost: 310
Youth wasted, minds degraded, honour
 lost,
These are thy fruits, successful Passion,
 these !
If, kindly cruel, early Hope is crost,
Still to the last it rankles, a disease,
Not to be cured when Love itself forgets
 to please.

XXXVI

Away ! nor let me loiter in my song,
For we have many a mountain-path to
tread,
And many a varied shore to sail along,
By pensive Sadness, not by Fiction, led, —
Climes, fair withal as ever mortal head
Imagined in its little schemes of thought;
Or e'er in new Utopias were ared, 322
To teach man what he might be, or he
ought;
If that corrupted thing could ever such be
taught.

XXXVII

Dear Nature is the kindest mother still,
Though alway changing, in her aspect
mild;
From her bare bosom let me take my fill,
Her never-wean'd, though not her fa-
vour'd child.
Oh, she is fairest in her features wild,
Where nothing polish'd dares pollute her
path ! 330
To me by day or night she ever smiled,
Though I have mark'd her when none
other hath,
And sought her more and more, and loved
her best in wrath.

XXXVIII

Land of Albania, where Iskander rose,
Theme of the young, and beacon of the
wise,
And he, his namesake, whose oft-baffled
foes
Shrunk from his deeds of chivalrous
emprize:
Land of Albania, let me bend mine eyes
On thee, thou rugged nurse of savage
men !
The cross descends, thy minarets arise,
And the pale crescent sparkles in the
glen, 341
Through many a cypress grove within each
city's ken.

XXXIX

Childe Harold sail'd, and pass'd the bar-
ren spot
Where sad Penelope o'erlook'd the wave;
And onward view'd the mount, not yet
forgot,
The lover's refuge, and the Lesbian's
grave.

Dark Sappho, could not verse immortal
save
That breast imbued with such immortal
fire ?
Could she not live who life eternal gave ?
If life eternal may await the lyre, 350
That only Heaven to which Earth's chil-
dren may aspire.

XL

'T was on a Grecian autumn's gentle eve
Childe Harold hail'd Leucadia's cape
afar,
A spot he long'd to see, nor cared to
leave:
Oft did he mark the scenes of vanish'd
war,
Actium, Lepanto, fatal Trafalgar,
Mark them unmoved, for he would not
delight
(Born beneath some remote inglorious
star)
In themes of bloody fray or gallant fight,
But loathed the bravo's trade and laugh'd
at marshal wight. 360

XLI

But when he saw the evening star above
Leucadia's far-projecting rock of woe,
And hail'd the last resort of fruitless
love,
He felt, or deem'd he felt, no common
glow:
And as the stately vessel glided slow
Beneath the shadow of that ancient
mount,
He watch'd the billows' melancholy flow;
And, sunk albeit in thought as he was
wont,
More placid seem'd his eye and smooth his
pallid front.

XLII

Morn dawns; and with it stern Albania's
hills, 370
Dark Suli's rocks, and Pindus' inland
peak,
Robed half in mist, bedew'd with snowy
rills,
Array'd in many a dun and purple streak,
Arise; and, as the clouds along them
break,
Disclose the dwelling of the mountaineer:
Here roams the wolf, the eagle whets his
beak,

Birds, beasts of prey, and wilder men
 appear,
And gathering storms around convulse the
 closing year.

XLIII

Now Harold felt himself at length alone,
And bade to Christian tongues a long
 adieu; 380
Now he adventured on a shore unknown,
Which all admire but many dread to view:
His breast was arm'd 'gainst fate, his
 wants were few;
Peril he sought not, but ne'er shrank to
 meet:
The scene was savage, but the scene was
 new;
This made the ceaseless toil of travel
 sweet,
Beat back keen winter's blast, and welcomed
 summer's heat.

XLIV

Here the red cross (for still the cross is
 here,
Though sadly scoff'd at by the circum-
 cised)
Forgets that pride to pamper'd priest-
 hood dear, — 390
Churchman and votary alike despised.
Foul Superstition! howsoe'er disguised,
Idol, saint, virgin, prophet, crescent,
 cross,
For whatsoever symbol thou art prized,
Thou sacerdotal gain, but general loss!
Who from true worship's gold can separate
 thy dross?

XLV

Ambracia's gulf behold, where once was
 lost
A world for woman, lovely, harmless
 thing!
In yonder rippling bay, their naval host
Did many a Roman chief and Asian
 king 400
To doubtful conflict, certain slaughter
 bring.
Look where the second Cæsar's trophies
 rose,
Now, like the hands that rear'd them,
 withering!
Imperial anarchs, doubling human woes!
God, was thy globe ordain'd for such to
 win and lose?

XLVI

From the dark barriers of that rugged
 clime,
Ev'n to the centre of Illyria's vales,
Childe Harold pass'd o'er many a mount
 sublime,
Through lands scarce noticed in historic
 tales;
Yet in famed Attica such lovely dales 410
Are rarely seen; nor can fair Tempe
 boast
A charm they know not; loved Par-
 nassus fails,
Though classic ground and consecrated
 most,
To match some spots that lurk within this
 lowering coast.

XLVII

He pass'd bleak Pindus, Acherusia's lake,
And left the primal city of the land,
And onwards did his further journey take
To greet Albania's chief, whose dread
 command
Is lawless law; for with a bloody hand
He sways a nation, turbulent and bold:
Yet here and there some daring moun-
 tain-band 421
Disdain his power, and from their rocky
 hold
Hurl their defiance far, nor yield, unless to
 gold.

XLVIII

Monastic Zitza, from thy shady brow,
Thou small, but favour'd spot of holy
 ground!
Where'er we gaze, around, above, below,
What rainbow tints, what magic charms
 are found!
Rock, river, forest, mountain, all abound,
And bluest skies that harmonise the
 whole;
Beneath, the distant torrent's rushing
 sound 430
Tells where the volumed cataract doth
 roll
Between those hanging rocks, that shock
 yet please the soul.

XLIX

Amidst the grove that crowns yon tufted
 hill,
Which, were it not for many a mountain
 nigh

Rising in lofty ranks, and loftier still
Might well itself be deem'd of dignity,
The convent's white walls glisten fair on
 high:
Here dwells the caloyer, nor rude is he,
Nor niggard of his cheer; the passer by
Is welcome still; nor heedless will he
 flee 440
From hence, if he delight kind Nature's
 sheen to see.

L

Here in the sultriest season let him
 rest,
Fresh is the green beneath those aged
 trees;
Here winds of gentlest wing will fan his
 breast,
From heaven itself he may inhale the
 breeze.
The plain is far beneath — oh ! let him
 seize
Pure pleasure while he can; the scorch-
 ing ray
Here pierceth not, impregnate with dis-
 ease:
Then let his length the loitering pilgrim
 lay,
And gaze, untired, the morn, the noon, the
 eve away. 450

LI

Dusky and huge, enlarging on the sight,
Nature's volcanic amphitheatre,
Chimæra's alps extend from left to right:
Beneath, a living valley seems to stir;
Flocks play, trees wave, streams flow, the
 mountain-fir
Nodding above; behold black Acheron,
Once consecrated to the sepulchre !
Pluto, if this be hell I look upon,
Close shamed Elysium's gates, my shade
 shall seek for none. 459

LII

Ne city's towers pollute the lovely view;
Unseen is Yanina, though not remote,
Veil'd by the screen of hills; here men
 are few,
Scanty the hamlet, rare the lonely cot:
But, peering down each precipice, the
 goat
Browseth; and, pensive o'er his scatter'd
 flock,
The little shepherd in his white capote

Doth lean his boyish form along the rock,
Or in his cave awaits the tempest's short-
 lived shock.

LIII

Oh ! where, Dodona, is thine aged grove,
Prophetic fount, and oracle divine ? 470
What valley echo'd the response of Jove ?
What trace remaineth of the Thunderer's
 shrine ?
All, all forgotten — and shall man repine
That his frail bonds to fleeting life are
 broke ?
Cease, fool, the fate of gods may well be
 thine !
Wouldst thou survive the marble or the
 oak,
When nations, tongues, and worlds must
 sink beneath the stroke ?

LIV

Epirus' bounds recede and mountains fail;
Tired of up-gazing still, the wearied eye
Reposes gladly on as smooth a vale 480
As ever Spring yclad in grassy dye.
Ev'n on a plain no humble beauties lie,
Where some bold river breaks the long
 expanse,
And woods along the banks are waving
 high,
Whose shadows in the glassy waters
 dance,
Or with the moonbeam sleep in midnight's
 solemn trance.

LV

The sun had sunk behind vast Tomerit,
And Laos wide and fierce came roaring by;
The shades of wonted night were gather-
 ing yet,
When, down the steep banks winding
 warily, 490
Childe Harold saw, like meteors in the
 sky,
The glittering minarets of Tepalen,
Whose walls o'erlook the stream; and
 drawing nigh,
He heard the busy hum of warrior-men
Swelling the breeze that sigh'd along the
 lengthening glen.

LVI

He pass'd the sacred Haram's silent
 tower,
And underneath the wide o'erarching gate

Survey'd the dwelling of this chief of
 power,
Where all around proclaim'd his high
 estate.
Amidst no common pomp the despot
 sate, 500
While busy preparation shook the court,
Slaves, eunuchs, soldiers, guests, and san-
 tons wait;
Within, a palace, and without, a fort:
Here men of every clime appear to make
 resort.

LVII

Richly caparison'd, a ready row
Of armèd horse and many a warlike store
Circled the wide extending court below;
Above, strange groups adorn'd the cor-
 ridor;
And oft-times through the area's echoing
 door
Some high-capp'd Tartar spurr'd his steed
 away: 510
The Turk, the Greek, the Albanian, and
 the Moor,
Here mingled in their many-hued array,
While the deep war-drum's sound an-
 nounced the close of day.

LVIII

The wild Albanian kirtled to his knee,
With shawl-girt head and ornamented
 gun,
And gold-embroider'd garments fair to
 see;
The crimson-scarfèd men of Macedon;
The Delhi with his cap of terror on,
And crooked glaive; the lively, supple
 Greek;
And swarthy Nubia's mutilated son; 520
The bearded Turk, that rarely deigns to
 speak,
Master of all around, too potent to be meek,

LIX

Are mix'd conspicuous: some recline in
 groups,
Scanning the motley scene that varies
 round;
There some grave Moslem to devotion
 stoops,
And some that smoke, and some that play,
 are found;
Here the Albanian proudly treads the
 ground;

Half-whispering there the Greek is heard
 to prate;
Hark! from the mosque the nightly sol-
 emn sound,
The Muezzin's call doth shake the min-
 aret, 530
'There is no god but God!—to prayer—
 lo! God is great!'

LX

Just at this season Ramazani's fast
Through the long day its penance did
 maintain;
But when the lingering twilight hour was
 past,
Revel and feast assumed the rule again.
Now all was bustle, and the menial train
Prepared and spread the plenteous board
 within;
The vacant gallery now seem'd made in
 vain,
But from the chambers came the min-
 gling din,
As page and slave anon were passing out
 and in. 540

LXI

Here woman's voice is never heard: apart,
And scarce permitted, guarded, veil'd, to
 move,
She yields to one her person and her heart,
Tamed to her cage, nor feels a wish to
 rove:
For, not unhappy in her master's love,
And joyful in a mother's gentlest cares,
Blest cares! all other feelings far above!
Herself more sweetly rears the babe she
 bears,
Who never quits the breast no meaner pas-
 sion shares.

LXII

In marble-paved pavilion, where a
 spring 550
Of living water from the centre rose,
Whose bubbling did a genial freshness
 fling,
And soft voluptuous couches breathed
 repose,
ALI reclined, a man of war and woes:
Yet in his lineaments ye cannot trace,
While Gentleness her milder radiance
 throws
Along that aged venerable face,
The deeds that lurk beneath and stain him
 with disgrace.

LXIII

It is not that yon hoary lengthening beard
Ill suits the passions which belong to
 youth; 560
Love conquers age — so Hafiz hath
 averr'd,
So sings the Teian, and he sings in sooth —
But crimes that scorn the tender voice of
 Ruth,
Beseeming all men ill but most the man
In years, have mark'd him with a tiger's
 tooth:
Blood follows blood, and, through their
 mortal span,
In bloodier acts conclude those who with
 blood began.

LXIV

'Mid many things most new to ear and
 eye
The pilgrim rested here his weary feet,
And gazed around on Moslem luxury,
Till quickly wearied with that spacious
 seat 571
Of Wealth and Wantonness, the choice
 retreat
Of sated Grandeur from the city's noise:
And were it humbler it in sooth were
 sweet;
But Peace abhorreth artificial joys,
And Pleasure, leagued with Pomp, the zest
 of both destroys.

LXV

Fierce are Albania's children, yet they
 lack
Not virtues, were those virtues more
 mature.
Where is the foe that ever saw their
 back ? 579
Who can so well the toil of war endure ?
Their native fastnesses not more secure
Than they in doubtful time of troublous
 need;
Their wrath how deadly! but their friend-
 ship sure,
When Gratitude or Valour bids them
 bleed,
Unshaken rushing on where'er their chief
 may lead.

LXVI

Childe Harold saw them in their chief-
 tain's tower,
Thronging to war in splendour and suc-
 cess;

And after view'd them, when, within
 their power,
Himself awhile the victim of distress, —
That saddening hour when bad men hot-
 lier press; 590
But these did shelter him beneath their
 roof,
When less barbarians would have cheer'd
 him less,
And fellow-countrymen have stood
 aloof —
In aught that tries the heart how few with-
 stand the proof !

LXVII

It chanced that adverse winds once drove
 his bark
Full on the coast of Suli's shaggy shore,
When all around was desolate and dark;
To land was perilous, to sojourn, more;
Yet for a while the mariners forbore,
Dubious to trust where treachery might
 lurk: 600
At length they ventured forth, though
 doubting sore
That those who loathe alike the Frank and
 Turk
Might once again renew their ancient
 butcher-work.

LXVIII

Vain fear ! the Suliotes stretch'd the
 welcome hand,
Led them o'er rocks and past the danger-
 ous swamp,
Kinder than polish'd slaves though not
 so bland,
And piled the hearth, and wrung their
 garments damp,
And fill'd the bowl, and trimm'd the
 cheerful lamp,
And spread their fare, though homely,
 all they had:
Such conduct bears Philanthropy's rare
 stamp — 610
To rest the weary and to soothe the sad,
Doth lesson happier men, and shames at
 least the bad.

LXIX

It came to pass that when he did address
Himself to quit at length this mountain-
 land,
Combined marauders, half-way, barr'd
 egress,

And wasted far and near with glaive and
 brand;
And therefore did he take a trusty band
To traverse Acarnania's forest wide,
In war well season'd, and with labours
 tann'd,
Till he did greet white Achelous' tide,
And from his further bank Ætolia's wolds
 espied. 621

LXX

Where lone Utraikey forms its circling
 cove,
And weary waves retire to gleam at rest,
How brown the foliage of the green hill's
 grove,
Nodding at midnight o'er the calm bay's
 breast,
As winds come lightly whispering from
 the west,
Kissing, not ruffling, the blue deep's
 serene: —
Here Harold was received a welcome
 guest;
Nor did he pass unmoved the gentle scene,
For many a joy could he from Night's soft
 presence glean. 630

LXXI

On the smooth shore the night-fires
 brightly blazed,
The feast was done, the red wine circling
 fast,
And he that unawares had there ygazed
With gaping wonderment had stared
 aghast;
For ere night's midmost, stillest hour
 was past,
The native revels of the troop began;
Each Palikar his sabre from him cast,
And bounding hand in hand, man link'd
 to man,
Yelling their uncouth dirge, long daunced
 the kirtled clan.

LXXII

Childe Harold at a little distance stood,
And view'd, but not displeased, the re-
 velrie, 641
Nor hated harmless mirth, however rude:
In sooth, it was no vulgar sight to see
Their barbarous, yet their not indecent,
 glee,
And, as the flames along their faces
 gleam'd,

Their gestures nimble, dark eyes flashing
 free,
The long wild locks that to their girdles
 stream'd,
While thus in concert they this lay half
 sang, half scream'd: —

1

Tambourgi! Tambourgi! thy 'larum afar
Gives hope to the valiant and promise of war;
All the sons of the mountains arise at the
 note, 651
Chimariot, Illyrian, and dark Suliote!

2

Oh! who is more brave than a dark Suliote,
In his snowy camese and his shaggy capote?
To the wolf and the vulture he leaves his wild
 flock,
And descends to the plain like the stream from
 the rock.

3

Shall the sons of Chimari, who never forgive
The fault of a friend, bid an enemy live?
Let those guns so unerring such vengeance
 forego?
What mark is so fair as the breast of a foe? 660

4

Macedonia sends forth her invincible race;
For a time they abandon the cave and the
 chase:
But those scarfs of blood-red shall be redder,
 before
The sabre is sheathed and the battle is o'er.

5

Then the pirates of Parga that dwell by the
 waves,
And teach the pale Franks what it is to be
 slaves,
Shall leave on the beach the long galley and oar,
And track to his covert the captive on shore.

6

I ask not the pleasures that riches supply,
My sabre shall win what the feeble must buy;
Shall win the young bride with her long flowing
 hair, 671
And many a maid from her mother shall tear.

7

I love the fair face of the maid in her youth,
Her caresses shall lull me, her music shall
 soothe;
Let her bring from the chamber her many-toned
 lyre,
And sing us a song on the fall of her sire.

8

Remember the moment when Previsa fell,
The shrieks of the conquer'd, the conquerors'
 yell;

The roofs that we fired, and the plunder we
 shared,
The wealthy we slaughter'd, the lovely we
 spared. 680

9

I talk not of mercy, I talk not of fear ;
He neither must know who would serve the
 Vizier :
Since the days of our prophet the Crescent ne'er
 saw
A chief ever glorious like Ali Pashaw.

10

Dark Muchtar his son to the Danube is sped,
Let the yellow-hair'd Giaours view his horse-
 tail with dread ;
When his Delhis come dashing in blood o'er the
 banks,
How few shall escape from the Muscovite
 ranks!

11

Selictar, unsheathe then our chief's scimitār :
Tambourgi, thy 'larum gives promise of war ;
Ye mountains, that see us descend to the
 shore, 691
Shall view us as victors, or view us no more !

LXXIII

Fair Greece, sad relic of departed worth !
Immortal, though no more ; though fallen,
 great !
Who now shall lead thy scatter'd children
 forth,
And long accustom'd bondage uncreate ?
Not such thy sons who whilome did
 await,
The hopeless warriors of a willing doom,
In bleak Thermopylæ's sepulchral
 strait —
Oh ! who that gallant spirit shall resume,
Leap from Eurotas' banks, and call thee
 from the tomb ? 701

LXXIV

Spirit of freedom ! when on Phyle's brow
Thou sat'st with Thrasybulus and his
 train,
Couldst thou forbode the dismal hour
 which now
Dims the green beauties of thine Attic
 plain ?
Not thirty tyrants now enforce the chain,
But every carle can lord it o'er thy land;
Nor rise thy sons, but idly rail in vain,
Trembling beneath the scourge of Turkish
 hand,
From birth till death enslaved; in word, in
 deed, unmann'd. 710

LXXV

In all save form alone, how changed !
 and who
That marks the fire still sparkling in each
 eye,
Who but would deem their bosoms
 burn'd anew
With thy unquenchèd beam, lost Liberty !
And many dream withal the hour is nigh
That gives them back their fathers'
 heritage:
For foreign arms and aid they fondly sigh,
Nor solely dare encounter hostile rage,
Or tear their name defiled from Slavery's
 mournful page.

LXXVI

Hereditary bondsmen ! know ye not 720
Who would be free themselves must
 strike the blow ?
By their right arms the conquest must be
 wrought ?
Will Gaul or Muscovite redress ye ? no !
True, they may lay your proud despoilers
 low,
But not for you will Freedom's altars
 flame.
Shades of the Helots, triumph o'er your
 foe !
Greece, change thy lords, thy state is still
 the same;
Thy glorious day is o'er, but not thine years
 of shame.

LXXVII

The city won for Allah from the Giaour,
The Giaour from Othman's race again
 may wrest; 730
And the Serai's impenetrable tower
Receive the fiery Frank, her former
 guest;
Or Wahab's rebel brood, who dared di-
 vest
The prophet's tomb of all its pious spoil,
May wind their path of blood along the
 West;
But ne'er will freedom seek this fated soil,
But slave succeed to slave through years
 of endless toil.

LXXVIII

Yet mark their mirth — ere lenten days
 begin,
That penance which their holy rites pre-
 pare

To shrive from man his weight of mortal
 sin 740
By daily abstinence and nightly prayer;
But ere his sackcloth garb Repentance
 wear,
Some days of joyaunce are decreed to all,
To take of pleasaunce each his secret
 share,
In motley robe to dance at masking ball,
And join the mimic train of merry Carnival.

LXXIX

And whose more rife with merriment
 than thine,
Oh Stamboul, once the empress of their
 reign?
Though turbans now pollute Sophia's
 shrine,
And Greece her very altars eyes in vain;
(Alas, her woes will still pervade my
 strain!) 751
Gay were her minstrels once, for free her
 throng,
All felt the common joy they now must
 feign,
Nor oft I've seen such sight nor heard
 such song,
As woo'd the eye and thrill'd the Bosphorus
 along.

LXXX

Loud was the lightsome tumult on the
 shore,
Oft Music changed but never ceased her
 tone,
And timely echo'd back the measured
 oar,
And rippling waters made a pleasant
 moan:
The Queen of tides on high consenting
 shone, 760
And when a transient breeze swept o'er
 the wave,
'T was, as if darting from her heavenly
 throne,
A brighter glance her form reflected
 gave,
Till sparkling billows seem'd to light the
 banks they lave.

LXXXI

Glanced many a light caïque along the
 foam,
Danced on the shore the daughters of the
 land,

Ne thought had man or maid of rest or
 home,
While many a languid eye and thrilling
 hand
Exchanged the look few bosoms may
 withstand,
Or gently prest, return'd the pressure
 still: 770
Oh Love! young Love! bound in thy
 rosy band,
Let sage or cynic prattle as he will,
These hours, and only these, redeem Life's
 years of ill!

LXXXII

But, midst the throng in merry mas-
 querade,
Lurk there no hearts that throb with
 secret pain,
Even through the closest searment half
 betray'd?
To such the gentle murmurs of the main
Seem to re-echo all they mourn in vain;
To such the gladness of the gamesome
 crowd
Is source of wayward thought and stern
 disdain: 780
How do they loathe the laughter idly
 loud,
And long to change the robe of revel for
 the shroud!

LXXXIII

This must he feel, the true-born son of
 Greece,
If Greece one true-born patriot still can
 boast, —
Not such as prate of war but skulk in
 peace,
The bondsman's peace, who sighs for all
 he lost,
Yet with smooth smile his tyrant can ac-
 cost,
And wield the slavish sickle, not the
 sword:
Ah, Greece, they love thee least who
 owe thee most —
Their birth, their blood, and that sublime
 record 790
Of hero sires who shame thy now degen-
 erated horde!

LXXXIV

When riseth Lacedæmon's hardihood,
When Thebes Epaminondas rears again,

When Athens' children are with hearts
 endued,
When Grecian mothers shall give birth
 to men,
Then may'st thou be restored, but not till
 then.
A thousand years scarce serve to form a
 state;
An hour may lay it in the dust; and
 when
Can man its shatter'd splendour reno-
 vate,
Recall its virtues back and vanquish Time
 and Fate ? 800

LXXXV

And yet how lovely in thine age of woe,
Land of lost gods and godlike men, art
 thou !
Thy vales of evergreen, thy hills of
 snow,
Proclaim thee Nature's varied favourite
 now;
Thy fanes, thy temples to thy surface
 bow,
Commingling slowly with heroic earth,
Broke by the share of every rustic
 plough
(So perish monuments of mortal birth,
So perish all in turn, save well-recorded
 Worth) ; 809

LXXXVI

Save where some solitary column mourns
Above its prostrate brethren of the cave;
Save where Tritonia's airy shrine adorns
Colonna's cliff, and gleams along the
 wave;
Save o'er some warrior's half-forgotten
 grave,
Where the gray stones and unmolested
 grass
Ages, but not oblivion, feebly brave,
While strangers only not regardless pass,
Lingering like me, perchance, to gaze, and
 sigh ' Alas ! '

LXXXVII

Yet are thy skies as blue, thy crags as
 wild;
Sweet are thy groves, and verdant are
 thy fields, 820
Thine olive ripe as when Minerva smiled,
And still his honied wealth Hymettus
 yields;

There the blithe bee his fragrant fortress
 builds,
The freeborn wanderer of thy mountain-
 air;
Apollo still thy long, long summer gilds,
Still in his beam Mendeli's marbles glare;
Art, Glory, Freedom fail, but Nature still
 is fair.

LXXXVIII

Where'er we tread 't is haunted, holy
 ground;
No earth of thine is lost in vulgar mould,
But one vast realm of wonder spreads
 around, 830
And all the Muse's tales seem truly
 told,
Till the sense aches with gazing to be-
 hold
The scenes our earliest dreams have
 dwelt upon:
Each hill and dale, each deepening glen
 and wold
Defies the power which crush'd thy tem-
 ples gone:
Age shakes Athena's tower but spares gray
 Marathon.

LXXXIX

The sun, the soil, but not the slave, the
 same;
Unchanged in all except its foreign
 lord —
Preserves alike its bounds and boundless
 fame
The Battle-field, where Persia's victim
 horde 840
First bow'd beneath the brunt of Hellas'
 sword,
As on the morn to distant Glory dear,
When Marathon became a magic word;
Which utter'd, to the hearer's eye appear
The camp, the host, the fight, the conquer-
 or's career,

XC

The flying Mede, his shaftless broken
 bow;
The fiery Greek, his red pursuing spear;
Mountains above, Earth's, Ocean's plain
 below;
Death in the front, Destruction in the
 rear !
Such was the scene — what now re-
 maineth here ? 850

What sacred trophy marks the hallow'd
 ground,
Recording Freedom's smile and Asia's
 tear ?
The rifled urn, the violated mound,
The dust thy courser's hoof, rude stranger,
 spurns around.

XCI

Yet to the remnants of thy splendour past
Shall pilgrims, pensive, but unwearied,
 throng;
Long shall the voyager, with th' Ionian
 blast,
Hail the bright clime of battle and of song;
Long shall thine annals and immortal
 tongue
Fill with thy fame the youth of many a
 shore; 860
Boast of the aged ! lesson of the young !
Which sages venerate and bards adore,
As Pallas and the Muse unveil their awful
 lore.

XCII

The parted bosom clings to wonted
 home,
If aught that's kindred cheer the wel-
 come hearth:
He that is lonely, hither let him roam,
And gaze complacent on congenial earth.
Greece is no lightsome land of social
 mirth;
But he whom Sadness sootheth may abide,
And scarce regret the region of his birth,
When wandering slow by Delphi's sacred
 side, 871
Or gazing o'er the plains where Greek and
 Persian died.

XCIII

Let such approach this consecrated land,
And pass in peace along the magic waste;
But spare its relics — let no busy hand
Deface the scenes, already how defaced !
Not for such purpose were these altars
 placed;
Revere the remnants nations once
 revered:
So may our country's name be undis-
 graced,
So may'st thou prosper where thy youth
 was rear'd, 880
By every honest joy of love and life en-
 dear'd !

XCIV

For thee, who thus in too protracted
 song
Hast soothed thine idlesse with inglorious
 lays,
Soon shall thy voice be lost amid the
 throng
Of louder minstrels in these later days:
To such resign the strife for fading
 bays;
Ill may such contest now the spirit move
Which heeds nor keen reproach nor partial
 praise,
Since cold each kinder heart that might
 approve,
And none are left to please when none are
 left to love. 890

XCV

Thou too art gone, thou loved and lovely
 one !
Whom youth and youth's affections bound
 to me;
Who did for me what none beside have
 done,
Nor shrank from one albeit unworthy
 thee.
What is my being ? thou hast ceased to
 be !
Nor staid to welcome here thy wanderer
 home,
Who mourns o'er hours which we no
 more shall see —
Would they had never been, or were to
 come !
Would he had ne'er return'd to find fresh
 cause to roam !

XCVI

Oh, ever loving, lovely, and beloved ! 900
How selfish Sorrow ponders on the past,
And clings to thoughts now better far
 removed !
But Time shall tear thy shadow from me
 last.
All thou couldst have of mine, stern
 Death, thou hast, —
The parent, friend, and now the more
 than friend;
Ne'er yet for one thine arrows flew so
 fast,
And grief with grief continuing still to
 blend,
Hath snatch'd the little joy that life had
 yet to lend.

XCVII

Then must I plunge again into the
crowd,
And follow all that Peace disdains to
seek ? 910
Where Revel calls, and Laughter, vainly
loud,
False to the heart, distorts the hollow
cheek,
To leave the flagging spirit doubly weak !
Still o'er the features, which perforce
they cheer,
To feign the pleasure or conceal the
pique,
Smiles form the channel of a future tear,
Or raise the writhing lip with ill-dissembled
sneer.

XCVIII

What is the worst of woes that wait on
age ?
What stamps the wrinkle deeper on the
brow ?
To view each loved one blotted from
life's page, 920
And be alone on earth, as I am now.
Before the Chastener humbly let me bow,
O'er hearts divided and o'er hopes de-
stroy'd:
Roll on, vain days ! full reckless may ye
flow,
Since Time hath reft whate'er my soul
enjoy'd,
And with the ills of Eld mine earlier years
alloy'd.

CANTO THE THIRD

Afin que cette application vous forçât de
penser à autre chose : il n'y a en vérité de re-
mède que celui-là et le temps. — *Lettre du
Roi de Prusse à D'Alembert*, Sept. 7, 1776.

I

Is thy face like thy mother's, my fair
child,
ADA, sole daughter of my house and
heart ?
When last I saw thy young blue eyes
they smiled,
And then we parted, — not as now we
part,
But with a hope. —
Awaking with a start,
The waters heave around me, and on high

The winds lift up their voices: I depart,
Whither I know not ; but the hour 's
gone by,
When Albion's lessening shores could grieve
or glad mine eye.

II

Once more upon the waters, yet once
more ! 10
And the waves bound beneath me as a steed
That knows his rider. Welcome to their
roar !
Swift be their guidance wheresoe'er it
lead !
Though the strain'd mast should quiver
as a reed,
And the rent canvass fluttering strew the
gale,
Still must I on; for I am as a weed,
Flung from the rock on Ocean's foam to
sail
Where'er the surge may sweep, the tem-
pest's breath prevail.

III

In my youth's summer I did sing of One,
The wandering outlaw of his own dark
mind; 20
Again I seize the theme, then but begun,
And bear it with me, as the rushing wind
Bears the cloud onwards: in that Tale I
find
The furrows of long thought, and dried-
up tears,
Which, ebbing, leave a sterile track be-
hind,
O'er which all heavily the journeying
years
Plod the last sands of life, — where not a
flower appears.

IV

Since my young days of passion — joy,
or pain,
Perchance my heart and harp have lost a
string,
And both may jar; it may be that in vain
I would essay as I have sung to sing. 31
Yet, though a dreary strain, to this I
cling,
So that it wean me from the weary dream
Of selfish grief or gladness — so it fling
Forgetfulness around me — it shall seem
To me, though to none else, a not ungrate-
ful theme.

V

He, who grown aged in this world of woe,
In deeds, not years, piercing the depths
　　of life,
So that no wonder waits him; nor below
Can love, or sorrow, fame, ambition,
　　strife,　　　　　　　　　　　　40
Cut to his heart again with the keen knife
Of silent, sharp endurance: he can tell
Why thought seeks refuge in lone caves,
　　yet rife
With airy images, and shapes which dwell
Still unimpair'd, though old, in the soul's
　　haunted cell.

VI

'T is to create, and in creating live
A being more intense, that we endow
With form our fancy, gaining as we give
The life we image, even as I do now.
What am I? Nothing: but not so art
　　thou,　　　　　　　　　　　　50
Soul of my thought! with whom I traverse
　　earth,
Invisible but gazing, as I glow
Mix'd with thy spirit, blended with thy
　　birth,
And feeling still with thee in my crush'd
　　feelings' dearth.

VII

Yet must I think less wildly: — I *have*
　　thought
Too long and darkly, till my brain be-
　　came,
In its own eddy boiling and o'erwrought,
A whirling gulf of phantasy and flame:
And thus, untaught in youth my heart to
　　tame,
My springs of life were poison'd. 'T is
　　too late!　　　　　　　　　　60
Yet am I changed; though still enough
　　the same
In strength to bear what time can not
　　abate,
And feed on bitter fruits without accusing
　　Fate.

VIII

Something too much of this: but now 't is
　　past,
And the spell closes with its silent seal.
Long absent HAROLD re-appears at last, —
He of the breast which fain no more would
　　feel,

Wrung with the wounds which kill not
　　but ne'er heal;
Yet Time, who changes all, had alter'd
　　him
In soul and aspect as in age: years steal
Fire from the mind as vigour from the
　　limb,　　　　　　　　　　　　71
And life's enchanted cup but sparkles near
　　the brim.

IX

His had been quaff'd too quickly, and he
　　found
The dregs were wormwood; but he fill'd
　　again,
And from a purer fount, on holier ground,
And deem'd its spring perpetual — but
　　in vain!
Still round him clung invisibly a chain
Which gall'd for ever, fettering though
　　unseen,
And heavy though it clank'd not; worn
　　with pain,
Which pined although it spoke not, and
　　grew keen,　　　　　　　　　80
Entering with every step he took through
　　many a scene.

X

Secure in guarded coldness, he had mix'd
Again in fancied safety with his kind,
And deem'd his spirit now so firmly
　　fix'd
And sheathed with an invulnerable mind,
That, if no joy, no sorrow lurk'd behind;
And he, as one, might 'midst the many
　　stand
Unheeded, searching through the crowd
　　to find
Fit speculation, such as in strange land
He found in wonder-works of God and Na-
　　ture's hand.　　　　　　　　90

XI

But who can view the ripen'd rose nor
　　seek
To wear it? who can curiously behold
The smoothness and the sheen of beauty's
　　cheek,
Nor feel the heart can never all grow
　　old?
Who can contemplate Fame through
　　clouds unfold
The star which rises o'er her steep, nor
　　climb?

Harold, once more within the vortex,
 roll'd
On with the giddy circle, chasing Time,
Yet with a nobler aim than in his youth's
 fond prime.

XII

But soon he knew himself the most unfit
Of men to herd with Man, with whom he
 held 101
Little in common; — untaught to submit
His thoughts to others, though his soul
 was quell'd
In youth by his own thoughts; still un-
 compell'd,
He would not yield dominion of his mind
To spirits against whom his own rebell'd;
Proud though in desolation; which could
 find
A life within itself, to breathe without
 mankind.

XIII

Where rose the mountains, there to him
 were friends;
Where roll'd the ocean, thereon was his
 home; 110
Where a blue sky, and glowing clime, ex-
 tends,
He had the passion and the power to
 roam;
The desert, forest, cavern, breaker's foam,
Were unto him companionship; they spake
A mutual language, clearer than the tome
Of his land's tongue, which he would oft
 forsake
For Nature's pages glass'd by sunbeams on
 the lake.

XIV

Like the Chaldean he could watch the
 stars,
Till he had peopled them with beings
 bright
As their own beams; and earth, and
 earth-born jars, 120
And human frailties, were forgotten quite.
Could he have kept his spirit to that flight
He had been happy; but this clay will
 sink
Its spark immortal, envying it the light
To which it mounts, as if to break the
 link
That keeps us from yon heaven which woos
 us to its brink.

XV

But in Man's dwellings he became a thing
Restless and worn, and stern and weari-
 some,
Droop'd as a wild-born falcon with clipt
 wing,
To whom the boundless air alone were
 home. 130
Then came his fit again, which to o'ercome,
As eagerly the barr'd-up bird will beat
His breast and beak against his wiry dome
Till the blood tinge his plumage, so the
 heat
Of his impeded soul would through his
 bosom eat.

XVI

Self-exiled Harold wanders forth again,
With nought of hope left, but with less
 of gloom;
The very knowledge that he lived in vain,
That all was over on this side the tomb,
Had made Despair a smilingness assume,
Which, though 't were wild, — as on the
 plunder'd wreck 141
When mariners would madly meet their
 doom
With draughts intemperate on the sink-
 ing deck, —
Did yet inspire a cheer which he forbore to
 check.

XVII

Stop! — for thy tread is on an Empire's
 dust!
An Earthquake's spoil is sepulchred be-
 low!
Is the spot mark'd with no colossal bust,
Nor column trophied for triumphal show?
None; but the moral's truth tells simpler
 so,
As the ground was before, thus let it
 be; — 150
How that red rain hath made the har-
 vest grow!
And is this all the world has gained by
 thee,
Thou first and last of fields, king-making
 Victory?

XVIII

And Harold stands upon this place of
 skulls,
The grave of France, the deadly Water-
 loo!

How in an hour the power which gave
 annuls
Its gifts, transferring fame as fleeting too !
In 'pride of place' here last the eagle
 flew,
Then tore with bloody talon the rent
 plain,
Pierced by the shaft of banded nations
 through ; 160
Ambition's life and labours all were vain ;
He wears the shatter'd links of the world's
 broken chain.

XIX

Fit retribution ! Gaul may champ the
 bit
And foam in fetters ;—but is Earth
 more free ?
Did nations combat to make *One* submit ;
Or league to teach all kings true sover-
 eignty ?
What ! shall reviving Thraldom again be
The patch'd-up idol of enlighten'd days ?
Shall we, who struck the Lion down, shall
 we
Pay the Wolf homage ? proffering lowly
 gaze 170
And servile knees to thrones ? No ; *prove*
 before ye praise !

XX

If not, o'er one fallen despot boast no
 more !
In vain fair cheeks were furrow'd with
 hot tears
For Europe's flowers long rooted up be-
 fore
The trampler of her vineyards ; in vain
 years
Of death, depopulation, bondage, fears,
Have all been borne, and broken by the
 accord
Of roused-up millions : all that most
 endears
Glory, is when the myrtle wreathes a
 sword
Such as Harmodius drew on Athens' tyrant
 lord. 180

XXI

There was a sound of revelry by night,
And Belgium's capital had gather'd then
Her Beauty and her Chivalry, and bright
The lamps shone o'er fair women and
 brave men ;

A thousand hearts beat happily ; and
 when
Music arose with its voluptuous swell,
Soft eyes look'd love to eyes which spake
 again,
And all went merry as a marriage-bell ;—
But hush ! hark ! a deep sound strikes
 like a rising knell !

XXII

Did ye not hear it ?—No ; 't was but the
 wind, 190
Or the car rattling o'er the stony street ;
On with the dance ! let joy be uncon-
 fined ;
No sleep till morn, when Youth and
 Pleasure meet
To chase the glowing Hours with flying
 feet—
But hark !—that heavy sound breaks in
 once more
As if the clouds its echo would repeat ;
And nearer, clearer, deadlier than be-
 fore !
Arm ! Arm ! it is—it is—the cannon's
 opening roar !

XXIII

Within a window'd niche of that high
 hall
Sate Brunswick's fated chieftain ; he did
 hear 200
That sound the first amidst the festival,
And caught its tone with Death's pro-
 phetic ear ;
And when they smiled because he deem'd
 it near,
His heart more truly knew that peal too
 well
Which stretch'd his father on a bloody
 bier,
And roused the vengeance blood alone
 could quell :
He rush'd into the field, and, foremost
 fighting, fell.

XXIV

Ah ! then and there was hurrying to and
 fro,
And gathering tears, and tremblings of
 distress,
And cheeks all pale, which but an hour
 ago 210
Blush'd at the praise of their own love-
 liness ;

And there were sudden partings, such as
 press
The life from out young hearts, and
 choking sighs
Which ne'er might be repeated; who
 could guess
If ever more should meet those mutual
 eyes,
Since upon night so sweet such awful morn
 could rise !

XXV

And there was mounting in hot haste:
 the steed,
The mustering squadron, and the clatter-
 ing car,
Went pouring forward with impetuous
 speed, 219
And swiftly forming in the ranks of war;
And the deep thunder peal on peal afar;
And near, the beat of the alarming drum
Roused up the soldier ere the morning
 star;
While throng'd the citizens with terror
 dumb,
Or whispering, with white lips — ' The foe !
 They come ! they come !'

XXVI

And wild and high the ' Cameron's
 gathering ' rose !
The war-note of Lochiel, which Albyn's
 hills
Have heard, and heard too have her
 Saxon foes: —
How in the noon of night that pibroch
 thrills,
Savage and shrill ! But with the breath
 which fills 230
Their mountain-pipe, so fill the moun-
 taineers
With the fierce native daring which in-
 stils
The stirring memory of a thousand years,
And Evan's, Donald's fame rings in each
 clansman's ears !

XXVII

And Ardennes waves above them her
 green leaves,
Dewy with nature's tear-drops, as they
 pass,
Grieving, if aught inanimate e'er grieves,
Over the unreturning brave, — alas !
Ere evening to be trodden like the grass

Which now beneath them, but above shall
 grow 240
In its next verdure, when this fiery mass
Of living valour, rolling on the foe
And burning with high hope, shall moulder
 cold and low.

XXVIII

Last noon beheld them full of lusty life,
Last eve in Beauty's circle proudly gay,
The midnight brought the signal-sound
 of strife,
The morn the marshalling in arms, — the
 day
Battle's magnificently-stern array !
The thunder-clouds close o'er it, which
 when rent
The earth is cover'd thick with other
 clay, 250
Which her own clay shall cover, heap'd
 and pent,
Rider and horse, — friend, foe, — in one
 red burial blent !

XXIX

Their praise is hymn'd by loftier harps
 than mine;
Yet one I would select from that proud
 throng,
Partly because they blend me with his
 line,
And partly that I did his sire some wrong,
And partly that bright names will hallow
 song;
And his was of the bravest, and when
 shower'd
The death-bolts deadliest the thinn'd files
 along,
Even where the thickest of war's tempest
 lower'd, 260
They reach'd no nobler breast than thine,
 young, gallant Howard !

XXX

There have been tears and breaking hearts
 for thee,
And mine were nothing, had I such to
 give;
But when I stood beneath the fresh green
 tree,
Which living waves where thou didst
 cease to live,
And saw around me the wide field revive
With fruits and fertile promise, and the
 Spring

Come forth her work of gladness to con-
trive,
With all her reckless birds upon the wing,
I turn'd from all she brought to those she
could not bring.　　　270

XXXI

I turn'd to thee, to thousands, of whom
each
And one as all a ghastly gap did make
In his own kind and kindred, whom to
teach
Forgetfulness were mercy for their sake;
The Archangel's trump, not Glory's, must
awake
Those whom they thirst for; though the
sound of Fame
May for a moment soothe, it cannot slake
The fever of vain longing, and the name
So honour'd but assumes a stronger, bit-
terer claim.

XXXII

They mourn, but smile at length; and,
smiling, mourn:　　　280
The tree will wither long before it fall;
The hull drives on, though mast and sail
be torn;
The roof-tree sinks, but moulders on the
hall
In massy hoariness; the ruin'd wall
Stands when its wind-worn battlements
are gone;
The bars survive the captive they enthral;
The day drags through though storms
keep out the sun;
And thus the heart will break, yet brokenly
live on:

XXXIII

Even as a broken mirror, which the
glass
In every fragment multiplies; and makes
A thousand images of one that was,　291
The same, and still the more, the more it
breaks;
And thus the heart will do which not for-
sakes,
Living in shatter'd guise, and still, and
cold,
And bloodless, with its sleepless sorrow
aches,
Yet withers on till all without is old,
Showing no visible sign, for such things are
untold.

XXXIV

There is a very life in our despair,
Vitality of poison, a quick root
Which feeds these deadly branches: for
it were　　　300
As nothing did we die; but Life will suit
Itself to Sorrow's most detested fruit,
Like to the apples on the Dead Sea's
shore,
All ashes to the taste. Did man com-
pute
Existence by enjoyment, and count o'er
Such hours 'gainst years of life, — say,
would he name threescore ?

XXXV

The Psalmist number'd out the years of
man:
They are enough, and if thy tale be *true*,
Thou, who didst grudge him even that
fleeting span,　　　309
More than enough, thou fatal Waterloo !
Millions of tongues record thee, and anew
Their children's lips shall echo them, and
say —
' Here, where the sword united nations
drew,
Our countrymen were warring on that
day ! '
And this is much, and all which will not
pass away.

XXXVI

There sunk the greatest, nor the worst of
men,
Whose spirit antithetically mixt
One moment of the mightiest, and again
On little objects with like firmness fixt,
Extreme in all things ! hadst thou been
betwixt,　　　320
Thy throne had still been thine, or never
been;
For daring made thy rise as fall: thou
seek'st
Even now to re-assume the imperial mien,
And shake again the world, the Thun-
derer of the scene !

XXXVII

Conqueror and captive of the earth art
thou !
She trembles at thee still, and thy wild
name
Was ne'er more bruited in men's minds
than now

That thou art nothing, save the jest of
Fame,
Who woo'd thee once, thy vassal, and
became
The flatterer of thy fierceness, till thou
wert 330
A god unto thyself; nor less the same
To the astounded kingdoms all inert,
Who deem'd thee for a time whate'er thou
didst assert.

XXXVIII

Oh, more or less than man — in high or
low,
Battling with nations, flying from the field;
Now making monarchs' necks thy foot-
stool, now
More than thy meanest soldier taught to
yield:
An empire thou couldst crush, command,
rebuild,
But govern not thy pettiest passion, nor,
However deeply in men's spirits skill'd,
Look through thine own, nor curb the
lust of war, 341
Nor learn that tempted Fate will leave the
loftiest star.

XXXIX

Yet well thy soul hath brook'd the turn-
ing tide
With that untaught innate philosophy,
Which, be it wisdom, coldness, or deep
pride,
Is gall and wormwood to an enemy.
When the whole host of hatred stood
hard by,
To watch and mock thee shrinking, thou
hast smiled
With a sedate and all-enduring eye;
When Fortune fled her spoil'd and favour-
ite child, 350
He stood unbow'd beneath the ills upon him
piled.

XL

Sager than in thy fortunes; for in them
Ambition steel'd thee on too far to show
That just habitual scorn, which could
contemn
Men and their thoughts; 't was wise to
feel, not so
To wear it ever on thy lip and brow,
And spurn the instruments thou wert to
use

Till they were turn'd unto thine over-
throw:
'T is but a worthless world to win or
lose,
So hath it proved to thee and all such lot
who choose. 360

XLI

If, like a tower upon a headlong rock,
Thou hadst been made to stand or fall
alone,
Such scorn of man had help'd to brave
the shock;
But men's thoughts were the steps which
paved thy throne,
Their admiration thy best weapon shone;
The part of Philip's son was thine, not
then
(Unless aside thy purple had been thrown)
Like stern Diogenes to mock at men;
For sceptred cynics earth were far too
wide a den.

XLII

But quiet to quick bosoms is a hell, 370
And *there* hath been thy bane; there is a
fire
And motion of the soul which will not
dwell
In its own narrow being, but aspire
Beyond the fitting medium of desire;
And, but once kindled, quenchless ever-
more,
Preys upon high adventure, nor can tire
Of aught but rest; a fever at the core,
Fatal to him who bears, to all who ever bore.

XLIII

This makes the madmen who have made
men mad
By their contagion, — Conquerors and
Kings, 380
Founders of sects and systems, to whom
add
Sophists, Bards, Statesmen, all unquiet
things
Which stir too strongly the soul's secret
springs,
And are themselves the fools to those
they fool;
Envied, yet how unenviable ! what stings
Are theirs ! One breast laid open were a
school
Which would unteach mankind the lust to
shine or rule.

XLIV

Their breath is agitation, and their life
A storm whereon they ride, to sink at
last;
And yet so nursed and bigoted to strife,
That should their days, surviving perils
past, 391
Melt to calm twilight, they feel overcast
With sorrow and supineness, and so die;
Even as a flame unfed which runs to
waste
With its own flickering, or a sword laid
by,
Which eats into itself and rusts inglori-
ously.

XLV

He who ascends to mountain-tops, shall
find
The loftiest peaks most wrapt in clouds
and snow;
He who surpasses or subdues mankind,
Must look down on the hate of those be-
low. 400
Though high *above* the sun of glory glow,
And far *beneath* the earth and ocean
spread,
Round him are icy rocks, and loudly blow
Contending tempests on his naked head,
And thus reward the toils which to those
summits led.

XLVI

Away with these ! true Wisdom's world
will be
Within its own creation, or in thine,
Maternal Nature ! for who teems like
thee,
Thus on the banks of thy majestic Rhine?
There Harold gazes on a work divine,
A blending of all beauties, — streams and
dells, 411
Fruit, foliage, crag, wood, cornfield,
mountain, vine,
And chiefless castles breathing stern fare-
wells
From gray but leafy walls, where Ruin
greenly dwells.

XLVII

And there they stand, as stands a lofty
mind,
Worn, but unstooping to the baser crowd,
All tenantless, save to the crannying
wind,

Or holding dark communion with the
cloud.
There was a day when they were young
and proud,
Banners on high, and battles pass'd be-
low; 420
But they who fought are in a bloody
shroud,
And those which waved are shredless dust
ere now,
And the bleak battlements shall bear no
future blow.

XLVIII

Beneath these battlements, within those
walls,
Power dwelt amidst her passions; in
proud state
Each robber chief upheld his armèd halls,
Doing his evil will, nor less elate
Than mightier heroes of a longer date.
What want these outlaws conquerors
should have,
But History's purchased page to call
them great ? 430
A wider space, an ornamented grave ?
Their hopes were not less warm, their souls
were full as brave.

XLIX

In their baronial feuds and single fields,
What deeds of prowess unrecorded died !
And Love, which lent a blazon to their
shields
With emblems well devised by amorous
pride,
Through all the mail of iron hearts would
glide:
But still their flame was fierceness, and
drew on
Keen contest and destruction near allied;
And many a tower for some fair mischief
won, 440
Saw the discolour'd Rhine beneath its ruin
run.

L

But Thou, exulting and abounding river !
Making thy waves a blessing as they flow
Through banks whose beauty would en-
dure for ever,
Could man but leave thy bright creation
so,
Nor its fair promise from the surface
mow

With the sharp scythe of conflict, — then
 to see
Thy valley of sweet waters, were to know
Earth paved like Heaven; and to seem
 such to me,
Even now what wants thy stream? — that it
 should Lethe be. 450

LI

A thousand battles have assail'd thy
 banks,
But these and half their fame have pass'd
 away,
And Slaughter heap'd on high his welter-
 ing ranks;
Their very graves are gone, and what are
 they ?
Thy tide wash'd down the blood of yester-
 day,
And all was stainless, and on thy clear
 stream
Glass'd with its dancing light the sunny
 ray;
But o'er the blacken'd memory's blight-
 ing dream
Thy waves would vainly roll, all sweeping
 as they seem.

LII

Thus Harold inly said, and pass'd along,
Yet not insensibly to all which here 461
Awoke the jocund birds to early song
In glens which might have made even
 exile dear.
Though on his brow were graven lines
 austere,
And tranquil sternness which had ta'en
 the place
Of feelings fierier far but less severe,
Joy was not always absent from his
 face,
But o'er it in such scenes would steal with
 transient trace.

LIII

Nor was all love shut from him, though
 his days
Of passion had consumed themselves to
 dust. 470
It is in vain that we would coldly gaze
On such as smile upon us; the heart must
Leap kindly back to kindness, though
 disgust
Hath wean'd it from all wordlings: thus
 he felt,

For there was soft remembrance, and
 sweet trust
In one fond breast to which his own would
 melt,
And in its tenderer hour on that his bosom
 dwelt.

LIV

And he had learn'd to love (I know not
 why,
For this in such as him seems strange of
 mood) 479
The helpless looks of blooming infancy,
Even in its earliest nurture; what subdued,
To change like this, a mind so far imbued
With scorn of man, it little boots to know;
But thus it was; and though in solitude
Small power the nipp'd affections have
 to grow,
In him this glow'd when all beside had
 ceased to glow.

LV

And there was one soft breast, as hath
 been said,
Which unto his was bound by stronger ties
Than the church links withal; and, though
 unwed,
That love was pure, and, far above dis-
 guise, 490
Had stood the test of mortal enmities
Still undivided, and cemented more
By peril, dreaded most in female eyes;
But this was firm, and from a foreign shore
Well to that heart might his these absent
 greetings pour !

1

The castled crag of Drachenfels
Frowns o'er the wide and winding Rhine,
Whose breast of waters broadly swells
Between the banks which bear the vine ;
And hills all rich with blossom'd trees, 500
And fields which promise corn and wine,
And scatter'd cities crowning these,
Whose far white walls along them shine,
Have strew'd a scene, which I should see
With double joy wert *thou* with me.

2

And peasant girls, with deep blue eyes
And hands which offer early flowers,
Walk smiling o'er this paradise ;
Above, the frequent feudal towers
Through green leaves lift their walls of gray ;
And many a rock which steeply lowers, 511
And noble arch in proud decay,
Look o'er this vale of vintage-bowers ;

But one thing want these banks of Rhine,—
Thy gentle hand to clasp in mine !

3

I send the lilies given to me ;
Though long before thy hand they touch,
I know that they must wither'd be,
But yet reject them not as such ;
For I have cherish'd them as dear,　　520
Because they yet may meet thine eye,
And guide thy soul to mine even here,
When thou behold'st them, drooping nigh,
And know'st them gather'd by the Rhine,
And offer'd from my heart to thine !

4

The river nobly foams and flows,
The charm of this enchanted ground,
And all its thousand turns disclose
Some fresher beauty varying round :
The haughtiest breast its wish might
　　bound　　530
Through life to dwell delighted here ;
Nor could on earth a spot be found
To nature and to me so dear,
Could thy dear eyes in following mine
Still sweeten more these banks of Rhine !

LVI

By Coblentz, on a rise of gentle ground,
There is a small and simple pyramid,
Crowning the summit of the verdant
　　mound;
Beneath its base are heroes' ashes hid,
Our enemy's, — but let not that forbid
Honour to Marceau ! o'er whose early
　　tomb　　541
Tears, big tears, gush'd from the rough
　　soldier's lid,
Lamenting and yet envying such a doom,
Falling for France whose rights he battled
　　to resume.

LVII

Brief, brave, and glorious was his young
　　career, —
His mourners were two hosts, his friends
　　and foes;
And fitly may the stranger lingering
　　here
Pray for his gallant spirit's bright repose;
For he was Freedom's champion, one of
　　those,
The few in number, who had not o'er-
　　stept　　550
The charter to chastise which she bestows
On such as wield her weapons; he had kept
The whiteness of his soul, and thus men
　　o'er him wept.

LVIII

Here Ehrenbreitstein, with her shatter'd
　　wall
Black with the miner's blast, upon her
　　height
Yet shows of what she was, when shell
　　and ball
Rebounding idly on her strength did
　　light, —
A tower of victory! from whence the flight
Of baffled foes was watch'd along the
　　plain:
But Peace destroy'd what War could
　　never blight,　　560
And laid those proud roofs bare to Sum-
　　mer's rain,
On which the iron shower for years had
　　pour'd in vain.

LIX

Adieu to thee, fair Rhine ! How long de-
　　lighted
The stranger fain would linger on his
　　way !
Thine is a scene alike where souls united
Or lonely Contemplation thus might
　　stray;
And could the ceaseless vultures cease to
　　prey
On self-condemning bosoms, it were here,
Where Nature, nor too sombre nor too
　　gay,
Wild but not rude, awful yet not austere,
Is to the mellow Earth as Autumn to the
　　year.　　571

LX

Adieu to thee again ! a vain adieu !
There can be no farewell to scene like
　　thine;
The mind is colour'd by thy every hue;
And if reluctantly the eyes resign
Their cherish'd gaze upon thee, lovely
　　Rhine,
'T is with the thankful glance of parting
　　praise;
More mighty spots may rise, more glaring
　　shine,
But none unite in one attaching maze
The brilliant, fair, and soft, — the glories
　　of old days,　　580

LXI

The negligently grand, the fruitful bloom
Of coming ripeness, the white city's sheen,

The rolling stream, the precipice's gloom,
The forest's growth, and Gothic walls be-
 tween,
The wild rocks shaped as they had turrets
 been
In mockery of man's art; and these
 withal
A race of faces happy as the scene,
Whose fertile bounties here extend to all,
Still springing o'er thy banks, though Em-
 pires near them fall.

LXII

But these recede. Above me are the
 Alps, 590
The palaces of Nature, whose vast walls
Have pinnacled in clouds their snowy
 scalps,
And throned Eternity in icy halls
Of cold sublimity, where forms and falls
The avalanche — the thunderbolt of snow!
All that expands the spirit, yet appals,
Gather around these summits, as to show
How Earth may pierce to Heaven, yet leave
 vain man below.

LXIII

But ere these matchless heights I dare to
 scan,
There is a spot should not be pass'd in
 vain, — 600
Morat! the proud, the patriot field!
 where man
May gaze on ghastly trophies of the slain,
Nor blush for those who conquer'd on
 that plain;
Here Burgundy bequeath'd his tombless
 host,
A bony heap, through ages to remain,
Themselves their monument; — the Sty-
 gian coast
Unsepulchred they roam'd, and shriek'd
 each wandering ghost.

LXIV

While Waterloo with Cannæ's carnage
 vies,
Morat and Marathon twin names shall
 stand;
They were true Glory's stainless victories,
Won by the unambitious heart and
 hand 611
Of a proud, brotherly, and civic band,
All unbought champions in no princely
 cause

Of vice-entail'd Corruption; they no land
Doom'd to bewail the blasphemy of laws
Making kings' rights divine, by some Dra-
 conic clause.

LXV

By a lone wall a lonelier column rears
A gray and grief-worn aspect of old
 days;
'T is the last remnant of the wreck of
 years,
And looks as with the wild-bewildered
 gaze 620
Of one to stone converted by amaze,
Yet still with consciousness; and there it
 stands
Making a marvel that it not decays,
When the coeval pride of human hands,
Levell'd Aventicum, hath strew'd her sub-
 ject lands.

LXVI

And there — oh! sweet and sacred be the
 name! —
Julia, the daughter, the devoted, gave
Her youth to Heaven; her heart, beneath
 a claim
Nearest to Heaven's, broke o'er a father's
 grave.
Justice is sworn 'gainst tears, and hers
 would crave 630
The life she lived in; but the judge was
 just,
And then she died on him she could not
 save.
Their tomb was simple, and without a
 bust,
And held within their urn one mind, one
 heart, one dust.

LXVII

But these are deeds which should not
 pass away,
And names that must not wither, though
 the earth
Forgets her empires with a just decay,
The enslavers and the enslaved, their
 death and birth;
The high, the mountain-majesty of worth
Should be, and shall, survivor of its
 woe, 640
And from its immortality look forth
In the sun's face, like yonder Alpine
 snow,
Imperishably pure beyond all things below.

LXVIII

Lake Leman woos me with its crystal
 face,
The mirror where the stars and mountains
 view
The stillness of their aspect in each trace
Its clear depth yields of their far height
 and hue.
There is too much of man here, to look
 through
With a fit mind the might which I be-
 hold;
But soon in me shall Loneliness renew
Thoughts hid, but not less cherish'd than
 of old, 651
Ere mingling with the herd had penn'd me
 in their fold.

LXIX

To fly from, need not be to hate, man-
 kind:
All are not fit with them to stir and toil,
Nor is it discontent to keep the mind
Deep in its fountain, lest it overboil
In the hot throng, where we become the
 spoil
Of our infection, till too late and long
We may deplore and struggle with the
 coil,
In wretched interchange of wrong for
 wrong 660
Midst a contentious world, striving where
 none are strong.

LXX

There, in a moment, we may plunge our
 years
In fatal penitence, and in the blight
Of our own soul turn all our blood to
 tears,
And colour things to come with hues of
 Night;
The race of life becomes a hopeless flight
To those that walk in darkness: on the
 sea,
The boldest steer but where their ports
 invite,
But there are wanderers o'er Eternity
Whose bark drives on and on, and anchor'd
 ne'er shall be. 670

LXXI

Is it not better, then, to be alone,
And love Earth only for its earthly sake?
By the blue rushing of the arrowy Rhone,

Or the pure bosom of its nursing lake,
Which feeds it as a mother who doth
 make
A fair but froward infant her own care,
Kissing its cries away as these awake; —
Is it not better thus our lives to wear,
Than join the crushing crowd, doom'd to
 inflict or bear?

LXXII

I live not in myself, but I become 680
Portion of that around me; and to me
High mountains are a feeling, but the
 hum
Of human cities torture: I can see
Nothing to loathe in nature, save to be
A link reluctant in a fleshly chain,
Class'd among creatures, when the soul
 can flee,
And with the sky, the peak, the heaving
 plain
Of ocean, or the stars, mingle, and not in
 vain.

LXXIII

And thus I am absorb'd, and this is life:
I look upon the peopled desert past, 690
As on a place of agony and strife,
Where, for some sin, to sorrow I was
 cast,
To act and suffer, but remount at last
With a fresh pinion; which I feel to
 spring,
Though young, yet waxing vigorous, as
 the blast
Which it would cope with, on delighted
 wing,
Spurning the clay-cold bonds which round
 our being cling.

LXXIV

And when at length the mind shall be
 all free
From what it hates in this degraded form,
Reft of its carnal life, save what shall
 be 700
Existent happier in the fly and worm, —
When elements to elements conform,
And dust is as it should be, shall I not
Feel all I see, less dazzling, but more
 warm?
The bodiless thought? the Spirit of each
 spot?
Of which, even now, I share at times the
 immortal lot?

LXXV

Are not the mountains, waves, and skies,
 a part
Of me and of my soul, as I of them?
Is not the love of these deep in my heart
With a pure passion? should I not con-
 temn 710
All objects, if compared with these? and
 stem
A tide of suffering, rather than forego
Such feelings for the hard and worldly
 phlegm
Of those whose eyes are only turn'd be-
 low,
Gazing upon the ground, with thoughts
 which dare not glow?

LXXVI

But this is not my theme; and I return
To that which is immediate, and require
Those who find contemplation in the urn,
To look on One whose dust was once all
 fire,
A native of the land where I respire 720
The clear air for a while (a passing guest,
Where he became a being) whose desire
Was to be glorious; — 't was a foolish
 quest,
The which to gain and keep he sacrificed all
 rest.

LXXVII

Here the self-torturing sophist, wild
 Rousseau,
The apostle of affliction, he who threw
Enchantment over passion, and from woe
Wrung overwhelming eloquence, first
 drew
The breath which made him wretched;
 yet he knew
How to make madness beautiful, and
 cast 730
O'er erring deeds and thoughts a heavenly
 hue
Of words, like sunbeams, dazzling as they
 past
The eyes, which o'er them shed tears feel-
 ingly and fast.

LXXVIII

His love was passion's essence — as a tree
On fire by lightning; with ethereal flame
Kindled he was, and blasted; for to be
Thus, and enamour'd, were in him the
 same.

But his was not the love of living dame,
Nor of the dead who rise upon our dreams,
But of ideal beauty, which became 740
In him existence, and o'erflowing teems
Along his burning page, distemper'd though
 it seems.

LXXIX

This breathed itself to life in Julie, *this*
Invested her with all that's wild and
 sweet;
This hallow'd, too, the memorable kiss
Which every morn his fever'd lip would
 greet,
From hers who but with friendship his
 would meet;
But to that gentle touch, through brain
 and breast
Flash'd the thrill'd spirit's love-devouring
 heat;
In that absorbing sigh perchance more
 blest 750
Than vulgar minds may be with all they
 seek possest.

LXXX

His life was one long war with self-sought
 foes,
Or friends by him self-banish'd; for his
 mind
Had grown Suspicion's sanctuary, and
 chose,
For its own cruel sacrifice, the kind
'Gainst whom he raged with fury strange
 and blind.
But he was phrensied, — wherefore, who
 may know?
Since cause might be which skill could
 never find;
But he was phrensied by disease or woe
To that worst pitch of all, which wears a
 reasoning show. 760

LXXXI

For then he was inspired, and from him
 came,
As from the Pythian's mystic cave of
 yore,
Those oracles which set the world in
 flame,
Nor ceased to burn till kingdoms were
 no more:
Did he not this for France, which lay be-
 fore
Bow'd to the inborn tyranny of years?

Broken and trembling to the yoke she
 bore,
Till by the voice of him and his compeers
Roused up to too much wrath, which follows
 o'ergrown fears?

LXXXII

They made themselves a fearful monu-
 ment! 770
The wreck of old opinions, things which
 grew,
Breathed from the birth of time: the veil
 they rent,
And what behind it lay, all earth shall
 view.
But good with ill they also overthrew,
Leaving but ruins, wherewith to rebuild
Upon the same foundation, and renew
Dungeons and thrones, which the same
 hour re-fill'd
As heretofore because ambition was self-
 will'd.

LXXXIII

But this will not endure, nor be en-
 dured;
Mankind have felt their strength, and
 made it felt! 780
They might have used it better, but, al-
 lured
By their new vigour, sternly have they
 dealt
On one another; pity ceased to melt
With her once natural charities. But they,
Who in oppression's darkness caved had
 dwelt,
They were not eagles, nourish'd with the
 day;
What marvel then, at times, if they mis-
 took their prey?

LXXXIV

What deep wounds ever closed without
 a scar?
The heart's bleed longest, and but heal
 to wear
That which disfigures it; and they who
 war 790
With their own hopes and have been van-
 quish'd, bear
Silence, but not submission. In his lair
Fix'd Passion holds his breath, until the
 hour
Which shall atone for years; none need
 despair:

It came, it cometh, and will come, — the
 power
To punish or forgive — in *one* we shall be
 slower.

LXXXV

Clear, placid Leman! thy contrasted lake,
With the wild world I dwelt in, is a
 thing
Which warns me with its stillness to for-
 sake
Earth's troubled waters for a purer
 spring. 800
This quiet sail is as a noiseless wing
To waft me from distraction; once I
 loved
Torn ocean's roar, but thy soft murmur-
 ing
Sounds sweet as if a Sister's voice re-
 proved,
That I with stern delights should e'er have
 been so moved.

LXXXVI

It is the hush of night, and all between
Thy margin and the mountains, dusk, yet
 clear,
Mellow'd and mingling, yet distinctly
 seen,
Save darken'd Jura, whose capt heights
 appear
Precipitously steep; and drawing near,
There breathes a living fragrance from
 the shore, 811
Of flowers yet fresh with childhood; on
 the ear
Drops the light drip of the suspended
 oar,
Or chirps the grasshopper one good-night
 carol more; —

LXXXVII

He is an evening reveller, who makes
His life an infancy, and sings his fill; —
At intervals, some bird from out the
 brakes
Starts into voice a moment, then is still.
There seems a floating whisper on the
 hill,
But that is fancy, for the starlight dews
All silently their tears of love instil, 821
Weeping themselves away, till they in-
 fuse
Deep into Nature's breast the spirit of her
 hues.

LXXXVIII

Ye stars, which are the poetry of heaven !
If in your bright leaves we would read
 the fate
Of men and empires, — 't is to be for-
 given,
That in our aspirations to be great,
Our destinies o'erleap their mortal state,
And claim a kindred with you; for ye are
A beauty and a mystery, and create 830
In us such love and reverence from afar
That fortune, fame, power, life, have named
 themselves a star.

LXXXIX

All heaven and earth are still — though
 not in sleep,
But breathless, as we grow when feeling
 most;
And silent, as we stand in thoughts too
 deep: —
All heaven and earth are still. From
 the high host
Of stars to the lull'd lake and mountain-
 coast,
All is concentred in a life intense,
Where not a beam nor air nor leaf is lost,
But hath a part of being, and a sense 840
Of that which is of all Creator and defence.

XC

Then stirs the feeling infinite, so felt
In solitude where we are *least* alone;
A truth, which through our being then
 doth melt
And purifies from self: it is a tone,
The soul and source of music, which
 makes known
Eternal harmony, and sheds a charm,
Like to the fabled Cytherea's zone,
Binding all things with beauty; —'t would
 disarm
The spectre Death, had he substantial power
 to harm. 850

XCI

Not vainly did the early Persian make
His altar the high places and the peak
Of earth-o'ergazing mountains, and thus
 take
A fit and unwall'd temple, there to seek
The Spirit, in whose honour shrines are
 weak
Uprear'd of human hands. Come, and
 compare

Columns and idol-dwellings, Goth or
 Greek,
With Nature's realms of worship, earth
 and air,
Nor fix on fond abodes to circumscribe thy
 pray'r !

XCII

The sky is changed ! — and such a
 change ! Oh night, 860
And storm, and darkness, ye are won-
 drous strong,
Yet lovely in your strength, as is the
 light
Of a dark eye in woman ! Far along,
From peak to peak the rattling crags
 among,
Leaps the live thunder ! Not from one
 lone cloud,
But every mountain now hath found a
 tongue,
And Jura answers, through her misty
 shroud,
Back to the joyous Alps who call to her
 aloud !

XCIII

And this is in the night: — Most glorious
 night !
Thou wert not sent for slumber ! let me
 be 870
A sharer in thy fierce and far delight,
A portion of the tempest and of thee !
How the lit lake shines, a phosphoric sea,
And the big rain comes dancing to the
 earth !
And now again 't is black, — and now,
 the glee
Of the loud hills shakes with its moun-
 tain-mirth,
As if they did rejoice o'er a young earth-
 quake's birth.

XCIV

Now, where the swift Rhone cleaves his
 way between
Heights which appear as lovers who have
 parted
In hate, whose mining depths so inter-
 vene 880
That they can meet no more, though
 broken-hearted !
Though in their souls, which thus each
 other thwarted,
Love was the very root of the fond rage

Which blighted their life's bloom and
 then departed —
Itself expired, but leaving them an age
Of years all winters, war within themselves
 to wage: —

XCV

Now, where the quick Rhone thus hath
 cleft his way,
The mightiest of the storms hath ta'en
 his stand:
For here, not one, but many, make their
 play,
And fling their thunder-bolts from hand
 to hand, 890
Flashing and cast around. Of all the
 band,
The brightest through these parted hills
 hath fork'd
His lightnings, as if he did understand,
That in such gaps as desolation work'd,
There the hot shaft should blast whatever
 therein lurk'd.

XCVI

Sky, mountains, river, winds, lake, light-
 nings ! ye,
With night, and clouds, and thunder, and
 a soul
To make these felt and feeling, well
 may be
Things that have made me watchful; the
 far roll
Of your departing voices, is the knoll 900
Of what in me is sleepless, — if I rest.
But where of ye, oh tempests, is the goal ?
Are ye like those within the human
 breast,
Or do ye find at length, like eagles, some
 high nest ?

XCVII

Could I embody and unbosom now
That which is most within me, — could I
 wreak
My thoughts upon expression, and thus
 throw
Soul, heart, mind, passions, feelings,
 strong or weak,
All that I would have sought, and all I
 seek,
Bear, know, feel and yet breathe — into
 one word, 910
And that one word were Lightning, I
 would speak;

But as it is, I live and die unheard,
With a most voiceless thought, sheathing
 it as a sword.

XCVIII

The morn is up again, the dewy morn,
With breath all incense and with cheek
 all bloom,
Laughing the clouds away with playful
 scorn,
And living as if earth contain'd no
 tomb, —
And glowing into day. We may resume
The march of our existence; and thus I,
Still on thy shores, fair Leman ! may
 find room 920
And food for meditation, nor pass by
Much that may give us pause if ponder'd
 fittingly.

XCIX

Clarens, sweet Clarens, birthplace of
 deep Love !
Thine air is the young breath of pas-
 sionate thought,
Thy trees take root in Love; the snows
 above,
The very Glaciers have his colours caught,
And sunset into rose-hues sees them
 wrought
By rays which sleep there lovingly: the
 rocks,
The permanent crags, tell here of Love,
 who sought
In them a refuge from the worldly
 shocks, 930
Which stir and sting the soul with hope
 that woos, then mocks.

C

Clarens ! by heavenly feet thy paths are
 trod, —
Undying Love's, who here ascends a
 throne
To which the steps are mountains; where
 the god
Is a pervading life and light, — so shown
Not on those summits solely, nor alone
In the still cave and forest; o'er the flower
His eye is sparkling and his breath hath
 blown,
His soft and summer breath, whose ten-
 der power
Passes the strength of storms in their most
 desolate hour. 940

CI

All things are here of *him;* from the
 black pines
Which are his shade on high, and the
 loud roar
Of torrents where he listeneth, to the vines
Which slope his green path downward to
 the shore,
Where the bow'd waters meet him, and
 adore,
Kissing his feet with murmurs; and the
 wood,
The covert of old trees with trunks all
 hoar,
But light leaves, young as joy, stands
 where it stood,
Offering to him and his a populous soli-
 tude, —

CII

A populous solitude of bees and birds, 950
And fairy - form'd and many - colour'd
 things,
Who worship him with notes more sweet
 than words,
And innocently open their glad wings,
Fearless and full of life: the gush of
 springs,
And fall of lofty fountains, and the bend
Of stirring branches, and the bud which
 brings
The swiftest thought of beauty, here ex-
 tend,
Mingling, and made by Love, unto one
 mighty end.

CIII

He who hath loved not, here would learn
 that lore,
And make his heart a spirit; he who
 knows 960
That tender mystery, will love the more,
For this is Love's recess, where vain men's
 woes
And the world's waste have driven him
 far from those,
For 't is his nature to advance or die;
He stands not still, but or decays or grows
Into a boundless blessing, which may vie
With the immortal lights in its eternity !

CIV

'T was not for fiction chose Rousseau this
 spot,
Peopling it with affections; but he found

It was the scene which passion must allot
To the mind's purified beings; 't was the
 ground 971
Where early Love his Psyche's zone un-
 bound,
And hallow'd it with loveliness. 'T is lone,
And wonderful, and deep, and hath a
 sound,
And sense, and sight of sweetness; here
 the Rhone
Hath spread himself a couch, the Alps have
 rear'd a throne.

CV

Lausanne and Ferney, ye have been the
 abodes
Of names which unto you bequeath'd a
 name;
Mortals, who sought and found, by dan-
 gerous roads,
A path to perpetuity of fame: 980
They were gigantic minds, and their
 steep aim
Was, Titan-like, on daring doubts to pile
Thoughts which should call down thunder
 and the flame
Of Heaven, again assail'd, if Heaven the
 while
On man and man's research could deign do
 more than smile.

CVI

The one was fire and fickleness, a child,
Most mutable in wishes, but in mind
A wit as various, — gay, grave, sage, or
 wild, —
Historian, bard, philosopher, combined.
He multiplied himself among mankind,
The Proteus of their talents; but his own
Breathed most in ridicule, — which, as
 the wind, 992
Blew where it listed, laying all things
 prone, —
Now to o'erthrow a fool, and now to shake
 a throne.

CVII

The other, deep and slow, exhausting
 thought,
And hiving wisdom with each studious
 year,
In meditation dwelt, with learning
 wrought,
And shaped his weapon with an edge
 severe,

Sapping a solemn creed with solemn
 sneer;
The lord of irony, — that master-spell,
Which stung his foes to wrath which grew
 from fear, 1001
And doom'd him to the zealot's ready
 Hell,
Which answers to all doubts so eloquently
 well.

CVIII

Yet, peace be with their ashes for by
 them,
If merited, the penalty is paid;
It is not ours to judge, far less condemn;
The hour must come when such things
 shall be made
Known unto all, — or hope and dread
 allay'd
By slumber, on one pillow, — in the dust,
Which, thus much we are sure, must lie
 decay'd; 1010
And when it shall revive, as is our trust,
'T will be to be forgiven, or suffer what is
 just.

CIX

But let me quit man's works again to
 read
His Maker's, spread around me, and sus-
 pend
This page, which from my reveries I
 feed
Until it seems prolonging without end.
The clouds above me to the white Alps
 tend,
And I must pierce them, and survey
 whate'er
May be permitted, as my steps I bend
To their most great and growing region,
 where 1020
The earth to her embrace compels the
 powers of air.

CX

Italia ! too, Italia ! looking on thee,
Full flashes on the soul the light of ages,
Since the fierce Carthaginian almost won
 thee,
To the last halo of the chiefs and sages
Who glorify thy consecrated pages;
Thou wert the throne and grave of em-
 pires; still
The fount, at which the panting mind
 assuages

Her thirst of knowledge, quaffing there
 her fill,
Flows from the eternal source of Rome's
 imperial hill. 1030

CXI

Thus far have I proceeded in a theme
Renew'd with no kind auspices: — to feel
We are not what we have been, and to
 deem
We are not what we should be, and to
 steel
The heart against itself; and to conceal,
With a proud caution, love, or hate, or
 aught, —
Passion or feeling, purpose, grief, or
 zeal, —
Which is the tyrant spirit of our thought,
Is a stern task of soul; — no matter — it
 is taught.

CXII

And for these words, thus woven into
 song, 1040
It may be that they are a harmless wile, —
The colouring of the scenes which fleet
 along,
Which I would seize, in passing, to be-
 guile
My breast, or that of others, for a while.
Fame is the thirst of youth, — but I am
 not
So young as to regard men's frown or
 smile
As loss or guerdon of a glorious lot;
I stood and stand alone, — remember'd or
 forgot.

CXIII

I have not loved the world, nor the world
 me;
I have not flatter'd its rank breath, nor
 bow'd 1050
To its idolatries a patient knee,
Nor coin'd my cheek to smiles, nor cried
 aloud
In worship of an echo; in the crowd
They could not deem me one of such: I
 stood
Among them, but not of them; in a
 shroud
Of thoughts which were not their
 thoughts, and still could,
Had I not filed my mind, which thus itself
 subdued.

CXIV

I have not loved the world, nor the world
 me, —
But let us part fair foes; I do believe,
Though I have found them not, that there
 may be 1060
Words which are things, hopes which will
 not deceive,
And virtues which are merciful nor weave
Snares for the failing: I would also deem
O'er others' griefs that some sincerely
 grieve;
That two, or one, are almost what they
 seem,
That goodness is no name and happiness
 no dream.

CXV

My daughter ! with thy name this song
 begun —
My daughter ! with thy name thus much
 shall end —
I see thee not, I hear thee not, but none
Can be so wrapt in thee; thou art the
 friend 1070
To whom the shadows of far years ex-
 tend:
Albeit my brow thou never shouldst be-
 hold,
My voice shall with thy future visions
 blend,
And reach into thy heart, — when mine
 is cold, —
A token and a tone even from thy father's
 mould.

CXVI

To aid thy mind's development, to watch
Thy dawn of little joys, to sit and see
Almost thy very growth, to view thee catch
Knowledge of objects, wonders yet to
 thee !
To hold thee lightly on a gentle knee,
And print on thy soft cheek a parent's
 kiss, — 1081
This, it should seem, was not reserved for
 me;
Yet this was in my nature: — as it is,
I know not what is there, yet something
 like to this.

CXVII

Yet, though dull Hate as duty should be
 taught,
I know that thou wilt love me; though
 my name

Should be shut from thee, as a spell still
 fraught
With desolation, and a broken claim;
Though the grave closed between us, —
 't were the same,
I know that thou wilt love me; though
 to drain 1090
My blood from out thy being were an
 aim
And an attainment, all would be in
 vain, —
Still thou wouldst love me, still that more
 than life retain.

CXVIII

The child of love, though born in bitter-
 ness
And nurtured in convulsion, — of thy sire
These were the elements, and thine no
 less.
As yet such are around thee, but thy
 fire
Shall be more temper'd and thy hope far
 higher.
Sweet be thy cradled slumbers ! O'er the
 sea,
And from the mountains where I now
 respire, 1100
Fain would I waft such blessing upon
 thee,
As, with a sigh, I deem thou mightst have
 been to me !

CANTO THE FOURTH

Visto ho Toscana, Lombardia, Romagna,
Quel Monte che divide, e quel che serra
Italia, e un mare e l' altro, che la bagna.
 ARIOSTO, *Satira* iii.

VENICE, *January* 2, 1818.

TO JOHN HOBHOUSE, ESQ., A. M., F. R. S., &c.

MY DEAR HOBHOUSE, —

After an interval of eight years between
the composition of the first and last cantos of
Childe Harold, the conclusion of the poem is
about to be submitted to the public. In part-
ing with so old a friend, it is not extraordinary
that I should recur to one still older and better,
— to one who has beheld the birth and death
of the other, and to whom I am far more in-
debted for the social advantages of an enlight-
ened friendship, than — though not ungrateful
— I can, or could be, to *Childe Harold*, for any
public favour reflected through the poem on
the poet, — to one, whom I have known long,

and accompanied far, whom I have found wakeful over my sickness and kind in my sorrow, glad in my prosperity and firm in my adversity, true in counsel and trusty in peril, — to a friend often tried and never found wanting ; — to yourself.

In so doing, I recur from fiction to truth ; and in dedicating to you, in its complete or at least concluded state, a poetical work which is the longest, the most thoughtful and comprehensive of my compositions, I wish to do honour to myself by the record of many years' intimacy with a man of learning, of talent, of steadiness, and of honour. It is not for minds like ours to give or to receive flattery ; yet the praises of sincerity have ever been permitted to the voice of friendship ; and it is not for you, nor even for others, but to relieve a heart which has not elsewhere, or lately, been so much accustomed to the encounter of good-will as to withstand the shock firmly, that I thus attempt to commemorate your good qualities, or rather the advantages which I have derived from their exertion. Even the recurrence of the date of this letter, the anniversary of the most unfortunate day of my past existence, but which cannot poison my future while I retain the resource of your friendship and of my own faculties, will henceforth have a more agreeable recollection for both, inasmuch as it will remind us of this my attempt to thank you for an indefatigable regard, such as few men have experienced, and no one could experience without thinking better of his species and of himself.

It has been our fortune to traverse together, at various periods, the countries of chivalry, history, and fable — Spain, Greece, Asia Minor, and Italy ; and what Athens and Constantinople were to us a few years ago, Venice and Rome have been more recently. The poem also, or the pilgrim, or both, have accompanied me from first to last ; and perhaps it may be a pardonable vanity which induces me to reflect with complacency on a composition which in some degree connects me with the spot where it was produced, and the objects it would fain describe ; and however unworthy it may be deemed of those magical and memorable abodes, however short it may fall of our distant conceptions and immediate impressions, yet as a mark of respect for what is venerable and of feeling for what is glorious, it has been to me a source of pleasure in the production, and I part with it with a kind of regret which I hardly suspected that events could have left me for imaginary objects.

With regard to the conduct of the last canto, there will be found less of the pilgrim than in any of the preceding, and that little slightly, if at all, separated from the author speaking in his own person. The fact is, that I had become weary of drawing a line which every one seemed determined not to perceive. Like the Chinese in Goldsmith's *Citizen of the World*, whom nobody would believe to be a Chinese, it was in vain that I asserted, and imagined that I had drawn, a distinction between the author and the pilgrim ; and the very anxiety to preserve this difference, and disappointment at finding it unavailing, so far crushed my efforts in the composition, that I determined to abandon it altogether — and have done so. The opinions which have been, or may be, formed on that subject, are *now* a matter of indifference ; the work is to depend on itself, and not on the writer ; and the author, who has no resources in his own mind beyond the reputation, transient or permanent, which is to arise from his literary efforts, deserves the fate of authors.

In the course of the following canto it was my intention, either in the text or in the notes, to have touched upon the present state of Italian literature, and perhaps of manners. But the text, within the limits I proposed, I soon found hardly sufficient for the labyrinth of external objects, and the consequent reflections ; and for the whole of the notes, excepting a few of the shortest, I am indebted to yourself, and these were necessarily limited to the elucidation of the text.

It is also a delicate, and no very grateful task, to dissert upon the literature and manners of a nation so dissimilar ; and requires an attention and impartiality which would induce us — though perhaps no inattentive observers, nor ignorant of the language or customs of the people amongst whom we have recently abode — to distrust, or at least defer our judgment, and more narrowly examine our information. The state of literary, as well as political party, appears to run, or to *have* run, so high, that for a stranger to steer impartially between them is next to impossible. It may be enough, then, at least for my purpose, to quote from their own beautiful language — ' Mi pare che in un paese tutto poetico, che vanta la lingua la più nobile ed insieme la più dolce, tutte tutte le vie diverse si possono tentare, e che sinche la patria di Alfieri e di Monti non ha perduto l' antico valore, in tutte essa dovrebbe essere la prima.' Italy has great names still : Canova, Monti, Ugo, Foscolo, Pindemonte, Visconti, Morelli, Cicognara, Albrizzi, Mezzofanti, Mai, Mustoxidi, Aglietti, and Vacca, will secure to the present generation an honourable place in most of the departments of Art, Science, and Belles Lettres, and in some the very highest ; Europe — the World — has but one Canova.

It has been somewhere said by Alfieri, that ' La pianta uomo nasce più robusta in Italia

che in qualunque altra terra — e che gli stessi atroci delitti che vi si commettono ne sono una prova.' Without subscribing to the latter part of his proposition, a dangerous doctrine, the truth of which may be disputed on better grounds, namely, that the Italians are in no respect more ferocious than their neighbours, that man must be wilfully blind, or ignorantly heedless, who is not struck with the extraordinary capacity of this people, or, if such a word be admissible, their *capabilities*, the facility of their acquisitions, the rapidity of their conceptions, the fire of their genius, their sense of beauty, and, amidst all the disadvantages of repeated revolutions, the desolation of battles, and the despair of ages, their still unquenched 'longing after immortality,' — the immortality of independence. And when we ourselves, in riding round the walls of Rome, heard the simple lament of the labourers' chorus, 'Roma! Roma! Roma! Roma non è più come era prima,' it was difficult not to contrast this melancholy dirge with the bacchanal roar of the songs of exultation still yelled from the London taverns, over the carnage of Mont St. Jean, and the betrayal of Genoa, of Italy, of France, and of the world, by men whose conduct you yourself have exposed in a work worthy of the better days of our history. For me, —

> 'Non movero mai corda
> Ove la turba di sue ciance assorda.'

What Italy has gained by the late transfer of nations, it were useless for Englishmen to enquire, till it becomes ascertained that England has acquired something more than a permanent army and a suspended Habeas Corpus: it is enough for them to look at home. For what they have done abroad, and especially in the South, 'Verily they *will have* their reward,' and at no very distant period.

Wishing you, my dear Hobhouse, a safe and agreeable return to that country whose real welfare can be dearer to none than to yourself, I dedicate to you this poem in its completed state; and repeat once more how truly I am ever,

Your obliged
And affectionate friend,
BYRON.

I

I stood in Venice on the Bridge of Sighs,
A palace and a prison on each hand;
I saw from out the wave her structures rise
As from the stroke of the enchanter's wand:
A thousand years their cloudy wings expand

Around me, and a dying Glory smiles
O'er the far times, when many a subject land
Look'd to the wingèd Lion's marble piles,
Where Venice sate in state, throned on her hundred isles!

II

She looks a sea Cybele, fresh from ocean, 10
Rising with her tiara of proud towers
At airy distance, with majestic motion,
A ruler of the waters and their powers.
And such she was; — her daughters had their dowers
From spoils of nations, and the exhaustless East
Pour'd in her lap all gems in sparkling showers:
In purple was she robed, and of her feast
Monarchs partook, and deem'd their dignity increased.

III

In Venice Tasso's echoes are no more, 19
And silent rows the songless gondolier;
Her palaces are crumbling to the shore,
And music meets not always now the ear;
Those days are gone, but Beauty still is here;
States fall, arts fade, but Nature doth not die,
Nor yet forget how Venice once was dear,
The pleasant place of all festivity,
The revel of the earth, the masque of Italy!

IV

But unto us she hath a spell beyond
Her name in story, and her long array
Of mighty shadows, whose dim forms despond 30
Above the dogeless city's vanish'd sway:
Ours is a trophy which will not decay
With the Rialto; Shylock and the Moor
And Pierre can not be swept or worn away,
The keystones of the arch! — though all were o'er,
For us repeopled were the solitary shore.

V

The beings of the mind are not of clay;
Essentially immortal, they create
And multiply in us a brighter ray

And more beloved existence. That which
 Fate 40
Prohibits to dull life in this our state
Of mortal bondage, by these spirits sup-
 plied,
First exiles, then replaces what we hate;
Watering the heart whose early flowers
 have died,
And with a fresher growth replenishing the
 void.

VI

Such is the refuge of our youth and age,
The first from Hope, the last from
 Vacancy;
And this worn feeling peoples many a
 page,
And, may be, that which grows beneath
 mine eye.
Yet there are things whose strong reality
Outshines our fairy-land; in shape and
 hues 51
More beautiful than our fantastic sky,
And the strange constellations which the
 Muse
O'er her wild universe is skilful to diffuse:

VII

I saw or dream'd of such, — but let them
 go, —
They came like truth, and disappear'd
 like dreams;
And whatsoe'er they were — are now but
 so.
I could replace them if I would; still
 teems
My mind with many a form which aptly
 seems
Such as I sought for, and at moments
 found: 60
Let these too go, for waking Reason deems
Such over-weening phantasies unsound,
And other voices speak and other sights sur-
 round.

VIII

I've taught me other tongues, and in
 strange eyes
Have made me not a stranger — to the
 mind
Which is itself, no changes bring sur-
 prise;
Nor is it harsh to make, nor hard to find
A country with — ay, or without man-
 kind;

Yet was I born where men are proud to
 be,
Not without cause; and should I leave
 behind 70
The inviolate island of the sage and free,
And seek me out a home by a remoter sea,

IX

Perhaps I loved it well; and should I
 lay
My ashes in a soil which is not mine,
My spirit shall resume it — if we may
Unbodied choose a sanctuary. I twine
My hopes of being remember'd in my
 line
With my land's language: if too fond and
 far
These aspirations in their scope incline, —
If my fame should be, as my fortunes
 are, 80
Of hasty growth and blight, and dull Obli-
 vion bar

X

My name from out the temple where the
 dead
Are honour'd by the nations — let it be,
And light the laurels on a loftier head!
And be the Spartan's epitaph on me,
'Sparta hath many a worthier son than
 he.'
Meantime I seek no sympathies, nor
 need;
The thorns which I have reap'd are of the
 tree
I planted, — they have torn me — and I
 bleed:
I should have known what fruit would
 spring from such a seed. 90

XI

The spouseless Adriatic mourns her lord;
And annual marriage now no more re-
 new'd,
The Bucentaur lies rotting unrestored,
Neglected garment of her widowhood!
St. Mark yet sees his lion where he stood
Stand, but in mockery of his wither'd
 power,
Over the proud Place where an Emperor
 sued,
And monarchs gazed and envied in the
 hour
When Venice was a queen with an un-
 equall'd dower.

XII

The Suabian sued, and now the Austrian
 reigns — 100
An Emperor tramples where an Emperor
 knelt;
Kingdoms are shrunk to provinces, and
 chains
Clank over sceptred cities; nations melt
From power's high pinnacle, when they
 have felt
The sunshine for a while, and downward
 go
Like lauwine loosen'd from the moun-
 tain's belt; —
Oh, for one hour of blind old Dan-
 dolo,
Th' octogenarian chief, Byzantium's con-
 quering foe !

XIII

Before St. Mark still glow his steeds of
 brass,
Their gilded collars glittering in the
 sun; 110
But is not Doria's menace come to pass ?
Are they not *bridled ?* — Venice, lost and
 won,
Her thirteen hundred years of freedom
 done,
Sinks, like a sea-weed, into whence she
 rose !
Better be whelm'd beneath the waves,
 and shun,
Even in destruction's depth, her foreign
 foes,
From whom submission wrings an infamous
 repose.

XIV

In youth she was all glory, a new Tyre,
Her very by-word sprung from victory,
The ' Planter of the Lion,' which through
 fire 120
And blood she bore o'er subject earth and
 sea;
Though making many slaves, herself still
 free,
And Europe's bulwark 'gainst the Otto-
 mite; —
Witness Troy's rival, Candia ! Vouch it,
 ye
Immortal waves that saw Lepanto's
 fight !
For ye are names no time nor tyranny can
 blight.

XV

Statues of glass — all shiver'd — the long
 file
Of her dead Doges are declined to dust;
But where they dwelt, the vast and
 sumptuous pile
Bespeaks the pageant of their splendid
 trust; 130
Their sceptre broken, and their sword in
 rust,
Have yielded to the stranger: empty
 halls,
Thin streets, and foreign aspects, such as
 must
Too oft remind her who and what en-
 thralls,
Have flung a desolate cloud o'er Venice'
 lovely walls.

XVI

When Athens' armies fell at Syracuse,
And fetter'd thousands bore the yoke of
 war,
Redemption rose up in the Attic Muse,
Her voice their only ransom from afar:
See ! as they chant the tragic hymn, the
 car 140
Of the o'ermaster'd victor stops, the reins
Fall from his hands — his idle scimitar
Starts from its belt — he rends his cap-
 tive's chains,
And bids him thank the bard for freedom
 and his strains.

XVII

Thus, Venice, if no stronger claim were
 thine,
Were all thy proud historic deeds for-
 got,
Thy choral memory of the Bard divine,
Thy love of Tasso, should have cut the
 knot
Which ties thee to thy tyrants; and thy
 lot
Is shameful to the nations, — most of
 all, 150
Albion, to thee: the Ocean queen should
 not
Abandon Ocean's children; in the fall
Of Venice think of thine, despite thy
 watery wall.

XVIII

I loved her from my boyhood; she to me
Was as a fairy city of the heart,

Rising like water-columns from the sea,
Of joy the sojourn, and of wealth the
 mart:
And Otway, Radcliffe, Schiller, Shak-
 speare's art,
Had stamp'd her image in me; and even
 so,
Although I found her thus, we did not
 part, 160
Perchance even dearer in her day of woe
Than when she was a boast, a marvel, and
 a show.

XIX

I can repeople with the past — and of
The present there is still for eye and
 thought,
And meditation chasten'd down, enough,
And more, it may be, than I hoped or
 sought;
And of the happiest moments which were
 wrought
Within the web of my existence, some
From thee, fair Venice, have their colours
 caught:
There are some feelings Time cannot
 benumb, 170
Nor Torture shake, or mine would now be
 cold and dumb.

XX

But from their nature will the tannen
 grow
Loftiest on loftiest and least shelter'd
 rocks,
Rooted in barrenness, where nought below
Of soil supports them 'gainst the Alpine
 shocks
Of eddying storms; yet springs the trunk,
 and mocks
The howling tempest, till its height and
 frame
Are worthy of the mountains from whose
 blocks
Of bleak, gray granite into life it came,
And grew a giant tree; — the mind may
 grow the same. 180

XXI

Existence may be borne, and the deep root
Of life and sufferance make its firm abode
In bare and desolated bosoms: mute
The camel labours with the heaviest load,
And the wolf dies in silence, — not be-
 stow'd

In vain should such example be; if they,
Things of ignoble or of savage mood,
Endure and shrink not, we of nobler clay
May temper it to bear, — it is but for a day.

XXII

All suffering doth destroy, or is de-
 stroy'd 190
Even by the sufferer; and, in each event,
Ends: — Some, with hope replenish'd and
 rebuoy'd,
Return to whence they came — with like
 intent,
And weave their web again; some, bow'd
 and bent,
Wax gray and ghastly, withering ere
 their time,
And perish with the reed on which they
 leant;
Some seek devotion, toil, war, good or
 crime,
According as their souls were form'd to sink
 or climb.

XXIII

But ever and anon of griefs subdued
There comes a token like a scorpion's
 sting, 200
Scarce seen, but with fresh bitterness
 imbued;
And slight withal may be the things which
 bring
Back on the heart the weight which it
 would fling
Aside for ever: it may be a sound, —
A tone of music, summer's eve, or spring,
A flower, the wind, the ocean, — which
 shall wound,
Striking the electric chain wherewith we
 are darkly bound;

XXIV

And how and why we know not, nor can
 trace
Home to its cloud this lightning of the
 mind,
But feel the shock renew'd, nor can
 efface 210
The blight and blackening which it leaves
 behind,
Which out of things familiar, undesign'd,
When least we deem of such, calls up to
 view
The spectres whom no exorcism can
 bind,

The cold — the changed — perchance the
 dead — anew,
The mourn'd, the loved, the lost — too
 many ! — yet how few !

XXV

But my soul wanders; I demand it back
To meditate amongst decay, and stand
A ruin amidst ruins; there to track
Fall'n states and buried greatness, o'er a
 land 220
Which *was* the mightiest in its old com-
 mand,
And *is* the loveliest, and must ever be
The master-mould of Nature's heavenly
 hand,
Wherein were cast the heroic and the
 free,
The beautiful, the brave — the lords of
 earth and sea,

XXVI

The commonwealth of kings, the men of
 Rome !
And even since, and now, fair Italy,
Thou art the garden of the world, the
 home 228
Of all Art yields, and Nature can decree;
Even in thy desert, what is like to thee ?
Thy very weeds are beautiful, thy waste
More rich than other climes' fertility;
Thy wreck a glory, and thy ruin graced
With an immaculate charm which cannot
 be defaced.

XXVII

The moon is up, and yet it is not night —
Sunset divides the sky with her, a sea
Of glory streams along the Alpine height
Of blue Friuli's mountains; Heaven is free
From clouds, but of all colours seems to
 be
Melted to one vast Iris of the West, 240
Where the Day joins the past Eternity;
While, on the other hand, meek Dian's
 crest
Floats through the azure air, an island of
 the blest !

XXVIII

A single star is at her side, and reigns
With her o'er half the lovely heaven; but
 still
Yon sunny sea heaves brightly, and re-
 mains

Roll'd o'er the peak of the far Rhætian
 hill,
As Day and Night contending were, until
Nature reclaim'd her order: gently flows
The deep-dyed Brenta, where their hues
 instil 250
The odorous purple of a new-born rose,
Which streams upon her stream, and glass'd
 within it glows,

XXIX

Fill'd with the face of heaven, which from
 afar
Comes down upon the waters; all its hues,
From the rich sunset to the rising star,
Their magical variety diffuse.
And now they change; a paler shadow
 strews
Its mantle o'er the mountains; parting
 day
Dies like the dolphin, whom each pang
 imbues
With a new colour as it gasps away, 260
The last still loveliest, till — 't is gone —
 and all is gray.

XXX

There is a tomb in Arqua; — rear'd in air,
Pillar'd in their sarcophagus, repose
The bones of Laura's lover: here repair
Many familiar with his well-sung woes,
The pilgrims of his genius. He arose
To raise a language, and his land reclaim
From the dull yoke of her barbaric foes;
Watering the tree which bears his lady's
 name
With his melodious tears, he gave himself
 to fame. 270

XXXI

They keep his dust in Arqua where he
 died,
The mountain-village where his latter
 days
Went down the vale of years; and 't is
 their pride —
An honest pride, and let it be their
 praise —
To offer to the passing stranger's gaze
His mansion and his sepulchre; both
 plain
And venerably simple, such as raise
A feeling more accordant with his strain
Than if a pyramid form'd his monumental
 fane.

XXXII

And the soft quiet hamlet where he
 dwelt 280
Is one of that complexion which seems
 made
For those who their mortality have felt,
And sought a refuge from their hopes
 decay'd
In the deep umbrage of a green hill's
 shade,
Which shows a distant prospect far away
Of busy cities, now in vain display'd
For they can lure no further; and the ray
Of a bright sun can make sufficient holiday,

XXXIII

Developing the mountains, leaves, and
 flowers,
And shining in the brawling brook,
 where-by, 290
Clear as its current, glide the sauntering
 hours
With a calm languor, which, though to
 the eye
Idlesse it seem, hath its morality.
If from society we learn to live,
'T is solitude should teach us how to die;
It hath no flatterers; vanity can give
No hollow aid; alone — man with his God
 must strive:

XXXIV

Or, it may be, with demons, who impair
The strength of better thoughts, and seek
 their prey
In melancholy bosoms, such as were 300
Of moody texture from their earliest day
And loved to dwell in darkness and dis-
 may,
Deeming themselves predestined to a
 doom
Which is not of the pangs that pass away;
Making the sun like blood, the earth a
 tomb,
The tomb a hell, and hell itself a murkier
 gloom.

XXXV

Ferrara, in thy wide and grass-grown
 streets,
Whose symmetry was not for solitude,
There seems as 't were a curse upon the
 seats
Of former sovereigns, and the antique
 brood 310

Of Este, which for many an age made
 good
Its strength within thy walls, and was of
 yore
Patron or tyrant, as the changing mood
Of petty power impell'd, of those who
 wore
The wreath which Dante's brow alone had
 worn before.

XXXVI

And Tasso is their glory and their shame:
Hark to his strain and then survey his
 cell !
And see how dearly earn'd Torquato's
 fame,
And where Alfonso bade his poet dwell.
The miserable despot could not quell 320
The insulted mind he sought to quench,
 and blend
With the surrounding maniacs, in the
 hell
Where he had plunged it. Glory with-
 out end
Scatter'd the clouds away, and on that name
 attend

XXXVII

The tears and praises of all time; while
 thine
Would rot in its oblivion — in the sink
Of worthless dust which from thy boasted
 line
Is shaken into nothing — but the link
Thou formest in his fortunes bids us think
Of thy poor malice, naming thee with
 scorn. 330
Alfonso ! how thy ducal pageants shrink
From thee ! if in another station born,
Scarce fit to be the slave of him thou madest
 to mourn: —

XXXVIII

Thou ! form'd to eat, and be despised,
 and die,
Even as the beasts that perish, save that
 thou
Hadst a more splendid trough and wider
 sty;
He ! with a glory round his furrow'd
 brow,
Which emanated then, and dazzles now,
In face of all his foes, the Cruscan quire,
And Boileau, whose rash envy could
 allow 340

No strain which shamed his country's
 creaking lyre,
That whetstone of the teeth — monotony in
 wire !

XXXIX

Peace to Torquato's injured shade ! 't was
 his
In life and death to be the mark where
 Wrong
Aim'd with her poison'd arrows, but to
 miss.
Oh, victor unsurpass'd in modern song !
Each year brings forth its millions; but
 how long
The tide of generations shall roll on,
And not the whole combined and count-
 less throng
Compose a mind like thine ? Though all
 in one 350
Condensed their scatter'd rays, they would
 not form a sun.

XL

Great as thou art, yet parallel'd by those,
Thy countrymen, before thee born to
 shine,
The Bards of Hell and Chivalry: first
 rose
The Tuscan father's comedy divine;
Then, not unequal to the Florentine
The southern Scott, the minstrel who
 call'd forth
A new creation with his magic line,
And, like the Ariosto of the North,
Sang ladye-love and war, romance and
 knightly worth. 360

XLI

The lightning rent from Ariosto's bust
The iron crown of laurel's mimic'd leaves;
Nor was the ominous element unjust,
For the true laurel-wreath which Glory
 weaves
Is of the tree no bolt of thunder cleaves,
And the false semblance but disgraced
 his brow;
Yet still, if fondly Superstition grieves,
Know, that the lightning sanctifies below
Whate'er it strikes; — yon head is doubly
 sacred now.

XLII

Italia ! oh, Italia ! thou who hast 370
The fatal gift of beauty, which became

A funeral dower of present woes and
 past,
On thy sweet brow is sorrow plough'd by
 shame,
And annals graved in characters of flame.
Oh, God ! that thou wert in thy naked-
 ness
Less lovely or more powerful, and couldst
 claim
Thy right, and awe the robbers back,
 who press
To shed thy blood and drink the tears of
 thy distress;

XLIII

Then mightst thou more appal; or, less
 desired,
Be homely and be peaceful, undeplored
For thy destructive charms; then, still
 untired, 381
Would not be seen the armèd torrents
 pour'd
Down the deep Alps; nor would the hos-
 tile horde
Of many-nation'd spoilers from the Po
Quaff blood and water; nor the stranger's
 sword
Be thy sad weapon of defence, and so,
Victor or vanquish'd, thou the slave of
 friend or foe.

XLIV

Wandering in youth, I traced the path
 of him,
The Roman friend of Rome's least-mor-
 tal mind,
The friend of Tully. As my bark did
 skim 390
The bright blue waters with a fanning
 wind,
Came Megara before me, and behind
Ægina lay, Piræus on the right,
And Corinth on the left; I lay reclined
Along the prow, and saw all these unite
In ruin, even as he had seen the desolate
 sight; —

XLV

For Time hath not rebuilt them, but up-
 rear'd
Barbaric dwellings on their shatter'd site,
Which only make more mourn'd and
 more endear'd
The few last rays of their far-scatter'd
 light 400

And the crush'd relics of their vanish'd
 might.
The Roman saw these tombs in his own
 age,
These sepulchres of cities which excite
Sad wonder, and his yet surviving page
The moral lesson bears, drawn from such
 pilgrimage.

XLVI

That page is now before me, and on mine
His country's ruin added to the mass
Of perish'd states he mourn'd in their
 decline,
And I in desolation. All that *was*
Of then destruction *is;* and now, alas ! 410
Rome — Rome imperial, bows her to the
 storm,
In the same dust and blackness, and we
 pass
The skeleton of her Titanic form,
Wrecks of another world whose ashes still
 are warm.

XLVII

Yet, Italy ! through every other land
Thy wrongs should ring, and shall, from
 side to side;
Mother of Arts, as once of arms; thy
 hand
Was then our guardian, and is still our
 guide;
Parent of our Religion, whom the wide
Nations have knelt to for the keys of
 heaven ! 420
Europe, repentant of her parricide,
Shall yet redeem thee, and, all backward
 driven,
Roll the barbarian tide, and sue to be for-
 given.

XLVIII

But Arno wins us to the fair white walls,
Where the Etrurian Athens claims and
 keeps
A softer feeling for her fairy halls.
Girt by her theatre of hills, she reaps
Her corn and wine and oil, and Plenty
 leaps
To laughing life with her redundant horn.
Along the banks where smiling Arno
 sweeps 430
Was modern Luxury of Commerce born,
And buried Learning rose, redeem'd to a
 new morn.

XLIX

There, too, the Goddess loves in stone,
 and fills
The air around with beauty. We inhale
The ambrosial aspect, which, beheld, in-
 stils
Part of its immortality; the veil
Of heaven is half undrawn; within the
 pale
We stand, and in that form and face
 behold .
What mind can make when Nature's self
 would fail;
And to the fond idolaters of old 440
Envy the innate flash which such a soul
 could mould.

L

We gaze and turn away, and know not
 where,
Dazzled and drunk with beauty, till the
 heart
Reels with its fulness; there — for ever
 there —
Chain'd to the chariot of triumphal Art,
We stand as captives and would not de-
 part.
Away ! — there need no words nor terms
 precise,
The paltry jargon of the marble mart
Where Pedantry gulls Folly — we have
 eyes:
Blood, pulse, and breast confirm the Dardan
 Shepherd's prize. 450

LI

Appear'dst thou not to Paris in this
 guise ?
Or to more deeply blest Anchises ? or,
In all thy perfect goddess-ship, when lies
Before thee thy own vanquish'd Lord of
 War ?
And gazing in thy face as toward a star,
Laid on thy lap, his eyes to thee upturn,
Feeding on thy sweet cheek; while thy
 lips are
With lava kisses melting while they burn,
Shower'd on his eyelids, brow, and mouth,
 as from an urn !

LII

Glowing and circumfused in speechless
 love, 460
Their full divinity inadequate
That feeling to express or to improve,

The gods become as mortals, and man's
 fate
Has moments like their brightest; but
 the weight
Of earth recoils upon us; — let it go !
We can recall such visions, and create,
From what has been or might be, things
 which grow
Into thy statue's form and look like gods
 below.

LIII

I leave to learnèd fingers and wise hands,
The artist and his ape, to teach and tell
How well his connoisseurship under-
 stands 471
The graceful bend and the voluptuous
 swell:
Let these describe the undescribable;
I would not their vile breath should crisp
 the stream
Wherein that image shall for ever dwell,
The unruffled mirror of the loveliest
 dream
That ever left the sky on the deep soul to
 beam.

LIV

In Santa Croce's holy precincts lie
Ashes which make it holier, dust which
 is
Even in itself an immortality, 480
Though there were nothing save the past,
 and this,
The particle of those sublimities
Which have relapsed to chaos: here re-
 pose
Angelo's, Alfieri's bones, and his,
The starry Galileo, with his woes;
Here Machiavelli's earth return'd to whence
 it rose.

LV

These are four minds, which, like the
 elements,
Might furnish forth creation. Italy !
Time, which hath wrong'd thee with ten
 thousand rents
Of thine imperial garment, shall deny,
And hath denied, to every other sky 491
Spirits which soar from ruin: — thy decay
Is still impregnate with divinity,
Which gilds it with revivifying ray;
Such as the great of yore, Canova is to-
 day.

LVI

But where repose the all Etruscan
 three —
Dante, and Petrarch, and, scarce less than
 they,
The Bard of Prose, creative spirit, he
Of the Hundred Tales of love — where
 did they lay
Their bones, distinguish'd from our com-
 mon clay 500
In death as life ? Are they resolved to
 dust,
And have their country's marbles nought
 to say ?
Could not her quarries furnish forth one
 bust ?
Did they not to her breast their filial earth
 intrust ?

LVII

Ungrateful Florence ! Dante sleeps afar,
Like Scipio, buried by the upbraiding
 shore;
Thy factions, in their worse than civil
 war,
Proscribed the bard whose name for
 evermore
Their children's children would in vain
 adore
With the remorse of ages ; and the
 crown 510
Which Petrarch's laureate brow su-
 premely wore,
Upon a far and foreign soil had grown,
His life, his fame, his grave, though rifled
 — not thine own.

LVIII

Boccaccio to his parent earth bequeath'd
His dust; and lies it not her Great
 among,
With many a sweet and solemn requiem
 breathed
O'er him who form'd the Tuscan's siren
 tongue ?
That music in itself, whose sounds are
 song,
The poetry of speech ? No; — even his
 tomb
Uptorn must bear the hyæna bigot's
 wrong, 520
No more amidst the meaner dead find
 room,
Nor claim a passing sigh, because it told
 for *whom* !

LIX

And Santa Croce wants their mighty dust, —
Yet for this want more noted, as of yore
The Cæsar's pageant, shorn of Brutus' bust,
Did but of Rome's best Son remind her more.
Happier Ravenna! on thy hoary shore,
Fortress of falling empire, honour'd sleeps
The immortal exile; Arqua, too, her store
Of tuneful relics proudly claims and keeps, 530
While Florence vainly begs her banish'd dead, and weeps.

LX

What is her pyramid of precious stones,
Of porphyry, jasper, agate, and all hues
Of gem and marble, to encrust the bones
Of merchant-dukes? The momentary dews
Which, sparkling to the twilight stars, infuse
Freshness in the green turf that wraps the dead,
Whose names are mausoleums of the Muse,
Are gently prest with far more reverent tread
Than ever paced the slab which paves the princely head. 540

LXI

There be more things to greet the heart and eyes
In Arno's dome of Art's most princely shrine,
Where Sculpture with her rainbow sister vies;
There be more marvels yet — but not for mine;
For I have been accustom'd to entwine
My thoughts with Nature rather in the fields,
Than Art in galleries: though a work divine
Calls for my spirit's homage, yet it yields
Less than it feels, because the weapon which it wields

LXII

Is of another temper, and I roam 550
By Thrasimene's lake, in the defiles
Fatal to Roman rashness, more at home;
For there the Carthaginian's warlike wiles
Come back before me, as his skill beguiles
The host between the mountains and the shore,
Where Courage falls in her despairing files,
And torrents, swoll'n to rivers with their gore,
Reek through the sultry plain with legions scatter'd o'er.

LXIII

Like to a forest fell'd by mountain winds;
And such the storm of battle on this day,
And such the frenzy, whose convulsion blinds 561
To all save carnage, that, beneath the fray,
An earthquake reel'd unheededly away!
None felt stern Nature rocking at his feet,
And yawning forth a grave for those who lay
Upon their bucklers for a winding sheet;
Such is the absorbing hate when warring nations meet!

LXIV

The Earth to them was as a rolling bark
Which bore them to Eternity; they saw
The Ocean round, but had no time to mark 570
The motions of their vessel; Nature's law,
In them suspended, reck'd not of the awe
Which reigns when mountains tremble, and the birds
Plunge in the clouds for refuge and withdraw
From their down-toppling nests; and bellowing herds
Stumble o'er heaving plains, and man's dread hath no words.

LXV

Far other scene is Thrasimene now;
Her lake a sheet of silver, and her plain
Rent by no ravage save the gentle plough;
Her aged trees rise thick as once the slain 580

Lay where their roots are; but a brook
 hath ta'en —
A little rill of scanty stream and bed —
A name of blood from that day's san-
 guine rain;
And Sanguinetto tells ye where the dead
Made the earth wet and turn'd the unwill-
 ing waters red.

LXVI

But thou, Clitumnus, in thy sweetest
 wave
Of the most living crystal that was e'er
The haunt of river nymph, to gaze and
 lave
Her limbs where nothing hid them, thou
 dost rear
Thy grassy banks whereon the milk-
 white steer 590
Grazes, — the purest god of gentle waters,
And most serene of aspect, and most
 clear !
Surely that stream was unprofaned by
 slaughters —
A mirror and a bath for Beauty's youngest
 daughters !

LXVII

And on thy happy shore a Temple still,
Of small and delicate proportion, keeps,
Upon a mild declivity of hill,
Its memory of thee; beneath it sweeps
Thy current's calmness; oft from out it
 leaps
The finny darter with the glittering
 scales, 600
Who dwells and revels in thy glassy
 deeps;
While, chance, some scatter'd water-lily
 sails
Down where the shallower wave still tells
 its bubbling tales.

LXVIII

Pass not unblest the Genius of the place !
If through the air a zephyr more serene
Win to the brow, 't is his; and if ye trace
Along his margin a more eloquent green,
If on the heart the freshness of the scene
Sprinkle its coolness, and from the dry
 dust
Of weary life a moment lave it clean 610
With Nature's baptism, — 't is to him ye
 must
Pay orisons for this suspension of disgust.

LXIX

The roar of waters ! — from the head-
 long height
Velino cleaves the wave-worn precipice;
The fall of waters ! rapid as the light
The flashing mass foams shaking the
 abyss;
The hell of waters ! where they howl and
 hiss,
And boil in endless torture; while the
 sweat
Of their great agony, wrung out from this
Their Phlegethon, curls round the rocks
 of jet 620
That gird the gulf around, in pitiless hor-
 ror set,

LXX

And mounts in spray the skies, and thence
 again
Returns in an unceasing shower, which
 round,
With its unemptied cloud of gentle rain,
Is an eternal April to the ground,
Making it all one emerald: — how pro-
 found
The gulf ! and how the giant element
From rock to rock leaps with delirious
 bound,
Crushing the cliffs, which, downward
 worn and rent
With his fierce footsteps, yield in chasms
 a fearful vent 630

LXXI

To the broad column which rolls on, and
 shows
More like the fountain of an infant sea
Torn from the womb of mountains by the
 throes
Of a new world, than only thus to be
Parent of rivers, which flow gushingly,
With many windings, through the vale: —
 Look back !
Lo, where it comes like an eternity,
As if to sweep down all things in its track,
Charming the eye with dread — a match-
 less cataract,

LXXII

Horribly beautiful ! but on the verge,
From side to side, beneath the glittering
 morn, 641
An Iris sits, amidst the infernal surge,
Like Hope upon a death-bed, and, unworn

Its steady dyes while all around is torn
By the distracted waters, bears serene
Its brilliant hues with all their beams
 unshorn;
Resembling, 'mid the torture of the scene,
Love watching Madness with unalterable
 mien.

LXXIII

Once more upon the woody Apennine,
The infant Alps, which — had I not before
Gazed on their mightier parents, where
 the pine 651
Sits on more shaggy summits, and where
 roar
The thundering lauwine — might be wor-
 shipp'd more;
But I have seen the soaring Jungfrau rear
Her never-trodden snow, and seen the
 hoar
Glaciers of bleak Mont Blanc both far
 and near,
And in Chimari heard the thunder-hills of
 fear,

LXXIV

Th' Acroceraunian mountains of old
 name;
And on Parnassus seen the eagles fly
Like spirits of the spot, as 't were for
 fame, 660
For still they soar'd unutterably high;
I 've look'd on Ida with a Trojan's eye;
Athos, Olympus, Ætna, Atlas, made
These hills seem things of lesser dignity,
All, save the lone Soracte's height, dis-
 play'd
Not *now* in snow, which asks the lyric Ro-
 man's aid

LXXV

For our remembrance, and from out the
 plain
Heaves like a long-swept wave about to
 break,
And on the curl hangs pausing. Not in
 vain 669
May he, who will, his recollections rake,
And quote in classic raptures, and awake
The hills with Latian echoes; I abhorr'd
Too much, to conquer for the poet's sake,
The drill'd dull lesson, forced down word
 by word
In my repugnant youth, with pleasure to
 record

LXXVI

Aught that recalls the daily drug which
 turn'd
My sickening memory; and, though Time
 hath taught
My mind to meditate what then it
 learn'd,
Yet such the fix'd inveteracy wrought
By the impatience of my early thought,
That, with the freshness wearing out be-
 fore 681
My mind could relish what it might have
 sought,
If free to choose, I cannot now restore
Its health; but what it then detested, still
 abhor.

LXXVII

Then farewell, Horace; whom I hated so,
Not for thy faults, but mine; it is a curse
To understand, not feel thy lyric flow,
To comprehend, but never love thy verse,
Although no deeper Moralist rehearse
Our little life, nor Bard prescribe his
 art, 690
Nor livelier Satirist the conscience pierce,
Awakening without wounding the touch'd
 heart; —
Yet fare thee well — upon Soracte's ridge
 we part.

LXXVIII

Oh Rome, my country ! city of the soul !
The orphans of the heart must turn to
 thee,
Lone mother of dead empires, and con-
 trol
In their shut breasts their petty misery.
What are our woes and sufferance ?
 Come and see
The cypress, hear the owl, and plod your
 way
O'er steps of broken thrones and temples,
 Ye ! 700
Whose agonies are evils of a day —
A world is at our feet as fragile as our clay.

LXXIX

The Niobe of nations ! there she stands,
Childless and crownless, in her voiceless
 woe;
An empty urn within her wither'd hands,
Whose holy dust was scatter'd long
 ago:
The Scipios' tomb contains no ashes now;

The very sepulchres lie tenantless
Of their heroic dwellers; — dost thou
 flow,
Old Tiber, through a marble wilderness?
Rise, with thy yellow waves, and mantle
 her distress! 711

LXXX

The Goth, the Christian, Time, War,
 Flood, and Fire,
Have dealt upon the seven-hill'd city's
 pride;
She saw her glories star by star expire,
And up the steep barbarian monarchs
 ride
Where the car climb'd the capitol; far
 and wide
Temple and tower went down, nor left a
 site: —
Chaos of ruins! who shall trace the void,
O'er the dim fragments cast a lunar light,
And say, 'here was, or is,' where all is
 doubly night? 720

LXXXI

The double night of ages, and of her,
Night's daughter, Ignorance, hath wrapt
 and wrap
All round us; we but feel our way to err:
The ocean hath his chart, the stars their
 map,
And Knowledge spreads them on her
 ample lap;
But Rome is as the desert where we steer
Stumbling o'er recollections; now we clap
Our hands, and cry 'Eureka!' it is
 clear —
When but some false mirage of ruin rises
 near.

LXXXII

Alas, the lofty city! and alas, 730
The trebly hundred triumphs! and the
 day
When Brutus made the dagger's edge
 surpass
The conqueror's sword in bearing fame
 away!
Alas, for Tully's voice, and Virgil's lay,
And Livy's pictured page! — but these
 shall be
Her resurrection; all beside — decay.
Alas, for Earth, for never shall we see
That brightness in her eye she bore when
 Rome was free!

LXXXIII

Oh thou, whose chariot roll'd on Fortune's
 wheel,
Triumphant Sylla! thou, who didst sub-
 due 740
Thy country's foes ere thou wouldst
 pause to feel
The wrath of thy own wrongs, or reap
 the due
Of hoarded vengeance till thine eagles flew
O'er prostrate Asia; — thou, who with
 thy frown
Annihilated senates — Roman, too,
With all thy vices, for thou didst lay
 down
With an atoning smile a more than earthly
 crown,

LXXXIV

The dictatorial wreath, — couldst thou
 divine
To what would one day dwindle that
 which made
Thee more than mortal? and that so
 supine 750
By aught than Romans Rome should
 thus be laid?
She who was named Eternal, and array'd
Her warriors but to conquer — she who
 veil'd
Earth with her haughty shadow, and dis-
 play'd,
Until the o'er-canopied horizon fail'd,
Her rushing wings — Oh, she who was
 Almighty hail'd!

LXXXV

Sylla was first of victors; but our own
The sagest of usurpers, Cromwell; he
Too swept off senates while he hew'd the
 throne 759
Down to a block — immortal rebel! See
What crimes it costs to be a moment free
And famous through all ages! but be-
 neath
His fate the moral lurks of destiny;
His day of double victory and death
Beheld him win two realms, and, happier,
 yield his breath.

LXXXVI

The third of the same moon whose for-
 mer course
Had all but crown'd him, on the self
 same day

Deposed him gently from his throne of
 force,
And laid him with the earth's preceding
 clay.
And show'd not Fortune thus how fame
 and sway, 770
And all we deem delightful and con-
 sume
Our souls to compass through each
 arduous way,
Are in her eyes less happy than the
 tomb?
Were they but so in man's, how different
 were his doom!

LXXXVII

And thou, dread statue, yet existent in
The austerest form of naked majesty!
Thou who beheldest, 'mid the assassins'
 din,
At thy bathed base the bloody Cæsar lie,
Folding his robe in dying dignity,
An offering to thine altar from the
 queen 780
Of gods and men, great Nemesis! did he
 die,
And thou, too, perish, Pompey? have ye
 been
Victors of countless kings, or puppets of a
 scene?

LXXXVIII

And thou, the thunder-stricken nurse of
 Rome!
She-wolf, whose brazen-imaged dugs
 impart
The milk of conquest yet within the
 dome
Where, as a monument of antique art,
Thou standest; mother of the mighty
 heart,
Which the great founder suck'd from
 thy wild teat,
Scorch'd by the Roman Jove's ethereal
 dart, 790
And thy limbs black with lightning —
 dost thou yet
Guard thine immortal cubs, nor thy fond
 charge forget?

LXXXIX

Thou dost; but all thy foster-babes are
 dead —
The men of iron; and the world hath
 rear'd

Cities from out their sepulchres. Men
 bled
In imitation of the things they fear'd
And fought and conquer'd, and the same
 course steer'd,
At apish distance; but as yet none have,
Nor could the same supremacy have
 near'd,
Save one vain man, who is not in the
 grave, 800
But vanquish'd by himself, to his own slaves
 a slave —

XC

The fool of false dominion — and a kind
Of bastard Cæsar, following him of old
With steps unequal; for the Roman's
 mind
Was modell'd in a less terrestrial mould,
With passions fiercer, yet a judgment cold,
And an immortal instinct which redeem'd
The frailties of a heart so soft, yet bold,
Alcides with the distaff now he seem'd
At Cleopatra's feet, — and now himself he
 beam'd, 810

XCI

And came — and saw — and conquer'd!
 But the man
Who would have tamed his eagles down
 to flee,
Like a train'd falcon, in the Gallic van,
Which he, in sooth, long led to victory,
With a deaf heart which never seem'd
 to be
A listener to itself, was strangely framed;
With but one weakest weakness — vanity,
Coquettish in ambition — still he aim'd —
At what? can he avouch — or answer what
 he claim'd? —

XCII

And would be all or nothing — nor could
 wait 820
For the sure grave to level him; few years
Had fix'd him with the Cæsars in his fate,
On whom we tread. For *this* the con-
 queror rears
The arch of triumph! and for this the tears
And blood of earth flow on as they have
 flow'd,
An universal deluge, which appears
Without an ark for wretched man's abode,
And ebbs but to reflow! — Renew thy rain-
 bow, God!

XCIII

What from this barren being do we reap?
Our senses narrow, and our reason frail,
Life short, and truth a gem which loves
 the deep, 831
And all things weigh'd in custom's falsest
 scale;
Opinion an omnipotence, — whose veil
Mantles the earth with darkness, until
 right
And wrong are accidents, and men grow
 pale
Lest their own judgments should become
 too bright,
And their free thoughts be crimes, and
 earth have too much light.

XCIV

And thus they plod in sluggish misery,
Rotting from sire to son, and age to
 age,
Proud of their trampled nature, and so
 die, 840
Bequeathing their hereditary rage
To the new race of inborn slaves, who
 wage
War for their chains, and rather than be
 free,
Bleed gladiator-like, and still engage
Within the same arena where they see
Their fellows fall before, like leaves of the
 same tree.

XCV

I speak not of men's creeds — they rest
 between
Man and his Maker — but of things al-
 low'd,
Averr'd, and known — and daily, hourly
 seen —
The yoke that is upon us doubly bow'd
And the intent of tyranny avow'd, 851
The edict of Earth's rulers, who are
 grown
The apes of him who humbled once the
 proud
And shook them from their slumbers on
 the throne;
Too glorious, were this all his mighty arm
 had done.

XCVI

Can tyrants but by tyrants conquer'd be,
And Freedom find no champion and no
 child

Such as Columbia saw arise when she
Sprung forth a Pallas, arm'd and unde-
 filed ?
Or must such minds be nourish'd in the
 wild, 860
Deep in the unpruned forest, 'midst the
 roar
Of cataracts, where nursing Nature
 smiled
On infant Washington? Has Earth no
 more
Such seeds within her breast, or Europe no
 such shore?

XCVII

But France got drunk with blood to
 vomit crime,
And fatal have her Saturnalia been
To Freedom's cause, in every age and
 clime;
Because the deadly days which we have
 seen,
And vile Ambition, that built up be-
 tween 869
Man and his hopes an adamantine wall,
And the base pageant last upon the scene,
Are grown the pretext for the eternal
 thrall
Which nips life's tree, and dooms man's
 worst — his second fall.

XCVIII

Yet, Freedom, yet thy banner, torn but
 flying,
Streams like the thunder-storm *against*
 the wind;
Thy trumpet voice, though broken now
 and dying,
The loudest still the tempest leaves be-
 hind:
Thy tree hath lost its blossoms, and the
 rind,
Chopp'd by the axe, looks rough and
 little worth,
But the sap lasts, — and still the seed we
 find 880
Sown deep, even in the bosom of the
 North;
So shall a better spring less bitter fruit
 bring forth.

XCIX

There is a stern round tower of other
 days,
Firm as a fortress, with its fence of stone,

Such as an army's baffled strength delays,
Standing with half its battlements alone,
And with two thousand years of ivy
grown,
The garland of eternity, where wave
The green leaves over all by time o'er-
thrown; —
What was this tower of strength ? within
its cave 890
What treasure lay so lock'd, so hid ? A
woman's grave.

C

But who was she, the lady of the dead,
Tomb'd in a palace ? Was she chaste
and fair ?
Worthy a king's — or more — a Roman's
bed ?
What race of chiefs and heroes did she
bear ?
What daughter of her beauties was the
heir ?
How lived, how loved, how died she ?
Was she not
So honour'd — and conspicuously there,
Where meaner relics must not dare to rot,
Placed to commemorate a more than mor-
tal lot ? 900

CI

Was she as those who love their lords, or
they
Who love the lords of others ? — such
have been
Even in the olden time, Rome's annals say.
Was she a matron of Cornelia's mien,
Or the light air of Egypt's graceful queen,
Profuse of joy — or 'gainst it did she war,
Inveterate in virtue ? Did she lean
To the soft side of the heart, or wisely
bar
Love from amongst her griefs ? — for such
the affections are.

CII

Perchance she died in youth: it may be,
bow'd 910
With woes far heavier than the ponder-
ous tomb
That weigh'd upon her gentle dust, a
cloud
Might gather o'er her beauty, and a gloom
In her dark eye, prophetic of the doom
Heaven gives its favourites — early
death; yet shed

A sunset charm around her, and illume
With hectic light, the Hesperus of the
dead,
Of her consuming cheek the autumnal leaf-
like red.

CIII

Perchance she died in age — surviving all,
Charms, kindred, children — with the
silver gray 920
On her long tresses, which might yet re-
call,
It may be, still a something of the day
When they were braided, and her proud
array
And lovely form were envied, praised,
and eyed
By Rome. — But whither would Conjec-
ture stray ?
Thus much alone we know — Metella
died,
The wealthiest Roman's wife. Behold his
love or pride !

CIV

I know not why, but standing thus by
thee,
It seems as if I had thine inmate known,
Thou tomb ! and other days come back
on me 930
With recollected music, though the tone
Is changed and solemn, like the cloudy
groan
Of dying thunder on the distant wind;
Yet could I seat me by this ivied stone
Till I had bodied forth the heated mind
Forms from the floating wreck which Ruin
leaves behind;

CV

And from the planks, far shatter'd o'er
the rocks,
Built me a little bark of hope, once more
To battle with the ocean and the shocks
Of the loud breakers, and the ceaseless
roar 940
Which rushes on the solitary shore
Where all lies founder'd that was ever
dear.
But could I gather from the wave-worn
store
Enough for my rude boat, where should
I steer ?
There woos no home, nor hope, nor life,
save what is here.

CVI

Then let the winds howl on ! their har-
 mony
Shall henceforth be my music, and the
 night
The sound shall temper with the owlets'
 cry,
As I now hear them, in the fading
 light
Dim o'er the bird of darkness' native
 site, 950
Answering each other on the Palatine,
With their large eyes all glistening gray
 and bright,
And sailing pinions. Upon such a shrine
What are our petty griefs ? — let me not
 number mine.

CVII

Cypress and ivy, weed and wallflower
 grown
Matted and mass'd together, hillocks
 heap'd
On what were chambers, arch crush'd,
 column strown
In fragments, choked up vaults, and
 frescos steep'd
In subterranean damps where the owl
 peep'd,
Deeming it midnight: — Temples, baths,
 or halls ? 960
Pronounce who can; for all that Learn-
 ing reap'd
From her research hath been, that these
 are walls —
Behold the Imperial Mount ! 't is thus the
 mighty falls.

CVIII

There is the moral of all human tales;
'T is but the same rehearsal of the
 past,
First Freedom and then Glory — when
 that fails,
Wealth, vice, corruption, — barbarism at
 last.
And History, with all her volumes vast,
Hath but *one* page, — 't is better written
 here
Where gorgeous Tyranny hath thus
 amass'd 970
All treasures, all delights, that eye or
 ear,
Heart, soul could seek, tongue ask. — Away
 with words, draw near,

CIX

Admire, exult — despise — laugh, weep,
 — for here
There is such matter for all feeling: —
 Man !
Thou pendulum betwixt a smile and tear,
Ages and realms are crowded in this span,
This mountain, whose obliterated plan
The pyramid of empires pinnacled,
Of Glory's gewgaws shining in the van
Till the sun's rays with added flame were
 fill'd ! 980
Where are its golden roofs ? where those
 who dared to build ?

CX

Tully was not so eloquent as thou,
Thou nameless column with the buried
 base !
What are the laurels of the Cæsar's
 brow ?
Crown me with ivy from his dwelling-
 place.
Whose arch or pillar meets me in the
 face,
Titus' or Trajan's ? No — 't is that of
 Time:
Triumph, arch, pillar, all he doth displace
Scoffing; and apostolic statues climb
To crush the imperial urn whose ashes slept
 sublime, 990

CXI

Buried in air, the deep blue sky of Rome,
And looking to the stars. They had con-
 tain'd
A spirit which with these would find a
 home,
The last of those who o'er the whole earth
 reign'd,
The Roman globe, for after none sus-
 tain'd
But yielded back his conquests: he was
 more
Than a mere Alexander, and, unstain'd
With household blood and wine, serenely
 wore
His sovereign virtues — still we Trajan's
 name adore.

CXII

Where is the rock of Triumph, the high
 place 1000
Where Rome embraced her heroes ?
 where the steep

Tarpeian, fittest goal of Treason's race,
The promontory whence the Traitor's
 Leap
Cured all ambition ? Did the conquerors
 heap
Their spoils here ? Yes; and in yon
 field below,
A thousand years of silenced factions
 sleep —
The Forum, where the immortal accents
 glow,
And still the eloquent air breathes — burns
 with Cicero !

CXIII

The field of freedom, faction, fame, and
 blood:
Here a proud people's passions were ex-
 haled, 1010
From the first hour of empire in the
 bud
To that when further worlds to conquer
 fail'd;
But long before had Freedom's face been
 veil'd,
And Anarchy assumed her attributes;
Till every lawless soldier who assail'd
Trod on the trembling senate's slavish
 mutes,
Or raised the venal voice of baser prosti-
 tutes.

CXIV

Then turn we to her latest tribune's
 name,
From her ten thousand tyrants turn to
 thee, 1019
Redeemer of dark centuries of shame —
The friend of Petrarch — hope of Italy —
Rienzi ! last of Romans ! While the
 tree
Of freedom's wither'd trunk puts forth a
 leaf,
Even for thy tomb a garland let it be —
The forum's champion, and the people's
 chief —
Her new-born Numa thou — with reign,
 alas, too brief.

CXV

Egeria, sweet creation of some heart
Which found no mortal resting-place so
 fair 1028
As thine ideal breast ! whate'er thou art
Or wert, — a young Aurora of the air,

The nympholepsy of some fond despair;
Or, it might be, a beauty of the earth,
Who found a more than common votary
 there
Too much adoring; whatsoe'er thy birth,
Thou wert a beautiful thought, and softly
 bodied forth.

CXVI

The mosses of thy fountain still are
 sprinkled
With thine Elysian water-drops; the face
Of thy cave-guarded spring, with years
 unwrinkled,
Reflects the meek-eyed genius of the
 place,
Whose green, wild margin now no more
 erase 1040
Art's works; nor must the delicate waters
 sleep,
Prison'd in marble; bubbling from the
 base
Of the cleft statue, with a gentle leap
The rill runs o'er, and round, fern, flowers,
 and ivy creep,

CXVII

Fantastically tangled. The green hills
Are clothed with early blossoms, through
 the grass
The quick-eyed lizard rustles, and the bills
Of summer-birds sing welcome as ye
 pass;
Flowers fresh in hue, and many in their
 class,
Implore the pausing step, and with their
 dyes 1050
Dance in the soft breeze in a fairy
 mass;
The sweetness of the violet's deep blue
 eyes,
Kiss'd by the breath of heaven, seems
 colour'd by its skies.

CXVIII

Here didst thou dwell, in this enchanted
 cover,
Egeria ! thy all heavenly bosom beating
For the far footsteps of thy mortal lover.
The purple Midnight veil'd that mystic
 meeting
With her most starry canopy; and seating
Thyself by thine adorer, what befell ?
This cave was surely shaped out for the
 greeting 1060

Of an enamour'd Goddess, and the cell
Haunted by holy Love — the earliest
 oracle !

CXIX

And didst thou not, thy breast to his re-
 plying,
Blend a celestial with a human heart;
And Love, which dies as it was born, in
 sighing,
Share with immortal transports ? Could
 thine art
Make them indeed immortal, and im-
 part
The purity of heaven to earthly joys,
Expel the venom and not blunt the dart —
The dull satiety which all destroys —
And root from out the soul the deadly weed
 which cloys ? 1071

CXX

Alas ! our young affections run to waste,
Or water but the desert; whence arise
But weeds of dark luxuriance, tares of
 haste,
Rank at the core, though tempting to the
 eyes,
Flowers whose wild odours breathe but
 agonies,
And trees whose gums are poison; — such
 the plants
Which spring beneath her steps as Pas-
 sion flies
O'er the world's wilderness, and vainly
 pants
For some celestial fruit forbidden to our
 wants. 1080

CXXI

Oh Love ! no habitant of earth thou
 art —
An unseen seraph, we believe in thee,
A faith whose martyrs are the broken
 heart,
But never yet hath seen, nor e'er shall
 see
The naked eye, thy form, as it should
 be;
The mind hath made thee, as it peopled
 heaven,
Even with its own desiring phantasy,
And to a thought such shape and image
 given,
As haunts the unquench'd soul — parch'd —
 wearied — wrung — and riven. 1089

CXXII

Of its own beauty is the mind diseased,
And fevers into false creation: — where,
Where are the forms the sculptor's soul
 hath seized ? —
In him alone. Can Nature show so fair ?
Where are the charms and virtues which
 we dare
Conceive in boyhood and pursue as men,
The unreach'd Paradise of our despair,
Which o'er-informs the pencil and the
 pen,
And overpowers the page where it would
 bloom again ?

CXXIII

Who loves, raves — 't is youth's frenzy;
 but the cure
Is bitterer still. As charm by charm un-
 winds 1100
Which robed our idols, and we see too
 sure
Nor worth nor beauty dwells from out
 the mind's
Ideal shape of such; yet still it binds
The fatal spell, and still it draws us on,
Reaping the whirlwind from the oft-
 sown winds;
The stubborn heart, its alchemy begun,
Seems ever near the prize, — wealthiest when
 most undone.

CXXIV

We wither from our youth, we gasp
 away —
Sick — sick; unfound the boon — unslaked
 the thirst,
Though to the last, in verge of our decay,
Some phantom lures, such as we sought
 at first — 1111
But all too late, — so are we doubly curst.
Love, fame, ambition, avarice — 't is the
 same,
Each idle, and all ill, and none the
 worst —
For all are meteors with a different name,
And Death the sable smoke where vanishes
 the flame.

CXXV

Few — none — find what they love or
 could have loved,
Though accident, blind contact, and the
 strong
Necessity of loving, have removed

Antipathies — but to recur, ere long, 1120
Envenom'd with irrevocable wrong;
And Circumstance, that unspiritual god
And miscreator, makes and helps along
Our coming evils with a crutch-like rod,
Whose touch turns Hope to dust, — the
 dust we all have trod.

CXXVI

Our life is a false nature, 't is not in
The harmony of things, — this hard decree,
This uneradicable taint of sin,
This boundless upas, this all-blasting tree
Whose root is earth, whose leaves and
 branches be 1130
The skies which rain their plagues on
 men like dew —
Disease, death, bondage — all the woes
 we see —
And worse, the woes we see not — which
 throb through
The immedicable soul, with heart-aches
 ever new.

CXXVII

Yet let us ponder boldly; 't is a base
Abandonment of reason to resign
Our right of thought, our last and only
 place
Of refuge — this, at least, shall still be
 mine.
Though from our birth the faculty divine
Is chain'd and tortured — cabin'd, cribb'd,
 confined, 1140
And bred in darkness, lest the truth should
 shine
Too brightly on the unprepare̒d mind,
The beam pours in, for time and skill will
 couch the blind.

CXXVIII

Arches on arches ! as it were that Rome,
Collecting the chief trophies of her line,
Would build up all her triumphs in one
 dome, —
Her Coliseum stands; the moonbeams
 shine
As 't were its natural torches, for divine
Should be the light which streams here,
 to illume
This long-explored but still exhaustless
 mine 1150
Of contemplation; and the azure gloom
Of an Italian night, where the deep skies
 assume

CXXIX

Hues which have words and speak to ye
 of heaven,
Floats o'er this vast and wondrous monu-
 ment,
And shadows forth its glory. There is
 given
Unto the things of earth, which Time
 hath bent,
A spirit's feeling; and where he hath
 leant
His hand, but broke his scythe, there is a
 power
And magic in the ruin'd battlement,
For which the palace of the present
 hour 1160
Must yield its pomp and wait till ages are
 its dower.

CXXX

Oh, Time ! the beautifier of the dead,
Adorner of the ruin, comforter
And only healer when the heart hath
 bled —
Time ! the corrector where our judgments
 err,
The test of truth, love, — sole philosopher,
For all besides are sophists, from thy
 thrift
Which never loses though it doth defer —
Time, the avenger ! unto thee I lift
My hands and eyes and heart, and crave of
 thee a gift: 1170

CXXXI

Amidst this wreck, where thou hast made
 a shrine
And temple more divinely desolate,
Among thy mightier offerings here are
 mine,
Ruins of years — though few, yet full of
 fate: —
If thou hast ever seen me too elate,
Hear me not; but if calmly I have borne
Good, and reserved my pride against the
 hate
Which shall not whelm me, let me not
 have worn
This iron in my soul in vain — shall *they*
 not mourn ?

CXXXII

And thou, who never yet of human
 wrong 1180
Left the unbalanced scale, great Nemesis!

Here, where the ancient paid thee homage
long —
Thou, who didst call the Furies from the
abyss,
And round Orestes bade them howl and
hiss
For that unnatural retribution — just,
Had it but been from hands less near — in
this
Thy former realm, I call thee from the
dust !
Dost thou not hear my heart ? — Awake !
thou shalt, and must.

CXXXIII

It is not that I may not have incurr'd
For my ancestral faults or mine the
wound 1190
I bleed withal, and, had it been conferr'd
With a just weapon, it had flow'd un-
bound;
But now my blood shall not sink in the
ground;
To thee I do devote it —*thou* shalt take
The vengeance, which shall yet be sought
and found,
Which if *I* have not taken for the sake—
But let that pass — I sleep, but thou shalt
yet awake.

CXXXIV

And if my voice break forth, 't is not
that now
I shrink from what is suffer'd; let him
speak
Who hath beheld decline upon my
brow, 1200
Or seen my mind's convulsion leave it
weak:
But in this page a record will I seek.
Not in the air shall these my words
disperse,
Though I be ashes; a far hour shall wreak
The deep prophetic fulness of this verse,
And pile on human heads the mountain of
my curse !

CXXXV

That curse shall be Forgiveness. Have I
not —
Hear me, my mother Earth ! behold it,
Heaven ! —
Have I not had to wrestle with my lot ?
Have I not suffer'd things to be for-
given ? 1210

Have I not had my brain sear'd, my heart
riven,
Hopes sapp'd, name blighted, Life's life
lied away ?
And only not to desperation driven,
Because not altogether of such clay
As rots into the souls of those whom I survey.

CXXXVI

From mighty wrongs to petty perfidy
Have I not seen what human things could
do ?
From the loud roar of foaming calumny
To the small whisper of the as paltry
few, 1219
And subtler venom of the reptile crew,
The Janus glance of whose significant eye,
Learning to lie with silence, would *seem*
true,
And without utterance, save the shrug
or sigh,
Deal round to happy fools its speechless
obloquy.

CXXXVII

But I have lived, and have not lived in
vain:
My mind may lose its force, my blood its
fire,
And my frame perish even in conquering
pain;
But there is that within me which shall
tire
Torture and Time, and breathe when I
expire;
Something unearthly which they deem
not of, 1230
Like the remember'd tone of a mute lyre,
Shall on their soften'd spirits sink, and
move
In hearts all rocky now the late remorse of
love.

CXXXVIII

The seal is set. — Now welcome, thou
dread power !
Nameless, yet thus omnipotent, which
here
Walk'st in the shadow of the midnight
hour
With a deep awe, yet all distinct from
fear;
Thy haunts are ever where the dead walls
rear
Their ivy mantles, and the solemn scene

Derives from thee a sense so deep and
 clear 1240
That we become a part of what has been,
And grow unto the spot, all-seeing but
 unseen.

CXXXIX

And here the buzz of eager nations ran,
In murmur'd pity or loud-roar'd applause,
As man was slaughter'd by his fellow man.
And wherefore slaughter'd? wherefore,
 but because
Such were the bloody Circus' genial laws,
And the imperial pleasure. — Wherefore
 not?
What matters where we fall to fill the
 maws
Of worms — on battle-plains or listed
 spot? 1250
Both are but theatres where the chief actors
 rot.

CXL

I see before me the Gladiator lie:
He leans upon his hand — his manly brow
Consents to death, but conquers agony,
And his droop'd head sinks gradually
 low —
And through his side the last drops, ebb-
 ing slow
From the red gash, fall heavy, one by
 one,
Like the first of a thunder-shower; and
 now
The arena swims around him — he is
 gone,
Ere ceased the inhuman shout which hail'd
 the wretch who won. 1260

CXLI

He heard it, but he heeded not — his eyes
Were with his heart and that was far
 away;
He reck'd not of the life he lost nor prize,
But where his rude hut by the Danube
 lay,
There were his young barbarians all at
 play,
There was their Dacian mother — he, their
 sire,
Butcher'd to make a Roman holiday —
All this rush'd with his blood. — Shall he
 expire
And unavenged? — Arise! ye Goths, and
 glut your ire!

CXLII

But here, where Murder breathed her
 bloody steam; 1270
And here, where buzzing nations choked
 the ways,
And roar'd or murmur'd like a mountain
 stream
Dashing or winding as its torrent strays;
Here, where the Roman millions' blame
 or praise
Was death or life, the playthings of a
 crowd,
My voice sounds much, and fall the stars'
 faint rays
On the arena void — seats crush'd — walls
 bow'd —
And galleries, where my steps seem echoes
 strangely loud.

CXLIII

A ruin — yet what ruin! From its mass
Walls, palaces, half-cities, have been
 rear'd; 1280
Yet oft the enormous skeleton ye pass,
And marvel where the spoil could have
 appear'd.
Hath it indeed been plunder'd, or but
 clear'd?
Alas! developed, opens the decay,
When the colossal fabric's form is near'd:
It will not bear the brightness of the day,
Which streams too much on all years, man,
 have reft away.

CXLIV

But when the rising moon begins to climb
Its topmost arch and gently pauses there;
When the stars twinkle through the loops
 of time, 1290
And the low night-breeze waves along
 the air
The garland forest, which the gray walls
 wear
Like laurels on the bald first Cæsar's
 head;
When the light shines serene but doth
 not glare,
Then in this magic circle raise the dead:
Heroes have trod this spot — 't is on their
 dust ye tread.

CXLV

'While stands the Coliseum, Rome shall
 stand;
When falls the Coliseum, Rome shall fall;

And when Rome falls — the World.'
From our own land
Thus spake the pilgrims o'er this mighty
wall 1300
In Saxon times, which we are wont to call
Ancient; and these three mortal things
are still
On their foundations, and unalter'd all;
Rome and her Ruin past Redemption's
skill,
The World, the same wide den — of thieves,
or what ye will.

CXLVI

Simple, erect, severe, austere, sublime —
Shrine of all saints and temple of all gods,
From Jove to Jesus — spared and blest
by time;
Looking tranquillity, while falls or nods
Arch, empire, each thing round thee, and
man plods 1310
His way through thorns to ashes —
glorious dome !
Shalt thou not last ? Time's scythe and
tyrants' rods
Shiver upon thee — sanctuary and home
Of art and piety — Pantheon ! — pride of
Rome !

CXLVII

Relic of nobler days and noblest arts !
Despoil'd, yet perfect, with thy circle
spreads
A holiness appealing to all hearts —
To art a model; and to him who treads
Rome for the sake of ages, Glory sheds
Her light through thy sole aperture; to
those 1320
Who worship, here are altars for their
beads;
And they who feel for genius may repose
Their eyes on honour'd forms whose busts
around them close.

CXLVIII

There is a dungeon, in whose dim drear
light
What do I gaze on ? Nothing: Look
again !
Two forms are slowly shadow'd on my
sight —
Two insulated phantoms of the brain:
It is not so; I see them full and plain —
An old man, and a female young and fair,
Fresh as a nursing mother, in whose vein

The blood is nectar; — but what doth she
there, 1331
With her unmantled neck, and bosom white
and bare ?

CXLIX

Full swells the deep pure fountain of
young life,
Where *on* the heart and *from* the heart
we took
Our first and sweetest nurture, when the
wife,
Blest into mother, in the innocent look
Or even the piping cry of lips that brook
No pain and small suspense, a joy per-
ceives
Man knows not, when from out its
cradled nook
She sees her little bud put forth its
leaves — 1340
What may the fruit be yet ? — I know not,
Cain was Eve's.

CL

But here youth offers to old age the food,
The milk of his own gift: — it is her
sire
To whom she renders back the debt of
blood
Born with her birth. No; he shall not
expire
While in those warm and lovely veins the
fire
Of health and holy feeling can provide
Great Nature's Nile, whose deep stream
rises higher
Than Egypt's river: — from that gentle
side
Drink, drink and live, old man ! Heaven's
realm holds no such tide. 1350

CLI

The starry fable of the milky way
Has not thy story's purity; it is
A constellation of a sweeter ray,
And sacred Nature triumphs more in
this
Reverse of her decree than in the abyss
Where sparkle distant worlds. Oh, holi-
est nurse !
No drop of that clear stream its way shall
miss
To thy sire's heart, replenishing its source
With life, as our freed souls rejoin the uni-
verse.

CLII

Turn to the Mole which Hadrian rear'd
on high, 1360
Imperial mimic of old Egypt's piles,
Colossal copyist of deformity,
Whose travell'd phantasy from the far
Nile's
Enormous model doom'd the artist's toils
To build for giants, and for his vain earth,
His shrunken ashes, raise this dome. How
smiles
The gazer's eye with philosophic mirth,
To view the huge design which sprung from
such a birth !

CLIII

But lo, the dome, the vast and wondrous
dome
To which Diana's marvel was a cell, 1370
Christ's mighty shrine above his martyr's
tomb !
I have beheld the Ephesian's miracle —
Its columns strew the wilderness, and
dwell
The hyæna and the jackal in their shade;
I have beheld Sophia's bright roofs swell
Their glittering mass i' the sun, and have
survey'd
Its sanctuary the while the usurping
Moslem pray'd;

CLIV

But thou, of temples old or altars new,
Standest alone, with nothing like to thee —
Worthiest of God, the holy and the true.
Since Zion's desolation, when that He 1381
Forsook his former city, what could be,
Of earthly structures, in his honour piled
Of a sublimer aspect ? Majesty,
Power, Glory, Strength, and Beauty, all
are aisled
In this eternal ark of worship undefiled.

CLV

Enter: its grandeur overwhelms thee not;
And why ? it is not lessen'd; but thy
mind,
Expanded by the genius of the spot,
Has grown colossal, and can only find 1390
A fit abode wherein appear enshrined
Thy hopes of immortality; and thou
Shalt one day, if found worthy, so defined,
See thy God face to face as thou dost now
His Holy of Holies, nor be blasted by his
brow.

CLVI

Thou movest — but increasing with the
advance,
Like climbing some great Alp, which still
doth rise,
Deceived by its gigantic elegance;
Vastness which grows, but grows to har-
monise —
All musical in its immensities; 1400
Rich marbles, richer painting, shrines
where flame
The lamps of gold, and haughty dome
which vies
In air with Earth's chief structures,
though their frame
Sits on the firm-set ground — and this the
clouds must claim.

CLVII

Thou seest not all; but piecemeal thou
must break
To separate contemplation the great
whole;
And as the ocean many bays will make,
That ask the eye — so here condense thy
soul
To more immediate objects, and control
Thy thoughts until thy mind hath got by
heart 1410
Its eloquent proportions, and unroll
In mighty graduations, part by part,
The glory which at once upon thee did not
dart,

CLVIII

Not by its fault — but thine. Our outward
sense
Is but of gradual grasp: and as it is
That what we have of feeling most in-
tense
Outstrips our faint expression; even so
this
Outshining and o'erwhelming edifice
Fools our fond gaze, and greatest of the
great
Defies at first our Nature's littleness, 1420
Till, growing with its growth, we thus
dilate
Our spirits to the size of that they con-
template.

CLIX

Then pause, and be enlighten'd; there is
more
In such a survey than the sating gaze

Of wonder pleased, or awe which would
　　adore
The worship of the place, or the mere
　　praise
Of art and its great masters, who could
　　raise
What former time, nor skill, nor thought
　　could plan;
The fountain of sublimity displays
Its depth, and thence may draw the mind
　　of man　　　　　　　　　　　1430
Its golden sands, and learn what great con-
　　ceptions can.

CLX

Or, turning to the Vatican, go see
Laocoon's torture dignifying pain —
A father's love and mortal's agony
With an immortal's patience blending. Vain
The struggle; vain, against the coiling
　　strain
And gripe and deepening of the dragon's
　　grasp,
The old man's clench; the long envenom'd
　　chain
Rivets the living links, the enormous asp
Enforces pang on pang, and stifles gasp on
　　gasp.　　　　　　　　　　　1440

CLXI

Or view the Lord of the unerring bow,
The God of life and poesy and light, —
The Sun in human limbs array'd, and brow
All radiant from his triumph in the fight;
The shaft hath just been shot — the arrow
　　bright
With an immortal's vengeance; in his eye
And nostril beautiful disdain and might
And majesty flash their full lightnings by,
Developing in that one glance the Deity.

CLXII

But in his delicate form — a dream of
　　Love,　　　　　　　　　　　1450
Shaped by some solitary nymph, whose
　　breast
Long'd for a deathless lover from above
And madden'd in that vision — are ex-
　　prest
All that ideal beauty ever bless'd
The mind with in its most unearthly
　　mood,
When each conception was a heavenly
　　guest —

A ray of immortality — and stood,
Starlike, around, until they gather'd to a
　　god !

CLXIII

And if it be Prometheus stole from
　　Heaven　　　　　　　　　　　1459
The fire which we endure, it was repaid
By him to whom the energy was given
Which this poetic marble hath array'd
With an eternal glory — which, if made
By human hands, is not of human thought;
And Time himself hath hallow'd it, nor
　　laid
One ringlet in the dust; nor hath it caught
A tinge of years, but breathes the flame
　　with which 't was wrought.

CLXIV

But where is he, the Pilgrim of my song,
The being who upheld it through the
　　past ?
Methinks he cometh late and tarries long.
He is no more — these breathings are his
　　last;　　　　　　　　　　　1471
His wanderings done, his visions ebbing
　　fast,
And he himself as nothing: — if he was
Aught but a phantasy, and could be
　　class'd
With forms which live and suffer — let
　　that pass —
His shadow fades away into Destruction's
　　mass,

CLXV

Which gathers shadow, substance, life,
　　and all
That we inherit in its mortal shroud,
And spreads the dim and universal pall
Through which all things grow phantoms;
　　and the cloud　　　　　　　　1480
Between us sinks and all which ever
　　glow'd,
Till Glory's self is twilight, and displays
A melancholy halo scarce allow'd
To hover on the verge of darkness; —
　　rays
Sadder than saddest night, for they distract
　　the gaze,

CLXVI

And send us prying into the abyss,
To gather what we shall be when the
　　frame

Shall be resolved to something less than
 this
Its wretched essence; and to dream of
 fame,
And wipe the dust from off the idle
 name 1490
We never more shall hear, — but never
 more,
Oh, happier thought! can we be made
 the same:
It is enough in sooth that *once* we bore
These fardels of the heart — the heart
 whose sweat was gore.

CLXVII

Hark! forth from the abyss a voice pro-
 ceeds,
A long low distant murmur of dread
 sound,
Such as arises when a nation bleeds
With some deep and immedicable wound;
Through storm and darkness yawns the
 rending ground;
The gulf is thick with phantoms, but the
 chief 1500
Seems royal still, though with her head
 discrown'd;
And pale, but lovely, with maternal
 grief
She clasps a babe to whom her breast yields
 no relief.

CLXVIII

Scion of chiefs and monarchs, where art
 thou?
Fond hope of many nations, art thou
 dead?
Could not the grave forget thee, and lay
 low
Some less majestic, less beloved head?
In the sad midnight, while thy heart still
 bled,
The mother of a moment, o'er thy boy,
Death hush'd that pang for ever; with
 thee fled 1510
The present happiness and promised joy
Which fill'd the imperial isles so full it
 seem'd to cloy.

CLXIX

Peasants bring forth in safety. — Can it
 be,
Oh thou that wert so happy, so adored!
Those who weep not for kings shall weep
 for thee,

And Freedom's heart, grown heavy, cease
 to hoard
Her many griefs for One; for she had
 pour'd
Her orisons for thee, and o'er thy head
Beheld her Iris. — Thou, too, lonely lord,
And desolate consort — vainly wert thou
 wed! 1520
The husband of a year! the father of the
 dead!

CLXX

Of sackcloth was thy wedding garment
 made;
Thy bridal's fruit is ashes; in the dust
The fair-hair'd Daughter of the Isles is
 laid,
The love of millions! How we did in-
 trust
Futurity to her! and, though it must
Darken above our bones, yet fondly
 deem'd
Our children should obey her child, and
 bless'd
Her and her hoped-for seed, whose pro-
 mise seem'd
Like stars to shepherds' eyes: — 't was but
 a meteor beam'd. 1530

CLXXI

Woe unto us, not her; for she sleeps
 well:
The fickle reek of popular breath, the
 tongue
Of hollow counsel, the false oracle,
Which from the birth of monarchy hath
 rung
Its knell in princely ears till the o'er-
 stung
Nations have arm'd in madness, the
 strange fate
Which tumbles mightiest sovereigns, and
 hath flung
Against their blind omnipotence a weight
Within the opposing scale which crushes
 soon or late, —

CLXXII

These might have been her destiny; but
 no, 1540
Our hearts deny it: and so young, so
 fair,
Good without effort, great without a foe;
But now a bride and mother — and now
 there!

How many ties did that stern moment
tear!
From thy Sire's to his humblest subject's
breast
Is link'd the electric chain of that despair,
Whose shock was as an earthquake's, and
opprest
The land which loved thee so that none
could love thee best.

CLXXIII

Lo, Nemi! navell'd in the woody hills
So far, that the uprooting wind which
tears 1550
The oak from his foundation, and which
spills
The ocean o'er its boundary, and bears
Its foam against the skies, reluctant
spares
The oval mirror of thy glassy lake; —
And, calm as cherish'd hate, its surface
wears
A deep cold settled aspect nought can
shake,
All coil'd into itself and round, as sleeps
the snake.

CLXXIV

And near Albano's scarce divided waves
Shine from a sister valley; and afar
The Tiber winds, and the broad ocean
laves 1560
The Latian coast where sprung the Epic
war,
'Arms and the Man,' whose re-ascend-
ing star
Rose o'er an empire: but beneath thy
right
Tully reposed from Rome; and where
yon bar
Of girdling mountains intercepts the
sight
The Sabine farm was till'd, the weary
bard's delight.

CLXXV

But I forget. — My Pilgrim's shrine is
won,
And he and I must part — so let it be:
His task and mine alike are nearly done;
Yet once more let us look upon the sea;
The midland ocean breaks on him and
me, 1571
And from the Alban Mount we now be-
hold

Our friend of youth, that ocean, which
when we
Beheld it last by Calpe's rock unfold
Those waves, we follow'd on till the dark
Euxine roll'd

CLXXVI

Upon the blue Symplegades. Long
years —
Long, though not very many — since
have done
Their work on both; some suffering and
some tears
Have left us nearly where we had begun:
Yet not in vain our mortal race hath
run; 1580
We have had our reward, and it is here, —
That we can yet feel gladden'd by the
sun,
And reap from earth, sea, joy almost as
dear
As if there were no man to trouble what is
clear.

CLXXVII

Oh that the Desert were my dwelling-
place,
With one fair Spirit for my minister,
That I might all forget the human race,
And, hating no one, love but only her!
Ye Elements, in whose ennobling stir
I feel myself exalted, can ye not 1590
Accord me such a being? Do I err
In deeming such inhabit many a spot,
Though with them to converse can rarely
be our lot?

CLXXVIII

There is a pleasure in the pathless woods,
There is a rapture on the lonely shore,
There is society where none intrudes,
By the deep Sea, and music in its roar:
I love not Man the less, but Nature more,
From these our interviews, in which I
steal 1599
From all I may be or have been before,
To mingle with the Universe, and feel
What I can ne'er express, yet can not all
conceal.

CLXXIX

Roll on, thou deep and dark blue Ocean,
roll!
Ten thousand fleets sweep over thee in
vain;

Man marks the earth with ruin, his con-
 trol
Stops with the shore; upon the watery
 plain
The wrecks are all thy deed, nor doth
 remain
A shadow of man's ravage, save his own,
When, for a moment, like a drop of rain,
He sinks into thy depths with bubbling
 groan, 1610
Without a grave, unknell'd, uncoffin'd, and
 unknown.

CLXXX

His steps are not upon thy paths, thy
 fields
Are not a spoil for him, — thou dost arise
And shake him from thee; the vile
 strength he wields
For earth's destruction thou dost all de-
 spise,
Spurning him from thy bosom to the skies,
And send'st him, shivering in thy playful
 spray
And howling, to his Gods, where haply
 lies
His petty hope in some near port or bay,
And dashest him again to earth: — there let
 him lay. 1620

CLXXXI

The armaments which thunderstrike the
 walls
Of rock-built cities, bidding nations quake
And monarchs tremble in their capitals,
The oak leviathans, whose huge ribs
 make
Their clay creator the vain title take
Of lord of thee and arbiter of war, —
These are thy toys, and, as the snowy
 flake,
They melt into thy yeast of waves, which
 mar
Alike the Armada's pride or spoils of Tra-
 falgar.

CLXXXII

Thy shores are empires, changed in all
 save thee — 1630
Assyria, Greece, Rome, Carthage, what
 are they ?
Thy waters wash'd them power while they
 were free,
And many a tyrant since; their shores
 obey

The stranger, slave, or savage; their
 decay
Has dried up realms to deserts: — not so
 thou,
Unchangeable save to thy wild waves'
 play;
Time writes no wrinkle on thine azure
 brow;
Such as creation's dawn beheld, thou rollest
 now.

CLXXXIII

Thou glorious mirror, where the Al-
 mighty's form
Glasses itself in tempests; in all time,
Calm or convulsed — in breeze, or gale,
 or storm, 1641
Icing the pole, or in the torrid clime
Dark-heaving; — boundless, endless, and
 sublime —
The image of Eternity — the throne
Of the Invisible; even from out thy
 slime
The monsters of the deep are made; each
 zone
Obeys thee; thou goest forth, dread, fath-
 omless, alone.

CLXXXIV

And I have loved thee, Ocean ! and my
 joy
Of youthful sports was on thy breast to
 be
Borne, like thy bubbles, onward. From
 a boy 1650
I wanton'd with thy breakers — they to
 me
Were a delight; and if the freshening sea
Made them a terror — 't was a pleasing
 fear,
For I was as it were a child of thee,
And trusted to thy billows far and near,
And laid my hand upon thy mane — as I
 do here.

CLXXXV

My task is done — my song hath ceased —
 my theme
Has died into an echo; it is fit
The spell should break of this protracted
 dream.
The torch shall be extinguish'd which hath
 lit 1660
My midnight lamp — and what is writ,
 is writ, —

Would it were worthier! but I am not now
That which I have been — and my visions
 flit
Less palpably before me — and the glow
Which in my spirit dwelt is fluttering,
 faint, and low.

CLXXXVI

Farewell! a word that must be, and hath
 been —
A sound which makes us linger; — yet
 — farewell!

Ye, who have traced the Pilgrim to the
 scene
Which is his last, if in your memories
 dwell
A thought which once was his, if on ye
 swell 1670
A single recollection, not in vain
He wore his sandal-shoon and scallop-
 shell;
Farewell! with *him* alone may rest the pain,
If such there were — with *you*, the moral of
 his strain!

ELEGY ON NEWSTEAD ABBEY

' It is the voice of years that are gone ! they
roll before me with all their deeds.' — OSSIAN.

NEWSTEAD ! fast-falling, once-resplendent
 dome !
 Religion's shrine ! repentant HENRY'S
 pride !
Of warriors, monks, and dames the clois-
 ter'd tomb,
 Whose pensive shades around thy ruins
 glide,

Hail to thy pile ! more honour'd in thy
 fall
 Than modern mansions in their pillar'd
 state;
Proudly majestic frowns thy vaulted hall,
 Scowling defiance on the blasts of fate.

No mail-clad serfs, obedient to their lord,
 In grim array the crimson cross de-
 mand; 10
Or gay assemble round the festive board
 Their chief's retainers, an immortal
 band:

Else might inspiring Fancy's magic eye
 Retrace their progress through the lapse
 of time,
Marking each ardent youth, ordain'd to
 die,
 A votive pilgrim in Judea's clime.

But not from thee, dark pile ! departs the
 chief;
 His feudal realm in other regions lay:
In thee the wounded conscience courts re-
 lief,
 Retiring from the garish blaze of day. 20

Yes ! in thy gloomy cells and shades pro-
 found
 The monk abjured a world he ne'er could
 view;
Or blood-stain'd guilt repenting solace
 found,
 Or innocence from stern oppression flew.

A monarch bade thee from that wild arise,
 Where Sherwood's outlaws once were
 wont to prowl;
And Superstition's crimes, of various dyes,

Sought shelter in the priest's protecting
 cowl.
Where now the grass exhales a murky
 dew, 29
 The humid pall of life-extinguish'd clay,
In sainted fame the sacred fathers grew,
 Nor raised their pious voices but to
 pray.

Where now the bats their wavering wings
 extend
 Soon as the gloaming spreads her waning
 shade,
The choir did oft their mingling vespers
 blend,
 Or matin orisons to Mary paid.

Years roll on years; to ages, ages yield;
 Abbots to abbots, in a line, succeed:
Religion's charter their protecting shield
 Till royal sacrilege their doom de-
 creed. 40

One holy HENRY rear'd the Gothic walls,
 And bade the pious inmates rest in peace ;
Another HENRY the kind gift recalls,
 And bids devotion's hallow'd echoes cease.

Vain is each threat or supplicating prayer;
 He drives them exiles from their blest
 abode,
To roam a dreary world in deep despair —
 No friend, no home, no refuge, but their
 God.

Hark how the hall, resounding to the
 strain, 49
 Shakes with the martial music's novel din !
The heralds of a warrior's haughty reign,
 High crested banners wave thy walls
 within.

Of changing sentinels the distant hum,
 The mirth of feasts, the clang of bur-
 nish'd arms,
The braying trumpet and the hoarser
 drum,
 Unite in concert with increased alarms.

An abbey once, a regal fortress now,
 Encircled by insulting rebel powers,
War's dread machines o'erhang thy threat-
 ening brow,
 And dart destruction in sulphureous
 showers. 60

Ah, vain defence! the hostile traitor's
 siege,
 Though oft repulsed, by guile o'ercomes
 the brave;
His thronging foes oppress the faithful
 liege,
 Rebellion's reeking standards o'er him
 wave.

Not unavenged the raging baron yields;
 The blood of traitors smears the purple
 plain;
Unconquer'd still, his falchion there he
 wields,
 And days of glory yet for him remain.

Still in that hour the warrior wish'd to
 strew
 Self-gather'd laurels on a self-sought
 grave; 70
But Charles' protecting genius hither flew,
 The monarch's friend, the monarch's
 hope, to save.

Trembling, she snatch'd him from th' un-
 equal strife,
 In other fields the torrent to repel;
For nobler combats, here, reserved his life,
 To lead the band where godlike FALK-
 LAND fell.

From thee, poor pile! to lawless plunder
 given,
 While dying groans their painful requiem
 sound,
Far different incense now ascends to heaven,
 Such victims wallow on the gory ground.

There many a pale and ruthless robber's
 corse, 81
 Noisome and ghast, defiles thy sacred
 sod;
O'er mingling man, and horse commix'd
 with horse,
 Corruption's heap, the savage spoilers
 trod.

Graves, long with rank and sighing weeds
 o'erspread,
 Ransack'd, resign perforce their mortal
 mould:
From ruffian fangs escape not e'en the dead,
 Raked from repose in search for buried
 gold.

Hush'd is the harp, unstrung the warlike
 lyre,
 The minstrel's palsied hand reclines in
 death; 90
No more he strikes the quivering chords
 with fire,
 Or sings the glories of the martial wreath.

At length the sated murderers, gorged with
 prey,
 Retire; the clamour of the fight is o'er;
Silence again resumes her awful sway,
 And sable Horror guards the massy
 door.

Here Desolation holds her dreary court:
 What satellites declare her dismal reign!
Shrieking their dirge, ill-omen'd birds re-
 sort,
 To flit their vigils in the hoary fane. 100

Soon a new morn's restoring beams dispel
 The clouds of anarchy from Britain's
 skies;
The fierce usurper seeks his native hell,
 And Nature triumphs as the tyrant dies.

With storms she welcomes his expiring
 groans,
 Whirlwinds, responsive, greet his labour-
 ing breath;
Earth shudders as her caves receive his
 bones,
 Loathing the offering of so dark a death.

The legal ruler now resumes the helm,
 He guides through gentle seas the prow
 of state; 110
Hope cheers with wonted smiles the peace-
 ful realm,
 And heals the bleeding wounds of wearied
 hate.

The gloomy tenants, Newstead! of thy
 cells,
 Howling, resign their violated nest;
Again the master on his tenure dwells,
 Enjoy'd, from absence, with enraptured
 zest.

Vassals, within thy hospitable pale,
 Loudly carousing, bless their lord's re-
 turn;
Culture again adorns the gladdening vale,

And matrons, once lamenting, cease to
 mourn. 120

A thousand songs on tuneful echo float,
 Unwonted foliage mantles o'er the trees;
And hark ! the horns proclaim a mellow
 note,
 The hunters' cry hangs lengthening on
 the breeze.

Beneath their coursers' hoofs the valleys
 shake:
 What fears, what anxious hopes, attend
 the chase !
The dying stag seeks refuge in the Lake;
 Exulting shouts announce the finish'd
 race.

Ah happy days ! too happy to endure !
 Such simple sports our plain forefathers
 knew; 130
No splendid vices glitter'd to allure;
 Their joys were many, as their cares were
 few.

From these descending, sons to sires suc-
 ceed;
 Time steals along, and Death uprears his
 dart;
Another chief impels the foaming steed,
 Another crowd pursue the panting hart.

Newstead ! what saddening change of
 scene is thine !
 Thy yawning arch betokens slow de-
 cay;
The last and youngest of a noble line
 Now holds thy mouldering turrets in his
 sway. 140

Deserted now, he scans thy gray worn
 towers;
 Thy vaults where dead of feudal ages
 sleep;
Thy cloisters, pervious to the wintry show-
 ers;
 These, these he views, and views them
 but to weep.

Yet are his tears no emblem of regret:
 Cherish'd affection only bids them flow;
Pride, hope, and love forbid him to forget,
 But warm his bosom with impassion'd
 glow.

Yet he prefers thee to the gilded domes
 Or gewgaw grottos of the vainly great;
Yet lingers 'mid thy damp and mossy tombs,
 Nor breathes a murmur 'gainst the will
 of fate. 152

Haply thy sun, emerging, yet may shine,
 Thee to irradiate with meridian ray;
Hours splendid as the past may still be
 thine,
 And bless thy future as thy former day.

TO A KNOT OF UNGENEROUS
CRITICS

[First printed in Edition of 1898 from a
manuscript in possession of Mr. Murray.]

RAIL on, Rail on, ye heartless Crew !
My strains were never meant for you;
Remorseless Rancour still reveal,
And damn the verse you cannot feel.
Invoke those kindred passions' aid,
Whose baleful stings your breasts pervade;
Crush, if you can, the hopes of youth,
Trampling regardless on the Truth.
Truth's Records you consult in vain,
She will not blast her native strain; 10
She will assist her votary's cause,
His will at least be her applause,
Your prayer the gentle Power will spurn.
To Fiction's motley altar turn,
Who joyful in the fond address
Her favour'd worshippers will bless:
And lo ! she holds a magic glass,
Where Images reflected pass,
Bent on your knees the Boon receive —
This will assist you to deceive — 20
The glittering gift was made for you,
Now hold it up to public view;
Lest evil unforeseen betide,
A Mask each canker'd brow shall hide
(Whilst Truth my sole desire is nigh,
Prepared the danger to defy),
'There is the Maid's perverted name,
And there the Poet's guilty Flame,
Gloaming a deep phosphoric fire,
Threatening — but ere it spreads, retire.' 30
Says Truth ' Up Virgins, do not fear !
The Comet rolls its Influence here;
'T is Scandal's Mirror you perceive,
These dazzling Meteors but deceive —
Approach and touch — Nay do not turn,
It blazes there but will not burn.' —

At once the shivering Mirror flies,
Teeming no more with varnish'd Lies;
The baffled friends of Fiction start,
Too late desiring to depart — 40
Truth poising high Ithuriel's spear
Bids every Fiend unmask'd appear,
The vizard tears from every face,
And dooms them to a dire disgrace.
For ere they compass their escape,
Each takes perforce a native shape —
The Leader of the wrathful Band,
Behold a portly Female stand !
She raves, impell'd by private pique,
This mean unjust revenge to seek; 50
From vice to save this virtuous Age,
Thus does she vent indecent rage !
What child has she of promise fair,
Who claims a fostering Mother's care ?
Whose Innocence requires defence,
Or forms at least a smooth pretence,
Thus to disturb a harmless Boy,
His humble hope, and peace annoy ?
She need not fear the amorous rhyme,
Love will not tempt her future time, 60
For her his wings have ceased to spread,
No more he flutters round her head;
Her day's Meridian now is past,
The clouds of Age her Sun o'ercast;
To her the strain was never sent,
For feeling Souls alone 't was meant —
The verse she seized, unask'd, unbade,
And damn'd, ere yet the whole was read !
Yes ! for one single erring verse,
Pronounced an unrelenting Curse; 70
Yes ! at a first and transient view,
Condemn'd a heart she never knew.
Can such a verdict then decide,
Which springs from disappointed pride ?
Without a wondrous share of Wit,
To judge is such a Matron fit ?
The rest of the censorious throng
Who to this zealous Band belong,
To her a general homage pay,
And right or wrong her wish obey: 80
Why should I point my pen of steel
To break 'such flies upon the wheel' ?
With minds to Truth and Sense unknown,
Who dare not call their words their own.
Rail on, Rail on, ye heartless Crew !
Your Leader's grand design pursue;
Secure behind her ample shield,
Yours is the harvest of the field.
My path with thorns you cannot strew,
Nay more, my warmest thanks are due; 90
When such as you revile my Name,

Bright beams the rising Sun of Fame,
Chasing the shades of envious night,
Outshining every critic Light.
Such, such as you will serve to show
Each radiant tint with higher glow.
Vain is the feeble cheerless toil,
Your efforts on yourselves recoil;
Then Glory still for me you raise,
Yours is the Censure, mine the Praise. 100
 December 1, 1806.

THE DUEL

[First published in the Edition of 1901 from
a manuscript in the possession of Mr. Murray.
These lines, addressed to Mary Chaworth, allude
to the duel fought between her granduncle,
William Chaworth, Esq., of Annesley, and the
poet's granduncle, the fifth Lord Byron, on
January 26, 1765. Mr. Chaworth fell in the
encounter, and his antagonist was tried before
the House of Lords on the charge of murder,
but acquitted by a verdict of 'manslaughter.']

'T is fifty years, and yet their fray
To us might seem but yesterday.
'T is fifty years, and three to boot,
Since, hand to hand, and foot to foot,
And heart to heart, and sword to sword,
One of our Ancestors was gored.
I've seen the sword that slew him; he,
The slain, stood in a like degree
To thee, as he, the Slayer, stood
(Oh had it been but other blood !) 10
In kin and Chieftainship to me.
Thus came the Heritage to thee.

To me the Lands of him who slew
 Came through a line of yore renown'd;
For I can boast a race as true
 To Monarchs crown'd, and some dis-
 crown'd,
As ever Britain's Annals knew:
For the first Conqueror gave us Ground,
 And the last Conquer'd own'd the line
 Which was my mother's, and is mine. 20

I loved thee — I will not say *how*,
 Since things like these are best forgot;
Perhaps thou mayst imagine now
 Who loved thee, and who loved thee not.
And thou wert wedded to another,
 And I at last another wedded:

I am a father, thou a mother,
 To Strangers vow'd, with strangers
 bedded.
For land to land, even blood to blood —
 Since leagued of yore our fathers were —
Our manors and our birthright stood; 31
And not unequal had I woo'd,
 If to have woo'd thee I could dare.
But this I never dared — even yet
When nought is left but to forget.
 I feel that I could only love:
To sue was never meant for me,
And least of all to sue to thee;
For many a bar, and many a feud,
Though never told, well understood, 40
 Roll'd like a river wide between —
And then there was the Curse of blood,
 Which even my Heart's cannot remove.
Alas! how many things have been!
Since we were friends; for I alone
Feel more for thee than can be shown.

How many things! I loved thee — thou
 Lovedst me not: another was
The Idol of thy virgin vow,
 And I was, what I am, Alas! 50
And what he is, and what thou art,
 And what we were, is like the rest:
 We must endure it as a test,
And old Ordeal of the Heart.
 VENICE, *December* 29, 1818.

STANZAS

[A friend of Lord Byron's, who was with
him at Ravenna when he wrote these Stanzas,
says: 'They were composed, like many others,
with no view of publication, but merely to re-
lieve himself in a moment of suffering. He
had been painfully excited by some circum-
stances which appeared to make it necessary
that he should immediately quit Italy, and in
the day and the hour that he wrote the song was
labouring under an access of fever.' — So reads
the note in the Edition of 1831. It is to be re-
marked, however, that Byron was not at Ra-
venna but at Venice on the date of the poem.]

 COULD Love for ever
 Run like a river,
 And Time's endeavour
 Be tried in vain —
 No other pleasure
 With this could measure,

 And like a treasure
 We 'd hug the chain.
 But since our sighing
 Ends not in dying, 10
 And, form'd for flying,
 Love plumes his wing;
 Then for this reason
 Let 's love a season;
But let that season be only Spring.

 When lovers parted
 Feel broken-hearted,
 And, all hopes thwarted,
 Expect to die;
 A few years older, 20
 Ah! how much colder
 They might behold her
 For whom they sigh!
 When link'd together,
 In every weather,
 They pluck Love's feather
 From out his wing —
 He 'll stay for ever,
 But sadly shiver
Without his plumage, when past the Spring.

 Like Chiefs of Faction, 31
 His life is action —
 A formal paction
 That curbs his reign,
 Obscures his glory,
 Despot no more, he
 Such territory
 Quits with disdain.
 Still, still advancing,
 With banners glancing, 40
 His power enhancing,
 He must move on —
 Repose but cloys him,
 Retreat destroys him,
Love brooks not a degraded throne.

 Wait not, fond lover!
 Till years are over,
 And then recover,
 As from a dream.
 While each bewailing 50
 The other's failing,
 With wrath and railing,
 All hideous seem —
 While first decreasing,
 Yet not quite ceasing,
 Wait not till teasing
 All passion blight:
 If once diminish'd

Love's reign is finish'd —
Then part in friendship, — and bid good-
night. 60

So shall Affection
To recollection
The dear connection
 Bring back with joy:
You had not waited
Till, tired or hated,
Your passions sated
 Began to cloy.
Your last embraces
Leave no cold traces — 70
The same fond faces
 As through the past;
And eyes, the mirrors
Of your sweet errors,
Reflect but rapture — not least though
last.

True, separations
Ask more than patience;
What desperations
 From such have risen!
But yet remaining, 80
What is 't but chaining
Hearts which, once waning,
 Beat 'gainst their prison?
Time can but cloy love,
And use destroy love:
The wingèd boy, Love,
 Is but for boys —
You 'll find it torture
Though sharper, shorter,
To wean, and not wear out your joys.
December 1, 1819. [First published, 1832.]

'SHE WALKS IN BEAUTY'

[These stanzas were written on returning
from a ball-room, where he had seen Lady
Wilmot Horton, who appeared in mourning
with numerous spangles on her dress.]

SHE walks in beauty, like the night
Of cloudless climes and starry skies;
And all that 's best of dark and bright
 Meet in her aspect and her eyes:
Thus mellow'd to that tender light
 Which heaven to gaudy day denies.

One shade the more, one ray the less,
 Had half impair'd the nameless grace

Which waves in every raven tress,
 Or softly lightens o'er her face;
Where thoughts serenely sweet express
 How pure, how dear their dwelling-place.

And on that cheek, and o'er that brow,
 So soft, so calm, yet eloquent,
The smiles that win, the tints that glow,
 But tell of days in goodness spent,
A mind at peace with all below,
 A heart whose love is innocent!
 June 12, 1814.

'OH! SNATCH'D AWAY IN BEAUTY'S BLOOM'

OH! snatch'd away in beauty's bloom,
On thee shall press no ponderous tomb;
 But on thy turf shall roses rear
 Their leaves, the earliest of the year;
And the wild cypress wave in tender gloom:

And oft by yon blue gushing stream
 Shall Sorrow lean her drooping head,
And feed deep thought with many a dream,
 And lingering pause and lightly tread;
 Fond wretch! as if her step disturb'd
 the dead!

Away! we know that tears are vain,
 That death nor heeds nor hears distress:
Will this unteach us to complain?
 Or make one mourner weep the less?
And thou — who tell'st me to forget,
Thy looks are wan, thine eyes are wet.

'DEAR DOCTOR, I HAVE READ YOUR PLAY'

[To John Murray, August 21, 1817. Mur-
ray had written to Byron: 'Polidori has sent
me his tragedy! Do me the kindness to send
by return of post a *delicate* declension of it,
which I engage faithfully to copy.' The fol-
lowing is Byron's 'civil and delicate declen-
sion for the medical tragedy.']

DEAR Doctor, I have read your play,
Which is a good one in its way, —
Purges the eyes and moves the bowels,
And drenches handkerchiefs like towels
With tears, that, in a flux of grief,
Afford hysterical relief

To shatter'd nerves and quicken'd pulses,
Which your catastrophe convulses.
 I like your moral and machinery;
Your plot, too, has such scope for Scenery;
Your dialogue is apt and smart; 11
The play's concoction full of art;
Your hero raves, your heroine cries,
All stab, and everybody dies.
In short, your tragedy would be
The very thing to hear and see;
And for a piece of publication,
If I decline on this occasion,
It is not that I am not sensible
To merits in themselves ostensible, 20
But — and I grieve to speak it — plays
Are drugs — mere drugs, Sir — now-a-days.
I had a heavy loss by *Manuel*, —
Too lucky if it prove not annual, —
And Sotheby, with his damn'd *Orestes*
(Which, by the way, the old Bore's best is),
Has lain so very long on hand
That I despair of all demand.
I 've advertised, but see my books,
Or only watch my Shopman's looks; — 30
Still *Ivan, Ina,* and such lumber,
My back-shop glut, my shelves encumber.
 There 's Byron, too, who once did better,
Has sent me, folded in a letter,
A sort of — it 's no more a drama
Than *Darnley, Ivan,* or *Kehama;*
So alter'd since last year his pen is,
I think he 's lost his wits at Venice,

.
.

In short, sir, what with one and t'other,
I dare not venture on another. 40
I write in haste; excuse each blunder;
The Coaches through the street so thunder!
My Room 's so full; we 've Gifford here
Reading MSS., with Hookham Frere,
Pronouncing on the nouns and particles
Of some of our forthcoming Articles.
 The *Quarterly* — Ah, Sir, if you
Had but the Genius to review ! —
A smart Critique upon St. Helena,
Or if you only would but tell in a 50
Short compass what — but, to resume:
As I was saying, Sir, the Room —
The Room 's so full of wits and bards,
Crabbes, Campbells, Crokers, Freres, and
 Wards
And others, neither bards nor wits: —
My humble tenement admits

All persons in the dress of gent.,
From Mr. Hammond to Dog Dent.

 A party dines with me to-day,
All clever men, who make their way; 60
Crabbe, Malcolm, Hamilton, and Chantrey,
Are all partakers of my pantry.
They 're at this moment in discussion
On poor De Staël's late dissolution.
Her book, they say, was in advance —
Pray Heaven ! she tell the truth of France !
'T is said she certainly was married
To Rocca, and had twice miscarried,
No — not miscarried, I opine, —
But brought to bed at forty-nine. 70
Some say she died a Papist; Some
Are of opinion *that*'s a Hum;
I don't know that — the fellow, Schlegel,
Was very likely to inveigle
A dying person in compunction
To try the extremity of Unction.
But peace be with her ! for a woman
Her talents surely were uncommon.
Her Publisher (and Public too)
The hour of her demise may rue — 80
For never more within his shop he —
Pray — was not she interr'd at Coppet ?
Thus run our time and tongues away. —
But, to return, Sir, to your play:
Sorry, Sir, but I cannot deal,
Unless 't were acted by O'Neill.
My hands are full, my head so busy,
I 'm almost dead, and always dizzy;
And so, with endless truth and hurry, 89
Dear Doctor, I am yours,
 JOHN MURRAY.

 August, 1817.

'MY DEAR MR. MURRAY'

[To John Murray, January 8, 1818. Byron
was sending home the fourth canto of *Childe
Harold* by his friend Hobhouse. The *Edin-
burgh Monthly Magazine* was begun in 1817.]

MY dear Mr. Murray,
You 're in a damn'd hurry
 To set up this ultimate Canto;
But (if they don't rob us)
You 'll see Mr. Hobhouse
 Will bring it safe in his portmanteau.

For the Journal you hint of,
As ready to print off,

No doubt you do right to commend it;
But as yet I have writ off 10
The devil a bit of
 Our *Beppo:* — when copied, I 'll send it.

In the mean time you 've ' Galley '
Whose verses all tally,
 Perhaps you may say he 's a Ninny,
But if you abash'd are
Because of *Alashtar*,
 He 'll drivel another *Phrosine*.

Then you 've Sotheby's tour,
No great things, to be sure, — 20
 You could hardly begin with a less work;
For the pompous rascallion,
Who don't speak Italian
 Nor French, must have scribbled by
 guess-work.

No doubt he 's a rare man
Without knowing German
 Translating his way up Parnassus,
And now still absurder
He meditates Murder
 As you 'll see in the trash he calls *Tasso's.*

But you 've others his betters 31
The real men of letters
 Your Orators — Critics — and Wits, —
And I 'll bet that your Journal
(Pray is it diurnal ?)
 Will pay with your luckiest hits.

You can make any loss up
With ' Spence ' and his gossip,
 A work which must surely succeed;
Then Queen Mary's Epistle-craft, 40
With the new ' Fytte ' of ' Whistlecraft,'
 Must make people purchase and read.

Then you 've General Gordon,
Who girded his sword on,
 To serve with a Muscovite Master;
And help him to polish
A nation so owlish,
 They thought shaving their beards a
 disaster.

For the man, ' *poor and shrewd*,'
With whom you 'd conclude 50
 A compact without more delay,
Perhaps some such pen is
Still extant in Venice;
 But please, sir, to mention *your pay.*

Now tell me some news
Of your friends and the Muse
 Of the Bar, or the Gown, or the House,
From Canning, the tall wit,
To Wilmot, the small wit,
 Ward's creeping Companion and *Louse*,

Who 's so damnably bit 61
With fashion and Wit,
 That he crawls on the surface like Vermin,
But an Insect in both, —
By his Intellect's growth
 Of what size you may quickly determine.

THE NEW VICAR OF BRAY

[George Frederick Nott (1767–1841) was
Rector of Harrietsham and Woodchurch.
While in Italy he preached in the basement
story of Shelley's house at Pisa. He attacked
the Satanic school, and especially Byron's
Cain.]

 Do you know Dr. Nott ?
 With ' a crook in his lot,'
Who seven years since tried to dish up
 A neat Codi*cil*
 To the Princess's Will,
Which made Dr. Nott *not* a bishop.

 So the Doctor being found
 A little unsound
In his doctrine, at least as a teacher,
 And kick'd from one stool 10
 As a knave or a fool,
He mounted another as preacher.

 In that Gown (like the Skin
 With no Lion within)
He still for the Bench would be driving;
 And roareth away,
 A new Vicar of *Bray*,
Except that *his bray* lost his living.

 ' 'Gainst Freethinkers,' he roars,
 ' You should all block your doors 20
Or be named in the Devil's indentures: '
 And here I agree,
 For *who* e'er would be
A Guest where old Simony enters ?

 Let the Priest, who beguiled
 His own Sovereign's child
To his own dirty views of promotion,
 Wear his Sheep's clothing still

Among flocks to his will,
And dishonour the Cause of devotion. 30

The Altar and Throne
Are in danger alone
From such as himself, who would render
The Altar itself
But a step up to Pelf,
And pray God to pay his defender.

But, Doctor, one word
Which perhaps you have heard:
' He should never throw stones who has
 windows
Of Glass to be broken, 40
And by this same token
As a sinner, you can't care what Sin does.

' But perhaps you do well:
Your own windows, they tell,
Have long ago suffered censure;
Not a fragment remains
Of your character's panes,
Since the Regent refused you a glazier.

' Though your visions of lawn
Have all been withdrawn, 50
And you miss'd your bold stroke for a mitre;
In a very snug way
You may still preach and pray,
And from bishop sink into backbiter! '
[First published, 1831.]

JOURNAL IN CEPHALONIA

[First published in the *Letters*, 1901.]

THE dead have been awaken'd — shall I
 sleep?
The World's at war with tyrants — shall
 I crouch?
The harvest's ripe — and shall I pause to
 reap?
I slumber not; the thorn is in my Couch;
Each day a trumpet soundeth in mine ear,
Its echo in my heart —
 June 19, 1823.

ENGLISH BARDS AND SCOTCH

REVIEWERS

A SATIRE

'I had rather be a kitten, and cry mew!
Than one of these same metre ballad-mongers.'
 SHAKSPEARE.

'Such shameless bards we have; and yet 't is true,
There are as mad, abandon'd critics too.'
 POPE.

PREFACE

All my friends, learned and unlearned, have urged me not to publish this Satire with my name. If I were to be 'turned from the career of my humour by quibbles quick, and paper bullets of the brain,' I should have complied with their counsel. But I am not to be terrified by abuse, or bullied by reviewers, with or without arms. I can safely say that I have attacked none personally, who did not commence on the offensive. An author's works are public property: he who purchases may judge, and publish his opinion if he pleases; and the authors I have endeavoured to commemorate may do by me as I have done by them. I dare say they will succeed better in condemning my scribblings, than in mending their own. But my object is not to prove that I can write well, but, if possible, to make others write better.

As the poem has met with far more success than I expected, I have endeavoured in this edition to make some additions and alterations, to render it more worthy of public perusal.

In the first edition of this satire, published anonymously, fourteen lines on the subject of Bowles's Pope were written by, and inserted at the request of, an ingenious friend of mine, who has now in the press a volume of poetry. In the present edition they are erased, and some of my own substituted in their stead, my only reason for this being that which I conceive would operate with any other person in the same manner, — a determination not to publish with my name any production, which was not entirely and exclusively my own composition.

With regard to the real talents of many of the poetical persons whose performances are mentioned or alluded to in the following pages, it is presumed by the author that there can be little difference of opinion in the public at large; though, like other sectaries, each has his separate tabernacle of proselytes, by whom his abilities are over-rated, his faults overlooked, and his metrical canons received without scruple and without consideration. But the unquestionable possession of considerable genius by several of the writers here censured renders their mental prostitution more to be regretted. Imbecility may be pitied, or, at worst, laughed at and forgotten; perverted powers demand the most decided reprehension. No one can wish more than the author that some known and able writer had undertaken their exposure; but Mr. Gifford has devoted himself to Massinger, and, in the absence of the regular physician, a country practitioner may, in cases of absolute necessity, be allowed to prescribe his nostrum to prevent the extension of so deplorable an epidemic, provided there be no quackery in his treatment of the malady. A caustic is here offered; as it is to be feared nothing short of actual cautery can recover the numerous patients afflicted with the present prevalent and distressing *rabies* for rhyming. — As to the Edinburgh Reviewers, it would indeed require an Hercules to crush the Hydra; but if the author succeeds in merely 'bruising one of the heads of the serpent,' though his own hand should suffer in the encounter, he will be amply satisfied.

STILL must I hear? — shall hoarse Fitz-
 gerald bawl
His creaking couplets in a tavern hall,
And I not sing, lest, haply, Scotch reviews
Should dub me scribbler and denounce my
 muse?
Prepare for rhyme — I 'll publish, right or
 wrong:
Fools are my theme, let satire be my song

Oh, nature's noblest gift, my grey goose-
quill !
Slave of my thoughts, obedient to my will,
Torn from thy parent bird to form a pen,
That mighty instrument of little men ! 10
The pen ! foredoom'd to aid the mental
throes
Of brains that labour, big with verse or
prose,
Though nymphs forsake, and critics may
deride,
The lover's solace and the author's pride.
What wits ! what poets dost thou daily
raise !
How frequent is thy use, how small thy
praise,
Condemn'd at length to be forgotten quite,
With all the pages which 't was thine to
write.
But thou, at least, mine own especial pen !
Once laid aside, but now assumed again, 20
Our task complete like Hamet's, shall be
free;
Though spurn'd by others, yet beloved by
me:
Then let us soar to-day; no common theme,
No eastern vision, no distemper'd dream
Inspires — our path, though full of thorns,
is plain;
Smooth be the verse, and easy be the strain.

When Vice triumphant holds her sov'-
reign sway,
Obey'd by all who nought beside obey;
When Folly, frequent harbinger of crime,
Bedecks her cap with bells of every clime;
When knaves and fools combined o'er all
prevail, 31
And weigh their justice in a golden scale;
E'en then the boldest start from public
sneers,
Afraid of shame, unknown to other fears,
More darkly sin, by satire kept in awe,
And shrink from ridicule though not from
law.

Such is the force of wit ! but not belong
To me the arrows of satiric song;
The royal vices of our age demand
A keener weapon and a mightier hand. 40
Still there are follies, e'en for me to
chase,
And yield at least amusement in the race.
Laugh when I laugh, I seek no other fame;
The cry is up, and scribblers are my game.

Speed, Pegasus ! — ye strains of great and
small,
Ode, epic, elegy, have at you all !
I too can scrawl, and once upon a time
I pour'd along the town a flood of rhyme,
A schoolboy freak, unworthy praise or
blame;
I printed — older children do the same. 50
'T is pleasant, sure, to see one's name in
print;
A book 's a book, although there 's nothing
in 't.
Not that a title's sounding charm can save
Or scrawl or scribbler from an equal grave:
This Lambe must own, since his patrician
name
Fail'd to preserve the spurious farce from
shame.
No matter, George continues still to write,
Though now the name is veil'd from pub-
lic sight.
Moved by the great example, I pursue
The self-same road, but make my own re-
view: 60
Not seek great Jeffrey's, yet like him will
be
Self-constituted judge of poesy.

A man must serve his time to ev'ry trade
Save censure — critics all are ready made.
Take hackney'd jokes from Miller, got by
rote,
With just enough of learning to misquote;
A mind well skill'd to find or forge a fault;
A turn for punning, call it Attic salt;
To Jeffrey go, be silent and discreet,
His pay is just ten sterling pounds per
sheet: 70
Fear not to lie, 't will seem a sharper hit;
Shrink not from blasphemy, 't will pass for
wit;
Care not for feeling—pass your proper jest,
And stand a critic, hated yet caress'd.

And shall we own such judgment? no—
as soon
Seek roses in December, ice in June;
Hope constancy in wind, or corn in chaff;
Believe a woman or an epitaph,
Or any other thing that 's false, before
You trust in critics, who themselves are
sore; 80
Or yield one single thought to be misled
By Jeffrey's heart or Lambe's Bœotian
head.

To these young tyrants, by themselves mis-
 placed,
Combined usurpers on the throne of taste;
To these, when authors bend in humble
 awe,
And hail their voice as truth, their word
 as law —
While these are censors, 't would be sin to
 spare;
While such are critics, why should I for-
 bear ?
But yet, so near all modern worthies run,
'T is doubtful whom to seek, or whom to
 shun; 90
Nor know we when to spare, or where to
 strike,
Our bards and censors are so much alike.

Then should you ask me, why I venture
 o'er
The path which Pope and Gifford trod be-
 fore;
If not yet sicken'd, you can still proceed:
Go on; my rhyme will tell you as you read.
'But hold !' exclaims a friend, 'here 's
 some neglect:
This, that, and t'other line seem incor-
 rect.'
What then ? the self-same blunder Pope
 has got,
And careless Dryden — 'Ay, but Pye has
 not: ' — 100
Indeed ! — 't is granted, faith ! — but what
 care I ?
Better to err with Pope than shine with
 Pye.

Time was, ere yet in these degenerate
 days
Ignoble themes obtain'd mistaken praise,
When sense and wit with poesy allied,
No fabled graces, flourish'd side by side;
From the same fount their inspiration drew,
And, rear'd by taste, bloom'd fairer as they
 grew.
Then, in this happy isle, a Pope's pure
 strain
Sought the rapt soul to charm, nor sought
 in vain; 110
A polish'd nation's praise aspired to claim,
And raised the people's, as the poet's fame.
Like him great Dryden pour'd the tide of
 song,
In stream less smooth, indeed, yet doubly
 strong.

Then Congreve's scenes could cheer, or
 Otway's melt —
For nature then an English audience felt.
But why these names, or greater still, re-
 trace,
When all to feebler bards resign their
 place ?
Yet to such times our lingering looks are
 cast,
When taste and reason with those times are
 past. 120
Now look around, and turn each trifling
 page,
Survey the precious works that please the
 age;
This truth at least let satire's self allow,
No dearth of bards can be complain'd of
 now.
The loaded press beneath her labour groans,
And printers' devils shake their weary
 bones;
While Southey's epics cram the creaking
 shelves,
And Little's lyrics shine in hot-press'd
 twelves.
Thus saith the preacher: 'Nought beneath
 the sun
Is new;' yet still from change to change
 we run: 130
What varied wonders tempt us as they
 pass !
The cow-pox, tractors, galvanism, and gas,
In turns appear, to make the vulgar stare,
Till the swoln bubble bursts — and all is
 air !
Nor less new schools of Poetry arise,
Where dull pretenders grapple for the
 prize:
O'er taste awhile these pseudo-bards pre-
 vail;
Each country book-club bows the knee to
 Baal,
And, hurling lawful genius from the throne,
Erects a shrine and idol of its own; 140
Some leaden calf — but whom it matters
 not,
From soaring Southey down to grovelling
 Stott.

Behold ! in various throngs the scribbling
 crew,
For notice eager, pass in long review:
Each spurs his jaded Pegasus apace,
And rhyme and blank maintain an equal
 race;

Sonnets on sonnets crowd, and ode on ode;
And tales of terror jostle on the road;
Immeasurable measures move along;
For simpering folly loves a varied song, 150
To strange mysterious dulness still the friend,
Admires the strain she cannot comprehend.
Thus Lays of Minstrels — may they be the last ! —
On half-strung harps whine mournful to the blast.
While mountain spirits prate to river sprites,
That dames may listen to the sound at nights;
And goblin brats, of Gilpin Horner's brood,
Decoy young border-nobles through the wood,
And skip at every step, Lord knows how high,
And frighten foolish babes, the Lord knows why; 160
While high-born ladies in their magic cell,
Forbidding knights to read who cannot spell,
Despatch a courier to a wizard's grave,
And fight with honest men to shield a knave.

Next view in state, proud prancing on his roan,
The golden-crested haughty Marmion,
Now forging scrolls, now foremost in the fight,
Not quite a felon, yet but half a knight,
The gibbet or the field prepared to grace;
A mighty mixture of the great and base.
And think'st thou, Scott ! by vain conceit perchance, 171
On public taste to foist thy stale romance,
Though Murray with his Miller may combine
To yield thy muse just half-a-crown per line ?
No ! when the sons of song descend to trade,
Their bays are sere, their former laurels fade.
Let such forego the poet's sacred name,
Who rack their brains for lucre, not for fame:
Still for stern Mammon may they toil in vain,
And sadly gaze on gold they cannot gain !

Such be their meed, such still the just reward 181
Of prostituted muse and hireling bard !
For this we spurn Apollo's venal son,
And bid a long ' good night to Marmion.'

These are the themes that claim our plaudits now;
These are the bards to whom the muse must bow;
While Milton, Dryden, Pope, alike forgot,
Resign their hallow'd bays to Walter Scott.

The time has been, when yet the muse was young,
When Homer swept the lyre, and Maro sung, 190
An epic scarce ten centuries could claim,
While awe-struck nations hail'd the magic name:
The work of each immortal bard appears
The single wonder of a thousand years.
Empires have moulder'd from the face of earth,
Tongues have expired with those who gave them birth,
Without the glory such a strain can give,
As even in ruin bids the language live.
Not so with us, though minor bards, content,
On one great work a life of labour spent:
With eagle pinion soaring to the skies, 201
Behold the ballad-monger Southey rise !
To him let Camoens, Milton, Tasso yield,
Whose annual strains, like armies, take the field.
First in the ranks see Joan of Arc advance,
The scourge of England and the boast of France !
Though burnt by wicked Bedford for a witch,
Behold her statue placed in glory's niche;
Her fetters burst, and just released from prison,
A virgin phœnix from her ashes risen. 210
Next see tremendous Thalaba come on,
Arabia's monstrous, wild, and wondrous son;
Domdaniel's dread destroyer, who o'erthrew
More mad magicians than the world e'er knew.
Immortal hero ! all thy foes o'ercome,
For ever reign — the rival of Tom Thumb !
Since startled metre fled before thy face,
Well wert thou doom'd the last of all thy race !

Well might triumphant genii bear thee hence,
Illustrious conqueror of common sense !
Now, last and greatest, Madoc spreads his sails, 221
Cacique in Mexico, and prince in Wales;
Tells us strange tales, as other travellers do,
More old than Mandeville's, and not so true.
Oh, Southey ! Southey ! cease thy varied song !
A bard may chant too often and too long:
As thou art strong in verse, in mercy, spare !
A fourth, alas ! were more than we could bear.
But if, in spite of all the world can say,
Thou still wilt verseward plod thy weary way; 230
If still in Berkley ballads most uncivil,
Thou wilt devote old women to the devil,
The babe unborn thy dread intent may rue:
' God help thee,' Southey, and thy readers too.

Next comes the dull disciple of thy school,
That mild apostate from poetic rule,
The simple Wordsworth, framer of a lay
As soft as evening in his favourite May,
Who warns his friend ' to shake off toil and trouble,
And quit his books, for fear of growing double; ' 240
Who, both by precept and example, shows
That prose is verse, and verse is merely prose;
Convincing all, by demonstration plain,
Poetic souls delight in prose insane;
And Christmas stories tortured into rhyme
Contain the essence of the true sublime.
Thus, when he tells the tale of Betty Foy,
The idiot mother of ' an idiot boy;'
A moon-struck, silly lad, who lost his way,
And, like his bard, confounded night with day; 250
So close on each pathetic part he dwells,
And each adventure so sublimely tells,
That all who view the ' idiot in his glory '
Conceive the bard the hero of the story.

Shall gentle Coleridge pass unnoticed here,
To turgid ode and tumid stanza dear ?
Though themes of innocence amuse him best,
Yet still obscurity 's a welcome guest.

If Inspiration should her aid refuse
To him who takes a pixy for a muse, 260
Yet none in lofty numbers can surpass
The bard who soars to elegise an ass.
So well the subject suits his noble mind,
He brays, the laureat of the long-ear'd kind.

Oh, wonder-working Lewis ! monk, or bard,
Who fain wouldst make Parnassus a churchyard !
Lo ! wreaths of yew, not laurel, bind thy brow,
Thy muse a sprite, Apollo's sexton thou !
Whether on ancient tombs thou takest thy stand,
By gibb'ring spectres hail'd, thy kindred band; 270
Or tracest chaste descriptions on thy page,
To please the females of our modest age;
All hail, M. P. ! from whose infernal brain
Thin sheeted phantoms glide, a grisly train;
At whose command ' grim women ' throng in crowds,
And kings of fire, of water, and of clouds,
With ' small grey men,' ' wild yagers,' and what not,
To crown with honour thee and Walter Scott.
Again all hail! if tales like thine may please,
St. Luke alone can vanquish the disease;
Even Satan's self with thee might dread to dwell, 281
And in thy skull discern a deeper hell.

Who in soft guise, surrounded by a choir
Of virgins melting, not to Vesta's fire,
With sparkling eyes, and cheek by passion flush'd,
Strikes his wild lyre, whilst listening dames are hush'd ?
'T is Little ! young Catullus of his day,
As sweet, but as immoral, in his lay !
Grieved to condemn, the muse must still be just,
Nor spare melodious advocates of lust. 290
Pure is the flame which o'er her altar burns;
From grosser incense with disgust she turns:
Yet kind to youth, this expiation o'er,
She bids thee ' mend thy line, and sin no more.'

For thee, translator of the tinsel song,
To whom such glittering ornaments belong,

Hibernian Strangford ! with thine eyes of
 blue,
And boasted locks of red or auburn hue,
Whose plaintive strain each love-sick miss
 admires,
And o'er harmonious fustian half expires,
Learn, if thou canst, to yield thine author's
 sense, 301
Nor vend thy sonnets on a false pretence.
Think'st thou to gain thy verse a higher
 place,
By dressing Camoëns in a suit of lace ?
Mend, Strangford ! mend thy morals and
 thy taste;
Be warm, but pure; be amorous, but be
 chaste:
Cease to deceive; thy pilfer'd harp re-
 store,
Nor teach the Lusian bard to copy Moore.

Behold ! — ye tarts ! one moment spare
 the text —
Hayley's last work, and worst — until his
 next; 310
Whether he spin poor couplets into plays,
Or damn the dead with purgatorial praise,
His style in youth or age is still the same,
For ever feeble and for ever tame.
Triumphant first see *Temper's Triumphs*
 shine !
At least I 'm sure they triumph'd over mine.
Of *Music's Triumphs*, all who read may
 swear
That luckless music never triumph'd there.

Moravians, rise ! bestow some meet re-
 ward
On dull devotion — Lo ! the Sabbath bard,
Sepulchral Grahame, pours his notes sub-
 lime 321
In mangled prose, nor e'en aspires to rhyme;
Breaks into blank the Gospel of St. Luke,
And boldly pilfers from the Pentateuch;
And, undisturb'd by conscientious qualms,
Perverts the Prophets, and purloins the
 Psalms.

Hail, Sympathy ! thy soft idea brings
A thousand visions of a thousand things,
And shows, still whimpering through three-
 score of years,
The maudlin prince of mournful sonneteers.
And art thou not their prince, harmonious
 Bowles ! 331
Thou first, great oracle of tender souls ?

Whether thou sing'st with equal ease, and
 grief,
The fall of empires or a yellow leaf;
Whether thy muse most lamentably tells
What merry sounds proceed from Oxford
 bells,
Or, still in bells delighting, finds a friend
In every chime that jingled from Ostend;
Ah ! how much juster were thy muse's hap,
If to thy bells thou wouldst but add a cap !
Delightful Bowles ! still blessing and still
 blest, 341
All love thy strain, but children like it best.
'T is thine, with gentle Little's moral song,
To soothe the mania of the amorous throng !
With thee our nursery damsels shed their
 tears,
Ere miss as yet completes her infant years:
But in her teens thy whining powers are
 vain;
She quits poor Bowles for Little's purer
 strain.
Now to soft themes thou scornest to con-
 fine
The lofty numbers of a harp like thine; 350
' Awake a louder and a lofter strain,'
Such as none heard before, or will again !
Where all Discoveries jumbled from the
 flood,
Since first the leaky ark reposed in mud,
By more or less, are sung in every book,
From Captain Noah down to Captain Cook.
Nor this alone; but, pausing on the road,
The bard sighs forth a gentle episode;
And gravely tells — attend, each beauteous
 miss ! —
When first Madeira trembled to a kiss. 360
Bowles ! in thy memory let this precept
 dwell,
Stick to thy sonnets, man ! — at least they
 sell.
But if some new-born whim, or larger bribe,
Prompt thy crude brain, and claim thee for
 a scribe;
If chance some bard, though once by dunces
 fear'd,
Now, prone in dust, can only be revered;
If Pope, whose fame and genius from the
 first
Have foil'd the best of critics, needs the
 worst,
Do thou essay: each fault, each failing scan;
The first of poets was, alas ! but man. 370
Rake from each ancient dunghill ev'ry pearl,
Consult Lord Fanny, and confide in Curll;

Let all the scandals of a former age
Perch on thy pen, and flutter o'er thy page;
Affect a candour which thou canst not feel,
Clothe envy in the garb of honest zeal;
Write, as if St. John's soul could still in-
 spire,
And do from hate what Mallet did for hire.
Oh ! hadst thou lived in that congenial time,
To rave with Dennis, and with Ralph to
 rhyme; 380
Throng'd with the rest around his living
 head,
Not raised thy hoof against the lion dead;
A meet reward had crown'd thy glorious
 gains,
And link'd thee to the Dunciad for thy
 pains.

Another epic ! Who inflicts again
More books of blank upon the sons of
 men ?
Bœotian Cottle, rich Bristowa's boast,
Imports old stories from the Cambrian
 coast,
And sends his goods to market — all alive !
Lines forty thousand, cantos twenty-five !
Fresh fish from Hippocrene ! who 'll buy ?
 who 'll buy ? 391
The precious bargain 's cheap — in faith,
 not I.
Your turtle-feeder's verse must needs be
 flat,
Though Bristol bloat him with the verdant
 fat;
If Commerce fills the purse, she clogs the
 brain,
And Amos Cottle strikes the lyre in vain.
In him an author's luckless lot behold,
Condemn'd to make the books which once
 he sold.
Oh, Amos Cottle ! — Phœbus ! what a name
To fill the speaking trump of future fame ! —
Oh, Amos Cottle ! for a moment think 401
What meagre profits spring from pen and
 ink !
When thus devoted to poetic dreams,
Who will peruse thy prostituted reams ?
Oh pen perverted ! paper misapplied !
Had Cottle still adorn'd the counter's side,
Bent o'er the desk, or, born to useful toils,
Been taught to make the paper which he
 soils,
Plough'd, delved, or plied the oar with
 lusty limb, 409
He had not sung of Wales, nor I of him.

As Sisyphus against the infernal steep
Rolls the huge rock whose motions ne'er
 may sleep,
So up thy hill, ambrosial Richmond, heaves
Dull Maurice all his granite weight of
 leaves:
Smooth, solid monuments of mental pain !
The petrifactions of a plodding brain,
That, ere they reach the top, fall lumbering
 back again.

With broken lyre and cheek serenely pale,
Lo ! sad Alcæus wanders down the vale;
Though fair they rose, and might have
 bloom'd at last, 420
His hopes have perish'd by the northern
 blast:
Nipp'd in the bud by Caledonian gales,
His blossoms wither as the blast prevails !
O'er his lost works let *classic* Sheffield
 weep;
May no rude hand disturb their early sleep!

Yet say ! why should the bard at once
 resign
His claim to favour from the sacred Nine ?
For ever startled by the mingled howl
Of northern wolves, that still in darkness
 prowl;
A coward brood, which mangle as they
 prey, 430
By hellish instinct, all that cross their way;
Aged or young, the living or the dead,
No mercy find — these harpies must be fed.
Why do the injured unresisting yield
The calm possession of their native field ?
Why tamely thus before their fangs retreat,
Nor hunt the bloodhounds back to Arthur's
 Seat ?

Health to immortal Jeffrey ! once, in
 name,
England could boast a judge almost the
 same;
In soul so like, so merciful, yet just, 440
Some think that Satan has resign'd his
 trust,
And given the spirit to the world again,
To sentence letters, as he sentenced men.
With hand less mighty, but with heart as
 black,
With voice as willing to decree the rack;
Bred in the courts betimes, though all that
 law
As yet hath taught him is to find a flaw;

Since well instructed in the patriot school
To rail at party, though a party tool —
Who knows, if chance his patrons snould
 restore 450
Back to the sway they forfeited before,
His scribbling toils some recompense may
 meet,
And raise this Daniel to the judgment-seat ?
Let Jeffries' shade indulge the pious hope,
And greeting thus, present him with a rope:
' Heir to my virtues ! man of equal mind !
Skill'd to condemn as to traduce mankind,
This cord receive, for thee reserved with
 care,
To wield in judgment, and at length to
 wear.'

 Health to great Jeffrey ! Heaven pre-
 serve his life 460
To flourish on the fertile shores of Fife,
And guard it sacred in its future wars,
Since authors sometimes seek the field of
 Mars !
Can none remember that eventful day,
That ever glorious, almost fatal fray,
When Little's leadless pistol met his eye,
And Bow-street myrmidons stood laughing
 by ?
Oh, day disastrous ! On her firm-set rock,
Dunedin's castle felt a secret shock;
Dark roll'd the sympathetic waves of Forth,
Low groan'd the startled whirlwinds of the
 north; 471
Tweed ruffled half his waves to form a tear,
The other half pursued its calm career;
Arthur's steep summit nodded to its base,
The surly Tolbooth scarcely kept her place.
The Tolbooth felt — for marble sometimes
 can,
On such occasions, feel as much as man —
The Tolbooth felt defrauded of his charms,
If Jeffrey died, except within her arms.
Nay last, not least, on that portentous
 morn, 480
The sixteenth story, where himself was born,
His patrimonial garret, fell to ground,
And pale Edina shudder'd at the sound.
Strew'd were the streets around with milk-
 white reams,
Flow'd all the Canongate with inky streams;
This of his candour seem'd the sable dew,
That of his valour show'd the bloodless hue;
And all with justice deem'd the two com-
 bined
The mingled emblems of his mighty mind.

But Caledonia's goddess hover'd o'er 490
The field, and saved him from the wrath of
 Moore;
From either pistol snatch'd the vengeful
 lead,
And straight restored it to her favourite's
 head;
That head, with greater than magnetic
 pow'r,
Caught it, as Danaë caught the golden
 show'r,
And, though the thickening dross will
 scarce refine,
Augments its ore, and is itself a mine.
' My son,' she cried, ' ne'er thirst for gore
 again,
Resign the pistol and resume the pen;
O'er politics and poesy preside, 500
Boast of thy country and Britannia's guide !
For long as Albion's heedless sons submit,
Or Scottish taste decides on English wit,
So long shall last thine unmolested reign,
Nor any dare to take thy name in vain.
Behold, a chosen band shall aid thy plan,
And own thee chieftain of the critic clan.
First in the oat-fed phalanx shall be seen
The travell'd thane, Athenian Aberdeen.
Herbert shall wield Thor's hammer, and
 sometimes, 510
In gratitude, thou 'lt praise his rugged
 rhymes.
Smug Sydney too thy bitter page shall seek,
And classic Hallam, much renown'd for
 Greek;
Scott may perchance his name and influence
 lend,
And paltry Pillans shall traduce his friend;
While gay Thalia's luckless votary, Lambe,
Damn'd like the devil, devil-like will damn.
Known be thy name, unbounded be thy
 sway !
Thy Holland's banquets shall each toil re-
 pay;
While grateful Britain yields the praise
 she owes 520
To Holland's hirelings and to learning's
 foes.
Yet mark one caution ere thy next Review
Spread its light wings of saffron and of
 blue,
Beware lest blundering Brougham destroy
 the sale,
Turn beef to bannocks, cauliflowers to kail.'
Thus having said, the kilted goddess kist
Her son, and vanish'd in a Scottish mist.

Then prosper, Jeffrey! pertest of the
 train
Whom Scotland pampers with her fiery
 grain! 529
Whatever blessing waits a genuine Scot,
In double portion swells thy glorious lot;
For thee Edina culls her evening sweets,
And showers their odours on thy candid
 sheets,
Whose hue and fragrance to thy work ad-
 here —
This scents its pages, and that gilds its rear.
Lo! blushing Itch, coy nymph, enamour'd
 grown,
Forsakes the rest, and cleaves to thee alone;
And, too unjust to other Pictish men,
Enjoys thy person, and inspires thy pen!

Illustrious Holland! hard would be his
 lot, 540
His hirelings mention'd, and himself for-
 got!
Holland, with Henry Petty at his back,
The whipper-in and huntsman of the pack.
Blest be the banquets spread at Holland
 House,
Where Scotchmen feed, and critics may
 carouse!
Long, long beneath that hospitable roof
Shall Grub-street dine, while duns are kept
 aloof.
See honest Hallam lay aside his fork, 548
Resume his pen, review his Lordship's work,
And, grateful for the dainties on his plate,
Declare his landlord can at least translate!
Dunedin! view thy children with delight,
They write for food — and feed because
 they write.
And lest, when heated with the unusual
 grape,
Some glowing thoughts should to the press
 escape,
And tinge with red the female reader's
 cheek,
My lady skims the cream of each critique;
Breathes o'er the page her purity of soul,
Reforms each error, and refines the whole.

Now to the Drama turn — Oh! motley
 sight! 560
What precious scenes the wondering eyes
 invite!
Puns, and a prince within a barrel pent,
And Dibdin's nonsense yield complete con-
 tent.

Though now, thank Heaven! the Roscio-
 mania's o'er,
And full-grown actors are endured once
 more;
Yet what avail their vain attempts to
 please,
While British critics suffer scenes like
 these;
While Reynolds vents his 'dammes!'
 'poohs!' and 'zounds!'
And common-place and common sense con-
 founds?
While Kenney's *World* — ah! where is
 Kenney's wit? — 570
Tires the sad gallery, lulls the listless pit;
And Beaumont's pilfer'd Caratach affords
A tragedy complete in all but words?
Who but must mourn, while these are all
 the rage,
The degradation of our vaunted stage!
Heavens! is all sense of shame and talent
 gone?
Have we no living bard of merit? — none!
Awake, George Colman! Cumberland,
 awake!
Ring the alarum bell! let folly quake!
Oh, Sheridan! if aught can move thy pen,
Let Comedy assume her throne again; 581
Abjure the mummery of the German
 schools;
Leave new Pizarros to translating fools;
Give, as thy last memorial to the age,
One classic drama, and reform the stage.
Gods! o'er those boards shall Folly rear
 her head,
Where Garrick trod, and Siddons lives to
 tread?
On those shall Farce display Buffoon'ry's
 mask,
And Hook conceal his heroes in a cask?
Shall sapient managers new scenes pro-
 duce 590
From Cherry, Skeffington, and Mother
 Goose?
While Shakspeare, Otway, Massinger, for-
 got,
On stalls must moulder, or in closets rot?
Lo! with what pomp the daily prints pro-
 claim
The rival candidates for Attic fame!
In grim array though Lewis' spectres rise,
Still Skeffington and Goose divide the prize.
And sure *great* Skeffington must claim our
 praise,
For skirtless coats and skeletons of plays

Renown'd alike; whose genius ne'er con-
fines 600
Her flight to garnish Greenwood's gay de-
signs;
Nor sleeps with *Sleeping Beauties*, but anon
In five facetious acts comes thundering on,
While poor John Bull, bewilder'd with the
scene,
Stares, wondering what the devil it can
mean;
But as some hands applaud, a venal few !
Rather than sleep, why John applauds it
too.

Such are we now. Ah ! wherefore should
we turn 608
To what our fathers were, unless to mourn ?
Degenerate Britons ! are ye dead to shame,
Or, kind to dulness, do you fear to blame ?
Well may the nobles of our present race
Watch each distortion of a Naldi's face;
Well may they smile on Italy's buffoons,
And worship Catalani's pantaloons,
Since their own drama yields no fairer trace
Of wit than puns, of humour than grimace.

Then let Ausonia, skill'd in every art
To soften manners, but corrupt the heart,
Pour her exotic follies o'er the town, 620
To sanction Vice, and hunt Decorum down.
Let wedded strumpets languish o'er De-
shayes,
And bless the promise which his form dis-
plays;
While Gayton bounds before th' enraptured
looks
Of hoary marquises and stripling dukes.
Let high-born lechers eye the lively Prêsle
Twirl her light limbs, that spurn the need-
less veil;
Let Angiolini bare her breast of snow,
Wave the white arm, and point the pliant
toe;
Collini trill her love-inspiring song, 630
Strain her fair neck, and charm the listen-
ing throng !
Whet not your scythe, suppressors of our
vice !
Reforming saints ! too delicately nice !
By whose decrees, our sinful souls to save,
No Sunday tankards foam, no barbers
shave;
And beer undrawn, and beards unmown,
display
Your holy reverence for the Sabbath-day.

Or hail at once the patron and the pile
Of vice and folly, Greville and Argyle !
Where yon proud palace, Fashion's hallow'd
fane, 640
Spreads wide her portals for the motley
train,
Behold the new Petronius of the day,
Our arbiter of pleasure and of play !
There the hired eunuch, the Hesperian
choir,
The melting lute, the soft lascivious lyre,
The song from Italy, the step from France,
The midnight orgy, and the mazy dance,
The smile of beauty, and the flush of wine,
For fops, fools, gamesters, knaves, and
lords combine:
Each to his humour — Comus all allows;
Champaign, dice, music, or your neigh-
bour's spouse. 651
Talk not to us, ye starving sons of trade !
Of piteous ruin which ourselves have
made;
In Plenty's sunshine Fortune's minions
bask,
Nor think of poverty, except 'en masque,'
When for the night some lately titled ass
Appears the beggar which his grandsire
was.
The curtain dropp'd, the gay burletta o'er,
The audience take their turn upon the
floor;
Now round the room the circling dow'gers
sweep, 660
Now in loose waltz the thin-clad daughters
leap;
The first in lengthen'd line majestic swim,
The last display the free unfetter'd limb !
Those for Hibernia's lusty sons repair
With art the charms which nature could not
spare;
These after husbands wing their eager flight,
Nor leave much mystery for the nuptial
night.

Oh ! blest retreats of infamy and ease,
Where, all forgotten but the power to
please,
Each maid may give a loose to genial
thought, 670
Each swain may teach new systems, or be
taught.
There the blithe youngster, just return'd
from Spain,
Cuts the light pack, or calls the rattling
main;

The jovial caster 's set, and seven 's the nick,
Or — done ! — a thousand on the coming
 trick !
If, mad with loss, existence 'gins to tire,
And all your hope or wish is to expire,
Here 's Powell's pistol ready for your life,
And, kinder still, two Pagets for your wife;
Fit consummation of an earthly race 680
Begun in folly, ended in disgrace;
While none but menials o'er the bed of
 death,
Wash thy red wounds, or watch thy waver-
 ing breath;
Traduced by liars, and forgot by all,
The mangled victim of a drunken brawl,
To live like Clodius and like Falkland fall.

 Truth ! rouse some genuine bard, and
 guide his hand
To drive this pestilence from out the land.
E'en I — least thinking of a thoughtless
 throng,
Just skill'd to know the right and choose
 the wrong, 690
Freed at that age when reason's shield is
 lost,
To fight my course through passion's count-
 less host,
Whom every path of pleasure's flow'ry way
Has lured in turn, and all have led astray —
E'en I must raise my voice, e'en I must feel
Such scenes, such men, destroy the public
 weal;
Although some kind, censorious friend will
 say,
'What art thou better, meddling fool,
 than they ? '
And every brother rake will smile to see
That miracle, a moralist in me. 700
No matter — when some bard in virtue
 strong,
Gifford perchance, shall raise the chasten-
 ing song,
Then sleep my pen for ever ! and my
 voice
Be only heard to hail him, and rejoice;
Rejoice, and yield my feeble praise, though I
May feel the lash that Virtue must apply.

 As for the smaller fry, who swarm in
 shoals
From silly Hafiz up to simple Bowles,
Why should we call them from their dark
 abode, 709
In broad St. Giles's or in Tottenham-road ?

Or (since some men of fashion nobly dare
To scrawl in verse) from Bond-street or the
 Square ?
If things of ton their harmless lays indite,
Most wisely doom'd to shun the public
 sight,
What harm ? In spite of every critic elf,
Sir T. may read his stanzas to himself;
Miles Andrews still his strength in couplets
 try,
And live in prologues, though his dramas
 die.
Lords too are bards, such things at times
 befall,
And 't is some praise in peers to write at
 all. 720
Yet, did or taste or reason sway the times,
Ah ! who would take their titles with their
 rhymes ?
Roscommon ! Sheffield ! with your spirits
 fled,
No future laurels deck a noble head;
No muse will cheer, with renovating smile,
The paralytic puling of Carlisle.
The puny schoolboy and his early lay
Men pardon, if his follies pass away;
But who forgives the senior's ceaseless
 verse,
Whose hairs grow hoary as his rhymes
 grow worse ! 730
What heterogeneous honours deck the peer !
Lord, rhymester, petit-maître, pamphlet-
 eer !
So dull in youth, so drivelling in his age,
His scenes alone had damn'd our sinking
 stage;
But managers for once cried, 'Hold,
 enough ! '
Nor drugg'd their audience with the tragic
 stuff.
Yet at their judgment let his lordship
 laugh,
And case his volumes in congenial calf:
Yes ! doff that covering, where morocco
 shines, 739
And hang a calf-skin on those recreant lines.

 With you, ye Druids ! rich in native lead,
Who daily scribble for your daily bread;
With you I war not: Gifford's heavy hand
Has crush'd, without remorse, your numer-
 ous band.
On 'all the talents' vent your venal
 spleen;
Want is your plea, let pity be your screen.

Let monodies on Fox regale your crew,
And Melville's Mantle prove a blanket too!
One common Lethe waits each hapless bard,
And, peace be with you! 't is your best
 reward. 750
Such damning fame as Dunciads only give
Could bid your lines beyond a morning
 live;
But now at once your fleeting labours
 close,
With names of greater note in blest re-
 pose.
Far be 't from me unkindly to upbraid
The lovely Rosa's prose in masquerade,
Whose strains, the faithful echoes of her
 mind,
Leave wondering comprehension far be-
 hind.
Though Crusca's bards no more our jour-
 nals fill,
Some stragglers skirmish round the col-
 umns still; 760
Last of the howling host which once was
 Bell's,
Matilda snivels yet, and Hafiz yells;
And Merry's metaphors appear anew,
Chain'd to the signature of O. P. Q.

When some brisk youth, the tenant of a
 stall,
Employs a pen less pointed than his awl,
Leaves his snug shop, forsakes his store of
 shoes,
St. Crispin quits, and cobbles for the muse,
Heavens! how the vulgar stare! how
 crowds applaud!
How ladies read, and literati laud! 770
If chance some wicked wag should pass his
 jest,
'T is sheer ill-nature — don't the world
 know best?
Genius must guide when wits admire the
 rhyme,
And Capel Lofft declares 't is quite sub-
 lime.
Hear, then, ye happy sons of needless
 trade!
Swains! quit the plough, resign the useless
 spade!
Lo! Burns and Bloomfield, nay, a greater
 far,
Gifford was born beneath an adverse star,
Forsook the labours of a servile state,
Stemm'd the rude storm, and triumph'd
 over fate: 780

Then why no more? if Phœbus smiled on
 you,
Bloomfield! why not on brother Nathan
 too?
Him too the mania, not the muse, has
 seized;
Not inspiration, but a mind diseased:
And now no boor can seek his last abode,
No common be enclosed without an ode.
Oh! since increased refinement deigns to
 smile
On Britain's sons and bless our genial isle,
Let poesy go forth, pervade the whole,
Alike the rustic and mechanic soul! 790
Ye tuneful cobblers! still your notes pro-
 long,
Compose at once a slipper and a song;
So shall the fair your handywork peruse,
Your sonnets sure shall please — perhaps
 your shoes.
May Moorland weavers boast Pindaric
 skill,
And tailors' lays be longer than their bill!
While punctual beaux reward the grateful
 notes,
And pay for poems — when they pay for
 coats.

To the famed throng now paid the trib-
 ute due,
Neglected genius! let me turn to you. 800
Come forth, oh Campbell! give thy talents
 scope;
Who dares aspire if thou must cease to
 hope?
And thou, melodious Rogers! rise at last,
Recall the pleasing memory of the past;
Arise! let blest remembrance still inspire,
And strike to wonted tones thy hallow'd
 lyre;
Restore Apollo to his vacant throne,
Assert thy country's honour and thine own.
What! must deserted Poesy still weep
Where her last hopes with pious Cowper
 sleep? 810
Unless, perchance, from his cold bier she
 turns,
To deck the turf that wraps her minstrel,
 Burns!
No! though contempt hath mark'd the
 spurious brood,
The race who rhyme from folly, or for food,
Yet still some genuine sons 't is hers to
 boast,
Who, least affecting, still affect the most:

Feel as they write, and write but as they
feel—
Bear witness Gifford, Sotheby, Macneil.

'Why slumbers Gifford?' once was ask'd
in vain; 819
Why slumbers Gifford? let us ask again.
Are there no follies for his pen to purge?
Are there no fools whose backs demand
the scourge?
Are there no sins for satire's bard to greet?
Stalks not gigantic Vice in every street?
Shall peers or princes tread pollution's
path,
And 'scape alike the law's and muse's
wrath?
Nor blaze with guilty glare through future
time,
Eternal beacons of consummate crime?
Arouse thee, Gifford! be thy promise
claim'd,
Make bad men better, or at least ashamed.

Unhappy White! while life was in its
spring, 831
And thy young muse just waved her joyous
wing,
The spoiler swept that soaring lyre away,
Which else had sounded an immortal lay.
Oh! what a noble heart was here undone,
When Science' self destroy'd her favourite
son!
Yes, she too much indulged thy fond pur-
suit,
She sow'd the seeds, but death has reap'd
the fruit.
'T was thine own genius gave the final
blow,
And help'd to plant the wound that laid
thee low: 840
So the struck eagle, stretch'd upon the
plain,
No more through rolling clouds to soar
again,
View'd his own feather on the fatal dart,
And wing'd the shaft that quiver'd in his
heart;
Keen were his pangs, but keener far to
feel
He nursed the pinion which impell'd the
steel;
While the same plumage that had warm'd
his nest
Drank the last life-drop of his bleeding
breast.

There be who say, in these enlighten'd
days, 849
That splendid lies are all the poet's praise;
That strain'd invention, ever on the wing,
Alone impels the modern bard to sing.
'T is true, that all who rhyme—nay, all
who write,
Shrink from that fatal word to genius—
trite;
Yet Truth sometimes will lend her noblest
fires,
And decorate the verse herself inspires:
This fact in Virtue's name let Crabbe
attest;
Though nature's sternest painter, yet the
best.

And here let Shee and Genius find a
place,
Whose pen and pencil yield an equal grace;
To guide whose hand the sister arts com-
bine, 861
And trace the poet's or the painter's line;
Whose magic touch can bid the canvass
glow,
Or pour the easy rhyme's harmonious flow;
While honours, doubly merited, attend
The poet's rival, but the painter's friend.

Blest is the man who dares approach the
bower
Where dwelt the muses at their natal hour;
Whose steps have press'd, whose eye has
mark'd afar,
The clime that nursed the sons of song and
war, 870
The scenes which glory still must hover
o'er,
Her place of birth, her own Achaian shore.
But doubly blest is he whose heart ex-
pands
With hallow'd feelings for those classic
lands;
Who rends the veil of ages long gone by,
And views their remnants with a poet's
eye!
Wright! 't was thy happy lot at once to view
Those shores of glory, and to sing them too;
And sure no common muse inspired thy pen
To hail the land of gods and godlike men.

And you, associate bards! who snatch'd
to light 881
Those gems too long withheld from modern
sight;

Whose mingling taste combined to cull the
 wreath
Where Attic flowers Aonian odours breathe,
And all their renovated fragrance flung,
To grace the beauties of your native tongue;
Now let those minds, that nobly could trans-
 fuse
The glorious spirit of the Grecian muse,
Though soft the echo, scorn a borrow'd tone:
Resign Achaia's lyre, and strike your own.

Let these, or such as these, with just
 applause, 891
Restore the muse's violated laws;
But not in flimsy Darwin's pompous chime,
That mighty master of unmeaning rhyme,
Whose gilded cymbals, more adorn'd than
 clear,
The eye delighted, but fatigued the ear;
In show the simple lyre could once surpass,
But now, worn down, appear in native brass;
While all his train of hovering sylphs around
Evaporate in similes and sound: 900
Him let them shun, with him let tinsel die:
False glare attracts, but more offends the eye.

Yet let them not to vulgar Wordsworth
 stoop,
The meanest object of the lowly group,
Whose verse, of all but childish prattle void,
Seems blessed harmony to Lamb and Lloyd.
Let them — but hold, my muse, nor dare
 to teach
A strain far, far beyond thy humble reach:
The native genius with their being given
Will point the path, and peal their notes to
 heaven. 910

And thou, too, Scott ! resign to minstrels
 rude
The wilder slogan of a border feud:
Let others spin their meagre lines for hire;
Enough for genius if itself inspire !
Let Southey sing, although his teeming
 muse,
Prolific every spring, be too profuse;
Let simple Wordsworth chime his childish
 verse,
And brother Coleridge lull the babe at nurse;
Let spectre-mongering Lewis aim, at most,
To rouse the galleries, or to raise a ghost;
Let Moore still sigh; let Strangford steal
 from Moore, 921
And swear that Camoëns sang such notes
 of yore;

Let Hayley hobble on, Montgomery rave,
And godly Grahame chant a stupid stave;
Let sonneteering Bowles his strains refine,
And whine and whimper to the fourteenth
 line;
Let Stott, Carlisle, Matilda, and the rest
Of Grub-street, and of Grosvenor-place the
 best,
Scrawl on, till death release us from the
 strain,
Or Common Sense assert her rights again.
But thou, with powers that mock the aid of
 praise, 931
Shouldst leave to humbler bards ignoble
 lays:
Thy country's voice, the voice of all the
 nine,
Demand a hallow'd harp — that harp is
 thine.
Say ! will not Caledonia's annals yield
The glorious record of some nobler field
Than the vile foray of a plundering clan,
Whose proudest deeds disgrace the name
 of man ?
Or Marmion's acts of darkness, fitter food
For Sherwood's outlaw tales of Robin
 Hood ? 940
Scotland ! still proudly claim thy native
 bard,
And be thy praise his first, his best re-
 ward !
Yet not with thee alone his name should
 live,
But own the vast renown a world can give;
Be known, perchance, when Albion is no
 more,
And tell the tale of what she was before;
To future times her faded fame recall,
And save her glory, though his country
 fall.

Yet what avails the sanguine poet's hope,
To conquer ages, and with time to cope ?
New eras spread their wings, new nations
 rise, 951
And other victors fill the applauding skies;
A few brief generations fleet along,
Whose sons forget the poet and his song:
E'en now, what once-loved minstrels scarce
 may claim
The transient mention of a dubious name !
When fame's loud trump hath blown its
 noblest blast,
Though long the sound, the echo sleeps at
 last;

And glory, like the phœnix 'midst her
 fires, 959
Exhales her odours, blazes, and expires.

Shall hoary Granta call her sable sons,
Expert in science, more expert at puns?
Shall these approach the muse? ah, no!
 she flies,
Even from the tempting ore of Seaton's
 prize;
Though printers condescend the press to soil
With rhyme by Hoare, and epic blank by
 Hoyle:
Not him whose page, if still upheld by
 whist,
Requires no sacred theme to bid us list.
Ye! who in Granta's honours would sur-
 pass, 969
Must mount her Pegasus, a full-grown ass;
A foal well worthy of her ancient dam,
Whose Helicon is duller than her Cam.

There Clarke, still striving piteously 'to
 please,'
Forgetting doggerel leads not to degrees,
A would-be satirist, a hired buffoon,
A monthly scribbler of some low lampoon,
Condemn'd to drudge, the meanest of the
 mean,
And furbish falsehoods for a magazine,
Devotes to scandal his congenial mind; 980

Oh! dark asylum of a Vandal race,
At once the boast of learning, and dis-
 grace!
So lost to Phœbus, that nor Hodgson's verse
Can make thee better, nor poor Hewson's
 worse.
But where fair Isis rolls her purer wave,
The partial muse delighted loves to lave;
On her green banks a greener wreath she
 wove,
To crown the bards that haunt her classic
 grove;
Where Richards wakes a genuine poet's
 fires,
And modern Britons glory in their sires.

For me, who, thus unask'd, have dared
 to tell 991
My country, what her sons should know
 too well,
Zeal for her honour bade me here engage
The host of idiots that infest her age;

No just applause her honour'd name shall
 lose,
As first in freedom, dearest to the muse.
Oh! would thy bards but emulate thy
 fame,
And rise more worthy, Albion, of thy name!
What Athens was in science, Rome in
 power,
What Tyre appear'd in her meridian hour,
'T is thine at once, fair Albion! to have
 been — 1001
Earth's chief dictatress, ocean's lovely
 queen.
But Rome decay'd, and Athens strew'd the
 plain,
And Tyre's proud piers lie shatter'd in the
 main;
Like these, thy strength may sink, in ruin
 hurl'd,
And Britain fall, the bulwark of the world.
But let me cease, and dread Cassandra's
 fate,
With warning ever scoff'd at, till too late;
To themes less lofty still my lay confine,
And urge thy bards to gain a name like
 thine. 1010

Then, hapless Britain! be thy rulers blest,
The senate's oracles, the people's jest!
Still hear thy motley orators dispense
The flowers of rhetoric, though not of
 sense,
While Canning's colleagues hate him for
 his wit,
And old dame Portland fills the place of
 Pitt.

Yet once again, adieu! ere this the sail
That wafts me hence is shivering in the
 gale;
And Afric's coast and Calpe's adverse
 height,
And Stamboul's minarets must greet my
 sight; 1020
Thence shall I stray through beauty's na-
 tive clime,
Where Kaff is clad in rocks and crown'd
 with snows sublime.
But should I back return, no tempting press
Shall drag my journal from the desk's
 recess.
Let coxcombs, printing as they come from
 far,
Snatch his own wreath of ridicule from
 Carr;

Let Aberdeen and Elgin still pursue
The shade of fame through regions of virtù;
Waste useless thousands on their Phidian
 freaks,
Misshapen monuments and maim'd antiques;
And make their grand saloons a general
 mart 1031
For all the mutilated blocks of art:
Of Dardan tours let dilettanti tell,
I leave topography to rapid Gell;
And, quite content, no more shall interpose
To stun the public ear — at least with
 prose.

Thus far I 've held my undisturb'd ca-
 reer,
Prepared for rancour, steel'd 'gainst selfish
 fear.
This thing of rhyme I ne'er disdain'd to
 own —
Though not obtrusive, yet not quite un-
 known: 1040
My voice was heard again, though not so
 loud,
My page, though nameless, never disa-
 vow'd;
And now at once I tear the veil away: —
Cheer on the pack ! the quarry stands at
 bay,
Unscared by all the din of Melbourne
 house,
By Lambe's resentment, or by Holland's
 spouse,
By Jeffrey's harmless pistol, Hallam's rage,
Edina's brawny sons and brimstone page.
Our men in buckram shall have blows
 enough,
And feel they too are ' penetrable stuff: '
And though I hope not thence unscathed to
 go, 1051
Who conquers me shall find a stubborn foe.
The time hath been, when no harsh sound
 would fall
From lips that now may seem imbued with
 gall;
Nor fools nor follies tempt me to despise
The meanest thing that crawl'd beneath
 my eyes:
But now, so callous grown, so changed
 since youth,
I 've learn'd to think and sternly speak
 the truth;
Learn'd to deride the critic's starch decree,
And break him on the wheel he meant for
 me; 1060

To spurn the rod a scribbler bids me kiss,
Nor care if courts and crowds applaud or
 hiss:
Nay more, though all my rival rhymesters
 frown,
I too can hunt a poetaster down;
And, arm'd in proof, the gauntlet cast at
 once
To Scotch marauder and to southern dunce.
Thus much I 've dared; if my incondite lay
Hath wrong'd these righteous times, let
 others say:
This, let the world, which knows not how
 to spare 1069
Yet rarely blames unjustly, now declare.

THE CORSAIR

A TALE

—I suoi pensieri in lui dormir non ponno.
Tasso, *Gerusalemme Liberata*, canto x. [stanza 78].

TO THOMAS MOORE, ESQ.

My dear Moore,

I dedicate to you the last production with
which I shall trespass on public patience, and
your indulgence, for some years; and I own
that I feel anxious to avail myself of this latest
and only opportunity of adorning my pages
with a name, consecrated by unshaken public
principle, and the most undoubted and various
talents. While Ireland ranks you among the
firmest of her patriots; while you stand alone
the first of her bards in her estimation, and
Britain repeats and ratifies the decree, permit
one, whose only regret, since our first acquaint-
ance, has been the years he had lost before it
commenced, to add the humble but sincere
suffrage of friendship, to the voice of more
than one nation. It will at least prove to you,
that I have neither forgotten the gratification
derived from your society, nor abandoned the
prospect of its renewal, whenever your leisure
or inclination allows you to atone to your
friends for too long an absence. It is said
among those friends, I trust truly, that you are
engaged in the composition of a poem whose
scene will be laid in the East; none can do
those scenes so much justice. The wrongs of
your own country, the magnificent and fiery
spirit of her sons, the beauty and feeling of her
daughters, may there be found; and Collins,
when he denominated his Oriental his Irish
Eclogues, was not aware how true, at least,
was a part of his parallel. Your imagination
will create a warmer sun, and less clouded
sky; but wildness, tenderness, and originality,

are part of your national claim of Oriental descent, to which you have already thus far proved your title more clearly than the most zealous of your country's antiquarians.

May I add a few words on a subject on which all men are supposed to be fluent, and none agreeable, — Self? I have written much, and published more than enough to demand a longer silence than I now meditate; but, for some years to come, it is my intention to tempt no further the award of 'Gods, men, nor columns.' In the present composition I have attempted not the most difficult, but, perhaps, the best adapted measure to our language, the good old and now neglected heroic couplet. The stanza of Spenser is perhaps too slow and dignified for narrative; though, I confess, it is the measure most after my own heart: Scott alone, of the present generation, has hitherto completely triumphed over the fatal facility of the octo-syllabic verse; and this is not the least victory of his fertile and mighty genius: in blank verse, Milton, Thomson, and our dramatists, are the beacons that shine along the deep, but warn us from the rough and barren rock on which they are kindled. The heroic couplet is not the most popular measure certainly; but as I did not deviate into the other from a wish to flatter what is called public opinion, I shall quit it without further apology, and take my chance once more with that versification, in which I have hitherto published nothing but compositions whose former circulation is part of my present, and will be of my future regret.

With regard to my story, and stories in general, I should have been glad to have rendered my personages more perfect and amiable, if possible, inasmuch as I have been sometimes criticised, and considered no less responsible for their deeds and qualities than if all had been personal. Be it so — if I have deviated into the gloomy vanity of 'drawing from self,' the pictures are probably like, since they are unfavourable; and if not, those who know me are undeceived, and those who do not, I have little interest in undeceiving. I have no particular desire that any but my acquaintance should think the author better than the beings of his imagining; but I cannot help a little surprise, and perhaps amusement, at some odd critical exceptions in the present instance, when I see several bards (far more deserving, I allow) in very reputable plight, and quite exempted from all participation in the faults of those heroes, who, nevertheless, might be found with little more morality than the Giaour, and perhaps — but no — I must admit Childe Harold to be a very repulsive personage; and as to his identity, those who like it must give him whatever 'alias' they please.

If, however, it were worth while to remove the impression, it might be of some service to me, that the man who is alike the delight of his readers and his friends, the poet of all circles, and the idol of his own, permits me here and elsewhere to subscribe myself,

Most truly,
And affectionately,
His obedient servant,
January 2, 1814. BYRON.

CANTO THE THIRD
Come vedi, ancor non m' abbandona.
DANTE. [*Inferno*, v. 105.]

I

SLOW sinks, more lovely ere his race be run,
Along Morea's hills the setting sun;
Not, as in northern climes, obscurely bright,
But one unclouded blaze of living light!
O'er the hush'd deep the yellow beam he throws,
Gilds the green wave that trembles as it glows.
On old Ægina's rock and Idra's isle
The god of gladness sheds his parting smile;
O'er his own regions lingering, loves to shine,
Though there his altars are no more divine. 10
Descending fast, the mountain shadows kiss
Thy glorious gulf, unconquer'd Salamis!
Their azure arches through the long expanse
More deeply purpled meet his mellowing glance,
And tenderest tints, along their summits driven,
Mark his gay course and own the hues of heaven;
Till, darkly shaded from the land and deep,
Behind his Delphian cliff he sinks to sleep.

On such an eve his palest beam he cast
When, Athens! here thy Wisest look'd his last. 20
How watch'd thy better sons his farewell ray,
That closed their murder'd sage's latest day!
Not yet — not yet — Sol pauses on the hill,
The precious hour of parting lingers still;
But sad his light to agonising eyes,
And dark the mountain's once delightful dyes:

Gloom o'er the lovely land he seem'd to
 pour,
The land where Phœbus never frown'd be-
 fore;
But here he sank below Cithæron's head,
The cup of woe was quaff'd — the spirit
 fled; 30
The soul of him who scorn'd to fear or fly,
Who lived and died as none can live or
 die !

But lo ! from high Hymettus to the plain,
The queen of night asserts her silent reign.
No murky vapour, herald of the storm,
Hides her fair face, nor girds her glowing
 form.
With cornice glimmering as the moonbeams
 play,
There the white column greets her grateful
 ray,
And, bright around with quivering beams
 beset,
Her emblem sparkles o'er the minaret: 40
The groves of olive, scatter'd dark and
 wide
Where meek Cephisus pours his scanty
 tide,
The cypress saddening by the sacred mosque,
The gleaming turret of the gay kiosk,
And, dun and sombre 'mid the holy calm,
Near Theseus' fane yon solitary palm;
All tinged with varied hues, arrest the
 eye —
And dull were his that pass'd them heed-
 less by.

Again the Ægean, heard no more afar,
Lulls his chafed breast from elemental
 war; 50
Again his waves in milder tints unfold
Their long array of sapphire and of gold,
Mix'd with the shades of many a distant
 isle
That frown, where gentler ocean seems to
 smile.

II

Not now my theme — why turn my thoughts
 to thee ?
Oh ! who can look along thy native sea,
Nor dwell upon thy name, whate'er the
 tale,
So much its magic must o'er all prevail ?
Who that beheld that sun upon thee set,
Fair Athens ! could thine evening face for-
 get ? 60

Not he, whose heart nor time nor distance
 frees,
Spell-bound within the clustering Cyclades !
Nor seems this homage foreign to his
 strain,
His Corsair's isle was once thine own do-
 main —
Would that with freedom it were thine
 again !

III

The sun hath sunk, and, darker than the
 night,
Sinks with its beam upon the beacon height
Medora's heart; the third day 's come and
 gone —
With it he comes not, sends not — faithless
 one !
The wind was fair though light ; and storms
 were none. 70
Last eve Anselmo's bark return'd, and yet
His only tidings that they had not met ! —
Though wild, as now, far different were the
 tale
Had Conrad waited for that single sail.

The night-breeze freshens; she that day had
 pass'd
In watching all that Hope proclaim'd a
 mast;
Sadly she sate on high — Impatience bore
At last her footsteps to the midnight shore,
And there she wander'd, heedless of the
 spray
That dash'd her garments oft, and warn'd
 away. 80
She saw not, felt not this, nor dared de-
 part,
Nor deem'd it cold — her chill was at her
 heart;
Till grew such certainty from that sus-
 pense,
His very sight had shock'd from life or
 sense !

It came at last — a sad and shatter'd boat,
Whose inmates first beheld whom first they
 sought;
Some bleeding — all most wretched — these
 the few —
Scarce knew they how escaped — this all
 they knew.
In silence, darkling, each appear'd to wait
His fellow's mournful guess at Conrad's
 fate. 90
Something they would have said; but
 seem'd to fear

To trust their accents to Medora's ear.
She saw at once, yet sunk not — trembled not;
Beneath that grief, that loneliness of lot,
Within that meek fair form, were feelings high,
That deem'd not till they found their energy.
While yet was Hope — they soften'd — flutter'd — wept;
All lost — that softness died not, but it slept;
And o'er its slumber rose that Strength which said,
' With nothing left to love, there 's nought to dread.' 100
'T is more than nature's; like the burning might
Delirium gathers from the fever's height.

' Silent you stand, nor would I hear you tell
What — speak not, breathe not — for I know it well —
Yet would I ask — almost my lip denies
The — quick your answer — tell me where he lies.'

' Lady ! we know not — scarce with life we fled;
But here is one denies that he is dead:
He saw him bound; and bleeding — but alive.'

She heard no further — 't was in vain to strive, 110
So throbb'd each vein, each thought, till then withstood;
Her own dark soul these words at once subdued:
She totters — falls — and senseless had the wave
Perchance but snatch'd her from another grave;
But that with hands though rude, yet weeping eyes,
They yield such aid as Pity's haste supplies:
Dash o'er her deathlike cheek the ocean dew,
Raise, fan, sustain — till life returns anew;
Awake her handmaids, with the matrons leave
That fainting form o'er which they gaze and grieve; 120
Then seek Anselmo's cavern, to report
The tale too tedious — when the triumph short.

IV

In that wild council words wax'd warm and strange,
With thoughts of ransom, rescue, and revenge;
All, save repose or flight. Still lingering there
Breathed Conrad's spirit, and forbade despair;
Whate'er his fate — the breasts he form'd and led
Will save him living or appease him dead.
Woe to his foes ! there yet survive a few,
Whose deeds are daring as their hearts are true. 130

V

Within the Haram's secret chamber sate
Stern Seyd, still pondering o'er his Captive's fate;
His thoughts on love and hate alternate dwell,
Now with Gulnare, and now in Conrad's cell.
Here at his feet the lovely slave reclined
Surveys his brow — would soothe his gloom of mind:
While many an anxious glance her large dark eye
Sends in its idle search for sympathy,
His only bends in seeming o'er his beads,
But inly views his victim as he bleeds. 140

' Pacha ! the day is thine; and on thy crest
Sits Triumph — Conrad taken, fall'n the rest !
His doom is fix'd — he dies: and well his fate
Was earn'd — yet much too worthless for thy hate:
Methinks, a short release, for ransom told
With all his treasure, not unwisely sold;
Report speaks largely of his pirate-hoard —
Would that of this my Pacha were the lord !
While baffled, weaken'd by this fatal fray —
Watch'd — follow'd — he were then an easier prey; 150
But once cut off — the remnant of his band
Embark their wealth and seek a safer strand.'

' Gulnare ! if for each drop of blood a gem
Were offer'd rich as Stamboul's diadem;
If for each hair of his a massy mine
Of virgin ore should supplicating shine;

If all our Arab tales divulge or dream
Of wealth were here — that gold should
 not redeem !
It had not now redeem'd a single hour; 159
But that I know him fetter'd, in my power;
And, thirsting for revenge, I ponder still
On pangs that longest rack and latest kill.'

'Nay, Seyd ! — I seek not to restrain thy
 rage,
Too justly moved for mercy to assuage;
My thoughts were only to secure for thee
His riches — thus released, he were not
 free:
Disabled, shorn of half his might and band,
His capture could but wait thy first com-
 mand.'

'His capture *could* ! — and shall I then re-
 sign
One day to him — the wretch already
 mine ? 170
Release my foe ! — at whose remonstrance ?
 — thine !
Fair suitor ! — to thy virtuous gratitude,
That thus repays this Giaour's relenting
 mood,
Which thee and thine alone of all could
 spare,
No doubt regardless if the prize were fair, —
My thanks and praise alike are due — now
 hear !
I have a counsel for thy gentler ear:
I do mistrust thee, woman ! and each word
Of thine stamps truth on all Suspicion
 heard.
Borne in his arms through fire from yon
 Serai — 180
Say, wert thou lingering there with him to
 fly ?
Thou need'st not answer — thy confession
 speaks,
Already reddening on thy guilty cheeks;
Then, lovely dame, bethink thee ! and be-
 ware:
'T is not *his* life alone may claim such care !
Another word and — nay — I need no more.
Accursèd was the moment when he bore
Thee from the flames, which better far —
 but — no —
I then had mourn'd thee with a lover's woe;
Now 't is thy lord that warns — deceitful
 thing ! 190
Know'st thou that I can clip thy wanton
 wing ?

In words alone I am not wont to chafe:
Look to thyself, nor deem thy falsehood
 safe !'

He rose — and slowly, sternly thence with-
 drew,
Rage in his eye and threats in his adieu:
Ah ! little reck'd that chief of womanhood,
Which frowns ne'er quell'd nor menaces
 subdued;
And little deem'd he what thy heart, Gul-
 nare,
When soft could feel, and when incensed
 could dare.
His doubts appear'd to wrong — nor yet she
 knew 200
How deep the root from whence compas-
 sion grew;
She was a slave — from such may captives
 claim
A fellow-feeling, differing but in name.
Still half unconscious, heedless of his wrath,
Again she ventured on the dangerous path,
Again his rage repell'd — until arose
That strife of thought, the source of wo-
 man's woes !

VI

Meanwhile long anxious, weary, still the
 same
Roll'd day and night: his soul, could terror
 tame,
This fearful interval of doubt and dread,
When every hour might doom him worse
 than dead, 211
When every step that echo'd by the gate
Might entering lead where axe and stake
 await;
When every voice that grated on his ear
Might be the last that he could ever hear; —
Could Terror tame, that spirit stern and
 high
Had proved unwilling as unfit to die.
'T was worn, perhaps decay'd, yet silent bore
That conflict, deadlier far than all before.
The heat of fight, the hurry of the gale,
Leave scarce one thought inert enough to
 quail: 221
But bound and fix'd in fetter'd solitude,
To pine, the prey of every changing mood;
To gaze on thine own heart, and meditate
Irrevocable faults and coming fate —
Too late the last to shun, the first to mend;
To count the hours that struggle to thine
 end,

With not a friend to animate, and tell
To other ears that death became thee well;
Around thee foes to forge the ready lie, 230
And blot life's latest scene with calumny;
Before thee tortures, which the soul can
 dare,
Yet doubts how well the shrinking flesh
 may bear,
But deeply feels a single cry would shame,
To valour's praise thy last and dearest
 claim;
The life thou leav'st below, denied above
By kind monopolists of heavenly love;
And more than doubtful paradise, thy
 heaven
Of earthly hope, thy loved one from thee
 riven; —
Such were the thoughts that outlaw must
 sustain, 240
And govern pangs surpassing mortal pain:
And those sustain'd he — boots it well or
 ill?
Since not to sink beneath, is something
 still!

VII

The first day pass'd; he saw not her, Gul-
 nare;
The second — third — and still she came
 not there;
But what her words avouch'd, her charms
 had done,
Or else he had not seen another sun.
The fourth day roll'd along, and with the
 night
Came storm and darkness in their mingling
 might. 249
Oh! how he listen'd to the rushing deep,
That ne'er till now so broke upon his sleep;
And his wild spirit wilder wishes sent,
Roused by the roar of his own element!
Oft had he ridden on that wingèd wave,
And loved its roughness for the speed it
 gave;
And now its dashing echo'd on his ear,
A long-known voice — alas! too vainly
 near!
Loud sung the wind above; and, doubly
 loud,
Shook o'er his turret cell the thunder-
 cloud;
And flash'd the lightning by the latticed
 bar, 260
To him more genial than the midnight
 star:

Close to the glimmering grate he dragg'd
 his chain,
And hoped *that* peril might not prove in
 vain.
He raised his iron hand to Heaven, and
 pray'd
One pitying flash to mar the form it made:
His steel and impious prayer attract alike —
The storm roll'd onward, and disdain'd to
 strike;
Its peal wax'd fainter — ceased — he felt
 alone,
As if some faithless friend had spurn'd his
 groan!

VIII

The midnight pass'd, and to the massy
 door 270
A light step came — it paused — it moved
 once more;
Slow turns the grating bolt and sullen key:
'T is as his heart foreboded — that fair
 she!
Whate'er her sins, to him a guardian saint,
And beauteous still as hermit's hope can
 paint;
Yet changed since last within that cell she
 came,
More pale her cheek, more tremulous her
 frame.
On him she cast her dark and hurried
 eye,
Which spoke before her accents — 'Thou
 must die!
Yes, thou must die; there is but one re-
 source, 280
The last — the worst — if torture were not
 worse.'

'Lady! I look to none; my lips proclaim
What last proclaim'd they — Conrad still
 the same.
Why should'st thou seek an outlaw's life
 to spare,
And change the sentence I deserve to
 bear?
Well have I earn'd — nor here alone —
 the meed
Of Seyd's revenge, by many a lawless
 deed.'

'Why should I seek? because — Oh! didst
 thou not
Redeem my life from worse than slavery's
 lot?

Why should I seek ? — hath misery made
 thee blind 290
To the fond workings of a woman's mind ?
And must I say ? albeit my heart rebel
With all that woman feels, but should not
 tell —
Because, despite thy crimes, that heart is
 moved :
It fear'd thee — thank'd thee — pitied —
 madden'd — loved.
Reply not, tell not now thy tale again,
Thou lov'st another — and I love in vain;
Though fond as mine her bosom, form more
 fair,
I rush through peril which she would not
 dare.
If that thy heart to hers were truly dear,
Were I thine own, thou wert not lonely
 here : 301
An outlaw's spouse — and leave her lord
 to roam !
What hath such gentle dame to do with
 home ?
But speak not now — o'er thine and o'er
 my head
Hangs the keen sabre by a single thread;
If thou hast courage still, and wouldst be
 free,
Receive this poinard — rise, and follow
 me !'

'Ay, in my chains ! my steps will gently
 tread,
With these adornments, o'er each slumber-
 ing head !
Thou hast forgot — is this a garb for
 flight ? 310
Or is that instrument more fit for fight ?'

'Misdoubting Corsair ! I have gain'd the
 guard,
Ripe for revolt, and greedy for reward.
A single word of mine removes that
 chain :
Without some aid how here could I re-
 main ?
Well, since we met, hath sped my busy
 time,
If in aught evil, for thy sake the crime :
The crime — 't is none to punish those of
 Seyd.
That hated tyrant, Conrad — he must bleed !
I see thee shudder, but my soul is changed —
Wrong'd, spurn'd, reviled — and it shall be
 avenged; 321

Accused of what till now my heart dis-
 dain'd —
Too faithful, though to bitter bondage
 chain'd.
Yes, smile ! — but he had little cause to
 sneer,
I was not treacherous then, nor thou too
 dear :
But he has said it, and the jealous well
(Those tyrants, teasing, tempting to rebel)
Deserve the fate their fretting lips foretell.
I never loved — he bought me — somewhat
 high,
Since with me came a heart he could not
 buy. 330
I was a slave unmurmuring : he hath said,
But for his rescue I with thee had fled.
'T was false thou know'st; but let such au-
 gurs rue,
Their words are omens Insult renders true.
Nor was thy respite granted to my prayer;
This fleeting grace was only to prepare
New torments for thy life, and my despair.
Mine too he threatens; but his dotage still
Would fain reserve me for his lordly
 will :
When wearier of these fleeting charms and
 me, 340
There yawns the sack — and yonder rolls
 the sea !
What, am I then a toy for dotard's play,
To wear but till the gilding frets away ?
I saw thee — loved thee — owe thee all —
 would save,
If but to show how grateful is a slave.
But had he not thus menaced fame and life
(And well he keeps his oaths pronounced in
 strife),
I still had saved thee — but the Pacha
 spared.
Now I am all thine own — for all pre-
 pared :
Thou lov'st me not — nor know'st — or but
 the worst. 350
Alas ! *this* love, *that* hatred are the first —
Oh ! couldst thou prove my truth, thou
 wouldst not start,
Nor fear the fire that lights an Eastern
 heart;
'T is now the beacon of thy safety — now
It points within the port a Mainote prow:
But in one chamber, where our path must
 lead,
There sleeps — he must not wake — the op-
 pressor Seyd !'

'Gulnare — Gulnare — I never felt till now
My abject fortune, wither'd fame so low !
Seyd is mine enemy, had swept my band
From earth with ruthless but with open
 hand; 361
And therefore came I, in my bark of war,
To smite the smiter with the scimitar;
Such is my weapon — not the secret knife;
Who spares a woman's seeks not slumber's
 life.
Thine saved I gladly, Lady, not for this —
Let me not deem that mercy shown amiss.
Now fare thee well — more peace be with
 thy breast !
Night wears apace, my last of earthly
 rest !'

'Rest ! rest ! by sunrise must thy sinews
 shake, 370
And thy limbs writhe around the ready
 stake.
I heard the order — saw — I will not see —
If thou wilt perish, I will fall with thee.
My life — my love — my hatred — all be-
 low
Are on this cast; Corsair ! 't is but a blow !
Without it flight were idle — how evade
His sure pursuit ? my wrongs too unrepaid,
My youth disgraced — the long, long
 wasted years,
One blow shall cancel with our future fears.
But since the dagger suits thee less than
 brand, 380
I'll try the firmness of a female hand.
The guards are gain'd — one moment all
 were o'er —
Corsair ! we meet in safety or no more;
If errs my feeble hand, the morning cloud
Will hover o'er thy scaffold, and my
 shroud.'

IX

She turn'd, and vanish'd ere he could reply,
But his glance follow'd far with eager eye;
And gathering, as he could, the links that
 bound
His form, to curl their length and curb
 their sound,
Since bar and bolt no more his steps pre-
 clude, 390
He, fast as fetter'd limbs allow, pursued.
'T was dark and winding, and he knew not
 where
That passage led; nor lamp nor guard was
 there.

He sees a dusky glimmering — shall he
 seek
Or shun that ray so indistinct and weak ?
Chance guides his steps — a freshness seems
 to bear
Full on his brow, as if from morning air;
He reach'd an open gallery — on his eye
Gleam'd the last star of night, the clearing
 sky: 399
Yet scarcely heeded these — another light
From a lone chamber struck upon his sight.
Towards it he moved; a scarcely closing
 door
Reveal'd the ray within, but nothing more.
With hasty step a figure outward pass'd,
Then paused — and turn'd — and paused —
 't is She at last !
No poniard in that hand, nor sign of ill —
'Thanks to that softening heart, she could
 not kill !'
Again he look'd, the wildness of her eye
Starts from the day abrupt and fearfully.
She stopp'd — threw back her dark far-
 floating hair, 410
That nearly veil'd her face and bosom fair:
As if she late had bent her leaning head
Above some object of her doubt or dread.
They meet — upon her brow, unknown, for-
 got,
Her hurrying hand had left — 't was but a
 spot —
Its hue was all he saw, and scarce with-
 stood —
Oh ! slight but certain pledge of crime —
 't is blood !

X

He had seen battle, he had brooded lone
O'er promised pangs to sentenced guilt
 foreshown;
He had been tempted, chasten'd, and the
 chain 420
Yet on his arms might ever there remain:
But ne'er from strife, captivity, remorse,
From all his feelings in their inmost force,
So thrill'd, so shudder'd every creeping
 vein,
As now they froze before that purple stain.
That spot of blood, that light but guilty
 streak,
Had banish'd all the beauty from her
 cheek !
Blood he had view'd — could view un-
 moved — but then
It flow'd in combat, or was shed by men !

XI

' 'T is done — he nearly waked — but it is
 done; 430
Corsair ! he perish'd — thou art dearly
 won.
All words would now be vain — away —
 away !
Our bark is tossing — 't is already day.
The few gain'd over, now are wholly mine,
And these thy yet surviving band shall
 join:
Anon my voice shall vindicate my hand,
When once our sail forsakes this hated
 strand ! '

XII

She clapp'd her hands, and through the
 gallery pour,
Equipp'd for flight, her vassals — Greek
 and Moor;
Silent but quick they stoop, his chains un-
 bind; 440
Once more his limbs are free as mountain
 wind !
But on his heavy heart such sadness sate,
As if they there transferr'd that iron
 weight.
No words are utter'd; at her sign, a door
Reveals the secret passage to the shore;
The city lies behind — they speed, they
 reach
The glad waves dancing on the yellow
 beach;
And Conrad following, at her beck, obey'd,
Nor cared he now if rescued or betray'd;
Resistance were as useless as if Seyd 450
Yet lived to view the doom his ire decreed.

XIII

Embark'd, the sail unfurl'd, the light breeze
 blew —
How much had Conrad's memory to re-
 view !
Sunk he in Contemplation, till the Cape
Where last he anchor'd rear'd its giant
 shape.
Ah ! since that fatal night, though brief
 the time,
Had swept an age of terror, grief, and
 crime.
As its far shadow frown'd above the mast,
He veil'd his face and sorrow'd as he pass'd;
He thought of all — Gonsalvo and his
 band, 460
His fleeting triumph and his failing hand;

He thought on her afar, his lonely bride:
He turn'd and saw — Gulnare, the homi-
 cide !

XIV

She watch'd his features till she could not
 bear
Their freezing aspect and averted air;
And that strange fierceness, foreign to her
 eye,
Fell quench'd in tears, too late to shed or
 dry.
She knelt beside him and his hand she
 press'd,
' Thou may'st forgive though Allah's self
 detest;
But for that deed of darkness what wert
 thou ? 470
Reproach me — but not yet — Oh ! spare
 me now !
I am not what I seem — this fearful night
My brain bewilder'd — do not madden
 quite !
If I had never loved — though less my guilt,
Thou hadst not lived to — hate me — if
 thou wilt.'

XV

She wrongs his thoughts, they more him-
 self upbraid
Than her, though undesign'd, the wretch
 he made;
But speechless all, deep, dark, and un-
 exprest,
They bleed within that silent cell — his
 breast.
Still onward, fair the breeze, nor rough
 the surge, 480
The blue waves sport around the stern
 they urge;
Far on the horizon's verge appears a speck,
A spot — a mast — a sail — an armèd deck !
Their little bark her men of watch descry,
And ampler canvass woos the wind from
 high;
She bears her down majestically near,
Speed on her prow, and terror in her tier;
A flash is seen — the ball beyond their bow
Booms harmless, hissing to the deep be-
 low. 489
Up rose keen Conrad from his silent trance,
A long, long absent gladness in his glance;
' 'T is mine — my blood-red flag ! again —
 again —
I am not all deserted on the main ! '

They own the signal, answer to the hail,
Hoist out the boat at once, and slacken
 sail.
' 'T is Conrad! Conrad!' shouting from the
 deck,
Command nor duty could their transport
 check!
With light alacrity and gaze of pride,
They view him mount once more his ves-
 sel's side;
A smile relaxing in each rugged face, 500
Their arms can scarce forbear a rough em-
 brace.
He, half forgetting danger and defeat,
Returns their greeting as a chief may
 greet,
Wrings with a cordial grasp Anselmo's
 hand,
And feels he yet can conquer and com-
 mand!

XVI

These greetings o'er, the feelings that o'er-
 flow,
Yet grieve to win him back without a blow;
They sail'd prepared for vengeance — had
 they known
A woman's hand secured that deed her own,
She were their queen; less scrupulous are
 they 510
Than haughty Conrad how they win their
 way.
With many an asking smile and wondering
 stare,
They whisper round and gaze upon Gulnare;
And her, — at once above, beneath her sex,
Whom blood appall'd not, — their regards
 perplex.
To Conrad turns her faint imploring eye,
She drops her veil, and stands in silence by;
Her arms are meekly folded on that breast,
Which — Conrad safe — to fate resign'd
 the rest.
Though worse than frenzy could that bosom
 fill, 520
Extreme in love or hate, in good or ill,
The worst of crimes had left her woman
 still!

XVII

This Conrad mark'd, and felt — ah! could
 he less? —
Hate of that deed but grief for her distress;
What she has done no tears can wash away,
And Heaven must punish on its angry day.

But — it was done: he knew, whate'er her
 guilt,
For him that poniard smote, that blood was
 spilt;
And he was free! — and she for him had
 given
Her all on earth and more than all in
 heaven! 530
And now he turn'd him to that dark-eyed
 slave,
Whose brow was bow'd beneath the glance
 he gave,
Who now seem'd changed and humbled: —
 faint and meek,
But varying oft the colour of her cheek
To deeper shades of paleness, all its red
That fearful spot which stain'd it from the
 dead!
He took that hand — it trembled — now too
 late —
So soft in love, so wildly nerved in hate;
He clasp'd that hand — it trembled — and
 his own
Had lost its firmness, and his voice its tone.
' Gulnare!' — but she replied not — 'dear
 Gulnare!' 541
She raised her eye, her only answer there;
At once she sought and sunk in his embrace:
If he had driven her from that resting-
 place,
His had been more or less than mortal
 heart,
But — good or ill — it bade her not depart.
Perchance, but for the bodings of his breast,
His latest virtue then had join'd the rest.
Yet even Medora might forgive the kiss
That ask'd from form so fair no more than
 this, 550
The first, the last that Frailty stole from
 Faith —
To lips where Love had lavish'd all his
 breath,
To lips whose broken sighs such fragrance
 fling,
As he had fann'd them freshly with his
 wing!

XVIII

They gain by twilight's hour their lonely
 isle.
To them the very rocks appear to smile;
The haven hums with many a cheering
 sound,
The beacons blaze their wonted stations
 round,

The boats are darting o'er the curly bay,
And sportive dolphins bend them through
 the spray; 560
Even the hoarse sea-bird's shrill, discordant
 shriek
Greets like the welcome of his tuneless
 beak !
Beneath each lamp that through its lattice
 gleams,
Their fancy paints the friends that trim the
 beams.
Oh ! what can sanctify the joys of home,
Like Hope's gay glance from Ocean's
 troubled foam ?

XIX

The lights are high on beacon and from
 bower,
And 'midst them Conrad seeks Medora's
 tower:
He looks in vain — 't is strange — and all
 remark,
Amid so many, hers alone is dark. 570
'T is strange — of yore its welcome never
 fail'd,
Nor now, perchance, extinguish'd, only
 veil'd.
With the first boat descends he for the shore,
And looks impatient on the lingering oar.
Oh ! for a wing beyond the falcon's flight,
To bear him like an arrow to that height !
With the first pause the resting rowers gave,
He waits not — looks not — leaps into the
 wave,
Strives through the surge, bestrides the
 beach, and high
Ascends the path familiar to his eye. 580

He reach'd his turret door; he paused —
 no sound
Broke from within, and all was night
 around.
He knock'd, and loudly — footstep nor re-
 ply
Announced that any heard or deem'd him
 nigh;
He knock'd — but faintly — for his trem-
 bling hand
Refused to aid his heavy heart's demand.
The portal opens — 't is a well-known
 face —
But not the form he panted to embrace.
Its lips are silent; twice his own essay'd,
And fail'd to frame the question they de-
 lay'd; 590

He snatch'd the lamp — its light will an-
 swer all —
It quits his grasp, expiring in the fall.
He would not wait for that reviving ray —
As soon could he have linger'd there for
 day;
But, glimmering through the dusky corri-
 dore,
Another chequers o'er the shadow'd floor;
His steps the chamber gain, his eyes behold
All that his heart believed not — yet fore-
 told !

XX

He turn'd not — spoke not — sunk not —
 fix'd his look,
And set the anxious frame that lately
 shook: 600
He gazed — how long we gaze despite of
 pain,
And know, but dare not own, we gaze in
 vain !
In life itself she was so still and fair,
That death with gentler aspect wither'd
 there;
And the cold flowers her colder hand con-
 tain'd,
In that last grasp as tenderly were strain'd
As if she scarcely felt, but feign'd a sleep,
And made it almost mockery yet to weep.
The long dark lashes fringed her lids of
 snow,
And veil'd — thought shrinks from all that
 lurk'd below — 610
Oh ! o'er the eye Death most exerts his
 might,
And hurls the spirit from her throne of
 light !
Sinks those blue orbs in that long last
 eclipse,
But spares, as yet, the charm around her
 lips;
Yet, yet they seem as they forebore to
 smile,
And wish'd repose — but only for a while;
But the white shroud, and each extended
 tress,
Long, fair, but spread in utter lifelessness,
Which, late the sport of every summer
 wind,
Escaped the baffled wreath that strove to
 bind; 620
These and the pale pure cheek became the
 bier —
But she is nothing — wherefore is he here ?

XXI

He ask'd no question — all were answer'd
 now
By the first glance on that still, marble
 brow.
It was enough — she died — what reck'd it
 how ?
The love of youth, the hope of better
 years,
The source of softest wishes, tenderest
 fears,
The only living thing he could not hate,
Was reft at once — and he deserved his
 fate,
But did not feel it less ; — the good ex-
 plore, 630
For peace, those realms where guilt can
 never soar:
The proud, the wayward, who have fix'd
 below
Their joy and find this earth enough for
 woe,
Lose in that one their all — perchance a
 mite —
But who in patience parts with all delight ?
Full many a stoic eye and aspect stern
Mask hearts where grief hath little left to
 learn;
And many a withering thought lies hid, not
 lost,
In smiles that least befit who wear them
 most.

XXII

By those that deepest feel is ill exprest 640
The indistinctness of the suffering breast;
Where thousand thoughts begin, to end in
 one
Which seeks from all the refuge found in
 none;
No words suffice the secret soul to show,
For Truth denies all eloquence to Woe.
On Conrad's stricken soul exhaustion prest,
And stupor almost lull'd it into rest;
So feeble now — his mother's softness crept
To those wild eyes, which like an infant's
 wept:
It was the very weakness of his brain, 650
Which thus confess'd without relieving pain.
None saw his trickling tears — perchance, if
 seen,
That useless flood of grief had never been:
Nor long they flow'd — he dried them to
 depart,
In helpless, hopeless, brokenness of heart:

The sun goes forth, but Conrad's day is
 dim;
And the night cometh, ne'er to pass from
 him.
There is no darkness like the cloud of mind
On Grief's vain eye — the blindest of the
 blind !
Which may not, dare not see, but turns
 aside 660
To blackest shade, nor will endure a guide !

XXIII

His heart was form'd for softness, warp'd
 to wrong;
Betray'd too early, and beguiled too long;
Each feeling pure — as falls the dropping
 dew
Within the grot, like that had harden'd
 too;
Less clear, perchance, its earthly trials
 pass'd,
But sunk, and chill'd, and petrified at last.
Yet tempests wear, and lightning cleaves the
 rock;
If such his heart, so shatter'd it the shock.
There grew one flower beneath its rugged
 brow; 670
Though dark the shade, it shelter'd, saved
 till now.
The thunder came; that bolt hath blasted
 both,
The Granite's firmness and the Lily's
 growth:
The gentle plant hath left no leaf to tell
Its tale, but shrunk and wither'd where it
 fell;
And of its cold protector, blacken round
But shiver'd fragments on the barren
 ground !

XXIV

'T is morn; to venture on his lonely hour
Few dare, though now Anselmo sought his
 tower.
He was not there, nor seen along the shore;
Ere night, alarm'd, their isle is traversed
 o'er. 681
Another morn — another bids them seek,
And shout his name till echo waxeth weak;
Mount, grotto, cavern, valley search'd in
 vain,
They find on shore a seaboat's broken
 chain:
Their hope revives, they follow o'er the
 main.

'T is idle all; moons roll on moons away,
And Conrad comes not, came not since that
 day:
Nor trace, nor tidings of his doom de-
 clare
Where lives his grief, or perish'd his de-
 spair ! 690
Long mourn'd his band whom none could
 mourn beside;
And fair the monument they gave his bride:
For him they raise not the recording
 stone —
His death yet dubious, deeds too widely
 known;
He left a Corsair's name to other times,
Link'd with one virtue and a thousand
 crimes.

THE PRISONER OF CHILLON

A FABLE

SONNET ON CHILLON

ETERNAL Spirit of the chainless Mind !
 Brightest in dungeons, Liberty ! thou
 art,
 For there thy habitation is the heart —
The heart which love of thee alone can
 bind;
And when thy sons to fetters are con-
 sign'd —
 To fetters, and the damp vault's dayless
 gloom,
 Their country conquers with their mar-
 tyrdom,
And Freedom's fame finds wings on every
 wind.
Chillon ! thy prison is a holy place,
 And thy sad floor an altar; for 't was
 trod,
Until his very steps have left a trace
 Worn, as if thy cold pavement were a
 sod,
By Bonnivard ! — May none those marks
 efface !
 For they appeal from tyranny to God.

I

My hair is grey, but not with years,
 Nor grew it white
 In a single night,
As men's have grown from sudden fears.

My limbs are bow'd, though not with toil,
 But rusted with a vile repose,
For they have been a dungeon's spoil,
 And mine has been the fate of those
To whom the goodly earth and air
Are bann'd, and barr'd — forbidden fare.
But this was for my father's faith, 11
I suffer'd chains and courted death;
That father perish'd at the stake
For tenets he would not forsake;
And for the same his lineal race
In darkness found a dwelling-place.
We were seven — who now are one,
 Six in youth, and one in age,
Finish'd as they had begun,
 Proud of Persecution's rage; 20
One in fire, and two in field,
Their belief with blood have seal'd,
Dying as their father died,
For the God their foes denied;
Three were in a dungeon cast,
Of whom this wreck is left the last.

II

There are seven pillars of Gothic mould
In Chillon's dungeons deep and old,
There are seven columns, massy and
 grey,
Dim with a dull imprison'd ray, 30
A sunbeam which hath lost its way,
And through the crevice and the cleft
Of the thick wall is fallen and left;
Creeping o'er the floor so damp,
Like a marsh's meteor lamp.
And in each pillar there is a ring,
 And in each ring there is a chain;
That iron is a cankering thing,
 For in these limbs its teeth remain,
With marks that will not wear away, 40
Till I have done with this new day,
Which now is painful to these eyes,
Which have not seen the sun so rise
For years — I cannot count them o'er,
I lost their long and heavy score
When my last brother droop'd and died,
And I lay living by his side.

III

They chain'd us each to a column stone,
And we were three — yet, each alone;
We could not move a single pace, 50
We could not see each other's face,
But with that pale and livid light
That made us strangers in our sight.
And thus together, yet apart,

Fetter'd in hand, but join'd in heart,
'T was still some solace, in the dearth
Of the pure elements of earth,
To hearken to each other's speech,
And each turn comforter to each
With some new hope or legend old, 60
Or song heroically bold;
But even these at length grew cold.
Our voices took a dreary tone,
An echo of the dungeon stone,
 A grating sound — not full and free
 As they of yore were wont to be:
 It might be fancy, but to me
They never sounded like our own.

IV

I was the eldest of the three,
 And to uphold and cheer the rest 70
 I ought to do — and did my best;
And each did well in his degree.
 The youngest, whom my father loved,
Because our mother's brow was given
To him, with eyes as blue as heaven —
 For him my soul was sorely moved.
And truly might it be distress'd
To see such bird in such a nest;
For he was beautiful as day
 (When day was beautiful to me 80
 As to young eagles being free) —
 A polar day, which will not see
A sunset till its summer's gone,
 Its sleepless summer of long light,
The snow-clad offspring of the sun:
 And thus he was as pure and bright,
And in his natural spirit gay,
With tears for nought but others' ills,
And then they flow'd like mountain rills,
Unless he could assuage the woe 90
Which he abhorr'd to view below.

V

The other was as pure of mind,
But form'd to combat with his kind;
Strong in his frame, and of a mood
Which 'gainst the world in war had stood,
And perish'd in the foremost rank
 With joy: — but not in chains to pine:
His spirit wither'd with their clank,
 I saw it silently decline —
 And so perchance in sooth did mine: 100
But yet I forced it on to cheer
Those relics of a home so dear.
He was a hunter of the hills,
 Had follow'd there the deer and wolf;

To him this dungeon was a gulf,
And fetter'd feet the worst of ills.

VI

Lake Leman lies by Chillon's walls:
A thousand feet in depth below
Its massy waters meet and flow;
Thus much the fathom-line was sent 110
From Chillon's snow-white battlement
 Which round about the wave inthrals:
A double dungeon wall and wave
Have made — and like a living grave.
Below the surface of the lake
The dark vault lies wherein we lay:
We heard it ripple night and day;
 Sounding o'er our heads it knock'd;
And I have felt the winter's spray
Wash through the bars when winds were high
And wanton in the happy sky; 121
 And then the very rock hath rock'd,
 And I have felt it shake, unshock'd,
Because I could have smiled to see
The death that would have set me free.

VII

I said my nearer brother pined,
I said his mighty heart declined,
He loathed and put away his food;
It was not that 't was coarse and rude,
For we were used to hunters' fare, 130
And for the like had little care.
The milk drawn from the mountain goat
Was changed for water from the moat,
Our bread was such as captives' tears
Have moisten'd many a thousand years,
Since man first pent his fellow men
Like brutes within an iron den;
But what were these to us or him?
These wasted not his heart or limb;
My brother's soul was of that mould 140
Which in a palace had grown cold,
Had his free breathing been denied
The range of the steep mountain's side.
But why delay the truth? — he died.
I saw, and could not hold his head,
Nor reach his dying hand — nor dead, —
Though hard I strove, but strove in
 vain,
To rend and gnash my bonds in twain.
He died — and they unlock'd his chain,
And scoop'd for him a shallow grave 150
Even from the cold earth of our cave.
I begg'd them, as a boon, to lay
His corse in dust whereon the day
Might shine — it was a foolish thought,

But then within my brain it wrought,
That even in death his freeborn breast
In such a dungeon could not rest.
I might have spared my idle prayer;
They coldly laugh'd — and laid him there:
The flat and turfless earth above 160
The being we so much did love;
His empty chain above it leant,
Such murder's fitting monument !

VIII

But he, the favourite and the flower,
Most cherish'd since his natal hour,
His mother's image in fair face,
The infant love of all his race,
His martyr'd father's dearest thought,
My latest care, for whom I sought
To hoard my life, that his might be 170
Less wretched now, and one day free;
He, too, who yet had held untired
A spirit natural or inspired —
He, too, was struck, and day by day
Was wither'd on the stalk away.
Oh, God ! it is a fearful thing
To see the human soul take wing
In any shape, in any mood : —
I 've seen it rushing forth in blood,
I 've seen it on the breaking ocean 180
Strive with a swoln convulsive motion,
I 've seen the sick and ghastly bed
Of Sin delirious with its dread:
But these were horrors — this was woe
Unmix'd with such — but sure and slow.
He faded, and so calm and meek,
So softly worn, so sweetly weak,
So tearless, yet so tender — kind,
And grieved for those he left behind;
With all the while a cheek whose bloom
Was as a mockery of the tomb, 191
Whose tints as gently sunk away
As a departing rainbow's ray;
An eye of most transparent light,
That almost made the dungeon bright;
And not a word of murmur, not
A groan o'er his untimely lot, —
A little talk of better days,
A little hope my own to raise,
For I was sunk in silence — lost 200
In this last loss, of all the most;
And then the sighs he would suppress
Of fainting nature's feebleness,
More slowly drawn, grew less and less.
I listen'd, but I could not hear —
I call'd, for I was wild with fear;
I knew 't was hopeless, but my dread

Would not be thus admonishèd.
I call'd, and thought I heard a sound —
I burst my chain with one strong bound, 210
And rush'd to him: — I found him not,
I only stirr'd in this black spot,
I only lived — *I* only drew
The accursèd breath of dungeon-dew;
The last — the sole — the dearest link
Between me and the eternal brink,
Which bound me to my failing race,
Was broken in this fatal place.
One on the earth, and one beneath —
My brothers — both had ceased to breathe:
I took that hand which lay so still, 221
Alas ! my own was full as chill,
I had not strength to stir, or strive,
But felt that I was still alive —
A frantic feeling, when we know
That what we love shall ne'er be so.
 I know not why
 I could not die,
I had no earthly hope — but faith,
And that forbade a selfish death. 230

IX

What next befell me then and there
 I know not well — I never knew;
First came the loss of light, and air,
 And then of darkness too.
I had no thought, no feeling — none —
Among the stones I stood a stone,
And was, scarce conscious what I wist,
As shrubless crags within the mist;
For all was blank, and bleak, and grey,
It was not night — it was not day, 240
It was not even the dungeon-light
So hateful to my heavy sight,
But vacancy absorbing space,
And fixedness — without a place;
There were no stars, no earth, no time,
No check, no change, no good, no
 crime —
But silence, and a stirless breath
Which neither was of life nor death;
A sea of stagnant idleness,
Blind, boundless, mute, and motionless ! 250

X

A light broke in upon my brain, —
 It was the carol of a bird;
It ceased, and then it came again,
 The sweetest song ear ever heard,
And mine was thankful till my eyes
Ran over with the glad surprise,
And they that moment could not see

I was the mate of misery.
But then by dull degrees came back
My senses to their wonted track; 260
I saw the dungeon walls and floor
Close slowly round me as before,
I saw the glimmer of the sun
Creeping as it before had done,
But through the crevice where it came
That bird was perch'd, as fond and tame,
 And tamer than upon the tree;
A lovely bird, with azure wings,
And song that said a thousand things,
 And seem'd to say them all for me ! 270
I never saw its like before,
I ne'er shall see its likeness more:
It seem'd like me to want a mate,
But was not half so desolate,
And it was come to love me when
None lived to love me so again,
And cheering from my dungeon's brink,
Had brought me back to feel and think.
I know not if it late were free,
 Or broke its cage to perch on mine, 280
But knowing well captivity,
 Sweet bird ! I could not wish for thine !
Or if it were, in wingèd guise,
A visitant from Paradise;
For — Heaven forgive that thought ! the
 while
Which made me both to weep and smile —
I sometimes deem'd that it might be
My brother's soul come down to me;
But then at last away it flew,
And then 't was mortal — well I knew, 290
For he would never thus have flown,
And left me twice so doubly lone, —
Lone — as the corse within its shroud,
Lone — as a solitary cloud,
 A single cloud on a sunny day,
While all the rest of heaven is clear,
A frown upon the atmosphere
That hath no business to appear
 When skies are blue and earth is gay.

XI

A kind of change came in my fate, 300
My keepers grew compassionate;
I know not what had made them so,
They were inured to sights of woe,
But so it was: — my broken chain
With links unfasten'd did remain,
And it was liberty to stride
Along my cell from side to side,
And up and down, and then athwart,
And tread it over every part;

And round the pillars one by one, 310
Returning where my walk begun,
Avoiding only, as I trod,
My brothers' graves without a sod;
For if I thought with heedless tread
My step profaned their lowly bed,
My breath came gaspingly and thick,
And my crush'd heart fell blind and sick.

XII

I made a footing in the wall,
 It was not therefrom to escape,
For I had buried one and all 320
 Who loved me in a human shape;
And the whole earth would henceforth
 be
A wider prison unto me.
No child, no sire, no kin had I,
No partner in my misery;
I thought of this, and I was glad,
For thought of them had made me mad;
But I was curious to ascend
To my barr'd windows, and to bend
Once more, upon the mountains high, 330
The quiet of a loving eye.

XIII

I saw them — and they were the same,
They were not changed like me in frame;
I saw their thousand years of snow
On high — their wide long lake below,
And the blue Rhone in fullest flow;
I heard the torrents leap and gush
O'er channell'd rock and broken bush;
I saw the white-wall'd distant town,
And whiter sails go skimming down. 340
And then there was a little isle,
 Which in my very face did smile,
 The only one in view;
A small green isle, it seem'd no more,
Scarce broader than my dungeon floor,
But in it there were three tall trees,
And o'er it blew the mountain breeze,
And by it there were waters flowing,
And on it there were young flowers growing
 Of gentle breath and hue. 350
The fish swam by the castle wall,
And they seem'd joyous each and all;
The eagle rode the rising blast,
Methought he never flew so fast
As then to me he seem'd to fly;
And then new tears came in my eye,
And I felt troubled and would fain
I had not left my recent chain.
And when I did descend again,

The darkness of my dim abode 360
Fell on me as a heavy load;
It was as is a new-dug grave,
Closing o'er one we sought to save;
And yet my glance, too much oppress'd,
Had almost need of such a rest.
 The monk abjured a world he ne'er could

XIV

It might be months, or years, or days —
 I kept no count, I took no note,
I had no hope my eyes to raise,
 And clear them of their dreary mote.
At last men came to set me free, 370
 I ask'd not why, and reck'd not where,
It was at length the same to me,
Fetter'd or fetterless to be,
 I learn'd to love despair.
And thus when they appear'd at last,
And all my bonds aside were cast,
These heavy walls to me had grown
A hermitage — and all my own !
And half I felt as they were come
To tear me from a second home. 380
With spiders I had friendship made,
And watch'd them in their sullen trade,
Had seen the mice by moonlight play,
And why should I feel less than they ?
We were all inmates of one place,
And I, the monarch of each race,
Had power to kill — yet, strange to
 tell !
In quiet we had learn'd to dwell —
My very chains and I grew friends,
So much a long communion tends 390
To make us what we are: — even I
Regain'd my freedom with a sigh.

MANFRED

A DRAMATIC POEM

' There are more things in heaven and earth, Horatio,
Than are dreamt of in your philosophy.'

DRAMATIS PERSONÆ

MANFRED	WITCH OF THE ALPS
CHAMOIS HUNTER	ARIMANES
ABBOT OF ST. MAURICE	NEMESIS
MANUEL	THE DESTINIES
HERMAN	SPIRITS, etc.

*The scene of the Drama is amongst the Higher Alps —
partly in the Castle of Manfred, and partly in the
Mountains.*

ACT I

SCENE I

MANFRED *alone. — Scene, a Gothic Gallery. — Time,
Midnight.*

Man. The lamp must be replenish'd,
 but even then
It will not burn so long as I must watch.
My slumbers — if I slumber — are not sleep,
But a continuance of enduring thought,
Which then I can resist not: in my heart
There is a vigil, and these eyes but close
To look within; and yet I live, and bear
The aspect and the form of breathing men.
But grief should be the instructor of the
 wise;
Sorrow is knowledge: they who know the
 most 10
Must mourn the deepest o'er the fatal
 truth,
The Tree of Knowledge is not that of Life.
Philosophy and science, and the springs
Of wonder, and the wisdom of the world,
I have essay'd, and in my mind there is
A power to make these subject to itself —
But they avail not: I have done men good,
And I have met with good even among
 men —
But this avail'd not: I have had my foes,
And none have baffled, many fallen before
 me — 20

But this avail'd not: — Good, or evil, life,
Powers, passions, all I see in other beings,
Have been to me as rain unto the sands,
Since that all-nameless hour. I have no
 dread,
And feel the curse to have no natural fear,
Nor fluttering throb, that beats with hopes
 or wishes,
Or lurking love of something on the earth.
Now to my task. —
 Mysterious Agency!
Ye spirits of the unbounded Universe,
Whom I have sought in darkness and in
 light! 30
Ye, who do compass earth about, and dwell
In subtler essence! ye, to whom the tops
Of mountains inaccessible are haunts,
And earth's and ocean's caves familiar
 things —
I call upon ye by the written charm
Which gives me power upon you — Rise!
 appear! [A pause.
They come not yet. — Now by the voice of
 him
Who is the first among you; by this sign,
Which makes you tremble; by the claims
 of him
Who is undying, — Rise! appear! — Ap-
 pear! [A pause.
If it be so. — Spirits of earth and air, 41
Ye shall not thus elude me: by a power,
Deeper than all yet urged, a tyrant-spell,
Which had its birthplace in a star con-
 demn'd,
The burning wreck of a demolish'd world,
A wandering hell in the eternal space;
By the strong curse which is upon my
 soul,
The thought which is within me and around
 me,
I do compel ye to my will. Appear!

[A star is seen at the darker end of the gallery: it is sta-
tionary; and a voice is heard singing.

FIRST SPIRIT.

Mortal! to thy bidding bow'd, 50
From my mansion in the cloud,
Which the breath of twilight builds,
And the summer's sunset gilds
With the azure and vermilion
Which is mix'd for my pavilion;
Though thy quest may be forbidden,
On a star-beam I have ridden,
To thine adjuration bow'd;
Mortal — be thy wish avow'd!

Voice of the SECOND SPIRIT.

Mont Blanc is the monarch of mountains;
 They crown'd him long ago 61
On a throne of rocks, in a robe of clouds,
 With a diadem of snow.
Around his waist are forests braced,
 The Avalanche in his hand;
But ere it fall, that thundering ball
 Must pause for my command.
The Glacier's cold and restless mass
 Moves onward day by day;
But I am he who bids it pass, 70
 Or with its ice delay.
I am the spirit of the place,
 Could make the mountain bow
And quiver to his cavern'd base —
 And what with me wouldst *Thou?*

Voice of the THIRD SPIRIT.

In the blue depth of the waters,
 Where the wave hath no strife,
Where the wind is a stranger,
 And the sea-snake hath life,
Where the Mermaid is decking 80
 Her green hair with shells;
Like the storm on the surface
 Came the sound of thy spells;
O'er my calm Hall of Coral
 The deep echo roll'd —
To the Spirit of Ocean
 Thy wishes unfold!

FOURTH SPIRIT.

Where the slumbering earthquake
 Lies pillow'd on fire,
And the lakes of bitumen 90
 Rise boilingly higher;
Where the roots of the Andes
 Strike deep in the earth,
As their summits to heaven
 Shoot soaringly forth;
I have quitted my birthplace,
 Thy bidding to bide —
Thy spell hath subdued me,
 Thy will be my guide!

FIFTH SPIRIT.

I am the Rider of the wind, 100
 The Stirrer of the storm;
The hurricane I left behind
 Is yet with lightning warm;
To speed to thee, o'er shore and sea
 I swept upon the blast:
The fleet I met sail'd well, and yet
 'T will sink ere night be past.

SIXTH SPIRIT.

My dwelling is the shadow of the night,
Why doth thy magic torture me with light?

SEVENTH SPIRIT.

The star which rules thy destiny 110
Was ruled, ere earth began, by me:
It was a world as fresh and fair
As e'er revolved round sun in air;
Its course was free and regular,
Space bosom'd not a lovelier star.
The hour arrived — and it became
A wandering mass of shapeless flame,
A pathless comet, and a curse,
The menace of the universe;
Still rolling on with innate force, 120
Without a sphere, without a course,
A bright deformity on high,
The monster of the upper sky !
And thou ! beneath its influence born —
Thou worm ! whom I obey and scorn —
Forced by a power (which is not thine,
And lent thee but to make thee mine)
For this brief moment to descend,
Where these weak spirits round thee bend
And parley with a thing like thee — 130
What wouldst thou, Child of Clay, with me?

The SEVEN SPIRITS.

Earth, ocean, air, night, mountains, winds,
 thy star,
 Are at thy beck and bidding, Child of
 Clay !
Before thee at thy quest their spirits are —
 What wouldst thou with us, son of mor-
 tals — say ?

Man. Forgetfulness —
First Spirit. Of what — of whom — and
 why ?
Man. Of that which is within me; read
 it there —
Ye know it, and I cannot utter it.
 Spirit. We can but give thee that which
 we possess:
Ask of us subjects, sovereignty, the power
O'er earth, the whole, or portion, or a
 sign 141
Which shall control the elements, whereof
We are the dominators, — each and all,
These shall be thine.
 Man. Oblivion, self-oblivion —
Can ye not wring from out the hidden
 realms
Ye offer so profusely what I ask ?

Spirit. It is not in our essence, in our
 skill;
But — thou mayst die.
 Man. Will death bestow it on me ?
 Spirit. We are immortal, and do not for-
 get;
We are eternal; and to us the past 150
Is as the future, present. Art thou
 answer'd ?
 Man. Ye mock me — but the power which
 brought ye here
Hath made you mine. Slaves, scoff not at
 my will !
The mind, the spirit, the Promethean spark,
The lightning of my being, is as bright,
Pervading, and far darting as your own,
And shall not yield to yours, though coop'd
 in clay !
Answer, or I will teach you what I am.
 Spirit. We answer as we answer'd; our
 reply
Is even in thine own words.
 Man. Why say ye so ?
 Spirit. If, as thou say'st, thine essence be
 as ours, 161
We have replied in telling thee, the thing
Mortals call death hath nought to do with
 us.
 Man. I then have call'd ye from your
 realms in vain;
Ye cannot, or ye will not, aid me.
 Spirit. Say;
What we possess we offer; it is thine:
Bethink ere thou dismiss us, ask again —
Kingdom, and sway, and strength, and
 length of days —
 Man. Accursèd ! what have I to do with
 days ?
They are too long already. — Hence — be-
 gone ! 170
 Spirit. Yet pause: being here, our will
 would do thee service;
Bethink thee, is there then no other gift
Which we can make not worthless in thine
 eyes ?
 Man. No, none: yet stay — one moment,
 ere we part —
I would behold ye face to face. I hear
Your voices, sweet and melancholy sounds,
As music on the waters; and I see
The steady aspect of a clear large star;
But nothing more. Approach me as ye are,
Or one, or all, in your accustom'd forms. 180
 Spirit. We have no forms, beyond the
 elements

Of which we are the mind and principle:
But choose a form — in that we will appear.
 Man. I have no choice; there is no form
 on earth
Hideous or beautiful to me. Let him,
Who is most powerful of ye, take such aspect
As unto him may seem most fitting — Come!
 Seventh Spirit (*appearing in the shape of*
 a beautiful female figure). Behold!
 Man. Oh God! if it be thus, and *thou*
Art not a madness and a mockery,
I yet might be most happy. I will clasp
 thee, 190
And we again will be — [*The figure vanishes.*
 My heart is crush'd!
 [MANFRED *falls senseless.*

(*A Voice is heard in the Incantation which follows.*)

 When the moon is on the wave,
 And the glow-worm in the grass,
 And the meteor on the grave,
 And the wisp on the morass;
 When the falling stars are shooting,
 And the answer'd owls are hooting,
 And the silent leaves are still
 In the shadow of the hill,
 Shall my soul be upon thine, 200
 With a power and with a sign.

 Though thy slumber may be deep,
 Yet thy spirit shall not sleep;
 There are shades which will not vanish,
 There are thoughts thou canst not banish;
 By a power to thee unknown,
 Thou canst never be alone;
 Thou art wrapt as with a shroud,
 Thou art gather'd in a cloud;
 And for ever shalt thou dwell 210
 In the spirit of this spell.

 Though thou seest me not pass by,
 Thou shalt feel me with thine eye
 As a thing that, though unseen,
 Must be near thee, and hath been;
 And when in that secret dread
 Thou hast turn'd around thy head,
 Thou shalt marvel I am not
 As thy shadow on the spot,
 And the power which thou dost feel 220
 Shall be what thou must conceal.

 And a magic voice and verse
 Hath baptized thee with a curse;
 And a spirit of the air
 Hath begirt thee with a snare;

 In the wind there is a voice
 Shall forbid thee to rejoice;
 And to thee shall Night deny
 All the quiet of her sky;
 And the day shall have a sun, 230
 Which shall make thee wish it done.

 From thy false tears I did distil
 An essence which hath strength to kill;
 From thy own heart I then did wring
 The black blood in its blackest spring;
 From thy own smile I snatch'd the snake,
 For there it coil'd as in a brake;
 From thy own lip I drew the charm
 Which gave all these their chiefest harm;
 In proving every poison known, 240
 I found the strongest was thine own.

 By thy cold breast and serpent smile,
 By thy unfathom'd gulfs of guile,
 By that most seeming virtuous eye,
 By thy shut soul's hypocrisy;
 By the perfection of thine art
 Which pass'd for human thine own heart;
 By thy delight in others' pain,
 And by thy brotherhood of Cain,
 I call upon thee! and compel 250
 Thyself to be thy proper Hell!

 And on thy head I pour the vial
 Which doth devote thee to this trial;
 Nor to slumber, nor to die,
 Shall be in thy destiny;
 Though thy death shall still seem near
 To thy wish, but as a fear;
 Lo! the spell now works around thee,
 And the clankless chain hath bound thee;
 O'er thy heart and brain together 260
 Hath the word been pass'd — now wither!

SCENE II

The Mountain of the Jungfrau. — Time, Morning. —
 MANFRED *alone upon the Cliffs.*

 Man. The spirits I have raised abandon
 me,
The spells which I have studied baffle me,
The remedy I reck'd of tortured me;
I lean no more on super-human aid,
It hath no power upon the past, and for
The future, till the past be gulf'd in dark-
 ness,
It is not of my search. — My mother Earth!
And thou fresh breaking Day, and you, ye
 Mountains, 269
Why are ye beautiful? I cannot love ye.

And thou, the bright eye of the universe,
That openest over all, and unto all
Art a delight — thou shin'st not on my
 heart.
And you, ye crags, upon whose extreme
 edge
I stand, and on the torrent's brink beneath
Behold the tall pines dwindled as to shrubs
In dizziness of distance; when a leap,
A stir, a motion, even a breath, would bring
My breast upon its rocky bosom's bed 279
To rest for ever — wherefore do I pause ?
I feel the impulse — yet I do not plunge;
I see the peril — yet do not recede;
And my brain reels — and yet my foot is
 firm.
There is a power upon me which withholds,
And makes it my fatality to live;
If it be life to wear within myself
This barrenness of spirit, and to be
My own soul's sepulchre, for I have ceased
To justify my deeds unto myself —
The last infirmity of evil. Ay, 290
Thou wingèd and cloud-cleaving minister,
 [An eagle passes.
Whose happy flight is highest into heaven,
Well may'st thou swoop so near me — I
 should be
Thy prey, and gorge thine eaglets; thou art
 gone
Where the eye cannot follow thee; but
 thine
Yet pierces downward, onward, or above,
With a pervading vision. — Beautiful !
How beautiful is all this visible world !
How glorious in its action and itself !
But we, who name ourselves its sovereigns,
 we, 300
Half dust, half deity, alike unfit
To sink or soar, with our mix'd essence make
A conflict of its elements, and breathe
The breath of degradation and of pride,
Contending with low wants and lofty will,
Till our mortality predominates,
And men are — what they name not to
 themselves,
And trust not to each other. Hark ! the note,
 [The Shepherd's pipe in the distance is heard.
The natural music of the mountain reed
(For here the patriarchal days are not 310
A pastoral fable) pipes in the liberal air,
Mix'd with the sweet bells of the saunter-
 ing herd;
My soul would drink those echoes. — Oh,
 that I were

The viewless spirit of a lovely sound,
A living voice, a breathing harmony,
A bodiless enjoyment — born and dying
With the blest tone which made me !

 Enter from below a CHAMOIS HUNTER.
Chamois Hunter. Even so
This way the chamois leapt : her nimble
 feet
Have baffled me; my gains to-day will
 scarce
Repay my break-neck travail. — What is
 here ? 320
Who seems not of my trade, and yet hath
 reach'd
A height which none even of our moun-
 taineers,
Save our best hunters, may attain: his garb
Is goodly, his mien manly, and his air
Proud as a freeborn peasant's, at this dis-
 tance —
I will approach him nearer.
 Man. (*not perceiving the other*). To be
 thus —
Grey-hair'd with anguish, like these blasted
 pines,
Wrecks of a single winter, barkless, branch-
 less,
A blighted trunk upon a cursèd root,
Which but supplies a feeling to decay —
And to be thus, eternally but thus, 331
Having been otherwise ! Now furrow'd
 o'er
With wrinkles, plough'd by moments, not
 by years
And hours — all tortured into ages — hours
Which I outlive ! — Ye toppling crags of
 ice !
Ye avalanches, whom a breath draws down
In mountainous o'erwhelming, come and
 crush me !
I hear ye momently above, beneath,
Crash with a frequent conflict; but ye pass,
And only fall on things that still would
 live; 340
On the young flourishing forest, or the hut
And hamlet of the harmless villager.
 C. Hun. The mists begin to rise from up
 the valley;
I 'll warn him to descend, or he may chance
To lose at once his way and life together.
 Man. The mists boil up around the gla-
 ciers; clouds
Rise curling fast beneath me, white and
 sulphury,

Like foam from the roused ocean of deep
 Hell,
Whose every wave breaks on a living
 shore
Heap'd with the damn'd like pebbles. — I
 am giddy. 350
 C. Hun. I must approach him cautiously;
 if near,
A sudden step will startle him, and he
Seems tottering already.
 Man. Mountains have fallen,
Leaving a gap in the clouds, and with the
 shock
Rocking their Alpine brethren; filling up
The ripe green valleys with destruction's
 splinters;
Damming the rivers with a sudden dash,
Which crush'd the waters into mist and
 made
Their fountains find another channel —
 thus,
Thus, in its old age, did Mount Rosen-
 berg — 360
Why stood I not beneath it ?
 C. Hun. Friend ! have a care,
Your next step may be fatal ! — for the
 love
Of him who made you, stand not on that
 brink !
 Man. (*not hearing him*). Such would have
 been for me a fitting tomb;
My bones had then been quiet in their
 depth;
They had not then been strewn upon the
 rocks
For the wind's pastime — as thus — thus
 they shall be —
In this one plunge. — Farewell, ye opening
 heavens !
Look not upon me thus reproachfully —
Ye were not meant for me — Earth ! take
 these atoms ! 370

[*As* MANFRED *is in act to spring from the cliff, the*
 CHAMOIS HUNTER *seizes and retains him with a sud-*
 den grasp.

 C. Hun. Hold, madman! — though aweary
 of thy life,
Stain not our pure vales with thy guilty
 blood !
Away with me — I will not quit my hold.
 Man. I am most sick at heart — nay,
 grasp me not —
I am all feebleness — the mountains whirl
Spinning around me — I grow blind —
 What art thou ?

 C. Hun. I 'll answer that anon. — Away
 with me !
The clouds grow thicker — there — now
 lean on me —
Place your foot here — here, take this staff,
 and cling
A moment to that shrub — now give me
 your hand, 380
And hold fast by my girdle — softly —
 well —
The Chalet will be gain'd within an hour.
Come on, we 'll quickly find a surer footing,
And something like a pathway, which the
 torrent
Hath wash'd since winter. — Come, 't is
 bravely done;
You should have been a hunter. — Follow
 me.

[*As they descend the rocks with difficulty, the scene
closes.*

ACT II

SCENE I

A Cottage amongst the Bernese Alps.

MANFRED *and the* CHAMOIS HUNTER.

 C. Hun. No, no, yet pause, thou must not
 yet go forth:
Thy mind and body are alike unfit
To trust each other, for some hours, at least;
When thou art better, I will be thy guide —
But whither ?
 Man. It imports not; I do know
My route full well and need no further guid-
 ance.
 C. Hun. Thy garb and gait bespeak thee
 of high lineage —
One of the many chiefs, whose castled crags
Look o'er the lower valleys — which of these
May call thee lord ? I only know their por-
 tals; 10
My way of life leads me but rarely down
To bask by the huge hearths of those old
 halls,
Carousing with the vassals; but the paths,
Which step from out our mountains to their
 doors,
I know from childhood — which of these is
 thine ?
 Man. No matter.
 C. Hun. Well, sir, pardon me the
 question,
And be of better cheer. Come, taste my
 wine;

'T is of an ancient vintage; many a day
'T has thaw'd my veins among our glaciers,
 now
Let it do thus for thine. Come, pledge me
 fairly. 20
 Man. Away, away! there 's blood upon
 the brim!
Will it then never — never sink in the earth?
 C. Hun. What dost thou mean? thy
 senses wander from thee.
 Man. I say 't is blood — my blood! the
 pure warm stream
Which ran in the veins of my fathers, and in
 ours
When we were in our youth, and had one
 heart,
And loved each other as we should not love,
And this was shed: but still it rises up,
Colouring the clouds, that shut me out from
 heaven,
Where thou art not — and I shall never be.
 C. Hun. Man of strange words, and some
 half-maddening sin, 31
Which makes thee people vacancy, whate'er
Thy dread and sufferance be, there 's com-
 fort yet —
The aid of holy men, and heavenly pa-
 tience —
 Man. Patience and patience! Hence —
 that word was made
For brutes of burthen, not for birds of prey;
Preach it to mortals of a dust like thine, —
I am not of thine order.
 C. Hun. Thanks to heaven!
I would not be of thine for the free fame
Of William Tell; but whatsoe'er thine ill,
It must be borne, and these wild starts are
 useless. 41
 Man. Do I not bear it? — Look on me
 — I live.
 C. Hun. This is convulsion, and no
 healthful life.
 Man. I tell thee, man! I have lived
 many years,
Many long years, but they are nothing now
To those which I must number: ages —
 ages —
Space and eternity — and consciousness,
With the fierce thirst of death — and still
 unslaked!
 C. Hun. Why, on thy brow the seal of
 middle age
Hath scarce been set; I am thine elder far.
 Man. Think'st thou existence doth de-
 pend on time? 51

It doth; but actions are our epochs: mine
Have made my days and nights imperish-
 able,
Endless, and all alike, as sands on the shore,
Innumerable atoms; and one desert,
Barren and cold, on which the wild waves
 break,
But nothing rests, save carcasses and wrecks,
Rocks, and the salt-surf weeds of bitter-
 ness.
 C. Hun. Alas! he 's mad — but yet I
 must not leave him.
 Man. I would I were, for then the things
 I see 60
Would be but a distemper'd dream.
 C. Hun. What is it
That thou dost see, or think thou look'st
 upon?
 Man. Myself, and thee — a peasant of
 the Alps,
Thy humble virtues, hospitable home,
And spirit patient, pious, proud and free;
Thy self-respect, grafted on innocent
 thoughts;
Thy days of health, and nights of sleep;
 thy toils,
By danger dignified, yet guiltless; hopes
Of cheerful old age and a quiet grave, 69
With cross and garland over its green turf,
And thy grandchildren's love for epitaph;
This do I see — and then I look within —
It matters not — my soul was scorch'd al-
 ready!
 C. Hun. And wouldst thou then exchange
 thy lot for mine?
 Man. No, friend! I would not wrong
 thee nor exchange
My lot with living being: I can bear —
However wretchedly, 't is still to bear —
In life what others could not brook to
 dream,
But perish in their slumber.
 C. Hun. And with this —
This cautious feeling for another's pain, 80
Canst thou be black with evil? — say not
 so.
Can one of gentle thoughts have wreak'd
 revenge
Upon his enemies?
 Man. Oh! no, no, no!
My injuries came down on those who loved
 me —
On those whom I best loved: I never quell'd
An enemy, save in my just defence —
But my embrace was fatal.

C. Hun. Heaven give thee rest !
And penitence restore thee to thyself;
My prayers shall be for thee.
 Man. I need them not,
But can endure thy pity. I depart — 90
'T is time — farewell ! — Here 's gold, and
 thanks for thee;
No words — it is thy due. Follow me not;
I know my path — the mountain peril 's past:
And once again, I charge thee, follow not !
 [*Exit* MANFRED.

SCENE II

A lower Valley in the Alps. — A Cataract.

Enter MANFRED.

It is not noon; the sunbow's rays still arch
The torrent with the many hues of heaven,
And roll the sheeted silver's waving column
O'er the crag's headlong perpendicular,
And fling its lines of foaming light along, 99
And to and fro, like the pale courser's tail,
The Giant steed, to be bestrode by Death,
As told in the Apocalypse. No eyes
But mine now drink this sight of loveliness;
I should be sole in this sweet solitude,
And with the Spirit of the place divide
The homage of these waters. — I will call
 her.

[MANFRED *takes some of the water into the palm of his
hand, and flings it in the air, muttering the adjuration.
After a pause, the* WITCH OF THE ALPS *rises beneath
the arch of the sunbow of the torrent.*

Beautiful Spirit ! with thy hair of light,
And dazzling eyes of glory, in whose form
The charms of earth's least mortal daugh-
 ters grow
To an unearthly stature, in an essence 110
Of purer elements; while the hues of youth
(Carnation'd like a sleeping infant's cheek
Rock'd by the beating of her mother's
 heart,
Or the rose tints, which summer's twilight
 leaves
Upon the lofty glacier's virgin snow,
The blush of earth embracing with her
 heaven)
Tinge thy celestial aspect, and make tame
The beauties of the sunbow which bends
 o'er thee.
Beautiful Spirit ! in thy calm clear brow,
Wherein is glass'd serenity of soul, 120
Which of itself shows immortality,
I read that thou wilt pardon to a Son
Of Earth, whom the abstruser powers per-
 mit

At times to commune with them — if that
 he
Avail him of his spells — to call thee thus,
And gaze on thee a moment.
 Witch. Son of Earth !
I know thee, and the powers which give
 thee power;
I know thee for a man of many thoughts,
And deeds of good and ill, extreme in both,
Fatal and fated in thy sufferings. 130
I have expected this — what wouldst thou
 with me ?
 Man. To look upon thy beauty — nothing
 further.
The face of the earth hath madden'd me,
 and I
Take refuge in her mysteries, and pierce
To the abodes of those who govern her —
But they can nothing aid me. I have sought
From them what they could not bestow, and
 now
I search no further.
 Witch. What could be the quest
Which is not in the power of the most
 powerful,
The rulers of the invisible ?
 Man. A boon; 140
But why should I repeat it ? 't were in vain.
 Witch. I know not that; let thy lips utter
 it.
 Man. Well, though it torture me, 't is
 but the same;
My pang shall find a voice. From my youth
 upwards
My spirit walk'd not with the souls of men,
Nor look'd upon the earth with human
 eyes;
The thirst of their ambition was not mine,
The aim of their existence was not mine;
My joys, my griefs, my passions, and my
 powers,
Made me a stranger; though I wore the
 form, 150
I had no sympathy with breathing flesh,
Nor midst the creatures of clay that girded
 me
Was there but one who — but of her anon.
I said, with men, and with the thoughts of
 men,
I held but slight communion; but instead,
My joy was in the Wilderness, to breathe
The difficult air of the iced mountain's top,
Where the birds dare not build, nor insect's
 wing
Flit o'er the herbless granite; or to plunge

Into the torrent, and to roll along 160
On the swift whirl of the new breaking
 wave
Of river-stream, or ocean, in their flow.
In these my early strength exulted; or
To follow through the night the moving
 moon,
The stars and their development; or catch
The dazzling lightnings till my eyes grew
 dim;
Or to look, list'ning, on the scatter'd leaves,
While Autumn winds were at their evening
 song.
These were my pastimes, and to be
 alone;
For if the beings, of whom I was one, — 170
Hating to be so, — cross'd me in my path,
I felt myself degraded back to them,
And was all clay again. And then I dived,
In my lone wanderings, to the caves of
 death,
Searching its cause in its effect; and drew
From wither'd bones, and skulls, and heap'd
 up dust,
Conclusions most forbidden. Then I pass'd
The nights of years in sciences, untaught
Save in the old time; and with time and
 toil,
And terrible ordeal, and such penance 180
As in itself hath power upon the air
And spirits that do compass air and earth,
Space, and the peopled infinite, I made
Mine eyes familiar with Eternity,
Such as, before me, did the Magi, and
He who from out their fountain dwellings
 raised
Eros and Anteros, at Gadara,
As I do thee; — and with my knowledge
 grew
The thirst of knowledge, and the power and
 joy
Of this most bright intelligence, until — 190
 Witch. Proceed.
 Man. Oh! I but thus prolong'd
 my words,
Boasting these idle attributes, because
As I approach the core of my heart's
 grief —
But to my task. I have not named to thee
Father or mother, mistress, friend, or being,
With whom I wore the chain of human
 ties;
If I had such, they seem'd not such to me —
Yet there was one —
 Witch. Spare not thyself — proceed.

Man. She was like me in lineaments —
 her eyes,
Her hair, her features, all, to the very
 tone 200
Even of her voice, they said were like to
 mine;
But soften'd all, and temper'd into beauty;
She had the same lone thoughts and wander-
 ings,
The quest of hidden knowledge, and a mind
To comprehend the universe: nor these
Alone, but with them gentler powers than
 mine,
Pity, and smiles, and tears — which I had
 not;
And tenderness — but that I had for her;
Humility — and that I never had.
Her faults were mine — her virtues were
 her own — 210
I loved her, and destroy'd her !
 Witch. With thy hand ?
Man. Not with my hand, but heart —
 which broke her heart;
It gazed on mine, and wither'd. I have shed
Blood, but not hers — and yet her blood
 was shed —
I saw, and could not stanch it.
 Witch. And for this —
A being of the race thou dost despise,
The order which thine own would rise
 above,
Mingling with us and ours, thou dost forego
The gifts of our great knowledge, and
 shrink'st back
To recreant mortality — Away ! 220
 Man. Daughter of Air ! I tell thee,
 since that hour —
But words are breath — look on me in my
 sleep,
Or watch my watchings — Come and sit by
 me !
My solitude is solitude no more,
But peopled with the Furies; — I have
 gnash'd
My teeth in darkness till returning morn,
Then cursed myself till sunset; — I have
 pray'd
For madness as a blessing — 't is denied me.
I have affronted death, but in the war
Of elements the waters shrunk from me, 230
And fatal things pass'd harmless — the
 cold hand
Of an all-pitiless demon held me back,
Back by a single hair, which would not
 break.

In fantasy, imagination, all
The affluence of my soul — which one day was
A Crœsus in creation — I plunged deep,
But, like an ebbing wave, it dash'd me back
Into the gulf of my unfathom'd thought.
I plunged amidst mankind — Forgetfulness
I sought in all, save where 't is to be found,
And that I have to learn — my sciences, 241
My long pursued and superhuman art,
Is mortal here; I dwell in my despair —
And live — and live for ever.

Witch. It may be
That I can aid thee.

Man. To do this thy power
Must wake the dead, or lay me low with them.
Do so — in any shape — in any hour —
With any torture — so it be the last.

Witch. That is not in my province; but if thou
Wilt swear obedience to my will, and do 250
My bidding, it may help thee to thy wishes.

Man. I will not swear — Obey! and whom? the spirits
Whose presence I command, and be the slave
Of those who served me — Never!

Witch. Is this all?
Hast thou no gentler answer? — Yet bethink thee,
And pause ere thou rejectest.

Man. I have said it.

Witch. Enough! — I may retire then — say!

Man. Retire! [*The* WITCH *disappears.*

Man. (*alone*). We are the fools of time and terror: Days
Steal on us and steal from us; yet we live,
Loathing our life, and dreading still to die.
In all the days of this detested yoke — 261
This vital weight upon the struggling heart,
Which sinks with sorrow, or beats quick with pain,
Or joy that ends in agony or faintness —
In all the days of past and future, for
In life there is no present, we can number
How few, how less than few, wherein the soul
Forbears to pant for death, and yet draws back
As from a stream in winter, though the chill
Be but a moment's. I have one resource 270
Still in my science — I can call the dead,

And ask them what it is we dread to be:
The sternest answer can but be the Grave,
And that is nothing; — if they answer not —
The buried Prophet answered to the Hag
Of Endor; and the Spartan Monarch drew
From the Byzantine maid's unsleeping spirit
An answer and his destiny — he slew
That which he loved, unknowing what he slew,
And died unpardon'd — though he call'd in aid 280
The Phyxian Jove, and in Phigalia roused
The Arcadian Evocators to compel
The indignant shadow to depose her wrath,
Or fix her term of vengeance — she replied
In words of dubious import, but fulfill'd.
If I had never lived, that which I love
Had still been living; had I never loved,
That which I love would still be beautiful —
Happy and giving happiness. What is she?
What is she now? — a sufferer for my sins — 290
A thing I dare not think upon — or nothing.
Within few hours I shall not call in vain —
Yet in this hour I dread the thing I dare:
Until this hour I never shrunk to gaze
On spirit, good or evil — now I tremble,
And feel a strange cold thaw upon my heart.
But I can act even what I most abhor,
And champion human fears. — The night approaches. [*Exit.*

SCENE III

The Summit of the Jungfrau Mountain.

Enter FIRST DESTINY.

The moon is rising broad, and round, and bright;
And here on snows, where never human foot 300
Of common mortal trod, we nightly tread,
And leave no traces; o'er the savage sea,
The glassy ocean of the mountain ice,
We skim its rugged breakers, which put on
The aspect of a tumbling tempest's foam,
Frozen in a moment — a dead whirlpool's image.
And this most steep fantastic pinnacle,
The fretwork of some earthquake — where the clouds
Pause to repose themselves in passing by —
Is sacred to our revels, or our vigils. 310
Here do I wait my sisters, on our way

To the Hall of Arimanes, for to-night
Is our great festival — 't is strange they
　　come not.

A Voice without, singing.

The Captive Usurper,
　　Hurl'd down from the throne,
Lay buried in torpor,
　　Forgotten and lone;
I broke through his slumbers,
　　I shiver'd his chain,
I leagued him with numbers —　　　320
　　He 's Tyrant again!
With the blood of a million he 'll answer
　　my care,
With a nation's destruction — his flight and
　　despair.

Second Voice, without.

The ship sail'd on, the ship sail'd fast,
But I left not a sail, and I left not a mast;
There is not a plank of the hull or the deck,
And there is not a wretch to lament o'er
　　his wreck;
Save one, whom I held, as he swam, by the
　　hair,
And he was a subject well worthy my
　　care;
A traitor on land, and a pirate at sea —　330
But I saved him to wreak further havoc
　　for me!

FIRST DESTINY, *answering.*

The city lies sleeping;
　　The morn, to deplore it,
May dawn on it weeping:
　　Sullenly, slowly,
The black plague flew o'er it, —
　　Thousands lie lowly;
Tens of thousands shall perish —
　　The living shall fly from
The sick they should cherish;　　　340
　　But nothing can vanquish
The touch that they die from.
　　Sorrow and anguish,
　　And evil and dread,
　　Envelope a nation —
　　The blest are the dead,
Who see not the sight
　　Of their own desolation;
This work of a night —
This wreck of a realm — this deed of my
　　doing —　　　350
For ages I 've done, and shall still be re-
　　newing!

Enter the Second *and* Third Destinies.

The Three.

Our hands contain the hearts of men,
　　Our footsteps are their graves;
We only give to take again
　　The spirits of our slaves!

First Des. Welcome! Where 's Neme-
　　sis?
Second Des. At some great work;
But what I know not, for my hands were
　　full.
Third Des. Behold she cometh.

Enter Nemesis.

First Des. Say, where hast thou been?
My sisters and thyself are slow to-night.
　Nem. I was detain'd repairing shatter'd
　　thrones,　　　360
Marrying fools, restoring dynasties,
Avenging men upon their enemies,
And making them repent their own re-
　　venge;
Goading the wise to madness; from the dull
Shaping out oracles to rule the world
Afresh, for they were waxing out of date,
And mortals dared to ponder for them-
　　selves,
To weigh kings in the balance, and to speak
Of freedom, the forbidden fruit. — Away!
We have outstay'd the hour — mount we
　　our clouds!　　　[*Exeunt.*

SCENE IV

*The Hall of Arimanes — Arimanes on his Throne, a
Globe of Fire, surrounded by the Spirits.*

Hymn of the SPIRITS.

Hail to our Master! — Prince of Earth and
　　Air!　　　371
　　Who walks the clouds and waters — in
　　　his hand
The sceptre of the elements which tear
　　Themselves to chaos at his high com-
　　　mand!
He breatheth — and a tempest shakes the
　　sea;
　　He speaketh — and the clouds reply in
　　　thunder;
He gazeth — from his glance the sunbeams
　　flee;
　　He moveth — earthquakes rend the world
　　　asunder.
Beneath his footsteps the volcanoes rise;
　　His shadow is the Pestilence; his path　380

The comets herald through the crackling
skies;
And planets turn to ashes at his wrath.
To him War offers daily sacrifice;
To him Death pays his tribute; Life is
his,
With all its infinite of agonies —
And his the spirit of whatever is !

Enter the DESTINIES *and* NEMESIS.

First Des. Glory to **Arimanes** ! on the
earth
His power increaseth — both my sisters did
His bidding, nor did I neglect my duty !
Second Des. Glory to Arimanes ! we who
bow 390
The necks of men, bow down before his
throne !
Third Des. Glory to Arimanes ! we await
His nod !
Nem. Sovereign of Sovereigns ! we are
thine,
And all that liveth, more or less, is ours,
And most things wholly so; still to increase
Our power, increasing thine, demands our
care,
And we are vigilant. — Thy late commands
Have been fulfill'd to the utmost.

Enter MANFRED.

A Spirit. What is here ?
A mortal ! — Thou most rash and fatal
wretch, 399
Bow down and worship !
Second Spirit. I do know the man —
A Magian of great power and fearful skill !
Third Spirit. Bow down and worship,
slave ! What, know'st thou not
Thine and our Sovereign ? — Tremble, and
obey !
All the Spirits. Prostrate thyself, and thy
condemnèd clay,
Child of the Earth ! or dread the worst.
Man. I know it;
And yet ye see I kneel not.
Fourth Spirit. 'T will be taught thee.
Man. 'T is taught already; — many a
night on the earth,
On the bare ground, have I bow'd down my
face,
And strew'd my head with ashes; I have
known
The fulness of humiliation, for 410
I sunk before my vain despair, and knelt
To my own desolation.

Fifth Spirit. Dost thou dare
Refuse to Arimanes on his throne
What the whole earth accords, beholding
not
The terror of his Glory ? — Crouch ! I say.
Man. Bid *him* bow down to that which is
above him,
The overruling Infinite, the Maker
Who made him not for worship — let him
kneel,
And we will kneel together.
The Spirits. Crush the worm !
Tear him in pieces ! —
First Des. Hence ! Avaunt ! — he 's
mine. 420
Prince of the Powers invisible ! This man
Is of no common order, as his port
And presence here denote. His sufferings
Have been of an immortal nature, like
Our own; his knowledge and his powers and
will,
As far as is compatible with clay,
Which clogs the ethereal essence, have been
such
As clay hath seldom borne; his aspirations
Have been beyond the dwellers of the earth,
And they have only taught him what we
know — 430
That knowledge is not happiness, and
science
But an exchange of ignorance for that
Which is another kind of ignorance.
This is not all; the passions, attributes
Of earth and heaven, from which no power,
nor being,
Nor breath from the worm upwards is ex-
empt,
Have pierced his heart; and in their con-
sequence
Made him a thing, which I, who pity not,
Yet pardon those who pity. He is mine,
And thine, it may be; — be it so, or not, 440
No other Spirit in this region hath
A soul like his — or power upon his soul.
Nem. What doth he here then ?
First Des. Let him answer that.
Man. Ye know what I have known; and
without power
I could not be amongst ye: but there are
Powers deeper still beyond — I come in
quest
Of such, to answer unto what I seek.
Nem. What wouldst thou ?
Man. Thou canst not reply to me.
Call up the dead — my question is for them.

Nem. Great Arimanes, doth thy will avouch 450
The wishes of this mortal?
Ari. Yea.
Nem. Whom wouldst thou Uncharnel?
Man. One without a tomb — call up Astarte.

NEMESIS.

Shadow! or Spirit!
 Whatever thou art,
Which still doth inherit
 The whole or a part
Of the form of thy birth,
 Of the mould of thy clay
Which return'd to the earth, — 460
 Re-appear to the day!
Bear what thou borest,
 The heart and the form,
And the aspect thou worest
 Redeem from the worm.
Appear! — Appear! — Appear!
Who sent thee there requires thee here!

[*The phantom of* ASTARTE *rises and stands in the midst.*

Man. Can this be death? there's bloom upon her cheek;
But now I see it is no living hue,
But a strange hectic — like the unnatural red 470
Which Autumn plants upon the perish'd leaf.
It is the same! Oh, God! that I should dread
To look upon the same — Astarte! — No,
I cannot speak to her — but bid her speak —
Forgive me or condemn me.

NEMESIS.

By the power which hath broken
 The grave which enthrall'd thee,
Speak to him who hath spoken,
 Or those who have call'd thee!

Man. She is silent,
And in that silence I am more than answer'd. 480
Nem. My power extends no further. Prince of air!
It rests with thee alone — command her voice.
Ari. Spirit — obey this sceptre!
Nem. Silent still!
She is not of our order, but belongs

To the other powers. Mortal! thy quest is vain,
And we are baffled also.
Man. Hear me, hear me —
Astarte! my belovèd! speak to me:
I have so much endured, so much endure —
Look on me! the grave hath not changed thee more
Than I am changed for thee. Thou lovèdst me 490
Too much, as I loved thee: we were not made
To torture thus each other, though it were
The deadliest sin to love as we have loved.
Say that thou loath'st me not, that I do bear
This punishment for both, that thou wilt be
One of the blessèd, and that I shall die;
For hitherto all hateful things conspire
To bind me in existence — in a life
Which makes me shrink from immortality —
A future like the past. I cannot rest. 500
I know not what I ask, nor what I seek:
I feel but what thou art — and what I am;
And I would hear yet once before I perish
The voice which was my music — Speak to me!
For I have call'd on thee in the still night,
Startled the slumbering birds from the hush'd boughs,
And woke the mountain wolves, and made the caves
Acquainted with thy vainly echo'd name,
Which answer'd me — many things answer'd me —
Spirits and men — but thou wert silent all.
Yet speak to me! I have outwatch'd the stars, 511
And gazed o'er heaven in vain in search of thee.
Speak to me! I have wander'd o'er the earth,
And never found thy likeness — Speak to me!
Look on the fiends around — they feel for me:
I fear them not, and feel for thee alone.
Speak to me! though it be in wrath; — but say —
I reck not what — but let me hear thee once —
This once — once more!
Phantom of Astarte. Manfred!
Man. Say on, say on —
I live but in the sound — it is thy voice!
Phan. Manfred! To-morrow ends thine earthly ills. 521
Farewell!

Man. Yet one word more — am I for-
given ?
Phan. Farewell !
Man. Say, shall we meet again ?
Phan. Farewell !
Man. One word for mercy ! Say, thou
lovest me.
Phan. Manfred !
 [*The Spirit of* ASTARTE *disappears.*
Nem. She 's gone, and will not be
recall'd ;
Her words will be fulfill'd. Return to the
earth.
A Spirit. He is convulsed — This is to be
a mortal
And seek the things beyond mortality.
Another Spirit. Yet, see, he mastereth
himself, and makes
His torture tributary to his will. 530
Had he been one of us, he would have
made
An awful spirit.
Nem. Hast thou further question
Of our great sovereign, or his worshippers ?
Man. None.
Nem. Then for a time farewell.
Man. We meet then ! Where ? On the
earth ? —
Even as thou wilt : and for the grace ac-
corded
I now depart a debtor. Fare ye well !
 [*Exit* MANFRED.
(*Scene closes.*)

ACT III

SCENE I

A Hall in the Castle of Manfred.

MANFRED *and* HERMAN.

Man. What is the hour ?
Her. It wants but one till sunset,
And promises a lovely twilight.
Man. Say,
Are all things so disposed of in the tower
As I directed ?
Her. All, my lord, are ready :
Here is the key and casket.
Man. It is well :
Thou may'st retire. [*Exit* HERMAN.
Man. (*alone*). There is a calm upon
me —
Inexplicable stillness ! which till now
Did not belong to what I knew of life.
If that I did not know philosophy

To be of all our vanities the motliest, 10
The merest word that ever fool'd the ear
From out the schoolman's jargon, I should
deem
The golden secret, the sought 'Kalon,'
found,
And seated in my soul. It will not last,
But it is well to have known it, though but
once :
It hath enlarged my thoughts with a new
sense,
And I within my tablets would note down
That there is such a feeling. Who is
there ?

Re-enter HERMAN.

Her. My lord, the abbot of St. Maurice
craves
To greet your presence.

Enter the ABBOT OF ST. MAURICE.

Abbot. Peace be with Count
Manfred ! 20
Man. Thanks, holy father ! welcome to
these walls ;
Thy presence honours them, and blesseth
those
Who dwell within them.
Abbot. Would it were so, Count ! —
But I would fain confer with thee alone.
Man. Herman, retire. — What would my
reverend guest ?
Abbot. Thus, without prelude : — Age and
zeal, my office,
And good intent, must plead my privilege ;
Our near, though not acquainted neighbour-
hood,
May also be my herald. Rumours strange,
And of unholy nature, are abroad, 30
And busy with thy name ; a noble name
For centuries : may he who bears it now
Transmit it unimpair'd !
Man. Proceed, I listen.
Abbot. 'T is said thou holdest converse
with the things
Which are forbidden to the search of man ;
That with the dwellers of the dark abodes,
The many evil and unheavenly spirits
Which walk the valley of the shade of
death,
Thou communest. I know that with man-
kind,
Thy fellows in creation, thou dost rarely 40
Exchange thy thoughts, and that thy soli-
tude
Is as an anchorite's, were it but holy.

Man. And what are they who do avouch
 these things ?
Abbot. My pious brethren, the scared
 peasantry,
Even thy own vassals, who do look on thee
With most unquiet eyes. Thy life 's in peril.
Man. Take it.
 Abbot. I come to save, and not
 destroy.
I would not pry into thy secret soul;
But if these things be sooth, there still is
 time
For penitence and pity: reconcile thee 50
With the true church, and through the
 church to heaven.
 Man. I hear thee. This is my reply:
 whate'er
I may have been, or am, doth rest between
Heaven and myself; I shall not choose a
 mortal
To be my mediator. Have I sinn'd
Against your ordinances ? prove and punish!
 Abbot. My son ! I did not speak of punish-
 ment,
But penitence and pardon; with thyself
The choice of such remains — and for the
 last,
Our institutions and our strong belief 60
Have given me power to smooth the path
 from sin
To higher hope and better thoughts; the first
I leave to heaven, — 'Vengeance is mine
 alone ! '
So saith the Lord, and with all humbleness
His servant echoes back the awful word.
 Man. Old man ! there is no power in holy
 men,
Nor charm in prayer, nor purifying form
Of penitence, nor outward look, nor fast,
Nor agony, nor, greater than all these,
The innate tortures of that deep despair, 70
Which is remorse without the fear of hell
But all in all sufficient to itself
Would make a hell of heaven, — can exor-
 cise
From out the unbounded spirit the quick
 sense
Of its own sins, wrongs, sufferance, and re-
 venge
Upon itself; there is no future pang
Can deal that justice on the self-condemn'd
He deals on his own soul.
 Abbot. All this is well;
For this will pass away, and be succeeded
By an auspicious hope, which shall look up 80

With calm assurance to that blessed place
Which all who seek may win, whatever be
Their earthly errors, so they be atoned:
And the commencement of atonement is
The sense of its necessity. — Say on —
And all our church can teach thee shall be
 taught;
And all we can absolve thee shall be par-
 don'd.
 Man. When Rome's sixth emperor was
 near his last,
The victim of a self-inflicted wound,
To shun the torments of a public death 90
From senates once his slaves, a certain sol-
 dier,
With show of loyal pity, would have
 stanch'd
The gushing throat with his officious robe;
The dying Roman thrust him back, and
 said —
Some empire still in his expiring glance —
' It is too late, is this fidelity ? '
 Abbot. And what of this ?
 Man. I answer with the Roman,
' It is too late ! '
 Abbot. It never can be so,
To reconcile thyself with thy own soul,
And thy own soul with heaven. Hast thou
 no hope ? 100
'T is strange — even those who do despair
 above,
Yet shape themselves some fantasy on earth,
To which frail twig they cling like drowning
 men.
 Man. Ay — father ! I have had those
 earthly visions
And noble aspirations in my youth,
To make my own the mind of other men,
The enlightener of nations; and to rise
I knew not whither — it might be to fall;
But fall, even as the mountain-cataract,
Which, having leapt from its more dazzling
 height, 110
Even in the foaming strength of its abyss
(Which casts up misty columns that become
Clouds raining from the re-ascended skies)
Lies low but mighty still. — But this is past,
My thoughts mistook themselves.
 Abbot. And wherefore so ?
 Man. I could not tame my nature down;
 for he
Must serve who fain would sway — and
 soothe, and sue,
And watch all time, and pry into all place,
And be a living lie, who would become

A mighty thing amongst the mean, and
 such 120
The mass are; I disdain'd to mingle with
A herd, though to be leader — and of
 wolves.
The lion is alone, and so am I.
 Abbot. And why not live and act with
 other men?
 Man. Because my nature was averse
 from life;
And yet not cruel; for I would not make,
But find a desolation. Like the wind,
The red-hot breath of the most lone Simoom,
Which dwells but in the desert and sweeps
 o'er
The barren sands which bear no shrubs to
 blast, 130
And revels o'er their wild and arid waves,
And seeketh not, so that it is not sought,
But being met is deadly, — such hath been
The course of my existence; but there came
Things in my path which are no more.
 Abbot. Alas!
I 'gin to fear that thou art past all aid
From me and from my calling; yet so young,
I still would —
 Man. Look on me! there is an order
Of mortals on the earth, who do become
Old in their youth, and die ere middle age,
Without the violence of warlike death; 141
Some perishing of pleasure, some of study,
Some worn with toil, some of mere weari-
 ness,
Some of disease, and some insanity,
And some of wither'd or of broken hearts;
For this last is a malady which slays
More than are number'd in the lists of Fate,
Taking all shapes and bearing many names.
Look upon me! for even of all these things
Have I partaken; and of all these things, 150
One were enough; then wonder not that I
Am what I am, but that I ever was,
Or having been, that I am still on earth.
 Abbot. Yet, hear me still —
 Man. Old man! I do respect
Thine order, and revere thine years; I deem
Thy purpose pious, but it is in vain.
Think me not churlish; I would spare thy-
 self,
Far more than me, in shunning at this time
All further colloquy; and so — farewell.
 [*Exit* MANFRED.
 Abbot. This should have been a noble
 creature: he 160
Hath all the energy which would have made

A goodly frame of glorious elements,
Had they been wisely mingled; as it is,
It is an awful chaos — light and darkness,
And mind and dust, and passions and pure
 thoughts,
Mix'd, and contending without end or order,
All dormant or destructive. He will perish,
And yet he must not; I will try once more,
For such are worth redemption; and my duty
Is to dare all things for a righteous end. 170
I 'll follow him — but cautiously, though
 surely. [*Exit* ABBOT.

<center>SCENE II</center>

<center>*Another Chamber.*</center>

<center>MANFRED *and* HERMAN.</center>

 Her. My lord, you bade me wait on you
 at sunset:
He sinks beyond the mountain.
 Man. Doth he so?
I will look on him.
 [MANFRED *advances to the Window of the Hall.*
 Glorious Orb! the idol
Of early nature, and the vigorous race
Of undiseased mankind, the giant sons
Of the embrace of angels with a sex
More beautiful than they, which did draw
 down
The erring spirits who can ne'er return; —
Most glorious orb! that wert a worship,
 ere 180
The mystery of thy making was reveal'd!
Thou earliest minister of the Almighty,
Which gladden'd, on their mountain tops,
 the hearts
Of the Chaldean shepherds, till they pour'd
Themselves in orisons! Thou material God!
And representative of the Unknown,
Who chose thee for his shadow! Thou chief
 star!
Centre of many stars! which mak'st our
 earth
Endurable, and temperest the hues
And hearts of all who walk within thy
 rays! 190
Sire of the seasons! Monarch of the climes,
And those who dwell in them! for near or far,
Our inborn spirits have a tint of thee,
Even as our outward aspects; — thou dost
 rise,
And shine, and set in glory. Fare thee well!
I ne'er shall see thee more. As my first
 glance
Of love and wonder was for thee, then take

My latest look: thou wilt not beam on one
To whom the gifts of life and warmth have
 been
Of a more fatal nature. He is gone; 200
I follow. [*Exit* MANFRED.

SCENE III

The Mountains — The Castle of Manfred at some dis-
tance — A Terrace before a Tower. — Time, Twilight.

HERMAN, MANUEL, *and other Dependants of*
MANFRED.

Her. 'T is strange enough; night after
 night, for years,
He hath pursued long vigils in this tower,
Without a witness. I have been within it, —
So have we all been oft-times; but from it,
Or its contents, it were impossible
To draw conclusions absolute of aught
His studies tend to. To be sure, there is
One chamber where none enter: I would
 give
The fee of what I have to come these three
 years, 210
To pore upon its mysteries.
Manuel. 'T were dangerous;
Content thyself with what thou know'st
 already.
Her. Ah, Manuel ! thou art elderly and
 wise,
And couldst say much; thou hast dwelt
 within the castle —
How many years is 't ?
Manuel. Ere Count Manfred's birth,
I served his father, whom he nought re-
 sembles.
Her. There be more sons in like predica-
 ment.
But wherein do they differ ?
Manuel. I speak not
Of features or of form, but mind and
 habits;
Count Sigismund was proud, but gay and
 free — 220
A warrior and a reveller; he dwelt not
With books and solitude, nor made the
 night
A gloomy vigil, but a festal time,
Merrier than day; he did not walk the
 rocks
And forests like a wolf, nor turn aside
From men and their delights.
Her. Beshrew the hour,
But those were jocund times ! I would that
 such

Would visit the old walls again; they look
As if they had forgotten them.
Manuel. These walls
Must change their chieftain first. Oh ! I
 have seen 230
Some strange things in them, Herman.
Her. Come, be friendly;
Relate me some to while away our watch:
I 've heard thee darkly speak of an event
Which happen'd hereabouts, by this same
 tower.
Manuel. That was a night indeed ! I do
 remember
'T was twilight, as it may be now, and such
Another evening; yon red cloud, which rests
On Eigher's pinnacle, so rested then, —
So like that it might be the same; the wind
Was faint and gusty, and the mountain
 snows 240
Began to glitter with the climbing moon.
Count Manfred was, as now, within his
 tower, —
How occupied, we knew not, but with him
The sole companion of his wanderings
And watchings — her, whom of all earthly
 things
That lived, the only thing he seem'd to
 love, —
As he, indeed, by blood was bound to do,
The Lady Astarte, his —
 Hush ! who comes here ?

Enter the ABBOT.

Abbot. Where is your master ?
Her. Yonder in the tower.
Abbot. I must speak with him.
Manuel. 'T is impossible; 250
He is most private, and must not be thus
Intruded on.
Abbot. Upon myself I take
The forfeit of my fault, if fault there be —
But I must see him.
Her. Thou hast seen him once
This eve already.
Abbot. Herman ! I command thee,
Knock, and apprize the Count of my ap-
 proach.
Her. We dare not.
Abbot. Then it seems I must be herald
Of my own purpose.
Manuel. Reverend father, stop —
I pray you pause.
Abbot. Why so ?
Manuel. But step this way,
And I will tell you further. [*Exeunt.*

SCENE IV

Interior of the Tower.

MANFRED *alone.*

The stars are forth, the moon above the
 tops 261
Of the snow-shining mountains. — Beauti-
 ful !
I linger yet with Nature, for the night
Hath been to me a more familiar face
Than that of man; and in her starry shade
Of dim and solitary loveliness,
I learn'd the language of another world.
I do remember me, that in my youth,
When I was wandering, — upon such a
 night
I stood within the Coliseum's wall, 270
Midst the chief relics of almighty Rome.
The trees which grew along the broken
 arches
Waved dark in the blue midnight, and the
 stars
Shone through the rents of ruin; from afar
The watch-dog bay'd beyond the Tiber; and
More near from out the Cæsars' palace came
The owl's long cry, and, interruptedly,
Of distant sentinels the fitful song
Begun and died upon the gentle wind.
Some cypresses beyond the time-worn
 breach 280
Appear'd to skirt the horizon, yet they stood
Within a bowshot. Where the Cæsars dwelt,
And dwell the tuneless birds of night,
 amidst
A grove which springs through levell'd
 battlements
And twines its roots with the imperial
 hearths,
Ivy usurps the laurel's place of growth; —
But the gladiators' bloody Circus stands,
A noble wreck in ruinous perfection !
While Cæsar's chambers and the Augustan
 halls
Grovel on earth in indistinct decay. 290
And thou didst shine, thou rolling moon,
 upon
All this, and cast a wide and tender light,
Which soften'd down the hoar austerity
Of rugged desolation, and fill'd up,
As 't were anew, the gaps of centuries;
Leaving that beautiful which still was so,
And making that which was not, till the
 place
Became religion, and the heart ran o'er
With silent worship of the great of old, —

The dead, but sceptred sovereigns, who
 still rule 300
Our spirits from their urns. —
 'T was such a night !
'T is strange that I recall it at this time;
But I have found our thoughts take wildest
 flight
Even at the moment when they should array
Themselves in pensive order.

Enter the ABBOT.

Abbot. My good lord !
I crave a second grace for this approach;
But yet let not my humble zeal offend
By its abruptness — all it hath of ill
Recoils on me; its good in the effect
May light upon your head — could I say
 heart — 310
Could I touch *that*, with words or prayers,
 I should
Recall a noble spirit which hath wander'd
But is not yet all lost.
Man. Thou know'st me not;
My days are number'd, and my deeds re-
 corded:
Retire, or 't will be dangerous — Away !
 Abbot. Thou dost not mean to menace
 me ?
Man. Not I;
I simply tell thee peril is at hand,
And would preserve thee.
 Abbot. What dost thou mean ?
Man. Look there !
What dost thou see ?
 Abbot. Nothing.
Man. Look there, I say,
And steadfastly; — now tell me what thou
 seest. 320
 Abbot. That which should shake me —
 but I fear it not:
I see a dusk and awful figure rise,
Like an infernal god, from out the earth;
His face wrapt in a mantle, and his form
Robed as with angry clouds: he stands be-
 tween
Thyself and me — but I do fear him not.
 Man. Thou hast no cause; he shall not
 harm thee, but
His sight may shock thine old limbs into
 palsy.
I say to thee — Retire !
 Abbot. And I reply,
Never — till I have battled with this
 fiend: — 330
What doth he here ?

Man. Why — ay — what doth he
 here ?
I did not send for him, — he is unbidden.
 Abbot. Alas ! lost mortal ! what with
 guests like these
Hast thou to do ? I tremble for thy sake :
Why doth he gaze on thee, and thou on
 him ?
Ah ! he unveils his aspect : on his brow
The thunder-scars are graven ; from his
 eye
Glares forth the immortality of hell —
Avaunt ! —
 Man. Pronounce — what is thy mis-
 sion ?
 Spirit. Come !
 Abbot. What art thou, unknown being ?
 answer ! — speak ! 340
 Spirit. The genius of this mortal. —
 Come ! 't is time.
 Man. I am prepared for all things, but
 deny
The power which summons me. Who sent
 thee here ?
 Spirit. Thou 'lt know anon — Come !
 Come !
 Man. I have commanded
Things of an essence greater far than thine,
And striven with thy masters. Get thee
 hence !
 Spirit. Mortal ! thine hour is come —
 Away ! I say.
 Man. I knew, and know my hour is come,
 but not
To render up my soul to such as thee : 349
Away ! I 'll die as I have lived — alone.
 Spirit. Then I must summon up my bre-
 thren. — Rise ! [*Other Spirits rise up.*
 Abbot. Avaunt ! ye evil ones ! — Avaunt !
 I say, —
Ye have no power where piety hath power,
And I do charge ye in the name —
 Spirit. Old man !
We know ourselves, our mission, and thine
 order ;
Waste not thy holy words on idle uses,
It were in vain : this man is forfeited.
Once more I summon him — Away ! away !
 Man. I do defy ye, — though I feel my
 soul
Is ebbing from me, yet I do defy ye ; 360
Nor will I hence, while I have earthly
 breath
To breathe my scorn upon ye — earthly
 strength

To wrestle, though with spirits ; what ye
 take
Shall be ta'en limb by limb.
 Spirit. Reluctant mortal !
In this the Magian who would so pervade
The world invisible, and make himself
Almost our equal ? — Can it be that thou
Art thus in love with life ? the very life
Which made thee wretched !
 Man. Thou false fiend, thou liest !
My life is in its last hour, — *that* I know, 370
Nor would redeem a moment of that hour.
I do not combat against death, but thee
And thy surrounding angels ; my past power
Was purchased by no compact with thy
 crew,
But by superior science, penance, daring,
And length of watching, strength of mind,
 and skill
In knowledge of our fathers when the earth
Saw men and spirits walking side by side
And gave ye no supremacy : I stand 379
Upon my strength — I do defy — deny —
Spurn back, and scorn ye ! —
 Spirit. But thy many crimes
Have made thee —
 Man. What are they to such as thee ?
Must crimes be punish'd but by other
 crimes,
And greater criminals ? — Back to thy hell !
Thou hast no power upon me, *that* I feel ;
Thou never shalt possess me, *that* I know :
What I have done is done ; I bear within
A torture which could nothing gain from
 thine.
The mind which is immortal makes itself
Requital for its good or evil thoughts, 390
Is its own origin of ill and end,
And its own place and time ; its innate sense,
When stripp'd of this mortality, derives
No colour from the fleeting things without,
But is absorb'd in sufferance or in joy,
Born from the knowledge of its own desert.
Thou didst not tempt me, and thou couldst
 not tempt me ;
I have not been thy dupe nor am thy prey,
But was my own destroyer, and will be
My own hereafter. — Back, ye baffled
 fiends ! 400
The hand of death is on me — but not
 yours ! [*The Demons disappear.*
 Abbot. Alas ! how pale thou art — thy
 lips are white —
And thy breast heaves — and in thy gasp-
 ing throat

The accents rattle. Give thy prayers to
 Heaven —
Pray — albeit but in thought, — but die not
 thus.
 Man. 'T is over — my dull eyes can fix
 thee not;
But all things swim around me, and the
 earth
Heaves as it were beneath me. Fare thee
 well —
Give me thy hand.
 Abbot. Cold — cold — even to the
 heart —
But yet one prayer — Alas ! how fares it
 with thee ? 410
 Man. Old man ! 't is not so difficult to
 die. [MANFRED *expires.*
 Abbot. He 's gone, his soul hath ta'en its
 earthless flight;
Whither ? I dread to think; but he is gone.

CAIN

A MYSTERY

'Now the Serpent was more subtil than any
beast of the field which the Lord God had
made.' — *Gen.* ch. iii. v. 1.

TO
SIR WALTER SCOTT, BART.
THIS MYSTERY OF CAIN
IS INSCRIBED,
BY HIS OBLIGED FRIEND,
AND FAITHFUL SERVANT,
THE AUTHOR.

PREFACE

The following scenes are entitled ' A Mys-
tery,' in conformity with the ancient title
annexed to dramas upon similar subjects, which
were styled ' Mysteries, or Moralities.' The
author has by no means taken the same liber-
ties with his subject which were common,
formerly, as may be seen by any reader curious
enough to refer to those very profane produc-
tions, whether in English, French, Italian, or
Spanish. The author has endeavoured to pre-
serve the language adapted to his characters;
and where it is (and this is but rarely) taken
from actual *Scripture*, he has made as little
alteration, even of words, as the rhythm would
permit. The reader will recollect that the
book of Genesis does not state that Eve was
tempted by a demon, but by 'the Serpent;'
and that only because he was ' the most subtil
of all the beasts of the field.' Whatever inter-
pretation the Rabbins and the Fathers may
have put upon this, I take the words as I find
them, and reply, with Bishop Watson upon
similar occasions, when the Fathers were quoted
to him, as Moderator in the schools of Cam-
bridge, ' Behold the Book ! ' — holding up
the Scripture. It is to be recollected that my
present subject has nothing to do with the
New Testament, to which no reference can be

here made without anachronism. With the poems upon similar topics, I have not been recently familiar. Since I was twenty I have never read Milton; but I had read him so frequently before, that this may make little difference. Gesner's *Death of Abel* I have never read since I was eight years of age, at Aberdeen. The general impression of my recollection is delight; but of the contents I remember only that Cain's wife was called Mahala, and Abel's Thirza: in the following pages I have called them 'Adah' and 'Zillah,' the earliest female names which occur in Genesis; they were those of Lamech's wives: those of Cain and Abel are not called by their names. Whether, then, a coincidence of subject may have caused the same in expression, I know nothing, and care as little.

The reader will please to bear in mind (what few choose to recollect), that there is no allusion to a future state in any of the books of Moses, nor indeed in the Old Testament. For a reason for this extraordinary omission he may consult Warburton's *Divine Legation;* whether satisfactory or not, no better has yet been assigned. I have therefore supposed it new to Cain, without, I hope, any perversion of Holy Writ.

With regard to the language of Lucifer, it was difficult for me to make him talk like a clergyman upon the same subjects; but I have done what I could to restrain him within the bounds of spiritual politeness. If he disclaims having tempted Eve in the shape of the Serpent, it is only because the book of Genesis has not the most distant allusion to any thing of the kind, but merely to the Serpent in his serpentine capacity.

Note. — The reader will perceive that the author has partly adopted in this poem the notion of Cuvier, that the world had been destroyed several times before the creation of man. This speculation, derived from the different strata and the bones of enormous and unknown animals found in them, is not contrary to the Mosaic account, but rather confirms it; as no human bones have yet been discovered in those strata, although those of many known animals are found near the remains of the unknown. The assertion of Lucifer, that the pre-Adamite world was also peopled by rational beings much more intelligent than man, and proportionably powerful to the mammoth, etc., etc., is, of course, a poetical fiction to help him to make out his case.

I ought to add, that there is a 'tramelogedia' of Alfieri, called *Abele.* — I have never read that, nor any other of the posthumous works of the writer, except his Life.

RAVENNA, *Sept.* 20, 1821.

DRAMATIS PERSONÆ

MEN $\left\{\begin{array}{l}\text{ADAM.}\\\text{CAIN.}\\\text{ABEL.}\end{array}\right.$

SPIRITS $\left\{\begin{array}{l}\text{ANGEL OF THE LORD.}\\\text{LUCIFER.}\end{array}\right.$

WOMEN $\left\{\begin{array}{l}\text{EVE.}\\\text{ADAH.}\\\text{ZILLAH.}\end{array}\right.$

ACT I

SCENE I

The Land without Paradise. — Time, Sunrise.

ADAM, EVE, CAIN, ABEL, ADAH, ZILLAH, *offering a Sacrifice.*

Adam. God, the Eternal! Infinite! All-
wise ! —
Who out of darkness on the deep didst make
Light on the waters with a word — all hail!
Jehovah, with returning light, all hail!
Eve. God! who didst name the day, and
separate
Morning from night, till then divided
never,
Who didst divide the wave from wave, and
call
Part of thy work the firmament — all hail!
Abel. God! who didst call the elements
into
Earth, ocean, air, and fire, and with the day
And night, and worlds which these illumi-
nate 11
Or shadow, madest beings to enjoy them,
And love both them and thee — all hail!
all hail!
Adah. God, the Eternal! Parent of all
things!
Who didst create these best and beauteous
beings,
To be belovèd more than all save thee —
Let me love thee and them: — all hail! all
hail!
Zillah. Oh, God! who loving, making,
blessing all,
Yet didst permit the Serpent to creep in, 19
And drive my father forth from Paradise,
Keep us from further evil: — Hail! all hail!
Adam. Son Cain, my first-born, where-
fore art thou silent ?

Cain. Why should I speak ?
Adam. To pray.
Cain. Have ye not pray'd ?
Adam. We have, most fervently.
Cain. And loudly : I
Have heard you.
Adam. So will God, I trust.
Abel. Amen !
Adam. But thou, my eldest born, art
 silent still.
Cain. 'T is better I should be so.
Adam. Wherefore so ?
Cain. I have nought to ask.
Adam. Nor aught to thank for ?
Cain. No.
Adam. Dost thou not live ?
Cain. Must I not die ?
Eve. Alas !
The fruit of our forbidden tree begins 30
To fall.
Adam. And we must gather it again.
Oh, God ! why didst thou plant the tree of
 knowledge !
Cain. And wherefore pluck'd ye not the
 tree of life ?
Ye might have then defied him.
Adam. Oh ! my son,
Blaspheme not: these are serpent's words.
Cain. Why not ?
The snake spoke *truth :* it *was* the tree of
 knowledge;
It *was* the tree of life: knowledge is good,
And life is good; and how can both be evil ?
Eve. My boy ! thou speakest as I spoke,
 in sin,
Before thy birth: let me not see renew'd 40
My misery in thine. I have repented.
Let me not see my offspring fall into
The snares beyond the walls of Paradise,
Which e'en in Paradise destroy'd his par-
 ents.
Content thee with what *is.* Had we been
 so,
Thou now hadst been contented. — Oh, my
 son !
Adam. Our orisons completed, let us
 hence,
Each to his task of toil — not heavy,
 though
Needful: the earth is young, and yields us
 kindly
Her fruits with little labour.
Eve. Cain, my son,
Behold thy father cheerful and resign'd, 51
And do as he doth. [*Exeunt* ADAM *and* EVE.

Zillah. Wilt thou not, my brother ?
Abel. Why wilt thou wear this gloom
 upon thy brow,
Which can avail thee nothing, save to
 rouse
The Eternal anger ?
Adah. My belovèd Cain,
Wilt thou frown even on me ?
Cain. No, Adah ! no;
I fain would be alone a little while.
Abel, I 'm sick at heart: but it will pass.
Precede me, brother — I will follow shortly.
And you, too, sisters, tarry not behind; 60
Your gentleness must not be harshly met:
I 'll follow you anon.
Adah. If not, I will
Return to seek you here.
Abel. The peace of God
Be on your spirit, brother !
 [*Exeunt* ABEL, ZILLAH, *and* ADAH.
Cain (solus). And this is
Life — Toil ! and wherefore should I toil ?
 — because
My father could not keep his place in Eden.
What had *I* done in this ? — I was unborn:
I sought not to be born; nor love the state
To which that birth has brought me. Why
 did he
Yield to the serpent and the woman ? or,
Yielding, why suffer ? What was there in
 this ? 71
The tree was planted, and why not for
 him ?
If not, why place him near it, where it
 grew,
The fairest in the centre ? They have but
One answer to all questions, ' 'T was *his*
 will,
And *he* is good.' How know I that ? Be-
 cause
He is all-powerful, must all-good, too, fol-
 low ?
I judge but by the fruits — and they are
 bitter —
Which I must feed on for a fault not mine.
Whom have we here ? — A shape like to
 the angels, 80
Yet of a sterner and a sadder aspect
Of spiritual essence: why do I quake ?
Why should I fear him more than other
 spirits,
Whom I see daily wave their fiery swords
Before the gates round which I linger oft,
In twilight's hour, to catch a glimpse of
 those

Gardens which are my just inheritance,
Ere the night closes o'er the inhibited walls
And the immortal trees which overtop
The cherubim-defended battlements ? 90
If I shrink not from these, the fire-arm'd
 angels,
Why should I quail from him who now
 approaches ?
Yet he seems mightier far than them, nor
 less
Beauteous, and yet not all as beautiful
As he hath been, and might be: sorrow
 seems
Half of his immortality. And is it
So ? and can aught grieve save humanity ?
He cometh.

Enter LUCIFER.

Lucifer. Mortal !
Cain. Spirit, who art thou ?
Lucifer. Master of spirits.
Cain. And being so, canst thou
Leave them, and walk with dust ?
Lucifer. I know the thoughts 100
Of dust, and feel for it, and with you.
Cain. How !
You know my thoughts ?
Lucifer. They are the thoughts of all
Worthy of thought; — 't is your immortal
 part
Which speaks within you.
Cain. What immortal part ?
This has not been reveal'd: the tree of life
Was withheld from us by my father's folly,
While that of knowledge, by my mother's
 haste,
Was pluck'd too soon; and all the fruit is
 death !
Lucifer. They have deceived thee; thou
 shalt live.
Cain. I live,
But live to die: and, living, see no thing 110
To make death hateful, save an innate
 clinging,
A loathsome, and yet all invincible
Instinct of life, which I abhor, as I
Despise myself, yet cannot overcome —
And so I live. Would I had never lived !
Lucifer. Thou livest, and must live for
 ever: think not
The earth, which is thine outward cov'ring,
 is
Existence — it will cease, and thou wilt be
No less than thou art now.
Cain. No *less !* and why 119
No more ?

Lucifer. It may be thou shalt be as we.
Cain. And ye ?
Lucifer. Are everlasting.
Cain. Are ye happy ?
Lucifer. We are mighty.
Cain. Are ye happy ?
Lucifer. No; art thou ?
Cain. How should I be so ? Look on me !
Lucifer. Poor clay !
And thou pretendest to be wretched !
 Thou !
Cain. I am: — and thou, with all thy
 might, what art thou ?
Lucifer. One who aspired to be what
 made thee, and
Would not have made thee what thou art.
Cain. Ah !
Thou look'st almost a god; and —
Lucifer. I am none:
And having fail'd to be one, would be nought
Save what I am. He conquer'd; let him
 reign ! 130
Cain. Who ?
Lucifer. Thy sire's Maker and the earth's.
Cain. And heaven's,
And all that in them is. So I have heard
His seraphs sing; and so my father saith.
Lucifer. They say — what they must sing
 and say on pain
Of being that which I am — and thou art —
Of spirits and of men.
Cain. And what is that ?
Lucifer. Souls who dare use their immor-
 tality —
Souls who dare look the Omnipotent tyrant
 in
His everlasting face, and tell him that
His evil is not good ! If he has made, 140
As he saith — which I know not, nor be-
 lieve —
But, if he made us — he cannot unmake:
We are immortal ! — nay, he 'd *have* us so,
That he may torture: — let him ! He is
 great —
But, in his greatness, is no happier than
We in our conflict ! Goodness would not
 make
Evil; and what else hath he made ? But
 let him
Sit on his vast and solitary throne,
Creating worlds, to make eternity
Less burthensome to his immense exist-
 ence 150
And unparticipated solitude;
Let him crowd orb on orb: he is alone

Indefinite, indissoluble tyrant;
Could he but crush himself, 't were the best
 boon
He ever granted: but let him reign on,
And multiply himself in misery!
Spirits and men, at least we sympathise —
And, suffering in concert, make our pangs,
Innumerable, more endurable,
By the unbounded sympathy of all 160
With all! But *He!* so wretched in his
 height,
So restless in his wretchedness, must still
Create, and re-create —
 Cain. Thou speak'st to me of things
 which long have swum
In visions through my thought: I never
 could
Reconcile what I saw with what I heard.
My father and my mother talk to me
Of serpents, and of fruits and trees: I see
The gates of what they call their Paradise
Guarded by fiery-sworded cherubim, 170
Which shut them out, and me: I feel the
 weight
Of daily toil and constant thought: I look
Around a world where I seem nothing, with
Thoughts which arise within me, as if they
Could master all things: — but I thought
 alone
This misery was *mine.* — My father is
Tamed down; my mother has forgot the
 mind
Which made her thirst for knowledge at
 the risk
Of an eternal curse; my brother is
A watching shepherd boy, who offers up
The firstlings of the flock to him who
 bids 181
The earth yield nothing to us without
 sweat;
My sister Zillah sings an earlier hymn
Than the birds' matins; and my Adah, my
Own and belovèd, she, too, understands not
The mind which overwhelms me: never till
Now met I aught to sympathise with me.
'T is well — I rather would consort with
 spirits.
 Lucifer. And hadst thou not been fit by
 thine own soul
For such companionship, I would not now
Have stood before thee as I am: a ser-
 pent 191
Had been enough to charm ye, as before.
 Cain. Ah! didst *thou* tempt my mother?
 Lucifer. I tempt none,

Save with the truth: was not the tree, the
 tree
Of knowledge? and was not the tree of life
Still fruitful? Did *I* bid her pluck them
 not?
Did *I* plant things prohibited within
The reach of beings innocent, and curious
By their own innocence? I would have
 made ye
Gods; and even He who thrust ye forth,
 so thrust ye 200
Because 'ye should not eat the fruits of
 life,
And become gods as we.' Were those his
 words?
 Cain. They were, as I have heard from
 those who heard them,
In thunder.
 Lucifer. Then who was the demon? He
Who would not let ye live, or he who would
Have made ye live for ever in the joy
And power of knowledge?
 Cain. Would they had snatch'd both
The fruits, or neither!
 Lucifer. One is yours already;
The other may be still.
 Cain. How so?
 Lucifer. By being
Yourselves, in your resistance. Nothing
 can 210
Quench the mind, if the mind will be itself
And centre of surrounding things — 't is
 made
To sway.
 Cain. But didst thou tempt my parents?
 Lucifer. I?
Poor clay! what should I tempt them for,
 or how?
 Cain. They say the serpent was a spirit.
 Lucifer. Who
Saith that? It is not written so on high:
The proud One will not so far falsify,
Though man's vast fears and little vanity
Would make him cast upon the spiritual
 nature
His own low failing. The snake *was* the
 snake — 220
No more; and yet not less than those he
 tempted,
In nature being earth also — *more* in *wisdom*,
Since he could overcome them, and fore-
 knew
The knowledge fatal to their narrow joys.
Think'st thou I 'd take the shape of things
 that die?

Cain. But the thing had a demon?
Lucifer. He but woke one
In those he spake to with his forky tongue.
I tell thee that the serpent was no more
Than a mere serpent: ask the cherubim
Who guard the tempting tree. When
 thousand ages 230
Have roll'd o'er your dead ashes, and your
 seed's,
The seed of the then world may thus array
Their earliest fault in fable, and attribute
To them a shape I scorn, as I scorn all
That bows to him who made things but to
 bend
Before his sullen, sole eternity;
But we, who see the truth, must speak it.
 Thy
Fond parents listen'd to a creeping thing,
And fell. For what should spirits tempt
 them? What
Was there to envy in the narrow bounds
Of Paradise, that spirits who pervade 241
Space — but I speak to thee of what thou
 know'st not,
With all thy tree of knowledge.
Cain. But thou canst not
Speak aught of knowledge which I would
 not know,
And do not thirst to know, and bear a mind
To know.
Lucifer. And heart to look on?
Cain. Be it proved.
Lucifer. Darest thou to look on Death?
Cain. He has not yet
Been seen.
Lucifer. But must be undergone.
Cain. My father
Says he is something dreadful, and my
 mother
Weeps when he's named; and Abel lifts his
 eyes 250
To heaven, and Zillah casts hers to the
 earth,
And sighs a prayer; and Adah looks on me,
And speaks not.
Lucifer. And thou?
Cain. Thoughts unspeakable
Crowd in my breast to burning, when I hear
Of this almighty Death, who is, it seems,
Inevitable. Could I wrestle with him?
I wrestled with the lion, when a boy,
In play, till he ran roaring from my gripe.
Lucifer. It has no shape; but will absorb
 all things
That bear the form of earth-born being.

Cain. Ah!
I thought it was a being: who could do 261
Such evil things to beings save a being?
Lucifer. Ask the Destroyer.
Cain. Who?
Lucifer. The Maker — call him
Which name thou wilt: he makes but to
 destroy.
Cain. I knew not that, yet thought it,
 since I heard
Of death; although I know not what it is,
Yet it seems horrible. I have look'd out
In the vast desolate night in search of him;
And when I saw gigantic shadows in 269
The umbrage of the walls of Eden, chequer'd
By the far-flashing of the cherubs' swords,
I watch'd for what I thought his coming; for
With fear rose longing in my heart to know
What 't was which shook us all — but no-
 thing came.
And then I turn'd my weary eyes from off
Our native and forbidden Paradise,
Up to the lights above us, in the azure,
Which are so beautiful: shall they, too,
 die?
Lucifer. Perhaps — but long outlive both
 thine and thee.
Cain. I'm glad of that: I would not have
 them die — 280
They are so lovely. What is death? I
 fear,
I feel, it is a dreadful thing; but what,
I cannot compass: 't is denounced against
 us,
Both them who sinn'd and sinn'd not, as an
 ill —
What ill?
Lucifer. To be resolved into the earth.
Cain. But shall I know it?
Lucifer. As I know not death,
I cannot answer.
Cain. Were I quiet earth
That were no evil: would I ne'er had been
Aught else but dust!
Lucifer. That is a grovelling wish,
Less than thy father's, for he wish'd to
 know. 290
Cain. But not to live, or wherefore
 pluck'd he not
The life-tree?
Lucifer. He was hinder'd.
Cain. Deadly error!
Not to snatch first that fruit: — but ere he
 pluck'd
The knowledge, he was ignorant of death.

Alas! I scarcely now know what it is,
And yet I fear it — fear I know not what!
 Lucifer. And I, who know all things, fear
 nothing: see
What is true knowledge.
 Cain. Wilt thou teach me all?
 Lucifer. Ay, upon one condition.
 Cain. Name it.
 Lucifer. That
Thou dost fall down and worship me — thy
 Lord. 300
 Cain. Thou art not the Lord my father
 worships.
 Lucifer. No.
 Cain. His equal?
 Lucifer. No; — I have nought in com-
 mon with him!
Nor would: I would be aught above —
 beneath —
Aught save a sharer or a servant of
His power. I dwell apart; but I am
 great: —
Many there are who worship me, and more
Who shall — be thou amongst the first.
 Cain. I never
As yet have bow'd unto my father's God,
Although my brother Abel oft implores 309
That I would join with him in sacrifice: —
Why should I bow to thee?
 Lucifer. Hast thou ne'er bow'd
 To him?
 Cain. Have I not said it? — need I say
 it?
Could not thy mighty knowledge teach thee
 that?
 Lucifer. He who bows not to him has
 bow'd to me!
 Cain. But I will bend to neither.
 Lucifer. Ne'er the less,
Thou art my worshipper: not worshipping
Him makes thee mine the same.
 Cain. And what is that?
 Lucifer. Thou 'lt know here — and here-
 after.
 Cain. Let me but
Be taught the mystery of my being.
 Lucifer. Follow
Where I will lead thee.
 Cain. But I must retire 320
To till the earth — for I had promised —
 Lucifer. What?
 Cain. To cull some first-fruits.
 Lucifer. Why?
 Cain. To offer up
With Abel on an altar.

 Lucifer. Saidst thou not
Thou ne'er hadst bent to him who made
 thee?
 Cain. Yes —
But Abel's earnest prayer has wrought
 upon me;
The offering is more his than mine — and
 Adah —
 Lucifer. Why dost thou hesitate?
 Cain. She is my sister,
Born on the same day, of the same womb;
 and
She wrung from me, with tears, this pro-
 mise; and
Rather than see her weep, I would, me-
 thinks, 330
Bear all — and worship aught.
 Lucifer. Then follow me!
 Cain. I will.
 Enter ADAH.
 Adah. My brother, I have come for
 thee;
It is our hour of rest and joy — and we
Have less without thee. Thou hast la-
 bour'd not
This morn; but I have done thy task: the
 fruits
Are ripe, and glowing as the light which
 ripens:
Come away.
 Cain. Seest thou not?
 Adah. I see an angel;
We have seen many: will he share our hour
Of rest? — he is welcome.
 Cain. But he is not like
The angels we have seen.
 Adah. Are there, then, others?
But he is welcome, as they were: they
 deign'd 341
To be our guests — will he?
 Cain (*to Lucifer*). Wilt thou?
 Lucifer. I ask
Thee to be mine.
 Cain. I must away with him.
 Adah. And leave us?
 Cain. Ay.
 Adah. And *me?*
 Cain. Belovèd Adah!
 Adah. Let me go with thee.
 Lucifer. No, she must not.
 Adah. Who
Art thou that steppest between heart and
 heart?
 Cain. He is a god.
 Adah. How know'st thou?

Cain. He speaks like
A god.
Adah. So did the serpent, and it lied.
Lucifer. Thou errest, Adah ! — was not
 the tree that
Of knowledge ?
Adah. Ay — to our eternal sorrow.
Lucifer. And yet that grief is knowledge
 — so he lied not: 351
And if he did betray you, 't was with truth;
And truth in its own essence cannot be
But good.
Adah. But all we know of it has
 gather'd
Evil on ill: expulsion from our home,
And dread, and toil, and sweat, and heavi-
 ness;
Remorse of that which was — and hope of
 that
Which cometh not. Cain ! walk not with
 this spirit.
Bear with what we have borne, and love
 me — I
Love thee.
Lucifer. More than thy mother and thy
 sire ? 360
Adah. I do. Is that a sin, too ?
Lucifer. No, not yet:
It one day will be in your children.
Adah. What !
Must not my daughter love her brother
 Enoch ?
Lucifer. Not as thou lovest Cain.
Adah. Oh, my God !
Shall they not love and bring forth things
 that love
Out of their love ? have they not drawn
 their milk
Out of this bosom ? was not he, their father,
Born of the same sole womb, in the same
 hour
With me ? did we not love each other ? and
In multiplying our being multiply 370
Things which will love each other as we
 love
Them ? — And as I love thee, my Cain ! go
 not
Forth with this spirit; he is not of ours.
Lucifer. The sin I speak of is not of my
 making,
And cannot be a sin in you — whate'er
It seem in those who will replace ye in
Mortality.
Adah. What is the sin which is not
Sin in itself ? Can circumstance make sin

Or virtue ? — if it doth, we are the slaves
Of —
Lucifer. Higher things than ye are slaves:
 and higher 380
Than them or ye would be so, did they
 not
Prefer an independency of torture
To the smooth agonies of adulation,
In hymns and harpings, and self-seeking
 prayers,
To that which is omnipotent, because
It is omnipotent, and not from love,
But terror and self-hope.
Adah. Omnipotence
Must be all goodness.
Lucifer. Was it so in Eden ?
Adah. Fiend ! tempt me not with beauty;
 thou art fairer
Than was the serpent, and as false.
Lucifer. As true.
Ask Eve, your mother: bears she not the
 knowledge 391
Of good and evil ?
Adah. Oh, my mother ! thou
Hast pluck'd a fruit more fatal to thine off-
 spring
Than to thyself ; thou at the least hast
 pass'd
Thy youth in Paradise, in innocent
And happy intercourse with happy spirits:
But we, thy children, ignorant of Eden,
Are girt about by demons, who assume
The words of God and tempt us with our
 own
Dissatisfied and curious thoughts — as thou
Wert work'd on by the snake in thy most
 flush'd 401
And heedless, harmless wantonness of bliss.
I cannot answer this immortal thing
Which stands before me; I cannot abhor
 him;
I look upon him with a pleasing fear,
And yet I fly not from him: in his eye
There is a fastening attraction which
Fixes my fluttering eyes on his; my heart
Beats quick; he awes me, and yet draws me
 near,
Nearer, and nearer: — Cain — Cain — save
 me from him ! 410
Cain. What dreads my Adah ? This is no
 ill spirit.
Adah. He is not God — nor God's: I have
 beheld
The cherubs and the seraphs; he looks not
Like them.

Cain. But there are spirits loftier still —
The archangels.
 Lucifer. And still loftier than the arch-
angels.
 Adah. Ay — but not blessèd.
 Lucifer. If the blessedness
Consists in slavery — no.
 Adah. I have heard it said,
The seraphs *love most* — cherubim *know
 most ;*
And this should be a cherub — since he
 loves not.
 Lucifer. And if the higher knowledge
 quenches love, 420
What must *he be* you cannot love when
 known ?
Since the all-knowing cherubim love least,
The seraphs' love can be but ignorance:
That they are not compatible, the doom
Of thy fond parents, for their daring, proves.
Choose betwixt love and knowledge — since
 there is
No other choice. Your sire has chosen al-
 ready;
His worship is but fear.
 Adah. Oh, Cain ! choose love.
 Cain. For thee, my Adah, I choose not —
 it was
Born with me — but I love nought else.
 Adah. Our parents ?
 Cain. Did they love us when they snatch'd
 from the tree 431
That which hath driven us all from Para-
 dise ?
 Adah. We were not born then — and if
 we had been,
Should we not love them and our children,
 Cain ?
 Cain. My little Enoch ! and his lisping
 sister !
Could I but deem them happy, I would
 half
Forget — but it can never be forgotten
Through thrice a thousand generations !
 never
Shall men love the remembrance of the
 man
Who sow'd the seed of evil and mankind
In the same hour ! They pluck'd the tree
 of science, 441
And sin — and not content with their own
 sorrow,
Begot *me* — *thee* — and all the few that are,
And all the unnumber'd and innumerable
Multitudes, millions, myriads, which may be,

To inherit agonies accumulated
By ages ! — and *I* must be sire of such
 things !
Thy beauty and thy love — my love and
 joy,
The rapturous moment and the placid hour,
All we love in our children and each other,
But lead them and ourselves through many
 years 451
Of sin and pain — or few, but still of sor-
 row,
Intercheck'd with an instant of brief plea-
 sure,
To Death — the unknown ! Methinks the
 tree of knowledge
Hath not fulfill'd its promise: — if they
 sinn'd,
At least they ought to have known all
 things that are
Of knowledge — and the mystery of death.
What do they know ? — that they are mis-
 erable.
What need of snakes and fruits to teach us
 that ?
 Adah. I am not wretched, Cain, and if
 thou 460
Wert happy —
 Cain. Be thou happy, then, alone —
I will have nought to do with happiness,
Which humbles me and mine.
 Adah. Alone I could not,
Nor *would* be happy: but with those around
 us,
I think I could be so, despite of death,
Which, as I know it not, I dread not,
 though
It seems an awful shadow — if I may
Judge from what I have heard.
 Lucifer. And thou couldst not
Alone, thou say'st, be happy ?
 Adah. Alone ! Oh, my God !
Who could be happy and alone, or good ?
To me my solitude seems sin; unless 471
When I think how soon I shall see my
 brother,
His brother, and our children, and our par-
 ents.
 Lucifer. Yet thy God is alone; and is he
 happy,
Lonely, and good ?
 Adah. He is not so; he hath
The angels and the mortals to make happy,
And thus becomes so in diffusing joy.
What else can joy be, but the spreading
 joy ?

Lucifer. Ask of your sire, the exile fresh
 from Eden;
Or of his first-born son: ask your own
 heart; 480
It is not tranquil.
 Adah. Alas, no ! and you —
Are you of heaven ?
 Lucifer. If I am not, enquire
The cause of this all-spreading happiness
(Which you proclaim) of the all-great and
 good
Maker of life and living things; it is
His secret, and he keeps it. *We* must bear,
And some of us resist, and both in vain,
His seraphs say; but it is worth the trial,
Since better may not be without. There is
A wisdom in the spirit, which directs 490
To right, as in the dim blue air the eye
Of you, young mortals, lights at once upon
The star which watches, welcoming the
 morn.
 Adah. It is a beautiful star ; I love it for
Its beauty.
 Lucifer. And why not adore ?
 Adah. Our father
Adores the Invisible only.
 Lucifer. But the symbols
Of the Invisible are the loveliest
Of what is visible; and yon bright star
Is leader of the host of heaven.
 Adah. Our father
Saith that he has beheld the God himself 500
Who made him and our mother.
 Lucifer. Hast *thou* seen him ?
 Adah. Yes — in his works.
 Lucifer. But in his being ?
 Adah. No —
Save in my father, who is God's own image;
Or in his angels, who are like to thee —
And brighter, yet less beautiful and power-
 ful
In seeming: as the silent sunny noon,
All light they look upon us ; but thou
 seem'st
Like an ethereal night, where long white
 clouds
Streak the deep purple, and unnumber'd
 stars
Spangle the wonderful mysterious vault
With things that look as if they would be
 suns; 511
So beautiful, unnumber'd, and endearing,
Not dazzling, and yet drawing us to them,
They fill my eyes with tears, and so dost
 thou.

Thou seem'st unhappy: do not make us so,
And I will weep for thee.
 Lucifer. Alas ! those tears !
Couldst thou but know what oceans will be
 shed —
 Adah. By me ?
 Lucifer. By all.
 Adah. What all ?
 Lucifer. The million millions —
The myriad myriads — the all - peopled
 earth —
The unpeopled earth — and the o'erpeopled
 Hell, 520
Of which thy bosom is the germ.
 Adah. O Cain !
This spirit curseth us.
 Cain. Let him say on;
Him will I follow.
 Adah. Whither ?
 Lucifer. To a place
Whence he shall come back to thee in an
 hour;
But in that hour see things of many days.
 Adah. How can that be ?
 Lucifer. Did not your Maker make
Out of old worlds this new one in few
 days ?
And cannot I, who aided in this work,
Show in an hour what he hath made in
 many,
Or hath destroy'd in few ?
 Cain. Lead on.
 Adah. Will he, 530
In sooth, return within an hour ?
 Lucifer. He shall.
With us acts are exempt from time, and we
Can crowd eternity into an hour,
Or stretch an hour into eternity:
We breathe not by a mortal measure-
 ment —
But that 's a mystery. Cain, come on with
 me.
 Adah. Will he return ?
 Lucifer. Ay, woman ! he alone
Of mortals from that place (the first and last
Who shall return, save ONE) shall come
 back to thee,
To make that silent and expectant world
As populous as this: at present there 540
Are few inhabitants.
 Adah. Where dwellest thou ?
 Lucifer. Throughout all space. Where
 should I dwell ? Where are
Thy God or Gods — there am I: all things
 are

Divided with me; life and death — and
time —
Eternity — and heaven and earth — and
that
Which is not heaven nor earth, but peopled
with
Those who once peopled or shall people
both —
These are my realms! So that I do
divide
His, and possess a kingdom which is not
His. If I were not that which I have
said, 551
Could I stand here? His angels are within
Your vision.
 Adah. So they were when the fair ser-
pent
Spoke with our mother first.
 Lucifer. Cain! thou hast heard.
If thou dost long for knowledge, I can
satiate
That thirst; nor ask thee to partake of
fruits
Which shall deprive thee of a single good
The conqueror has left thee. Follow me.
 Cain. Spirit, I have said it.
 [*Exeunt* LUCIFER *and* CAIN.
 Adah (*follows, exclaiming*). Cain! my
brother! Cain!

ACT II

SCENE I

The Abyss of Space.

 Cain. I tread on air, and sink not; yet I
fear
To sink.
 Lucifer. Have faith in me, and thou shalt
be
Borne on the air, of which I am the prince.
 Cain. Can I do so without impiety?
 Lucifer. Believe — and sink not! doubt
— and perish! thus
Would run the edict of the other God,
Who names me demon to his angels; they
Echo the sound to miserable things,
Which, knowing nought beyond their
shallow senses,
Worship the word which strikes their ear,
and deem 10
Evil or good what is proclaim'd to them
In their abasement. I will have none such:
Worship or worship not, thou shalt behold

The worlds beyond thy little world, nor be
Amerced for doubts beyond thy little life,
With torture of *my* dooming. There will
come
An hour, when, toss'd upon some water-
drops,
A man shall say to a man, 'Believe in me,
And walk the waters;' and the man shall
walk
The billows and be safe. *I* will not say, 20
Believe in *me*, as a conditional creed
To save thee; but fly with me o'er the
gulf
Of space an equal flight, and I will show
What thou dar'st not deny, — the history
Of past, and present, and of future worlds.
 Cain. Oh, god, or demon, or whate'er
thou art,
Is yon our earth?
 Lucifer. Dost thou not recognise
The dust which form'd your father?
 Cain. Can it be?
Yon small blue circle, swinging in far ether,
With an inferior circlet near it still, 30
Which looks like that which lit our earthly
night?
Is this our Paradise? Where are its walls,
And they who guard them?
 Lucifer. Point me out the site
Of Paradise.
 Cain. How should I? As we move
Like sunbeams onward, it grows small and
smaller,
And as it waxes little, and then less,
Gathers a halo round it, like the light
Which shone the roundest of the stars,
when I
Beheld them from the skirts of Paradise.
Methinks they both, as we recede from
them, 40
Appear to join the innumerable stars
Which are around us; and, as we move on,
Increase their myriads.
 Lucifer. And if there should be
Worlds greater than thine own, inhabited
By greater things, and they themselves far
more
In number than the dust of thy dull earth,
Though multiplied to animated atoms,
All living, and all doom'd to death, and
wretched,
What wouldst thou think?
 Cain. I should be proud of thought
Which knew such things.
 Lucifer. But if that high thought were

Link'd to a servile mass of matter, and, 51
Knowing such things, aspiring to such
 things,
And science still beyond them, were chain'd
 down
To the most gross and petty paltry wants,
All foul and fulsome, and the very best
Of thine enjoyments a sweet degradation,
A most enervating and filthy cheat
To lure thee on to the renewal of
Fresh souls and bodies, all foredoom'd to
 be
As frail and few so happy —
 Cain. Spirit ! I 60
Know nought of death, save as a dreadful
 thing
Of which I have heard my parents speak,
 as of
A hideous heritage I owe to them
No less than life; a heritage not happy,
If I may judge, till now. But, spirit ! if
It be as thou hast said (and I within
Feel the prophetic torture of its truth),
Here let me die: for to give birth to those
Who can but suffer many years, and die,
Methinks is merely propagating death, 70
And multiplying murder.
 Lucifer. Thou canst not
All die — there is what must survive.
 Cain. The Other
Spake not of this unto my father, when
He shut him forth from Paradise, with
 death
Written upon his forehead. But at least
Let what is mortal of me perish, that
I may be in the rest as angels are.
 Lucifer. I am angelic: wouldst thou be
 as I am ?
 Cain. I know not what thou art: I see
 thy power,
And see thou show'st me things beyond
 my power, 80
Beyond all power of my born faculties,
Although inferior still to my desires
And my conceptions.
 Lucifer. What are they which dwell
So humbly in their pride as to sojourn
With worms in clay ?
 Cain. And what art thou who dwellest
So haughtily in spirit, and canst range
Nature and immortality — and yet
Seem'st sorrowful ?
 Lucifer. I seem that which I am;
And therefore do I ask of thee, if thou
Wouldst be immortal ?

 Cain. Thou hast said, I must be 90
Immortal in despite of me. I knew not
This until lately — but since it must be,
Let me, or happy or unhappy, learn
To anticipate my immortality.
 Lucifer. Thou didst before I came upon
 thee.
 Cain. How ?
 Lucifer. By suffering.
 Cain. And must torture be immortal ?
 Lucifer. We and thy sons will try. But
 now, behold !
Is it not glorious ?
 Cain. Oh, thou beautiful
And unimaginable ether ! and
Ye multiplying masses of increased 100
And still increasing lights ! what are ye ?
 what
Is this blue wilderness of interminable
Air, where ye roll along, as I have seen
The leaves along the limpid streams of
 Eden ?
Is your course measured for ye ? Or do ye
Sweep on in your unbounded revelry
Through an aërial universe of endless
Expansion — at which my soul aches to
 think —
Intoxicated with eternity ?
Oh God ! Oh Gods ! or whatsoe'er ye are ! 110
How beautiful ye are ! how beautiful
Your works, or accidents, or whatsoe'er
They may be ! Let me die as atoms die
(If that they die), or know ye in your might
And knowledge ! My thoughts are not in
 this hour
Unworthy what I see, though my dust is; —
Spirit ! let me expire, or see them nearer. —
 Lucifer. Art thou not nearer ? look back
 to thine earth !
 Cain. Where is it ? I see nothing save a
 mass
Of most innumerable lights.
 Lucifer. Look there ! 120
 Cain. I cannot see it.
 Lucifer. Yet it sparkles still.
 Cain. That ! — yonder !
 Lucifer. Yea.
 Cain. And wilt thou tell me so ?
Why, I have seen the fire-flies and fire-
 worms
Sprinkle the dusky groves and the green
 banks
In the dim twilight, brighter than yon
 world
Which bears them.

Lucifer. Thou hast seen both worms and
 worlds,
Each bright and sparkling — what dost
 think of them ?
Cain. That they are beautiful in their own
 sphere,
And that the night, which makes both beau-
 tiful,
The little shining fire-fly in its flight, 130
And the immortal star in its great course,
Must both be guided.
 Lucifer. But by whom or what ?
 Cain. Show me.
 Lucifer. Dar'st thou behold ?
 Cain. How know I what
I *dare* behold ? As yet, thou hast shown
 nought
I dare not gaze on further.
 Lucifer. On, then, with me.
Wouldst thou behold things mortal or im-
 mortal ?
 Cain. Why, what are things ?
 Lucifer. *Both* partly; but what doth
Sit next thy heart ?
 Cain. The things I see.
 Lucifer. But what
Sate nearest it ?
 Cain. The things I have not seen,
Nor ever shall — the mysteries of death.
 Lucifer. What, if I show to thee things
 which have died, 141
As I have shown thee much which cannot
 die ?
 Cain. Do so.
 Lucifer. Away, then, on our mighty
 wings !
 Cain. Oh, how we cleave the blue ! The
 stars fade from us !
The earth ! where is my earth ? Let me
 look on it,
For I was made of it.
 Lucifer. 'T is now beyond thee,
Less, in the universe, than thou in it;
Yet deem not that thou canst escape it; thou
Shalt soon return to earth and all its dust:
'T is part of thy eternity, and mine. 150
 Cain. Where dost thou lead me ?
 Lucifer. To what was before thee !
The phantasm of the world; of which thy
 world
Is but the wreck.
 Cain. What ! is it not then new ?
 Lucifer. No more than life is; and that
 was ere thou
Or *I* were, or the things which seem to us

Greater than either. Many things will have
No end; and some, which would pretend to
 have
Had no beginning, have had one as mean
As thou; and mightier things have been
 extinct
To make way for much meaner than we
 can 160
Surmise; for *moments* only and the *space*
Have been and must be all *unchangeable.*
But changes make not death, except to clay;
But thou art clay, and canst but compre-
 hend
That which was clay, and such thou shalt
 behold.
 Cain. Clay, spirit ! what thou wilt, I can
 survey.
 Lucifer. Away, then !
 Cain. But the lights fade from me fast,
And some till now grew larger as we
 approach'd
And wore the look of worlds.
 Lucifer. And such they are.
 Cain. And Edens in them ?
 Lucifer. It may be.
 Cain. And men ? 170
 Lucifer. Yea, or things higher.
 Cain. Ay, and serpents too ?
 Lucifer. Wouldst thou have men without
 them ? must no reptiles
Breathe save the erect ones ?
 Cain. How the lights recede !
Where fly we ?
 Lucifer. To the world of phantoms, which
Are beings past, and shadows still to come.
 Cain. But it grows dark and dark — the
 stars are gone !
 Lucifer. And yet thou seest.
 Cain. 'T is a fearful light !
No sun, no moon, no lights innumerable —
The very blue of the empurpled night
Fades to a dreary twilight, yet I see 180
Huge dusky masses: but unlike the worlds
We were approaching, which, begirt with
 light,
Seem'd full of life even when their atmo-
 sphere
Of light gave way, and show 'd them taking
 shapes
Unequal, of deep valleys and vast mountains;
And some emitting sparks, and some
 displaying
Enormous liquid plains, and some begirt
With luminous belts, and floating moons,
 which took

Like them the features of fair earth: —
 instead,
All here seems dark and dreadful.
 Lucifer. But distinct.
Thou seekest to behold death and dead
 things ? 191
 Cain. I seek it not; but as I know there
 are
Such, and that my sire's sin makes him and
 me,
And all that we inherit, liable
To such, I would behold at once what I
Must one day see perforce.
 Lucifer. Behold !
 Cain. 'T is darkness.
 Lucifer. And so it shall be ever; but we
 will
Unfold its gates !
 Cain. Enormous vapours roll
Apart — what 's this ?
 Lucifer. Enter !
 Cain. Can I return ?
 Lucifer. Return! be sure: how else should
 death be peopled ? 200
Its present realm is thin to what it will be,
Through thee and thine.
 Cain. The clouds still open wide
And wider, and make widening circles
 round us.
 Lucifer. Advance !
 Cain. And thou ?
 Lucifer. Fear not — without me thou
Couldst not have gone beyond thy world.
 On ! on !

 [*They disappear through the clouds.*

SCENE II

Hades.

Enter LUCIFER *and* CAIN.

 Cain. How silent and how vast are these
 dim worlds !
For they seem more than one, and yet more
 peopled
Than the huge brilliant luminous orbs which
 swung
So thickly in the upper air, that I
Had deem'd them rather the bright popu-
 lace 210
Of some all unimaginable heaven
Than things to be inhabited themselves,
But that on drawing near them I beheld
Their swelling into palpable immensity
Of matter, which seem'd made for life to
 dwell on,

Rather than life itself. But here, all is
So shadowy and so full of twilight, that
It speaks of a day past.
 Lucifer. It is the realm
Of death. — Wouldst have it present ?
 Cain. Till I know
That which it really is, I cannot answer. 220
But if it be as I have heard my father
Deal out in his long homilies, 't is a thing —
Oh God ! I dare not think on 't ! Cursèd be
He who invented life that leads to death !
Or the dull mass of life, that, being life,
Could not retain, but needs must forfeit it —
Even for the innocent !
 Lucifer. Dost thou curse thy father ?
 Cain. Cursed he not me in giving me my
 birth ?
Cursed he not me before my birth, in daring
To pluck the fruit forbidden ?
 Lucifer. Thou say'st well:
The curse is mutual 'twixt thy sire and
 thee — 231
But for thy sons and brother ?
 Cain. Let them share it
With me, their sire and brother ! What
 else is
Bequeath'd to me ? I leave them my inherit-
 ance.
Oh, ye interminable gloomy realms
Of swimming shadows and enormous shapes,
Some fully shown, some indistinct, and all
Mighty and melancholy — what are ye ?
Live ye, or have ye lived ?
 Lucifer. Somewhat of both.
 Cain. Then what is death ?
 Lucifer. What ? Hath not he who made ye
Said 't is another life ?
 Cain. Till now he hath 241
Said nothing, save that all shall die.
 Lucifer. Perhaps
He one day will unfold that further secret.
 Cain. Happy the day !
 Lucifer. Yes; happy ! when unfolded,
Through agonies unspeakable, and clogg'd
With agonies eternal, to innumerable
Yet unborn myriads of unconscious atoms,
All to be animated for this only !
 Cain. What are these mighty phantoms
 which I see
Floating around me ? — They wear not the
 form 250
Of the intelligences I have seen
Round our regretted and unenter'd Eden,
Nor wear the form of man as I have view'd
 it

In Adam's, and in Abel's, and in mine,
Nor in my sister-bride's, nor in my chil-
 dren's:
And yet they have an aspect, which, though
 not
Of men nor angels, looks like something
 which,
If not the last, rose higher than the first,
Haughty, and high, and beautiful, and full
Of seeming strength, but of inexplicable 260
Shape; for I never saw such. They bear
 not
The wing of seraph, nor the face of man,
Nor form of mightiest brute, nor aught that
 is
Now breathing; mighty yet and beautiful
As the most beautiful and mighty which
Live, and yet so unlike them, that I scarce
Can call them living.

 Lucifer. Yet they lived.
 Cain. Where ?
 Lucifer. Where
Thou livest.
 Cain. When ?
 Lucifer. On what thou callest earth
They did inhabit.
 Cain. Adam is the first.
 Lucifer. Of thine, I grant thee — but too
 mean to be 270
The last of these.
 Cain. And what are they ?
 Lucifer. That which
Thou shalt be.
 Cain. But what *were* they ?
 Lucifer. Living, high,
Intelligent, good, great, and glorious things,
As much superior unto all thy sire,
Adam, could e'er have been in Eden, as
The sixty-thousandth generation shall be,
In its dull damp degeneracy, to
Thee and thy son; — and how weak they
 are, judge
By thy own flesh.
 Cain. Ah me ! and did *they* perish ?
 Lucifer. Yes, from their earth, as thou
 wilt fade from thine. 280
 Cain. But was *mine* theirs ?
 Lucifer. It was.
 Cain. But not as now.
It is too little and too lowly to
Sustain such creatures.
 Lucifer. True, it was more glorious.
 Cain. And wherefore did it fall ?
 Lucifer. Ask him who fells.
 Cain. But how ?

 Lucifer. By a most crushing and inexor-
 able
Destruction and disorder of the elements,
Which struck a world to chaos, as a chaos
Subsiding has struck out a world: such
 things,
Though rare in time, are frequent in eter-
 nity. —
Pass on, and gaze upon the past.
 Cain. 'T is awful !
 Lucifer. And true. Behold these phan-
 toms ! they were once 291
Material as thou art.
 Cain. And must I be
Like them ?
 Lucifer. Let He who made thee answer
 that.
I show thee what thy predecessors are,
And what they *were* thou feelest, in degree
Inferior as thy petty feelings and
Thy pettier portion of the immortal part
Of high intelligence and earthly strength.
What ye in common have with what they
 had
Is life, and what ye *shall* have — death : the
 rest 300
Of your poor attributes is such as suits
Reptiles engender'd out of the subsiding
Slime of a mighty universe, crush'd into
A scarcely-yet shaped planet, peopled with
Things whose enjoyment was to be in
 blindness —
A Paradise of Ignorance, from which
Knowledge was barr'd as poison. But be-
 hold
What these superior beings are or were;
Or, if it irk thee, turn thee back and till
The earth, thy task — I 'll waft thee there
 in safety. 310
 Cain. No; I 'll stay here.
 Lucifer. How long ?
 Cain. For ever ! Since
I must one day return here from the earth,
I rather would remain; I am sick of all
That dust has shown me — let me dwell in
 shadows.
 Lucifer. It cannot be: thou now behold-
 est as
A vision that which is reality.
To make thyself fit for this dwelling, thou
Must pass through what the things thou
 seest have pass'd —
The gates of death —
 Cain. By what gate have we enter'd
Even now ?

Lucifer. By mine ! But, plighted to re-
 turn, 320
My spirit buoys thee up to breathe in
 regions
Where all is breathless save thyself. Gaze
 on;
But do not think to dwell here till thine
 hour
Is come.
 Cain. And these, too; can they ne'er
 repass
To earth again ?
 Lucifer. *Their* earth is gone for ever —
So changed by its convulsion, they would
 not
Be conscious to a single present spot
Of its new scarcely harden'd surface —
 't was —
Oh, what a beautiful world it *was !*
 Cain. And is.
It is not with the earth, though I must till
 it, 330
I feel at war, but that I may not profit
By what it bears of beautiful, untoiling,
Nor gratify my thousand swelling thoughts
With knowledge, nor allay my thousand
 fears
Of death and life.
 Lucifer. What thy world is, thou seest,
But canst not comprehend the shadow of
That which it was.
 Cain. And those enormous creatures,
Phantoms inferior in intelligence
(At least so seeming) to the things we have
 pass'd,
Resembling somewhat the wild habitants 340
Of the deep woods of earth, the hugest
 which
Roar nightly in the forest, but ten-fold
In magnitude and terror; taller than
The cherub-guarded walls of Eden, with
Eyes flashing like the fiery swords which
 fence them,
And tusks projecting like the trees stripp'd
 of
Their bark and branches — what were
 they ?
 Lucifer. That which
The Mammoth is in thy world; — but these
 lie
By myriads underneath its surface.
 Cain. But
None on it ?
 Lucifer. No; for thy frail race to
 war 350

With them would render the curse on it
 useless —
'T would be destroy'd so early.
 Cain. But why *war ?*
 Lucifer. You have forgotten the denun-
 ciation
Which drove your race from Eden — war
 with all things,
And death to all things, and disease to most
 things,
And pangs, and bitterness; these were the
 fruits
Of the forbidden tree.
 Cain. But animals —
Did they, too, eat of it, that they must die ?
 Lucifer. Your Maker told ye, *they* were
 made for you,
As you for him. You would not have their
 doom 360
Superior to your own ? Had Adam not
Fallen, all had stood.
 Cain. Alas, the hopeless wretches !
They too must share my sire's fate, like his
 sons;
Like them, too, without having shared the
 apple;
Like them, too, without the so dear-bought
 knowledge !
It was a lying tree — for we *know* no-
 thing.
At least it *promised knowledge* at the *price*
Of death — but *knowledge* still: but what
 knows man ?
 Lucifer. It may be death leads to the
 highest knowledge;
And being of all things the sole thing cer-
 tain, 370
At least leads to the *surest* science: there-
 fore
The tree was true, though deadly.
 Cain. These dim realms !
I see them, but I know them not.
 Lucifer. Because
Thy hour is yet afar, and matter cannot
Comprehend spirit wholly — but 't is some-
 thing
To know there are such realms.
 Cain. We knew already
That there was death.
 Lucifer. But not what was beyond it.
 Cain. Nor know I now.
 Lucifer. Thou knowest that there is
A state, and many states beyond thine
 own —
And this thou knewest not this morn.

Cain. But all ₃₈₀
Seems dim and shadowy.
 Lucifer. Be content; it will
Seem clearer to thine immortality.
 Cain. And yon immeasurable liquid space
Of glorious azure which floats on beyond us,
Which looks like water, and which I should
 deem
The river which flows out of Paradise
Past my own dwelling, but that it is bank-
 less
And boundless, and of an ethereal hue —
What is it?
 Lucifer. There is still some such on earth,
Although inferior, and thy children shall ₃₉₀
Dwell near it — 't is the phantasm of an
 ocean.
 Cain. 'T is like another world; a liquid
 sun —
And those inordinate creatures sporting o'er
Its shining surface?
 Lucifer. Are its habitants,
The past leviathans.
 Cain. And yon immense
Serpent, which rears his dripping mane and
 vasty
Head ten times higher than the haughtiest
 cedar
Forth from the abyss, looking as he could
 coil
Himself around the orbs we lately look'd
 on —
Is he not of the kind which bask'd be-
 neath ₄₀₀
The tree in Eden?
 Lucifer. Eve, thy mother, best
Can tell what shape of serpent tempted her.
 Cain. This seems too terrible. No doubt
 the other
Had more of beauty.
 Lucifer. Hast thou ne'er beheld him?
 Cain. Many of the same kind (at least
 so call'd),
But never that precisely which persuaded
The fatal fruit, nor even of the same aspect.
 Lucifer. Your father saw him not?
 Cain. No; 't was my mother
Who tempted him — she tempted by the
 serpent.
 Lucifer. Good man, whene'er thy wife, or
 thy sons' wives, ₄₁₀
Tempt thee or them to aught that 's new or
 strange,
Be sure thou seest first who hath tempted
 them.

 Cain. Thy precept comes too late: there
 is no more
For serpents to tempt woman to.
 Lucifer. But there
Are some things still which woman may
 tempt man to,
And man tempt woman: — let thy sons
 look to it!
My counsel is a kind one; for 't is even
Given chiefly at my own expense: 't is true,
'T will not be follow'd, so there 's little lost.
 Cain. I understand not this.
 Lucifer. The happier thou —
Thy world and thou are still too young!
 Thou thinkest ₄₂₁
Thyself most wicked and unhappy: is it
Not so?
 Cain. For crime, I know not; but for
 pain,
I have felt much.
 Lucifer. First-born of the first man!
Thy present state of sin — and thou art
 evil,
Of sorrow — and thou sufferest, are both
 Eden
In all its innocence compared to what
Thou shortly may'st be; and that state again,
In its redoubled wretchedness, a Paradise
To what thy sons' sons' sons, accumulat-
 ing ₄₃₀
In generations like to dust (which they
In fact but add to), shall endure and do. —
Now let us back to earth!
 Cain. And wherefore didst thou
Lead me only to inform me this?
 Lucifer. Was not thy quest for know-
 ledge?
 Cain. Yes, as being
The road to happiness.
 Lucifer. If truth be so,
Thou hast it.
 Cain. Then my father's God did well
When he prohibited the fatal tree.
 Lucifer. But had done better in not plant-
 ing it.
But ignorance of evil doth not save ₄₄₀
From evil; it must still roll on the same,
A part of all things.
 Cain. Not of all things. No;
I 'll not believe it — for I thirst for good.
 Lucifer. And who and what doth not?
 Who covets evil
For its own bitter sake? *None*—nothing!
 't is
The leaven of all life, and lifelessness.

Cain. Within those glorious orbs which
 we beheld,
Distant, and dazzling, and innumerable,
Ere we came down into this phantom realm,
Ill cannot come: they are too beautiful. 450
 Lucifer. Thou hast seen them from afar.
 Cain. And what of that ?
Distance can but diminish glory — they,
When nearer, must be more ineffable.
 Lucifer. Approach the things of earth
 most beautiful,
And judge their beauty near.
 Cain. I have done this —
The loveliest thing I know is loveliest
 nearest.
 Lucifer. Then there must be delusion. —
 What is that,
Which being nearest to thine eyes is still
More beautiful than beauteous things
 remote ?
 Cain. My sister Adah. — All the stars of
 heaven, 460
The deep blue noon of night, lit by an orb
Which looks a spirit, or a spirit's world —
The hues of twilight — the sun's gorgeous
 coming —
His setting indescribable, which fills
My eyes with pleasant tears as I behold
Him sink, and feel my heart float softly
 with him
Along that western paradise of clouds —
The forest shade — the green bough — the
 bird's voice,
The vesper bird's which seems to sing of
 love,
And mingles with the song of cherubim, 470
As the day closes over Eden's walls; —
All these are nothing, to my eyes and heart,
Like Adah's face: I turn from earth and
 heaven
To gaze on it.
 Lucifer. 'T is fair as frail mortality,
In the first dawn and bloom of young
 creation,
And earliest embraces of earth's parents
Can make its offspring; still it is delusion.
 Cain. You think so, being not her brother.
 Lucifer. Mortal !
My brotherhood 's with those who have no
 children.
 Cain. Then thou canst have no fellowship
 with us. 480
 Lucifer. It may be that thine own shall
 be for me.
But if thou dost possess a beautiful

Being beyond all beauty in thine eyes,
Why art thou wretched ?
 Cain. Why do I exist ?
Why art *thou* wretched ? why are all things
 so ?
Ev'n he who made us must be, as the maker
Of things unhappy ! To produce destruc-
 tion
Can surely never be the task of joy,
And yet my sire says he 's omnipotent: 489
Then why is evil — he being good ? I ask'd
This question of my father; and he said,
Because this evil only was the path
To good. Strange good, that must arise
 from out
Its deadly opposite. I lately saw
A lamb stung by a reptile: the poor suckling
Lay foaming on the earth, beneath the vain
And piteous bleating of its restless dam;
My father pluck'd some herbs, and laid them
 to
The wound: and by degrees the helpless
 wretch 499
Resumed its careless life, and rose to drain
The mother's milk, who o'er it tremulous
Stood licking its reviving limbs with joy.
Behold, my son ! said Adam, how from evil
Springs good !
 Lucifer. What didst thou answer ?
 Cain. Nothing; for
He is my father; but I thought, that 't were
A better portion for the animal
Never to have been *stung at all*, than to
Purchase renewal of its little life
With agonies unutterable, though
Dispell'd by antidotes.
 Lucifer. But as thou saidst
Of all belovèd things thou lovest her 511
Who shared thy mother's milk, and giveth
 hers
Unto thy children —
 Cain. Most assuredly:
What should I be without her ?
 Lucifer. What am I ?
 Cain. Dost thou love nothing ?
 Lucifer. What does thy God love ?
 Cain. All things, my father says; but I
 confess
I see it not in their allotment here.
 Lucifer. And, therefore, thou canst not
 see if *I* love
Or no, except some vast and general pur-
 pose,
To which particular things must melt like
 snows. 520

Cain. Snows ! what are they ?

Lucifer. Be happier in not knowing
What thy remoter offspring must encounter;
But bask beneath the clime which knows no
 winter !

Cain. But dost thou not love something
 like thyself ?

Lucifer. And dost thou love *thyself ?*

Cain. Yes, but love more
What makes my feelings more endurable,
And is more than myself because I love it.

Lucifer. Thou lovest it, because 't is beau-
 tiful,
As was the apple in thy mother's eye;
And when it ceases to be so, thy love 530
Will cease, like any other appetite.

Cain. Cease to be beautiful ! how can
 that be ?

Lucifer. With time.

Cain. But time has past, and hitherto
Even Adam and my mother both are fair:
Not like fair Adah and the seraphim —
But very fair.

Lucifer. All that must pass away
In them and her.

Cain. I 'm sorry for it; but
Cannot conceive my love for her the less.
And when her beauty disappears, methinks
He who creates all beauty will lose more
Than me in seeing perish such a work. 541

Lucifer. I pity thee who lovest what must
 perish.

Cain. And I thee who lov'st nothing.

Lucifer. And thy brother —
Sits he not near thy heart ?

Cain. Why should he not ?

Lucifer. Thy father loves him well — so
 does thy God.

Cain. And so do I.

Lucifer. 'T is well and meekly done.

Cain. Meekly !

Lucifer. He is the second born of flesh,
And is his mother's favourite.

Cain. Let him keep
Her favour, since the serpent was the first
To win it.

Lucifer. And his father's ?

Cain. What is that 550
To me ? should I not love that which all love ?

Lucifer. And the Jehovah — the indul-
 gent Lord
And bounteous planter of barr'd Paradise —
He, too, looks smilingly on Abel.

Cain. I
Ne'er saw him, and I know not if he smiles.

Lucifer. But you have seen his angels.

Cain. Rarely.

Lucifer. But
Sufficiently to see they love your brother:
His sacrifices are acceptable.

Cain. So be they ! wherefore speak to me
 of this ?

Lucifer. Because thou hast thought of this
 ere now.

Cain. And if 560
I *have* thought, why recall a thought that —
 (*he pauses, as agitated*) — Spirit !
Here we are in *thy* world; speak not of *mine.*
Thou hast shown me wonders; thou hast
 shown me those
Mighty pre-Adamites who walk'd the earth
Of which ours is the wreck; thou hast
 pointed out
Myriads of starry worlds, of which our
 own
Is the dim and remote companion, in
Infinity of life; thou hast shown me shadows
Of that existence with the dreaded name
Which my sire brought us — Death; thou
 hast shown me much — 570
But not all : show me where Jehovah
 dwells,
In his especial Paradise, — or *thine :*
Where is it ?

Lucifer. *Here,* and o'er all space.

Cain. But ye
Have some allotted dwelling — as all things:
Clay has its earth, and other worlds their
 tenants;
All temporary breathing creatures their
Peculiar element; and things which have
Long ceased to breathe *our* breath, have
 theirs, thou say'st;
And the Jehovah and thyself have thine —
Ye do not dwell together ?

Lucifer. No, we reign 580
Together; but our dwellings are asunder.

Cain. Would there were only one of ye !
 perchance
An unity of purpose might make union
In elements which seem now jarr'd in
 storms.
How came ye, being spirits wise and infi-
 nite,
To separate ? Are ye not as brethren in
Your essence, and your nature, and your
 glory ?

Lucifer. Art thou not Abel's brother ?

Cain. We are brethren,
And so we shall remain; but were it not so,

Is spirit like to flesh ? can it fall out — 590
Infinity with Immortality ?
Jarring and turning space to misery —
For what ?
 Lucifer. To reign.
 Cain. Did ye not tell me that
Ye are both eternal ?
 Lucifer. Yea !
 Cain. And what I have seen,
Yon blue immensity, is boundless ?
 Lucifer. Ay.
 Cain. And cannot ye both *reign* then ? —
 is there not
Enough ? — why should ye differ ?
 Lucifer. We *both* reign.
 Cain. But one of you makes evil.
 Lucifer. Which ?
 Cain. Thou ! for
If thou canst do man good, why dost thou
 not ?
 Lucifer. And why not he who made ? *I*
 made ye not; 600
Ye are *his* creatures, and not mine.
 Cain. Then leave us
His creatures, as thou say'st we are, or
 show me
Thy dwelling, or *his* dwelling.
 Lucifer. I could show thee
Both; but the time will come thou shalt see
 one
Of them for evermore.
 Cain. And why not now ?
 Lucifer. Thy human mind hath scarcely
 grasp to gather
The little I have shown thee into calm
And clear thought; and *thou* wouldst go on
 aspiring
To the great double Mysteries ! the *two*
 Principles !
And gaze upon them on their secret thrones !
Dust ! limit thy ambition; for to see 611
Either of these, would be for thee to per-
 ish !
 Cain. And let me perish, so I see them !
 Lucifer. There
The son of her who snatch'd the apple
 spake !
But thou wouldst only perish, and not see
 them;
That sight is for the other state.
 Cain. Of death ?
 Lucifer. That is the prelude.
 Cain. Then I dread it less,
Now that I know it leads to something def-
 inite.

 Lucifer. And now I will convey thee to
 thy world,
Where thou shalt multiply the race of
 Adam, 620
Eat, drink, toil, tremble, laugh, weep, sleep,
 and die.
 Cain. And to what end have I beheld
 these things
Which thou hast shown me ?
 Lucifer. Didst thou not require
Knowledge ? And have I not, in what I
 show'd,
Taught thee to know thyself ?
 Cain. Alas ! I seem
Nothing
 Lucifer. And this should be the human
 sum
Of knowledge, to know mortal nature's
 nothingness:
Bequeath that science to thy children, and
'T will spare them many tortures.
 Cain. Haughty spirit !
Thou speak'st it proudly; but thyself,
 though proud, 630
Hast a superior.
 Lucifer. No ! by Heaven, which He
Holds, and the abyss, and the immensity
Of worlds and life, which I hold with him —
 No !
I have a victor — true; but no superior.
Homage he has from all — but none from
 me:
I battle it against him, as I battled
In highest heaven. Through all eternity,
And the unfathomable gulfs of Hades,
And the interminable realms of space,
And the infinity of endless ages, 640
All, all, will I dispute ! And world by
 world,
And star by star, and universe by uni-
 verse,
Shall tremble in the balance, till the great
Conflict shall cease, if ever it shall cease,
Which it ne'er shall, till he or I be
 quench'd !
And what can quench our immortality,
Or mutual and irrevocable hate ?
He as a conqueror will call the conquer'd
Evil ; but what will be the *good* he gives ?
Were I the victor, *his* works would be
 deem'd 650
The only evil ones. And you, ye new
And scarce-born mortals, what have been
 his gifts
To you already, in your little world ?

Cain. But few ! and some of those but
bitter.
Lucifer. Back
With me, then, to thine earth, and try the
rest
Of his celestial boons to you and yours.
Evil and good are things in their own es-
sence,
And not made good or evil by the giver ;
But if he gives you good — so call him : if
Evil springs from *him*, do not name it *mine*,
Till ye know better its true fount ; and
judge 661
Not by words, though of spirits, but the
fruits
Of your existence, such as it must be.
One good gift has the fatal apple given —
Your *reason :* — let it not be over-sway'd
By tyrannous threats to force you into faith
'Gainst all external sense and inward feel-
ing :
Think and endure, and form an inner
world
In your own bosom — where the outward
fails ;
So shall you nearer be the spiritual 670
Nature, and war triumphant with your own.
 [*They disappear.*

ACT III

Scene I

The Earth near Eden, as in Act I.

Enter Cain *and* Adah.

Adah. Hush ! tread softly, Cain.
Cain. I will ; but wherefore ?
Adah. Our little Enoch sleeps upon yon
bed
Of leaves, beneath the cypress.
Cain. Cypress ! 't is
A gloomy tree, which looks as if it mourn'd
O'er what it shadows ; wherefore didst thou
choose it
For our child's canopy ?
Adah. Because its branches
Shut out the sun like night, and therefore
seem'd
Fitting to shadow slumber.
Cain. Ay, the last —
And longest ; but no matter — lead me to
him. [*They go up to the child.*
How lovely he appears ! his little cheeks,
In their pure incarnation, vying with 11
The rose leaves strewn beneath them.

Adah. And his lips, too,
How beautifully parted ! No ; you shall not
Kiss him, at least not now : he will awake
soon,
His hour of mid-day rest is nearly over ;
But it were pity to disturb him till
'T is closed.
Cain. You have said well ; I will contain
My heart till then. He smiles and sleeps !
— Sleep on
And smile, thou little, young inheritor
Of a world scarce less young : sleep on, and
smile ! 20
Thine are the hours and days when both
are cheering
And innocent ! *thou* hast not pluck'd the
fruit —
Thou know'st not that thou art naked !
Must the time
Come thou shalt be amerced for sins un-
known,
Which were not thine nor mine ? But now
sleep on !
His cheeks are reddening into deeper smiles,
And shining lids are trembling o'er his long
Lashes, dark as the cypress which waves
o'er them ;
Half open, from beneath them the clear
blue
Laughs out, although in slumber. He must
dream — 30
Of what ? Of Paradise ! — Ay ! dream
of it,
My disinherited boy ! 'T is but a dream ;
For never more thyself, thy sons, nor
fathers,
Shall walk in that forbidden place of joy !
Adah. Dear Cain ! Nay, do not whisper
o'er our son
Such melancholy yearnings o'er the past :
Why wilt thou always mourn for Paradise ?
Can we not make another ?
Cain. Where ?
Adah. Here, or
Where'er thou wilt : where'er thou art, I
feel not
The want of this so much regretted Eden.
Have I not thee, our boy, our sire, and
brother, 41
And Zillah — our sweet sister, and our Eve,
To whom we owe so much besides our birth ?
Cain. Yes — death, too, is amongst the
debts we owe her.
Adah. Cain ! that proud spirit who with-
drew thee hence,

Hath sadden'd thine still deeper. I had
 hoped
The promised wonders which thou hast
 beheld,
Visions, thou say'st, of past and present
 worlds,
Would have composed thy mind into the
 calm
Of a contented knowledge; but I see 50
Thy guide hath done thee evil: still I thank
 him,
And can forgive him all, that he so soon
Hath given thee back to us.
 Cain. So soon ?
 Adah. 'T is scarcely
Two hours since ye departed: two *long*
 hours
To *me*, but only *hours* upon the sun.
 Cain. And yet I have approach'd that
 sun, and seen
Worlds which he once shone on, and never
 more
Shall light; and worlds he never lit:
 methought
Years had roll'd o'er my absence.
 Adah. Hardly hours.
 Cain. The mind then hath capacity of
 time 60
And measures it by that which it beholds,
Pleasing or painful, little or almighty.
I had beheld the immemorial works
Of endless beings; skirr'd extinguish'd
 worlds;
And, gazing on eternity, methought
I had borrow'd more by a few drops of ages
From its immensity; but now I feel
My littleness again. Well said the spirit,
That I was nothing !
 Adah. Wherefore said he so ?
Jehovah said not that.
 Cain. No; *he* contents him 70
With making us the *nothing* which we are;
And after flattering dust with glimpses of
Eden and Immortality, resolves
It back to dust again — for what ?
 Adah. Thou know'st —
Even for our parents' error.
 Cain. What is that
To us ? they sinn'd, then *let them* die !
 Adah. Thou hast not spoken well, nor is
 that thought
Thy own, but of the spirit who was with
 thee.
Would *I* could die for them, so *they* might
 live !

 Cain. Why, so say I — provided that one
 victim 80
Might satiate the insatiable of life,
And that our little rosy sleeper there
Might never taste of death nor human sor-
 row,
Nor hand it down to those who spring from
 him.
 Adah. How know we that some such
 atonement one day
May not redeem our race ?
 Cain. By sacrificing
The harmless for the guilty ? what atone-
 ment
Were there ? Why, *we* are innocent: what
 have we
Done, that we must be victims for a deed
Before our birth, or need have victims to 90
Atone for this mysterious, nameless sin —
If it be such a sin to seek for knowledge ?
 Adah. Alas ! thou sinnest now, my Cain:
 thy words
Sound impious in mine ears.
 Cain. Then leave me !
 Adah. Never,
Though thy God left thee.
 Cain. Say, what have we here ?
 Adah. Two altars, which our brother Abel
 made
During thine absence, whereupon to offer
A sacrifice to God on thy return.
 Cain. And how knew *he*, that *I* would be
 so ready
With the burnt offerings, which he daily
 brings 100
With a meek brow, whose base humility
Shows more of fear than worship, as a bribe
To the Creator ?
 Adah. Surely, 't is well done.
 Cain. One altar may suffice; *I* have no
 offering.
 Adah. The fruits of the earth, the early,
 beautiful
Blossom and bud, and bloom of flowers and
 fruits,
These are a goodly offering to the Lord,
Given with a gentle and a contrite spirit.
 Cain. I have toil'd, and till'd, and sweaten
 in the sun 109
According to the curse: — must I do more ?
For what should I be gentle ? for a war
With all the elements ere they will yield
The bread we eat ? For what must I be
 grateful ?
For being dust, and grovelling in the dust,

Till I return to dust ? If I am nothing —
For nothing shall I be an hypocrite,
And seem well-pleased with pain ? For
 what should I
Be contrite ? for my father's sin, already
Expiate with what we all have undergone,
And to be more than expiated by 120
The ages prophesied, upon our seed.
Little deems our young blooming sleeper
 there,
The germs of an eternal misery
To myriads is within him ! better 't were
I snatch'd him in his sleep, and dash'd him
 'gainst
The rocks, than let him live to —
 Adah. Oh, my God !
Touch not the child — my child ! *thy* child !
 Oh, Cain !
 Cain. Fear not ! for all the stars, and all
 the power
Which sways them, I would not accost yon
 infant
With ruder greeting than a father's kiss. 130
 Adah. Then, why so awful in thy speech ?
 Cain. I said,
'T were better that he ceased to live, than
 give
Life to so much of sorrow as he must
Endure, and, harder still, bequeath; but
 since
That saying jars you, let us only say —
'T were better that he never had been born.
 Adah. Oh, do not say so ! Where were
 then the joys,
The mother's joys of watching, nourish-
 ing,
And loving him ? Soft ! he awakes. Sweet
 Enoch ! [*She goes to the child.*
Oh Cain ! look on him; see how full of
 life, 140
Of strength, of bloom, of beauty, and of
 joy,
How like to me — how like to thee, when
 gentle,
For *then* we are *all* alike; is 't not so, Cain ?
Mother, and sire, and son, our features are
Reflected in each other; as they are
In the clear waters, when *they* are *gentle*,
 and
When *thou* art *gentle*. Love us, then, my
 Cain !
And love thyself for our sakes, for we love
 thee.
Look ! how he laughs and stretches out his
 arms,

And opens wide his blue eyes upon thine, 150
To hail his father; while his little form
Flutters as wing'd with joy. Talk not of
 pain !
The childless cherubs well might envy thee
The pleasures of a parent ! Bless him, Cain !
As yet he hath no words to thank thee,
 but
His heart will, and thine own too.
 Cain. Bless thee, boy !
If that a mortal blessing may avail thee,
To save thee from the serpent's curse !
 Adah. It shall.
Surely a father's blessing may avert
A reptile's subtlety.
 Cain. Of that I doubt; 160
But bless him ne'er the less.
 Adah. Our brother comes.
 Cain. Thy brother Abel.

 Enter ABEL.

 Abel. Welcome, Cain ! My brother,
The peace of God be on thee !
 Cain. Abel, hail !
 Abel. Our sister tells me that thou hast
 been wandering,
In high communion with a spirit, far
Beyond our wonted range. Was he of
 those
We have seen and spoken with, like to our
 father ?
 Cain. No.
 Abel. Why then commune with him ?
 he may be
A foe to the Most High.
 Cain. And friend to man.
Has the Most High been so — if so you
 term him ? 170
 Abel. Term him ! your words are strange
 to-day, my brother.
My sister Adah, leave us for awhile —
We mean to sacrifice.
 Adah. Farewell, my Cain;
But first embrace thy son. May his soft
 spirit,
And Abel's pious ministry, recall thee
To peace and holiness !
 [*Exit* ADAH, *with her child.*
 Abel. Where hast thou been ?
 Cain. I know not.
 Abel. Nor what thou hast seen ?
 Cain. The dead,
The immortal, the unbounded, the omnipo-
 tent,
The overpowering mysteries of space —

The innumerable worlds that were and
are —　　　　　　　　　　　　　180
A whirlwind of such overwhelming things,
Suns, moons, and earths, upon their loud-
voiced spheres
Singing in thunder round me, as have made
me
Unfit for mortal converse: leave me, Abel.
 Abel. Thine eyes are flashing with un-
natural light,
Thy cheek is flush'd with an unnatural hue,
Thy words are fraught with an unnatural
sound —
What may this mean?
 Cain.　It means — I pray thee, leave
me.
 Abel. Not till we have pray'd and sacri-
ficed together.　　　　　　　189
 Cain. Abel, I pray thee, sacrifice alone —
Jehovah loves thee well.
 Abel.　　　　　　*Both* well, I hope.
 Cain. But thee the better: I care not for
that;
Thou art fitter for his worship than I am;
Revere him, then — but let it be alone —
At least, without me.
 Abel.　　　　Brother, I should ill
Deserve the name of our great father's son,
If, as my elder, I revered thee not,
And in the worship of our God call'd not
On thee to join me, and precede me in　199
Our priesthood — 't is thy place.
 Cain.　　　　But I have ne'er
Asserted it.
 Abel.　The more my grief; I pray thee
To do so now: thy soul seems labouring in
Some strong delusion; it will calm thee.
 Cain.　　　　　　No;
Nothing can calm me more. *Calm!* say I?
Never
Knew I what calm was in the soul, although
I have seen the elements still'd. My Abel,
leave me!
Or let me leave thee to thy pious purpose.
 Abel. Neither; we must perform our task
together.
Spurn me not.
 Cain.　If it must be so — well, then,
What shall I do?
 Abel.　Choose one of those two altars.
 Cain. Choose for me: they to me are so
much turf　　　　　　　211
And stone.
 Abel.　Choose thou!
 Cain.　　I have chosen.

 Abel.　　　　　　'T is the highest,
And suits thee, as the elder. Now prepare
Thine offerings.
 Cain.　　Where are thine?
 Abel.　　　Behold them here,
The firstlings of the flock, and fat thereof —
A shepherd's humble offering.
 Cain.　　　I have no flocks;
I am a tiller of the ground, and must
Yield what it yieldeth to my toil — its
fruit:　　　　　[*He gathers fruits.*
Behold them in their various bloom and
ripeness.
 [*They dress their altars, and kindle a flame upon them.*
 Abel. My brother, as the elder, offer
first　　　　　　　　　220
Thy prayer and thanksgiving with sacrifice.
 Cain. No — I am new to this; lead thou
the way,
And I will follow — as I may.
 Abel (*kneeling*).　　Oh God!
Who made us, and who breathed the breath
of life
Within our nostrils, who hath blessèd us,
And spared, despite our father's sin, to
make
His children all lost, as they might have
been,
Had not thy justice been so temper'd with
The mercy which is thy delight as to
Accord a pardon like a Paradise　　230
Compared with our great crimes: — Sole
Lord of light!
Of good, and glory, and eternity;
Without whom all were evil, and with whom
Nothing can err, except to some good end
Of thine omnipotent benevolence —
Inscrutable, but still to be fulfill'd —
Accept from out thy humble first of shep-
herd's
First of the first-born flocks — an offering,
In itself nothing — as what offering can be
Aught unto thee? but yet accept it for　240
The thanksgiving of him who spreads it in
The face of thy high heaven, bowing his
own
Even to the dust, of which he is, in honour
Of thee, and of thy name, for evermore!
 Cain (*standing erect during this speech*).
 　Spirit! whate'er or whosoe'er thou
art,
Omnipotent, it may be — and, if good,
Shown in the exemption of thy deeds from
evil;
Jehovah upon earth! and God in heaven!

And it may be with other names, because
Thine attributes seem many, as thy works —
If thou must be propitiated with prayers, 251
Take them ! If thou must be induced with
 altars,
And soften'd with a sacrifice, receive them !
Two beings here erect them unto thee.
If thou lov'st blood, the shepherd's shrine,
 which smokes
On my right hand, hath shed it for thy ser-
 vice
In the first of his flock whose limbs now
 reek
In sanguinary incense to thy skies;
Or if the sweet and blooming fruits of earth
And milder seasons, which the unstain'd
 turf 260
I spread them on now offers in the face
Of the broad sun which ripen'd them, may
 seem
Good to thee, inasmuch as they have not
Suffer'd in limb or life, and rather form
A sample of thy works than supplication
To look on ours ! If a shrine without vic-
 tim,
And altar without gore, may win thy favour,
Look on it ! and for him who dresseth it,
He is — such as thou mad'st him; and seeks
 nothing
Which must be won by kneeling; if he's
 evil, 270
Strike him ! thou art omnipotent and
 may'st —
For what can he oppose ? If he be good,
Strike him, or spare him, as thou wilt ! since
 all
Rests upon thee; and good and evil seem
To have no power themselves, save in thy
 will;
And whether that be good or ill I know
 not,
Not being omnipotent, nor fit to judge
Omnipotence, but merely to endure
Its mandate; which thus far I have endured.

[*The fire upon the altar of* ABEL *kindles into a column
 of the brightest flame, and ascends to heaven; while a
 whirlwind throws down the altar of* CAIN, *and scatters
 the fruits abroad upon the earth.*

Abel (*kneeling*). Oh, brother, pray ! Je-
 hovah's wroth with thee. 280
Cain. Why so ?
Abel. Thy fruits are scatter'd on the
 earth.
Cain. From earth they came, to earth
 let them return;

Their seed will bear fresh fruit there ere
 the summer:
Thy burnt flesh-off'ring prospers better; see
How heav'n licks up the flames when thick
 with blood !
Abel. Think not upon my offering's ac-
 ceptance,
But make another of thine own before
It is too late.
Cain. I will build no more altars,
Nor suffer any.
Abel (*rising*). Cain ! what meanest thou ?
Cain. To cast down yon vile flatt'rer of
 the clouds, 290
The smoky harbinger of thy dull pray'rs —
Thine altar, with its blood of lambs and
 kids,
Which fed on milk, to be destroy'd in blood.
Abel (*opposing him*). Thou shalt not: —
 add not impious works to impious
Words ! let that altar stand — 't is hallow'd
 now
By the immortal pleasure of Jehovah,
In his acceptance of the victims.
Cain. His !
His pleasure ! what was his high pleasure
 in
The fumes of scorching flesh and smoking
 blood,
To the pain of the bleating mothers
 which 300
Still yearn for their dead offspring ? or the
 pangs
Of the sad ignorant victims underneath
Thy pious knife ? Give way ! this bloody
 record
Shall not stand in the sun, to shame crea-
 tion !
Abel. Brother, give back ! thou shalt not
 touch my altar
With violence: if that thou wilt adopt it,
To try another sacrifice, 't is thine.
Cain. Another sacrifice ! Give way, or
 else
That sacrifice may be —
Abel. What mean'st thou ?
Cain. Give —
Give way ! — thy God loves blood ! — then
 look to it: 310
Give way, ere he hath *more !*
Abel. In *his* great name,
I stand between thee and the shrine which
 hath
Had his acceptance.
Cain. If thou lov'st thyself,

Stand back till I have strew'd this turf
 along
Its native soil: — else —
 Abel (opposing him). I love God far more
Than life.
 *Cain (striking him with a brand, on the
 temples, which he snatches from the
 altar).* Then take thy life unto thy
 God,
Since he loves lives.
 Abel (falls). What hast thou done, my
 brother?
 Cain. Brother!
 Abel. Oh, God! receive thy servant, and
Forgive his slayer, for he knew not what
He did — Cain, give me — give me thy
 hand; and tell 320
Poor Zillah —
 Cain (after a moment's stupefaction). My
 hand! 't is all red, and with —
What? [*A long pause. — Looking slowly round.*
 Where am I? alone! Where's Abel?
 where
Cain? Can it be that I am he? My brother,
Awake! — why liest thou so on the green
 earth?
'T is not the hour of slumber: — why so pale?
What hast thou! — thou wert full of life
 this morn!
Abel! I pray thee, mock me not! I smote
Too fiercely, but not fatally. Ah, why
Wouldst thou oppose me? This is mockery;
And only done to daunt me: — 't was a
 blow — 330
And but a blow. Stir — stir — nay, only
 stir!
Why, so — that's well — thou breath'st!
 breathe upon me!
Oh God! Oh God!
 Abel (very faintly). What's he who
 speaks of God?
 Cain. Thy murderer.
 Abel. Then may God forgive him! Cain,
Comfort poor Zillah: — she has but one
 brother
Now. [*Abel dies.*
 Cain. And I none! — Who makes me
 brotherless?
His eyes are open! then he is not dead!
Death is like sleep, and sleep shuts down
 our lids.
His lips, too, are apart; why then he
 breathes!
And yet I feel it not. — His heart! his
 heart! 340

Let me see, doth it beat? methinks — No!
 — no!
This is a vision, else I am become
The native of another and worse world.
The earth swims round me: — what is this?
 — 't is wet;
 [*Puts his hand to his brow, and then looks at it.*
And yet there are no dews! 'T is blood —
 my blood —
My brother's and my own, and shed by me!
Then what have I further to do with life,
Since I have taken life from my own flesh?
But he cannot be dead! — Is silence
 death?
No; he will wake; then let me watch by
 him. 350
Life cannot be so slight, as to be quench'd
Thus quickly! — he hath spoken to me
 since —
What shall I say to him? — My brother!
 No:
He will not answer to that name; for
 brethren
Smite not each other. Yet — yet — speak
 to me.
Oh, for a word more of that gentle voice,
That I may bear to hear my own again!

 Enter ZILLAH.

 Zillah. I heard a heavy sound; what can
 it be?
'T is Cain; and watching by my husband.
 What
Dost thou there, brother? Doth he sleep?
 Oh, heav'n! 360
What means this paleness, and yon stream?
 — No, no!
It is not blood; for who would shed his
 blood?
Abel! what's this? — who hath done this?
 He moves not;
He breathes not; and his hands drop down
 from mine
With stony lifelessness! Ah, cruel Cain!
Why cam'st thou not in time to save him
 from
This violence? Whatever hath assail'd
 him,
Thou wert the stronger, and shouldst have
 stepp'd in
Between him and aggression! Father! —
 Eve! —
Adah! — come hither! Death is in the
 world! 370
 [*Exit* ZILLAH, *calling on her Parents, etc.*

Cain (solus). And who hath brought him
 there ? — I — who abhor
The name of Death so deeply, that the
 thought
Empoison'd all my life before I knew
His aspect — I have led him here, and giv'n
My brother to his cold and still embrace,
As if he would not have asserted his
Inexorable claim without my aid.
I am awake at last — a dreary dream
Had madden'd me; — but *he* shall ne'er
 awake !

 Enter ADAM, EVE, ADAH, *and* ZILLAH.

Adam. A voice of woe from Zillah brings
 me here. 380
What do I see ? — 'T is true ! — My son !
 my son !
Woman, behold the serpent's work, and
 thine ! [*To* EVE.
Eve. Oh ! speak not of it now; the ser-
 pent's fangs
Are in my heart. My best beloved, Abel !
Jehovah ! this is punishment beyond
A mother's sin, to take *him* from me !
Adam. Who,
Or what hath done this deed ? — speak,
 Cain, since thou
Wert present; was it some more hostile
 angel,
Who walks not with Jehovah? or some wild
Brute of the forest ?
Eve. Ah ! a livid light 390
Breaks through, as from a thunder-cloud !
Massy and bloody ! snatch'd from off the
 altar,
And black with smoke, and red with —
Adam. Speak, my son !
Speak, and assure us, wretched as we are,
That we are not more miserable still.
Adah. Speak, Cain ! and say it was not
 thou !
Eve. It was,
I see it now — he hangs his guilty head,
And covers his ferocious eye with hands
Incarnadine.
Adah. Mother, thou dost him wrong —
Cain ! clear thee from this horrible ac-
 cusal, 400
Which grief wrings from our parent.
Eve. Hear, Jehovah !
May the eternal serpent's curse be on him !
For he was fitter for his seed than ours.
May all his days be desolate ! May —

Adah. Hold !
Curse him not, mother, for he is thy son —
Curse him not, mother, for he is my bro-
 ther,
And my betroth'd.
Eve. He hath left thee no brother —
Zillah no husband — me *no son !* — for thus
I curse him from my sight for evermore !
All bonds I break between us, as he broke
That of his nature, in yon — Oh death !
 death ! 411
Why didst thou not take *me*, who first in-
 curr'd thee ?
Why dost thou not so now ?
Adam. Eve ! let not this,
Thy natural grief, lead to impiety !
A heavy doom was long forespoken to us;
And now that it begins, let it be borne
In such sort as may show our God that we
Are faithful servants to his holy will.
Eve (pointing to Cain). His will ! the
 will of yon incarnate spirit
Of death, whom I have brought upon the
 earth 420
To strew it with the dead. May all the
 curses
Of life be on him ! and his agonies
Drive him forth o'er the wilderness, like
 us
From Eden, till his children do by him
As he did by his brother ! May the swords
And wings of fiery cherubim pursue him
By day and night — snakes spring up in his
 path —
Earth's fruits be ashes in his mouth — the
 leaves
On which he lays his head to sleep be
 strew'd
With scorpions ! May his dreams be of his
 victim ! 430
His waking a continual dread of death !
May the clear rivers turn to blood as he
Stoops down to stain them with his raging
 lip !
May every element shun or change to
 him !
May he live in the pangs which others die
 with !
And death itself wax something worse than
 death
To him who first acquainted him with man !
Hence, fratricide ! henceforth that word is
 Cain,
Through all the coming myriads of man-
 kind,

Who shall abhor thee though thou wert
 their sire ! 440
May the grass wither from thy feet ! the
 woods
Deny thee shelter ! earth a home ! the dust
A grave ! the sun his light ! and heaven her
 God ! [*Exit* EVE.
 Adam. Cain ! get thee forth: we dwell
 no more together.
Depart and leave the dead to me — I am
Henceforth alone — we never must meet
 more.
 Adah. Oh, part not with him thus, my
 father: do not
Add thy deep curse to Eve's upon his head !
 Adam. I curse him not: his spirit be his
 curse.
Come, Zillah !
 Zillah. I must watch my husband's
 corse. 450
 Adam. We will return again, when he is
 gone
Who hath provided for us this dread office.
Come, Zillah !
 Zillah. Yet one kiss on yon pale clay,
And those lips once so warm — my heart !
 my heart !
 [*Exeunt* ADAM *and* ZILLAH, *weeping.*
 Adah. Cain ! thou hast heard, we must
 go forth. I am ready,
So shall our children be. I will bear Enoch,
And you his sister. Ere the sun declines
Let us depart, nor walk the wilderness
Under the cloud of night. — Nay, speak to
 me,
To *me — thine own.*
 Cain. Leave me !
 Adah. Why, all have left thee.
 Cain. And wherefore lingerest thou ?
 Dost thou not fear 461
To dwell with one who hath done this ?
 Adah. I fear
Nothing except to leave thee, much as I
Shrink from the deed which leaves thee
 brotherless.
I must not speak of this — it is between
 thee
And the great God.
 A Voice from within exclaims, Cain ! Cain !
 Adah. Hear'st thou that voice ?
 The Voice within. Cain ! Cain !
 Adah. It soundeth like an angel's tone.

 Enter the ANGEL *of the Lord.*

 Angel. Where is thy brother Abel ?

 Cain. Am I then
My brother's keeper ?
 Angel. Cain ! what hast thou done ?
The voice of thy slain brother's blood cries
 out, 470
Even from the ground, unto the Lord ! —
 Now art thou
Cursed from the earth, which open'd late
 her mouth
To drink thy brother's blood from thy rash
 hand.
Henceforth, when thou shalt till the ground,
 it shall not
Yield thee her strength; a fugitive shalt
 thou
Be from this day, and vagabond on earth !
 Adah. This punishment is more than he
 can bear.
Behold, thou drivest him from the face of
 earth,
And from the face of God shall he be hid.
A fugitive and vagabond on earth, 480
'T will come to pass, that whoso findeth him
Shall slay him.
 Cain. Would they could ! but
 who are they
Shall slay me ? Where are these on the
 lone earth
As yet unpeopled ?
 Angel. Thou hast slain thy brother,
And who shall warrant thee against thy
 son ?
 Adah. Angel of Light ! be merciful, nor
 say
That this poor aching breast now nour-
 ishes
A murderer in my boy, and of his father.
 Angel. Then he would but be what his
 father is.
Did not the milk of Eve give nutriment 490
To him thou now see'st so besmear'd with
 blood ?
The fratricide might well engender parri-
 cides. —
But it shall not be so — the Lord thy God
And mine commandeth me to set his seal
On Cain, so that he may go forth in safety.
Who slayeth Cain, a sevenfold vengeance
 shall
Be taken on his head. Come hither !
 Cain. What
Wouldst thou with me ?
 Angel. To mark upon thy brow
Exemption from such deeds as thou hast
 done.

Cain. No, let me die!

Angel. It must not be.

[*The* ANGEL *sets the mark on* CAIN's *brow.*

Cain. It burns
My brow, but nought to that which is within
 it. 501
Is there more? let me meet it as I may.

Angel. Stern hast thou been and stubborn
 from the womb,
As the ground thou must henceforth till;
 but he
Thou slew'st was gentle as the flocks he
 tended.

Cain. After the fall too soon was I be-
 gotten;
Ere yet my mother's mind subsided from
The serpent, and my sire still mourn'd for
 Eden.
That which I am, I am; I did not seek
For life, nor did I make myself; but could I
With my own death redeem him from the
 dust — 511
And why not so? let him return to-day,
And I lie ghastly! so shall be restored
By God the life to him he loved; and taken
From me a being I ne'er loved to bear.

Angel. Who shall heal murder? what is
 done is done;
Go forth! fulfil thy days! and be thy deeds
Unlike the last! [*The* ANGEL *disappears.*

Adah. He's gone, let us go forth;
I hear our little Enoch cry within
Our bower.

Cain. Ah, little knows he what he weeps
 for! 520
And I who have shed blood cannot shed
 tears!
But the four rivers would not cleanse my
 soul.
Think'st thou my boy will bear to look on
 me?

Adah. If I thought that he would not, I
 would —

Cain (*interrupting her*). No,
No more of threats: we have had too many
 of them:
Go to our children; I will follow thee.

Adah. I will not leave thee lonely with
 the dead;
Let us depart together.

Cain. Oh, thou dead ·
And everlasting witness! whose unsinking
Blood darkens earth and heaven! what thou
 now art 530
I know not! but if *thou* see'st what *I* am,

I think thou wilt forgive him, whom his
 God
Can ne'er forgive, nor his own soul. — Fare-
 well!
I must not, dare not touch what I have made
 thee.
I, who sprung from the same womb with
 thee, drain'd
The same breast, clasp'd thee often to my
 own,
In fondness brotherly and boyish, I
Can never meet thee more, nor even dare
To do that for thee, which thou shouldst
 have done
For me — compose thy limbs into their
 grave — 540
The first grave yet dug for mortality.
But who hath dug that grave? Oh, earth!
 Oh, earth!
For all the fruits thou hast render'd to me, I
Give thee back this. — Now for the wilder-
 ness.

[ADAH *stoops down and kisses the body of* ABEL.

Adah. A dreary, and an early doom, my
 brother,
Has been thy lot! Of all who mourn for
 thee,
I alone must not weep. My office is
Henceforth to dry up tears, and not to shed
 them:
But yet, of all who mourn, none mourn like
 me,
Not only for thyself, but him who slew
 thee. 550
Now, Cain! I will divide thy burden with
 thee.

Cain. Eastward from Eden will we take
 our way;
'T is the most desolate, and suits my steps.

Adah. Lead! thou shalt be my guide, and
 may our God
Be thine! Now let us carry forth our chil-
 dren.

Cain. And *he* who lieth there was child-
 less. I
Have dried the fountain of a gentle race,
Which might have graced his recent mar-
 riage couch,
And might have temper'd this stern blood
 of mine, 559
Uniting with our children Abel's offspring!
O Abel!

Adah. Peace be with him!

Cain. But with *me*! —

[*Exeunt.*

DON JUAN

[The composition of *Don Juan* began in the autumn of 1818 and extended, with intermissions, until a few months before Byron's death. The fragment of the seventeenth Canto, which is here reproduced from the new Murray edition, was actually carried with him to Greece. The dates of composition and publication are as follows : Canto I. was written in September, 1818; Canto II. in December, 1818, and January, 1819; Cantos I. and II. were published July 15, 1819; Cantos III. and IV. were written in the following winter; Canto V. in October and November of 1820; Cantos III., IV., and V. were published August 8, 1821; Cantos VI. to XVI. were written between June, 1822, and March, 1823; Cantos VI., VII., VIII. were published July 15, 1823; Cantos IX., X., XI., August 29, 1823; Cantos XII., XIII., XIV., December 17, 1823; Cantos XV., XVI., March 26, 1824. The first five cantos were issued by Murray without name of either author or publisher — and wisely, for the storm of obloquy roused by their mingled voluptuousness and scepticism was tremendous. Naturally the authorship was an open secret, for who but Byron could have written them ? The remaining cantos were prudently declined by Mr. Murray, and were finally brought out by John Hunt. — Byron shows no particular knowledge of the *Don Juan* story as treated by earlier poets, and the subject was manifestly a mere pretext in his hands for writing indiscriminately on whatever came into his mind. He speaks somewhere as intending to follow the regular epic tradition, with a picture of hell and the like; but it is hard to see how any miraculous conclusion could have been tacked on to the plot as it was progressing in the sixteenth and seventeenth cantos. Were this the proper place for such a discussion, it might be argued that *Don Juan*, in its actual form, was the only epic manner left for a poet of the nineteenth century to adopt with power of conviction. In one sense *Don Juan* is a satire, to many critics the greatest satire ever written; but it is something still more than that. It is the epic of modern life.]

Difficile est proprie communia dicere. — Hor.

' Dost thou think, because thou art virtuous,
there shall be no more cakes and ale ? — Yes,
by Saint Anne, and ginger shall be hot i' the
mouth, too ! ' — Shakspeare, *Twelfth Night,
or What You Will.*

FRAGMENT

On the back of the Poet's MS. of Canto I

I would to heaven that I were so much clay,
 As I am blood, bone, marrow, passion, feeling —
Because at least the past were pass'd away —
 And for the future — (but I write this reeling,
Having got drunk exceedingly to-day,
 So that I seem to stand upon the ceiling)
I say — the future is a serious matter —
And so — for God's sake — hock and soda-water !

DEDICATION

I

Bob Southey ! You 're a poet — Poet-
 laureate,
 And representative of all the race,
Although 't is true that you turn'd out a
 Tory at
 Last, — yours has lately been a common
 case ;
And now, my Epic Renegade ! what are ye
 at ?
 With all the Lakers, in and out of place ?
A nest of tuneful persons, to my eye
Like ' four and twenty Blackbirds in a pye ; '

II

' Which pye being open'd they began to
 sing '
 (This old song and new simile holds
 good), 10
' A dainty dish to set before the King,'
 Or Regent, who admires such kind of
 food ; —
And Coleridge, too, has lately taken wing,
 But like a hawk encumber'd with his
 hood, —
Explaining metaphysics to the nation —
I wish he would explain his Explanation.

III

You, Bob ! are rather insolent, you know,
 At being disappointed in your wish
To supersede all warblers here below,
 And be the only Blackbird in the dish ;
And then you overstrain yourself, or so, 21
 And tumble downward like the flying
 fish

Gasping on deck, because you soar too high,
 Bob,
And fall, for lack of moisture, quite a-dry,
 Bob !

IV

And Wordsworth, in a rather long *Excur-
 sion*
 (I think the quarto holds five hundred
 pages),
Has given a sample from the vasty version
 Of his new system to perplex the sages ;
'T is poetry — at least by his assertion,
 And may appear so when the dog-star
 rages — 30
And he who understands it would be able
To add a story to the Tower of Babel.

V

You — Gentlemen ! by dint of long seclu-
 sion
 From better company, have kept your
 own
At Keswick, and, through still continued
 fusion
 Of one another's minds, at last have
 grown
To deem as a most logical conclusion,
 That Poesy has wreaths for you alone :
There is a narrowness in such a notion,
Which makes me wish you 'd change your
 lakes for ocean. 40

VI

I would not imitate the petty thought,
 Nor coin my self-love to so base a vice,
For all the glory your conversion brought,
 Since gold alone should not have been its
 price.
You have your salary ; was 't for that you
 wrought ?
 And Wordsworth has his place in the
 Excise.
You 're shabby fellows — true — but poets
 still,
And duly seated on the immortal hill.

VII

Your bays may hide the baldness of your
 brows —
 Perhaps some virtuous blushes ; — let
 them go — 50
To you I envy neither fruit nor boughs —
 And for the fame you would engross
 below,

The field is universal, and allows
 Scope to all such as feel the inherent glow:
Scott, Rogers, Campbell, Moore, and
 Crabbe will try
'Gainst you the question with posterity.

VIII

For me, who, wandering with pedestrian
 Muses,
 Contend not with you on the wingèd
 steed,
I wish your fate may yield ye, when she
 chooses,
 The fame you envy and the skill you
 need; 60
And recollect a poet nothing loses
 In giving to his brethren their full meed
Of merit, and complaint of present days
Is not the certain path to future praise.

IX

He that reserves his laurels for posterity
 (Who does not often claim the bright
 reversion)
Has generally no great crop to spare it, he
 Being only injured by his own assertion;
And although here and there some glorious
 rarity
 Arise like Titan from the sea's immer-
 sion, 70
The major part of such appellants go
To — God knows where — for no one else
 can know.

X

If, fallen in evil days on evil tongues,
 Milton appeal'd to the Avenger, Time,
If Time, the Avenger, execrates his wrongs,
 And makes the word 'Miltonic' mean
 'sublime,'
He deign'd not to belie his soul in songs,
 Nor turn his very talent to a crime;
He did not loathe the Sire to laud the
 Son,
But closed the tyrant-hater he begun. 80

XI

Think'st thou, could he — the blind Old
 Man — arise
 Like Samuel from the grave, to freeze
 once more
The blood of monarchs with his prophecies,
 Or be alive again — again all hoar
With time and trials, and those helpless
 eyes,

And heartless daughters — worn — and
 pale — and poor;
Would *he* adore a sultan? *he* obey
The intellectual eunuch Castlereagh?

XII

Cold-blooded, smooth-faced, placid mis-
 creant!
 Dabbling its sleek young hands in Erin's
 gore, 90
And thus for wider carnage taught to pant,
 Transferr'd to gorge upon a sister shore,
The vulgarest tool that Tyranny could
 want,
 With just enough of talent, and no
 more,
To lengthen fetters by another fix'd,
And offer poison long already mix'd.

XIII

An orator of such set trash of phrase
 Ineffably — legitimately vile,
That even its grossest flatterers dare not
 praise,
 Nor foes — all nations — condescend to
 smile, — 100
Not even a sprightly blunder's spark can
 blaze
 From that Ixion grindstone's ceaseless
 toil,
That turns and turns to give the world a
 notion
Of endless torments and perpetual motion.

XIV

A bungler even in its disgusting trade,
 And botching, patching, leaving still be-
 hind
Something of which its masters are afraid,
 States to be curb'd and thoughts to be
 confined,
Conspiracy or Congress to be made —
 Cobbling at manacles for all mankind —
A tinkering slave-maker, who mends old
 chains, 111
With God and man's abhorrence for its
 gains.

XV

If we may judge of matter by the mind,
 Emasculated to the marrow *It*
Hath but two objects, how to serve and
 bind,
 Deeming the chain it wears even men
 may fit,

Eutropius of its many masters, — blind
 To worth as freedom, wisdom as to wit,
Fearless — because *no* feeling dwells in ice,
Its very courage stagnates to a vice. 120

XVI

Where shall I turn me not to *view* its bonds,
 For I will never *feel* them ? — Italy !
Thy late reviving Roman soul desponds
 Beneath the lie this State-thing breathed
 o'er thee —
Thy clanking chain, and Erin's yet green
 wounds,
 Have voices, tongues to cry aloud for me.
Europe has slaves, allies, kings, armies
 still,
And Southey lives to sing them very ill.

XVIII

Meantime, Sir Laureate, I proceed to dedi-
 cate,
 In honest simple verse, this song to you.
And, if in flattering strains I do not predi-
 cate, 131
 'T is that I still retain my ' buff and
 blue;'
My politics as yet are all to educate:
 Apostasy 's so fashionable, too,
To keep *one* creed 's a task grown quite
 Herculean;
Is it not so, my Tory, ultra-Julian ?

VENICE, *September* 16, 1818.

CANTO THE FIRST

I

I WANT a hero : an uncommon want,
 When every year and month sends forth
 a new one,
Till, after cloying the gazettes with cant,
 The age discovers he is not the true one;
Of such as these I should not care to vaunt,
 I 'll therefore take our ancient friend
 Don Juan —
We all have seen him, in the pantomime,
Sent to the devil somewhat ere his time.

II

Vernon, the butcher Cumberland, Wolfe,
 Hawke,
 Prince Ferdinand, Granby, Burgoyne,
 Keppel, Howe, 10
Evil and good, have had their tithe of talk,
 And fill'd their sign posts then, like
 Wellesley now;

Each in their turn like Banquo's monarchs
 stalk,
 Followers of fame, ' nine farrow ' of that
 sow:
France, too, had Buonaparté and Dumou-
 rier
Recorded in the Moniteur and Courier.

III

Barnave, Brissot, Condorcet, Mirabeau,
 Petion, Clootz, Danton, Marat, La Fay-
 ette,
Were French, and famous people, as we
 know:
 And there were others, scarce forgotten
 yet, 20
Joubert, Hoche, Marceau, Lannes, Desaix,
 Moreau,
 With many of the military set,
Exceedingly remarkable at times,
But not at all adapted to my rhymes.

IV

Nelson was once Britannia's god of war,
 And still should be so, but the tide is
 turn'd;
There 's no more to be said of Trafalgar,
 'T is with our hero quietly inurn'd;
Because the army 's grown more popular, 29
 At which the naval people are concern'd;
Besides, the prince is all for the land-service,
Forgetting Duncan, Nelson, Howe, and
 Jervis.

V

Brave men were living before Agamem-
 non
 And since, exceeding valorous and sage,
A good deal like him too, though quite the
 same none;
 But then they shone not on the poet's
 page,
And so have been forgotten: — I condemn
 none,
 But can 't find any in the present age
Fit for my poem (that is, for my new one);
So, as I said, I 'll take my friend Don Juan.

VI

Most epic poets plunge ' in medias res ' 41
 (Horace makes this the heroic turn-
 pike road),
And then your hero tells, whene'er you
 please,
 What went before — by way of episode,

While seated after dinner at his ease,
 Beside his mistress in some soft abode,
Palace, or garden, paradise, or cavern,
Which serves the happy couple for a tavern.

VII

That is the usual method, but not mine —
 My way is to begin with the beginning; 50
The regularity of my design
 Forbids all wandering as the worst of
 sinning,
And therefore I shall open with a line
 (Although it cost me half an hour in spin-
 ning)
Narrating somewhat of Don Juan's father,
And also of his mother, if you 'd rather.

VIII

In Seville was he born, a pleasant city,
 Famous for oranges and women — he
Who has not seen it will be much to pity,
 So says the proverb — and I quite agree;
Of all the Spanish towns is none more
 pretty, 61
 Cadiz perhaps — but that you soon may
 see;
Don Juan's parents lived beside the river,
A noble stream, and call'd the Guadalquivir.

IX

His father's name was José — *Don*, of
 course, —
 A true Hidalgo, free from every stain
Of Moor or Hebrew blood, he traced his
 source
 Through the most Gothic gentlemen of
 Spain;
A better cavalier ne'er mounted horse,
 Or, being mounted, e'er got down again,
Than José, who begot our hero, who 71
Begot — but that 's to come — Well, to re-
 new:

X

His mother was a learned lady, famed
 For every branch of every science known
In every Christian language ever named,
 With virtues equall'd by her wit alone,
She made the cleverest people quite
 ashamed,
 And even the good with inward envy
 groan,
Finding themselves so very much exceeded
In their own way by all the things that she
 did. 80

XI

Her memory was a mine: she knew by heart
 All Calderon and greater part of Lopé,
So that if any actor miss'd his part
 She could have served him for the promp-
 ter's copy;
For her Feinagle's were an useless art,
 And he himself obliged to shut up shop
 — he
Could never make a memory so fine as
That which adorn'd the brain of Donna Inez.

XII

Her favourite science was the mathematical,
 Her noblest virtue was her magnanimity,
Her wit (she sometimes tried at wit) was
 Attic all, 91
 Her serious sayings darken'd to sublim-
 ity;
In short, in all things she was fairly what I
 call
 A prodigy — her morning dress was dim-
 ity,
Her evening silk, or, in the summer, mus-
 lin,
And other stuffs, with which I won't stay
 puzzling.

XIII

She knew the Latin — that is, 'the Lord's
 prayer,'
 And Greek — the alphabet — I 'm nearly
 sure;
She read some French romances here and
 there,
 Although her mode of speaking was not
 pure; 100
For native Spanish she had no great care,
 At least her conversation was obscure;
Her thoughts were theorems, her words a
 problem,
As if she deem'd that mystery would enno-
 ble 'em.

XIV

She liked the English and the Hebrew
 tongue,
 And said there was analogy between 'em;
She proved it somehow out of sacred song,
 But I must leave the proofs to those
 who 've seen 'em;
But this I heard her say, and can't be
 wrong,
 And all may think which way their judg-
 ments lean 'em, 110

' 'T is strange — the Hebrew noun which
 means " I am,"
The English always use to govern d—n.'

XV

Some women use their tongues — she *look'd*
 a lecture,
 Each eye a sermon, and her brow a hom-
 ily,
An all-in-all sufficient self-director,
 Like the lamented late Sir Samuel Ro-
 milly,
The Law's expounder, and the State's cor-
 rector,
 Whose suicide was almost an anomaly —
One sad example more, that ' All is van-
 ity '
(The jury brought their verdict in ' In-
 sanity '). 120

XVI

In short, she was a walking calculation,
 Miss Edgeworth's novels stepping from
 their covers,
Or Mrs. Trimmer's books on education,
 Or ' Cœlebs' Wife ' set out in quest of
 lovers,
Morality's prim personification,
 In which not Envy's self a flaw discov-
 ers;
To others' share let ' female errors fall,'
For she had not even one — the worst of all.

XVII

Oh ! she was perfect past all parallel — 129
 Of any modern female saint's comparison;
So far above the cunning powers of hell,
 Her guardian angel had given up his gar-
 rison;
Even her minutest motions went as well
 As those of the best time-piece made by
 Harrison:
In virtues nothing earthly could surpass her,
Save thine ' incomparable oil,' Macassar !

XVIII

Perfect she was, but as perfection is
 Insipid in this naughty world of ours,
Where our first parents never learn'd to kiss
 Till they were exiled from their earlier
 bowers, 140
Where all was peace, and innocence, and
 bliss
 (I wonder how they got through the
 twelve hours),

Don José, like a lineal son of Eve,
Went plucking various fruit without her
 leave.

XIX

He was a mortal of the careless kind,
 With no great love for learning, or the
 learn'd,
Who chose to go where'er he had a mind,
 And never dream'd his lady was con-
 cern'd;
The world, as usual, wickedly inclined
 To see a kingdom or a house o'erturn'd,
Whisper'd he had a mistress, some said
 two — 151
But for domestic quarrels *one* will do.

XX

Now Donna Inez had, with all her merit,
 A great opinion of her own good quali-
 ties;
Neglect, indeed, requires a saint to bear it,
 And such, indeed, she was in her morali-
 ties;
But then she had a devil of a spirit,
 And sometimes mix'd up fancies with
 realities,
And let few opportunities escape
Of getting her liege lord into a scrape. 160

XXI

This was an easy matter with a man
 Oft in the wrong, and never on his
 guard;
And even the wisest, do the best they can,
 Have moments, hours, and days, so un-
 prepared,
That you might ' brain them with their
 lady's fan;'
 And sometimes ladies hit exceeding hard,
And fans turn into falchions in fair hands,
And why and wherefore no one under-
 stands.

XXII

'T is pity learned virgins ever wed
 With persons of no sort of education, 170
Or gentlemen, who, though well born and
 bred,
 Grow tired of scientific conversation:
I don't choose to say much upon this head,
 I 'm a plain man, and in a single station,
But — Oh ! ye lords of ladies intellectual,
Inform us truly, have they not hen-peck'd
 you all ?

XXIII

Don José and his lady quarrell'd — *why*,
 Not any of the many could divine,
Though several thousand people chose to try,
 'T was surely no concern of theirs nor
 mine; 180
I loathe that low vice — curiosity;
 But if there 's anything in which I shine,
'T is in arranging all my friends' affairs,
Not having of my own domestic cares.

XXIV

And so I interfered, and with the best
 Intentions, but their treatment was not
 kind;
I think the foolish people were possess'd,
 For neither of them could I ever find,
Although their porter afterwards con-
 fess'd —
 But that 's no matter, and the worst 's
 behind, 190
For little Juan o'er me threw, down stairs,
A pail of housemaid's water unawares.

XXV

A little curly-headed, good-for-nothing,
 And mischief-making monkey from his
 birth;
His parents ne'er agreed except in doting
 Upon the most unquiet imp on earth;
Instead of quarrelling, had they been but
 both in
 Their senses, they 'd have sent young
 master forth
To school, or had him soundly whipp'd at
 home, 199
To teach him manners for the time to come.

XXVI

Don José and the Donna Inez led
 For some time an unhappy sort of life,
Wishing each other, not divorced, but dead;
 They lived respectably as man and wife,
Their conduct was exceedingly well-bred,
 And gave no outward signs of inward
 strife,
Until at length the smother'd fire broke
 out,
And put the business past all kind of doubt.

XXVII

For Inez call'd some druggists and physi-
 cians,
 And tried to prove her loving lord was
 mad ; 210

But as he had some lucid intermissions,
 She next decided he was only *bad;*
Yet when they ask'd her for her deposi-
 tions,
 No sort of explanation could be had,
Save that her duty both to man and God
Required this conduct — which seem'd very
 odd.

XXVIII

She kept a journal, where his faults were
 noted,
 And open'd certain trunks of books and
 letters,
All which might, if occasion served, be
 quoted;
 And then she had all Seville for abet-
 tors, 220
Besides her good old grandmother (who
 doted);
 The hearers of her case became re-
 peaters,
Then advocates, inquisitors, and judges,
Some for amusement, others for old
 grudges.

XXIX

And then this best and weakest woman
 bore
 With such serenity her husband's woes,
Just as the Spartan ladies did of yore,
 Who saw their spouses kill'd, and nobly
 chose
Never to say a word about them more —
 Calmly she heard each calumny that
 rose, 230
And saw *his* agonies with such sublimity,
That all the world exclaim'd, 'What mag-
 nanimity !'

XXX

No doubt this patience, when the world is
 damning us,
 Is philosophic in our former friends;
'T is also pleasant to be deem'd magnani-
 mous,
 The more so in obtaining our own
 ends;
And what the lawyers call a '*malus ani-
 mus*'
 Conduct like this by no means compre-
 hends;
Revenge in person 's certainly no virtue,
But then 't is not *my* fault, if *others* hurt
 you. 240

XXXI

And if your quarrels should rip up old
 stories,
 And help them with a lie or two addi-
 tional,
I 'm not to blame, as you well know — no
 more is
 Any one else — they were become tradi-
 tional;
Besides, their resurrection aids our glories
 By contrast, which is what we just were
 wishing all:
And science profits by this resurrection —
Dead scandals form good subjects for dis-
 section.

XXXII

Their friends had tried at reconciliation,
 Then their relations, who made matters
 worse. 250
('T were hard to tell upon a like occasion
 To whom it may be best to have re-
 course —
I can't say much for friend or yet relation):
 The lawyers did their utmost for divorce,
But scarce a fee was paid on either side
Before, unluckily, Don José died.

XXXIII

He died: and most unluckily, because,
 According to all hints I could collect
From counsel learned in those kinds of laws
 (Although their talk 's obscure and cir-
 cumspect), 260
His death contrived to spoil a charming
 cause;
 A thousand pities also with respect
To public feeling, which on this occasion
Was manifested in a great sensation.

XXXIV

But, ah ! he died; and buried with him lay
 The public feeling and the lawyers' fees:
His house was sold, his servants sent away,
 A Jew took one of his two mistresses,
A priest the other — at least so they say:
 I ask'd the doctors after his disease —
He died of the slow fever call'd the tertian,
And left his widow to her own aversion.

XXXV

Yet José was an honourable man, 273
 That I must say who knew him very well;
Therefore his frailties I 'll no further scan
 Indeed there were not many more to tell;

And if his passions now and then outran
 Discretion, and were not so peaceable
As Numa's (who was also named Pompi-
 lius),
He had been ill brought up, and was born
 bilious. 280

XXXVI

Whate'er might be his worthlessness or
 worth,
 Poor fellow ! he had many things to
 wound him.
Let 's own — since it can do no good on
 earth —
 It was a trying moment that which found
 him
Standing alone beside his desolate hearth,
 Where all his household gods lay shiv-
 er'd round him:
No choice was left his feelings or his pride,
Save death or Doctors' Commons — so he
 died.

XXXVII

Dying intestate, Juan was sole heir
 To a chancery suit, and messuages, and
 lands, 290
Which, with a long minority and care,
 Promised to turn out well in proper
 hands:
Inez became sole guardian, which was fair,
 And answer'd but to nature's just de-
 mands;
An only son left with an only mother
Is brought up much more wisely than an-
 other.

XXXVIII

Sagest of women, even of widows, she
 Resolved that Juan should be quite a
 paragon,
And worthy of the noblest pedigree
 (His sire was of Castile, his dam from
 Aragon): 300
Then for accomplishments of chivalry,
 In case our lord the king should go to
 war again,
He learn'd the arts of riding, fencing, gun-
 nery,
And how to scale a fortress — or a nunnery.

XXXIX

But that which Donna Inez most desired,
 And saw into herself each day before
 all

The learned tutors whom for him she hired,
 Was, that his breeding should be strictly
 moral:
Much into all his studies she inquired,
 And so they were submitted first to her,
 all, 310
Arts, sciences, no branch was made a mys-
 tery
To Juan's eyes, excepting natural history.

XL

The languages, especially the dead,
 The sciences, and most of all the abstruse,
The arts, at least all such as could be said
 To be the most remote from common use,
In all these he was much and deeply read;
 But not a page of any thing that 's loose,
Or hints continuation of the species,
Was ever suffer'd, lest he should grow vi-
 cious. 320

XLI

His classic studies made a little puzzle,
 Because of filthy loves of gods and god-
 desses,
Who in the earlier ages raised a bustle,
 But never put on pantaloons or bodices;
His reverend tutors had at times a tussle,
 And for their Æneids, Iliads, and Odys-
 seys,
Were forced to make an odd sort of apol-
 ogy,
For Donna Inez dreaded the Mythology.

XLII

Ovid 's a rake, as half his verses show him,
 Anacreon's morals are a still worse sam-
 ple, 330
Catullus scarcely has a decent poem,
 I don't think Sappho's Ode a good example,
Although Longinus tells us there is no hymn
 Where the sublime soars forth on wings
 more ample:
But Virgil's songs are pure, except that hor-
 rid one
Beginning with 'Formosum Pastor Cory-
 don.'

XLIII

Lucretius' irreligion is too strong,
 For early stomachs, to prove wholesome
 food;
I can't help thinking Juvenal was wrong,
 Although no doubt his real intent was
 good, 340

For speaking out so plainly in his song,
 So much indeed as to be downright rude;
And then what proper person can be partial
To all those nauseous epigrams of Martial ?

XLIV

Juan was taught from out the best edition,
 Expurgated by learned men, who place,
Judiciously, from out the schoolboy's vi-
 sion,
 The grosser parts; but, fearful to deface
Too much their modest bard by this omis-
 sion,
 And pitying sore his mutilated case, 350
They only add them all in an appendix,
Which saves, in fact, the trouble of an in-
 dex;

XLV

For there we have them all 'at one fell
 swoop,'
 Instead of being scatter'd through the
 pages;
They stand forth marshall'd in a handsome
 troop,
 To meet the ingenuous youth of future
 ages,
Till some less rigid editor shall stoop
 To call them back into their separate
 cages,
Instead of standing staring all together,
Like garden gods — and not so decent
 either. 360

XLVI

The Missal too (it was the family Missal)
 Was ornamented in a sort of way
Which ancient mass-books often are, and
 this all
 Kinds of grotesques illumined; and how
 they,
Who saw those figures on the margin kiss
 all,
 Could turn their optics to the text and
 pray,
Is more than I know — But Don Juan's
 mother
Kept this herself, and gave her son another.

XLVII

Sermons he read, and lectures he endured,
 And homilies, and lives of all the saints;
To Jerome and to Chrysostom inured, 371
 He did not take such studies for re-
 straints;

But how faith is acquired, and then en-
sured,
 So well not one of the aforesaid paints
As Saint Augustine in his fine Confessions,
 Which make the reader envy his trans-
gressions.

XLVIII

This, too, was a seal'd book to little Juan —
 I can't but say that his mamma was right,
If such an education was the true one.
 She scarcely trusted him from out her
sight; 380
Her maids were old, and if she took a new
one,
 You might be sure she was a perfect
fright;
She did this during even her husband's
life —
I recommend as much to every wife.

XLIX

Young Juan wax'd in goodliness and grace;
 At six a charming child, and at eleven
With all the promise of as fine a face
 As e'er to man's maturer growth was
given:
He studied steadily, and grew apace,
 And seem'd, at least, in the right road
to heaven, 390
For half his days were pass'd at church,
the other
Between his tutors, confessor, and mother.

L

At six, I said, he was a charming child,
 At twelve he was a fine, but quiet boy;
Although in infancy a little wild,
 They tamed him down amongst them: to
destroy
His natural spirit not in vain they toil'd,
 At least it seem'd so; and his mother's
joy
Was to declare how sage, and still, and
steady, 399
Her young philosopher was grown already.

LI

I had my doubts, perhaps I have them still,
 But what I say is neither here nor there:
I knew his father well, and have some
skill
 In character — but it would not be fair
From sire to son to augur good or ill:
 He and his wife were an ill-sorted pair —

But scandal's my aversion — I protest
Against all evil speaking, even in jest.

LII

For my part I say nothing — nothing —
but
 This I will say — my reasons are my
own — 410
That if I had an only son to put
 To school (as God be praised that I have
none),
'T is not with Donna Inez I would shut
 Him up to learn his catechism alone,
No — no — I'd send him out betimes to
college,
For there it was I pick'd up my own know-
ledge.

LIII

For there one learns — 't is not for me to
boast,
 Though I acquired — but I pass over
that,
As well as all the Greek I since have lost:
 I say that there's the place — but ' *Ver-
bum sat*,' 420
I think I pick'd up too, as well as most,
 Knowledge of matters — but no matter
what —
I never married — but, I think, I know
That sons should not be educated so.

LIV

Young Juan now was sixteen years of
age,
 Tall, handsome, slender, but well knit:
he seem'd
Active, though not so sprightly, as a page;
 And everybody but his mother deem'd
Him almost man; but she flew in a rage
 And bit her lips (for else she might have
scream'd) 430
If any said so, for to be precocious
Was in her eyes a thing the most atrocious.

LV

Amongst her numerous acquaintance, all
 Selected for discretion and devotion,
There was the Donna Julia, whom to call
 Pretty were but to give a feeble notion
Of many charms in her as natural
 As sweetness to the flower, or salt to
ocean,
Her zone to Venus, or his bow to Cupid
(But this last simile is trite and stupid).

LVI

The darkness of her Oriental eye 441
 Accorded with her Moorish origin
(Her blood was not all Spanish, by the by;
 In Spain, you know, this is a sort of sin);
When proud Granada fell, and, forced to fly,
 Boabdil wept, of Donna Julia's kin
Some went to Africa, some stay'd in Spain,
Her great-great-grandmamma chose to re-
 main.

LVII

She married (I forget the pedigree)
 With an Hidalgo, who transmitted down
His blood less noble than such blood should
 be; 451
 At such alliances his sires would frown,
In that point so precise in each degree
 That they bred *in and in*, as might be
 shown,
Marrying their cousins — nay, their aunts,
 and nieces,
Which always spoils the breed, if it in-
 creases.

LVIII

This heathenish cross restored the breed
 again,
 Ruin'd its blood, but much improved its
 flesh;
For from a root the ugliest in Old Spain
 Sprung up a branch as beautiful as fresh;
The sons no more were short, the daughters
 plain: 461
 But there's a rumour which I fain would
 hush,
'T is said that Donna Julia's grandmamma
Produced her Don more heirs at love than
 law.

LIX

However this might be, the race went on
 Improving still through every generation,
Until it centred in an only son,
 Who left an only daughter; my narration
May have suggested that this single one 469
 Could be but Julia (whom on this occasion
I shall have much to speak about), and she
Was married, charming, chaste, and twenty-
 three.

LX

Her eye (I'm very fond of handsome eyes)
 Was large and dark, suppressing half its
 fire

Until she spoke, then through its soft dis-
 guise
 Flash'd an expression more of pride than
 ire,
And love than either; and there would
 arise
 A something in them which was not de-
 sire,
But would have been, perhaps, but for the
 soul
Which struggled through and chasten'd
 down the whole. 480

LXI

Her glossy hair was cluster'd o'er a brow
 Bright with intelligence, and fair, and
 smooth;
Her eyebrow's shape was like th' aërial bow,
 Her cheek all purple with the beam of
 youth,
Mounting at times to a transparent glow,
 As if her veins ran lightning; she, in
 sooth,
Possess'd an air and grace by no means
 common:
Her stature tall — I hate a dumpy woman.

LXII

Wedded she was some years, and to a man
 Of fifty, and such husbands are in plenty;
And yet, I think, instead of such a ONE 491
 'T were better to have TWO of five-and-
 twenty,
Especially in countries near the sun:
 And now I think on 't, 'mi vien in
 mente,'
Ladies even of the most uneasy virtue
Prefer a spouse whose age is short of
 thirty.

LXIII

'T is a sad thing, I cannot choose but say,
 And all the fault of that indecent sun,
Who cannot leave alone our helpless clay,
 But will keep baking, broiling, burning
 on, 500
That howsoever people fast and pray,
 The flesh is frail, and so the soul undone:
What men call gallantry, and gods adultery,
Is much more common where the climate's
 sultry.

LXIV

Happy the nations of the moral North !
 Where all is virtue, and the winter season

Sends sin, without a rag on, shivering forth
 ('T was snow that brought St. Anthony
 to reason);
Where juries cast up what a wife is worth,
 By laying whate'er sum in mulct they
 please on 510
The lover, who must pay a handsome price,
Because it is a marketable vice.

LXV

Alfonso was the name of Julia's lord,
 A man well looking for his years, and
 who
Was neither much beloved nor yet abhorr'd:
 They lived together, as most people do,
Suffering each other's foibles by accord,
 And not exactly either *one* or *two;*
Yet he was jealous, though he did not show
 it, 519
For jealousy dislikes the world to know it.

LXVI

Julia was — yet I never could see why —
 With Donna Inez quite a favourite friend;
Between their tastes there was small sym-
 pathy,
 For not a line had Julia ever penn'd:
Some people whisper (but no doubt they
 lie,
 For malice still imputes some private end)
That Inez had, ere Don Alfonso's marriage,
Forgot with him her very prudent carriage;

LXVII

And that still keeping up the old connection,
 Which time had lately render'd much
 more chaste, 530
She took his lady also in affection,
 And certainly this course was much the
 best:
She flatter'd Julia with her sage protection,
 And complimented Don Alfonso's taste;
And if she could not (who can ?) silence
 scandal,
At least she left it a more slender handle.

LXVIII

I can't tell whether Julia saw the affair
 With other people's eyes, or if her own
Discoveries made, but none could be aware
 Of this, at least no symptom e'er was
 shown; 540
Perhaps she did not know, or did not care,
 Indifferent from the first or callous
 grown:

I 'm really puzzled what to think or say,
She kept her counsel in so close a way.

LXIX

Juan she saw, and, as a pretty child,
 Caress'd him often — such a thing might
 be
Quite innocently done, and harmless styled,
 When she had twenty years, and thirteen
 he;
But I am not so sure I should have smiled
 When he was sixteen, Julia twenty-
 three; 550
These few short years make wondrous
 alterations,
Particularly amongst sun-burnt nations.

LXX

Whate'er the cause might be, they had
 become
 Changed; for the dame grew distant, the
 youth shy,
Their looks cast down, their greetings
 almost dumb,
 And much embarrassment in either eye;
There surely will be little doubt with some
 That Donna Julia knew the reason why,
But as for Juan, he had no more notion 559
Than he who never saw the sea of ocean.

LXXI

Yet Julia's very coldness still was kind,
 And tremulously gentle her small hand
Withdrew itself from his, but left behind
 A little pressure, thrilling, and so bland
And slight, so very slight, that to the mind
 'T was but a doubt ; but ne'er magician's
 wand
Wrought change with all Armida's fairy art
Like what this light touch left on Juan's
 heart.

LXXII

And if she met him, though she smiled no
 more,
 She look'd a sadness sweeter than her
 smile, 570
As if her heart had deeper thoughts in
 store
 She must not own, but cherish'd more the
 while
For that compression in its burning core;
 Even innocence itself has many a wile,
And will not dare to trust itself with truth,
And love is taught hypocrisy from youth.

LXXIII

But passion most dissembles, yet betrays
　Even by its darkness; as the blackest
　　sky
Foretells the heaviest tempest, it displays
　Its workings through the vainly guarded
　　eye,　　　　　　　　　　　　　　580
And in whatever aspect it arrays
　Itself, 't is still the same hypocrisy;
Coldness or anger, even disdain or hate,
Are masks it often wears, and still too late.

LXXIV

Then there were sighs, the deeper for sup-
　　pression,
　And stolen glances, sweeter for the theft,
And burning blushes, though for no trans-
　　gression,
　Tremblings when met, and restlessness
　　when left;
All these are little preludes to possession,
　Of which young passion cannot be be-
　　reft,　　　　　　　　　　　　　　590
And merely tend to show how greatly love
　is
Embarrass'd at first starting with a novice.

LXXV

Poor Julia's heart was in an awkward state;
　She felt it going, and resolved to make
The noblest efforts for herself and mate,
　For honour's, pride's, religion's, virtue's
　　sake;
Her resolutions were most truly great,
　And almost might have made a Tarquin
　　quake:
She pray'd the Virgin Mary for her grace,
As being the best judge of a lady's case.　600

LXXVI

She vow'd she never would see Juan more,
　And next day paid a visit to his mother,
And look'd extremely at the opening door,
　Which, by the Virgin's grace, let in an-
　　other;
Grateful she was, and yet a little sore —
　Again it opens, it can be no other,
'T is surely Juan now — No! I'm afraid
That night the Virgin was no further pray'd.

LXXVII

She now determined that a virtuous wo-
　　man
　Should rather face and overcome tempta-
　　tion,　　　　　　　　　　　　　　610

That flight was base and dastardly, and no
　　man
　Should ever give her heart the least sen-
　　sation;
That is to say, a thought beyond the common
　Preference, that we must feel upon occa-
　　sion
For people who are pleasanter than others,
But then they only seem so many brothers.

LXXVIII

And even if by chance — and who can tell?
　The devil's so very sly — she should dis-
　　cover
That all within was not so very well,
　And, if still free, that such or such a
　　lover　　　　　　　　　　　　　　620
Might please perhaps, a virtuous wife can
　　quell
　Such thoughts, and be the better when
　　they 're over;
And if the man should ask, 't is but denial:
I recommend young ladies to make trial.

LXXIX

And then there are such things as love di-
　　vine,
　Bright and immaculate, unmix'd and pure,
Such as the angels think so very fine,
　And matrons who would be no less se-
　　cure,
Platonic, perfect, 'just such love as mine;'
　Thus Julia said — and thought so, to be
　　sure;　　　　　　　　　　　　　　630
And so I'd have her think, were I the man
On whom her reveries celestial ran.

LXXX

Such love is innocent, and may exist
　Between young persons without any dan-
　　ger.
A hand may first, and then a lip be kist;
　For my part, to such doings I 'm a stran-
　　ger,
But hear these freedoms form the utmost
　　list
　Of all o'er which such love may be a
　　ranger:
If people go beyond, 't is quite a crime,　639
But not my fault — I tell them all in time.

LXXXI

Love, then, but love within its proper limits,
　Was Julia's innocent determination
In young Don Juan's favour, and to him its

Exertion might be useful on occasion;
 And, lighted at too pure a shrine to dim its
 Ethereal lustre, with what sweet persua-
 sion
He might be taught, by love and her to-
 gether —
I really don't know what, nor Julia either.

LXXXII

Fraught with this fine intention, and well
 fenced 649
 In mail of proof — her purity of soul —
She, for the future of her strength convinced,
 And that her honour was a rock, or mole,
Exceeding sagely from that hour dispensed
 With any kind of troublesome control;
But whether Julia to the task was equal
Is that which must be mention'd in the
 sequel.

LXXXIII

Her plan she deem'd both innocent and fea-
 sible,
 And, surely, with a stripling of sixteen
Not scandal's fangs could fix on much that 's
 seizable,
 Or if they did so, satisfied to mean 660
Nothing but what was good, her breast was
 peaceable —
 A quiet conscience makes one so serene!
Christians have burnt each other, quite per-
 suaded
That all the Apostles would have done as
 they did.

LXXXIV

And if in the mean time her husband died,
 But Heaven forbid that such a thought
 should cross
Her brain, though in a dream! (and then
 she sigh'd)
 Never could she survive that common
 loss;
But just suppose that moment should betide,
 I only say suppose it — *inter nos.* 670
(This should be *entre nous*, for Julia thought
In French, but then the rhyme would go
 for naught.)

LXXXV

I only say suppose this supposition:
 Juan being then grown up to man's estate
Would fully suit a widow of condition,
 Even seven years hence it would not be
 too late;

And in the interim (to pursue this vision)
 The mischief, after all, could not be great,
For he would learn the rudiments of love,
I mean the seraph way of those above. 680

LXXXVI

So much for Julia. Now we 'll turn to Juan.
 Poor little fellow! he had no idea
Of his own case, and never hit the true one;
 In feelings quick as Ovid's Miss Medea,
He puzzled over what he found a new one,
 But not as yet imagined it could be a
Thing quite in course, and not at all alarm-
 ing,
Which, with a little patience, might grow
 charming.

LXXXVII

Silent and pensive, idle, restless, slow, 689
 His home deserted for the lonely wood,
Tormented with a wound he could not know,
 His, like all deep grief, plunged in solitude:
I 'm fond myself of solitude or so,
 But then, I beg it may be understood,
By solitude I mean a sultan's, not
A hermit's, with a haram for a grot.

LXXXVIII

'Oh Love! in such a wilderness as this,
 Where transport and security entwine,
Here is the empire of thy perfect bliss, 699
 And here thou art a god indeed divine.'
The bard I quote from does not sing amiss,
 With the exception of the second line,
For that same twining 'transport and secu-
 rity'
Are twisted to a phrase of some obscurity.

LXXXIX

The poet meant, no doubt, and thus appeals
 To the good sense and senses of mankind,
The very thing which every body feels,
 As all have found on trial, or may find,
That no one likes to be disturb'd at meals
 Or love. — I won't say more about 'en-
 twined' 710
Or 'transport,' as we knew all that before,
But beg 'Security' will bolt the door.

XC

Young Juan wander'd by the glassy brooks,
 Thinking unutterable things; he threw
Himself at length within the leafy nooks
 Where the wild branch of the cork forest
 grew;

There poets find materials for their books,
 And every now and then we read them
 through,
So that their plan and prosody are eligible,
 Unless, like Wordsworth, they prove unin-
 telligible. 720

XCI

He, Juan (and not Wordsworth), so pursued
 His self-communion with his own high
 soul,
Until his mighty heart, in its great mood,
 Had mitigated part, though not the whole
Of its disease; he did the best he could
 With things not very subject to control,
And turn'd, without perceiving his condition,
Like Coleridge, into a metaphysician.

XCII

He thought about himself, and the whole
 earth,
 Of man the wonderful, and of the stars,
And how the deuce they ever could have
 birth; 731
 And then he thought of earthquakes, and
 of wars,
How many miles the moon might have in
 girth,
 Of air-balloons, and of the many bars
To perfect knowledge of the boundless
 skies; —
And then he thought of Donna Julia's eyes.

XCIII

In thoughts like these true wisdom may
 discern
Longings sublime, and aspirations high,
 Which some are born with, but the most
 part learn
 To plague themselves withal, they know
 not why: 740
'T was strange that one so young should
 thus concern
 His brain about the action of the sky;
If *you* think 't was philosophy that this did,
I can't help thinking puberty assisted.

XCIV

He pored upon the leaves, and on the flowers,
 And heard a voice in all the winds; and
 then
He thought of wood-nymphs and immortal
 bowers,
 And how the goddesses came down to
 men:

He miss'd the pathway, he forgot the hours,
 And when he look'd upon his watch
 again, 750
He found how much old Time had been a
 winner —
He also found that he had lost his dinner.

XCV

Sometimes he turn'd to gaze upon his book,
 Boscan, or Garcilasso; — by the wind
Even as the page is rustled while we look,
 So by the poesy of his own mind
Over the mystic leaf his soul was shook,
 As if 't were one whereon magicians bind
Their spells, and give them to the passing
 gale, 759
According to some good old woman's tale.

XCVI

Thus would he while his lonely hours away
 Dissatisfied, nor knowing what he wanted;
Nor glowing reverie, nor poet's lay,
 Could yield his spirit that for which it
 panted,
A bosom whereon he his head might lay,
 And hear the heart beat with the love it
 granted,
With — several other things, which I forget,
Or which, at least, I need not mention yet.

XCVII

Those lonely walks, and lengthening rev-
 eries, 769
 Could not escape the gentle Julia's eyes;
She saw that Juan was not at his ease;
 But that which chiefly may, and must
 surprise,
Is, that the Donna Inez did not tease
 Her only son with question or surmise:
Whether it was she did not see, or would not,
Or, like all very clever people, could not.

XCVIII

This may seem strange, but yet 't is very
 common;
 For instance — gentlemen, whose ladies
 take
Leave to o'erstep the written rights of
 woman,
 And break the — Which commandment
 is 't they break ? 780
(I have forgot the number, and think no
 man
 Should rashly quote, for fear of a mis-
 take.)

I say, when these same gentlemen are
jealous,
They make some blunder, which their ladies
tell us.

XCIX

A real husband always is suspicious,
But still no less suspects in the wrong
place,
Jealous of some one who had no such
wishes,
Or pandering blindly to his own disgrace,
By harbouring some dear friend extremely
vicious;
The last indeed 's infallibly the case: 790
And when the spouse and friend are gone
off wholly,
He wonders at their vice, and not his folly.

C

Thus parents also are at times short-sighted;
Though watchful as the lynx, they ne'er
discover,
The while the wicked world beholds de-
lighted,
Young Hopeful's mistress, or Miss
Fanny's lover,
Till some confounded escapade has blighted
The plan of twenty years, and all is
over;
And then the mother cries, the father
swears,
And wonders why the devil he got heirs. 800

CI

But Inez was so anxious, and so clear
Of sight, that I must think, on this occa-
sion,
She had some other motive much more
near
For leaving Juan to this new temptation;
But what that motive was, I sha'n't say
here;
Perhaps to finish Juan's education,
Perhaps to open Don Alfonso's eyes,
In case he thought his wife too great a
prize.

CII

It was upon a day, a summer's day; —
Summer 's indeed a very dangerous sea-
son, 810
And so is spring about the end of May;
The sun, no doubt, is the prevailing rea-
son;

But whatsoe'er the cause is, one may say,
And stand convicted of more truth than
treason,
That there are months which nature grows
more merry in, —
March has its hares, and May must have its
heroine.

CIII

'T was on a summer's day — the sixth of
June: —
I like to be particular in dates,
Not only of the age, and year, but moon;
They are a sort of post-house, where
the Fates 820
Change horses, making history change its
tune,
Then spur away o'er empires and o'er
states,
Leaving at last not much besides chronology,
Excepting the post-obits of theology.

CIV

'T was on the sixth of June, about the hour
Of half-past six — perhaps still nearer
seven —
When Julia sate within as pretty a bower
As e'er held houri in that heathenish
heaven
Described by Mahomet, and Anacreon
Moore,
To whom the lyre and laurels have been
given, 830
With all the trophies of triumphant song —
He won them well, and may he wear them
long !

CV

She sate, but not alone; I know not well
How this same interview had taken place,
And even if I knew, I should not tell —
People should hold their tongues in any
case;
No matter how or why the thing befell,
But there were she and Juan, face to
face —
When two such faces are so, 't would be
wise,
But very difficult, to shut their eyes. 840

CVI

How beautiful she look'd ! her conscious
heart
Glow'd in her cheek, and yet she felt no
wrong.

Oh Love ! how perfect is thy mystic art,
 Strengthening the weak, and trampling
 on the strong,
How self-deceitful is the sagest part
 Of mortals whom thy lure hath led
 along —
The precipice she stood on was immense,
So was her creed in her own innocence.

CVII

She thought of her own strength, and Juan's
 youth,
 And of the folly of all prudish fears, 850
Victorious virtue, and domestic truth,
 And then of Don Alfonso's fifty years:
I wish these last had not occurr'd, in sooth,
 Because that number rarely much en-
 dears,
And through all climes, the snowy and the
 sunny,
Sounds ill in love, whate'er it may in money.

CVIII

When people say, ' I 've told you *fifty* times,'
 They mean to scold, and very often do;
When poets say, ' I 've written *fifty* rhymes,'
 They make you dread that they 'll recite
 them too; 860
In gangs of *fifty*, thieves commit their
 crimes;
 At *fifty* love for love is rare, 't is true,
But then, no doubt, it equally as true is,
A good deal may be bought for *fifty* Louis.

CIX

Julia had honour, virtue, truth, and love,
 For Don Alfonso; and she inly swore,
By all the vows below to powers above,
 She never would disgrace the ring she
 wore,
Nor leave a wish which wisdom might re-
 prove;
 And while she ponder'd this, besides
 much more, 870
One hand on Juan's carelessly was thrown,
Quite by mistake — she thought it was her
 own;

CX

Unconsciously she lean'd upon the other,
 Which play'd within the tangles of her
 hair:
And to contend with thoughts she could
 not smother
 She seem'd by the distraction of her air.

'T was surely very wrong in Juan's mo-
 ther
 To leave together this imprudent pair,
She who for many years had watch'd her son
 so —
I 'm very certain *mine* would not have done
 so. 880

CXI

The hand which still held Juan's, by de-
 grees
 Gently, but palpably confirm'd its grasp,
As if it said, ' Detain me, if you please;'
 Yet there 's no doubt she only meant to
 clasp
His fingers with a pure Platonic squeeze:
 She would have shrunk as from a toad,
 or asp,
Had she imagined such a thing could rouse
A feeling dangerous to a prudent spouse.

CXII

I cannot know what Juan thought of this,
 But what he did, is much what you would
 do; 890
His young lip thank'd it with a grateful
 kiss,
 And then, abash'd at its own joy, with-
 drew
In deep despair, lest he had done amiss, —
 Love is so very timid when 't is new:
She blush'd, and frown'd not, but she
 strove to speak,
And held her tongue, her voice was grown
 so weak.

CXIII

The sun set, and up rose the yellow moon:
 The devil 's in the moon for mischief;
 they
Who call'd her CHASTE, methinks, began too
 soon 899
 Their nomenclature; there is not a day,
The longest, not the twenty-first of June,
 Sees half the business in a wicked way
On which three single hours of moonshine
 smile —
And then she looks so modest all the while.

CXIV

There is a dangerous silence in that hour,
 A stillness, which leaves room for the full
 soul
To open all itself, without the power
 Of calling wholly back its self-control;

The silver light which, hallowing tree and
 tower,
 Sheds beauty and deep softness o'er the
 whole, 910
Breathes also to the heart, and o'er it throws
A loving languor, which is not repose.

CXV

And Julia sate with Juan, half embraced
 And half retiring from the glowing arm,
Which trembled like the bosom where 't was
 placed;
 Yet still she must have thought there was
 no harm,
Or else 't were easy to withdraw her waist;
 But then the situation had its charm,
And then — God knows what next — I can't
 go on;
I 'm almost sorry that I e'er begun. 920

CXVI

Oh Plato ! Plato ! you have paved the way,
 With your confounded fantasies, to more
Immoral conduct by the fancied sway
 Your system feigns o'er the controulless
 core
Of human hearts, than all the long array
 Of poets and romancers: — You 're a bore,
A charlatan, a coxcomb — and have been,
At best, no better than a go-between.

CXVII

And Julia's voice was lost, except in sighs,
 Until too late for useful conversation; 930
The tears were gushing from her gentle
 eyes,
 I wish indeed they had not had occasion,
But who, alas ! can love, and then be wise ?
 Not that remorse did not oppose tempta-
 tion;
A little still she strove, and much repented,
And whispering ' I will ne'er consent ' —
 consented.

CXVIII

'T is said that Xerxes offer'd a reward
 To those who could invent him a new
 pleasure:
Methinks the requisition 's rather hard,
 And must have cost his majesty a trea-
 sure: 940
For my part, I 'm a moderate-minded bard,
 Fond of a little love (which I call leisure);
I care not for new pleasures, as the old
Are quite enough for me, so they but hold.

CXIX

Oh Pleasure! you are indeed a pleasant
 thing,
 Although one must be damn'd for you,
 no doubt:
I make a resolution every spring
 Of reformation, ere the year run out,
But somehow, this my vestal vow takes
 wing,
 Yet still, I trust it may be kept through-
 out: 950
I 'm very sorry, very much ashamed,
And mean, next winter, to be quite re-
 claim'd.

CXX

Here my chaste Muse a liberty must take —
 Start not! still chaster reader — she 'll
 be nice hence-
Forward, and there is no great cause to
 quake;
 This liberty is a poetic licence,
Which some irregularity may make
 In the design, and as I have a high sense
Of Aristotle and the Rules, 't is fit
To beg his pardon when I err a bit. 960

CXXI

This licence is to hope the reader will
 Suppose from June the sixth (the fatal
 day,
Without whose epoch my poetic skill
 For want of facts would all be thrown
 away),
But keeping Julia and Don Juan still
 In sight, that several months have pass'd;
 we 'll say
'T was in November, but I 'm not so sure
About the day — the era 's more obscure.

CXXII

We 'll talk of that anon. — 'T is sweet to
 hear
 At midnight on the blue and moonlit
 deep 970
The song and oar of Adria's gondolier,
 By distance mellow'd, o'er the waters
 sweep;
'T is sweet to see the evening star appear;
 'T is sweet to listen as the night-winds
 creep
From leaf to leaf; 't is sweet to view on
 high
The rainbow, based on ocean, span the
 sky.

CXXIII

'T is sweet to hear the watch-dog's honest
 bark
 Bay deep-mouth'd welcome as we draw
 near home;
'T is sweet to know there is an eye will mark
 Our coming, and look brighter when we
 come; 980
'T is sweet to be awaken'd by the lark,
 Or lull'd by falling waters; sweet the hum
Of bees, the voice of girls, the song of birds,
The lisp of children, and their earliest words.

CXXIV

Sweet is the vintage, when the showering
 grapes
 In Bacchanal profusion reel to earth,
Purple and gushing: sweet are our escapes
 From civic revelry to rural mirth;
Sweet to the miser are his glittering heaps,
 Sweet to the father is his first-born's
 birth, 990
Sweet is revenge — especially to women,
Pillage to soldiers, prize-money to seamen.

CXXV

Sweet is a legacy, and passing sweet
 The unexpected death of some old lady
Or gentleman of seventy years complete,
 Who 've made 'us youth' wait too — too
 long already
For an estate, or cash, or country seat,
 Still breaking, but with stamina so steady
That all the Israelites are fit to mob its
Next owner for their double-damn'd post-
 obits. 1000

CXXVI

'T is sweet to win, no matter how, one's
 laurels,
 By blood or ink; 't is sweet to put an end
To strife; 't is sometimes sweet to have our
 quarrels,
 Particularly with a tiresome friend:
Sweet is old wine in bottles, ale in barrels;
 Dear is the helpless creature we defend
Against the world; and dear the schoolboy
 spot
We ne'er forget, though there we are forgot.

CXXVII

But sweeter still than this, than these, than
 all,
 Is first and passionate love — it stands
 alone, 1010

Like Adam's recollection of his fall;
 The tree of knowledge has been pluck'd
 — all 's known —
And life yields nothing further to recall
 Worthy of this ambrosial sin, so shown,
No doubt in fable, as the unforgiven
Fire which Prometheus filch'd for us from
 heaven.

CXXVIII

Man 's a strange animal, and makes strange
 use
 Of his own nature, and the various arts,
And likes particularly to produce
 Some new experiment to show his parts;
This is the age of oddities let loose, 1021
 Where different talents find their different
 marts;
You 'd best begin with truth, and when
 you 've lost your
Labour, there 's a sure market for imposture.

CXXIX

What opposite discoveries we have seen !
 (Signs of true genius, and of empty
 pockets.)
One makes new noses, one a guillotine,
 One breaks your bones, one sets them in
 their sockets;
But vaccination certainly has been 1029
 A kind antithesis to Congreve's rockets,
With which the Doctor paid off an old pox,
By borrowing a new one from an ox.

CXXX

Bread has been made (indifferent) from
 potatoes;
 And galvanism has set some corpses
 grinning,
But has not answer'd like the apparatus
 Of the Humane Society's beginning
By which men are unsuffocated gratis:
 What wondrous new machines have late
 been spinning ! 1038
I said the small-pox has gone out of late;
Perhaps it may be follow'd by the great.

CXXXI

'T is said the great came from America;
 Perhaps it may set out on its return, —
The population there so spreads, they say
 'T is grown high time to thin it in its
 turn,
With war, or plague, or famine, any way,
 So that civilisation they may learn;

And which in ravage the more loathsome
 evil is —
Their real lues, or our pseudo-syphilis?

CXXXII

This is the patent-age of new inventions 1049
 For killing bodies, and for saving souls,
All propagated with the best intentions;
 Sir Humphry Davy's lantern, by which
 coals
Are safely mined for in the mode he men-
 tions,
 Tombuctoo travels, voyages to the Poles,
Are ways to benefit mankind, as true,
Perhaps, as shooting them at Waterloo.

CXXXIII

Man 's a phenomenon, one knows not what,
 And wonderful beyond all wondrous
 measure;
'T is pity though, in this sublime world, that
 Pleasure 's a sin, and sometimes sin 's a
 pleasure; 1060
Few mortals know what end they would be
 at,
 But whether glory, power, or love, or
 treasure,
The path is through perplexing ways, and
 when
The goal is gain'd, we die, you know — and
 then —

CXXXIV

What then? — I do not know, no more do
 you —
 And so good night. — Return we to our
 story:
'T was in November, when fine days are
 few,
 And the far mountains wax a little hoary,
And clap a white cape on their mantles
 blue;
 And the sea dashes round the promon-
 tory, 1070
And the loud breaker boils against the
 rock,
And sober suns must set at five o'clock.

CXXXV

'T was, as the watchmen say, a cloudy
 night;
 No moon, no stars, the wind was low or
 loud
By gusts, and many a sparkling hearth was
 bright

With the piled wood, round which the
 family crowd;
There 's something cheerful in that sort of
 light,
 Even as a summer sky 's without a
 cloud:
I 'm fond of fire, and crickets, and all
 that, 1079
A lobster salad, and champagne, and chat.

CXXXVI

'T was midnight — Donna Julia was in
 bed,
 Sleeping, most probably, — when at her
 door
Arose a clatter might awake the dead,
 If they had never been awoke before,
And that they have been so we all have
 read,
 And are to be so, at the least, once
 more; —
The door was fasten'd, but with voice and
 fist
First knocks were heard, then 'Madam —
 Madam — hist!

CXXXVII

'For God's sake, Madam — Madam —
 here 's my master,
 With more than half the city at his
 back — 1090
Was ever heard of such a curst disaster!
 'T is not my fault — I kept good watch —
 Alack!
Do pray undo the bolt a little faster —
 They 're on the stair just now, and in
 a crack
Will all be here; perhaps he yet may
 fly —
Surely the window 's not so *very* high!'

CXXXVIII

By this time Don Alfonso was arrived,
 With torches, friends, and servants in
 great number;
The major part of them had long been
 wived,
 And therefore paused not to disturb the
 slumber 1100
Of any wicked woman, who contrived
 By stealth her husband's temples to en-
 cumber:
Examples of this kind are so contagious,
Were *one* not punish'd, *all* would be outra-
 geous.

CXXXIX

I can't tell how, or why, or what suspicion
 Could enter into Don Alfonso's head;
But for a cavalier of his condition
 It surely was exceedingly ill-bred,
Without a word of previous admonition,
 To hold a levee round his lady's bed, 1110
And summon lackeys, arm'd with fire and
 sword,
 To prove himself the thing he most ab-
 horr'd.

CXL

Poor Donna Julia, starting as from sleep
 (Mind — that I do not say — she had not
 slept),
Began at once to scream, and yawn, and
 weep;
 Her maid Antonia, who was an adept,
Contrived to fling the bed-clothes in a heap,
 As if she had just now from out them
 crept:
I can't tell why she should take all this
 trouble
To prove her mistress had been sleeping
 double. 1120

CXLI

But Julia mistress, and Antonia maid,
 Appear'd like two poor harmless women,
 who
Of goblins, but still more of men afraid,
 Had thought one man might be deterr'd
 by two,
And therefore side by side were gently
 laid,
 Until the hours of absence should run
 through,
And truant husband should return, and say,
'My dear, I was the first who came away.'

CXLII

Now Julia found at length a voice, and
 cried,
 'In heaven's name, Don Alfonso, what
 d' ye mean? 1130
Has madness seized you? would that I had
 died
 Ere such a monster's victim I had been!
What may this midnight violence betide,
 A sudden fit of drunkenness or spleen?
Dare you suspect me, whom the thought
 would kill?
Search, then, the room!' — Alfonso said,
 'I will.'

CXLIII

He search'd, *they* search'd, and rummaged
 everywhere,
 Closet and clothes' press, chest and win-
 dow-seat,
And found much linen, lace, and several pair
 Of stockings, slippers, brushes, combs,
 complete, 1140
With other articles of ladies fair,
 To keep them beautiful, or leave them
 neat:
Arras they prick'd and curtains with their
 swords,
And wounded several shutters, and some
 boards.

CXLIV

Under the bed they search'd, and there
 they found —
 No matter what — it was not that they
 sought;
They open'd windows, gazing if the ground
 Had signs or footmarks, but the earth
 said nought;
And then they stared each other's faces
 round:
 'T is odd, not one of all these seekers
 thought, 1150
And seems to me almost a sort of blunder,
Of looking *in* the bed as well as under.

CXLV

During this inquisition, Julia's tongue
 Was not asleep — 'Yes, search and
 search,' she cried,
'Insult on insult heap, and wrong on wrong!
 It was for this that I became a bride!
For this in silence I have suffer'd long
 A husband like Alfonso at my side; 1158
But now I 'll bear no more, nor here remain,
If there be law or lawyers in all Spain.

CXLVI

'Yes, Don Alfonso! husband now no more,
 If ever you indeed deserved the name,
Is 't worthy of your years? — you have
 threescore —
 Fifty, or sixty, it is all the same —
Is 't wise or fitting, causeless to explore
 For facts against a virtuous woman's
 fame?
Ungrateful, perjured, barbarous Don Al-
 fonso,
How dare you think your lady would go on
 so?

CXLVII

'Is it for this I have disdain'd to hold
 The common privileges of my sex ? 1170
That I have chosen a confessor so old
 And deaf, that any other it would vex,
And never once he has had cause to scold,
 But found my very innocence perplex
So much, he always doubted I was mar-
 ried —
How sorry you will be when I 've miscar-
 ried !

CXLVIII

'Was it for this that no Cortejo e'er
 I yet have chosen from out the youth of
 Seville ?
Is it for this I scarce went anywhere,
 Except to bull-fights, mass, play, rout,
 and revel ? 1180
Is it for this, whate'er my suitors were,
 I favor'd none — nay, was almost uncivil ?
Is it for this that General Count O'Reilly,
Who took Algiers, declares I used him
 vilely ?

CXLIX

'Did not the Italian Musico Cazzani
 Sing at my heart six months at least in
 vain ?
Did not his countryman, Count Corniani,
 Call me the only virtuous wife in Spain ?
Were there not also Russians, English,
 many ? 1189
 The Count Strongstroganoff I put in pain,
And Lord Mount Coffeehouse, the Irish peer,
 Who kill'd himself for love (with wine)
 last year.

CL

'Have I not had two bishops at my feet,
 The Duke of Ichar, and Don Fernan
 Nunez ?
And is it thus a faithful wife you treat ?
 I wonder in what quarter now the moon is:
I praise your vast forbearance not to beat
 Me also, since the time so opportune is —
Oh, valiant man ! with sword drawn and
 cock'd trigger,
Now, tell me, don't you cut a pretty fig-
 ure ? 1200

CLI

'Was it for this you took your sudden
 journey,
 Under pretence of business indispensable

With that sublime of rascals your attor-
 ney,
 Whom I see standing there, and looking
 sensible
Of having play'd the fool ? though both I
 spurn, he
 Deserves the worst, his conduct 's less
 defensible,
Because, no doubt, 't was for his dirty fee,
And not from any love to you nor me.

CLII

'If he comes here to take a deposition,
 By all means let the gentleman pro-
 ceed; 1210
You 've made the apartment in a fit condi-
 tion:
 There 's pen and ink for you, sir, when
 you need —
Let every thing be noted with precision,
 I would not you for nothing should be
 fee'd —
But, as my maid 's undrest, pray turn your
 spies out.'
' Oh ! ' sobb'd Antonia, ' I could tear their
 eyes out.'

CLIII

'There is the closet, there the toilet, there
 The antechamber — search them under,
 over;
There is the sofa, there the great arm-chair,
 The chimney — which would really hold
 a lover. 1220
I wish to sleep, and beg you will take care
 And make no further noise, till you dis-
 cover
The secret cavern of this lurking treasure —
And when 't is found, let me, too, have that
 pleasure.

CLIV

'And now, Hidalgo ! now that you have
 thrown
 Doubt upon me, confusion over all,
Pray have the courtesy to make it known
 Who is the man you search for ? how
 d' ye call
Him ? what 's his lineage ? let him but be
 shown —
 I hope he 's young and handsome — is he
 tall ? 1230
Tell me — and be assured, that since you
 stain
My honour thus, it shall not be in vain.

CLV

' At least, perhaps, he has not sixty years,
 At that age he would be too old for
 slaughter,
Or for so young a husband's jealous fears
 (Antonia ! let me have a glass of water).
I am ashamed of having shed these tears,
 They are unworthy of my father's
 daughter;
My mother dream'd not in my natal hour
That I should fall into a monster's power.

CLVI

' Perhaps 't is of Antonia you are jealous,
 You saw that she was sleeping by my
 side 1242
When you broke in upon us with your
 fellows:
 Look where you please — we 've nothing,
 sir, to hide;
Only another time, I trust, you 'll tell us,
 Or for the sake of decency abide
A moment at the door, that we may be
Drest to receive so much good company.

CLVII

' And now, sir, I have done, and say no
 more;
 The little I have said may serve to show
The guileless heart in silence may grieve
 o'er 1251
 The wrongs to whose exposure it is
 slow:
I leave you to your conscience as before,
 'T will one day ask you *why* you used me
 so ?
God grant you feel not then the bitterest
 grief ! —
Antonia ! where 's my pocket-handker-
 chief ? '

CLVIII

She ceased, and turn'd upon her pillow; pale
 She lay, her dark eyes flashing through
 their tears,
Like skies that rain and lighten; as a veil,
 Waved and o'ershading her wan cheek,
 appears 1260
Her streaming hair; the black curls strive,
 but fail,
 To hide the glossy shoulder, which uprears
Its snow through all; — her soft lips lie
 apart,
And louder than her breathing beats her
 heart.

CLIX

The Senhor Don Alfonso stood confused;
 Antonia bustled round the ransack'd
 room,
And, turning up her nose, with looks abused
 Her master and his myrmidons, of whom
Not one, except the attorney, was amused;
 He, like Achates, faithful to the tomb,
So there were quarrels, cared not for the
 cause, 1271
Knowing they must be settled by the laws.

CLX

With prying snub-nose, and small eyes, he
 stood,
 Following Antonia's motions here and
 there,
With much suspicion in his attitude;
 For reputations he had little care;
So that a suit or action were made good,
 Small pity had he for the young and fair,
And ne'er believed in negatives, till these
Were proved by competent false witnesses.

CLXI

But Don Alfonso stood with downcast
 looks, 1281
 And, truth to say, he made a foolish figure;
When, after searching in five hundred nooks,
 And treating a young wife with so much
 rigour,
He gain'd no point, except some self-
 rebukes,
 Added to those his lady with such vigour
Had pour'd upon him for the last half-hour,
Quick, thick, and heavy — as a thunder-
 shower.

CLXII

At first he tried to hammer an excuse,
 To which the sole reply was tears and
 sobs, 1290
And indications of hysterics, whose
 Prologue is always certain throes, and
 throbs,
Gasps, and whatever else the owners choose:
 Alfonso saw his wife, and thought of
 Job's;
He saw too, in perspective, her relations,
And then he tried to muster all his patience.

CLXIII

He stood in act to speak, or rather stam-
 mer,
 But sage Antonia cut him short before

The anvil of his speech received the hammer,
 With 'Pray, sir, leave the room, and say
 no more, 1300
Or madam dies.' — Alfonso mutter'd, 'D—n
 her,'
 But nothing else, the time of words was
 o'er;
He cast a rueful look or two, and did,
He knew not wherefore, that which he was
 bid.

CLXIV

With him retired his '*posse comitatus*,'
 The attorney last, who linger'd near the
 door
Reluctantly, still tarrying there as late as
 Antonia let him — not a little sore
At this most strange and unexplain'd '*hiatus*'
 In Don Alfonso's facts, which just now
 wore 1310
An awkward look; as he revolved the case,
The door was fasten'd in his legal face.

CLXV

No sooner was it bolted, than — Oh shame!
 Oh sin! Oh sorrow! and oh womankind!
How can you do such things and keep your
 fame,
 Unless this world, and t' other too, be
 blind?
Nothing so dear as an unfilch'd good name!
 But to proceed — for there is more behind:
With much heartfelt reluctance be it said,
Young Juan slipp'd half-smother'd, from
 the bed. 1320

CLXVI

He had been hid — I don't pretend to say
 How, nor can I indeed describe the
 where —
Young, slender, and pack'd easily, he lay,
 No doubt, in little compass, round or
 square;
But pity him I neither must nor may
 His suffocation by that pretty pair;
'T were better, sure, to die so, than be shut
With maudlin Clarence in his Malmsey
 butt.

CLXVII

And, secondly, I pity not, because
 He had no business to commit a sin, 1330

Forbid by heavenly, fined by human laws,
 At least 't was rather early to begin;
But at sixteen the conscience rarely gnaws
 So much as when we call our old debts in
At sixty years, and draw the accompts of
 evil,
And find a deucèd balance with the devil.

CLXVIII

Of his position I can give no notion:
 'T is written in the Hebrew Chronicle,
How the physicians, leaving pill and potion,
 Prescribed, by way of blister, a young
 belle, 1340
When old King David's blood grew dull in
 motion,
 And that the medicine answer'd very
 well;
Perhaps 't was in a different way applied,
For David lived, but Juan nearly died.

CLXIX

What 's to be done? Alfonso will be back
 The moment he has sent his fools away.
Antonia's skill was put upon the rack,
 But no device could be brought into
 play —
And how to parry the renew'd attack?
 Besides, it wanted but few hours of day:
Antonia puzzled; Julia did not speak, 1351
But press'd her bloodless lip to Juan's
 cheek.

CLXX

He turn'd his lip to hers, and with his hand
 Call'd back the tangles of her wandering
 hair;
Even then their love they could not all
 command,
 And half forgot their danger and despair:
Antonia's patience now was at a stand —
 'Come, come, 't is no time now for fooling there,'
She whisper'd, in great wrath — 'I must
 deposit
This pretty gentleman within the closet:

CLXXI

'Pray, keep your nonsense for some luckier
 night — 1361
 Who can have put my master in this
 mood?
What will become on 't — I 'm in such a
 fright,
The devil 's in the urchin, and no good —

Is this a time for giggling ? this a plight ?
　Why, don't you know that it may end in
　　blood ?
You 'll lose your life, and I shall lose my
　　place,
My mistress all, for that half-girlish face.

CLXXII

' Had it but been for a stout cavalier
　Of twenty-five or thirty (come, make
　　haste) —　　　　　　　　　　　1370
But for a child, what piece of work is here !
　I really, madam, wonder at your taste
(Come, sir, get in) — my master must be
　　near:
　There, for the present, at the least, he 's
　　fast,
And if we can but till the morning keep
Our counsel — (Juan, mind, you must not
　　sleep.) '

CLXXIII

Now, Don Alfonso entering, but alone,
　Closed the oration of the trusty maid:
She loiter'd, and he told her to be gone,
　An order somewhat sullenly obey'd;　1380
However, present remedy was none,
　And no great good seem'd answer'd if
　　she staid:
Regarding both with slow and sidelong
　　view,
She snuff'd the candle, curtsied, and with-
　　drew.

CLXXIV

Alfonso paused a minute — then begun
　Some strange excuses for his late pro-
　　ceeding;
He would not justify what he had done,
　To say the best, it was extreme ill-
　　breeding;
But there were ample reasons for it, none
　Of which he specified in this his plead-
　　ing:　　　　　　　　　　　　　1390
His speech was a fine sample, on the whole,
Of rhetoric, which the learn'd call ' rigma-
　role.'

CLXXV

Julia said nought ; though all the while
　　there rose
　A ready answer, which at once enables
A matron, who her husband's foible knows,
　By a few timely words to turn the ta-
　　bles,

Which, if it does not silence, still must
　　pose, —
　Even if it should comprise a pack of
　　fables;
'T is to retort with firmness, and when
　　he
Suspects with *one*, do you reproach with
　　three.　　　　　　　　　　　1400

CLXXVI

Julia, in fact, had tolerable grounds, —
　Alfonso's loves with Inez were well
　　known,
But whether 't was that one's own guilt
　　confounds —
But that can't be, as has been often shown,
　A lady with apologies abounds; —
　It might be that her silence sprang alone
From delicacy to Don Juan's ear,
To whom she knew his mother's fame was
　　dear.

CLXXVII

There might be one more motive, which
　　makes two;
　Alfonso ne'er to Juan had alluded, — 1410
Mention'd his jealousy, but never who
　Had been the happy lover, he concluded,
Conceal'd amongst his premises; 't is true,
　His mind the more o'er this its mystery
　　brooded;
To speak of Inez now were, one may say,
Like throwing Juan in Alfonso's way.

CLXXVIII

A hint, in tender cases, is enough;
　Silence is best, besides there is a *tact*
(That modern phrase appears to me sad
　　stuff,
　But it will serve to keep my verse com-
　　pact) —　　　　　　　　　　　1420
Which keeps, when push'd by questions
　　rather rough,
　A lady always distant from the fact:
The charming creatures lie with such a
　　grace,
There 's nothing so becoming to the face.

CLXXIX

They blush, and we believe them; at least I
　Have always done so; 't is of no great
　　use,
In any case, attempting a reply,
　For then their eloquence grows quite
　　profuse;

And when at length they 're out of breath,
 they sigh,
 And cast their languid eyes down, and
 let loose 1430
A tear or two, and then we make it up;
And then — and then — and then — sit
 down and sup.

CLXXX

Alfonso closed his speech, and begg'd her
 pardon,
 Which Julia half withheld, and then half
 granted,
And laid conditions he thought very hard
 on,
 Denying several little things he wanted:
He stood like Adam lingering near his
 garden,
 With useless penitence perplex'd and
 haunted,
Beseeching she no further would refuse,
When, lo! he stumbled o'er a pair of
 shoes. 1440

CLXXXI

A pair of shoes! — what then? not much,
 if they
 Are such as fit with ladies' feet, but these
(No one can tell how much I grieve to say)
 Were masculine; to see them, and to seize,
Was but a moment's act. — Ah! well-a-
 day!
 My teeth begin to chatter, my veins
 freeze —
Alfonso first examined well their fashion,
And then flew out into another passion.

CLXXXII

He left the room for his relinquish'd sword,
 And Julia instant to the closet flew. 1450
'Fly, Juan, fly! for heaven's sake — not a
 word —
 The door is open — you may yet slip
 through
The passage you so often have explored —
 Here is the garden-key — Fly — fly —
 Adieu!
Haste — haste! I hear Alfonso's hurrying
 feet —
Day has not broke — there 's no one in the
 street.'

CLXXXIII

None can say that this was not good advice,
 The only mischief was, it came too late;

Of all experience 't is the usual price,
 A sort of income-tax laid on by fate: 1460
Juan had reach'd the room-door in a trice,
 And might have done so by the garden-
 gate,
But met Alfonso in his dressing-gown,
Who threaten'd death — so Juan knock'd
 him down.

CLXXXIV

Dire was the scuffle, and out went the
 light;
 Antonia cried out 'Rape!' and Julia
 'Fire!'
But not a servant stirr'd to aid the fight.
 Alfonso, pommell'd to his heart's de-
 sire,
Swore lustily he 'd be revenged this night;
 And Juan, too, blasphemed an octave
 higher; 1470
His blood was up: though young, he was a
 Tartar,
And not at all disposed to prove a martyr.

CLXXXV

Alfonso's sword had dropp'd ere he could
 draw it,
 And they continued battling hand to hand,
For Juan very luckily ne'er saw it;
 His temper not being under great com-
 mand,
If at that moment he had chanced to claw
 it,
 Alfonso's days had not been in the land
Much longer. — Think of husbands', lovers'
 lives!
And how ye may be doubly widows — wives!

CLXXXVI

Alfonso grappled to detain the foe, 1481
 And Juan throttled him to get away,
And blood ('t was from the nose) began to
 flow;
 At last, as they more faintly wrestling
 lay,
Juan contrived to give an awkward blow,
 And then his only garment quite gave
 way;
He fled, like Joseph, leaving it; but there,
I doubt, all likeness ends between the pair.

CLXXXVII

Lights came at length, and men, and maids,
 who found
 An awkward spectacle their eyes before;

Antonia in hysterics, Julia swoon'd, 1491
 Alfonso leaning, breathless, by the door;
Some half-torn drapery scatter'd on the
 ground,
 Some blood, and several footsteps, but no
 more:
Juan the gate gain'd, turn'd the key about,
And liking not the inside, lock'd the out.

CLXXXVIII

Here ends this canto. — Need I sing, or say,
 How Juan naked, favour'd by the night,
Who favours what she should not, found his
 way,
 And reach'd his home in an unseemly
 plight? 1500
The pleasant scandal which arose next day,
 The nine days' wonder which was brought
 to light,
And how Alfonso sued for a divorce,
Were in the English newspapers, of course.

CLXXXIX

If you would like to see the whole proceed-
 ings,
 The depositions, and the cause at full,
The names of all the witnesses, the plead-
 ings
 Of counsel to nonsuit, or to annul,
There's more than one edition, and the
 readings
 Are various, but they none of them are
 dull; 1510
The best is that in short-hand ta'en by Gur-
 ney,
Who to Madrid on purpose made a journey.

CXC

But Donna Inez, to divert the train
 Of one of the most circulating scandals
That had for centuries been known in Spain,
 At least since the retirement of the Van-
 dals,
First vow'd (and never had she vow'd in
 vain)
 To Virgin Mary several pounds of can-
 dles;
And then, by the advice of some old ladies,
She sent her son to be shipp'd off from
 Cadiz. 1520

CXCI

She had resolved that he should travel
 through
 All European climes, by land or sea,

To mend his former morals, and get new,
 Especially in France and Italy
(At least this is the thing most people do).
 Julia was sent into a convent: she
Grieved, but, perhaps, her feelings may be
 better
Shown in the following copy of her Let-
 ter: —

CXCII

'They tell me 't is decided; you depart:
 'T is wise — 't is well, but not the less a
 pain; 1530
I have no further claim on your young heart,
 Mine is the victim, and would be again;
To love too much has been the only art
 I used; — I write in haste, and if a stain
Be on this sheet, 't is not what it appears;
My eyeballs burn and throb, but have no
 tears.

CXCIII

'I loved, I love you, for this love have
 lost
 State, station, heaven, mankind's, my own
 esteem,
And yet can not regret what it hath cost,
 So dear is still the memory of that dream;
Yet, if I name my guilt, 't is not to boast,
 None can deem harshlier of me than I
 deem: 1542
I trace this scrawl because I cannot rest —
I 've nothing to reproach, or to request.

CXCIV

'Man's love is of man's life a thing apart,
 'T is woman's whole existence; man may
 range
The court, camp, church, the vessel, and the
 mart;
 Sword, gown, gain, glory, offer in ex-
 change
Pride, fame, ambition, to fill up his heart,
 And few there are whom these cannot
 estrange; 1550
Men have all these resources, we but one,
To love again, and be again undone.

CXCV

'You will proceed in pleasure, and in
 pride,
 Beloved and loving many; all is o'er
For me on earth, except some years to hide
 My shame and sorrow deep in my heart's
 core;

These I could bear, but cannot cast aside
 The passion which still rages as before —
And so farewell — forgive me, love me —
 No,
That word is idle now — but let it go. 1560

CXCVI

'My breast has been all weakness, is so yet;
 But still I think I can collect my mind;
My blood still rushes where my spirit 's set,
 As roll the waves before the settled
 wind;
My heart is feminine, nor can forget —
 To all, except one image, madly blind;
So shakes the needle, and so stands the pole,
As vibrates my fond heart to my fix'd soul.

CXCVII

' I have no more to say, but linger still,
 And dare not set my seal upon this sheet,
And yet I may as well the task fulfil, 1571
 My misery can scarce be more complete:
I had not lived till now, could sorrow kill;
 Death shuns the wretch who fain the blow
 would meet,
And I must even survive this last adieu,
And bear with life, to love and pray for
 you !'

CXCVIII

This note was written upon gilt-edged paper
 With a neat little crow-quill, slight and
 new:
Her small white hand could hardly reach
 the taper,
 It trembled as magnetic needles do, 1580
And yet she did not let one tear escape her;
 The seal a sun-flower; ' *Elle vous suit
 partout*,'
The motto cut upon a white cornelian;
The wax was superfine, its hue vermilion.

CXCIX

This was Don Juan's earliest scrape; but
 whether
 I shall proceed with his adventures is
Dependent on the public altogether;
 We 'll see, however, what they say to
 this:
Their favour in an author's cap 's a feather,
 And no great mischief 's done by their
 caprice; 1590
And if their approbation we experience,
Perhaps they 'll have some more about a
 year hence.

CC

My poem 's epic, and is meant to be
 Divided in twelve books; each book con-
 taining,
With love, and war, a heavy gale at sea,
 A list of ships, and captains, and kings
 reigning,
New characters; the episodes are three:
 A panoramic view of hell 's in training,
After the style of Virgil and of Homer,
So that my name of Epic 's no misnomer. 1600

CCI

All these things will be specified in time,
 With strict regard to Aristotle's rules,
The *Vade Mecum* of the true sublime,
 Which makes so many poets, and some
 fools:
Prose poets like blank-verse, I 'm fond of
 rhyme,
 Good workmen never quarrel with their
 tools;
I 've got new mythological machinery,
And very handsome supernatural scenery.

CCII

There 's only one slight difference be-
 tween 1609
Me and my epic brethren gone before,
And here the advantage is my own, I ween
 (Not that I have not several merits
 more,
But this will more peculiarly be seen);
 They so embellish, that 't is quite a bore
Their labyrinth of fables to thread through,
Whereas this story 's actually true.

CCIII

If any person doubt it, I appeal
 To history, tradition, and to facts,
To newspapers, whose truth all know and
 feel,
 To plays in five, and operas in three acts;
All these confirm my statement a good
 deal, 1621
 But that which more completely faith
 exacts
Is that myself, and several now in Seville,
Saw Juan's last elopement with the devil.

CCIV

If ever I should condescend to prose,
 I 'll write poetical commandments, which
Shall supersede beyond all doubt all those
 That went before; in these I shall enrich

My text with many things that no one
 knows, 1629
And carry precept to the highest pitch:
I 'll call the work ' Longinus o'er a Bottle,
Or, Every Poet his *own* Aristotle.'

CCV

Thou shalt believe in Milton, Dryden, Pope;
 Thou shalt not set up Wordsworth, Cole-
 ridge, Southey;
Because the first is crazed beyond all hope,
 The second drunk, the third so quaint
 and mouthy:
With Crabbe it may be difficult to cope,
 And Campbell's Hippocrene is somewhat
 drouthy:
Thou shalt not steal from Samuel Rogers,
 nor
Commit — flirtation with the muse of
 Moore. 1640

CCVI

Thou shalt not covet Mr. Sotheby's Muse,
 His Pegasus, nor anything that 's his;
Thou shalt not bear false witness like ' the
 Blues '
 (There 's one, at least, is very fond of
 this);
Thou shalt not write, in short, but what I
 choose:
 This is true criticism, and you may kiss —
Exactly as you please, or not, — the rod;
But if you don't, I 'll lay it on, by G—d !

CCVII

If any person should presume to assert
 This story is not moral, first, I pray,
That they will not cry out before they 're
 hurt, 1651
 Then that they 'll read it o'er again, and
 say
(But, doubtless, nobody will be so pert)
 That this is not a moral tale, though
 gay;
Besides, in Canto Twelfth, I mean to show
The very place where wicked people go.

CCVIII

If, after all, there should be some so blind
 To their own good this warning to despise,
Led by some tortuosity of mind,
 Not to believe my verse and their own
 eyes, 1660
And cry that they ' the moral cannot find,'
 I tell him, if a clergyman, he lies;

Should captains the remark, or critics, make,
They also lie too — under a mistake.

CCIX

The public approbation I expect,
 And beg they 'll take my word about the
 moral,
Which I with their amusement will connect
 (So children cutting teeth receive a coral);
Meantime, they 'll doubtless please to
 recollect
 My epical pretensions to the laurel: 1670
For fear some prudish readers should grow
 skittish,
I 've bribed my grandmother's review —
 the British.

CCX

I sent it in a letter to the Editor,
 Who thank'd me duly by return of post —
I 'm for a handsome article his creditor;
 Yet, if my gentle Muse he please to
 roast,
And break a promise after having made it
 her,
Denying the receipt of what it cost,
And smear his page with gall instead of
 honey, 1679
All I can say is — that he had the money.

CCXI

I think that with this holy new alliance
 I may ensure the public, and defy
All other magazines of art or science,
 Daily, or monthly, or three monthly; I
Have not essay'd to multiply their clients,
 Because they tell me 't were in vain to
 try,
And that the Edinburgh Review and Quar-
 terly
Treat a dissenting author very martyrly.

CCXII

' *Non ego hoc ferrem calidâ juventâ*
 Consule Planco,' Horace said, and so 1690
Say I; by which quotation there is meant a
 Hint that some six or seven good years
 ago
(Long ere I dreamt of dating from the
 Brenta)
 I was most ready to return a blow,
And would not brook at all this sort of
 thing
In my hot youth — when George the Third
 was King.

CCXIII

But now at thirty years my hair is grey
 (I wonder what it will be like at forty ?
I thought of a peruke the other day) —
 My heart is not much greener; and, in
 short, I 1700
Have squander'd my whole summer while
 't was May,
 And feel no more the spirit to retort; I
Have spent my life, both interest and prin-
 cipal,
And deem not, what I deem'd, my soul
 invincible.

CCXIV

No more — no more — Oh ! never more on
 me
 The freshness of the heart can fall like
 dew,
Which out of all the lovely things we see
 Extracts emotions beautiful and new,
Hived in our bosoms like the bag o' the
 bee:
 Think'st thou the honey with those ob-
 jects grew ? 1710
Alas ! 't was not in them, but in thy power
To double even the sweetness of a flower.

CCXV

No more — no more — Oh ! never more,
 my heart,
 Canst thou be my sole world, my uni-
 verse !
Once all in all, but now a thing apart,
 Thou canst not be my blessing or my
 curse:
The illusion 's gone for ever, and thou art
 Insensible, I trust, but none the worse,
And in thy stead I 've got a deal of judg-
 ment,
 Though heaven knows how it ever found a
 lodgment. 1720

CCXVI

My days of love are over; me no more
 The charms of maid, wife, and still less
 of widow,
Can make the fool of which they made be-
 fore, —
 In short, I must not lead the life I did
 do;
The credulous hope of mutual minds is o'er,
 The copious use of claret is forbid too,
So for a good old-gentlemanly vice,
I think I must take up with avarice.

CCXVII

Ambition was my idol, which was broken
 Before the shrines of Sorrow, and of
 Pleasure; 1730
And the two last have left me many a token
 O'er which reflection may be made at
 leisure:
Now, like Friar Bacon's brazen head, I 've
 spoken,
 ' Time is, Time was, Time 's past: ' — a
 chymic treasure
Is glittering youth, which I have spent be-
 times —
My heart in passion, and my head on rhymes.

CCXVIII

What is the end of Fame ? 't is but to fill
 A certain portion of uncertain paper:
Some liken it to climbing up a hill,
 Whose summit, like all hills, is lost in
 vapour; 1740
For this men write, speak, preach, and
 heroes kill,
 And bards burn what they call their
 ' midnight taper,'
To have, when the original is dust,
A name, a wretched picture, and worse bust.

CCXIX

What are the hopes of man ? Old Egypt's
 King
 Cheops erected the first pyramid
And largest, thinking it was just the thing
 To keep his memory whole, and mummy
 hid;
But somebody or other rummaging,
 Burglariously broke his coffin's lid: 1750
Let not a monument give you or me hopes,
Since not a pinch of dust remains of Cheops.

CCXX

But I being fond of true philosophy,
 Say very often to myself, ' Alas !
All things that have been born were born
 to die,
 And flesh (which Death mows down to
 hay) is grass;
You 've pass'd your youth not so unplea-
 santly,
 And if you had it o'er again — 't would
 pass —
So thank your stars that matters are no
 worse,
And read your Bible, sir, and mind your
 purse.' 1760

CCXXI

But for the present, gentle reader ! and
 Still gentler purchaser ! the bard — that 's
 I —
Must, with permission, shake you by the
 hand,
 And so ' Your humble servant, and good-
 b'ye ! '
We meet again, if we should understand
 Each other; and if not, I shall not try
Your patience further than by this short
 sample —
'T were well if others follow'd my exam-
 ple.

CCXXII

' Go, little book, from this my solitude !
 I cast thee on the waters — go thy
 ways ! 1770
And if, as I believe, thy vein be good,
 The world will find thee after many
 days.'
When Southey 's read, and Wordsworth
 understood,
 I can't help putting in my claim to
 praise —
The four first rhymes are Southey's every
 line:
For God's sake, reader ! take them not for
 mine.

CANTO THE SECOND

I

Oh ye ! who teach the ingenuous youth of
 nations,
 Holland, France, England, Germany, or
 Spain,
I pray ye flog them upon all occasions,
 It mends their morals, never mind the
 pain:
The best of mothers and of educations
 In Juan's case were but employ'd in
 vain,
Since, in a way that 's rather of the odd-
 est, he
Became divested of his native modesty.

II

Had he but been placed at a public school,
 In the third form, or even in the fourth,
His daily task had kept his fancy cool, 11
 At least, had he been nurtured in the
 north;

Spain may prove an exception to the rule,
 But then exceptions always prove its
 worth —
A lad of sixteen causing a divorce
Puzzled his tutors very much, of course.

III

I can't say that it puzzles me at all,
 If all things be consider'd: first, there was
His lady-mother, mathematical, 19
 A — never mind; his tutor, an old ass;
A pretty woman (that 's quite natural,
 Or else the thing had hardly come to
 pass);
A husband rather old, not much in unity
With his young wife — a time, and oppor-
 tunity.

IV

Well — well, the world must turn upon its
 axis,
 And all mankind turn with it, heads or
 tails,
And live and die, make love and pay our
 taxes,
 And as the veering wind shifts, shift our
 sails;
The king commands us, and the doctor
 quacks us,
 The priest instructs, and so our life ex-
 hales, 30
A little breath, love, wine, ambition, fame,
Fighting, devotion, dust, — perhaps a name.

V

I said that Juan had been sent to Cadiz —
 A pretty town, I recollect it well —
'T is there the mart of the colonial trade is
 (Or was, before Peru learn'd to rebel),
And such sweet girls — I mean, such grace-
 ful ladies,
 Their very walk would make your bosom
 swell;
I can't describe it, though so much it strike,
Nor liken it — I never saw the like: 40

VI

An Arab horse, a stately stag, a barb
 New broke, a cameleopard, a gazelle,
No — none of these will do; — and then
 their garb !
 Their veil and petticoat — Alas ! to dwell
Upon such things would very near absorb
 A canto — then their feet and ankles, —
 well,

Thank Heaven I 've got no metaphor quite
 ready
(And so, my sober Muse — come, let 's be
 steady —

VII

Chaste Muse! — well, if you must, you
 must) — the veil
 Thrown back a moment with the glanc-
 ing hand, 50
While the o'erpowering eye, that turns you
 pale,
 Flashes into the heart: — All sunny land
Of love! when I forget you, may I fail
 To — say my prayers — but never was
 there plann'd
A dress through which the eyes give such
 a volley,
Excepting the Venetian Fazzioli.

VIII

But to our tale: the Donna Inez sent
 Her son to Cadiz only to embark;
To stay there had not answer'd her intent,
 But why? — we leave the reader in the
 dark — 60
'T was for a voyage that the young man
 was meant,
 As if a Spanish ship were Noah's ark,
To wean him from the wickedness of earth,
And send him like a dove of promise forth.

IX

Don Juan bade his valet pack his things
 According to direction, then received
A lecture and some money: for four
 springs
 He was to travel; and though Inez
 grieved
(As every kind of parting has its stings),
 She hoped he would improve — perhaps
 believed: 70
A letter, too, she gave (he never read it)
Of good advice — and two or three of
 credit.

X

In the mean time, to pass her hours away,
 Brave Inez now set up a Sunday school
For naughty children, who would rather
 play
 (Like truant rogues) the devil, or the
 fool;
Infants of three years old were taught that
 day,

Dunces were whipt, or set upon a stool:
The great success of Juan's education,
Spurr'd her to teach another generation. 80

XI

Juan embark'd — the ship got under way,
 The wind was fair, the water passing
 rough:
A devil of a sea rolls in that bay,
 As I, who've cross'd it oft, know well
 enough;
And, standing upon deck, the dashing spray
 Flies in one's face, and makes it weather-
 tough:
And there he stood to take, and take
 again,
His first — perhaps his last — farewell of
 Spain.

XII

I can't but say it is an awkward sight 89
 To see one's native land receding through
The growing waters; it unmans one quite,
 Especially when life is rather new:
I recollect Great Britain's coast looks
 white,
 But almost every other country's blue,
When gazing on them, mystified by dis-
 tance,
We enter on our nautical existence.

XIII

So Juan stood, bewilder'd on the deck:
 The wind sung, cordage strain'd, and
 sailors swore,
And the ship creak'd, the town became a
 speck,
 From which away so fair and fast they
 bore. 100
The best of remedies is a beef-steak
 Against sea-sickness: try it, sir, before
You sneer, and I assure you this is true,
For I have found it answer — so may you.

XIV

Don Juan stood, and, gazing from the stern,
 Beheld his native Spain receding far:
First partings form a lesson hard to learn,
 Even nations feel this when they go to
 war;
There is a sort of unexprest concern,
 A kind of shock that sets one's heart
 ajar: 110
At leaving even the most unpleasant people
And places, one keeps looking at the steeple.

XV

But Juan had got many things to leave,
 His mother, and a mistress, and no wife,
So that he had much better cause to grieve
 Than many persons more advanced in
 life;
And if we now and then a sigh must heave
 At quitting even those we quit in strife,
No doubt we weep for those the heart
 endears — 119
That is, till deeper griefs congeal our tears.

XVI

So Juan wept, as wept the captive Jews
 By Babel's waters, still remembering
 Sion:
I 'd weep, — but mine is not a weeping
 Muse,
 And such light griefs are not a thing to
 die on;
Young men should travel, if but to amuse
 Themselves; and the next time their ser-
 vants tie on
Behind their carriages their new portman-
 teau,
Perhaps it may be lined with this my canto.

XVII

And Juan wept, and much he sigh'd and
 thought,
 While his salt tears dropp'd into the salt
 sea, 130
'Sweets to the sweet' (I like so much to
 quote;
 You must excuse this extract, 't is where
 she,
The Queen of Denmark, for Ophelia brought
 Flowers to the grave); and, sobbing often,
 he
Reflected on his present situation,
And seriously resolved on reformation.

XVIII

'Farewell, my Spain! a long farewell!'
 he cried,
 'Perhaps I may revisit thee no more,
But die, as many an exiled heart hath died,
 Of its own thirst to see again thy shore:
Farewell, where Guadalquivir's waters
 glide! 141
 Farewell, my mother! and, since all is
 o'er,
Farewell, too, dearest Julia! — (Here he
 drew
Her letter out again, and read it through.)

XIX

'And, oh! if e'er I should forget, I swear—
 But that 's impossible, and cannot be —
Sooner shall this blue ocean melt to air,
 Sooner shall earth resolve itself to sea,
Than I resign thine image, oh, my fair!
 Or think of any thing excepting thee; 150
A mind diseased no remedy can physic
(Here the ship gave a lurch, and he grew
 sea-sick).

XX

'Sooner shall heaven kiss earth (here he
 fell sicker),
 Oh, Julia! what is every other wo?
(For God's sake let me have a glass of
 liquor;
 Pedro, Battista, help me down below.)
Julia, my love! (you rascal, Pedro,
 quicker) —
 Oh, Julia! (this curst vessel pitches
 so) —
Beloved Julia, hear me still beseeching!'
(Here he grew inarticulate with retching.)

XXI

He felt that chilling heaviness of heart, 161
 Or rather stomach, which, alas! attends,
Beyond the best apothecary's art,
 The loss of love, the treachery of friends,
Or death of those we dote on, when a part
 Of us dies with them as each fond hope
 ends:
No doubt he would have been much more
 pathetic,
But the sea acted as a strong emetic.

XXII

Love 's a capricious power: I 've known it
 hold
 Out through a fever caused by its own
 heat, 170
But be much puzzled by a cough and cold,
 And find a quinsy very hard to treat;
Against all noble maladies he 's bold,
 But vulgar illnesses don't like to meet,
Nor that a sneeze should interrupt his sigh,
Nor inflammations redden his blind eye.

XXIII

But worst of all is nausea, or a pain
 About the lower region of the bowels;
Love, who heroically breathes a vein,
 Shrinks from the application of hot tow-
 els, 180

And purgatives are dangerous to his reign,
 Sea-sickness death: his love was perfect,
 how else
Could Juan's passion, while the billows roar,
Resist his stomach, ne'er at sea before?

XXIV

The ship, call'd the most holy ' Trinidada,'
 Was steering duly for the port Leghorn;
For there the Spanish family Moncada
 Were settled long ere Juan's sire was
 born:
They were relations, and for them he had a
 Letter of introduction, which the morn
Of his departure had been sent him by 191
His Spanish friends for those in Italy.

XXV

His suite consisted of three servants and
 A tutor, the licentiate Pedrillo,
Who several languages did understand,
 But now lay sick and speechless on his
 pillow,
And rocking in his hammock, long'd for
 land,
 His headache being increased by every
 billow;
And the waves oozing through the port-hole
 made
His berth a little damp, and him afraid. 200

XXVI

'T was not without some reason, for the
 wind
 Increased at night, until it blew a gale;
And though 't was not much to a naval
 mind,
 Some landsmen would have look'd a little
 pale,
For sailors are, in fact, a different kind:
 At sunset they began to take in sail,
For the sky show'd it would come on to
 blow,
And carry away, perhaps, a mast or so.

XXVII

At one o'clock the wind with sudden shift
 Threw the ship right into the trough of
 the sea, 210
Which struck her aft, and made an awk-
 ward rift,
 Started the stern-post, also shatter'd the
Whole of her stern-frame, and, ere she
 could lift
 Herself from out her present jeopardy,

The rudder tore away: 't was time to sound
The pumps, and there were four feet water
 found.

XXVIII

One gang of people instantly was put
 Upon the pumps and the remainder set
To get up part of the cargo, and what not;
 But they could not come at the leak as
 yet; 220
At last they did get at it really, but
 Still their salvation was an even bet:
The water rush'd through in a way quite
 puzzling,
While they thrust sheets, shirts, jackets,
 bales of muslin,

XXIX

Into the opening; but all such ingredients
 Would have been vain, and they must
 have gone down,
Despite of all their efforts and expedients,
 But for the pumps: I 'm glad to make
 them known
To all the brother tars who may have need
 hence,
 For fifty tons of water were upthrown
By them per hour, and they had all been
 undone, 231
But for the maker, Mr. Mann, of London.

XXX

As day advanced the weather seem'd to
 abate,
 And then the leak they reckon'd to re-
 duce,
And keep the ship afloat, though three feet
 yet
 Kept two hand and one chain-pump still
 in use.
The wind blew fresh again: as it grew late
 A squall came on, and while some guns
 broke loose,
A gust — which all descriptive power tran-
 scends —
Laid with one blast the ship on her beam
 ends. 240

XXXI

There she lay motionless, and seem'd upset;
 The water left the hold, and wash'd the
 decks,
And made a scene men do not soon forget;
 For they remember battles, fires, and
 wrecks,

Or any other thing that brings regret,
 Or breaks their hopes, or hearts, or heads,
 or necks:
Thus drownings are much talk'd of by the
 divers,
And swimmers, who may chance to be sur-
 vivors.

XXXII

Immediately the masts were cut away,
 Both main and mizen; first the mizen
 went, 250
The main-mast follow'd: but the ship still
 lay
Like a mere log, and baffled our intent.
Foremast and bowsprit were cut down, and
 they
 Eased her at last (although we never
 meant
To part with all till every hope was blighted),
And then with violence the old ship righted.

XXXIII

It may be easily supposed, while this
 Was going on, some people were unquiet,
That passengers would find it much amiss
 To lose their lives, as well as spoil their
 diet; 260
That even the able seaman, deeming his
 Days nearly o'er, might be disposed to
 riot,
As upon such occasions tars will ask
For grog, and sometimes drink rum from
 the cask.

XXXIV

There 's nought, no doubt, so much the spirit
 calms
 As rum and true religion: thus it was,
Some plunder'd, some drank spirits, some
 sung psalms,
 The high wind made the treble, and as bass
The hoarse harsh waves kept time; fright
 cured the qualms
 Of all the luckless landsmen's sea-sick
 maws: 270
Strange sounds of wailing, blasphemy, de-
 votion,
Clamour'd in chorus to the roaring ocean.

XXXV

Perhaps more mischief had been done, but
 for
 Our Juan, who, with sense beyond his
 years,

Got to the spirit-room, and stood before
 It with a pair of pistols; and their fears,
As if Death were more dreadful by his door
 Of fire than water, spite of oaths and tears,
Kept still aloof the crew, who, ere they sunk,
Thought it would be becoming to die drunk.

XXXVI

'Give us more grog,' they cried, 'for it will
 be 281
 All one an hour hence.' Juan answer'd,
 'No!
'T is true that death awaits both you and me,
 But let us die like men, not sink below
Like brutes;' — and thus his dangerous post
 kept he,
 And none liked to anticipate the blow;
And even Pedrillo, his most reverend tutor,
Was for some rum a disappointed suitor.

XXXVII

The good old gentleman was quite aghast,
 And made a loud and pious lamentation;
Repented all his sins, and made a last 291
 Irrevocable vow of reformation;
Nothing should tempt him more (this peril
 past)
 To quit his academic occupation,
In cloisters of the classic Salamanca,
To follow Juan's wake, like Sancho Panca.

XXXVIII

But now there came a flash of hope once
 more;
 Day broke, and the wind lull'd: the
 masts were gone,
The leak increased; shoals round her, but
 no shore,
 The vessel swam, yet still she held her
 own. 300
They tried the pumps again, and though
 before
 Their desperate efforts seem'd all useless
 grown,
A glimpse of sunshine set some hands to
 bale —
The stronger pump'd, the weaker thrumm'd
 a sail.

XXXIX

Under the vessel's keel the sail was past,
 And for the moment it had some effect;
But with a leak, and not a stick of mast,
 Nor rag of canvas, what could they ex-
 pect?

But still 't is best to struggle to the last,
 'T is never too late to be wholly wreck'd:
And though 't is true that man can only die
 once, 311
'T is not so pleasant in the Gulf of Lyons.

XL

There winds and waves had hurl'd them,
 and from thence,
 Without their will, they carried them
 away;
For they were forced with steering to dis-
 pense,
 And never had as yet a quiet day
On which they might repose, or even com-
 mence
 A jurymast or rudder, or could say
The ship would swim an hour, which, by
 good luck, 319
Still swam — though not exactly like a duck.

XLI

The wind, in fact, perhaps was rather less,
 But the ship labour'd so, they scarce could
 hope
To weather out much longer; the distress
 Was also great with which they had to
 cope
For want of water, and their solid mess
 Was scant enough: in vain the telescope
Was used — nor sail nor shore appear'd in
 sight,
Nought but the heavy sea, and coming
 night.

XLII

Again the weather threaten'd, — again blew
 A gale, and in the fore and after hold 330
Water appear'd; yet, though the people
 knew
 All this, the most were patient, and some
 bold,
Until the chains and leathers were worn
 through
 Of all our pumps: — a wreck complete
 she roll'd,
At mercy of the waves, whose mercies are
Like human beings during civil war.

XLIII

Then came the carpenter, at last, with tears
 In his rough eyes, and told the captain he
Could do no more: he was a man in years,
 And long had voyaged through many a
 stormy sea, 340

And if he wept at length, they were not
 fears
 That made his eyelids as a woman's be,
But he, poor fellow, had a wife and chil-
 dren, —
Two things for dying people quite bewil-
 dering.

XLIV

The ship was evidently settling now
 Fast by the head; and, all distinction gone,
Some went to prayers again, and made a
 vow
 Of candles to their saints — but there
 were none
To pay them with; and some look'd o'er
 the bow;
 Some hoisted out the boats; and there
 was one 350
That begg'd Pedrillo for an absolution,
Who told him to be damn'd — in his confu-
 sion.

XLV

Some lash'd them in their hammocks; some
 put on
 Their best clothes, as if going to a fair;
Some cursed the day on which they saw the
 sun,
 And gnash'd their teeth, and, howling,
 tore their hair;
And others went on as they had begun,
 Getting the boats out, being well aware
That a tight boat will live in a rough sea,
Unless with breakers close beneath her lee.

XLVI

The worst of all was, that in their condi-
 tion, 361
 Having been several days in great dis-
 tress,
'T was difficult to get out such provision
 As now might render their long suffering
 less:
Men, even when dying, dislike inanition;
 Their stock was damaged by the weath-
 er's stress:
Two casks of biscuit and a keg of butter
Were all that could be thrown into the
 cutter.

XLVII

But in the long-boat they contrived to stow
 Some pounds of bread, though injured by
 the wet; 370

Water, a twenty-gallon cask or so;
 Six flasks of wine; and they contrived to
 get
A portion of their beef up from below,
 And with a piece of pork, moreover,
 met,
But scarce enough to serve them for a
 luncheon —
 Then there was rum, eight gallons in a
 puncheon.

XLVIII

The other boats, the yawl and pinnace, had
 Been stove in the beginning of the gale;
And the long-boat's condition was but
 bad,
 As there were but two blankets for a
 sail, 380
And one oar for a mast, which a young
 lad
 Threw in by good luck over the ship's
 rail;
And two boats could not hold, far less be
 stored,
 To save one half the people then on board.

XLIX

'T was twilight, and the sunless day went
 down
 Over the waste of waters; like a veil,
Which, if withdrawn, would but disclose
 the frown
 Of one whose hate is mask'd but to
 assail,
Thus to their hopeless eyes the night was
 shown,
 And grimly darkled o'er the faces pale,
And the dim desolate deep: twelve days
 had Fear 391
 Been their familiar, and now Death was
 here.

L

Some trial had been making at a raft,
 With little hope in such a rolling sea,
A sort of thing at which one would have
 laugh'd,
 If any laughter at such times could be,
Unless with people who too much have
 quaff'd,
 And have a kind of wild and horrid
 glee,
Half epileptical and half hysterical: —
 Their preservation would have been a
 miracle. 400

LI

At half-past eight o'clock, booms, hencoops,
 spars,
 And all things, for a chance, had been
 cast loose,
That still could keep afloat the struggling
 tars,
 For yet they strove, although of no great
 use:
There was no light in heaven but a few
 stars,
 The boats put off o'ercrowded with their
 crews;
She gave a heel, and then a lurch to port,
And, going down head foremost — sunk, in
 short.

LII

Then rose from sea to sky the wild fare-
 well —
 Then shriek'd the timid, and stood still
 the brave, 410
Then some leap'd overboard with dreadful
 yell,
 As eager to anticipate their grave;
And the sea yawn'd around her like a hell,
 And down she suck'd with her the whirl-
 ing wave,
Like one who grapples with his enemy,
And strives to strangle him before he die.

LIII

And first one universal shriek there rush'd,
 Louder than the loud ocean, like a crash
Of echoing thunder; and then all was
 hush'd,
 Save the wild wind and the remorseless
 dash 420
Of billows; but at intervals there gush'd,
 Accompanied with a convulsive splash,
A solitary shriek, the bubbling cry
Of some strong swimmer in his agony.

LIV

The boats, as stated, had got off before,
 And in them crowded several of the
 crew;
And yet their present hope was hardly
 more
 Than what it had been, for so strong it
 blew
There was slight chance of reaching any
 shore;
 And then they were too many, though so
 few — 430

Nine in the cutter, thirty in the boat,
Were counted in them when they got
afloat.

LV

All the rest perish'd; near two hundred
souls
 Had left their bodies; and what's worse,
alas !
When over Catholics the ocean rolls,
 They must wait several weeks before a
mass
Takes off one peck of purgatorial coals,
 Because, till people know what's come
to pass,
They won't lay out their money on the
dead —
It costs three francs for every mass that's
said. 440

LVI

Juan got into the long-boat, and there
 Contrived to help Pedrillo to a place;
It seem'd as if they had exchanged their
care,
 For Juan wore the magisterial face
Which courage gives, while poor Pedrillo's
pair
 Of eyes were crying for their owner's
case:
Battista, though (a name call'd shortly
Tita),
Was lost by getting at some aqua-vita.

LVII

Pedro, his valet, too, he tried to save,
 But the same cause, conducive to his
loss, 450
Left him so drunk, he jump'd into the wave
 As o'er the cutter's edge he tried to cross,
And so he found a wine-and-watery grave;
 They could not rescue him although so
close,
Because the sea ran higher every minute,
And for the boat — the crew kept crowding
in it.

LVIII

A small old spaniel, — which had been Don
José's,
 His father's, whom he loved, as ye may
think,
For on such things the memory reposes
 With tenderness — stood howling on the
brink, 460

Knowing (dogs have such intellectual
noses !),
 No doubt, the vessel was about to sink;
And Juan caught him up, and ere he stepp'd
Off, threw him in, then after him he leap'd.

LIX

He also stuff'd his money where he could
 About his person, and Pedrillo's too,
Who let him do, in fact, whate'er he would,
 Not knowing what himself to say, or do,
As every rising wave his dread renew'd;
 But Juan, trusting they might still get
through, 470
And deeming there were remedies for any
ill,
Thus re-embark'd his tutor and his spaniel.

LX

'T was a rough night, and blew so stiffly yet,
 That the sail was becalm'd between the
seas,
Though on the wave's high top too much
to set,
 They dared not take it in for all the
breeze:
Each sea curl'd o'er the stern, and kept
them wet,
 And made them bale without a moment's
ease,
So that themselves as well as hopes were
damp'd,
And the poor little cutter quickly swamp'd.

LXI

Nine souls more went in her: the long-boat
still 481
 Kept above water, with an oar for mast,
Two blankets stitch'd together, answering
ill
 Instead of sail, were to the oar made fast:
Though every wave roll'd menacing to fill,
 And present peril all before surpass'd,
They grieved for those who perish'd with
the cutter,
And also for the biscuit-casks and butter.

LXII

The sun rose red and fiery, a sure sign
 Of the continuance of the gale: to run 490
Before the sea until it should grow fine,
 Was all that for the present could be
done:
A few tea-spoonfuls of their rum and wine
 Were served out to the people, who begun

To faint, and damaged bread wet through
 the bags,
And most of them had little clothes but rags.

LXIII

They counted thirty, crowded in a space
 Which left scarce room for motion or
 exertion;
They did their best to modify their case,
 One half sate up, though numb'd with the
 immersion, 500
While t'other half were laid down in their
 place
 At watch and watch; thus, shivering like
 the tertian
Ague in its cold fit, they fill'd their boat,
With nothing but the sky for a great coat.

LXIV

'T is very certain the desire of life
 Prolongs it: this is obvious to physicians,
When patients, neither plagued with friends
 nor wife,
 Survive through very desperate condi-
 tions,
Because they still can hope, nor shines the
 knife 509
 Nor shears of Atropos before their visions:
Despair of all recovery spoils longevity,
And makes men's miseries of alarming
 brevity.

LXV

'T is said that persons living on annuities
 Are longer lived than others, — God
 knows why,
Unless to plague the grantors, — yet so
 true it is,
 That some, I really think, *do* never die;
Of any creditors the worst a Jew it is,
 And *that*'s their mode of furnishing sup-
 ply:
In my young days they lent me cash that
 way,
Which I found very troublesome to pay. 520

LXVI

'T is thus with people in an open boat,
 They live upon the love of life, and bear
More than can be believed, or even thought,
 And stand like rocks the tempest's wear
 and tear;
And hardship still has been the sailor's lot,
 Since Noah's ark went cruising here and
 there;

She had a curious crew as well as cargo,
Like the first old Greek privateer, the Argo.

LXVII

But man is a carnivorous production,
 And must have meals, at least one meal
 a day; 530
He cannot live, like woodcocks, upon suc-
 tion,
 But, like the shark and tiger, must have
 prey;
Although his anatomical construction
 Bears vegetables, in a grumbling way,
Your labouring people think beyond all
 question,
Beef, veal, and mutton, better for digestion.

LXVIII

And thus it was with this our hapless crew;
 For on the third day there came on a
 calm,
And though at first their strength it might
 renew, 539
 And lying on their weariness like balm,
Lull'd them like turtles sleeping on the blue
 Of ocean, when they woke they felt a
 qualm,
And fell all ravenously on their provision,
Instead of hoarding it with due precision.

LXIX

The consequence was easily foreseen —
 They ate up all they had, and drank their
 wine,
In spite of all remonstrances, and then
 On what, in fact, next day were they to
 dine?
They hoped the wind would rise, these fool-
 ish men!
 And carry them to shore; these hopes
 were fine, 550
But as they had but one oar, and that brit-
 tle,
It would have been more wise to save their
 victual.

LXX

The fourth day came, but not a breath of
 air,
 And Ocean slumber'd like an unwean'd
 child:
The fifth day, and their boat lay floating
 there,
 The sea and sky were blue, and clear, and
 mild —

With their one oar (I wish they had had a
 pair)
 What could they do ? and hunger's rage
 grew wild:
So Juan's spaniel, spite of his entreating,
Was kill'd and portion'd out for present
 eating. 560

LXXI

On the sixth day they fed upon his hide,
 And Juan, who had still refused, because
The creature was his father's dog that died,
 Now feeling all the vulture in his jaws,
With some remorse received (though first
 denied)
 As a great favour one of the fore-paws,
Which he divided with Pedrillo, who
Devour'd it, longing for the other too.

LXXII

The seventh day, and no wind — the burn-
 ing sun
 Blister'd and scorch'd, and, stagnant on
 the sea, 570
They lay like carcasses; and hope was none,
 Save in the breeze that came not; savagely
They glared upon each other — all was done,
 Water, and wine, and food, — and you
 might see
The longings of the cannibal arise
(Although they spoke not) in their wolfish
 eyes.

LXXIII

At length one whisper'd his companion, who
 Whisper'd another, and thus it went round,
And then into a hoarser murmur grew,
 An ominous, and wild, and desperate
 sound; 580
And when his comrade's thought each suf-
 ferer knew,
 'T was but his own, suppress'd till now,
 he found:
And out they spoke of lots for flesh and
 blood,
And who should die to be his fellow's food.

LXXIV

But ere they came to this, they that day
 shared
 Some leathern caps, and what remain'd
 of shoes ;
And then they look'd around them and
 despair'd,
 And none to be the sacrifice would choose;

At length the lots were torn up, and pre-
 pared,
 But of materials that much shock the
 Muse — 590
Having no paper, for the want of better,
They took by force from Juan Julia's letter.

LXXV

The lots were made, and mark'd, and mix'd,
 and handed,
 In silent horror, and their distribution
Lull'd even the savage hunger which de-
 manded,
 Like the Promethean vulture, this pollu-
 tion;
None in particular had sought or plann'd
 it,
 'T was nature gnaw'd them to this reso-
 lution,
By which none were permitted to be neu-
 ter —
And the lot fell on Juan's luckless tutor.

LXXVI

He but requested to be bled to death: 601
 The surgeon had his instruments, and bled
Pedrillo, and so gently ebb'd his breath,
 You hardly could perceive when he was
 dead.
He died as born, a Catholic in faith,
 Like most in the belief in which they 're
 bred,
And first a little crucifix he kiss'd,
And then held out his jugular and wrist.

LXXVII

The surgeon, as there was no other fee,
 Had his first choice of morsels for his
 pains; 610
But being thirstiest at the moment, he
 Preferr'd a draught from the fast-flow-
 ing veins:
Part was divided, part thrown in the sea,
 And such things as the entrails and the
 brains
Regaled two sharks, who follow'd o'er the
 billow —
The sailors ate the rest of poor Pedrillo.

LXXVIII

The sailors ate him, all save three or four,
 Who were not quite so fond of animal
 food;
To these was added Juan, who, before 619
 Refusing his own spaniel, hardly could

Feel now his appetite increased much more;
 'T was not to be expected that he should,
Even in extremity of their disaster,
Dine with them on his pastor and his mas-
 ter.

LXXIX

'T was better that he did not; for, in fact,
 The consequence was awful in the ex-
 treme;
For they, who were most ravenous in the
 act,
 Went raging mad — Lord ! how they did
 blaspheme !
And foam and roll, with strange convulsions
 rack'd,
 Drinking salt-water like a mountain-
 stream, 630
Tearing, and grinning, howling, screeching,
 swearing,
And, with hyæna-laughter, died despairing.

LXXX

Their numbers were much thinn'd by this
 infliction,
 And all the rest were thin enough, Heaven
 knows;
And some of them had lost their recollec-
 tion,
 Happier than they who still perceived
 their woes;
But others ponder'd on a new dissection,
 As if not warn'd sufficiently by those
Who had already perish'd, suffering madly,
For having used their appetites so sadly.

LXXXI

And next they thought upon the master's
 mate, 641
 As fattest; but he saved himself, because,
Besides being much averse from such a fate,
 There were some other reasons: the first
 was,
He had been rather indisposed of late;
 And that which chiefly proved his saving
 clause
Was a small present made to him at Cadiz,
By general subscription of the ladies.

LXXXII

Of poor Pedrillo something still remain'd,
 But was used sparingly, — some were
 afraid, 650
And others still their appetites constrain'd,
 Or but at times a little supper made;

All except Juan, who throughout abstain'd,
 Chewing a piece of bamboo and some
 lead:
At length they caught two boobies and a
 noddy,
And then they left off eating the dead body.

LXXXIII

And if Pedrillo's fate should shocking be,
 Remember Ugolino condescends
To eat the head of his arch-enemy
 The moment after he politely ends 660
His tale: if foes be food in hell, at sea
 'T is surely fair to dine upon our friends,
When shipwreck's short allowance grows
 too scanty,
Without being much more horrible than
 Dante.

LXXXIV

And the same night there fell a shower of rain,
 For which their mouths gaped, like the
 cracks of earth
When dried to summer dust; till taught by
 pain
 Men really know not what good water 's
 worth;
If you had been in Turkey or in Spain,
 Or with a famish'd boat's-crew had your
 berth, 670
Or in the desert heard the camel's bell,
You 'd wish yourself where Truth is — in a
 well.

LXXXV

It pour'd down torrents, but they were no
 richer
 Until they found a ragged piece of sheet,
Which served them as a sort of spongy
 pitcher,
 And when they deem'd its moisture was
 complete
They wrung it out, and though a thirsty
 ditcher
 Might not have thought the scanty
 draught so sweet
As a full pot of porter, to their thinking
They ne'er till now had known the joys of
 drinking. 680

LXXXVI

And their baked lips, with many a bloody
 crack,
 Suck'd in the moisture, which like nectar
 stream'd;

Their throats were ovens, their swoln
 tongues were black,
 As the rich man's in hell, who vainly
 scream'd
To beg the beggar, who could not rain back
 A drop of dew, when every drop had
 seem'd
To taste of heaven — If this be true, indeed
Some Christians have a comfortable creed.

LXXXVII

There were two fathers in this ghastly crew,
 And with them their two sons, of whom
 the one 690
Was more robust and hardy to the view,
 But he died early; and when he was gone,
His nearest messmate told his sire, who
 threw
 One glance at him, and said, ' Heaven's
 will be done !
I can do nothing,' and he saw him thrown
Into the deep without a tear or groan.

LXXXVIII

The other father had a weaklier child,
 Of a soft cheek and aspect delicate;
But the boy bore up long, and with a mild
 And patient spirit held aloof his fate; 700
Little he said, and now and then he smiled,
 As if to win a part from off the weight
He saw increasing on his father's heart,
 With the deep deadly thought that they
 must part.

LXXXIX

And o'er him bent his sire, and never raised
 His eyes from off his face, but wiped the
 foam
From his pale lips, and ever on him gazed,
 And when the wish'd-for shower at length
 was come,
And the boy's eyes, which the dull film half
 glazed,
 Brighten'd, and for a moment seem'd to
 roam, 710
He squeezed from out a rag some drops of
 rain
Into his dying child's mouth — but in vain.

XC

The boy expired — the father held the clay,
 And look'd upon it long, and when at
 last
Death left no doubt, and the dead burthen
 lay

Stiff on his heart, and pulse and hope
 were past,
He watch'd it wistfully, until away
 'T was borne by the rude wave wherein
 't was cast;
Then he himself sunk down all dumb and
 shivering,
And gave no sign of life, save his limbs
 quivering. 720

XCI

Now overhead a rainbow, bursting through
 The scattering clouds, shone, spanning
 the dark sea,
Resting its bright base on the quivering
 blue;
 And all within its arch appear'd to be
Clearer than that without, and its wide hue
 Wax'd broad and waving, like a banner
 free,
Then changed like to a bow that 's bent,
 and then
Forsook the dim eyes of these shipwreck'd
 men.

XCII

It changed, of course; a heavenly chame-
 leon,
 The airy child of vapour and the sun, 730
Brought forth in purple, cradled in ver-
 milion,
 Baptized in molten gold, and swathed in
 dun,
Glittering like crescents o'er a Turk's pa-
 vilion,
 And blending every colour into one,
Just like a black eye in a recent scuffle
(For sometimes we must box without the
 muffle).

XCIII

Our shipwreck'd seamen thought it a good
 omen —
 It is as well to think so, now and then;
'T was an old custom of the Greek and
 Roman,
 And may become of great advantage
 when 740
Folks are discouraged; and most surely no
 men
 Had greater need to nerve themselves
 again
Than these, and so this rainbow look'd like
 hope —
Quite a celestial kaleidoscope.

XCIV

About this time a beautiful white bird,
 Webfooted, not unlike a dove in size
And plumage (probably it might have err'd
 Upon its course), pass'd oft before their
 eyes,
And tried to perch, although it saw and
 heard
 The men within the boat, and in this
 guise 750
It came and went, and flutter'd round them
 till
Night fell: this seem'd a better omen still.

XCV

But in this case I also must remark,
 'T was well this bird of promise did not
 perch,
Because the tackle of our shatter'd bark
 Was not so safe for roosting as a church;
And had it been the dove from Noah's ark,
 Returning there from her successful
 search,
Which in their way that moment chanced
 to fall,
They would have eat her, olive-branch and
 all. 760

XCVI

With twilight it again came on to blow,
 But not with violence; the stars shone
 out,
The boat made way; yet now they were so
 low,
 They knew not where nor what they
 were about;
Some fancied they saw land, and some said
 'No!'
 The frequent fog-banks gave them cause
 to doubt —
Some swore that they heard breakers,
 others guns,
And all mistook about the latter once.

XCVII

As morning broke, the light wind died away,
 When he who had the watch sung out
 and swore, 770
If 't was not land that rose with the sun's
 ray,
 He wish'd that land he never might see
 more;
And the rest rubb'd their eyes and saw a bay,
 Or thought they saw, and shaped their
 course for shore;

For shore it was, and gradually grew
Distinct, and high, and palpable to view.

XCVIII

And then of these some part burst into
 tears,
 And others, looking with a stupid stare,
Could not yet separate their hopes from
 fears,
 And seem'd as if they had no further
 care; 780
While a few pray'd (the first time for some
 years) —
 And at the bottom of the boat three were
Asleep: they shook them by the hand and
 head,
And tried to awaken them, but found them
 dead.

XCIX

The day before, fast sleeping on the water
 They found a turtle of the hawk's-bill
 kind,
And by good fortune, gliding softly, caught
 her,
 Which yielded a day's life, and to their
 mind
Proved even still a more nutritious matter,
 Because it left encouragement behind:
They thought that in such perils, more than
 chance 791
Had sent them this for their deliverance.

C

The land appear'd a high and rocky coast,
 And higher grew the mountains as they
 drew,
Set by a current, toward it: they were lost
 In various conjectures, for none knew
To what part of the earth they had been
 tost,
 So changeable had been the winds that
 blew;
Some thought it was Mount Ætna, some
 the highlands, 799
Of Candia, Cyprus, Rhodes, or other islands.

CI

Meantime the current, with a rising gale,
 Still set them onwards to the welcome
 shore,
Like Charon's bark of spectres, dull and
 pale:
 Their living freight was now reduced to
 four,

And three dead, whom their strength
 could not avail
 To heave into the deep with those be-
 fore,
Though the two sharks still follow'd them,
 and dash'd
The spray into their faces as they splash'd.

CII

Famine, despair, cold, thirst, and heat, had
 done
 Their work on them by turns, and thinn'd
 them to 810
Such things a mother had not known her
 son
 Amidst the skeletons of that gaunt crew;
By night chill'd, by day scorch'd, thus one
 by one
 They perish'd, until wither'd to these
 few,
But chiefly by a species of self-slaughter,
In washing down Pedrillo with salt water.

CIII

As they drew nigh the land, which now was
 seen
 Unequal in its aspect here and there,
They felt the freshness of its growing green,
 That waved in forest-tops, and smooth'd
 the air, 820
And fell upon their glazed eyes like a screen
 From glistening waves, and skies so hot
 and bare —
Lovely seem'd any object that should sweep
Away the vast, salt, dread, eternal deep.

CIV

The shore look'd wild, without a trace of
 man,
 And girt by formidable waves; but they
Were mad for land, and thus their course
 they ran,
 Though right ahead the roaring breakers
 lay:
A reef between them also now began
 To show its boiling surf and bounding
 spray, 830
But finding no place for their landing better,
They ran the boat for shore, — and over-
 set her.

CV

But in his native stream, the Guadalquivir,
 Juan to lave his youthful limbs was
 wont;

And having learnt to swim in that sweet
 river,
 Had often turn'd the art to some account:
A better swimmer you could scarce see
 ever,
 He could, perhaps, have pass'd the
 Hellespont,
As once (a feat on which ourselves we
 prided)
Leander, Mr. Ekenhead, and I did. 840

CVI

So here, though faint, emaciated, and stark,
 He buoy'd his boyish limbs, and strove to
 ply
With the quick wave, and gain, ere it was
 dark,
 The beach which lay before him, high
 and dry:
The greatest danger here was from a shark,
 That carried off his neighbour by the
 thigh;
As for the other two, they could not swim,
So nobody arrived on shore but him.

CVII

Nor yet had he arrived but for the oar,
 Which, providentially for him, was
 wash'd 850
Just as his feeble arms could strike no
 more,
 And the hard wave o'erwhelm'd him as
 't was dash'd
Within his grasp; he clung to it, and sore
 The waters beat while he thereto was
 lash'd;
At last, with swimming, wading, scrambling,
 he
Roll'd on the beach, half-senseless, from the
 sea:

CVIII

There, breathless, with his digging nails he
 clung
 Fast to the sand, lest the returning wave,
From whose reluctant roar his life he
 wrung,
 Should suck him back to her insatiate
 grave: 860
And there he lay, full length, where he was
 flung,
 Before the entrance of a cliff-worn cave,
With just enough of life to feel its pain,
And deem that it was saved, perhaps, in
 vain.

CIX

With slow and staggering effort he arose,
 But sunk again upon his bleeding knee
And quivering hand; and then he look'd
 for those
 Who long had been his mates upon the
 sea;
But none of them appear'd to share his
 woes,
 Save one, a corpse, from out the famish'd
 three, 870
Who died two days before, and now had
 found
An unknown barren beach for burial ground.

CX

And as he gazed, his dizzy brain spun fast,
 And down he sunk; and as he sunk, the
 sand
Swam round and round, and all his senses
 pass'd:
 He fell upon his side, and his stretch'd
 hand
Droop'd dripping on the oar (their jury-
 mast),
 And, like a wither'd lily, on the land
His slender frame and pallid aspect lay,
As fair a thing as e'er was form'd of clay.

CXI

How long in his damp trance young Juan
 lay 881
 He knew not, for the earth was gone for
 him,
And Time had nothing more of night nor
 day
 For his congealing blood, and senses dim;
And how this heavy faintness pass'd away
 He knew not, till each painful pulse and
 limb,
And tingling vein, seem'd throbbing back
 to life,
For Death, though vanquish'd, still retired
 with strife.

CXII

His eyes he open'd, shut, again unclosed,
 For all was doubt and dizziness; he
 thought 890
He still was in the boat and had but dozed,
 And felt again with his despair o'er-
 wrought,
And wish'd it death in which he had reposed;
 And then once more his feelings back
 were brought,

And slowly by his swimming eyes was seen
A lovely female face of seventeen.

CXIII

'T was bending close o'er his, and the small
 mouth
 Seem'd almost prying into his for breath;
And chafing him, the soft warm hand of
 youth
 Recall'd his answering spirits back from
 death; 900
And, bathing his chill temples, tried to
 soothe
 Each pulse to animation, till beneath
Its gentle touch and trembling care, a sigh
To these kind efforts made a low reply.

CXIV

Then was the cordial pour'd, and mantle
 flung
 Around his scarce-clad limbs; and the
 fair arm
Raised higher the faint head which o'er it
 hung;
 And her transparent cheek, all pure and
 warm,
Pillow'd his death-like forehead; then she
 wrung
 His dewy curls, long drench'd by every
 storm; 910
And watch'd with eagerness each throb that
 drew
A sigh from his heaved bosom — and hers,
 too.

CXV

And lifting him with care into the cave,
 The gentle girl and her attendant, — one
Young, yet her elder, and of brow less
 grave,
 And more robust of figure, — then begun
To kindle fire, and as the new flames gave
 Light to the rocks that roof'd them, which
 the sun
Had never seen, the maid, or whatsoe'er 919
She was, appear'd distinct, and tall, and fair.

CXVII

Her brow was overhung with coins of gold,
 That sparkled o'er the auburn of her
 hair —
Her clustering hair, whose longer locks
 were roll'd
 In braids behind; and though her stature
 were

Even of the highest for a female mould,
 They nearly reach'd her heel; and in her
 air
There was a something which bespoke com-
 mand,
As one who was a lady in the land.

CXVII

Her hair, I said, was auburn; but her eyes
 Were black as death, their lashes the
 same hue, 930
Of downcast length, in whose silk shadow
 lies
Deepest attraction; for when to the view
Forth from its raven fringe the full glance
 flies,
Ne'er with such force the swiftest arrow
 flew;
'T is as the snake late coil'd, who pours his
 length,
And hurls at once his venom and his strength.

CXVIII

Her brow was white and low, her cheek's
 pure dye
 Like twilight rosy still with the set sun;
Short upper lip — sweet lips ! that make us
 sigh
 Ever to have seen such; for she was one
Fit for the model of a statuary 941
 (A race of mere impostors, when all 's
 done —
I 've seen much finer women, ripe and real,
Than all the nonsense of their stone ideal).

CXIX

I 'll tell you why I say so, for 't is just
 One should not rail without a decent cause:
There was an Irish lady, to whose bust
 I ne'er saw justice done, and yet she was
A frequent model; and if e'er she must
 Yield to stern Time and Nature's wrin-
 kling laws, 950
They will destroy a face which mortal
 thought
Ne'er compass'd, nor less mortal chisel
 wrought.

CXX

And such was she, the lady of the cave:
 Her dress was very different from the
 Spanish,
Simpler, and yet of colours not so grave;
 For, as you know, the Spanish women
 banish

Bright hues when out of doors, and yet,
 while wave
 Around them (what I hope will never
 vanish)
The basquina and the mantilla, they 959
Seem at the same time mystical and gay.

CXXI

But with our damsel this was not the case:
 Her dress was many-colour'd, finely spun;
Her locks curl'd negligently round her face,
 But through them gold and gems pro-
 fusely shone:
Her girdle sparkled, and the richest lace
 Flow'd in her veil, and many a precious
 stone
Flash'd on her little hand; but, what was
 shocking,
Her small snow feet had slippers, but no
 stocking.

CXXII

The other female's dress was not unlike,
 But of inferior materials: she 970
Had not so many ornaments to strike,
 Her hair had silver only, bound to be
Her dowry; and her veil, in form alike,
 Was coarser; and her air, though firm,
 less free;
Her hair was thicker, but less long; her eyes
As black, but quicker, and of smaller size.

CXXIII

And these two tended him, and cheer'd him
 both
 With food and raiment, and those soft
 attentions,
Which are (as I must own) of female
 growth,
 And have ten thousand delicate inven-
 tions: 980
They made a most superior mess of broth,
 A thing which poesy but seldom mentions,
But the best dish that e'er was cook'd since
 Homer's
Achilles ordered dinner for new comers.

CXXIV

I 'll tell you who they were, this female
 pair,
 Lest they should seem princesses in dis-
 guise;
Besides, I hate all mystery, and that air
 Of clap-trap which your recent poets
 prize;

And so, in short, the girls they really were
 They shall appear before your curious
 eyes, 990
Mistress and maid; the first was only
 daughter
Of an old man who lived upon the water.

CXXV

A fisherman he had been in his youth,
 And still a sort of fisherman was he;
But other speculations were, in sooth,
 Added to his connection with the sea,
Perhaps not so respectable, in truth:
 A little smuggling, and some piracy,
Left him, at last, the sole of many masters
Of an ill-gotten million of piastres. 1000

CXXVI

A fisher, therefore, was he, — though of
 men,
 Like Peter the Apostle, — and he fish'd
For wandering merchant-vessels, now and
 then,
 And sometimes caught as many as he
 wish'd;
The cargoes he confiscated, and gain
 He sought in the slave-market too, and
 dish'd
Full many a morsel for that Turkish trade,
By which, no doubt, a good deal may be
 made.

CXXVII

He was a Greek, and on his isle had built
 (One of the wild and smaller Cyclades)
A very handsome house from out his
 guilt, 1011
 And there he lived exceedingly at ease;
Heaven knows what cash he got or blood
 he spilt,
 A sad old fellow was he, if you please;
But this I know, it was a spacious build-
 ing,
Full of barbaric carving, paint, and gilding.

CXXVIII

He had an only daughter, call'd Haidée,
 The greatest heiress of the Eastern Isles;
Besides, so very beautiful was she, 1019
 Her dowry was as nothing to her smiles:
Still in her teens, and like a lovely tree
 She grew to womanhood, and between
 whiles
Rejected several suitors, just to learn
How to accept a better in his turn.

CXXIX

And walking out upon the beach, below
 The cliff, towards sunset, on that day she
 found,
Insensible, — not dead, but nearly so, —
 Don Juan, almost famish'd, and half
 drown'd;
But being naked, she was shock'd, you
 know,
 Yet deem'd herself in common pity
 bound, 1030
As far as in her lay, 'to take him in,
A stranger' dying, with so white a skin.

CXXX

But taking him into her father's house
 Was not exactly the best way to save,
But like conveying to the cat the mouse,
 Or people in a trance into their grave;
Because the good old man had so much
 'νοῦς,'
 Unlike the honest Arab thieves so brave,
He would have hospitably cured the
 stranger,
And sold him instantly when out of danger.

CXXXI

And therefore, with her maid, she thought
 it best 1041
 (A virgin always on her maid relies)
To place him in the cave for present rest:
 And when, at last, he open'd his black
 eyes,
Their charity increased about their guest;
 And their compassion grew to such a
 size,
It open'd half the turnpike-gates to heaven
(St. Paul says, 't is the toll which must be
 given).

CXXXII

They made a fire, — but such a fire as
 they
 Upon the moment could contrive with
 such 1050
Materials as were cast up round the bay, —
 Some broken planks, and oars, that to
 the touch
Were nearly tinder, since so long they
 lay
 A mast was almost crumbled to a crutch;
But, by God's grace, here wrecks were in
 such plenty,
That there was fuel to have furnish'd
 twenty.

CXXXIII

He had a bed of furs, and a pelisse,
 For Haidée stripped her sables off to
 make
His couch; and, that he might be more at
 ease,
 And warm, in case by chance he should
 awake, 1060
They also gave a petticoat apiece,
 She and her maid — and promised by
 daybreak
To pay him a fresh visit, with a dish
For breakfast, of eggs, coffee, bread, and
 fish.

CXXXIV

And thus they left him to his lone repose:
 Juan slept like a top, or like the dead,
Who sleep at last, perhaps (God only
 knows),
 Just for the present; and in his lull'd
 head
Not even a vision of his former woes
 Throbb'd in accursèd dreams, which
 sometimes spread 1070
Unwelcome visions of our former years,
Till the eye, cheated, opens thick with
 tears.

CXXXV

Young Juan slept all dreamless: — but the
 maid,
 Who smooth'd his pillow, as she left the
 den
Look'd back upon him, and a moment
 stay'd,
 And turn'd, believing that he call'd
 again.
He slumber'd; yet she thought, at least
 she said
 (The heart will slip, even as the tongue
 and pen),
He had pronounced her name — but she
 forgot
That at this moment Juan knew it not.

CXXXVI

And pensive to her father's house she
 went, 1081
 Enjoining silence strict to Zoe, who
Better than her knew what, in fact, she
 meant,
 She being wiser by a year or two:
A year or two 's an age when rightly spent,
 And Zoe spent hers, as most women do,

In gaining all that useful sort of know-
 ledge
Which is acquired in Nature's good old
 college.

CXXXVII

The morn broke, and found Juan slumber-
 ing still
 Fast in his cave, and nothing clash'd
 upon 1090
His rest; the rushing of the neighbouring
 rill,
 And the young beams of the excluded
 sun,
Troubled him not, and he might sleep his
 fill;
 And need he had of slumber yet, for
 none
Had suffer'd more — his hardships were
 comparative
To those related in my grand-dad's 'Nar-
 rative.'

CXXXVIII

Not so Haidée: she sadly toss'd and tum-
 bled,
 And started from her sleep, and, turning
 o'er
Dream'd of a thousand wrecks, o'er which
 she stumbled,
 And handsome corpses strew'd upon the
 shore; 1100
And woke her maid so early that she
 grumbled,
 And call'd her father's old slaves up,
 who swore
In several oaths — Armenian, Turk, and
 Greek —
They knew not what to think of such a
 freak.

CXXXIX

But up she got, and up she made them get,
 With some pretence about the sun, that
 makes
Sweet skies just when he rises, or is set;
 And 't is, no doubt, a sight to see when
 breaks
Bright Phœbus, while the mountains still
 are wet
 With mist, and every bird with him
 awakes, 1110
And night is flung off like a mourning suit
Worn for a husband, — or some other
 brute.

CXL

I say, the sun is a most glorious sight,
 I 've seen him rise full oft, indeed of late
I have sat up on purpose all the night,
 Which hastens, as physicians say, one's
 fate;
And so all ye, who would be in the right
 In health and purse, begin your day to
 date
From daybreak, and when coffin'd at four-
 score, 1119
Engrave upon the plate, you rose at four.

CXLI

And Haidée met the morning face to face;
 Her own was freshest, though a feverish
 flush
Had dyed it with the headlong blood, whose
 race
 From heart to cheek is curb'd into a
 blush,
Like to a torrent which a mountain's base,
 That overpowers some Alpine river's rush,
Checks to a lake, whose waves in circles
 spread;
Or the Red Sea — but the sea is not red.

CXLII

And down the cliff the island virgin came,
 And near the cave her quick light foot-
 steps drew, 1130
While the sun smiled on her with his first
 flame,
 And young Aurora kiss'd her lips with
 dew,
Taking her for a sister; just the same
 Mistake you would have made on seeing
 the two,
Although the mortal, quite as fresh and
 fair,
Had all the advantage, too, of not being air.

CXLIII

And when into the cavern Haidée stepp'd
 All timidly, yet rapidly, she saw
That like an infant Juan sweetly slept;
 And then she stopp'd, and stood as if in
 awe 1140
(For sleep is awful), and on tiptoe crept
 And wrapt him closer, lest the air, too
 raw,
Should reach his blood, then o'er him still as
 death
Bent with hush'd lips, that drank his scarce-
 drawn breath.

CXLIV

And thus like to an angel o'er the dying
 Who die in righteousness, she lean'd; and
 there
All tranquilly the shipwreck'd boy was ly-
 ing,
 As o'er him lay the calm and stirless air:
But Zoe the meantime some eggs was frying,
 Since, after all, no doubt the youthful
 pair 1150
Must breakfast — and betimes, lest they
 should ask it,
She drew out her provision from the basket.

CXLV

She knew that the best feelings must have
 victual,
 And that a shipwreck'd youth would hun-
 gry be;
Besides, being less in love, she yawn'd a
 little,
 And felt her veins chill'd by the neigh-
 bouring sea;
And so, she cook'd their breakfast to a tittle;
 I can't say that she gave them any tea,
But there were eggs, fruit, coffee, bread,
 fish, honey,
With Scio wine, — and all for love, not
 money. 1160

CXLVI

And Zoe, when the eggs were ready, and
 The coffee made, would fain have waken'd
 Juan;
But Haidée stopp'd her with her quick
 small hand,
 And without word, a sign her finger drew
 on
Her lip, which Zoe needs must understand;
 And, the first breakfast spoilt, prepared
 a new one,
Because her mistress would not let her break
That sleep which seem'd as it would ne'er
 awake.

CXLVII

For still he lay, and on his thin worn
 cheek 1169
 A purple hectic play'd like dying day
On the snow-tops of distant hills; the streak
 Of sufferance yet upon his forehead lay,
Where the blue veins look'd shadowy,
 shrunk, and weak;
 And his black curls were dewy with the
 spray,

Which weigh'd upon them yet, all damp
and salt,
Mix'd with the stony vapours of the vault.

CXLVIII

And she bent o'er him, and he lay beneath,
 Hush'd as the babe upon its mother's
 breast,
Droop'd as the willow when no winds can
 breathe,
 Lull'd like the depth of ocean when at
 rest, 1180
Fair as the crowning rose of the whole
 wreath,
 Soft as the callow cygnet in its nest;
In short, he was a very pretty fellow,
Although his woes had turn'd him rather
 yellow.

CXLIX

He woke and gazed, and would have slept
 again,
 But the fair face which met his eyes
 forbade
Those eyes to close, though weariness and
 pain
 Had further sleep a further pleasure
 made;
For woman's face was never form'd in
 vain
 For Juan, so that even when he pray'd
He turn'd from grisly saints, and martyrs
 hairy, 1191
To the sweet portraits of the Virgin Mary.

CL

And thus upon his elbow he arose,
 And look'd upon the lady, in whose cheek
The pale contended with the purple rose,
 As with an effort she began to speak;
Her eyes were eloquent, her words would
 pose,
 Although she told him, in good modern
 Greek,
With an Ionian accent, low and sweet,
That he was faint, and must not talk, but
 eat. 1200

CLI

Now Juan could not understand a word,
 Being no Grecian; but he had an ear,
And her voice was the warble of a bird,
 So soft, so sweet, so delicately clear,
That finer, simpler music ne'er was heard;
 The sort of sound we echo with a tear,

Without knowing why — an overpowering
 tone,
Whence Melody descends as from a throne.

CLII

And Juan gazed as one who is awoke 1209
 By a distant organ, doubting if he be
Not yet a dreamer, till the spell is broke
 By the watchman, or some such reality,
Or by one's early valet's cursèd knock;
 At least it is a heavy sound to me,
Who like a morning slumber — for the
 night
Shows stars and women in a better light.

CLIII

And Juan, too, was help'd out from his
 dream,
 Or sleep, or whatsoe'er it was, by feel-
 ing
A most prodigious appetite: the steam
 Of Zoe's cookery no doubt was steal-
 ing 1220
Upon his senses, and the kindling beam
 Of the new fire, which Zoe kept up,
 kneeling
To stir her viands, made him quite awake
And long for food, but chiefly a beef-steak.

CLIV

But beef is rare within these oxless isles;
 Goat's flesh there is, no doubt, and kid,
 and mutton;
And, when a holiday upon them smiles,
 A joint upon their barbarous spits they
 put on:
But this occurs but seldom, between whiles,
 For some of these are rocks with scarce
 a hut on; 1230
Others are fair and fertile, among which
This, though not large, was one of the most
 rich.

CLV

I say that beef is rare, and can't help think-
 ing
 That the old fable of the Minotaur —
From which our modern morals rightly
 shrinking
 Condemn the royal lady's taste who wore
A cow's shape for a mask — was only
 (sinking
 The allegory) a mere type, no more,
That Pasiphae promoted breeding cattle,
To make the Cretans bloodier in battle. 1240

CLVI

For we all know that English people are
 Fed upon beef — I won't say much of
 beer,
Because 't is liquor only, and being far
 From this my subject, has no business
 here;
We know, too, they are very fond of war,
 A pleasure — like all pleasures — rather
 dear;
So were the Cretans — from which I infer
That beef and battles both were owing to
 her.

CLVII

But to resume. The languid Juan raised
 His head upon his elbow, and he saw 1250
A sight on which he had not lately gazed,
 As all his latter meals had been quite raw,
Three or four things, for which the Lord he
 praised,
 And, feeling still the famish'd vulture
 gnaw,
He fell upon whate'er was offer'd, like
A priest, a shark, an alderman, or pike.

CLVIII

He ate, and he was well supplied: and she,
 Who watch'd him like a mother, would
 have fed
Him past all bounds, because she smiled to
 see
 Such appetite in one she had deem'd
 dead; 1260
But Zoe, being older than Haidée,
 Knew (by tradition, for she ne'er had
 read)
That famish'd people must be slowly nurst,
And fed by spoonfuls, else they always
 burst.

CLIX

And so she took the liberty to state,
 Rather by deeds than words, because
 the case
Was urgent, that the gentleman, whose fate
 Had made her mistress quit her bed to
 trace
The sea-shore at this hour, must leave his
 plate,
 Unless he wish'd to die upon the place —
She snatch'd it, and refused another mor-
 sel, 1271
Saying, he had gorged enough to make a
 horse ill.

CLX

Next they — he being naked, save a tat-
 ter'd
 Pair of scarce decent trowsers — went to
 work,
And in the fire his recent rags they scat-
 ter'd,
 And dress'd him, for the present, like a
 Turk,
Or Greek — that is, although it not much
 matter'd,
 Omitting turban, slippers, pistols, dirk, —
They furnish'd him, entire, except some
 stitches,
With a clean shirt, and very spacious
 breeches. 1280

CLXI

And then fair Haidée tried her tongue at
 speaking,
 But not a word could Juan comprehend,
Although he listen'd so that the young
 Greek in
 Her earnestness would ne'er have made
 an end;
And, as he interrupted not, went eking
 Her speech out to her protégé and friend,
Till pausing at the last her breath to take,
She saw he did not understand Romaic.

CLXII

And then she had recourse to nods, and
 signs,
 And smiles, and sparkles of the speaking
 eye, 1290
And read (the only book she could) the
 lines
 Of his fair face, and found, by sympathy,
The answer eloquent, where the soul shines
 And darts in one quick glance a long reply;
And thus in every look she saw exprest
A world of words, and things at which she
 guess'd.

CLXIII

And now, by dint of fingers and of eyes,
 And words repeated after her, he took
A lesson in her tongue; but by surmise,
 No doubt, less of her language than her
 look: 1300
As he who studies fervently the skies
 Turns oftener to the stars than to his
 book,
Thus Juan learn'd his alpha beta better
From Haidée's glance than any graven letter.

CLXIV

'T is pleasing to be school'd in a strange
 tongue
 By female lips and eyes — that is, I
 mean,
When both the teacher and the taught are
 young,
 As was the case, at least, where I have
 been;
They smile so when one 's right, and when
 one 's wrong
 They smile still more, and then there
 intervene 1310
Pressure of hands, perhaps even a chaste
 kiss; —
I learn'd the little that I know by this:

CLXV

That is, some words of Spanish, Turk, and
 Greek,
 Italian not at all, having no teachers;
Much English I cannot pretend to speak,
 Learning that language chiefly from its
 preachers,
Barrow, South, Tillotson, whom every week
 I study, also Blair, the highest reachers
Of eloquence in piety and prose —
I hate your poets, so read none of those. 1320

CLXVI

As for the ladies, I have nought to say,
 A wanderer from the British world of
 fashion,
Where I, like other 'dogs, have had my
 day,'
 Like other men, too, may have had my
 passion —
But that, like other things, has pass'd
 away,
 And all her fools whom I *could* lay the
 lash on:
Foes, friends, men, women, now are nought
 to me
But dreams of what has been, no more to be.

CLXVII

Return we to Don Juan. He begun
 To hear new words, and to repeat them ;
 but 1330
Some feelings, universal as the sun,
 Were such as could not in his breast be
 shut
More than within the bosom of a nun :
 He was in love, — as you would be, no
 doubt,

With a young benefactress, — so was she,
Just in the way we very often see.

CLXVIII

And every day by daybreak — rather early
 For Juan, who was somewhat fond of
 rest —
She came into the cave, but it was merely
 To see her bird reposing in his nest ; 1340
And she would softly stir his locks so curly,
 Without disturbing her yet slumbering
 guest,
Breathing all gently o'er his cheek and
 mouth,
As o'er a bed of roses the sweet south.

CLXIX

And every morn his colour freshlier came,
 And every day help'd on his convales-
 cence ;
'T was well, because health in the human
 frame
 Is pleasant, besides being true love's es-
 sence,
For health and idleness to passion's flame
 Are oil and gunpowder; and some good
 lessons 1350
Are also learnt from Ceres and from Bac-
 chus,
Without whom Venus will not long attack
 us.

CLXX

While Venus fills the heart (without heart
 really
 Love, though good always, is not quite
 so good),
Ceres presents a plate of vermicelli, —
 For love must be sustain'd like flesh and
 blood, —
While Bacchus pours out wine, or hands a
 jelly :
 Eggs, oysters, too, are amatory food ;
But who is their purveyor from above
Heaven knows, — it may be Neptune, Pan,
 or Jove. 1360

CLXXI

When Juan woke he found some good
 things ready,
 A bath, a breakfast, and the finest eyes
That ever made a youthful heart less
 steady,
 Besides her maid's as pretty for their
 size ;

But I have spoken of all this already —
　And repetition 's tiresome and unwise, —
Well — Juan, after bathing in the sea,
Came always back to coffee and Haidée.

CLXXII

Both were so young, and one so innocent,
　That bathing pass'd for nothing ; Juan
　　seem'd　　　　　　　　　　　　　1370
To her, as 'twere, the kind of being sent,
　Of whom these two years she had nightly
　　dream'd,
A something to be loved, a creature meant
　To be her happiness, and whom she
　　deem'd
To render happy ; all who joy would win
Must share it, — Happiness was born a
　twin.

CLXXIII

It was such pleasure to behold him, such
　Enlargement of existence to partake
Nature with him, to thrill beneath his
　touch,
　To watch him slumbering, and to see
　　him wake:　　　　　　　　　　　1380
To live with him forever were too much;
　But then the thought of parting made
　　her quake;
He was her own, her ocean-treasure, cast
Like a rich wreck — her first love, and her
　last.

CLXXIV

And thus a moon roll'd on, and fair Hai-
　dée
　Paid daily visits to her boy, and took
Such plentiful precautions, that still he
　Remain'd unknown within his craggy
　　nook;
At last her father's prows put out to sea
　For certain merchantmen upon the look,
Not as of yore to carry off an Io,　　1391
But three Ragusan vessels, bound for Scio.

CLXXV

Then came her freedom, for she had no
　mother,
　So that, her father being at sea, she was
Free as a married woman, or such other
　Female, as where she likes may freely
　　pass,
Without even the incumbrance of a brother,
　The freest she that ever gazed on
　　glass;

I speak of Christian lands in this compari-
　son,
　Where wives, at least, are seldom kept in
　　garrison.　　　　　　　　　　　1400

CLXXVI

Now she prolong'd her visits and her talk
　(For they must talk), and he had learnt
　　to say
So much as to propose to take a walk, —
　For little had he wander'd since the day
On which, like a young flower snapp'd from
　the stalk,
　Drooping and dewy on the beach he lay, —
And thus they walk'd out in the after-
　noon,
And saw the sun set opposite the moon.

CLXXVII

It was a wild and breaker-beaten coast,
　With cliffs above, and a broad sandy
　　shore,　　　　　　　　　　　　1410
Guarded by shoals and rocks as by an host,
　With here and there a creek, whose aspect
　　wore
A better welcome to the tempest-tost;
　And rarely ceased the haughty billow's
　　roar,
Save on the dead long summer days, which
　make
The outstretch'd ocean glitter like a lake.

CLXXVIII

And the small ripple spilt upon the beach
　Scarcely o'erpass'd the cream of your
　　champagne,
When o'er the brim the sparkling bumpers
　reach,
　That spring-dew of the spirit ! the heart's
　　rain !　　　　　　　　　　　　1420
Few things surpass old wine; and they may
　preach
　Who please, — the more because they
　　preach in vain, —
Let us have wine and women, mirth and
　laughter,
Sermons and soda-water the day after.

CLXXIX

Man, being reasonable, must get drunk;
　The best of life is but intoxication:
Glory, the grape, love, gold, in these are
　sunk
　The hopes of all men, and of every na-
　　tion;

Without their sap, how branchless were the
 trunk
 Of life's strange tree, so fruitful on oc-
 casion: 1430
But to return, — Get very drunk; and when
You wake with headache, you shall see
 what then.

CLXXX

Ring for your valet — bid him quickly bring
 Some hock and soda-water, then you'll
 know
A pleasure worthy Xerxes the great king;
 For not the bless'd sherbet, sublimed
 with snow,
Nor the first sparkle of the desert-spring,
 Nor Burgundy in all its sunset glow,
After long travel, ennui, love, or slaughter,
Vie with that draught of hock and soda-
 water. 1440

CLXXXI

The coast — I think it was the coast that I
 Was just describing — Yes, it *was* the
 coast —
Lay at this period quiet as the sky,
 The sands untumbled, the blue waves
 untost,
And all was stillness, save the sea-bird's cry,
 And dolphin's leap, and little billow crost
By some low rock or shelve, that made it
 fret
Against the boundary it scarcely wet.

CLXXXII

And forth they wander'd, her sire being
 gone,
 As I have said, upon an expedition; 1450
And mother, brother, guardian, she had
 none,
 Save Zoe, who, although with due pre-
 cision
She waited on her lady with the sun,
 Thought daily service was her only mis-
 sion,
Bringing warm water, wreathing her long
 tresses,
And asking now and then for cast-off
 dresses.

CLXXXIII

It was the cooling hour, just when the
 rounded
 Red sun sinks down behind the azure
 hill,

Which then seems as if the whole earth it
 bounded,
 Circling all nature, hush'd, and dim, and
 still, 1460
With the far mountain-crescent half sur-
 rounded
 On one side, and the deep sea calm and
 chill
Upon the other, and the rosy sky,
With one star sparkling through it like an
 eye.

CLXXXIV

And thus they wander'd forth, and hand in
 hand,
 Over the shining pebbles and the shells,
Glided along the smooth and harden'd sand,
 And in the worn and wild receptacles
Work'd by the storms, yet work'd as it were
 plann'd,
 In hollow halls, with sparry roofs and
 cells, 1470
They turn'd to rest; and, each clasp'd by an
 arm,
Yielded to the deep twilight's purple charm.

CLXXXV

They look'd up to the sky, whose floating
 glow
 Spread like a rosy ocean, vast and bright;
They gazed upon the glittering sea be-
 low,
 Whence the broad moon rose circling into
 sight;
They heard the wave's splash, and the wind
 so low,
 And saw each other's dark eyes darting
 light
Into each other — and, beholding this,
Their lips drew near, and clung into a
 kiss; 1480

CLXXXVI

A long, long kiss, a kiss of youth, and
 love,
 And beauty, all concentrating like rays
Into one focus, kindled from above;
 Such kisses as belong to early days,
Where heart, and soul, and sense, in concert
 move,
 And the blood's lava, and the pulse a
 blaze,
Each kiss a heart-quake, — for a kiss's
 strength,
I think, it must be reckon'd by its length.

CLXXXVII

By length I mean duration; theirs endured
 Heaven knows how long — no doubt they
 never reckon'd; 1490
And if they had, they could not have
 secured
The sum of their sensations to a second:
They had not spoken; but they felt allured,
 As if their souls and lips each other
 beckon'd,
Which, being join'd, like swarming bees
 they clung —
Their hearts the flowers from whence the
 honey sprung.

CLXXXVIII

They were alone, but not alone as they
 Who shut in chambers think it loneliness;
The silent ocean, and the starlight bay,
 The twilight glow which momently grew
 less, 1500
The voiceless sands and dropping caves,
 that lay
 Around them, made them to each other
 press,
As if there were no life beneath the sky
Save theirs, and that their life could never
 die.

CLXXXIX

They fear'd no eyes nor ears on that lone
 beach,
 They felt no terrors from the night, they
 were
All in all to each other: though their
 speech
 Was broken words, they *thought* a lan-
 guage there,—
And all the burning tongues the passions
 teach 1509
 Found in one sigh the best interpreter
Of nature's oracle — first love, — that all
Which Eve has left her daughters since her
 fall.

CXC

Haidée spoke not of scruples, ask'd no vows,
 Nor offer'd any; she had never heard
Of plight and promises to be a spouse,
 Or perils by a loving maid incurr'd;
She was all which pure ignorance allows,
 And flew to her young mate like a young
 bird;
And, never having dreamt of falsehood, she
Had not one word to say of constancy. 1520

CXCI

She loved, and was belovèd — she adored,
 And she was worshipp'd; after nature's
 fashion,
Their intense souls, into each other pour'd,
 If souls could die, had perish'd in that
 passion, —
But by degrees their senses were restored,
 Again to be o'ercome, again to dash on;
And, beating 'gainst *his* bosom, Haidée's
 heart
Felt as if never more to beat apart. 1528

CXCII

Alas ! they were so young, so beautiful,
 So lonely, loving, helpless, and the hour
Was that in which the heart is always full,
 And, having o'er itself no further power,
Prompts deeds eternity can not annul,
 But pays off moments in an endless
 shower
Of hell-fire — all prepared for people giving
Pleasure or pain to one another living.

CXCIII

Alas ! for Juan and Haidée ! they were
 So loving and so lovely — till then never,
Excepting our first parents, such a pair
 Had run the risk of being damn'd for
 ever; 1540
And Haidée, being devout as well as fair,
 Had, doubtless, heard about the Stygian
 river,
And hell and purgatory — but forgot
Just in the very crisis she should not.

CXCIV

They look upon each other, and their eyes
 Gleam in the moonlight; and her white
 arm clasps
Round Juan's head, and his around her lies
 Half buried in the tresses which it grasps;
She sits upon his knee, and drinks his sighs,
 He hers, until they end in broken gasps;
And thus they form a group that's quite
 antique, 1551
Half naked, loving, natural, and Greek.

CXCV

And when those deep and burning moments
 pass'd,
 And Juan sunk to sleep within her arms,
She slept not, but all tenderly, though fast,
 Sustain'd his head upon her bosom's
 charms;

'Stop!' cried Philosophy, with air so
 Grecian
(Though she was masqued then as a fair
 Venetian); 1680

CCXI

'Stop!' so I stopp'd. — But to return: that
 which
Men call inconstancy is nothing more
Than admiration due where nature's rich
 Profusion with young beauty covers o'er
Some favour'd object; and as in the niche
 A lovely statue we almost adore,
This sort of adoration of the real
Is but a heightening of the 'beau ideal.'

CCXII

'T is the perception of the beautiful,
 A fine extension of the faculties, 1690
Platonic, universal, wonderful,
 Drawn from the stars, and filter'd through
 the skies,
Without which life would be extremely
 dull;
 In short, it is the use of our own eyes,
With one or two small senses added, just
To hint that flesh is form'd of fiery dust.

CCXIII

Yet 't is a painful feeling, and unwilling,
 For surely if we always could perceive
In the same object graces quite as killing
 As when she rose upon us like an Eve, 1700
'T would save us many a heartache, many
 a shilling
 (For we must get them any how or
 grieve),
Whereas if one sole lady pleased for ever,
How pleasant for the heart as well as liver!

CCXIV

The heart is like the sky, a part of heaven,
 But changes night and day, too, like the
 sky;
Now o'er it clouds and thunder must be
 driven,
 And darkness and destruction as on high:
But when it hath been scorch'd, and pierced,
 and riven,
 Its storms expire in water-drops; the
 eye 1710
Pours forth at last the heart's blood turn'd
 to tears,
Which make the English climate of our
 years.

CCXV

The liver is the lazaret of bile,
 But very rarely executes its function,
For the first passion stays there such a while,
 That all the rest creep in and form a
 junction,
Life knots of vipers on a dunghill's soil, —
 Rage, fear, hate, jealousy, revenge, com-
 punction, —
So that all mischiefs spring up from this
 entrail,
Like earthquakes from the hidden fire
 call'd 'central,' 1720

CCXVI

In the mean time, without proceeding more
 In this anatomy, I 've finish'd now
Two hundred and odd stanzas as before,
 That being about the number I 'll allow
Each canto of the twelve, or twenty-four;
 And, laying down my pen, I make my
 bow,
Leaving Don Juan and Haidée to plead
For them and theirs with all who deign to
 read.

CANTO THE THIRD

I

HAIL, Muse! *et cetera.* — We left Juan
 sleeping,
 Pillow'd upon a fair and happy breast,
And watch'd by eyes that never yet knew
 weeping,
 And loved by a young heart, too deeply
 blest
To feel the poison through her spirit creep-
 ing,
 Or know who rested there, a foe to rest,
Had soil'd the current of her sinless years,
And turn'd her pure heart's purest blood
 to tears!

II

Oh, Love! what is it in this world of ours
 Which makes it fatal to be loved? Ah,
 why 10
With cypress branches hast thou wreathed
 thy bowers,
 And made thy best interpreter a sigh?
As those who dote on odours pluck the
 flowers,
 And place them on their breast — but
 place to die —

Thus the frail beings we would fondly
 cherish
Are laid within our bosoms but to perish.

III

In her first passion woman loves her lover,
 In all the others all she loves is love,
Which grows a habit she can ne'er get over,
 And fits her loosely — like an easy glove,
As you may find, whene'er you like to
 prove her: 21
 One man alone at first her heart can
 move;
She then prefers him in the plural number,
Not finding that the additions much en-
 cumber.

IV

I know not if the fault be men's or theirs;
 But one thing's pretty sure; a woman
 planted
(Unless at once she plunge for life in
 prayers)
 After a decent time must be gallanted;
Although, no doubt, her first of love affairs
 Is that to which her heart is wholly
 granted; 30
Yet there are some, they say, who have
 had *none*,
But those who have ne'er end with only
 one.

V

'T is melancholy, and a fearful sign
 Of human frailty, folly, also crime,
That love and marriage rarely can combine,
 Although they both are born in the same
 clime;
Marriage from love, like vinegar from
 wine —
 A sad, sour, sober beverage — by time
Is sharpen'd from its high celestial flavour
Down to a very homely household savour. 40

VI

There's something of antipathy, as 't were,
 Between their present and their future
 state;
A kind of flattery that's hardly fair
 Is used until the truth arrives too late —
Yet what can people do, except despair?
 The same things change their names at
 such a rate;
For instance — passion in a lover's glorious,
But in a husband is pronounced uxorious.

VII

Men grow ashamed of being so very fond;
 They sometimes also get a little tired 50
(But that, of course, is rare), and then de-
 spond:
 The same things cannot always be ad-
 mired,
Yet 't is 'so nominated in the bond,'
 That both are tied till one shall have
 expired.
Sad thought! to lose the spouse that was
 adorning
Our days, and put one's servants into mourn-
 ing.

VIII

There's doubtless something in domestic
 doings
 Which forms, in fact, true love's antithe-
 sis;
Romances paint at full length people's woo-
 ings,
 But only give a bust of marriages; 60
For no one cares for matrimonial cooings,
 There's nothing wrong in a connubial
 kiss:
Think you, if Laura had been Petrarch's
 wife,
He would have written sonnets all his life?

IX

All tragedies are finish'd by a death,
 All comedies are ended by a marriage;
The future states of both are left to faith,
 For authors fear description might dis-
 parage
The worlds to come of both, or fall be-
 neath,
 And then both worlds would punish their
 miscarriage; 70
So leaving each their priest and prayer-
 book ready,
They say no more of Death or of the Lady.

X

The only two that in my recollection
 Have sung of heaven and hell, or mar-
 riage, are
Dante and Milton, and of both the affec-
 tion
 Was hapless in their nuptials, for some
 bar
Of fault or temper ruin'd the connection
 (Such things, in fact, it don't ask much
 to mar);

But Dante's Beatrice and Milton's Eve
Were not drawn from their spouses, you
 conceive. 80

XI

Some persons say that Dante meant the-
 ology
By Beatrice, and not a mistress — I,
Although my opinion may require apology,
 Deem this a commentator's fantasy,
Unless indeed it was from his own know-
 ledge he
 Decided thus, and show'd good reason
 why;
I think that Dante's more abstruse ecstatics
Meant to personify the mathematics.

XII

Haidée and Juan were not married, but
 The fault was theirs, not mine; it is not
 fair. 90
Chaste reader, then, in any way to put
 The blame on me, unless you wish they
 were;
Then if you'd have them wedded, please to
 shut
 The book which treats of this erroneous
 pair,
Before the consequences grow too awful;
'T is dangerous to read of loves unlawful.

XIII

Yet they were happy, — happy in the illicit
 Indulgence of their innocent desires;
But more imprudent grown with every visit,
 Haidée forgot the island was her sire's;
When we have what we like, 't is hard to
 miss it, 101
 At least in the beginning, ere one tires;
Thus she came often, not a moment losing,
Whilst her piratical papa was cruising.

XIV

Let not his mode of raising cash seem
 strange,
 Although he fleeced the flags of every
 nation,
For into a prime minister but change
 His title, and 't is nothing but taxation;
But he, more modest, took an humbler
 range
 Of life, and in an honester vocation 110
Pursued o'er the high seas his watery jour-
 ney,
And merely practised as a sea-attorney.

XV

The good old gentleman had been detain'd
 By winds and waves, and some impor-
 tant captures;
And, in the hope of more, at sea re-
 main'd,
 Although a squall or two had damp'd his
 raptures,
By swamping one of the prizes; he had
 chain'd
 His prisoners, dividing them like chap-
 ters
In number'd lots; they all had cuffs and
 collars,
And averaged each from ten to a hundred
 dollars. 120

XVI

Some he disposed of off Cape Matapan,
 Among his friends the Mainots; some he
 sold
To his Tunis correspondents, save one man
 Toss'd overboard unsaleable (being old);
The rest — save here and there some richer
 one,
 Reserved for future ransom — in the hold
Were link'd alike, as for the common peo-
 ple he
Had a large order from the Dey of Tripoli.

XVII

The merchandise was served in the same
 way,
 Pieced out for different marts in the Le-
 vant; 130
Except some certain portions of the prey,
 Light classic articles of female want,
French stuffs, lace, tweezers, toothpicks,
 teapot, tray,
 Guitars and castanets from Alicant,
All which selected from the spoil he gath-
 ers,
Robb'd for his daughter by the best of fa-
 thers.

XVIII

A monkey, a Dutch mastiff, a mackaw,
 Two parrots, with a Persian cat and
 kittens,
He chose from several animals he saw —
 A terrier, too, which once had been a
 Briton's, 140
Who dying on the coast of Ithaca,
 The peasants gave the poor dumb thing
 a pittance;

These to secure in this strong blowing
 weather,
He caged in one huge hamper altogether.

XIX

Then having settled his marine affairs,
 Despatching single crusiers here and
 there,
His vessel having need of some repairs,
 He shaped his course to where his
 daughter fair
Continued still her hospitable cares;
 But that part of the coast being shoal and
 bare, 150
And rough with reefs which ran out many
 a mile,
His port lay on the other side o' the isle.

XX

And there he went ashore without delay,
 Having no custom-house nor quarantine
To ask him awkward questions on the
 way
 About the time and place where he had
 been:
He left his ship to be hove down next day,
 With orders to the people to careen;
So that all hands were busy beyond measure,
In getting out goods, ballast, guns, and
 treasure. 160

XXI

Arriving at the summit of a hill
 Which overlook'd the white walls of his
 home,
He stopp'd. — What singular emotions fill
 Their bosoms who have been induced to
 roam !
With fluttering doubts if all be well or ill —
 With love for many, and with fears for
 some;
All feelings which o'erleap the years long
 lost,
And bring our hearts back to their starting-
 post.

XXII

The approach of home to husbands and to
 sires, 169
 After long travelling by land or water,
Most naturally some small doubt inspires —
 A female family 's a serious matter
(None trusts the sex more, or so much
 admires —
 But they hate flattery, so I never flatter);

Wives in their husbands' absences grow
 subtler,
And daughters sometimes run off with the
 butler.

XXIII

An honest gentleman at his return
 May not have the good fortune of Ulysses;
Not all lone matrons for their husbands
 mourn, 179
 Or show the same dislike to suitors' kisses;
The odds are that he finds a handsome urn
 To his memory — and two or three young
 misses
Born to some friend, who holds his wife and
 riches, —
And that *his* Argus — bites him by the
 breeches.

XXIV

If single, probably his plighted fair
 Has in his absence wedded some rich
 miser;
But all the better, for the happy pair
 May quarrel, and the lady growing wiser,
He may resume his amatory care
 As cavalier servente, or despise her; 190
And that his sorrow may not be a dumb one,
Write odes on the Inconstancy of Woman.

XXV

And oh ! ye gentlemen who have already
 Some chaste *liaison* of the kind — I mean
An honest friendship with a married lady —
 The only thing of this sort ever seen
To last — of all connections the most steady,
 And the true Hymen (the first 's but a
 screen) —
Yet for all that keep not too long away,
I 've known the absent wrong'd four times
 a day. 200

XXVI

Lambro, our sea-solicitor, who had
 Much less experience of dry land than
 ocean,
On seeing his own chimney-smoke, felt glad;
 But not knowing metaphysics, had no
 notion
Of the true reason of his not being sad,
 Or that of any other strong emotion;
He loved his child, and would have wept
 the loss of her,
But knew the cause no more than a philoso-
 pher.

XXVII

He saw his white walls shining in the sun,
　His garden trees all shadowy and green;
He heard his rivulet's light bubbling run, 211
　The distant dog-bark; and perceived between
The umbrage of the wood so cool and dun
　The moving figures, and the sparkling sheen
Of arms (in the East all arm) — and various dyes
Of colour'd garbs, as bright as butterflies.

XXVIIII

And as the spot where they appear he nears,
　Surprised at these unwonted signs of idling,
He hears — alas ! no music of the spheres,
　But an unhallow'd, earthly sound of fiddling ! 220
A melody which made him doubt his ears,
　The cause being past his guessing or unriddling;
A pipe, too, and a drum, and shortly after,
A most unoriental roar of laughter.

XXIX

And still more nearly to the place advancing,
　Descending rather quickly the declivity,
Through the waved branches o'er the greensward glancing,
　'Midst other indications of festivity,
Seeing a troop of his domestics dancing
　Like dervises, who turn as on a pivot, he 230
Perceived it was the Pyrrhic dance so martial,
To which the Levantines are very partial.

XXX

And further on a group of Grecian girls,
　The first and tallest her white kerchief waving,
Were strung together like a row of pearls,
　Link'd hand in hand, and dancing; each too having
Down her white neck long floating auburn curls
　(The least of which would set ten poets raving);
Their leader sang — and bounded to her song,
With choral step and voice, the virgin throng. 240

XXXI

And here, assembled cross-legg'd round their trays,
　Small social parties just begun to dine;
Pilaus and meats of all sorts met the gaze,
　And flasks of Samian and of Chian wine,
And sherbet cooling in the porous vase;
　Above them their dessert grew on its vine,
The orange and pomegranate nodding o'er
Dropp'd in their laps, scarce pluck'd, their mellow store.

XXXII

A band of children, round a snow-white ram,
　There wreathe his venerable horns with flowers; 250
While peaceful as if still an unwean'd lamb,
　The patriarch of the flock all gently cowers
His sober head, majestically tame,
　Or eats from out the palm, or playful lowers
His brow, as if in act to butt, and then
Yielding to their small hands, draws back again.

XXXIII

Their classical profiles, and glittering dresses,
　Their large black eyes, and soft seraphic cheeks,
Crimson as cleft pomegranates, their long tresses,
　The gesture which enchants, the eye that speaks, 260
The innocence which happy childhood blesses,
　Made quite a picture of these little Greeks;
So that the philosophical beholder
Sigh'd for their sakes — that they should e'er grow older.

XXXIV

Afar, a dwarf buffoon stood telling tales
　To a sedate grey circle of old smokers,
Of secret treasures found in hidden vales,
　Of wonderful replies from Arab jokers,
Of charms to make good gold and cure bad ails,
　Of rocks bewitch'd that open to the knockers, 270
Of magic ladies who, by one sole act,
Transform'd their lords to beasts (but that's a fact).

XXXV

Here was no lack of innocent diversion
 For the imagination or the senses,
Song, dance, wine, music, stories from the
 Persian,
 All pretty pastimes in which no offence is;
But Lambro saw all these things with aver-
 sion,
 Perceiving in his absence such expenses,
Dreading that climax of all human ills,
The inflammation of his weekly bills. 280

XXXVI

Ah ! what is man ? what perils still environ
 The happiest mortals even after dinner —
A day of gold from out an age of iron
 Is all that life allows the luckiest sinner;
Pleasure (whene'er she sings, at least) 's a
 siren,
 That lures, to flay alive, the young
 beginner;
Lambro's reception at his people's banquet
Was such as fire accords to a wet blanket.

XXXVII

He — being a man who seldom used a word
 Too much, and wishing gladly to surprise
(In general he surprised men with the
 sword) 291
 His daughter — had not sent before to
 advise
Of his arrival, so that no one stirr'd;
 And long he paused to re-assure his eyes
In fact much more astonish'd than delighted,
To find so much good company invited.

XXXVIII

He did not know (alas ! how men will lie)
 That a report (especially the Greeks)
Avouch'd his death (such people never die),
 And put his house in mourning several
 weeks, — 300
But now their eyes and also lips were
 dry;
 The bloom, too, had return'd to Haidée's
 cheeks.
Her tears, too, being return'd into their
 fount,
She now kept house upon her own account.

XXXIX

Hence all this rice, meat, dancing, wine, and
 fiddling,
 Which turn'd the isle into a place of
 pleasure;

The servants all were getting drunk or idling,
 A life which made them happy beyond
 measure.
Her father's hospitality seem'd middling,
 Compared with what Haidée did with his
 treasure; 310
'T was wonderful how things went on im-
 proving,
While she had not one hour to spare from
 loving.

XL

Perhaps you think in stumbling on this feast
 He flew into a passion, and in fact
There was no mighty reason to be pleased;
 Perhaps you prophesy some sudden act,
The whip, the rack, or dungeon at the least,
 To teach his people to be more exact,
And that, proceeding at a very high rate,
He show'd the royal *penchants* of a pirate.

XLI

You 're wrong. — He was the mildest
 manner'd man 321
 That ever scuttled ship or cut a throat:
With such true breeding of a gentleman,
 You never could divine his real thought;
No courtier could, and scarcely woman can
 Gird more deceit within a petticoat;
Pity he loved adventurous life's variety,
He was so great a loss to good society.

XLII

Advancing to the nearest dinner tray, 329
 Tapping the shoulder of the nighest guest,
With a peculiar smile, which, by the way,
 Boded no good, whatever it express'd,
He ask'd the meaning of this holiday;
 The vinous Greek to whom he had ad-
 dress'd
His question, much too merry to divine
The questioner, fill'd up a glass of wine,

XLIII

And without turning his facetious head,
 Over his shoulder, with a Bacchant air,
Presented the o'erflowing cup, and said,
 'Talking 's dry work, I have no time to
 spare.' 340
A second hiccup'd, 'Our old master 's dead,
 You 'd better ask our mistress who 's his
 heir.'
'Our mistress !' quoth a third: 'Our mis-
 tress ! — pooh ! —
You mean our master — not the old, but new.'

XLIV

These rascals, being new comers, knew not
 whom
 They thus address'd — and Lambro's vis-
 age fell —
And o'er his eye a momentary gloom
 Pass'd, but he strove quite courteously to
 quell
The expression, and endeavouring to resume
 His smile, requested one of them to
 tell 350
The name and quality of his new patron,
Who seem'd to have turn'd Haidée into a
 matron.

XLV

'I know not,' quoth the fellow, ' who or
 what
 He is, nor whence he came — and little
 care;
But this I know, that this roast capon 's fat,
 And that good wine ne'er wash'd down
 better fare;
And if you are not satisfied with that,
 Direct your questions to my neighbour
 there;
He 'll answer all for better or for worse,
 For none likes more to hear himself con-
 verse.' 360

XLVI

I said that Lambro was a man of patience,
 And certainly he show'd the best of
 breeding,
Which scarce even France, the paragon of
 nations,
 E'er saw her most polite of sons exceed-
 ing;
He bore these sneers against his near re-
 lations,
 His own anxiety, his heart, too, bleeding,
The insults, too, of every servile glutton,
Who all the time was eating up his mutton.

XLVII

Now in a person used to much command —
 To bid men come, and go, and come
 again — 370
To see his orders done, too, out of hand —
 Whether the word was death, or but the
 chain —
It may seem strange to find his manners
 bland;
 Yet such things are, which I can not ex-
 plain,

Though doubtless he who can command
 himself
Is good to govern — almost as a Guelf.

XLVIII

Not that he was not sometimes rash or so,
 But never in his real and serious mood;
Then calm, concentrated, and still, and
 slow, 379
 He lay coil'd like the boa in the wood;
With him it never was a word and blow,
 His angry word once o'er, he shed no
 blood,
But in his silence there was much to rue,
And his *one* blow left little work for *two*.

XLIX

He ask'd no further questions, and pro-
 ceeded
 On to the house, but by a private way,
So that the few who met him hardly heeded,
 So little they expected him that day;
If love paternal in his bosom pleaded
 For Haidée's sake, is more than I can
 say, 390
But certainly to one deem'd dead, returning,
This revel seem'd a curious mode of mourn-
 ing.

L

If all the dead could now return to life
 (Which God forbid !) or some, or a great
 many,
For instance, if a husband or his wife
 (Nuptial examples are as good as any),
No doubt whate'er might be their former
 strife,
 The present weather would be much
 more rainy —
Tears shed into the grave of the connection
Would share most probably its resurrec-
 tion. 400

LI

He enter'd in the house no more his home,
 A thing to human feelings the most try-
 ing,
And harder for the heart to overcome,
 Perhaps, than even the mental pangs of
 dying;
To find our hearthstone turn'd into a tomb,
 And round its once warm precincts palely
 lying
The ashes of our hopes, is a deep grief,
Beyond a single gentleman's belief.

LII

He enter'd in the house — his home no
 more,
 For without hearts there is no home;
 and felt 410
The solitude of passing his own door
 Without a welcome; *there* he long had
 dwelt,
There his few peaceful days Time had
 swept o'er,
 There his worn bosom and keen eye
 would melt
Over the innocence of that sweet child,
His only shrine of feelings undefiled.

LIII

He was a man of a strange tempera-
 ment,
 Of mild demeanour though of savage
 mood,
Moderate in all his habits, and content
 With temperance in pleasure, as in food,
Quick to perceive, and strong to bear, and
 meant 421
 For something better, if not wholly good;
His country's wrongs and his despair to
 save her
Had stung him from a slave to an enslaver.

LIV

The love of power, and rapid gain of
 gold,
 The hardness by long habitude produced,
The dangerous life in which he had grown
 old,
 The mercy he had granted oft abused,
The sights he was accustom'd to behold,
 The wild seas, and wild men with whom
 he cruised, 430
Had cost his enemies a long repentance,
And made him a good friend, but bad ac-
 quaintance.

LV

But something of the spirit of old Greece
 Flash'd o'er his soul a few heroic rays,
Such as lit onward to the Golden Fleece
 His predecessors in the Colchian days;
'T is true he had no ardent love for peace —
 Alas! his country show'd no path to
 praise:
Hate to the world and war with every
 nation
He waged, in vengeance of her degrada-
 tion. 440

LVI

Still o'er his mind the influence of the
 clime
 Shed its Ionian elegance, which show'd
Its power unconsciously full many a time, —
 A taste seen in the choice of his abode,
A love of music and of scenes sublime,
 A pleasure in the gentle stream that flow'd
Past him in crystal, and a joy in flowers,
Bedew'd his spirit in his calmer hours.

LVII

But whatsoe'er he had of love reposed
 On that belovèd daughter; she had been
The only thing which kept his heart un-
 closed 451
 Amidst the savage deeds he had done and
 seen;
A lonely pure affection unopposed:
 There wanted but the loss of this to wean
His feelings from all milk of human kind-
 ness,
And turn him like the Cyclops mad with
 blindness.

LVIII

The cubless tigress in her jungle raging
 Is dreadful to the shepherd and the flock;
The ocean when its yeasty war is waging
 Is awful to the vessel near the rock; 460
But violent things will sooner bear assua-
 ging,
 Their fury being spent by its own shock,
Than the stern, single, deep, and wordless
 ire
Of a strong human heart, and in a sire.

LIX

It is a hard although a common case
 To find our children running restive —
 they
In whom our brightest days we would re-
 trace,
 Our little selves re-form'd in finer clay,
Just as old age is creeping on apace,
 And clouds come o'er the sunset of our
 day, 470
They kindly leave us, though not quite
 alone,
But in good company — the gout or stone.

LX

Yet a fine family is a fine thing
 (Provided they don't come in after din-
 ner);

'T is beautiful to see a matron bring
 Her children up (if nursing them don't
 thin her);
Like cherubs round an altar-piece they
 cling
 To the fire-side (a sight to touch a sinner).
A lady with her daughters or her nieces
 Shines like a guinea and seven-shilling
 pieces. 480

LXI

Old Lambro pass'd unseen a private gate,
 And stood within his hall at eventide;
Meantime the lady and her lover sate
 At wassail in their beauty and their pride:
An ivory inlaid table spread with state
 Before them, and fair slaves on every side;
Gems, gold, and silver, form'd the service
 mostly,
Mother of pearl and coral the less costly.

LXII

The dinner made about a hundred dishes;
 Lamb and pistachio nuts — in short, all
 meats, 490
And saffron soups, and sweetbreads; and
 the fishes
 Were of the finest that e'er flounced in
 nets,
Drest to a Sybarite's most pamper'd wishes;
 The beverage was various sherbets
Of raisin, orange, and pomegranate juice,
Squeezed through the rind, which makes it
 best for use.

LXIII

These were ranged round, each in its crystal
 ewer,
 And fruits, and date-bread loaves closed
 the repast,
And Mocha's berry, from Arabia pure,
 In small fine China cups, came in at
 last; 500
Cold cups of filigree made to secure
 The hand from burning underneath them
 placed,
Cloves, cinnamon, and saffron too were
 boil'd
Up with the coffee, which (I think) they
 spoil'd.

LXIV

The hangings of the room were tapestry,
 made
 Of velvet panels, each of different hue,
And thick with damask flowers of silk in-
 laid;
 And round them ran a yellow border too;
The upper border, richly wrought, display'd,
 Embroider'd delicately o'er with blue,
Soft Persian sentences, in lilac letters, 511
From poets, or the moralists their betters.

LXV

These Oriental writings on the wall,
 Quite common in those countries, are a
 kind
Of monitors adapted to recall,
 Like skulls at Memphian banquets, to
 the mind
The words which shook Belshazzar in his
 hall,
 And took his kingdom from him: You
 will find,
Though sages may pour out their wisdom's
 treasure,
There is no sterner moralist than Pleasure.

LXVI

A beauty at the season's close grown hec-
 tic, 521
 A genius who has drunk himself to death,
A rake turn'd methodistic, or Eclectic
 (For that 's the name they like to pray
 beneath) —
But most, an alderman struck apoplectic,
 Are things that really take away the
 breath, —
And show that late hours, wine, and love
 are able
To do not much less damage than the table.

LXVII

Haidée and Juan carpeted their feet
 On crimson satin, border'd with pale
 blue; 530
Their sofa occupied three parts complete
 Of the apartment — and appear'd quite
 new;
The velvet cushions (for a throne more
 meet)
 Were scarlet, from whose glowing centre
 grew
A sun emboss'd in gold, whose rays of tissue,
Meridian-like, were seen all light to issue.

LXVIII

Crystal and marble, plate and porcelain,
 Had done their work of splendour; Indian
 mats

And Persian carpets, which the heart bled
 to stain,
 Over the floors were spread; gazelles and
 cats, 540
And dwarfs and blacks, and such like
 things, that gain
 Their bread as ministers and favourites
 (that's
To say, by degradation) mingled there
As plentiful as in a court, or fair.

LXIX

There was no want of lofty mirrors, and
 The tables, most of ebony inlaid
With mother of pearl or ivory, stood at hand,
 Or were of tortoise-shell or rare woods
 made,
Fretted with gold or silver: — by command,
 The greater part of these were ready
 spread 550
With viands and sherbets in ice — and
 wine —
Kept for all comers at all hours to dine.

LXX

Of all the dresses I select Haidée's:
 She wore two jelicks — one was of pale
 yellow;
Of azure, pink, and white was her chemise —
 'Neath which her breast heaved like a
 little billow;
With buttons form'd of pearls as large as
 peas,
 All gold and crimson shone her jelick's
 fellow,
And the striped white gauze baracan that
 bound her,
Like fleecy clouds about the moon, flow'd
 round her. 560

LXXI

One large gold bracelet clasp'd each lovely
 arm,
 Lockless — so pliable from the pure gold
That the hand stretch'd and shut it without
 harm,
 The limb which it adorn'd its only mould;
So beautiful — its very shape would charm;
 And, clinging as if loath to lose its hold,
The purest ore enclosed the whitest skin
That e'er by precious metal was held in.

LXXII

Around, as princess of her father's land,
 A like gold bar above her instep roll'd

Announced her rank; twelve rings were on
 her hand; 571
 Her hair was starr'd with gems; her veil's
 fine fold
Below her breast was fasten'd with a band
 Of lavish pearls, whose worth could scarce
 be told;
Her orange silk full Turkish trousers furl'd
About the prettiest ankle in the world.

LXXIII

Her hair's long auburn waves down to her
 heel
 Flow'd like an Alpine torrent which the
 sun
Dyes with his morning light, — and would
 conceal
 Her person if allow'd at large to run,
And still they seem resentfully to feel 581
 The silken fillet's curb, and sought to
 shun
Their bonds whene'er some Zephyr caught
 began
To offer his young pinion as her fan.

LXXIV

Round her she made an atmosphere of life,
 The very air seem'd lighter from her eyes,
They were so soft and beautiful, and rife
 With all we can imagine of the skies,
And pure as Psyche ere she grew a wife —
 Too pure even for the purest human ties;
Her overpowering presence made you feel
It would not be idolatry to kneel. 592

LXXV

Her eyelashes, though dark as night, were
 tinged
 (It is the country's custom), but in vain;
For those large black eyes were so blackly
 fringed,
 The glossy rebels mock'd the jetty stain,
And in their native beauty stood avenged:
 Her nails were touch'd with henna; but
 again
The power of art was turn'd to nothing, for
They could not look more rosy than before.

LXXVI

The henna should be deeply dyed to make
 The skin relieved appear more fairly
 fair; 602
She had no need of this, day ne'er will break
 On mountain tops more heavenly white
 than her:

The eye might doubt if it were well awake,
 She was so like a vision; I might err,
But Shakspeare also says, 't is very silly
 'To gild refinèd gold, or paint the lily.'

LXXVII

Juan had on a shawl of black and gold,
 But a white baracan, and so transparent
The sparkling gems beneath you might be-
 hold, 611
 Like small stars through the milky way
 apparent;
His turban, furl'd in many a graceful fold,
 An emerald aigrette with Haidée's hair
 in 't
Surmounted as its clasp — a glowing cres-
 cent,
Whose rays shone ever trembling, but in-
 cessant.

LXXVIII

And now they were diverted by their suite,
 Dwarfs, dancing girls, black eunuchs,
 and a poet,
Which made their new establishment com-
 plete;
 The last was of great fame, and liked to
 show it: 620
His verses rarely wanted their due feet;
 And for his theme — he seldom sung be-
 low it,
He being paid to satirize or flatter,
As the psalm says, 'inditing a good matter.'

LXXIX

He praised the present, and abused the
 past,
 Reversing the good custom of old days,
An Eastern anti-jacobin at last
 He turn'd, preferring pudding to *no*
 praise —
For some few years his lot had been o'er-
 cast 629
 By his seeming independent in his lays,
But now he sung the Sultan and the Pacha
With truth like Southey, and with verse
 like Crashaw.

LXXX

He was a man who had seen many changes,
 And always changed as true as any
 needle;
His polar star being one which rather ranges,
 And not the fix'd — he knew the way to
 wheedle:

So vile he 'scaped the doom which oft
 avenges;
 And being fluent (save indeed when fee'd
 ill),
He lied with such a fervour of intention —
There was no doubt he earn'd his laureate
 pension. 640

LXXXI

But he had genius, — when a turncoat has it,
 The 'Vates irritabilis' takes care
That without notice few full moons shall
 pass it;
 Even good men like to make the public
 stare: —
But to my subject — let me see — what
 was it ? —
 Oh ! — the third canto — and the pretty
 pair —
Their loves, and feasts, and house, and
 dress, and mode
Of living in their insular abode.

LXXXII

Their poet, a sad trimmer, but no less
 In company a very pleasant fellow, 650
Had been the favourite of full many a mess
 Of men, and made them speeches when
 half mellow;
And though his meaning they could rarely
 guess,
 Yet still they deign'd to hiccup or to bel-
 low
The glorious meed of popular applause,
Of which the first ne'er knows the second
 cause.

LXXXIII

But now being lifted into high society,
 And having pick'd up several odds and
 ends
Of free thoughts in his travels for variety,
 He deem'd, being in a lone isle, among
 friends, 660
That, without any danger of a riot, he
 Might for long lying make himself
 amends;
And, singing as he sung in his warm youth,
Agree to a short armistice with truth.

LXXXIV

He had travell'd 'mongst the Arabs, Turks,
 and Franks,
 And knew the self-loves of the different
 nations;

And having lived with people of all ranks,
 Had something ready upon most occa-
 sions —
Which got him a few presents and some
 thanks.
He varied with some skill his adulations;
To 'do at Rome as Romans do,' a piece 671
Of conduct was which he observed in
 Greece.

LXXXV

Thus, usually, when he was ask'd to sing,
 He gave the different nations something
 national;
'T was all the same to him — 'God save
 the king,'
Or ' Ça ira,' according to the fashion all:
His muse made increment of any thing,
 From the high lyric down to the low ra-
 tional:
If Pindar sang horse-races, what should
 hinder
Himself from being as pliable as Pindar ?

LXXXVI

In France, for instance, he would write a
 chanson; 681
 In England a six canto quarto tale;
In Spain, he 'd make a ballad or romance
 on
The last war — much the same in Por-
 tugal;
In Germany, the Pegasus he 'd prance on
 Would be old Goethe's (see what says
 De Staël);
In Italy he 'd ape the ' Trecentisti; '
In Greece, he 'd sing some sort of hymn
 like this t' ye:

1

The isles of Greece, the Isles of Greece !
 Where burning Sappho loved and sung, 690
Where grew the arts of war and peace,
 Where Delos rose, and Phœbus sprung !
Eternal summer gilds them yet,
But all, except their sun, is set.

2

The Scian and the Teian muse,
 The hero's harp, the lover's lute,
Have found the fame your shores refuse;
 Their place of birth alone is mute
To sounds which echo further west
Than your sires' ' Islands of the Blest.' 700

3

The mountains look on Marathon —
 And Marathon looks on the sea ;

And musing there an hour alone,
 I dream'd that Greece might still be free ;
For standing on the Persians' grave,
I could not deem myself a slave.

4

A king sate on the rocky brow
 Which looks o'er sea-born Salamis ;
And ships, by thousands, lay below,
 And men in nations ; — all were his ! 710
He counted them at break of day —
And when the sun set where were they ?

5

And where are they ? and where art thou,
 My country ? On thy voiceless shore
The heroic lay is tuneless now —
 The heroic bosom beats no more !
And must thy lyre, so long divine,
Degenerate into hands like mine ?

6

'T is something, in the dearth of fame,
 Though link'd among a fetter'd race, 720
To feel at least a patriot's shame,
 Even as I sing, suffuse my face ;
For what is left the poet here ?
For Greeks a blush — for Greece a tear.

7

Must we but weep o'er days more blest ?
 Must we but blush ? — Our fathers bled.
Earth ! render back from out thy breast
 A remnant of our Spartan dead !
Of the three hundred grant but three,
To make a new Thermopylæ ! 730

8

What, silent still ? and silent all ?
 Ah ! no ; — the voices of the dead
Sound like a distant torrent's fall,
 And answer, ' Let one living head,
But one arise, — we come, we come ! '
'T is but the living who are dumb.

9

In vain — in vain : strike other chords;
 Fill high the cup with Samian wine !
Leave battles to the Turkish hordes,
 And shed the blood of Scio's vine ! 740
Hark ! rising to the ignoble call —
How answers each bold Bacchanal !

10

You have the Pyrrhic dance as yet,
 Where is the Pyrrhic phalanx gone ?
Of two such lessons, why forget
 The nobler and the manlier one ?
You have the letters Cadmus gave —
Think ye he meant them for a slave ?

11

Fill high the bowl with Samian wine !
 We will not think of themes like these ! 750
It made Anacreon's song divine:
 He served — but served Polycrates —

A tyrant ; but our masters then
Were still, at least, our countrymen.

12

The tyrant of the Chersonese
 Was freedom's best and bravest friend ;
 That tyrant was Miltiades !
 Oh ! that the present hour would lend
Another despot of the kind !
Such chains as his were sure to bind. 760

13

Fill high the bowl with Samian wine !
 On Suli's rock, and Parga's shore,
 Exists the remnant of a line
 Such as the Doric mothers bore ;
And there, perhaps, some seed is sown,
The Heracleidan blood might own.

14

Trust not for freedom to the Franks —
 They have a king who buys and sells :
 In native swords, and native ranks,
 The only hope of courage dwells ; 770
But Turkish force, and Latin fraud,
Would break your shield, however broad.

15

Fill high the bowl with Samian wine !
 Our virgins dance beneath the shade —
 I see their glorious black eyes shine ;
 But gazing on each glowing maid,
My own the burning tear-drop laves,
To think such breasts must suckle slaves.

16

Place me on Sunium's marbled steep,
 Where nothing, save the waves and I, 780
 May hear our mutual murmurs sweep ;
 There, swan-like, let me sing and die :
A land of slaves shall ne'er be mine —
Dash down yon cup of Samian wine !

LXXXVII

Thus sung, or would, or could, or should
 have sung,
 The modern Greek, in tolerable verse ;
If not like Orpheus quite, when Greece was
 young,
 Yet in these times he might have done
 much worse :
His strain display'd some feeling — right or
 wrong ;
 And feeling, in a poet, is the source 790
Of others' feeling ; but they are such liars,
And take all colours — like the hands of
 dyers.

LXXXVIII

But words are things, and a small drop of ink,
 Falling like dew, upon a thought, pro-
 duces

That which makes thousands, perhaps mil-
 lions, think ;
 'T is strange, the shortest letter which
 man uses
Instead of speech, may form a lasting link
 Of ages ; to what straits old Time re-
 duces
Frail man, when paper — even a rag like
 this,
Survives himself, his tomb, and all that 's
 his. 800

LXXXIX

And when his bones are dust, his grave a
 blank,
 His station, generation, even his nation,
Become a thing, or nothing, save to rank
 In chronological commemoration,
Some dull MS. oblivion long has sank,
 Or graven stone found in a barrack's
 station
In digging the foundation of a closet,
May turn his name up, as a rare deposit.

XC

And glory long has made the sages smile ;
 'T is something, nothing, words, illusion,
 wind — 810
Depending more upon the historian's style
 Than on the name a person leaves be-
 hind :
Troy owes to Homer what whist owes to
 Hoyle :
 The present century was growing blind
To the great Marlborough's skill in giving
 knocks,
Until his late Life by Archdeacon Coxe.

XCI

Milton 's the prince of poets — so we say ;
 A little heavy, but no less divine :
An independent being in his day —
 Learn'd, pious, temperate in love and
 wine ; 820
But, his life falling into Johnson's way,
 We 're told this great high priest of all
 the Nine
Was whipt at college — a harsh sire — odd
 spouse,
For the first Mrs. Milton left his house.

XCII

All these are, *certes*, entertaining facts,
 Like Shakspeare's stealing deer, Lord
 Bacon's bribes ;

Like Titus' youth, and Cæsar's earliest acts;
 Like Burns (whom Doctor Currie well
 describes);
Like Cromwell's pranks; — but although
 truth exacts
 These amiable descriptions from the
 scribes, 830
As most essential to their hero's story,
They do not much contribute to his glory.

XCIII

All are not moralists, like Southey, when
 He prated to the world of ' Pantiso-
 cracy;'
Or Wordsworth unexcised, unhired, who
 then
 Season'd his pedlar poems with demo-
 cracy;
Or Coleridge, long before his flighty pen
Let to the *Morning Post* its aristocracy;
When he and Southey, following the same
 path, 839
Espoused two partners (milliners of Bath).

XCIV

Such names at present cut a convict figure,
 The very Botany Bay in moral geography;
Their loyal treason, renegado rigour,
 Are good manure for their more bare
 biography.
Wordsworth's last quarto, by the way, is
 bigger
 Than any since the birthday of typo-
 graphy;
A drowsy frowzy poem, call'd the ' *Excur-
 sion,*'
Writ in a manner which is my aversion.

XCV

He there builds up a formidable dyke
 Between his own and others' intellect;
But Wordsworth's poem, and his followers,
 like 851
 Joanna Southcote's Shiloh, and her sect,
Are things which in this century don't
 strike
 The public mind, — so few are the elect;
And the new births of both their stale vir-
 ginities
Have proved but dropsies, taken for divin-
 ities.

XCVI

But let me to my story: I must own,
 If I have any fault, it is digression —

Leaving my people to proceed alone, 859
 While I soliloquize beyond expression;
But these are my addresses from the throne,
 Which put off business to the ensuing
 session:
Forgetting each omission is a loss to
The world, not quite so great as Ariosto.

XCVII

I know that what our neighbours call ' *lon-
 gueurs* '
 (We 've not so good a *word*, but have the
 thing
In that complete perfection which ensures
 An epic from Bob Southey every
 spring),
Form not the true temptation which allures
 The reader; but 't would not be hard to
 bring 870
Some fine examples of the *epopée*,
To prove its grand ingredient is *ennui*.

XCVIII

We learn from Horace, ' Homer sometimes
 sleeps;'
 We feel without him, Wordsworth some-
 times wakes, —
To show with what complacency he creeps,
 With his dear ' *Waggoners*,' around his
 lakes.
He wishes for ' a boat ' to sail the deeps —
 Of ocean ? — No, of air; and then he
 makes
Another outcry for ' a little boat,'
And drivels seas to set it well afloat. 880

XCIX

If he must fain sweep o'er the ethereal plain,
 And Pegasus runs restive in his ' Wag-
 gon,'
Could he not beg the loan of Charles's
 Wain ?
 Or pray Medea for a single dragon ?
Or if, too classic for his vulgar brain,
 He fear'd his neck to venture such a nag
 on,
And he must needs mount nearer to the
 moon,
Could not the blockhead ask for a balloon ?

C

' Pedlars,' and ' Boats,' and ' Waggons ! '
 Oh ! ye shades
 Of Pope and Dryden, are we come to
 this ? 890

That trash of such sort not alone evades
 Contempt, but from the bathos' vast
 abyss
Floats scumlike uppermost, and these Jack
 Cades
 Of sense and song above your graves may
 hiss —
The 'little boatman' and his ' Peter Bell'
Can sneer at him who drew ' Achitophel' !

CI

T' our tale. — The feast was over, the
 slaves gone,
 The dwarfs and dancing girls had all re-
 tired;
The Arab lore and poet's song were done,
 And every sound of revelry expired; 900
The lady and her lover, left alone,
 The rosy flood of twilight's sky ad-
 mired; —
Ave Maria! o'er the earth and sea,
That heavenliest hour of Heaven is wor-
 thiest thee !

CII

Ave Maria ! blessèd be the hour !
 The time, the clime, the spot, where I
 so oft
Have felt that moment in its fullest power
 Sink o'er the earth so beautiful and
 soft,
While swung the deep bell in the distant
 tower,
 Or the faint dying day-hymn stole aloft,
And not a breath crept through the rosy
 air, 911
And yet the forest leaves seem'd stirr'd
 with prayer.

CIII

Ave Maria ! 't is the hour of prayer !
 Ave Maria ! 't is the hour of love !
Ave Maria ! may our spirits dare
 Look up to thine and to thy Son's above !
Ave Maria ! oh that face so fair !
 Those downcast eyes beneath the Al-
 mighty dove —
What though 't is but a pictured image ? —
 strike —
That painting is no idol, — 't is too like. 920

CIV

Some kinder casuists are pleased to say,
 In nameless print — that I have no devo-
 tion;

But set those persons down with me to
 pray,
 And you shall see who has the properest
 notion
Of getting into heaven the shortest way;
 My altars are the mountains and the
 ocean,
Earth, air, stars, — all that springs from
 the great Whole,
Who hath produced, and will receive the
 soul.

CV

Sweet hour of twilight ! — in the solitude
 Of the pine forest, and the silent shore
Which bounds Ravenna's immemorial wood,
 Rooted where once the Adrian wave
 flow'd o'er, 932
To where the last Cæsarean fortress stood,
 Evergreen forest ! which Boccaccio's lore
And Dryden's lay made haunted ground to
 me,
How have I loved the twilight hour and
 thee !

CVI

The shrill cicalas, people of the pine,
 Making their summer lives one ceaseless
 song,
Were the sole echoes, save my steed's and
 mine,
 And vesper bell's that rose the boughs
 along; 940
The spectre huntsman of Onesti's line,
 His hell-dogs, and their chase, and the
 fair throng
Which learn'd from this example not to fly
From a true lover, — shadow'd my mind's
 eye.

CVII

Oh, Hesperus ! thou bringest all good
 things —
 Home to the weary, to the hungry cheer,
To the young bird the parent's brooding
 wings,
 The welcome stall to the o'erlabour'd
 steer;
Whate'er of peace about our hearthstone
 clings,
 Whate'er our household gods protect of
 dear, 950
Are gather'd round us by thy look of rest;
Thou bring'st the child, too, to the mother's
 breast.

CVIII

Soft hour ! which wakes the wish and melts
 the heart
 Of those who sail the seas, on the first
 day
When they from their sweet friends are
 torn apart;
 Or fills with love the pilgrim on his
 way
As the far bell of vesper makes him
 start,
 Seeming to weep the dying day's decay;
Is this a fancy which our reason scorns ?
Ah ! surely nothing dies but something
 mourns ! 960

CIX

When Nero perish'd by the justest doom
 Which ever the destroyer yet destroy'd,
Amidst the roar of liberated Rome,
 Of nations freed, and the world over-
 joy'd,
Some hands unseen strew'd flowers upon
 his tomb:
 Perhaps the weakness of a heart not
 void
Of feeling for some kindness done, when
 power
Had left the wretch an uncorrupted hour.

CX

But I 'm digressing ; what on earth has
 Nero,
 Or any such like sovereign buffoons, 970
To do with the transactions of my hero,
 More than such madmen's fellow man —
 the moon's ?
Sure my invention must be down at zero,
 And I grown one of many ' wooden
 spoons '
Of verse (the name with which we Cantabs
 please
To dub the last of honours in degrees).

CXI

I feel this tediousness will never do —
 'T is being *too* epic, and I must cut down
(In copying) this long canto into two; 979
 They 'll never find it out, unless I own
The fact, excepting some experienced few;
 And then as an improvement 't will be
 shown:
I 'll prove that such the opinion of the
 critic is
From Aristotle *passim.* — See Ποιητικης.

CANTO THE FOURTH

I

Nothing so difficult as a beginning
 In poesy, unless perhaps the end;
For oftentimes when Pegasus seems win-
 ning
 The race, he sprains a wing, and down
 we tend,
Like Lucifer when hurl'd from heaven for
 sinning;
 Our sin the same, and hard as his to
 mend,
Being pride, which leads the mind to soar
 too far,
Till our own weakness shows us what we are.

II

But Time, which brings all beings to their
 level,
 And sharp Adversity, will teach at last 10
Man, — and, as we would hope, — perhaps
 the devil,
 That neither of their intellects are vast:
While youth's hot wishes in our red veins
 revel,
 We know not this — the blood flows on
 too fast;
But as the torrent widens towards the
 ocean,
We ponder deeply on each past emotion.

III

As boy, I thought myself a clever fellow,
 And wish'd that others held the same
 opinion;
They took it up when my days grew more
 mellow,
 And other minds acknowledged my do-
 minion: 20
Now my sere fancy ' falls into the yellow
 Leaf,' and Imagination droops her pinion,
And the sad truth which hovers o'er my
 desk
Turns what was once romantic to burlesque.

IV

And if I laugh at any mortal thing,
 'T is that I may not weep; and if I weep,
'T is that our nature cannot always bring
 Itself to apathy, for we must steep
Our hearts first in the depths of Lethe's
 spring,
 Ere what we least wish to behold will
 sleep: 30

Thetis baptized her mortal son in Styx;
A mortal mother would on Lethe fix.

V

Some have accused me of a strange design
 Against the creed and morals of the land,
And trace it in this poem every line:
 I don't pretend that I quite understand
My own meaning when I would be *very* fine;
 But the fact is that I have nothing plann'd,
Unless it were to be a moment merry,
A novel word in my vocabulary. 40

VI

To the kind reader of our sober clime
 This way of writing will appear exotic;
Pulci was sire of the half-serious rhyme,
 Who sang when chivalry was more Quix-
 otic,
And revell'd in the fancies of the time,
 True knights, chaste dames, huge giants,
 kings despotic;
But all these, save the last, being obsolete,
I chose a modern subject as more meet.

VII

How I have treated it, I do not know;
 Perhaps no better than they have treated
 me 50
Who have imputed such designs as show
 Not what they saw, but what they wish'd
 to see:
But if it gives them pleasure, be it so;
 This is a liberal age, and thoughts are
 free:
Meantime Apollo plucks me by the ear,
And tells me to resume my story here.

VIII

Young Juan and his lady-love were left
 To their own hearts' most sweet society;
Even Time the pitiless in sorrow cleft
 With his rude scythe such gentle bosoms;
 he 60
Sigh'd to behold them of their hours bereft,
 Though foe to love; and yet they could
 not be
Meant to grow old, but die in happy spring,
Before one charm or hope had taken wing.

IX

Their faces were not made for wrinkles, their
 Pure blood to stagnate, their great hearts
 to fail;

The blank grey was not made to blast their
 hair,
 But like the climes that know nor snow
 nor hail
They were all summer: lightning might
 assail
 And shiver them to ashes, but to trail 70
A long and snake-like life of dull decay
Was not for them — they had too little clay.

X

They were alone once more; for them to be
 Thus was another Eden; they were never
Weary, unless when separate: the tree
 Cut from its forest root of years — the
 river
Damm'd from its fountain — the child from
 the knee
 And breast maternal wean'd at once for
 ever, —
Would wither less than these two torn
 apart;
Alas ! there is no instinct like the heart —

XI

The heart — which may be broken: happy
 they ! 81
 Thrice fortunate ! who of that fragile
 mould,
The precious porcelain of human clay,
 Break with the first fall: they can ne'er
 behold
The long year link'd with heavy day on day,
 And all which must be borne, and never
 told;
While life's strange principle will often
 lie
Deepest in those who long the most to die.

XII

' Whom the gods love die young,' was said
 of yore,
 And many deaths do they escape by this:
The death of friends, and that which slays
 even more — 91
 The death of friendship, love, youth, all
 that is,
Except mere breath; and since the silent
 shore
 Awaits at last even those who longest
 miss
The old archer's shafts, perhaps the early
 grave
Which men weep over may be meant to
 save.

XIII

Haidée and Juan thought not of the dead —
 The heavens, and earth, and air, seem'd
 made for them:
They found no fault with Time, save that
 he fled;
 They saw not in themselves aught to
 condemn: 100
Each was the other's mirror, and but read
 Joy sparkling in their dark eyes like a
 gem,
And knew such brightness was but the re-
 flection
Of their exchanging glances of affection.

XIV

The gentle pressure, and the thrilling touch,
 The least glance better understood than
 words,
Which still said all, and ne'er could say too
 much;
 A language, too, but like to that of birds,
Known but to them, at least appearing such
 As but to lovers a true sense affords; 110
Sweet playful phrases, which would seem
 absurd
To those who have ceased to hear such, or
 ne'er heard, —

XV

All these were theirs, for they were chil-
 dren still,
 And children still they should have ever
 been;
They were not made in the real world to
 fill
 A busy character in the dull scene,
But like two beings born from out a rill,
 A nymph and her belovèd, all unseen
To pass their lives in fountains and on
 flowers,
And never know the weight of human hours.

XVI

Moons changing had roll'd on, and change-
 less found 121
 Those their bright rise had lighted to
 such joys
As rarely they beheld throughout their
 round;
 And these were not of the vain kind which
 cloys,
For theirs were buoyant spirits, never bound
 By the mere senses; and that which de-
 stroys

Most love, possession, unto them appear'd
A thing which each endearment more en-
 dear'd.

XVII

Oh beautiful! and rare as beautiful!
 But theirs was love in which the mind
 delights 130
To lose itself when the old world grows dull,
 And we are sick of its hack sounds and
 sights,
Intrigues, adventures of the common school,
 Its petty passions, marriages, and flights,
Where Hymen's torch but brands one strum-
 pet more,
Whose husband only knows her not a
 wh—re.

XVIII

Hard words; harsh truth; a truth which
 many know.
 Enough. — The faithful and the fairy
 pair,
Who never found a single hour too slow,
 What was it made them thus exempt
 from care? 140
Young innate feelings all have felt below,
 Which perish in the rest, but in them
 were
Inherent — what we mortals call romantic,
And always envy, though we deem it fran-
 tic.

XIX

This is in others a factitious state,
 An opium dream of too much youth and
 reading,
But was in them their nature or their fate:
 No novels e'er had set their young hearts
 bleeding,
For Haidée's knowledge was by no means
 great,
 And Juan was a boy of saintly breed-
 ing; 150
So that there was no reason for their loves
More than for those of nightingales or
 doves.

XX

They gazed upon the sunset; 't is an hour
 Dear unto all, but dearest to *their* eyes,
For it had made them what they were: the
 power
 Of love had first o'erwhelm'd them from
 such skies,

When happiness had been their only dower,
 And twilight saw them link'd in passion's
 ties;
Charm'd with each other, all things charm'd
 that brought
The past still welcome as the present
 thought. 160

XXI

I know not why, but in that hour to-night,
 Even as they gazed, a sudden tremor came,
And swept, as 't were, across their hearts'
 delight,
 Like the wind o'er a harp-string, or a
 flame,
When one is shook in sound, and one in
 sight;
 And thus some boding flash'd through
 either frame,
And call'd from Juan's breast a faint low
 sigh,
While one new tear arose in Haidée's eye.

XXII

That large black prophet eye seem'd to
 dilate
 And follow far the disappearing sun, 170
As if their last day of a happy date
 With his broad, bright, and dropping orb
 were gone;
Juan gazed on her as to ask his fate —
 He felt a grief, but knowing cause for
 none,
His glance inquired of hers for some ex-
 cuse
For feelings causeless, or at least abstruse.

XXIII

She turn'd to him, and smiled, but in that
 sort
 Which makes not others smile; then
 turn'd aside:
Whatever feeling shook her, it seem'd short,
 And master'd by her wisdom or her
 pride; 180
When Juan spoke, too — it might be in
 sport —
 Of this their mutual feeling, she re-
 plied —
'If it should be so, — but — it cannot be —
Or I at least shall not survive to see.'

XXIV

Juan would question further, but she press'd
 His lip to hers, and silenced him with this,
And then dismiss'd the omen from her
 breast,
 Defying augury with that fond kiss;
And no doubt of all methods 't is the best:
 Some people prefer wine — 't is not
 amiss; 190
I have tried both; so those who would
 a part take
May choose between the headache and the
 heartache.

XXV

One of the two, according to your choice,
 Woman or wine, you 'll have to undergo;
Both maladies are taxes on our joys:
 But which to choose, I really hardly
 know;
And if I had to give a casting voice,
 For both sides I could many reasons
 show,
And then decide, without great wrong to
 either,
It were much better to have both than
 neither. 200

XXVI

Juan and Haidée gazed upon each other
 With swimming looks of speechless ten-
 derness,
Which mix'd all feelings, friend, child,
 lover, brother,
 All that the best can mingle and ex-
 press
When two pure hearts are pour'd in one
 another,
 And love too much, and yet can not love
 less;
But almost sanctify the sweet excess
By the immortal wish and power to bless.

XXVII

Mix'd in each other's arms, and heart in
 heart,
 Why did they not then die? — they had
 lived too long 210
Should an hour come to bid them breathe
 apart;
 Years could but bring them cruel things
 or wrong;
The world was not for them, nor the world's
 art
 For beings passionate as Sappho's song;
Love was born *with* them, *in* them, so in-
 tense,
It was their very spirit — not a sense.

XXVIII

They should have lived together deep in
 woods,
 Unseen as sings the nightingale; they
 were
Unfit to mix in these thick solitudes
 Call'd social, haunts of Hate, and Vice,
 and Care: 220
How lonely every freeborn creature broods !
 The sweetest song-birds nestle in a pair;
The eagle soars alone; the gull and crow
Flock o'er their carrion, just like men be-
 low.

XXIX

Now pillow'd cheek to cheek, in loving
 sleep,
 Haidée and Juan their siesta took,
A gentle slumber, but it was not deep,
 For ever and anon a something shook
Juan, and shuddering o'er his frame would
 creep;
 And Haidée's sweet lips murmur'd like
 a brook 230
A wordless music, and her face so fair
Stirr'd with her dream, as rose-leaves with
 the air.

XXX

Or as the stirring of a deep clear stream
 Within an Alpine hollow, when the wind
Walks o'er it, was she shaken by the dream,
 The mystical usurper of the mind —
O'erpowering us to be whate'er may seem
 Good to the soul which we no more can
 bind;
Strange state of being ! (for 't is still to be)
Senseless to feel, and with seal'd eyes to
 see. 240

XXXI

She dream'd of being alone on the sea-shore,
 Chain'd to a rock; she knew not how, but
 stir
She could not from the spot, and the loud
 roar
 Grew, and each wave rose roughly,
 threatening her;
And o'er her upper lip they seem'd to pour,
 Until she sobb'd for breath, and soon
 they were
Foaming o'er her lone head, so fierce and
 high —
Each broke to drown her, yet she could not
 die.

XXXII

Anon — she was released, and then she
 stray'd
 O'er the sharp shingles with her bleed-
 ing feet, 250
And stumbled almost every step she made;
 And something roll'd before her in a
 sheet,
Which she must still pursue howe'er afraid:
 'T was white and indistinct, nor stopp'd
 to meet
Her glance nor grasp, for still she gazed,
 and grasp'd,
And ran, but it escaped her as she clasp'd.

XXXIII

The dream changed: — in a cave she stood,
 its walls
 Were hung with marble icicles, the work
Of ages on its water-fretted halls,
 Where waves might wash, and seals might
 breed and lurk; 260
Her hair was dripping, and the very balls
 Of her black eyes seem'd turn'd to tears,
 and mirk
The sharp rocks look'd below each drop
 they caught,
Which froze to marble as it fell, — she
 thought.

XXXIV

And wet, and cold, and lifeless at her feet,
 Pale as the foam that froth'd on his dead
 brow,
Which she essay'd in vain to clear (how
 sweet
 Were once her cares, how idle seem'd
 they now !),
Lay Juan, nor could aught renew the beat
 Of his quench'd heart; and the sea dirges
 low 270
Rang in her sad ears like a mermaid's song,
And that brief dream appear'd a life too long.

XXXV

And gazing on the dead, she thought his
 face
 Faded, or alter'd into something new —
Like to her father's features, till each trace
 More like and like to Lambro's aspect
 grew —
With all his keen worn look and Grecian
 grace;
 And starting, she awoke, and what to
 view ?

Oh! Powers of Heaven! what dark eye
 meets she there?
'T is — 't is her father's — fix'd upon the
 pair! 280

XXXVI

Then shrieking, she arose, and shrieking
 fell,
 With joy and sorrow, hope and fear, to
 see
Him whom she deem'd a habitant where
 dwell
The ocean-buried, risen from death, to be
Perchance the death of one she loved too
 well:
 Dear as her father had been to Haidée,
It was a moment of that awful kind —
I have seen such — but must not call to
 mind.

XXXVII

Up Juan sprung to Haidée's bitter shriek,
 And caught her falling, and from off the
 wall 290
Snatch'd down his sabre, in hot haste to
 wreak
 Vengeance on him who was the cause of
 all:
Then Lambro, who till now forbore to
 speak,
 Smiled scornfully, and said, ' Within my
 call,
A thousand scimitars await the word;
Put up, young man, put up your silly sword.'

XXXVIII

And Haidée clung around him; ' Juan,
 't is —
 'T is Lambro — 't is my father! Kneel
 with me —
He will forgive us — yes — it must be —
 yes.
Oh! dearest father, in this agony 300
Of pleasure and of pain — even while I kiss
 Thy garment's hem with transport, can
 it be
That doubt should mingle with my filial
 joy?
Deal with me as thou wilt, but spare this
 boy.'

XXXIX

High and inscrutable the old man stood,
 Calm in his voice, and calm within his
 eye —

Not always signs with him of calmest mood:
 He look'd upon her, but gave no reply;
Then turn'd to Juan, in whose cheek the
 blood
 Oft came and went, as there resolved to
 die; 310
In arms, at least, he stood, in act to spring
On the first foe whom Lambro's call might
 bring.

XL

' Young man, your sword;' so Lambro once
 more said :
 Juan replied, ' Not while this arm is
 free.'
The old man's cheek grew pale, but not
 with dread,
 And drawing from his belt a pistol, he
Replied, ' Your blood be then on your own
 head.'
Then look'd close at the flint, as if to see
'T was fresh — for he had lately used the
 lock —
And next proceeded quietly to cock. 320

XLI

It has a strange quick jar upon the ear,
 That cocking of a pistol, when you know
A moment more will bring the sight to
 bear
 Upon your person, twelve yards off, or
 so;
A gentlemanly distance, not too near,
 If you have got a former friend for foe;
But after being fired at once or twice,
The ear becomes more Irish, and less nice.

XLII

Lambro presented, and one instant more
 Had stopp'd this Canto, and Don Juan's
 breath, 330
When Haidée threw herself her boy before;
 Stern as her sire : ' On me,' she cried,
 ' let death
Descend — the fault is mine; this fatal
 shore
 He found — but sought not. I have
 pledged my faith;
I love him — I will die with him: I knew
Your nature's firmness — know your daugh-
 ter's too.'

XLIII

A minute past, and she had been all tears,
 And tenderness, and infancy; but now

She stood as one who champion'd human
 fears —
 Pale, statue-like, and stern, she woo'd the
 blow; 340
And tall beyond her sex, and their compeers,
 She drew up to her height, as if to show
A fairer mark; and with a fix'd eye scann'd
Her father's face — but never stopp'd his
 hand.

XLIV

He gazed on her, and she on him; 't was
 strange
 How like they look'd ! the expression was
 the same;
Serenely savage, with a little change
 In the large dark eye's mutual-darted
 flame;
For she, too, was as one who could avenge,
 If cause should be — a lioness, though
 tame. 350
Her father's blood before her father's face
Boil'd up, and proved her truly of his race.

XLV

I said they were alike, their features and
 Their stature, differing but in sex and
 years;
Even to the delicacy of their hand
 There was resemblance, such as true
 blood wears;
And now to see them, thus divided, stand
 In fix'd ferocity, when joyous tears
And sweet sensations should have welcomed
 both,
Show what the passions are in their full
 growth. 360

XLVI

The father paused a moment, then withdrew
 His weapon, and replaced it; but stood
 still,
And looking on her, as to look her through,
 'Not I,' he said, 'have sought this
 stranger's ill;
Not I have made this desolation: few
 Would bear such outrage, and forbear to
 kill;
But I must do my duty — how thou hast
Done thine, the present vouches for the past.

XLVII

'Let him disarm; or, by my father's head,
 His own shall roll before you like a
 ball !' 370

He raised his whistle, as the word he said,
 And blew; another answer'd to the call,
And rushing in disorderly, though led,
 And arm'd from boot to turban, one and
 all,
Some twenty of his train came, rank on rank;
He gave the word, — ' Arrest or slay the
 Frank.'

XLVIII

Then, with a sudden movement, he with-
 drew
 His daughter; while compress'd within
 his clasp,
'Twixt her and Juan interposed the crew;
 In vain she struggled in her father's
 grasp — 380
His arms were like a serpent's coil: then
 flew
 Upon their prey, as darts an angry asp,
The file of pirates; save the foremost, who
Had fallen, with his right shoulder half cut
 through.

XLIX

The second had his cheek laid open; but
 The third, a wary, cool old sworder, took
The blows upon his cutlass, and then put
 His own well in; so well, ere you could
 look,
His man was floor'd, and helpless at his
 foot,
 With the blood running like a little brook
From two smart sabre gashes, deep and
 red — 391
One on the arm, the other on the head.

L

And then they bound him where he fell,
 and bore
 Juan from the apartment: with a sign
Old Lambro bade them take him to the
 shore,
 Where lay some ships which were to sail
 at nine.
They laid him in a boat, and plied the oar
 Until they reach'd some galliots, placed
 in line;
On board of one of these, and under hatches,
They stow'd him, with strict orders to the
 watches. 400

LI

The world is full of strange vicissitudes,
 And here was one exceedingly unpleasant:

A gentleman so rich in the world's goods,
　Handsome and young, enjoying all the
　　present,
Just at the very time when he least broods
　On such a thing is suddenly to sea sent,
Wounded and chain'd, so that he cannot
　move,
And all because a lady fell in love.

LII

Here I must leave him, for I grow pathetic,
　Moved by the Chinese nymph of tears,
　　green tea !　　　　　　　　　　410
Than whom Cassandra was not more pro-
　phetic;
For if my pure libations exceed three,
　I feel my heart become so sympathetic,
That I must have recourse to black
　Bohea:
'T is pity wine should be so deleterious,
For tea and coffee leave us much more
　serious,

LIII

Unless when qualified with thee, Cogniac !
　Sweet Naïad of the Phlegethontic rill !
Ah ! why the liver wilt thou thus attack,
　And make, like other nymphs, thy lovers
　　ill ?　　　　　　　　　　　　　420
I would take refuge in weak punch, but *rack*
　(In each sense of the word), whene'er I fill
My mild and midnight beakers to the brim,
Wakes me next morning with its synonym.

LIV

I leave Don Juan for the present, safe —
　Not sound, poor fellow, but severely
　　wounded;
Yet could his corporal pangs amount to half
　Of those with which his Haidée's bosom
　　bounded ?
She was not one to weep, and rave, and
　chafe,
　And then give way, subdued because our
　　rounded;　　　　　　　　　　430
Her mother was a Moorish maid, from Fez,
Where all is Eden, or a wilderness.

LV

There the large olive rains its amber store
　In marble fonts; there grain, and flower,
　　and fruit,
Gush from the earth until the land runs o'er;
　But there, too, many a poison-tree has
　　root,

And midnight listens to the lion's roar,
　And long, long deserts scorch the camel's
　　foot,
Or heaving whelm the helpless caravan;
And as the soil is, so the heart of man.　440

LVI

Afric is all the sun's, and as her earth
　Her human clay is kindled; full of power
For good or evil, burning from its birth,
　The Moorish blood partakes the planet's
　　hour,
And like the soil beneath it will bring forth:
　Beauty and love were Haidée's mother's
　　dower;
But her large dark eye show'd deep Pas-
　sion's force,
Though sleeping like a lion near a source.

LVII

Her daughter, temper'd with a milder ray,
　Like summer clouds all silvery, smooth,
　　and fair,　　　　　　　　　　450
Till slowly charged with thunder they dis-
　play
Terror to earth, and tempest to the air,
　Had held till now her soft and milky way;
　But overwrought with passion and de-
　　spair,
The fire burst forth from her Numidian
　veins,
Even as the Simoom sweeps the blasted
　plains.

LVIII

The last sight which she saw was Juan's
　gore,
　And he himself o'ermaster'd and cut
　　down;
His blood was running on the very floor
　Where late he trod, her beautiful, her
　　own;　　　　　　　　　　　　460
Thus much she view'd an instant and no
　more, —
　Her struggles ceased with one convulsive
　　groan;
On her sire's arm, which until now scarce
　held
Her writhing, fell she like a cedar fell'd.

LIX

A vein had burst, and her sweet lips' pure
　dyes
　Were dabbled with the deep blood which
　　ran o'er;

And her head droop'd as when the lily
lies
 O'ercharged with rain: her summon'd
handmaids bore
Their lady to her couch with gushing eyes;
 Of herbs and cordials they produced their
store, 470
But she defied all means they could employ,
Like one life could not hold, nor death
destroy.

LX

Days lay she in that state unchanged, though
chill —
 With nothing livid, still her lips were
red;
She had no pulse, but death seem'd absent
still;
 No hideous sign proclaim'd her surely
dead;
Corruption came not in each mind to kill
 All hope; to look upon her sweet face
bred
New thoughts of life, for it seem'd full of
soul —
She had so much, earth could not claim the
whole. 480

LXI

The ruling passion, such as marble shows
 When exquisitely chisell'd, still lay there,
But fix'd as marble's unchanged aspect
throws
 O'er the fair Venus, but for ever fair;
O'er the Laocoon's all eternal throes,
 And ever-dying Gladiator's air,
Their energy like life forms all their fame,
Yet looks not life, for they are still the
same.

LXII

She woke at length, but not as sleepers
wake,
 Rather the dead, for life seem'd something new, 490
A strange sensation which she must par-
take
Perforce, since whatsoever met her view
Struck not on memory, though a heavy
ache
 Lay at her heart, whose earliest beat still
true
Brought back the sense of pain without the
cause,
For, for a while, the furies made a pause.

LXIII

She look'd on many a face with vacant eye,
 On many a token without knowing what;
She saw them watch her without asking
why,
 And reck'd not who around her pillow
sat; 500
Not speechless, though she spoke not; not
a sigh
 Relieved her thoughts; dull silence and
quick chat
Were tried in vain by those who served;
she gave
No sign, save breath, of having left the
grave.

LXIV

Her handmaids tended, but she heeded not;
 Her father watch'd, she turn'd her eyes
away;
She recognized no being, and no spot,
 However dear or cherish'd in their day;
They changed from room to room — but
all forgot —
 Gentle, but without memory she lay; 510
At length those eyes, which they would
fain be weaning
Back to old thoughts, wax'd full of fearful
meaning.

LXV

And then a slave bethought her of a harp;
 The harper came, and tuned his instru-
ment;
At the first notes, irregular and sharp,
 On him her flashing eyes a moment bent,
Then to the wall she turn'd as if to warp
 Her thoughts from sorrow through her
heart re-sent;
And he begun a long low island song 519
Of ancient days, ere tyranny grew strong.

LXVI

Anon her thin wan fingers beat the wall
 In time to his old tune; he changed the
theme,
And sung of love; the fierce name struck
through all
 Her recollection; on her flash'd the dream
Of what she was, and is, if ye could call
 To be so being; in a gushing stream
The tears rush'd forth from her o'erclouded
brain,
Like mountain mists at length dissolved in
rain.

LXVII

Short solace, vain relief ! — thought came
 too quick,
 And whirl'd her brain to madness; she
 arose 530
As one who ne'er had dwelt among the sick,
 And flew at all she met, as on her foes;
But no one ever heard her speak or shriek,
 Although her paroxysm drew towards its
 close; —
Hers was a phrensy which disdain'd to rave,
Even when they smote her, in the hope to
 save.

LXVIII

Yet she betray'd at times a gleam of sense;
 Nothing could make her meet her father's
 face,
 Though on all other things with looks in-
 tense
 She gazed, but none she ever could re-
 trace; 540
Food she refused, and raiment; no pretence
 Avail'd for either; neither change of
 place,
Nor time, nor skill, nor remedy, could give
 her
Senses to sleep — the power seem'd gone
 for ever.

LXIX

Twelve days and nights she wither'd thus;
 at last,
 Without a groan, or sigh, or glance, to
 show
A parting pang, the spirit from her past:
 And they who watch'd her nearest could
 not know
The very instant, till the change that cast
 Her sweet face into shadow, dull and slow,
Glazed o'er her eyes — the beautiful, the
 black — 551
Oh ! to possess such lustre — and then lack !

LXX

She died, but not alone; she held within
 A second principle of life, which might
Have dawn'd a fair and sinless child of sin;
 But closed its little being without light,
And went down to the grave unborn, wherein
 Blossom and bough lie wither'd with one
 blight;
In vain the dews of Heaven descend above
The bleeding flower and blasted fruit of
 love. 560

LXXI

Thus lived — thus died she; never more on
 her
 Shall sorrow light, or shame. She was
 not made
Through years or moons the inner weight
 to bear,
 Which colder hearts endure till they are
 laid
By age in earth: her days and pleasures
 were
 Brief, but delightful — such as had not
 staid
Long with her destiny; but she sleeps well
By the sea-shore, whereon she loved to
 dwell.

LXXII

That isle is now all desolate and bare,
 Its dwellings down, its tenants pass'd
 away; 570
None but her own and father's grave is
 there,
 And nothing outward tells of human clay;
Ye could not know where lies a thing so
 fair,
 No stone is there to show, no tongue to
 say
What was; no dirge, except the hollow
 sea's,
Mourns o'er the beauty of the Cyclades.

LXXIII

But many a Greek maid in a loving song
 Sighs o'er her name; and many an
 islander
With his sire's story makes the night less
 long;
 Valour was his, and beauty dwelt with
 her: 580
If she loved rashly, her life paid for
 wrong —
 A heavy price must all pay who thus err,
In some shape; let none think to fly the
 danger,
For soon or late Love is his own avenger.

LXXIV

But let me change this theme which grows
 too sad,
 And lay this sheet of sorrows on the
 shelf;
I don't much like describing people mad,
 For fear of seeming rather touch'd my-
 self —

Besides, I 've no more on this head to add;
 And as my Muse is a capricious elf, 590
We 'll put about, and try another tack
With Juan, left half-kill'd some stanzas
 back.

LXXV

Wounded and fetter'd, ' cabin'd, cribb'd,
 confined,'
 Some days and nights elapsed before that
 he
Could altogether call the past to mind;
 And when he did, he found himself at
 sea,
Sailing six knots an hour before the wind;
 The shores of Ilion lay beneath their
 lee —
Another time he might have liked to see
 'em,
But now was not much pleased with Cape
 Sigæum. 600

LXXVI

There, on the green and village-cotted hill,
 is
 (Flank'd by the Hellespont and by the
 sea)
Entomb'd the bravest of the brave, Achilles;
 They say so (Bryant says the contrary):
And further downward, tall and towering
 still, is
 The tumulus — of whom ? Heaven knows!
 't may be
Patroclus, Ajax, or Protesilaus —
All heroes, who if living still would slay
 us.

LXXVII

High barrows, without marble or a name,
 A vast, untill'd, and mountain-skirted
 plain, 610
And Ida in the distance, still the same,
 And old Scamander (if 't is he) remain;
The situation seems still form'd for fame —
 A hundred thousand men might fight
 again
With ease; but where I sought for Ilion's
 walls,
The quiet sheep feeds, and the tortoise
 crawls;

LXXVIII

Troops of untended horses; here and there
 Some little hamlets, with new names un-
 couth;

Some shepherds (unlike Paris) led to stare
 A moment at the European youth 620
Whom to the spot their school-boy feelings
 bear;
 A Turk, with beads in hand and pipe in
 mouth,
Extremely taken with his own religion,
Are what I found there — but the devil a
 Phrygian.

LXXIX

Don Juan, here permitted to emerge
 From his dull cabin, found himself a
 slave;
Forlorn, and gazing on the deep blue surge,
 O'ershadow'd there by many a hero's
 grave;
Weak still with loss of blood, he scarce
 could urge
 A few brief questions; and the answers
 gave 630
No very satisfactory information
About his past or present situation.

LXXX

He saw some fellow captives, who appear'd
 To be Italians, as they were in fact;
From them, at least, *their* destiny he heard,
 Which was an odd one; a troop going to
 act
In Sicily (all singers, duly rear'd
 In their vocation) had not been attack'd
In sailing from Livorno by the pirate, 639
But sold by the impresario at no high rate.

LXXXI

By one of these, the buffo of the party,
 Juan was told about their curious case;
For although destined to the Turkish mart,
 he
 Still kept his spirits up — at least his
 face;
The little fellow really look'd quite hearty,
 And bore him with some gaiety and
 grace,
Showing a much more reconciled demean-
 our,
Than did the prima donna and the tenor.

LXXXII

In a few words he told their hapless story,
 Saying, ' Our Machiavelian impresario,
Making a signal off some promontory, 651
 Hail'd a strange brig — Corpo di Caio
 Mario !

We were transferr'd on board her in a
 hurry,
 Without a single scudo of salario;
But if the Sultan has a taste for song,
 We will revive our fortunes before long.

LXXXIII

'The prima donna, though a little old,
 And haggard with a dissipated life,
And subject, when the house is thin, to
 cold,
 Has some good notes; and then the
 tenor's wife, 660
With no great voice, is pleasing to behold;
 Last carnival she made a deal of strife
By carrying off Count Cesare Cicogna
From an old Roman princess at Bologna.

LXXXIV

'And then there are the dancers; there 's
 the Nini,
 With more than one profession, gains by
 all;
Then there 's that laughing slut the Pele-
 grini,
 She, too, was fortunate last carnival,
And made at least five hundred good zec-
 chini,
 But spends so fast, she has not now a
 paul; 670
And then there 's the Grotesca — such a
 dancer !
Where men have souls or bodies she must
 answer.

LXXXV

'As for the figuranti, they are like
 The rest of all that tribe; with here and
 there
A pretty person, which perhaps may strike,
 The rest are hardly fitted for a fair;
There 's one, though tall and stiffer than a
 pike,
 Yet has a sentimental kind of air
Which might go far, but she don't dance
 with vigour.
The more 's the pity, with her face and
 figure. 680

LXXXVI

'As for the men, they are a middling
 set;
 The musico is but a crack'd old basin,
But being qualified in one way yet,
 May the seraglio do to set his face in,

And as a servant some preferment get;
 His singing I no further trust can place
 in:
From all the Pope makes yearly 't would
 perplex
To find three perfect pipes of the *third* sex.

LXXXVII

'The tenor's voice is spoilt by affectation,
 And for the bass, the beast can only bel-
 low; 690
In fact, he had no singing education,
 An ignorant, noteless, timeless, tuneless
 fellow;
But being the prima donna's near relation,
 Who swore his voice was very rich and
 mellow,
They hired him, though to hear him you 'd
 believe
An ass was practising recitative.

LXXXVIII

'T would not become myself to dwell upon
 My own merits, and though young — I
 see, Sir — you
Have got a travell'd air, which speaks you
 one
 To whom the opera is by no means new:
You 've heard of Raucocanti ? — I 'm the
 man; 701
 The time may come when you may hear
 me too;
You was not last year at the fair of Lugo,
But next, when I 'm engaged to sing there
 — do go.

LXXXIX

'Our baritone I almost had forgot,
 A pretty lad, but bursting with conceit;
With graceful action, science not a jot,
 A voice of no great compass, and not
 sweet,
He always is complaining of his lot,
 Forsooth, scarce fit for ballads in the
 street; 710
In lovers' parts his passion more to breathe,
Having no heart to show, he shows his
 teeth.'

XC

Here Raucocanti's eloquent recital
 Was interrupted by the pirate crew,
Who came at stated moments to invite all
 The captives back to their sad berths;
 each threw

A rueful glance upon the waves (which bright all
 From the blue skies derived a double blue,
Dancing all free and happy in the sun),
And then went down the hatchway one by one. 720

XCI

They heard next day — that in the Dardanelles,
 Waiting for his Sublimity's firmān,
The most imperative of sovereign spells,
 Which every body does without who can,
More to secure them in their naval cells,
 Lady to lady, well as man to man,
Were to be chain'd and lotted out per couple,
For the slave market of Constantinople.

XCII

It seems when this allotment was made out,
 There chanced to be an odd male, and odd female, 730
Who (after some discussion and some doubt,
 If the soprano might be deem'd to be male,
They placed him o'er the women as a scout)
 Were link'd together, and it happen'd the male
Was Juan, — who, an awkward thing at his age,
Pair'd off with a Bacchante blooming visage.

XCIII

With Raucocanti lucklessly was chain'd
 The tenor; these two hated with a hate
Found only on the stage, and each more pain'd
 With this his tuneful neighbour than his fate; 740
Sad strife arose, for they were so crossgrain'd,
 Instead of bearing up without debate,
That each pull'd different ways with many an oath,
'Arcades ambo,' id est — blackguards both.

XCIV

Juan's companion was a Romagnole,
 But bred within the March of old Ancona,
With eyes that look'd into the very soul
 (And other chief points of a 'bella donna'),
Bright — and as black and burning as a coal;
 And through her clear brunette complexion shone a 750
Great wish to please — a most attractive dower,
Especially when added to the power.

XCV

But all that power was wasted upon him,
 For sorrow o'er each sense held stern command;
Her eye might flash on his, but found it dim;
 And though thus chain'd, as natural her hand
Touch'd his, nor that — nor any handsome limb
 (And she had some not easy to withstand)
Could stir his pulse, or make his faith feel brittle;
Perhaps his recent wounds might help a little. 760

XCVI

No matter; we should ne'er too much enquire,
 But facts are facts: no knight could be more true,
And firmer faith no ladye-love desire;
 We will omit the proofs, save one or two:
'T is said no one in hand ' can hold a fire
 By thought of frosty Caucasus;' but few,
I really think; yet Juan's then ordeal
Was more triumphant, and not much less real.

XCVII

Here I might enter on a chaste description,
 Having withstood temptation in my youth, 770
But hear that several people take exception
 At the first two books having too much truth;
Therefore I 'll make Don Juan leave the ship soon,
 Because the publisher declares, in sooth,
Through needles' eyes it easier for the camel is
To pass, than those two cantos into families.

XCVIII

'T is all the same to me; I 'm fond of yield-
ing,
　And therefore leave them to the purer
　　page
Of Smollett, Prior, Ariosto, Fielding,
　Who say strange things for so correct an
　　age;　　　　　　　　　　　　780
I once had great alacrity in wielding
　My pen, and liked poetic war to wage,
And recollect the time when all this cant
Would have provoked remarks which now
　it shan't.

XCIX

As boys love rows, my boyhood liked a
　squabble;
　But at this hour I wish to part in peace,
Leaving such to the literary rabble:
　Whether my verse's fame be doom'd to
　　cease
While the right hand which wrote it still is
　able,
　Or of some centuries to take a lease,　790
The grass upon my grave will grow as long,
And sigh to midnight winds, but not to
　song.

C

Of poets who come down to us through
　distance
　Of time and tongues, the foster-babes of
　　Fame,
Life seems the smallest portion of existence;
　Where twenty ages gather o'er a name,
'T is as a snowball which derives assistance
　From every flake, and yet rolls on the
　　same,
Even till an iceberg it may chance to grow;
But, after all, 't is nothing but cold snow.

CI

And so great names are nothing more than
　nominal,　　　　　　　　　　801
　And love of glory 's but an airy lust,
Too often in its fury overcoming all
　Who would as 't were identify their dust
From out the wide destruction, which, en-
　tombing all,
　Leaves nothing till 'the coming of the
　　just'—
Save change: I 've stood upon Achilles'
　tomb,
And heard Troy doubted; time will doubt
　of Rome.

CII

The very generations of the dead
　Are swept away, and tomb inherits tomb,
Until the memory of an age is fled,　　811
　And, buried, sinks beneath its offspring's
　　doom:
Where are the epitaphs our fathers read?
　Save a few glean'd from the sepulchral
　　gloom
Which once-named myriads nameless lie
　beneath,
And lose their own in universal death.

CIII

I canter by the spot each afternoon
　Where perish'd in his fame the hero-
　　boy,
Who lived too long for men, but died too
　soon
　For human vanity, the young De Foix!
A broken pillar, not uncouthly hewn,　821
　But which neglect is hastening to de-
　　stroy,
Records Ravenna's carnage on its face,
While weeds and ordure rankle round the
　base.

CIV

I pass each day where Dante's bones are
　laid:
　A little cupola, more neat than solemn,
Protects his dust, but reverence here is
　paid
　To the bard's tomb, and not the warrior's
　　column.
The time must come, when both alike de-
　cay'd,
　The chieftain's trophy, and the poet's
　　volume,　　　　　　　　　　830
Will sink where lie the songs and wars of
　earth,
Before Pelides' death, or Homer's birth.

CV

With human blood that column was ce-
　mented,
　With human filth that column is defiled,
As if the peasant's coarse contempt were
　vented
　To show his loathing of the spot he soil'd:
Thus is the trophy used, and thus lamented
　Should ever be those blood-hounds, from
　　whose wild
Instinct of gore and glory earth has known
Those sufferings Dante saw in hell alone.

CVI

Yet there will still be bards: though fame
 is smoke, 841
 Its fumes are frankincense to human
 thought;
And the unquiet feelings, which first woke
 Song in the world, will seek what then
 they sought;
As on the beach the waves at last are broke,
 Thus to their extreme verge the passions
 brought
Dash into poetry, which is but passion,
Or at least was so ere it grew a fashion.

CVII

If in the course of such a life as was 849
 At once adventurous and contemplative,
Men, who partake all passions as they pass,
 Acquire the deep and bitter power to give
 Their images again as in a glass,
 And in such colours that they seem to live;
You may do right forbidding them to show
 'em,
But spoil (I think) a very pretty poem.

CVIII

Oh! ye, who make the fortunes of all
 books!
 Benign Ceruleans of the second sex!
Who advertise new poems by your looks,
 Your 'imprimatur' will ye not annex?
What! must I go to the oblivious cooks,
 Those Cornish plunderers of Parnassian
 wrecks? 862
Ah! must I then the only minstrel be,
Proscribed from tasting your Castalian tea!

CIX

What! can I prove 'a lion' then no more?
 A ball-room bard, a foolscap, hot-press
 darling?
To bear the compliments of many a bore,
 And sigh, 'I can't get out,' like Yorick's
 starling;
Why then I'll swear, as poet Wordy swore
 (Because the world won't read him, al-
 ways snarling), 870
That taste is gone, that fame is but a lot-
 tery,
Drawn by the blue-coat misses of a coterie.

CX

Oh! 'darkly, deeply, beautifully blue,'
 As some one somewhere sings about the
 sky,
And I, ye learned ladies, say of you;
 They say your stockings are so (Heaven
 knows why,
I have examined few pair of that hue);
 Blue as the garters which serenely lie
Round the Patrician left-legs, which adorn
The festal midnight, and the levee morn.

CXI

Yet some of you are most seraphic crea-
 tures — 881
 But times are alter'd since, a rhyming
 lover,
You read my stanzas, and I read your
 features:
 And — but no matter, all those things are
 over;
Still I have no dislike to learned natures,
 For sometimes such a world of virtues
 cover;
I knew one woman of that purple school,
The loveliest, chastest, best, but — quite a
 fool.

CXII

Humboldt, 'the first of travellers,' but not
 The last, if late accounts be accurate, 890
Invented, by some name I have forgot,
 As well as the sublime discovery's date,
An airy instrument, with which he sought
 To ascertain the atmospheric state,
By measuring 'the *intensity of blue*:'
Oh, Lady Daphne! let me measure you!

CXIII

But to the narrative: — The vessel bound
 With slaves to sell off in the capital,
After the usual process, might be found
 At anchor under the seraglio wall; 900
Her cargo, from the plague being safe and
 sound,
 Were landed in the market, one and all,
And there with Georgians, Russians, and
 Circassians,
Bought up for different purposes and
 passions.

CXIV

Some went off dearly; fifteen hundred
 dollars
 For one Circassian, a sweet girl, were
 given,
Warranted virgin; beauty's brightest colours
 Had deck'd her out in all the hues of
 heaven:

Her sale sent home some disappointed
 bawlers,
 Who bade on till the hundreds reach'd
 eleven; 910
But when the offer went beyond, they knew
'T was for the Sultan, and at once withdrew.

CXV

Twelve negresses from Nubia brought a
 price
 Which the West Indian market scarce
 would bring;
Though Wilberforce, at last, has made it
 twice
What 't was ere Abolition; and the thing
Need not seem very wonderful, for vice
 Is always much more splendid than a king:
The virtues, even the most exalted, Charity,
Are saving — vice spares nothing for a
 rarity. 920

CXVI

But for the destiny of this young troop,
 How some were bought by pachas, some
 by Jews,
How some to burdens were obliged to stoop,
 And others rose to the command of crews
As renegadoes; while in hapless group,
 Hoping no very old vizier might choose,
The females stood, as one by one they
 pick'd 'em,
To make a mistress, or fourth wife, or
 victim:

CXVII

All this must be reserved for further song;
 Also our hero's lot, howe'er unpleasant
(Because this Canto has become too long),
 Must be postponed discreetly for the
 present; 932
I 'm sensible redundancy is wrong,
 But could not for the muse of me put
 less in 't:
And now delay the progress of Don Juan,
Till what is call'd in Ossian the fifth Duan.

CANTO THE FIFTH

I

WHEN amatory poets sing their loves
 In liquid lines mellifluously bland,
And pair their rhymes as Venus yokes her
 doves,
 They little think what mischief is in hand;

The greater their success the worse it
 proves,
 As Ovid's verse may give to understand;
Even Petrarch's self, if judged with due
 severity,
Is the Platonic pimp of all posterity.

II

I therefore do denounce all amorous writ-
 ing,
 Except in such a way as not to attract; 10
Plain — simple — short, and by no means
 inviting,
 But with a moral to each error tack'd,
Form'd rather for instructing than delight-
 ing,
 And with all passions in their turn at-
 tack'd;
Now, if my Pegasus should not be shod ill,
This poem will become a moral model.

III

The European with the Asian shore
 Sprinkled with palaces; the ocean stream
Here and there studded with a seventy-four;
 Sophia's cupola with golden gleam; 20
The cypress groves ; Olympus high and
 hoar;
 The twelve isles, and the more than I
 could dream,
Far less describe, present the very view
Which charm'd the charming Mary Mon-
 tagu.

IV

I have a passion for the name of ' Mary,'
 For once it was a magic sound to me;
And still it half calls up the realms of fairy,
 Where I beheld what never was to be;
All feelings changed, but this was last to
 vary,
 A spell from which even yet I am not
 quite free: 30
But I grow sad — and let a tale grow cold,
Which must not be pathetically told.

V

The wind swept down the Euxine, and the
 wave
 Broke foaming o'er the blue Symple-
 gades;
'T is a grand sight from off ' the Giant's
 Grave '
 To watch the progress of those rolling
 seas

Between the Bosphorus, as they lash and
 lave
 Europe and Asia, you being quite at ease;
There's not a sea the passenger e'er pukes
 in,
 Turns up more dangerous breakers than the
 Euxine. 40

VI

'T was a raw day of Autumn's bleak be-
 ginning,
 When nights are equal, but not so the
 days;
The Parcæ then cut short the further spin-
 ning
 Of seamen's fates, and the loud tempests
 raise
The waters, and repentance for past sinning
 In all, who o'er the great deep take their
 ways:
They vow to amend their lives, and yet
 they don't;
Because if drown'd, they can't — if spared,
 they won't.

VII

A crowd of shivering slaves of every nation,
 And age, and sex, were in the market
 ranged; 50
Each bevy with the merchant in his station:
 Poor creatures ! their good looks were
 sadly changed.
All save the blacks seem'd jaded with vex-
 ation,
 From friends, and home, and freedom
 far estranged;
The negroes more philosophy display'd, —
Used to it, no doubt, as eels are to be flay'd.

VIII

Juan was juvenile, and thus was full,
 As most at his age are, of hope and
 health;
Yet I must own he looked a little dull,
 And now and then a tear stole down by
 stealth; 60
Perhaps his recent loss of blood might pull
 His spirit down; and then the loss of
 wealth,
A mistress, and such comfortable quarters,
To be put up for auction amongst Tartars,

IX

Were things to shake a stoic; ne'ertheless,
 Upon the whole his carriage was serene:

His figure, and the splendour of his dress,
 Of which some gilded remnants still were
 seen,
Drew all eyes on him, giving them to guess
 He was above the vulgar by his mien; 70
And then, though pale, he was so very hand-
 some;
And then — they calculated on his ransom.

X

Like a backgammon board the place was
 dotted
 With whites and blacks, in groups on
 show for sale,
Though rather more irregularly spotted:
 Some bought the jet, while others chose
 the pale.
It chanced amongst the other people lotted,
 A man of thirty rather stout and hale,
With resolution in his dark grey eye,
Next Juan stood, till some might choose to
 buy. 80

XI

He had an English look; that is, was square
 In make, of a complexion white and
 ruddy,
Good teeth, with curling rather dark brown
 hair,
 And, it might be from thought or toil
 or study,
An open brow a little mark'd with care:
 One arm had on a bandage rather bloody;
And there he stood with such *sang-froid*,
 that greater
Could scarce be shown even by a mere
 spectator.

XII

But seeing at his elbow a mere lad,
 Of a high spirit evidently, though 90
At present weigh'd down by a doom which
 had
 O'erthrown even men, he soon began to
 show
A kind of blunt compassion for the sad
 Lot of so young a partner in the woe,
Which for himself he seem'd to deem no
 worse
Than any other scrape, a thing of course.

XIII

' My boy ! ' said he, ' amidst this motley crew
 Of Georgians, Russians, Nubians, and
 what not,

All ragamuffins differing but in hue,
 With whom it is our luck to cast our
 lot, 100
The only gentlemen seem I and you;
 So let us be acquainted, as we ought:
If I could yield you any consolation,
 'T would give me pleasure. — Pray, what
 is your nation ? '

XIV

When Juan answer'd — ' Spanish ! ' he re-
 plied,
 ' I thought, in fact, you could not be a
 Greek;
Those servile dogs are not so proudly eyed:
 Fortune has play'd you here a pretty
 freak,
But that 's her way with all men, till
 they 're tried;
 But never mind, — she 'll turn, perhaps,
 next week; 110
She has served me also much the same as
 you,
Except that I have found it nothing new.'

XV

' Pray, sir,' said Juan, ' if I may presume,
 What brought you here ? ' — ' Oh ! no-
 thing very rare —
Six Tartars and a drag-chain.' ' To this
 doom
But what conducted, if the question 's fair,
Is that which I would learn.' — ' I served
 for some
 Months with the Russian army here and
 there,
And taking lately, by Suwarrow's bidding,
A town, was ta'en myself instead of Wid-
 din.' 120

XVI

' Have you no friends ? ' — ' I had — but,
 by God's blessing,
 Have not been troubled with them lately.
 Now
I have answer'd all your questions without
 pressing,
 And you an equal courtesy should show.'
' Alas ! ' said Juan, ' 't were a tale distress-
 ing,
 And long besides.' — ' Oh ! if 't is really
 so,
You 're right on both accounts to hold your
 tongue;
A sad tale saddens doubly, when 't is long.

XVII

' But droop not: Fortune at your time of
 life,
 Although a female moderately fickle, 130
Will hardly leave you (as she 's not your
 wife)
 For any length of days in such a pickle.
To strive, too, with our fate were such a
 strife
 As if the corn-sheaf should oppose the
 sickle:
Men are the sport of circumstances, when
The circumstances seem the sport of men.'

XVIII

' 'T is not,' said Juan, ' for my present
 doom
 I mourn, but for the past; — I loved a
 maid: ' —
He paused, and his dark eye grew full of
 gloom;
 A single tear upon his eyelash staid 140
A moment, and then dropp'd; ' but to re-
 sume,
 'T is not my present lot, as I have said,
Which I deplore so much; for I have
 borne
Hardships which have the hardiest over-
 worn,

XIX

' On the rough deep. But this last blow — '
 and here
 He stopp'd again, and turn'd away his
 face.
' Ay,' quoth his friend, ' I thought it would
 appear
 That there had been a lady in the case;
And these are things which ask a tender
 tear,
 Such as I, too, would shed if in your
 place: 150
I cried upon my first wife's dying day,
And also when my second ran away:

XX

' My third — ' — ' Your third ! ' quoth Juan,
 turning round;
 ' You scarcely can be thirty: have you
 three ? '
' No — only two at present above ground:
 Surely 't is nothing wonderful to see
One person thrice in holy wedlock bound ! '
 ' Well, then, your third,' said Juan;
 ' what did she ?

She did not run away, too, — did she, sir ? '
'No, faith.' — 'What then ? ' — ' I ran
 away from her.' 160

XXI

'You take things coolly, sir,' said Juan.
 'Why,'
Replied the other, 'what can a man do ?
There still are many rainbows in your sky,
 But mine have vanish'd. All, when life
 is new,
Commence with feelings warm, and pros-
 pects high;
But time strips our illusions of their hue,
And one by one in turn, some grand mistake
Casts off its bright skin yearly like the
 snake.

XXII

' 'T is true, it gets another bright and fresh,
 Or fresher, brighter; but the year gone
 through, 170
This skin must go the way, too, of all flesh,
 Or sometimes only wear a week or
 two; —
Love 's the first net which spreads its deadly
 mesh;
 Ambition, Avarice, Vengeance, Glory,
 glue
The glittering lime-twigs of our latter days,
Where still we flutter on for pence or
 praise.'

XXIII

' All this is very fine, and may be true,'
 Said Juan; ' but I really don't see how
It betters present times with me or you.'
 ' No ? ' quoth the other; ' yet you will
 allow 180
By setting things in their right point of
 view,
 Knowledge, at least, is gain'd; for
 instance, now,
We know what slavery is, and our disasters
May teach us better to behave when
 masters.'

XXIV

' Would we were masters now, if but to try
 Their present lessons on our Pagan
 friends here,'
Said Juan, — swallowing a heart-burning
 sigh:
 ' Heaven help the scholar whom his
 fortune sends here ! '

' Perhaps we shall be one day, by and
 by,'
 Rejoin'd the other, ' when our bad luck
 mends here; 190
Meantime (yon old black eunuch seems to
 eye us)
I wish to G—d that somebody would buy
 us !

XXV

' But after all, what *is* our present state ?
 'T is bad, and may be better — all men's
 lot:
Most men are slaves, none more so than the
 great,
 To their own whims and passions, and
 what not;
Society itself, which should create
 Kindness, destroys what little we had got:
To feel for none is the true social art
Of the world's stoics — men without a
 heart.' 200

XXVI

Just now a black old neutral personage
 Of the third sex stept up, and peering
 over
The captives, seem'd to mark their looks
 and age,
 And capabilities, as to discover
If they were fitted for the purposed cage:
 No lady e'er is ogled by a lover,
Horse by a blackleg, broadcloth by a tailor,
Fee by a counsel, felon by a jailor,

XXVII

As is a slave by his intended bidder.
 'T is pleasant purchasing our fellow-
 creatures; 210
And all are to be sold, if you consider
 Their passions, and are dext'rous; some
 by features
Are bought up, others by a warlike leader,
 Some by a place — as tend their years or
 natures;
The most by ready cash — but all have
 prices,
From crowns to kicks, according to their
 vices.

XXVIII

The eunuch, having eyed them o'er with
 care,
 Turn'd to the merchant, and begun to
 bid

First but for one, and after for the pair;
 They haggled, wrangled, swore, too — so
 they did ! 220
As though they were in a mere Christian fair
 Cheapening an ox, an ass, a lamb, or kid;
So that their bargain sounded like a battle
For this superior yoke of human cattle.

XXIX

At last they settled into simple grumbling,
 And pulling out reluctant purses, and
Turning each piece of silver o'er, and tum-
 bling
 Some down, and weighing others in their
 hand,
And by mistake sequins with paras jum-
 bling,
 Until the sum was accurately scann'd, 230
And then the merchant giving change, and
 signing
Receipts in full, began to think of dining.

XXX

I wonder if his appetite was good ?
 Or, if it were, if also his digestion ?
Methinks at meals some odd thoughts might
 intrude,
 And conscience ask a curious sort of
 question,
About the right divine how far we should
 Sell flesh and blood. When dinner has
 opprest one,
I think it is perhaps the gloomiest hour
Which turns up out of the sad twenty-four.

XXXI

Voltaire says 'No:' he tells you that Can-
 dide 241
 Found life most tolerable after meals;
He 's wrong — unless man were a pig, in-
 deed,
 Repletion rather adds to what he feels,
Unless he 's drunk, and then no doubt he 's
 freed
 From his own brain's oppression while it
 reels.
Of food I think with Philip's son, or rather
Ammon's (ill pleased with one world and
 one father);

XXXII

I think with Alexander, that the act
 Of eating, with another act or two, 250
Makes us feel our mortality in fact
 Redoubled; when a roast and a ragout,

And fish, and soup, by some side dishes
 back'd,
 Can give us either pain or pleasure, who
Would pique himself on intellects, whose
 use
Depends so much upon the gastric juice ?

XXXIII

The other evening ('t was on Friday last) —
 This is a fact and no poetic fable —
Just as my great coat was about me cast,
 My hat and gloves still lying on the
 table, 260
I heard a shot — 't was eight o'clock scarce
 past —
 And, running out as fast as I was able,
I found the military commandant
Stretch'd in the street, and able scarce to
 pant.

XXXIV

Poor fellow ! for some reason, surely bad,
 They had slain him with five slugs; and
 left him there
To perish on the pavement: so I had
 Him borne into the house and up the stair,
And stripp'd and look'd to — But why
 should I add 269
 More circumstances ? vain was every care;
The man was gone : in some Italian quarrel
Kill'd by five bullets from an old gun-barrel.

XXXV

I gazed upon him, for I knew him well;
 And though I have seen many corpses,
 never
Saw one, whom such an accident befell,
 So calm; though pierced through stomach,
 heart, and liver,
He seem'd to sleep, — for you could scarcely
 tell
 (As he bled inwardly, no hideous river
Of gore divulged the cause) that he was
 dead:
So as I gazed on him, I thought or said —

XXXVI

'Can this be death ? then what is life or
 death ? 281
 Speak !' but he spoke not: 'Wake !' but
 still he slept : —
'But yesterday and who had mightier
 breath ?
 A thousand warriors by his word were
 kept

In awe: he said, as the centurion saith,
 "Go," and he goeth; " come," and forth
 he stepp'd.
The trump and bugle till he spake were
 dumb —
And now nought left him but the muffled
 drum.'

XXXVII

And they who waited once and worshipp'd —
 they
 With their rough faces throng'd about
 the bed 290
To gaze once more on the commanding
 clay
 Which for the last, though not the first,
 time bled:
And such an end! that he who many a day
 Had faced Napoleon's foes until they
 fled, —
The foremost in the charge or in the sally,
Should now be butcher'd in a civic alley.

XXXVIII

The scars of his old wounds were near his
 new,
 Those honourable scars which brought
 him fame;
And horrid was the contrast to the view —
 But let me quit the theme; as such
 things claim 300
Perhaps even more attention than is due
 From me: I gazed (as oft I have gazed
 the same)
To try if I could wrench aught out of death
Which should confirm, or shake, or make a
 faith;

XXXIX

But it was all a mystery. Here we are,
 And there we go: — but *where?* five bits
 of lead,
Or three, or two, or one, send very far!
 And is this blood, then, form'd but to be
 shed?
Can every element our elements mar?
 And air — earth — water — fire live —
 and we dead? 310
We whose minds comprehend all things?
 No more;
But let us to the story as before.

XL

The purchaser of Juan and acquaintance
 Bore off his bargains to a gilded boat,

Embark'd himself and them, and off they
 went thence
 As fast as oars could pull and water float;
They look'd like persons being led to sen-
 tence,
 Wondering what next, till the caïque was
 brought
Up in a little creek below a wall
O'ertopp'd with cypresses, dark-green and
 tall. 320

XLI

Here their conductor tapping at the wicket
 Of a small iron door, 't was open'd, and
He led them onward, first through a low
 thicket
 Flank'd by large groves, which tower'd
 on either hand:
They almost lost their way, and had to pick
 it —
 For night was closing ere they came to
 land.
The eunuch made a sign to those on board,
Who row'd off, leaving them without a
 word.

XLII

As they were plodding on their winding
 way
 Through orange bowers, and jasmine, and
 so forth 330
(Of which I might have a good deal to say,
 There being no such profusion in the
 North
Of oriental plants, 'et cetera,'
 But that of late your scribblers think it
 worth
Their while to rear whole hotbeds in *their*
 works
Because one poet travell'd 'mongst the
 Turks) —

XLIII

As they were threading on their way, there
 came
 Into Don Juan's head a thought, which
 he
Whisper'd to his companion: — 't was the
 same
 Which might have then occurr'd to you
 or me. 340
' Methinks,' said he, ' it would be no great
 shame
 If we should strike a stroke to set us
 free;

Let's knock that old black fellow on the
 head,
And march away — 't were easier done than
 said.'

XLIV

'Yes,' said the other, 'and when done, what
 then ?
How get out ? how the devil got we in ?
And when we once were fairly out, and when
 From Saint Bartholomew we have saved
 our skin,
To-morrow 'd see us in some other den,
 And worse off than we hitherto have
 been; 350
Besides, I 'm hungry, and just now would
 take,
Like Esau, for my birthright a beef-steak.

XLV

'We must be near some place of man's
 abode; —
 For the old negro's confidence in creeping,
With his two captives, by so queer a road,
 Shows that he thinks his friends have not
 been sleeping;
A single cry would bring them all abroad:
 'T is therefore better looking before leap-
 ing —
And there, you see, this turn has brought
 us through,
By Jove, a noble palace ! — lighted too.' 360

XLVI

It was indeed a wide extensive building
 Which open'd on their view, and o'er the
 front
There seem'd to be besprent a deal of gild-
 ing
 And various hues, as is the Turkish
 wont, —
A gaudy taste ; for they are little skill'd in
 The arts of which these lands were once
 the font :
Each villa on the Bosphorus looks a screen
New painted, or a pretty opera-scene.

XLVII

And nearer as they came, a genial savour
 Of certain stews, and roast-meats, and
 pilaus, 370
Things which in hungry mortals' eyes find
 favour,
 Made Juan in his harsh intentions pause,

And put himself upon his good behaviour :
 His friend, too, adding a new saving
 clause,
Said, 'In Heaven's name let 's get some
 supper now,
And then I 'm with you, if you 're for a
 row.'

XLVIII

Some talk of an appeal unto some passion,
 Some to men's feelings, others to their
 reason ;
The last of these was never much the fash-
 ion,
 For reason thinks all reasoning out of sea-
 son. 380
Some speakers whine, and others lay the
 lash on,
 But more or less continue still to tease on,
With arguments according to their 'forte;'
But no one dreams of ever being short. —

XLIX

But I digress : of all appeals, — although
 I grant the power of pathos, and of gold,
Of beauty, flattery, threats, a shilling, — no
 Method 's more sure at moments to take
 hold
Of the best feelings of mankind, which
 grow
 More tender, as we every day behold, 390
Than that all-softening, overpowering knell,
The tocsin of the soul — the dinner-bell.

L

Turkey contains no bells, and yet men dine;
 And Juan and his friend, albeit they
 heard
No Christian knoll to table, saw no line
 Of lackeys usher to the feast prepared,
Yet smelt roast-meat, beheld a huge fire
 shine,
 And cooks in motion with their clean
 arms bared,
And gazed around them to the left and
 right
With the prophetic eye of appetite. 400

LI

And giving up all notions of resistance,
 They follow'd close behind their sable
 guide,
Who little thought that his own crack'd ex-
 istence
 Was on the point of being set aside :

He motion'd them to stop at some small
 distance,
 And knocking at the gate, 't was open'd
 wide,
And a magnificent large hall display'd
The Asian pomp of Ottoman parade.

LII

I won't describe ; description is my forte,
 But every fool describes in these bright
 days 410
His wondrous journey to some foreign
 court,
 And spawns his quarto, and demands
 your praise —
Death to his publisher, to him 't is sport ;
 While Nature, tortured twenty thousand
 ways,
Resigns herself with exemplary patience
To guide-books, rhymes, tours, sketches,
 illustrations.

LIII

Along this hall, and up and down, some,
 squatted
 Upon their hams, were occupied at chess;
Others in monosyllable talk chatted,
 And some seem'd much in love with
 their own dress. 420
And divers smoked superb pipes decorated
 With amber mouths of greater price or
 less;
And several strutted, others slept, and some
Prepared for supper with a glass of rum.

LIV

As the black eunuch enter'd with his brace
 Of purchased Infidels, some raised their
 eyes
A moment without slackening from their
 pace;
 But those who sate ne'er stirr'd in any-
 wise :
One or two stared the captives in the face,
 Just as one views a horse to guess his
 price ; 430
Some nodded to the negro from their sta-
 tion,
But no one troubled him with conversation.

LV

He leads them through the hall, and, with-
 out stopping,
 On through a farther range of goodly
 rooms,

Splendid but silent, save in *one*, where,
 dropping,
 A marble fountain echoes through the
 glooms
Of night which robe the chamber, or where
 popping
 Some female head most curiously pre-
 sumes
To thrust its black eyes through the door
 or lattice,
As wondering what the devil a noise that is.

LVI

Some faint lamps gleaming from the lofty
 walls 441
 Gave light enough to hint their farther
 way,
But not enough to show the imperial halls,
 In all the flashing of their full array;
Perhaps there's nothing — I 'll not say appals,
 But saddens more by night as well as day,
Than an enormous room without a soul
To break the lifeless splendour of the
 whole.

LVII

Two or three seem so little, *one* seems
 nothing:
 In deserts, forests, crowds, or by the
 shore, 450
There solitude, we know, has her full
 growth in
 The spots which were her realms for
 evermore;
But in a mighty hall or gallery, both in
 More modern buildings and those built
 of yore,
A kind of death comes o'er us all alone,
Seeing what 's meant for many with but one.

LVIII

A neat, snug study on a winter's night,
 A book, friend, single lady, or a glass
Of claret, sandwich, and an appetite,
 Are things which make an English
 evening pass; 460
Though *certes* by no means so grand a sight
 As is a theatre lit up by gas.
I pass my evenings in long galleries solely,
And that 's the reason I 'm so melancholy.

LIX

Alas ! man makes that great which makes
 him little:
 I grant you in a church 't is very well:

What speaks of Heaven should by no means
 be brittle,
But strong and lasting, till no tongue can
 tell
Their names who rear'd it; but huge houses
 fit ill —
 And huge tombs worse — mankind, since
 Adam fell: 470
Methinks the story of the tower of Babel
 Might teach them this much better than
 I 'm able.

LX

Babel was Nimrod's hunting-box, and then
 A town of gardens, walls, and wealth
 amazing,
Where Nabuchadonosor, king of men,
 Reign'd, till one summer's day he took to
 grazing,
And Daniel tamed the lions in their den,
 The people's awe and admiration rais-
 ing;
'T was famous, too, for Thisbe and for
 Pyramus,
And the calumniated queen Semiramis. 480

LXI

That injured Queen by chroniclers so coarse
 Has been accused (I doubt not by con-
 spiracy)
Of an improper friendship for her horse
 (Love, like religion, sometimes runs to
 heresy):
This monstrous tale had probably its source
 (For such exaggerations here and there
 I see)
In writing 'Courser' by mistake for
 'Courier:'
I wish the case could come before a jury
 here.

LXII

But to resume, — should there be (what may
 not
 Be in these days?) some infidels, who
 don't, 490
Because they can't find out the very spot
 Of that same Babel, or because they
 won't
(Though Claudius Rich, Esquire, some
 bricks has got,
 And written lately two memoirs upon't),
Believe the Jews, those unbelievers, who
Must be believed, though they believe not
 you,

LXIII

Yet let them think that Horace has ex-
 prest
 Shortly and sweetly the masonic folly
Of those, forgetting the great place of
 rest,
 Who give themselves to architecture
 wholly; 500
We know where things and men must end
 at best:
 A moral (like all morals) melancholy,
And 'Et sepulchri immemor struis domos'
 Shows that we build when we should but
 entomb us.

LXIV

At last they reach'd a quarter most retired,
 Where echo woke as if from a long
 slumber;
Though full of all things which could be
 desired,
 One wonder'd what to do with such a
 number
Of articles which nobody required;
 Here wealth had done its utmost to en-
 cumber 510
With furniture an exquisite apartment,
Which puzzled Nature much to know what
 Art meant.

LXV

It seem'd, however, but to open on
 A range or suite of further chambers,
 which
Might lead to heaven knows where; but in
 this one
 The movables were prodigally rich:
Sofas 't was half a sin to sit upon,
 So costly were they; carpets every stitch
Of workmanship so rare, they made you
 wish
You could glide o'er them like a golden fish.

LXVI

The black, however, without hardly deign-
 ing 521
 A glance at that which wrapt the slaves
 in wonder,
Trampled what they scarce trod for fear of
 staining,
 As if the milky way their feet was under
With all its stars; and with a stretch at-
 taining
 A certain press or cupboard niched in
 yonder —

In that remote recess which you may see —
Or if you don't the fault is not in me, —

LXVII

I wish to be perspicuous; and the black,
 I say, unlocking the recess, pull'd forth
A quantity of clothes fit for the back 531
 Of any Mussulman, whate'er his worth;
And of variety there was no lack —
 And yet, though I have said there was no
 dearth,
He chose himself to point out what he
 thought
Most proper for the Christians he had
 bought.

LXVIII

The suit he thought most suitable to each
 Was, for the elder and the stouter, first
A Candiote cloak, which to the knee might
 reach,
 And trousers not so tight that they would
 burst, 540
But such as fit an Asiatic breech;
 A shawl, whose folds in Cashmire had
 been nurst,
Slippers of saffron, dagger rich and handy;
In short, all things which form a Turkish
 Dandy.

LXIX

While he was dressing, Baba, their black
 friend,
 Hinted the vast advantages which they
Might probably attain both in the end,
 If they would but pursue the proper
 way
Which fortune plainly seem'd to recom-
 mend;
 And then he added, that he needs must
 say, 550
 ''T would greatly tend to better their con-
 dition,
If they would condescend to circumcision.

LXX

'For his own part, he really should re-
 joice
 To see them true believers, but no less
Would leave his proposition to their choice.'
 The other, thanking him for this excess
Of goodness, in thus leaving them a voice
 In such a trifle, scarcely could express
'Sufficiently' (he said) 'his approbation
Of all the customs of this polish'd nation. 560

LXXI

'For his own share — he saw but small ob-
 jection
 To so respectable an ancient rite;
And, after swallowing down a slight refec-
 tion,
 For which he own'd a present appetite,
He doubted not a few hours of reflection
 Would reconcile him to the business
 quite.'
'Will it ?' said Juan, sharply: 'Strike me
 dead,
But they as soon shall circumcise my
 head !

LXXII

'Cut off a thousand heads, before —'
 — 'Now, pray,'
 Replied the other, 'do not interrupt: 570
You put me out in what I had to say.
 Sir ! — as I said, as soon as I have supt,
I shall perpend if your proposal may
 Be such as I can properly accept;
Provided always your great goodness still
Remits the matter to our own free-will.'

LXXIII

Baba eyed Juan, and said, 'Be so good
 As dress yourself —' and pointed out a
 suit
In which a Princess with great pleasure
 would
 Array her limbs; but Juan standing mute,
As not being in a masquerading mood, 581
 Gave it a slight kick with his Christian
 foot;
And when the old negro told him to 'Get
 ready,'
Replied, 'Old gentleman, I 'm not a lady.'

LXXIV

'What you may be, I neither know nor
 care,'
 Said Baba; 'but pray do as I desire:
I have no more time nor many words to
 spare.'
 'At least,' said Juan, 'sure I may
 enquire
The cause of this odd travesty ?' — 'For-
 bear,'
 Said Baba, 'to be curious; 't will tran-
 spire, 590
No doubt, in proper place, and time, and
 season:
I have no authority to tell the reason.'

LXXV

'Then if I do,' said Juan, 'I 'll be —'
 — 'Hold !'
 Rejoin'd the negro, ' pray be not provok-
 ing;
This spirit 's well, but it may wax too bold,
 And you will find us not too fond of jok-
 ing.'
'What, sir !' said Juan, ' shall it e'er be
 told
 That I unsex'd my dress ? ' But Baba,
 stroking
The things down, said, ' Incense me, and I
 call
Those who will leave you of no sex at all.

LXXVI

' I offer you a handsome suit of clothes: 601
 A woman's, true; but then there is a cause
Why you should wear them.' — ' What,
 though my soul loathes
 The effeminate garb ? ' — thus, after a
 short pause,
Sigh'd Juan, muttering also some slight
 oaths,
 ' What the devil shall I do with all this
 gauze ? '
Thus he profanely term'd the finest lace
Which e'er set off a marriage-morning face.

LXXVII

And then he swore; and, sighing, on he
 slipp'd 609
 A pair of trousers of flesh-colour'd silk;
Next with a virgin zone he was equipp'd,
 Which girt a slight chemise as white as
 milk;
But tugging on his petticoat, he tripp'd,
 Which — as we say — or, as the Scotch
 say, whilk
(The rhyme obliges me to this; sometimes
Monarchs are less imperative than
 rhymes) —

LXXVIII

Whilk, which (or what you please), was
 owing to
 His garment's novelty, and his being
 awkward:
And yet at last he managed to get through
 His toilet, though no doubt a little back-
 ward: 620
The negro Baba help'd a little too,
 When some untoward part of raiment
 stuck hard;

And, wrestling both his arms into a gown,
He paused, and took a survey up and down.

LXXIX

One difficulty still remain'd — his hair
 Was hardly long enough; but Baba found
So many false long tresses all to spare,
 That soon his head was most completely
 crown'd,
After the manner then in fashion there;
 And this addition with such gems was
 bound 630
As suited the ensemble of his toilet,
While Baba made him comb his head and
 oil it.

LXXX

And now being femininely all array'd,
 With some small aid from scissors, paint,
 and tweezers,
He look'd in almost all respects a maid,
 And Baba smilingly exclaim'd, ' You see,
 sirs,
A perfect transformation here display'd;
 And now, then, you must come along
 with me, sirs,
That is — the Lady: ' clapping his hands
 twice,
Four blacks were at his elbow in a trice. 640

LXXXI

' You, sir,' said Baba, nodding to the one,
 ' Will please to accompany those gentle-
 men
To supper; but you, worthy Christian nun,
 Will follow me : no trifling, sir ; for
 when
I say a thing, it must at once be done.
 What fear you ? think you this a lion's
 den ?
Why, 't is a palace; where the truly wise
Anticipate the Prophet's paradise.

LXXXII

' You fool ! I tell you no one means you
 harm.'
 ' So much the better,' Juan said, ' for
 them ; 650
Else they shall feel the weight of this my
 arm,
 Which is not quite so light as you may
 deem.
I yield thus far ; but soon will break the
 charm
 If any take me for that which I seem :

So that I trust for everybody's sake,
That this disguise may lead to no mistake.'

LXXXIII

'Blockhead! come on, and see,' quoth Baba;
 while
Don Juan, turning to his comrade, who
Though somewhat grieved, could scarce for-
 bear a smile
 Upon the metamorphosis in view, — 660
'Farewell!' they mutually exclaim'd:
 'this soil
 Seems fertile in adventures strange and
 new;
One's turn'd half Mussulman, and one a maid,
By this old black enchanter's unsought aid.'

LXXXIV

'Farewell!' said Juan: 'should we meet
 no more,
 I wish you a good appetite.' — 'Fare-
 well!'
Replied the other; 'though it grieves me
 sore;
 When we next meet we'll have a tale
 to tell:
We needs must follow when Fate puts from
 shore.
 Keep your good name; though Eve her-
 self once fell.' 670
'Nay,' quoth the maid, 'the Sultan's self
 shan't carry me,
Unless his highness promises to marry me.'

LXXXV

And thus they parted, each by separate
 doors;
 Baba led Juan onward room by room
Through glittering galleries and o'er mar-
 ble floors,
 Till a gigantic portal through the gloom,
Haughty and huge, along the distance low-
 ers;
 And wafted far arose a rich perfume:
It seem'd as though they came upon a shrine,
For all was vast, still, fragrant, and divine.

LXXXVI

The giant door was broad, and bright, and
 high, 681
 Of gilded bronze, and carved in curious
 guise;
Warriors thereon were battling furiously;
 Here stalks the victor, there the van-
 quish'd lies;

There captives led in triumph droop the
 eye,
 And in perspective many a squadron flies:
It seems the work of times before the
 line
Of Rome transplanted fell with Constan-
 tine.

LXXXVII

This massy portal stood at the wide close
 Of a huge hall, and on its either side 690
Two little dwarfs, the least you could sup-
 pose,
 Were sate, like ugly imps, as if allied
In mockery to the enormous gate which
 rose
 O'er them in almost pyramidic pride:
The gate so splendid was in all its *features*,
You never thought about those little crea-
 tures,

LXXXVIII

Until you nearly trod on them, and then
 You started back in horror to survey
The wondrous hideousness of those small
 men,
 Whose colour was not black, nor white,
 nor grey, 700
But an extraneous mixture, which no pen
 Can trace, although perhaps the pencil
 may;
They were mis-shapen pigmies, deaf and
 dumb —
Monsters, who cost a no less monstrous
 sum.

LXXXIX

Their duty was — for they were strong, and
 though
 They look'd so little, did strong things
 at times —
To ope this door, which they could really
 do,
 The hinges being as smooth as Rogers'
 rhymes;
And now and then, with tough strings of
 the bow,
 As is the custom of those Eastern climes,
To give some rebel Pacha a cravat; 711
For mutes are generally used for that.

XC

They spoke by signs — that is, not spoke at
 all;
 And looking like two incubi, they glared

As Baba with his fingers made them fall
 To heaving back the portal folds: it
 scared
Juan a moment, as this pair so small
 With shrinking serpent optics on him
 stared;
It was as if their little looks could poison
Or fascinate whome'er they fix'd their eyes
 on. 720

XCI

Before they enter'd, Baba paused to hint
 To Juan some slight lessons as his guide:
' If you could just contrive,' he said, ' to
 stint
 That somewhat manly majesty of stride,
'T would be as well, and (though there's
 not much in 't)
 To swing a little less from side to side,
Which has at times an aspect of the
 oddest;—
And also could you look a little modest,

XCII

' 'T would be convenient; for these mutes
 have eyes
 Like needles, which may pierce those
 petticoats; 730
And if they should discover your disguise,
 You know how near us the deep Bos-
 phorus floats;
And you and I may chance, ere morning
 rise,
 To find our way to Marmora without
 boats,
Stitch'd up in sacks — a mode of naviga-
 tion
A good deal practised here upon occasion.'

XCIII

With this encouragement, he led the way
 Into a room still nobler than the last;
A rich confusion form'd a disarray
 In such sort, that the eye along it cast
Could hardly carry anything away, 741
 Object on object flash'd so bright and
 fast;
A dazzling mass of gems, and gold, and
 glitter,
Magnificently mingled in a litter.

XCIV

Wealth had done wonders — taste not much;
 such things
 Occur in Orient palaces, and even

In the more chasten'd domes of Western
 kings
 (Of which I have also seen some six or
 seven),
Where I can't say or gold or diamond flings
 Great lustre, there is much to be for-
 given; 750
Groups of bad statues, tables, chairs, and
 pictures,
On which I cannot pause to make my
 strictures.

XCV

In this imperial hall, at distance lay
 Under a canopy, and there reclined
Quite in a confidential queenly way,
 A lady; Baba stopp'd, and kneeling
 sign'd
To Juan, who though not much used to
 pray,
 Knelt down by instinct, wondering in his
 mind,
What all this meant: while Baba bow'd and
 bended
His head, until the ceremony ended. 760

XCVI

The lady rising up with such an air
 As Venus rose with from the wave, on
 them
Bent like an antelope a Paphian pair
 Of eyes, which put out each surrounding
 gem;
And raising up an arm as moonlight fair,
 She sign'd to Baba, who first kiss'd the
 hem
Of her deep purple robe, and speaking low,
Pointed to Juan who remain'd below.

XCVII

Her presence was as lofty as her state; 769
 Her beauty of that overpowering kind,
Whose force description only would abate:
 I'd rather leave it much to your own
 mind,
Than lessen it by what I could relate
 Of forms and features; it would strike
 you blind
Could I do justice to the full detail;
So, luckily for both, my phrases fail.

XCVIII

Thus much however I may add, — her years
 Were ripe, they might make six-and-
 twenty springs;

But there are forms which Time to touch
 forbears,
 And turns aside his scythe to vulgar
 things, 780
Such as was Mary's Queen of Scots; true —
 tears
And love destroy; and sapping sorrow
 wrings
Charms from the charmer, yet some never
 grow
Ugly; for instance — Ninon de l'Enclos.

XCIX

She spake some words to her attendants,
 who
Composed a choir of girls, ten or a dozen,
And were all clad alike; like Juan, too,
 Who wore their uniform, by Baba chosen;
They form'd a very nymph-like looking
 crew,
 Which might have call'd Diana's chorus
 'cousin,' 790
As far as outward show may correspond;
I won't be bail for anything beyond.

C

They bow'd obeisance and withdrew, re-
 tiring,
 But not by the same door through which
 came in
Baba and Juan, which last stood admiring,
 At some small distance, all he saw within
This strange saloon, much fitted for in-
 spiring
 Marvel and praise; for both or none
 things win;
And I must say, I ne'er could see the very
Great happiness of the 'Nil Admirari.' 800

CI

'Not to admire is all the art I know
 (Plain truth, dear Murray, needs few
 flowers of speech)
To make men happy, or to keep them so'
 (So take it in the very words of Creech) —
Thus Horace wrote we all know long ago;
 And thus Pope quotes the precept to
 re-teach
From his translation; but had *none admired*,
Would Pope have sung, or Horace been
 inspired?

CII

Baba, when all the damsels were withdrawn,
 Motion'd to Juan to approach, and then

A second time desired him to kneel down,
 And kiss the lady's foot; which maxim
 when 812
He heard repeated, Juan with a frown
 Drew himself up to his full height again,
And said, 'It grieved him, but he could
 not stoop
To any shoe, unless it shod the Pope.'

CIII

Baba, indignant at this ill-timed pride,
 Made fierce remonstrances, and then a
 threat
He mutter'd (but the last was given aside)
 About a bow-string — quite in vain; not
 yet 820
Would Juan bend, though 't were to Ma-
 homet's bride:
 There's nothing in the world like *eti-
 quette*
In kingly chambers or imperial halls,
As also at the race and county balls.

CIV

He stood like Atlas, with a world of words
 About his ears, and nathless would not
 bend:
The blood of all his line's Castilian lords
 Boil'd in his veins, and rather than de-
 scend
To stain his pedigree a thousand swords
 A thousand times of him had made an
 end; 830
At length perceiving the '*foot*' could not
 stand,
Baba proposed that he should kiss the hand.

CV

Here was an honourable compromise,
 A half-way house of diplomatic rest,
Where they might meet in much more
 peaceful guise;
 And Juan now his willingness exprest
To use all fit and proper courtesies,
 Adding, that this was commonest and
 best,
For through the South the custom still
 commands
The gentleman to kiss the lady's hands. 840

CVI

And he advanced, though with but a bad
 grace,
 Though on more *thorough-bred* or fairer
 fingers

No lips e'er left their transitory trace;
 On such as these the lip too fondly lin-
 gers,
And for one kiss would fain imprint a
 brace,
 As you will see, if she you love shall
 bring hers
In contact ; and sometimes even a fair
 stranger's
An almost twelvemonth's constancy en-
 dangers.

CVII

The lady eyed him o'er and o'er, and bade
 Baba retire, which he obey'd in style,
As if well used to the retreating trade; 851
 And taking hints in good part all the
 while,
He whisper'd Juan not to be afraid,
 And looking on him with a sort of smile,
Took leave, with such a face of satisfaction
As good men wear who have done a virtu-
 ous action.

CVIII

When he was gone, there was a sudden
 change:
 I know not what might be the lady's
 thought,
But o'er her bright brow flash'd a tumult
 strange,
 And into her clear cheek the blood was
 brought, 860
Blood-red as sunset summer clouds which
 range
 The verge of Heaven; and in her large
 eyes wrought,
A mixture of sensations might be scann'd,
Of half voluptuousness and half command.

CIX

Her form had all the softness of her sex,
 Her features all the sweetness of the
 devil,
When he put on the cherub to perplex
 Eve, and paved (God knows how) the
 road to evil;
The sun himself was scarce more free from
 specks
 Than she from aught at which the eye
 could cavil; 870
Yet, somehow, there was something some-
 where wanting,
As if she rather *order'd* than was *grant-
 ing.*

CX

Something imperial, or imperious, threw
 A chain o'er all she did; that is, a chain
Was thrown as 't were about the neck of
 you, —
 And rapture's self will seem almost a
 pain
With aught which looks like despotism in
 view:
 Our souls at least are free, and 't is in
 vain
We would against them make the flesh
 obey —
The spirit in the end will have its way. 880

CXI

Her very smile was haughty, though so
 sweet;
 Her very nod was not an inclination;
There was a self-will even in her small feet,
 As though they were quite conscious of
 her station —
They trod as upon necks; and to complete
 Her state (it is the custom of her nation),
A poniard deck'd her girdle, as the sign
She was a sultan's bride (thank Heaven,
 not mine!).

CXII

'To hear and to obey' had been from birth
 The law of all around her; to fulfil 890
All phantasies which yielded joy or mirth,
 Had been her slaves' chief pleasure, as
 her will;
Her blood was high, her beauty scarce of
 earth:
 Judge, then, if her caprices e'er stood
 still;
Had she but been a Christian, I 've a notion
We should have found out the 'perpetual
 motion.'

CXIII

Whate'er she saw and coveted was brought;
 Whate'er she did *not* see, if she sup-
 posed
It might be seen, with diligence was sought,
 And when 't was found straightway the
 bargain closed; 900
There was no end unto the things she
 bought,
 Nor to the trouble which her fancies
 caused;
Yet even her tyranny had such a grace,
The women pardon'd all except her face.

CXIV

Juan, the latest of her whims, had caught
 Her eye in passing on his way to sale;
She order'd him directly to be bought,
 And Baba, who had ne'er been known to
 fail
In any kind of mischief to be wrought, 909
 At all such auctions knew how to prevail:
She had no prudence, but he had; and this
Explains the garb which Juan took amiss.

CXV

His youth and features favour'd the dis-
 guise,
 And, should you ask how she, a sultan's
 bride,
Could risk or compass such strange phan-
 tasies,
 This I must leave sultanas to decide :
Emperors are only husbands in wives' eyes,
 And kings and consorts oft are mysti-
 fied,
As we may ascertain with due precision,
Some by experience, others by tradition. 920

CXVI

But to the main point, where we have been
 tending : —
 She now conceived all difficulties past,
And deem'd herself extremely condescend-
 ing
 When, being made her property at last,
Without more preface, in her blue eyes
 blending
 Passion and power, a glance on him she
 cast,
And merely saying, ' Christian, canst thou
 love ? '
Conceived that phrase was quite enough to
 move.

CXVII

And so it was, in proper time and place;
 But Juan, who had still his mind o'er-
 flowing 930
With Haidée's isle and soft Ionian face,
 Felt the warm blood, which in his face
 was glowing,
Rush back upon his heart, which fill'd
 apace,
 And left his cheeks as pale as snowdrops
 blowing;
These words went through his soul like
 Arab-spears,
So that he spoke not, but burst into tears.

CXVIII

She was a good deal shock'd; not shock'd at
 tears,
 For women shed and use them at their
 liking;
But there is something when man's eye
 appears
 Wet, still more disagreeable and striking;
A woman's tear-drop melts, a man's half
 sears, 941
 Like molten lead, as if you thrust a pike
 in
His heart to force it out, for (to be shorter)
To them 't is a relief, to us a torture.

CXIX

And she would have consoled, but knew not
 how :
 Having no equals, nothing which had e'er
Infected her with sympathy till now,
 And never having dreamt what 't was to
 bear
Aught of a serious, sorrowing kind, although
 There might arise some pouting petty
 care 950
To cross her brow, she wonder'd how so
 near
Her eyes another's eye could shed a tear.

CXX

But nature teaches more than power can
 spoil,
 And, when a *strong* although a strange
 sensation
Moves — female hearts are such a genial
 soil
 For kinder feelings, whatsoe'er their na-
 tion,
They naturally pour the ' wine and oil,'
 Samaritans in every situation;
And thus Gulbeyaz, though she knew not
 why,
Felt an odd glistening moisture in her eye.

CXXI

But tears must stop like all things else;
 and soon 961
 Juan, who for an instant had been moved
To such a sorrow by the intrusive tone
 Of one who dared to ask if ' he *had*
 loved,'
Call'd back the stoic to his eyes, which
 shone
 Bright with the very weakness he re-
 proved;

And although sensitive to beauty, he
Felt most indignant still at not being free.

CXXII

Gulbeyaz, for the first time in her days,
 Was much embarrass'd, never having met
In all her life with aught save prayers and
 praise; 971
 And as she also risk'd her life to get
Him whom she meant to tutor in love's
 ways
Into a comfortable tête-à-tête,
To lose the hour would make her quite a
 martyr,
And they had wasted now almost a quarter.

CXXIII

I also would suggest the fitting time
 To gentlemen in any such like case,
That is to say in a meridian clime —
 With us there is more law given to the
 chase, 980
But here a small delay forms a great crime:
 So recollect that the extremest grace
Is just two minutes for your declaration —
A moment more would hurt your reputation.

CXXIV

Juan's was good; and might have been still
 better,
 But he had got Haidée into his head:
However strange, he could not yet forget
 her,
 Which made him seem exceedingly ill-
 bred.
Gulbeyaz, who look'd on him as her debtor
 For having had him to her palace led, 990
Began to blush up to the eyes, and then
Grow deadly pale, and then blush back
 again.

CXXV

At length, in an imperial way, she laid
 Her hand on his, and bending on him
 eyes
Which needed not an empire to persuade,
 Look'd into his for love, where none
 replies:
Her brow grew black, but she would not
 upbraid,
 That being the last thing a proud woman
 tries;
She rose, and pausing one chaste moment,
 threw 999
Herself upon his breast, and there she grew.

CXXVI

This was an awkward test, as Juan found,
 But he was steel'd by sorrow, wrath, and
 pride:
With gentle force her white arms he
 unwound,
 And seated her all drooping by his side,
Then rising haughtily he glanced around,
 And looking coldly in her face, he cried,
' The prison'd eagle will not pair, nor I
Serve a Sultana's sensual phantasy.

CXXVII

' Thou ask'st if I can love ? be this the proof
 How much I *have* loved — that I love not
 thee ! 1010
In this vile garb, the distaff, web, and woof,
 Were fitter for me: Love is for the free !
I am not dazzled by this splendid roof,
 Whate'er thy power, and great it seems
 to be;
Heads bow, knees bend, eyes watch around
 a throne,
And hands obey — our hearts are still our
 own.'

CXXVIII

This was a truth to us extremely trite;
 Not so to her, who ne'er had heard such
 things:
She deem'd her least command must yield
 delight,
 Earth being only made for queens and
 kings. 1020
If hearts lay on the left side or the right
 She hardly knew, to such perfection brings
Legitimacy its born votaries, when
Aware of their due royal rights o'er men.

CXXIX

Besides, as has been said, she was so fair
 As even in a much humbler lot had made
A kingdom or confusion anywhere,
 And also, as may be presumed, she laid
Some stress on charms, which seldom are,
 if e'er,
 By their possessors thrown into the shade:
She thought hers gave a double ' right
 divine;' 1031
And half of that opinion 's also mine.

CXXX

Remember, or (if you can not) imagine,
 Ye, who have kept your chastity when
 young,

While some more desperate dowager has
 been waging
 Love with you, and been in the dog-days
 stung
By your refusal, recollect her raging !
 Or recollect all that was said or sung 1038
On such a subject; then suppose the face
Of a young downright beauty in this case.

CXXXI

Suppose, — but you already have supposed,
 The spouse of Potiphar, the Lady Booby,
Phædra, and all which story has disclosed
 Of good examples; pity that so few by
Poets and private tutors are exposed,
 To educate — ye youth of Europe — you
 by !
But when you have supposed the few we
 know,
You can't suppose Gulbeyaz' angry brow.

CXXXII

A tigress robb'd of young, a lioness,
 Or any interesting beast of prey, 1050
Are similes at hand for the distress
 Of ladies who can not have their own
 way;
But though my turn will not be served
 with less,
 These don't express one half what I
 should say:
For what is stealing young ones, few or
 many,
To cutting short their hopes of having any ?

CXXXIII

The love of offspring 's nature's general law,
 From tigresses and cubs to ducks and
 ducklings;
There 's nothing whets the beak, or arms the
 claw
 Like an invasion of their babes and
 sucklings; 1060
And all who have seen a human nursery,
 saw
 How mothers love their children's squalls
 and chucklings;
This strong extreme effect (to tire no longer
Your patience) shows the cause must still
 be stronger.

CXXXIV

If I said fire flash'd from Gulbeyaz' eyes,
 ' T were nothing — for her eyes flash'd
 always fire;

Or said her cheeks assumed the deepest dyes,
 I should but bring disgrace upon the
 dyer,
So supernatural was her passion's rise;
 For ne'er till now she knew a check'd
 desire: 1070
Even ye who know what a check'd woman
 is
(Enough, God knows !) would much fall
 short of this.

CXXXV

Her rage was but a minute's, and 't was
 well —
 A moment's more had slain her; but the
 while
It lasted 't was like a short glimpse of hell:
 Nought 's more sublime than energetic
 bile,
Though horrible to see yet grand to tell,
 Like ocean warring 'gainst a rocky isle;
And the deep passions flashing through her
 form
Made her a beautiful embodied storm. 1080

CXXXVI

A vulgar tempest 't were to a typhoon
 To match a common fury with her rage,
And yet she did not want to reach the moon,
 Like moderate Hotspur on the immortal
 page;
Her anger pitch'd into a lower tune,
 Perhaps the fault of her soft sex and
 age —
Her wish was but to ' kill, kill, kill,' like
 Lear's,
And then her thirst of blood was quench'd
 in tears.

CXXXVII

A storm it raged, and like the storm it pass'd,
 Pass'd without words — in fact she could
 not speak; 1090
And then her sex's shame broke in at last,
 A sentiment till then in her but weak,
But now it flow'd in natural and fast,
 As water through an unexpected leak;
For she felt humbled — and humiliation
Is sometimes good for people in her station.

CXXXVIII

It teaches them that they are flesh and
 blood,
 It also gently hints to them that
 others,

Although of clay, are yet not quite of mud;
 That urns and pipkins are but fragile
 brothers, 1100
And works of the same pottery, bad or good,
 Though not all born of the same sires and
 mothers:
It teaches — Heaven knows only what it
 teaches,
But sometimes it may mend, and often
 reaches.

CXXXIX

Her first thought was to cut off Juan's head;
 Her second, to cut only his — acquaint-
 ance;
Her third, to ask him where he had been
 bred;
 Her fourth, to rally him into repent-
 ance;
Her fifth, to call her maids and go to bed;
 Her sixth, to stab herself; her seventh,
 to sentence 1110
The lash to Baba: — but her grand resource
Was to sit down again, and cry of course.

CXL

She thought to stab herself, but then she
 had
 The dagger close at hand, which made it
 awkward;
For Eastern stays are little made to pad,
 So that a poniard pierces if 't is stuck
 hard:
She thought of killing Juan — but, poor
 lad!
 Though he deserved it well for being so
 backward, 1118
The cutting off his head was not the art
Most likely to attain her aim — his heart.

CXLI

Juan was moved; he had made up his mind
 To be impaled, or quarter'd as a dish
For dogs, or to be slain with pangs refined,
 Or thrown to lions, or made baits for fish,
And thus heroically stood resign'd,
 Rather than sin — except to his own wish:
But all his great preparatives for dying
Dissolved like snow before a woman cry-
 ing.

CXLII

As through his palms Bob Acres' valour
 oozed,
 So Juan's virtue ebb'd, I know not how;

And first he wonder'd why he had re-
 fused; 1131
 And then, if matters could be made up
 now;
And next his savage virtue he accused,
 Just as a friar may accuse his vow,
Or as a dame repents her of her oath,
Which mostly ends in some small breach
 of both.

CXLIII

So he began to stammer some excuses;
 But words are not enough in such a
 matter,
Although you borrow'd all that e'er the
 muses
 Have sung, or even a Dandy's dandiest
 chatter, 1140
Or all the figures Castlereagh abuses;
 Just as a languid smile began to flat-
 ter
His peace was making, but before he ven-
 tured
Further, old Baba rather briskly enter'd.

CXLIV

'Bride of the Sun! and Sister of the Moon!'
 ('T was thus he spake) 'and Empress of
 the Earth!
Whose frown would put the spheres all out
 of tune,
 Whose smile makes all the planets dance
 with mirth,
Your slave brings tidings — he hopes not
 too soon —
 Which your sublime attention may be
 worth: 1150
The Sun himself has sent me like a ray,
To hint that he is coming up this way.'

CXLV

'Is it,' exclaim'd Gulbeyaz, 'as you say?
 I wish to heaven he would not shine till
 morning!
But bid my women form the milky way.
 Hence, my old comet! give the stars due
 warning —
And, Christian! mingle with them as you
 may,
 And as you'd have me pardon your past
 scorning —'
Here they were interrupted by a hum-
 ming
Sound, and then by a cry, 'The Sultan's
 coming!' 1160

CXLVI

First came her damsels, a decorous file,
 And then his Highness' eunuchs, black
 and white;
The train might reach a quarter of a mile:
 His majesty was always so polite
As to announce his visits a long while
 Before he came, especially at night;
For being the last wife of the Emperour,
She was of course the favorite of the four.

CXLVII

His Highness was a man of solemn port,
 Shawl'd to the nose, and bearded to the
 eyes, 1170
Snatch'd from a prison to preside at court,
 His lately bowstrung brother caused his
 rise;
He was as good a sovereign of the sort
 As any mention'd in the histories
Of Cantemir, or Knölles, where few shine
Save Solyman, the glory of their line.

CXLVIII

He went to mosque in state, and said his
 prayers
 With more than ' Oriental scrupulosity;'
He left to his vizier all state affairs,
 And show'd but little royal curiosity:
I know not if he had domestic cares — 1181
 No process proved connubial animosity;
Four wives and twice five hundred maids,
 unseen,
Were ruled as calmly as a Christian queen.

CXLIX

If now and then there happen'd a slight slip,
 Little was heard of criminal or crime;
The story scarcely pass'd a single lip —
 The sack and sea had settled all in time,
From which the secret nobody could rip:
 The Public knew no more than does this
 rhyme; 1190
No scandals made the daily press a curse —
Morals were better, and the fish no worse.

CL

He saw with his own eyes the moon was
 round,
 Was also certain that the earth was square,
Because he had journey'd fifty miles, and
 found
 No sign that it was circular anywhere;
His empire also was without a bound:
 'T is true, a little troubled here and there,

By rebel pachas, and encroaching giaours,
But then they never came to ' the Seven
 Towers;' 1200

CLI

Except in shape of envoys, who were sent
 To lodge there when a war broke out,
 according
To the true law of nations, which ne'er meant
 Those scoundrels, who have never had a
 sword in
Their dirty diplomatic hands, to vent
 Their spleen in making strife, and safely
 wording
Their lies, yclep'd despatches, without risk
 or
The singeing of a single inky whisker.

CLII

He had fifty daughters and four dozen sons,
 Of whom all such as came of age were
 stow'd, 1210
The former in a palace, where like nuns
 They lived till some Bashaw was sent
 abroad,
When she, whose turn it was, was wed at
 once,
 Sometimes at six years old — though it
 seems odd,
'T is true; the reason is, that the Bashaw
Must make a present to his sire in law.

CLIII

His sons were kept in prison, till they grew
 Of years to fill a bowstring or the
 throne,
One or the other, but which of the two 1219
 Could yet be known unto the fates alone;
Meantime the education they went through
 Was princely, as the proofs have always
 shown:
So that the heir apparent still was found
No less deserving to be hang'd than crown'd.

CLIV

His majesty saluted his fourth spouse
 With all the ceremonies of his rank,
Who clear'd her sparkling eyes and
 smooth'd her brows,
 As suits a matron who has play'd a
 prank;
These must seem doubly mindful of their
 vows,
 To save the credit of their breaking
 bank: 1230

To no men are such cordial greetings given
As those whose wives have made them fit
 for heaven.

CLV

His Highness cast around his great black
 eyes,
 And looking, as he always look'd, per-
 ceived
Juan amongst the damsels in disguise,
 At which he seem'd no whit surprised
 nor grieved,
But just remark'd with air sedate and
 wise,
 While still a fluttering sigh Gulbeyaz
 heaved,
'I see you 've bought another girl; 't is
 pity
That a mere Christian should be half so
 pretty.' 1240

CLVI

This compliment, which drew all eyes upon
 The new-bought virgin, made her blush
 and shake.
Her comrades, also, thought themselves
 undone:
 Oh! Mahomet! that his majesty should
 take
Such notice of a giaour, while scarce to
 one
 Of them his lips imperial ever spake !
There was a general whisper, toss, and
 wriggle,
But etiquette forbade them all to giggle.

CLVII

The Turks do well to shut — at least, some-
 times —
 The women up, because, in sad reality,
Their chastity in these unhappy climes 1251
 Is not a thing of that astringent quality
Which in the North prevents precocious
 crimes,
 And makes our snow less pure than our
 morality;
The sun, which yearly melts the polar ice,
Has quite the contrary effect on vice.

CLVIII

Thus in the East they are extremely strict,
 And *Wedlock* and a *Padlock* mean the
 same; 1258
Excepting only when the former 's pick'd
 It ne'er can be replaced in proper frame;

Spoilt, as a pipe of claret is when prick'd:
 But then their own Polygamy 's to blame;
Why don't they knead two virtuous souls
 for life
Into that moral centaur, man and wife ?

CLIX

Thus far our chronicle; and now we pause,
 Though not for want of matter; but 't is
 time
According to the ancient epic laws,
 To slacken sail, and anchor with our
 rhyme.
Let this fifth canto meet with due applause,
 The sixth shall have a touch of the sub-
 lime; 1270
Meanwhile, as Homer sometimes sleeps,
 perhaps
You 'll pardon to my muse a few short naps.

PREFACE

TO CANTOS VI, VII, AND VIII

The details of the siege of Ismail in **two of**
the following cantos (*i. e.* the seventh **and**
eighth) are taken from a French Work, en-
titled *Histoire de la Nouvelle Russie.* Some of
the incidents attributed to Don Juan really
occurred, particularly the circumstance of his
saving the infant, which was the actual case of
the late Duc de Richelieu, then a young volun-
teer in the Russian service, and afterward the
founder and benefactor of Odessa, where his
name and memory can never cease to be re-
garded with reverence.

In the course of these cantos, a stanza or two
will be found relative to the late Marquis of
Londonderry, but written some time before his
decease. Had that person's oligarchy died
with him, they would have been suppressed;
as it is, I am aware of nothing in the manner
of his death or of his life to prevent the free
expression of the opinions of all whom his
whole existence was consumed in endeavouring
to enslave. That he was an amiable man in
private life, may or may not be true : but with
this the public have nothing to do; and as to
lamenting his death, it will be time enough
when Ireland has ceased to mourn for his birth.
As a minister, I, for one of millions, looked
upon him as the most despotic in intention,
and the weakest in intellect, that ever tyran-
nised over a country. It is the first time in-
deed since the Normans that England has been
insulted by a *minister* (at least) who could not
speak English, and that parliament permitted

itself to be dictated to in the language of Mrs. Malaprop.

Of the manner of his death little need be said, except that if a poor radical, such as Waddington or Watson, had cut his throat, he would have been buried in a cross-road, with the usual appurtenances of the stake and mallet. But the minister was an elegant lunatic — a sentimental suicide — he merely cut the 'carotid artery' (blessings on their learning!) and lo! the pageant and the Abbey! and 'the syllables of dolour yelled forth' by the newspapers — and the harangue of the Coroner in a eulogy over the bleeding body of the deceased (an Anthony worthy of such a Cæsar) — and the nauseous and atrocious cant of a degraded crew of conspirators against all that is sincere and honourable. In his death he was necessarily one of two things by the *law*[1] — a felon or a madman — and in either case no great subject for panegyric. In his life he was — what all the world knows, and half of it will feel for years to come, unless his death prove a 'moral lesson' to the surviving Sejani[2] of Europe. It may at least serve as some consolation to the nations, that their oppressors are not happy, and in some instances judge so justly of their own actions as to anticipate the sentence of mankind. — Let us hear no more of this man; and let Ireland remove the ashes of her Grattan from the sanctuary of Westminster. Shall the patriot of humanity repose by the Werther of politics!!!

With regard to the objections which have been made on another score to the already published cantos of this poem, I shall content myself with two quotations from Voltaire: — 'La pudeur s'est enfuite des cœurs, et s'est refugiée sur les lèvres' . . . 'Plus les mœurs sont dépravés, plus les expressions deviennent mesurées; on croit regagner en langage ce qu'on a perdu en vertu.'

This is the real fact, as applicable to the degraded and hypocritical mass which leavens the present English generation, and is the only answer they deserve. The hackneyed and lavished title of Blasphemer — which, with Radical, Liberal, Jacobin, Reformer, etc., are the changes which the hirelings are daily ringing in the ears of those who will listen — should be welcome to all who recollect on *whom* it was originally bestowed. Socrates and Jesus Christ

were put to death publicly as *blasphemers*, and so have been and may be many who dare to oppose the most notorious abuses of the name of God and the mind of man. But persecution is not refutation, nor even triumph: the 'wretched infidel,' as he is called, is probably happier in his prison than the proudest of his assailants. With his opinions I have nothing to do — they may be right or wrong — but he has suffered for them, and that very suffering for conscience' sake will make more proselytes to deism than the example of heterodox[1] Prelates to Christianity, suicide statesmen to oppression, or over-pensioned homicides to the impious alliance which insults the world with the name of 'Holy!' I have no wish to trample on the dishonoured or the dead; but it would be well if the adherents to the classes from whence those persons sprung should abate a little of the *cant* which is the crying sin of this double-dealing and false-speaking time of selfish spoilers, and — but enough for the present.

PISA, *July*, 1822.

CANTO THE SIXTH

I

'There is a tide in the affairs of men
 Which, — taken at the flood,' — you know
 the rest,
And most of us have found it now and then;
 At least we think so, though but few
 have guess'd
The moment, till too late to come again.
 But no doubt every thing is for the best —
Of which the surest sign is in the end:
When things are at the worst they sometimes mend.

II

There is a tide in the affairs of women
 Which, taken at the flood, leads — God
 knows where: 10
Those navigators must be able seamen
 Whose charts lay down its current to a
 hair;
Not all the reveries of Jacob Behmen
 With its strange whirls and eddies can
 compare:

[1] I say by the *law* of the land — the laws of humanity judge more gently; but as the legitimates have always the *law* in their mouths, let them here make the most of it.

[2] From this number must be excepted Canning. Canning is a genius, almost a universal one, an orator, a wit, a poet, a statesman; and no man of talent can long pursue the path of his late predecessor, Lord C. If ever man saved his country, Canning *can*, but *will* he? I, for one, hope so.

[1] When Lord Sandwich said 'he did not know the difference between orthodoxy and heterodoxy,' Warburton, the bishop, replied, 'Orthodoxy, my lord, is *my doxy*, and heterodoxy is *another man's doxy*.' A prelate of the present day has discovered, it seems, a *third* kind of doxy, which has not greatly exalted in the eyes of the elect that which Bentham calls 'Church-of-Englandism.'

Men with their heads reflect on this and
 that —
But women with their hearts on heaven
 knows what !

III

And yet a headlong, headstrong, downright
 she,
 Young, beautiful, and daring — who
 would risk
A throne, the world, the universe, to be
 Beloved in her own way, and rather
 whisk 20
The stars from out the sky, than not be
 free
 As are the billows when the breeze is
 brisk —
Though such a she's a devil (if that there
 be one),
Yet she would make full many a Manichean.

IV

Thrones, worlds, et cetera, are so oft upset
 By commonest ambition, that when pas-
 sion
O'erthrows the same, we readily forget,
 Or at the least forgive, the loving rash
 one.
If Anthony be well remember'd yet,
 'T is not his conquests keep his name in
 fashion, 30
But Actium, lost for Cleopatra's eyes,
Outbalances all Cæsar's victories.

V

He died at fifty for a queen of forty;
 I wish their years had been fifteen and
 twenty,
For then wealth, kingdoms, worlds are but
 a sport — I
 Remember when, though I had no great
 plenty
Of worlds to lose, yet still, to pay my court,
 I
 Gave what I had — a heart: as the world
 went, I
Gave what was worth a world; for worlds
 could never
Restore me those pure feelings, gone for-
 ever. 40

VI

'T was the boy's ' mite,' and, like the ' wid-
 ow's,' may
 Perhaps be weigh'd hereafter, if not now;

But whether such things do or do not weigh,
 All who have loved, or love, will still
 allow
Life has nought like it. God is love, they
 say,
 And Love's a god, or was before the brow
Of earth was wrinkled by the sins and tears
Of — but Chronology best knows the years.

VII

We left our hero and third heroine in
 A kind of state more awkward than un-
 common, 50
For gentlemen must sometimes risk their
 skin
 For that sad tempter, a forbidden woman:
Sultans too much abhor this sort of sin,
 And don't agree at all with the wise Ro-
 man,
Heroic, stoic Cato, the sententious,
Who lent his lady to his friend Hortensius.

VIII

I know Gulbeyaz was extremely wrong;
 I own it, I deplore it, I condemn it;
But I detest all fiction even in song,
 And so must tell the truth, howe'er you
 blame it. 60
Her reason being weak, her passions strong,
 She thought that her lord's heart (even
 could she claim it)
Was scarce enough; for he had fifty-nine
Years, and a fifteen-hundredth concubine.

IX

I am not, like Cassio, ' an arithmetician,'
 But by ' the bookish theoric ' it appears,
If 't is summ'd up with feminine precision,
 That, adding to the account his Highness'
 years,
The fair Sultana err'd from inanition;
 For, were the Sultan just to all his dears,
She could but claim the fifteen-hundredth
 part 71
Of what should be monopoly — the heart.'

X

It is observed that ladies are litigious
 Upon all legal objects of possession,
And not the least so when they are religious,
 Which doubles what they think of the
 transgression:
With suits and prosecutions they besiege us,
 As the tribunals show through many a
 session,

XI

When they suspect that any one goes
shares
In that to which the law makes them sole
heirs. 80

Now, if this holds good in a Christian land,
 The heathen also, though with lesser
 latitude,
Are apt to carry things with a high hand,
 And take what kings call 'an imposing
 attitude,'
And for their rights connubial make a stand,
 When their liege husbands treat them
 with ingratitude:
And as four wives must have quadruple
 claims,
The Tigris hath its jealousies like Thames.

XII

Gulbeyaz was the fourth, and (as I said)
 The favourite; but what's favour amongst
 four? 90
Polygamy may well be held in dread,
 Not only as a sin, but as a *bore*:
Most wise men, with *one* moderate woman
 wed,
 Will scarcely find philosophy for more;
And all (except Mahometans) forbear
To make the nuptial couch a ' Bed of Ware.'

XIII

His Highness, the sublimest of mankind, —
 So styled according to the usual forms
Of every monarch, till they are consign'd
 To those sad hungry jacobins the worms,
Who on the very loftiest kings have
 dined, — 101
 His Highness gazed upon Gulbeyaz'
 charms,
Expecting all the welcome of a lover
(A ' Highland welcome ' all the wide world
 over).

XIV

Now here we should distinguish; for how-
 e'er
 Kisses, sweet words, embraces, and all
 that,
May look like what is — neither here nor
 there,
 They are put on as easily as a hat,
Or rather bonnet, which the fair sex wear,
 Trimm'd either heads or hearts to deco-
 rate, 110

Which form an ornament, but no more part
Of heads, than their caresses of the heart.

XV

A slight blush, a soft tremor, a calm kind
 Of gentle feminine delight, and shown
More in the eyelids than the eyes, resign'd
 Rather to hide what pleases most un-
 known,
Are the best tokens (to a modest mind)
 Of love, when seated on his loveliest
 throne,
A sincere woman's breast, — for over-*warm*
Or over-*cold* annihilates the charm. 120

XVI

For over-warmth, if false, is worse than
 truth;
 If true, 't is no great lease of its own
 fire;
For no one, save in very early youth,
 Would like (I think) to trust all to desire,
Which is but a precarious bond, in sooth,
 And apt to be transferr'd to the first
 buyer
At a sad discount: while your over chilly
Women, on t'other hand, seem somewhat
 silly.

XVII

That is, we cannot pardon their bad taste,
 For so it seems to lovers swift or slow,
Who fain would have a mutual flame con-
 fess'd, 131
 And see a sentimental passion glow,
Even were St. Francis' paramour their
 guest,
 In his monastic concubine of snow; —
In short, the maxim for the amorous tribe is
Horatian, 'Medio tu tutissimus ibis.'

XVIII

The 'tu' 's *too* much, — but let it stand, —
 the verse
 Requires it, that 's to say, the English
 rhyme,
And not the pink of old hexameters;
 But, after all, there 's neither tune nor
 time 140
In the last line, which cannot well be worse,
 And was thrust in to close the octave's
 chime:
I own no prosody can ever rate it
As a rule, but *truth* may, if you translate
 it.

XIX

If fair Gulbeyaz overdid her part,
　I know not — it succeeded, and success
Is much in most things, not less in the heart
　Than other articles of female dress.
Self-love in man, too, beats all female art;
　They lie, we lie, all lie, but love no less;
And no one virtue yet, except starvation, 151
　Could stop that worst of vices — propaga-
　　tion.

XX

We leave this royal couple to repose:
　A bed is not a throne, and they may sleep,
Whate'er their dreams be, if of joys or woes:
　Yet disappointed joys are woes as deep
As any man's clay mixture undergoes.
　Our least of sorrows are such as we weep;
'T is the vile daily drop on drop which wears
The soul out (like the stone) with petty
　cares. 160

XXI

A scolding wife, a sullen son, a bill
　To pay, unpaid, protested, or discounted
At a per-centage; a child cross, dog ill,
　A favourite horse fallen lame just as he 's
　　mounted,
A bad old woman making a worse will,
　Which leaves you minus of the cash you
　　counted
As certain; — these are paltry things, and
　yet
I 've rarely seen the man they did not fret.

XXII

I 'm a philosopher ; confound them all !
　Bills, beasts, and men, and — no ! not
　　womankind ! 170
With one good hearty curse I vent my gall,
　And then my stoicism leaves nought be-
　　hind
Which it can either pain or evil call,
　And I can give my whole soul up to mind;
Though what is soul or mind, their birth or
　growth,
Is more than I know — the deuce take them
　both !

XXIII

So now all things are d—n'd one feels at
　ease,
　As after reading Athanasius' curse,
Which doth your true believer so much
　please:

I doubt if any now could make it worse
O'er his worst enemy when at his knees, 181
'T is so sententious, positive, and terse,
　And decorates the book of Common Prayer,
As doth a rainbow the just clearing air.

XXIV

Gulbeyaz and her lord were sleeping, or
　At least one of them ! — Oh, the heavy
　　night,
When wicked wives, who love some bachelor,
　Lie down in dudgeon to sigh for the light
Of the gray morning, and look vainly for
　Its twinkle through the lattice dusky
　　quite — 190
To toss, to tumble, doze, revive, and quake
Lest their too lawful bed-fellow should
　wake !

XXV

These are beneath the canopy of heaven,
　Also beneath the canopy of beds
Four-posted and silk curtain'd, which are
　given
　For rich men and their brides to lay their
　　heads
Upon, in sheets white as what bards call
　'driven
Snow.' Well ! 't is all hap-hazard when
　one weds.
Gulbeyaz was an empress, but had been
Perhaps as wretched if a peasant's quean. 200

XXVI

Don Juan in his feminine disguise,
　With all the damsels in their long array,
Had bow'd themselves before th' imperial
　eyes,
　And at the usual signal ta'en their way
Back to their chambers, those long galleries
　In the seraglio, where the ladies lay
Their delicate limbs; a thousand bosoms
　there
Beating for love, as the caged bird's for air.

XXVII

I love the sex, and sometimes would re-
　verse
　The tyrant's wish, 'that mankind only
　　had 210
One neck, which he with one fell stroke
　might pierce:'
　My wish is quite as wide, but not so bad,
And much more tender on the whole than
　fierce;

It being (not *now*, but only while a lad)
That womankind had but one rosy mouth,
To kiss them all at once from North to
South.

XXVIII

Oh, enviable Briareus ! with thy hands
 And heads, if thou hadst all things mul-
 tiplied
In such proportion ! — But my Muse with-
 stands
 The giant thought of being a Titan's
 bride, 220
Or travelling in Patagonian lands;
 So let us back to Lilliput, and guide
Our hero through the labyrinth of love
In which we left him several lines above.

XXIX

He went forth with the lovely Odalisques,
 At the given signal join'd to their array;
And though he certainly ran many risks,
 Yet he could not at times keep, by the
 way
(Although the consequences of such frisks
 Are worse than the worst damages men
 pay 230
In moral England, where the thing's a tax),
From ogling all their charms from breasts
 to backs.

XXX

Still he forgot not his disguise: — along
 The galleries from room to room they
 walk'd,
A virgin-like and edifying throng,
 By eunuchs flank'd; while at their head
 there stalk'd
A dame who kept up discipline among
 The female ranks, so that none stirr'd or
 talk'd
Without her sanction on their she-parades:
Her title was 'the Mother of the Maids.' 240

XXXI

Whether she was a ' mother,' I know not,
 Or whether they were ' maids ' who call'd
 her mother;
But this is her seraglio title, got
 I know not how, but good as any other;
So Cantemir can tell you, or De Tott:
 Her office was to keep aloof or smother
All bad propensities in fifteen hundred
Young women, and correct them when they
 blunder'd.

XXXII

A goodly sinecure, no doubt ! but made
 More easy by the absence of all men —
Except his majesty, who, with her aid, 251
 And guards, and bolts, and walls, and now
 and then
A slight example, just to cast a shade
 Along the rest, contrived to keep this den
Of beauties cool as an Italian convent,
Where all the passions have, alas ! but one
 vent.

XXXIII

And what is that ? Devotion, doubtless —
 how
 Could you ask such a question ? — but
 we will
Continue. As I said, this goodly row
 Of ladies of all countries at the will 260
Of one good man, with stately march and
 slow,
 Like water-lilies floating down a rill —
Or rather lake, for *rills* do *not* run *slowly* —
Paced on most maiden-like and melancholy.

XXXIV

But when they reach'd their own apart-
 ments, there,
 Like birds, or boys, or bedlamites broke
 loose,
Waves at spring-tide, or women anywhere
 When freed from bonds (which are of
 no great use
After all), or like Irish at a fair,
 Their guards being gone, and as it were
 a truce 270
Establish'd between them and bondage, they
Began to sing, dance, chatter, smile, and
 play.

XXXV

Their talk, of course, ran most on the new
 comer;
 Her shape, her hair, her air, her every-
 thing:
Some thought her dress did not so much
 become her,
 Or wonder'd at her ears without a ring;
Some said her years were getting nigh their
 summer,
 Others contended they were but in spring;
Some thought her rather masculine in
 height,
While others wish'd that she had been so
 quite. 280

XXXVI

But no one doubted on the whole, that she
 Was what her dress bespoke, a damsel
 fair,
And fresh, and 'beautiful exceedingly,'
 Who with the brightest Georgians might
 compare:
They wonder'd how Gulbeyaz, too, could
 be
So silly as to buy slaves who might share
(If that his Highness wearied of his bride)
Her throne and power, and every thing be-
 side.

XXXVII

But what was strangest in this virgin crew,
 Although her beauty was enough to vex,
After the first investigating view, 291
 They all found out as few, or fewer,
 specks
In the fair form of their companion new,
 Than is the custom of the gentle sex,
When they survey, with Christian eyes or
 Heathen,
In a new face 'the ugliest creature breath-
 ing.'

XXXVIII

And yet they had their little jealousies,
 Like all the rest; but upon this occasion,
Whether there are such things as sympa-
 thies
 Without our knowledge or our approba-
 tion, 300
Although they could not see through his
 disguise,
 All felt a soft kind of concatenation,
Like magnetism, or devilism, or what
You please — we will not quarrel about
 that:

XXXIX

But certain 't is they all felt for their new
 Companion something newer still, as
 't were
A sentimental friendship through and
 through,
 Extremely pure, which made them all
 concur
In wishing her their sister, save a few
 Who wish'd they had a brother just like
 her, 310
Whom, if they were at home in sweet Cir-
 cassia,
They would prefer to Padisha or Pacha.

XL

Of those who had most genius for this sort
 Of sentimental friendship, there were
 three,
Lolah, Katinka, and Dudù; in short
 (To save description), fair as fair can be
Were they, according to the best report,
 Though differing in stature and degree,
And clime and time, and country and com-
 plexion;
They all alike admired their new connec-
 tion. 320

XLI

Lolah was dusk as India and as warm;
 Katinka was a Georgian, white and red,
With great blue eyes, a lovely hand and
 arm,
 And feet so small they scarce seem'd
 made to tread,
But rather skim the earth; while Dudù's
 form
 Look'd more adapted to be put to bed,
Being somewhat large, and languishing, and
 lazy,
Yet of a beauty that would drive you crazy.

XLII

A kind of sleepy Venus seem'd Dudù,
 Yet very fit to 'murder sleep' in those
Who gazed upon her cheek's transcendent
 hue, 331
 Her Attic forehead, and her Phidian
 nose:
Few angles were there in her form, 't is
 true,
 Thinner she might have been, and yet
 scarce lose;
Yet, after all, 't would puzzle to say where
It would not spoil some separate charm to
 pare.

XLIII

She was not violently lively, but
 Stole on your spirit like a May-day
 breaking;
Her eyes were not too sparkling, yet, half-
 shut,
 They put beholders in a tender taking;
She look'd (this simile 's quite new) just
 cut 341
 From marble, like Pygmalion's statue
 waking,
The mortal and the marble still at strife,
And timidly expanding into life.

XLIV

Lolah demanded the new damsel's name —
 'Juanna.' — Well, a pretty name enough.
Katinka ask'd her also whence she came —
 'From Spain.' — ' But where *is* Spain ? ' —
 ' Don't ask such stuff,
Nor show your Georgian ignorance — for
 shame ! ' 349
 Said Lolah, with an accent rather rough,
To poor Katinka: ' Spain 's an island near
Morocco, betwixt Egypt and Tangier.'

XLV

Dudù said nothing, but sat down beside
 Juanna, playing with her veil or hair;
And looking at her steadfastly, she sigh'd,
 As if she pitied her for being there,
A pretty stranger without friend or guide,
 And all abash'd, too, at the general stare
Which welcomes hapless strangers in all
 places,
With kind remarks upon their mien and
 faces. 360

XLVI

But here the Mother of the Maids drew near,
 With, ' Ladies, it is time to go to rest.
I 'm puzzled what to do with you, my dear,'
 She added to Juanna, their new guest:
' Your coming has been unexpected here,
 And every couch is occupied; you had best
Partake of mine; but by to-morrow early
We will have all things settled for you
 fairly.'

XLVII

Here Lolah interposed — ' Mamma, you
 know
 You don't sleep soundly, and I cannot
 bear 370
That anybody should disturb you so;
 I 'll take Juanna; we 're a slenderer pair
Than you would make the half of; — don't
 say no;
 And I of your young charge will take
 due care.'
But here Katinka interfered, and said,
' She also had compassion and a bed.

XLVIII

' Besides, I hate to sleep alone,' quoth she.
 The matron frown'd: ' Why so ? ' —
 ' For fear of ghosts,'
Replied Katinka; ' I am sure I see
 A phantom upon each of the four posts;

And then I have the worst dreams that can
 be, 381
 Of Guebres, Giaours, and Ginns, and Gouls
 in hosts.'
The dame replied, ' Between your dreams
 and you,
I fear Juanna's dreams would be but few.

XLIX

' You, Lolah, must continue still to lie
 Alone, for reasons which don't matter;
 you
The same, Katinka, until by and by;
 And I shall place Juanna with Dudù,
Who 's quiet, inoffensive, silent, shy,
 And will not toss and chatter the night
 through. 390
What say you, child ? ' — Dudù said
 nothing, as
Her talents were of the more silent class;

L

But she rose up, and kiss'd the matron's
 brow
 Between the eyes, and Lolah on both
 cheeks,
Katinka, too; and with a gentle bow
 (Curt'sies are neither used by Turks nor
 Greeks)
She took Juanna by the hand to show
 Their place of rest, and left to both their
 piques,
The others pouting at the matron's prefer-
 ence
Of Dudù, though they held their tongues
 from deference. 400

LI

It was a spacious chamber (Oda is
 The Turkish title), and ranged round the
 wall
Were couches, toilets — and much more
 than this
 I might describe, as I have seen it all,
But it suffices — little was amiss;
 'T was on the whole a nobly furnish'd
 hall,
With all things ladies want, save one or two,
And even those were nearer than they knew.

LII

Dudú, as has been said, was a sweet crea-
 ture,
 Not very dashing, but extremely win-
 ning, 410

With the most regulated charms of feature,
 Which painters cannot catch like faces
 sinning
Against proportion — the wild strokes of
 nature
 Which they hit off at once in the beginning,
Full of expression, right or wrong, that
 strike,
And pleasing or unpleasing, still are like.

LIII

But she was a soft landscape of mild earth,
 Where all was harmony, and calm, and
 quiet,
Luxuriant, budding; cheerful without mirth,
 Which, if not happiness, is much more
 nigh it 420
Than are your mighty passions and so forth,
 Which some call 'the sublime:' I wish
 they 'd try it:
I 've seen your stormy seas and stormy
 women,
And pity lovers rather more than seamen.

LIV

But she was pensive more than melancholy,
 And serious more than pensive, and se-
 rene,
It may be, more than either — not unholy
 Her thoughts, at least till now, appear to
 have been.
The strangest thing was, beauteous, she was
 wholly
 Unconscious, albeit turn'd of quick seven-
 teen, 430
That she was fair, or dark, or short, or tall;
She never thought about herself at all.

LV

And therefore was she kind and gentle as
 The Age of Gold (when gold was yet un-
 known,
By which its nomenclature came to pass;
 Thus most appropriately has been shown
'Lucus à non lucendo,' not what was,
 But what was not; a sort of style that 's
 grown
Extremely common in this age, whose metal
The devil may decompose, but never settle:

LVI

I think it may be of 'Corinthian Brass,' 441
 Which was a mixture of all metals, but
The brazen uppermost). Kind reader! pass
 This long parenthesis: I could not shut

It sooner for the soul of me, and class
 My faults even with your own! which
 meaneth, Put
A kind construction upon them and me:
 But that you won't — then don't — I am
 not less free.

LVII

'T is time we should return to plain narra-
 tion,
 And thus my narrative proceeds: — Dudù,
With every kindness short of ostentation, 451
 Show'd Juan, or Juanna, through and
 through
This labyrinth of females, and each station
 Described — what 's strange — in words
 extremely few:
I have but one simile, and that 's a blunder,
For wordless woman, which is silent thunder.

LVIII

And next she gave her (I say her, because
 The gender still was epicene, at least
In outward show, which is a saving clause)
 An outline of the customs of the East, 460
With all their chaste integrity of laws,
 By which the more a haram is increased,
The stricter doubtless grow the vestal duties
Of any supernumerary beauties.

LIX

And then she gave Juanna a chaste kiss:
 Dudù was fond of kissing — which I 'm
 sure
That nobody can ever take amiss,
 Because 't is pleasant, so that it be pure,
And between females means no more than
 this —
 That they have nothing better near, or
 newer. 470
'Kiss' rhymes to 'bliss' in fact as well as
 verse —
I wish it never led to something worse.

LX

In perfect innocence she then unmade
 Her toilet, which cost little, for she was
A child of Nature, carelessly array'd:
 If fond of a chance ogle at her glass,
'T was like the fawn, which, in the lake dis-
 play'd,
 Beholds her own shy, shadowy image pass,
When first she starts, and then returns to
 peep,
Admiring this new native of the deep. 480

LXI

And one by one her articles of dress
 Were laid aside; but not before she
 offer'd
Her aid to fair Juanna, whose excess
 Of modesty declined the assistance prof-
 fer'd:
Which pass'd well off — as she could do no
 less;
 Though by this politesse she rather
 suffer'd,
Pricking her fingers with those cursèd pins,
Which surely were invented for our sins, —

LXII

Making a woman like a porcupine,
 Not to be rashly touch'd. But still more
 dread, 490
Oh ye! whose fate it is, as once 't was
 mine,
 In early youth, to turn a lady's maid; —
I did my very boyish best to shine
 In tricking her out for a masquerade;
The pins were placed sufficiently, but not
Stuck all exactly in the proper spot.

LXIII

But these are foolish things to all the wise,
 And I love wisdom more than she loves
 me;
My tendency is to philosophise
 On most things, from a tyrant to a
 tree; 500
But still the spouseless virgin *Knowledge*
 flies.
 What are we? and whence came we?
 what shall be
Our *ultimate* existence? what's our present?
Are questions answerless, and yet inces-
 sant.

LXIV

There was deep silence in the chamber:
 dim
 And distant from each other burn'd the
 lights,
And slumber hover'd o'er each lovely limb
 Of the fair occupants: if there be sprites,
They should have walk'd there in their
 sprightliest trim,
 By way of change from their sepulchral
 sites, 510
And shown themselves as ghosts of better
 taste
Than haunting some old ruin or wild waste.

LXV

Many and beautiful lay those around,
 Like flowers of different hue, and clime,
 and root,
In some exotic garden sometimes found,
 With cost, and care, and warmth induced
 to shoot.
One with her auburn tresses lightly bound,
 And fair brows gently drooping, as the
 fruit
Nods from the tree, was slumbering with
 soft breath,
And lips apart, which show'd the pearls
 beneath. 520

LXVI

One with her flush'd cheek laid on her
 white arm,
 And raven ringlets gather'd in dark
 crowd
Above her brow, lay dreaming soft and
 warm;
 And smiling through her dream, as
 through a cloud
The moon breaks, half unveil'd each further
 charm,
 As, slightly stirring in her snowy shroud,
Her beauties seized the unconscious hour
 of night
All bashfully to struggle into light.

LXVII

This is no bull, although it sounds so; for
 'T was night, but there were lamps, as
 hath been said. 530
A third's all pallid aspect offer'd more
 The traits of sleeping sorrow, and be-
 tray'd
Through the heaved breast the dream of
 some far shore
 Belovèd and deplored; while slowly
 stray'd
(As night-dew, on a cypress glittering,
 tinges
The black bough) tear-drops through her
 eyes' dark fringes.

LXVIII

A fourth as marble, statue-like and still,
 Lay in a breathless, hush'd, and stony
 sleep;
White, cold, and pure, as looks a frozen
 rill,
 Or the snow minaret on an Alpine
 steep, 540

Or Lot's wife done in salt, — or what you
 will; —
 My similes are gather'd in a heap,
So pick and choose — perhaps you 'll be
 content
 With a carved lady on a monument.

LXIX

And lo! a fifth appears; — and what is she ?
 A lady of a ' certain age,' which means
Certainly agèd — what her years might be
 I know not, never counting past their
 teens;
But there she slept, not quite so fair to
 see,
 As ere that awful period intervenes 550
Which lays both men and women on the
 shelf,
To meditate upon their sins and self.

LXX

But all this time how slept, or dream'd,
 Dudù ?
 With strict inquiry I could ne'er discover,
And scorn to add a syllable untrue;
 But ere the middle watch was hardly
 over,
Just when the fading lamps waned dim and
 blue,
 And phantoms hover'd, or might seem to
 hover,
To those who like their company, about
The apartment, on a sudden she scream'd
 out: 560

LXXI

And that so loudly, that upstarted all
 The Oda, in a general commotion:
Matron and maids, and those whom you
 may call
 Neither, came crowding like the waves
 of ocean,
One on the other, throughout the whole
 hall,
 All trembling, wondering, without the
 least notion
More than I have myself of what could
 make
The calm Dudù so turbulently wake.

LXXII

But wide awake she was, and round her
 bed,
 With floating draperies and with flying
 hair,
 570

With eager eyes, and light but hurried tread,
 And bosoms, arms, and ankles glancing
 bare,
And bright as any meteor ever bred
 By the North Pole, — they sought her
 cause of care,
For she seem'd agitated, flush'd, and
 frighten'd,
 Her eye dilated and her colour heighten'd.

LXXIII

But what was strange — and a strong proof
 how great
 A blessing is sound sleep — Juanna lay
As fast as ever husband by his mate
 In holy matrimony snores away. 580
Not all the clamour broke her happy state
 Of slumber, ere they shook her, — so
 they say
At least, — and then she, too, unclosed her
 eyes,
And yawn'd a good deal with discreet sur-
 prise.

LXXIV

And now commenced a strict investigation,
 Which, as all spoke at once and more
 than once,
Conjecturing, wondering, asking a narra-
 tion,
 Alike might puzzle either wit or dunce
To answer in a very clear oration.
 Dudù had never pass'd for wanting sense,
But, being ' no orator as Brutus is,' 591
Could not at first expound what was amiss.

LXXV

At length she said, that in a slumber sound
 She dream'd a dream, of walking in a
 wood —
A ' wood obscure,' like that where Dante
 found
 Himself in at the age when all grow
 good;
Life's half-way house, where dames with
 virtue crown'd
 Run much less risk of lovers turning rude;
And that this wood was full of pleasant
 fruits,
And trees of goodly growth and spreading
 roots; 600

LXXVI

And in the midst a golden apple grew, —
 A most prodigious pippin, — but it hung

Rather too high and distant; that she threw
　　Her glances on it, and then, longing,
　　　　flung
Stones and whatever she could pick up, to
　　Bring down the fruit, which still per-
　　　　versely clung
To its own bough, and dangled yet in
　　sight,
But always at a most provoking height; —

LXXVII

That on a sudden, when she least had hope,
　　It fell down of its own accord before 610
Her feet; that her first movement was to
　　stoop
And pick it up, and bite it to the core;
　　That just as her young lip began to ope
Upon the golden fruit the vision bore,
　　A bee flew out and stung her to the heart,
And so — she awoke with a great scream
　　and start.

LXXVIII

All this she told with some confusion and
　　Dismay, the usual consequence of dreams
Of the unpleasant kind, with none at hand
　　To expound their vain and visionary
　　　　gleams.　　　　　　　　　　　　　620
I 've known some odd ones which seem'd
　　really plann'd
Prophetically, or that which one deems
　　A ' strange coincidence,' to use a phrase
By which such things are settled now-a-
　　days.

LXXIX

The damsels, who had thoughts of some
　　great harm,
　　Began, as is the consequence of fear,
To scold a little at the false alarm
　　That broke for nothing on their sleeping
　　　　ear.
The matron, too, was wroth to leave her
　　warm
　　Bed for the dream she had been obliged
　　　　to hear,　　　　　　　　　　　　　630
And chafed at poor Dudù, who only sigh'd,
And said that she was sorry she had cried.

LXXX

' I 've heard of stories of a cock and bull;
　　But visions of an apple and a bee,
To take us from our natural rest, and pull
　　The whole Oda from their beds at half-
　　　　past three,

Would make us think the moon is at its
　　full.
　　You surely are unwell, child ! we must
　　　　see,
To-morrow, what his Highness's physician
Will say to this hysteric of a vision.　640

LXXXI

' And poor Juanna, too — the child's first
　　night
　　Within these walls to be broke in upon
With such a clamour ! I had thought it
　　right
　　That the young stranger should not lie
　　　　alone,
And, as the quietest of all, she might
　　With you, Dudù, a good night's rest have
　　　　known;
But now I must transfer her to the charge
Of Lolah — though her couch is not so
　　large.'

LXXXII

Lolah's eyes sparkled at the proposition;
　　But poor Dudù, with large drops in her
　　　　own,　　　　　　　　　　　　　　650
Resulting from the scolding or the vision,
　　Implored that present pardon might be
　　　　shown
For this first fault, and that on no condition
　　(She added in a soft and piteous tone)
Juanna should be taken from her, and
　　Her future dreams should all be kept in
　　　　hand.

LXXXIII

She promised never more to have a dream,
　　At least to dream so loudly as just now;
She wonder'd at herself how she could
　　scream —
　　'T was foolish, nervous, as she must
　　　　allow,　　　　　　　　　　　　　660
A fond hallucination, and a theme
　　For laughter — but she felt her spirits
　　　　low,
And begg'd they would excuse her; she 'd
　　get over
This weakness in a few hours, and recover.

LXXXIV

And here Juanna kindly interposed,
　　And said she felt herself extremely well
Where she then was, as her sound sleep dis-
　　closed
　　When all around rang like a tocsin bell:

She did not find herself the least disposed
 To quit her gentle partner, and to dwell
Apart from one who had no sin to show, 671
Save that of dreaming once ' mal-à-propos.'

LXXXV

As thus Juanna spoke, Dudù turn'd round
 And hid her face within Juanna's breast:
Her neck alone was seen, but that was found
 The colour of a budding rose's crest.
I can't tell why she blush'd, nor can expound
 The mystery of this rupture of their rest;
All that I know is, that the facts I state
Are true as truth has ever been of late. 680

LXXXVI

And so good night to them, — or, if you will,
 Good morrow — for the cock had crown, and light
Began to clothe each Asiatic hill,
 And the mosque crescent struggled into sight
Of the long caravan, which in the chill
 Of dewy dawn wound slowly round each height
That stretches to the stony belt, which girds
Asia, where Kaff looks down upon the Kurds.

LXXXVII

With the first ray, or rather grey of morn,
 Gulbeyaz rose from restlessness; and pale
As passion rises, with its bosom worn, 691
 Array'd herself with mantle, gem, and veil.
The nightingale that sings with the deep thorn,
 Which fable places in her breast of wail,
Is lighter far of heart and voice than those
Whose headlong passions form their proper woes.

LXXXVIII

And that 's the moral of this composition,
 If people would but see its real drift; —
But *that* they will not do without suspicion,
 Because all gentle readers have the gift
Of closing 'gainst the light their orbs of vision; 701
 While gentle writers also love to lift
Their voices 'gainst each other, which is natural,
The numbers are too great for them to flatter all.

LXXXIX

Rose the sultana from a bed of splendour,
 Softer than the soft Sybarite's, who cried
Aloud because his feelings were too tender
 To brook a ruffled rose-leaf by his side, —
So beautiful that art could little mend her,
 Though pale with conflicts between love and pride; — 710
So agitated was she with her error,
She did not even look into the mirror.

XC

Also arose about the self-same time,
 Perhaps a little later, her great lord,
Master of thirty kingdoms so sublime,
 And of a wife by whom he was abhorr'd;
A thing of much less import in that clime —
 At least to those of incomes which afford
The filling up their whole connubial cargo —
Than where two wives are under an embargo. 720

XCI

He did not think much on the matter, nor
 Indeed on any other: as a man
He liked to have a handsome paramour
 At hand, as one may like to have a fan,
And therefore of Circassians had good store,
 As an amusement after the Divan;
Though an unusual fit of love, or duty,
Had made him lately bask in his bride's beauty.

XCII

And now he rose; and after due ablutions
 Exacted by the customs of the East, 730
And prayers and other pious evolutions,
 He drank six cups of coffee at the least,
And then withdrew to hear about the Russians,
 Whose victories had recently increased
In Catherine's reign, whom glory still adores,
Aε greatest of all sovereigns and w——s.

XCIII

But oh, thou grand legitimate Alexander !
 Her son's son, let not this last phrase offend
Thine ear, if it should reach — and now rhymes wander
 Almost as far as Petersburgh and lend 740
A dreadful impulse to each loud meander
 Of murmuring Liberty's wide waves, which blend

Their roar even with the Baltic's — so you
 be
Your father's son, 't is quite enough for me.

XCIV

To call men love-begotten or proclaim
 Their mothers as the antipodes of Timon,
That hater of mankind, would be a shame,
 A libel, or whate'er you please to rhyme
 on:
But people's ancestors are history's game;
 And if one lady's slip could leave a crime
 on 750
All generations, I should like to know
What pedigree the best would have to
 show ?

XCV

Had Catherine and the sultan understood
 Their own true interests, which kings
 rarely know
Until 't is taught by lessons rather rude,
 There was a way to end their strife,
 although
Perhaps precarious, had they but thought
 good,
 Without the aid of prince or plenipo:
She to dismiss her guards and he his haram,
And for their other matters, meet and share
 'em. 760

XCVI

But as it was, his Highness had to hold
 His daily council upon ways and means
How to encounter with this martial scold,
 This modern Amazon and queen of queans;
And the perplexity could not be told
 Of all the pillars of the state, which leans
Sometimes a little heavy on the backs
Of those who cannot lay on a new tax.

XCVII

Meantime Gulbeyaz, when her king was
 gone,
 Retired into her boudoir, a sweet place
For love or breakfast; private, pleasing,
 lone, 771
 And rich with all contrivances which
 grace
Those gay recesses: — many a precious
 stone
 Sparkled along its roof, and many a
 vase
Of porcelain held in the fetter'd flowers,
Those captive soothers of a captive's hours.

XCVIII

Mother of pearl, and porphyry, and marble,
 Vied with each other on this costly spot;
And singing birds without were heard to
 warble;
 And the stain'd glass which lighted this
 fair grot 780
Varied each ray; — but all descriptions
 garble
The true effect, and so we had better not
Be too minute; an outline is the best, —
A lively reader's fancy does the rest.

XCIX

And here she summon'd Baba, and required
 Don Juan at his hands, and information
Of what had pass'd since all the slaves
 retired,
 And whether he had occupied their
 station;
If matters had been managed as desired,
 And his disguise with due consideration
Kept up; and above all, the where and how
He had pass'd the night, was what she
 wish'd to know. 792

C

Baba, with some embarrassment, replied
 To this long catechism of questions, ask'd
More easily than answer'd, — that he had
 tried
 His best to obey in what he had been
 task'd;
But there seem'd something that he wish'd
 to hide,
 Which hesitation more betray'd than
 mask'd;
He scratch'd his ear, the infallible resource
To which embarrass'd people have recourse.

CI

Gulbeyaz was no model of true patience,
 Nor much disposed to wait in word or
 deed; 802
She liked quick answers in all conversations;
 And when she saw him stumbling like a
 steed
In his replies, she puzzled him for fresh
 ones;
 And as his speech grew still more broken-
 kneed,
Her cheek began to flush, her eyes to
 sparkle,
And her proud brow's blue veins to swell
 and darkle.

CII

When Baba saw these symptoms, which he
 knew
 To bode him no great good, he deprecated
Her anger, and beseech'd she 'd hear him
 through — 811
 He could not help the thing which he
 related:
Then out it came at length, that to Dudù
 Juan was given in charge, as hath been
 stated;
But not by Baba's fault, he said, and swore on
The holy camel's hump, besides the Koran.

CIII

The chief dame of the Oda, upon whom
 The discipline of the whole haram bore,
As soon as they re-enter'd their own room,
 For Baba's function stopt short at the
 door, 820
Had settled all; nor could he then presume
 (The aforesaid Baba) just then to do
 more,
Without exciting such suspicion as
Might make the matter still worse than it
 was.

CIV

He hoped, indeed he thought, he could be
 sure
 Juan had not betray'd himself; in fact
'T was certain that his conduct had been
 pure,
 Because a foolish or imprudent act
Would not alone have made him insecure,
 But ended in his being found out and
 sack'd,
And thrown into the sea. — Thus Baba
 spoke 831
Of all save Dudù's dream, which was no
 joke.

CV

This he discreetly kept in the background,
 And talk'd away — and might have talk'd
 till now,
For any further answer that he found,
 So deep an anguish wrung Gulbeyaz'
 brow:
Her cheek turn'd ashes, ears rung, brain
 whirl'd round,
 As if she had received a sudden blow,
And the heart's dew of pain sprang fast and
 chilly 839
O'er her fair front, like Morning's on a lily.

CVI

Although she was not of the fainting sort,
 Baba thought she would faint, but there
 he err'd —
It was but a convulsion, which though
 short
 Can never be described; we all have
 heard,
And some of us have felt thus ' all amort,'
 When things beyond the common have
 occurr'd; —
Gulbeyaz proved in that brief agony
What she could ne'er express — then how
 should I ?

CVII

She stood a moment as a Pythoness
 Stands on her tripod, agonised, and full
Of inspiration gather'd from distress, 851
 When all the heart-strings like wild
 horses pull
The heart asunder ; — then, as more or less
 Their speed abated or their strength grew
 dull,
She sunk down on her seat by slow degrees,
And bow'd her throbbing head o'er trem-
 bling knees.

CVIII

Her face declined and was unseen; her hair
 Fell in long tresses like the weeping wil-
 low,
Sweeping the marble underneath her chair,
 Or rather sofa (for it was all pillow, 860
A low soft ottoman), and black despair
 Stirr'd up and down her bosom like a bil-
 low,
Which rushes to some shore whose shingles
 check
Its farther course, but must receive its
 wreck.

CIX

Her head hung down, and her long hair in
 stooping
 Conceal'd her features better than a veil;
And one hand o'er the ottoman lay droop-
 ing,
 White, waxen, and as alabaster pale :
Would that I were a painter! to be grouping
 All that a poet drags into detail ! 870
Oh that my words were colours ! but their
 tints
May serve perhaps as outlines or slight
 hints.

CX

Baba, who knew by experience when to
talk
 And when to hold his tongue, now held
 it till
This passion might blow o'er, nor dared to
balk
 Gulbeyaz' taciturn or speaking will.
At length she rose up, and began to walk
 Slowly along the room, but silent still,
And her brow clear'd, but not her troubled
eye;
The wind was down, but still the sea ran
high. 880

CXI

She stopp'd, and raised her head to speak —
 but paused,
 And then moved on again with rapid
 pace;
Then slacken'd it, which is the march most
 caused
 By deep emotion: — you may sometimes
 trace
A feeling in each footstep, as disclosed
 By Sallust in his Catiline, who, chased
By all the demons of all passions, show'd
Their work even by the way in which he
trode.

CXII

Gulbeyaz stopp'd and beckon'd Baba: —
 'Slave !
 Bring the two slaves !' she said in a low
 tone, 890
But one which Baba did not like to brave,
 And yet he shudder'd, and seem'd rather
 prone
To prove reluctant, and begg'd leave to
 crave
 (Though he well knew the meaning) to
 be shown
What slaves her highness wish'd to indi-
cate,
For fear of any error, like the late.

CXIII

'The Georgian and her paramour,' replied
 The imperial bride — and added, 'Let
 the boat
Be ready by the secret portal's side:
 You know the rest.' The words stuck in
 her throat, 900
Despite her injured love and fiery pride;
 And of this Baba willingly took note,

And begg'd by every hair of Mahomet's
beard,
She would revoke the order he had heard.

CXIV

'To hear is to obey,' he said; 'but still,
 Sultana, think upon the consequence:
It is not that I shall not all fulfil
 Your orders, even in their severest sense;
But such precipitation may end ill, 909
 Even at your own imperative expense:
I do not mean destruction and exposure,
In case of any premature disclosure;

CXV

'But your own feelings. Even should all
 the rest
 Be hidden by the rolling waves, which hide
Already many a once love-beaten breast
 Deep in the caverns of the deadly tide —
You love this boyish, new, seraglio guest,
 And if this violent remedy be tried —
Excuse my freedom, when I here assure you,
That killing him is not the way to cure
 you.' 920

CXVI

'What dost thou know of love or feeling ?
 — Wretch !
 Begone !' she cried, with kindling eyes
 — 'and do
My bidding !' Baba vanish'd, for to stretch
 His own remonstrance further he well
 knew
Might end in acting as his own 'Jack
 Ketch;'
 And though he wish'd extremely to get
 through
This awkward business without harm to
 others,
He still preferr'd his own neck to another's.

CXVII

Away he went then upon his commission,
 Growling and grumbling in good Turk-
 ish phrase 930
Against all women of whate'er condition,
 Especially sultanas and their ways;
Their obstinacy, pride, and indecision,
 Their never knowing their own mind two
 days,
The trouble that they gave, their immor-
ality,
Which made him daily bless his own neu-
trality.

CXVIII

And then he call'd his brethren to his aid,
 And sent one on a summons to the pair,
That they must instantly be well array'd,
 And above all be comb'd even to a hair,
And brought before the empress, who had
 made 941
 Inquiries after them with kindest care:
At which Dudù look'd strange, and Juan
 silly;
But go they must at once, and will I —
 nill I.

CXIX

And here I leave them at their preparation
 For the imperial presence, wherein
 whether
Gulbeyaz show'd them both commiseration,
 Or got rid of the parties altogether,
Like other angry ladies of her nation, —
 Are things the turning of a hair or fea-
 ther 950
May settle; but far be 't from me to antici-
 pate
In what way feminine caprice may dissipate.

CXX

I leave them for the present with good
 wishes,
 Though doubts of their well doing, to
 arrange
Another part of history; for the dishes
 Of this our banquet we must sometimes
 change;
And trusting Juan may escape the fishes,
 Although his situation now seems strange
And scarce secure, as such digressions *are*
 fair,
The Muse will take a little touch at war-
 fare. 960

CANTO THE SEVENTH

I

O LOVE! O Glory! what are ye who fly
 Around us ever, rarely to alight?
There 's not a meteor in the polar sky
 Of such transcendent and more fleeting
 flight.
Chill, and chain'd to cold earth, we lift on
 high
 Our eyes in search of either lovely light;
A thousand and a thousand colours they
Assume, then leave us on our freezing way.

II

And such as they are, such my present tale
 is,
 A non-descript and ever-varying rhyme,
A versified Aurora Borealis, 11
 Which flashes o'er a waste and icy clime.
When we know what all are, we must be-
 wail us,
 But ne'ertheless I hope it is no crime
To laugh at *all* things — for I wish to know
What, after *all*, are *all* things — but a *show?*

III

They accuse me — *Me* — the present writer
 of
 The present poem — of — I know not
 what —
A tendency to under-rate and scoff 19
 At human power and virtue, and all that;
And this they say in language rather rough.
 Good God! I wonder what they would be
 at!
I say no more than hath been said in Dante's
Verse, and by Solomon and by Cervantes;

IV

By Swift, by Machiavel, by Rochefoucault,
 By Fénelon, by Luther, and by Plato;
By Tillotson, and Wesley, and Rousseau,
 Who knew this life was not worth a potato.
'T is not their fault, nor mine, if this be
 so —
 For my part, I pretend not to be Cato, 30
Nor even Diogenes. — We live and die,
But which is best, you know no more than I.

V

Socrates said, our only knowledge was
 'To know that nothing could be known;'
 a pleasant
Science enough, which levels to an ass
 Each man of wisdom, future, past, or
 present.
Newton (that proverb of the mind), alas!
 Declared, with all his grand discoveries
 recent,
That he himself felt only 'like a youth
Picking up shells by the great ocean —
 Truth.' 40

VI

Ecclesiastes said, 'that all is vanity' —
 Most modern preachers say the same, or
 show it
By their examples of true Christianity:

In short, all know, or very soon may know
 it;
And in this scene of all-confess'd inanity,
 By saint, by sage, by preacher, and by
 poet,
Must I restrain me, through the fear of
 strife,
From holding up the nothingness of life ?

VII

Dogs, or men ! — for I flatter you in saying
 That ye are dogs — your betters far — ye
 may 50
Read, or read not, what I am now essaying
 To show ye what ye are in every way.
As little as the moon stops for the baying
 Of wolves, will the bright muse withdraw
 one ray
From out her skies — then howl your idle
 wrath !
While she still silvers o'er your gloomy path.

VIII

' Fierce loves and faithless wars ' — I am not
 sure
 If this be the right reading — 't is no
 matter;
The fact 's about the same, I am secure; 59
 I sing them both, and am about to batter
A town which did a famous siege endure,
 And was beleaguer'd both by land and
 water
By Souvaroff, or Anglicè Suwarrow,
Who loved blood as an alderman loves
 marrow.

IX

The fortress is call'd Ismail, and is placed
 Upon the Danube's left branch and left
 bank,
With buildings in the Oriental taste,
 But still a fortress of the foremost rank,
Or was at least, unless 't is since defaced,
 Which with your conquerors is a common
 prank: 70
It stands some eighty versts from the high
 sea,
And measures round of toises thousands
 three.

X

Within the extent of this fortification
 A borough is comprised along the height
Upon the left, which from its loftier station
 Commands the city, and upon its site

A Greek had raised around this elevation
 A quantity of palisades *upright,*
So placed as to *impede* the fire of those
Who held the place, and to *assist* the foe's.

XI

This circumstance may serve to give a
 notion 81
 Of the high talents of this new Vauban:
But the town ditch below was deep as ocean,
 The rampart higher than you 'd wish to
 hang:
But then there was a great want of pre-
 caution
 (Prithee, excuse this engineering slang),
Nor work advanced, nor cover'd way was
 there,
To hint at least ' Here is no thoroughfare.'

XII

But a stone bastion, with a narrow gorge,
 And walls as thick as most skulls born as
 yet; 90
Two batteries, cap-à-pie, as our St. George,
 Case-mated one, and t' other 'à barbette,'
Of Danube's bank took formidable charge;
 While two and twenty cannon duly set
Rose over the town's right side, in bristling
 tier,
Forty feet high, upon a cavalier.

XIII

But from the river the town 's open quite,
 Because the Turks could never be per-
 suaded
A Russian vessel e'er would heave in sight;
 And such their creed was, till they were
 invaded, 100
When it grew rather late to set things
 right.
 But as the Danube could not well be
 waded,
They look'd upon the Muscovite flotilla,
And only shouted, ' Allah !' and ' Bis
 Millah ! '

XIV

The Russians now were ready to attack:
 But oh, ye goddesses of war and glory !
How shall I spell the name of each Cos-
 sacque
 Who were immortal, could one tell their
 story ?
Alas ! what to their memory can lack ?
 Achilles' self was not more grim and gory

Than thousands of this new and polish'd nation, 111
Whose names want nothing but — pronunciation.

XV

Still I 'll record a few, if but to increase
 Our euphony: there was Strongenoff, and Strokonoff,
Meknop, Serge Lwow, Arsniew of modern Greece,
 And Tschitsshakoff, and Roguenoff, and Chokenoff,
And others of twelve consonants apiece;
 And more might be found out, if I could poke enough
Into gazettes; but Fame (capricious strumpet),
It seems, has got an ear as well as trumpet, 120

XVI

And cannot tune those discords of narration,
 Which may be names at Moscow, into rhyme;
Yet there were several worth commemoration,
 As e'er was virgin of a nuptial chime;
Soft words, too, fitted for the peroration
 Of Londonderry drawling against time,
Ending in 'ischskin,' 'ousckin,' 'iffskchy,' 'ouski,'
Of whom we can insert but Rousamouski,

XVII

Scherematoff and Chrematoff, Koklophti,
 Koclobski, Kourakin, and Mouskin Pouskin, 130
All proper men of weapons, as e'er scoff'd high
 Against a foe, or ran a sabre through skin:
Little cared they for Mahomet or Mufti,
 Unless to make their kettle-drums a new skin
Out of their hides, if parchment had grown dear,
And no more handy substitute been near.

XVIII

Then there were foreigners of much renown,
 Of various nations, and all volunteers;
Not fighting for their country or its crown,
 But wishing to be one day brigadiers; 140

Also to have the sacking of a town, —
 A pleasant thing to young men at their years.
'Mongst them were several Englishmen of pith,
Sixteen call'd Thomson, and nineteen named Smith.

XIX

Jack Thomson and Bill Thomson; all the rest
 Had been call'd ' Jemmy,' after the great bard ;
I don't know whether they had arms or crest,
 But such a godfather's as good a card.
Three of the Smiths were Peters; but the best
 Amongst them all, hard blows to inflict or ward, 150
Was he, since so renown'd ' in country quarters
At Halifax;' but now he served the Tartars.

XX

The rest were Jacks and Gills and Wills and Bills;
 But when I 've added that the elder Jack Smith
Was born in Cumberland among the hills,
 And that his father was an honest blacksmith,
I 've said all I know of a name that fills
 Three lines of the despatch in taking ' Schmacksmith,'
A village of Moldavia's waste, wherein
He fell, immortal in a bulletin. 160

XXI

I wonder (although Mars no doubt 's a god I
 Praise) if a man's name in a bulletin
May make up for a bullet in his body ?
 I hope this little question is no sin,
Because, though I am but a simple noddy,
 I think one Shakspeare puts the same thought in
The mouth of some one in his plays so doting,
Which many people pass for wits by quoting.

XXII

Then there were Frenchmen, gallant, young, and gay :
 But I 'm too great a patriot to record 170

Their Gallic names upon a glorious day;
 I 'd rather tell ten lies than say a word
Of truth; — such truths are treason; they
 betray
 Their country; and as traitors are ab-
 horr'd
Who name the French in English, save to
 show
How Peace should make John Bull the
 Frenchman's foe.

XXIII

The Russians, having built two batteries on
 An isle near Ismail, had two ends in
 view;
The first was to bombard it, and knock
 down
 The public buildings and the private
 too, 180
No matter what poor souls might be un-
 done.
 The city's shape suggested this, 't is true;
Form'd like an amphitheatre, each dwell-
 ing
Presented a fine mark to throw a shell in.

XXIV

The second object was to profit by
 The moment of the general consterna-
 tion,
To attack the Turk's flotilla, which lay
 nigh
 Extremely tranquil, anchor'd at its sta-
 tion:
But a third motive was as probably
 To frighten them into capitulation; 190
A phantasy which sometimes seizes war-
 riors,
Unless they are game as bull-dogs and fox-
 terriers.

XXV

A habit rather blamable, which is
 That of despising those we combat with,
Common in many cases, was in this
 The cause of killing Tchitchitzkoff and
 Smith;
One of the valorous ' Smiths' whom we
 shall miss
 Out of those nineteen who late rhymed
 to ' pith;'
But 't is a name so spread o'er ' Sir' and
 ' Madam,'
That one would think the first who bore it
 ' Adam.' 200

XXVI

The Russian batteries were incomplete,
 Because they were constructed in a hurry;
Thus the same cause which makes a verse
 want feet,
 And throws a cloud o'er Longman and
 John Murray,
When the sale of new books is not so fleet
 As they who print them think is neces-
 sary,
May likewise put off for a time what story
Sometimes calls ' murder,' and at others
 ' glory.'

XXVII

Whether it was their engineer's stupidity,
 Their haste, or waste, I neither know nor
 care, 210
Or some contractor's personal cupidity,
 Saving his soul by cheating in the ware
Of homicide, but there was no solidity
 In the new batteries erected there;
They either miss'd, or they were never
 miss'd,
And added greatly to the missing list.

XXVIII

A sad miscalculation about distance
 Made all their naval matters incorrect;
Three fireships lost their amiable existence
 Before they reach'd a spot to take
 effect: 220
The match was lit too soon, and no assist-
 ance
 Could remedy this lubberly defect;
They blew up in the middle of the river,
While, though 't was dawn, the Turks slept
 fast as ever.

XXIX

At seven they rose, however, and survey'd
 The Russ flotilla getting under way;
'T was nine, when still advancing undis-
 may'd,
 Within a cable's length their vessels lay
Off Ismail, and commenced a cannonade,
 Which was return'd with interest, I may
 say, 230
And by a fire of musketry and grape,
And shells and shot of every size and
 shape.

XXX

For six hours bore they without intermission
 The Turkish fire, and aided by their own

Land batteries, work'd their guns with great
 precision:
 At length they found mere cannonade
 alone
By no means would produce the town's
 submission,
 And made a signal to retreat at one.
One bark blew up, a second near the works
Running aground, was taken by the
 Turks. 240

XXXI

The Moslem, too, had lost both ships and
 men;
 But when they saw the enemy retire,
Their Delhis mann'd some boats, and sail'd
 again,
 And gall'd the Russians with a heavy
 fire,
And tried to make a landing on the main;
 But here the effect fell short of their
 desire:
Count Damas drove them back into the water
Pell-mell, and with a whole gazette of
 slaughter.

XXXII

'If' (says the historian here) 'I could
 report
 All that the Russians did upon this day, 250
I think that several volumes would fall
 short,
 And I should still have many things to
 say;'
And so he says no more — but pays his
 court
 To some distinguish'd strangers in that
 fray;
The Prince de Ligne, and Langeron, and
 Damas,
Names great as any that the roll of Fame
 has.

XXXIII

This being the case, may show us what
 Fame *is*:
 For out of these three '*preux Chevaliers*,'
 how
Many of common readers give a guess
 That such existed? (and they may live
 now 260
For aught we know.) Renown's all hit or
 miss;
 There's fortune even in fame, we must
 allow.

'Tis true the Memoirs of the Prince de
 Ligne
Have half withdrawn from *him* oblivion's
 screen.

XXXIV

But here are men who fought in gallant
 actions
 As gallantly as ever heroes fought,
But buried in the heap of such transactions
 Their names are rarely found, nor often
 sought.
Thus even good fame may suffer sad con-
 tractions,
 And is extinguish'd sooner than she
 ought: 270
Of all our modern battles, I will bet
You can't repeat nine names from each
 Gazette.

XXXV

In short, this last attack, though rich in
 glory,
 Show'd that *somewhere, somehow*, there
 was a fault,
And Admiral Ribas (known in Russian
 story)
 Most strongly recommended an assault;
In which he was opposed by young and
 hoary,
 Which made a long debate; but I must
 halt,
For if I wrote down every warrior's speech,
I doubt few readers e'er would mount the
 breach. 280

XXXVI

There was a man, if that he was a man,
 Not that his manhood could be call'd in
 question,
For had he not been Hercules, his span
 Had been as short in youth as indigestion
Made his last illness, when, all worn and
 wan,
 He died beneath a tree, as much unblest
 on
The soil of the green province he had
 wasted,
As e'er was locust on the land it blasted.

XXXVII

This was Potemkin — a great thing in days
 When homicide and harlotry made great;
If stars and titles could entail long praise,
 His glory might half equal his estate. 292

This fellow, being six foot high, could raise
 A kind of phantasy proportionate
In the then sovereign of the Russian people,
 Who measured men as you would do a
 steeple.

XXXVIII

While things were in abeyance, Ribas sent
 A courier to the prince, and he succeeded
In ordering matters after his own bent;
 I cannot tell the way in which he pleaded,
But shortly he had cause to be content. 301
 In the mean time, the batteries proceeded,
And fourscore cannon on the Danube's
 border
Were briskly fired and answer'd in due
 order.

XXXIX

But on the thirteenth, when already part
 Of the troops were embark'd, the siege
 to raise,
A courier on the spur inspired new heart
 Into all panters for newspaper praise,
As well as dilettanti in war's art,
 By his despatches couch'd in pithy phrase;
Announcing the appointment of that lover
 of 311
Battles to the command, Field-Marshal Sou-
 varoff.

XL

The letter of the prince to the same marshal
 Was worthy of a Spartan, had the cause
Been one to which a good heart could be
 partial —
Defence of freedom, country, or of laws;
But as it was mere lust of power to o'er-
 arch all
 With its proud brow, it merits slight ap-
 plause,
Save for its style, which said, all in a trice,
' You will take Ismail at whatever price.'

XLI

' Let there be light ! said God, and there
 was light !' 321
 ' Let there be blood !' says man, and
 there 's a sea !
The fiat of this spoil'd child of the Night
 (For Day ne'er saw his merits) could de-
 cree
More evil in an hour, than thirty bright
 Summers could renovate, though they
 should be

Lovely as those which ripen'd Eden's fruit;
For war cuts up not only branch, but root.

XLII

Our friends the Turks, who with loud ' Al-
 lahs ' now
 Began to signalise the Russ retreat, 330
Were damnably mistaken; few are slow
 In thinking that their enemy is beat
(Or *beaten*, if *you* insist on grammar, though
 I never think about it in a heat),
But here I say the Turks were much mis-
 taken,
Who hating hogs, yet wish'd to save their
 bacon.

XLIII

For, on the sixteenth, at full gallop, drew
 In sight two horsemen, who were deem'd
 Cossacques
For some time, till they came in nearer
 view.
 They had but little baggage at their
 backs, 340
For there were but *three* shirts between the
 two;
 But on they rode upon two Ukraine
 hacks,
Till, in approaching, were at length descried
In this plain pair, Suwarrow and his guide.

XLIV

' Great joy to London now !' says some great
 fool,
 When London had a grand illumination,
Which to that bottle-conjurer, John Bull,
 Is of all dreams the first hallucination;
So that the streets of colour'd lamps are
 full,
 That Sage (*said* John) surrenders at dis-
 cretion 350
His purse, his soul, his sense, and even his
 nonsense,
To gratify, like a huge moth, this *one* sense.

XLV

'T is strange that he should farther ' damn
 his eyes,'
 For they are damn'd; that once all-fa-
 mous oath
Is to the devil now no farther prize,
 Since John has lately lost the use of both.
Debt he calls wealth, and taxes Paradise;
 And Famine, with her gaunt and bony
 growth,

Which stare him in the face, he won't ex-
amine,
Or swears that Ceres hath begotten Fam-
ine. 360

XLVI

But to the tale: — great joy unto the camp!
 To Russian, Tartar, English, French,
 Cossacque,
O'er whom Suwarrow shone like a gas lamp,
 Presaging a most luminous attack;
Or like a wisp along the marsh so damp,
 Which leads beholders on a boggy walk,
He flitted to and fro a dancing light,
Which all who saw it follow'd, wrong or
 right.

XLVII

But certes matters took a different face;
 There was enthusiasm and much ap-
 plause, 370
The fleet and camp saluted with great
 grace,
 And all presaged good fortune to their
 cause.
Within a cannon-shot length of the place
 They drew, constructed ladders, repair'd
 flaws
In former works, made new, prepared fas-
 cines,
And all kinds of benevolent machines.

XLVIII

'T is thus the spirit of a single mind
 Makes that of multitudes take one direc-
 tion,
As roll the waters to the breathing wind,
 Or roams the herd beneath the bull's pro-
 tection; 380
Or as a little dog will lead the blind,
 Or a bell-wether form the flock's connec-
 tion
By tinkling sounds, when they go forth to
 victual;
Such is the sway of your great men o'er
 little.

XLIX

The whole camp rung with joy; you would
 have thought
 That they were going to a marriage
 feast
(This metaphor, I think, holds good as
 aught,
 Since there is discord after both at least):

There was not now a luggage boy but sought
 Danger and spoil with ardour much in-
 creased; 390
And why? because a little — odd — old
 man,
 Stript to his shirt, was come to lead the van.

L

But so it was; and every preparation
 Was made with all alacrity: the first
Detachment of three columns took its sta-
 tion,
 And waited but the signal's voice to burst
Upon the foe: the second's ordination
 Was also in three columns, with a thirst
For glory gaping o'er a sea of slaughter:
The third, in columns two, attack'd by
 water. 400

LI

New batteries were erected, and was held
 A general council, in which unanimity,
That stranger to most councils, here pre-
 vail'd,
 As sometimes happens in a great extrem-
 ity;
And every difficulty being dispell'd,
 Glory began to dawn with due sublimity,
While Souvaroff, determined to obtain it,
Was teaching his recruits to use the bayonet.

LII

It is an actual fact, that he, commander
 In chief, in proper person deign'd to
 drill 410
The awkward squad, and could afford to
 squander
 His time, a corporal's duty to fulfil:
Just as you 'd break a sucking salamander
 To swallow flame, and never take it ill:
He show'd them how to mount a ladder
 (which
Was not like Jacob's) or to cross a ditch.

LIII

Also he dress'd up, for the nonce, fascines
 Like men with turbans, scimitars, and
 dirks,
And made them charge with bayonet these
 machines,
 By way of lesson against actual Turks:
And when well practised in these mimic
 scenes, 421
 He judged them proper to assail the
 works;

At which your wise men sneer'd in phrases
witty:
He made no answer; but he took the city.

LIV

Most things were in this posture on the eve
Of the assault, and all the camp was in
A stern repose; which you would scarce con-
ceive;
Yet men resolved to dash through thick
and thin
Are very silent when they once believe
That all is settled: — there was little din,
For some were thinking of their home and
friends, 431
And others of themselves and latter ends.

LV

Suwarrow chiefly was on the alert,
Surveying, drilling, ordering, jesting, pon-
dering;
For the man was, we safely may assert,
A thing to wonder at beyond most won-
dering;
Hero, buffoon, half-demon, and half-dirt,
Praying, instructing, desolating, plunder-
ing;
Now Mars, now Momus; and when bent to
storm
A fortress, Harlequin in uniform. 440

LVI

The day before the assault, while upon drill —
For this great conqueror play'd the cor-
poral —
Some Cossacques, hovering like hawks
round a hill,
Had met a party towards the twilight's
fall,
One of whom spoke their tongue — or well
or ill,
'T was much that he was understood at all;
But whether from his voice, or speech, or
manner,
They found that he had fought beneath
their banner.

LVII

Whereon immediately at his request
They brought him and his comrades to
head-quarters; 450
Their dress was Moslem, but you might
have guess'd
That these were merely masquerading
Tartars,

And that beneath each Turkish-fashion'd
vest
Lurk'd Christianity; which sometimes
barters
Her inward grace for outward show, and
makes
It difficult to shun some strange mistakes.

LVIII

Suwarrow, who was standing in his shirt
Before a company of Calmucks, drilling,
Exclaiming, fooling, swearing at the inert,
And lecturing on the noble art of kill-
ing, — 460
For deeming human clay but common dirt,
This great philosopher was thus instilling
His maxims, which to martial comprehen-
sion
Proved death in battle equal to a pension; —

LIX

Suwarrow, when he saw this company
Of Cossacques and their prey, turn'd
round and cast
Upon them his slow brow and piercing
eye :—
'Whence come ye?' — 'From Constanti-
nople last,
Captives just now escaped,' was the reply.
'What are ye?' — 'What you see us.'
Briefly pass'd 470
This dialogue; for he who answer'd knew
To whom he spoke, and made his words
but few.

LX

'Your names?' — 'Mine's Johnson, and
my comrade's Juan;
The other two are women, and the third
Is neither man nor woman.' The chief
threw on
The party a slight glance, then said, 'I
have heard
Your name before, the second is a new one:
To bring the other three here was absurd:
But let that pass: — I think I have heard
your name
In the Nikolaiew regiment?' — 'The
same.' 480

LXI

'You served at Widdin?' — 'Yes.' — 'You
led the attack?'
'I did.' — 'What next?' — 'I really
hardly know.'

You were the first i' the breach ? ' — ' I was
 not slack
 At least to follow those who might be so.'
' What follow'd ? ' — ' A shot laid me on my
 back,
 And I became a prisoner to the foe.'
' You shall have vengeance, for the town
 surrounded
Is twice as strong as that where you were
 wounded.

LXII

' Where will you serve ? ' — ' Where'er you
 please.' — ' I know
 You like to be the hope of the forlorn,
And doubtless would be foremost on the
 foe 491
 After the hardships you 've already borne.
And this young fellow — say what can he
 do ?
 He with the beardless chin and garments
 torn ? '
' Why, general, if he hath no greater fault
In war than love, he had better lead the
 assault.'

LXIII

' He shall if that he dare.' Here Juan
 bow'd
 Low as the compliment deserved. Suwar-
 row
Continued: ' Your old regiment 's allow'd,
 By special providence, to lead to-morrow,
Or it may be to-night, the assault: I have
 vow'd 501
 To several saints, that shortly plough or
 harrow
Shall pass o'er what was Ismail, and its tusk
Be unimpeded by the proudest mosque.

LXIV

' So now, my lads, for glory ! ' — Here he
 turn'd
 And drill'd away in the most classic
 Russian,
Until each high, heroic bosom burn'd
 For cash and conquest, as if from a
 cushion
A preacher had held forth (who nobly
 spurn'd
 All earthly goods save tithes) and bade
 them push on 510
To slay the Pagans who resisted, battering
The armies of the Christian Empress
 Catherine.

LXV

Johnson, who knew by this long colloquy
 Himself a favourite, ventured to ad-
 dress
Suwarrow, though engaged with accents
 high
 In his resumed amusement. ' I confess
My debt in being thus allow'd to die
 Among the foremost; but if you 'd ex-
 press
Explicitly our several posts, my friend 519
And self would know what duty to attend.'

LXVI

' Right ! I was busy, and forgot. Why, you
 Will join your former regiment, which
 should be
Now under arms. Ho ! Katskoff, take him
 to
 (Here he call'd up a Polish orderly)
His post, I mean the regiment Nikolaiew:
 The stranger stripling may remain with
 me;
He 's a fine boy. The women may be
 sent
To the other baggage, or to the sick tent.'

LXVII

But here a sort of scene began to ensue:
 The ladies, — who by no means had been
 bred 530
To be disposed of in a way so new,
 Although their haram education led
Doubtless to that of doctrines the most
 true,
 Passive obedience, — now raised up the
 head,
With flashing eyes and starting tears, and
 flung
Their arms, as hens their wings about their
 young,

LXVIII

O'er the promoted couple of brave men
 Who were thus honour'd by the greatest
 chief
That ever peopled hell with heroes slain,
 Or plunged a province or a realm in grief.
Oh, foolish mortals ! Always taught in
 vain ! 541
 Oh, glorious laurel ! since for one sole
 leaf
Of thine imaginary deathless tree,
Of blood and tears must flow the unebbing
 sea.

LXIX

Suwarrow, who had small regard for tears,
　And not much sympathy for blood, sur-
　　vey'd
The women with their hair about their
　ears
　And natural agonies, with a slight shade
Of feeling: for however habit sears
　Men's hearts against whole millions, when
　　their trade　　　　　　　　　　550
Is butchery, sometimes a single sorrow
Will touch even heroes — and such was
　Suwarrow.

LXX

He said, — and in the kindest Calmuck
　tone, —
　'Why, Johnson, what the devil do you
　mean
By bringing women here ? They shall be
　shown
　All the attention possible, and seen
In safety to the waggons, where alone
　In fact they can be safe. You should
　have been
Aware this kind of baggage never thrives:
Save wed a year, I hate recruits with
　wives.'　　　　　　　　　　560

LXXI

'May it please your excellency,' thus re-
　plied
　Our British friend, 'these are the wives
　of others,
And not our own. I am too qualified
　By service with my military brothers
To break the rules by bringing one's own
　bride
　Into a camp: I know that nought so
　bothers
The hearts of the heroic on a charge,
As leaving a small family at large.

LXXII

'But these are but two Turkish ladies,
　who
　With their attendant aided our escape, 570
And afterwards accompanied us through
　A thousand perils in this dubious shape.
To me this kind of life is not so new;
　To them, poor things, it is an awkward
　scrape.
I therefore, if you wish me to fight freely,
Request that they may both be used gen-
　teelly.'

LXXIII

Meantime these two poor girls, with swim-
　ming eyes,
　Look'd on as if in doubt if they could trust
Their own protectors; nor was their surprise
　Less than their grief (and truly not less
　just)　　　　　　　　　　580
To see an old man, rather wild than wise
　In aspect, plainly clad, besmear'd with
　dust,
Stript to his waistcoat, and *that not* too clean,
More fear'd than all the sultans ever seen.

LXXIV

For every thing seem'd resting on his nod,
　As they could read in all eyes. Now to
　them,
Who were accustom'd, as a sort of god,
　To see the sultan, rich in many a gem,
Like an imperial peacock stalk abroad 589
　(That royal bird, whose tail's a diadem),
With all the pomp of power, it was a doubt
How power could condescend to do without.

LXXV

John Johnson, seeing their extreme dismay,
　Though little versed in feelings oriental,
Suggested some slight comfort in his way:
　Don Juan, who was much more senti-
　mental,
Swore they should see him by the dawn of
　day,
　Or that the Russian army should repent all:
And, strange to say, they found some con-
　solation
In this — for females like exaggeration. 600

LXXVI

And then with tears, and sighs, and some
　slight kisses,
　They parted for the present — these to
　await,
According to the artillery's hits or misses,
　What sages call Chance, Providence, or
　Fate
(Uncertainty is one of many blisses,
　A mortgage on Humanity's estate) —
While their beloved friends began to arm,
To burn a town which never did them harm.

LXXVII

Suwarrow, — who but saw things in the
　gross,
　Being much too gross to see them in de-
　tail,　　　　　　　　　　610

Who calculated life as so much dross,
 And as the wind a widow'd nation's wail,
And cared as little for his army's loss
 (So that their efforts should at length
 prevail)
As wife and friends did for the boils of
 Job, —
What was 't to him to hear two women sob ?

LXXVIII

Nothing. — The work of glory still went on
 In preparations for a cannonade
As terrible as that of Ilion,
 If Homer had found mortars ready made;
But now, instead of slaying Priam's son, 621
 We only can but talk of escalade,
Bombs, drums, guns, bastions, batteries,
 bayonets, bullets, —
Hard words, which stick in the soft Muses'
 gullets.

LXXIX

Oh, thou eternal Homer ! who couldst
 charm
 All ears, though long; all ages, though so
 short,
By merely wielding with poetic arm
 Arms to which men will never more re-
 sort,
Unless gunpowder should be found to harm
 Much less than is the hope of every court,
Which now is leagued young Freedom to
 annoy; 631
But they will not find Liberty a Troy: —

LXXX

Oh, thou eternal Homer ! I have now
 To paint a siege, wherein more men were
 slain,
With deadlier engines and a speedier blow,
 Than in thy Greek gazette of that cam-
 paign;
And yet, like all men else, I must allow,
 To vie with thee would be about as
 vain
As for a brook to cope with ocean's flood;
But still we moderns equal you in blood; 640

LXXXI

If not in poetry, at least in fact;
 And fact is truth, the grand desideratum !
Of which, howe'er the Muse describes each
 act,
 There should be ne'ertheless a slight
 substratum.

But now the town is going to be attack'd;
 Great deeds are doing — how shall I
 relate 'em ?
Souls of immortal generals ! Phœbus
 watches
To colour up his rays from your despatches.

LXXXII

Oh, ye great bulletins of Bonaparte !
 Oh, ye less grand long lists of kill'd and
 wounded ! 650
Shade of Leonidas, who fought so hearty,
 When my poor Greece was once, as now,
 surrounded !
Oh, Cæsar's Commentaries ! now impart, ye
 Shadows of glory ! (lest I be confounded)
A portion of your fading twilight hues,
So beautiful, so fleeting, to the Muse.

LXXXIII

When I call 'fading' martial immortality,
 I mean, that every age and every year,
And almost every day, in sad reality, 659
 Some sucking hero is compell'd to rear,
Who, when we come to sum up the totality
 Of deeds to human happiness most dear,
Turns out to be a butcher in great busi-
 ness,
Afflicting young folks with a sort of dizzi-
 ness.

LXXXIV

Medals, rank, ribands, lace, embroidery,
 scarlet,
 Are things immortal to immortal man,
As purple to the Babylonian harlot:
 An uniform to boys is like a fan
To women; there is scarce a crimson varlet
 But deems himself the first in Glory's
 van. 670
But Glory's glory; and if you would find
What that is — ask the pig who sees the
 wind !

LXXXV

At least *he feels it*, and some say he *sees*,
 Because he runs before it like a pig;
Or, if that simple sentence should displease,
 Say, that he scuds before it like a brig,
A schooner, or — but it is time to ease
 This Canto, ere my Muse perceives
 fatigue.
The next shall ring a peal to shake all
 people,
Like a bob-major from a village steeple.

LXXXVI

Hark ! through the silence of the cold, dull
 night, 681
 The hum of armies gathering rank on
 rank !
Lo ! dusky masses steal in dubious sight
 Along the leaguer'd wall and bristling
 bank
Of the arm'd river, while with straggling
 light
 The stars peep through the vapours dim
 and dank,
Which curl in curious wreaths: — how soon
 the smoke
Of Hell shall pall them in a deeper cloak !

LXXXVII

Here pause we for the present — as even
 then
 That awful pause, dividing life from
 death, 690
Struck for an instant on the hearts of
 men,
 Thousands of whom were drawing their
 last breath !
A moment — and all will be life again !
 The march ! the charge ! the shouts of
 either faith !
Hurra ! and Allah ! and — one moment
 more,
The death-cry drowning in the battle's roar.

CANTO THE EIGHTH

I

OH blood and thunder ! and oh blood and
 wounds !
 These are but vulgar oaths, as you may
 deem,
Too gentle reader ! and most shocking
 sounds :
 And so they are; yet thus is Glory's
 dream
Unriddled, and as my true Muse expounds
 At present such things, since they are her
 theme,
So be they her inspirers ! Call them Mars,
Bellona, what you will — they mean but
 wars.

II

All was prepared — the fire, the sword, the
 men
 To wield them in their terrible array. 10

The army, like a lion from his den,
 March'd forth with nerve and sinews
 bent to slay, —
A human Hydra, issuing from its fen
 To breathe destruction on its winding
 way,
Whose heads were heroes, which cut off in
 vain
Immediately in others grew again.

III

History can only take things in the gross;
 But could we know them in detail, per-
 chance
In balancing the profit and the loss,
 War's merit it by no means might
 enhance, 20
To waste so much gold for a little dross,
 As hath been done, mere conquest to
 advance.
The drying up a single tear has more
Of honest fame, than shedding seas of gore.

IV

And why ? — because it brings self-appro-
 bation;
 Whereas the other, after all its glare,
Shouts, bridges, arches, pensions from a
 nation,
 Which (it may be) has not much left to
 spare,
A higher title, or a loftier station,
 Though they may make Corruption gape
 or stare, 30
Yet, in the end, except in Freedom's battles,
Are nothing but a child of Murder's rattles.

V

And such they are — and such they will be
 found :
 Not so Leonidas and Washington,
Whose every battle-field is holy ground,
 Which breathes of nations saved, not
 worlds undone.
How sweetly on the ear such echoes sound !
 While the mere victor's may appal or
 stun
The servile and the vain, such names will be
A watchword till the future shall be free.

VI

The night was dark, and the thick mist
 allow'd 41
 Nought to be seen save the artillery's
 flame,

Which arch'd the horizon like a fiery cloud,
 And in the Danube's waters shone the
 same —
A mirror'd hell! the volleying roar, and
 loud
 Long booming of each peal on peal, o'er-
 came
The ear far more than thunder; for Heaven's
 flashes
Spare, or smite rarely — man's make mil-
 lions ashes!

VII

The column order'd on the assault scarce
 pass'd 49
 Beyond the Russian batteries a few toises,
When up the bristling Moslem rose at
 last,
 Answering the Christian thunders with
 like voices:
Then one vast fire, air, earth, and stream
 embraced,
 Which rock'd as 't were beneath the
 mighty noises;
While the whole rampart blazed like Etna,
 when
The restless Titan hiccups in his den.

VIII

And one enormous shout of ' Allah!' rose
 In the same moment, loud as even the
 roar
Of war's most mortal engines, to their foes
 Hurling defiance: city, stream, and shore
Resounded ' Allah!' and the clouds which
 close 61
 With thick'ning canopy the conflict o'er,
Vibrate to the Eternal name. Hark!
 through
All sounds it pierceth ' Allah! Allah! Hu!'

IX

The columns were in movement one and
 all,
 But of the portion which attack'd by
 water,
Thicker than leaves the lives began to
 fall,
 Though led by Arseniew, that great son
 of slaughter,
As brave as ever faced both bomb and ball.
 ' Carnage ' (so Wordsworth tells you) ' is
 God's daughter:' 70
If *he* speak truth, she is Christ's sister, and
Just now behaved as in the Holy Land.

X

The Prince de Ligne was wounded in the
 knee;
 Count Chapeau-Bras, too, had a ball be-
 tween
His cap and head, which proves the head
 to be
 Aristocratic as was ever seen,
Because it then received no injury
 More than the cap; in fact, the ball could
 mean
No harm unto a right legitimate head:
' Ashes to ashes ' — why not lead to lead?

XI

Also the General Markow, Brigadier, 81
 Insisting on removal of *the prince*
Amidst some groaning thousands dying
 near, —
 All common fellows, who might writhe
 and wince,
And shriek for water into a deaf ear, —
 The General Markow, who could thus
 evince
His sympathy for rank, by the same token,
To teach him greater, had his own leg
 broken.

XII

Three hundred cannon threw up their
 emetic,
 And thirty thousand muskets flung their
 pills 90
Like hail, to make a bloody diuretic.
 Mortality! thou hast thy monthly bills;
Thy plagues, thy famines, thy physicians,
 yet tick,
 Like the death-watch, within our ears
 the ills
Past, present, and to come; — but all may
 yield
To the true portrait of one battle-field.

XIII

There the still varying pangs, which mul-
 tiply
 Until their very number makes men
 hard
By the infinities of agony,
 Which meet the gaze whate'er it may
 regard — 100
The groan, the roll in dust, the all-white
 eye
 Turn'd back within its socket, — these
 reward

Your rank and file by thousands, while the
 rest
May win perhaps a riband at the breast !

XIV

Yet I love glory; — glory 's a great thing: —
 Think what it is to be in your old age
Maintain'd at the expense of your good
 king:
 A moderate pension shakes full many a
 sage,
And heroes are but made for bards to sing,
 Which is still better; thus in verse to
 wage 110
Your wars eternally, besides enjoying
Half-pay for life, make mankind worth de-
 stroying.

XV

The troops, already disembark'd, push'd on
 To take a battery on the right; the oth-
 ers,
Who landed lower down, their landing done,
 Had set to work as briskly as their bro-
 thers:
Being grenadiers, they mounted one by
 one,
 Cheerful as children climb the breasts of
 mothers,
O'er the entrenchment and the palisade,
Quite orderly, as if upon parade. 120

XVI

And this was admirable; for so hot
 The fire was, that were red Vesuvius
 loaded,
Besides its lava, with all sorts of shot
 And shells or hells, it could not more
 have goaded.
Of officers a third fell on the spot,
 A thing which victory by no means boded
To gentlemen engaged in the assault:
Hounds, when the huntsman tumbles, are
 at fault.

XVII

But here I leave the general concern,
 To track our hero on his path of fame:
He must his laurels separately earn; 131
 For fifty thousand heroes, name by name,
Though all deserving equally to turn
 A couplet, or an elegy to claim,
Would form a lengthy lexicon of glory,
And what is worse still, a much longer
 story:

XVIII

And therefore we must give the greater
 number
 To the Gazette — which doubtless fairly
 dealt
By the deceased, who lie in famous slum-
 ber
 In ditches, fields, or wheresoe'er they
 felt
Their clay for the last time their souls en-
 cumber; — 141
 Thrice happy he whose name has been well
 spelt
In the despatch: I knew a man whose loss
Was printed *Grove*, although his name was
 Grose.

XIX

Juan and Johnson join'd a certain corps,
 And fought away with might and main,
 not knowing
The way which they had never trod be-
 fore,
 And still less guessing where they might
 be going;
But on they march'd, dead bodies trampling
 o'er,
 Firing, and thrusting, slashing, sweating,
 glowing, 150
But fighting thoughtlessly enough to win,
To their *two* selves, *one* whole bright bulle-
 tin.

XX

Thus on they wallow'd in the bloody mire
 Of dead and dying thousands, — some-
 times gaining
A yard or two of ground, which brought
 them nigher
 To some odd angle for which all were
 straining;
At other times, repulsed by the close fire,
 Which really pour'd as if all hell were
 raining
Instead of heaven, they stumbled backwards
 o'er
A wounded comrade, sprawling in his gore.

XXI

Though 't was Don Juan's first of fields, and
 though 161
 The nightly muster and the silent march
In the chill dark, when courage does not
 glow
 So much as under a triumphal arch,

Perhaps might make him shiver, yawn, or
 throw
A glance on the dull clouds (as thick as
 starch,
Which stiffen'd heaven) as if he wish'd for
 day; —
Yet for all this he did not run away.

XXII

Indeed he could not. But what if he had?
 There *have been* and *are* heroes who begun
With something not much better, or as
 bad: 171
Frederic the Great from Molwitz deign'd
 to run,
For the first and last time; for, like a pad,
 Or hawk, or bride, most mortals after one
Warm bout are broken into their new tricks,
And fight like fiends for pay or politics.

XXIII

He was what Erin calls, in her sublime
 Old Erse or Irish, or it may be *Punic*
(The antiquarians who can settle time,
 Which settles all things, Roman, Greek,
 or Runic, 180
Swear that Pat's language sprung from the
 same clime
 With Hannibal, and wears the Tyrian
 tunic
Of Dido's alphabet; and this is rational
As any other notion, and not national); —

XXIV

But Juan was quite 'a broth of a boy,'
 A thing of impulse and a child of song;
Now swimming in the sentiment of joy,
 Or the *sensation* (if that phrase seem
 wrong),
And afterward, if he must needs destroy,
 In such good company as always throng
To battles, sieges, and that kind of plea-
 sure, 191
No less delighted to employ his leisure;

XXV

But always without malice: if he warr'd
 Or loved, it was with what we call 'the
 best
Intentions,' which form all mankind's *trump
 card,*
 To be produced when brought up to the
 test.
The statesman, hero, harlot, lawyer — ward
 Off each attack, when people are in quest

Of their designs, by saying they *meant well;*
'T is pity 'that such meaning should pave
 hell.' 200

XXVI

I almost lately have begun to doubt
 Whether hell's pavement — if it be so
 paved —
Must not have latterly been quite worn out,
 Not by the numbers good intent hath
 saved,
But by the mass who go below without
 Those ancient good intentions, which once
 shaved
And smooth'd the brimstone of that street
 of hell
Which bears the greatest likeness to Pall
 Mall.

XXVII

Juan, by some strange chance, which oft
 divides
 Warrior from warrior in their grim ca-
 reer, 210
Like chastest wives from constant husbands'
 sides
Just at the close of the first bridal year,
By one of those odd turns of Fortune's tides,
 Was on a sudden rather puzzled here,
When, after a good deal of heavy firing,
He found himself alone, and friends retir-
 ing.

XXVIII

I don't know how the thing occurr'd — it
 might
 Be that the greater part were kill'd or
 wounded,
And that the rest had faced unto the right
 About; a circumstance which has con-
 founded 220
Cæsar himself, who, in the very sight
 Of his whole army, which so much
 abounded
In courage, was obliged to snatch a shield,
And rally back his Romans to the field.

XXIX

Juan, who had no shield to snatch, and
 was
 No Cæsar, but a fine young lad, who
 fought
He knew not why, arriving at this pass,
 Stopp'd for a minute, as perhaps he
 ought

For a much longer time; then, like an
 ass
 (Start not, kind reader; since great Ho-
 mer thought 230
This simile enough for Ajax, Juan
Perhaps may find it better than a new
 one) —

XXX

Then, like an ass, he went upon his way,
 And, what was stranger, never look'd be-
 hind;
But seeing, flashing forward, like the day
 Over the hills, a fire enough to blind
Those who dislike to look upon a fray,
 He stumbled on, to try if he could find
A path, to add his own slight arm and
 forces
To corps, the greater part of which were
 corses. 240

XXXI

Perceiving then no more the commandant
 Of his own corps, nor even the corps,
 which had
Quite disappear'd — the gods know how!
 (I can't
 Account for every thing which may look
 bad
In history; but we at least may grant
 It was not marvellous that a mere lad,
In search of glory, should look on before,
Nor care a pinch of snuff about his corps): —

XXXII

Perceiving nor commander nor commanded,
 And left at large, like a young heir, to
 make 250
His way to — where he knew not — single
 handed;
 As travellers follow over bog and brake
An 'ignis fatuus;' or as sailors stranded
 Unto the nearest hut themselves betake;
So Juan, following honour and his nose,
Rush'd where the thickest fire announced
 most foes.

XXXIII

He knew not where he was, nor greatly
 cared,
 For he was dizzy, busy, and his veins
Fill'd as with lightning — for his spirit
 shared
 The hour, as is the case with lively
 brains; 260

And where the hottest fire was seen and
 heard,
 And the loud cannon peal'd his hoarsest
 strains,
He rush'd, while earth and air were sadly
 shaken
By thy humane discovery, Friar Bacon!

XXXIV

And as he rush'd along, it came to pass he
 Fell in with what was late the second
 column,
Under the orders of the General Lascy,
 But now reduced, as is a bulky volume
Into an elegant extract (much less massy)
 Of heroism, and took his place with sol-
 emn 270
Air 'midst the rest, who kept their valiant
 faces
And levell'd weapons still against the gla-
 cis.

XXXV

Just at this crisis up came Johnson too,
 Who had 'retreated,' as the phrase is
 when
Men run away much rather than go through
 Destruction's jaws into the devil's den;
But Johnson was a clever fellow, who
 Knew when and how 'to cut and come
 again,'
And never ran away, except when running
Was nothing but a valorous kind of cun-
 ning. 280

XXXVI

And so, when all his corps were dead or
 dying,
 Except Don Juan, a mere novice, whose
More virgin valour never dreamt of flying
 From ignorance of danger, which indues
Its votaries, like innocence relying
 On its own strength, with careless nerves
 and thews, —
Johnson retired a little, just to rally
Those who catch cold in 'shadows of Death's
 valley.'

XXXVII

And there, a little shelter'd from the shot,
 Which rain'd from bastion, battery, para-
 pet, 290
Rampart, wall, casement, house, — for there
 was not
 In this extensive city, sore beset

By Christian soldiery, a single spot
　Which did not combat like the devil, as
　　yet,
He found a number of Chasseurs, all scat-
　ter'd
By the resistance of the chase they batter'd.

XXXVIII

And these he call'd on; and, what 's strange,
　they came
　Unto his call, unlike 'the spirits from
The vasty deep,' to whom you may exclaim,
　Says Hotspur, long ere they will leave
　　their home.　　　　　　　　　　300
Their reasons were uncertainty, or shame
　At shrinking from a bullet or a bomb,
And that odd impulse, which in wars or
　creeds
Makes men, like cattle, follow him who
　leads.

XXXIX

By Jove! he was a noble fellow, Johnson,
　And though his name, than Ajax or
　　Achilles,
Sounds less harmonious, underneath the sun
　　soon
　We shall not see his likeness: he could
　　kill his
Man quite as quietly as blows the monsoon
　Her steady breath (which some months
　　the same *still* is):　　　　　　310
Seldom he varied feature, hue, or muscle,
And could be very busy without bustle;

XL

And therefore, when he ran away, he did so
　Upon reflection, knowing that behind
He would find others who would fain be rid so
　Of idle apprehensions, which like wind
Trouble heroic stomachs. Though their lids
　　so
　Oft are soon closed, all heroes are not
　　blind,
But when they light upon immediate death,
Retire a little, merely to take breath.　　320

XLI

But Johnson only ran off, to return
　With many other warriors, as we said,
Unto that rather somewhat misty bourn,
　Which Hamlet tells us is a pass of dread.
To Jack howe'er this gave but slight con-
　cern:
　His soul (like galvanism upon the dead)

Acted upon the living as on wire,
And led them back into the heaviest fire.

XLII

Egad! they found the second time what
　they
　The first time thought quite terrible
　　enough　　　　　　　　　　　330
To fly from, malgré all which people say
　Of glory, and all that immortal stuff
Which fills a regiment (besides their pay,
　That daily shilling which makes warriors
　　tough) —
They found on their return the self-same
　welcome,
Which made some *think*, and others *know*,
　a *hell* come.

XLIII

They fell as thick as harvests beneath
　hail,
　Grass before scythes, or corn below the
　　sickle,
Proving that trite old truth, that life 's as
　frail
　As any other boon for which men stickle.
The Turkish batteries thrash'd them like a
　flail,　　　　　　　　　　　　341
　Or a good boxer, into a sad pickle
Putting the very bravest, who were knock'd
Upon the head, before their guns were
　cock'd.

XLIV

The Turks, behind the traverses and flanks
　Of the next bastion, fired away like devils,
And swept, as gales sweep foam away, whole
　ranks:
　However, Heaven knows how, the Fate
　　who levels
Towns, nations, worlds, in her revolving
　pranks,
　So order'd it, amidst these sulphury re-
　　vels,　　　　　　　　　　　350
That Johnson and some few who had not
　scamper'd,
Reach'd the interior talus of the rampart.

XLV

First one or two, then five, six, and a dozen,
　Came mounting quickly up, for it was
　　now
All neck or nothing, as, like pitch or rosin,
　Flame was shower'd forth above, as well 's
　　below,

So that you scarce could say who best had
 chosen,
 The gentlemen that were the first to show
Their martial faces on the parapet,
 Or those who thought it brave to wait as
 yet. 360

XLVI

But those who scaled, found out that their
 advance
 Was favour'd by an accident or blunder:
The Greek or Turkish Cohorn's ignorance
 Had palisado'd in a way you'd wonder
To see in forts of Netherlands or France
 (Though these to our Gibraltar must
 knock under) —
Right in the middle of the parapet
Just named, these palisades were primly
 set:

XLVII

So that on either side some nine or ten
 Paces were left, whereon you could con-
 trive 370
To march; a great convenience to our men,
 At least to all those who were left alive,
Who thus could form a line and fight again;
 And that which farther aided them to
 strive
Was, that they could kick down the pali-
 sades,
Which scarcely rose much higher than grass
 blades.

XLVIII

Among the first, — I will not say the *first*,
 For such precedence upon such occa-
 sions
Will oftentimes make deadly quarrels burst
 Out between friends as well as allied na-
 tions: 380
The Briton must be bold who really durst
 Put to such trial John Bull's partial pa-
 tience,
As say that Wellington at Waterloo
Was beaten — though the Prussians say so
 too; —

XLIX

And that if Blucher, Bulow, Gneisenau,
 And God knows who besides in 'au' and
 .'ow,'
Had not come up in time to cast an awe
 Into the hearts of those who fought till
 now

As tigers combat with an empty craw,
 The Duke of Wellington had ceased to
 show 390
His orders, also to receive his pensions,
Which are the heaviest that our history
 mentions.

L

But never mind; — 'God save the king!'
 and kings!
 For if *he* don't, I doubt if *men* will
 longer —
I think I hear a little bird, who sings
 The people by and by will be the stronger:
The veriest jade will wince whose harness
 wrings
So much into the raw as quite to wrong her
Beyond the rules of posting, — and the mob
At last fall sick of imitating Job. 400

LI

At first it grumbles, then it swears, and then,
 Like David, flings smooth pebbles 'gainst
 a giant;
At last it takes to weapons such as men
 Snatch when despair makes human hearts
 less pliant.
Then comes 'the tug of war;' — 't will come
 again,
 I rather doubt; and I would fain say 'fie
 on 't,'
If I had not perceived that revolution
Alone can save the earth from hell's pollu-
 tion.

LII

But to continue: — I say not *the* first,
 But of the first, our little friend Don
 Juan 410
Walk'd o'er the walls of Ismail, as if nursed
 Amidst such scenes — though this was
 quite a new one
To him, and I should hope to *most*. The
 thirst
 Of glory, which so pierces through and
 through one,
Pervaded him — although a generous
 creature,
As warm in heart as feminine in feature.

LIII

And here he was — who upon woman's
 breast,
 Even from a child, felt like a child;
 howe'er

The man in all the rest might be confest,
 To him it was Elysium to be there; 420
And he could even withstand that awkward
 test
 Which Rousseau points out to the dubious
 fair,
'Observe your lover when he *leaves* your
 arms;'
But Juan never left them, while they had
 charms,

LIV

Unless compell'd by fate, or wave, or
 wind,
 Or near relations, who are much the
 same.
But *here* he was ! — where each tie that can
 bind
 Humanity must yield to steel and flame:
And *he* whose very body was all mind,
 Flung here by fate or circumstance,
 which tame 430
The loftiest, hurried by the time and place,
Dash'd on like a spurr'd blood-horse in a
 race.

LV

So was his blood stirr'd while he found re-
 sistance,
 As is the hunter's at the five-bar gate,
Or double post and rail, where the exist-
 ence
 Of Britain's youth depends upon their
 weight,
The lightest being the safest: at a distance
 He hated cruelty, as all men hate
Blood, until heated — and even then his
 own
At times would curdle o'er some heavy
 groan. 440

LVI

The General Lascy, who had been hard
 press'd,
 Seeing arrive an aid so opportune
As were some hundred youngsters all
 abreast,
 Who came as if just dropp'd down from
 the moon,
To Juan, who was nearest him, address'd
 His thanks, and hopes to take the city
 soon,
Not reckoning him to be a 'base Bezo-
 nian'
(As Pistol calls it), but a young Livonian.

LVII

Juan, to whom he spoke in German, knew
 As much of German as of Sanscrit,
 and 450
In answer made an inclination to
 The general who held him in command;
For seeing one with ribands, black and
 blue,
 Stars, medals, and a bloody sword in
 hand,
Addressing him in tones which seem'd to
 thank,
He recognised an officer of rank.

LVIII

Short speeches pass between two men who
 speak
 No common language; and besides, in
 time
Of war and taking towns, when many a
 shriek
 Rings o'er the dialogue, and many a
 crime 460
Is perpetrated ere a word can break
 Upon the ear, and sounds of horror chime
In like church-bells, with sigh, howl, groan,
 yell, prayer,
There cannot be much conversation there.

LIX

And therefore all we have related in
 Two long octaves, pass'd in a little
 minute;
But in the same small minute, every sin
 Contrived to get itself comprised within
 it.
The very cannon, deafen'd by the din,
 Grew dumb, for you might almost hear
 a linnet, 470
As soon as thunder, 'midst the general
 noise
Of human nature's agonising voice !

LX

The town was enter'd. Oh eternity ! —
 'God made the country and man made
 the town,'
So Cowper says — and I begin to be
 Of his opinion, when I see cast down
Rome, Babylon, Tyre, Carthage, Nineveh,
 All walls men know, and many never
 known;
And pondering on the present and the past,
To deem the woods shall be our home at
 last. 480

LXI

Of all men, saving Sylla the man-slayer,
 Who passes for in life and death most
 lucky,
Of the great names which in our faces
 stare,
 The General Boon, back-woodsman of
 Kentucky,
Was happiest amongst mortals anywhere;
 For killing nothing but a bear or buck,
 he
Enjoy'd the lonely, vigorous, harmless days
Of his old age in wilds of deepest maze.

LXII

Crime came not near him — she is not the
 child
 Of solitude; Health shrank not from him
 — for 490
Her home is in the rarely trodden wild,
 Where if men seek her not, and death be
 more
Their choice than life, forgive them, as be-
 guiled
 By habit to what their own hearts ab-
 hor —
In cities caged. The present case in point I
Cite is, that Boon lived hunting up to
 ninety;

LXIII

And what's still stranger, left behind a name
 For which men vainly decimate the
 throng,
Not only famous, but of that *good* fame,
 Without which glory 's but a tavern
 song — 500
Simple, serene, the antipodes of shame,
 Which hate nor envy e'er could tinge
 with wrong;
An active hermit, even in age the child
Of Nature, or the man of Ross run wild.

LXIV

'T is true he shrank from men even of his
 nation,
 When they built up unto his darling
 trees, —
He moved some hundred miles off, for a
 station
 Where there were fewer houses and more
 ease;
The inconvenience of civilisation
 Is, that you neither can be pleased nor
 please; 510

But where he met the individual man,
He show'd himself as kind as mortal can.

LXV

He was not all alone: around him grew
 A sylvan tribe of children of the chase,
Whose young, unwaken'd world was ever
 new,
 Nor sword nor sorrow yet had left a
 trace
On her unwrinkled brow, nor could you
 view
 A frown on Nature's or on human face;
The free-born forest found and kept them
 free,
And fresh as is a torrent or a tree. 520

LXVI

And tall, and strong, and swift of foot were
 they,
 Beyond the dwarfing city's pale abor-
 tions,
Because their thoughts had never been the
 prey
 Of care or gain: the green woods were
 their portions;
No sinking spirits told them they grew grey,
 No fashion made them apes of her distor-
 tions;
Simple they were, not savage; and their
 rifles,
Though very true, were not yet used for
 trifles.

LXVII

Motion was in their days, rest in their
 slumbers,
 And cheerfulness the handmaid of their
 toil; 530
Nor yet too many nor too few their num-
 bers;
 Corruption could not make their hearts
 her soil;
The lust which stings, the splendour which
 encumbers,
 With the free foresters divide no spoil;
Serene, not sullen, were the solitudes
Of this unsighing people of the woods.

LXVIII

So much for Nature: —by way of variety,
 Now back to thy great joys, Civilisation !
And the sweet consequence of large society,
 War, pestilence, the despot's desola-
 tion, 540

The kingly scourge, the lust of notoriety,
　The millions slain by soldiers for their
　　ration,
The scenes like Catherine's boudoir at
　threescore,
With Ismail's storm to soften it the more.

LXIX

The town was enter'd: first one column
　made
　Its sanguinary way good — then another;
The reeking bayonet and the flashing blade
　Clash'd 'gainst the scimitar, and babe
　　and mother
With distant shrieks were heard Heaven to
　upbraid:
　Still closer sulphury clouds began to
　　smother　　　　　　　　　　　　550
The breath of morn and man, where foot by
　foot
The madden'd Turks their city still dis-
　pute.

LXX

Koutousow, he who afterward beat back
　(With some assistance from the frost and
　　snow)
Napoleon on his bold and bloody track,
　It happen'd was himself beat back just
　　now;
He was a jolly fellow, and could crack
　His jest alike in face of friend or foe,
Though life, and death, and victory were at
　stake;
But here it seem'd his jokes had ceased to
　take:　　　　　　　　　　　　　560

LXXI

For having thrown himself into a ditch,
　Follow'd in haste by various grenadiers,
Whose blood the puddle greatly did en-
　rich,
　He climb'd to where the parapet appears;
But there his project reach'd its utmost
　pitch
　('Mongst other deaths the General Ri-
　　baupierre's
Was much regretted), for the Moslem men
Threw them all down into the ditch again.

LXXII

And had it not been for some stray troops
　landing
　They knew not where, being carried by
　　the stream　　　　　　　　　570

To some spot, where they lost their under-
　standing,
　And wander'd up and down as in a dream,
Until they reach'd, as daybreak was ex-
　panding,
　That which a portal to their eyes did
　　seem, —
The great and gay Koutousow might have
　lain
Where three parts of his column yet re-
　main.

LXXIII

And scrambling round the rampart, these
　same troops,
　After the taking of the 'Cavalier,'
Just as Koutousow's most 'forlorn' of
　' hopes '
　Took like chameleons some slight tinge
　　of fear,　　　　　　　　　　　580
Open'd the gate call'd ' Kilia', to the groups
　Of baffled heroes, who stood shyly near,
Sliding knee-deep in lately frozen mud,
Now thaw'd into a marsh of human blood.

LXXIV

The Kozacks, or, if so you please, Cos-
　sacques
　(I don't much pique myself upon ortho-
　　graphy,
So that I do not grossly err in facts,
　Statistics, tactics, politics, and geo-
　　graphy) —
Having been used to serve on horses' backs,
　And no great dilettanti in topography 590
Of fortresses, but fighting where it pleases
Their chiefs to order, — were all cut to
　pieces.

LXXV

Their column, though the Turkish batteries
　thunder'd
　Upon them, ne'ertheless had reach'd the
　　rampart,
And naturally thought they could have
　plunder'd
　The city, without being farther hamper'd;
But as it happens to brave men, they
　blunder'd —
　The Turks at first pretended to have
　　scamper'd,
Only to draw them 'twixt two bastion cor-
　ners,
From whence they sallied on those Chris-
　tian scorners.　　　　　　　　600

LXXVI

Then being taken by the tail — a taking
 Fatal to bishops as to soldiers — these
Cossacques were all cut off as day was
 breaking,
 And found their lives were let at a short
 lease —
But perish'd without shivering or shaking,
 Leaving as ladders their heap'd carcasses,
O'er which Lieutenant-Colonel Yesouskoi
March'd with the brave battalion of Pol-
 ouzki: —

LXXVII

This valiant man kill'd all the Turks he
 met,
 But could not eat them, being in his
 turn 610
Slain by some Mussulmans, who would not
 yet,
 Without resistance, see their city burn.
The walls were won, but 't was an even bet
 Which of the armies would have cause
 to mourn:
'T was blow for blow, disputing inch by
 inch,
For one would not retreat, nor t' other
 flinch.

LXXVIII

Another column also suffer'd much: —
 And here we may remark with the his-
 torian,
You should but give few cartridges to such
 Troops as are meant to march with
 greatest glory on: 620
When matters must be carried by the touch
 Of the bright bayonet, and they all should
 hurry on,
They sometimes, with a hankering for ex-
 istence,
Keep merely firing at a foolish distance.

LXXIX

A junction of the General Meknop's men
 (Without the General, who had fallen
 some time
Before, being badly seconded just then)
 Was made at length with those who dared
 to climb
The death-disgorging rampart once again;
 And though the Turk's resistance was
 sublime, 630
They took the bastion, which the Seraskier
Defended at a price extremely dear.

LXXX

Juan and Johnson, and some volunteers,
 Among the foremost, offer'd him good
 quarter,
A word which little suits with Seraskiers,
 Or at least suited not this valiant Tar-
 tar.
He died, deserving well his country's
 tears,
 A savage sort of military martyr.
An English naval officer, who wish'd
To make him prisoner, was also dish'd: 640

LXXXI

For all the answer to his proposition
 Was from a pistol-shot that laid him
 dead;
On which the rest, without more intermis-
 sion,
 Began to lay about with steel and lead —
The pious metals most in requisition
 On such occasions: not a single head
Was spared; — three thousand Moslems
 perish'd here,
And sixteen bayonets pierced the Seraskier.

LXXXII

The city's taken — only part by part —
 And death is drunk with gore: there's
 not a street 650
Where fights not to the last some desperate
 heart
 For those for whom it soon shall cease to
 beat.
Here War forgot his own destructive art
 In more destroying Nature; and the
 heat
Of carnage, like the Nile's sun-sodden
 slime,
Engender'd monstrous shapes of every
 crime.

LXXXIII

A Russian officer, in martial tread
 Over a heap of bodies, felt his heel
Seized fast, as if 't were by the serpent's
 head
 Whose fangs Eve taught her human seed
 to feel: 660
In vain he kick'd, and swore, and writhed,
 and bled,
 And howl'd for help as wolves do for a
 meal —
The teeth still kept their gratifying hold,
As do the subtle snakes described of old.

LXXXIV

A dying Moslem, who had felt the foot
　Of a foe o'er him, snatch'd at it, and bit
The very tendon which is most acute
　(That which some ancient Muse or mod-
　　ern wit
Named after thee, Achilles), and quite
　　through 't
　He made the teeth meet, nor relinquish'd
　　it　　　　　　　　　　　　　　　　670
Even with his life — for (but they lie) 't is
　　said
To the live leg still clung the sever'd head.

LXXXV

However this may be, 't is pretty sure
　The Russian officer for life was lamed,
For the Turk's teeth stuck faster than a
　　skewer,
　And left him 'midst the invalid and
　　maim'd:
The regimental surgeon could not cure
　His patient, and perhaps was to be
　　blamed
More than the head of the inveterate foe,
Which was cut off, and scarce even then
　　let go.　　　　　　　　　　　　680

LXXXVI

But then the fact 's a fact — and 't is the
　　part
　Of a true poet to escape from fiction
Whene'er he can; for there is little art
　In leaving verse more free from the re-
　　striction
Of truth than prose, unless to suit the mart
　For what is sometimes called poetic
　　diction,
And that outrageous appetite for lies
Which Satan angles with for souls, like
　　flies.

LXXXVII

The city 's taken, but not render'd ! — No !
　There 's not a Moslem that hath yielded
　　sword:　　　　　　　　　　　690
The blood may gush out, as the Danube's
　　flow
　Rolls by the city wall; but deed nor
　　word
Acknowledge aught of dread of death or
　　foe:
　In vain the yell of victory is roar'd
By the advancing Muscovite — the groan
Of the last foe is echoed by his own.

LXXXVIII

The bayonet pierces and the sabre cleaves,
　And human lives are lavish'd everywhere,
As the year closing whirls the scarlet
　　leaves
　When the stripp'd forest bows to the
　　bleak air,　　　　　　　　　　700
And groans; and thus the peopled city
　　grieves,
　Shorn of its best and loveliest, and left
　　bare;
But still it falls in vast and awful splinters,
As oaks blown down with all their thousand
　　winters.

LXXXIX

It is an awful topic — but 't is not
　My cue for any time to be terrific:
For checker'd as is seen our human lot
　With good, and bad, and worse, alike
　　prolific
Of melancholy merriment, to quote
　Too much of one sort would be sopo-
　　rific; —　　　　　　　　　　710
Without, or with, offence to friends or
　　foes,
I sketch your world exactly as it goes.

XC

And one good action in the midst of crimes
　Is 'quite refreshing,' in the affected
　　phrase
Of these ambrosial, Pharisaic times,
　With all their pretty milk-and-water
　　ways,
And may serve therefore to bedew these
　　rhymes,
　A little scorch'd at present with the
　　blaze
Of conquest and its consequences, which
Make epic poesy so rare and rich.　　720

XCI

Upon a taken bastion, where there lay
　Thousands of slaughter'd men, a yet
　　warm group
Of murder'd women, who had found their
　　way
　To this vain refuge, made the good heart
　　droop
And shudder; — while, as beautiful as May,
　A female child of ten years tried to
　　stoop
And hide her little palpitating breast
Amidst the bodies lull'd in bloody rest.

XCII

Two villanous Cossacques pursued the child
 With flashing eyes and weapons: match'd
 with them, 730
The rudest brute that roams Siberia's wild
 Has feelings pure and polish'd as a
 gem, —
The bear is civilised, the wolf is mild;
 And whom for this at last must we con-
 demn ?
Their natures ? or their sovereigns, who
 employ
All arts to teach their subjects to destroy ?

XCIII

Their sabres glitter'd o'er her little head,
 Whence her fair hair rose twining with
 affright,
Her hidden face was plunged amidst the
 dead:
 When Juan caught a glimpse of this sad
 sight, 740
I shall not say exactly what he *said*,
 Because it might not solace ' ears polite;'
But what he *did*, was to lay on their backs,
The readiest way of reasoning with Cos-
 sacques.

XCIV

One's hip he slash'd, and split the other's
 shoulder,
 And drove them with their brutal yells
 to seek
If there might be chirurgeons who could
 solder
 The wounds they richly merited, and
 shriek
Their baffled rage and pain; while waxing
 colder
 As he turn'd o'er each pale and gory
 cheek, 750
Don Juan raised his little captive from
The heap a moment more had made her
 tomb.

XCV

And she was chill as they, and on her face
 A slender streak of blood announced how
 near
Her fate had been to that of all her race;
 For the same blow which laid her mother
 here
Had scarr'd her brow, and left its crimson
 trace,
 As the last link with all she had held dear;

But else unhurt, she open'd her large eyes,
And gazed on Juan with a wild surprise.

XCVI

Just at this instant, while their eyes were
 fix'd 761
 Upon each other, with dilated glance,
In Juan's look, pain, pleasure, hope, fear,
 mix'd
 With joy to save, and dread of some mis-
 chance
Unto his protégée; while hers, transfix'd
 With infant terrors, glared as from a
 trance,
A pure, transparent, pale, yet radiant face,
Like to a lighted alabaster vase; —

XCVII

Up came John Johnson (I will not say
 ' *Jack*,'
 For that were vulgar, cold, and common-
 place 770
On great occasions, such as an attack
 On cities, as hath been the present case):
Up Johnson came, with hundreds at his
 back,
 Exclaiming; — ' Juan ! Juan ! On, boy !
 brace
Your arm, and I 'll bet Moscow to a dollar
That you and I will win St. George's
 collar.

XCVIII

' The Seraskier is knock'd upon the head,
 But the stone bastion still remains,
 wherein
The old Pacha sits among some hundreds
 dead,
 Smoking his pipe quite calmly 'midst the
 din 780
Of our artillery and his own: 't is said
 Our kill'd, already piled up to the chin,
Lie round the battery; but still it batters,
And grape in volleys, like a vineyard,
 scatters.

XCIX

' Then up with me ! ' — But Juan answer'd,
 ' Look
 Upon this child — I saved her — must
 not leave
Her life to chance; but point me out some
 nook
 Of safety, where she less may shrink and
 grieve,

And I am with you.' — Whereon Johnson took
 A glance around — and shrugg'd — and twitch'd his sleeve 790
And black silk neckcloth — and replied, ' You 're right;
Poor thing! what 's to be done? I 'm puzzled quite.'

C

Said Juan: ' Whatsoever is to be
 Done, I 'll not quit her till she seems secure
Of present life a good deal more than we.'
 Quoth Johnson: ' *Neither* will I quite ensure;
But at the least *you* may die gloriously.'
 Juan replied: ' At least I will endure
Whate'er is to be borne — but not resign
This child, who is parentless, and therefore mine.' 800

CI

Johnson said: ' Juan, we 've no time to lose;
 The child 's a pretty child — a very pretty —
I never saw such eyes — but hark! now choose
 Between your fame and feelings, pride and pity; —
Hark! how the roar increases! — no excuse
 Will serve when there is plunder in a city; —
I should be loth to march without you, but,
By God! we 'll be too late for the first cut.'

CII

But Juan was immoveable; until
 Johnson, who really loved him in his way,
Pick'd out amongst his followers with some skill 811
 Such as he thought the least given up to prey; —
And swearing if the infant came to ill
 That they should all be shot on the next day;
But if she were deliver'd safe and sound,
They should at least have fifty rubles round,

CIII

And all allowances besides of plunder
 In fair proportion with their comrades;— then

Juan consented to march on through thunder,
 Which thinn'd at every step their ranks of men: 820
And yet the rest rush'd eagerly — no wonder,
 For they were heated by the hope of gain,
A thing which happens everywhere each day —
No hero trusteth wholly to half pay.

CIV

And such is victory, and such is man!
 At least nine tenths of what we call so; — God
May have another name for half we scan
 As human beings, or his ways are odd.
But to our subject: a brave Tartar khan —
 Or ' sultan,' as the author (to whose nod
In prose I bend my humble verse) doth call 831
This chieftain — somehow would not yield at all:

CV

But flank'd by *five* brave sons (such is polygamy,
 That she spawns warriors by the score, where none
Are prosecuted for that false crime bigamy),
 He never would believe the city won
While courage clung but to a single twig. — Am I
 Describing Priam's, Peleus', or Jove's son?
Neither — but a good, plain, old, temperate man,
Who fought with his five children in the van. 840

CVI

To *take* him was the point. The truly brave,
 When they behold the brave oppress'd with odds,
Are touch'd with a desire to shield and save; —
 A mixture of wild beasts and demigods
Are they — now furious as the sweeping wave,
 Now moved with pity: even as sometimes nods
The rugged tree unto the summer wind,
Compassion breathes along the savage mind.

CVII

But he would *not* be *taken,* and replied
 To all the propositions of surrender 850
By mowing Christians down on every side,
 As obstinate as Swedish Charles at
 Bender.
His five brave boys no less the foe defied;
 Whereon the Russian pathos grew less
 tender,
As being a virtue, like terrestrial patience,
Apt to wear out on trifling provocations.

CVIII

And spite of Johnson and of Juan, who
 Expended all their Eastern phraseology
In begging him, for God's sake, just to show
 So much less fight as might form an
 apology 860
For *them* in saving such a desperate foe —
 He hew'd away, like doctors of theology
When they dispute with sceptics; and with
 curses
Struck at his friends, as babies beat their
 nurses.

CIX

Nay, he had wounded, though but slightly,
 both
 Juan and Johnson; whereupon they fell,
The first with sighs, the second with an
 oath,
 Upon his angry sultanship, pell-mell,
And all around were grown exceeding wroth
 At such a pertinacious infidel, 870
And pour'd upon him and his sons like rain,
Which they resisted like a sandy plain

CX

That drinks and still is dry. At last they
 perish'd —
 His second son was levell'd by a shot ;
His third was sabred; and the fourth, most
 cherish'd
 Of all the five, on bayonets met his lot ;
The fifth, who, by a Christian mother nour-
 ish'd,
 Had been neglected, ill-used, and what not,
Because deform'd, yet died all game and
 bottom,
To save a sire who blush'd that he begot
 him. 880

CXI

The eldest was a true and tameless Tartar,
 As great a scorner of the Nazarene

As ever Mahomet pick'd out for a martyr,
 Who only saw the black-eyed girls in
 green,
Who make the beds of those who won't
 take quarter
 On earth, in Paradise ; and when once
 seen,
Those houris, like all other pretty creatures,
Do just whate'er they please, by dint of
 features.

CXII

And what they pleased to do with the young
 khan
 In heaven I know not, nor pretend to
 guess ; 890
But doubtless they prefer a fine young man
 To tough old heroes, and can do no less;
And that's the cause no doubt why, if we
 scan
 A field of battle's ghastly wilderness,
For one rough, weather-beaten, veteran
 body,
You'll find ten thousand handsome cox-
 combs bloody.

CXIII

Your houris also have a natural pleasure
 In lopping off your lately married men,
Before the bridal hours have danced their
 measure
 And the sad, second moon grows dim
 again, 900
Or dull repentance hath had dreary leisure
 To wish him back a bachelor now and
 then.
And thus your houri (it may be) disputes
Of these brief blossoms the immediate
 fruits.

CXIV

Thus the young khan, with houris in his
 sight,
 Thought not upon the charms of four
 young brides,
But bravely rush'd on his first heavenly
 night.
 In short, howe'er *our* better faith derides,
These black-eyed virgins make the Mos-
 lems fight,
 As though there were one heaven and
 none besides, — 910
Whereas, if all be true we hear of heaven
And hell, there must at least be six or
 seven.

CXV

So fully flash'd the phantom on his eyes,
 That when the very lance was in his
 heart,
He shouted ' Allah ! ' and saw Paradise
 With all its veil of mystery drawn apart,
And bright eternity without disguise
 On his soul, like a ceaseless sunrise,
 dart : —
With prophets, houris, angels, saints, de-
 scried
In one voluptuous blaze, — and then he
 died, 920

CXVI

But with a heavenly rapture on his face.
 The good old khan, who long had ceased
 to see
Houris, or aught except his florid race
 Who grew like cedars round him glori-
 ously —
When he beheld his latest hero grace
 The earth, which he became like a fell'd
 tree,
Paused for a moment, from the fight, and
 cast
A glance on that slain son, his first and last.

CXVII

The soldiers, who beheld him drop his
 point,
 Stopp'd as if once more willing to con-
 cede 930
Quarter, in case he bade them not ' aroynt !'
 As he before had done. He did not heed
Their pause nor signs : his heart was out of
 joint,
 And shook (till now unshaken) like a
 reed,
As he look'd down upon his children gone,
And felt — though done with life — he was
 alone.

CXVIII

But 't was a transient tremor : — with a
 spring
 Upon the Russian steel his breast he
 flung,
As carelessly as hurls the moth her wing
 Against the light wherein she dies : he
 clung 940
Closer, that all the deadlier they might
 wring,
 Unto the bayonets which had pierced his
 young ;

And throwing back a dim look on his sons,
In one wide wound pour'd forth his soul at
 once.

CXIX

'T is strange enough — the rough, tough
 soldiers, who
 Spared neither sex nor age in their career
Of carnage, when this old man was pierced
 through,
 And lay before them with his children
 near,
Touch'd by the heroism of him they slew,
 Were melted for a moment : though no
 tear 950
Flow'd from their bloodshot eyes, all red
 with strife,
They honour'd such determined scorn of
 life.

CXX

But the stone bastion still kept up its fire,
 Where the chief pacha calmly held his
 post :
Some twenty times he made the Russ re-
 tire,
 And baffled the assaults of all their host;
At length he condescended to inquire
 If yet the city's rest were won or lost;
And being told the latter, sent a bey
To answer Ribas' summons to give way. 960

CXXI

In the mean time, cross-legg'd, with great
 sang-froid,
 Among the scorching ruins he sat smok-
 ing
Tobacco on a little carpet; — Troy
 Saw nothing like the scene around : — yet
 looking
With martial stoicism, nought seem'd to
 annoy
 His stern philosophy; but gently strok-
 ing
His beard, he puff'd his pipe's ambrosial
 gales,
As if he had three lives, as well as tails.

CXXII

The town was taken — whether he might
 yield 969
 Himself or bastion, little matter'd now :
His stubborn valour was no future shield.
 Ismail 's no more ! The crescent's silver
 bow

Sunk, and the crimson cross glared o'er the
field,
But red with no *redeeming* gore: the glow
Of burning streets, like moonlight on the
water,
Was imaged back in blood, the sea of
slaughter.

CXXIII

All that the mind would shrink from of
excesses;
All that the body perpetrates of bad;
All that we read, hear, dream, of man's
distresses;
All that the devil would do if run stark
mad; 980
All that defies the worst which pen ex-
presses;
All by which hell is peopled, or as sad
As hell — mere mortals who their power
abuse —
Was here (as heretofore and since) let loose.

CXXIV

If here and there some transient trait of pity
Was shown, and some more noble heart
broke through
Its bloody bond, and saved perhaps some
pretty
Child, or an aged, helpless man or two —
What's this in one annihilated city,
Where thousand loves, and ties, and duties
grew? 990
Cockneys of London! Muscadins of Paris!
Just ponder what a pious pastime war is.

CXXV

Think how the joys of reading a Gazette
Are purchased by all agonies and crimes:
Or if these do not move you, don't forget
Such doom may be your own in after-
times.
Meantime the Taxes, Castlereagh, and
Debt,
Are hints as good as sermons, or as
rhymes.
Read your own hearts and Ireland's present
story,
Then feed her famine fat with Wellesley's
glory. 1000

CXXVI

But still there is unto a patriot nation,
Which loves so well its country and its
king,

A subject of sublimest exultation —
Bear it, ye Muses, on your brightest wing!
Howe'er the mighty locust, Desolation,
Strip your green fields, and to your har-
vests cling,
Gaunt famine never shall approach the
throne —
Though Ireland starve, great George
weighs twenty stone.

CXXVII

But let me put an end unto my theme:
There was an end of Ismail — hapless
town! 1010
Far flash'd her burning towers o'er Dan-
ube's stream,
And redly ran his blushing waters down.
The horrid war-whoop and the shriller
scream
Rose still; but fainter were the thunders
grown:
Of forty thousand who had mann'd the wall,
Some hundreds breathed — the rest were
silent all!

CXXVIII

In one thing ne'ertheless 't is fit to praise
The Russian army upon this occasion,
A virtue much in fashion now-a-days, 1019
And therefore worthy of commemoration:
The topic 's tender, so shall be my phrase —
Perhaps the season's chill, and their long
station
In winter's depth, or want of rest and victual,
Had made them chaste; — they ravish'd
very little.

CXXIX

Much did they slay, more plunder, and no
less
Might here and there occur some violation
In the other line; — but not to such excess
As when the French, that dissipated na-
tion,
Take towns by storm: no causes can I guess,
Except cold weather and commisera-
tion; 1030
But all the ladies, save some twenty score,
Were almost as much virgins as before.

CXXX

Some odd mistakes, too, happen'd in the
dark,
Which show'd a want of lanterns, or of
taste —

Indeed the smoke was such they scarce could
 mark
 Their friends from foes, — besides such
 things from haste
Occur, though rarely, when there is a spark
 Of light to save the venerably chaste:
But six old damsels, each of seventy years,
Were all deflower'd by different grena-
 diers. 1040

CXXXI

But on the whole their continence was great;
 So that some disappointment there ensued
To those who had felt the inconvenient state
 Of 'single blessedness,' and thought it
 good
(Since it was not their fault, but only fate,
 To bear these crosses) for each waning
 prude
To make a Roman sort of Sabine wedding,
Without the expense and the suspense of
 bedding.

CXXXII

Some voices of the buxom middle-aged
 Were also heard to wonder in the din 1050
(Widows of forty were these birds long
 caged)
 'Wherefore the ravishing did not begin !'
But while the thirst for gore and plunder
 raged,
 There was small leisure for superfluous sin;
But whether they escaped or no, lies hid
In darkness — I can only hope they did.

CXXXIII

Suwarrow now was conqueror — a match
 For Timour or for Zinghis in his trade.
While mosques and streets, beneath his eyes,
 like thatch
 Blazed, and the cannon's roar was scarce
 allay'd, 1060
With bloody hands he wrote his first de-
 spatch;
 And here exactly follows what he said: —
'Glory to *God* and to the Empress !'
 (*Powers
Eternal ! such names mingled !*) 'Ismail 's
 ours.'

CXXXIV

Methinks these are the most tremendous
 words,
 Since 'Menè, Menè, Tekel,' and 'Uphar-
 sin,'

Which hands or pens have ever traced of
 swords.
 Heaven help me ! I 'm but little of a
 parson:
What Daniel read was short-hand of the
 Lord's,
 Severe, sublime; the prophet wrote no
 farce on 1070
The fate of nations ; — but this Russ so
 witty
Could rhyme, like Nero, o'er a burning city.

CXXXV

He wrote this Polar melody, and set it,
 Duly accompanied by shrieks and groans,
Which few will sing, I trust, but none for-
 get it —
 For I will teach, if possible, the stones
To rise against earth's tyrants. Never let
 it
 Be said that we still truckle unto
 thrones; —
But ye — our children's children ! think
 how we
Show'd *what things were* before the world
 was free ! 1080

CXXXVI

That hour is not for us, but 't is for you:
 And as, in the great joy of your mil-
 lennium,
You hardly will believe such things were
 true
 As now occur, I thought that I would
 pen you 'em;
But may their very memory perish too ! —
 Yet if perchance remember'd, still dis-
 dain you 'em
More than you scorn the savages of yore,
Who *painted* their *bare* limbs, but *not* with
 gore.

CXXXVII

And when you hear historians talk of
 thrones,
 And those that sate upon them, let it
 be 1090
As we now gaze upon the mammoth's
 bones,
 And wonder what old world such things
 could see,
Or hieroglyphics on Egyptian stones,
 The pleasant riddles of futurity —
Guessing at what shall happily be hid,
As the real purpose of a pyramid.

CXXXVIII

Reader! I have kept my word, — at least
 so far
 As the first Canto promised. You have
 now
Had sketches of love, tempest, travel, war —
 All very accurate, you must allow, 1100
And *epic*, if plain truth should prove no
 bar;
 For I have drawn much less with a long
 bow
Than my forerunners. Carelessly I sing,
But Phœbus lends me now and then a
 string,

CXXXIX

With which I still can harp, and carp, and
 fiddle.
 What farther hath befallen or may befall
The hero of this grand poetic riddle,
 I by and by may tell you, if at all:
But now I choose to break off in the mid-
 dle,
 Worn out with battering Ismail's stub-
 born wall, 1110
While Juan is sent off with the despatch,
For which all Petersburgh is on the watch.

CXL

This special honour was conferr'd, because
 He had behaved with courage and hu-
 manity —
Which *last* men like, when they have time
 to pause
From their ferocities produced by vanity.
His little captive gain'd him some applause
 For saving her amidst the wild insanity
Of carnage, — and I think he was more
 glad in her
Safety, than his new order of St. Vladimir.

CXLI

The Moslem orphan went with her pro-
 tector, 1121
 For she was homeless, houseless, helpless;
 all
Her friends, like the sad family of Hector,
 Had perish'd in the field or by the wall:
Her very place of birth was but a spectre
 Of what it had been; there the Muezzin's
 call
To prayer was heard no more! — and Juan
 wept,
And made a vow to shield her, which he
 kept.

CANTO THE NINTH

I

OH, Wellington! (or ' Villainton ' — for
 Fame
 Sounds the heroic syllables both ways;
France could not even conquer your great
 name,
 But punn'd it down to this facetious
 phrase —
Beating or beaten she will laugh the same),
 You have obtain'd great pensions and
 much praise:
Glory like yours should any dare gainsay,
Humanity would rise, and thunder ' Nay ! '

II

I don't think that you used Kinnaird quite
 well
 In Marinèt's affair — in fact, 't was
 shabby, 10
And like some other things won't do to tell
 Upon your tomb in Westminster's old
 abbey.
Upon the rest 't is not worth while to dwell,
 Such tales being for the tea-hours of some
 tabby;
But though your years as *man* tend fast to
 zero,
In fact your grace is still but a *young hero*.

III

Though Britain owes (and pays you too) so
 much,
 Yet Europe doubtless owes you greatly
 more:
You have repair'd Legitimacy's crutch,
 A prop not quite so certain as before: 20
The Spanish, and the French, as well as
 Dutch,
 Have seen, and felt, how strongly you
 restore ;
And Waterloo has made the world your
 debtor
(I wish your bards would sing it rather
 better).

IV

You are ' the best of cut-throats: ' — do not
 start ;
 The phrase is Shakspeare's, and not mis-
 applied:
War 's a brain-spattering, windpipe-slitting
 art,
 Unless her cause by right be sanctified.

If you have acted *once* a generous part,
 The world, not the world's masters, will
 decide, 30
And I shall be delighted to learn who,
Save you and yours, have gain'd by Water-
 loo ?

V

I am no flatterer — you 've supp'd full of
 flattery:
 They say you like it too — 't is no great
 wonder.
He whose whole life has been assault and
 battery,
 At last may get a little tired of thunder;
And swallowing eulogy much more than
 satire, he
 May like being praised for every lucky
 blunder,
Call'd 'Saviour of the Nations ' — not yet
 saved,
And ' Europe's Liberator ' — still enslaved.

VI

I 've done. Now go and dine from off the
 plate 41
Presented by the Prince of the Brazils,
And send the sentinel before your gate
 A slice or two from your luxurious meals:
He fought, but has not fed so well of late.
 Some hunger, too, they say the people
 feels: —
There is no doubt that you deserve your
 ration,
But pray give back a little to the nation.

VII

I don't mean to reflect — a man so great as
 You, my lord duke ! is far above reflec-
 tion: 50
The high Roman fashion, too, of Cincin-
 natus,
 With modern history has but small con-
 nection:
Though as an Irishman you love potatoes,
 You need not take them under your di-
 rection;
And half a million for your Sabine farm
Is rather dear ! — I 'm sure I mean no
 harm.

VIII

Great men have always scorn'd great re-
 compenses:
 Epaminondas saved his Thebes, and died,

Not leaving even his funeral expenses:
 George Washington had thanks and
 nought beside, 60
Except the all-cloudless glory (which few
 men's is)
 To free his country: Pitt too had his
 pride,
And as a high-soul'd minister of state is
Renown'd for ruining Great Britain gratis.

IX

Never had mortal man such opportunity,
 Except Napoleon, or abused it more:
You might have freed fallen Europe from
 the unity
 Of tyrants, and been blest from shore to
 shore:
And *now* — what *is* your fame ? Shall the
 Muse tune it ye ?
 Now — that the rabble 's first vain shouts
 are o'er ? 70
Go ! hear it in your famish'd country's
 cries !
Behold the world ! and curse your vic-
 tories !

X

As these new cantos touch on warlike feats,
 To *you* the unflattering Muse deigns to
 inscribe
Truths, that you will not read in the Ga-
 zettes,
 But which 't is time to teach the hireling
 tribe
Who fatten on their country's gore, and
 debts,
 Must be recited, and — without a bribe.
You *did great* things; but not being *great*
 in mind,
Have left *undone* the *greatest* — and man-
 kind. 80

XI

Death laughs — Go ponder o'er the skel-
 eton
 With which men image out the unknown
 thing
That hides the past world, like to a set
 sun
 Which still elsewhere may rouse a
 brighter spring —
Death laughs at all you weep for: — look
 upon
 This hourly dread of all ! whose *threat-
 en'd sting*

Turns life to terror, even though in its
 sheath:
Mark how its lipless mouth grins without
 breath !

XII

Mark how it laughs and scorns at all you
 are !
 And yet *was* what you are: from *ear* to
 ear 90
It *laughs not* — there is now no fleshy bar
 So call'd; the Antic long hath ceased to
 hear,
But still he *smiles;* and whether near or
 far,
 He strips from man that mantle (far
 more dear
Than even the tailor's), his incarnate skin,
White, black, or copper — the dead bones
 will grin.

XIII

And thus Death laughs, — it is sad merri-
 ment,
 But still it *is* so; and with such example
Why should not Life be equally content
 With his superior, in a smile to tram-
 ple 100
Upon the nothings which are daily spent
 Like bubbles on an ocean much less am-
 ple
Than the eternal deluge, which devours
Suns as rays — worlds like atoms — years
 like hours ?

XIV

'To be, or not to be ? that is the question,'
 Says Shakspeare, who just now is much
 in fashion.
I am neither Alexander nor Hephæstion,
 Nor ever had for *abstract* fame much
 passion;
But would much rather have a sound
 digestion
 Than Buonaparte's cancer: could I dash
 on 110
Through fifty victories to shame or fame —
Without a stomach what were a good
 name ?

XV

'O dura ilia messorum !' —'Oh
 Ye rigid guts of reapers !' I translate
For the great benefit of those who know
 What indigestion is — that inward fate

Which makes all Styx through one small
 liver flow.
 A peasant's sweat is worth his lord's
 estate :
Let *this* one toil for bread — *that* rack for
 rent,
He who sleeps best may be the most con-
 tent. 120

XVI

'To be, or not to be ? ' — Ere I decide,
 I should be glad to know that which *is
 being ?*
'T is true we speculate both far and wide,
 And deem, because we *see*, we are *all-
 seeing :*
For my part, I 'll enlist on neither side,
 Until I see both sides for once agreeing.
For me, I sometimes think that life is death,
Rather than life a mere affair of breath.

XVII

'Que scais-je ? ' was the motto of Mon-
 taigne,
 As also of the first academicians: 130
That all is dubious which man may attain,
 Was one of their most favourite positions.
There 's no such thing as certainty, that 's
 plain
 As any of Mortality's conditions;
So little do we know what we 're about in
This world, I doubt if doubt itself be doubt-
 ing.

XVIII

It is a pleasant voyage perhaps to float,
 Like Pyrrho, on a sea of speculation;
But what if carrying sail capsize the boat ?
 Your wise men don't know much of navi-
 gation; 140
And swimming long in the abyss of thought
 Is apt to tire: a calm and shallow station
Well nigh the shore, where one stoops down
 and gathers
Some pretty shell, is best for moderate
 bathers.

XIX

'But heaven,' as Cassio says, 'is above all —
 No more of this, then, — let us pray ! '
 We have
Souls to save, since Eve's slip and Adam's
 fall,
 Which tumbled all mankind into the
 grave,

Besides fish, beasts, and birds. 'The spar-
 row's fall
 Is special providence,' though how it
 gave 150
Offence, we know not; probably it perch'd
Upon the tree which Eve so fondly search'd.

XX

Oh, ye immortal gods ! what is theogony ?
 Oh, thou too, mortal man ! what is
 philanthropy ?
Oh, world ! which was and is, what is cos-
 mogony ?
 Some people have accused me of misan-
 thropy;
And yet I know no more than the mahogany
 That forms this desk, of what they mean;
 lykanthropy
I comprehend, for without transformation
Men become wolves on any slight occasion.

XXI

But I, the mildest, meekest of mankind, 161
 Like Moses, or Melancthon, who have
 ne'er
Done anything exceedingly unkind, —
 And (though I could not now and then
 forbear
Following the bent of body or of mind)
 Have always had a tendency to spare, —
Why do they call me misanthrope ? Be-
 cause
They hate me, not I them : — and here we 'll
 pause.

XXII

'T is time we should proceed with our good
 poem, —
 For I maintain that it is really good, 170
Not only in the body but the proem,
 However little both are understood
Just now, — but by and by the Truth will
 show 'em
 Herself in her sublimest attitude:
And till she doth, I fain must be content
To share her beauty and her banishment.

XXIII

Our hero (and, I trust, kind reader,
 yours)
 Was left upon his way to the chief city
Of the immortal Peter's polish'd boors
 Who still have shown themselves more
 brave than witty. 180
I know its mighty empire now allures

Much flattery — even Voltaire's, and
 that 's a pity.
For me, I deem an absolute autocrat
Not a barbarian, but much worse than that.

XXIV

And I will war, at least in words (and —
 should
 My chance so happen — deeds), with all
 who war
With Thought; — and of Thought's foes by
 far most rude,
 Tyrants and sycophants have been and are.
I know not who may conquer : if I could
 Have such a prescience, it should be no
 bar 190
To this my plain, sworn, downright detes-
 tation
Of every depotism in every nation.

XXV

It is not that I adulate the people:
 Without *me*, there are demagogues
 enough,
And infidels, to pull down every steeple,
 And set up in their stead some proper
 stuff.
Whether they may sow scepticism to reap
 hell,
 As is the Christian dogma rather rough,
I do not know; — I wish men to be free
As much from mobs as kings — from you
 as me. 200

XXVI

The consequence is, being of no party,
 I shall offend all parties: never mind !
My words, at least, are more sincere and
 hearty
 Than if I sought to sail before the wind.
He who has nought to gain can have small
 art: he
 Who neither wishes to be bound nor bind,
May still expatiate freely, as will I,
Nor give my voice to slavery's jackal cry.

XXVII

That 's an appropriate simile, *that jackal ;* —
 I 've heard them in the Ephesian ruins
 howl 210
By night, as do that mercenary pack all,
 Power's base purveyors, who for pickings
 prowl,
And scent the prey their masters would
 attack all.

However, the poor jackals are less foul
(As being the brave lions' keen providers)
Than human insects, catering for spiders.

XXVIII

Raise but an arm ! 't will brush their web
 away,
 And without *that*, their poison and their
 claws
Are useless. Mind, good people ! what I
 say
 (Or rather peoples) — *go on* without
 pause ! 220
The web of these tarantulas each day
 Increases, till you shall make common
 cause:
None, save the Spanish fly and Attic bee,
As yet are strongly stinging to be free.

XXIX

Don Juan, who had shone in the late slaugh-
 ter,
 Was left upon his way with the despatch,
Where blood was talk'd of as we would of
 water;
 And carcasses that lay as thick as thatch
O'er silenced cities, merely served to flatter
 Fair Catherine's pastime — who look'd
 on the match 230
Between these nations as a main of cocks,
Wherein she liked her own to stand like
 rocks.

XXX

And there in a *kibitka* he roll'd on
 (A cursed sort of carriage without
 springs,
Which on rough roads leaves scarcely a
 whole bone),
 Pondering on glory, chivalry, and kings,
And orders, and on all that he had done —
 And wishing that post-horses had the
 wings
Of Pegasus, or at the least post-chaises
Had feathers, when a traveller on deep
 ways is. 240

XXXI

At every jolt — and they were many — still
 He turn'd his eyes upon his little charge,
As if he wish'd that she should fare less ill
 Than he, in these sad highways left at
 large
To ruts, and flints, and lovely Nature's skill,
 Who is no paviour, nor admits a barge

On *her* canals, where God takes sea and
 land,
Fishery and farm, both into his own hand.

XXXII

At least he pays no rent, and has best right
 To be the first of what we used to call
'Gentlemen farmers' — a race worn out
 quite, 251
 Since lately there have been no rents at
 all,
And 'gentlemen' are in a piteous plight,
 And 'farmers' can't raise Ceres from her
 fall :
She fell with Buonaparte — What strange
 thoughts
Arise, when we see emperors fall with
 oats !

XXXIII

But Juan turn'd his eyes on the sweet child
 Whom he had saved from slaughter —
 what a trophy !
Oh ! ye who build up monuments, defiled
 With gore, like Nadir Shah, that costive
 sophy, 260
Who, after leaving Hindostan a wild,
 And scarce to the Mogul a cup of coffee
To soothe his woes withal, was slain, the
 sinner !
Because he could no more digest his din-
 ner ; —

XXXIV

Oh ye ! or we ! or he ! or she ! reflect,
 That *one* life saved, especially if young
Or pretty, is a thing to recollect
 Far sweeter than the greenest laurels
 sprung
From the manure of human clay, though
 deck'd
With all the praises ever said or sung: 270
Though hymn'd by every harp, unless with-
 in
Your heart joins chorus, Fame is but a din.

XXXV

Oh! ye great authors luminous, volumi-
 nous !
 Ye twice ten hundred thousand daily
 scribes !
Whose pamphlets, volumes, newspapers,
 illumine us !
 Whether you 're paid by government in
 bribes,

To prove the public debt is not consuming
 us —
 Or, roughly treading on the ' courtier's
 kibes '
With clownish heel, your popular circula-
 tion
Feeds you by printing half the realm's star-
 vation; — 280

XXXVI

Oh, ye great authors! — ' Apropos des
 bottes,' —
I have forgotten what I meant to say,
 As sometimes have been greater sages'
 lots;
'T was something calculated to allay
All wrath in barracks, palaces, or cots:
 Certes it would have been but thrown
 away,
And that 's one comfort for my lost advice,
Although no doubt it was beyond all price.

XXXVII

But let it go: — it will one day be found
 With other relics of ' a former world,'
When this world shall be *former*, under-
 ground, 291
 Thrown topsy-turvy, twisted, crisp'd,
 and curl'd,
Baked, fried, or burnt, turn'd inside-out, or
 drown'd,
 Like all the worlds before, which have
 been hurl'd
First out of, and then back again to chaos,
The superstratum which will overlay us.

XXXVIII

So Cuvier says; — and then shall come
 again
 Unto the new creation, rising out
From our old crash, some mystic, ancient
 strain
 Of things destroy'd and left in airy
 doubt: 300
Like to the notions we now entertain
 Of Titans, giants, fellows of about
Some hundred feet in height, *not* to say
 miles,
And mammoths, and your wingèd crocodiles.

XXXIX

Think if then George the Fourth should be
 dug up !
 How the new worldlings of the then new
 East

Will wonder where such animals could
 sup !
 (For they themselves will be but of the
 least:
Even worlds miscarry, when too oft they
 pup, 309
 And every new creation hath decreased
In size, from overworking the material —
Men are but maggots of some huge Earth's
 burial.)

XL

How will — to these young people, just
 thrust out
 From some fresh Paradise, and set to
 plough,
And dig, and sweat, and turn themselves
 about,
 And plant, and reap, and spin, and grind,
 and sow,
Till all the arts at length are brought
 about,
 Especially of war and taxing, — how,
I say, will these great relics, when they
 see 'em,
Look like the monsters of a new museum ?

XLI

But I am apt to grow too metaphysical: 321
 ' The time is out of joint,' — and so
 am I;
I quite forget this poem 's merely quiz-
 zical,
 And deviate into matters rather dry.
I ne'er decide what I shall say, and this I
 call
 Much too poetical: men should know
 why
They write, and for what end; but, note or
 text,
I never know the word which will come
 next.

XLII

So on I ramble, now and then narrating,
 Now pondering: — it is time we should
 narrate. 330
I left Don Juan with his horses baiting —
 Now we 'll get o'er the ground at a great
 rate.
I shall not be particular in stating
 His journey, we 've so many tours of
 late:
Suppose him then at Petersburgh; suppose
That pleasant capital of painted snows;

XLIII

Suppose him in a handsome uniform, —
 A scarlet coat, black facings, a long
 plume,
Waving, like sails new shiver'd in a storm,
 Over a cock'd hat in a crowded room, 340
And brilliant breeches, bright as a Cairn
 Gorme,
Of yellow casimere we may presume,
White stocking drawn uncurdled as new
 milk
O'er limbs whose symmetry set off the
 silk;

XLIV

Suppose him sword by side, and hat in
 hand,
 Made up by youth, fame, and an army
 tailor —
That great enchanter, at whose rod's com-
 mand
 Beauty springs forth, and Nature's self
 turns paler,
Seeing how Art can make her work more
 grand
 (When she don't pin men's limbs in like
 a gaoler), — 350
Behold him placed as if upon a pillar! He
Seems Love turn'd a lieutenant of artil-
 lery: —

XLV

His bandage slipp'd down into a cravāt;
 His wings subdued to epaulettes; his
 quiver
Shrunk to a scabbard, with his arrows at
 His side as a small sword, but sharp as
 ever;
His bow converted into a cock'd hat;
 But still so like, that Psyche were more
 clever
Than some wives (who make blunders no
 less stupid),
If she had not mistaken him for Cupid. 360

XLVI

The courtiers stared, the ladies whisper'd,
 and
 The empress smiled: the reigning favour-
 ite frown'd —
I quite forget which of them was in hand
 Just then; as they are rather numerous
 found,
Who took by turns that difficult command
 Since first her majesty was singly crown'd:

But they were mostly nervous six-foot fel-
 lows,
All fit to make a Patagonian jealous.

XLVII

Juan was none of these, but slight and slim,
 Blushing and beardless; and yet ne'er-
 theless 370
There was a something in his turn of limb,
 And still more in his eye, which seem'd
 to express,
That though he look'd one of the sera-
 phim,
 There lurk'd a man beneath the spirit's
 dress.
Besides, the empress sometimes liked a
 boy,
And had just buried the fair-faced Lan-
 skoi.

XLVIII

No wonder then that Yermoloff, or Momo-
 noff,
 Or Scherbatoff, or any other *off*
Or *on*, might dread her majesty had not
 room enough
 Within her bosom (which was not too
 tough) 380
For a new flame; a thought to cast of
 gloom enough
 Along the aspect, whether smooth or
 rough,
Of him who, in the language of his station,
Then held that 'high official situation.'

XLIX

O, gentle ladies! should you seek to know
 The import of this diplomatic phrase,
Bid Ireland's Londonderry's Marquess show
 His parts of speech; and in the strange
 displays
Of that odd string of words, all in a row,
 Which none divine, and every one obeys,
Perhaps you may pick out some queer *no*
 meaning, 391
Of that weak wordy harvest the sole glean-
 ing.

L

I think I can explain myself without
 That sad inexplicable beast of prey —
That Sphinx, whose words would ever be a
 doubt,
 Did not his deeds unriddle them each
 day —

That monstrous hieroglyphic — that long
 spout
Of blood and water, leaden Castlereagh !
And here I must an anecdote relate,
But luckily of no great length or weight.

LI

An English lady ask'd of an Italian, 401
 What were the actual and official duties
Of the strange thing some women set a
 value on,
 Which hovers oft about some married
 beauties,
Called ' Cavalier servente ? ' — a Pygmalion
 Whose statues warm (I fear, alas ! too
 true 't is)
Beneath his art. The dame, press'd to dis-
 close them,
Said — ' Lady, I beseech you to *suppose
 them.*'

LII

And thus I supplicate your supposition,
 And mildest, matron-like interpretation,
Of the imperial favourite's condition. 411
 'T was a high place, the highest in the
 nation
In fact, if not in rank; and the suspicion
 Of any one's attaining to his station,
No doubt gave pain, where each new pair
 of shoulders,
If rather broad, made stocks rise and their
 holders.

LIII

Juan, I said, was a most beauteous boy,
 And had retain'd his boyish look be-
 yond
The usual hirsute seasons which destroy,
 With beards and whiskers, and the like,
 the fond 420
Parisian aspect which upset old Troy
 And founded Doctors' Commons: — I
 have conn'd
The history of divorces, which, though
 chequer'd,
Calls Ilion's the first damages on record.

LIV

And Catherine, who loved all things (save
 her lord,
 Who was gone to his place), and pass'd
 for much
Admiring those (by dainty dames abhorr'd)
 Gigantic gentlemen, yet had a touch

Of sentiment; and he she most adored
 Was the lamented Lanskoi, who was such
A lover as had cost her many a tear, 431
 And yet but made a middling grenadier.

LV

Oh thou ' teterrima causa ' of all ' belli ' —
 Thou gate of life and death — thou non-
 descript !
Whence is our exit and our entrance, —
 well I
 May pause in pondering how all souls are
 dipt
In thy perennial fountain: — how man *fell* I
 Know not, since knowledge saw her
 branches stript
Of her first fruit; but how he falls and
 rises
Since, thou hast settled beyond all sur-
 mises. 440

LVI

Some call thee ' the worst cause of war,'
 but I
 Maintain thou art the *best :* for after all
From thee we come, to thee we go, and
 why
 To get at thee not batter down a wall,
Or waste a world ? since no one can deny
 Thou dost replenish worlds both great
 and small:
With, or without thee, all things at a stand
Are, or would be, thou sea of life's dry
 land !

LVII

Catherine, who was the grand epitome
 Of that great cause of war, or peace, or
 what 450
You please (it causes all the things which be,
 So you may take your choice of this or
 that) —
Catherine, I say, was very glad to see
 The handsome herald, on whose plumage
 sat
Victory; and pausing as she saw him kneel
With his despatch, forgot to break the seal.

LVIII

Then recollecting the whole empress, nor
 Forgetting quite the woman (which com-
 posed
At least three parts of this great whole),
 she tore
 The letter open with an air which posed

The court, that watch'd each look her visage
 wore, 461
Until a royal smile at length disclosed
Fair weather for the day. Though rather
 spacious,
Her face was noble, her eyes fine, mouth
 gracious.

LIX

Great joy was hers, or rather joys: the first
 Was a ta'en city, thirty thousand slain.
Glory and triumph o'er her aspect burst,
 As an East Indian sunrise on the main.
These quench'd a moment her ambition's
 thirst —
 So Arab deserts drink in summer's rain:
In vain ! — As fall the dews on quenchless
 sands, 471
Blood only serves to wash Ambition's
 hands !

LX

Her next amusement was more fanciful;
 She smiled at mad Suwarrow's rhymes,
 who threw
Into a Russian couplet rather dull
 The whole gazette of thousands whom he
 slew.
Her third was feminine enough to annul
 The shudder which runs naturally
 through
Our veins, when things call'd sovereigns
 think it best
To kill, and generals turn it into jest. 480

LXI

The two first feelings ran their course com-
 plete,
 And lighted first her eye, and then her
 mouth:
The whole court look'd immediately most
 sweet,
 Like flowers well water'd after a long
 drouth.
But when on the lieutenant at her feet
 Her majesty, who liked to gaze on youth
Almost as much as on a new despatch,
Glanced mildly, all the world was on the
 watch.

LXII

Though somewhat large, exuberant, and
 truculent,
 When *wroth* — while *pleased*, she was as
 fine a figure 490

As those who like things rosy, ripe, and suc-
 culent,
 Would wish to look on, while they are in
 vigour.
She could repay each amatory look you
 lent
 With interest, and in turn was wont with
 rigour
To exact of Cupid's bills the full amount
At sight, nor would permit you to discount.

LXIII

With her the latter, though at times con-
 venient,
 Was not so necessary; for they tell
That she was handsome, and though fierce
 look'd lenient,
 And always used her favourites too well.
If once beyond her boudoir's precincts in ye
 went, 501
 Your ' fortune ' was in a fair way ' to swell
A man ' (as Giles says); for though she
 would widow all
Nations, she liked man as an individual.

LXIV

What a strange thing is man! and what a
 stranger
 Is woman! What a whirlwind is her head,
And what a whirlpool full of depth and
 danger
 Is all the rest about her ! Whether wed
Or widow, maid or mother, she can change
 her
 Mind like the wind: whatever she has
 said 510
Or done, is light to what she 'll say or do; —
The oldest thing on record, and yet new !

LXV

Oh Catherine ! (for of all interjections,
 To thee both *oh !* and *ah !* belong of
 right
In love and war) how odd are the connec-
 tions
 Of human thoughts, which jostle in their
 flight !
Just now *yours* were cut out in different sec-
 tions:
 First Ismail's capture caught your fancy
 quite;
Next of new knights, the fresh and glori-
 ous batch;
And *thirdly* he who brought you the de-
 spatch ! 520

LXVI

Shakspeare talks of 'the herald Mercury
 New lighted on a heaven-kissing hill;'
And some such visions cross'd her majesty,
 While her young herald knelt before her
 still.
'T is very true the hill seem'd rather high,
 For a lieutenant to climb up; but skill
Smooth'd even the Simplon's steep, and by
 God's blessing
With youth and health all kisses are 'hea-
 ven-kissing.'

LXVII

Her majesty look'd down, the youth look'd
 up —
 And so they fell in love; — she with his
 face, 530
His grace, his God-knows-what: for Cupid's
 cup
 With the first draught intoxicates apace,
A quintessential laudanum or 'black drop,'
 Which makes one drunk at once, without
 the base
Expedient of full bumpers; for the eye
In love drinks all life's fountains (save
 tears) dry.

LXVIII

He, on the other hand, if not in love,
 Fell into that no less imperious passion,
Self-love — which, when some sort of thing
 above
 Ourselves, a singer, dancer, much in fash-
 ion, 540
Or duchess, princess, empress, 'deigns to
 prove'
 ('T is Pope's phrase) a great longing,
 though a rash one,
For one especial person out of many,
Makes us believe ourselves as good as any.

LXIX

Besides, he was of that delighted age
 Which makes all female ages equal —
 when
We don't much care with whom we may
 engage,
 As bold as Daniel in the lion's den,
So that we can our native sun assuage
 In the next ocean, which may flow just
 then, 550
To make a twilight in, just as Sol's heat
 is
Quench'd in the lap of the salt sea, or Thetis.

LXX

And Catherine (we must say thus much for
 Catherine),
 Though bold and bloody, was the kind of
 thing
Whose temporary passion was quite flatter-
 ing,
 Because each lover look'd a sort of king,
Made up upon an amatory pattern,
 A royal husband in all save the *ring* —
Which, being the damn'dest part of matri-
 mony,
Seem'd taking out the sting to leave the
 honey. 560

LXXI

And when you add to this, her womanhood
 In its meridian, her blue eyes or gray
(The last, if they have soul, are quite as
 good,
 Or better, as the best examples say:
Napoleon's, Mary's (queen of Scotland),
 should
 Lend to that colour a transcendent ray;
And Pallas also sanctions the same hue,
Too wise to look through optics black or
 blue) —

LXXII

Her sweet smile, and her then majestic
 figure,
 Her plumpness, her imperial condescen-
 sion, 570
Her preference of a boy to men much
 bigger
 (Fellows whom Messalina's self would
 pension),
Her prime of life, just now in juicy vigour,
 With other *extras*, which we need not
 mention, —
All these, or any one of these, explain
Enough to make a stripling very vain.

LXXIII

And that's enough, for love is vanity,
 Selfish in its beginning as its end,
Except where 't is a mere insanity,
 A maddening spirit which would strive to
 blend 580
Itself with beauty's frail inanity,
 On which the passion's self seems to de-
 pend:
And hence some heathenish philosophers
Make love the main spring of the uni-
 verse.

LXXIV

Besides Platonic love, besides the love
 Of God, the love of sentiment, the loving
Of faithful pairs (I needs must rhyme with
 dove,
 That good old steam-boat which keeps
 verses moving
'Gainst reason — Reason ne'er was hand-
 and-glove
 With rhyme, but always leant less to
 improving 590
The sound than sense) — beside all these
 pretences
To love, there are those things which words
 name senses;

LXXV

Those movements, those improvements in
 our bodies
Which make all bodies anxious to get out
Of their own sand-pits, to mix with a god-
 dess,
 For such all women are at first no doubt.
How beautiful that moment ! and how odd
 is
 That fever which precedes the languid
 rout
Of our sensations ! What a curious way 599
The whole thing is of clothing souls in clay !

LXXVI

The noblest kind of love is love Platonical,
 To end or to begin with; the next grand
Is that which may be christen'd love canon-
 ical,
 Because the clergy take the thing in hand;
The third sort to be noted in our chronicle
 As flourishing in every Christian land,
Is when chaste matrons to their other ties
Add what may be call'd *marriage in disguise*.

LXXVII

Well, we won't analyse — our story must
 Tell for itself: the sovereign was smitten,
Juan much flatter'd by her love, or lust; —
 I cannot stop to alter words once writ-
 ten, 612
And the two are so mix'd with human
 dust,
 That he who *names one*, both perchance
 may hit on:
But in such matters Russia's mighty em-
 press
Behaved no better than a common semp-
 stress.

LXXVIII

The whole court melted into one wide
 whisper,
 And all lips were applied unto all ears !
The elder ladies' wrinkles curl'd much
 crisper
 As they beheld; the younger cast some
 leers 620
On one another, and each lovely lisper
 Smiled as she talk'd the matter o'er; but
 tears
Of rivalship rose in each clouded eye
Of all the standing army who stood by.

LXXIX

All the ambassadors of all the powers
 Enquired, Who was this very new young
 man,
Who promised to be great in some few
 hours ?
 Which is full soon — though life is but a
 span.
Already they beheld the silver showers
 Of rubles rain, as fast as specie can, 630
Upon his cabinet, besides the presents
Of several ribands, and some thousand pea-
 sants.

LXXX

Catherine was generous, — all such ladies
 are:
 Love, that great opener of the heart and
 all
The ways that lead there, be they near or
 far,
 Above, below, by turnpikes great or
 small, —
Love (though she had a cursèd taste for
 war,
 And was not the best wife, unless we call
Such Clytemnestra, though perhaps 't is
 better
That one should die, than two drag on the
 fetter) — 640

LXXXI

Love had made Catherine make each lover's
 fortune,
 Unlike our own half-chaste Elizabeth,
Whose avarice all disbursements did im-
 portune,
 If history, the grand liar, ever saith
The truth; and though grief her old age
 might shorten,
 Because she put a favourite to death,

Her vile, ambiguous method of flirtation,
And stinginess, disgrace her sex and sta-
tion.

LXXXII

But when the levee rose, and all was
bustle
In the dissolving circle, all the nations'
Ambassadors began as 't were to hustle 651
Round the young man with their congrat-
ulations.
Also the softer silks were heard to rustle
Of gentle dames, among whose recrea-
tions
It is to speculate on handsome faces,
Especially when such lead to high places.

LXXXIII

Juan, who found himself, he knew not
how,
A general object of attention, made
His answers with a very graceful bow,
As if born for the ministerial trade. 660
Though modest, on his unembarrass'd brow
Nature had written 'gentleman.' He
said
Little, but to the purpose; and his man-
ner
Flung hovering graces o'er him like a
banner.

LXXXIV

An order from her majesty consign'd
Our young lieutenant to the genial care
Of those in office: all the world look'd
kind
(As it will look sometimes with the first
stare,
Which youth would not act ill to keep in
mind),
As also did Miss Protasoff then there,
Named from her mystic office 'l'Eprou-
veuse,' 671
A term inexplicable to the Muse.

LXXXV

With *her* then, as in humble duty bound,
Juan retired, — and so will I, until
My Pegasus shall tire of touching ground.
We have just lit on a 'heaven-kissing
hill,'
So lofty that I feel my brain turn round,
And all my fancies whirling like a mill;
Which is a signal to my nerves and brain,
To take a quiet ride in some green lane. 680

CANTO THE TENTH

I

WHEN Newton saw an apple fall, he found
In that slight startle from his contem-
plation —
'T is *said* (for I 'll not answer above ground
For any sage's creed or calculation) —
A mode of proving that the earth turn'd
round
In a most natural whirl, called 'gravita-
tion;'
And this is the sole mortal who could grap-
ple,
Since Adam, with a fall or with an apple.

II

Man fell with apples, and with apples rose,
If this be true; for we must deem the
mode 10
In which Sir Isaac Newton could disclose
Through the then unpaved stars the turn-
pike road,
A thing to counterbalance human woes:
For ever since immortal man hath glow'd
With all kinds of mechanics, and full soon
Steam-engines will conduct him to the
moon.

III

And wherefore this exordium? — Why, just
now,
In taking up this paltry sheet of paper,
My bosom underwent a glorious glow,
And my internal spirit cut a caper: 20
And though so much inferior, as I know,
To those who, by the dint of glass and
vapour,
Discover stars and sail in the wind's eye,
I wish to do as much by poesy.

IV

In the wind's eye I have sail'd, and sail;
but for
The stars, I own my telescope is dim:
But at least I have shunn'd the common
shore,
And leaving land far out of sight, would
skim
The ocean of eternity: the roar
Of breakers has not daunted my slight,
trim, 30
But *still* sea-worthy skiff; and she may float
Where ships have founder'd, as doth many
a boat.

V

We left our hero, Juan, in the *bloom*
 Of favouritism, but not yet in the
 blush ;
And far be it from my *Muses* to presume
 (For I have more than one Muse at a
 push)
To follow him beyond the drawing-room:
 It is enough that Fortune found him
 flush
Of youth, and vigour, beauty, and those
 things
Which for an instant clip enjoyment's
 wings. 40

VI

But soon they grow again and leave their
 nest.
 'Oh !' saith the Psalmist, 'that I had a
 dove's
Pinions to flee away, and be at rest !'
 And who that recollects young years and
 loves, —
Though hoary now, and with a withering
 breast,
 And palsied fancy, which no longer roves
Beyond its dimm'd eye's sphere, — but
 would much rather
Sigh like his son, than cough like his grand-
 father?

VII

But sighs subside, and tears (even widows')
 shrink, 49
 Like Arno in the summer, to a shallow,
So narrow as to shame their wintry brink,
 Which threatens inundations deep and
 yellow !
Such difference doth a few months make.
 You'd think
 Grief a rich field which never would lie
 fallow;
No more it doth, its ploughs but change
 their boys,
Who furrow some new soil to sow for joys.

VIII

But coughs will come when sighs depart —
 and now
 And then before sighs cease; for oft the
 one
Will bring the other, ere the lake-like brow
 Is ruffled by a wrinkle, or the sun 60
Of life reach'd ten o'clock: and while a
 glow,

Hectic and brief as summer's day nigh
 done,
O'erspreads the cheek which seems too
 pure for clay,
Thousands blaze, love, hope, die, — how
 happy they !

IX

But Juan was not meant to die so soon.
 We left him in the focus of such glory
As may be won by favour of the moon
 Or ladies' fancies — rather transitory
Perhaps; but who would scorn the month
 of June,
 Because December, with his breath so
 hoary, 70
Must come ? Much rather should he court
 the ray,
To hoard up warmth against a wintry day.

X

Besides, he had some qualities which fix
 Middle-aged ladies even more than
 young :
The former know what's what; while new-
 fledged chicks
 Know little more of love than what is
 sung
In rhymes, or dreamt (for fancy will play
 tricks)
 In visions of those skies from whence
 Love sprung.
Some reckon women by their suns or
 years,
I rather think the moon should date the
 dears. 80

XI

And why ? because she's changeable and
 chaste.
 I know no other reason, whatsoe'er
Suspicious people, who find fault in haste,
 May choose to tax me with; which is not
 fair,
Nor flattering to 'their temper or their
 taste,'
 As my friend Jeffrey writes with such an
 air:
However, I forgive him, and I trust
He will forgive himself; — if not, I must.

XII

Old enemies who have become new friends
 Should so continue — 't is a point of
 honour; 90

And I know nothing which could make
amends
 For a return to hatred: I would shun her
Like garlic, howsoever she extends
 Her hundred arms and legs, and fain
 outrun her.
Old flames, new wives, become our bitterest
 foes —
Converted foes should scorn to join with
 those.

XIII

This were the worst desertion: — rene-
 gadoes,
 Even shuffling Southey, that incarnate lie,
Would scarcely join again the 'reformadoes,'
 Whom he forsook to fill the laureate's
 sty: 100
And honest men from Iceland to Barbadoes,
 Whether in Caledon or Italy,
Should not veer round with every breath,
 nor seize
To pain, the moment when you cease to
 please.

XIV

The lawyer and the critic but behold
 The baser sides of literature and life,
And nought remains unseen, but much un-
 told,
 By those who scour those double vales of
 strife.
While common men grow ignorantly old,
 The lawyer's brief is like the surgeon's
 knife, 110
Dissecting the whole inside of a question,
And with it all the process of digestion.

XV

A legal broom's a moral chimney-sweeper,
 And that's the reason he himself's so
 dirty;
The endless soot bestows a tint far deeper
 Than can be hid by altering his shirt, he
Retains the sable stains of the dark creeper,
 At least some twenty-nine do out of thirty,
In all their habits; — not so you, I own;
As Cæsar wore his robe you wear your
 gown. 120

XVI

And all our little feuds, at least all mine,
 Dear Jeffrey, once my most redoubted foe
(As far as rhyme and criticism combine
 To make such puppets of us things below),

Are over: Here's a health to 'Auld Lang
 Syne!'
 I do not know you, and may never know
Your face — but you have acted on the
 whole
Most nobly, and I own it from my soul.

XVII

And when I use the phrase of 'Auld Lang
 Syne!'
 'T is not address'd to you — the more's
 the pity 130
For me, for I would rather take my wine
 With you, than aught (save Scott) in your
 proud city.
But somehow, — it may seem a schoolboy's
 whine,
 And yet I seek not to be grand nor
 witty,
But I am half a Scot by birth, and bred
A whole one, and my heart flies to my
 head, —

XVIII

As 'Auld Lang Syne' brings Scotland, one
 and all,
 Scotch plaids, Scotch snoods, the blue
 hills, and clear streams,
The Dee, the Don, Balgounie's brig's black
 wall,
 All my boy feelings, all my gentler
 dreams 140
Of what I then dreamt, clothed in their own
 pall,
 Like Banquo's offspring; — floating past
 me seems
My childhood in this childishness of mine:
I care not — 't is a glimpse of 'Auld Lang
 Syne.'

XIX

And though, as you remember, in a fit
 Of wrath and rhyme, when juvenile and
 curly,
I rail'd at Scots to show my wrath and
 wit,
 Which must be own'd was sensitive and
 surly,
Yet 't is in vain such sallies to permit,
 They cannot quench young feelings fresh
 and early: 150
I 'scotch'd' not kill'd' the Scotchman in my
 blood,
And love the land of 'mountain and of
 flood.'

XX

Don Juan, who was real, or ideal, —
 For both are much the same, since what
 men think
Exists when the once thinkers are less real
 Than what they thought, for mind can
 never sink,
And 'gainst the body makes a strong appeal;
 And yet 't is very puzzling on the brink
Of what is call'd eternity, to stare,
And know no more of what is here, than
 there; — 160

XXI

Don Juan grew a very polish'd Russian —
 How we won't mention, *why* we need not
 say:
Few youthful minds can stand the strong
 concussion
 Of any slight temptation in their way;
But *his* just now were spread as is a cushion
 Smooth'd for a monarch's seat of honour;
 gay
Damsels, and dances, revels, ready money,
Made ice seem paradise, and winter sunny.

XXII

The favour of the empress was agreeable;
 And though the duty wax'd a little hard,
Young people at his time of life should be
 able 171
 To come off handsomely in that regard.
He was now growing up like a green tree,
 able
 For love, war, or ambition, which reward
Their luckier votaries, till old age's tedium
Make some prefer the circulating medium.

XXIII

About this time, as might have been antici-
 pated,
 Seduced by youth and dangerous ex-
 amples,
Don Juan grew, I fear, a little dissipated;
 Which is a sad thing, and not only
 tramples 180
On our fresh feelings, but — as being par-
 ticipated
 With all kinds of incorrigible samples
Of frail humanity — must make us selfish,
And shut our souls up in us like a shell-fish.

XXIV

This we pass over. We will also pass
 The usual progress of intrigues between

Unequal matches, such as are, alas !
 A young lieutenant's with a *not old* queen,
But one who is not so youthful as she was
 In all the royalty of sweet seventeen. 190
Sovereigns may sway materials, but not
 matter,
And wrinkles, the d——d democrats, won't
 flatter.

XXV

And Death, the sovereign's sovereign,
 though the great
 Gracchus of all mortality, who levels
With his *Agrarian* laws the high estate
 Of him who feasts, and fights, and roars,
 and revels,
To one small grass-grown patch (which
 must await
 Corruption for its crop) with the poor
 devils
Who never had a foot of land till now, —
Death 's a reformer, all men must allow. 200

XXVI

He lived (not Death, but Juan) in a hurry
 Of waste, and haste, and glare, and gloss,
 and glitter,
In this gay clime of bear-skins black and
 furry —
 Which (though I hate to say a thing
 that 's bitter)
Peep out sometimes, when things are in a
 flurry,
 Through all the 'purple and fine linen,'
 fitter
For Babylon's than Russia's royal harlot —
And neutralize her outward show of scarlet.

XXVII

And this same state we won't describe: we
 would
 Perhaps from hearsay, or from recollec-
 tion; 210
But getting nigh grim Dante's 'obscure
 wood,'
 That horrid equinox, that hateful sec-
 tion
Of human years, that half-way house, that
 rude
 Hut, whence wise travellers drive with
 circumspection
Life's sad post-horses o'er the dreary fron-
 tier
Of age, and looking back to youth, give
 one tear; —

XXVIII

I won't describe, — that is, if I can help
 Description; and I won't reflect, — that
 is,
If I can stave off thought, which — as a
 whelp
Clings to its teat — sticks to me through
 the abyss 220
Of this odd labyrinth; or as the kelp
 Holds by the rock; or as a lover's kiss
Drains its first draught of lips: — but, as I
 said,
I *won't* philosophise, and *will* be read.

XXIX

Juan, instead of courting courts, was
 courted, —
 A thing which happens rarely: this he
 owed
Much to his youth, and much to his reported
 Valour; much also to the blood he show'd,
Like a race-horse; much to each dress he
 sported,
 Which set the beauty off in which he
 glow'd, 230
As purple clouds befringe the sun; but
 most
He owed to an old woman and his post.

XXX

He wrote to Spain: — and all his near rela-
 tions,
 Perceiving he was in a handsome way
Of getting on himself, and finding stations
 For cousins also, answer'd the same
 day.
Several prepared themselves for emigra-
 tions;
 And eating ices, were o'erheard to say,
That with the addition of a slight pelisse,
Madrid's and Moscow's climes were of a
 piece. 240

XXXI

His mother, Donna Inez, finding, too,
 That in the lieu of drawing on his banker,
Where his assets were waxing rather few,
 He had brought his spending to a hand-
 some anchor, —
Replied, ' that she was glad to see him
 through
 Those pleasures after which wild youth
 will hanker;
As the sole sign of man's being in his senses
Is, learning to reduce his past expenses.

XXXII

' She also recommended him to God,
 And no less to God's Son, as well as
 Mother, 250
Warn'd him against Greek worship, which
 looks odd
 In Catholic eyes; but told him, too, to
 smother
Outward dislike, which don't look well
 abroad;
 Inform'd him that he had a little brother
Born in a second wedlock; and above
All, praised the empress's *maternal* love.

XXXIII

' She could not too much give her approbation
 Unto an empress, who preferr'd young
 men
Whose age, and what was better still, whose
 nation
 And climate, stopp'd all scandal (now
 and then): — 260
At home it might have given her some
 vexation;
 But where thermometers sunk down to
 ten,
Or five, or one, or zero, she could never
Believe that virtue thaw'd before the river.'

XXXIV

Oh for a *forty-parson power* to chant
 Thy praise, Hypocrisy ! Oh for a hymn
Loud as the virtues thou dost loudly vaunt,
 Not practise ! Oh for trumps of cheru-
 bim !
Or the ear-trumpet of my good old aunt,
 Who, though her spectacles at last grew
 dim, 270
Drew quiet consolation through its hint,
When she no more could read the pious
 print.

XXXV

She was no hypocrite at least, poor soul,
 But went to heaven in as sincere a way
As any body on the elected roll,
 Which portions out upon the judgment
 day
Heaven's freeholds, in a sort of doomsday
 scroll,
 Such as the conqueror William did re-
 pay
His knights with, lotting others' properties
Into some sixty thousand new knights'
 fees. 280

XXXVI

I can't complain, whose ancestors are there,
 Erneis, Radulphus — eight-and-forty ma-
 nors
(If that my memory doth not greatly err)
 Were their reward for following Billy's
 banners:
And though I can't help thinking 't was
 scarce fair
 To strip the Saxons of their *hydes*, like
 tanners;
Yet as they founded churches with the pro-
 duce,
 You 'll deem, no doubt, they put it to a
 good use.

XXXVII

The gentle Juan flourish'd, though at times
 He felt like other plants called sensitive,
Which shrink from touch, as monarchs do
 from rhymes, 291
 Save such as Southey can afford to give.
Perhaps he long'd in bitter frosts for climes
 In which the Neva's ice would cease to
 live
Before May-day: perhaps, despite his duty,
In royalty's vast arms he sigh'd for beauty:

XXXVIII

Perhaps — but, sans perhaps, we need not
 seek
 For causes young or old: the canker-
 worm
Will feed upon the fairest, freshest cheek,
 As well as further drain the wither'd
 form: 300
Care, like a housekeeper, brings every week
 His bills in, and however we may storm,
They must be paid : though six days
 smoothly run,
The seventh will bring blue devils or a dun.

XXXIX

I don't know how it was, but he grew sick:
 The empress was alarm'd, and her physi-
 cian
(The same who physick'd Peter) found the
 tick
 Of his fierce pulse betoken a condition
Which augur'd of the dead, however *quick*
 Itself, and show'd a feverish disposition;
At which the whole court was extremely
 troubled, 311
The sovereign shock'd, and all his medi-
 cines doubled.

XL

Low were the whispers, manifold the ru-
 mours:
 Some said he had been poison'd by Po-
 temkin;
Others talk'd learnedly of certain tu-
 mours,
 Exhaustion, or disorders of the same kin;
Some said 't was a concoction of the hu-
 mours,
 Which with the blood too readily will
 claim kin;
Others again were ready to maintain,
' 'T was only the fatigue of last cam-
 paign.' 320

XLI

But here is one prescription out of many:
' Sodæ sulphat. ℨvj. ℥fs. Mannæ optim.
Aq. fervent. f. ℨifs. ℨij. tinct. Sennæ
 Haustus' (And here the surgeon came
 and cupp'd him)
' ℞ Pulv. Com. gr. iij. Ipecacuanhæ '
(With more beside if Juan had not stopp'd
 'em).
' Bolus Potassæ Sulphuret. sumendus,
Et haustus ter in die capiendus.'

XLII

This is the way physicians mend or end
 us,
 Secundum artem: but although we sneer
In health — when ill, we call them to at-
 tend us, 331
 Without the least propensity to jeer:
While that ' hiatus maxime deflendus '
 To be fill'd up by spade or mattock's
 near,
Instead of gliding graciously down Lethe,
We tease mild Baillie, or soft Abernethy.

XLIII

Juan demurr'd at this first notice to
 Quit; and though death had threaten'd
 an ejection,
His youth and constitution bore him
 through,
 And sent the doctors in a new direc-
 tion. 340
But still his state was delicate: the hue
 Of health but flicker'd with a faint reflec-
 tion
Along his wasted cheek, and seem'd to
 gravel
The faculty — who said that he must travel.

XLIV

The climate was too cold, they said, for
him,
Meridian-born, to bloom in. This opinion
Made the chaste Catherine look a little grim,
Who did not like at first to lose her min-
ion:
But when she saw his dazzling eye wax dim,
And drooping like an eagle's with clipt
pinion, 350
She then resolved to send him on a mission,
But in a style becoming his condition.

XLV

There was just then a kind of a discussion,
A sort of treaty or negotiation
Between the British cabinet and Russian,
Maintain'd with all the due prevarication
With which great states such things are apt
to push on;
Something about the Baltic's navigation,
Hides, train-oil, tallow, and the rights of
Thetis, 359
Which Britons deem their ' uti possidetis.'

XLVI

So Catherine, who had a handsome way
Of fitting out her favourites, conferr'd
This secret charge on Juan, to display
At once her royal splendour, and reward
His services. He kiss'd hands the next day,
Received instructions how to play his card,
Was laden with all kinds of gifts and
honours,
Which show'd what great discernment was
the donor's.

XLVII

But she was lucky, and luck's all. Your
queens
Are generally prosperous in reigning; 370
Which puzzles us to know what Fortune
means.
But to continue: though her years were
waning
Her climacteric teased her like her teens;
And though her dignity brook'd no com-
plaining,
So much did Juan's setting off distress her,
She could not find at first a fit successor.

XLVIII

But time, the comforter, will come at last;
And four-and-twenty hours, and twice
that number

Of candidates requesting to be placed,
Made Catherine taste next night a quiet
slumber: — 380
Not that she meant to fix again in haste,
Nor did she find the quantity encumber,
But always choosing with deliberation,
Kept the place open for their emulation.

XLIX

While this high post of honour 's in abeyance,
For one or two days, reader, we request
You 'll mount with our young hero the con-
veyance
Which wafted him from Petersburgh:
the best
Barouche, which had the glory to display
once
The fair czarina's autocratic crest, 390
When, a new Iphigene, she went to Tauris,
Was given to her favourite, and now *bore*
his.

L

A bull-dog, and a bullfinch, and an ermine,
All private favourites of Don Juan; —
for
(Let deeper sages the true cause determine)
He had a kind of inclination, or
Weakness, for what most people deem mere
vermin,
Live animals: an old maid of threescore
For cats and birds more penchant ne'er dis-
play'd,
Although he was not old, nor even a
maid; — 400

LI

The animals aforesaid occupied
Their station: there were valets, secre-
taries,
In other vehicles; but at his side
Sat little Leila, who survived the parries
He made 'gainst Cossacque sabres, in the
wide
Slaughter of Ismail. Though my wild
Muse varies
Her note, she don't forget the infant girl
Whom he preserved, a pure and living pearl.

LII

Poor little thing ! She was as fair as docile,
And with that gentle, serious character,
As rare in living beings as a fossile 411
Man, 'midst thy mouldy mammoths,
' grand Cuvier !'

Ill fitted was her ignorance to jostle
　　With this o'erwhelming world, where all
　　　　must err:
But she was yet but ten years old, and
　　　　therefore
Was tranquil, though she knew not why or
　　wherefore.

LIII

Don Juan loved her, and she loved him, as
　　Nor brother, father, sister, daughter love.
I cannot tell exactly what it was;　　419
　　He was not yet quite old enough to prove
Parental feelings, and the other class,
　　Call'd brotherly affection, could not move
His bosom, — for he never had a sister:
Ah! if he had, how much he would have
　　miss'd her!

LIV

And still less was it sensual; for besides
　　That he was not an ancient debauchee
(Who like sour fruit, to stir their veins' salt
　　　　tides,
　　As acids rouse a dormant alkali),
Although ('t *will* happen as our planet
　　　　guides)
　　His youth was not the chastest that might
　　　　be,　　430
There was the purest Platonism at bottom
Of all his feelings — only he forgot 'em.

LV

Just now there was no peril of tempta-
　　　　tion;
　　He loved the infant orphan he had saved,
As patriots (now and then) may love a
　　　　nation;
　　His pride, too, felt that she was not en-
　　　　slaved
Owing to him; — as also her salvation
　　Through his means and the church's
　　　　might be paved.
But one thing 's odd, which here must be
　　　　inserted,
The little Turk refused to be converted. 440

LVI

'T was strange enough she should retain the
　　　　impression
　　Through such a scene of change, and
　　　　dread, and slaughter;
But though three bishops told her the trans-
　　　　gression,
　　She show'd a great dislike to holy water:

She also had no passion for confession;
　　Perhaps she had nothing to confess : — no
　　　　matter,
Whate'er the cause, the church made little
　　of it —
She still held out that Mahomet was a pro-
　　phet.

LVII

In fact, the only Christian she could bear
　　Was Juan; whom she seem'd to have
　　　　selected　　450
In place of what her home and friends once
　　were.
　　He *naturally* loved what he protected:
And thus they form'd a rather curious
　　　　pair,
　　A guardian green in years, a ward con-
　　　　nected
In neither clime, time, blood, with her
　　defender;
And yet this want of ties made theirs more
　　tender.

LVIII

They journey'd on through Poland and
　　　　through Warsaw,
　　Famous for mines of salt and yokes of
　　　　iron:
Through Courland also, which that famous
　　　　farce saw
　　Which gave her dukes the graceless
　　　　name of ' Biron.'　　460
'T is the same landscape which the modern
　　Mars saw,
　　Who march'd to Moscow, led by Fame,
　　　　the siren!
To lose by one month's frost some twenty
　　　　years
Of conquest, and his guard of grenadiers.

LIX

Let this not seem an anti - climax: —
　　　　' Oh!
　　My guard! my old guard!' exclaim'd
　　　　that god of clay.
Think of the Thunderer's falling down
　　　　below
Carotid-artery-cutting Castlereagh!
Alas, that glory should be chill'd by snow!
　　But should we wish to warm us on our
　　　　way　　470
Through Poland, there is Kosciusko's name
Might scatter fire through ice, like Hecla's
　　flame.

LX

From Poland they came on through Prussia
Proper,
 And Königsberg the capital, whose vaunt,
Besides some veins of iron, lead, or cop-
per,
 Has lately been the great Professor
Kant.
Juan, who cared not a tobacco-stopper
 About philosophy, pursued his jaunt
To Germany, whose somewhat tardy mil-
lions
Have princes who spur more than their pos-
tilions. 480

LXI

And thence through Berlin, Dresden, and
the like,
 Until he reach'd the castellated Rhine: —
Ye glorious Gothic scenes! how much ye
strike
 All phantasies, not even excepting mine;
A grey wall, a green ruin, rusty pike,
 Make my soul pass the equinoctial line
Between the present and past worlds, and
hover
Upon their airy confine, half-seas-over.

LXII

But Juan posted on through Manheim,
Bonn,
 Which Drachenfels frowns over like a
spectre 490
Of the good feudal times forever gone,
 On which I have not time just now to
lecture.
From thence he was drawn onwards to
Cologne,
 A city which presents to the inspector
Eleven thousand maidenheads of bone,
The greatest number flesh hath ever known.

LXIII

From thence to Holland's Hague and Hel-
voetsluys,
 That water-land of Dutchmen and of
ditches,
Where juniper expresses its best juice,
 The poor man's sparkling substitute for
riches. 500
Senates and sages have condemn'd its use —
 But to deny the mob a cordial, which is
Too often all the clothing, meat, or fuel,
Good government has left them, seems but
cruel.

LXIV

Here he embark'd, and with a flowing sail
 Went bounding for the island of the free,
Towards which the impatient wind blew
half a gale;
 High dash'd the spray, the bows dipp'd
in the sea,
And sea-sick passengers turn'd somewhat
pale; 509
 But Juan, season'd, as he well might be,
By former voyages, stood to watch the skiffs
Which pass'd, or catch the first glimpse of
the cliffs.

LXV

At length they rose, like a white wall along
 The blue sea's border; and Don Juan
felt —
What even young strangers feel a little
strong
 At the first sight of Albion's chalky
belt —
A kind of pride that he should be among
 Those haughty shopkeepers, who sternly
dealt
Their goods and edicts out from pole to pole,
And made the very billows pay them toll. 520

LXVI

I 've no great cause to love that spot of earth,
 Which holds what *might have been* the no-
blest nation;
But though I owe it little but my birth,
 I feel a mix'd regret and veneration
For its decaying fame and former worth.
 Seven years (the usual term of transpor-
tation)
Of absence lay one's old resentments level,
When a man's country 's going to the devil.

LXVII

Alas! could she but fully, truly, know
 How her great name is now throughout
abhorr'd: 530
How eager all the earth is for the blow
 Which shall lay bare her bosom to the
sword;
How all the nations deem her their worst
foe,
 That worse than *worst of foes*, the once
adored
False friend, who held out freedom to man-
kind,
And now would chain them, to the very
mind: —

LXVIII

Would she be proud, or boast herself the free,
 Who is but first of slaves? The nations are
In prison, — but the gaoler, what is he?
 No less a victim to the bolt and bar. 540
Is the poor privilege to turn the key
 Upon the captive, freedom? He's as far
From the enjoyment of the earth and air
Who watches o'er the chain, as they who wear.

LXIX

Don Juan now saw Albion's earliest beauties,
 Thy cliffs, *dear* Dover! harbour, and hotel;
Thy custom-house, with all its delicate duties;
 Thy waiters running mucks at every bell;
Thy packets, all whose passengers are booties
 To those who upon land or water dwell;
And last, not least, to strangers uninstructed, 551
Thy long, long bills, whence nothing is deducted.

LXX

Juan, though careless, young, and magnifique,
 And rich in rubles, diamonds, cash, and credit,
Who did not limit much his bills per week,
 Yet stared at this a little, though he paid it
(His Maggior Duomo, a smart, subtle Greek,
 Before him summ'd the awful scroll and read it);
But doubtless as the air, though seldom sunny,
Is free, the respiration's worth the money.

LXXI

On with the horses! Off to Canterbury! 561
 Tramp, tramp o'er pebble, and splash, splash through puddle;
Hurrah! how swiftly speeds the post so merry!
 Not like slow Germany, wherein they muddle
Along the road, as if they went to bury
 Their fare; and also pause besides, to fuddle

With 'schnapps' — sad dogs! whom 'Hundsfot,' or 'Verflucter,'
Affect no more than lightning a conductor.

LXXII

Now there is nothing gives a man such spirits,
 Leavening his blood as cayenne doth a curry, 570
As going at full speed — no matter where its
 Direction be, so 't is but in a hurry,
And merely for the sake of its own merits;
 For the less cause there is for all this flurry,
The greater is the pleasure in arriving
At the great *end* of travel — which is driving.

LXXIII

They saw at Canterbury the cathedral;
 Black Edward's helm, and Becket's bloody stone,
Were pointed out as usual by the bedral,
 In the same quaint, uninterested tone: —
There's glory again for you, gentle reader! All 681
 Ends in a rusty casque and dubious bone,
Half-solved into these sodas or magnesias;
Which form that bitter draught, the human species.

LXXIV

The effect on Juan was of course sublime:
 He breathed a thousand Cressys, as he saw
That casque, which never stoop'd except to Time.
 Even the bold Churchman's tomb excited awe,
Who died in the then great attempt to climb
 O'er kings, who *now* at least *must talk* of law
Before they butcher. Little Leila gazed, 590
And ask'd why such a structure had been raised:

LXXV

And being told it was 'God's house,' she said
 He was well lodged, but only wonder'd how
He suffer'd Infidels in his homestead,
 The cruel Nazarenes, who had laid low

His holy temples in the lands which bred
　The True Believers:—and her infant brow
Was bent with grief that Mahomet should
　resign
A mosque so noble, flung like pearls to
　swine.　　　　　　　　　　　　600

LXXVI

On! on! through meadows managed like a
　garden,
　A paradise of hops and high production;
For after years of travel by a bard in
　Countries of greater heat, but lesser suc-
　　tion,
A green field is a sight which makes him
　pardon
　The absence of that more sublime con-
　　struction,
Which mixes up vines, olives, precipices,
Glaciers, volcanos, oranges, and ices.

LXXVII

And when I think upon a pot of beer —
　But I won't weep!—and so drive on,
　　postilions!　　　　　　　　　610
As the smart boys spurr'd fast in their ca-
　reer,
　Juan admired these highways of free mil-
　　lions;
A country in all senses the most dear
　To foreigner or native, save some silly
　　ones,
Who 'kick against the pricks' just at this
　juncture,
And for their pains get only a fresh punc-
　ture.

LXXVIII

What a delightful thing 's a turnpike road!
　So smooth, so level, such a mode of shav-
　　ing
The earth, as scarce the eagle in the broad
　Air can accomplish, with his wide wings
　　waving.　　　　　　　　　　620
Had such been cut in Phaeton's time, the
　god
　Had told his son to satisfy his craving
With the York mail;—but onward as we
　roll,
'Surgit amari aliquid'—the toll!

LXXIX

Alas, how deeply painful is all payment!
　Take lives, take wives, take aught except
　　men's purses:

As Machiavel shows those in purple rai-
　ment,
　Such is the shortest way to general
　　curses.
They hate a murderer much less than a
　claimant
　On that sweet ore which every body
　　nurses;—　　　　　　　　　630
Kill a man's family, and he may brook it,
But keep your hands out of his breeches'
　pocket.

LXXX

So said the Florentine: ye monarchs, hearken
　To your instructor. Juan now was borne,
Just as the day began to wane and darken,
　O'er the high hill, which looks with pride
　　or scorn
Toward the great city.—Ye who have a
　spark in
　Your veins of Cockney spirit, smile or
　　mourn
According as you take things well or ill;—
Bold Britons, we are now on Shooter's Hill!

LXXXI

The sun went down, the smoke rose up, as
　from　　　　　　　　　　　641
　A half-unquench'd volcano, o'er a space
Which well beseem'd the 'Devil's drawing-
　room,'
　As some have qualified that wondrous
　　place:
But Juan felt, though not approaching
　home,
　As one who, though he were not of the
　　race,
Revered the soil, of those true sons the
　mother,
Who butcher'd half the earth, and bullied
　t' other.

LXXXII

A mighty mass of brick, and smoke, and
　shipping,
　Dirty and dusky, but as wide as eye　650
Could reach, with here and there a sail
　just skipping
　In sight, then lost amidst the forestry
Of masts; a wilderness of steeples peep-
　ing
　On tiptoe through their sea-coal canopy;
A huge, dun cupola, like a foolscap crown
On a fool's head—and there is London
　Town!

LXXXIII

But Juan saw not this: each wreath of smoke
Appear'd to him but as the magic vapour
Of some alchymic furnace, from whence broke
The wealth of worlds (a wealth of tax and paper): 660
The gloomy clouds, which o'er it as a yoke
Are bow'd, and put the sun out like a taper,
Were nothing but the natural atmosphere,
Extremely wholesome, though but rarely clear.

LXXXIV

He paused — and so will I; as doth a crew
Before they give their broadside. By and by,
My gentle countrymen, we will renew
Our old acquaintance; and at least I'll try
To tell you truths *you* will not take as true,
Because they are so; — a male Mrs. Fry, 670
With a soft besom will I sweep your halls,
And brush a web or two from off the walls.

LXXXV

Oh Mrs. Fry! Why go to Newgate? Why
Preach to poor rogues? And wherefore not begin
With Carlton, or with other houses? Try
Your head at harden'd and imperial sin.
To mend the people's an absurdity,
A jargon, a mere philanthropic din,
Unless you make their betters better: — Fy!
I thought you had more religion, Mrs. Fry. 680

LXXXVI

Teach them the decencies of good three-score;
Cure them of tours, hussar and highland dresses;
Tell them that youth once gone returns no more,
That hired huzzas redeem no land's distresses;
Tell them Sir William Curtis is a bore,
Too dull even for the dullest of excesses,
The witless Falstaff of a hoary Hal,
A fool whose bells have ceased to ring at all.

LXXXVII

Tell them, though it may be perhaps too late,
On life's worn confine, jaded, bloated, sated, 690
To set up vain pretence of being great,
'T is not so to be good; and be it stated,
The worthiest kings have ever loved least state;
And tell them — But you won't, and I have prated
Just now enough; but by and by I'll prattle
Like Roland's horn in Roncesvalles' battle.

CANTO THE ELEVENTH

I

WHEN Bishop Berkeley said 'there was no matter,'
And proved it — 't was no matter what he said:
They say his system 't is in vain to batter,
Too subtle for the airiest human head;
And yet who can believe it? I would shatter
Gladly all matters down to stone or lead,
Or adamant, to find the world a spirit,
And wear my head, denying that I wear it.

II

What a sublime discovery 't was to make the
Universe universal egotism, 10
That all 's ideal — *all ourselves:* I'll stake the
World (be it what you will) that *that* 's no schism.
Oh Doubt! — if thou be'st Doubt, for which some take thee,
But which I doubt extremely — thou sole prism
Of the Truth's rays, spoil not my draught of spirit!
Heaven's brandy, though our brain can hardly bear it.

III

For ever and anon comes Indigestion,
(Not the most 'dainty Ariel') and perplexes
Our soarings with another sort of question:
And that which after all my spirit vexes,
Is, that I find no spot where man can rest eye on, 21
Without confusion of the sorts and sexes,

Of beings, stars, and this unriddled wonder,
 The world, which at the worst 's a glorious
 blunder —

IV

If it be chance; or if it be according
 To the old text, still better:—lest it should
Turn out so, we 'll say nothing 'gainst the
 wording,
 As several people think such hazards
 rude.
They 're right; our days are too brief for
 affording
 Space to dispute what *no one* ever could
Decide, and *every body one day* will 31
Know very clearly — or at least lie still.

V

And therefore will I leave off metaphysical
 Discussion, which is neither here nor
 there:
If I agree that what is, is; then this I call
 Being quite perspicuous and extremely
 fair;
The truth is, I 've grown lately rather
 phthisical:
 I don't know what the reason is — the air
Perhaps; but as I suffer from the shocks
Of illness, I grow much more orthodox. 40

VI

The first attack at once proved the Divinity
 (But *that* I never doubted, nor the Devil);
The next, the Virgin's mystical virginity;
 The third, the usual Origin of Evil;
The fourth at once establish'd the whole
 Trinity
 On so uncontrovertible a level,
That I devoutly wish'd the three were four,
On purpose to believe so much the more.

VII

To our theme. — The man who has stood on
 the Acropolis,
 And look'd down over Attica; or he 50
Who has sail'd where picturesque Constan-
 tinople is,
 Or seen Timbuctoo, or hath taken tea
In small-eyed China's crockery-ware me-
 tropolis,
 Or sat amidst the bricks of Nineveh,
May not think much of London's first ap-
 pearance —
 But ask him what he thinks of it a year
 hence ?

VIII

Don Juan had got out on Shooter's Hill;
 Sunset the time, the place the same de-
 clivity
Which looks along that vale of good and ill
 Where London streets ferment in full
 activity; 60
While every thing around was calm and
 still,
 Except the creak of wheels, which on their
 pivot he
Heard, — and that bee-like, bubbling, busy
 hum
Of cities, that boil over with their scum: —

IX

I say, Don Juan, wrapt in contemplation,
 Walk'd on behind his carriage, o'er the
 summit,
And lost in wonder of so great a nation,
 Gave way to 't, since he could not over-
 come it.
' And here,' he cried, ' is Freedom's chosen
 station;
 Here peals the people's voice, nor can
 entomb it 70
Racks, prisons, inquisitions; resurrection
Awaits it, each new meeting or election.

X

' Here are chaste wives, pure lives; here
 people pay
 But what they please; and if that things
 be dear,
'T is only that they love to throw away
 Their cash, to show how much they have
 a-year.
Here laws are all inviolate; none lay
 Traps for the traveller; every highway 's
 clear:
Here — ' he was interrupted by a knife,
With, — ' Damn your eyes ! your money or
 your life ! ' 80

XI

These freeborn sounds proceeded from four
 pads
 In ambush laid, who had perceived him
 loiter
Behind his carriage; and, like handy lads,
 Had seized the lucky hour to reconnoitre,
In which the heedless gentleman who gads
 Upon the road, unless he prove a fighter,
May find himself within that isle of riches
Exposed to lose his life as well as breeches.

XII

Juan, who did not understand a word
 Of English, save their shibboleth, 'God
 damn!' 90
And even that he had so rarely heard,
 He sometimes thought 't was only their
 'Salām,'
Or 'God be with you!'—and 't is not
 absurd
 To think so: for half English as I am
(To my misfortune), never can I say
I heard them wish 'God with you,' save
 that way;—

XIII

Juan yet quickly understood their ges-
 ture,
 And being somewhat choleric and sud-
 den,
Drew forth a pocket pistol from his vesture,
 And fired it into one assailant's pud-
 ding— 100
Who fell, as rolls an ox o'er in his pasture,
 And roar'd out, as he writhed his native
 mud in,
Unto his nearest follower or henchman,
'Oh Jack! I 'm floor'd by that 'ere bloody
 Frenchman!'

XIV

On which. Jack and his train set off at
 speed,
 And Juan's suite, late scatter'd at a dis-
 tance,
Came up, all marvelling at such a deed,
 And offering, as usual, late assistance.
Juan, who saw the moon's late minion
 bleed
 As if his veins would pour out his exist-
 ence, 110
Stood calling out for bandages and lint,
And wish'd he had been less hasty with his
 flint.

XV

'Perhaps,' thought he, 'it is the country's
 wont
 To welcome foreigners in this way: now
I recollect some innkeepers who don't
 Differ, except in robbing with a bow,
In lieu of a bare blade and brazen front.
 But what is to be done? I can't allow
The fellow to lie groaning on the road:
So take him up; I 'll help you with the
 load.' 120

XVI

But ere they could perform this pious duty,
 The dying man cried, 'Hold! I 've got
 my gruel!
Oh for a glass of *max!* We 've miss'd our
 booty;
 Let me die where I am!' And as the
 fuel
Of life shrunk in his heart, and thick and
 sooty
 The drops fell from his death-wound, and
 he drew ill
His breath,—he from his swelling throat
 untied
A kerchief, crying, 'Give Sal that!'—and
 died.

XVII

The cravat stain'd with bloody drops fell
 down
 Before Don Juan's feet: he could not
 tell 130
Exactly why it was before him thrown,
 Nor what the meaning of the man's fare-
 well.
Poor Tom was once a kiddy upon town,
 A thorough varmint, and a *real* swell,
Full flash, all fancy, until fairly diddled,
His pockets first and then his body riddled.

XVIII

Don Juan, having done the best he could
 In all the circumstances of the case,
As soon as 'Crowner's quest' allow'd, pur-
 sued
 His travels to the capital apace;— 140
Esteeming it a little hard he should
 In twelve hours' time, and very little
 space,
Have been obliged to slay a freeborn na-
 tive
In self-defence: this made him meditative.

XIX

He from the world had cut off a great
 man,
 Who in his time had made heroic bustle.
Who in a row like Tom could lead the
 van,
 Booze in the ken, or at the spellken
 hustle?
Who queer a flat? Who (spite of Bow-
 street's ban)
 On the high toby-spice so flash the
 muzzle? 150

Who on a lark, with black-eyed Sal (his
 blowing),
So prime, so swell, so nutty, and so know-
 ing ?

XX

But Tom 's no more — and so no more of
 Tom.
 Heroes must die; and by God's blessing
 't is
Not long before the most of them go home.
Hail ! Thamis, hail ! Upon thy verge it is
That Juan's chariot, rolling like a drum
 In thunder, holds the way it can't well
 miss,
Through Kennington and all the other
 'tons,'
Which makes us wish ourselves in town at
 once; — 160

XXI

Through Groves, so call'd as being void of
 trees
 (Like *lucus* from *no* light); through pros-
 pects named
Mount Pleasant, as containing nought to
 please,
 Nor much to climb; through little boxes
 framed
Of bricks, to let the dust in at your ease,
 With 'To be let' upon their doors pro-
 claim'd;
Through 'Rows' most modestly call'd
 'Paradise,'
Which Eve might quit without much sacri-
 fice; —

XXII

Through coaches, drays, choked turnpikes,
 and a whirl
 Of wheels, and roar of voices, and con-
 fusion; 170
Here taverns wooing to a pint of 'purl,'
 There mails fast flying off like a delu-
 sion;
There barbers' blocks with periwigs in curl
 In windows; here the lamplighter's in-
 fusion
Slowly distill'd into the glimmering glass
(For in those days we had not got to gas);—

XXIII

Through this, and much, and more, is the
 approach
 Of travellers to mighty Babylon:

Whether they come by horse, or chaise, or
 coach,
 With slight exceptions, all the ways seem
 one. 180
I could say more, but do not choose to
 encroach
Upon the Guide-book's privilege. The sun
Had set some time, and night was on the
 ridge
Of twilight, as the party cross'd the bridge, —

XXIV

That 's rather fine. The gentle sound of
 Thamis —
 Who vindicates a moment, too, his
 stream,
Though hardly heard through multifarious
 'damme's ' —
 The lamps of Westminster's more regu-
 lar gleam,
The breadth of pavement, and yon shrine
 where fame is
A spectral resident — whose pallid beam
In shape of moonshine hovers o'er the
 pile — 191
Make this a sacred part of Albion's isle.

XXV

The Druids' groves are gone — so much the
 better:
 Stone-Henge is not — but what the devil
 is it ? —
But Bedlam still exists with its sage fetter,
 That madmen may not bite you on a visit;
The Bench too seats or suits full many a
 debtor;
 The Mansion House too (though some
 people quiz it)
To me appears a stiff yet grand erection;
But then the Abbey's worth the whole col-
 lection. 200

XXVI

The line of lights too up to Charing Cross,
 Pall Mall, and so forth, have a coruscation
Like gold as in comparison to dross,
 Match'd with the Continent's illumination,
Whose cities Night by no means deigns to
 gloss.
 The French were not yet a lamp-lighting
 nation,
And when they grew so — on their new-
 found lantern,
Instead of wicks, they made a wicked man
 turn.

XXVII

A row of gentlemen along the streets
 Suspended may illuminate mankind, 210
As also bonfires made of country seats;
 But the old way is best for the purblind:
The other looks like phosphorus on sheets,
 A sort of ignis fatuus to the mind,
Which, though 't is certain to perplex and
 frighten,
Must burn more mildly ere it can enlighten.

XXVIII

But London 's so well lit, that if Diogenes
 Could recommence to hunt his *honest
 man,*
And found him not amidst the various pro-
 genies
 Of this enormous city's spreading span,
'T were not for want of lamps to aid his
 dodging his 221
 Yet undiscover'd treasure. What *I* can,
I 've done to find the same throughout life's
 journey,
But see the world is only one attorney.

XXIX

Over the stones still rattling up Pall Mall,
 Through crowds and carriages, but wax-
 ing thinner
As thunder'd knockers broke the long seal'd
 spell
 Of doors 'gainst duns, and to an early
 dinner
Admitted a small party as night fell, —
 Don Juan, our young diplomatic sinner,
Pursued his path, and drove past some ho-
 tels, 231
St. James's Palace and St. James's 'Hells.'

XXX

They reach'd the hotel: forth stream'd from
 the front door
 A tide of well-clad waiters, and around
The mob stood, and as usual several score
 Of those pedestrian Paphians who abound
In decent London when the daylight 's o'er;
 Commodious but immoral, they are
 found
Useful, like Malthus, in promoting mar-
 riage. —
But Juan now is stepping from his carriage

XXXI

Into one of the sweetest of hotels, 241
 Especially for foreigners — and mostly
For those whom favour or whom fortune
 swells,
 And cannot find a bill's small items costly.
There many an envoy either dwelt or
 dwells
 (The den of many a diplomatic lost lie),
Until to some conspicuous square they pass,
And blazon o'er the door their names in
 brass.

XXXII

Juan, whose was a delicate commission,
 Private, though publicly important, bore
No title to point out with due precision 251
 The exact affair on which he was sent
 o'er.
'T was merely known, that on a secret mis-
 sion
 A foreigner of rank had graced our shore,
Young, handsome, and accomplish'd, who
 was said
(In whispers) to have turn'd his sovereign's
 head.

XXXIII

Some rumour also of some strange adven-
 tures
 Had gone before him, and his wars and
 loves;
And as romantic heads are pretty painters,
 And, above all, an Englishwoman's roves
Into the excursive, breaking the indentures
 Of sober reason wheresoe'er it moves, 262
He found himself extremely in the fashion,
Which serves our thinking people for a
 passion.

XXXIV

I don't mean that they are passionless, but
 quite
 The contrary; but then 't is in the head;
Yet as the consequences are as bright
 As if they acted with the heart instead,
What after all can signify the site
 Of ladies' lucubrations? So they lead 270
In safety to the place for which you start,
What matters if the road be head or heart?

XXXV

Juan presented in the proper place,
 To proper placemen, every Russ creden-
 tial;
And was received with all the due grimace
 By those who govern in the mood poten-
 tial,

Who, seeing a handsome stripling with
 smooth face,
 Thought (what in state affairs is most
 essential)
That they as easily might *do* the youngster,
As hawks may pounce upon a woodland
 songster. 280

XXXVI

They err'd, as aged men will do; but by
 And by we 'll talk of that; and if we
 don't,
'T will be because our notion is not high
 Of politicians and their double front,
Who live by lies, yet dare not boldly lie: —
 Now what I love in women is, they won't
Or can't do otherwise than lie, but do it
So well, the very truth seems falsehood to
 it.

XXXVII

And, after all, what is a lie ? 'T is but
 The truth in masquerade; and I defy 290
Historians, heroes, lawyers, priests, to put
 A fact without some leaven of a lie.
The very shadow of true Truth would shut
 Up annals, revelations, poesy,
And prophecy — except it should be dated
Some years before the incidents related.

XXXVIII

Praised be all liars and all lies ! Who now
 Can tax my mild Muse with misan-
 thropy?
She rings the world's ' Te Deum,' and her
 brow
 Blushes for those who will not: — but to
 sigh 300
Is idle; let us like most others bow,
 Kiss hands, feet, any part of majesty,
After the good example of ' Green Erin,'
Whose shamrock now seems rather worse
 for wearing.

XXXIX

Don Juan was presented, and his dress
 And mien excited general admiration —
I don't know which was more admired or
 less:
 One monstrous diamond drew much ob-
 servation, 308
Which Catherine in a moment of ' ivresse '
 (In love or brandy's fervent fermentation)
Bestow'd upon him, as the public learn'd;
And, to say truth, it had been fairly earn'd.

XL

Besides the ministers and underlings,
 Who must be courteous to the accredited
Diplomatists of rather wavering kings,
 Until their royal riddle 's fully read,
The very clerks, — those somewhat dirty
 springs
 Of office, or the house of office, fed
By foul corruption into streams, — even
 they
Were hardly rude enough to earn their
 pay: 320

XLI

And insolence no doubt is what they are
 Employ'd for, since it is their daily la-
 bour,
In the dear offices of peace or war;
 And should you doubt, pray ask of your
 next neighbour,
When for a passport, or some other bar
 To freedom, he applied (a grief and a
 bore),
If he found not his spawn of taxborn riches,
Like lap-dogs, the least civil sons of b—s.

XLII

But Juan was received with much ' em-
 pressement: ' —
 These phrases of refinement I must bor-
 row 330
From our next neighbours' land, where,
 like a chessman,
 There is a move set down for joy or sor-
 row
Not only in mere talking, but the press.
 Man
 In islands is, it seems, downright and
 thorough,
More than on continents — as if the sea
(See Billingsgate) made even the tongue
 more free.

XLIII

And yet the British ' Damme ' 's rather
 Attic:
 Your continental oaths are but inconti-
 nent,
And turn on things which no aristocratic
 Spirit would name, and therefore even I
 won't anent 340
This subject quote; as it would be schis-
 matic
 In politesse, and have a sound affronting
 in 't: —

But ' Damme ' 's quite ethereal, though too
 daring —
Platonic blasphemy, the soul of swearing.

XLIV

For downright rudeness, ye may stay at
 home;
 For true or false politeness (and scarce
 that
Now) you may cross the blue deep and
 white foam —
 The first the emblem (rarely though) of
 what
You leave behind, the next of much you
 come
 To meet. However, 't is no time to chat
On general topics: poems must confine 351
Themselves to unity, like this of mine.

XLV

In the great world, — which, being inter-
 preted,
 Meaneth the west or worst end of a city,
And about twice two thousand people bred
 By no means to be very wise or witty,
But to sit up while others lie in bed,
 And look down on the universe with
 pity, —
Juan, as an inveterate patrician,
Was well received by persons of condi-
 tion. 360

XLVI

He was a bachelor, which is a matter
 Of import both to virgin and to bride,
The former's hymeneal hopes to flatter;
 And (should she not hold fast by love or
 pride)
'T is also of some moment to the latter:
 A rib 's a thorn in a wed gallant's side,
Requires decorum, and is apt to double
The horrid sin — and what 's still worse,
 the trouble.

XLVII

But Juan was a bachelor — of arts,
 And parts, and hearts: he danced and
 sung, and had 370
An air as sentimental as Mozart's
 Softest of melodies; and could be sad
Or cheerful, without any ' flaws or starts,'
 Just at the proper time; and though a lad,
Had seen the world — which is a curious
 sight,
And very much unlike what people write.

XLVIII

Fair virgins blush'd upon him; wedded dames
 Bloom'd also in less transitory hues;
For both commodities dwell by the Thames,
 The painting and the painted; youth,
 ceruse, 380
Against his heart preferr'd their usual
 claims,
 Such as no gentleman can quite refuse:
Daughters admired his dress, and pious
 mothers
Inquired his income, and if he had brothers.

XLIX

The milliners who furnish ' drapery Misses '
 Throughout the season, upon speculation
Of payment ere the honey-moon's last kisses
 Have waned into a crescent's coruscation,
Thought such an opportunity as this is,
 Of a rich foreigner's initiation, 390
Not to be overlook'd — and gave such credit,
That future bridegrooms swore, and sigh'd,
 and paid it.

L

The Blues, that tender tribe who sigh o'er
 sonnets,
 And with the pages of the last Review
Line the interior of their heads or bonnets,
 Advanced in all their azure's highest hue:
They talk'd bad French or Spanish, and
 upon its
 Late authors ask'd him for a hint or two;
And which was softest, Russian or Cas-
 tilian ?
And whether in his travels he saw Ilion ?

LI

Juan, who was a little superficial, 401
 And not in literature a great Drawcansir,
Examined by this learned and especial
 Jury of matrons, scarce knew what to
 answer:
His duties warlike, loving or official,
 His steady application as a dancer,
Had kept him from the brink of Hippocrene,
Which now he found was blue instead of
 green.

LII

However, he replied at hazard, with 409
 A modest confidence and calm assurance,
Which lent his learned lucubrations pith,
 And pass'd for arguments of good en-
 durance.

That prodigy, Miss Araminta Smith
　　(Who at sixteen translated 'Hercules
　　　Furens'
Into as furious English), with her best look,
Set down his sayings in her common-place
　　book.

LIII

Juan knew several languages — as well
　　He might — and brought them up with
　　　skill, in time
To save his fame with each accomplish'd
　　belle,
　　Who still regretted that he did not rhyme.
There wanted but this requisite to swell 421
　　His qualities (with them) into sublime:
Lady Fitz-Frisky, and Miss Mævia Man-
　　nish,
Both long'd extremely to be sung in Spanish.

LIV

However, he did pretty well, and was
　　Admitted as an aspirant to all
The coteries, and, as in Banquo's glass,
　　At great assemblies or in parties small,
He saw ten thousand living authors pass,
　　That being about their average numeral;
Also the eighty 'greatest living poets,' 431
As every paltry magazine can show its.

LV

In twice five years the 'greatest living
　　poet,'
　　Like to the champion in the fisty ring,
Is call'd on to support his claim, or show it,
　　Although 't is an imaginary thing.
Even I — albeit I 'm sure I did not know it,
　　Nor sought of foolscap subjects to be
　　　king —
Was reckon'd a considerable time,
　　The grand Napoleon of the realms of
　　　rhyme. 440

LVI

But Juan was my Moscow, and Faliero
　　My Leipsic, and my Mount Saint Jean
　　　seems Cain:
'La Belle Alliance' of dunces down at zero,
　　Now that the Lion's fall'n, may rise
　　　again:
But I will fall at least as fell my hero;
　　Nor reign at all, or as a monarch reign;
Or to some lonely isle of gaolers go,
With turncoat Southey for my turnkey
　　Lowe.

LVII

Sir Walter reign'd before me; Moore and
　　Campbell
　　Before and after; but now grown more
　　　holy, 450
The Muses upon Sion's hill must ramble
　　With poets almost clergymen, or wholly;
And Pegasus hath a psalmodic amble
　　Beneath the very Reverend Rowley
　　　Powley,
Who shoes the glorious animal with stilts,
A modern Ancient Pistol — by the hilts !

LVIII

Then there 's my gentle Euphues, who,
　　they say,
　　Sets up for being a sort of moral me;
He 'll find it rather difficult some day
　　To turn out both, or either, it may be. 460
Some persons think that Coleridge hath
　　the sway;
　　And Wordsworth has supporters, two or
　　　three;
And that deep-mouth'd Bœotian 'Savage
　　Landor'
Has taken for a swan rogue Southey's
　　gander.

LIX

John Keats, who was kill'd off by one
　　critique,
　　Just as he really promised something
　　　great,
If not intelligible, without Greek
　　Contrived to talk about the gods of late,
Much as they might have been supposed to
　　speak.
　　Poor fellow ! His was an untoward fate;
'T is strange the mind, that very fiery
　　particle, 471
Should let itself be snuff'd out by an ar-
　　ticle.

LX

The list grows long of live and dead pre-
　　tenders
　　To that which none will gain — or none
　　　will know
The conqueror at least; who, ere Time
　　renders
　　His last award, will have the long grass
　　　grow
Above his burnt-out brain, and sapless
　　cinders.
　　If I might augur, I should rate but low

Their chances; they 're too numerous, like
 the thirty
Mock tyrants, when Rome's annals wax'd
 but dirty. 480

LXI

This is the literary *lower* empire,
 Where the prætorian bands take up the
 matter; —
A ' dreadful trade,' like his who ' gathers
 samphire,'
 The insolent soldiery to soothe and flat-
 ter,
With the same feelings as you 'd coax a
 vampire.
 Now, were I once at home, and in good
 satire,
I 'd try conclusions with those Janizaries,
And show them *what* an intellectual war is.

LXII

I think I know a trick or two, would turn
 Their flanks; — but it is hardly worth
 my while 490
With such small gear to give myself con-
 cern:
 Indeed I 've not the necessary bile;
My natural temper 's really aught but stern,
 And even my Muse's worst reproof 's a
 smile;
And then she drops a brief and modern
 curtsy,
And glides away, assured she never hurts
 ye.

LXIII

My Juan, whom I left in deadly peril
 Amongst live poets and blue ladies, past
With some small profit through that field
 so sterile,
 Being tired in time, and, neither least nor
 last, 500
Left it before he had been treated very ill;
 And henceforth found himself more gaily
 class'd
Amongst the higher spirits of the day,
The sun's true son, no vapour, but a ray.

LXIV

His morns he pass'd in business — which,
 dissected,
 Was like all business a laborious nothing
That leads to lassitude, the most infected
 And Centaur Nessus garb of mortal
 clothing,

And on our sofas makes us lie dejected,
 And talk in tender horrors of our loath-
 ing 510
All kinds of toil, save for our country's
 good —
Which grows no better, though 't is time it
 should.

LXV

His afternoons he pass'd in visits, luncheons,
 Lounging and boxing; and the twilight
 hour
In riding round those vegetable puncheons
 Call'd ' Parks,' where there is neither
 fruit nor flower
Enough to gratify a bee's slight munchings;
 But after all it is the only ' bower '
(In Moore's phrase), where the fashionable
 fair
Can form a slight acquaintance with fresh
 air. 520

LXVI

Then dress, then dinner, then awakes the
 world !
 Then glare the lamps, then whirl the
 wheels, then roar
Through street and square fast flashing
 chariots hurl'd
 Like harness'd meteors; then along the
 floor
Chalk mimics painting; then festoons are
 twirl'd;
 Then roll the brazen thunders of the door,
Which opens to the thousand happy few
An earthly paradise of ' Or Molu.'

LXVII

There stands the noble hostess, nor shall
 sink
 With the three-thousandth curtsy; there
 the waltz, 530
The only dance which teaches girls to think,
 Makes one in love even with its very
 faults.
Saloon, room, hall, o'erflow beyond their
 brink,
 And long the latest of arrivals halts,
'Midst royal dukes and dames condemn'd
 to climb,
And gain an inch of staircase at a time.

LXVIII

Thrice happy he who, after a survey
 Of the good company, can win a corner,

The House of Commons turn'd to a tax-
 trap —
 I have seen that sad affair of the late
 Queen — 660
I have seen crowns worn instead of a fool's
 cap —
 I have seen a Congress doing all that 's
 mean —
I have seen some nations like o'erloaded
 asses
Kick off their burthens, meaning the high
 classes.

LXXXIV

I have seen small poets, and great prosers,
 and
 Interminable — *not eternal* — speakers —
I have seen the funds at war with house
 and land —
 I have seen the country gentlemen turn
 squeakers —
I have seen the people ridden o'er like sand
 By slaves on horseback — I have seen
 malt liquors 670
Exchanged for 'thin potations' by John
 Bull —
I have seen John half detect himself a
 fool. —

LXXXV

But 'carpe diem,' Juan, 'carpe, carpe!'
 To-morrow sees another race as gay
And transient, and devour'd by the same
 harpy.
 'Life's a poor player,' — then 'play out
 the play,
Ye villains!' and above all keep a sharp eye
 Much less on what you do than what you
 say:
Be hypocritical, be cautious, be
 Not what you *seem*, but always what you
 see. 680

LXXXVI

But how shall I relate in other cantos
 Of what befell our hero in the land,
Which 't is the common cry and lie to
 vaunt as
 A moral country? But I hold my
 hand —
For I disdain to write an Atalantis;
 But 't is as well at once to understand,
You are *not* a moral people, and you know
 it
Without the aid of too sincere a poet.

LXXXVII

What Juan saw and underwent shall be
 My topic, with of course the due restric-
 tion 690
Which is required by proper courtesy;
 And recollect the work is only fiction,
And that I sing of neither mine nor me,
 Though every scribe, in some slight turn
 of diction,
Will hint allusions never *meant*. Ne'er
 doubt
This — when I speak, I *don't hint*, but *speak
 out.*

LXXXVIII

Whether he married with the third or
 fourth
 Offspring of some sage husband-hunting
 countess,
Or whether with some virgin of more worth
 (I mean in Fortune's matrimonial boun-
 ties) 700
He took to regularly peopling Earth,
 Of which your lawful awful wedlock
 fount is, —
Or whether he was taken in for damages,
For being too excursive in his homages, —

LXXXIX

Is yet within the unread events of time.
 Thus far, go forth, thou lay, which I will
 back
Against the same given quantity of rhyme,
 For being as much the subject of at-
 tack
As ever yet was any work sublime,
 By those who love to say that white is
 black. 710
So much the better! — I may stand alone,
But would not change my free thoughts for
 a throne.

CANTO THE TWELFTH

I

OF all the barbarous middle ages, that
 Which is most barbarous is the middle
 age
Of man; it is — I really scarce know what;
 But when we hover between fool and
 sage,
And don't know justly what we would be
 at —
 A period something like a printed page,

Black letter upon foolscap, while our hair
 Grows grizzled, and we are not what we
 were; —

II

Too old for youth, — too young, at thirty-
 five,
 To herd with boys, or hoard with good
 threescore, — 10
I wonder people should be left alive;
 But since they are, that epoch is a bore:
Love lingers still, although 't were late to
 wive;
 And as for other love, the illusion 's o'er;
And money, that most pure imagination,
Gleams only through the dawn of its cre-
 ation.

III

O Gold ! Why call we misers miserable ?
 Theirs is the pleasure that can never
 pall;
Theirs is the best bower anchor, the chain
 cable
 Which holds fast other pleasures great
 and small. 20
Ye who but see the saving man at table,
 And scorn his temperate board, as none
 at all,
And wonder how the wealthy can be sparing,
Know not what visions spring from each
 cheese-paring.

IV

Love or lust makes man sick, and wine
 much sicker;
 Ambition rends, and gaming gains a
 loss;
But making money, slowly first, then
 quicker,
 And adding still a little through each
 cross
 Which *will* come over things), beats love
 or liquor,
 The gamester's counter, or the states-
 man's *dross.* 30
O Gold ! I still prefer thee unto paper,
Which makes bank credit like a bank of
 vapour.

V

Who hold the balance of the world ? Who
 reign
 O'er congress, whether royalist or lib-
 eral ?

Who rouse the shirtless patriots of Spain ?
 (That make old Europe's journals squeak
 and gibber all.)
Who keep the world, both old and new, in
 pain
 Or pleasure ? Who make politics run
 glibber all ?
The shade of Buonaparte's noble daring ? —
Jew Rothschild, and his fellow-Christian,
 Baring. 40

VI

Those, and the truly liberal Lafitte,
 Are the true lords of Europe. Every
 loan
Is not a merely speculative hit,
 But seats a nation or upsets a throne.
Republics also get involved a bit;
 Columbia's stock hath holders not un-
 known
On 'Change; and even thy silver soil, Peru,
Must get itself discounted by a Jew.

VII

Why call the miser miserable ? as
 I said before: the frugal life is his, 50
Which in a saint or cynic ever was
 The theme of praise: a hermit would not
 miss
Canonization for the self-same cause,
 And wherefore blame gaunt wealth's
 austerities ?
Because, you 'll say, nought calls for such
 a trial; —
Then there 's more merit in his self-denial.

VIII

He is your only poet; — passion, pure
 And sparkling on from heap to heap, dis-
 plays,
Possess'd, the ore, of which *mere hopes* al-
 lure
 Nations athwart the deep: the golden
 rays 60
Flash up in ingots from the mine obscure;
 On him the diamond pours its brilliant
 blaze,
While the mild emerald's beam shades
 down the dies
Of other stones, to soothe the miser's eyes.

IX

The lands on either side are his; the ship
 From Ceylon, Inde, or far Cathay, un-
 loads

For him the fragrant produce of each trip;
 Beneath his cars of Ceres groan the
 roads,
And the vine blushes like Aurora's lip;
 His very cellars might be kings' abodes;
While he, despising every sensual call, 71
Commands — the intellectual lord of all.

X

Perhaps he hath great projects in his mind,
 To build a college, or to found a race,
A hospital, a church, — and leave behind
 Some dome surmounted by his meagre
 face:
Perhaps he fain would liberate mankind
 Even with the very ore which makes
 them base;
Perhaps he would be wealthiest of his na-
 tion,
Or revel in the joys of calculation. 80

XI

But whether all, or each, or none of these
 May be the hoarder's principle of action,
The fool will call such mania a disease: —
 What is his *own*? Go — look at each
 transaction,
Wars, revels, loves — do these bring men
 more ease
 Than the mere plodding through each
 'vulgar fraction?'
Or do they benefit mankind? Lean miser!
Let spendthrifts' heirs enquire of yours —
 who's wiser?

XII

How beauteous are rouleaus! how charm-
 ing chests
 Containing ingots, bags of dollars, coins
(Not of old victors, all whose heads and
 crests 91
 Weigh not the thin ore where their vis-
 age shines,
But) of fine unclipt gold, where dully rests
 Some likeness, which the glittering
 cirque confines,
Of modern, reigning, sterling, stupid
 stamp: —
Yes! ready money *is* Aladdin's lamp.

XIII

'Love rules the camp, the court, the
 grove,' — 'for love
 Is heaven, and heaven is love:' — so
 sings the bard;

Which it were rather difficult to prove
 (A thing with poetry in general hard). 100
Perhaps there may be something in 'the
 grove,'
 At least it rhymes to 'love;' but I'm
 prepared
To doubt (no less than landlords of their
 rental)
If 'courts' and 'camps' be quite so senti-
 mental.

XIV

But if Love don't, *Cash* does, and Cash
 alone:
 Cash rules the grove, and fells it too
 besides;
Without cash, camps were thin, and courts
 were none;
 Without cash, Malthus tells you — 'take
 no brides.'
So Cash rules Love the ruler, on his own
 High ground, as virgin Cynthia sways
 the tides: 110
And as for 'Heaven being Love,' why not
 say honey
Is wax? Heaven is not Love, 't is Matri-
 mony.

XV

Is not all love prohibited whatever,
 Excepting marriage? which is love, no
 doubt,
After a sort; but somehow people never
 With the same thought the two words
 have help'd out:
Love may exist *with* marriage, and *should*
 ever,
 And marriage also may exist without;
But love *sans* bans is both a sin and shame,
And ought to go by quite another name. 120

XVI

Now if the 'court,' and 'camp,' and 'grove,'
 be not
 Recruited all with constant married men,
Who never coveted their neighbour's lot,
 I say *that* line's a lapsus of the pen; —
Strange too in my 'buon camerado' Scott,
 So celebrated for his morals, when
My Jeffrey held him up as an example
To me; — of whom these morals are a
 sample.

XVII

Well, if I don't succeed, I *have* succeeded,
 And that's enough; succeeded in my
 youth, 130

The only time when much success is needed:
 And my success produced what I, in
 sooth,
Cared most about; it need not now be
 pleaded —
 Whate'er it was, 't was mine; I' ve paid,
 in truth,
Of late the penalty of such success,
But have not learn'd to wish it any less.

XVIII

That suit in Chancery, — which some per-
 sons plead
 In an appeal to the unborn, whom they,
In the faith of their procreative creed,
 Baptize posterity, or future clay, — 140
To me seems but a dubious kind of reed
 To lean on for support in any way;
Since odds are that posterity will know
No more of them, than they of her, I trow.

XIX

Why, I 'm posterity — and so are you;
 And whom do we remember ? Not a
 hundred.
Were every memory written down all
 true,
 The tenth or twentieth name would be
 but blunder'd;
Even Plutarch's Lives have but pick'd out
 a few,
 And 'gainst those few your annalists have
 thunder'd; 150
And Mitford in the nineteenth century
Gives, with Greek truth, the good old Greek
 the lie.

XX

Good people all, of every degree,
 Ye gentle readers and ungentle writers,
In this twelfth Canto 't is my wish to be
 As serious as if I had for inditers
Malthus and Wilberforce: — the last set
 free
 The Negroes, and is worth a million
 fighters;
While Wellington has but enslaved the
 Whites,
And Malthus does the thing 'gainst which
 he writes. 160

XXI

I 'm serious — so are all men upon paper;
 And why should I not form my specula-
 tion,

And hold up to the sun my little taper ?
 Mankind just now seem wrapt in media-
 tion
On constitutions and steam-boats of va-
 pour;
 While sages write against all procreation,
Unless a man can calculate his means
Of feeding brats the moment his wife
 weans.

XXII

That 's noble ! That 's romantic ! For my
 part,
 I think that ' Philo-genitiveness ' is 170
(Now here's a word quite after my own
 heart,
 Though there 's a shorter a good deal
 than this,
If that politeness set it not apart;
 But I 'm resolved to say nought that 's
 amiss) —
I say, methinks that ' Philo-genitiveness '
Might meet from men a little more forgive-
 ness.

XXIII

And now to business. — O my gentle Juan !
 Thou art in London — in that pleasant
 place,
Where every kind of mischief's daily brew-
 ing,
 Which can await warm youth in its wild
 race. 180
'T is true, that thy career is not a new one;
 Thou art no novice in the headlong chase
Of early life; but this is a new land,
Which foreigners can never understand.

XXIV

What with a small diversity of climate,
 Of hot or cold, mercurial or sedate,
I could send forth my mandate like a
 primate
 Upon the rest of Europe's social state;
But thou art the most difficult to rhyme at,
 Great Britain, which the Muse may pene-
 trate. 190
All countries have their ' Lions,' but in thee
There is but one superb menagerie.

XXV

But I am sick of politics. Begin,
 ' Paulo Majora.' Juan, undecided
Amongst the paths of being ' taken in,'
 Above the ice had like a skater glided:

When tired of play, he flirted without sin
 With some of those fair creatures who
 have prided
Themselves on innocent tantalisation,
And hate all vice except its reputation. ₂₀₀

XXVI

But these are few, and in the end they make
 Some devilish escapade or stir, which
 shows
That even the purest people may mistake
 Their way through virtue's primrose paths
 of snows;
And then men stare, as if a new ass spake
 To Balaam, and from tongue to ear
 o'erflows
Quicksilver small talk, ending (if you note
 it)
With the kind world's amen — ' Who would
 have thought it ? '

XXVII

The little Leila, with her orient eyes,
 And taciturn Asiatic disposition ₂₁₀
(Which saw all western things with small
 surprise,
 To the surprise of people of condition,
Who think that novelties are butterflies
 To be pursued as food for inanition),
Her charming figure and romantic history
Became a kind of fashionable mystery.

XXVIII

The women much divided — as is usual
 Amongst the sex in little things or great.
Think not, fair creatures, that I mean to
 abuse you all — ₂₁₉
 I have always liked you better than I
 state:
Since I 've grown moral, still I must accuse
 you all
 Of being apt to talk at a great rate;
And now there was a general sensation
Amongst you, about Leila's education.

XXIX

In one point only were you settled — and
 You had reason; 't was that a young child
 of grace,
As beautiful as her own native land,
 And far away, the last bud of her race,
Howe'er our friend Don Juan might com-
 mand
 Himself for five, four, three, or two
 years' space, ₂₃₀

Would be much better taught beneath the
 eye
Of peeresses whose follies had run dry.

XXX

So first there was a generous emulation,
 And then there was a general competi-
 tion,
To undertake the orphan's education.
 As Juan was a person of condition,
It had been an affront on this occasion
 To talk of a subscription or petition;
But sixteen dowagers, ten unwed she sages,
Whose tale belongs to ' Hallam's Middle
 Ages,' ₂₄₀

XXXI

And one or two sad, separate wives, without
 A fruit to bloom upon their withering
 bough —
Begg'd to bring *up* the little girl and ' *out*,' —
 For that 's the phrase that settles all
 things now,
Meaning a virgin's first blush at a rout,
 And all her points as thorough-bred to
 show:
And I assure you, that like virgin honey
Tastes their first season (mostly if they
 have money).

XXXII

How all the needy honourable misters,
 Each out-at-elbow peer, or desperate
 dandy, ₂₅₀
The watchful mothers, and the careful
 sisters
 (Who, by the by, when clever, are more
 handy
At making matches, where ' 't is gold that
 glisters,'
 Than their *he* relatives), like flies o'er
 candy
Buzz round ' *the* Fortune ' with their busy
 battery,
To turn her head with waltzing and with
 flattery !

XXXIII

Each aunt, each cousin, hath her specula-
 tion;
 Nay, married dames will now and then
 discover
Such pure disinterestedness of passion,
 I 've known them court an heiress for
 their lover. ₂₆₀

'Tantæne !' Such the virtues of high sta-
tion,
 Even in the hopeful Isle, whose outlet's
 'Dover !'
While the poor rich wretch, object of these
cares,
Has cause to wish her sire had had male
heirs.

XXXIV

Some are soon bagg'd, and some reject three
dozen.
 'T is fine to see them scattering refusals
And wild dismay o'er every angry cousin
 (Friends of the party), who begin accusals,
Such as — 'Unless Miss (Blank) meant to
have chosen
 Poor Frederick, why did she accord
 perusals 270
To his billets ? *Why* waltz with him ?
Why, I pray,
Look *yes* last night, and yet say *no* to-day ?

XXXV

'Why ? — Why ? — Besides, Fred really
was *attach'd;*
 'T was not her fortune — he has enough
 without:
The time will come she 'll wish that she
had snatch'd
 So good an opportunity, no doubt: —
But the old marchioness some plan had
hatch'd,
 As I 'll tell Aurea at to-morrow's rout:
And after all poor Frederick may do
better — 279
Pray did you see her answer to his letter ? '

XXXVI

Smart uniforms and sparkling coronets
 Are spurn'd in turn, until her turn arrives,
After male loss of time, and hearts, and bets
 Upon the sweepstakes for substantial
 wives;
And when at last the pretty creature gets
 Some gentleman, who fights, or writes,
 or drives,
It soothes the awkward squad of the re-
jected
To find how very badly she selected.

XXXVII

For sometimes they accept some long pur-
suer,
 Worn out with importunity; or fall 290

(But here perhaps the instances are fewer)
 To the lot of him who scarce pursued at
 all.
A hazy widower turn'd of forty 's sure
 (If 't is not vain examples to recall)
To draw a high prize: now, howe'er he got
her, I
See nought more strange in this than
t' other lottery.

XXXVIII

I, for my part (one 'modern instance'
more,
 'True, 't is a pity — pity 't is, 't is true '),
Was chosen from out an amatory score,
 Albeit my years were less discreet than
 few; 300
But though I also had reform'd before
 Those became one who soon were to be
 two,
I 'll not gainsay the generous public's voice,
That the young lady made a monstrous
choice.

XXXIX

Oh, pardon my digression — or at least
 Peruse ! 'T is always with a moral end
That I dissert, like grace before a feast:
 For like an aged aunt, or tiresome friend,
A rigid guardian, or a zealous priest, 309
 My Muse by exhortation means to mend
All people, at all times, and in most places,
Which puts my Pegasus to these grave
paces.

XL

But now I 'm going to be immoral; now
 I mean to show things really as they are,
Not as they ought to be: for I avow,
 That till we see what 's what in fact,
 we 're far
From much improvement with that vir-
tuous plough
 Which skims the surface, leaving scarce
 a scar
Upon the black loam long manured by Vice,
Only to keep its corn at the old price. 320

XLI

But first of little Leila we 'll dispose;
 For like a day-dawn she was young and
 pure,
Or like the old comparison of snows,
 Which are more pure than pleasant to be
 sure.

Like many people everybody knows,
　Don Juan was delighted to secure
A goodly guardian for his infant charge,
Who might not profit much by being at
　　large.

XLII

Besides, he had found out he was no tutor
　(I wish that others would find out the
　　same); 330
And rather wish'd in such things to stand
　neuter,
　For silly wards will bring their guardians
　　blame:
So when he saw each ancient dame a suitor
　To make his little wild Asiatic tame,
Consulting 'the Society for Vice
Suppression,' Lady Pinchbeck was his
　choice.

XLIII

Olden she was — but had been very young;
　Virtuous she was — and had been, I
　　believe;
Although the world has such an evil
　tongue
　That — but my chaster ear will not
　　receive 340
An echo of a syllable that 's wrong:
　In fact, there 's nothing makes me so
　　much grieve,
As that abominable tittle-tattle,
Which is the cud eschew'd by human cattle.

XLIV

Moreover I 've remark'd (and I was once
　A slight observer in a modest way),
And so may every one except a dunce,
　That ladies in their youth a little gay,
Besides their knowledge of the world, and
　sense
　Of the sad consequence of going astray, 350
Are wiser in their warnings 'gainst the
　woe
Which the mere passionless can never know.

XLV

While the harsh prude indemnifies her
　virtue
　By railing at the unknown and envied
　　passion,
Seeking far less to save you than to hurt
　you,
　Or, what 's still worse, to put you out of
　　fashion, —

The kinder veteran with calm words will
　court you,
　Entreating you to pause before you dash
　　on;
Expounding and illustrating the riddle 359
Of epic Love's beginning, end, and middle.

XLVI

Now whether it be thus, or that they are
　stricter,
　As better knowing why they should be so,
I think you 'll find from many a family pic-
　ture,
　That daughters of such mothers as may
　　know
The world by experience rather than by
　lecture,
　Turn out much better for the Smithfield
　　Show
Of vestals brought into the marriage mart,
Than those bred up by prudes without a
　heart.

XLVII

I said that Lady Pinchbeck had been talk'd
　about —
　As who has not, if female, young, and
　　pretty? 370
But now no more the ghost of Scandal
　stalk'd about;
　She merely was deem'd amiable and
　　witty,
And several of her best bon-mots were
　hawk'd about:
　Then she was given to charity and pity,
And pass'd (at least the latter years of life)
For being a most exemplary wife.

XLVIII

High in high circles, gentle in her own,
　She was the mild reprover of the young,
Whenever — which means every day —
　they 'd shown
　An awkward inclination to go wrong. 380
The quantity of good she did 's unknown,
　Or at the least would lengthen out my
　　song:
In brief, the little orphan of the East
Had raised an interest in her, which in-
　creased.

XLIX

Juan, too, was a sort of favourite with her,
　Because she thought him a good heart at
　　bottom,

A little spoil'd, but not so altogether;
 Which was a wonder, if you think who
 got him,
And how he had been toss'd, he scarce knew
 whither:
 Though this might ruin others, it did
 not him, 390
At least entirely — for he had seen too
 many
Changes in youth, to be surprised at any.

L

And these vicissitudes tell best in youth;
 For when they happen at a riper age,
People are apt to blame the Fates, forsooth,
 And wonder Providence is not more sage.
Adversity is the first path to truth:
 He who hath proved war, storm, or wo-
 man's rage,
Whether his winters be eighteen or eighty,
Hath won the experience which is deem'd
 so weighty. 400

LI

How far it profits is another matter. —
 Our hero gladly saw his little charge
Safe with a lady, whose last grown-up
 daughter
 Being long married, and thus set at large,
Had left all the accomplishments she taught
 her
 To be transmitted, like the Lord Mayor's
 barge,
To the next comer; or — as it will tell
More Muse-like — like to Cytherea's shell.

LII

I call such things transmission; for there is
 A floating balance of accomplishment 410
Which forms a pedigree from Miss to Miss,
 According as their minds or backs are
 bent.
Some waltz; some draw; some fathom the
 abyss
 Of metaphysics; others are content
With music; the most moderate shine as
 wits;
While others have a genius turn'd for fits.

LIII

But whether fits, or wits, or harpsichords,
 Theology, fine arts, or finer stays,
May be the baits for gentlemen or lords
 With regular descent, in these our
 days, 420

The last year to the new transfers its
 hoards;
 New vestals claim men's eyes with the
 same praise
Of 'elegant' *et cætera*, in fresh batches —
All matchless creatures, and yet bent on
 matches.

LIV

But now I will begin my poem. 'T is
 Perhaps a little strange, if not quite new,
That from the first of Cantos up to this
 I 've not begun what we have to go
 through.
These first twelve books are merely flour-
 ishes,
 Preludios, trying just a string or two 430
Upon my lyre, or making the pegs sure;
And when so, you shall have the overture.

LV

My Muses do not care a pinch of rosin
 About what 's call'd success, or not suc-
 ceeding:
Such thoughts are quite below the strain
 they have chosen;
 'T is a 'great moral lesson' they are
 reading.
I thought, at setting off, about two dozen
 Cantos would do; but at Apollo's pleading,
If that my Pegasus should not be founder'd,
I think to canter gently through a hun-
 dred. 440

LVI

Don Juan saw that microcosm on stilts,
 Yclept the Great World; for it is the
 least,
Although the highest: but as swords have
 hilts
 By which their power of mischief is in-
 creased,
When man in battle or in quarrel tilts,
 Thus the low world, north, south, or west,
 or east,
Must still obey the high — which is their
 handle,
Their moon, their sun, their gas, their far-
 thing candle.

LVII

He had many friends who had many wives,
 and was
 Well look'd upon by both, to that ex-
 tent 450

Of friendship which you may accept or
 pass,
 It does nor good nor harm; being merely
 meant
To keep the wheels going of the higher
 class,
 And draw them nightly when a ticket's
 sent:
And what with masquerades, and fêtes, and
 balls,
For the first season such a life scarce
 palls.

LVIII

A young unmarried man, with a good name
 And fortune, has an awkward part to
 play;
For good society is but a game,
 'The royal game of Goose,' as I may
 say, 460
Where every body has some separate aim,
 An end to answer, or a plan to lay —
The single ladies wishing to be double,
The married ones to save the virgins
 trouble.

LIX

I don't mean this as general, but particular
 Examples may be found of such pur-
 suits:
Though several also keep their perpendicu-
 lar
 Like poplars, with good principles for
 roots;
Yet many have a method more *reticular* —
 'Fishers for men,' like sirens with soft
 lutes: 470
For talk six times with the same single
 lady,
And you may get the wedding dresses ready.

LX

Perhaps you'll have a letter from the
 mother,
 To say her daughter's feelings are tre-
 pann'd;
Perhaps you'll have a visit from the brother,
 All strut, and stays, and whiskers, to de-
 mand
What 'your intentions are?' — One way or
 other
 It seems the virgin's heart expects your
 hand:
And between pity for her case and yours,
You'll add to Matrimony's list of cures. 480

LXI

I've known a dozen weddings made even
 thus,
 And some of them high names: I have
 also known
Young men who — though they hated to
 discuss
 Pretensions which they never dream'd to
 have shown —
Yet neither frighten'd by a female fuss,
 Nor by mustachios moved, were let
 alone,
And lived, as did the broken-hearted
 fair,
In happier plight than if they form'd a
 pair.

LXII

There's also nightly, to the uninitiated,
 A peril — not indeed like love or mar-
 riage, 490
But not the less for this to be depre-
 ciated:
 It is — I meant and mean not to dispar-
 age
The show of virtue even in the vitiated —
 It adds an outward grace unto their car-
 riage —
But to denounce the amphibious sort of har-
 lot,
'Couleur de rose,' who's neither white nor
 scarlet.

LXIII

Such is your cold coquette, who can't say
 'No,'
 And won't say 'Yes,' and keeps you on
 and off-ing
On a lee-shore, till it begins to blow —
 Then sees your heart wreck'd, with an
 inward scoffing. 500
This works a world of sentimental woe,
 And sends new Werters yearly to their
 coffin;
But yet is merely innocent flirtation,
Not quite adultery, but adulteration.

LXIV

'Ye gods, I grow a talker!' Let us prate.
 The next of perils, though I place it
 *stern*est,
Is when, without regard to 'church or
 state,'
 A wife makes or takes love in upright
 earnest.

Abroad, such things decide few women's
 fate —
 (Such, early traveller! is the truth thou
 learnest) — 510
But in old England, when a young bride
 errs,
Poor thing! Eve's was a trifling case to
 hers.

LXV

For 't is a low, newspaper, humdrum, law-
 suit
 Country, where a young couple of the
 same ages
Can't form a friendship, but the world o'er-
 awes it.
 Then there 's the vulgar trick of those
 d—d damages!
A verdict — grievous foe to those who cause
 it! —
 Forms a sad climax to romantic hom-
 ages;
Besides those soothing speeches of the
 pleaders,
And evidences which regale all readers. 520

LXVI

But they who blunder thus are raw begin-
 ners;
 A little genial sprinkling of hypocrisy
Has saved the fame of thousand splendid
 sinners,
 The loveliest oligarchs of our gynocracy;
You may see such at all the balls and din-
 ners,
 Among the proudest of our aristocracy,
So gentle, charming, charitable, chaste —
And all by having *tact* as well as taste.

LXVII

Juan, who did not stand in the predicament
 Of a mere novice, had one safeguard
 more; 530
For he was sick ——no, 't was not the word
 sick I meant —
 But he had seen so much good love be-
 fore,
That he was not in heart so very weak; —
 I meant
 But thus much, and no sneer against the
 shore
Of white cliffs, white necks, blue eyes,
 bluer stockings,
Tithes, taxes, duns, and doors with double
 knockings.

LXVIII

But coming young from lands and scenes
 romantic,
 Where lives, not lawsuits, must be risk'd
 for Passion,
And Passion's self must have a spice of
 frantic,
 Into a country where 't is half a fashion,
Seem'd to him half commercial, half pedan-
 tic, 541
 Howe'er he might esteem this moral na-
 tion:
Besides (alas! his taste — forgive and pity!)
At first he did not think the women pretty.

LXIX

I say at *first* — for he found out at *last*,
 But by degrees, that they were fairer far
Than the more glowing dames whose lot is
 cast
 Beneath the influence of the eastern star.
A further proof we should not judge in
 haste;
 Yet inexperience could not be his bar 550
To taste: — the truth is, if men would con-
 fess,
That novelties *please* less than they *impress*.

LXX

Though travell'd, I have never had the
 luck to
 Trace up those shuffling negroes, Nile or
 Niger,
To that impracticable place, Timbuctoo,
 Where Geography finds no one to oblige
 her
With such a chart as may be safely stuck
 to —
 For Europe ploughs in Afric like 'bos
 piger:'
But if I *had been* at Timbuctoo, there
No doubt I should be told that black is
 fair. 560

LXXI

It is. I will not swear that black is white;
 But I suspect in fact that white is
 black,
And the whole matter rests upon eye-
 sight.
 Ask a blind man, the best judge. You 'll
 attack
Perhaps this new position — but I 'm right;
 Or if I 'm wrong, I 'll not be ta'en
 aback: —

He hath no morn nor night, but all is dark
Within; and what seest thou ? A dubious
 spark.

LXXII

But I 'm relapsing into metaphysics,
 That labyrinth, whose clue is of the
 same 570
Construction as your cures for hectic
 phthisics,
 Those bright moths fluttering round a
 dying flame;
And this reflection brings me to plain
 physics,
And to the beauties of a foreign dame,
Compared with those of our pure pearls of
 price,
Those polar summers, *all* sun, and some
 ice.

LXXIII

Or say they are like virtuous mermaids,
 whose
 Beginnings are fair faces, ends mere
 fishes; —
Not that there 's not a quantity of those
 Who have a due respect for their own
 wishes. 580
Like Russians rushing from hot baths to
 snows
 Are they, at bottom virtuous even when
 vicious:
They warm into a scrape, but keep of
 course,
As a reserve, a plunge into remorse.

LXXIV

But this has nought to do with their out-
 sides.
 I said that Juan did not think them
 pretty
At the first blush; for a fair Briton hides
 Half her attractions — probably from
 pity —
And rather calmly into the heart glides,
 Than storms it as a foe would take a
 city; 590
But once there (if you doubt this, prithee
 try)
She keeps it for you like a true ally.

LXXV

She cannot step as does an Arab barb,
 Or Andalusian girl from mass return-
 ing,

Nor wear as gracefully as Gauls her garb,
 Nor in her eye Ausonia's glance is burn-
 ing;
Her voice, though sweet, is not so fit to warb-
 le those bravuras (which I still am learn-
 ing
To like, though I have been seven years in
 Italy,
And have, or had, an ear that served me
 prettily); — 600

LXXVI

She cannot do these things, nor one or two
 Others, in that off-hand and dashing style
Which takes so much — to give the devil
 his due;
 Nor is she quite so ready with her smile,
Nor settles all things in one interview
 (A thing approved as saving time and
 toil); —
But though the soil may give you time and
 trouble,
Well cultivated, it will render double.

LXXVII

And if in fact she takes to a ' grande pas-
 sion,'
 It is a very serious thing indeed: 610
Nine times in ten 't is but caprice or fash-
 ion,
 Coquetry, or a wish to take the lead,
The pride of a mere child with a new sash
 on,
 Or wish to make a rival's bosom bleed:
But the tenth instance will be a tornado,
For there 's no saying what they will or
 may do.

LXXVIII

The reason 's obvious; if there 's an éclat,
 They lose their caste at once, as do the
 Parias;
And when the delicacies of the law
 Have fill'd their papers with their com-
 ments various, 620
Society, that china without flaw
 (The hypocrite !), will banish them like
 Marius,
To sit amidst the ruins of their guilt:
For Fame 's a Carthage not so soon rebuilt.

LXXIX

Perhaps this is as it should be; — it is
 A comment on the Gospel's 'Sin no
 more,

And be thy sins forgiven:' — but upon
 this
 I leave the saints to settle their own
 score.
Abroad, though doubtless they do much
 amiss,
 An erring woman finds an opener door 630
For her return to Virtue — as they call
That lady, who should be at home to all.

LXXX

For me, I leave the matter where I find it,
 Knowing that such uneasy virtue leads
People some ten times less in fact to mind
 it,
 And care but for discoveries and not
 deeds.
And as for chastity, you 'll never bind it
 By all the laws the strictest lawyer
 pleads,
But aggravate the crime you have not pre-
 vented,
By rendering desperate those who had else
 repented.　　　　　　　　　640

LXXXI

But Juan was no casuist, nor had ponder'd
 Upon the moral lessons of mankind:
Besides, he had not seen of several hundred
 A lady altogether to his mind.
A little 'blasé' — 't is not to be wonder'd
 At, that his heart had got a tougher
 rind:
And though not vainer from his past success,
No doubt his sensibilities were less.

LXXXII

He also had been busy seeing sights —
 The Parliament and all the other houses;
Had sat beneath the gallery at nights, 651
 To hear debates whose thunder *roused*
 (not *rouses*)
The world to gaze upon those northern
 lights
 Which flash'd as far as where the musk-
 bull browses;
He had also stood at times behind the
 throne —
But Grey was not arrived, and Chatham
 gone.

LXXXIII

He saw, however, at the closing session,
 That noble sight, when *really* free the
 nation,

A king in constitutional possession
 Of such a throne as is the proudest sta-
 tion,　　　　　　　660
Though despots know it not — till the pro-
 gression
 Of freedom shall complete their educa-
 tion.
'T is not mere splendour makes the show
 august
To eye or heart — it is the people's trust.

LXXXIV

There, too, he saw (whate'er he may be
 now)
 A Prince, the prince of princes at the
 time,
With fascination in his very bow,
 And full of promise, as the spring of
 prime.
Though royalty was written on his brow,
 He had *then* the grace, too, rare in every
 clime,　　　　　　　670
Of being, without alloy of fop or beau,
A finish'd gentleman from top to toe.

LXXXV

And Juan was received, as hath been said,
 Into the best society: and there
Occurr'd what often happens, I 'm afraid,
 However disciplined and debonnaire: —
The talent and good humour he display'd,
 Besides the mark'd distinction of his air,
Exposed him, as was natural, to tempta-
 tion,
Even though himself avoided the occa-
 sion.　　　　　　　680

LXXXVI

But what, and where, with whom, and
 when, and why,
 Is not to be put hastily together;
And as my object is morality
 (Whatever people say), I don't know
 whether
I 'll leave a single reader's eyelid dry,
 But harrow up his feelings till they
 wither,
And hew out a huge monument of pathos,
As Philip's son proposed to do with Athos.

LXXXVII

Here the twelfth Canto of our introduc-
 tion
 Ends. When the body of the book 's
 begun,　　　　　　　690

You 'll find it of a different construction
 From what some people say 't will be
 when done:
The plan at present 's simply in concoction,
 I can't oblige you, reader, to read on;
That 's your affair, not mine: a real spirit
Should neither court neglect, nor dread to
 bear it.

LXXXVIII

And if my thunderbolt not always rattles,
 Remember, reader ! you have had before
The worst of tempests and the best of bat-
 tles
 That e'er were brew'd from elements or
 gore, 700
Besides the most sublime of — Heaven
 knows what else:
 An usurer could scarce expect much
 more —
But my best canto, save one on astronomy,
Will turn upon ' political economy.'

LXXXIX

That is your present theme for popularity:
 Now that the public hedge hath scarce a
 stake,
It grows an act of patriotic charity,
 To show the people the best way to break.
My plan (but I, if but for singularity,
 Reserve it) will be very sure to take. 710
Meantime, read all the national debt-sinkers,
And tell me what you think of your great
 thinkers.

CANTO THE THIRTEENTH

I

I NOW mean to be serious; — it is time,
 Since laughter now-a-days is deem'd too
 serious.
A jest at Vice by Virtue 's call'd a crime,
 And critically held as deleterious:
Besides, the sad 's a source of the sublime,
 Although when long a little apt to weary
 us;
And therefore shall my lay soar high and
 solemn,
As an old temple dwindled to a column.

II

The Lady Adeline Amundeville
 ('T is an old Norman name, and to be
 found 10

In pedigrees, by those who wander still
 Along the last fields of that Gothic
 ground)
Was high-born, wealthy by her father's will,
 And beauteous, even where beauties most
 abound,
In Britain — which of course true patriots
 find
The goodliest soil of body and of mind.

III

I 'll not gainsay them; it is not my cue;
 I 'll leave them to their taste, no doubt
 the best:
An eye 's an eye, and whether black or
 blue,
 Is no great matter, so 't is in request, 20
'T is nonsense to dispute about a hue —
 The kindest may be taken as a test.
The fair sex should be always fair; and no
 man,
Till thirty, should perceive there 's a plain
 woman.

IV

And after that serene and somewhat dull
 Epoch, that awkward corner turn'd for
 days
More quiet, when our moon 's no more at
 full,
 We may presume to criticise or praise;
Because indifference begins to lull
 Our passions, and we walk in wisdom's
 ways; 30
Also because the figure and the face
Hint, that 't is time to give the younger
 place.

V

I know that some would fain postpone this
 era,
 Reluctant as all placemen to resign
Their post; but theirs is merely a chimera,
 For they have pass'd life's equinoctial
 line:
But then they have their claret and Madeira
 To irrigate the dryness of decline;
And county meetings, and the parliament,
And debt, and what not, for their solace
 sent. 40

VI

And is there not religion, and reform,
 Peace, war, the taxes, and what 's call'd
 the ' Nation ' ?

The struggle to be pilots in a storm ?
 The landed and the monied speculation ?
The joys of mutual hate to keep them
 warm,
 Instead of love, that mere hallucination ?
Now hatred is by far the longest pleasure;
Men love in haste, but they detest at leisure.

VII

Rough Johnson, the great moralist, pro-
 fess'd,
 Right honestly, 'he liked an honest
 hater !'— 50
The only truth that yet has been confest
 Within these latest thousand years or
 later.
Perhaps the fine old fellow spoke in jest:—
 For my part, I am but a mere spectator,
And gaze where'er the palace or the hovel is,
Much in the mode of Goethe's Mephisto-
 pheles;

VIII

But neither love nor hate in much excess;
 Though 't was not once so. If I sneer
 sometimes,
It is because I cannot well do less,
 And now and then it also suits my
 rhymes. 60
I should be very willing to redress
 Men's wrongs, and rather check than
 punish crimes,
Had not Cervantes, in that too true tale
Of Quixote, shown how all such efforts
 fail.

IX

Of all tales 't is the saddest — and more sad,
 Because it makes us smile: his hero's
 right,
And still pursues the right;— to curb the
 bad
 His only object, and 'gainst odds to fight
His guerdon: 't is his virtue makes him
 mad !
 But his adventures form a sorry sight;
A sorrier still is the great moral taught 71
By that real epic unto all who have thought.

X

Redressing injury, revenging wrong,
 To aid the damsel and destroy the caitiff;
Opposing singly the united strong,
 From foreign yoke to free the helpless
 native:—

Alas ! must noblest views, like an old song,
 Be for mere fancy 's sport a theme crea-
 tive,
A jest, a riddle, Fame through thin and
 thick sought !
And Socrates himself but Wisdom's
 Quixote ? 80

XI

Cervantes smiled Spain's chivalry away;
 A single laugh demolish'd the right arm
Of his own country;— seldom since that
 day
 Has Spain had heroes. While Romance
 could charm,
The world gave ground before her bright
 array;
 And therefore have his volumes done
 such harm,
That all their glory, as a composition,
Was dearly purchased by his land's perdi-
 tion.

XII

I 'm ' at my old lunes '— digression, and
 forget
 The Lady Adeline Amundeville; 90
The fair most fatal Juan ever met,
 Although she was not evil nor meant ill;
But Destiny and Passion spread the net
 (Fate is a good excuse for our own will),
And caught them;— what do they not
 catch, methinks ?
But I 'm not Œdipus, and life 's a Sphinx.

XIII

I tell the tale as it is told, nor dare
 To venture a solution: ' Davus sum !'
And now I will proceed upon the pair.
 Sweet Adeline, amidst the gay world's
 hum, 100
Was the Queen-Bee, the glass of all that 's
 fair;
 Whose charms made all men speak, and
 women dumb.
The last 's a miracle, and such was reckon'd,
And since that time there has not been a
 second.

XIV

Chaste was she, to detraction's desperation,
 And wedded unto one she had loved
 well —
A man known in the councils of the nation,
 Cool, and quite English, imperturbable,

Though apt to act with fire upon occasion,
 Proud of himself and her: the world
 could tell 110
Nought against either, and both seem'd
 secure —
She in her virtue, he in his hauteur.

XV

It chanced some diplomatical relations,
 Arising out of business, often brought
Himself and Juan in their mutual stations
 Into close contact. Though reserved, nor
 caught
By specious seeming, Juan's youth, and
 patience,
 And talent, on his haughty spirit wrought,
And form'd a basis of esteem, which ends
In making men what courtesy calls friends.

XVI

And thus Lord Henry, who was cautious
 as 121
 Reserve and pride could make him, and
 full slow
In judging men — when once his judgment
 was
 Determined, right or wrong, on friend or
 foe,
Had all the pertinacity pride has,
 Which knows no ebb to its imperious
 flow,
And loves or hates, disdaining to be guided,
Because its own good pleasure hath decided.

XVII

His friendships, therefore, and no less aver-
 sions,
 Though oft well founded, which confirm'd
 but more 130
His prepossessions, like the laws of Per-
 sians
 And Medes, would ne'er revoke what
 went before.
His feelings had not those strange fits, like
 tertians,
 Of common likings, which make some
 deplore
What they should laugh at — the mere ague
 still
Of men's regard, the fever or the chill.

XVIII

' 'T is not in mortals to command success:
 But *do you more*, Sempronius — *don't* de-
 serve it,'

And take my word, you won't have any
 less.
Be wary, watch the time, and always
 serve it; 140
Give gently way, when there 's too great a
 press;
 And for your conscience, only learn to
 nerve it,
For, like a racer, or a boxer training,
'T will make, if proved, vast efforts with-
 out paining.

XIX

Lord Henry also liked to be superior,
 As most men do, the little or the great;
The very lowest find out an inferior,
 At least they think so, to exert their state
Upon: for there are very few things wea-
 rier
 Than solitary Pride's oppressive weight,
Which mortals generously would divide, 151
By bidding others carry while they ride.

XX

In birth, in rank, in fortune likewise equal,
 O'er Juan he could no distinction claim;
In years he had the advantage of time's
 sequel;
 And, as he thought, in country much the
 same —
Because bold Britons have a tongue and
 free quill,
 At which all modern nations vainly
 aim;
And the Lord Henry was a great debater,
So that few members kept the house up
 later. 160

XXI

These were advantages: and then he
 thought —
 It was his foible, but by no means sinis-
 ter —
That few or none more than himself had
 caught
 Court mysteries, having been himself a
 minister:
He liked to teach that which he had been
 taught,
 And greatly shone whenever there had
 been a stir;
And reconciled all qualities which grace
 man,
Always a patriot, and sometimes a place-
 man.

XXII

He liked the gentle Spaniard for his grav-
 ity;
He almost honour'd him for his docility;
Because, though young, he acquiesced with
 suavity, 171
 Or contradicted but with proud humility.
He knew the world, and would not see de-
 pravity
 In faults which sometimes show the soil's
 fertility,
If that the weeds o'erlive not the first
 crop —
For then they are very difficult to stop.

XXIII

And then he talk'd with him about Ma-
 drid,
Constantinople, and such distant places;
Where people always did as they were
 bid,
 Or did what they should not with foreign
 graces. 180
Of coursers also spake they: Henry rid
 Well, like most Englishmen, and loved
 the races;
And Juan, like a true-born Andalusian,
Could back a horse, as despots ride a Rus-
 sian.

XXIV

And thus acquaintance grew, at noble routs,
 And diplomatic dinners, or at other —
For Juan stood well both with Ins and Outs,
 As in freemasonry a higher brother.
Upon his talent Henry had no doubts;
 His manner show'd him sprung from a
 high mother; 190
And all men like to show their hospitality
To him whose breeding matches with his
 quality.

XXV

At Blank-Blank Square; — for we will
 break no squares
 By naming streets: since men are so cen-
 sorious,
And apt to sow an author's wheat with tares,
 Reaping allusions private and inglorious,
Where none were dreamt of, unto love's
 affairs,
 Which were, or are, or are to be notorious,
That therefore do I previously declare,
Lord Henry's mansion was in Blank-Blank
 Square. 200

XXVI

Also there bin another pious reason
 For making squares and streets anony-
 mous;
Which is, that there is scarce a single sea-
 son
 Which doth not shake some very splendid
 house
With some slight heart-quake of domestic
 treason —
A topic scandal doth delight to rouse:
Such I might stumble over unawares,
Unless I knew the very chastest squares.

XXVII

'T is true, I might have chosen Picca-
 dilly,
 A place where peccadillos are un-
 known; 210
But I have motives, whether wise or silly,
 For letting that pure sanctuary alone.
Therefore I name not square, street, place,
 until I
 Find one where nothing naughty can be
 shown,
A vestal shrine of innocence of heart:
Such are —— but I have lost the London
 Chart.

XXVIII

At Henry's mansion then, in Blank-Blank
 Square,
 Was Juan a recherché, welcome guest,
As many other noble scions were;
 And some who had but talent for their
 crest; 220
Or wealth, which is a passport every
 where;
 Or even mere fashion, which indeed 's the
 best
Recommendation; and to be well drest
Will very often supersede the rest.

XXIX

And since ' there 's safety in a multitude
 Of counsellors,' as Solomon has said,
Or some one for him, in some sage, grave
 mood; —
 Indeed we see the daily proof display'd
In senates, at the bar, in wordy feud,
 Where'er collective wisdom can parade,
Which is the only cause that we can
 guess 231
Of Britain's present wealth and happi-
 ness; —

XXX

But as 'there's safety' grafted in the
 number
 'Of counsellors' for men, thus for the
 sex
A large acquaintance lets not Virtue slum-
 ber;
 Or should it shake, the choice will more
 perplex —
Variety itself will more encumber.
 'Midst many rocks we guard more against
 wrecks;
And thus with women: howsoe'er it shocks
 some's
Self-love, there's safety in a crowd of cox-
 combs. 240

XXXI

But Adeline had not the least occasion
 For such a shield, which leaves but little
 merit
To virtue proper, or good education.
 Her chief resource was in her own high
 spirit,
Which judged mankind at their due estima-
 tion;
 And for coquetry, she disdain'd to wear
 it:
Secure of admiration, its impression
Was faint, as of an every-day possession.

XXXII

To all she was polite without parade;
 To some she show'd attention of that
 kind
Which flatters, but is flattery convey'd 251
 In such a sort as cannot leave behind
A trace unworthy either wife or maid; —
 A gentle, genial courtesy of mind,
To those who were, or pass'd for merito-
 rious,
Just to console sad glory for being glorious;

XXXIII

Which is in all respects, save now and
 then,
 A dull and desolate appendage. Gaze
Upon the shades of those distinguish'd men
 Who were or are the puppet-shows of
 praise, 260
The praise of persecution; gaze again
 On the most favour'd; and amidst the
 blaze
Of sunset halos o'er the laurel-brow'd,
What can ye recognise? — a gilded cloud.

XXXIV

There also was of course in Adeline
 That calm patrician polish in the address,
Which ne'er can pass the equinoctial line
 Of any thing which nature would ex-
 press;
Just as a mandarin finds nothing fine, —
 At least his manner suffers not to guess
That any thing he views can greatly please.
Perhaps we have borrow'd this from the
 Chinese — 272

XXXV

Perhaps from Horace: his '*Nil admirari*'
 Was what he call'd the 'Art of Happi-
 ness;'
An art on which the artists greatly vary,
 And have not yet attain'd to much success.
However, 't is expedient to be wary:
 Indifference certes don't produce distress;
And rash enthusiasm in good society
Were nothing but a moral inebriety. 280

XXXVI

But Adeline was not indifferent: for
 (*Now* for a common-place !) beneath the
 snow,
As a volcano holds the lava more
 Within — *et cætera*. Shall I go on ? — No!
I hate to hunt down a tired metaphor,
 So let the often-used volcano go.
Poor thing ! How frequently, by me and
 others,
It hath been stirr'd up till its smoke quite
 smothers !

XXXVII

I 'll have another figure in a trice: —
 What say you to a bottle of champagne ?
Frozen into a very vinous ice, 291
 Which leaves few drops of that immortal
 rain,
Yet in the very centre, past all price,
 About a liquid glassful will remain;
And this is stronger than the strongest grape
Could e'er express in its expanded shape:

XXXVIII

'T is the whole spirit brought to a quintes-
 sence;
 And thus the chilliest aspects may con-
 centre
A hidden nectar under a cold presence.
 And such are many — though I only
 meant her 300

From whom I now deduce these moral les-
sons,
 On which the Muse has always sought to
 enter.
And your cold people are beyond all price,
When once you have broken their con-
 founded ice.

XXXIX

But after all they are a North-West Passage
 Unto the glowing India of the soul;
And as the good ships sent upon that message
 Have not exactly ascertain'd the Pole
(Though Parry's efforts look a lucky pre-
 sage),
 Thus gentlemen may run upon a shoal;
For if the Pole 's not open, but all frost 311
(A chance still), 't is a voyage or vessel
 lost.

XL

And young beginners may as well com-
 mence
 With quiet cruising o'er the ocean wo-
 man;
While those who are not beginners should
 have sense
 Enough to make for port, ere time shall
 summon
With his grey signal-flag; and the past
 tense,
 The dreary ' Fuimus ' of all things human,
Must be declined, while life's thin thread 's
 spun out 319
Between the gaping heir and gnawing gout.

XLI

But heaven must be diverted; its diver-
 sion
 Is sometimes truculent — but never mind:
The world upon the whole is worth the as-
 sertion
 (If but for comfort) that all things are
 kind:
And that same devilish doctrine of the Per-
 sian,
 Of the two principles, but leaves behind
As many doubts as any other doctrine
 Has ever puzzled Faith withal, or yoked
 her in.

XLII

The English winter — ending in July,
 To recommence in August — now was
 done. 330

'T is the postilion's paradise: wheels fly;
 On roads, east, south, north, west, there
 is a run.
But for post-horses who finds sympathy ?
 Man's pity 's for himself, or for his son,
Always premising that said son at college
 Has not contracted much more debt than
 knowledge.

XLIII

The London winter 's ended in July —
 Sometimes a little later. I don't err
In this : whatever other blunders lie
 Upon my shoulders, here I must aver 340
My Muse a glass of weatherology;
 For parliament is our barometer:
Let radicals its other acts attack,
Its sessions form our only almanack.

XLIV

When its quicksilver 's down at zero, — lo !
 Coach, chariot, luggage, baggage, equi-
 page !
Wheels whirl from Carlton palace to Soho,
 And happiest they who horses can engage;
The turnpikes glow with dust; and Rotten
 Row
 Sleeps from the chivalry of this bright
 age; 350
And tradesmen, with long bills and longer
 faces,
Sigh — as the postboys fasten on the traces.

XLV

They and their bills, ' Arcadians both,' are
 left
 To the Greek kalends of another ses-
 sion.
Alas ! to them of ready cash bereft,
 What hope remains ? Of hope the full
 possession,
Or generous draft, conceded as a gift,
 At a long date — till they can get a fresh
 one —
Hawk'd about at a discount, small or large;
Also the solace of an overcharge. 360

XLVI

But these are trifles. Downward flies my
 lord,
 Nodding beside my lady in his carriage.
Away ! away ! ' Fresh horses !' are the
 word,
 And changed as quickly as hearts after
 marriage;

The obsequious landlord hath the change
restored;
 The postboys have no reason to disparage
Their fee; but ere the water'd wheels may
hiss hence,
 The ostler pleads too for a reminiscence.

XLVII

'T is granted ; and the valet mounts the
dickey —
 That gentleman of lords and gentlemen;
Also my lady's gentlewoman, tricky, 371
 Trick'd out, but modest more than poet's
pen
Can paint, — ' Cosi viaggino i Ricchi ! '
 (Excuse a foreign slipslop now and then,
If but to show I 've travell'd; and what 's
travel,
Unless it teaches one to quote and cavil ?)

XLVIII

The London winter and the country summer
 Were well nigh over. 'T is perhaps a
pity,
When nature wears the gown that doth be-
come her,
 To lose those best months in a sweaty
city, 380
And wait until the nightingale grows
dumber,
 Listening debates not very wise or witty,
Ere patriots their true country can re-
member; —
But there 's no shooting (save grouse) till
September.

XLIX

I 've done with my tirade. The world was
gone;
 The twice two thousand, for whom earth
was made,
Were vanish'd to be what they call alone —
 That is, with thirty servants for parade,
As many guests, or more; before whom
groan
 As many covers, duly, daily, laid. 390
Let none accuse Old England's hospital-
ity —
Its quantity is but condensed to quality.

L

Lord Henry and the Lady Adeline
 Departed like the rest of their compeers,
The peerage, to a mansion very fine;
 The Gothic Babel of a thousand years.

None than themselves could boast a longer
line,
 Where time through heroes and through
beauties steers;
And oaks as olden as their pedigree
Told of their sires, a tomb in every tree.

LI

A paragraph in every paper told 401
 Of their departure: such is modern
fame:
'T is pity that it takes no farther hold
 Than an advertisement, or much the
same;
When, ere the ink be dry, the sound grows
cold.
 The Morning Post was foremost to pro-
proclaim —
' Departure, for his country seat, to-day,
Lord H. Amundeville and Lady A.

LII

' We understand the splendid host intends
 To entertain, this autumn, a select 410
And numerous party of his noble friends;
 Midst whom we have heard, from sources
quite correct,
The Duke of D—— the shooting season
spends,
 With many more by rank and fashion
deck'd;
Also a foreigner of high condition,
The envoy of the secret Russian mission.'

LIII

And thus we see — who doubts the Morn-
ing Post ?
 (Whose articles are like the 'Thirty-nine,'
Which those most swear to who believe
them most) —
 Our gay Russ Spaniard was ordain'd to
shine, 420
Deck'd by the rays reflected from his host,
 With those who, Pope says, ' greatly
daring dine.'
'T is odd, but true, — last war the News
abounded
More with these dinners than the kill'd or
wounded; —

LIV

As thus: ' On Thursday there was a grand
dinner;
 Present, Lords A. B. C.' — Earls, dukes,
by name

Announced with no less pomp than victory's
 winner:
 Then underneath, and in the very same
Column; date, 'Falmouth. There has
 lately been here
 The Slap-dash regiment, so well known
 to fame, 430
Whose loss in the late action we regret:
The vacancies are fill'd up — see Gazette.'

LV

To Norman Abbey whirl'd the noble pair, —
 An old, old monastery once, and now
Still older mansion; of a rich and rare
 Mix'd Gothic, such as artists all allow
Few specimens yet left us can compare
 Withal: it lies perhaps a little low,
Because the monks preferr'd a hill behind,
To shelter their devotion from the wind.

LVI

It stood embosom'd in a happy valley, 441
 Crown'd by high woodlands, where the
 Druid oak
Stood like Caractacus in act to rally
 His host, with broad arms 'gainst the
 thunderstroke;
And from beneath his boughs were seen to
 sally
 The dappled foresters — as day awoke,
The branching stag swept down with all
 his herd,
To quaff a brook which murmur'd like a
 bird.

LVII

Before the mansion lay a lucid lake,
 Broad as transparent, deep, and freshly
 fed 450
By a river, which its soften'd way did
 take
 In currents through the calmer water
 spread
Around: the wildfowl nestled in the brake
 And sedges, brooding in their liquid bed:
The woods sloped downwards to its brink,
 and stood
With their green faces fix'd upon the flood.

LVIII

Its outlet dash'd into a deep cascade,
 Sparkling with foam, until again subsid-
 ing,
Its shriller echoes — like an infant made
 Quiet — sank into softer ripples, gliding

Into a rivulet; and thus allay'd, 461
 Pursued its course, now gleaming, and
 now hiding
Its windings through the woods; now clear,
 now blue,
According as the skies their shadows threw.

LIX

A glorious remnant of the Gothic pile
 (While yet the church was Rome's) stood
 half apart
In a grand arch, which once screen'd many
 an aisle.
 These last had disappear'd — a loss to
 art:
The first yet frown'd superbly o'er the soil,
 And kindled feelings in the roughest
 heart, 470
Which mourn'd the power of time's or
 tempest's march,
In gazing on that venerable arch.

LX

Within a niche, nigh to its pinnacle,
 Twelve saints had once stood sanctified
 in stone;
But these had fallen, not when the friars
 fell,
 But in the war which struck Charles from
 his throne,
When each house was a fortalice, as tell
 The annals of full many a line undone, —
The gallant cavaliers, who fought in vain
For those who knew not to resign or reign.

LXI

But in a higher niche, alone, but crown'd,
 The Virgin Mother of the God-born
 Child, 482
With her Son in her blessed arms, look'd
 round,
 Spared by some chance when all beside
 was spoil'd;
She made the earth below seem holy ground.
 This may be superstition, weak or wild,
But even the faintest relics of a shrine
Of any worship wake some thoughts divine.

LXII

A mighty window, hollow in the centre,
 Shorn of its glass of thousand colourings,
Through which the deepen'd glories once
 could enter, 491
 Streaming from off the sun like seraph's
 wings,

Now yawns all desolate: now loud, now
 fainter,
 The gale sweeps through its fretwork,
 and oft sings
The owl his anthem, where the silenced
 quire
Lie with their hallelujahs quench'd like
 fire.

LXIII

But in the noontide of the moon, and when
 The wind is wingèd from one point of
 heaven,
There moans a strange unearthly sound,
 which then
Is musical — a dying accent driven 500
Through the huge arch, which soars and
 sinks again.
 Some deem it but the distant echo given
Back to the night wind by the waterfall,
And harmonised by the old choral wall:

LXIV

Others, that some original shape, or form
 Shaped by decay perchance, hath given
 the power
(Though less than that of Memnon's statue,
 warm
In Egypt's rays, to harp at a fix'd hour)
To this grey ruin, with a voice to charm.
 Sad, but serene, it sweeps o'er tree or
 tower; 510
The cause I know not, nor can solve; but
 such
The fact: — I 've heard it — once perhaps
 too much.

LXV

Amidst the court a Gothic fountain play'd,
 Symmetrical, but deck'd with carvings
 quaint —
Strange faces, like to men in masquerade,
 And here perhaps a monster, there a
 saint:
The spring gush'd through grim mouths of
 granite made,
 And sparkled into basins, where it spent
Its little torrent in a thousand bubbles,
Like man's vain glory, and his vainer
 troubles. 520

LXVI

The mansion's self was vast and venera-
 ble,
 With more of the monastic than has been

Elsewhere preserved : the cloisters still
 were stable,
 The cells, too, and refectory, I ween:
An exquisite small chapel had been able,
 Still unimpair'd, to decorate the scene;
The rest had been reform'd, replaced, or
 sunk,
And spoke more of the baron than the monk.

LXVII

Huge halls, long galleries, spacious cham-
 bers, join'd
 By no quite lawful marriage of the arts,
Might shock a connoisseur; but when com-
 bined, 531
 Form'd a whole which, irregular in parts,
Yet left a grand impression on the mind,
 At least of those whose eyes are in their
 hearts:
We gaze upon a giant for his stature,
Nor judge at first if all be true to nature.

LXVIII

Steel barons, molten the next generation
 To silken rows of gay and garter'd earls,
Glanced from the walls in goodly preserva-
 tion;
 And Lady Marys blooming into girls, 540
With fair long locks, had also kept their
 station;
 And countesses mature in robes and
 pearls:
Also some beauties of Sir Peter Lely,
Whose drapery hints we may admire them
 freely.

LXIX

Judges in very formidable ermine
 Were there, with brows that did not
 much invite
The accused to think their lordships would
 determine
 His cause by leaning much from might
 to right:
Bishops, who had not left a single sermon:
 Attorneys-general, awful to the sight, 550
As hinting more (unless our judgments
 warp us)
Of the 'Star Chamber' than of 'Habeas
 Corpus.'

LXX

Generals, some all in armour, of the old
 And iron time, ere lead had ta'en the
 lead;

Others in wigs of Marlborough's martial
 fold,
 Huger than twelve of our degenerate
 breed:
Lordlings, with staves of white or keys of
 gold:
 Nimrods, whose canvass scarce contain'd
 the steed;
And here and there some stern high patriot
 stood,
Who could not get the place for which he
 sued. 560

LXXI

But ever and anon, to soothe your vision,
 Fatigued with these hereditary glories,
There rose a Carlo Dolce or a Titian,
 Or wilder group of savage Salvatore's;
Here danced Albano's boys, and here the
 sea shone
 In Vernet's ocean lights; and there the
 stories
Of martyrs awed, as Spagnoletto tainted
His brush with all the blood of all the
 sainted.

LXXII

Here sweetly spread a landscape of Lor-
 raine;
 There Rembrandt made his darkness
 equal light, 570
Or gloomy Caravaggio's gloomier stain
 Bronzed o'er some lean and stoic ancho-
 rite: —
But, lo ! a Teniers woos, and not in vain,
 Your eyes to revel in a livelier sight:
His bell-mouth'd goblet makes me feel
 quite Danish
Or Dutch with thirst — What, ho ! a flask
 of Rhenish.

LXXIII

O reader ! if that thou canst read, — and
 know,
 'T is not enough to spell, or even to
 read,
To constitute a reader; there must go
 Virtues of which both you and I have
 need; — 580
Firstly, begin with the beginning (though
 That clause is hard); and secondly, pro-
 ceed;
Thirdly, commence not with the end — or,
 sinning
In this sort, end at least with the beginning.

LXXIV

But, reader, thou hast patient been of late,
 While I, without remorse of rhyme, or
 fear,
Have built and laid out ground at such a
 rate,
 Dan Phœbus takes me for an auctioneer.
That poets were so from their earliest date,
 By Homer's 'Catalogue of ships' is
 clear; 590
But a mere modern must be moderate —
I spare you then the furniture and plate.

LXXV

The mellow autumn came, and with it came
 The promised party, to enjoy its sweets.
The corn is cut, the manor full of game;
 The pointer ranges, and the sportsman
 beats
In russet jacket: — lynx-like is his aim;
 Full grows his bag, and wonder*ful* his
 feats.
Ah, nut-brown partridges ! Ah, brilliant
 pheasants !
And ah, ye poachers ! — 'T is no sport for
 peasants. 600

LXXVI

An English autumn, though it hath no
 vines,
 Blushing with Bacchant coronals along
The paths, o'er which the far festoon en-
 twines
 The red grape in the sunny lands of
 song,
Hath yet a purchased choice of choicest
 wines;
 The claret light, and the Madeira strong.
If Britain mourn her bleakness, we can tell
 her,
The very best of vineyards is the cellar.

LXXVII

Then, if she hath not that serene decline
 Which makes the southern autumn's day
 appear 610
As if 't would to a second spring resign
 The season, rather than to winter drear,
Of in-door comforts still she hath a mine, —
 The sea-coal fires the 'earliest of the
 year;'
Without doors, too, she may compete in
 mellow,
As what is lost in green is gain'd in yel-
 low.

LXXVIII

And for the effeminate *villeggiatura* —
 Rife with more horns than hounds — she
 hath the chase,
So animated that it might allure a
 Saint from his beads to join the jocund
 race; 620
Even Nimrod's self might leave the plains
 of Dura,
 And wear the Melton jacket for a space:
If she hath no wild boars, she hath a tame
Preserve of bores, who ought to be made
 game.

LXXIX

The noble guests, assembled at the Abbey,
 Consisted of — we give the sex the *pas* —
The Duchess of Fitz-Fulke; the Countess
 Crabby;
 The Ladies Scilly, Busey; — Miss Eclat,
Miss Bombazeen, Miss Mackstay, Miss
 O'Tabby,
 And Mrs. Rabbi, the rich banker's
 squaw; 630
Also the honourable Mrs. Sleep,
Who look'd a white lamb, yet was a black
 sheep:

LXXX

With other Countesses of Blank — but
 rank;
 At once the 'lie' and the 'élite' of
 crowds;
Who pass like water filter'd in a tank,
 All purged and pious from their native
 clouds;
Or paper turn'd to money by the Bank:
 No matter how or why, the passport
 shrouds
The 'passée' and the past; for good society
Is no less famed for tolerance than
 piety, — 640

LXXXI

That is, up to a certain point; which point
 Forms the most difficult in punctuation.
Appearances appear to form the joint
 On which it hinges in a higher station;
And so that no explosion cry 'Aroint
 Thee, witch!' or each Medea has her
 Jason;
Or (to the point with Horace and with
 Pulci)
' *Omne tulit punctum*, quæ *miscuit utile
 dulci*.'

LXXXII

I can't exactly trace their rule of right, 649
 Which hath a little leaning to a lottery.
I 've seen a virtuous woman put down quite
 By the mere combination of a coterie;
Also a so-so matron boldly fight
 Her way back to the world by dint of
 plottery,
And shine the very *Siria* of the spheres,
Escaping with a few slight, scarless sneers.

LXXXIII

I have seen more than I 'll say: — but we
 will see
 How our *villeggiatura* will get on.
The party might consist of thirty-three
 Of highest caste — the Brahmins of the
 ton. 660
I have named a few, not foremost in de-
 gree,
 But ta'en at hazard as the rhyme may
 run.
By way of sprinkling, scatter'd amongst
 these,
There also were some Irish absentees.

LXXXIV

There was Parolles, too, the legal bully,
 Who limits all his battles to the bar
And senate: when invited elsewhere, truly,
 He shows more appetite for words than
 war.
There was the young bard Rackrhyme, who
 had newly
 Come out and glimmer'd as a six weeks'
 star. 670
There was Lord Pyrrho, too, the great free-
 thinker;
 And Sir John Pottledeep, the mighty
 drinker.

LXXXV

There was the Duke of Dash, who was a —
 duke,
 'Ay,' every inch a' duke; there were
 twelve peers
Like Charlemagne's — and all such peers in
 look
 And intellect, that neither eyes nor ears
For commoners had ever them mistook.
 There were the six Miss Rawbolds —
 pretty dears !
All song and sentiment; whose hearts were
 set
Less on a convent than a coronet. 680

LXXXVI

There were four Honourable Misters, whose
 Honour was more before their names than
 after;
There was the preux Chevalier de la Ruse,
 Whom France and Fortune lately deign'd
 to waft here,
Whose chiefly harmless talent was to amuse;
 But the clubs found it rather serious
 laughter,
Because — such was his magic power to
 please —
The dice seem'd charm'd, too, with his re-
 partees.

LXXXVII

There was Dick Dubious, the metaphysi-
 cian,
 Who loved philosophy and a good dinner;
Angle, the soi-disant mathematician; 691
 Sir Henry Silvercup, the great race-
 winner.
There was the Reverend Rodomont Pre-
 cisian,
 Who did not hate so much the sin as sin-
 ner;
And Lord Augustus Fitz-Plantagenet,
Good at all things, but better at a bet.

LXXXVIII

There was Jack Jargon, the gigantic
 guardsman;
 And General Fireface, famous in the
 field,
A great tactician, and no less a swordsman,
 Who ate, last war, more Yankees than he
 kill'd. 700
There was the waggish Welsh Judge, Jef-
 feries Hardsman,
 In his grave office so completely skill'd,
That when a culprit came for condemnation,
He had his judge's joke for consolation.

LXXXIX

Good company's a chess-board — there are
 kings,
 Queens, bishops, knights, rooks, pawns;
 the world's a game;
Save that the puppets pull at their own
 strings,
 Methinks gay Punch hath something of
 the same.
My Muse, the butterfly hath but her wings,
 Not stings, and flits through ether with-
 out aim, 710

Alighting rarely: — were she but a hor-
 net,
Perhaps there might be vices which would
 mourn it.

XC

I had forgotten — but must not forget —
 An orator, the latest of the session,
Who had deliver'd well a very set
 Smooth speech, his first and maidenly
 transgression
Upon debate: the papers echoed yet
 With his début, which made a strong im-
 pression,
And rank'd with what is every day dis-
 play'd —
'The best first speech that ever yet was
 made.' 720

XCI

Proud of his 'Hear hims!' proud, too, of
 his vote
 And lost virginity of oratory,
Proud of his learning (just enough to
 quote),
 He revell'd in his Ciceronian glory:
With memory excellent to get by rote,
 With wit to hatch a pun or tell a story,
Graced with some merit, and with more
 effrontery,
'His country's pride,' he came down to the
 country.

XCII

There also were two wits by acclamation,
 Longbow from Ireland, Strongbow from
 the Tweed, 730
Both lawyers and both men of educa-
 tion;
 But Strongbow's wit was of more polish'd
 breed:
Longbow was rich in an imagination
 As beautiful and bounding as a steed,
But sometimes stumbling over a potato, —
While Strongbow's best things might have
 come from Cato.

XCIII

Strongbow was like a new-tuned harpsi-
 chord;
 But Longbow wild as an Æolian harp,
With which the winds of heaven can claim
 accord,
 And make a music, whether flat or
 sharp. 740

Of Strongbow's talk you would not change
 a word:
 At Longbow's phrases you might some-
 times carp:
Both wits — one born so, and the other
 bred —
This by his heart, his rival by his head.

XCIV

If all these seem a heterogeneous mass
 To be assembled at a country seat,
Yet think, a specimen of every class
 Is better than a humdrum tête-à-tête.
The days of Comedy are gone, alas !
 When Congreve's fool could vie with
 Molière's *bête :* 750
Society is smooth'd to that excess,
That manners hardly differ more than
 dress.

XCV

Our ridicules are kept in the back-ground —
 Ridiculous enough, but also dull;
Professions, too, are no more to be found
 Professional; and there is nought to cull
Of folly's fruit; for though your fools
 abound,
 They 're barren, and not worth the pains
 to pull.
Society is now one polish'd horde,
Form'd of two mighty tribes, the *Bores* and
 Bored. 760

XCVI

But from being farmers, we turn gleaners,
 gleaning
 The scanty but right-well thresh'd ears
 of truth;
And, gentle reader ! when you gather mean-
 ing,
 You may be Boaz, and I — modest Ruth.
Farther I 'd quote, but Scripture intervening
 Forbids. A great impression in my youth
Was made by Mrs. Adams, where she cries,
' That Scriptures out of church are blasphe-
 mies.'

XCVII

But what we can we glean in this vile age
 Of chaff, although our gleanings be not
 grist. 770
I must not quite omit the talking sage,
 Kit-Cat, the famous Conversationist,
Who, in his common-place book, had a page
 Prepared each morn for evenings. ' List,
 oh, list ! ' —

' Alas, poor ghost ! ' — What unexpected
 woes
Await those who have studied their bon-
 mots !

XCVIII

Firstly, they must allure the conversation
 By many windings to their clever clinch;
And secondly, must let slip no occasion,
 Nor *bate* (abate) their hearers of an
 inch, 780
But take an ell — and make a great sensa-
 tion,
 If possible; and thirdly, never flinch
When some smart talker puts them to the
 test,
But seize the last word, which no doubt 's
 the best.

XCIX

Lord Henry and his lady were the hosts;
 The party we have touch'd on were the
 guests:
Their table was a board to tempt even
 ghosts
 To pass the Styx for more substantial
 feasts.
I will not dwell upon ragoûts or roasts,
 Albeit all human history attests 790
That happiness for man — the hungry
 sinner ! —
Since Eve ate apples, much depends on
 dinner.

C

Witness the lands which ' flow'd with milk
 and honey,'
 Held out unto the hungry Israelites;
To this we have added since, the love of
 money,
 The only sort of pleasure which requites.
Youth fades, and leaves our days no longer
 sunny;
 We tire of mistresses and parasites;
But oh, ambrosial cash ! Ah ! who would
 lose thee ?
When we no more can use, or even abuse
 thee ! 800

CI

The gentlemen got up betimes to shoot,
 Or hunt: the young, because they liked
 the sport —
The first thing boys like after play and
 fruit;

The middle-aged to make the day more
short;
For *ennui* is a growth of English root,
 Though nameless in our language: — we
 retort
The fact for words, and let the French
translate
That awful yawn which sleep can not abate.

CII

The elderly walk'd through the library,
 And tumbled books, or criticised the
 pictures, 810
Or saunter'd through the gardens piteously,
 And made upon the hot-house several
 strictures,
Or rode a nag which trotted not too high,
 Or on the morning papers read their
 lectures,
Or on the watch their longing eyes would
 fix,
Longing at sixty for the hour of six.

CIII

But none were 'gêné:' the great hour of
 union
 Was rung by dinner's knell; till then all
 were
Masters of their own time — or in com-
 munion,
 Or solitary, as they chose to bear 820
The hours, which how to pass is but to few
 known.
 Each rose up at his own, and had to
 spare
What time he chose for dress, and broke his
fast
When, where, and how he chose for that
repast.

CIV

The ladies — some rouged, some a little
 pale —
 Met the morn as they might. If fine,
 they rode,
Or walk'd; if foul, they read, or told a
 tale,
 Sung, or rehearsed the last dance from
 abroad;
Discuss'd the fashion which might next
 prevail,
 And settled bonnets by the newest code,
Or cramm'd twelve sheets into one little
 letter, 831
To make each correspondent a new debtor.

CV

For some had absent lovers, all had friends.
 The earth has nothing like a she epistle,
And hardly heaven — because it never ends.
 I love the mystery of a female missal,
Which, like a creed, ne'er says all it intends,
 But full of cunning as Ulysses' whistle,
When he allured poor Dolon: — you had
 better
Take care what you reply to such a letter.

CVI

Then there were billiards; cards, too, but
 no dice; — 841
 Save in the clubs no man of honour
 plays; —
Boats when 't was water, skating when 't was
 ice,
 And the hard frost destroy'd the scenting
 days:
And angling, too, that solitary vice,
 Whatever Izaak Walton sings or says;
The quaint, old, cruel coxcomb, in his gul-
 let
Should have a hook, and a small trout to
pull it.

CVII

With evening came the banquet and the
 wine;
 The conversazione; the duet, 850
Attuned by voices more or less divine
 (My heart or head aches with the mem-
 ory yet).
The four Miss Rawbolds in a glee would
 shine;
 But the two youngest loved more to be
 set
Down to the harp — because to music's
 charms
They added graceful necks, white hands
and arms.

CVIII

Sometimes a dance (though rarely on field
 days,
 For then the gentlemen were rather
 tired)
Display'd some sylph-like figures in its
 maze;
 Then there was small-talk ready when
 required; 860
Flirtation — but decorous; the mere praise
 Of charms that should or should not be
 admired.

The hunters fought their fox-hunt o'er
 again,
And then retreated soberly — at ten.

CIX

The politicians, in a nook apart,
 Discuss'd the world, and settled all the
 spheres;
The wits watch'd every loophole for their
 art,
 To introduce a bon-mot head and ears;
Small is the rest of those who would be
 smart,
 A moment's good thing may have cost
 them years 870
Before they find an hour to introduce it;
And then, even *then*, some bore may make
 them lose it.

CX

But all was gentle and aristocratic
 In this our party; polish'd, smooth, and
 cold,
As Phidian forms cut out of marble At-
 tic.
 There now are no Squire Westerns as of
 old;
And our Sophias are not so emphatic,
 But fair as then, or fairer to behold.
We have no accomplish'd blackguards, like
 Tom Jones,
But gentlemen in stays, as stiff as stones.

CXI

They separated at an early hour; 881
 That is, ere midnight — which is Lon-
 don's noon:
But in the country ladies seek their bower
 A little earlier than the waning moon.
Peace to the slumbers of each folded
 flower —
 May the rose call back its true colour
 soon !
Good hours of fair cheeks are the fairest
 tinters,
And lower the price of rouge — at least
 some winters.

CANTO THE FOURTEENTH

I

IF from great nature's or our own abyss
 Of thought we could but snatch a cer-
 tainty,

Perhaps mankind might find the path they
 miss —
 But then 't would spoil much good philo-
 sophy.
One system eats another up, and this
 Much as old Saturn ate his progeny;
For when his pious consort gave him stones
In lieu of sons, of these he made no bones.

II

But System doth reverse the Titan's break-
 fast,
 And eats her parents, albeit the diges-
 tion 10
Is difficult. Pray tell me, can you make
 fast,
 After due search, your faith to any ques-
 tion ?
Look back o'er ages, ere unto the stake
 fast
 You bind yourself, and call some mode
 the best one.
Nothing more true than *not* to trust your
 senses;
And yet what are your other evidences ?

III

For me, I know nought; nothing I deny,
 Admit, reject, contemn; and what know
 you,
Except perhaps that you were born to die ?
 And both may after all turn out untrue.
An age may come, Font of Eternity, 21
 When nothing shall be either old or new.
Death, so call'd, is a thing which makes
 men weep,
And yet a third of life is pass'd in sleep.

IV

A sleep without dreams, after a rough day
 Of toil, is what we covet most; and yet
How clay shrinks back from more quiescent
 clay !
 The very Suicide that pays his debt
At once without instalments (an old way
 Of paying debts, which creditors regret)
Lets out impatiently his rushing breath, 31
Less from disgust of life than dread of
 death.

V

'T is round him, near him, here, there,
 every where;
 And there 's a courage which grows out
 of fear,

Perhaps of all most desperate, which will
　　dare
　　The worst to *know* it : — when the moun-
　　　　tains rear
Their peaks beneath your human foot, and
　　there
　　You look down o'er the precipice, and
　　　　drear
The gulf of rock yawns, — you can't gaze
　　a minute
Without an awful wish to plunge within it.

VI

'T is true, you don't — but, pale and struck
　　with terror,　　　　　　　　　　　41
　　Retire: but look into your past impres-
　　　　sion !
And you will find, though shuddering at the
　　mirror
　　Of your own thoughts, in all their self-
　　　　confession,
The lurking bias, be it truth or error,
　　To the *unknown ;* a secret prepossession,
To plunge with all your fears — but where?
　　　　You know not,
And that's the reason why you do — or do
　　not.

VII

But what's this to the purpose ? you will
　　say.
　　Gent. reader, nothing; a mere specula-
　　　　tion,　　　　　　　　　　　　　　50
For which my sole excuse is — 't is my
　　way;
　　Sometimes *with* and sometimes without
　　　　occasion
I write what's uppermost, without delay:
　　This narrative is not meant for narration,
But a mere airy and fantastic basis,
　　To build up common things with common
　　　　places.

VIII

You know, or don't know, that great Bacon
　　saith,
　　'Fling up a straw, 't will show the way
　　　　the wind blows;'
And such a straw, borne on by human
　　breath,
　　Is poesy, according as the mind glows;
A paper kite which flies 'twixt life and
　　death,　　　　　　　　　　　　　　61
　　A shadow which the onward soul behind
　　　　throws:

And mine's a bubble, not blown up for
　　praise,
But just to play with, as an infant plays.

IX

The world is all before me — or behind;
　　For I have seen a portion of that same,
And quite enough for me to keep in mind; —
　　Of passions, too, I have proved enough to
　　　　blame,
To the great pleasure of our friends, man-
　　kind,
　　Who like to mix some slight alloy with
　　　　fame;　　　　　　　　　　　　70
For I was rather famous in my time,
Until I fairly knock'd it up with rhyme.

X

I have brought this world about my ears,
　　and eke
　　The other; that's to say, the clergy, who
Upon my head have bid their thunders
　　break
　　In pious libels by no means a few.
And yet I can't help scribbling once a
　　week,
　　Tiring old readers, nor discovering new.
In youth I wrote because my mind was
　　full,
And now because I feel it growing dull.　80

XI

But 'why then publish ? ' — There are no
　　rewards
　　Of fame or profit when the world grows
　　　　weary.
I ask in turn, — Why do you play at cards?
　　Why drink ?　Why read ? — To make
　　　　some hour less dreary.
It occupies me to turn back regards
　　On what I've seen or ponder'd, sad or
　　　　cheery;
And what I write I cast upon the stream,
　　To swim or sink — I have had at least my
　　　　dream.

XII

I think that were I *certain* of success,
　　I hardly could compose another line:　90
So long I've battled either more or less,
　　That no defeat can drive me from the
　　　　Nine.
This feeling 't is not easy to express,
　　And yet 't is not affected, I opine.

In play, there are two pleasures for your
 choosing —
The one is winning, and the other losing.

XIII

Besides, my Muse by no means deals in
 fiction:
 She gathers a repertory of facts,
Of course with some reserve and slight re-
 striction,
 But mostly sings of human things and
 acts — 100
And that's one cause she meets with con-
 tradiction;
 For too much truth, at first sight, ne'er
 attracts;
And were her object only what's call'd
 glory,
With more ease too she'd tell a different
 story.

XIV

Love, war, a tempest — surely there's va-
 riety;
 Also a seasoning slight of lucubration;
A bird's-eye view, too, of that wild, Society;
 A slight glance thrown on men of every
 station.
If you have nought else, here's at least sa-
 tiety
 Both in performance and in prepara-
 tion; 110
And though these lines should only line
 portmanteaus,
Trade will be all the better for these Cantos.

XV

The portion of this world which I at present
 Have taken up to fill the following ser-
 mon,
Is one of which there's no description re-
 cent.
The reason why is easy to determine:
Although it seems both prominent and
 pleasant,
 There is a sameness in its gems and er-
 mine,
A dull and family likeness through all ages,
Of no great promise for poetic pages. 120

XVI

With much to excite, there's little to ex-
 alt;
 Nothing that speaks to all men and all
 times;

A sort of varnish over every fault;
 A kind of common-place, even in their
 crimes;
Factitious passions, wit without much salt,
 A want of that true nature which sublimes
Whate'er it shows with truth; a smooth
 monotony
Of character, in those at least who have
 got any.

XVII

Sometimes, indeed, like soldiers off parade,
 They break their ranks and gladly leave
 the drill; 130
But then the roll-call draws them back
 afraid,
 And they must be or seem what they
 were: still
Doubtless it is a brilliant masquerade;
 But when of the first sight you have had
 your fill,
It palls — at least it did so upon me,
This paradise of pleasure and ennui.

XVIII

When we have made our love, and gamed
 our gaming,
 Drest, voted, shone, and, may be, some-
 thing more;
With dandies dined; heard senators de-
 claiming;
 Seen beauties brought to market by the
 score, 140
Sad rakes to sadder husbands chastely
 taming;
 There's little left but to be bored or
 bore.
Witness those 'ci-devant jeunes hommes'
 who stem
The stream, nor leave the world which
 leaveth them.

XIX

'T is said — indeed a general complaint —
 That no one has succeeded in describing
The monde, exactly as they ought to paint:
 Some say, that authors only snatch, by
 bribing
The porter, some slight scandals strange
 and quaint,
 To furnish matter for their moral gibing;
And that their books have but one style in
 common — 151
My lady's prattle, filter'd through her
 woman.

XX

But this can't well be true, just now; for writers
　Are grown of the beau monde a part potential:
I've seen them balance even the scale with fighters,
　Especially when young, for that's essential.
Why do their sketches fail them as inditers
　Of what they deem themselves most consequential,
The *real* portrait of the highest tribe ?
'T is that, in fact, there's little to describe.

XXI

'*Haud ignara loquor ;*' these are *Nugœ,*
　'*quarum*　　　　　　　　　　　　161
　Pars parva *fui,*' but still art and part.
Now I could much more easily sketch a harem,
　A battle, wreck, or history of the heart,
Than these things; and besides, I wish to spare 'em,
　For reasons which I choose to keep apart.
'*Vetabo Cereris sacrum qui vulgarit*' —
Which means that vulgar people must not share it.

XXII

And therefore what I throw off is ideal —
　Lower'd, leaven'd, like a history of freemasons;　　　　　　　　　　　170
Which bears the same relation to the real,
　As Captain Parry's voyage may do to Jason's.
The grand arcanum's not for men to see all;
　My music has some mystic diapasons;
And there is much which could not be appreciated
In any manner by the uninitiated.

XXIII

Alas ! worlds fall — and woman, since she fell'd
　The world (as, since that history less polite
Than true, hath been a creed so strictly held)　　　　　　　　　　　179
　Has not yet given up the practice quite.
Poor thing of usages ! coerced, compell'd,
　Victim when wrong, and martyr oft when right,

Condemn'd to child-bed, as men for their sins
Have shaving too entail'd upon their chins, —

XXIV

A daily plague, which in the aggregate
　May average on the whole with parturition.
But as to women, who can penetrate
　The real sufferings of their she condition ?
Man's very sympathy with their estate
　Has much of selfishness, and more suspicion.　　　　　　　　　　　190
Their love, their virtue, beauty, education,
But form good housekeepers, to breed a nation.

XXV

All this were very well, and can't be better;
　But even this is difficult, Heaven knows,
So many troubles from her birth beset her,
　Such small distinction between friends and foes,
The gilding wears so soon from off her fetter,
　That — but ask any woman if she'd choose
(Take her at thirty, that is) to have been
Female or male ? a schoolboy or a queen ?

XXVI

'Petticoat influence' is a great reproach,
　Which even those who obey would fain be thought　　　　　　　　　　202
To fly from, as from hungry pikes a roach;
　But since beneath it upon earth we are brought,
By various joltings of life's hackney coach,
　I for one venerate a petticoat —
A garment of a mystical sublimity,
No matter whether russet, silk, or dimity.

XXVII

Much I respect, and much I have adored,
　In my young days, that chaste and goodly veil,　　　　　　　　210
Which holds a treasure, like a miser's hoard,
　And more attracts by all it doth conceal —
A golden scabbard on a Damasque sword,
　A loving letter with a mystic seal,

A cure for grief — for what can ever rankle
Before a petticoat and peeping ankle ?

XXVIII

And when upon a silent, sullen day,
 With a sirocco, for example, blowing,
When even the sea looks dim with all its
 spray, 219
 And sulkily the river's ripple 's flowing,
And the sky shows that very ancient gray,
 The sober, sad antithesis to glowing, —
'T is pleasant, if *then* any thing is pleasant,
To catch a glimpse even of a pretty peasant.

XXIX

We left our heroes and our heroines
 In that fair clime which don't depend on
 climate,
Quite independent of the Zodiac's signs,
 Though certainly more difficult to rhyme
 at,
Because the sun, and stars, and aught that
 shines,
 Mountains, and all we can be most sub-
 lime at, 230
Are there oft dull and dreary as a *dun* —
Whether a sky's or tradesman's is all one.

XXX

An in-door life is less poetical;
 And out of door hath showers, and mists,
 and sleet,
With which I could not brew a pastoral.
 But be it as it may, a bard must meet
All difficulties, whether great or small,
 To spoil his undertaking or complete,
And work away like spirit upon matter,
Embarrass'd somewhat both with fire and
 water. 240

XXXI

Juan — in this respect, at least, like saints —
 Was all things unto people of all sorts,
And lived contentedly, without complaints,
 In camps, in ships, in cottages, or courts —
Born with that happy soul which seldom
 faints,
 And mingling modestly in toils or sports.
He likewise could be most things to all
 women,
Without the coxcombry of certain *she* men.

XXXII

A fox-hunt to a foreigner is strange;
 'T is also subject to the double danger 250

Of tumbling first, and having in exchange
 Some pleasant jesting at the awkward
 stranger:
But Juan had been early taught to range
 The wilds, as doth an Arab turn'd
 avenger,
So that his horse, or charger, hunter, hack,
Knew that he had a rider on his back.

XXXIII

And now in this new field, with some ap-
 plause,
 He clear'd hedge, ditch, and double post,
 and rail,
And never *craned*, and made but few '*faux
 pas,*'
 And only fretted when the scent 'gan
 fail. 260
He broke, 't is true, some statutes of the
 laws
 Of hunting — for the sagest youth is
 frail;
Rode o'er the hounds, it may be, now and
 then,
And once o'er several country gentlemen.

XXXIV

But on the whole, to general admiration
 He acquitted both himself and horse: the
 squires
Marvell'd at merit of another nation;
 The boors cried ' Dang it ! who 'd have
 thought it ? '— Sires,
The Nestors of the sporting generation,
 Swore praises, and recall'd their former
 fires; 270
The huntsman's self relented to a grin,
And rated him almost a whipper-in.

XXXV

Such were his trophies — not of spear and
 shield,
 But leaps, and bursts, and sometimes
 foxes' brushes;
Yet I must own, — although in this I
 yield
 To patriot sympathy a Briton's blushes,—
He thought at heart like courtly Chester-
 field,
 Who, after a long chase o'er hills, dales,
 bushes,
And what not, though he rode beyond all
 price,
Ask'd next day, ' If men ever hunted
 twice ? ' 280

XXXVI

He also had a quality uncommon
 To early risers after a long chase,
Who wake in winter ere the cock can summon
 December's drowsy day to his dull
 race, —
A quality agreeable to woman,
 When her soft, liquid words run on
 apace,
Who likes a listener, whether saint or
 sinner, —
He did not fall asleep just after dinner;

XXXVII

But, light and airy, stood on the alert,
 And shone in the best part of dialogue,
By humouring always what they might
 assert, 291
 And listening to the topics most in
 vogue;
Now grave, now gay, but never dull or
 pert;
 And smiling but in secret — cunning
 rogue!
He ne'er presumed to make an error
 clearer; —
In short, there never was a better hearer.

XXXVIII

And then he danced; — all foreigners excel
 The serious Angles in the eloquence
Of pantomime; — he danced, I say, right
 well,
 With emphasis, and also with good
 sense — 300
A thing in footing indispensable;
 He danced without theatrical pretence,
Not like a ballet-master in the van
Of his drill'd nymphs, but like a gentleman.

XXXIX

Chaste were his steps, each kept within due
 bound,
 And elegance was sprinkled o'er his
 figure;
Like swift Camilla, he scarce skimm'd the
 ground,
 And rather held in than put forth his
 vigour;
And then he had an ear for music's sound,
 Which might defy a crotchet critic's
 rigour. 310

Such classic pas — sans flaws — set off our
 hero,
He glanced like a personified Bolero;

XL

Or, like a flying Hour before Aurora,
 In Guido's famous fresco which alone
Is worth a tour to Rome, although no more a
 Remnant were there of the old world's
 sole throne.
The 'tout ensemble' of his movements wore a
 Grace of the soft ideal, seldom shown,
And ne'er to be described; for to the dolour
Of bards and prosers, words are void of
 colour. 320

XLI

No marvel then he was a favourite;
 A full-grown Cupid, very much admired;
A little spoilt, but by no means so quite;
 At least he kept his vanity retired.
Such was his tact, he could alike delight
 The chaste, and those who are not so
 much inspired.
The Duchess of Fitz-Fulke, who loved
 'tracasserie,'
Began to treat him with some small
 'agacerie.'

XLII

She was a fine and somewhat full-blown
 blonde,
 Desirable, distinguish'd, celebrated 330
For several winters in the grand, grand
 monde.
 I'd rather not say what might be related
Of her exploits, for this were ticklish
 ground;
 Besides there might be falsehood in
 what's stated:
Her late performance had been a dead
 set
At Lord Augustus Fitz-Plantagenet.

XLIII

This noble personage began to look
 A little black upon this new flirtation;
But such small licences must lovers brook,
 Mere freedoms of the female corporation. 340
Woe to the man who ventures a rebuke!
 'T will but precipitate a situation
Extremely disagreeable, but common
To calculators when they count on woman.

XLIV

The circle smiled, then whisper'd, and then
 sneer'd;
 The Misses bridled, and the matrons
 frown'd;
Some hoped things might not turn out as
 they fear'd;
 Some would not deem such women could
 be found;
Some ne'er believed one half of what they
 heard;
 Some look'd perplex'd, and others look'd
 profound; 350
And several pitied with sincere regret
Poor Lord Augustus Fitz-Plantagenet.

XLV

But what is odd, none ever named the duke,
 Who, one might think, was something in
 the affair:
True, he was absent, and, 't was rumour'd,
 took
 But small concern about the when, or
 where,
Or what his consort did: if he could brook
 Her gaieties, none had a right to stare:
Theirs was that best of unions, past all
 doubt,
Which never meets, and therefore can't
 fall out. 360

XLVI

But, oh! that I should ever pen so sad a
 line!
 Fired with an abstract love of virtue, she,
My Dian of the Ephesians, Lady Adeline,
 Began to think the duchess' conduct
 free;
Regretting much that she had chosen so bad
 a line,
 And waxing chiller in her courtesy,
Look'd grave and pale to see her friend's
 fragility,
For which most friends reserve their sensi-
 bility.

XLVII

There's nought in this bad world like sym-
 pathy:
 'T is so becoming to the soul and face,
Sets to soft music the harmonious sigh, 371
 And robes sweet friendship in a Brussels
 lace.
Without a friend, what were humanity,
 To hunt our errors up with a good grace?

Consoling us with — 'Would you had
 thought twice!
Ah, if you had but follow'd my advice!'

XLVIII

O Job! you had two friends: one's quite
 enough,
 Especially when we are ill at ease;
They are but bad pilots when the weather's
 rough,
 Doctors less famous for their cures than
 fees. 380
Let no man grumble when his friends fall
 off,
 As they will do like leaves at the first
 breeze:
When your affairs come round, one way or
 t' other,
Go to the coffee-house, and take another.

XLIX

But this is not my maxim: had it been,
 Some heart-aches had been spared me:
 yet I care not —
I would not be a tortoise in his screen
 Of stubborn shell, which waves and
 weather wear not.
'T is better on the whole to have felt and
 seen
 That which humanity may bear, or bear
 not: 390
'T will teach discernment to the sensi-
 tive,
And not to pour their ocean in a sieve.

L

Of all the horrid, hideous notes of woe,
 Sadder than owl-songs or the midnight
 blast,
Is that portentous phrase, 'I told you
 so,'
 Utter'd by friends, those prophets of the
 past,
Who, 'stead of saying what you now should
 do,
 Own they foresaw that you would fall at
 last,
And solace your slight lapse 'gainst ' bonos
 mores,'
With a long memorandum of old stories.

LI

The Lady Adeline's serene severity 401
 Was not confined to feeling for her
 friend,

Whose fame she rather doubted with pos-
　　terity,
　　Unless her habits should begin to mend:
But Juan also shared in her austerity,
　　But mix'd with pity, pure as e'er was
　　penn'd:
His inexperience moved her gentle ruth,
And (as her junior by six weeks) his youth.

LII

These forty days' advantage of her years —
　　And hers were those which can face cal-
　　culation, 410
Boldly referring to the list of peers
　　And noble births, nor dread the enumer-
　　ation —
Gave her a right to have maternal fears
　　For a young gentleman's fit education,
Though she was far from that leap year,
　　whose leap,
In female dates, strikes Time all of a
　　heap.

LIII

This may be fix'd at somewhere before
　　thirty —
　　Say seven-and-twenty; for I never knew
The strictest in chronology and virtue
　　Advance beyond, while they could pass
　　for new. 420
O Time! why dost not pause? Thy scythe,
　　so dirty
　　With rust, should surely cease to hack
　　and hew.
Reset it; shave more smoothly, also slower,
If but to keep thy credit as a mower.

LIV

But Adeline was far from that ripe age,
　　Whose ripeness is but bitter at the best:
'T was rather her experience made her
　　sage,
　　For she had seen the world and stood its
　　test,
As I have said in — I forget what page;
　　My Muse despises reference, as you have
　　guess'd 430
By this time; — but strike six from seven-
　　and-twenty,
And you will find her sum of years in
　　plenty.

LV

At sixteen she came out; presented, vaunted,
　　She put all coronets into commotion:

At seventeen, too, the world was still en-
　　chanted
　　With the new Venus of their brilliant
　　ocean:
At eighteen, though below her feet still
　　panted
　　A hecatomb of suitors with devotion,
She had consented to create again
That Adam, call'd 'The happiest of men.'

LVI

Since then she had sparkled through three
　　glowing winters, 441
　　Admired, adored; but also so correct,
That she had puzzled all the acutest hinters,
　　Without the apparel of being circum-
　　spect:
They could not even glean the slightest
　　splinters
　　From off the marble, which had no defect.
She had also snatch'd a moment since her
　　marriage
To bear a son and heir — and one miscar-
　　riage.

LVII

Fondly the wheeling fire-flies flew around
　　her,
　　Those little glitterers of the London
　　night; 450
But none of these possess'd a sting to
　　wound her —
　　She was a pitch beyond a coxcomb's
　　flight.
Perhaps she wish'd an aspirant profounder;
　　But whatsoe'er she wish'd, she acted
　　right;
And whether coldness, pride, or virtue
　　dignify
A woman, so she's good, what does it
　　signify?

LVIII

I hate a motive, like a lingering bottle
　　Which with the landlord makes too long
　　a stand,
Leaving all-claretless the unmoisten'd
　　throttle,
　　Especially with politics on hand; 460
I hate it, as I hate a drove of cattle,
　　Who whirl the dust as simooms whirl the
　　sand;
I hate it, as I hate an argument,
A laureate's ode, or servile peer's 'con-
　　tent.'

LIX

'T is sad to hack into the roots of things,
　They are so much intertwisted with the
　　earth;
So that the branch a goodly verdure flings,
　I reck not if an acorn gave it birth.
To trace all actions to their secret springs
　Would make indeed some melancholy
　　mirth;　　　　　　　　　　　　　470
But this is not at present my concern,
And I refer you to wise Oxenstiern.

LX

With the kind view of saving an éclat,
　Both to the duchess and diplomatist,
The Lady Adeline, as soon 's she saw
　That Juan was unlikely to resist
(For foreigners don't know that a *faux pas*
　In England ranks quite on a different list
From those of other lands unblest with
　juries,
Whose verdict for such sin a certain cure
　is); —　　　　　　　　　　　　480

LXI

The Lady Adeline resolved to take
　Such measures as she thought might best
　　impede
The farther progress of this sad mistake.
　She thought with some simplicity indeed;
But innocence is bold even at the stake,
　And simple in the world, and doth not
　　need
Nor use those palisades by dames erected,
Whose virtue lies in never being detected.

LXII

It was not that she fear'd the very worst:
　His Grace was an enduring, married
　　man,　　　　　　　　　　　　490
And was not likely all at once to burst
　Into a scene, and swell the clients' clan
Of Doctors' Commons: but she dreaded first
　The magic of her Grace's talisman,
And next a quarrel (as he seem'd to fret)
With Lord Augustus Fitz-Plantagenet.

LXIII

Her Grace, too, pass'd for being an intri-
　gante,
　And somewhat *méchante* in her amorous
　　sphere;
One of those pretty, precious plagues, which
　haunt
　A lover with caprices soft and dear,　500

That like to *make* a quarrel, when they
　can't
Find one, each day of the delightful year;
Bewitching, torturing, as they freeze or
　glow,
And — what is worst of all — won't let you
　go:

LXIV

The sort of thing to turn a young man's
　head,
　Or make a Werter of him in the end.
No wonder then a purer soul should dread
　This sort of chaste *liaison* for a friend;
It were much better to be wed or dead,
　Than wear a heart a woman loves to
　　rend.　　　　　　　　　　　510
'T is best to pause, and think, ere you rush
　on,
If that a ' *bonne fortune* ' be really ' *bonne*.'

LXV

And first, in the o'erflowing of her heart,
　Which really knew or thought it knew
　　no guile,
She call'd her husband now and then apart,
　And bade him counsel Juan. With a
　　smile
Lord Henry heard her plans of artless art
　To wean Don Juan from the siren's wile;
And answer'd, like a statesman or a pro-
　phet,
In such guise that she could make nothing
　of it.　　　　　　　　　　　520

LXVI

Firstly, he said, ' he never interfered
　In any body's business but the king's: '
Next, that ' he never judged from what ap-
　pear'd,
　Without strong reason, of those sort of
　　things: '
Thirdly, that ' Juan had more brain than
　heard,
　And was not to be held in leading
　　strings; '
And fourthly, what need hardly be said
　twice,
' That good but rarely came from good ad-
　vice.'

LXVII

And, therefore, doubtless to approve the
　truth
　Of the last axiom, he advised his spouse

To leave the parties to themselves, for-
 sooth — 531
 At least as far as *bienséance* allows:
That time would temper Juan's faults of
 youth;
 That young men rarely made monastic
 vows;
That opposition only more attaches —
But here a messenger brought in de-
 spatches:

LXVIII

And being of the council call'd ' the Privy,'
 Lord Henry walk'd into his cabinet,
To furnish matter for some future Livy 539
 To tell how he reduced the nation's debt;
And if their full contents I do not give ye,
 It is because I do not know them yet;
But I shall add them in a brief appen-
 dix,
To come between mine epic and its index.

LXIX

But ere he went, he added a slight hint,
 Another gentle common-place or two,
Such as are coin'd in conversation's mint,
 And pass, for want of better, though not
 new:
Then broke his packet, to see what was
 in 't,
 And having casually glanced it through,
Retired; and, as went out, calmly kiss'd
 her, 551
Less like a young wife than an aged sister.

LXX

He was a cold, good, honourable man,
 Proud of his birth, and proud of every
 thing;
A goodly spirit for a state divan,
 A figure fit to walk before a king;
Tall, stately, form'd to lead the courtly van
 On birthdays, glorious with a star and
 string;
The very model of a chamberlain —
And such I mean to make him when I reign.

LXXI

But there was something wanting on the
 whole — 561
 I don't know what, and therefore cannot
 tell —
Which pretty women — the sweet souls !
 — call *soul.*
 Certes it was not body; he was well

Proportion'd, as a poplar or a pole,
 A handsome man, that human miracle;
And in each circumstance of love or war
Had still preserved his perpendicular.

LXXII

Still there was something wanting, as I 've
 said —
 That undefinable ' *Je ne sçais quoi,*' 570
Which, for what I know, may of yore have
 led
 To Homer's Iliad, since it drew to Troy
The Greek Eve, Helen, from the Spartan's
 bed;
 Though on the whole, no doubt, the Dar-
 dan boy
Was much inferior to King Menelaüs : —
But thus it is some women will betray us.

LXXIII

There is an awkward thing which much
 perplexes,
 Unless like wise Tiresias we had proved
By turns the difference of the several sexes;
 Neither can show quite *how* they would
 be loved. 580
The sensual for a short time but connects us,
 The sentimental boasts to be unmoved;
But both together form a kind of centaur,
Upon whose back 't is better not to venture.

LXXIV

A something all-sufficient for the *heart*
 Is that for which the sex are always
 seeking:
But how to fill up that same vacant part ?
 There lies the rub — and this they are
 but weak in.
Frail mariners afloat without a chart,
 They run before the wind through high
 seas breaking; 590
And when they have made the shore through
 every shock,
'T is odd, or odds, it may turn out a rock.

LXXV

There is a flower call'd ' Love in Idleness,'
 For which see Shakspeare's ever blooming
 garden; —
I will not make his great description less,
 And beg his British godship's humble
 pardon,
If in my extremity of rhyme's distress,
 I touch a single leaf where he is war-
 den; —

But though the flower is different, with the
 French
Or Swiss Rousseau, cry ' *Voilà la Per-*
 venche ! ' 600

LXXVI

Eureka ! I have found it ! What I mean
 To say is, not that love is idleness,
But that in love such idleness has been
 An accessory, as I have cause to guess.
Hard labour 's an indifferent go-between ;
 Your men of business are not apt to ex-
 press
Much passion, since the merchant-ship, the
 Argo,
Convey'd Medea as her supercargo.

LXXVII

' *Beatus ille procul !* ' from ' *negotiis*,'
 Saith Horace ; the great little poet 's
 wrong ; 610
His other maxim, ' *Noscitur à sociis*,'
 Is much more to the purpose of his song ;
Though even that were sometimes too
 ferocious,
 Unless good company be kept too long ;
But, in his teeth, whate'er their state or
 station,
Thrice happy they who *have* an occupa-
 tion !

LXXVIII

Adam exchanged his Paradise for plough-
 ing,
 Eve made up millinery with fig leaves —
The earliest knowledge from the tree so
 knowing,
 As far as I know, that the church
 receives : 620
And since that time it need not cost much
 showing,
 That many of the ills o'er which man
 grieves,
And still more women, spring from not
 employing
Some hours to make the remnant worth en-
 joying.

LXXIX

And hence high life is oft a dreary void,
 A rack of pleasures, where we must
 invent
A something wherewithal to be annoy'd.
 Bards may sing what they please about
 Content ;

Contented, when translated, means but
 cloy'd ;
 And hence arise the woes of sentiment,
Blue devils, and blue-stockings, and
 romances 631
Reduced to practice, and perform'd like
 dances.

LXXX

I do declare, upon an affidavit,
 Romances I ne'er read like those I have
 seen ;
Nor, if unto the world I ever gave it,
 Would some believe that such a tale had
 been :
But such intent I never had, nor have it ;
 Some truths are better kept behind a
 screen,
Especially when they would look like lies ;
I therefore deal in generalities. 640

LXXXI

' An oyster may be cross'd in love,' — and
 why ?
 Because he mopeth idly in his shell,
And heaves a lonely subterraqueous sigh,
 Much as a monk may do within his
 cell :
And *à-propos* of monks, their piety
 With sloth hath found it difficult to
 dwell ;
Those vegetables of the Catholic creed
Are apt exceedingly to run to seed.

LXXXII

O Wilberforce ! thou man of black renown,
 Whose merit none enough can sing or
 say, 650
Thou hast struck one immense Colossus
 down,
 Thou moral Washington of Africa !
But there 's another little thing, I own,
 Which you should perpetrate some sum-
 mer's day,
And set the other half of earth to rights ;
You have freed the *blacks* — now pray shut
 up the whites.

LXXXIII

Shut up the bald-coot bully Alexander !
 Ship off the Holy Three to Senegal ;
Teach them that ' sauce for goose is sauce
 for gander,'
 And ask them how *they* like to be in
 thrall ? 660

Shut up each high heroic salamander,
 Who eats fire gratis (since the pay's but
 small);
Shut up — no, *not* the King, but the Pavil-
 ion,
Or else 't will cost us all another million.

LXXXIV

Shut up the world at large, let Bedlam out;
 And you will be perhaps surprised to find
All things pursue exactly the same route,
 As now with those of *soi-disant* sound
 mind.
This I could prove beyond a single doubt,
 Were there a jot of sense among man-
 kind; 670
But till that *point d'appui* is found, alas !
Like Archimedes, I leave earth as 't was.

LXXXV

Our gentle Adeline had one defect —
 Her heart was vacant, though a splendid
 mansion;
Her conduct had been perfectly correct,
 As she had seen nought claiming its ex-
 pansion.
A wavering spirit may be easier wreck'd,
 Because 't is frailer, doubtless, than a
 stanch one;
But when the latter works its own undoing,
Its inner crash is like an earthquake's ruin.

LXXXVI

She loved her lord, or thought so; but *that*
 love 681
 Cost her an effort, which is a sad toil,
The stone of Sysiphus, if once we move
 Our feelings 'gainst the nature of the
 soil.
She had nothing to complain of, or re-
 prove,
 No bickerings, no connubial turmoil:
Their union was a model to behold,
Serene and noble, — conjugal, but cold.

LXXXVII

There was no great disparity of years,
 Though much in temper; but they never
 clash'd: 690
They moved like stars united in their
 spheres,
 Or like the Rhone by Leman's waters
 wash'd,
Where mingled and yet separate appears
 The river from the lake, all bluely dash'd

Through the serene and placid glassy deep,
Which fain would lull its river-child to
 sleep.

LXXXVIII

Now when she once had ta'en an interest
 In any thing, however she might flat-
 ter
Herself that her intentions were the best,
 Intense intentions are a dangerous mat-
 ter: 700
Impressions were much stronger than she
 guess'd,
 And gather'd as they run like growing
 water
Upon her mind; the more so, as her breast
Was not at first too readily impress'd.

LXXXIX

But when it was, she had that lurking de-
 mon
 Of double nature, and thus doubly
 named —
Firmness yclept in heroes, kings, and sea-
 men,
 That is, when they succeed; but greatly
 blamed
As *obstinacy*, both in men and women,
 Whene'er their triumph pales, or star is
 tamed: — 710
And 't will perplex the casuist in morality
To fix the due bounds of this dangerous
 quality.

XC

Had Buonaparte won at Waterloo,
 It had been firmness; now 't is pertina-
 city:
Must the event decide between the two ?
 I leave it to your people of sagacity
To draw the line between the false and
 true,
 If such can e'er be drawn by man's ca-
 pacity:
My business is with Lady Adeline,
Who in her way too was a heroine. 720

XCI

She knew not her own heart; then how
 should I ?
 I think not she was *then* in love with
 Juan:
If so, she would have had the strength to
 fly
 The wild sensation, unto her a new one:

She merely felt a common sympathy
 (I will not say it was a false or true one)
In him, because she thought he was in
 danger, —
 Her husband's friend, her own, young, and
 a stranger,

XCII

She was, or thought she was, his friend —
 and this
 Without the farce of friendship, or ro-
 mance 730
Of Platonism, which leads so oft amiss
 Ladies who have studied friendship but
 in France,
 Or Germany, where people *purely* kiss.
 To thus much Adeline would not advance;
But of such friendship as man's may to
 man be
She was as capable as woman can be.

XCIII

No doubt the secret influence of the sex
 Will there, as also in the ties of blood,
An innocent predominance annex,
 And tune the concord to a finer mood.
If free from passion, which all friendship
 checks, 741
 And your true feelings fully understood,
No friend like to a woman earth discovers,
So that you have not been nor will be lov-
 ers.

XCIV

Love bears within its breast the very germ
 Of change; and how should this be other-
 wise ?
That violent things more quickly find a
 term
 Is shown through nature's whole anal-
 ogies;
And how should the most fierce of all be
 firm ?
 Would you have endless lightning in the
 skies ? 750
Methinks Love's very title says enough:
How should 'the *tender* passion' e'er be
 tough ?

XCV

Alas ! by all experience, seldom yet
 (I merely quote what I have heard from
 many)
Had lovers not some reason to regret
 The passion which made Solomon a zany.

I 've also seen some wives (not to forget
 The marriage state, the best or worst of
 any)
Who were the very paragons of wives,
Yet made the misery of at least two lives.

XCVI

I 've also seen some female *friends* ('t is
 odd, 761
 But true — as, if expedient, I could
 prove)
That faithful were through thick and thin,
 abroad,
 At home, far more than ever yet was
 Love —
Who did not quit me when Oppression
 trod
 Upon me; whom no scandal could re-
 move;
Who fought, and fight, in absence, too, my
 battles,
Despite the snake Society's loud rattles.

XCVII

Whether Don Juan and chaste Adeline
 Grew friends in this or any other sense,
Will be discuss'd hereafter, I opine: 771
 At present I am glad of a pretence
To leave them hovering, as the effect is
 fine,
 And keeps the atrocious reader in *sus-
 pense ;*
The surest way for ladies and for books
To bait their tender, or their tenter, hooks.

XCVIII

Whether they rode, or walk'd, or studied
 Spanish
 To read Don Quixote in the original,
A pleasure before which all others vanish;
 Whether their talk was of the kind
 call'd 'small,' 780
Or serious, are the topics I must banish
 To the next Canto; where perhaps I
 shall
Say something to the purpose, and display
Considerable talent in my way.

XCIX

Above all, I beg all men to forbear
 Anticipating aught about the matter:
They 'll only make mistakes about the fair,
 And Juan too, especially the latter.
And I shall take a much more serious air
 Than I have yet done, in this epic satire.

It is not clear that Adeline and Juan 791
Will fall; but if they do, 't will be their
 ruin.

C

But great things spring from little: —
 Would you think,
 That in our youth, as dangerous a pas-
 sion
As e'er brought man and woman to the
 brink
Of ruin, rose from such a slight occasion,
As few would ever dream could form the
 link
Of such a sentimental situation?
You 'll never guess, I 'll bet you millions,
 milliards —
It all sprung from a harmless game at bil-
 liards. 800

CI

'T is strange, — but true; for truth is al-
 ways strange;
 Stranger than fiction; if it could be told,
How much would novels gain by the ex-
 change!
 How differently the world would men
 behold!
How oft would vice and virtue places
 change!
 The new world would be nothing to the
 old,
If some Columbus of the moral seas
Would show mankind their souls' antipodes.

CII

What 'antres vast and deserts idle' then
 Would be discover'd in the human soul!
What icebergs in the hearts of mighty
 men, 811
 With self-love in the centre as their pole!
What Anthropophagi are nine of ten
 Of those who hold the kingdoms in con-
 trol!
Were things but only call'd by their right
 name,
Cæsar himself would be ashamed of fame.

CANTO THE FIFTEENTH

I

Ah! — What should follow slips from my
 reflection;
 Whatever follows ne'ertheless may be

As à-propos of hope or retrospection,
 As though the lurking thought had fol-
 low'd free.
All present life is but an interjection,
 An 'Oh!' or 'Ah!' of joy or misery,
Or a 'Ha! ha!' or 'Bah!' — a yawn, or
 'Pooh!'
Of which perhaps the latter is most true.

II

But, more or less, the whole 's a syncopé
 Or a singultus — emblems of emotion, 10
The grand antithesis to great ennui,
 Wherewith we break our bubbles on the
 ocean, —
That watery outline of eternity,
 Or miniature at least, as is my notion,
Which ministers unto the soul's delight,
In seeing matters which are out of sight.

III

But all are better than the sigh supprest,
 Corroding in the cavern of the heart,
Making the countenance a masque of rest,
 And turning human nature to an art. 20
Few men dare show their thoughts of worst
 or best;
 Dissimulation always sets apart
A corner for herself; and therefore fiction
Is that which passes with least contradiction.

IV

Ah! who can tell? Or rather, who can not
 Remember, without telling, passion's
 errors?
The drainer of oblivion, even the sot,
 Hath got blue devils for his morning
 mirrors:
What though on Lethe's stream he seem to
 float,
 He cannot sink his tremors or his
 terrors; 30
The ruby glass that shakes within his hand
Leaves a sad sediment of Time's worst
 sand.

V

And as for love — O love! — We will pro-
 ceed.
 The Lady Adeline Amundeville,
A pretty name as one would wish to read,
 Must perch harmonious on my tuneful
 quill.
There 's music in the sighing of a reed;
 There 's music in the gushing of a rill;

There's music in all things, if men had
 ears:
Their earth is but an echo of the spheres. 40

VI

The Lady Adeline, right honourable,
 And honour'd, ran a risk of growing less
 so;
For few of the soft sex are very stable
 In their resolves — alas! that I should
 say so!
They differ as wine differs from its label,
 When once decanted; — I presume to
 guess so,
But will not swear: yet both upon occasion,
Till old, may undergo adulteration.

VII

But Adeline was of the purest vintage,
 The unmingled essence of the grape; and
 yet 50
Bright as a new Napoleon from its mint-
 age,
 Or glorious as a diamond richly set;
A page where Time should hesitate to print
 age,
 And for which Nature might forego her
 debt —
Sole creditor whose process doth involve
 in 't
The luck of finding every body solvent.

VIII

O Death! thou dunnest of all duns! thou
 daily
 Knockest at doors, at first with modest
 tap,
Like a meek tradesman when, approaching
 palely,
 Some splendid debtor he would take by
 sap: 60
But oft denied, as patience 'gins to fail, he
 Advances with exasperated rap,
And (if let in) insists, in terms unhandsome,
On ready money, or 'a draft on Ransom.'

IX

Whate'er thou takest, spare a while poor
 Beauty!
 She is so rare, and thou hast so much
 prey.
What though she now and then may slip
 from duty,
 The more 's the reason why you ought to
 stay.

Gaunt Gourmand! with whole nations for
 your booty,
 You should be civil in a modest way: 70
Suppress, then, some slight feminine dis-
 eases,
And take as many heroes as Heaven
 pleases.

X

Fair Adeline, the more ingenuous
 Where she was interested (as was said),
Because she was not apt, like some of us,
 To like too readily, or too high bred
To show it (points we need not now dis-
 cuss) —
 Would give up artlessly both heart and
 head
Unto such feelings as seem'd innocent,
For objects worthy of the sentiment. 80

XI

Some parts of Juan's history, which Ru-
 mour,
 That live gazette, had scatter'd to dis-
 figure,
She had heard; but women hear with more
 good humour
 Such aberrations than we men of rig-
 our:
Besides, his conduct, since in England, grew
 more
 Strict, and his mind assumed a manlier
 vigour;
Because he had, like Alcibiades,
The art of living in all climes with ease.

XII

His manner was perhaps the more seduc-
 tive,
 Because he ne'er seem'd anxious to se-
 duce; 90
Nothing affected, studied, or constructive
 Of coxcombry or conquest: no abuse
Of his attractions marr'd the fair perspec-
 tive,
 To indicate a Cupidon broke loose,
And seem to say, 'Resist us if you can' —
Which makes a dandy while it spoils a
 man.

XIII

They are wrong — that's not the way to set
 about it;
 As, if they told the truth, could well be
 shown.

But, right or wrong, Don Juan was without
 it;
 In fact, his manner was his own alone;
Sincere he was — at least you could not
 doubt it, 101
 In listening merely to his voice's tone.
The devil hath not in all his quiver's choice
An arrow for the heart like a sweet voice.

XIV

By nature soft, his whole address held off
 Suspicion: though not timid, his regard
Was such as rather seem'd to keep aloof,
 To shield himself than put you on your
 guard:
Perhaps 't was hardly quite assured enough,
 But modesty's at times its own re-
 ward, 110
Like virtue; and the absence of pretension
Will go much farther than there's need to
 mention.

XV

Serene, accomplish'd, cheerful but not loud;
 Insinuating without insinuation;
Observant of the foibles of the crowd,
 Yet ne'er betraying this in conversation;
Proud with the proud, yet courteously
 proud,
 So as to make them feel he knew his sta-
 tion
And theirs: — without a struggle for pri-
 ority,
He neither brook'd nor claim'd superiority.

XVI

That is, with men: with women he was
 what 121
 They pleased to make or take him for;
 and their
Imagination's quite enough for that:
 So that the outline's tolerably fair,
They fill the canvass up — and 'verbum
 sat.'
If once their phantasies be brought to bear
Upon an object, whether sad or playful,
They can transfigure brighter than a Ra-
 phael.

XVII

Adeline, no deep judge of character,
 Was apt to add a colouring from her own:
'T is thus the good will amiably err, 131
 And eke the wise, as has been often
 shown.

Experience is the chief philosopher,
 But saddest when his science is well
 known:
And persecuted sages teach the schools
Their folly in forgetting there are fools.

XVIII

Was it not so, great Locke? and greater
 Bacon?
 Great Socrates? And thou, Diviner still,
Whose lot it is by man to be mistaken,
 And thy pure creed made sanction of all
 ill? 140
Redeeming worlds to be by bigots shaken,
 How was thy toil rewarded? We might
 fill
Volumes with similar sad illustrations,
But leave them to the conscience of the na-
 tions.

XIX

I perch upon an humbler promontory,
 Amidst life's infinite variety:
With no great care for what is nicknamed
 glory,
 But speculating as I cast mine eye
On what may suit or may not suit my story,
 And never straining hard to versify, 150
I rattle on exactly as I'd talk
With any body in a ride or walk.

XX

I don't know that there may be much abil-
 ity
 Shown in this sort of desultory rhyme;
But there's a conversational facility,
 Which may round off an hour upon a
 time.
Of this I'm sure at least, there's no servil-
 ity
 In mine irregularity of chime,
Which rings what's uppermost of new or
 hoary,
Just as I feel the 'Improvvisatore.' 160

XXI

'Omnia vult belle Matho dicere — dic ali-
 quando
 Et bene, dic neutrum, dic aliquando male.'
The first is rather more than mortal can
 do;
 The second may be sadly done or gaily;
The third is still more difficult to stand to;
 The fourth we hear, and see, and say too,
 daily:

The whole together is what I could wish
To serve in this conundrum of a dish.

XXII

A modest hope — but modesty 's my forte,
 And pride my feeble: — let us ramble
 on. 170
I meant to make this poem very short,
 But now I can't tell where it may not
 run.
No doubt, if I had wish'd to pay my court
 To critics, or to hail the *setting* sun
Of tyranny of all kinds, my concision
Were more; — but I was born for opposi-
 tion.

XXIII

But then 't is mostly on the weaker side;
 So that I verily believe if they
Who now are basking in their full-blown
 pride
 Were shaken down, and ' dogs had had
 their day,' 180
Though at the first I might perchance de-
 ride
 Their tumble, I should turn the other
 way,
And wax an ultra-royalist in loyalty,
Because I hate even democratic royalty.

XXIV

I think I should have made a decent spouse,
 If I had never proved the soft condition;
I think I should have made monastic vows,
 But for my own peculiar superstition:
'Gainst rhyme I never should have knock'd
 my brows,
 Nor broken my own head, nor that of
 Priscian, 190
Nor worn the motley mantle of a poet,
If some one had not told me to forego it.

XXV

But ' laissez aller ' — knights and dames I
 sing,
 Such as the times may furnish. 'T is a
 flight
Which seems at first to need no lofty wing,
 Plumed by Longinus or the Stagyrite:
The difficulty lies in colouring
 (Keeping the due proportions still in
 sight)
With nature manners which are artificial,
And rend'ring general that which is espe-
 cial. 200

XXVI

The difference is, that in the days of old
 Men made the manners; manners now
 make men —
Pinn'd like a flock, and fleeced too in their
 fold,
 At least nine, and a ninth beside of ten.
Now this at all events must render cold
 Your writers, who must either draw again
Days better drawn before, or else assume
The present, with their common-place cos-
 tume.

XXVII

We 'll do our best to make the best on 't: —
 March !
 March, my Muse ! If you cannot fly, yet
 flutter; 210
And when you may not be sublime, be arch,
 Or starch, as are the edicts statesmen
 utter.
We surely may find something worth re-
 search:
 Columbus found a new world in a cutter,
Or brigantine, or pink, of no great tonnage,
While yet America was in her non-age.

XXVIII

When Adeline, in all her growing sense
 Of Juan's merits and his situation,
Felt on the whole an interest intense, —
 Partly perhaps because a fresh sensation,
Or that he had an air of innocence, 221
 Which is for innocence a sad tempta-
 tion, —
As women hate half measures, on the whole,
She 'gan to ponder how to save his soul.

XXIX

She had a good opinion of advice,
 Like all who give and eke receive it
 gratis,
For which small thanks are still the market
 price,
 Even where the article at highest rate is:
She thought upon the subject twice or
 thrice,
 And morally decided, the best state is
For morals, marriage; and this question
 carried, 231
She seriously advised him to get married.

XXX

Juan replied, with all becoming deference,
 He had a predilection for that tie;

But that, at present, with immediate refer-
ence
To his own circumstances, there might lie
Some difficulties, as in his own preference,
Or that of her to whom he might apply:
That still he 'd wed with such or such a lady,
If that they were not married all already.

XXXI

Next to the making matches for herself,
And daughters, brothers, sisters, kith or
kin, 242
Arranging them like books on the same
shelf,
There 's nothing women love to dabble in
More (like a stock-holder in growing pelf)
Than match-making in general: 't is no
sin
Certes, but a preventative, and therefore
That is, no doubt, the only reason wherefore.

XXXII

But never yet (except of course a miss
Unwed, or mistress never to be wed, 250
Or wed already, who object to this)
Was there chaste dame who had not in
her head
Some drama of the marriage unities,
Observed as strictly both at board and
bed
As those of Aristotle, though sometimes
They turn out melodrames or pantomimes.

XXXIII

They generally have some only son,
Some heir to a large property, some
friend
Of an old family, some gay Sir John,
Or grave Lord George, with whom per-
haps might end 260
A line, and leave posterity undone,
Unless a marriage was applied to mend
The prospect and their morals: and besides,
They have at hand a blooming glut of brides.

XXXIV

From these they will be careful to select,
For this an heiress, and for that a beauty;
For one a songstress who hath no defect,
For t' other one who promises much duty;
For this a lady no one can reject,
Whose sole accomplishments were quite
a booty; 270
A second for her excellent connections;
A third, because there can be no objections.

XXXV

When Rapp the Harmonist embargo'd mar-
riage
In his harmonious settlement (which
flourishes
Strangely enough as yet without miscar-
riage,
Because it breeds no more mouths than
it nourishes,
Without those sad expenses which dispar-
age
What Nature naturally most encour-
ages) —
Why call'd he ' Harmony ' a state sans wed-
lock ?
Now here I 've got the preacher at a dead
lock. 280

XXXVI

Because he either meant to sneer at har-
mony
Or marriage, by divorcing them thus
oddly.
But whether reverend Rapp learn'd this in
Germany
Or no, 't is said his sect is rich and godly,
Pious and pure, beyond what I can term
any
Of ours, although they propagate more
broadly.
My objection 's to his title, not his ritual,
Although I wonder how it grew habitual.

XXXVII

But Rapp is the reverse of zealous ma-
trons,
Who favour, malgré Malthus, genera-
tion — 290
Professors of that genial art, and patrons
Of all the modest part of propagation;
Which after all at such a desperate rate
runs,
That half its produce tends to emigra-
tion,
That sad result of passions and potatoes —
Two weeds which pose our economic Catos.

XXXVIII

Had Adeline read Malthus ? I can't tell;
I wish she had: his book 's the eleventh
commandment,
Which says, ' Thou shalt not marry,' unless
well:
This he (as far as I can understand)
meant. 300

'T is not my purpose on his views to dwell
Nor canvass what so ' eminent a hand '
 meant;
But certes it conducts to lives ascetic,
Or turning marriage into arithmetic.

XXXIX

But Adeline, who probably presumed
 That Juan had enough of maintenance,
Or *separate* maintenance, in case 't was
 doom'd —
As on the whole it is an even chance
That bridegrooms, after they are fairly
 groom'd,
May retrograde a little in the dance 310
Of marriage (which might form a painter's
 fame,
Like Holbein's ' Dance of Death ' — but
 't is the same); —

XL

But Adeline determined Juan's wedding
 In her own mind, and that 's enough for
 woman:
But then, with whom ? There was the
 sage Miss Reading,
 Miss Raw, Miss Flaw, Miss Showman,
 and Miss Knowman,
And the two fair co-heiresses Giltbedding.
 She deem'd his merits something more
 than common:
All these were unobjectionable matches,
And might go on, if well wound up, like
 watches. 320

XLI

There was Miss Millpond, smooth as sum-
 mer's sea,
 That usual paragon, an only daughter,
Who seem'd the cream of equanimity
 Till skimm'd — and then there was some
 milk and water,
With a slight shade of blue too, it might be,
 Beneath the surface; but what did it
 matter ?
Love 's riotous, but marriage should have
 quiet,
And being consumptive, live on a milk diet.

XLII

And then there was the Miss Audacia
 Shoestring,
 A dashing demoiselle of good estate, 330
Whose heart was fix'd upon a star or blue
 string;

But whether English dukes grew rare of
 late,
Or that she had not harp'd upon the true
 string,
 By which such sirens can attract our
 great,
She took up with some foreign younger
 brother,
A Russ or Turk — the one 's as good as
 t' other.

XLIII

And then there was — but why should I go
 on,
 Unless the ladies should go off ? — there
 was
Indeed a certain fair and fairy one,
 Of the best class, and better than her
 class, — 340
Aurora Raby, a young star who shone
 O'er life, too sweet an image for such
 glass,
A lovely being, scarcely form'd or moulded,
A rose with all its sweetest leaves yet
 folded;

XLIV

Rich, noble, but an orphan; left an only
 Child to the care of guardians good and
 kind;
But still her aspect had an air so lonely !
 Blood is not water; and where shall we
 find
Feelings of youth like those which over-
 thrown lie
 By death, when we are left, alas !
 behind, 350
To feel, in friendless palaces, a home
Is wanting, and our best ties in the tomb ?

XLV

Early in years, and yet more infantine
 In figure, she had something of sub-
 lime
In eyes which sadly shone, as seraphs'
 shine.
 All youth — but with an aspect beyond
 time;
Radiant and grave — as pitying man's de-
 cline;
 Mournful — but mournful of another's
 crime,
She look'd as if she sat by Eden's door,
And grieved for those who could return no
 more. 360

XLVI

She was a Catholic, too, sincere, austere,
 As far as her own gentle heart allow'd,
And deem'd that fallen worship far more
 dear
 Perhaps because 't was fallen: her sires
 were proud
Of deeds and days when they had fill'd the
 ear
Of nations, and had never bent or bow'd
To novel power; and as she was the last,
She held their old faith and old feelings
 fast. 368

LXVII

She gazed upon a world she scarcely knew,
 As seeking not to know it; silent, lone,
As grows a flower, thus quietly she grew,
 And kept her heart serene within its zone.
There was awe in the homage which she
 drew;
 Her spirit seem'd as seated on a throne
Apart from the surrounding world, and
 strong
In its own strength — most strange in one
so young !

XLVIII

Now it so happen'd, in the catalogue
 Of Adeline, Aurora was omitted,
Although her birth and wealth had given
 her vogue
 Beyond the charmers we have already
 cited; 380
Her beauty also seem'd to form no clog
 Against her being mention'd as well fitted,
By many virtues, to be worth the trouble
Of single gentlemen who would be double.

XLIX

And this omission, like that of the bust
 Of Brutus at the pageant of Tiberius,
Made Juan wonder, as no doubt he must.
 This he express'd half smiling and half
 serious;
When Adeline replied with some disgust,
 And with an air, to say the least, imperi-
 ous, 390
She marvell'd ' what he saw in such a baby
As that prim, silent, cold Aurora Raby ? '

L

Juan rejoin'd — ' She was a Catholic,
 And therefore fittest, as of his persua-
 sion;

Since he was sure his mother would fall
 sick,
 And the Pope thunder excommunication,
If — ' But here Adeline, who seem'd to
 pique
 Herself extremely on the inoculation
Of others with her own opinions, stated —
As usual — the same reason which she late
 did. 400

LI

And wherefore not ? A reasonable reason,
 If good, is none the worse for repetition;
If bad, the best way 's certainly to tease on,
 And amplify: you lose much by conci-
 sion,
Whereas insisting in or out of season
 Convinces all men, even a politician;
Or — what is just the same — it wearies out.
So the end 's gain'd, what signifies the
 route ?

LII

Why Adeline had this slight prejudice —
 For prejudice it was — against a creature
As pure as sanctity itself from vice, 411
 With all the added charm of form and
 feature,
For me appears a question far too nice,
 Since Adeline was liberal by nature;
But nature 's nature, and has more caprices
Than I have time, or will, to take to pieces.

LIII

Perhaps she did not like the quiet way
 With which Aurora on those baubles
 look'd,
Which charm most people in their earlier
 day:
 For there are few things by mankind less
 brook'd, 420
And womankind too, if we so may say,
 Than finding thus their genius stand re-
 buked,
Like ' Anthony's by Cæsar,' by the few
Who look upon them as they ought to do.

LIV

It was not envy — Adeline had none;
 Her place was far beyond it, and her
 mind.
It was not scorn — which could not light
 on one
 Whose greatest *fault* was leaving few to
 find.

It was not jealousy, I think: but shun
 Following the 'ignes fatui' of mankind.
It was not — but 't is easier far, alas ! 431
 To say what it was not than what it was.

LV

Little Aurora deem'd she was the theme
 Of such discussion. She was there a
 guest;
A beauteous ripple of the brilliant stream
 Of rank and youth, though purer than
 the rest,
Which flow'd on for a moment in the beam
 Time sheds a moment o'er each sparkling
 crest.
Had she known this, she would have calmly
 smiled —
She had so much, or little, of the child. 440

LVI

The dashing and proud air of Adeline
 Imposed not upon her: she saw her blaze
Much as she would have seen a glow-worm
 shine,
 Then turn'd unto the stars for loftier
 rays.
Juan was something she could not divine,
 Being no sibyl in the new world's ways;
Yet she was nothing dazzled by the meteor,
Because she did not pin her faith on feature.

LVII

His fame too, — for he had that kind of
 fame
 Which sometimes plays the deuce with
 womankind,
 450
A heterogeneous mass of glorious blame,
 Half virtues and whole vices being com-
 bined;
Faults which attract because they are not
 tame;
 Follies trick'd out so brightly that they
 blind: —
These seals upon her wax made no impres-
 sion,
Such was her coldness or her self-possession.

LVIII

Juan knew nought of such a character —
 High, yet resembling not his lost Haidée;
Yet each was radiant in her proper sphere:
 The island girl, bred up by the lone
 sea,
More warm, as lovely, and not less sincere,
 Was Nature's all: Aurora could not be, 460

Nor would be thus: — the difference in them
Was such as lies between a flower and
 gem.

LIX

Having wound up with this sublime com-
 parison,
 Methinks we may proceed upon our nar-
 rative,
And, as my friend Scott says, 'I sound my
 warison;'
 Scott, the superlative of my compara-
 tive —
Scott, who can paint your Christian knight
 or Saracen,
 Serf, lord, man, with such skill as none
 would share it, if 470
There had not been one Shakspeare and
 Voltaire,
Of one or both of whom he seems the heir.

LX

I say, in my slight way I may proceed
 To play upon the surface of humanity.
I write the world, nor care if the world
 read,
 At least for this I cannot spare its vanity.
My Muse hath bred, and still perhaps may
 breed
 More foes by this same scroll: when I
 began it, I
Thought that it might turn out so — now I
 know it,
But still I am, or was, a pretty poet. 480

LXI

The conference or congress (for it ended
 As congresses of late do) of the Lady
Adeline and Don Juan rather blended
 Some acids with the sweets — for she
 was heady;
But, ere the matter could be marr'd or
 mended,
 The silvery bell rang, not for 'dinner
 ready,'
But for that hour, call'd half-hour, given to
 dress,
Though ladies' robes seem scant enough for
 less.

LXII

Great things were now to be achieved at
 table,
 With massy plate for armour, knives and
 forks
 490

For weapons; but what Muse since Homer's
 able
 (His feasts are not the worst part of his
 works)
To draw up in array a single day-bill
 Of modern dinners? where more mys-
 tery lurks,
In soups or sauces, or a sole ragoût,
Than witches, b—ches, or physicians brew.

LXIII

There was a goodly 'soupe à la *bonne
 femme*,'
 Though God knows whence it came from;
 there was, too,
A turbot for relief of those who cram, ₄₉₉
 Relieved with 'dindon à la Parigeux;'
There also was —— the sinner that I am!
 How shall I get this gourmand stanza
 through? —
'Soupe à la Beauveau,' whose relief was
 dory,
Relieved itself by pork, for greater glory.

LXIV

But I must crowd all into one grand
 mess
 Or mass; for should I stretch into de-
 tail,
My Muse would run much more into ex-
 cess,
 Than when some squeamish people deem
 her frail.
But though a 'bonne vivante,' I must con-
 fess
 Her stomach's not her peccant part;
 this tale ₅₁₀
However doth require some slight refec-
 tion,
Just to relieve her spirits from dejection.

LXV

Fowls 'à la Condé,' slices eke of salmon,
 With 'sauces Génévoises,' and haunch of
 venison;
Wines too, which might again have slain
 young Ammon —
 A man like whom I hope we shan't see
 many soon;
They also set a glazed Westphalian ham on,
 Whereon Apicius would bestow his beni-
 son;
And then there was champagne with foam-
 ing whirls,
As white as Cleopatra's melted pearls. ₅₂₀

LXVI

Then there was God knows what 'à l'Alle-
 mande,'
 'A l'Espagnole,' 'timballe,' and 'salpi-
 con' —
With things I can't withstand or under-
 stand,
 Though swallow'd with much zest upon
 the whole;
And 'entremets' to piddle with at hand,
 Gently to lull down the subsiding soul;
While great Lucullus' *Robe triumphal*
 muffles
(*There's fame*) young partridge fillets,
 deck'd with truffles.

LXVII

What are the *fillets* on the victor's brow
 To these? They are rags or dust.
 Where is the arch ₅₃₀
Which nodded to the nation's spoils below?
 Where the triumphal chariots' haughty
 march?
Gone to where victories must like dinners
 go.
Farther I shall not follow the research:
But oh! ye modern heroes with your car-
 tridges,
When will your names lend lustre e'en to
 partridges?

LXVIII

Those truffles too are no bad accessaries,
 Follow'd by 'petits puits d'amour' — a
 dish
Of which perhaps the cookery rather varies,
 So every one may dress it to his wish, ₅₄₀
According to the best of dictionaries,
 Which encyclopedize both flesh and fish;
But even sans 'confitures,' it no less true is,
There's pretty picking in those 'petits
 puits.'

LXIX

The mind is lost in mighty contemplation
 Of intellect expanded on two courses;
And indigestion's grand multiplication
 Requires arithmetic beyond my forces.
Who would suppose, from Adam's simple
 ration,
 That cookery could have call'd forth
 such resources, ₅₅₀
As form a science and a nomenclature
From out the commonest demands of
 nature?

LXX

The glasses jingled, and the palates tingled;
 The diners of celebrity dined well;
The ladies with more moderation mingled
 In the feast, pecking less than I can tell;
Also the younger men too: for a springald
 Can't, like ripe age, in gormandize excel,
But thinks less of good eating than the
 whisper
(When seated next him) of some pretty
 lisper. 560

LXXI

Alas! I must leave undescribed the gibier,
 The salmi, the consommé, the purée,
All which I use to make my rhymes run
 glibber
 Than could roast beef in our rough John
 Bull way:
I must not introduce even a spare rib here,
 'Bubble and squeak' would spoil my
 liquid lay:
But I have dined, and must forego, alas!
The chaste description even of a 'bécasse;'

LXXII

And fruits, and ice, and all that art refines
 From nature for the service of the
 goût — 570
Taste or the gout, — pronounce it as inclines
 Your stomach! Ere you dine, the French
 will do;
But after, there are sometimes certain signs
 Which prove plain English truer of the
 two.
Hast ever had the gout? I have not had it —
But I may have, and you too, reader, dread
 it.

LXXIII

The simple olives, best allies of wine,
 Must I pass over in my bill of fare?
I must, although a favourite 'plat' of mine
 In Spain, and Lucca, Athens, every
 where: 580
On them and bread 't was oft my luck to
 dine,
 The grass my table-cloth, in open-air,
On Sunium or Hymettus, like Diogenes,
Of whom half my philosophy the progeny
 is.

LXXIV

Amidst this tumult of fish, flesh, and fowl,
 And vegetables, all in masquerade,
The guests were placed according to their
 roll,
 But various as the various meats dis-
 play'd:
Don Juan sat next an 'à l'Espagnole' —
 No damsel, but a dish, as hath been said;
But so far like a lady, that 't was drest 591
Superbly, and contain'd a world of zest.

LXXV

By some odd chance too, he was placed be-
 tween
 Aurora and the Lady Adeline —
A situation difficult, I ween,
 For man therein, with eyes and heart, to
 dine.
Also the conference which we have seen
 Was not such as to encourage him to shine;
For Adeline, addressing few words to him,
With two transcendent eyes seem'd to look
 through him. 600

LXXVI

I sometimes almost think that eyes have
 ears:
 This much is sure, that, out of earshot,
 things
Are somehow echoed to the pretty dears,
 Of which I can't tell whence their know-
 ledge springs.
Like that same mystic music of the spheres,
 Which no one hears, so loudly though it
 rings,
'T is wonderful how oft the sex have heard
Long dialogues — which pass'd without a
 word!

LXXVII

Aurora sat with that indifference
 Which piques a preux chevalier — as it
 ought: 610
Of all offences that 's the worst offence,
 Which seems to hint you are not worth
 a thought.
Now Juan, though no coxcomb in pretence,
 Was not exactly pleased to be so caught;
Like a good ship entangled among ice,
And after so much excellent advice.

LXXVIII

To his gay nothings, nothing was replied,
 Or something which was nothing, as ur-
 banity
Required. Aurora scarcely look'd aside,
 Nor even smiled enough for any vanity.

The devil was in the girl! Could it be
 pride? 621
Or modesty, or absence, or inanity?
Heaven knows! But Adeline's malicious
 eyes
Sparkled with her successful prophecies,

LXXIX

And look'd as much as if to say, ' I said it;'
 A kind of triumph I 'll not recommend,
Because it sometimes, as I have seen or
 read it,
 Both in the case of lover and of friend,
Will pique a gentleman, for his own credit,
 To bring what was a jest to a serious
 end: 630
For all men prophesy what *is* or *was*,
And hate those who won't let them come to
 pass.

LXXX

Juan was drawn thus into some attentions,
 Slight but select, and just enough to ex-
 press,
To females of perspicuous comprehensions,
 That he would rather make them more
 than less.
Aurora at the last (so history mentions,
 Though probably much less a fact than
 guess)
So far relax'd her thoughts from their
 sweet prison,
As once or twice to smile, if not to listen.

LXXXI

From answering she began to question;
 this 641
 With her was rare: and Adeline, who as
 yet
Thought her predictions went not much
 amiss,
 Began to dread she 'd thaw to a
 coquette —
So very difficult, they say, it is
 To keep extremes from meeting, when
 once set
In motion; but she here too much refined —
Aurora's spirit was not of that kind.

LXXXII

But Juan had a sort of winning way,
 A proud humility, if such there be, 650
Which show'd such deference to what
 females say,
 As if each charming word were a decree.

His tact, too, temper'd him from grave to
 gay,
 And taught him when to be reserved or
 free:
He had the art of drawing people out,
Without their seeing what he was about.

LXXXIII

Aurora, who in her indifference
 Confounded him in common with the
 crowd
Of flatterers, though she deem'd he had
 more sense
 Than whispering foplings, or than
 witlings loud — 660
Commenced (from such slight things will
 great commence)
 To feel that flattery which attracts the
 proud
Rather by deference than compliment,
And wins even by a delicate dissent.

LXXXIV

And then he had good looks; — that point
 was carried
 Nem. con. amongst the women, which I
 grieve
To say leads oft to *crim. con.* with the
 married —
 A case which to the juries we may leave,
Since with digressions we too long have
 tarried.
 Now though we know of old that looks
 deceive, 670
And always have done, somehow these
 good looks
Make more impression than the best of
 books.

LXXXV

Aurora, who look'd more on books than
 faces,
 Was very young, although so very sage,
Admiring more Minerva than the Graces,
 Especially upon a printed page.
But Virtue's self, with all her tightest laces,
 Has not the natural stays of strict old
 age;
And Socrates, that model of all duty,
 Own'd to a penchant, though discreet, for
 beauty. 680

LXXXVI

And girls of sixteen are thus far Socratic,
 But innocently so, as Socrates;

And really, if the sage sublime and Attic
 At seventy years had phantasies like
 these,
Which Plato in his dialogues dramatic
 Has shown, I know not why they should
 displease
In virgins — always in a modest way,
Observe; for that with me 's a ' sine quâ.'

LXXXVII

Also observe, that, like the great Lord
 Coke
 (See Littleton), whene'er I have ex-
 press'd 690
Opinions two, which at first sight may look
 Twin opposites, the second is the best.
Perhaps I have a third, too, in a nook,
 Or none at all — which seems a sorry
 jest:
But if a writer should be quite consistent,
How could he possibly show things existent?

LXXXVIII

If people contradict themselves, can I
 Help contradicting them, and every body,
Even my veracious self? — But that's a
 a lie:
 I never did so, never will — how should
 I ? 700
He who doubts all things nothing can deny:
 Truth's fountains may be clear — her
 streams are muddy,
And cut through such canals of contradic-
 tion,
That she must often navigate o'er fiction.

LXXXIX

Apologue, fable, poesy, and parable,
 Are false, but may be render'd also true,
By those who sow them in a land that's
 arable.
'T is wonderful what fable will not do !
'T is said it makes reality more bearable:
 But what's reality ? Who has its clue ?
Philosophy ? No: she too much rejects. 711
Religion ? *Yes;* but which of all her sects ?

XC

Some millions must be wrong, that's pretty
 clear;
 Perhaps it may turn out that all were
 right.
God help us ! Since we have need on our
 career
 To keep our holy beacons always bright,

'T is time that some new prophet should
 appear,
 Or old indulge man with a second sight.
Opinions wear out in some thousand years,
 Without a small refreshment from the
 spheres. 720

XCI

But here again, why will I thus entangle
 Myself with metaphysics ? None can
 hate
So much as I do any kind of wrangle;
 And yet, such is my folly, or my fate,
I always knock my head against some
 angle
 About the present, past, or future state:
Yet I wish well to Trojan and to Tyrian,
For I was bred a moderate Presbyterian.

XCII

But though I am a temperate theologian,
 And also meek as a metaphysician, 730
Impartial between Tyrian and Trojan,
 As Eldon on a lunatic commission, —
In politics my duty is to show John
 Bull something of the lower world's
 condition.
It makes my blood boil like the springs of
 Hecla,
To see men let these scoundrel sovereigns
 break law.

XCIII

But politics, and policy, and piety,
 Are topics which I sometimes intro-
 duce,
Not only for the sake of their variety,
 But as subservient to a moral use; 740
Because my business is to *dress* society,
 And stuff with *sage* that very verdant
 goose.
And now, that we may furnish with some
 matter all
Tastes, we are going to try the super-
 natural.

XCIV

And now I will give up all argument;
 And positively henceforth no tempta-
 tion
Shall ' fool me to the top up of my bent:' —
 Yes, I 'll begin a thorough reformation.
Indeed, I never knew what people meant
 By deeming that my Muse's conversa-
 tion
 750

Was dangerous; — I think she is as harm-
less
As some who labour more and yet may
charm less.

XCV

Grim reader! did you ever see a ghost?
 No; but you have heard — I understand
 — be dumb!
And don't regret the time you may have
 lost,
 For you have got that pleasure still to
 come:
And do not think I mean to sneer at most
 Of these things, or by ridicule benumb
That source of the sublime and the myste-
 rious: —
For certain reasons my belief is serious. 760

XCVI

Serious? You laugh; — you may: that will
 I not;
 My smiles must be sincere or not at all.
I say I do believe a haunted spot
 Exists — and where? That shall I not
 recall,
Because I'd rather it should be forgot,
 'Shadows the soul of Richard' may appal.
In short, upon that subject I've some
 qualms very
Like those of the philosopher of Malms-
 bury.

XCVII

The night (I sing by night — sometimes an
 owl, 769
 And now and then a nightingale) is dim,
And the loud shriek of sage Minerva's fowl
 Rattles around me her discordant hymn:
Old portraits from old walls upon me
 scowl —
 I wish to heaven they would not look so
 grim;
The dying embers dwindle in the grate —
I think too that I have sate up too late:

XCVIII

And therefore, though 't is by no means my
 way
 To rhyme at noon — when I have other
 things
To think of, if I ever think — I say
 I feel some chilly midnight shudderings,
And prudently postpone, until mid-day, 781
 Treating a topic which, alas! but brings

Shadows; — but you must be in my condi-
 tion
Before you learn to call this superstition.

XCIX

Between two worlds life hovers like a star,
 'Twixt night and morn, upon the hori-
 zon's verge.
How little do we know that which we are!
 How less what we may be! The eternal
 surge
Of time and tide rolls on, and bears afar
 Our bubbles; as the old burst, new
 emerge, 790
Lash'd from the foam of ages; while the
 graves
Of empires heave but like some passing
 waves.

CANTO THE SIXTEENTH

I

THE antique Persians taught three useful
 things,
 To draw the bow, to ride, and speak the
 truth.
This was the mode of Cyrus, best of kings —
 A mode adopted since by modern youth.
Bows have they, generally with two strings;
 Horses they ride without remorse or
 ruth;
At speaking truth perhaps they are less
 clever,
But draw the long bow better now than ever.

II

The cause of this effect, or this defect, —
 'For this effect defective comes by
 cause,' — 10
Is what I have not leisure to inspect;
 But this I must say in my own applause,
Of all the Muses that I recollect,
 Whate'er may be her follies or her flaws
In some things, mine's beyond all contra-
 diction
The most sincere that ever dealt in fiction.

III

And as she treats all things, and ne'er re-
 treats
 From any thing, this epic will contain
A wilderness of the most rare conceits,
 Which you might elsewhere hope to find
 in vain. 20

'T is true there be some bitters with the
 sweets,
 Yet mix'd so slightly, that you can't com-
 plain,
But wonder they so few are, since my tale is
' De rebus cunctis et quibusdam aliis.'

IV

But of all truths which she has told, the
 most
 True is that which she is about to tell.
I said it was a story of a ghost —
 What then ? I only know it so befell.
Have you explored the limits of the coast,
 Where all the dwellers of the earth must
 dwell ? 30
'T is time to strike such puny doubters
 dumb as
The sceptics who would not believe Colum-
 bus.

V

Some people would impose now with au-
 thority,
 Turpin's or Monmouth Geoffry's Chroni-
 cle;
Men whose historical superiority
 Is always greatest at a miracle.
But Saint Augustine has the great priority,
 Who bids all men believe the impossible,
Because 't is so. Who nibble, scribble, quib-
 ble, he
Quiets at once with ' *quia* impossibile.' 40

VI

And therefore, mortals, cavil not at all;
 Believe: — if 't is improbable you *must*,
And if it is impossible, you *shall*:
 'T is always best to take things upon
 trust.
I do not speak profanely, to recall
 Those holier mysteries which the wise
 and just
Receive as gospel, and which grow more
 rooted,
As all truths must, the more they are dis-
 puted:

VII

I merely mean to say what Johnson said,
 That in the course of some six thousand
 years, 50
All nations have believed that from the
 dead
 A visitant at intervals appears;

And what is strangest upon this strange
 head,
 Is, that whatever bar the reason rears
'Gainst such belief, there 's something
 stronger still
In its behalf, let those deny who will.

VIII

The dinner and the soirée too were done,
 The supper too discuss'd, the dames ad-
 mired,
The banqueteers had dropp'd off one by
 one —
 The song was silent, and the dance ex-
 pired: 60
The last thin petticoats were vanish'd, gone
 Like fleecy clouds into the sky retired,
And nothing brighter gleam'd through the
 saloon
Than dying tapers — and the peeping moon.

IX

The evaporation of a joyous day
 Is like the last glass of champagne, with-
 out
The foam which made its virgin bumper
 gay;
 Or like a system coupled with a doubt;
Or like a soda bottle when its spray
 Has sparkled and let half its spirit out;
Or like a billow left by storms behind, 71
Without the animation of the wind;

X

Or like an opiate, which brings troubled
 rest,
 Or none; or like — like nothing that I
 know
Except itself; — such is the human breast;
 A thing, of which similitudes can show
No real likeness, — like the old Tyrian vest
 Dyed purple, none at present can tell
 how,
If from a shell-fish or from cochineal.
So perish every tyrant's robe piece-meal! 80

XI

But next to dressing for a rout or ball,
 Undressing is a woe; our robe de chambre
May sit like that of Nessus, and recall
 Thoughts quite as yellow, but less clear
 than amber.
Titus exclaim'd, ' I 've lost a day ! ' Of all
 The nights and days most people can re-
 member

(I have had of both, some not to be dis-
 dain'd),
I wish they 'd state how many they have
 gain'd.

XII

And Juan, on retiring for the night,
 Felt restless, and perplex'd, and compro-
 mised: 90
He thought Aurora Raby's eyes more
 bright
 Than Adeline (such is advice) advised;
If he had known exactly his own plight,
 He probably would have philosophised:
A great resource to all, and ne'er denied
Till wanted; therefore Juan only sigh'd.

XIII

He sigh'd; — the next resource is the full
 moon,
 Where all sighs are deposited; and now
It happen'd luckily, the chaste orb shone
 As clear as such a climate will allow; 100
And Juan's mind was in the proper tone
 To hail her with the apostrophe — ' O
 thou ! '
Of amatory egotism the *Tuism*,
Which further to explain would be a truism.

XIV

But lover, poet, or astronomer,
 Shepherd, or swain, whoever may be-
 hold,
Feel some abstraction when they gaze on
 her:
 Great thoughts we catch from thence
 (besides a cold
Sometimes, unless my feelings rather err);
 Deep secrets to her rolling light are
 told; 110
The ocean's tides and mortals' brains she
 sways,
And also hearts, if there be truth in lays.

XV

Juan felt somewhat pensive, and disposed
 For contemplation rather than his pil-
 low:
The Gothic chamber, where he was en-
 closed,
 Let in the rippling sound of the lake's
 billow,
With all the mystery by midnight caused;
 Below his window waved (of course) a
 willow;

And he stood gazing out on the cascade
That flash'd and after darken'd in the
 shade. 120

XVI

Upon his table or his toilet, — *which*
 Of these is not exactly ascertain'd
(I state this, for I am cautious to a pitch
 Of nicety, where a fact is to be gain'd), —
A lamp burn'd high, while he leant from a
 niche,
 Where many a Gothic ornament re-
 main'd,
In chisell'd stone and painted glass, and all
That time has left our fathers of their
 hall.

XVII

Then, as the night was clear though cold, he
 threw
 His chamber door wide open — and went
 forth 130
Into a gallery, of a sombre hue,
 Long, furnish'd with old pictures of great
 worth,
Of knights and dames heroic and chaste too,
 As doubtless should be people of high
 birth.
But by dim lights the portraits of the dead
Have something ghastly, desolate, and
 dread.

XVIII

The forms of the grim knight and pictured
 saint
 Look living in the moon; and as you turn
Backward and forward to the echoes faint
 Of your own footsteps — voices from the
 urn 140
Appear to wake, and shadows wild and
 quaint
 Start from the frames which fence their
 aspects stern,
As if to ask how you can dare to keep
A vigil there, where all but death should
 sleep.

XIX

And the pale smile of beauties in the grave,
 The charms of other days, in starlight
 gleams,
Glimmer on high; their buried locks still
 wave
 Along the canvass; their eyes glance like
 dreams

On ours, or spars within some dusky cave,
 But death is imaged in their shadowy
 beams. 150
A picture is the past; even ere its frame
Be gilt, who sate hath ceased to be the
 same.

XX

As Juan mused on mutability,
 Or on his mistress — terms synonymous —
No sound except the echo of his sigh
 Or step ran sadly through that antique
 house;
When suddenly he heard, or thought so,
 nigh,
A supernatural agent — or a mouse,
Whose little nibbling rustle will embar-
 rass
Most people as it plays along the arras. 160

XXI

It was no mouse, but lo ! a monk, ar-
 ray'd
 In cowl and beads and dusky garb, ap-
 pear'd,
Now in the moonlight, and now lapsed in
 shade,
 With steps that trod as heavy, yet un-
 heard;
His garments only a slight murmur made;
 He moved as shadowy as the sisters
 weird,
But slowly; and as he pass'd Juan by,
Glanced, without pausing, on him a bright
 eye.

XXII

Juan was petrified; he had heard a hint
 Of such a spirit in these halls of old, 170
But thought, like most men, there was
 nothing in 't
 Beyond the rumour which such spots un-
 fold,
Coin'd from surviving superstition's mint,
 Which passes ghosts in currency like
 gold,
But rarely seen, like gold compared with
 paper.
And did he see this ? or was it a vapour ?

XXIII

Once, twice, thrice pass'd, repass'd — the
 thing of air,
 Or earth beneath, or heaven, or t' other
 place;

And Juan gazed upon it with a stare,
 Yet could not speak or move; but, on its
 base 180
As stands a statue, stood: he felt his hair
 Twine like a knot of snakes around his
 face;
He tax'd his tongue for words, which were
 not granted,
To ask the reverend person what he wanted.

XXIV

The third time, after a still longer pause,
 The shadow pass'd away — but where ?
 the hall
Was long, and thus far there was no great
 cause
 To think his vanishing unnatural:
Doors there were many, through which, by
 the laws 189
 Of physics, bodies whether short or tall
Might come or go; but Juan could not state
Through which the spectre seem'd to evap-
 orate.

XXV

He stood — how long he knew not, but it
 seem'd
 An age — expectant, powerless, with his
 eyes
Strain'd on the spot where first the figure
 gleam'd;
 Then by degrees recall'd his energies,
And would have pass'd the whole off as a
 dream,
 But could not wake; he was, he did sur-
 mise,
Waking already, and return'd at length
Back to his chamber, shorn of half his
 strength. 200

XXVI

All there was as he left it: still his taper
 Burnt, and not *blue*, as modest tapers use,
Receiving sprites with sympathetic vapour;
 He rubb'd his eyes, and they did not re-
 fuse
Their office; he took up an old newspaper;
 The paper was right easy to peruse;
He read an article the king attacking,
And a long eulogy of ' patent blacking.'

XXVII

This savour'd of this world; but his hand
 shook — 207
 He shut his door, and after having read

A paragraph, I think about Horne Tooke,
 Undrest, and rather slowly went to bed.
There, couch'd all snugly on his pillow's
 nook,
 With what he had seen his phantasy he
 fed;
And though it was no opiate, slumber crept
Upon him by degrees, and so he slept.

XXVIII

He woke betimes; and, as may be supposed,
 Ponder'd upon his visitant or vision,
And whether it ought not to be disclosed,
 At risk of being quizz'd for supersti-
 tion. 220
The more he thought, the more his mind
 was posed:
 In the mean time, his valet, whose pre-
 cision
Was great, because his master brook'd no
 less,
Knock'd to inform him it was time to dress.

XXIX

He dress'd; and like young people he was
 wont
 To take some trouble with his toilet, but
This morning rather spent less time upon 't;
 Aside his very mirror soon was put;
His curls fell negligently o'er his front,
 His clothes were not curb'd to their usual
 cut, 230
His very neckcloth's Gordian knot was
 tied
Almost an hair's breadth too much on one
 side.

XXX

And when he walk'd down into the saloon,
 He sate him pensive o'er a dish of tea,
Which he perhaps had not discover'd soon,
 Had it not happen'd scalding hot to be,
Which made him have recourse unto his
 spoon;
 So much distrait he was, that all could
 see
That something was the matter — Adeline
The first — but *what* she could not well
 divine. 240

XXXI

She look'd, and saw him pale, and turn'd as
 pale
 Herself; then hastily look'd down, and
 mutter'd

Something, but what's not stated in my
 tale.
 Lord Henry said his muffin was ill
 butter'd;
The Duchess of Fitz-Fulke play'd with her
 veil,
 And look'd at Juan hard, but nothing
 utter'd.
Aurora Raby with her large dark eyes
Survey'd him with a kind of calm sur-
 prise.

XXXII

But seeing him all cold and silent still, 249
 And everybody wondering more or less,
Fair Adeline enquired, 'If he were ill?'
 He started, and said, 'Yes — no — rather
 — yes.'
The family physician had great skill,
 And being present, now began to ex-
 press
His readiness to feel his pulse and tell
The cause, but Juan said, 'He was quite
 well.'

XXXIII

'Quite well; yes, — no.' — These answers
 were mysterious,
 And yet his looks appear'd to sanction
 both,
However they might savour of delirious;
 Something like illness of a sudden
 growth 260
Weigh'd on his spirit, though by no means
 serious:
 But for the rest, as he himself seem'd
 loth
To state the case, it might be ta'en for
 granted
It was not the physician that he wanted.

XXXIV

Lord Henry, who had now discuss'd his
 chocolate,
 Also the muffin whereof he complain'd,
Said, Juan had not got his usual look
 elate,
 At which he marvell'd, since it had not
 rain'd;
Then ask'd her Grace what news were of
 the duke of late?
 Her Grace replied, *his* Grace was rather
 pain'd 270
With some slight, light, hereditary twinges
Of gout, which rusts aristocratic hinges.

XXXV

Then Henry turn'd to Juan, and address'd
 A few words of condolence on his state:
'You look,' quoth he, 'as if you had had
 your rest
 Broke in upon by the Black Friar of late.'
'What friar?' said Juan; and he did his
 best
 To put the question with an air sedate,
Or careless; but the effort was not valid
To hinder him from growing still more
 pallid. 280

XXXVI

'Oh! have you never heard of the Black
 Friar?
 The spirit of these walls?' — 'In truth
 not I.'
'Why Fame — but Fame you know's
 sometimes a liar —
 Tells an odd story, of which by and by:
Whether with time the spectre has grown
 shyer,
 Or that our sires had a more gifted eye
For such sights, though the tale is half be-
 lieved,
The friar of late has not been oft perceived.

XXXVII

'The last time was —— ' — 'I pray,' said
 Adeline
 (Who watch'd the changes of Don Juan's
 brow, 290
And from its context thought she could
 divine
 Connexions stronger then he chose to
 avow
With this same legend) — 'if you but de-
 sign
 To jest, you'll choose some other theme
 just now,
Because the present tale has oft been told,
And is not much improved by growing old.'

XXXVIII

'Jest!' quoth Milor; 'why, Adeline, you
 know
 That we ourselves — 'twas in the honey
 moon —
Saw —— ' — 'Well, no matter, 't was so
 long ago; 299
 But, come, I'll set your story to a tune.'
Graceful as Dian, when she draws her bow,
 She seized her harp, whose strings were
 kindled soon

As touch'd, and plaintively began to play
The air of ' 'T was a Friar of Orders Gray.'

XXXIX

'But add the words,' cried Henry, 'which
 you made;
 For Adeline is half a poetess,'
Turning round to the rest, he smiling said.
 Of course the others could not but ex-
 press
In courtesy their wish to see display'd
 By one *three* talents, for there were no
 less — 310
The voice, the words, the harper's skill, at
 once
Could hardly be united by a dunce.

XL

After some fascinating hesitation, —
 The charming of these charmers, who
 seem bound,
I can't tell why, to this dissimulation, —
 Fair Adeline, with eyes fix'd on the ground
At first, then kindling into animation,
 Added her sweet voice to the lyric sound,
And sang with much simplicity, — a merit
Not the less precious, that we seldom hear
 it. 320

1

Beware! beware! of the Black Friar,
 Who sitteth by Norman stone,
For he mutters his prayer in the midnight air,
 And his mass of the days that are gone.
When the Lord of the Hill, Amundeville,
 Made Norman Church his prey,
And expell'd the friars, one friar still
 Would not be driven away.

2

Though he came in his might, with King Hen-
 ry's right,
 To turn church lands to lay, 330
With sword in hand, and torch to light
 Their walls, if they said nay;
A monk remain'd, unchased, unchain'd,
 And he did not seem form'd of clay,
For he's seen in the porch, and he's seen in the
 church,
 Though he is not seen by day.

3

And whether for good, or whether for ill,
 It is not mine to say;
But still with the house of Amundeville
 He abideth night and day. 340
By the marriage-bed of their lords, 't is said,
 He flits on the bridal eve;
And 't is held as faith, to their bed of death
 He comes — but not to grieve.

4

When an heir is born, he 's heard to mourn,
 And when aught is to befall
That ancient line, in the pale moonshine
 He walks from hall to hall.
His form you may trace, but not his face,
 'T is shadow'd by his cowl; 350
But his eyes may be seen from the folds be-
 tween,
 And they seem of a parted soul.

5

But beware! beware! of the Black Friar,
 He still retains his sway,
For he is yet the church's heir
 Whoever may be the lay.
Amundeville is lord by day,
 But the monk is lord by night;
Nor wine nor wassail could raise a vassal
 To question that friar's right. 360

6

Say nought to him as he walks the hall,
 And he 'll say nought to you;
He sweeps along in his dusky pall,
 As o'er the grass the dew.
Then grammercy! for the Black Friar;
 Heaven sain him, fair or foul!
And whatsoe'er may be his prayer,
 Let ours be for his soul.

XLI

The lady's voice ceased, and the thrilling
 wires
 Died from the touch that kindled them
 to sound; 370
And the pause follow'd, which when song
 expires
 Pervades a moment those who listen
 round;
And then of course the circle much admires,
 Nor less applauds, as in politeness bound,
The tones, the feeling, and the execution,
To the performer's diffident confusion.

XLII

Fair Adeline, though in a careless way,
 As if she rated such accomplishment
As the mere pastime of an idle day,
 Pursued an instant for her own content,
Would now and then as 't were *without* dis-
 play, 381
 Yet *with* display in fact, at times relent
To such performances with haughty smile,
To show she *could*, if it were worth her
 while.

XLIII

Now this (but we will whisper it aside)
 Was — pardon the pedantic illustration —

Trampling on Plato's pride with greater
 pride,
 As did the Cynic on some like occasion;
Deeming the sage would be much mortified,
 Or thrown into a philosophic passion, 390
For a spoil'd carpet — but the 'Attic Bee'
Was much consoled by his own repartee.

XLIV

Thus Adeline would throw into the shade
 (By doing easily, whene'er she chose,
What dilettanti do with vast parade)
 Their sort of *half profession;* for it grows
To something like this when too oft dis-
 play'd;
 And that it is so everybody knows
Who have heard Miss That or This, or
 Lady T'other,
Show off — to please their company or mo-
 ther. 400

XLV

Oh! the long evenings of duets and trios!
 The admirations and the speculations;
The 'Mamma Mia's!' and the 'Amor
 Mio's!'
 The 'Tanti palpiti's' on such occasions:
The 'Lasciami's,' and quavering 'Ad-
 dio's!'
 Amongst our own most musical of na-
 tions;
With 'Tu mi chamas's' from Portingale,
To soothe our ears, lest Italy should fail.

XLVI

In Babylon's bravuras — as the home
 Heart-ballads of Green Erin or Gray
 Highlands, 410
That bring Lochaber back to eyes that roam
 O'er far Atlantic continents or islands,
The calentures of music which o'ercome
 All mountaineers with dreams that they
 are nigh lands,
No more to be beheld but in such visions —
Was Adeline well versed, as compositions.

XLVII

She also had a twilight tinge of '*Blue*,'
 Could write rhymes, and compose more
 than she wrote,
Made epigrams occasionally too
 Upon her friends, as everybody ought.
But still from that sublimer azure hue, 421
 So much the present dye, she was re-
 mote;

Was weak enough to deem Pope a great
 poet,
And what was worse, was not ashamed to
 show it.

XLVIII

Aurora — since we are touching upon taste,
 Which now-a-days is the thermometer
By whose degrees all characters are
 class'd —
 Was more Shakspearian, if I do not err.
The worlds beyond this world's perplexing
 waste
 Had more of her existence, for in her 430
There was a depth of feeling to embrace
Thoughts, boundless, deep, but silent too as
 Space.

XLIX

Not so her gracious, graceful, graceless
 Grace,
 The full-grown Hebe of Fitz-Fulke,
 whose mind,
If she had any, was upon her face,
 And that was of a fascinating kind.
A little turn for mischief you might trace
 Also thereon, — but that 's not much; we
 find
Few females without some such gentle
 leaven,
For fear we should suppose us quite in
 heaven. 440

L

I have not heard she was at all poetic,
 Though once she was seen reading the
 ' Bath Guide,'
And ' Hayley's Triumphs,' which she
 deem'd pathetic,
 Because she said *her temper* had been
 tried
So much, the bard had really been pro-
 phetic
 Of what she had gone through with —
 since a bride.
But of all verse, what most ensured her
 praise
Were sonnets to herself, or ' bouts rimés.'

LI

'T were difficult to say what was the object
 Of Adeline, in bringing this same lay 450
To bear on what appear'd to her the sub-
 ject
 Of Juan's nervous feelings on that day.

Perhaps she merely had the simple project
 To laugh him out of his supposed dis-
 may;
Perhaps she might wish to confirm him in it,
 Though why I cannot say — at least this
 minute.

LII

But so far the immediate effect
 Was to restore him to his self-propriety,
A thing quite necessary to the elect,
 Who wish to take the tone of their soci-
 ety: 460
In which you cannot be too circumspect,
 Whether the mode be persiflage or piety,
But wear the newest mantle of hypocrisy,
On pain of much displeasing the gynocracy.

LIII

And therefore Juan now began to rally
 His spirits, and without more explanation
To jest upon such themes in many a sally.
 Her Grace, too, also seized the same oc-
 casion,
With various similar remarks to tally,
 But wish'd for a still more detail'd nar-
 ration 470
Of this same mystic friar's curious doings,
About the present family's deaths and woo-
 ings.

LIV

Of these few could say more than has been
 said;
 They pass'd as such things do, for super-
 stition
With some, while others, who had more in
 dread
 The theme, half credited the strange
 tradition;
And much was talk'd on all sides on that
 head:
 But Juan, when cross-question'd on the
 vision,
Which some supposed (though he had not
 avow'd it)
Had stirr'd him, answer'd in a way to cloud
 it. 480

LV

And then, the mid-day having worn to one,
 The company prepared to separate;
Some to their several pastimes, or to none,
 Some wondering 't was so early, some so
 late.

There was a goodly match too, to be run
 Between some greyhounds on my lord's
 estate,
And a young race-horse of old pedigree
Match'd for the spring, whom several went
 to see.

LVI

There was a picture-dealer who had brought
 A special Titian, warranted original, 490
So precious that it was not to be bought,
 Though princes the possessor were be-
 sieging all.
The king himself had cheapen'd it, but
 thought
 The civil list he deigns to accept (oblig-
 ing all
His subjects by his gracious acceptation)
Too scanty, in these times of low taxa-
 tion.

LVII

But as Lord Henry was a connoisseur, —
 The friend of artists, if not arts, — the
 owner,
With motives the most classical and pure,
 So that he would have been the very
 donor, 500
Rather than seller, had his wants been
 fewer,
 So much he deem'd his patronage an
 honour,
Had brought the capo d'opera, not for sale,
But for his judgment — never known to
 fail.

LVIII

There was a modern Goth, I mean a Gothic
 Bricklayer of Babel, call'd an architect,
Brought to survey these grey walls, which
 though so thick,
 Might have from time acquired some
 slight defect;
Who after rummaging the Abbey through
 thick
 And thin, produced a plan whereby to
 erect 510
New buildings of correctest conformation,
And throw down old — which he call'd
 restoration.

LIX

The cost would be a trifle — an ' old song,'
 Set to some thousands ('t is the usual bur-
 den

Of that same tune, when people hum it
 long) —
 The price would speedily repay its worth
 in
An edifice no less sublime than strong,
 By which Lord Henry's good taste would
 go forth in
Its glory, through all ages shining sunny,
For Gothic daring shown in English money.

LX

There were two lawyers busy on a mort-
 gage 521
 Lord Henry wish'd to raise for a new
 purchase;
Also a lawsuit upon tenures burgage,
 And one on tithes, which sure are Dis-
 cord's torches,
Kindling Religion till she throws down *her*
 gage,
 ' Untying ' squires ' to fight against the
 churches; '
There was a prize ox, a prize pig, and
 ploughman,
For Henry was a sort of Sabine showman.

LXI

There were two poachers caught in a steel
 trap,
 Ready for gaol, their place of convales-
 cence; 530
There was a country girl in a close cap
 And scarlet cloak (I hate the sight to
 see, since —
Since — since — in youth, I had the sad
 mishap —
 But luckily I have paid few parish fees
 since):
That scarlet cloak, alas ! unclosed with rig-
 our,
Presents the problem of a double figure.

LXII

A reel within a bottle is a mystery,
 One can't tell how it e'er got in or out;
Therefore the present piece of natural his-
 tory
 I leave to those who are fond of solving
 doubt; 540
And merely state, though not for the consis-
 tory,
 Lord Henry was a justice, and that Scout
The constable, beneath a warrant's banner,
Had bagg'd this poacher upon Nature's
 manor.

LXIII

Now justices of peace must judge all
 pieces
 Of mischief of all kinds, and keep the
 game
And morals of the country from caprices
 Of those who have not a license for the
 same;
And of all things, excepting tithes and
 leases, 549
 Perhaps these are most difficult to tame:
Preserving partridges and pretty wenches
Are puzzles to the most precautious
 benches.

LXIV

The present culprit was extremely pale,
 Pale as if painted so; her cheek being
 red
By nature, as in higher dames less hale
 'T is white, at least when they just rise
 from bed.
Perhaps she was ashamed of seeming frail,
 Poor soul ! for she was country born and
 bred,
And knew no better in her immorality
Than to wax white — for blushes are for
 quality. 560

LXV

Her black, bright, downcast, yet espiègle
 eye,
 Had gather'd a large tear into its cor-
 ner,
Which the poor thing at times essay'd to
 dry,
 For she was not a sentimental mourner
Parading all her sensibility,
 Nor insolent enough to scorn the scorner,
But stood in trembling, patient tribula-
 tion,
To be call'd up for her examination.

LXVI

Of course these groups were scatter'd here
 and there,
 Not nigh the gay saloon of ladies gent.
The lawyers in the study; and in air 571
 The prize pig, ploughman, poachers; the
 men sent
From town, viz., architect and dealer, were
 Both busy (as a general in his tent
Writing despatches) in their several sta-
 tions,
Exulting in their brilliant lucubrations.

LXVII

But this poor girl was left in the great
 hall,
 While Scout, the parish guardian of the
 frail,
Discuss'd (he hated beer yclept the ' small ')
 A mighty mug of *moral* double ale. 580
She waited until Justice could recall
 Its kind attentions to their proper pale,
To name a thing in nomenclature rather
Perplexing for most virgins — a child's
 father.

LXVIII

You see here was enough of occupation
 For the Lord Henry, link'd with dogs
 and horses.
There was much bustle too, and prepara-
 tion
 Below stairs on the score of second
 courses;
Because, as suits their rank and situation,
 Those who in counties have great land
 resources 590
Have ' public days,' when all men may
 carouse,
Though not exactly what 's call'd ' open
 house.'

LXIX

But once a week or fortnight, *un*invited
 (Thus we translate a *general invitation*)
All country gentlemen, esquired or
 knighted,
 May drop in without cards, and take their
 station
At the full board, and sit alike delighted
 With fashionable wines and conversa-
 tion;
And, as the isthmus of the grand connec-
 tion,
Talk o'er themselves the past and next
 election. 600

LXX

Lord Henry was a great electioneerer,
 Burrowing for boroughs like a rat or
 rabbit;
But county contests cost him rather dearer,
 Because the neighbouring Scotch Earl of
 Giftgabbit
Had English influence in the self-same
 sphere here;
 His son, the Honourable Dick Dicedrab-
 bit,

Was member for the 'other interest'
 (meaning
The same self-interest, with a different
 leaning).

LXXI

Courteous and cautious therefore in his
 county,
 He was all things to all men, and dis-
 pensed 610
To some civility, to others bounty,
 And promises to all — which last com-
 menced
To gather to a somewhat large amount, he
 Not calculating how much they con-
 densed;
But what with keeping some, and breaking
 others,
His word had the same value as another's.

LXXII

A friend to freedom and freeholders — yet
 No less a friend to government — he
 held,
That he exactly the just medium hit
 'Twixt place and patriotism — albeit com-
 pell'd, 620
Such was his sovereign's pleasure (though
 unfit,
 He added modestly, when rebels rail'd),
To hold some sinecures he wish'd abolish'd,
But that with them all law would be de-
 molish'd.

LXXIII

He was 'free to confess' (whence comes
 this phrase ?
 Is 't English ? No — 't is only parlia-
 mentary)
That innovation's spirit now-a-days
 Had made more progress than for the
 last century.
He would not tread a factious path to
 praise,
 Though for the public weal disposed to
 venture high; 630
As for his place, he could but say this of
 it,
That the fatigue was greater than the profit.

LXXIV

Heaven, and his friends, knew that a pri-
 vate life
 Had ever been his sole and whole ambi-
 tion;

But could he quit his king in times of
 strife,
 Which threaten'd the whole country with
 perdition ?
When demagogues would with a butcher's
 knife
 Cut through and through (oh ! damnable
 incision !)
The Gordian or the Geordi-an knot, whose
 strings
Have tied together commons, lords, and
 kings. 640

LXXV

Sooner ' come place into the civil list
 And champion him to the utmost ' — he
 would keep it,
Till duly disappointed or dismiss'd:
 Profit he cared not for, let others reap
 it;
But should the day come when place ceased
 to exist,
 The country would have far more cause
 to weep it:
For how could it go on ? Explain who can !
He gloried in the name of Englishman.

LXXVI

He was as independent — ay, much more —
 Than those who were not paid for inde-
 pendence, 650
As common soldiers, or a common ——
 shore,
 Have in their several arts or parts ascend-
 ance
O'er the irregulars in lust or gore,
 Who do not give professional attendance.
Thus on the mob all statesmen are as
 eager
To prove their pride, as footmen to a
 beggar.

LXXVII

All this (save the last stanza) Henry said,
 And thought. I say no more — I 've
 said too much;
For all of us have either heard or read —
 Off — or *upon* the hustings — some slight
 such 660
Hints from the independent heart or head
 Of the official candidate. I 'll touch
No more on this — the dinner-bell hath
 rung,
And grace is said; the grace I *should* have
 sung —

LXXVIII

But I 'm too late, and therefore must make
 play.
 'T was a great banquet, such as Albion
 old
Was wont to boast — as if a glutton's
 tray
Were something very glorious to behold.
But 't was a public feast and public day, —
 Quite full, right dull, guests hot, and
 dishes cold, 670
Great plenty, much formality, small cheer,
And every body out of their own sphere.

LXXIX

The squires familiarly formal, and
 My lords and ladies proudly condescend-
 ing;
The very servants puzzling how to hand
 Their plates — without it might be too
 much bending
From their high places by the sideboard's
 stand —
 Yet, like their masters, fearful of offend-
 ing.
For any deviation from the graces
Might cost both man and master too — their
 places. 680

LXXX

There were some hunters bold, and coursers
 keen,
 Whose hounds ne'er err'd, nor grey-
 hounds deign'd to lurch;
Some deadly shots too, Septembrizers, seen
 Earliest to rise, and last to quit the search
Of the poor partridge through his stubble
 screen.
 There were some massy members of the
 church,
Takers of tithes, and makers of good
 matches,
And several who sung fewer psalms than
 catches.

LXXXI

There were some country wags too — and,
 alas !
 Some exiles from the town, who had been
 driven 690
To gaze, instead of pavement, upon grass,
 And rise at nine in lieu of long eleven.
And lo ! upon that day it came to pass,
 I sate next that o'erwhelming son of
 heaven,

The very powerful parson, Peter Pith,
The loudest wit I e'er was deafen'd with.

LXXXII

I knew him in his livelier London days,
 A brilliant diner out, though but a cu-
 rate;
And not a joke he cut but earn'd its
 praise,
 Until preferment, coming at a sure rate
(O Providence ! how wondrous are thy
 ways ! 701
 Who would suppose thy gifts sometimes
 obdurate ?),
Gave him, to lay the devil who looks o'er
 Lincoln,
A fat fen vicarage, and nought to think on.

LXXXIII

His jokes were sermons, and his sermons
 jokes;
 But both were thrown away amongst the
 fens;
For wit hath no great friend in aguish folks.
 No longer ready ears and short-hand
 pens
Imbibed the gay bon mot, or happy hoax:
 The poor priest was reduced to common
 sense, 710
Or to coarse efforts very loud and long,
To hammer a horse laugh from the thick
 throng.

LXXXIV

There *is* a difference, says the song, 'be-
 tween
 A beggar and a queen,' or *was* (of late
The latter worse used of the two we 've
 seen —
 But we 'll say nothing of affairs of state);
A difference ' 'twixt a bishop and a dean,'
 A difference between crockery ware and
 plate,
As between English beef and Spartan
 broth —
And yet great heroes have been bred by
 both. 720

LXXXV

But of all nature's discrepancies, none
 Upon the whole is greater than the dif-
 ference
Beheld between the country and the town,
 Of which the latter merits every prefer-
 ence

From those who have few resources of
their own,
 And only think, or act, or feel, with refer-
 ence
To some small plan of interest or ambi-
tion —
Both which are limited to no condition.

LXXXVI

But 'en avant !' The light loves languish
o'er
 Long banquets and too many guests,
 although 730
A slight repast makes people love much
more,
 Bacchus and Ceres being, as we know
Even from our grammar upwards, friends
of yore
 With vivifying Venus, who doth owe
To these the invention of champagne and
truffles:
Temperance delights her, but long fasting
ruffles.

LXXXVII

Dully past o'er the dinner of the day;
 And Juan took his place, he knew not
 where,
Confused, in the confusion, and distrait,
 And sitting as if nail'd upon his chair:
Though knives and forks clank'd round as
in a fray, 741
 He seem'd unconscious of all passing
 there,
Till some one, with a groan, exprest a
wish
(Unheeded twice) to have a fin of fish.

LXXXVIII

On which, at the *third* asking of the bans,
 He started; and perceiving smiles around
Broadening to grins, he colour'd more than
once,
 And hastily — as nothing can confound
A wise man more than laughter from a
dunce —
 Inflicted on the dish a deadly wound, 750
And with such hurry, that ere he could
curb it
He had paid his neighbour's prayer with half
a turbot.

LXXXIX

This was no bad mistake, as it occurr'd,
 The supplicator being an amateur;

But others, who were left with scarce a
third,
 Were angry — as they well might, to be
 sure.
They wonder'd how a young man so absurd
 Lord Henry at his table should endure;
And this, and his not knowing how much
oats
Had fallen last market, cost his host three
votes. 760

XC

They little knew, or might have sympa-
thised,
 That he the night before had seen a ghost,
A prologue which but slightly harmonised
 With the substantial company engross'd
By matter, and so much materialised,
 That one scarce knew at what to marvel
 most
Of two things — how (the question rather
odd is)
Such bodies could have souls, or souls such
bodies.

XCI

But what confused him more than smile or
stare
 From all the 'squires and 'squiresses
 around, 770
Who wonder'd at the abstraction of his air,
 Especially as he had been renown'd
For some vivacity among the fair,
 Even in the country circle's narrow bound
(For little things upon my lord's estate
Were good small talk for others still less
great) —

XCII

Was, that he caught Aurora's eye on his,
 And something like a smile upon her
 cheek.
Now this he really rather took amiss:
 In those who rarely smile, their smiles
 bespeak 780
A strong external motive; and in this
 Smile of Aurora's there was nought to
 pique
Or hope, or love, with any of the wiles
Which some pretend to trace in ladies'
smiles.

XCIII

'T was a mere quiet smile of contemplation,
 Indicative of some surprise and pity;

And Juan grew carnation with vexation,
 Which was not very wise, and still less
 witty,
Since he had gain'd at least her observa-
 tion,
 A most important outwork of the city —
As Juan should have known, had not his
 senses 791
By last night's ghost been driven from their
 defences.

XCIV

But what was bad, she did not blush in
 turn,
 Nor seem embarrass'd — quite the con-
 trary;
Her aspect was as usual, still — *not* stern —
 And she withdrew, but cast not down, her
 eye,
Yet grew a little pale — with what? con-
 cern ?
 I know not; but her colour ne'er was
 high —
Though sometimes faintly flush'd — and
 always clear,
As deep seas in a sunny atmosphere. 800

XCV

But Adeline was occupied by fame
 This day; and watching, witching, con-
 descending
To the consumers of fish, fowl, and game,
 And dignity with courtesy so blending,
As all must blend whose part it is to aim
 (Especially as the sixth year is ending)
At their lord's, son's, or similar connection's
Safe conduct through the rocks of re-elec-
 tions.

XCVI

Though this was most expedient on the
 whole, 809
 And usual — Juan, when he cast a glance
On Adeline while playing her grand rôle,
 Which she went through as though it
 were a dance,
Betraying only now and then her soul
 By a look scarce perceptibly askance
(Of weariness or scorn), began to feel
Some doubt how much of Adeline was
 real;

XCVII

So well she acted all and every part
 By turns — with that vivacious versatility,

Which many people take for want of heart.
 They err — 't is merely what is call'd
 mobility, 820
A thing of temperament and not of art,
 Though seeming so, from its supposed
 facility;
And false — though true; for surely they 're
 sincerest
Who are strongly acted on by what is
 nearest.

XCVIII

This makes your actors, artists, and ro-
 mancers,
 Heroes sometimes, though seldom —
 sages never;
But speakers, bards, diplomatists, and
 dancers,
 Little that 's great, but much of what is
 clever;
Most orators, but very few financiers,
 Though all Exchequer chancellors en-
 deavour, 830
Of late years, to dispense with Cocker's
 rigours,
And grow quite figurative with their figures.

XCIX

The poets of arithmetic are they
 Who, though they prove not two and two
 to be
Five, as they might do in a modest way,
 Have plainly made it out that four are
 three,
Judging by what they take, and what they
 pay.
 The Sinking Fund's unfathomable sea,
That most unliquidating liquid, leaves
The debt unsunk, yet sinks all it receives. 840

C

While Adeline dispensed her airs and
 graces,
 The fair Fitz-Fulke seem'd very much at
 ease;
Though too well bred to quiz men to their
 faces,
 Her laughing blue eyes with a glance
 could seize
The ridicules of people in all places —
 That honey of your fashionable bees —
And store it up for mischievous enjoy-
 ment;
And this at present was her kind employ-
 ment.

CI

However, the day closed, as days must
 close;
 The evening also waned — and coffee
 came. 850
Each carriage was announced, and ladies
 rose,
 And curtsying off, as curtsies country
 dame,
Retired: with most unfashionable bows
 Their docile esquires also did the same,
Delighted with their dinner and their host,
But with the Lady Adeline the most.

CII

Some praised her beauty; others her great
 grace;
 The warmth of her politeness, whose sin-
 cerity
Was obvious in each feature of her face,
 Whose traits were radiant with the rays
 of verity. 860
Yes; *she* was truly worthy *her* high place !
 No one could envy her deserved pros-
 perity.
And then her dress — what beautiful sim-
 plicity
Draperied her form with curious felicity !

CIII

Meanwhile sweet Adeline deserved their
 praises,
 By an impartial indemnification
For all her past exertion and soft phrases,
 In a most edifying conversation,
Which turn'd upon their late guests' miens
 and faces,
 And families, even to the last relation; 870
Their hideous wives, their horrid selves and
 dresses,
And truculent distortion of their tresses.

CIV

True, *she* said little — 't was the rest that
 broke
 Forth into universal epigram;
But then 't was to the purpose what she
 spoke:
 Like Addison's 'faint praise,' so wont to
 damn,
Her own but served to set off every joke,
 As music chimes in with a melodrame.
How sweet the task to shield an absent
 friend !
I ask but this of mine, to — *not* defend. 880

CV

There were but two exceptions to this keen
 Skirmish of wits o'er the departed; one
Aurora, with her pure and placid mien;
 And Juan, too, in general behind none
In gay remark on what he had heard or
 seen,
 Sate silent now, his usual spirits gone:
In vain he heard the others rail or rally,
He would not join them in a single sally.

CVI

'T is true he saw Aurora look as though
 She approved his silence; she perhaps
 mistook 890
Its motive for that charity we owe
 But seldom pay the absent, nor would
 look
Farther — it might or might not be so.
 But Juan, sitting silent in his nook,
Observing little in his reverie,
Yet saw this much, which he was glad to
 see.

CVII

The ghost at least had done him this much
 good,
 In making him as silent as a ghost,
If in the circumstances which ensued
 He gain'd esteem where it was worth the
 most. 900
And certainly Aurora had renew'd
 In him some feelings he had lately lost,
Or harden'd; feelings which, perhaps ideal,
Are so divine, that I must deem them
 real: —

CVIII

The love of higher things and better days;
 The unbounded hope, and heavenly igno-
 rance
Of what is call'd the world, and the world's
 ways;
 The moments when we gather from a
 glance
More joy than from all future pride or
 praise,
 Which kindle manhood, but can ne'er en-
 trance 910
The heart in an existence of its own,
Of which another's bosom is the zone.

CIX

Who would not sigh Αι αι ταν Κυθερειαν,
 That *hath* a memory, or that *had* a heart?

Alas ! *her* star must fade like that of
Dian:
 Ray fades on ray, as years on years de-
part.
Anacreon only had the soul to tie an
 Unwithering myrtle round the unblunted
dart
Of Eros: but though thou hast play'd us
many tricks,
Still we respect thee, ' Alma Venus Gene-
trix !' 920

CX

And full of sentiments, sublime as billows
 Heaving between this world and worlds
beyond,
Don Juan, when the midnight hour of pil-
lows
 Arrived, retired to his; but to despond
Rather than rest. Instead of poppies, wil-
lows
 Waved o'er his couch; he meditated, fond
Of those sweet bitter thoughts which ban-
ish sleep,
And make the worldling sneer, the young-
ling weep.

CXI

The night was as before: he was undrest,
 Saving his night-gown, which is an un-
dress; 930
Completely ' sans culotte,' and without vest;
 In short, he hardly could be clothed with
less:
But apprehensive of his spectral guest,
 He sate with feelings awkward to ex-
press
(By those who have not had such visita-
tions),
Expectant of the ghost's fresh operations.

CXII

And not in vain he listen'd; — Hush !
what 's that ?
 I see — I see — Ah, no ! — 't is not — yet
't is —
Ye powers ! it is the — the — the — Pooh !
the cat !
 The devil may take that stealthy pace of
his ! 940
So like a spiritual pit-a-pat,
 Or tiptoe of an amatory Miss,
Gliding the first time to a rendezvous,
And dreading the chaste echoes of her
shoe.

CXIII

Again — what is 't ? The wind ? No, no
— this time
 It is the sable friar as before,
With awful footsteps regular as rhyme,
 Or (as rhymes may be in these days)
much more.
Again through shadows of the night sub-
lime,
 When deep sleep fell on men, and the
world wore 950
The starry darkness round her like a girdle
Spangled with gems — the monk made his
blood curdle.

CXIV

A noise like to wet fingers drawn on glass,
 Which sets the teeth on edge; and a
slight clatter,
Like showers which on the midnight gusts
will pass,
 Sounding like very supernatural water,
Came over Juan's ear, which throbb'd, alas!
 For immaterialism 's a serious matter;
So that even those whose faith is the most
great
In souls immortal, shun them tête-à-tête.

CXV

Were his eyes open ? — Yes ! and his mouth
too. 961
 Surprise has this effect — to make one
dumb,
Yet leave the gate which eloquence slips
through
 As wide as if a long speech were to come.
Nigh and more nigh the awful echoes drew,
 Tremendous to a mortal tympanum:
His eyes were open, and (as was before
Stated) his mouth. What open'd next ? —
the door.

CXVI

It open'd with a most infernal creak,
 Like that of hell. ' Lasciate ogni spe-
ranza 970
Voi che entrate !' The hinge seem'd to
speak,
 Dreadful as Dante's rhima, or this stanza;
Or — but all words upon such themes are
weak:
 A single shade 's sufficient to entrance a
Hero — for what is substance to a spirit ?
Or how is 't *matter* trembles to come near
it ?

CXVII

The door flew wide, — not swiftly, but, as
 fly
 The sea-gulls, with a steady, sober
 flight, —
And then swung back; nor close — but
 stood awry,
 Half letting in long shadows on the
 light, 980
Which still in Juan's candlesticks burn'd
 high,
 For he had two, both tolerably bright,
And in the door-way, darkening darkness,
 stood
The sable friar in his solemn hood.

CXVIII

Don Juan shook, as erst he had been shaken
 The night before ; but being sick of
 shaking,
He first inclined to think he had been mis-
 taken;
 And then to be ashamed of such mistak-
 ing;
His own internal ghost began to awaken
 Within him, and to quell his corporal
 quaking — 990
Hinting that soul and body on the whole
Were odds against a disembodied soul.

CXIX

And then his dread grew wrath, and his
 wrath fierce,
 And he arose, advanced — the shade re-
 treated;
But Juan, eager now the truth to pierce,
 Follow'd, his veins no longer cold, but
 heated,
Resolved to thrust the mystery carte and
 tierce,
 At whatsoever risk of being defeated:
The ghost stopp'd, menaced, then retired,
 until
He reach'd the ancient wall, then stood
 stone still. 1000

CXX

Juan put forth one arm — Eternal powers !
 It touch'd no soul, nor body, but the wall,
On which the moonbeams fell in silvery
 showers,
 Chequer'd with all the tracery of the hall;
He shudder'd, as no doubt the bravest cowers
 When he can't tell what 't is that doth
 appal.

How odd, a single hobgoblin's non-entity
Should cause more fear than a whole host's
 identity.

CXXI

But still the shade remain'd: the blue eyes
 glared,
 And rather variably for stony death: 1010
Yet one thing rather good the grave had
 spared,
 The ghost had a remarkably sweet breath.
A straggling curl show'd he had been fair-
 hair'd;
 A red lip, with two rows of pearls beneath,
Gleam'd forth, as through the casement's
 ivy shroud
The moon peep'd, just escaped from a grey
 cloud.

CXXII

And Juan, puzzled, but still curious, thrust
 His other arm forth — Wonder upon
 wonder !
It press'd upon a hard but glowing bust,
 Which beat as if there was a warm heart
 under. 1020
He found, as people on most trials must,
 That he had made at first a silly blunder,
And that in his confusion he had caught
Only the wall, instead of what he sought.

CXXIII

The ghost, if ghost it were, seem'd a sweet
 soul
 As ever lurk'd beneath a holy hood:
A dimpled chin, a neck of ivory, stole
 Forth into something much like flesh and
 blood;
Back fell the sable frock and dreary cowl,
 And they reveal'd — alas ! that e'er they
 should ! 1030
In full, voluptuous, but *not o'er*grown bulk,
The phantom of her frolic Grace — Fitz-
 Fulke !

CANTO THE SEVENTEENTH

[First printed in the edition of 1903 from a
manuscript in the possession of Lady Dorches-
ter, the daughter of John Cam Hobhouse.]

I

The world is full of orphans: firstly, those
 Who are so in the strict sense of the
 phrase;

But many a lonely tree the loftier grows
 Than others crowded in the Forest's
 maze. —
The next are such as are not doomed to
 lose
 Their tender parents in their budding days,
But, merely, their parental tenderness,
Which leaves them orphans of the heart no
 less.

II

The next are ' *only* Children,' as they are
 styled,
 Who grow up *Children* only, since th' old
 saw 10
Pronounces that an ' only 's ' a spoilt child —
But not to go too far, I hold it law,
That where their education, harsh or mild,
 Transgresses the great bounds of love or
 awe,
The sufferers — be 't in heart or intellect —
Whate'er the *cause*, are orphans in *effect*.

III

But to return unto the stricter rule —
 As far as words make rules — our com-
 mon notion
Of orphan paints at once a parish school,
 A half-starved babe, a wreck upon Life's
 ocean, 20
A human (what the Italians nickname)
 ' Mule ' !
A theme for Pity or some worse emotion;
 Yet, if examined, it might be admitted
The wealthiest orphans are to be more
 pitied.

IV

Too soon they are Parents to themselves:
 for what
 Are Tutors, Guardians, and so forth,
 compared
With Nature's genial Genitors ? so that
 A child of Chancery, that Star-Chamber
 ward
(I 'll take the likeness I can first come at),
 Is like — a duckling by Dame Partlett
 rear'd, 30
And frights — especially if 't is a daughter,
Th' old Hen — by running headlong to the
 water.

V

There is a common-place book argument,
 Which glibly glides from every tongue;

When any dare a new light to present,
 ' If you are right, then everybody 's
 wrong ' !
Suppose the converse of this precedent
 So often urged, so loudly and so long;
' If you are wrong, then everybody 's right ' !
Was ever everybody yet so quite ? 40

VI

Therefore I would solicit free discussion
 Upon all points — no matter what, or
 whose —
Because as Ages upon Ages push on,
 The last is apt the former to accuse
Of pillowing its head on a pin-cushion,
 Heedless of pricks because it was obtuse:
What was a paradox becomes a truth or
A something like it — witness Luther !

VII

The Sacraments have been reduced to two,
 And Witches unto none, though some-
 what late 50
Since burning aged women (save a few —
 Not witches only b——ches — who create
Mischief in families, as some know or
 knew,
 Should still be singed, but lightly, let me
 state)
Has been declared an act of inurbanity
Malgré Sir Matthew Hales's great human-
 ity.

VIII

Great Galileo was debarr'd the Sun,
 Because he fix'd it; and, to stop his talk-
 ing,
How Earth could round the solar orbit
 run,
 Found his own legs embargo'd from mere
 walking: 60
The man was well-nigh dead, ere men
 begun
 To think his skull had not some need of
 caulking;
But now, it seems, he 's right — his notion
 just:
No doubt a consolation to his dust.

IX

Pythagoras, Locke, Socrates — but pages
 Might be fill'd up, as vainly as before,
With the sad usage of all sorts of sages,
 Who, in his life-time, each, was deem'd
 a Bore !

The loftiest minds outrun their tardy ages:
 This they must bear with and, perhaps,
 much more; 70
The wise man 's sure when he no more can
 share it, he
Will have a firm Post Obit on posterity.

X

If such doom waits each intellectual Giant,
 We little people in our lesser way,
In Life's small rubs should surely be more
 pliant,
 And so for one will I — as well I may —
Would that I were less bilious — but, oh,
 fie on 't !
Just as I make my mind up every day,
To be a ' *totus, teres,*' Stoic, Sage,
The wind shifts and I fly into a rage. 80

XI

Temperate I am — yet never had a tem-
 per;
 Modest I am — yet with some slight
 assurance;
Changeable too — yet somehow ' *Idem sem-*
 per ; '
 Patient — but not enamour'd of endur-
 ance;
Cheerful — but, sometimes, rather apt to
 whimper;
 Mild — but at times a sort of ' *Hercules*
 furens ; '
So that I almost think that the same skin
For one without — has two or three within.

XII

Our Hero was, in Canto the Sixteenth,
 Left in a tender moonlight situation, 90

Such as enables **Man** to show his strength
 Moral or physical: on this occasion
Whether his virtue triumph'd — or, at
 length,
 His vice — for he was of a kindling
 nation —
Is more than I shall venture to describe; —
Unless some Beauty with a kiss should bribe.

XIII

I leave the thing a problem, like all
 things: —
 The morning came — and breakfast, tea
 and toast,
Of which most men partake, but no one
 sings.
 The company whose birth, wealth, worth,
 has cost 100
My trembling Lyre already several strings,
 Assembled with our hostess, and mine
 host;
The guests dropp'd in — the last but one,
 Her Grace,
The latest, Juan, with his virgin face.

XIV

Which best it is to encounter — Ghost, or
 none,
 'T were difficult to say; but Juan look'd
As if he had combated with more than one,
 Being wan and worn, with eyes that
 hardly brook'd
The light that through the Gothic window
 shone:
 Her Grace, too, had a sort of air re-
 buked — 110
Seem'd pale and shiver'd, as if she had kept
A vigil, or dreamt rather more than slept.

A SELECTION OF BYRON'S LETTERS

✳

TO ROBERT CHARLES DALLAS [AN AUTHOR RELATED TO BYRON BY MARRIAGE]

Dorant's, January 21, 1808

Sir,

Whenever leisure and inclination permit me the pleasure of a visit, I shall feel truly gratified in a personal acquaintance with one whose mind has been long known to me in his writings.

You are so far correct in your conjecture, that I am a member of the University of Cambridge, where I shall take my degree of A.M. this term; but were reasoning, eloquence, or virtue, the objects of my search, Granta is not their metropolis, nor is the place of her situation an "El Dorado," far less an Utopia. The intellects of her children are as stagnant as her Cam, and their pursuits limited to the church—not of Christ, but of the nearest benefice.

As to my reading, I believe I may aver, without hyperbole, it has been tolerably extensive in the historical department; so that few nations exist, or have existed, with whose records I am not in some degree acquainted, from Herodotus down to Gibbon. Of the classics I know about as much as most schoolboys after a discipline of thirteen years; of the Law of the Land, as much as enables me to keep "within the statute"—to use the poacher's vocabulary. I did study the "Spirit of Laws," and the Law of Nations; but when I saw the latter violated every month, I gave up my attempts at so useless an accomplishment:—of geography, I have seen more land on maps than I should wish to traverse on foot;—of mathematics, enough to give me the head-ache without clearing the part affected;—of philosophy, astronomy, and metaphysics, more than I can comprehend; and of common sense so little, that I mean to leave a Byronian prize at each of our "Almae Matres" for the first discovery,—though I rather fear that of the longitude will precede it.

I once thought myself a philosopher, and talked nonsense with great decorum: I defied pain, and preached up equanimity. For some time this did very well, for no one was in *pain* for me but my friends, and none lost their patience but my hearers. At last, a fall from my horse convinced me bodily suffering was an evil; and the worst of an argument overset my maxims and my temper at the same moment: so I quitted Zeno for Aristippus, and conceive that pleasure constitutes the *το καλον*.

In morality, I prefer Confucius to the Ten Commandments, and Socrates to St. Paul (though the two latter agree in their opinion of marriage). In religion, I favour the Catholic emancipation, but do not acknowledge the Pope; and I have refused to take the sacrament, because I do not think eating bread or drinking wine from the hand of an earthly vicar will make me an inheritor of heaven. I hold virtue, in general, or the virtues severally, to be only in the disposition, each a *feeling*, not a principle. I believe truth the prime attribute of the Deity, and death an eternal sleep, at least of the body. You have here a brief compendium of the sentiments of the *wicked* George, Lord Byron; and, till I get a new suit, you will perceive I am badly cloathed.

I remain yours, etc.,
BYRON

✳

TO HIS MOTHER

Falmouth, June 22, 1809

Dear Mother,

I am about to sail in a few days; probably before this reaches you. Fletcher [Byron's valet] begged so hard, that I have continued him in my service. If he does not behave well abroad, I will send him back in a *transport*. I have a German servant (who has been with Mr. Wilbraham in Persia before, and

was strongly recommended to me by Dr. Butler of Harrow), Robert and William; they constitute my whole suite. I have letters in plenty:—you shall hear from me at the different ports I touch upon; but you must not be alarmed if my letters miscarry. The Continent is in a fine state—an insurrection has broken out at Paris, and the Austrians are beating Buonaparte—the Tyrolese have risen.

There is a picture of me in oil, to be sent down to Newstead soon.—I wish the Miss Pigots had something better to do than carry my miniatures to Nottingham to copy. Now they have done it, you may ask them to copy the others, which are greater favourites than my own. As to money matters, I am ruined—at least till Rochdale [Byron's Lancashire property] is sold; and if that does not turn out well, I shall enter into the Austrian or Russian service—perhaps the Turkish, if I like their manners. The world is all before me, and I leave England without regret, and without a wish to revisit any thing it contains, except *yourself*, and your present residence.

Believe me, yours ever
sincerely.

P.S.—Pray tell Mr. Rushton his son is well, and doing well; so is Murray [Byron's servant], indeed better than I ever saw him; he will be back in about a month. I ought to add the leaving Murray to my few regrets, as his age perhaps will prevent my seeing him again. Robert I take with me; I like him, because, like myself, he seems a friendless animal.

<div align="center">✳</div>

TO FRANCIS HODGSON [A POET AND TUTOR AT CAMBRIDGE]

Patras, Morea, October 3, 1810

As I have just escaped from a physician and a fever, which confined me five days to bed, you won't expect much *allegrezza* in the ensuing letter. In this place is an indigenous distemper, which when the wind blows from the Gulf of Corinth (as it does five months out of six), attacks great and small, and makes woful work with visitors. Here be also two physicians, one of whom trusts to his genius (never having studied)—the other to a campaign of eighteen months against the sick of Otranto, which he made in his youth with great effect.

When I was seized with my disorder, I protested against both these assassins;—but what can a helpless, feverish, toasted-and-watered poor wretch do? In spite of my teeth and tongue, the English consul, my Tartar, Albanians, dragoman, forced a physician upon me, and in three days vomited and glystered me to the last gasp. In this state I made my epitaph—take it:—

> Youth, Nature and relenting Jove,
> To keep my lamp *in* strongly strove;
> But Romanelli was so stout,
> He beat all three—and blew it *out*.

But Nature and Jove, being piqued at my doubts, did, in fact, at last, beat Romanelli, and here I am, well but weakly, at your service. . . .

As for England, it is long since I have heard from it. Every one at all connected with my concerns is asleep, and you are my only correspondent, agents excepted. I have really no friends in the world; though all my old school companions are gone forth into that world, and walk about there in monstrous disguises, in the garb of guardsmen, lawyers, parsons, fine gentlemen, and such other masquerade dresses. So, I have shaken hands and cut with all these busy people, none of whom write to me. Indeed I asked it not;—and here I am, a poor traveller and heathenish philosopher, who hath perambulated the greatest part of the Levant, and seen a great quantity of very improvable land and sea, and, after all, am no better than when I set out—Lord help me! . . .

<div align="center">✳</div>

TO FRANCIS HODGSON

8, St. James's Street, February 16, 1812

Dear Hodgson,

I send you a proof. Last week I was very ill and confined to bed with stone in the kidney, but I am now quite recovered. If the stone had got into my heart instead of my kidneys, it would have been all the better. The women are gone to their relatives, after many attempts to explain what was already too clear. However, I have quite recovered that also, and only wonder at my folly in excepting my own strumpets from the general corruption,—albeit a two months' weakness is better than ten years. I have one request to make, which is, never mention a woman again in any letter to me, or even allude to the existence of the sex. I won't even read a word of the feminine gender;—it must all be *propria quae maribus.*

In the spring of 1813 I shall leave England for ever. Every thing in my affairs tends to this, and my inclinations and health do not discourage it. Neither my habits nor constitution are improved by your customs or your climate. I shall find employment in making myself a good Oriental scholar. I shall retain a mansion in one of the fairest islands, and retrace, at intervals, the most interesting portions of the East. In the mean time, I am adjusting my concerns, which will (when arranged) leave me with wealth sufficient even for home, but enough for a principality in Turkey. At present they are involved, but I hope, by taking some necessary but unpleasant steps, to clear every thing. Hobhouse is expected daily in London: we shall be very glad to see him; and, perhaps, you will come up and "drink deep ere he depart," if not, "Mahomet must go to the mountain";—but Cambridge will bring sad recollections to him, and worse to me, though for very different reasons. I believe the only human being that ever loved me in truth and entirely, was of, or belonging to, Cambridge, and, in that, no change can now take place. There is one consolation in death—where he sets his seal, the impression can neither be melted or broken, but endureth for ever.

Yours always,
B.

＊

TO THOMAS MOORE [A POET AND ONE OF BYRON'S CLOSEST FRIENDS]

Venice, Feburary 28, 1817

You will, perhaps, complain as much of the frequency of my letters now, as you were wont to do of their rarity. I think this is the fourth within as many moons. I feel anxious to hear from you, even more than usual, because your last indicated that you were unwell. At present, I am on the invalid regiment myself. The Carnival—that is, the latter part of it, and sitting up late o' nights, had knocked me up a little. But it is over—and it is now Lent, with all its abstinence and sacred music.

The mumming closed with a masked ball at the Fenice, where I went, as also to most of the ridottos, etc., etc.; and, though I did not dissipate much upon the whole, yet I find "the sword wearing out the scabbard," though I have but just turned the corner of twenty-nine.

> So we'll go no more a roving
> So late into the night,
> Though the heart be still as loving,
> And the moon be still as bright.
>
> For the sword outwears its sheath,
> And the soul wears out the breast,
> And the heart must pause to breathe,
> And Love itself have rest.

Though the night was made for loving,
And the day returns too soon,
Yet we'll go no more a roving
By the light of the moon.

I have lately had some news of litterа*toor*, as I heard the editor of the *Monthly* pronounce it once upon a time. I hear that W.[edderburn] W.[ebster] has been publishing and responding to the attacks of the *Quarterly*, in the learned Perry's *Chronicle*. I read his poesies last autumn, and amongst them found an epitaph on his bull-dog, and another on *myself*. But I beg leave to assure him (like the astrologer Partridge) that I am not only alive now, but was alive also at the time he wrote it. . . . Hobhouse has (I hear, also) expectorated a letter against the *Quarterly*, addressed to me. I feel awkwardly situated between him and Gifford, both being my friends.

And this is your month of going to press—by the body of Diana! (a Venetian oath,) I feel as anxious—but not fearful for you—as if it were myself coming out in a work of humour, which would, you know, be the antipodes of all my previous publications. I don't think you have any thing to dread but your own reputation. You must keep up to that. As you never showed me a line of your work, I do not even know your measure; but you must send me a copy by Murray forthwith, and then you shall hear what I think. I dare say you are in a pucker. Of all authors, you are the only really *modest* one I ever met with,—which would sound oddly enough to those who recollect your morals when you were young— that is, when you were *extremely* young—I don't mean to stigmatize you either with years or morality.

I believe I told you that the *E[dinburgh] R[eview]* had attacked me, in an article on Coleridge (I have not seen it)—"Et tu, Jeffrey?"—"there is nothing but roguery in villanous man." But I absolve him of all attacks, present and future; for I think he had already pushed his clemency in my behoof to the utmost, and I shall always think well of him. I only wonder he did not begin before, as my domestic destruction was a fine opening for all the world, of which all who could did well to avail themselves.

If I live ten years longer, you will see, however, that it is not over with me—I don't mean in literature, for that is nothing; and it may seem odd enough to say, I do not think it my vocation. But you will see that I shall do something or other—the times and fortune permitting—that, "like the cosmogony, or creation of the world, will puzzle the philosophers of all ages." But I doubt whether my constitution will hold out. I have, at intervals, exo*r*cised it most devilishly.

I have not yet fixed a time of return, but I think of the spring. I shall have been away a year in April next. You never mention Rogers, nor Hodgson, your clerical neighbour, who has lately got a living near you. Has he also got a child yet?—his desideratum, when I saw him last. . . .

Pray let me hear from you, at your time and leisure, believing me ever and truly and affectionately, etc.

*

TO LADY BYRON

Venice, March 5, 1817

A letter from Mr. Hanson apprizes me of the result of his correspondence with Sir Ralph Noel (of which he has transmitted a copy), and of his interviews with Dr. Lushington [lawyer advising the separation] on the subject of our daughter. I am also informed of a bill in Chancery filed against me last Spring by Sir Ralph Noel, of which this is the first intimation, and of the subject of which I am ignorant.

Whatever may be the result of these discussions and the measures, which had led to them, and to which they may lead, remember, that I have not been the first to begin; but, being begun, neither shall I be the first to recede. I feel at length convinced that the feeling which I had cherished through all and in spite of all, namely—the hope of a reconciliation and reunion, however remote,—is indubitably useless; and although, all things considered, it could not be very sanguine, still it was sincere, and I cherished it as a sickly infatuation: and now I part with it with a regret, perhaps bitterer of [than] that which I felt in parting with yourself.

It was generally understood, if not expressed, that all legal proceedings were to terminate in the act

of our separation: to what then I am to attribute the bill, of which I am apprized, I am at a loss to conjecture. The object, however, is evident: it is to deprive me of my paternal right over my child, which I have the less merited, as I neither abused nor intended to abuse it. You and yours might have been satisfied with the outrages I have already suffered, if not by your design, at least by your means. I know your defence and your apology—duty and Justice; but *Qui n'est que juste, est dur:* or if the French aphorism should seem light in the balance, I could refer you to an older language and a higher authority for the condemnation of conduct, which you may yet live to condemn in your own heart.

Throughout the whole of this unhappy business, I have done my best to avoid the bitterness, which, however, is yet amongst us; and it would be as well if even you at times recollected, that the man who has been sacrificed in fame, in feelings, in every thing, to the convenience of your family, was he whom you once loved, and who—whatever you may imagine to the contrary—loved you. If you conceive that I could be actuated by revenge against you, you are mistaken: I am not humble enough to be vindictive. Irritated I may have been, and may be—is it a wonder? but upon such irritation, beyond its momentary expression, I have not acted, from the hour that you quitted me to that in which I am made aware that our daughter is to be the entail of our disunion, the inheritor of our bitterness. If you think to reconcile yourself to yourself by accumulating harshness against me, you are again mistaken: you are not happy, nor even tranquil, nor will you ever be so, even to the very moderate degree which is permitted to general humanity. For myself, I have a confidence in my Fortune, which will yet bear me through. Ταὐτόματον ἡμῶν κάλλιον βουλεύεται. The reverses, which have occurred, were what I should have expected; and, in considering you and yours merely as the instruments of my more recent adversity, it would be difficult for me to blame you, did not every thing appear to intimate a deliberate intention of as wilful malice on your part as could well be digested into a system. However, time and Nemesis will do that, which I would not, even were it in my power remote or immediate. You will smile at this piece of prophecy—do so, but recollect it: it is justified by all human experience. No one was ever even the involuntary cause of great evils to others, without a requital: I have paid and am paying for mine—so will you.

<p align="center">*</p>

TO JOHN MURRAY

Venice, May 30, 1817

Dear Sir,

I returned from Rome two days ago, and have received your letter; but no sign nor tidings of the parcel sent through Sir —— Stuart, which you mention. After an interval of months, a packet of *Tales*, etc., found me at Rome; but this is all, and may be all that ever will find me. The post seems to be the only sane conveyance; and *that only for letters*. From Florence I sent you a poem on Tasso, and from Rome the new third act of *Manfred*, and by Dr. Polidori two pictures for my sister. I left Rome, and made a rapid journey home. You will continue to direct here as usual. Mr. Hobhouse is gone to Naples: I should have run down there too for a week, but for the quantity of English whom I heard of there. I prefer hating them at a distance; unless an earthquaker, or a good real eruption of Vesuvius, were insured to reconcile me to their vicinity.

I know no other situation except Hell which I should feel inclined to participate with them—as a race, always excepting several individuals. There were few of them in Rome, and I believe none whom you know, except that old Blue-*bore* Sotheby, who will give a fine account of Italy, in which he will be greatly assisted by his total ignorance of Italian, and yet this is the translator of Tasso.

The day before I left Rome I saw three robbers guillotined. The ceremony—including the *masqued* priests; the half-naked executioners; the bandaged criminals; the black Christ and his banner; the scaffold; the soldiery; the slow procession, and the quick rattle and heavy fall of the axe; the splash of the blood, and the ghastliness of the exposed heads—is altogether more impressive than the vulgar and ungentlemanly dirty "new drop," and dog-like agony of infliction upon the sufferers of the English sentence. Two of these men behaved calmly enough, but the first of the three died with great terror and reluctance, which was very horrible. He would not lie down; then his neck was too large for the aperture, and the priest was obliged to drown his exclamations by still louder exhortations. The head was off

before the eye could trace the blow; but from an attempt to draw back the head, nowithstanding it was held forward by the hair, the first head was cut off close to the ears: the other two were taken off more cleanly. It is better than the oriental way, and (I should think) than the axe of our ancestors. The pain seems little; and yet the effect to the spectator, and the preparation to the criminal, are very striking and chilling. The first turned me quite hot and thirsty, and made me shake so that I could hardly hold the opera-glass (I was close, but determined to see, as one should see every thing, once, with attention); the second and third (which shows how dreadfully soon things grow indifferent), I am ashamed to say, had no effect on me as a horror, though I would have saved them if I could.

It is some time since I heard from you—the *12th April* I believe.

Yours ever truly,
B.

✳

TO JOHN MURRAY

September 15, 1817

Dear Sir,

I enclose a sheet for correction, if you ever get to another edition [of *The Prisoner of Chillon*]. You will observe that the blunder in printing makes it appear as if the Chateau was *over* St. Gingo, instead of being on the opposite shore of the Lake, over Clarens. So, separate the paragraphs, otherwise my *to*pography will seem as inaccurate as your *ty*pography on this occasion.

The other day I wrote to convey my proposition with regard to the 4th and concluding canto. I have gone over and extended it to one hundred and fifty stanzas, which is almost as long as the two first were originally, and longer by itself than any of the small poems except *The Corsair*. Mr. Hobhouse has made some very valuable and accurate notes of considerable length, and you may be sure I will do for the text all that I can to finish with decency. I look upon *Childe Harold* as my best; and as I begun, I think of concluding with it. But I make no resolutions on that head, as I broke my former intention with regard to *The Corsair*. However, I fear that I shall never do better; and yet, not being thirty years of age, for some moons to come, one ought to be progressive as far as Intellect goes for many a good year. But I have had a devilish deal of wear and tear of mind and body in my time, besides having published too often and much already. God grant me some judgement! to do what may be most fitting in that and every thing else, for I doubt my own exceedingly. . . .

With regard to poetry in general, I am convinced, the more I think of it, that he and *all* of us— Scott, Southey, Wordsworth, Moore, Campbell, I,—are all in the wrong, one as much as another; that we are upon a wrong revolutionary poetical system, or systems, not worth a damn in itself, and from which none but Rogers and Crabbe are free; and that the present and next generations will finally be of this opinion. I am the more confirmed in this by having lately gone over some of our classics, particularly *Pope*, whom I tried in this way,—I took Moore's poems and my own and some others, and went over them side by side with Pope's, and I was really astonished (I ought not to have been so) and mortified at the ineffable distance in point of sense, harmony, effect, and even *Imagination*, passion, and *Invention*, between the little Queen Anne's man, and us of the Lower Empire. Depend upon it, it is all Horace then, and Claudian now, among us; and if I had to begin again, I would model myself accordingly. Crabbe's the man, but he has got a coarse and impracticable subject, and Rogers, the Grandfather of living poetry, is retired upon half-pay, (I don't mean as a Banker). . . .

✳

TO AUGUSTA LEIGH [BYRON'S SISTER]

Venice, August 3, 1818

Dearest Augusta,

I am not uncomfortable, but have been obliged to scold Hobhouse, etc., for not doing a thing or two for me in England in the way of business. At present they are done, and I am graciously appeased.

My little girl, Allegra (the child I spoke to you of), has been with me these three months: she is very pretty, remarkably intelligent, and a great favourite with every body; but, what is remarkable, much more like Lady Byron than her mother—so much so as to stupefy the learned Fletcher and astonish me. Is it not odd? I suppose she must also resemble her sister, Ada: she has very blue eyes, and that singular forehead, fair curly hair, and a devil of a Spirit—but that is Papa's.

I am in health, and yours,
B.

*

TO RICHARD BELGRAVE HOPPNER [ENGLISH CONSUL IN VENICE]

Ravenna, April 3, 1821

Thanks for the translation. I have sent you some books, which I do not know whether you have read or no—you need not return them, in any case. I enclose you also a letter from Pisa. I have neither spared trouble nor expense in the care of the child [Allegra]; and as she was now four years old complete, and quite above the control of the servants—and as a *man* living without any woman at the head of his house cannot much attend to a nursery—I had no resource but to place her for a time (at a high pension too) in the convent of Bagna-Cavalli (twelve miles off), where the air is good, and where she will, at least, have her learning advanced, and her morals and religion inculcated. I had also another reason;—things were and are in such a state here, that I had no reason to look upon my own personal safety as particularly insurable; and I thought the infant best out of harm's way, for the present.

It is also fit that I should add that I by no means intended, nor intend, to give a *natural* child an *English* education, because with the disadvantages of her birth, her after-settlement would be doubly difficult. Abroad, with a fair foreign education and a portion of five or six thousand pounds, she might and may marry very respectably. In England such a dowry would be a pittance, while elsewhere it is a fortune. It is, besides, my wish that she should be a Roman Catholic, which I look upon as the best religion, as it is assuredly the oldest of the various branches of Christianity. I have now explained my notions as to the place where she now is—it is the best I could find for the present; but I have no prejudices in its favour.

I do not speak of politics, because it seems a hopeless subject, as long as those scoundrels are to be permitted to bully states out of their independence. Believe me,

Yours ever and truly,

P.S. —There is a report here of a change in France; but with what truth is not yet known.

P.S. —My respects to Mrs. H. I *have* the "best opinion" of her countrywomen [Swiss]; and at my time of life, (three and thirty, 22nd January, 1821), that is to say, after the life I have led, a *good* opinion is the only rational one which a man should entertain of the whole sex—up to *thirty*, the worst possible opinion a man can have of them in *general*, the better for himself. Afterwards, it is a matter of no importance to *them*, nor to him either, *what opinion* he entertains—his day is over, or at least, should be.

You see how sober I am become.

*

TO JOHN MURRAY

Ravenna, September 12, 1821

Dear Sir,

By Tuesday's post, I forwarded, in three packets, the drama of "*Cain*," in three acts, of which I request the acknowledgement when arrived. To the last speech of *Eve*, in the last act (i.e. where she curses Cain), add these three lines to the concluding one—

> May the Grass wither from the foot! the Woods
> Deny thee shelter! Earth a home! the Dust
> A Grave! the Sun his light! and Heaven her God!

There's as pretty a piece of Imprecation for you, when joined to lines already sent, as you may wish to meet with in the course of your business. But don't forget the addition of the above three lines, which are clinchers to Eve's speech. . . .

Why don't you publish my *Pulci?* The best thing I ever wrote, with the Italian to it. I wish I was alongside of you: nothing is ever done in a man's absence; every body runs counter, because they *can*. If ever I *do* return to England (which I shan't though), I will write a poem to which *English Bards*, etc., shall be New Milk, in comparison. Your present literary world of mountebanks stands in need of such an Avatar; but I am not yet quite bilious enough: a season or two more, and a provocation or two, will wind me up to the point, and then, have at the whole set!

I have no patience with the sort of trash you send me out by way of books; except Scott's novels, and three or four other things, I never saw such work or works. Campbell is lecturing, Moore idling, Southey twaddling, Wordsworth driveling, Coleridge muddling, Joanna Baillie piddling, Bowles quibbling, squabbling, and sniveling. Milman will *do*, if he don't cant too much, nor imitate Southey: the fellow has poesy in him; but he is envious, and unhappy, as all the envious are. Still he is among the best of the day. Barry Cornwall will do better by and bye, I dare say, if he don't get spoilt by green tea, and the praises of Pentonville and Paradise Row. The pity of these men is, that they never lived either in *high life*, nor in *solitude:* there is no medium for the knowledge of the *busy* or the *still* world. If admitted into high life for a season, it is merely as *spectators*—they form no part of the Mechanism thereof. Now Moore and I, the one by circumstances, and the other by birth, happened to be free of the corporation, and to have entered into its pulses and passions, *quarum partes fuimus*. Both of us have learnt by this much which nothing else could have taught us.

Yours,
B.

＊

TO EDWARD JOHN TRELAWNY [AUTHOR, ADVENTURER, FRIEND OF SHELLEY]

June 15, 1823

My Dear T.,

You must have heard that I am going to Greece. Why do you not come to me? I want your aid, and am exceedingly anxious to see you. Pray come, for I am at last determined to go to Greece; it is the only place I was ever contented in. I am serious, and did not write before, as I might have given you a journey for nothing; they all say I can be of use in Greece. I do not know how, nor do they; but at all events let us go.

Yours, etc., truly,
N. BYRON

P B Shelley

SELECTED POEMS

PERCY BYSSHE SHELLEY

PERCY BYSSHE SHELLEY was born in 1792 in Sussex, the son of a member of Parliament. He was educated at Eton, where he was taunted and called "Mad Shelley" by his peers, and at the University College of Oxford, which expelled him in 1811 for distributing a pamphlet called "The Necessity of Atheism." After his expulsion, he travelled to Scotland with 16-year-old Harriet Westbrook, whom he married in August 1811. During the three years of Shelley's marriage to Harriet, he continued to issue pamphlets on various radical topics, attempted to establish communes in England and North Wales, fathered two children, and in 1813 wrote the polemical poem "Queen Mab."

By 1814, his marriage to Harriet effectively over, Shelley travelled in Europe with Mary Godwin and her teenage stepsister, Jane (Claire) Clairmont. In 1816, he settled in London, where his poem "Alastor" was well received. While summering at Lake Geneva later that year, he formed a friendship with Lord Byron. That fall, Harriet drowned herself, and Shelley married Mary Godwin soon after. The Shelleys moved abroad in 1818, journeying from town to town in Italy. Haunted by the death of his children Clara and William and by Mary's breakdown, Shelley began in 1819 the most productive period of his literary life. During the next year, he wrote "Ode to the West Wind," "Peter Bell the Third," and "To a Skylark." Later the Shelleys settled in Pisa, where he wrote "The Two Spirits: An Allegory," "To the Moon," and "Adonais," an elegy for Keats. In 1822, the Shelleys moved again, this time to a house on the bay of Lerici. In August, while returning from a visit to Byron at Livorno, Shelley's schooner capsized during a storm and he drowned.

QUEEN MAB

A PHILOSOPHICAL POEM

WITH NOTES

ECRASEZ L'INFAME!
Corréspondance de Voltaire.

Avia Pieridum peragro loca, nullius ante
Trita solo, juvat integros accedere fonteis;
Atque haurire: juvatque novos decerpere flores.
.
Unde prius nulli velarint tempora Musæ.
Primum quod magnis doceo de rebus; et arctis
Religionum animos nodis exsolvere pergo.
LUCRETIUS, lib. iv.

Δὸς ποῦ στῶ, καὶ κόσμον κινήσω.
ARCHIMEDES.

'During my existence I have incessantly speculated, thought and read.' So Shelley wrote when he was yet not quite twenty years old; and the statement fairly represents the history of his boyhood and youth. *Queen Mab* was composed in 1812–13, in its present form, and issued during the summer of the latter year, when Shelley was just twenty-one. It embodies substantially the contents of his mind at that period, especially those speculative, religious and philanthropic opinions to the expression of which his 'passion for reforming the world' was the incentive; and, poetically, it is his first work of importance. Much of its subject-matter had been previously treated by him. The figure of Ahasuerus, which was a permanent imaginative motive for him, had been the centre of a juvenile poem, *The Wandering Jew*, in which Medwin claims to have collaborated with him, as early as 1809–10; and youthful verse written before 1812 is clearly incorporated in *Queen Mab*. It may fairly be regarded, poetically and intellectually, as the result of the three preceding years, from the eighteenth to the twenty-first of the poet's life.

The poem owes much to Shelley's studies in the Latin and French authors. The limitations of his poetical training and taste in English verse are justly stated by Mrs. Shelley, in her note:

'Our earlier English poetry was almost unknown to him. The love and knowledge of nature developed by Wordsworth — the lofty melody and mysterious beauty of Coleridge's poetry — and the wild fantastic machinery and gorgeous scenery adopted by Southey, composed his favorite reading. The rhythm of *Queen Mab* was founded on that of *Thalaba*, and the first few lines bear a striking resemblance in spirit, though not in idea, to the opening of that poem. His fertile imagination, and ear tuned to the finest sense of harmony, preserved him from imitation. Another of his favorite books was the poem of *Gebir*, by Walter Savage Landor.'

Queen Mab is, in form, what would be expected from such preferences. His own *Notes* indicate the prose sources of his thought. He dissented from all that was established in society, for the most part very radically, and was a believer in the perfectibility of man by moral means. Here, again, Mrs. Shelley's note is most just:

'He was animated to greater zeal by compassion for his fellow-creatures. His sympathy was excited by the misery with which the world is bursting. He witnessed the sufferings of the poor, and was aware of the evils of ignorance. He desired to induce every rich man to despoil himself of superfluity, and to create a brotherhood of property and service, and was ready to be the first to lay down the advantages of his birth. He was of too uncompromising a disposition to join any party

437

He did not in his youth look forward to grad-
ual improvement: nay, in those days of intol
erance, now almost forgotten, it seemed as easy
to look forward to the sort of millennium of
freedom and brotherhood, which he thought
the proper state of mankind, as to the present
reign of moderation and improvement. Ill
health made him believe that his race would
soon be run; that a year or two was all he had
of life. He desired that these years should be
useful and illustrious. He saw, in a fervent
call on his fellow-creatures to share alike the
blessings of the creation, to love and serve
each other, the noblest work that life and time
permitted him. In this spirit he composed
Queen Mab.'

Shelley's own opinion of the poem changed
in later years. He always referred to it as
written in his nineteenth year, when it was ap-
parently begun, though its final form at any
rate dates from the next year. In 1817 he
wrote of it as follows:

. . . 'Full of those errors which belong to
youth, as far as imagery and language and a
connected plan is concerned. But it was a sin-
cere overflowing of the heart and mind, and that
at a period when they are most uncorrupted and
pure. It is the author's boast, and it consti-
tutes no small portion of his happiness, that,
after six years [this period supports the date
1811] of added experience and reflection, the
doctrine of equality, and liberty, and disinter-
estedness, and entire unbelief in religion of any
sort, to which this poem is devoted, have
gained rather than lost that beauty and that
grandeur which first determined him to devote
his life to the investigation and inculcation of
them.'

In 1821, when the poem was printed by W.
Clark, Shelley, in a letter of protest to the edi-
tor of the *Examiner*, describes it in a different
strain:

'A poem, entitled *Queen Mab*, was written
by me, at the age of eighteen, I dare say in a
sufficiently intemperate spirit — but even then
was not intended for publication, and a few
copies only were struck off, to be distributed
among my personal friends. I have not seen
this production for several years; I doubt not
but that it is perfectly worthless in point of
literary composition; and that in all that con-
cerns moral and political speculation, as well
as in the subtler discriminations of metaphysi-
cal and religious doctrine, it is still more crude
and immature. I am a devoted enemy to re-
ligious, political, and domestic oppression; and
I regret this publication not so much from lit-
erary vanity, as because I fear it is better fitted
to injure than to serve the sacred cause of
freedom.'

Queen Mab, as Shelley here states, was pri-
vately issued. The name of the printer was
cut out of nearly all copies, for fear of prose-
cution. The edition was of two hundred and
fifty copies, of which about seventy were put
in circulation by gift. Many pirated editions
were issued after Shelley's death both in Eng-
land and America, and the poem was especially
popular with the Owenites. By it Shelley was
long most widely known, and it remains one
of the most striking of his works in popular
apprehension. Though at last he abandoned
it, because of its crudities, he had felt inter-
est in it after its first issue and had partly
recast it, and included a portion of this re-
vision in his next volume, *Alastor,* 1816, as the
Dæmon of the World. The radical character
of *Queen Mab,* which was made a part of the
evidence against his character, on the occasion
of the trial which resulted in his being de-
prived of the custody of his children by Lord
Eldon, was a main element in the contempo-
rary obloquy in which his name was involved in
England, though very few persons could ever
have read the poem then; but it may be
doubted whether in the end it did not help his
fame by the fascination it exercises over a cer-
tain class of minds in the first stages of social
and intellectual revolt or angry unrest so wide-
spread in this century.

The dedication *To Harriet* ***** is to his
first wife.

TO HARRIET *****

WHOSE is the love that, gleaming through
　　the world,
Wards off the poisonous arrow of its scorn?
　　Whose is the warm and partial praise,
　　Virtue's most sweet reward?

Beneath whose looks did my reviving soul
Riper in truth and virtuous daring grow?
　　Whose eyes have I gazed fondly on,
　　And loved mankind the more?

Harriet! on thine: — thou wert my purer
　　mind;
Thou wert the inspiration of my song;
　　Thine are these early wilding flowers,
　　Though garlanded by me.

Then press into thy breast this pledge of
　　love;
And know, though time may change and
　　years may roll,
　　Each floweret gathered in my heart
　　It consecrates to thine.

I

How wonderful is Death,
Death, and his brother Sleep !
One pale as yonder waning moon
 With lips of lurid blue ;
 The other, rosy as the morn
When throned on ocean's wave
 It blushes o'er the world ;
Yet both so passing wonderful !

Hath then the gloomy Power
Whose reign is in the tainted sepulchres 10
 Seized on her sinless soul ?
 Must then that peerless form
Which love and admiration cannot view
Without a beating heart, those azure veins
Which steal like streams along a field of
 snow,
 That lovely outline which is fair
 As breathing marble, perish ?
 Must putrefaction's breath
Leave nothing of this heavenly sight
 But loathsomeness and ruin ? 20
Spare nothing but a gloomy theme,
On which the lightest heart might moral-
 ize?
 Or is it only a sweet slumber
 Stealing o'er sensation,
Which the breath of roseate morning
 Chaseth into darkness ?
 Will Ianthe wake again,
 And give that faithful bosom joy
Whose sleepless spirit waits to catch
Light, life and rapture, from her smile ?

 Yes ! she will wake again, 31
Although her glowing limbs are motionless,
 And silent those sweet lips,
 Once breathing eloquence
That might have soothed a tiger's rage
Or thawed the cold heart of a conqueror.
 Her dewy eyes are closed,
And on their lids, whose texture fine
Scarce hides the dark blue orbs beneath,
 The baby Sleep is pillowed ; 40
 Her golden tresses shade
 The bosom's stainless pride,
Curling like tendrils of the parasite
 Around a marble column.

 Hark ! whence that rushing sound ?
 'T is like the wondrous strain
That round a lonely ruin swells,
Which, wandering on the echoing shore,
 The enthusiast hears at evening ;

'T is softer than the west wind's sigh ;
'T is wilder than the unmeasured notes
Of that strange lyre whose strings 52
 The genii of the breezes sweep ;
 Those lines of rainbow light
Are like the moonbeams when they
 fall
Through some cathedral window, but the
 tints
 Are such as may not find
 Comparison on earth.

Behold the chariot of the Fairy Queen !
Celestial coursers paw the unyielding
 air; 60
Their filmy pennons at her word they
 furl,
And stop obedient to the reins of light ;
 These the Queen of Spells drew in ;
 She spread a charm around the spot,
And, leaning graceful from the ethereal
 car,
 Long did she gaze, and silently,
 Upon the slumbering maid.

Oh ! not the visioned poet in his dreams,
When silvery clouds float through the wil-
 dered brain,
When every sight of lovely, wild and
 grand 70
 Astonishes, enraptures, elevates,
 When fancy at a glance combines
The wondrous and the beautiful, —
 So bright, so fair, so wild a shape
 Hath ever yet beheld,
As that which reined the coursers of the
 air
 And poured the magic of her gaze
 Upon the maiden's sleep.

 The broad and yellow moon
 Shone dimly through her form — 80
That form of faultless symmetry;
The pearly and pellucid car
 Moved not the moonlight's line.
 'T was not an earthly pageant.
Those, who had looked upon the sight
 Passing all human glory,
 Saw not the yellow moon,
 Saw not the mortal scene,
 Heard not the night-wind's rush,
 Heard not an earthly sound, 90
 Saw but the fairy pageant,
 Heard but the heavenly strains
That filled the lonely dwelling.

The Fairy's frame was slight — yon fibrous
 cloud,
That catches but the palest tinge of even,
And which the straining eye can hardly
 seize
When melting into eastern twilight's shad-
 ow,
Were scarce so thin, so slight ; but the fair
 star
That gems the glittering coronet of morn,
Sheds not a light so mild, so powerful, 100
As that which, bursting from the Fairy's
 form,
Spread a purpureal halo round the scene,
 Yet with an undulating motion,
 Swayed to her outline gracefully.

 From her celestial car
 The Fairy Queen descended,
 And thrice she waved her wand
 Circled with wreaths of amaranth;
 Her thin and misty form
 Moved with the moving air, 110
 And the clear silver tones,
 As thus she spoke, were such
As are unheard by all but gifted ear.

FAIRY

' Stars ! your balmiest influence shed !
Elements ! your wrath suspend !
Sleep, Ocean, in the rocky bounds
 That circle thy domain !
Let not a breath be seen to stir
Around yon grass-grown ruin's height !
 Let even the restless gossamer 120
 Sleep on the moveless air !
 Soul of Ianthe ! thou,
Judged alone worthy of the envied boon
That waits the good and the sincere ; that
 waits
Those who have struggled, and with reso-
 lute will
Vanquished earth's pride and meanness,
 burst the chains,
The icy chains of custom, and have shone
The day-stars of their age; — Soul of
 Ianthe !
 Awake ! arise ! '

 Sudden arose 130
 Ianthe's Soul; it stood
All beautiful in naked purity,
The perfect semblance of its bodily frame;
Instinct with inexpressible beauty and
 grace —

 Each stain of earthliness
 Had passed away — it reassumed
 Its native dignity and stood
 Immortal amid ruin.

 Upon the couch the body lay,
 Wrapt in the depth of slumber; 140
Its features were fixed and meaningless,
 Yet animal life was there,
 And every organ yet performed
Its natural functions; 'twas a sight
Of wonder to behold the body and the soul.
 The self-same lineaments, the same
 Marks of identity were there;
Yet, oh, how different ! One aspires to
 Heaven,
Pants for its sempiternal heritage,
And, ever changing, ever rising still, 150
 Wantons in endless being:
The other, for a time the unwilling sport
Of circumstance and passion, struggles on;
Fleets through its sad duration rapidly;
Then like an useless and worn-out machine,
Rots, perishes, and passes.

FAIRY

' Spirit ! who hast dived so deep;
 Spirit ! who hast soared so high;
 Thou the fearless, thou the mild,
Accept the boon thy worth hath earned,
 Ascend the car with me ! ' 161

SPIRIT

' Do I dream ? Is this new feeling
 But a visioned ghost of slumber ?
 If indeed I am a soul,
 A free, a disembodied soul,
 Speak again to me.'

FAIRY

' I am the Fairy MAB: to me 'tis given
The wonders of the human world to keep;
The secrets of the immeasurable past,
In the unfailing consciences of men, 170
Those stern, unflattering chroniclers, I
 find;
The future, from the causes which arise
In each event, I gather; not the sting
Which retributive memory implants
In the hard bosom of the selfish man,
Nor that ecstatic and exulting throb
Which virtue's votary feels when he
 sums up
The thoughts and actions of a well-spent
 day,

Are unforeseen, unregistered by me;
And it is yet permitted me to rend 180
The veil of mortal frailty, that the spirit,
Clothed in its changeless purity, may
 know
How soonest to accomplish the great
 end
For which it hath its being, and may
 taste
That peace which in the end all life will
 share.
This is the meed of virtue; happy Soul,
 Ascend the car with me ! '

The chains of earth's immurement
 Fell from Ianthe's spirit;
They shrank and brake like bandages of
 straw 190
Beneath a wakened giant's strength.
 She knew her glorious change,
And felt in apprehension uncontrolled
 New raptures opening round;
Each day-dream of her mortal life,
Each frenzied vision of the slumbers
 That closed each well-spent day,
 Seemed now to meet reality.
The Fairy and the Soul proceeded;
 The silver clouds disparted; 200
And as the car of magic they ascended,
 Again the speechless music swelled,
 Again the coursers of the air
Unfurled their azure pennons, and the
 Queen,
 Shaking the beamy reins,
 Bade them pursue their way.

The magic car moved on.
The night was fair, and countless stars
Studded heaven's dark blue vault;
 Just o'er the eastern wave 210
Peeped the first faint smile of morn.
 The magic car moved on —
 From the celestial hoofs
The atmosphere in flaming sparkles flew,
 And where the burning wheels
Eddied above the mountain's loftiest peak,
 Was traced a line of lightning.
Now it flew far above a rock,
 The utmost verge of earth, 219
The rival of the Andes, whose dark brow
 Lowered o'er the silver sea.

Far, far below the chariot's path,
 Calm as a slumbering babe,
 Tremendous Ocean lay.

The mirror of its stillness showed
 The pale and waning stars,
 The chariot's fiery track,
 And the gray light of morn
 Tinging those fleecy clouds
 That canopied the dawn. 230

Seemed it that the chariot's way
Lay through the midst of an immense con-
 cave
Radiant with million constellations, tinged
 With shades of infinite color,
 And semicircled with a belt
 Flashing incessant meteors.

The magic car moved on.
 As they approached their goal, 238
 The coursers seemed to gather speed;
The sea no longer was distinguished; earth
 Appeared a vast and shadowy sphere;
 The sun's unclouded orb
 Rolled through the black concave;
 Its rays of rapid light
Parted around the chariot's swifter course,
 And fell, like ocean's feathery spray
 Dashed from the boiling surge
 Before a vessel's prow.

The magic car moved on.
 Earth's distant orb appeared 250
The smallest light that twinkles in the
 heaven;
 Whilst round the chariot's way
 Innumerable systems rolled
 And countless spheres diffused
 An ever-varying glory.
It was a sight of wonder: some
 Were hornèd like the crescent moon;
 Some shed a mild and silver beam
Like Hesperus o'er the western sea; 259
Some dashed athwart with trains of flame,
 Like worlds to death and ruin driven;
Some shone like suns, and as the chariot
 passed,
 Eclipsed all other light.

 Spirit of Nature ! here —
In this interminable wilderness
Of worlds, at whose immensity
 Even soaring fancy staggers,
 Here is thy fitting temple!
 Yet not the lightest leaf 269
 That quivers to the passing breeze
 Is less instinct with thee;
 Yet not the meanest worm

That lurks in graves and fattens on the
 dead,
 Less shares thy eternal breath!
 Spirit of Nature! thou,
 Imperishable as this scene —
 Here is thy fitting temple!

II

If solitude hath ever led thy steps
 To the wild ocean's echoing shore,
 And thou hast lingered there,
 Until the sun's broad orb
Seemed resting on the burnished wave,
 Thou must have marked the lines
Of purple gold that motionless
 Hung o'er the sinking sphere;
Thou must have marked the billowy
 clouds,
 Edged with intolerable radiancy, 10
 Towering like rocks of jet
 Crowned with a diamond wreath;
 And yet there is a moment,
 When the sun's highest point
Peeps like a star o'er ocean's western edge,
When those far clouds of feathery gold,
 Shaded with deepest purple, gleam
 Like islands on a dark blue sea;
Then has thy fancy soared above the earth
 And furled its wearied wing 20
 Within the Fairy's fane.

 Yet not the golden islands
 Gleaming in yon flood of light,
 Nor the feathery curtains
 Stretching o'er the sun's bright couch,
 Nor the burnished ocean-waves
 Paving that gorgeous dome,
So fair, so wonderful a sight
As Mab's ethereal palace could afford. 29
Yet likest evening's vault, that faëry Hall!
As Heaven, low resting on the wave, it
 spread
 Its floors of flashing light,
 Its vast and azure dome,
 Its fertile golden islands
 Floating on a silver sea;
Whilst suns their mingling beamings darted
Through clouds of circumambient darkness,
 And pearly battlements around
 Looked o'er the immense of Heaven.

The magic car no longer moved. 40
 The Fairy and the Spirit
 Entered the Hall of Spells.
 Those golden clouds

 That rolled in glittering billows
 Beneath the azure canopy,
With the ethereal footsteps trembled not;
 The light and crimson mists,
Floating to strains of thrilling melody
 Through that unearthly dwelling,
Yielded to every movement of the will; 50
Upon their passive swell the Spirit leaned,
And, for the varied bliss that pressed
 around,
 Used not the glorious privilege
 Of virtue and of wisdom.

 'Spirit!' the Fairy said,
 And pointed to the gorgeous dome,
 'This is a wondrous sight
 And mocks all human grandeur;
But, were it virtue's only meed to dwell
In a celestial palace, all resigned 60
To pleasurable impulses, immured
Within the prison of itself, the will
Of changeless Nature would be unfulfilled.
Learn to make others happy. Spirit, come!
This is thine high reward: — the past shall
 rise;
Thou shalt behold the present; I will teach
 The secrets of the future.'

 The Fairy and the Spirit
Approached the overhanging battlement.
 Below lay stretched the universe! 70
 There, far as the remotest line
 That bounds imagination's flight,
 Countless and unending orbs
 In mazy motion intermingled,
 Yet still fulfilled immutably
 Eternal Nature's law.
 Above, below, around,
 The circling systems formed
 A wilderness of harmony;
 Each with undeviating aim, 80
In eloquent silence, through the depths of
 space
 Pursued its wondrous way.

 There was a little light
 That twinkled in the misty distance.
 None but a spirit's eye
 Might ken that rolling orb.
 None but a spirit's eye,
 And in no other place
But that celestial dwelling, might behold
Each action of this earth's inhabitants. 90
 But matter, space, and time,
 In those aërial mansions cease to act;

And all-prevailing wisdom, when it reaps
The harvest of its excellence, o'erbounds
Those obstacles of which an earthly soul
 Fears to attempt the conquest.

 The Fairy pointed to the earth.
 The Spirit's intellectual eye
 Its kindred beings recognized. 99
The thronging thousands, to a passing view,
 Seemed like an ant-hill's citizens.
 How wonderful! that even
 The passions, prejudices, interests,
That sway the meanest being — the weak touch
 That moves the finest nerve
 And in one human brain
Causes the faintest thought, becomes a link
 In the great chain of Nature!

 'Behold,' the Fairy cried,
 'Palmyra's ruined palaces! 110
 Behold where grandeur frowned!
 Behold where pleasure smiled!
What now remains? — the memory
 Of senselessness and shame.
 What is immortal there?
 Nothing — it stands to tell
 A melancholy tale, to give
 An awful warning; soon
Oblivion will steal silently
 The remnant of its fame. 120
 Monarchs and conquerors there
Proud o'er prostrate millions trod —
The earthquakes of the human race;
Like them, forgotten when the ruin
 That marks their shock is past.

 'Beside the eternal Nile
 The Pyramids have risen.
Nile shall pursue his changeless way;
 Those Pyramids shall fall.
Yea! not a stone shall stand to tell 130
 The spot whereon they stood;
Their very site shall be forgotten,
 As is their builder's name!

 'Behold yon sterile spot,
Where now the wandering Arab's tent
 Flaps in the desert blast!
There once old Salem's haughty fane
Reared high to heaven its thousand golden domes,
 And in the blushing face of day
 Exposed its shameful glory. 140
Oh! many a widow, many an orphan cursed

The building of that fane; and many a father,
Worn out with toil and slavery, implored
The poor man's God to sweep it from the earth
And spare his children the detested task
Of piling stone on stone and poisoning
 The choicest days of life
 To soothe a dotard's vanity.
There an inhuman and uncultured race 149
Howled hideous praises to their Demon-God;
They rushed to war, tore from the mother's womb
The unborn child — old age and infancy
Promiscuous perished; their victorious arms
Left not a soul to breathe. Oh! they were fiends!
But what was he who taught them that the God
Of Nature and benevolence had given
A special sanction to the trade of blood?
His name and theirs are fading, and the tales
Of this barbarian nation, which imposture
Recites till terror credits, are pursuing 160
 Itself into forgetfulness.

 'Where Athens, Rome, and Sparta stood,
 There is a moral desert now.
 The mean and miserable huts,
 The yet more wretched palaces,
 Contrasted with those ancient fanes
 Now crumbling to oblivion, —
 The long and lonely colonnades
Through which the ghost of Freedom stalks, —
 Seem like a well-known tune, 170
Which in some dear scene we have loved to hear,
 Remembered now in sadness.
But, oh! how much more changed,
How gloomier is the contrast
 Of human nature there!
Where Socrates expired, a tyrant's slave,
A coward and a fool, spreads death around —
 Then, shuddering, meets his own.
Where Cicero and Antoninus lived,
A cowled and hypocritical monk 180
 Prays, curses and deceives.

 'Spirit! ten thousand years
 Have scarcely passed away,

Since in the waste, where now the savage
 drinks
His enemy's blood, and, aping Europe's
 sons,
 Wakes the unholy song of war,
 Arose a stately city,
Metropolis of the western continent.
 There, now, the mossy column-stone,
Indented by time's unrelaxing grasp, 190
 Which once appeared to brave
 All, save its country's ruin, —
 There the wide forest scene,
Rude in the uncultivated loveliness
 Of gardens long run wild, —
Seems, to the unwilling sojourner whose steps
Chance in that desert has delayed,
Thus to have stood since earth was what
 it is.
Yet once it was the busiest haunt, 199
Whither, as to a common centre, flocked
 Strangers, and ships, and merchandise ;
 Once peace and freedom blest
 The cultivated plain;
 But wealth, that curse of man,
 Blighted the bud of its prosperity;
Virtue and wisdom, truth and liberty,
Fled, to return not, until man shall know
 That they alone can give the bliss
 Worthy a soul that claims
 Its kindred with eternity. 210

 ' There 's not one atom of yon earth
 But once was living man;
 Nor the minutest drop of rain,
 That hangeth in its thinnest cloud,
 But flowed in human veins;
 And from the burning plains
 Where Libyan monsters yell,
 From the most gloomy glens
 Of Greenland's sunless clime,
 To where the golden fields 220
 Of fertile England spread
 Their harvest to the day,
 Thou canst not find one spot
 Whereon no city stood.

 ' How strange is human pride !
I tell thee that those living things,
To whom the fragile blade of grass
 That springeth in the morn
 And perisheth ere noon,
 Is an unbounded world; 230
I tell thee that those viewless beings,
 Whose mansion is the smallest particle
 Of the impassive atmosphere,

 Think, feel and live like man;
That their affections and antipathies,
 Like his, produce the laws
 Ruling their moral state;
 And the minutest throb
That through their frame diffuses
 The slightest, faintest motion, 240
 Is fixed and indispensable
 As the majestic laws
 That rule yon rolling orbs.'

 The Fairy paused. The Spirit,
In ecstasy of admiration, felt
All knowledge of the past revived; the
 events
 Of old and wondrous times,
Which dim tradition interruptedly
Teaches the credulous vulgar, were un-
 folded
 In just perspective to the view; 250
 Yet dim from their infinitude.
The Spirit seemed to stand
High on an isolated pinnacle;
The flood of ages combating below,
The depth of the unbounded universe
 Above, and all around
 Nature's unchanging harmony.

III

 ' Fairy !' the Spirit said,
 And on the Queen of Spells
 Fixed her ethereal eyes,
 ' I thank thee. Thou hast given
A boon which I will not resign, and taught
A lesson not to be unlearned. I know
The past, and thence I will essay to glean
A warning for the future, so that man
May profit by his errors and derive
 Experience from his folly; 10
For, when the power of imparting joy
Is equal to the will, the human soul
 Requires no other heaven.'

MAB

 ' Turn thee, surpassing Spirit !
 Much yet remains unscanned.
 Thou knowest how great is man,
 Thou knowest his imbecility;
 Yet learn thou what he is;
 Yet learn the lofty destiny
 Which restless Time prepares 20
 For every living soul.

 ' Behold a gorgeous palace that amid
Yon populous city rears its thousand towers

And seems itself a city. Gloomy troops
Of sentinels in stern and silent ranks
Encompass it around; the dweller there
Cannot be free and happy; hearest thou
 not
The curses of the fatherless, the groans
Of those who have no friend? He passes
 on —
The King, the wearer of a gilded chain 30
That binds his soul to abjectness, the fool
Whom courtiers nickname monarch, whilst
 a slave
Even to the basest appetites — that man
Heeds not the shriek of penury; he smiles
At the deep curses which the destitute
Mutter in secret, and a sullen joy
Pervades his bloodless heart when thou-
 sands groan
But for those morsels which his wantonness
Wastes in unjoyous revelry, to save
All that they love from famine ; when he
 hears 40
The tale of horror, to some ready-made
 face
Of hypocritical assent he turns,
Smothering the glow of shame, that, spite
 of him,
Flushes his bloated cheek.

 Now to the meal
Of silence, grandeur and excess he drags
His palled unwilling appetite. If gold,
Gleaming around, and numerous viands
 culled
From every clime could force the loathing
 sense
To overcome satiety, — if wealth
The spring it draws from poisons not, — or
 vice, 50
Unfeeling, stubborn vice, converteth not
Its food to deadliest venom ; then that king
Is happy ; and the peasant who fulfils
His unforced task, when he returns at even
And by the blazing fagot meets again
Her welcome for whom all his toil is sped,
Tastes not a sweeter meal.

 Behold him now
Stretched on the gorgeous couch ; his fe-
 vered brain
Reels dizzily awhile ; but ah ! too soon
The slumber of intemperance subsides, 60
And conscience, that undying serpent, calls
Her venomous brood to their nocturnal
 task.

Listen ! he speaks ! oh ! mark that frenzied
 eye —
Oh ! mark that deadly visage !'

KING

 'No cessation !
Oh ! must this last forever ! Awful death,
I wish, yet fear to clasp thee ! — Not one
 moment
Of dreamless sleep ! O dear and blessèd
 Peace,
Why dost thou shroud thy vestal purity
In penury and dungeons ? Wherefore
 lurkest
With danger, death, and solitude ; yet
 shun'st 70
The palace I have built thee ? Sacred
 Peace !
Oh, visit me but once, — but pitying shed
One drop of balm upon my withered soul !'

THE FAIRY

'Vain man ! that palace is the virtuous
 heart,
And Peace defileth not her snowy robes
In such a shed as thine. Hark ! yet he
 mutters ;
His slumbers are but varied agonies ;
They prey like scorpions on the springs of
 life.
There needeth not the hell that bigots
 frame
To punish those who err ; earth in itself 80
Contains at once the evil and the cure ;
And all-sufficing Nature can chastise
Those who transgress her law ; she only
 knows
How justly to proportion to the fault
The punishment it merits.

 Is it strange
That this poor wretch should pride him in
 his woe ?
Take pleasure in his abjectness, and hug
The scorpion that consumes him ? Is it
 strange
That, placed on a conspicuous throne of
 thorns,
Grasping an iron sceptre, and immured 90
Within a splendid prison whose stern
 bounds
Shut him from all that's good or dear on
 earth,
His soul asserts not its humanity ?
That man's mild nature rises not in war

Against a king's employ ? No — 'tis not
 strange.
He, like the vulgar, thinks, feels, acts, and
 lives
Just as his father did ; the unconquered
 powers
Of precedent and custom interpose
Between a *king* and virtue. Stranger yet,
To those who know not Nature nor de-
 duce 100
The future from the present, it may seem,
That not one slave, who suffers from the
 crimes
Of this unnatural being, not one wretch,
Whose children famish and whose nuptial
 bed
Is earth's unpitying bosom, rears an arm
To dash him from his throne !

 Those gilded flies
That, basking in the sunshine of a court,
Fatten on its corruption ! what are they ? —
The drones of the community ; they feed
On the mechanic's labor ; the starved
 hind 110
For them compels the stubborn glebe to
 yield
Its unshared harvests ; and yon squalid
 form,
Leaner than fleshless misery, that wastes
A sunless life in the unwholesome mine,
Drags out in labor a protracted death
To glut their grandeur ; many faint with
 toil
That few may know the cares and woe of
 sloth.

Whence, thinkest thou, kings and parasites
 arose ?
Whence that unnatural line of drones who
 heap
Toil and unvanquishable penury 120
On those who build their palaces and bring
Their daily bread ? — From vice, black
 loathsome vice ;
From rapine, madness, treachery, and
 wrong ;
From all that genders misery, and makes
Of earth this thorny wilderness ; from lust,
Revenge, and murder. — And when reason's
 voice,
Loud as the voice of Nature, shall have
 waked
The nations ; and mankind perceive that
 vice

Is discord, war and misery ; that virtue
Is peace and happiness and harmony ; 130
When man's maturer nature shall disdain
The playthings of its childhood ; — kingly
 glare
Will lose its power to dazzle ; its authority
Will silently pass by ; the gorgeous throne
Shall stand unnoticed in the regal hall,
Fast falling to decay ; whilst falsehood's
 trade
Shall be as hateful and unprofitable
As that of truth is now.

 Where is the fame
Which the vain-glorious mighty of the earth
Seek to eternize ? Oh ! the faintest
 sound 140
From time's light footfall, the minutest
 wave
That swells the flood of ages, whelms in
 nothing
The unsubstantial bubble. Ay ! to-day
Stern is the tyrant's mandate, red the gaze
That flashes desolation, strong the arm
That scatters multitudes. To - morrow
 comes !
That mandate is a thunder-peal that died
In ages past ; that gaze, a transient flash
On which the midnight closed ; and on that
 arm 149
The worm has made his meal.
 The virtuous man,
Who, great in his humility as kings
Are little in their grandeur; he who leads
Invincibly a life of resolute good
And stands amid the silent dungeon-depths
More free and fearless than the trembling
 judge
Who, clothed in venal power, vainly strove
To bind the impassive spirit; — when he
 falls,
His mild eye beams benevolence no more;
Withered the hand outstretched but to re-
 lieve; 159
Sunk reason's simple eloquence that rolled
But to appall the guilty. Yes! the grave
Hath quenched that eye and death's relent-
 less frost
Withered that arm; but the unfading fame
Which virtue hangs upon its votary's tomb,
The deathless memory of that man whom
 kings
Call to their minds and tremble, the re-
 membrance
With which the happy spirit contemplates

Its well-spent pilgrimage on earth,
Shall never pass away. 169

'Nature rejects the monarch, not the man;
The subject, not the citizen; for kings
And subjects, mutual foes, forever play
A losing game into each other's hands,
Whose stakes are vice and misery. The man
Of virtuous soul commands not, nor obeys.
Power, like a desolating pestilence,
Pollutes whate'er it touches; and obedience,
Bane of all genius, virtue, freedom, truth,
Makes slaves of men, and of the human
 frame 179
A mechanized automaton.

 When Nero
High over flaming Rome with savage joy
Lowered like a fiend, drank with enrap-
 tured ear
The shrieks of agonizing death, beheld
The frightful desolation spread, and felt
A new-created sense within his soul
Thrill to the sight and vibrate to the
 sound, —
Thinkest thou his grandeur had not over-
 come
The force of human kindness? And when
 Rome
With one stern blow hurled not the tyrant
 down,
Crushed not the arm red with her dearest
 blood, 190
Had not submissive abjectness destroyed
Nature's suggestions?

 Look on yonder earth:
The golden harvests spring; the unfailing
 sun
Sheds light and life; the fruits, the flowers,
 the trees,
Arise in due succession; all things speak
Peace, harmony and love. The universe,
In Nature's silent eloquence, declares
That all fulfil the works of love and joy, —
All but the outcast, Man. He fabricates
The sword which stabs his peace; he
 cherisheth 200
The snakes that gnaw his heart; he raiseth
 up
The tyrant whose delight is in his woe,
Whose sport is in his agony. Yon sun,
Lights it the great alone? Yon silver
 beams,
Sleep they less sweetly on the cottage thatch

Than on the dome of kings? Is mother
 earth
A step-dame to her numerous sons who earn
Her unshared gifts with unremitting toil;
A mother only to those puling babes 209
Who, nursed in ease and luxury, make men
The playthings of their babyhood and mar
In self-important childishness that peace
Which men alone appreciate?

 'Spirit of Nature, no!
The pure diffusion of thy essence throbs
Alike in every human heart.
 Thou aye erectest there
Thy throne of power unappealable;
Thou art the judge beneath whose nod
Man's brief and frail authority 220
 Is powerless as the wind
 That passeth idly by;
Thine the tribunal which surpasseth
 The show of human justice
 As God surpasses man!

 'Spirit of Nature! thou
Life of interminable multitudes;
Soul of those mighty spheres
Whose changeless paths through Heaven's
 deep silence lie;
Soul of that smallest being, 230
 The dwelling of whose life
 Is one faint April sun-gleam; —
 Man, like these passive things,
Thy will unconsciously fulfilleth;
Like theirs, his age of endless peace,
 Which time is fast maturing,
 Will swiftly, surely, come;
And the unbounded frame which thou per-
 vadest,
 Will be without a flaw
Marring its perfect symmetry! 240

 IV
'How beautiful this night! the balmiest
 sigh,
Which vernal zephyrs breathe in evening's
 ear,
Were discord to the speaking quietude
That wraps this moveless scene. Heaven's
 ebon vault,
Studded with stars unutterably bright,
Through which the moon's unclouded gran-
 deur rolls,
Seems like a canopy which love had spread
To curtain her sleeping world. Yon gentle
 hills.

Robed in a garment of untrodden snow; 9
Yon darksome rocks, whence icicles depend
So stainless that their white and glittering
　　spires
Tinge not the moon's pure beam ; yon
　　castled steep
Whose banner hangeth o'er the time-worn
　　tower
So idly that rapt fancy deemeth it
A metaphor of peace; — all form a scene
Where musing solitude might love to lift
Her soul above this sphere of earthliness;
Where silence undisturbed might watch
　　alone —
So cold, so bright, so still.

　　　　　　　　　The orb of day
In southern climes o'er ocean's waveless
　　field　　　　　　　　　　　　　　　20
Sinks sweetly smiling ; not the faintest
　　breath
Steals o'er the unruffled deep ; the clouds
　　of eve
Reflect unmoved the lingering beam of day;
And Vesper's image on the western main
Is beautifully still.　To-morrow comes:
Cloud upon cloud, in dark and deepening
　　mass,
Roll o'er the blackened waters; the deep
　　roar
Of distant thunder mutters awfully;
Tempest unfolds its pinion o'er the gloom
That shrouds the boiling surge; the pitiless
　　fiend,　　　　　　　　　　　　　　30
With all his winds and lightnings, tracks
　　his prey;
The torn deep yawns, — the vessel finds a
　　grave
Beneath its jagged gulf.

　　　　　　　　　Ah ! whence yon glare
That fires the arch of heaven ? that dark
　　red smoke
Blotting the silver moon?　The stars are
　　quenched
In darkness, and the pure and spangling
　　snow
Gleams faintly through the gloom that
　　gathers round.
Hark to that roar whose swift and deafen-
　　ing peals
In countless echoes through the mountains
　　ring,
Startling pale Midnight on her starry
　　throne !　　　　　　　　　　　　　40

Now swells the intermingling din; the jar
Frequent and frightful of the bursting
　　bomb;
The falling beam, the shriek, the groan,
　　the shout,
The ceaseless clangor, and the rush of men
Inebriate with rage: — loud and more loud
The discord grows; till pale Death shuts
　　the scene
And o'er the conqueror and the conquered
　　draws
His cold and bloody shroud. — Of all the
　　men
Whom day's departing beam saw blooming
　　there
In proud and vigorous health; of all the
　　hearts　　　　　　　　　　　　　50
That beat with anxious life at sunset there;
How few survive, how few are beating
　　now !
All is deep silence, like the fearful calm
That slumbers in the storm's portentous
　　pause;
Save when the frantic wail of widowed love
Comes shuddering on the blast, or the faint
　　moan
With which some soul bursts from the
　　frame of clay
Wrapt round its struggling powers.

　　　　　　　　　The gray morn
Dawns on the mournful scene; the sulphur-
　　ous smoke
Before the icy wind slow rolls away,　　60
And the bright beams of frosty morning
　　dance
Along the spangling snow.　There tracks
　　of blood
Even to the forest's depth, and scattered
　　arms,
And lifeless warriors, whose hard linea-
　　ments
Death's self could change not, mark the
　　dreadful path
Of the outsallying victors; far behind
Black ashes note where their proud city
　　stood.
Within yon forest is a gloomy glen —
Each tree which guards its darkness from
　　the day,　　　　　　　　　　　　69
Waves o'er a warrior's tomb.

　　　　　　　　　I see thee shrink,
Surpassing Spirit ! — wert thou human
　　else ?

I see a shade of doubt and horror fleet
Across thy stainless features; yet fear not;
This is no unconnected misery,
Nor stands uncaused and irretrievable.
Man's evil nature, that apology
Which kings who rule, and cowards who
 crouch, set up
For their unnumbered crimes, sheds not
 the blood
Which desolates the discord-wasted land.
From kings and priests and statesmen war
 arose, 80
Whose safety is man's deep unbettered
 woe,
Whose grandeur his debasement. Let the
 axe
Strike at the root, the poison-tree will fall;
And where its venomed exhalations spread
Ruin, and death, and woe, where millions
 lay
Quenching the serpent's famine, and their
 bones
Bleaching unburied in the putrid blast,
A garden shall arise, in loveliness
Surpassing fabled Eden.

 Hath Nature's soul, —
That formed this world so beautiful, that
 spread 90
Earth's lap with plenty, and life's smallest
 chord
Strung to unchanging unison, that gave
The happy birds their dwelling in the
 grove,
That yielded to the wanderers of the deep
The lovely silence of the unfathomed main,
And filled the meanest worm that crawls in
 dust
With spirit, thought and love, — on Man
 alone,
Partial in causeless malice, wantonly
Heaped ruin, vice, and slavery; his soul 99
Blasted with withering curses; placed afar
The meteor-happiness, that shuns his grasp,
But serving on the frightful gulf to glare
Rent wide beneath his footsteps?

 Nature! — no!
Kings, priests and statesmen blast the hu-
 man flower
Even in its tender bud; their influence
 darts
Like subtle poison through the bloodless
 veins
Of desolate society. The child,

Ere he can lisp his mother's sacred name,
Swells with the unnatural pride of crime,
 and lifts
His baby-sword even in a hero's mood. 110
This infant arm becomes the bloodiest
 scourge
Of devastated earth; whilst specious names,
Learnt in soft childhood's unsuspecting
 hour,
Serve as the sophisms with which manhood
 dims
Bright reason's ray and sanctifies the sword
Upraised to shed a brother's innocent
 blood.
Let priest-led slaves cease to proclaim that
 man
Inherits vice and misery, when force
And falsehood hang even o'er the cradled
 babe, 119
Stifling with rudest grasp all natural good.

'Ah! to the stranger-soul, when first it
 peeps
From its new tenement and looks abroad
For happiness and sympathy, how stern
And desolate a tract is this wide world!
How withered all the buds of natural good!
No shade, no shelter from the sweeping
 storms
Of pitiless power! On its wretched frame
Poisoned, perchance, by the disease and
 woe
Heaped on the wretched parent whence it
 sprung 129
By morals, law and custom, the pure winds
Of heaven, that renovate the insect tribes,
May breathe not. The untainting light of
 day
May visit not its longings. It is bound
Ere it has life; yea, all the chains are
 forged
Long ere its being; all liberty and love
And peace is torn from its defencelessness;
Cursed from its birth, even from its cradle
 doomed
To abjectness and bondage!

'Throughout this varied and eternal world
Soul is the only element, the block 140
That for uncounted ages has remained.
The moveless pillar of a mountain's weight
Is active living spirit. Every grain
Is sentient both in unity and part,
And the minutest atom comprehends
A world of loves and hatreds; these beget

Evil and good; hence truth and falsehood
 spring;
Hence will and thought and action, all the
 germs
Of pain or pleasure, sympathy or hate,
That variegate the eternal universe. 150
Soul is not more polluted than the beams
Of heaven's pure orb ere round their rapid
 lines
The taint of earth-born atmospheres arise.

' Man is of soul and body, formed for deeds
Of high resolve; on fancy's boldest wing
To soar unwearied, fearlessly to turn
The keenest pangs to peacefulness, and
 taste
The joys which mingled sense and spirit
 yield;
Or he is formed for abjectness and woe,
To grovel on the dunghill of his fears, 160
To shrink at every sound, to quench the
 flame
Of natural love in sensualism, to know
That hour as blest when on his worthless
 days
The frozen hand of death shall set its seal,
Yet fear the cure, though hating the disease.
The one is man that shall hereafter be;
The other, man as vice has made him now.

' War is the statesman's game, the priest's
 delight,
The lawyer's jest, the hired assassin's trade,
And to those royal murderers whose mean
 thrones 170
Are bought by crimes of treachery and gore,
The bread they eat, the staff on which they
 lean.
Guards, garbed in blood-red livery, sur-
 round
Their palaces, participate the crimes
That force defends and from a nation's rage
Secures the crown, which all the curses
 reach
That famine, frenzy, woe and penury
 breathe.
These are the hired bravos who defend
The tyrant's throne—the bullies of his fear;
These are the sinks and channels of worst
 vice, 180
The refuse of society, the dregs
Of all that is most vile; their cold hearts
 blend
Deceit with sternness, ignorance with pride,
All that is mean and villainous with rage

Which hopelessness of good and self-con-
 tempt
Alone might kindle; they are decked in
 wealth,
Honor and power, then are sent abroad
To do their work. The pestilence that
 stalks
In gloomy triumph through some eastern
 land 189
Is less destroying. They cajole with gold
And promises of fame the thoughtless youth
Already crushed with servitude; he knows
His wretchedness too late, and cherishes
Repentance for his ruin, when his doom
Is sealed in gold and blood !
Those too the tyrant serve, who, skilled to
 snare
The feet of justice in the toils of law,
Stand ready to oppress the weaker still,
And right or wrong will vindicate for gold,
Sneering at public virtue, which beneath
Their pitiless tread lies torn and trampled
 where 201
Honor sits smiling at the sale of truth.

' Then grave and hoary-headed hypocrites,
Without a hope, a passion or a love,
Who through a life of luxury and lies
Have crept by flattery to the seats of power,
Support the system whence their honors
 flow.
They have three words — well tyrants know
 their use,
Well pay them for the loan with usury
Torn from a bleeding world ! — God, Hell
 and Heaven: 210
A vengeful, pitiless, and almighty fiend,
Whose mercy is a nickname for the rage
Of tameless tigers hungering for blood;
Hell, a red gulf of everlasting fire,
Where poisonous and undying worms pro-
 long
Eternal misery to those hapless slaves
Whose life has been a penance for its
 crimes;
And Heaven, a meed for those who dare
 belie
Their human nature, quake, believe and
 cringe
Before the mockeries of earthly power. 220

' These tools the tyrant tempers to his
 work,
Wields in his wrath, and as he wills de-
 stroys,

Omnipotent in wickedness; the while
Youth springs, age moulders, manhood
 tamely does
His bidding, bribed by short-lived joys to
 lend
Force to the weakness of his trembling
 arm.
They rise, they fall; one generation comes
Yielding its harvest to destruction's scythe.
It fades, another blossoms; yet behold !
Red glows the tyrant's stamp-mark on its
 bloom, 230
Withering and cankering deep its passive
 prime.
He has invented lying words and modes,
Empty and vain as his own coreless heart;
Evasive meanings, nothings of much sound,
To lure the heedless victim to the toils
Spread round the valley of its paradise.

'Look to thyself, priest, conqueror or
 prince!
Whether thy trade is falsehood, and thy
 lusts
Deep wallow in the earnings of the poor,
With whom thy master was; or thou de-
 light'st 240
In numbering o'er the myriads of thy slain,
All misery weighing nothing in the scale
Against thy short-lived fame; or thou dost
 load
With cowardice and crime the groaning
 land,
A pomp-fed king. Look to thy wretched
 self !
Ay, art thou not the veriest slave that e'er
Crawled on the loathing earth ? Are not
 thy days
Days of unsatisfying listlessness ?
Dost thou not cry, ere night's long rack is
 o'er,
" When will the morning come ? " Is not
 thy youth 250
A vain and feverish dream of sensualism ?
Thy manhood blighted with unripe disease ?
Are not thy views of unregretted death
Drear, comfortless and horrible ? Thy
 mind,
Is it not morbid as thy nerveless frame,
Incapable of judgment, hope or love ?
And dost thou wish the errors to survive,
That bar thee from all sympathies of good,
After the miserable interest
Thou hold'st in their protraction ? When
 the grave 260

Has swallowed up thy memory and thyself,
Dost thou desire the bane that poisons
 earth
To twine its roots around thy coffined clay,
Spring from thy bones, and blossom on thy
 tomb,
That of its fruit thy babes may eat and
 die ?

V

'Thus do the generations of the earth
Go to the grave and issue from the womb,
Surviving still the imperishable change
That renovates the world ; even as the
 leaves
Which the keen frost-wind of the waning
 year
Has scattered on the forest-soil and heaped
For many seasons there — though long they
 choke,
Loading with loathsome rottenness the land,
All germs of promise, yet when the tall
 trees
From which they fell, shorn of their lovely
 shapes, 10
Lie level with the earth to moulder there,
They fertilize the land they long deformed;
Till from the breathing lawn a forest
 springs
Of youth, integrity and loveliness,
Like that which gave it life, to spring and
 die.
Thus suicidal selfishness, that blights
The fairest feelings of the opening heart,
Is destined to decay, whilst from the soil
Shall spring all virtue, all delight, all love,
And judgment cease to wage unnatural
 war 20
With passion's unsubduable array.
Twin-sister of Religion, Selfishness !
Rival in crime and falsehood, aping all
The wanton horrors of her bloody play;
Yet frozen, unimpassioned, spiritless,
Shunning the light, and owning not its
 name,
Compelled by its deformity to screen
With flimsy veil of justice and of right
Its unattractive lineaments that scare
All save the brood of ignorance; at once 30
The cause and the effect of tyranny;
Unblushing, hardened, sensual and vile;
Dead to all love but of its abjectness,
With heart impassive by more noble powers
Than unshared pleasure, sordid gain, or
 fame;

Despising its own miserable being,
Which still it longs, yet fears, to disen-
thrall.

'Hence commerce springs, the venal inter-
change
Of all that human art or Nature yield ;
Which wealth should purchase not, but
want demand, 40
And natural kindness hasten to supply
From the full fountain of its boundless
love,
Forever stifled, drained and tainted now.
Commerce ! beneath whose poison-breath-
ing shade
No solitary virtue dares to spring,
But poverty and wealth with equal hand
Scatter their withering curses, and unfold
The doors of premature and violent death
To pining famine and full-fed disease,
To all that shares the lot of human life, 50
Which, poisoned body and soul, scarce
drags the chain
That lengthens as it goes and clanks be-
hind.

'Commerce has set the mark of selfishness,
The signet of its all-enslaving power,
Upon a shining ore, and called it gold ;
Before whose image bow the vulgar great,
The vainly rich, the miserable proud,
The mob of peasants, nobles, priests and
kings,
And with blind feelings reverence the
power
That grinds them to the dust of misery. 60
But in the temple of their hireling hearts
Gold is a living god and rules in scorn
All earthly things but virtue.

'Since tyrants by the sale of human life
Heap luxuries to their sensualism, and
fame
To their wide-wasting and insatiate pride,
Success has sanctioned to a credulous world
The ruin, the disgrace, the woe of war.
His hosts of blind and unresisting dupes
The despot numbers ; from his cabinet 70
These puppets of his schemes he moves at
will,
Even as the slaves by force or famine
driven,
Beneath a vulgar master, to perform
A task of cold and brutal drudgery ;—
Hardened to hope, insensible to fear,

Scarce living pulleys of a dead machine,
Mere wheels of work and articles of trade,
That grace the proud and noisy pomp of
wealth !

'The harmony and happiness of man
Yields to the wealth of nations; that which
lifts 80
His nature to the heaven of its pride,
Is bartered for the poison of his soul;
The weight that drags to earth his tower-
ing hopes,
Blighting all prospect but of selfish gain,
Withering all passion but of slavish fear,
Extinguishing all free and generous love
Of enterprise and daring, even the pulse
That fancy kindles in the beating heart
To mingle with sensation, it destroys,—
Leaves nothing but the sordid lust of
self, 90
The grovelling hope of interest and gold,
Unqualified, unmingled, unredeemed
Even by hypocrisy.

 And statesmen boast
Of wealth ! The wordy eloquence that
lives
After the ruin of their hearts, can gild
The bitter poison of a nation's woe;
Can turn the worship of the servile mob
To their corrupt and glaring idol, fame,
From virtue, trampled by its iron tread,—
Although its dazzling pedestal be raised 100
Amid the horrors of a limb-strewn field,
With desolated dwellings smoking round.
The man of ease, who, by his warm fire-
side,
To deeds of charitable intercourse
And bare fulfilment of the common laws
Of decency and prejudice confines
The struggling nature of his human heart,
Is duped by their cold sophistry; he sheds
A passing tear perchance upon the wreck
Of earthly peace, when near his dwelling's
door 110
The frightful waves are driven,—when his
son
Is murdered by the tyrant, or religion
Drives his wife raving mad. But the poor
man
Whose life is misery, and fear and care;
Whom the morn wakens but to fruitless
toil;
Who ever hears his famished offspring's
scream;

Whom their pale mother's uncomplaining
 gaze
Forever meets, and the proud rich man's
 eye
Flashing command, and the heart-breaking
 scene
Of thousands like himself ; — he little heeds
The rhetoric of tyranny ; his hate 121
Is quenchless as his wrongs ; he laughs to
 scorn
The vain and bitter mockery of words,
Feeling the horror of the tyrant's deeds,
And unrestrained but by the arm of power,
That knows and dreads his enmity.

' The iron rod of penury still compels
Her wretched slave to bow the knee to
 wealth,
And poison, with unprofitable toil,
A life too void of solace to confirm 130
The very chains that bind him to his doom.
Nature, impartial in munificence,
Has gifted man with all-subduing will.
Matter, with all its transitory shapes,
Lies subjected and plastic at his feet,
That, weak from bondage, tremble as they
 tread.
How many a rustic Milton has passed by,
Stifling the speechless longings of his heart,
In unremitting drudgery and care !
How many a vulgar Cato has compelled 140
His energies, no longer tameless then,
To mould a pin or fabricate a nail !
How many a Newton, to whose passive ken
Those mighty spheres that gem infinity
Were only specks of tinsel fixed in heaven
To light the midnights of his native town !

' Yet every heart contains perfection's
 germ.
The wisest of the sages of the earth,
That ever from the stores of reason drew
Science and truth, and virtue's dreadless
 tone, 150
Were but a weak and inexperienced boy,
Proud, sensual, unimpassioned, unimbued
With pure desire and universal love,
Compared to that high being, of cloudless
 brain,
Untainted passion, elevated will,
Which death (who even would linger long
 in awe
Within his noble presence and beneath
His changeless eye-beam) might alone sub-
 due.

Him, every slave now dragging through
 the filth
Of some corrupted city his sad life, 160
Pining with famine, swoln with luxury,
Blunting the keenness of his spiritual sense
With narrow schemings and unworthy
 cares,
Or madly rushing through all violent crime
To move the deep stagnation of his soul, —
Might imitate and equal.

 But mean lust
Has bound its chains so tight about the
 earth
That all within it but the virtuous man
Is venal ; gold or fame will surely reach
The price prefixed by Selfishness to all 170
But him of resolute and unchanging will ;
Whom nor the plaudits of a servile crowd,
Nor the vile joys of tainting luxury,
Can bribe to yield his elevated soul
To Tyranny or Falsehood, though they
 wield
With blood-red hand the sceptre of the
 world.

' All things are sold : the very light of
 heaven
Is venal ; earth's unsparing gifts of love,
The smallest and most despicable things
That lurk in the abysses of the deep, 180
All objects of our life, even life itself,
And the poor pittance which the laws al-
 low
Of liberty, the fellowship of man,
Those duties which his heart of human love
Should urge him to perform instinctively,
Are bought and sold as in a public mart
Of undisguising Selfishness, that sets
On each its price, the stamp-mark of her
 reign.
Even love is sold ; the solace of all woe
Is turned to deadliest agony, old age 190
Shivers in selfish beauty's loathing arms,
And youth's corrupted impulses prepare
A life of horror from the blighting bane
Of commerce ; whilst the pestilence that
 springs
From unenjoying sensualism, has filled
All human life with hydra-headed woes.

' Falsehood demands but gold to pay the
 pangs
Of outraged conscience; for the slavish
 priest

Sets no great value on his hireling faith ;
A little passing pomp, some servile
 souls, 200
Whom cowardice itself might safely chain
Or the spare mite of avarice could bribe
To deck the triumph of their languid zeal,
Can make him minister to tyranny.
More daring crime requires a loftier meed.
Without a shudder the slave-soldier lends
His arm to murderous deeds, and steels his
 heart,
When the dread eloquence of dying men,
Low mingling on the lonely field of fame,
Assails that nature whose applause he
 sel'fs 210
For the gross blessings of the patriot mob,
For the vile gratitude of heartless kings,
And for a cold world's good word, — viler
 still !

' There is a nobler glory which survives
Until our being fades, and, solacing
All human care, accompanies its change;
Deserts not virtue in the dungeon's gloom,
And in the precincts of the palace guides
Its footsteps through that labyrinth of
 crime ;
Imbues his lineaments with dauntless-
 ness, 220
Even when from power's avenging hand he
 takes
Its sweetest, last and noblest title — death ;
— The consciousness of good, which neither
 gold,
Nor sordid fame, nor hope of heavenly
 bliss,
Can purchase ; but a life of resolute good,
Unalterable will, quenchless desire
Of universal happiness, the heart
That beats with it in unison, the brain
Whose ever-wakeful wisdom toils to change
Reason's rich stores for its eternal weal. 230

' This commerce of sincerest virtue needs
No meditative signs of selfishness,
No jealous intercourse of wretched gain,
No balancings of prudence, cold and long ;
In just and equal measure all is weighed,
One scale contains the sum of human weal,
And one, the good man's heart.

 How vainly seek
The selfish for that happiness denied
To aught but virtue ! Blind and hardened,
 they,

Who hope for peace amid the storms of
 care, 240
Who covet power they know not how to
 use,
And sigh for pleasure they refuse to give, —
Madly they frustrate still their own de-
 signs;
And, where they hope that quiet to en-
 joy
Which virtue pictures, bitterness of soul,
Pining regrets, and vain repentances,
Disease, disgust and lassitude pervade
Their valueless and miserable lives.

' But hoary-headed selfishness has felt
Its death-blow and is tottering to the
 grave; 250
A brighter morn awaits the human day,
When every transfer of earth's natural
 gifts
Shall be a commerce of good words and
 works;
When poverty and wealth, the thirst of
 fame,
The fear of infamy, disease and woe,
War with its million horrors, and fierce
 hell,
Shall live but in the memory of time,
Who, like a penitent libertine, shall start,
Look back, and shudder at his younger
 years.'

VI

All touch, all eye, all ear,
The Spirit felt the Fairy's burning speech.
O'er the thin texture of its frame
The varying periods painted changing
 glows,
 As on a summer even,
When soul-enfolding music floats around,
 The stainless mirror of the lake
 Re-images the eastern gloom,
Mingling convulsively its purple hues
 With sunset's burnished gold. 10
 Then thus the Spirit spoke :
' It is a wild and miserable world !
 Thorny, and full of care,
Which every fiend can make his prey at
 will !
 O Fairy ! in the lapse of years,
 Is there no hope in store ?
 Will yon vast suns roll on
 Interminably, still illuming
 The night of so many wretched souls,
 And see no hope for them ? 20

Will not the universal Spirit e'er
Revivify this withered limb of Heaven?'

 The Fairy calmly smiled
In comfort, and a kindling gleam of hope
Suffused the Spirit's lineaments.
'Oh! rest thee tranquil; chase those fear-
 ful doubts
Which ne'er could rack an everlasting soul
That sees the chains which bind it to its
 doom.
Yes! crime and misery are in yonder earth,
 Falsehood, mistake and lust; 30
 But the eternal world
Contains at once the evil and the cure.
Some eminent in virtue shall start up,
 Even in perversest time;
The truths of their pure lips, that never
 die,
Shall bind the scorpion falsehood with a
 wreath
 Of ever-living flame,
Until the monster sting itself to death.

 'How sweet a scene will earth become!
Of purest spirits a pure dwelling-place, 40
Symphonious with the planetary spheres;
When man, with changeless Nature coa-
 lescing,
Will undertake regeneration's work,
When its ungenial poles no longer point
 To the red and baleful sun
 That faintly twinkles there!

 'Spirit, on yonder earth,
Falsehood now triumphs; deadly power
Has fixed its seal upon the lip of truth!
 Madness and misery are there! 50
The happiest is most wretched! Yet con-
 fide
Until pure health-drops from the cup of
 joy
Fall like a dew of balm upon the world.
Now, to the scene I show, in silence turn,
And read the blood-stained charter of all
 woe,
Which Nature soon with recreating hand
Will blot in mercy from the book of earth.
How bold the flight of passion's wandering
 wing,
How swift the step of reason's firmer tread,
How calm and sweet the victories of life,
How terrorless the triumph of the grave!
How powerless were the mightiest mon-
 arch's arm, 62

Vain his loud threat, and impotent his
 frown!
How ludicrous the priest's dogmatic roar!
The weight of his exterminating curse
How light! and his affected charity,
To suit the pressure of the changing times,
What palpable deceit!—but for thy aid,
Religion! but for thee, prolific fiend,
Who peoplest earth with demons, hell with
 men, 70
And heaven with slaves!

'Thou taintest all thou lookest upon!—
 the stars,
Which on thy cradle beamed so brightly
 sweet,
Were gods to the distempered playfulness
Of thy untutored infancy; the trees,
The grass, the clouds, the mountains and the
 sea,
All living things that walk, swim, creep or
 fly,
Were gods; the sun had homage, and the
 moon
Her worshipper. Then thou becamest, a
 boy, 79
More daring in thy frenzies; every shape,
Monstrous or vast, or beautifully wild,
Which from sensation's relics fancy culls,
The spirits of the air, the shuddering ghost,
The genii of the elements, the powers
That give a shape to Nature's varied
 works,
Had life and place in the corrupt belief
Of thy blind heart; yet still thy youthful
 hands
Were pure of human blood. Then man-
 hood gave
Its strength and ardor to thy frenzied
 brain;
Thine eager gaze scanned the stupendous
 scene, 90
Whose wonders mocked the knowledge of
 thy pride;
Their everlasting and unchanging laws
Reproached thine ignorance. Awhile thou
 stood'st
Baffled and gloomy; then thou didst sum
 up
The elements of all that thou didst know;
The changing seasons, winter's leafless
 reign,
The budding of the heaven-breathing trees,
The eternal orbs that beautify the night,
The sunrise, and the setting of the moon,

Earthquakes and wars, and poisons and
disease, 100
And all their causes, to an abstract point
Converging thou didst bend, and called it
God !
The self-sufficing, the omnipotent,
The merciful, and the avenging God !
Who, prototype of human misrule, sits
High in heaven's realm, upon a golden
throne,
Even like an earthly king; and whose dread
work,
Hell, gapes forever for the unhappy slaves
Of fate, whom he created in his sport
To triumph in their torments when they
fell ! 110
Earth heard the name; earth trembled as
the smoke
Of his revenge ascended up to heaven,
Blotting the constellations; and the cries
Of millions butchered in sweet confidence
And unsuspecting peace, even when the
bonds
Of safety were confirmed by wordy oaths
Sworn in his dreadful name, rung through
the land;
Whilst innocent babes writhed on thy stub-
born spear,
And thou didst laugh to hear the mother's
shriek
Of maniac gladness, as the sacred steel 120
Felt cold in her torn entrails !

'Religion ! thou wert then in manhood's
prime;
But age crept on; one God would not suf-
fice
For senile puerility; thou framedst
A tale to suit thy dotage and to glut
Thy misery-thirsting soul, that the mad
fiend
Thy wickedness had pictured might afford
A plea for sating the unnatural thirst
For murder, rapine, violence and crime, 129
That still consumed thy being, even when
Thou heard'st the step of fate; that flames
might light
Thy funeral scene; and the shrill horrent
shrieks
Of parents dying on the pile that burned
To light their children to thy paths, the roar
Of the encircling flames, the exulting cries
Of thine apostles loud commingling there,
Might sate thine hungry ear
Even on the bed of death !

'But now contempt is mocking thy gray
hairs;
Thou art descending to the darksome
grave, 140
Unhonored and unpitied but by those
Whose pride is passing by like thine, and
sheds,
Like thine, a glare that fades before the
sun
Of truth, and shines but in the dreadful
night
That long has lowered above the ruined
world.

'Throughout these infinite orbs of mingling
light
Of which yon earth is one, is wide diffused
A Spirit of activity and life,
That knows no term, cessation or decay;
That fades not when the lamp of earthly
life, 150
Extinguished in the dampness of the grave,
Awhile there slumbers, more than when
the babe
In the dim newness of its being feels
The impulses of sublunary things,
And all is wonder to unpractised sense;
But, active, steadfast and eternal, still
Guides the fierce whirlwind, in the tempest
roars,
Cheers in the day, breathes in the balmy
groves,
Strengthens in health, and poisons in dis-
ease;
And in the storm of change, that cease-
lessly 160
Rolls round the eternal universe and shakes
Its undecaying battlement, presides,
Apportioning with irresistible law
The place each spring of its machine shall
fill;
So that, when waves on waves tumultuous
heap
Confusion to the clouds, and fiercely driven
Heaven's lightnings scorch the uprooted
ocean-fords —
Whilst, to the eye of shipwrecked mariner,
Lone sitting on the bare and shuddering
rock,
All seems unlinked contingency and
chance — 170
No atom of this turbulence fulfils
A vague and unnecessitated task
Or acts but as it must and ought to act.
Even the minutest molecule of light,

That in an April sunbeam's fleeting glow
Fulfils its destined though invisible work,
The universal Spirit guides; nor less
When merciless ambition, or mad zeal,
Has led two hosts of dupes to battle-field,
That, blind, they there may dig each other's
 graves 180
And call the sad work glory, does it rule
All passions; not a thought, a will, an
 act,
No working of the tyrant's moody mind,
Nor one misgiving of the slaves who boast
Their servitude to hide the shame they
 feel,
Nor the events enchaining every will,
That from the depths of unrecorded time
Have drawn all-influencing virtue, pass
Unrecognized or unforeseen by thee,
Soul of the Universe! eternal spring 190
Of life and death, of happiness and woe,
Of all that chequers the phantasmal scene
That floats before our eyes in wavering
 light,
Which gleams but on the darkness of our
 prison
 Whose chains and massy walls
 We feel but cannot see.

'Spirit of Nature! all-sufficing Power,
Necessity! thou mother of the world!
Unlike the God of human error, thou
Requirest no prayers or praises; the ca-
 price 200
Of man's weak will belongs no more to
 thee
Than do the changeful passions of his
 breast
To thy unvarying harmony; the slave,
Whose horrible lusts spread misery o'er
 the world,
And the good man, who lifts with virtuous
 pride
His being in the sight of happiness
That springs from his own works; the
 poison-tree,
Beneath whose shade all life is withered
 up,
And the fair oak, whose leafy dome affords
A temple where the vows of happy love 210
Are registered, are equal in thy sight;
No love, no hate thou cherishest; revenge
And favoritism, and worst desire of fame
Thou knowest not; all that the wide world
 contains
Are but thy passive instruments, and thou

Regard'st them all with an impartial eye,
Whose joy or pain thy nature cannot feel,
 Because thou hast not human sense,
 Because thou art not human mind.

'Yes! when the sweeping storm of
 time 220
Has sung its death-dirge o'er the ruined
 fanes
And broken altars of the almighty fiend,
Whose name usurps thy honors, and the
 blood
Through centuries clotted there has floated
 down
The tainted flood of ages, shalt thou live
Unchangeable! A shrine is raised to thee,
Which nor the tempest breath of time,
Nor the interminable flood
Over earth's slight pageant rolling,
 Availeth to destroy, — 230
The sensitive extension of the world;
 That wondrous and eternal fane,
Where pain and pleasure, good and evil
 join,
To do the will of strong necessity,
 And life, in multitudinous shapes,
Still pressing forward where no term can be,
 Like hungry and unresting flame
Curls round the eternal columns of its
 strength.'

VII

SPIRIT

'I was an infant when my mother went
To see an atheist burned. She took me
 there.
The dark-robed priests were met around
 the pile;
The multitude was gazing silently;
And as the culprit passed with dauntless
 mien,
Tempered disdain in his unaltering eye,
Mixed with a quiet smile, shone calmly
 forth;
The thirsty fire crept round his manly
 limbs;
His resolute eyes were scorched to blind-
 ness soon;
His death-pang rent my heart! the insen-
 sate mob 10
Uttered a cry of triumph, and I wept
"Weep not, child!" cried my mother, "for
 that man
Has said, There is no God."'

FAIRY

'There is no God!
Nature confirms the faith his death-groan
 sealed.
Let heaven and earth, let man's revolving
 race,
His ceaseless generations, tell their tale;
Let every part depending on the chain
That links it to the whole, point to the
 hand
That grasps its term! Let every seed that
 falls
In silent eloquence unfold its store 20
Of argument; infinity within,
Infinity without, belie creation;
The exterminable spirit it contains
Is Nature's only God; but human pride
Is skilful to invent most serious names
To hide its ignorance.

 ' The name of God
Has fenced about all crime with holiness,
Himself the creature of his worshippers,
Whose names and attributes and passions
 change, 29
Seeva, Buddh, Foh, Jehovah, God, or Lord,
Even with the human dupes who build his
 shrines,
Still serving o'er the war-polluted world
For desolation's watchword; whether hosts
Stain his death-blushing chariot-wheels, as
 on
Triumphantly they roll, whilst Brahmins
 raise
A sacred hymn to mingle with the groans;
Or countless partners of his power divide
His tyranny to weakness; or the smoke
Of burning towns, the cries of female help-
 lessness, 39
Unarmed old age, and youth, and infancy,
Horribly massacred, ascend to heaven
In honor of his name; or, last and worst,
Earth groans beneath religion's iron age,
And priests dare babble of a God of peace,
Even whilst their hands are red with guilt-
 less blood,
Murdering the while, uprooting every germ
Of truth, exterminating, spoiling all,
Making the earth a slaughter-house!

 ' O Spirit! through the sense
By which thy inner nature was apprised 50
Of outward shows, vague dreams have
 rolled,
And varied reminiscences have waked

 Tablets that never fade;
All things have been imprinted there,
The stars, the sea, the earth, the sky,
Even the unshapeliest lineaments
 Of wild and fleeting visions
 Have left a record there
 To testify of earth.

' These are my empire, for to me is given 60
The wonders of the human world to keep,
And fancy's thin creations to endow
With manner, being and reality;
Therefore a wondrous phantom from the
 dreams
Of human error's dense and purblind faith
I will evoke, to meet thy questioning.
 Ahasuerus, rise!'

 A strange and woe-worn wight
 Arose beside the battlement,
 And stood unmoving there. 70
His inessential figure cast no shade
 Upon the golden floor;
His port and mien bore mark of many
 years,
And chronicles of untold ancientness
Were legible within his beamless eye;
Yet his cheek bore the mark of youth;
Freshness and vigor knit his manly frame;
The wisdom of old age was mingled there
 With youth's primeval dauntlessness;
 And inexpressible woe, 80
Chastened by fearless resignation, gave
An awful grace to his all-speaking brow.

SPIRIT

'Is there a God ? '

AHASUERUS

'Is there a God!—ay, an almighty God,
And vengeful as almighty! Once his voice
Was heard on earth; earth shuddered at
 the sound;
The fiery-visaged firmament expressed
Abhorrence, and the grave of Nature
 yawned
To swallow all the dauntless and the good
That dared to hurl defiance at his throne,
Girt as it was with power. None but
 slaves 91
Survived,—cold-blooded slaves, who did
 the work
Of tyrannous omnipotence; whose souls
No honest indignation ever urged
To elevated daring, to one deed

Which gross and sensual self did not pol-
lute.
These slaves built temples for the omnipo-
tent fiend,
Gorgeous and vast; the costly altars smoked
With human blood, and hideous pæans rung
Through all the long-drawn aisles. A mur-
derer heard 100
His voice in Egypt, one whose gifts and arts
Had raised him to his eminence in power,
Accomplice of omnipotence in crime
And confidant of the all-knowing one.
 These were Jehovah's words.

'" From an eternity of idleness
I, God, awoke ; in seven days' toil made
earth
From nothing; rested, and created man;
I placed him in a paradise, and there
Planted the tree of evil, so that he 110
Might eat and perish, and my soul procure
Wherewith to sate its malice and to turn,
Even like a heartless conqueror of the
earth,
All misery to my fame. The race of men,
Chosen to my honor, with impunity
May sate the lusts I planted in their heart.
Here I command thee hence to lead them
on,
Until with hardened feet their conquering
troops
Wade on the promised soil through wo-
man's blood,
And make my name be dreaded through
the land. 120
Yet ever-burning flame and ceaseless woe
Shall be the doom of their eternal souls,
With every soul on this ungrateful earth,
Virtuous or vicious, weak or strong, —
even all
Shall perish, to fulfil the blind revenge
(Which you, to men, call justice) of their
God.''

 ' The murderer's brow
Quivered with horror.

 '" God omnipotent,
Is there no mercy ? must our punishment
Be endless ? will long ages roll away, 130
And see no term ? Oh ! wherefore hast
thou made
In mockery and wrath this evil earth ?
Mercy becomes the powerful — be but just !
O God ! repent and save !"

 '" One way remains:
I will beget a son and he shall bear
The sins of all the world; he shall arise
In an unnoticed corner of the earth,
And there shall die upon a cross, and purge
The universal crime; so that the few
On whom my grace descends, those who are
marked 140
As vessels to the honor of their God,
May credit this strange sacrifice and save
Their souls alive. Millions shall live and
die,
Who ne'er shall call upon their Saviour's
name,
But, unredeemed, go to the gaping grave,
Thousands shall deem it an old woman's
tale,
Such as the nurses frighten babes withal;
These in a gulf of anguish and of flame
Shall curse their reprobation endlessly,
Yet tenfold pangs shall force them to
avow, 150
Even on their beds of torment where they
howl,
My honor and the justice of their doom.
What then avail their virtuous deeds, their
thoughts
Of purity, with radiant genius bright
Or lit with human reason's earthly ray ?
Many are called, but few will I elect.
Do thou my bidding, Moses !"

 ' Even the murderer's cheek
Was blanched with horror, and his quiver-
ing lips
Scarce faintly uttered — " O almighty one,
I tremble and obey !" 160

'O Spirit ! centuries have set their seal
On this heart of many wounds, and loaded
brain,
Since the Incarnate came ; humbly he came,
Veiling his horrible Godhead in the shape
Of man, scorned by the world, his name
unheard
Save by the rabble of his native town,
Even as a parish demagogue. He led
The crowd ; he taught them justice, truth
and peace,
In semblance ; but he lit within their souls
The quenchless flames of zeal, and blessed
the sword 170
He brought on earth to satiate with the
blood
Of truth and freedom his malignant soul

At length his mortal frame was led to
 death.
I stood beside him; on the torturing cross
No pain assailed his unterrestrial sense;
And yet he groaned. Indignantly I summed
The massacres and miseries which his name
Had sanctioned in my country, and I cried,
"Go ! go !" in mockery.
A smile of godlike malice reillumined 180
His fading lineaments. "I go," he cried,
"But thou shalt wander o'er the unquiet
 earth
Eternally." The dampness of the grave
Bathed my imperishable front. I fell,
And long lay tranced upon the charmèd
 soil.
When I awoke hell burned within my brain
Which staggered on its seat; for all around
The mouldering relics of my kindred lay,
Even as the Almighty's ire arrested them,
And in their various attitudes of death 190
My murdered children's mute and eyeless
 skulls
Glared ghastily upon me.

 But my soul,
From sight and sense of the polluting woe
Of tyranny, had long learned to prefer
Hell's freedom to the servitude of heaven.
Therefore I rose, and dauntlessly began
My lonely and unending pilgrimage,
Resolved to wage unweariable war
With my almighty tyrant and to hurl
Defiance at his impotence to harm 200
Beyond the curse I bore. The very hand,
That barred my passage to the peaceful
 grave,
Has crushed the earth to misery, and given
Its empire to the chosen of his slaves.
These I have seen, even from the earliest
 dawn
Of weak, unstable and precarious power,
Then preaching peace, as now they practise
 war;
So, when they turned but from the mas-
 sacre
Of unoffending infidels to quench
Their thirst for ruin in the very blood 210
That flowed in their own veins, and pitiless
 zeal
Froze every human feeling as the wife
Sheathed in her husband's heart the sacred
 steel,
Even whilst its hopes were dreaming of her
 love;

And friends to friends, brothers to brothers
 stood
Opposed in bloodiest battle-field, and war,
Scarce satiable by fate's last death-draught,
 waged,
Drunk from the wine-press of the Al-
 mighty's wrath;
Whilst the red cross, in mockery of peace,
Pointed to victory! When the fray was
 done, 220
No remnant of the exterminated faith
Survived to tell its ruin, but the flesh,
With putrid smoke poisoning the atmo-
 sphere,
That rotted on the half-extinguished pile.

'Yes ! I have seen God's worshippers un-
 sheathe
The sword of his revenge, when grace de-
 scended,
Confirming all unnatural impulses,
To sanctify their desolating deeds;
And frantic priests waved the ill-omened
 cross
O'er the unhappy earth ; then shone the
 sun 230
On showers of gore from the upflashing
 steel
Of safe assassination, and all crime
Made stingless by the spirits of the Lord,
And blood-red rainbows canopied the land.

'Spirit! no year of my eventful being
Has passed unstained by crime and misery,
Which flows from God's own faith. I've
 marked his slaves
With tongues, whose lies are venomous,
 beguile
The insensate mob, and, whilst one hand
 was red 239
With murder, feign to stretch the other out
For brotherhood and peace; and that they
 now
Babble of love and mercy, whilst their deeds
Are marked with all the narrowness and
 crime
That freedom's young arm dare not yet
 chastise,
Reason may claim our gratitude, who now,
Establishing the imperishable throne
Of truth and stubborn virtue, maketh vain
The unprevailing malice of my foe,
Whose bootless rage heaps torments for the
 brave,
Adds impotent eternities to pain, 250

Whilst keenest disappointment racks his
 breast
To see the smiles of peace around them
 play,
To frustrate or to sanctify their doom.

'Thus have I stood, — through a wild waste
 of years
Struggling with whirlwinds of mad agony,
Yet peaceful, and serene, and self-en-
 shrined,
Mocking my powerless tyrant's horrible
 curse
With stubborn and unalterable will,
Even as a giant oak, which heaven's fierce
 flame
Had scathèd in the wilderness, to stand 260
A monument of fadeless ruin there;
Yet peacefully and movelessly it braves
The midnight conflict of the wintry storm,
 As in the sunlight's calm it spreads
 Its worn and withered arms on high
To meet the quiet of a summer's noon.'

 The Fairy waved her wand;
 Ahasuerus fled
Fast as the shapes of mingled shade and
 mist, 269
That lurk in the glens of a twilight grove,
 Flee from the morning beam; —
 The matter of which dreams are made
 Not more endowed with actual life
 Than this phantasmal portraiture
 Of wandering human thought.

VIII

THE FAIRY

'The present and the past thou hast beheld.
It was a desolate sight. Now, Spirit, learn,
 The secrets of the future. — Time!
Unfold the brooding pinion of thy gloom,
Render thou up thy half-devoured babes,
And from the cradles of eternity,
Where millions lie lulled to their portioned
 sleep
By the deep murmuring stream of passing
 things,
Tear thou that gloomy shroud. — Spirit,
 behold
 Thy glorious destiny!' 10

 Joy to the Spirit came.
Through the wide rent in Time's eternal
 veil,

Hope was seen beaming through the mists
 of fear;
 Earth was no longer hell;
 Love, freedom, health had given
Their ripeness to the manhood of its prime,
 And all its pulses beat
Symphonious to the planetary spheres;
 Then dulcet music swelled 19
Concordant with the life-strings of the soul;
It throbbed in sweet and languid beatings
 there,
Catching new life from transitory death;
Like the vague sighings of a wind at even
That wakes the wavelets of the slumbering
 sea
And dies on the creation of its breath,
And sinks and rises, falls and swells by
 fits,
 Was the pure stream of feeling
 That sprung from these sweet notes,
And o'er the Spirit's human sympathies 29
With mild and gentle motion calmly flowed.

 Joy to the Spirit came, —
 Such joy as when a lover sees
The chosen of his soul in happiness
 And witnesses her peace
Whose woe to him were bitterer than death;
 Sees her unfaded cheek
Glow mantling in first luxury of health,
 Thrills with her lovely eyes,
Which like two stars amid the heaving
 main
 Sparkle through liquid bliss. 40

Then in her triumph spoke the Fairy Queen
'I will not call the ghost of ages gone
To unfold the frightful secrets of its
 lore;
 The present now is past,
And those events that desolate the earth
Have faded from the memory of Time,
Who dares not give reality to that
Whose being I annul. To me is given
The wonders of the human world to keep,
Space, matter, time and mind. Futurity 50
Exposes now its treasure; let the sight
Renew and strengthen all thy failing hope.
O human Spirit! spur thee to the goal
Where virtue fixes universal peace,
And, 'midst the ebb and flow of human
 things,
Show somewhat stable, somewhat certain
 still,
A light-house o'er the wild of dreary waves,

'The habitable earth is full of bliss;
Those wastes of frozen billows that were
 hurled
By everlasting snow-storms round the
 poles, 60
Where matter dared not vegetate or live,
But ceaseless frost round the vast solitude
Bound its broad zone of stillness, are un-
 loosed;
And fragrant zephyrs there from spicy
 isles
Ruffle the placid ocean-deep, that rolls
Its broad, bright surges to the sloping sand,
Whose roar is wakened into echoings sweet
To murmur through the heaven-breathing
 groves
And melodize with man's blest nature
 there.

'Those deserts of immeasurable sand, 70
Whose age-collected fervors scarce allowed
A bird to live, a blade of grass to spring,
Where the shrill chirp of the green lizard's
 love
Broke on the sultry silentness alone,
Now teem with countless rills and shady
 woods,
Cornfields and pastures and white cottages;
And where the startled wilderness beheld
A savage conqueror stained in kindred
 blood,
A tigress sating with the flesh of lambs
The unnatural famine of her toothless
 cubs, 80
Whilst shouts and howlings through the
 desert rang, —
Sloping and smooth the daisy-spangled
 lawn,
Offering sweet incense to the sunrise, smiles
To see a babe before his mother's door,
 Sharing his morning's meal
 With the green and golden basilisk
 That comes to lick his feet.

'Those trackless deeps, where many a weary
 sail
Has seen above the illimitable plain
Morning on night and night on morning
 rise, 90
Whilst still no land to greet the wanderer
 spread
Its shadowy mountains on the sun-bright
 sea,
Where the loud roarings of the tempest-
 waves

So long have mingled with the gusty wind
In melancholy loneliness, and swept
The desert of those ocean solitudes
But vocal to the sea-bird's harrowing shriek,
The bellowing monster, and the rushing
 storm;
Now to the sweet and many-mingling
 sounds
Of kindliest human impulses respond. 100
Those lonely realms bright garden-isles
 begem,
With lightsome clouds and shining seas
 between,
And fertile valleys, resonant with bliss,
Whilst green woods overcanopy the wave,
Which like a toil-worn laborer leaps to
 shore
To meet the kisses of the flowrets there.

'All things are recreated, and the flame
Of consentaneous love inspires all life.
The fertile bosom of the earth gives suck
To myriads, who still grow beneath her
 care, 110
Rewarding her with their pure perfectness;
The balmy breathings of the wind inhale
Her virtues and diffuse them all abroad;
Health floats amid the gentle atmosphere,
Glows in the fruits and mantles on the
 stream;
No storms deform the beaming brow of
 heaven,
Nor scatter in the freshness of its pride
The foliage of the ever-verdant trees;
But fruits are ever ripe, flowers ever fair,
And autumn proudly bears her matron
 grace, 120
Kindling a flush on the fair cheek of spring,
Whose virgin bloom beneath the ruddy
 fruit
Reflects its tint and blushes into love.

'The lion now forgets to thirst for blood;
There might you see him sporting in the
 sun
Beside the dreadless kid; his claws are
 sheathed,
His teeth are harmless, custom's force has
 made
His nature as the nature of a lamb.
Like passion's fruit, the nightshade's tempt-
 ing bane
Poisons no more the pleasure it be-
 stows; 130
All bitterness is past; the cup of joy

Unmingled mantles to the goblet's brim
And courts the thirsty lips it fled before.

But chief, ambiguous man, he that can
 know
More misery, and dream more joy than
 all;
Whose keen sensations thrill within his
 breast
To mingle with a loftier instinct there,
Lending their power to pleasure and to
 pain,
Yet raising, sharpening, and refining each;
Who stands amid the ever-varying world,
The burden or the glory of the earth; 141
He chief perceives the change; his being
 notes
The gradual renovation and defines
Each movement of its progress on his
 mind.

' Man, where the gloom of the long polar
 night
Lowers o'er the snow-clad rocks and
 frozen soil,
Where scarce the hardiest herb that braves
 the frost
Basks in the moonlight's ineffectual glow,
Shrank with the plants, and darkened with
 the night;
His chilled and narrow energies, his
 heart 150
Insensible to courage, truth or love,
His stunted stature and imbecile frame,
Marked him for some abortion of the earth,
Fit compeer of the bears that roamed
 around,
Whose habits and enjoyments were his
 own;
His life a feverish dream of stagnant woe,
Whose meagre wants, but scantily ful-
 filled,
Apprised him ever of the joyless length
Which his short being's wretchedness had
 reached;
His death a pang which famine, cold and
 toil 160
Long on the mind, whilst yet the vital
 spark
Clung to the body stubbornly, had brought:
All was inflicted here that earth's revenge
Could wreak on the infringers of her law;
One curse alone was spared — the name of
 God.

' Nor, where the tropics bound the realms
 of day
With a broad belt of mingling cloud and
 flame,
Where blue mists through the unmoving
 atmosphere
Scattered the seeds of pestilence and fed
Unnatural vegetation, where the land 170
Teemed with all earthquake, tempest and
 disease,
Was man a nobler being; slavery
Had crushed him to his country's blood-
 stained dust;
Or he was bartered for the fame of power,
Which, all internal impulses destroying,
Makes human will an article of trade;
Or he was changed with Christians for their
 gold
And dragged to distant isles, where to the
 sound
Of the flesh-mangling scourge he does the
 work
Of all-polluting luxury and wealth, 180
Which doubly visits on the tyrants' heads
The long-protracted fulness of their woe;
Or he was led to legal butchery,
To turn to worms beneath that burning sun
Where kings first leagued against the rights
 of men
And priests first traded with the name of
 God.

' Even where the milder zone afforded man
A seeming shelter, yet contagion there,
Blighting his being with unnumbered ills,
Spread like a quenchless fire; nor truth till
 late 190
Availed to arrest its progress or create
That peace which first in bloodless victory
 waved
Her snowy standard o'er this favored clime;
There man was long the train-bearer of
 slaves,
The mimic of surrounding misery,
The jackal of ambition's lion-rage,
The bloodhound of religion's hungry zeal.

' Here now the human being stands adorn-
 ing
This loveliest earth with taintless body and
 mind;
Blest from his birth with all bland im-
 pulses, 200
Which gently in his noble bosom wake

All kindly passions and all pure desires.
Him, still from hope to hope the bliss pur-
　　suing
Which from the exhaustless store of human
　　weal
Draws on the virtuous mind, the thoughts
　　that rise
In time-destroying infiniteness gift
With self-enshrined eternity, that mocks
The unprevailing hoariness of age;
And man, once fleeting o'er the transient
　　scene
Swift as an unremembered vision, stands 210
Immortal upon earth; no longer now
He slays the lamb that looks him in the
　　face,
And horribly devours his mangled flesh,
Which, still avenging Nature's broken
　　law,
Kindled all putrid humors in his frame,
All evil passions and all vain belief,
Hatred, despair and loathing in his mind,
The germs of misery, death, disease and
　　crime.
No longer now the wingèd habitants,
That in the woods their sweet lives sing
　　away, 220
Flee from the form of man ; but gather
　　round,
And prune their sunny feathers on the
　　hands
Which little children stretch in friendly
　　sport
Towards these dreadless partners of their
　　play.
All things are void of terror; man has
　　lost
His terrible prerogative, and stands
An equal amidst equals; happiness
And science dawn, though late, upon the
　　earth;
Peace cheers the mind, health renovates
　　the frame; 229
Disease and pleasure cease to mingle here,
Reason and passion cease to combat there;
Whilst each unfettered o'er the earth ex-
　　tend
Their all-subduing energies, and wield
The sceptre of a vast dominion there;
Whilst every shape and mode of matter
　　lends
Its force to the omnipotence of mind,
Which from its dark mine drags the gem
　　of truth
To decorate its paradise of peace.'

IX

'O happy Earth, reality of Heaven!
To which those restless souls that cease-
　　lessly
Throng through the human universe, aspire!
Thou consummation of all mortal hope!
Thou glorious prize of blindly working will,
Whose rays, diffused throughout all space
　　and time,
Verge to one point and blend forever there!
Of purest spirits thou pure dwelling-place
Where care and sorrow, impotence and
　　crime,
Languor, disease and ignorance dare not
　　come! 10
O happy Earth, reality of Heaven!

'Genius has seen thee in her passionate
　　dreams;
And dim forebodings of thy loveliness,
Haunting the human heart, have there en-
　　twined
Those rooted hopes of some sweet place of
　　bliss,
Where friends and lovers meet to part no
　　more.
Thou art the end of all desire and will,
The product of all action; and the souls,
That by the paths of an aspiring change 19
Have reached thy haven of perpetual peace,
There rest from the eternity of toil
That framed the fabric of thy perfectness.

'Even Time, the conqueror, fled thee in his
　　fear;
That hoary giant, who in lonely pride
So long had ruled the world that nations
　　fell
Beneath his silent footstep. Pyramids,
That for millenniums had withstood the tide
Of human things, his storm-breath drove in
　　sand
Across that desert where their stones sur-
　　vived
The name of him whose pride had heaped
　　them there. 30
Yon monarch, in his solitary pomp,
Was but the mushroom of a summer day,
That his light-wingèd footstep pressed to
　　dust;
Time was the king of earth; all things gave
　　way
Before him but the fixed and virtuous will,
The sacred sympathies of soul and sense,
That mocked his fury and prepared his fall.

'Yet slow and gradual dawned the morn of
love;
Long lay the clouds of darkness o'er the
scene,
Till from its native heaven they rolled
away: 40
First, crime triumphant o'er all hope ca-
reered
Unblushing, undisguising, bold and strong,
Whilst falsehood, tricked in virtue's attri-
butes,
Long sanctified all deeds of vice and woe,
Till, done by her own venomous sting to
death,
She left the moral world without a law,
No longer fettering passion's fearless wing,
Nor searing reason with the brand of God.
Then steadily the happy ferment worked;
Reason was free; and wild though passion
went 50
Through tangled glens and wood-embos-
omed meads,
Gathering a garland of the strangest flow-
ers,
Yet, like the bee returning to her queen,
She bound the sweetest on her sister's brow,
Who meek and sober kissed the sportive
child,
No longer trembling at the broken rod.

'Mild was the slow necessity of death.
The tranquil spirit failed beneath its grasp,
Without a groan, almost without a fear,
Calm as a voyager to some distant land, 60
And full of wonder, full of hope as he.
The deadly germs of languor and disease
Died in the human frame, and purity
Blessed with all gifts her earthly worship-
pers.
How vigorous then the athletic form of
age !
How clear its open and unwrinkled brow !
Where neither avarice, cunning, pride or
care
Had stamped the seal of gray deformity
On all the mingling lineaments of time.
How lovely the intrepid front of youth, 70
Which meek-eyed courage decked with
freshest grace;
Courage of soul, that dreaded not a name,
And elevated will, that journeyed on
Through life's phantasmal scene in fear-
lessness,
With virtue, love and pleasure, hand in
hand !

'Then, that sweet bondage which is free-
dom's self,
And rivets with sensation's softest tie
The kindred sympathies of human souls,
Needed no fetters of tyrannic law.
Those delicate and timid impulses 80
In Nature's primal modesty arose,
And with undoubting confidence disclosed
The growing longings of its dawning love,
Unchecked by dull and selfish chastity,
That virtue of the cheaply virtuous,
Who pride themselves in senselessness and
frost.
No longer prostitution's venomed bane
Poisoned the springs of happiness and
life;
Woman and man, in confidence and love,
Equal and free and pure together trod 90
The mountain - paths of virtue, which no
more
Were stained with blood from many a pil-
grim's feet.

'Then, where, through distant ages, long
in pride
The palace of the monarch - slave had
mocked
Famine's faint groan and penury's silent
tear,
A heap of crumbling ruins stood, and
threw
Year after year their stones upon the field,
Wakening a lonely echo; and the leaves
Of the old thorn, that on the topmost tower
Usurped the royal ensign's grandeur, shook
In the stern storm that swayed the topmost
tower, 101
And whispered strange tales in the whirl-
wind's ear.

'Low through the lone cathedral's roofless
aisles
The melancholy winds a death-dirge sung.
It were a sight of awfulness to see
The works of faith and slavery, so vast,
So sumptuous, yet so perishing withal,
Even as the corpse that rests beneath its
wall !
A thousand mourners deck the pomp of
death 109
To-day, the breathing marble glows above
To decorate its memory, and tongues
Are busy of its life; to-morrow, worms
In silence and in darkness seize their
prey.

' Within the massy prison's mouldering
 courts,
Fearless and free the ruddy children played,
Weaving gay chaplets for their innocent
 brows
With the green ivy and the red wall-flower
That mock the dungeon's unavailing gloom;
The ponderous chains and gratings of
 strong iron 119
There rusted amid heaps of broken stone
That mingled slowly with their native
 earth;
There the broad beam of day, which feebly
 once
Lighted the cheek of lean captivity
With a pale and sickly glare, then freely
 shone
On the pure smiles of infant playfulness;
No more the shuddering voice of hoarse
 despair
Pealed through the echoing vaults, but
 soothing notes
Of ivy-fingered winds and gladsome birds
And merriment were resonant around. 129

' These ruins soon left not a wreck behind;
Their elements, wide-scattered o'er the
 globe,
To happier shapes were moulded, and be-
 came
Ministrant to all blissful impulses;
Thus human things were perfected, and
 earth,
Even as a child beneath its mother's love,
Was strengthened in all excellence, and
 grew
Fairer and nobler with each passing year.

' Now Time his dusky pennons o'er the
 scene
Closes in steadfast darkness, and the past
Fades from our charmèd sight. My task
 is done; 140
Thy lore is learned. Earth's wonders are
 thine own
With all the fear and all the hope they
 bring.
My spells are passed; the present now re-
 curs.
Ah me ! a pathless wilderness remains
Yet unsubdued by man's reclaiming hand.

' Yet, human Spirit ! bravely hold thy
 course;
Let virtue teach thee firmly to pursue

The gradual paths of an aspiring change;
For birth and life and death, and that
 strange state 149
Before the naked soul has found its home,
All tend to perfect happiness, and urge
The restless wheels of being on their
 way,
Whose flashing spokes, instinct with infi-
 nite life,
Bicker and burn to gain their destined
 goal;
For birth but wakes the spirit to the sense
Of outward shows, whose unexperienced
 shape
New modes of passion to its frame may
 lend;
Life is its state of action, and the store
Of all events is aggregated there
That variegate the eternal universe; 160
Death is a gate of dreariness and gloom,
That leads to azure isles and beaming
 skies
And happy regions of eternal hope.
Therefore, O Spirit ! fearlessly bear on.
Though storms may break the primrose on
 its stalk,
Though frosts may blight the freshness of
 its bloom,
Yet spring's awakening breath will woo
 the earth
To feed with kindliest dews its favorite
 flower,
That blooms in mossy bank and darksome
 glens,
Lighting the greenwood with its sunny
 smile. 170

' Fear not then, Spirit, death's disrobing
 hand,
So welcome when the tyrant is awake,
So welcome when the bigot's hell-torch
 burns;
'T is but the voyage of a darksome hour,
The transient gulf-dream of a startling
 sleep.
Death is no foe to virtue; earth has seen
Love's brightest roses on the scaffold bloom,
Mingling with freedom's fadeless laurels
 there,
And presaging the truth of visioned bliss.
Are there not hopes within thee, which this
 scene 180
Of linked and gradual being has confirmed ?
Whose stingings bade thy heart look further
 still,

When, to the moonlight walk by Henry led,
Sweetly and sadly thou didst talk of death ?
And wilt thou rudely tear them from thy
 breast,
Listening supinely to a bigot's creed,
Or tamely crouching to the tyrant's rod,
Whose iron thongs are red with human
 gore ?
Never : but bravely bearing on, thy will
Is destined an eternal war to wage 190
With tyranny and falsehood, and uproot
The germs of misery from the human heart.
Thine is the hand whose piety would soothe
The thorny pillow of unhappy crime,
Whose impotence an easy pardon gains,
Watching its wanderings as a friend's dis-
 ease ;
Thine is the brow whose mildness would
 defy
Its fiercest rage, and brave its sternest
 will,
When fenced by power and master of the
 world.
Thou art sincere and good ; of resolute
 mind, 200
Free from heart-withering custom's cold
 control,
Of passion lofty, pure and unsubdued.
Earth's pride and meanness could not van-
 quish thee,
And therefore art thou worthy of the boon
Which thou hast now received ; virtue shall
 keep
Thy footsteps in the path that thou hast
 trod,
And many days of beaming hope shall bless
Thy spotless life of sweet and sacred love.
Go, happy one, and give that bosom joy,
 Whose sleepless spirit waits to catch 210
Light, life and rapture from thy smile ! '

The Fairy waves her wand of charm.
Speechless with bliss the Spirit mounts the
 car,
That rolled beside the battlement,
Bending her beamy eyes in thankfulness.
 Again the enchanted steeds were yoked ;
 Again the burning wheels inflame
The steep descent of heaven's untrodden
 way.
 Fast and far the chariot flew ;
 The vast and fiery globes that rolled 220
 Around the Fairy's palace-gate
Lessened by slow degrees, and soon ap-
 peared
Such tiny twinklers as the planet orbs
That there attendant on the solar power
With borrowed light pursued their nar-
 rower way.

 Earth floated then below ;
 The chariot paused a moment there ;
 The Spirit then descended ;
The restless coursers pawed the ungenial
 soil,
Snuffed the gross air, and then, their errand
 done, 230
Unfurled their pinions to the winds of
 heaven.

The Body and the Soul united then.
A gentle start convulsed Ianthe's frame ;
Her veiny eyelids quietly unclosed ;
Moveless awhile the dark blue orbs re-
 mained.
She looked around in wonder, and beheld
Henry, who kneeled in silence by her couch,
Watching her sleep with looks of speech-
 less love,
 And the bright beaming stars
 That through the casement shone. 240

ALASTOR

OR

THE SPIRIT OF SOLITUDE

Nondum amabam, et amare amabam,
quærebam quid amarem, amans amare.
 Confess. St. August.

Alastor was published nearly three years
after the issue of *Queen Mab*, in 1816, in a thin
volume with a few other poems. It is strongly
opposed to the earlier poem, and begins that
series of ideal portraits, — in the main, incar-
nations of Shelley's own aspiring and melan-
choly spirit, — which contain his personal charm
and shadow forth his own history of isolation
in the world ; they are interpretations of the
hero rather than pronunciamentos of the cause.

and are free from the entanglements of political and social reform and religious strife. The poetical antecedents of *Alastor* are Wordsworth and Coleridge. The deepening of the poet's self-consciousness is evident in every line, and the growth of his genius in grace and strength, in the element of expression, is so marked as to give a different cadence to his verse. He composed the poem in the autumn of 1815, when he was twenty-three years old and after the earlier misfortunes of his life had befallen him. Mrs. Shelley's account of the poem is the best, and nothing has since been added to it :

'*Alastor* is written in a very different tone from *Queen Mab*. In the latter, Shelley poured out all the cherished speculations of his youth — all the irrepressible emotions of sympathy, censure, and hope, to which the present suffering, and what he considers the proper destiny of his fellow - creatures, gave birth. *Alastor*, on the contrary, contains an individual interest only. A very few years, with their attendant events, had checked the ardor of Shelley's hopes, though he still thought them well-grounded, and that to advance their fulfilment was the noblest task man could achieve.

' This is neither the time nor place to speak of the misfortunes that checkered his life. It will be sufficient to say, that in all he did, he at the time of doing it believed himself justified to his own conscience ; while the various ills of poverty and loss of friends brought home to him the sad realities of life. Physical suffering had also considerable influence in causing him to turn his eyes inward ; inclining him rather to brood over the thoughts and emotions of his own soul, than to glance abroad, and to make, as in *Queen Mab*, the whole universe the object and subject of his song. In the spring of 1815, an eminent physician pronounced that he was dying rapidly of a consumption ; abscesses were formed on his lungs, and he suffered acute spasms. Suddenly a complete change took place ; and though through life he was a martyr to pain and debility, every symptom of pulmonary disease vanished. His nerves, which nature had formed sensitive to an unexampled degree, were rendered still more susceptible by the state of his health.

' As soon as the peace of 1814 had opened the Continent, he went abroad. He visited some of the more magnificent scenes of Switzerland, and returned to England from Lucerne by the Reuss and the Rhine. This river-navigation enchanted him. In his favorite poem of *Thalaba* his imagination had been excited by a description of such a voyage. In the summer of 1815, after a tour along the southern coast of Devonshire and a visit to Clifton, he rented a house on Bishopgate Heath, on the borders of Windsor Forest, where he enjoyed

several months of comparative health and tranquil happiness. The later summer months were warm and dry. Accompanied by a few friends, he visited the source of the Thames, making a voyage in a wherry from Windsor to Crichlade. His beautiful stanzas in the churchyard of Lechlade were written on that occasion. *Alastor* was composed on his return. He spent his days under the oak-shades of Windsor Great Park ; and the magnificent woodland was a fitting study to inspire the various descriptions of forest scenery we find in the poem.

' None of Shelley's poems is more characteristic than this. The solemn spirit that reigns throughout, the worship of the majesty of nature, the broodings of a poet's heart in solitude — the mingling of the exulting joy which the various aspect of the visible universe inspires, with the sad and struggling pangs which human passion imparts, give a touching interest to the whole. The death which he had often contemplated during the last months as certain and near, he here represented in such colors as had, in his lonely musings, soothed his soul to peace. The versification sustains the solemn spirit which breathes throughout : it is peculiarly melodious. The poem ought rather to be considered didactic than narrative : it was the outpouring of his own emotions, embodied in the purest form he could conceive, painted in the ideal hues which his brilliant imagination inspired, and softened by the recent anticipation of death.'

Peacock explains the title : ' At this time Shelley wrote his *Alastor*. He was at a loss for a title, and I proposed that which he adopted : *Alastor ; or, the Spirit of Solitude*. The Greek word, 'Αλάστωρ, is an evil genius, κακοδαίμων, though the sense of the two words is somewhat different, as in the Φανεὶς 'Αλάστωρ ἢ κακὸς δαίμων πόθεν of Æschylus. The poem treated the spirit of solitude as a spirit of evil. I mention the true meaning of the word because many have supposed *Alastor* to be the name of the hero of the poem.'

In his *Preface* Shelley thus describes the main character, and draws its moral :

' The poem entitled *Alastor* may be considered as allegorical of one of the most interesting situations of the human mind. It represents a youth of uncorrupted feelings and adventurous genius led forth by an imagination inflamed and purified through familiarity with all that is excellent and majestic to the contemplation of the universe. He drinks deep of the fountains of knowledge and is still insatiate. The magnificence and beauty of the external world sinks profoundly into the frame of his conceptions and affords to their modifications a variety not to be exhausted. So long

as it is possible for his desires to point towards objects thus infinite and unmeasured, he is joyous and tranquil and self-possessed. But the period arrives when these objects cease to suffice. His mind is at length suddenly awakened and thirsts for intercourse with an intelligence similar to itself. He images to himself the Being whom he loves. Conversant with speculations of the sublimest and most perfect natures, the vision in which he embodies his own imaginations unites all of wonderful or wise or beautiful, which the poet, the philosopher or the lover could depicture. The intellectual faculties, the imagination, the functions of sense have their respective requisitions on the sympathy of corresponding powers in other human beings. The Poet is represented as uniting these requisitions and attaching them to a single image. He seeks in vain for a prototype of his conception. Blasted by his disappointment, he descends to an untimely grave.

'The picture is not barren of instruction to actual men. The Poet's self-centred seclusion was avenged by the furies of an irresistible passion pursuing him to speedy ruin. But that Power, which strikes the luminaries of the world with sudden darkness and extinction by awakening them to too exquisite a perception of its influences, dooms to a slow and poisonous decay those meaner spirits that dare to abjure its dominion. Their destiny is more abject and inglorious as their delinquency is more contemptible and pernicious. They who, deluded by no generous error, instigated by no sacred thirst of doubtful knowledge, duped by no illustrious superstition, loving nothing on this earth, and cherishing no hopes beyond, yet keep aloof from sympathies with their kind, rejoicing neither in human joy nor mourning with human grief; these, and such as they, have their apportioned curse. They languish, because none feel with them their common nature. They are morally dead. They are neither friends, nor lovers, nor fathers, nor citizens of the world, nor benefactors of their country. Among those who attempt to exist without human sympathy, the pure and tenderhearted perish through the intensity and passion of their search after its communities, when the vacancy of their spirit suddenly makes itself felt. All else, selfish, blind and torpid, are those unforeseeing multitudes who constitute, together with their own, the lasting misery and loneliness of the world. Those who love not their fellow-beings live unfruitful lives and prepare for their old age a miserable grave.

> 'The good die first,
> And those whose hearts are dry as summer dust
> Burn to the socket!

'*December* 14, 1815.'

EARTH, Ocean, Air, belovèd brotherhood!
If our great Mother has imbued my soul
With aught of natural piety to feel
Your love, and recompense the boon with
 mine;
If dewy morn, and odorous noon, and even,
With sunset and its gorgeous ministers,
And solemn midnight's tingling silent-
 ness;
If Autumn's hollow sighs in the sere wood,
And Winter robing with pure snow and
 crowns
Of starry ice the gray grass and bare
 boughs; 10
If Spring's voluptuous pantings when she
 breathes
Her first sweet kisses, — have been dear to
 me;
If no bright bird, insect, or gentle beast
I consciously have injured, but still loved
And cherished these my kindred; then for-
 give
This boast, belovèd brethren, and with-
 draw
No portion of your wonted favor now!

Mother of this unfathomable world!
Favor my solemn song, for I have loved 15
Thee ever, and thee only; I have watched
Thy shadow, and the darkness of thy steps,
And my heart ever gazes on the depth
Of thy deep mysteries. I have made my
 bed
In charnels and on coffins, where black
 death
Keeps record of the trophies won from
 thee,
Hoping to still these obstinate questionings
Of thee and thine, by forcing some lone
 ghost,
Thy messenger, to render up the tale
Of what we are. In lone and silent hours,
When night makes a weird sound of its
 own stillness, 30
Like an inspired and desperate alchemist
Staking his very life on some dark hope,
Have I mixed awful talk and asking looks
With my most innocent love, until strange
 tears,
Uniting with those breathless kisses, made
Such magic as compels the charmèd night

To render up thy charge; and, though
ne'er yet
Thou hast unveiled thy inmost sanctuary,
Enough from incommunicable dream,
And twilight phantasms, and deep noonday
thought, 40
Has shone within me, that serenely now
And moveless, as a long-forgotten lyre
Suspended in the solitary dome
Of some mysterious and deserted fane,
I wait thy breath, Great Parent, that my
strain
May modulate with murmurs of the air,
And motions of the forests and the sea,
And voice of living beings, and woven
hymns
Of night and day, and the deep heart of
man. 49

There was a Poet whose untimely tomb
No human hands with pious reverence
reared,
But the charmed eddies of autumnal winds
Built o'er his mouldering bones a pyra-
mid
Of mouldering leaves in the waste wilder-
ness :
A lovely youth, — no mourning maiden
decked
With weeping flowers, or votive cypress
wreath,
The lone couch of his everlasting sleep :
Gentle, and brave, and generous, — no lorn
bard
Breathed o'er his dark fate one melodious
sigh :
He lived, he died, he sung in solitude. 60
Strangers have wept to hear his passionate
notes,
And virgins, as unknown he passed, have
pined
And wasted for fond love of his wild eyes.
The fire of those soft orbs has ceased to
burn,
And Silence, too enamoured of that voice,
Locks its mute music in her rugged cell.

By solemn vision and bright silver dream
His infancy was nurtured. Every sight
And sound from the vast earth and ambient
air
Sent to his heart its choicest impulses. 70
The fountains of divine philosophy
Fled not his thirsting lips, and all of great,
Or good, or lovely, which the sacred past

In truth or fable consecrates, he felt
And knew. When early youth had passed,
he left
His cold fireside and alienated home
To seek strange truths in undiscovered
lands.
Many a wide waste and tangled wilder-
ness
Has lured his fearless steps; and he has
bought
With his sweet voice and eyes, from savage
men, 80
His rest and food. Nature's most secret
steps
He like her shadow has pursued, where'er
The red volcano overcanopies
Its fields of snow and pinnacles of ice
With burning smoke, or where bitumen
lakes
On black bare pointed islets ever beat
With sluggish surge, or where the secret
caves,
Rugged and dark, winding among the
springs
Of fire and poison, inaccessible
To avarice or pride, their starry domes 90
Of diamond and of gold expand above
Numberless and immeasurable halls,
Frequent with crystal column, and clear
shrines
Of pearl, and thrones radiant with chryso-
lite.
Nor had that scene of ampler majesty
Than gems or gold, the varying roof of
heaven
And the green earth, lost in his heart its
claims
To love and wonder; he would linger long
In lonesome vales, making the wild his
home,
Until the doves and squirrels would par-
take 100
From his innocuous hand his bloodless food,
Lured by the gentle meaning of his looks,
And the wild antelope, that starts when-
e'er
The dry leaf rustles in the brake, suspend
Her timid steps, to gaze upon a form
More graceful than her own.

His wandering step,
Obedient to high thoughts, has visited
The awful ruins of the days of old :
Athens, and Tyre, and Balbec, and the
waste 109

Where stood Jerusalem, the fallen towers
Of Babylon, the eternal pyramids,
Memphis and Thebes, and whatsoe'er of
 strange,
Sculptured on alabaster obelisk
Or jasper tomb or mutilated sphinx,
Dark Æthiopia in her desert hills
Conceals. Among the ruined temples
 there,
Stupendous columns, and wild images
Of more than man, where marble daemons
 watch
The Zodiac's brazen mystery, and dead
 men
Hang their mute thoughts on the mute
 walls around, 120
He lingered, poring on memorials
Of the world's youth: through the long
 burning day
Gazed on those speechless shapes; nor,
 when the moon
Filled the mysterious halls with floating
 shades
Suspended he that task, but ever gazed
And gazed, till meaning on his vacant
 mind
Flashed like strong inspiration, and he saw
The thrilling secrets of the birth of time.

Meanwhile an Arab maiden brought his
 food, 129
Her daily portion, from her father's tent,
And spread her matting for his couch, and
 stole
From duties and repose to tend his steps,
Enamoured, yet not daring for deep awe
To speak her love, and watched his nightly
 sleep,
Sleepless herself, to gaze upon his lips
Parted in slumber, whence the regular
 breath
Of innocent dreams arose; then, when red
 morn
Made paler the pale moon, to her cold
 home
Wildered, and wan, and panting, she re-
 turned.

The Poet, wandering on, through Ara-
 bie, 140
And Persia, and the wild Carmanian waste,
And o'er the aërial mountains which pour
 down
Indus and Oxus from their icy caves,
In joy and exultation held his way;

Till in the vale of Cashmire, far within
Its loneliest dell, where odorous plants en-
 twine
Beneath the hollow rocks a natural bower,
Beside a sparkling rivulet he stretched
His languid limbs. A vision on his sleep
There came, a dream of hopes that never
 yet 150
Had flushed his cheek. He dreamed a
 veilèd maid
Sate near him, talking in low solemn tones.
Her voice was like the voice of his own
 soul
Heard in the calm of thought; its music
 long,
Like woven sounds of streams and breezes,
 held
His inmost sense suspended in its web
Of many-colored woof and shifting hues.
Knowledge and truth and virtue were her
 theme,
And lofty hopes of divine liberty, 159
Thoughts the most dear to him, and poesy,
Herself a poet. Soon the solemn mood
Of her pure mind kindled through all her
 frame
A permeating fire; wild numbers then
She raised, with voice stifled in tremulous
 sobs
Subdued by its own pathos; her fair hands
Were bare alone, sweeping from some
 strange harp
Strange symphony, and in their branching
 veins
The eloquent blood told an ineffable tale.
The beating of her heart was heard to fill
The pauses of her music, and her breath
Tumultuously accorded with those fits 171
Of intermitted song. Sudden she rose,
As if her heart impatiently endured
Its bursting burden; at the sound he turned,
And saw by the warm light of their own
 life
Her glowing limbs beneath the sinuous veil
Of woven wind, her outspread arms now
 bare,
Her dark locks floating in the breath of
 night,
Her beamy bending eyes, her parted lips
Outstretched, and pale, and quivering
 eagerly. 180
His strong heart sunk and sickened with
 excess
Of love. He reared his shuddering limbs,
 and quelled

His gasping breath, and spread his arms to
meet
Her panting bosom : — she drew back
awhile,
Then, yielding to the irresistible joy,
With frantic gesture and short breathless
cry
Folded his frame in her dissolving arms.
Now blackness veiled his dizzy eyes, and
night
Involved and swallowed up the vision;
sleep, 189
Like a dark flood suspended in its course,
Rolled back its impulse on his vacant brain.

Roused by the shock, he started from his
trance —
The cold white light of morning, the blue
moon
Low in the west, the clear and garish hills,
The distinct valley and the vacant woods,
Spread round him where he stood. Whither
have fled
The hues of heaven that canopied his
bower
Of yesternight ? The sounds that soothed
his sleep,
The mystery and the majesty of Earth,
The joy, the exultation ? His wan eyes 200
Gaze on the empty scene as vacantly
As ocean's moon looks on the moon in
heaven.
The spirit of sweet human love has sent
A vision to the sleep of him who spurned
Her choicest gifts. He eagerly pursues
Beyond the realms of dream that fleeting
shade;
He overleaps the bounds. Alas ! alas !
Were limbs and breath and being inter-
twined
Thus treacherously ? Lost, lost, forever
lost 209
In the wide pathless desert of dim sleep,
That beautiful shape ! Does the dark gate
of death
Conduct to thy mysterious paradise,
O Sleep ? Does the bright arch of rain-
bow clouds
And pendent mountains seen in the calm
lake
Lead only to a black and watery depth,
While death's blue vault with loathliest
vapors hung,
Where every shade which the foul grave
exhales

Hides its dead eye from the detested day,
Conducts, O Sleep, to thy delightful realms?
This doubt with sudden tide flowed on his
heart; 220
The insatiate hope which it awakened
stung
His brain even like despair.

 While daylight held
The sky, the Poet kept mute conference
With his still soul. At night the passion
came,
Like the fierce fiend of a distempered
dream,
And shook him from his rest, and led him
forth
Into the darkness. As an eagle, grasped
In folds of the green serpent, feels her
breast
Burn with the poison, and precipitates
Through night and day, tempest, and calm,
and cloud, 230
Frantic with dizzying anguish, her blind
flight
O'er the wide aëry wilderness: thus driven
By the bright shadow of that lovely dream,
Beneath the cold glare of the desolate
night,
Through tangled swamps and deep preci-
pitous dells,
Startling with careless step the moon-light
snake,
He fled. Red morning dawned upon his
flight,
Shedding the mockery of its vital hues
Upon his cheek of death. He wandered
on 239
Till vast Aornos seen from Petra's steep
Hung o'er the low horizon like a cloud;
Through Balk, and where the desolated
tombs
Of Parthian kings scatter to every wind
Their wasting dust, wildly he wandered on,
Day after day, a weary waste of hours,
Bearing within his life the brooding care
That ever fed on its decaying flame.
And now his limbs were lean; his scattered
hair,
Sered by the autumn of strange suffering,
Sung dirges in the wind; his listless hand
Hung like dead bone within its withered
skin; 251
Life, and the lustre that consumed it,
shone,
As in a furnace burning secretly,

From his dark eyes alone. The cottagers,
Who ministered with human charity
His human wants, beheld with wondering
 awe
Their fleeting visitant. The mountaineer,
Encountering on some dizzy precipice
That spectral form, deemed that the Spirit
 of Wind,
With lightning eyes, and eager breath, and
 feet 260
Disturbing not the drifted snow, had paused
In its career; the infant would conceal
His troubled visage in his mother's robe
In terror at the glare of those wild eyes,
To remember their strange light in many a
 dream
Of after times; but youthful maidens,
 taught
By nature, would interpret half the woe
That wasted him, would call him with false
 names
Brother and friend, would press his pallid
 hand
At parting, and watch, dim through tears,
 the path 270
Of his departure from their father's door.

At length upon the lone Chorasmian shore
He paused, a wide and melancholy waste
Of putrid marshes. A strong impulse urged
His steps to the sea-shore. A swan was
 there,
Beside a sluggish stream among the reeds.
It rose as he approached, and, with strong
 wings
Scaling the upward sky, bent its bright
 course
High over the immeasurable main.
His eyes pursued its flight: — 'Thou hast a
 home, 280
Beautiful bird! thou voyagest to thine
 home,
Where thy sweet mate will twine her downy
 neck
With thine, and welcome thy return with
 eyes
Bright in the lustre of their own fond joy.
And what am I that I should linger here,
With voice far sweeter than thy dying
 notes,
Spirit more vast than thine, frame more
 attuned
To beauty, wasting these surpassing powers
In the deaf air, to the blind earth, and
 heaven

That echoes not my thoughts?' A gloomy
 smile 290
Of desperate hope wrinkled his quivering
 lips.
For sleep, he knew, kept most relentlessly
Its precious charge, and silent death ex-
 posed,
Faithless perhaps as sleep, a shadowy lure,
With doubtful smile mocking its own
 strange charms.

Startled by his own thoughts, he looked
 around.
There was no fair fiend near him, not a
 sight
Or sound of awe but in his own deep mind.
A little shallop floating near the shore
Caught the impatient wandering of his
 gaze. 300
It had been long abandoned, for its sides
Gaped wide with many a rift, and its frail
 joints
Swayed with the undulations of the tide.
A restless impulse urged him to embark
And meet lone Death on the drear ocean's
 waste;
For well he knew that mighty Shadow
 loves
The slimy caverns of the populous deep.

The day was fair and sunny; sea and sky
Drank its inspiring radiance, and the wind
Swept strongly from the shore, blackening
 the waves. 310
Following his eager soul, the wanderer
Leaped in the boat; he spread his cloak
 aloft
On the bare mast, and took his lonely seat,
And felt the boat speed o'er the tranquil
 sea
Like a torn cloud before the hurricane.

As one that in a silver vision floats
Obedient to the sweep of odorous winds
Upon resplendent clouds, so rapidly
Along the dark and ruffled waters fled
The straining boat. A whirlwind swept it
 on, 320
With fierce gusts and precipitating force,
Through the white ridges of the chafèd sea.
The waves arose. Higher and higher still
Their fierce necks writhed beneath the
 tempest's scourge
Like serpents struggling in a vulture's
 grasp.

Calm and rejoicing in the fearful war
Of wave ruining on wave, and blast on blast
Descending, and black flood on whirlpool
 driven
With dark obliterating course, he sate:
As if their genii were the ministers 330
Appointed to conduct him to the light
Of those belovèd eyes, the Poet sate,
Holding the steady helm. Evening came
 on;
The beams of sunset hung their rainbow
 hues
High 'mid the shifting domes of sheeted
 spray
That canopied his path o'er the waste deep;
Twilight, ascending slowly from the east,
Entwined in duskier wreaths her braided
 locks
O'er the fair front and radiant eyes of Day;
Night followed, clad with stars. On every
 side 340
More horribly the multitudinous streams
Of ocean's mountainous waste to mutual
 war
Rushed in dark tumult thundering, as to
 mock
The calm and spangled sky. The little
 boat
Still fled before the storm; still fled, like
 foam
Down the steep cataract of a wintry river;
Now pausing on the edge of the riven wave;
Now leaving far behind the bursting mass
That fell, convulsing ocean; safely fled —
As if that frail and wastèd human form 350
Had been an elemental god.

 At midnight
The moon arose; and lo! the ethereal cliffs
Of Caucasus, whose icy summits shone
Among the stars like sunlight, and around
Whose caverned base the whirlpools and
 the waves
Bursting and eddying irresistibly
Rage and resound forever. — Who shall
 save ? —
The boat fled on, — the boiling torrent
 drove, —
The crags closed round with black and
 jagged arms, 359
The shattered mountain overhung the sea,
And faster still, beyond all human speed,
Suspended on the sweep of the smooth
 wave,
The little boat was driven. A cavern there

Yawned, and amid its slant and winding
 depths
Ingulfed the rushing sea. The boat fled on
With unrelaxing speed. — ' Vision and
 Love ! '
The Poet cried aloud, ' I have beheld
The path of thy departure. Sleep and
 death
Shall not divide us long.'

 The boat pursued
The windings of the cavern. Daylight
 shone 370
At length upon that gloomy river's flow;
Now, where the fiercest war among the
 waves
Is calm, on the unfathomable stream
The boat moved slowly. Where the moun-
 tain, riven,
Exposed those black depths to the azure
 sky,
Ere yet the flood's enormous volume fell
Even to the base of Caucasus, with sound
That shook the everlasting rocks, the mass
Filled with one whirlpool all that ample
 chasm: 379
Stair above stair the eddying waters rose,
Circling immeasurably fast, and laved
With alternating dash the gnarlèd roots
Of mighty trees, that stretched their giant
 arms
In darkness over it. I' the midst was left,
Reflecting yet distorting every cloud,
A pool of treacherous and tremendous
 calm.
Seized by the sway of the ascending stream,
With dizzy swiftness, round and round and
 round,
Ridge after ridge the straining boat arose,
Till on the verge of the extremest curve,
Where through an opening of the rocky
 bank 391
The waters overflow, and a smooth spot
Of glassy quiet 'mid those battling tides
Is left, the boat paused shuddering. —
Shall it sink
Down the abyss ? Shall the reverting
 stress
Of that resistless gulf embosom it ?
Now shall it fall ? — A wandering stream
 of wind
Breathed from the west, has caught the
 expanded sail,
And, lo ! with gentle motion between banks
Of mossy slope, and on a placid stream, 400

Beneath a woven grove, it sails, and, hark!
The ghastly torrent mingles its far roar
With the breeze murmuring in the musical
 woods.
Where the embowering trees recede, and
 leave
A little space of green expanse, the cove
Is closed by meeting banks, whose yellow
 flowers
Forever gaze on their own drooping eyes,
Reflected in the crystal calm. The wave
Of the boat's motion marred their pensive
 task,
Which naught but vagrant bird, or wanton
 wind, 410
Or falling spear-grass, or their own decay
Had e'er disturbed before. The Poet
 longed
To deck with their bright hues his withered
 hair,
But on his heart its solitude returned,
And he forbore. Not the strong impulse
 hid
In those flushed cheeks, bent eyes, and
 shadowy frame,
Had yet performed its ministry; it hung
Upon his life, as lightning in a cloud
Gleams, hovering ere it vanish, ere the
 floods 419
Of night close over it.

 The noonday sun
Now shone upon the forest, one vast mass
Of mingling shade, whose brown magnifi-
 cence
A narrow vale embosoms. There, huge
 caves,
Scooped in the dark base of their aëry
 rocks,
Mocking its moans, respond and roar for-
 ever.
The meeting boughs and implicated leaves
Wove twilight o'er the Poet's path, as, led
By love, or dream, or god, or mightier
 Death,
He sought in Nature's dearest haunt some
 bank, 429
Her cradle and his sepulchre. More dark
And dark the shades accumulate. The oak,
Expanding its immense and knotty arms,
Embraces the light beech. The pyramids
Of the tall cedar overarching frame
Most solemn domes within, and far below,
Like clouds suspended in an emerald sky,
The ash and the acacia floating hang

Tremulous and pale. Like restless ser-
 pents, clothed
In rainbow and in fire, the parasites,
Starred with ten thousand blossoms, flow
 around 440
The gray trunks, and, as gamesome infants'
 eyes,
With gentle meanings, and most innocent
 wiles,
Fold their beams round the hearts of those
 that love,
These twine their tendrils with the wedded
 boughs,
Uniting their close union; the woven leaves
Make network of the dark blue light of day
And the night's noontide clearness, mutable
As shapes in the weird clouds. Soft mossy
 lawns
Beneath these canopies extend their swells,
Fragrant with perfumed herbs, and eyed
 with blooms 450
Minute yet beautiful. One darkest glen
Sends from its woods of musk-rose twined
 with jasmine
A soul-dissolving odor to invite
To some more lovely mystery. Through
 the dell
Silence and Twilight here, twin-sisters,
 keep
Their noonday watch, and sail among the
 shades,
Like vaporous shapes half-seen; beyond, a
 well,
Dark, gleaming, and of most translucent
 wave,
Images all the woven boughs above, 459
And each depending leaf, and every speck
Of azure sky darting between their chasms;
Nor aught else in the liquid mirror laves
Its portraiture, but some inconstant star,
Between one foliaged lattice twinkling fair,
Or painted bird, sleeping beneath the moon,
Or gorgeous insect floating motionless,
Unconscious of the day, ere yet his wings
Have spread their glories to the gaze of
 noon.

Hither the Poet came. His eyes beheld
Their own wan light through the reflected
 lines 470
Of his thin hair, distinct in the dark depth
Of that still fountain; as the human heart,
Gazing in dreams over the gloomy grave,
Sees its own treacherous likeness there. He
 heard

The motion of the leaves — the grass that sprung
Startled and glanced and trembled even to feel
An unaccustomed presence — and the sound
Of the sweet brook that from the secret springs
Of that dark fountain rose. A Spirit seemed
To stand beside him — clothed in no bright robes 480
Of shadowy silver or enshrining light,
Borrowed from aught the visible world affords
Of grace, or majesty, or mystery;
But undulating woods, and silent well,
And leaping rivulet, and evening gloom
Now deepening the dark shades, for speech assuming,
Held commune with him, as if he and it
Were all that was; only — when his regard
Was raised by intense pensiveness — two eyes,
Two starry eyes, hung in the gloom of thought, 490
And seemed with their serene and azure smiles
To beckon him.

　　　　Obedient to the light
That shone within his soul, he went, pursuing
The windings of the dell. The rivulet,
Wanton and wild, through many a green ravine
Beneath the forest flowed. Sometimes it fell
Among the moss with hollow harmony
Dark and profound. Now on the polished stones
It danced, like childhood laughing as it went ;
Then, through the plain in tranquil wanderings crept, 500
Reflecting every herb and drooping bud
That overhung its quietness. — 'O stream !
Whose source is inaccessibly profound,
Whither do thy mysterious waters tend ?
Thou imagest my life. Thy darksome stillness,
Thy dazzling waves, thy loud and hollow gulfs,
Thy searchless fountain and invisible course,
Have each their type in me ; and the wide sky

And measureless ocean may declare as soon
What oozy cavern or what wandering cloud 510
Contains thy waters, as the universe
Tell where these living thoughts reside,
when stretched
Upon thy flowers my bloodless limbs shall waste
I' the passing wind !'

　　　　　　Beside the grassy shore
Of the small stream he went ; he did impress
On the green moss his tremulous step, that caught
Strong shuddering from his burning limbs. As one
Roused by some joyous madness from the couch
Of fever, he did move ; yet not like him
Forgetful of the grave, where, when the flame 520
Of his frail exultation shall be spent,
He must descend. With rapid steps he went
Beneath the shade of trees, beside the flow
Of the wild babbling rivulet ; and now
The forest's solemn canopies were changed
For the uniform and lightsome evening sky.
Gray rocks did peep from the spare moss, and stemmed
The struggling brook ; tall spires of windlestrae
Threw their thin shadows down the rugged slope,
And nought but gnarlèd roots of ancient pines 530
Branchless and blasted, clenched with grasping roots
The unwilling soil. A gradual change was here
Yet ghastly. For, as fast years flow away,
The smooth brow gathers, and the hair grows thin
And white, and where irradiate dewy eyes
Had shone, gleam stony orbs : — so from his steps
Bright flowers departed, and the beautiful shade
Of the green groves, with all their odorous winds
And musical motions. Calm he still pursued
The stream, that with a larger volume now 540

Rolled through the labyrinthine dell ; and
 there
Fretted a path through its descending
 curves
With its wintry speed. On every side now
 rose
Rocks, which, in unimaginable forms,
Lifted their black and barren pinnacles
In the light of evening, and its preci-
 pice
Obscuring the ravine, disclosed above,
'Mid toppling stones, black gulfs and yawn-
 ing caves,
Whose windings gave ten thousand various
 tongues
To the loud stream. Lo ! where the pass
 expands 550
Its stony jaws, the abrupt mountain breaks,
And seems with its accumulated crags
To overhang the world ; for wide expand
Beneath the wan stars and descending moon
Islanded seas, blue mountains, mighty
 streams,
Dim tracts and vast, robed in the lustrous
 gloom
Of leaden-colored even, and fiery hills
Mingling their flames with twilight, on the
 verge
Of the remote horizon. The near scene,
In naked and severe simplicity, 560
Made contrast with the universe. A pine,
Rock-rooted, stretched athwart the vacancy
Its swinging boughs, to each inconstant blast
Yielding one only response at each pause
In most familiar cadence, with the howl,
The thunder and the hiss of homeless
 streams
Mingling its solemn song, whilst the broad
 river
Foaming and hurrying o'er its rugged path,
Fell into that immeasurable void,
Scattering its waters to the passing
 winds. 570

Yet the gray precipice and solemn pine
And torrent were not all; — one silent nook
Was there. Even on the edge of that vast
 mountain,
Upheld by knotty roots and fallen rocks,
It overlooked in its serenity
The dark earth and the bending vault of
 stars.
It was a tranquil spot that seemed to smile
Even in the lap of horror. Ivy clasped
The fissured stones with its entwining arms,

And did embower with leaves forever
 green 580
And berries dark the smooth and even
 space
Of its inviolated floor ; and here
The children of the autumnal whirlwind
 bore
In wanton sport those bright leaves whose
 decay,
Red, yellow, or ethereally pale,
Rivals the pride of summer. 'T is the haunt
Of every gentle wind whose breath can
 teach
The wilds to love tranquillity. One step,
One human step alone, has ever broken
The stillness of its solitude ; one voice 590
Alone inspired its echoes ; — even that voice
Which hither came, floating among the
 winds,
And led the loveliest among human forms
To make their wild haunts the depository
Of all the grace and beauty that endued
Its motions, render up its majesty,
Scatter its music on the unfeeling storm,
And to the damp leaves and blue cavern
 mould,
Nurses of rainbow flowers and branching
 moss,
Commit the colors of that varying cheek, 600
That snowy breast, those dark and droop-
 ing eyes.

 The dim and hornèd moon hung low, and
 poured
A sea of lustre on the horizon's verge
That overflowed its mountains. Yellow
 mist
Filled the unbounded atmosphere, and
 drank
Wan moonlight even to fulness ; not a star
Shone, not a sound was heard ; the very
 winds,
Danger's grim playmates, on that precipice
Slept, clasped in his embrace. — O storm
 of death,
Whose sightless speed divides this sullen
 night ! 610
And thou, colossal Skeleton, that, still
Guiding its irresistible career
In thy devastating omnipotence,
Art king of this frail world ! from the red
 field
Of slaughter, from the reeking hospital,
The patriot's sacred couch, the snowy bed
Of innocence, the scaffold and the throne,

A mighty voice invokes thee ! Ruin calls
His brother Death ! A rare and regal prey
He hath prepared, prowling around the
 world ; 620
Glutted with which thou mayst repose, and
 men
Go to their graves like flowers or creeping
 worms,
Nor ever more offer at thy dark shrine
The unheeded tribute of a broken heart.

When on the threshold of the green
 recess
The wanderer's footsteps fell, he knew that
 death
Was on him. Yet a little, ere it fled,
Did he resign his high and holy soul
To images of the majestic past, 629
That paused within his passive being now,
Like winds that bear sweet music, when
 they breathe
Through some dim latticed chamber. He
 did place
His pale lean hand upon the rugged trunk
Of the old pine; upon an ivied stone
Reclined his languid head; his limbs did
 rest,
Diffused and motionless, on the smooth
 brink
Of that obscurest chasm; — and thus he
 lay,
Surrendering to their final impulses
The hovering powers of life. Hope and
 Despair,
The torturers, slept; no mortal pain or
 fear 640
Marred his repose; the influxes of sense
And his own being, unalloyed by pain,
Yet feebler and more feeble, calmly fed
The stream of thought, till he lay breath-
 ing there
At peace, and faintly smiling. His last
 sight
Was the great moon, which o'er the western
 line
Of the wide world her mighty horn sus-
 pended,
With whose dun beams inwoven darkness
 seemed
To mingle. Now upon the jagged hills
It rests; and still as the divided frame 650
Of the vast meteor sunk, the Poet's blood,
That ever beat in mystic sympathy
With Nature's ebb and flow, grew feebler
 still;

And when two lessening points of ligh'
 alone
Gleamed through the darkness, the altei
 nate gasp
Of his faint respiration scarce did stir
The stagnate night : — till the minutest ray
Was quenched, the pulse yet lingered in
 his heart.
It paused — it fluttered. But when hea-
 ven remained 659
Utterly black, the murky shades involved
An image silent, cold, and motionless,
As their own voiceless earth and vacant
 air.
Even as a vapor fed with golden beams
That ministered on sunlight, ere the west
Eclipses it, was now that wondrous frame —
No sense, no motion, no divinity —
A fragile lute, on whose harmonious strings
The breath of heaven did wander — a bright
 stream
Once fed with many-voicèd waves — a
 dream
Of youth, which night and time have
 quenched forever — 670
Still, dark, and dry, and unremembered
 now.

Oh, for Medea's wondrous alchemy,
Which wheresoe'er it fell made the earth
 gleam
With bright flowers, and the wintry boughs
 exhale
From vernal blooms fresh fragrance ! Oh,
 that God,
Profuse of poisons, would concede the
 chalice
Which but one living man has drained, wh(
 now,
Vessel of deathless wrath, a slave that feel
No proud exemption in the blighting curse
He bears, over the world wanders for-
 ever, 680
Lone as incarnate death ! Oh, that the
 dream
Of dark magician in his visioned cave,
Raking the cinders of a crucible
For life and power, even when his feeble
 hand
Shakes in its last decay, were the true law
Of this so lovely world ! But thou art fled,
Like some frail exhalation, which the dawn
Robes in its golden beams, — ah ! thou
 hast fled !
The brave, the gentle and the beautiful,

The child of grace and genius. Heartless
 things 690
Are done and said i' the world, and many
 worms
And beasts and men live on, and mighty
 Earth
From sea and mountain, city and wilder-
 ness,
In vesper low or joyous orison,
Lifts still its solemn voice : — but thou art
 fled —
Thou canst no longer know or love the
 shapes
Of this phantasmal scene, who have to thee
Been purest ministers, who are, alas !
Now thou art not ! Upon those pallid lips
So sweet even in their silence, on those
 eyes 700
That image sleep in death, upon that form
Yet safe from the worm's outrage, let no
 tear
Be shed — not even in thought. Nor, when
 those hues
Are gone, and those divinest lineaments,
Worn by the senseless wind, shall live alone

In the frail pauses of this simple strain,
Let not high verse, mourning the memory
Of that which is no more, or painting's
 woe
Or sculpture, speak in feeble imagery
Their own cold powers. Art and elo-
 quence, 710
And all the shows o' the world, are frail
 and vain
To weep a loss that turns their lights to
 shade.
It is a woe "too deep for tears," when
 all
Is reft at once, when some surpassing
 Spirit,
Whose light adorned the world around it
 leaves
Those who remain behind, not sobs or
 groans,
The passionate tumult of a clinging hope;
But pale despair and cold tranquillity,
Nature's vast frame, the web of human
 things,
Birth and the grave, that are not as they
 were. 720

ROSALIND

AND

HELEN

A MODERN ECLOGUE

Rosalind and Helen was begun at Marlow as early as the summer of 1817, and was sufficiently far advanced to lead Shelley to send copy to the publisher just before leaving England in March, 1818; it was finished in August, at the Baths of Lucca, and published in the spring of 1819. Shelley's original *Advertisement* to the volume, dated Naples, December 20, 1818, opens with the following :

'The story of *Rosalind and Helen* is, un-

doubtedly, not an attempt in the highest style of poetry. It is in no degree calculated to excite profound meditation; and if, by interesting the affections and amusing the imagination, it awaken a certain ideal melancholy favorable to the reception of more important impressions, it will produce in the reader all that the writer experienced in the composition. I resigned myself, as I wrote, to the impulse of the feelings which moulded the conception

of the story ; and this impulse determined the
pauses of a measure, which only pretends to
be regular inasmuch as it corresponds with,
and expresses, the irregularity of the imagin-
ations which inspired it.'

The feelings here spoken of ' which moulded
the conception of the story ' were suggested, in
part, by the relation of Mrs. Shelley with a
friend of her girlhood, Isabel Baxter, who fell
away from her early attachment in consequence
of Mrs. Shelley's flight with Shelley in July,
1814, and was afterward reconciled with her.
(Dowden, *Life*, ii. 130, 131.) Forman (Type
Facsimile of the original edition, Shelley Soci-
ety's Publications, Second Series, No. 17, In-
troduction) discusses the matter at length,
together with the reflection of political events
in England possibly to be detected in the
poem. Shelley wrote to Peacock, ' I lay no
stress on it one way or the other.' Mrs.
Shelley's note develops the reason for this
indifference :

' *Rosalind and Helen* was begun at Marlow,
and thrown aside, till I found it ; and, at my

request, it was completed. Shelley had no
care for any of his poems that did not ema-
nate from the depths of his mind, and develop
some high or abstruse truth. When he does
touch on human life and the human heart, no
pictures can be more faithful, more delicate,
more subtle, or more pathetic. He never men-
tioned Love, but he shed a grace, borrowed
from his own nature, that scarcely any other
poet has bestowed on that passion. When he
spoke of it as the law of life, which inasmuch
as we rebel against, we err and injure ourselves
and others, he promulgated that which he con-
sidered an irrefragable truth. In his eyes it
was the essence of our being, and all woe and
pain arose from the war made against it by
selfishness, or insensibility, or mistake. By
reverting in his mind to this first principle, he
discovered the source of many emotions, and
could disclose the secrets of all hearts, and his
delineations of passion and emotion touch the
finest chords in our nature. *Rosalind and Helen*
was finished during the summer of 1818, while
we were at the Baths of Lucca.'

ROSALIND AND HELEN

ROSALIND, HELEN, *and her Child.*

SCENE. *The Shore of the Lake of Como.*

HELEN

COME hither, my sweet Rosalind.
'T is long since thou and I have met;
And yet methinks it were unkind
Those moments to forget.
Come, sit by me. I see thee stand
By this lone lake, in this far land,
Thy loose hair in the light wind flying,
Thy sweet voice to each tone of even
United, and thine eyes replying
To the hues of yon fair heaven. 10
Come, gentle friend ! wilt sit by me ?
And be as thou wert wont to be
Ere we were disunited ?
None doth behold us now; the power
That led us forth at this lone hour
Will be but ill requited
If thou depart in scorn. Oh, come,
And talk of our abandoned home !
Remember, this is Italy,
And we are exiles. Talk with me 20
Of that our land, whose wilds and floods,
Barren and dark although they be,
Were dearer than these chestnut woods;
Those heathy paths, that inland stream,
And the blue mountains, shapes which seem
Like wrecks of childhood's sunny dream;

Which that we have abandoned now,
Weighs on the heart like that remorse
Which altered friendship leaves. I seek
No more our youthful intercourse. 30
That cannot be ! Rosalind, speak,
Speak to me ! Leave me not ! When morn
 did come,
When evening fell upon our common home,
When for one hour we parted, — do not
 frown;
I would not chide thee, though thy faith is
 broken;
But turn to me. Oh! by this cherished
 token
Of woven hair, which thou wilt not disown,
Turn, as 't were but the memory of me,
And not my scornèd self who prayed to thee !

ROSALIND

Is it a dream, or do I see 40
And hear frail Helen ? I would flee
Thy tainting touch; but former years
Arise, and bring forbidden tears;
And my o'erburdened memory
Seeks yet its lost repose in thee.
I share thy crime. I cannot choose
But weep for thee; mine own strange grief
But seldom stoops to such relief;
Nor ever did I love thee less,
Though mourning o'er thy wickedness 50
Even with a sister's woe. I knew
What to the evil world is due,

And therefore sternly did refuse
To link me with the infamy
Of one so lost as Helen. Now,
Bewildered by my dire despair,
Wondering I blush, and weep that thou
Shouldst love me still — thou only ! —
 There,
Let us sit on that gray stone
Till our mournful talk be done. 60

HELEN

Alas ! not there; I cannot bear
The murmur of this lake to hear.
A sound from there, Rosalind dear,
Which never yet I heard elsewhere
But in our native land, recurs,
Even here where now we meet. It stirs
Too much of suffocating sorrow !
In the dell of yon dark chestnut wood
Is a stone seat, a solitude
Less like our own. The ghost of peace 70
Will not desert this spot. To-morrow,
If thy kind feelings should not cease,
We may sit here.

ROSALIND

 Thou lead, my sweet,
And I will follow.

HENRY

 'T is Fenici's seat
Where you are going? This is not the
 way,
Mamma; it leads behind those trees that
 grow
Close to the little river.

HELEN

 Yes, I know;
I was bewildered. Kiss me and be gay,
Dear boy; why do you sob ?

HENRY

 I do not know;
But it might break any one's heart to see 80
You and the lady cry so bitterly.

HELEN

It is a gentle child, my friend. Go home,
Henry, and play with Lilla till I come.
We only cried with joy to see each other;
We are quite merry now. Good night.

 The boy
Lifted a sudden look upon his mother,

And, in the gleam of forced and hollow
 joy
Which lightened o'er her face, laughed with
 the glee
Of light and unsuspecting infancy,
And whispered in her ear, 'Bring home
 with you 90
That sweet strange lady-friend.' Then off
 he flew,
But stopped, and beckoned with a meaning
 smile,
Where the road turned. Pale Rosalind
 the while,
Hiding her face, stood weeping silently.

In silence then they took the way
Beneath the forest's solitude.
It was a vast and antique wood,
Through which they took their way;
And the gray shades of evening
O'er that green wilderness did fling 100
Still deeper solitude.
Pursuing still the path that wound
The vast and knotted trees around,
Through which slow shades were wander-
 ing,
To a deep lawny dell they came,
To a stone seat beside a spring,
O'er which the columned wood did frame
A roofless temple, like the fane
Where, ere new creeds could faith ob-
 tain,
Man's early race once knelt beneath 110
The overhanging deity.
O'er this fair fountain hung the sky,
Now spangled with rare stars. The snake,
The pale snake, that with eager breath
Creeps here his noontide thirst to slake,
Is beaming with many a mingled hue,
Shed from yon dome's eternal blue,
When he floats on that dark and lucid
 flood
In the light of his own loveliness;
And the birds, that in the fountain dip 120
Their plumes, with fearless fellowship
Above and round him wheel and hover.
The fitful wind is heard to stir
One solitary leaf on high;
The chirping of the grasshopper
Fills every pause. There is emotion
In all that dwells at noontide here;
Then through the intricate wild wood
A maze of life and light and motion
Is woven. But there is stillness now — 130
Gloom, and the trance of Nature now.

The snake is in his cave asleep;
The birds are on the branches dreaming;
Only the shadows creep;
Only the glow-worm is gleaming;
Only the owls and the nightingales
Wake in this dell when daylight fails,
And gray shades gather in the woods;
And the owls have all fled far away
In a merrier glen to hoot and play, 140
For the moon is veiled and sleeping now.
The accustomed nightingale still broods
On her accustomed bough,
But she is mute; for her false mate
Has fled and left her desolate.

This silent spot tradition old
Had peopled with the spectral dead.
For the roots of the speaker's hair felt cold
And stiff, as with tremulous lips he told
That a hellish shape at midnight led 150
The ghost of a youth with hoary hair,
And sate on the seat beside him there,
Till a naked child came wandering by,
When the fiend would change to a lady
 fair !
A fearful tale ! the truth was worse;
For here a sister and a brother
Had solemnized a monstrous curse,
Meeting in this fair solitude;
For beneath yon very sky,
Had they resigned to one another 160
Body and soul. The multitude,
Tracking them to the secret wood,
Tore limb from limb their innocent child,
And stabbed and trampled on its mother;
But the youth, for God's most holy grace,
A priest saved to burn in the market-place.

Duly at evening Helen came
To this lone silent spot,
From the wrecks of a tale of wilder sorrow
So much of sympathy to borrow 170
As soothed her own dark lot.
Duly each evening from her home,
With her fair child would Helen come
To sit upon that antique seat,
While the hues of day were pale;
And the bright boy beside her feet
Now lay, lifting at intervals
His broad blue eyes on her;
Now, where some sudden impulse calls,
Following. He was a gentle boy 180
And in all gentle sports took joy.
Oft in a dry leaf for a boat,
With a small feather for a sail,

His fancy on that spring would float,
If some invisible breeze might stir
Its marble calm; and Helen smiled
Through tears of awe on the gay child,
To think that a boy as fair as he,
In years which never more may be,
By that same fount, in that same wood, 190
The like sweet fancies had pursued;
And that a mother, lost like her,
Had mournfully sate watching him.
Then all the scene was wont to swim
Through the mist of a burning tear.
For many months had Helen known
This scene; and now she thither turned
Her footsteps, not alone.
The friend whose falsehood she had
 mourned
Sate with her on that seat of stone. 200
Silent they sate; for evening,
And the power its glimpses bring,
Had with one awful shadow quelled
The passion of their grief. They sate
With linkèd hands, for unrepelled
Had Helen taken Rosalind's.
Like the autumn wind, when it unbinds
The tangled locks of the nightshade's hair
Which is twined in the sultry summer air
Round the walls of an outworn sepulchre,
Did the voice of Helen, sad and sweet, 211
And the sound of her heart that ever beat
As with sighs and words she breathed on
 her,
Unbind the knots of her friend's despair,
Till her thoughts were free to float and flow;
And from her laboring bosom now,
Like the bursting of a prisoned flame,
The voice of a long-pent sorrow came.

ROSALIND

I saw the dark earth fall upon
The coffin; and I saw the stone 220
Laid over him whom this cold breast
Had pillowed to his nightly rest !
Thou knowest not, thou canst not know
My agony. Oh ! I could not weep.
The sources whence such blessings flow
Were not to be approached by me !
But I could smile, and I could sleep,
Though with a self-accusing heart.
In morning's light, in evening's gloom,
I watched — and would not thence de-
 part — 230
My husband's unlamented tomb.
My children knew their sire was gone;
But when I told them, 'He is dead,'

They laughed aloud in frantic glee,
They clapped their hands and leaped about,
Answering each other's ecstasy
With many a prank and merry shout.
But I sate silent and alone,
Wrapped in the mock of mourning weed.

They laughed, for he was dead; but I 240
Sate with a hard and tearless eye,
And with a heart which would deny
The secret joy it could not quell,
Low muttering o'er his loathèd name;
Till from that self-contention came
Remorse where sin was none; a hell
Which in pure spirits should not dwell.

I 'll tell thee truth. He was a man
Hard, selfish, loving only gold,
Yet full of guile; his pale eyes ran 250
With tears which each some falsehood told,
And oft his smooth and bridled tongue
Would give the lie to his flushing cheek;
He was a coward to the strong;
He was a tyrant to the weak,
On whom his vengeance he would wreak;
For scorn, whose arrows search the heart,
From many a stranger's eye would dart,
And on his memory cling, and follow
His soul to its home so cold and hollow. 260
He was a tyrant to the weak,
And we were such, alas the day!
Oft, when my little ones at play
Were in youth's natural lightness gay,
Or if they listened to some tale
Of travellers, or of fairyland,
When the light from the wood-fire's dying
 brand
Flashed on their faces, — if they heard
Or thought they heard upon the stair
His footstep, the suspended word 270
Died on my lips; we all grew pale;
The babe at my bosom was hushed with
 fear
If it thought it heard its father near;
And my two wild boys would near my knee
Cling, cowed and cowering fearfully.

I 'll tell thee truth: I loved another.
His name in my ear was ever ringing,
His form to my brain was ever clinging;
Yet, if some stranger breathed that name,
My lips turned white, and my heart beat
 fast. 280
My nights were once haunted by dreams of
 flame,

My days were dim in the shadow cast
By the memory of the same!
Day and night, day and night,
He was my breath and life and light,
For three short years, which soon were
 passed.
On the fourth, my gentle mother
Led me to the shrine, to be
His sworn bride eternally.
And now we stood on the altar stair, 290
When my father came from a distant land,
And with a loud and fearful cry
Rushed between us suddenly.
I saw the stream of his thin gray hair,
I saw his lean and lifted hand,
And heard his words — and live! O God!
Wherefore do I live? — 'Hold, hold!'
He cried, 'I tell thee 't is her brother!
Thy mother, boy, beneath the sod
Of yon churchyard rests in her shroud so
 cold; 300
I am now weak, and pale, and old;
We were once dear to one another,
I and that corpse! Thou art our child!'
Then with a laugh both long and wild
The youth upon the pavement fell.
They found him dead! All looked on
 me,
The spasms of my despair to see;
But I was calm. I went away;
I was clammy-cold like clay.
I did not weep; I did not speak; 310
But day by day, week after week,
I walked about like a corpse alive.
Alas! sweet friend, you must believe
This heart is stone — it did not break.

My father lived a little while,
But all might see that he was dying,
He smiled with such a woful smile.
When he was in the churchyard lying
Among the worms, we grew quite poor,
So that no one would give us bread; 320
My mother looked at me, and said
Faint words of cheer, which only meant
That she could die and be content;
So I went forth from the same church door
To another husband's bed.
And this was he who died at last,
When weeks and months and years had
 passed,
Through which I firmly did fulfil
My duties, a devoted wife,
With the stern step of vanquished will 330
Walking beneath the night of life,

Whose hours extinguished, like slow rain
Falling forever, pain by pain,
The very hope of death's dear rest;
Which, since the heart within my breast
Of natural life was dispossessed,
Its strange sustainer there had been.

When flowers were dead, and grass was
 green
Upon my mother's grave — that mother
Whom to outlive, and cheer, and make 340
My wan eyes glitter for her sake,
Was my vowed task, the single care
Which once gave life to my despair —
When she was a thing that did not stir,
And the crawling worms were cradling her
To a sleep more deep and so more sweet
Than a baby's rocked on its nurse's knee,
I lived; a living pulse then beat
Beneath my heart that awakened me.
What was this pulse so warm and free ? 350
Alas ! I knew it could not be
My own dull blood. 'T was like a thought
Of liquid love, that spread and wrought
Under my bosom and in my brain,
And crept with the blood through every
 vein,
And hour by hour, day after day,
The wonder could not charm away
But laid in sleep my wakeful pain,
Until I knew it was a child,
And then I wept. For long, long years 360
These frozen eyes had shed no tears;
But now — 't was the season fair and mild
When April has wept itself to May;
I sate through the sweet sunny day
By my window bowered round with leaves,
And down my cheeks the quick tears ran
Like twinkling rain-drops from the eaves,
When warm spring showers are passing
 o'er.
O Helen, none can ever tell
The joy it was to weep once more ! 370

I wept to think how hard it were
To kill my babe, and take from it
The sense of light, and the warm air,
And my own fond and tender care,
And love and smiles; ere I knew yet
That these for it might, as for me,
Be the masks of a grinning mockery.
And haply, I would dream, 't were sweet
To feed it from my faded breast,
Or mark my own heart's restless beat 380
Rock it to its untroubled rest,

And watch the growing soul beneath
Dawn in faint smiles; and hear its breath,
Half interrupted by calm sighs,
And search the depth of its fair eyes
For long departed memories !
And so I lived till that sweet load
Was lightened. Darkly forward flowed
The stream of years, and on it bore
Two shapes of gladness to my sight; 39c
Two other babes, delightful more,
In my lost soul's abandoned night,
Than their own country ships may be
Sailing towards wrecked mariners
Who cling to the rock of a wintry sea.
For each, as it came, brought soothing
 tears;
And a loosening warmth, as each one lay
Sucking the sullen milk away,
About my frozen heart did play,
And weaned it, oh, how painfully — 400
As they themselves were weaned each one
From that sweet food — even from the
 thirst
Of death, and nothingness, and rest,
Strange inmate of a living breast,
Which all that I had undergone
Of grief and shame, since she who first
The gates of that dark refuge closed
Came to my sight, and almost burst
The seal of that Lethean spring —
But these fair shadows interposed. 410
For all delights are shadows now !
And from my brain to my dull brow
The heavy tears gather and flow.
I cannot speak — oh, let me weep !

The tears which fell from her wan eyes
Glimmered among the moonlight dew.
Her deep hard sobs and heavy sighs
Their echoes in the darkness threw.
When she grew calm, she thus did keep
The tenor of her tale: —

 He died; 420
I know not how; he was not old,
If age be numbered by its years;
But he was bowed and bent with fears,
Pale with the quenchless thirst of gold,
Which, like fierce fever, left him weak;
And his strait lip and bloated cheek
Were warped in spasms by hollow sneers;
And selfish cares with barren plough,
Not age, had lined his narrow brow,
And foul and cruel thoughts, which feed 430
Upon the withering life within,

Like vipers on some poisonous weed.
Whether his ill were death or sin
None knew, until he died indeed,
And then men owned they were the same.

Seven days within my chamber lay
That corse, and my babes made holiday.
At last, I told them what is death.
The eldest, with a kind of shame,
Came to my knees with silent breath, 440
And sate awe-stricken at my feet;
And soon the others left their play,
And sate there too. It is unmeet
To shed on the brief flower of youth
The withering knowledge of the grave.
From me remorse then wrung that truth.
I could not bear the joy which gave
Too just a response to mine own.
In vain. I dared not feign a groan;
And in their artless looks I saw, 450
Between the mists of fear and awe,
That my own thought was theirs; and they
Expressed it not in words, but said,
Each in its heart, how every day
Will pass in happy work and play,
Now he is dead and gone away !

After the funeral all our kin
Assembled, and the will was read.
My friend, I tell thee, even the dead
Have strength, their putrid shrouds within,
To blast and torture. Those who live 461
Still fear the living, but a corse
Is merciless, and Power doth give
To such pale tyrants half the spoil
He rends from those who groan and toil,
Because they blush not with remorse
Among their crawling worms. Behold,
I have no child ! my tale grows old
With grief, and staggers; let it reach
The limits of my feeble speech, 470
And languidly at length recline
On the brink of its own grave and mine.

Thou knowest what a thing is Poverty
Among the fallen on evil days.
'T is Crime, and Fear, and Infamy,
And houseless Want in frozen ways
Wandering ungarmented, and Pain,
And, worse than all, that inward stain,
Foul Self-contempt, which drowns in sneers
Youth's starlight smile, and makes its
 tears 480
First like hot gall, then dry forever !
And well thou knowest a mother never

Could doom her children to this ill,
And well he knew the same. The will
Imported that, if e'er again
I sought my children to behold,
Or in my birthplace did remain
Beyond three days, whose hours were told,
They should inherit nought; and he,
To whom next came their patrimony, 490
A sallow lawyer, cruel and cold,
Aye watched me, as the will was read,
With eyes askance, which sought to see
The secrets of my agony;
And with close lips and anxious brow
Stood canvassing still to and fro
The chance of my resolve, and all
The dead man's caution just did call;
For in that killing lie 't was said —
' She is adulterous, and doth hold 500
In secret that the Christian creed
Is false, and therefore is much need
That I should have a care to save
My children from eternal fire.'
Friend, he was sheltered by the grave,
And therefore dared to be a liar !
In truth, the Indian on the pyre
Of her dead husband, half consumed,
As well might there be false as I
To those abhorred embraces doomed, 510
Far worse than fire's brief agony.
As to the Christian creed, if true
Or false, I never questioned it;
I took it as the vulgar do;
Nor my vexed soul had leisure yet
To doubt the things men say, or deem
That they are other than they seem.

All present who those crimes did hear,
In feigned or actual scorn and fear,
Men, women, children, slunk away, 520
Whispering with self-contented pride
Which half suspects its own base lie.
I spoke to none, nor did abide,
But silently I went my way,
Nor noticed I where joyously
Sate my two younger babes at play
In the courtyard through which I passed;
But went with footsteps firm and fast
Till I came to the brink of the ocean
 green,
And there, a woman with gray hairs, 530
Who had my mother's servant been,
Kneeling, with many tears and prayers,
Made me accept a purse of gold,
Half of the earnings she had kept
To refuge her when weak and old.

With woe, which never sleeps or slept,
I wander now. 'Tis a vain thought —
But on yon Alp, whose snowy head
'Mid the azure air is islanded,
(We see it — o'er the flood of cloud, 540
Which sunrise from its eastern caves
Drives, wrinkling into golden waves,
Hung with its precipices proud —
From that gray stone where first we met)
There — now who knows the dead feel
 nought ? —
Should be my grave; for he who yet
Is my soul's soul once said: ''T were sweet
'Mid stars and lightnings to abide,
And winds, and lulling snows that beat
With their soft flakes the mountain wide,
Where weary meteor lamps repose, 551
And languid storms their pinions close,
And all things strong and bright and pure,
And ever during, aye endure.
Who knows, if one were buried there,
But these things might our spirits make,
Amid the all-surrounding air,
Their own eternity partake ?'
Then 't was a wild and playful saying
At which I laughed or seemed to laugh. 560
They were his words — now heed my pray-
 ing,
And let them be my epitaph.
Thy memory for a term may be
My monument. Wilt remember me ?
I know thou wilt; and canst forgive,
Whilst in this erring world to live
My soul disdained not, that I thought
Its lying forms were worthy aught,
And much less thee.

<div style="text-align:center">HELEN</div>

 Oh, speak not so !
But come to me and pour thy woe 570
Into this heart, full though it be,
Aye overflowing with its own.
I thought that grief had severed me
From all beside who weep and groan,
Its likeness upon earth to be —
Its express image; but thou art
More wretched. Sweet, we will not part
Henceforth, if death be not division;
If so, the dead feel no contrition.
But wilt thou hear, since last we parted, 580
All that has left me broken-hearted ?

<div style="text-align:center">ROSALIND</div>

Yes, speak. The faintest stars are scarcely
 shorn

Of their thin beams by that delusive morn
Which sinks again in darkness, like the
 light
Of early love, soon lost in total night.

<div style="text-align:center">HELEN</div>

Alas ! Italian winds are mild,
But my bosom is cold — wintry cold;
When the warm air weaves, among the
 fresh leaves,
Soft music, my poor brain is wild,
And I am weak like a nursling child, 590
Though my soul with grief is gray and
 old.

<div style="text-align:center">ROSALIND</div>

Weep not at thine own words, though they
 must make
Me weep. What is thy tale ?

<div style="text-align:center">HELEN</div>

 I fear 't will shake
Thy gentle heart with tears. Thou well
Rememberest when we met no more;
And, though I dwelt with Lionel,
That friendless caution pierced me sore
With grief; a wound my spirit bore
Indignantly — but when he died,
With him lay dead both hope and pride.

Alas ! all hope is buried now. 601
But then men dreamed the aged earth
Was laboring in that mighty birth
Which many a poet and a sage
Has aye foreseen — the happy age
When truth and love shall dwell below
Among the works and ways of men;
Which on this world not power but will
Even now is wanting to fulfil.

Among mankind what thence befell 610
Of strife, how vain, is known too well;
When Liberty's dear pæan fell
'Mid murderous howls. To Lionel,
Though of great wealth and lineage high,
Yet through those dungeon walls there
 came
Thy thrilling light, O Liberty !
And as the meteor's midnight flame
Startles the dreamer, sun-like truth
Flashed on his visionary youth,
And filled him, not with love, but faith, 620
And hope, and courage mute in death;
For love and life in him were twins,
Born at one birth. In every other

First life, then love, its course begins,
Though they be children of one mother;
And so through this dark world they fleet
Divided, till in death they meet;
But he loved all things ever. Then
He passed amid the strife of men,
And stood at the throne of armèd power
Pleading for a world of woe. 631
Secure as one on a rock-built tower
O'er the wrecks which the surge trails to
 and fro,
'Mid the passions wild of humankind
He stood, like a spirit calming them;
For, it was said, his words could bind
Like music the lulled crowd, and stem
That torrent of unquiet dream
Which mortals truth and reason deem,
But is revenge and fear and pride. 640
Joyous he was; and hope and peace
On all who heard him did abide,
Raining like dew from his sweet talk,
As where the evening star may walk
Along the brink of the gloomy seas,
Liquid mists of splendor quiver.
His very gestures touched to tears
The unpersuaded tyrant, never
So moved before; his presence stung
The torturers with their victim's pain, 650
And none knew how; and through their
 ears
The subtle witchcraft of his tongue
Unlocked the hearts of those who keep
Gold, the world's bond of slavery.
Men wondered, and some sneered to see
One sow what he could never reap;
For he is rich, they said, and young,
And might drink from the depths of luxury.
If he seeks fame, fame never crowned
The champion of a trampled creed; 660
If he seeks power, power is enthroned
'Mid ancient rights and wrongs, to feed
Which hungry wolves with praise and spoil
Those who would sit near power must toil;
And such, there sitting, all may see.
What seeks he ? All that others seek
He casts away, like a vile weed
Which the sea casts unreturningly.
That poor and hungry men should break
The laws which wreak them toil and scorn
We understand; but Lionel, 671
We know, is rich and nobly born.
So wondered they; yet all men loved
Young Lionel, though few approved;
All but the priests, whose hatred fell
Like the unseen blight of a smiling day,

The withering honey-dew which clings
Under the bright green buds of May
Whilst they unfold their emerald wings;
For he made verses wild and queer 680
On the strange creeds priests hold so dear
Because they bring them land and gold.
Of devils and saints and all such gear
He made tales which whoso heard or read
Would laugh till he were almost dead.
So this grew a proverb: ' Don't get old
Till Lionel's *Banquet in Hell* you hear,
And then you will laugh yourself young
 again.'
So the priests hated him, and he
Repaid their hate with cheerful glee. 690

Ah, smiles and joyance quickly died,
For public hope grew pale and dim
In an altered time and tide,
And in its wasting withered him,
As a summer flower that blows too soon
Droops in the smile of the waning moon,
When it scatters through an April night
The frozen dews of wrinkling blight.
None now hoped more. Gray Power was
 seated
Safely on her ancestral throne; 700
And Faith, the Python, undefeated
Even to its blood-stained steps dragged on
Her foul and wounded train; and men
Were trampled and deceived again,
And words and shows again could bind
The wailing tribes of humankind
In scorn and famine. Fire and blood
Raged round the raging multitude,
To fields remote by tyrants sent
To be the scornèd instrument 710
With which they drag from mines of gore
The chains their slaves yet ever wore;
And in the streets men met each other,
And by old altars and in halls,
And smiled again at festivals.
But each man found in his heart's brother
Cold cheer; for all, though half deceived,
The outworn creeds again believed,
And the same round anew began
Which the weary world yet ever ran. 720

Many then wept, not tears, but gall,
Within their hearts, like drops which fall
Wasting the fountain-stone away.
And in that dark and evil day
Did all desires and thoughts that claim
Men's care — ambition, friendship, fame,
Love, hope, though hope was now despair —

Indue the colors of this change,
As from the all-surrounding air 729
The earth takes hues obscure and strange,
When storm and earthquake linger there.

And so, my friend, it then befell
To many, — most to Lionel,
Whose hope was like the life of youth
Within him, and when dead became
A spirit of unresting flame,
Which goaded him in his distress
Over the world's vast wilderness.
Three years he left his native land,
And on the fourth, when he returned, 740
None knew him; he was stricken deep
With some disease of mind, and turned
Into aught unlike Lionel.
On him — on whom, did he pause in sleep,
Serenest smiles were wont to keep,
And, did he wake, a wingèd band
Of bright Persuasions, which had fed
On his sweet lips and liquid eyes,
Kept their swift pinions half outspread
To do on men his least command — 750
On him, whom once 't was paradise
Even to behold, now misery lay.
In his own heart 't was merciless —
To all things else none may express
Its innocence and tenderness.

'T was said that he had refuge sought
In love from his unquiet thought
In distant lands, and been deceived
By some strange show; for there were
 found,
Blotted with tears — as those relieved 760
By their own words are wont to do —
These mournful verses on the ground,
By all who read them blotted too.

' How am I changed ! my hopes were once
 like fire;
I loved, and I believed that life was love.
How am I lost ! on wings of swift desire
 Among Heaven's winds my spirit once
 did move.
I slept, and silver dreams did aye inspire
 My liquid sleep; I woke, and did approve
All Nature to my heart, and thought to
 make 770
A paradise of earth for one sweet sake.

' I love, but I believe in love no more.
 I feel desire, but hope not. Oh, from
 sleep

Most vainly must my weary brain implore
 Its long lost flattery now ! I wake to
 weep,
And sit through the long day gnawing the
 core
 Of my bitter heart, and, like a miser,
 keep —
Since none in what I feel take pain or
 pleasure —
To my own soul its self-consuming trea-
 sure.'

He dwelt beside me near the sea; 780
And oft in evening did we meet,
When the waves, beneath the starlight,
 flee
O'er the yellow sands with silver feet,
And talked. Our talk was sad and sweet,
Till slowly from his mien there passed
The desolation which it spoke;
And smiles — as when the lightning's blast
Has parched some heaven-delighting oak,
The next spring shows leaves pale and
 rare,
But like flowers delicate and fair, 790
On its rent boughs — again arrayed
His countenance in tender light;
His words grew subtle fire, which made
The air his hearers breathed delight;
His motions, like the winds, were free,
Which bend the bright grass gracefully,
Then fade away in circlets faint;
And wingèd Hope — on which upborne
His soul seemed hovering in his eyes,
Like some bright spirit newly born 800
Floating amid the sunny skies —
Sprang forth from his rent heart anew.
Yet o'er his talk, and looks, and mien,
Tempering their loveliness too keen,
Past woe its shadow backward threw;
Till, like an exhalation spread
From flowers half drunk with evening dew,
They did become infectious — sweet
And subtle mists of sense and thought,
Which wrapped us soon, when we might
 meet, 810
Almost from our own looks and aught
The wild world holds. And so his mind
Was healed, while mine grew sick with
 fear;
For ever now his health declined,
Like some frail bark which cannot bear
The impulse of an altered wind,
Though prosperous; and my heart grew
 full,

'Mid its new joy, of a new care;
For his cheek became, not pale, but fair,
As rose-o'ershadowed lilies are; 820
And soon his deep and sunny hair,
In this alone less beautiful,
Like grass in tombs grew wild and rare.
The blood in his translucent veins
Beat, not like animal life, but love
Seemed now its sullen springs to move,
When life had failed, and all its pains;
And sudden sleep would seize him oft
Like death, so calm, — but that a tear,
His pointed eye-lashes between, 830
Would gather in the light serene
Of smiles whose lustre bright and soft
Beneath lay undulating there.
His breath was like inconstant flame
As eagerly it went and came;
And I hung o'er him in his sleep,
Till, like an image in the lake
Which rains disturb, my tears would break
The shadow of that slumber deep.
Then he would bid me not to weep, 840
And say, with flattery false yet sweet,
That death and he could never meet,
If I would never part with him.
And so we loved, and did unite
All that in us was yet divided;
For when he said, that many a rite,
By men to bind but once provided,
Could not be shared by him and me,
Or they would kill him in their glee,
I shuddered, and then laughing said —
'We will have rites our faith to bind, 851
But our church shall be the starry night,
Our altar the grassy earth outspread,
And our priest the muttering wind.'

'T was sunset as I spoke. One star
Had scarce burst forth, when from afar
The ministers of misrule sent
Seized upon Lionel, and bore
His chained limbs to a dreary tower,
In the midst of a city vast and wide. 860
For he, they said, from his mind had
 bent
Against their gods keen blasphemy,
For which, though his soul must roasted
 be
In hell's red lakes immortally,
Yet even on earth must he abide
The vengeance of their slaves: a trial,
I think, men call it. What avail
Are prayers and tears, which chase de-
 nial

From the fierce savage nursed in hate ?
What the knit soul that pleading and
 pale 870
Makes wan the quivering cheek which
 late
It painted with its own delight ?
We were divided. As I could,
I stilled the tingling of my blood,
And followed him in their despite,
As a widow follows, pale and wild,
The murderers and corse of her only child;
And when we came to the prison door,
And I prayed to share his dungeon floor
With prayers which rarely have been
 spurned, 880
And when men drove me forth, and I
Stared with blank frenzy on the sky, —
A farewell look of love he turned,
Half calming me; then gazed awhile,
As if through that black and massy pile,
And through the crowd around him there,
And through the dense and murky air,
And the thronged streets, he did espy
What poets know and prophesy;
And said, with voice that made them
 shiver 890
And clung like music in my brain,
And which the mute walls spoke again
Prolonging it with deepened strain —
'Fear not the tyrants shall rule forever,
Or the priests of the bloody faith;
They stand on the brink of that mighty
 river,
Whose waves they have tainted with death;
It is fed from the depths of a thousand
 dells,
Around them it foams, and rages, and
 swells,
And their swords and their sceptres I float-
 ing see, 900
Like wrecks, in the surge of eternity.'

I dwelt beside the prison gate;
And the strange crowd that out and in
Passed, some, no doubt, with mine own
 fate,
Might have fretted me with its ceaseless
 din,
But the fever of care was louder within.
Soon but too late, in penitence
Or fear, his foes released him thence.
I saw his thin and languid form,
As leaning on the jailor's arm, 910
Whose hardened eyes grew moist the while
To meet his mute and faded smile

And hear his words of kind farewell,
He tottered forth from his damp cell.
Many had never wept before,
From whom fast tears then gushed and
 fell;
Many will relent no more,
Who sobbed like infants then; ay, all
Who thronged the prison's stony hall,
The rulers or the slaves of law, 920
Felt with a new surprise and awe
That they were human, till strong shame
Made them again become the same.
The prison bloodhounds, huge and grim,
From human looks the infection caught,
And fondly crouched and fawned on him;
And men have heard the prisoners say,
Who in their rotting dungeons lay,
That from that hour, throughout one
 day,
The fierce despair and hate which kept 930
Their trampled bosoms almost slept,
Where, like twin vultures, they hung feed-
 ing
On each heart's wound, wide torn and
 bleeding, —
Because their jailors' rule, they thought,
Grew merciful, like a parent's sway.

I know not how, but we were free;
And Lionel sate alone with me,
As the carriage drove through the streets
 apace;
And we looked upon each other's face;
And the blood in our fingers intertwined 940
Ran like the thoughts of a single mind,
As the swift emotions went and came
Through the veins of each united frame.
So through the long, long streets we passed
Of the million-peopled City vast;
Which is that desert, where each one
Seeks his mate yet is alone,
Beloved and sought and mourned of none;
Until the clear blue sky was seen,
And the grassy meadows bright and
 green. 950
And then I sunk in his embrace
Enclosing there a mighty space
Of love; and so we travelled on
By woods, and fields of yellow flowers,
And towns, and villages, and towers,
Day after day of happy hours.
It was the azure time of June,
When the skies are deep in the stainless
 noon,
And the warm and fitful breezes shake

The fresh green leaves of the hedge-row
 briar; 960
And there were odors then to make
The very breath we did respire
A liquid element, whereon
Our spirits, like delighted things
That walk the air on subtle wings,
Floated and mingled far away
'Mid the warm winds of the sunny day.
And when the evening star came forth
Above the curve of the new bent moon,
And light and sound ebbed from the
 earth, 970
Like the tide of the full and the weary
 sea
To the depths of its own tranquillity,
Our natures to its own repose
Did the earth's breathless sleep attune;
Like flowers, which on each other close
Their languid leaves when daylight 's gone,
We lay, till new emotions came,
Which seemed to make each mortal frame
One soul of interwoven flame,
A life in life, a second birth 980
In worlds diviner far than earth; —
Which, like two strains of harmony
That mingle in the silent sky,
Then slowly disunite, passed by
And left the tenderness of tears,
A soft oblivion of all fears,
A sweet sleep: — so we travelled on
Till we came to the home of Lionel,
Among the mountains wild and lone,
Beside the hoary western sea, 990
Which near the verge of the echoing shore
The massy forest shadowed o'er.

The ancient steward with hair all hoar,
As we alighted, wept to see
His master changed so fearfully;
And the old man's sobs did waken me
From my dream of unremaining gladness;
The truth flashed o'er me like quick mad-
 ness
When I looked, and saw that there was
 death
On Lionel. Yet day by day 1000
He lived, till fear grew hope and faith,
And in my soul I dared to say,
Nothing so bright can pass away;
Death is dark, and foul, and dull,
But he is — oh, how beautiful !
Yet day by day he grew more weak,
And his sweet voice, when he might
 speak,

Which ne'er was loud, became more low;
And the light which flashed through his
 waxen cheek
Grew faint, as the rose-like hues which
 flow 1010
From sunset o'er the Alpine snow;
And death seemed not like death in him,
For the spirit of life o'er every limb
Lingered, a mist of sense and thought.
When the summer wind faint odors
 brought
From mountain flowers, even as it passed,
His cheek would change, as the noonday
 sea
Which the dying breeze sweeps fitfully.
If but a cloud the sky o'ercast, 1019
You might see his color come and go,
And the softest strain of music made
Sweet smiles, yet sad, arise and fade
Amid the dew of his tender eyes;
And the breath, with intermitting flow,
Made his pale lips quiver and part.
You might hear the beatings of his heart,
Quick but not strong ; and with my
 tresses
When oft he playfully would bind
In the bowers of mossy lonelinesses
His neck, and win me so to mingle 1030
In the sweet depth of woven caresses,
And our faint limbs were intertwined, —
Alas ! the unquiet life did tingle
From mine own heart through every
 vein,
Like a captive in dreams of liberty,
Who beats the walls of his stony cell.
But his, it seemed already free,
Like the shadow of fire surrounding me !
On my faint eyes and limbs did dwell
That spirit as it passed, till soon — 1040
As a frail cloud wandering o'er the moon,
Beneath its light invisible,
Is seen when it folds its gray wings
 again
To alight on midnight's dusky plain —
I lived and saw, and the gathering soul
Passed from beneath that strong control,
And I fell on a life which was sick with
 fear
Of all the woe that now I bear.

Amid a bloomless myrtle wood,
On a green and sea-girt promontory 1050
Not far from where we dwelt, there
 stood,
In record of a sweet sad story,

An altar and a temple bright
Circled by steps, and o'er the gate
Was sculptured, ' To Fidelity; '
And in the shrine an image sate
All veiled; but there was seen the light
Of smiles which faintly could express
A mingled pain and tenderness
Through that ethereal drapery. 1060
The left hand held the head, the right —
Beyond the veil, beneath the skin,
You might see the nerves quivering
 within —
Was forcing the point of a barbèd dart
Into its side-convulsing heart.
An unskilled hand, yet one informed
With genius, had the marble warmed
With that pathetic life. This tale
It told: A dog had from the sea,
When the tide was raging fearfully, 1070
Dragged Lionel's mother, weak and pale,
Then died beside her on the sand,
And she that temple thence had planned;
But it was Lionel's own hand
Had wrought the image. Each new moon
That lady did, in this lone fane,
The rites of a religion sweet
Whose god was in her heart and brain.
The seasons' loveliest flowers were strewn
On the marble floor beneath her feet, 1080
And she brought crowns of sea-buds
 white
Whose odor is so sweet and faint,
And weeds, like branching chrysolite,
Woven in devices fine and quaint;
And tears from her brown eyes did stain
The altar; need but look upon
That dying statue, fair and wan,
If tears should cease, to weep again;
And rare Arabian odors came,
Through the myrtle copses, steaming
 thence 1090
From the hissing frankincense,
Whose smoke, wool-white as ocean foam,
Hung in dense flocks beneath the dome —
That ivory dome, whose azure night
With golden stars, like heaven, was bright
O'er the split cedar's pointed flame;
And the lady's harp would kindle there
The melody of an old air,
Softer than sleep; the villagers
Mixed their religion up with hers, 1100
And, as they listened round, shed tears.

One eve he led me to this fane.
Daylight on its last purple cloud

Was lingering gray, and soon her strain
The nightingale began; now loud,
Climbing in circles the windless sky,
Now dying music; suddenly
'T is scattered in a thousand notes;
And now to the hushed ear it floats
Like field-smells known in infancy, 1110
Then, failing, soothes the air again.
We sate within that temple lone,
Pavilioned round with Parian stone;
His mother's harp stood near, and oft
I had awakened music soft
Amid its wires; the nightingale
Was pausing in her heaven-taught tale.
' Now drain the cup,' said Lionel,
' Which the poet-bird has crowned so
 well
With the wine of her bright and liquid
 song ! 1120
Heard'st thou not sweet words among
That heaven-resounding minstrelsy ?
Heard'st thou not that those who die
Awake in a world of ecstasy ?
That love, when limbs are interwoven,
And sleep, when the night of life is cloven,
And thought, to the world's dim bound-
 aries clinging,
And music, when one beloved is singing,
Is death ? Let us drain right joyously
The cup which the sweet bird fills for
 me.' 1130
He paused, and to my lips he bent
His own; like spirit his words went
Through all my limbs with the speed of
 fire;
And his keen eyes, glittering through
 mine,
Filled me with the flame divine
Which in their orbs was burning far,
Like the light of an unmeasured star
In the sky of midnight dark and deep;
Yes, 't was his soul that did inspire 1139
Sounds which my skill could ne'er awaken;
And first, I felt my fingers sweep
The harp, and a long quivering cry
Burst from my lips in symphony;
The dusk and solid air was shaken,
As swift and swifter the notes came
From my touch, that wandered like quick
 flame,
And from my bosom, laboring
With some unutterable thing.
The awful sound of my own voice made
My faint lips tremble; in some mood 1150
Of wordless thought Lionel stood

So pale, that even beside his cheek
The snowy column from its shade
Caught whiteness; yet his countenance,
Raised upward, burned with radiance
Of spirit-piercing joy whose light,
Like the moon struggling through the night
Of whirlwind-rifted clouds, did break
With beams that might not be confined.
I paused, but soon his gestures kindled
New power, as by the moving wind 1161
The waves are lifted; and my song
To low soft notes now changed and dwin-
 dled,
And, from the twinkling wires among,
My languid fingers drew and flung
Circles of life-dissolving sound,
Yet faint; in aëry rings they bound
My Lionel, who, as every strain
Grew fainter but more sweet, his mien
Sunk with the sound relaxedly; 1170
And slowly now he turned to me,
As slowly faded from his face
That awful joy; with look serene
He was soon drawn to my embrace,
And my wild song then died away
In murmurs; words I dare not say
We mixed, and on his lips mine fed
Till they methought felt still and cold.
' What is it with thee, love ? ' I said;
No word, no look, no motion ! yes, 1180
There was a change, but spare to guess,
Nor let that moment's hope be told.
I looked, — and knew that he was dead;
And fell, as the eagle on the plain
Falls when life deserts her brain,
And the mortal lightning is veiled again.

Oh, that I were now dead ! but such —
Did they not, love, demand too much,
Those dying murmurs ? — he forbade.
Oh, that I once again were mad ! 1190
And yet, dear Rosalind, not so,
For I would live to share thy woe.
Sweet boy ! did I forget thee too ?
Alas, we know not what we do
When we speak words.

 No memory more
Is in my mind of that sea-shore.
Madness came on me, and a troop
Of misty shapes did seem to sit
Beside me, on a vessel's poop, 1199
And the clear north wind was driving it.
Then I heard strange tongues, and saw
 strange flowers,

And the stars methought grew unlike ours,
And the azure sky and the stormless sea
Made me believe that I had died
And waked in a world which was to me
Drear hell, though heaven to all beside.
Then a dead sleep fell on my mind,
Whilst animal life many long years
Had rescued from a chasm of tears;
And, when I woke, I wept to find 1210
That the same lady, bright and wise,
With silver locks and quick brown eyes,
The mother of my Lionel,
Had tended me in my distress,
And died some months before. Nor less
Wonder, but far more peace and joy,
Brought in that hour my lovely boy.
For through that trance my soul had well
The impress of thy being kept;
And if I waked or if I slept, 1220
No doubt, though memory faithless be,
Thy image ever dwelt on me;
And thus, O Lionel, like thee
Is our sweet child. 'T is sure most strange
I knew not of so great a change
As that which gave him birth, who now
Is all the solace of my woe.

That Lionel great wealth had left
By will to me, and that of all
The ready lies of law bereft 1230
My child and me, — might well befall.
But let me think not of the scorn
Which from the meanest I have borne,
When, for my child's belovèd sake,
I mixed with slaves, to vindicate
The very laws themselves do make;
Let me not say scorn is my fate,
Lest I be proud, suffering the same
With those who live in deathless fame.

She ceased. — ' Lo, where red morning
 through the woods 1240
Is burning o'er the dew ! ' said Rosalind.
And with these words they rose, and
 towards the flood
Of the blue lake, beneath the leaves, now
 wind
With equal steps and fingers intertwined.
Thence to a lonely dwelling, where the
 shore
Is shadowed with steep rocks, and cypresses
Cleave with their dark green cones the
 silent skies
And with their shadows the clear depths
 below,

And where a little terrace from its bowers
Of blooming myrtle and faint lemon
 flowers 1250
Scatters its sense-dissolving fragrance o'er
The liquid marble of the windless lake;
And where the aged forest's limbs look
 hoar
Under the leaves which their green gar-
 ments make,
They come. 'T is Helen's home, and clean
 and white,
Like one which tyrants spare on our own
 land
In some such solitude; its casements bright
Shone through their vine-leaves in the
 morning sun,
And even within 't was scarce like Italy.
And when she saw how all things there
 were planned 1260
As in an English home, dim memory
Disturbed poor Rosalind; she stood as one
Whose mind is where his body cannot
 be,
Till Helen led her where her child yet
 slept,
And said, ' Observe, that brow was Lionel's,
Those lips were his, and so he ever kept
One arm in sleep, pillowing his head with
 it.
You cannot see his eyes — they are two
 wells
Of liquid love. Let us not wake him yet.'
But Rosalind could bear no more, and
 wept 1270
A shower of burning tears which fell upon
His face, and so his opening lashes shone
With tears unlike his own, as he did leap
In sudden wonder from his innocent sleep.

So Rosalind and Helen lived together
Thenceforth — changed in all else, yet
 friends again,
Such as they were, when o'er the mountain
 heather
They wandered in their youth through sun
 and rain.
And after many years, for human things
Change even like the ocean and the wind,
Her daughter was restored to Rosalind, 1281
And in their circle thence some visitings
Of joy 'mid their new calm would inter-
 vene.
A lovely child she was, of looks serene,
And motions which o'er things indifferent
 shed

The grace and gentleness from whence
 they came.
And Helen's boy grew with her, and they
 fed
From the same flowers of thought, until
 each mind
Like springs which mingle in one flood
 became; 1289
And in their union soon their parents saw
The shadow of the peace denied to them.
And Rosalind — for when the living stem
Is cankered in its heart, the tree must
 fall —
Died ere her time; and with deep grief and
 awe
The pale survivors followed her remains
Beyond the region of dissolving rains,
Up the cold mountain she was wont to
 call
Her tomb; and on Chiavenna's precipice
They raised a pyramid of lasting ice,
Whose polished sides, ere day had yet
 begun, 1300
Caught the first glow of the unrisen sun,
The last, when it had sunk; and through
 the night

The charioteers of Arctos wheelèd round
Its glittering point, as seen from Helen's
 home,
Whose sad inhabitants each year would
 come,
With willing steps climbing that rugged
 height,
And hang long locks of hair, and garlands
 bound
With amaranth flowers, which, in the
 clime's despite,
Filled the frore air with unaccustomed
 light;
Such flowers as in the wintry memory
 bloom 131c
Of one friend left adorned that frozen
 tomb.

Helen, whose spirit was of softer mould,
Whose sufferings too were less, death slow-
 lier led
Into the peace of his dominion cold.
She died among her kindred, being old.
And know, that if love die not in the dead
As in the living, none of mortal kind
Are blessed as now Helen and Rosalind.

JULIAN AND MADDALO

A CONVERSATION

The meadows with fresh streams, the bees with thyme,
The goats with the green leaves of budding Spring,
Are saturated not — nor Love with tears.

<div align="right">VIRGIL'S <i>Gallus.</i></div>

Julian and Maddalo is the fruit of Shelley's first visit to Venice in 1818, where he found Byron, and the poem is a reflection of their companionship, *Julian* standing for Shelley, *Maddalo* for Byron, and the child being Byron's daughter, Allegra. It was written in the fall, at Este, and received its last revision in May, 1819, but was not published, notwithstanding some efforts of Shelley to bring it out, until after his death, when it was included in the *Posthumous Poems*, 1824. Shelley had it in mind to write three other similar poems, laying the scenes at Rome, Florence and Naples, but he did not carry out the plan. He once refers to the tale, or 'conversation' as among 'his saddest verses;' but his important comment on it is contained in a letter to Hunt, August 15, 1819 :

'I send you a little poem to give to Ollier for publication, but *without my name*. Peacock will correct the proofs. I wrote it with the idea of offering it to the *Examiner*, but I find it is too long. It was composed last year at Este ; two of the characters you will recognize ; and the third is also in some degree a painting from nature, but, with respect to time and place, ideal. You will find the little piece, I think, in some degree consistent with your own ideas of the manner in which poetry ought to be written. I have employed a certain familiar style of language to express the actual way in which people talk with each other, whom education and a certain refinement of sentiment have placed above the use of vulgar idioms. I use the word *vulgar* in its most extensive sense. The vulgarity of rank and fashion is as gross in its way as that of poverty, and its cant terms equally expressive of base conceptions, and, therefore, equally unfit for poetry. Not that the familiar style is to be admitted in the treatment of a subject wholly ideal, or in that part of any subject

which relates to common life, where the passion, exceeding a certain limit, touches the boundaries of that which is ideal. Strong passion expresses itself in metaphor, borrowed from objects alike remote or near, and casts over all the shadow of its own greatness. But what am I about? If my grandmother sucks eggs, was it I who taught her?

'If *you* would really correct the proof, I need not trouble Peacock, who, I suppose, has enough. Can you take it as a compliment that I prefer to trouble you?

'I do not particularly wish this poem to be known as mine; but, at all events, I would not put my name to it. I leave you to judge whether it is best to throw it into the fire, or to publish it. So much for self — *self*, that burr that will stick to one.'

PREFACE

COUNT MADDALO is a Venetian nobleman of ancient family and of great fortune, who, without mixing much in the society of his countrymen, resides chiefly at his magnificent palace in that city. He is a person of the most consummate genius, and capable, if he would direct his energies to such an end, of becoming the redeemer of his degraded country. But it is his weakness to be proud. He derives, from a comparison of his own extraordinary mind with the dwarfish intellects that surround him, an intense apprehension of the nothingness of human life. His passions and his powers are incomparably greater than those of other men; and, instead of the latter having been employed in curbing the former, they have mutually lent each other strength. His ambition preys upon itself, for want of objects which it can consider worthy of exertion. I say that Maddalo is proud, because I can find no other word to express the concentred and impatient feelings which consume him; but it is on his own hopes and affections only that he seems to trample, for in social life no human being can be more gentle, patient and unassuming than Maddalo. He is cheerful, frank and witty. His more serious conversation is a sort of intoxication; men are held by it as by a spell. He has travelled much; and there is an inexpressible charm in his relation of his adventures in different countries.

Julian is an Englishman of good family, passionately attached to those philosophical notions which assert the power of man over his own mind, and the immense improvements of which. by the extinction of certain moral superstitions, human society may be yet susceptible. Without concealing the evil in the world he is forever speculating how good may be made superior. He is a complete infidel and a scoffer at all things reputed holy; and Maddalo takes a wicked pleasure in drawing out his taunts against religion. What Maddalo thinks on these matters is not exactly known. Julian, in spite of his heterodox opinions, is conjectured by his friends to possess some good qualities. How far this is possible the pious reader will determine. Julian is rather serious.

Of the Maniac I can give no information. He seems, by his own account, to have been disappointed in love. He was evidently a very cultivated and amiable person when in his right senses. His story, told at length, might be like many other stories of the same kind. The unconnected exclamations of his agony will perhaps be found a sufficient comment for the text of every heart.

I RODE one evening with Count Maddalo
Upon the bank of land which breaks the flow
Of Adria towards Venice. A bare strand
Of hillocks, heaped from ever-shifting sand,
Matted with thistles and amphibious weeds,
Such as from earth's embrace the salt ooze breeds,
Is this; an uninhabited sea-side,
Which the lone fisher, when his nets are dried,
Abandons; and no other object breaks
The waste but one dwarf tree and some few stakes 10
Broken and unrepaired, and the tide makes
A narrow space of level sand thereon,
Where 't was our wont to ride while day went down.

This ride was my delight. I love all waste
And solitary places; where we taste
The pleasure of believing what we see
Is boundless, as we wish our souls to be;
And such was this wide ocean, and this shore
More barren than its billows; and yet more
Than all, with a remembered friend I love 20
To ride as then I rode; — for the winds drove
The living spray along the sunny air
Into our faces; the blue heavens were bare,
Stripped to their depths by the awakening north;
And from the waves sound like delight broke forth
Harmonizing with solitude, and sent
Into our hearts aërial merriment.

So, as we rode, we talked; and the swift
 thought,
Winging itself with laughter, lingered not,
But flew from brain to brain, — such glee
 was ours, 30
Charged with light memories of remem-
 bered hours,
None slow enough for sadness; till we came
Homeward, which always makes the spirit
 tame.
This day had been cheerful but cold, and
 now
The sun was sinking, and the wind also.
Our talk grew somewhat serious, as may be
Talk interrupted with such raillery
As mocks itself, because it cannot scorn
The thoughts it would extinguish. 'T was
 forlorn,
Yet pleasing; such as once, so poets tell, 40
The devils held within the dales of Hell,
Concerning God, freewill and destiny;
Of all that earth has been, or yet may be,
All that vain men imagine or believe,
Or hope can paint, or suffering may achieve,
We descanted; and I (for ever still
Is it not wise to make the best of ill?)
Argued against despondency, but pride
Made my companion take the darker side.
The sense that he was greater than his
 kind 50
Had struck, methinks, his eagle spirit blind
By gazing on its own exceeding light.
Meanwhile the sun paused ere it should
 alight,
Over the horizon of the mountains. Oh,
How beautiful is sunset, when the glow
Of Heaven descends upon a land like thee,
Thou Paradise of exiles, Italy!
Thy mountains, seas and vineyards and the
 towers
Of cities they encircle! — It was ours
To stand on thee, beholding it; and then, 60
Just where we had dismounted, the Count's
 men
Were waiting for us with the gondola.
As those who pause on some delightful way
Though bent on pleasant pilgrimage, we
 stood
Looking upon the evening, and the flood,
Which lay between the city and the shore,
Paved with the image of the sky. The
 hoar
And aëry Alps towards the north appeared,
Through mist, an heaven-sustaining bul-
 wark reared

Between the east and west; and half the
 sky 70
Was roofed with clouds of rich emblazonry,
Dark purple at the zenith, which still grew
Down the steep west into a wondrous hue
Brighter than burning gold, even to the rent
Where the swift sun yet paused in his
 descent
Among the many-folded hills. They were
Those famous Euganean hills, which bear,
As seen from Lido through the harbor piles,
The likeness of a clump of peakèd isles; 79
And then, as if the earth and sea had been
Dissolved into one lake of fire, were seen
Those mountains towering as from waves
 of flame
Around the vaporous sun, from which there
 came
The inmost purple spirit of light, and made
Their very peaks transparent. 'Ere it
 fade,'
Said my companion, 'I will show you soon
A better station.' So, o'er the lagune
We glided; and from that funereal bark
I leaned, and saw the city, and could mark
How from their many isles, in evening's
 gleam, 90
Its temples and its palaces did seem
Like fabrics of enchantment piled to
 Heaven.
I was about to speak, when — 'We are
 even
Now at the point I meant,' said Maddalo,
And bade the gondolieri cease to row.
'Look, Julian, on the west, and listen well
If you hear not a deep and heavy bell.'
I looked, and saw between us and the sun
A building on an island, — such a one
As age to age might add, for uses vile, 100
A windowless, deformed and dreary pile;
And on the top an open tower, where hung
A bell, which in the radiance swayed and
 swung;
We could just hear its hoarse and iron
 tongue;
The broad sun sunk behind it, and it tolled
In strong and black relief. 'What we
 behold
Shall be the madhouse and its belfry
 tower,'
Said Maddalo; 'and ever at this hour
Those who may cross the water hear that
 bell,
Which calls the maniacs each one from his
 cell 110

To vespers.' — 'As much skill as need to
pray
In thanks or hope for their dark lot have
they
To their stern Maker,' I replied. ' O ho !
You talk as in years past,' said Maddalo.
' 'T is strange men change not. You were
ever still
Among Christ's flock a perilous infidel,
A wolf for the meek lambs — if you can't
swim,
Beware of Providence.' I looked on him,
But the gay smile had faded in his eye, —
' And such,' he cried, 'is our mortality; 120
And this must be the emblem and the sign
Of what should be eternal and divine !
And, like that black and dreary bell, the
soul,
Hung in a heaven-illumined tower, must
toll
Our thoughts and our desires to meet below
Round the rent heart and pray — as mad-
men do
For what ? they know not, till the night of
death,
As sunset that strange vision, severeth 128
Our memory from itself, and us from all
We sought, and yet were baffled.' I recall
The sense of what he said, although I mar
The force of his expressions. The broad
star
Of day meanwhile had sunk behind the hill,
And the black bell became invisible,
And the red tower looked gray, and all
between,
The churches, ships and palaces were seen
Huddled in gloom; into the purple sea
The orange hues of heaven sunk silently.
We hardly spoke, and soon the gondola
Conveyed me to my lodgings by the way.
The following morn was rainy, cold, and
dim. 141
Ere Maddalo arose, I called on him,
And whilst I waited, with his child I played.
A lovelier toy sweet Nature never made;
A serious, subtle, wild, yet gentle being,
Graceful without design, and unforeseeing,
With eyes — oh, speak not of her eyes ! —
which seem
Twin mirrors of Italian heaven, yet gleam
With such deep meaning as we never see
But in the human countenance. With me
She was a special favorite; I had nursed
Her fine and feeble limbs when she came
first 152

To this bleak world; and she yet seemed
to know
On second sight her ancient playfellow,
Less changed than she was by six months or
so;
For, after her first shyness was worn out,
We sate there, rolling billiard balls about,
When the Count entered. Salutations
past —
' The words you spoke last night might well
have cast
A darkness on my spirit. If man be 160
The passive thing you say, I should not see
Much harm in the religions and old saws,
(Though I may never own such leaden
laws)
Which break a teachless nature to the
yoke.
Mine is another faith.' Thus much I spoke,
And noting he replied not, added: ' See
This lovely child, blithe, innocent and free;
She spends a happy time with little care,
While we to such sick thoughts subjected
are 169
As came on you last night. It is our will
That thus enchains us to permitted ill.
We might be otherwise; we might be all
We dream of happy, high, majestical.
Where is the love, beauty and truth we
seek,
But in our mind ? and if we were not weak,
Should we be less in deed than in desire ? '
' Ay, if we were not weak — and we aspire
How vainly to be strong !' said Maddalo;
' You talk Utopia.' ' It remains to know,'
I then rejoined, 'and those who try may
find 180
How strong the chains are which our spirit
bind;
Brittle perchance as straw. We are assured
Much may be conquered, much may be
endured
Of what degrades and crushes us. We
know
That we have power over ourselves to do
And suffer — what, we know not till we try;
But something nobler than to live and die.
So taught those kings of old philosophy,
Who reigned before religion made men
blind;
And those who suffer with their suffering
kind 190
Yet feel this faith religion.' ' My dear
friend,'
Said Maddalo, ' my judgment will not bend

To your opinion, though I think you might
Make such a system refutation-tight
As far as words go. I knew one like you,
Who to this city came some months ago,
With whom I argued in this sort, and he
Is now gone mad, — and so he answered
me, —
Poor fellow ! but if you would like to go,
We 'll visit him, and his wild talk will
show 200
How vain are such aspiring theories.'
' I hope to prove the induction otherwise,
And that a want of that true theory still,
Which seeks " a soul of goodness " in things
ill,
Or in himself or others, has thus bowed
His being. There are some by nature
proud,
Who patient in all else demand but this —
To love and be beloved with gentleness;
And, being scorned, what wonder if they die
Some living death ? this is not destiny 210
But man's own wilful ill.'

 As thus I spoke,
Servants announced the gondola, and we
Through the fast-falling rain and high-
wrought sea
Sailed to the island where the madhouse
stands.
We disembarked. The clap of tortured
hands,
Fierce yells and howlings and lamentings
keen,
And laughter where complaint had merrier
been,
Moans, shrieks, and curses, and blasphem-
ing prayers, 218
Accosted us. We climbed the oozy stairs
Into an old courtyard. I heard on high,
Then, fragments of most touching melody,
But looking up saw not the singer there.
Through the black bars in the tempestuous
air
I saw, like weeds on a wrecked palace
growing,
Long tangled locks flung wildly forth, and
flowing,
Of those who on a sudden were beguiled
Into strange silence, and looked forth and
smiled
Hearing sweet sounds. Then I: ' Methinks
there were
A cure of these with patience and kind
care, 229

If music can thus move. But what is he,
Whom we seek here ? ' ' Of his sad history
I know but this,' said Maddalo: ' he came
To Venice a dejected man, and fame
Said he was wealthy, or he had been so.
Some thought the loss of fortune wrought
him woe;
But he was ever talking in such sort
As you do — far more sadly; he seemed
hurt,
Even as a man with his peculiar wrong,
To hear but of the oppression of the strong,
Or those absurd deceits (I think with you
In some respects, you know) which carry
through 241
The excellent impostors of this earth
When they outface detection. He had
worth,
Poor fellow ! but a humorist in his way.'
' Alas, what drove him mad ? ' ' I cannot
say;
A lady came with him from France, and
when
She left him and returned, he wandered
then
About yon lonely isles of desert sand
Till he grew wild. He had no cash or land
Remaining; the police had brought him
here; 250
Some fancy took him and he would not bear
Removal; so I fitted up for him
Those rooms beside the sea, to please his
whim,
And sent him busts and books and urns for
flowers,
Which had adorned his life in happier
hours,
And instruments of music. You may guess
A stranger could do little more or less
For one so gentle and unfortunate;
And those are his sweet strains which
charm the weight
From madmen's chains, and make this Hell
appear 260
A heaven of sacred silence, hushed to hear.'
' Nay, this was kind of you; he had no
claim,
As the world says.' ' None — but the very
same
Which I on all mankind, were I as he
Fallen to such deep reverse. His melody
Is interrupted; now we hear the din
Of madmen, shriek on shriek, again begin.
Let us now visit him; after this strain
He ever communes with himself again,

And sees nor hears not any.' Having said
These words, we called the keeper, and he
led 271
To an apartment opening on the sea.
There the poor wretch was sitting mourn-
fully
Near a piano, his pale fingers twined
One with the other, and the ooze and wind
Rushed through an open casement, and did
sway
His hair, and starred it with the brackish
spray;
His head was leaning on a music-book,
And he was muttering, and his lean limbs
shook; 279
His lips were pressed against a folded leaf,
In hue too beautiful for health, and grief
Smiled in their motions as they lay apart.
As one who wrought from his own fervid
heart
The eloquence of passion, soon he raised
His sad meek face, and eyes lustrous and
glazed,
And spoke — sometimes as one who wrote,
and thought
His words might move some heart that
heeded not,
If sent to distant lands; and then as one
Reproaching deeds never to be undone
With wondering self-compassion; then his
speech 290
Was lost in grief, and then his words came
each
Unmodulated, cold, expressionless,
But that from one jarred accent you might
guess
It was despair made them so uniform;
And all the while the loud and gusty storm
Hissed through the window, and we stood
behind
Stealing his accents from the envious wind
Unseen. I yet remember what he said
Distinctly; such impression his words made.

'Month after month,' he cried, 'to bear
this load, 300
And, as a jade urged by the whip and goad,
To drag life on — which like a heavy chain
Lengthens behind with many a link of
pain ! —
And not to speak my grief — oh, not to dare
To give a human voice to my despair,
But live, and move, and, wretched thing !
smile on
As if I never went aside to groan;

And wear this mask of falsehood even to
those
Who are most dear — not for my own re-
pose —
Alas, no scorn or pain or hate could be 310
So heavy as that falsehood is to me !
But that I cannot bear more altered faces
Than needs must be, more changed and
cold embraces,
More misery, disappointment and mistrust
To own me for their father. Would the
dust
Were covered in upon my body now !
That the life ceased to toil within my brow !
And then these thoughts would at the least
be fled;
Let us not fear such pain can vex the dead.

'What Power delights to torture us ? I
know 320
That to myself I do not wholly owe
What now I suffer, though in part I may.
Alas ! none strewed sweet flowers upon the
way
Where, wandering heedlessly, I met pale
Pain,
My shadow, which will leave me not
again.
If I have erred, there was no joy in error,
But pain and insult and unrest and terror;
I have not, as some do, bought penitence
With pleasure, and a dark yet sweet of-
fence;
For then — if love and tenderness and
truth 330
Had overlived hope's momentary youth,
My creed should have redeemed me from
repenting;
But loathèd scorn and outrage unrelenting
Met love excited by far other seeming
Until the end was gained; as one from
dreaming
Of sweetest peace, I woke, and found my
state
Such as it is —

 ' O Thou my spirit's mate !
Who, for thou art compassionate and wise,
Wouldst pity me from thy most gentle eyes
If this sad writing thou shouldst ever
see — 340
My secret groans must be unheard by thee;
Thou wouldst weep tears bitter as blood to
know
Thy lost friend's incommunicable woe.

'Ye few by whom my nature has been
 weighed
In friendship, let me not that name de-
 grade
By placing on your hearts the secret load
Which crushes mine to dust. There is one
 road
To peace, and that is truth, which follow
 ye !
Love sometimes leads astray to misery.
Yet think not, though subdued — and I may
 well 350
Say that I am subdued — that the full
 hell
Within me would infect the untainted
 breast
Of sacred Nature with its own unrest;
As some perverted beings think to find
In scorn or hate a medicine for the mind
Which scorn or hate have wounded — oh,
 how vain !
The dagger heals not, but may rend again !
Believe that I am ever still the same
In creed as in resolve; and what may tame
My heart must leave the understanding
 free, 360
Or all would sink in this keen agony;
Nor dream that I will join the vulgar cry;
Or with my silence sanction tyranny;
Or seek a moment's shelter from my pain
In any madness which the world calls gain,
Ambition or revenge or thoughts as stern
As those which make me what I am; or
 turn
To avarice or misanthropy or lust.
Heap on me soon, O grave, thy welcome
 dust !
Till then the dungeon may demand its
 prey, 370
And Poverty and Shame may meet and
 say,
Halting beside me on the public way,
" That love-devoted youth is ours; let 's sit
Beside him; he may live some six months
 yet."
Or the red scaffold, as our country bends,
May ask some willing victim; or ye, friends,
May fall under some sorrow, which this
 heart
Or hand may share or vanquish or avert;
I am prepared — in truth, with no proud
 joy,
To do or suffer aught, as when a boy 380
I did devote to justice and to love
My nature, worthless now ! —

' I must remove
A veil from my pent mind. 'T is torn
 aside !
O pallid as Death's dedicated bride,
Thou mockery which art sitting by my
 side,
Am I not wan like thee ? at the grave's
 call
I haste, invited to thy wedding-ball,
To greet the ghastly paramour for whom
Thou hast deserted me — and made the
 tomb
Thy bridal bed — but I beside your feet 390
Will lie and watch ye from my winding-
 sheet —
Thus — wide-awake though dead — yet
 stay, oh, stay !
Go not so soon — I know not what I say —
Hear but my reasons — I am mad, I fear,
My fancy is o'erwrought — thou art not
 here;
Pale art thou, 't is most true — but thou
 art gone,
Thy work is finished — I am left alone.

' Nay, was it I who wooed thee to this
 breast,
Which like a serpent thou envenomest
As in repayment of the warmth it lent ? 400
Didst thou not seek me for thine own con-
 tent ?
Did not thy love awaken mine ? I thought
That thou wert she who said " You kiss me
 not
Ever; I fear you do not love me now " —
In truth I loved even to my overthrow
Her who would fain forget these words;
 but they
Cling to her mind, and cannot pass away.

' You say that I am proud — that when I
 speak
My lip is tortured with the wrongs which
 break
The spirit it expresses. — Never one 410
Humbled himself before, as I have done !
Even the instinctive worm on which we
 tread
Turns, though it wound not — then with
 prostrate head
Sinks in the dust and writhes like me —
 and dies ?
No: wears a living death of agonies !
As the slow shadows of the pointed grass
Mark the eternal periods, his pangs pass,

Slow, ever-moving, making moments be
As mine seem, — each an immortality !

.

'That you had never seen me — never
 heard 420
My voice, and more than all had ne'er en-
 dured
The deep pollution of my loathed em-
 brace —
That your eyes ne'er had lied love in my
 face —
That, like some maniac monk, I had torn out
The nerves of manhood by their bleeding
 root
With mine own quivering fingers, so that
 ne'er
Our hearts had for a moment mingled there
To disunite in horror — these were not
With thee like some suppressed and hideous
 thought
Which flits athwart our musings but can
 find 430
No rest within a pure and gentle mind;
Thou sealedst them with many a bare
 broad word,
And sear'dst my memory o'er them, — for
 I heard
And can forget not; — they were ministered
One after one, those curses. Mix them up
Like self-destroying poisons in one cup,
And they will make one blessing, which
 thou ne'er
Didst imprecate for on me, — death.

.

 'It were
A cruel punishment for one most cruel,
If such can love, to make that love the
 fuel 440
Of the mind's hell — hate, scorn, remorse,
 despair;
But *me*, whose heart a stranger's tear might
 wear
As water-drops the sandy fountain-stone,
Who loved and pitied all things, and could
 moan
For woes which others hear not, and could
 see
The absent with the glance of fantasy,
And with the poor and trampled sit and
 weep,
Following the captive to his dungeon deep;
Me — who am as a nerve o'er which do
 creep 449
The else unfelt oppressions of this earth,
And was to thee the flame upon thy hearth,

When all beside was cold: — that thou on me
Shouldst rain these plagues of blistering
 agony !
Such curses are from lips once eloquent
With love's too partial praise ! Let none
 relent
Who intend deeds too dreadful for a name
Henceforth, if an example for the same
They seek: — for thou on me look'dst so,
 and so —
And didst speak thus — and thus. I live
 to show 459
How much men bear and die not !

.

 'Thou wilt tell
With the grimace of hate how horrible
It was to meet my love when thine grew
 less;
Thou wilt admire how I could e'er address
Such features to love's work. This taunt,
 though true,
(For indeed Nature nor in form nor hue
Bestowed on me her choicest workmanship)
Shall not be thy defence; for since thy lip
Met mine first, years long past, — since
 thine eye kindled
With soft fire under mine, — I have not
 dwindled,
Nor changed in mind or body, or in aught
But as love changes what it loveth not 471
After long years and many trials.

 'How vain
Are words ! I thought never to speak
 again,
Not even in secret, not to mine own heart;
But from my lips the unwilling accents
 start,
And from my pen the words flow as I write,
Dazzling my eyes with scalding tears ; my
 sight
Is dim to see that charactered in vain
On this unfeeling leaf, which burns the
 brain
And eats into it, blotting all things fair 480
And wise and good which time had written
 there.

Those who inflict must suffer, for they see
The work of their own hearts, and this
 must be
Our chastisement or recompense. — O
 child !
I would that thine were like to be more
 mild

For both our wretched sakes, — for thine
 the most
Who feelest already all that thou hast lost
Without the power to wish it thine again;
And as slow years pass, a funereal train,
Each with the ghost of some lost hope or
 friend 490
Following it like its shadow, wilt thou bend
No thought on my dead memory ?

.
 ' Alas, love !
Fear me not — against thee I would not
 move
A finger in despite. Do I not live
That thou mayst have less bitter cause to
 grieve ?
I give thee tears for scorn, and love for
 hate;
And that thy lot may be less desolate
Than his on whom thou tramplest, I refrain
From that sweet sleep which medicines all
 pain. 499
Then, when thou speakest of me, never say
" He could forgive not." Here I cast away
All human passions, all revenge, all pride;
I think, speak, act no ill; I do but hide
Under these words, like embers, every
 spark
Of that which has consumed me. Quick
 and dark
The grave is yawning — as its roof shall
 cover
My limbs with dust and worms under and
 over,
So let Oblivion hide this grief — the air
Closes upon my accents as despair 509
Upon my heart — let death upon despair ! '

He ceased, and overcome leant back
 awhile;
Then rising, with a melancholy smile,
Went to a sofa, and lay down, and slept
A heavy sleep, and in his dreams he wept,
And muttered some familiar name, and we
Wept without shame in his society.
I think I never was impressed so much;
The man who were not must have lacked a
 touch 518
Of human nature. — Then we lingered not,
Although our argument was quite forgot;
But, calling the attendants, went to dine
At Maddalo's; yet neither cheer nor wine
Could give us spirits, for we talked of him
And nothing else, till daylight made stars
 dim;

And we agreed his was some dreadful ill
Wrought on him boldly, yet unspeakable,
By a dear friend; some deadly change in
 love
Of one vowed deeply, which he dreamed
 not of;
For whose sake he, it seemed, had fixed a
 blot
Of falsehood on his mind which flourished
 not 530
But in the light of all-beholding truth;
And having stamped this canker on his
 youth
She had abandoned him — and how much
 more
Might be his woe, we guessed not; he had
 store
Of friends and fortune once, as we could
 guess
From his nice habits and his gentleness;
These were now lost — it were a grief
 indeed
If he had changed one unsustaining reed
For all that such a man might else adorn.
The colors of his mind seemed yet unworn;
For the wild language of his grief was
 high — 541
Such as in measure were called poetry.
And I remember one remark which then
Maddalo made. He said — ' Most wretched
 men
Are cradled into poetry by wrong;
They learn in suffering what they teach in
 song.'

If I had been an unconnected man,
I, from this moment, should have formed
 some plan
Never to leave sweet Venice, — for to me
It was delight to ride by the lone sea; 550
And then the town is silent — one may
 write
Or read in gondolas by day or night,
Having the little brazen lamp alight,
Unseen, uninterrupted; books are there,
Pictures, and casts from all those statues
 fair
Which were twin-born with poetry, and all
We seek in towns, with little to recall
Regrets for the green country. I might sit
In Maddalo's great palace, and his wit
And subtle talk would cheer the winter
 night 560
And make me know myself, and the fire-
 light

Would flash upon our faces, till the day
Might dawn and make me wonder at my
 stay.
But I had friends in London too. The
 chief
Attraction here was that I sought relief
From the deep tenderness that maniac
 wrought
Within me — 't was perhaps an idle thought,
But I imagined that if day by day 568
I watched him, and but seldom went away,
And studied all the beatings of his heart
With zeal, as men study some stubborn art
For their own good, and could by patience
 find
An entrance to the caverns of his mind,
I might reclaim him from this dark estate.
In friendships I had been most fortunate,
Yet never saw I one whom I would call
More willingly my friend; and this was all
Accomplished not; such dreams of baseless
 good
Oft come and go in crowds and solitude
And leave no trace, — but what I now de-
 signed 580
Made, for long years, impression on my
 mind.
The following morning, urged by my
 affairs,
I left bright Venice.

 After many years,
And many changes, I returned; the name
Of Venice, and its aspect, was the same;
But Maddalo was travelling far away
Among the mountains of Armenia.
His dog was dead. His child had now be-
 come 588
A woman; such as it has been my doom
To meet with few, a wonder of this earth,
Where there is little of transcendent worth,

Like one of Shakespeare's women. Kindly
 she,
And with a manner beyond courtesy,
Received her father's friend; and, when I
 asked
Of the lorn maniac, she her memory tasked,
And told, as she had heard, the mournful
 tale:
'That the poor sufferer's health began to
 fail
Two years from my departure, but that
 then
The lady, who had left him, came again.
Her mien had been imperious, but she now
Looked meek — perhaps remorse had
 brought her low. 601
Her coming made him better, and they
 stayed
Together at my father's — for I played
As I remember with the lady's shawl;
I might be six years old — but after all
She left him.' ' Why, her heart must have
 been tough.
How did it end?' 'And was not this
 enough?
They met — they parted.' ' Child, is there
 no more?'
' Something within that interval which bore
The stamp of *why* they parted, *how* they
 met; 610
Yet if thine aged eyes disdain to wet
Those wrinkled cheeks with youth's re-
 membered tears,
Ask me no more, but let the silent years
Be closed and cered over their memory,
As yon mute marble where their corpses
 lie.'
I urged and questioned still; she told me
 how
All happened — but the cold world shall
 not know.

PROMETHEUS UNBOUND

A LYRICAL DRAMA

IN FOUR ACTS

AUDISNE HÆC, AMPHIARÆ, SUB TERRAM ABDITE?

Prometheus Unbound best combines the va-
rious elements of Shelley's genius in their most
complete expression, and unites harmoniously
his lyrically creative power of imagination and

his 'passion for reforming the world.' It is
the fruit of an outburst of poetic energy un-
der the double stimulus of his enthusiastic
Greek studies, begun under Peacock's influ-

ence, and of his delight in the beauty of Italy, whither he had removed for health and rest. It marks his full mastery of his powers. It is, not less than *Queen Mab* and *The Revolt of Islam*, a poem of the moral perfection of man ; and, not less than *Alastor* and *Epipsychidion*, a poem of spiritual ideality. He was himself in love with it : 'a poem of a higher character than anything I have yet attempted and perhaps less an imitation of anything that has gone before it,' he writes to Ollier ; and again, 'a poem in my best style, whatever that may amount to, . . . the most perfect of my productions,' and 'the best thing I ever wrote;' and finally he says, '*Prometheus Unbound*, I must tell you, is my favorite poem ; I charge you, therefore, especially to pet him and feed him with fine ink and good paper. . . . I think, if I can judge by its merits, the *Prometheus* cannot sell beyond twenty copies.' Nor did he lose his affection for it. Trelawny records him as saying, 'If that is not durable poetry, tried by the severest test, I do not know what is. It is a lofty subject, not inadequately treated, and should not perish with me.' . . . 'My friends say my *Prometheus* is too wild, ideal, and perplexed with imagery. It may be so. It has no resemblance to the Greek drama. It is original ; and cost me severe mental labor. Authors, like mothers, prefer the children who have given them most trouble.'

The drama was begun in the summer-house of his garden at Este about September, 1818, and the first Act had been finished as early as October 8 ; it was apparently laid aside, and again taken up at Rome in the spring of 1819, where, under the circumstances described in the preface, the second and third Acts were added, and the work in its first form, was thus completed by April 6. The fourth Act was an afterthought, and was composed at Florence toward the end of the year. The whole was published, with other poems, in the summer of 1820.

The following extracts from Mrs. Shelley's long and admirable note show the progress of the poem during its composition, the atmosphere of its creation, and its general scheme :

'The first autumn of Italy enchanted Shelley ; it seemed a garden of delight placed beneath a clearer and brighter heaven than any he had lived under before. He wrote long descriptive letters during the first year of his residence in Italy, which, as compositions, are the most beautiful in the world, and show how truly he appreciated and studied the wonders of nature and art in that divine land.

'The poetical spirit within him speedily revived with all the power and with more than all the beauty of his first attempts. He meditated three subjects as the groundwork for

lyrical Dramas. One was the story of Tasso : of this a slight fragment of a song of Tasso remains. The other was one founded on the book of Job, which he never abandoned in idea, but of which no trace remains among his papers. The third was the *Prometheus Unbound*. The Greek tragedians were now his most familiar companions in his wanderings, and the sublime majesty of Æschylus filled him with wonder and delight. The father of Greek tragedy does not possess the pathos of Sophocles, nor the variety and tenderness of Euripides ; the interest on which he founds his dramas is often elevated above human vicissitudes into the mighty passions and throes of gods and demigods — such fascinated the abstract imagination of Shelley.

'We spent a month at Milan, visiting the Lake of Como during that interval. Thence we passed in succession to Pisa, Leghorn, the Baths of Lucca, Venice, Este, Rome, Naples, and back again to Rome, whither we returned early in March, 1819. During all this time Shelley meditated the subject of his drama, and wrote portions of it. Other poems were composed during this interval, and while at the Bagni di Lucca he translated Plato's *Symposium*. But though he diversified his studies, his thoughts centred in the *Prometheus*. At last, when at Rome, during a bright and beautiful spring, he gave up his whole time to the composition. The spot selected for his study was, as he mentions in his preface, the mountainous ruins of the Baths of Caracalla. These are little known to the ordinary visitor at Rome. He describes them in a letter, with that poetry, and delicacy, and truth of description, which rendered his narrated impressions of scenery of unequalled beauty and interest.

'At first he completed the drama in three acts. It was not till several months after, when at Florence, that he conceived that a fourth act, a sort of hymn of rejoicing in the fulfilment of the prophecies with regard to Prometheus, ought to be added to complete the composition.

'The prominent feature of Shelley's theory of the destiny of the human species was, that evil is not inherent in the system of the creation, but an accident that might be expelled. This also forms a portion of Christianity ; God made earth and man perfect, till he, by his fall,

' " Brought death into the world and all our woe."

Shelley believed that mankind had only to will that there should be no evil, and there would be none. It is not my part in these notes to notice the arguments that have been urged against this opinion, but to mention the fact that he entertained it, and was indeed attached to it with fervent enthusiasm. That man could

be so perfectionized as to be able to expel evil from his own nature, and from the greater part of the creation, was the cardinal point of his system. And the subject he loved best to dwell on, was the image of One warring with the Evil Principle, oppressed not only by it, but by all, even the good, who were deluded into considering evil a necessary portion of humanity; a victim full of fortitude and hope, and the spirit of triumph emanating from a reliance in the ultimate omnipotence of good. Such he had depicted in his last poem, when he made Laon the enemy and the victim of tyrants. He now took a more idealized image of the same subject. He followed certain classical authorities in figuring Saturn as the good principle, Jupiter the usurping evil one, and Prometheus as the regenerator, who, unable to bring mankind back to primitive innocence, used knowledge as a weapon to defeat evil, by leading mankind beyond the state wherein they are sinless through ignorance, to that in which they are virtuous through wisdom. Jupiter punished the temerity of the Titan by chaining him to a rock of Caucasus, and causing a vulture to devour his still-renewed heart. There was a prophecy afloat in heaven portending the fall of Jove, the secret of averting which was known only to Prometheus; and the god offered freedom from torture on condition of its being communicated to him. According to the mythological story, this referred to the offspring of Thetis, who was destined to be greater than his father. Prometheus at last bought pardon for his crime of enriching mankind with his gifts, by revealing the prophecy. Hercules killed the vulture and set him free, and Thetis was married to Peleus the father of Achilles.

'Shelley adapted the catastrophe of this story to his peculiar views. The son, greater than his father, born of the nuptials of Jupiter and Thetis, was to dethrone Evil and bring back a happier reign than that of Saturn. Prometheus defies the power of his enemy, and endures centuries of torture, till the hour arrives when Jove, blind to the real event, but darkly guessing that some great good to himself will flow, espouses Thetis. At the moment, the Primal Power of the world drives him from his usurped throne, and Strength, in the person of Hercules, liberates Humanity, typified in Prometheus, from the tortures generated by evil done or suffered. Asia, one of the Oceanides, is the wife of Prometheus — she was, according to other mythological interpretations, the same as Venus and Nature. When the Benefactor of Mankind is liberated, Nature resumes the beauty of her prime, and is united to her husband, the emblem of the human race, in perfect and happy union. In the

fourth Act, the poet gives further scope to his imagination, and idealizes the forms of creation, such as we know them, instead of such as they appeared to the Greeks. Maternal Earth, the mighty Parent, is superseded by the Spirit of the Earth — the guide of our planet through the realms of sky — while his fair and weaker companion and attendant, the Spirit of the Moon, receives bliss from the annihilation of Evil in the superior sphere.

'Shelley develops, more particularly in the lyrics of this drama, his abstruse and imaginative theories with regard to the Creation. It requires a mind as subtle and penetrating as his own to understand the mystic meanings scattered throughout the poem. They elude the ordinary reader by their abstraction and delicacy of distinction, but they are far from vague. It was his design to write prose metaphysical essays on the nature of Man, which would have served to explain much of what is obscure in his poetry; a few scattered fragments of observations and remarks alone remain. He considered these philosophical views of mind and nature to be instinct with the intensest spirit of poetry.

'More popular poets clothe the ideal with familiar and sensible imagery. Shelley loved to idealize the real — to gift the mechanism of the material universe with a soul and a voice, and to bestow such also on the most delicate and abstract emotions and thoughts of the mind. . . .

'Through the whole Poem there reigns a sort of calm and holy spirit of love; it soothes the tortured, and is hope to the expectant, till the prophecy is fulfilled, and Love, untainted by any evil, becomes the law of the world. . . .

'The charm of the Roman climate helped to clothe his thoughts in greater beauty than they had ever worn before; and as he wandered among the ruins, made one with nature in their decay, or gazed on the Praxitelean shapes that throng the Vatican, the Capitol, and the palaces of Rome, his soul imbibed forms of loveliness which became a portion of itself. There are many passages in the *Prometheus* which show the intense delight he received from such studies, and give back the impression with a beauty of poetical description peculiarly his own.'

PREFACE

The Greek tragic writers, in selecting as their subject any portion of their national history or mythology, employed in their treatment of it a certain arbitrary discretion. They by no means conceived themselves bound to adhere to the common interpretation or to imitate in story as in title their rivals and predecessors.

Such a system would have amounted to a resignation of those claims to preference over their competitors which incited the composition. The Agamemnonian story was exhibited on the Athenian theatre with as many variations as dramas.

I have presumed to employ a similar license. The *Prometheus Unbound* of Æschylus supposed the reconciliation of Jupiter with his victim as the price of the disclosure of the danger threatened to his empire by the consummation of his marriage with Thetis. Thetis, according to this view of the subject, was given in marriage to Peleus, and Prometheus, by the permission of Jupiter, delivered from his captivity by Hercules. Had I framed my story on this model, I should have done no more than have attempted to restore the lost drama of Æschylus; an ambition which, if my preference to this mode of treating the subject had incited me to cherish, the recollection of the high comparison such an attempt would challenge might well abate. But, in truth, I was averse from a catastrophe so feeble as that of reconciling the Champion with the Oppressor of mankind. The moral interest of the fable, which is so powerfully sustained by the sufferings and endurance of Prometheus, would be annihilated if we could conceive of him as unsaying his high language and quailing before his successful and perfidious adversary. The only imaginary being, resembling in any degree Prometheus, is Satan; and Prometheus is, in my judgment, a more poetical character than Satan, because, in addition to courage, and majesty, and firm and patient opposition to omnipotent force, he is susceptible of being described as exempt from the taints of ambition, envy, revenge, and a desire for personal aggrandizement, which, in the hero of *Paradise Lost*, interfere with the interest. The character of Satan engenders in the mind a pernicious casuistry which leads us to weigh his faults with his wrongs, and to excuse the former because the latter exceed all measure. In the minds of those who consider that magnificent fiction with a religious feeling it engenders something worse. But Prometheus is, as it were, the type of the highest perfection of moral and intellectual nature impelled by the purest and the truest motives to the best and noblest ends.

This Poem was chiefly written upon the mountainous ruins of the Baths of Caracalla, among the flowery glades and thickets of odoriferous blossoming trees, which are extended in ever winding labyrinths upon its immense platforms and dizzy arches suspended in the air. The bright blue sky of Rome, and the effect of the vigorous awakening spring in that divinest climate, and the new life with which

it drenches the spirits even to intoxication, were the inspiration of this drama.

The imagery which I have employed will be found, in many instances, to have been drawn from the operations of the human mind, or from those external actions by which they are expressed. This is unusual in modern poetry, although Dante and Shakespeare are full of instances of the same kind; Dante indeed more than any other poet, and with greater success. But the Greek poets, as writers to whom no resource of awakening the sympathy of their contemporaries was unknown, were in the habitual use of this power; and it is the study of their works (since a higher merit would probably be denied me) to which I am willing that my readers should impute this singularity.

One word is due in candor to the degree in which the study of contemporary writings may have tinged my composition, for such has been a topic of censure with regard to poems far more popular, and indeed more deservedly popular, than mine. It is impossible that any one, who inhabits the same age with such writers as those who stand in the foremost ranks of our own, can conscientiously assure himself that his language and tone of thought may not have been modified by the study of the productions of those extraordinary intellects. It is true that, not the spirit of their genius, but the forms in which it has manifested itself, are due less to the peculiarities of their own minds than to the peculiarity of the moral and intellectual condition of the minds among which they have been produced. Thus a number of writers possess the form, whilst they want the spirit of those whom, it is alleged, they imitate; because the former is the endowment of the age in which they live, and the latter must be the uncommunicated lightning of their own mind.

The peculiar style of intense and comprehensive imagery which distinguishes the modern literature of England has not been, as a general power, the product of the imitation of any particular writer. The mass of capabilities remains at every period materially the same; the circumstances which awaken it to action perpetually change. If England were divided into forty republics, each equal in population and extent to Athens, there is no reason to suppose but that, under institutions not more perfect than those of Athens, each would produce philosophers and poets equal to those who (if we except Shakespeare) have never been surpassed. We owe the great writers of the golden age of our literature to that fervid awakening of the public mind which shook to dust the oldest and most oppressive form of the Christian religion. We owe Milton to the

progress and development of the same spirit: the sacred Milton was, let it ever be remembered, a republican and a bold inquirer into morals and religion. The great writers of our own age are, we have reason to suppose, the companions and forerunners of some unimagined change in our social condition or the opinions which cement it. The cloud of mind is discharging its collected lightning, and the equilibrium between institutions and opinions is now restoring or is about to be restored.

As to imitation, poetry is a mimetic art. It creates, but it creates by combination and representation. Poetical abstractions are beautiful and new, not because the portions of which they are composed had no previous existence in the mind of man or in Nature, but because the whole produced by their combination has some intelligible and beautiful analogy with those sources of emotion and thought and with the contemporary condition of them. One great poet is a masterpiece of Nature which another not only ought to study but must study. He might as wisely and as easily determine that his mind should no longer be the mirror of all that is lovely in the visible universe as exclude from his contemplation the beautiful which exists in the writings of a great contemporary. The pretence of doing it would be a presumption in any but the greatest; the effect, even in him, would be strained, unnatural and ineffectual. A poet is the combined product of such internal powers as modify the nature of others, and of such external influences as excite and sustain these powers; he is not one, but both. Every man's mind is, in this respect, modified by all the objects of Nature and art; by every word and every suggestion which he ever admitted to act upon his consciousness; it is the mirror upon which all forms are reflected and in which they compose one form. Poets, not otherwise than philosophers, painters, sculptors and musicians, are, in one sense, the creators, and, in another, the creations, of their age. From this subjection the loftiest do not escape. There is a similarity between Homer and Hesiod, between Æschylus and Euripides, between Virgil and Horace, between Dante and Petrarch, between Shakespeare and Fletcher, between Dryden and Pope; each has a generic resemblance under which their specific distinctions are arranged. If this similarity be the result of imitation, I am willing to confess that I have imitated.

Let this opportunity be conceded to me of acknowledging that I have what a Scotch philosopher characteristically terms a ' passion for reforming the world : ' what passion incited him to write and publish his book he omits to explain. For my part I had rather be damned with Plato and Lord Bacon than go to Heaven with Paley and Malthus. But it is a mistake to suppose that I dedicate my poetical compositions solely to the direct enforcement of reform, or that I consider them in any degree as containing a reasoned system on the theory of human life. Didactic poetry is my abhorrence ; nothing can be equally well expressed in prose that is not tedious and supererogatory in verse. My purpose has hitherto been simply to familiarize the highly refined imagination of the more select classes of poetical readers with beautiful idealisms of moral excellence ; aware that, until the mind can love, and admire, and trust, and hope, and endure, reasoned principles of moral conduct are seeds cast upon the highway of life which the unconscious passenger tramples into dust, although they would bear the harvest of his happiness. Should I live to accomplish what I purpose, that is, produce a systematical history of what appear to me to be the genuine elements of human society, let not the advocates of injustice and superstition flatter themselves that I should take Æschylus rather than Plato as my model.

The having spoken of myself with unaffected freedom will need little apology with the candid ; and let the uncandid consider that they injure me less than their own hearts and minds by misrepresentation. Whatever talents a person may possess to amuse and instruct others, be they ever so inconsiderable, he is yet bound to exert them : if his attempt be ineffectual, let the punishment of an unaccomplished purpose have been sufficient ; let none trouble themselves to heap the dust of oblivion upon his efforts ; the pile they raise will betray his grave which might otherwise have been unknown.

PROMETHEUS UNBOUND

DRAMATIS PERSONÆ

PROMETHEUS.	ASIA
DEMOGORGON.	PANTHEA } Oceanides.
JUPITER.	IONE
THE EARTH.	THE PHANTASM OF JUPITER.
OCEAN.	THE SPIRIT OF THE EARTH.
APOLLO.	THE SPIRIT OF THE MOON.
MERCURY.	SPIRITS OF THE HOURS.
HERCULES.	SPIRITS. ECHOES. FAUNS.
	FURIES.

ACT I

SCENE, *a Ravine of Icy Rocks in the Indian
Caucasus.* PROMETHEUS *is discovered bound
to the Precipice.* PANTHEA *and* IONE *are
seated at his feet. Time, Night. During the
Scene morning slowly breaks.*

PROMETHEUS

MONARCH of Gods and Dæmons, and all
 Spirits
But One, who throng those bright and roll-
 ing worlds
Which Thou and I alone of living things
Behold with sleepless eyes! regard this
 Earth
Made multitudinous with thy slaves, whom
 thou
Requitest for knee-worship, prayer, and
 praise,
And toil, and hecatombs of broken hearts,
With fear and self-contempt and barren
 hope;
Whilst me, who am thy foe, eyeless in hate,
Hast thou made reign and triumph, to thy
 scorn, 10
O'er mine own misery and thy vain re-
 venge.
Three thousand years of sleep-unsheltered
 hours,
And moments aye divided by keen pangs
Till they seemed years, torture and soli-
 tude,
Scorn and despair — these are mine em-
 pire:
More glorious far than that which thou
 surveyest
From thine unenvied throne, O Mighty
 God!
Almighty, had I deigned to share the shame
Of thine ill tyranny, and hung not here
Nailed to this wall of eagle-baffling moun-
 tain, 20

Black, wintry, dead, unmeasured; without
 herb,
Insect, or beast, or shape or sound of life.
Ah me! alas, pain, pain ever, forever!

No change, no pause, no hope! Yet I
 endure.
I ask the Earth, have not the mountains
 felt?
I ask yon Heaven, the all-beholding Sun,
Has it not seen? The Sea, in storm or
 calm,
Heaven's ever-changing shadow, spread
 below,
Have its deaf waves not heard my agony?
Ah me! alas, pain, pain ever, forever! 30

The crawling glaciers pierce me with the
 spears
Of their moon-freezing crystals; the bright
 chains
Eat with their burning cold into my bones.
Heaven's wingèd hound, polluting from thy
 lips
His beak in poison not his own, tears up
My heart; and shapeless sights come wan-
 dering by,
The ghastly people of the realm of dream,
Mocking me; and the Earthquake-fiends
 are charged
To wrench the rivets from my quivering
 wounds
When the rocks split and close again be-
 hind; 40
While from their loud abysses howling
 throng
The genii of the storm, urging the rage
Of whirlwind, and afflict me with keen
 hail.
And yet to me welcome is day and night,
Whether one breaks the hoar-frost of the
 morn,
Or starry, dim, and slow, the other climbs
The leaden-colored east; for then they
 lead
The wingless, crawling hours, one among
 whom —
As some dark Priest hales the reluctant
 victim —
Shall drag thee, cruel King, to kiss the
 blood 50
From these pale feet, which then might
 trample thee
If they disdained not such a prostrate
 slave.

Disdain! Ah, no! I pity thee. What ruin
Will hunt thee undefended through the
 wide Heaven!
How will thy soul, cloven to its depth with
 terror,
Gape like a hell within! I speak in grief,
Not exultation, for I hate no more,
As then ere misery made me wise. The
 curse
Once breathed on thee I would recall. Ye
 Mountains,
Whose many-voicèd Echoes, through the
 mist 60
Of cataracts, flung the thunder of that
 spell!
Ye icy Springs, stagnant with wrinkling
 frost,
Which vibrated to hear me, and then crept
Shuddering through India! Thou serenest
 Air
Through which the Sun walks burning
 without beams!
And ye swift Whirlwinds, who on poisèd
 wings
Hung mute and moveless o'er yon hushed
 abyss,
As thunder, louder than your own, made
 rock
The orbèd world! If then my words had
 power,
Though I am changed so that aught evil
 wish 70
Is dead within; although no memory be
Of what is hate, let them not lose it now!
What was that curse? for ye all heard me
 speak.

FIRST VOICE: *from the Mountains*

Thrice three hundred thousand years
 O'er the earthquake's couch we stood;
Oft, as men convulsed with fears,
 We trembled in our multitude.

SECOND VOICE: *from the Springs*

Thunderbolts had parched our water,
 We had been stained with bitter blood,
And had run mute, 'mid shrieks of
 slaughter 80
 Through a city and a solitude.

THIRD VOICE: *from the Air*

I had clothed, since Earth uprose,
 Its wastes in colors not their own,
And oft had my serene repose
 Been cloven by many a rending groan.

FOURTH VOICE: *from the Whirlwinds*

We had soared beneath these mountains
 Unresting ages; nor had thunder,
Nor yon volcano's flaming fountains,
 Nor any power above or under
 Ever made us mute with wonder. 90

FIRST VOICE

But never bowed our snowy crest
As at the voice of thine unrest.

SECOND VOICE

Never such a sound before
To the Indian waves we bore.
A pilot asleep on the howling sea
Leaped up from the deck in agony,
And heard, and cried, 'Ah, woe is me!'
And died as mad as the wild waves be.

THIRD VOICE

By such dread words from Earth to Heaven
My still realm was never riven; 100
When its wound was closed, there stood
Darkness o'er the day like blood.

FOURTH VOICE

And we shrank back: for dreams of ruin
To frozen caves our flight pursuing
Made us keep silence — thus — and thus —
Though silence is a hell to us.

THE EARTH

The tongueless caverns of the craggy hills
Cried, 'Misery!' then; the hollow Heaven
 replied,
'Misery!' And the Ocean's purple waves,
Climbing the land, howled to the lashing
 winds, 110
And the pale nations heard it, 'Misery!'

PROMETHEUS

I hear a sound of voices; not the voice
Which I gave forth. Mother, thy sons and
 thou
Scorn him, without whose all-enduring will
Beneath the fierce omnipotence of Jove,
Both they and thou had vanished, like thin
 mist
Unrolled on the morning wind. Know ye
 not me,
The Titan? He who made his agony
The barrier to your else all-conquering foe?
O rock-embosomed lawns and snow-fed
 streams, 120
Now seen athwart frore vapors, deep below,

Through whose o'ershadowing woods I
 wandered once
With Asia, drinking life from her loved
 eyes;
Why scorns the spirit, which informs ye,
 now
To commune with me? me alone who
 checked,
As one who checks a fiend-drawn charioteer,
The falsehood and the force of him who
 reigns
Supreme, and with the groans of pining
 slaves
Fills your dim glens and liquid wildernesses:
Why answer ye not, still? Brethren!

THE EARTH
 They dare not. 130

PROMETHEUS

Who dares? for I would hear that curse
 again.
Ha, what an awful whisper rises up!
'T is scarce like sound; it tingles through
 the frame
As lightning tingles, hovering ere it strike.
Speak, Spirit! from thine inorganic voice
I only know that thou art moving near
And love. How cursed I him?

THE EARTH
 How canst thou hear
Who knowest not the language of the dead?

PROMETHEUS

Thou art a living spirit; speak as they.

THE EARTH

I dare not speak like life, lest Heaven's
 fell King 140
Should hear, and link me to some wheel of
 pain
More torturing than the one whereon I roll.
Subtle thou art and good; and though the
 Gods
Hear not this voice, yet thou art more than
 God,
Being wise and kind: earnestly hearken
 now.

PROMETHEUS

Obscurely through my brain, like shadows
 dim,
Sweep awful thoughts, rapid and thick.
 I feel

Faint, like one mingled in entwining love;
Yet 't is not pleasure.

THE EARTH
 No, thou canst not hear;
Thou art immortal, and this tongue is
 known 150
Only to those who die.

PROMETHEUS
 And what art thou,
O melancholy Voice?

THE EARTH
 I am the Earth,
Thy mother; she within whose stony veins,
To the last fibre of the loftiest tree
Whose thin leaves trembled in the frozen
 air,
Joy ran, as blood within a living frame,
When thou didst from her bosom, like a
 cloud
Of glory, arise, a spirit of keen joy!
And at thy voice her pining sons uplifted
Their prostrate brows from the polluting
 dust, 160
And our almighty Tyrant with fierce dread
Grew pale, until his thunder chained thee
 here.
Then — see those million worlds which burn
 and roll
Around us — their inhabitants beheld
My sphered light wane in wide Heaven;
 the sea
Was lifted by strange tempest, and new fire
From earthquake-rifted mountains of
 bright snow
Shook its portentous hair beneath Heaven's
 frown;
Lightning and Inundation vexed the plains;
Blue thistles bloomed in cities; foodless
 toads 170
Within voluptuous chambers panting
 crawled.
When Plague had fallen on man and beast
 and worm,
And Famine; and black blight on herb and
 tree;
And in the corn, and vines, and meadow-
 grass,
Teemed ineradicable poisonous weeds
Draining their growth, for my wan breast
 was dry
With grief, and the thin air, my breath,
 was stained

With the contagion of a mother's hate
Breathed on her child's destroyer; ay, I
 heard
Thy curse, the which, if thou rememberest
 not, 180
Yet my innumerable seas and streams,
Mountains, and caves, and winds, and yon
 wide air,
And the inarticulate people of the dead,
Preserve, a treasured spell. We meditate
In secret joy and hope those dreadful
 words,
But dare not speak them.

<div align="center">PROMETHEUS</div>

 Venerable mother !
All else who live and suffer take from thee
Some comfort; flowers, and fruits, and
 happy sounds,
And love, though fleeting; these may not
 be mine.
But mine own words, I pray, deny me
 not. 190

<div align="center">THE EARTH</div>

They shall be told. Ere Babylon was dust,
The Magus Zoroaster, my dead child,
Met his own image walking in the gar-
 den.
That apparition, sole of men, he saw.
For know there are two worlds of life and
 death:
One that which thou beholdest; but the
 other
Is underneath the grave, where do inhabit
The shadows of all forms that think and
 live,
Till death unite them and they part no
 more; 199
Dreams and the light imaginings of men,
And all that faith creates or love desires,
Terrible, strange, sublime and beauteous
 shapes.
There thou art, and dost hang, a writhing
 shade,
'Mid whirlwind-peopled mountains; all the
 gods
Are there, and all the powers of nameless
 worlds,
Vast, sceptred phantoms; heroes, men, and
 beasts;
And Demogorgon, a tremendous gloom;
And he, the supreme Tyrant, on his throne
Of burning gold. Son, one of these shall
 utter

The curse which all remember. Call at
 will 210
Thine own ghost, or the ghost of Jupiter,
Hades or Typhon, or what mightier Gods
From all-prolific Evil, since thy ruin,
Have sprung, and trampled on my prostrate
 sons.
Ask, and they must reply: so the revenge
Of the Supreme may sweep through vacant
 shades,
As rainy wind through the abandoned gate
Of a fallen palace.

<div align="center">PROMETHEUS</div>

 Mother, let not aught
Of that which may be evil pass again
My lips, or those of aught resembling me.
Phantasm of Jupiter, arise, appear ! 221

<div align="center">IONE</div>

 My wings are folded o'er mine ears;
 My wings are crossèd o'er mine eyes;
 Yet through their silver shade appears,
 And through their lulling plumes arise,
 A Shape, a throng of sounds.
 May it be no ill to thee
 O thou of many wounds !
Near whom, for our sweet sister's sake,
Ever thus we watch and wake. 230

<div align="center">PANTHEA</div>

 The sound is of whirlwind underground,
 Earthquake, and fire, and mountains
 cloven;
 The shape is awful, like the sound,
 Clothed in dark purple, star-inwoven.
 A sceptre of pale gold,
 To stay steps proud, o'er the slow
 cloud,
 His veinèd hand doth hold.
Cruel he looks, but calm and strong,
Like one who does, not suffers wrong.

<div align="center">PHANTASM OF JUPITER</div>

Why have the secret powers of this strange
 world 240
Driven me, a frail and empty phantom,
 hither
On direst storms ? What unaccustomed
 sounds
Are hovering on my lips, unlike the voice
With which our pallid race hold ghastly
 talk
In darkness ? And, proud sufferer, who
 art thou ?

PROMETHEUS

Tremendous Image ! as thou art must be
He whom thou shadowest forth. I am his
 foe,
The Titan. Speak the words which I would
 hear,
Although no thought inform thine empty
 voice.

THE EARTH

Listen ! And though your echoes must be
 mute, 250
Gray mountains, and old woods, and
 haunted springs,
Prophetic caves, and isle - surrounding
 streams,
Rejoice to hear what yet ye cannot speak.

PHANTASM

A spirit seizes me and speaks within;
It tears me as fire tears a thunder-cloud.

PANTHEA

See how he lifts his mighty looks ! the
 Heaven
Darkens above.

IONE

 He speaks ! Oh, shelter me !

PROMETHEUS

I see the curse on gestures proud and cold,
And looks of firm defiance, and calm hate,
And such despair as mocks itself with
 smiles, 260
Written as on a scroll: yet speak ! Oh,
 speak !

PHANTASM

Fiend, I defy thee ! with a calm, fixed
 mind,
All that thou canst inflict I bid thee
 do;
Foul tyrant both of Gods and human-
 kind,
One only being shalt thou not sub-
 due.
 Rain then thy plagues upon me here,
 Ghastly disease, and frenzying fear ;
 And let alternate frost and fire
 Eat into me, and be thine ire
Lightning, and cutting hail, and legioned
 forms 270
Of furies, driving by upon the wounding
 storms.

Ay, do thy worst ! Thou art omnipotent.
O'er all things but thyself I gave thee
 power,
And my own will. Be thy swift mis-
 chiefs sent
To blast mankind, from yon ethereal
 tower.
Let thy malignant spirit move
In darkness over those I love;
On me and mine I imprecate
The utmost torture of thy hate;
And thus devote to sleepless agony, 280
This undeclining head while thou must
 reign on high.

But thou, who art the God and Lord: O
 thou
Who fillest with thy soul this world of
 woe,
To whom all things of Earth and Heaven
 do bow
In fear and worship — all-prevailing
 foe !
I curse thee ! let a sufferer's curse
Clasp thee, his torturer, like remorse;
Till thine Infinity shall be
A robe of envenomed agony; 289
And thine Omnipotence a crown of pain,
To cling like burning gold round thy dis-
 solving brain !

Heap on thy soul, by virtue of this Curse,
Ill deeds; then be thou damned, be-
 holding good;
Both infinite as is the universe,
And thou, and thy self-torturing soli-
 tude.
An awful image of calm power
Though now thou sittest, let the hour
Come, when thou must appear to be
That which thou art internally;
And after many a false and fruitless
 crime, 300
Scorn track thy lagging fall through
 boundless space and time !

PROMETHEUS

Were these my words, O Parent ?

THE EARTH

 They were thine.

PROMETHEUS

It doth repent me; words are quick and
 vain;

Grief for awhile is blind, and so was mine.
I wish no living thing to suffer pain.

THE EARTH

Misery, oh, misery to me,
That Jove at length should vanquish
 thee !
Wail, howl aloud, Land and Sea, 308
The Earth's rent heart shall answer ye !
Howl, Spirits of the living and the dead,
Your refuge, your defence, lies fallen and
 vanquishèd !

FIRST ECHO

Lies fallen and vanquishèd !

SECOND ECHO

 Fallen and vanquishèd !

IONE

Fear not: 't is but some passing spasm,
 The Titan is unvanquished still.
But see, where through the azure chasm
 Of you forked and snowy hill,
Trampling the slant winds on high
 With golden-sandalled feet, that glow
 Under plumes of purple dye, 320
 Like rose-ensanguined ivory,
 A Shape comes now,
Stretching on high from his right hand
 A serpent-cinctured wand.

PANTHEA

'T is Jove's world-wandering herald, Mer-
 cury.

IONE

And who are those with hydra tresses
 And iron wings, that climb the wind,
Whom the frowning God represses, —
 Like vapors steaming up behind,
Clanging loud, an endless crowd ? 330

PANTHEA

These are Jove's tempest-walking
 hounds,
Whom he gluts with groans and blood,
When charioted on sulphurous cloud
 He bursts Heaven's bounds.

IONE

Are they now led from the thin dead
 On new pangs to be fed ?

PANTHEA

The Titan looks as ever, firm, not proud.

FIRST FURY

Ha ! I scent life !

SECOND FURY

 Let me but look into his eyes !

THIRD FURY

The hope of torturing him smells like a
 heap
Of corpses to a death-bird after battle. 340

FIRST FURY

Darest thou delay, O Herald ! take cheer,
 Hounds
Of Hell: what if the Son of Maia soon
Should make us food and sport — who can
 please long
The Omnipotent ?

MERCURY

 Back to your towers of iron,
And gnash, beside the streams of fire and
 wail,
Your foodless teeth. Geryon, arise ! and
 Gorgon,
Chimæra, and thou Sphinx, subtlest of
 fiends,
Who ministered to Thebes Heaven's poi-
 soned wine, 348
Unnatural love, and more unnatural hate:
These shall perform your task.

FIRST FURY

 Oh, mercy ! mercy !
We die with our desire ! drive us not back !

MERCURY

Crouch then in silence.
 Awful Sufferer !
To thee unwilling, most unwillingly
I come, by the great Father's will driven
 down,
To execute a doom of new revenge.
Alas ! I pity thee, and hate myself
That I can do no more; aye from thy sight
Returning, for a season, Heaven seems
 Hell,
So thy worn form pursues me night and day,
Smiling reproach. Wise art thou, firm and
 good, 360

But vainly wouldst stand forth alone in
 strife
Against the Omnipotent; as yon clear
 lamps,
That measure and divide the weary years
From which there is no refuge, long have
 taught
And long must teach. Even now thy Tor-
 turer arms
With the strange might of unimagined
 pains
The powers who scheme slow agonies in
 Hell,
And my commission is to lead them here,
Or what more subtle, foul, or savage fiends
People the abyss, and leave them to their
 task. 370
Be it not so ! there is a secret known
To thee, and to none else of living things,
Which may transfer the sceptre of wide
 Heaven,
The fear of which perplexes the Supreme.
Clothe it in words, and bid it clasp his
 throne
In intercession; bend thy soul in prayer,
And like a suppliant in some gorgeous fane,
Let the will kneel within thy haughty
 heart,
For benefits and meek submission tame
The fiercest and the mightiest.

PROMETHEUS

 Evil minds
Change good to their own nature. I gave
 all 381
He has; and in return he chains me here
Years, ages, night and day; whether the
 Sun
Split my parched skin, or in the moony
 night
The crystal-wingèd snow cling round my
 hair;
Whilst my belovèd race is trampled down
By his thought-executing ministers.
Such is the tyrant's recompense. 'T is just.
He who is evil can receive no good;
And for a world bestowed, or a friend
 lost,
He can feel hate, fear, shame; not grati-
 tude. 391
He but requites me for his own misdeed.
Kindness to such is keen reproach, which
 breaks
With bitter stings the light sleep of Re-
 venge.

Submission thou dost know I cannot try.
For what submission but that fatal word,
The death-seal of mankind's captivity,
Like the Sicilian's hair-suspended sword,
Which trembles o'er his crown, would he
 accept,
Or could I yield ? Which yet I will not
 yield. 400
Let others flatter Crime where it sits
 throned
In brief Omnipotence; secure are they;
For Justice, when triumphant, will weep
 down
Pity, not punishment, on her own wrongs,
Too much avenged by those who err. I
 wait,
Enduring thus, the retributive hour
Which since we spake is even nearer
 now.
But hark, the hell-hounds clamor: fear
 delay:
Behold ! Heaven lowers under thy Father's
 frown. 409

MERCURY

Oh, that we might be spared; I to inflict,
And thou to suffer ! Once more answer
 me.
Thou knowest not the period of Jove's
 power ?

PROMETHEUS

I know but this, that it must come.

MERCURY

 Alas !
Thou canst not count thy years to come of
 pain !

PROMETHEUS

They last while Jove must reign; nor
 more, nor less
Do I desire or fear.

MERCURY

 Yet pause, and plunge
Into Eternity, where recorded time,
Even all that we imagine, age on age,
Seems but a point, and the reluctant mind
Flags wearily in its unending flight, 420
Till it sink, dizzy, blind, lost, shelterless;
Perchance it has not numbered the slow
 years
Which thou must spend in torture, unre-
 prieved ?

PROMETHEUS

Perchance no thought can count them, yet
they pass.

MERCURY

If thou mightst dwell among the Gods the
while,
Lapped in voluptuous joy ?

PROMETHEUS

I would not quit
This bleak ravine, these unrepentant pains.

MERCURY

Alas ! I wonder at, yet pity thee.

PROMETHEUS

Pity the self-despising slaves of Heaven,
Not me, within whose mind sits peace
serene, 430
As light in the sun, throned. How vain is
talk !
Call up the fiends.

IONE

Oh, sister, look ! White fire
Has cloven to the roots you huge snow-
loaded cedar;
How fearfully God's thunder howls be-
hind !

MERCURY

I must obey his words and thine. Alas !
Most heavily remorse hangs at my heart !

PANTHEA

See where the child of Heaven, with wingèd
feet,
Runs down the slanted sunlight of the
dawn.

IONE

Dear sister, close thy plumes over thine
eyes
Lest thou behold and die; they come —
they come — 440
Blackening the birth of day with countless
wings,
And hollow underneath, like death.

FIRST FURY

Prometheus !

SECOND FURY

Immortal Titan !

THIRD FURY

Champion of Heaven's slaves !

PROMETHEUS

He whom some dreadful voice invokes is
here,
Prometheus, the chained Titan. Horrible
forms,
What and who are ye ? Never yet there
came
Phantasms so foul through monster-teeming
Hell
From the all-miscreative brain of Jove.
Whilst I behold such execrable shapes,
Methinks I grow like what I contemplate,
And laugh and stare in loathsome sym-
pathy. 451

FIRST FURY

We are the ministers of pain, and fear,
And disappointment, and mistrust, and
hate,
And clinging crime; and as lean dogs pur-
sue
Through wood and lake some struck and
sobbing fawn,
We track all things that weep, and bleed,
and live,
When the great King betrays them to our
will.

PROMETHEUS

O many fearful natures in one name,
I know ye; and these lakes and echoes
know
The darkness and the clangor of your
wings ! 460
But why more hideous than your loathèd
selves
Gather ye up in legions from the deep ?

SECOND FURY

We knew not that. Sisters, rejoice, re-
joice !

PROMETHEUS

Can aught exult in its deformity ?

SECOND FURY

The beauty of delight makes lovers glad,
Gazing on one another: so are we.
As from the rose which the pale priestess
kneels
To gather for her festal crown of flowers
The aërial crimson falls, flushing her cheek,

So from our victim's destined agony 470
The shade which is our form invests us
 round;
Else we are shapeless as our mother Night.

PROMETHEUS

I laugh your power, and his who sent you
 here,
To lowest scorn. Pour forth the cup of
 pain.

FIRST FURY

Thou thinkest we will rend thee bone from
 bone
And nerve from nerve, working like fire
 within?

PROMETHEUS

Pain is my element, as hate is thine;
Ye rend me now; I care not.

SECOND FURY

 Dost imagine
We will but laugh into thy lidless eyes?

PROMETHEUS

I weigh not what ye do, but what ye
 suffer,
Being evil. Cruel was the power which
 called 481
You, or aught else so wretched, into light.

THIRD FURY

Thou think'st we will live through thee,
 one by one,
Like animal life, and though we can obscure
 not
The soul which burns within, that we will
 dwell
Beside it, like a vain loud multitude,
Vexing the self-content of wisest men;
That we will be dread thought beneath thy
 brain,
And foul desire round thine astonished
 heart,
And blood within thy labyrinthine veins 490
Crawling like agony?

PROMETHEUS

 Why, ye are thus now;
Yet am I king over myself, and rule
The torturing and conflicting throngs
 within,
As Jove rules you when Hell grows muti-
 nous.

CHORUS OF FURIES

From the ends of the earth, from the ends
 of the earth,
Where the night has its grave and the
 morning its birth,
 Come, come, come!
O ye who shake hills with the scream of
 your mirth
When cities sink howling in ruin; and ye
Who with wingless footsteps trample the
 sea, 500
And close upon Shipwreck and Famine's
 track
Sit chattering with joy on the foodless
 wreck;
 Come, come, come!
 Leave the bed, low, cold, and red,
 Strewed beneath a nation dead;
 Leave the hatred, as in ashes
 Fire is left for future burning;
 It will burst in bloodier flashes
 When ye stir it, soon returning;
 Leave the self-contempt implanted 510
 In young spirits, sense-enchanted,
 Misery's yet unkindled fuel;
 Leave Hell's secrets half unchanted
 To the maniac dreamer; cruel
 More than ye can be with hate
 Is he with fear.
 Come, come, come!
We are steaming up from Hell's wide gate
 And we burden the blasts of the atmo-
 sphere,
But vainly we toil till ye come here. 520

IONE

Sister, I hear the thunder of new wings.

PANTHEA

These solid mountains quiver with the sound
Even as the tremulous air; their shadows
 make
The space within my plumes more black
 than night.

FIRST FURY

Your call was as a wingèd car,
Driven on whirlwinds fast and far;
It rapt us from red gulfs of war.

SECOND FURY

From wide cities, famine-wasted;

THIRD FURY

Groans half heard, and blood untasted;

FOURTH FURY

Kingly conclaves stern and cold, 530
Where blood with gold is bought and sold;

FIFTH FURY

From the furnace, white and hot,
In which —

A FURY

 Speak not; whisper not;
I know all that ye would tell,
But to speak might break the spell
Which must bend the Invincible,
 The stern of thought;
He yet defies the deepest power of Hell.

FURY

Tear the veil !

ANOTHER FURY

It is torn.

CHORUS

 The pale stars of the morn
Shine on a misery, dire to be borne. 540
Dost thou faint, mighty Titan ? We
 laugh thee to scorn.
Dost thou boast the clear knowledge thou
 waken'dst for man ?
Then was kindled within him a thirst
 which outran
Those perishing waters; a thirst of fierce
 fever,
Hope, love, doubt, desire, which consume
 him forever.
One came forth of gentle worth,
Smiling on the sanguine earth;
His words outlived him, like swift poison
 Withering up truth, peace, and pity.
Look ! where round the wide horizon 550
 Many a million-peopled city
Vomits smoke in the bright air !
Mark that outcry of despair !
'T is his mild and gentle ghost
 Wailing for the faith he kindled.
Look again ! the flames almost
 To a glow-worm's lamp have dwindled;
The survivors round the embers
 Gather in dread.
 Joy, joy, joy ! 560
Past ages crowd on thee, but each one re-
 members,
And the future is dark, and the present is
 spread

Like a pillow of thorns for thy slumberless
 head.

SEMICHORUS I

Drops of bloody agony flow
From his white and quivering brow.
Grant a little respite now.
See ! a disenchanted nation
Springs like day from desolation;
To Truth its state is dedicate,
And Freedom leads it forth, her mate;
A legioned band of linkèd brothers, 571
Whom Love calls children —

SEMICHORUS II

 'T is another's.
See how kindred murder kin !
'T is the vintage-time for Death and Sin;
Blood, like new wine, bubbles within;
 Till Despair smothers
The struggling world, which slaves and
 tyrants win.

 [*All the* FURIES *vanish, except one.*

IONE

Hark, sister ! what a low yet dreadful groan
Quite unsuppressed is tearing up the heart
Of the good Titan, as storms tear the deep,
And beasts hear the sea moan in inland
 caves. 581
Darest thou observe how the fiends torture
 him ?

PANTHEA

Alas ! I looked forth twice, but will no
 more.

IONE

What didst thou see ?

PANTHEA

 A woful sight: a youth
With patient looks nailed to a crucifix.

IONE

What next ?

PANTHEA

 The heaven around, the earth below,
Was peopled with thick shapes of human
 death,
All horrible, and wrought by human hands;
And some appeared the work of human
 hearts, 589

For men were slowly killed by frowns and
 smiles;
And other sights too foul to speak and live
Were wandering by. Let us not tempt
 worse fear
By looking forth; those groans are grief
 enough.

FURY

Behold an emblem: those who do endure
Deep wrongs for man, and scorn, and chains,
 but heap
Thousand-fold torment on themselves and
 him.

PROMETHEUS

Remit the anguish of that lighted stare;
Close those wan lips; let that thorn-wounded
 brow
Stream not with blood; it mingles with
 thy tears !
Fix, fix those tortured orbs in peace and
 death, 600
So thy sick throes shake not that crucifix,
So those pale fingers play not with thy
 gore.
Oh, horrible ! Thy name I will not speak —
It hath become a curse. I see, I see
The wise, the mild, the lofty, and the just,
Whom thy slaves hate for being like to
 thee,
Some hunted by foul lies from their heart's
 home,
An early-chosen, late-lamented home,
As hooded ounces cling to the driven hind;
Some linked to corpses in unwholesome
 cells; 610
Some — hear I not the multitude laugh
 loud ? —
Impaled in lingering fire; and mighty
 realms
Float by my feet, like sea-uprooted isles,
Whose sons are kneaded down in common
 blood
By the red light of their own burning
 homes.

FURY

Blood thou canst see, and fire; and canst
 hear groans:
Worse things unheard, unseen, remain be-
 hind.

PROMETHEUS

Worse ?

FURY

In each human heart terror survives
The ruin it has gorged: the loftiest fear
All that they would disdain to think were
 true. 620
Hypocrisy and custom make their minds
The fanes of many a worship, now outworn.
They dare not devise good for man's es-
 tate,
And yet they know not that they do not
 dare.
The good want power, but to weep barren
 tears.
The powerful goodness want; worse need
 for them.
The wise want love; and those who love
 want wisdom;
And all best things are thus confused to
 ill.
Many are strong and rich, and would be
 just, 629
But live among their suffering fellow-men
As if none felt; they know not what they
 do.

PROMETHEUS

Thy words are like a cloud of wingèd
 snakes;
And yet I pity those they torture not.

FURY

Thou pitiest them ? I speak no more !
 [*Vanishes.*

PROMETHEUS

 Ah woe !
Ah woe ! Alas ! pain, pain ever, forever !
I close my tearless eyes, but see more clear
Thy works within my woe-illumèd mind,
Thou subtle tyrant ! Peace is in the
 grave.
The grave hides all things beautiful and
 good.
I am a God and cannot find it there, 640
Nor would I seek it ; for, though dread
 revenge,
This is defeat, fierce king, not victory.
The sights with which thou torturest gird
 my soul
With new endurance, till the hour arrives
When they shall be no types of things
 which are.

PANTHEA

Alas ! what sawest thou ?

PROMETHEUS

There are two woes —
To speak and to behold; thou spare me
 one.
Names are there, Nature's sacred watch-
 words, they
Were borne aloft in bright emblazonry;
The nations thronged around, and cried
 aloud, 650
As with one voice, Truth, Liberty, and
 Love !
Suddenly fierce confusion fell from heaven
Among them; there was strife, deceit, and
 fear;
Tyrants rushed in, and did divide the spoil.
This was the shadow of the truth I saw.

THE EARTH

I felt thy torture, son, with such mixed
 joy
As pain and virtue give. To cheer thy
 state
I bid ascend those subtle and fair spirits,
Whose homes are the dim caves of human
 thought, 659
And who inhabit, as birds wing the wind,
Its world-surrounding ether; they behold
Beyond that twilight realm, as in a glass,
The future; may they speak comfort to
 thee !

PANTHEA

Look, sister, where a troop of spirits ga-
 ther,
Like flocks of clouds in spring's delightful
 weather,
Thronging in the blue air !

IONE

 And see ! more come,
Like fountain-vapors when the winds are
 dumb,
That climb up the ravine in scattered lines.
And hark ! is it the music of the pines ?
Is it the lake ? Is it the waterfall ? 670

PANTHEA

'T is something sadder, sweeter far than
 all.

CHORUS OF SPIRITS

From unremembered ages we
Gentle guides and guardians be
Of heaven-oppressed mortality;

And we breathe, and sicken not,
The atmosphere of human thought:
Be it dim, and dank, and gray,
Like a storm-extinguished day,
Travelled o'er by dying gleams;
 Be it bright as all between 680
Cloudless skies and windless streams,
 Silent, liquid, and serene ;
As the birds within the wind,
 As the fish within the wave,
As the thoughts of man's own mind
 Float through all above the grave;
We make there our liquid lair,
Voyaging cloudlike and unpent
Through the boundless element:
Thence we bear the prophecy 690
Which begins and ends in thee !

IONE

More yet come, one by one; the air around
 them
Looks radiant as the air around a star.

FIRST SPIRIT

On a battle-trumpet's blast
I fled hither, fast, fast, fast,
'Mid the darkness upward cast.
From the dust of creeds outworn,
From the tyrant's banner torn,
Gathering round me, onward borne,
There was mingled many a cry — 700
Freedom ! Hope ! Death ! Victory !
Till they faded through the sky;
And one sound above, around,
One sound beneath, around, above,
Was moving; 't was the soul of love;
'T was the hope, the prophecy,
Which begins and ends in thee.

SECOND SPIRIT

A rainbow's arch stood on the sea,
Which rocked beneath, immovably;
And the triumphant storm did flee, 710
Like a conqueror, swift and proud,
Begirt with many a captive cloud,
A shapeless, dark and rapid crowd,
Each by lightning riven in half.
I heard the thunder hoarsely laugh.
Mighty fleets were strewn like chaff
And spread beneath a hell of death
O'er the white waters. I alit
On a great ship lightning-split,
And speeded hither on the sigh 720
Of one who gave an enemy
His plank, then plunged aside to die.

I sat beside a sage's bed,
And the lamp was burning red
Near the book where he had fed,
When a Dream with plumes of flame
To his pillow hovering came,
And I knew it was the same
Which had kindled long ago
Pity, eloquence, and woe; 730
And the world awhile below
Wore the shade its lustre made.
It has borne me here as fleet
As Desire's lightning feet;
I must ride it back ere morrow,
Or the sage will wake in sorrow.

On a poet's lips I slept
Dreaming like a love-adept
In the sound his breathing kept;
Nor seeks nor finds he mortal blisses, 740
But feeds on the aërial kisses
Of shapes that haunt thought's wilder-
 nesses.
He will watch from dawn to gloom
The lake-reflected sun illume
The yellow bees in the ivy-bloom,
Nor heed nor see what things they be;
But from these create he can
Forms more real than living man,
Nurslings of immortality !
One of these awakened me, 750
And I sped to succor thee.

Behold'st thou not two shapes from the
 east and west
Come, as two doves to one belovèd nest,
Twin nurslings of the all-sustaining air,
On swift still wings glide down the at-
 mosphere ?
And, hark ! their sweet sad voices ! 't is
 despair
Mingled with love and then dissolved in
 sound.

Canst thou speak, sister ? all my words are
 drowned.

Their beauty gives me voice. See how
 they float
On their sustaining wings of skyey grain, 760

Orange and azure deepening into gold !
Their soft smiles light the air like a star's
 fire.

Hast thou beheld the form of Love ?

 As over wide dominions
I sped, like some swift cloud that wings
 the wide air's wildernesses,
That planet-crested Shape swept by on
 lightning-braided pinions,
Scattering the liquid joy of life from his
 ambrosial tresses.
His footsteps paved the world with light;
 but as I passed 't was fading,
And hollow Ruin yawned behind; great
 sages bound in madness,
And headless patriots, and pale youths who
 perished, unupbraiding,
Gleamed in the night. I wandered o'er,
 till thou, O King of sadness, 770
Turned by thy smile the worst I saw to
 recollected gladness.

Ah, sister ! Desolation is a delicate thing:
It walks not on the earth, it floats not on
 the air,
But treads with killing footstep, and fans
 with silent wing
The tender hopes which in their hearts the
 best and gentlest bear;
Who, soothed to false repose by the fan-
 ning plumes above
And the music-stirring motion of its soft
 and busy feet,
Dream visions of aërial joy, and call the
 monster, Love,
And wake, and find the shadow Pain, as
 he whom now we greet.

Though Ruin now Love's shadow be, 780
Following him, destroyingly,
 On Death's white and wingèd steed,
Which the fleetest cannot flee,
 Trampling down both flower and weed,
Man and beast, and foul and fair,
Like a tempest through the air;
Thou shalt quell this horseman grim,
Woundless though in heart or limb.

PROMETHEUS

Spirits ! how know ye this shall be ?

CHORUS

In the atmosphere we breathe, 790
As buds grow red, when the snow-storms
 flee,
From spring gathering up beneath,
Whose mild winds shake the elder-brake,
And the wandering herdsmen know
That the white-thorn soon will blow:
Wisdom, Justice, Love, and Peace,
When they struggle to increase,
Are to us as soft winds be
To shepherd boys, the prophecy
Which begins and ends in thee. 800

IONE

Where are the Spirits fled ?

PANTHEA

 Only a sense
Remains of them, like the omnipotence
Of music, when the inspired voice and lute
Languish, ere yet the responses are mute,
Which through the deep and labyrinthine
 soul,
Like echoes through long caverns, wind
 and roll.

PROMETHEUS

How fair these air-born shapes ! and yet I
 feel
Most vain all hope but love; and thou art
 far,
Asia who, when my being overflowed, 809
Wert like a golden chalice to bright wine
Which else had sunk into the thirsty dust.
All things are still. Alas ! how heavily
This quiet morning weighs upon my heart;
Though I should dream I could even
 sleep with grief,
If slumber were denied not. I would fain
Be what it is my destiny to be,
The saviour and the strength of suffering
 man,
Or sink into the original gulf of things.
There is no agony, and no solace left;
Earth can console, Heaven can torment no
 more. 820

PANTHEA

Hast thou forgotten one who watches thee
The cold dark night, and never sleeps but
 when
The shadow of thy spirit falls on her ?

PROMETHEUS

I said all hope was vain but love; thou
 lovest.

PANTHEA

Deeply in truth; but the eastern star looks
 white,
And Asia waits in that far Indian vale,
The scene of her sad exile; rugged once
And desolate and frozen, like this ravine;
But now invested with fair flowers and
 herbs,
And haunted by sweet airs and sounds,
 which flow 830
Among the woods and waters, from the
 ether
Of her transforming presence, which would
 fade
If it were mingled not with thine. Fare-
 well !

ACT II

SCENE I. — *Morning. A lovely Vale in the
Indian Caucasus.* ASIA, *alone.*

ASIA

FROM all the blasts of heaven thou hast
 descended;
Yes, like a spirit, like a thought, which
 makes
Unwonted tears throng to the horny eyes,
And beatings haunt the desolated heart,
Which should have learned repose; thou
 hast descended
Cradled in tempests; thou dost wake, O
 Spring !
O child of many winds ! As suddenly
Thou comest as the memory of a dream,
Which now is sad because it hath been
 sweet;
Like genius, or like joy which riseth up 10
As from the earth, clothing with golden
 clouds
The desert of our life.
This is the season, this the day, the hour;
At sunrise thou shouldst come, sweet sister
 mine,
Too long desired, too long delaying, come !
How like death-worms the wingless mo-
 ments crawl !
The point of one white star is quivering
 still
Deep in the orange light of widening morn
Beyond the purple mountains; through a
 chasm

Of wind-divided mist the darker lake 20
Reflects it; now it wanes; it gleams again
As the waves fade, and as the burning
 threads
Of woven cloud unravel in pale air;
'T is lost ! and through yon peaks of cloud-
 like snow
The roseate sunlight quivers; hear I not
The Æolian music of her sea-green plumes
Winnowing the crimson dawn ?

<div align="center">PANTHEA enters</div>

 I feel, I see
Those eyes which burn through smiles that
 fade in tears,
Like stars half-quenched in mists of silver
 dew. 29
Belovèd and most beautiful, who wearest
The shadow of that soul by which I live,
How late thou art ! the spherèd sun had
 climbed
The sea; my heart was sick with hope,
 before
The printless air felt thy belated plumes.

<div align="center">PANTHEA</div>

Pardon, great Sister ! but my wings were
 faint
With the delight of a remembered dream,
As are the noontide plumes of summer
 winds
Satiate with sweet flowers. I was wont to
 sleep
Peacefully, and awake refreshed and calm,
Before the sacred Titan's fall and thy 40
Unhappy love had made, through use and
 pity,
Both love and woe familiar to my heart
As they had grown to thine: erewhile I
 slept
Under the glaucous caverns of old Ocean
Within dim bowers of green and purple
 moss,
Our young Ione's soft and milky arms
Locked then, as now, behind my dark,
 moist hair,
While my shut eyes and cheek were pressed
 within
The folded depth of her life-breathing
 bosom: 49
But not as now, since I am made the
 wind
Which fails beneath the music that I bear
Of thy most wordless converse; since dis-
 solved

Into the sense with which love talks, my
 rest
Was troubled and yet sweet; my waking
 hours
Too full of care and pain.

<div align="center">ASIA</div>

 Lift up thine eyes,
And let me read thy dream.

<div align="center">PANTHEA</div>

 As I have said,
With our sea-sister at his feet I slept.
The mountain mists, condensing at our
 voice
Under the moon, had spread their snowy
 flakes,
From the keen ice shielding our linkèd
 sleep. 60
Then two dreams came. One I remember
 not.
But in the other his pale wound-worn limbs
Fell from Prometheus, and the azure night
Grew radiant with the glory of that form
Which lives unchanged within, and his
 voice fell
Like music which makes giddy the dim
 brain,
Faint with intoxication of keen joy:
'Sister of her whose footsteps pave the
 world
With loveliness — more fair than aught
 but her,
Whose shadow thou art — lift thine eyes
 on me.' 70
I lifted them; the overpowering light
Of that immortal shape was shadowed o'er
By love; which, from his soft and flowing
 limbs,
And passion-parted lips, and keen, faint
 eyes,
Steamed forth like vaporous fire; an at-
 mosphere
Which wrapped me in its all-dissolving
 power,
As the warm ether of the morning sun
Wraps ere it drinks some cloud of wander-
 ing dew.
I saw not, heard not, moved not, only felt
His presence flow and mingle through my
 blood 80
Till it became his life, and his grew mine,
And I was thus absorbed, until it passed,
And like the vapors when the sun sinks
 down,

Gathering again in drops upon the pines,
And tremulous as they, in the deep night
My being was condensed; and as the rays
Of thought were slowly gathered, I could
 hear
His voice, whose accents lingered ere they
 died
Like footsteps of weak melody; thy name
Among the many sounds alone I heard 90
Of what might be articulate; though still
I listened through the night when sound
 was none.
Ione wakened then, and said to me:
'Canst thou divine what troubles me to-
 night?
I always knew what I desired before,
Nor ever found delight to wish in vain.
But now I cannot tell thee what I seek;
I know not; something sweet, since it is
 sweet
Even to desire ; it is thy sport, false sis-
 ter;
Thou hast discovered some enchantment
 old, 100
Whose spells have stolen my spirit as I
 slept
And mingled it with thine; for when just
 now
We kissed, I felt within thy parted lips
The sweet air that sustained me; and the
 warmth
Of the life-blood, for loss of which I
 faint,
Quivered between our intertwining arms.'
I answered not, for the Eastern star grew
 pale,
But fled to thee.

<div align="center">ASIA</div>

 Thou speakest, but thy words
Are as the air; I feel them not. Oh, lift
Thine eyes, that I may read his written
 soul ! 110

<div align="center">PANTHEA</div>

I lift them, though they droop beneath the
 load
Of that they would express; what canst
 thou see
But thine own fairest shadow imaged there ?

<div align="center">ASIA</div>

Thine eyes are like the deep, blue, bound-
 less heaven
Contracted to two circles underneath

Their long, fine lashes; dark, far, measure-
 less,
Orb within orb, and line through line in-
 woven.

<div align="center">PANTHEA</div>

Why lookest thou as if a spirit passed ?

<div align="center">ASIA</div>

There is a change; beyond their inmost
 depth
I see a shade, a shape: 't is He, arrayed 120
In the soft light of his own smiles, which
 spread
Like radiance from the cloud-surrounded
 moon.
Prometheus, it is thine ! depart not yet !
Say not those smiles that we shall meet
 again
Within that bright pavilion which their
 beams
Shall build on the waste world ? The dream
 is told.
What shape is that between us ? Its rude
 hair
Roughens the wind that lifts it, its regard
Is wild and quick, yet 't is a thing of air,
For through its gray robe gleams the golden
 dew 130
Whose stars the noon has quenched not.

<div align="center">DREAM</div>

 Follow ! Follow !

<div align="center">PANTHEA</div>

It is mine other dream.

<div align="center">ASIA</div>

 It disappears.

<div align="center">PANTHEA</div>

It passes now into my mind. Methought
As we sate here, the flower-infolding buds
Burst on yon lightning - blasted almond
 tree;
When swift from the white Scythian wil-
 derness
A wind swept forth wrinkling the Earth
 with frost;
I looked, and all the blossoms were blown
 down;
But on each leaf was stamped, as the blue
 bells
Of Hyacinth tell Apollo's written grief, 140
OH, FOLLOW, FOLLOW !

ASIA

As you speak, your words
Fill, pause by pause, my own forgotten
 sleep
With shapes. Methought among the lawns
 together
We wandered, underneath the young gray
 dawn,
And multitudes of dense white fleecy clouds
Were wandering in thick flocks along the
 mountains,
Shepherded by the slow, unwilling wind;
And the white dew on the new-bladed
 grass,
Just piercing the dark earth, hung silently;
And there was more which I remember
 not; 150
But on the shadows of the morning clouds,
Athwart the purple mountain slope, was
 written
FOLLOW, OH, FOLLOW! as they vanished
 by;
And on each herb, from which Heaven's
 dew had fallen,
The like was stamped, as with a withering
 fire;
A wind arose among the pines; it shook
The clinging music from their boughs, and
 then
Low, sweet, faint sounds, like the farewell
 of ghosts,
Were heard: OH, FOLLOW, FOLLOW, FOLLOW
 ME!
And then I said, 'Panthea, look on me.' 160
But in the depth of those belovèd eyes
Still I saw, FOLLOW, FOLLOW!

ECHO
 Follow, follow!

PANTHEA
The crags, this clear spring morning, mock
 our voices,
As they were spirit-tongued.

ASIA
 It is some being
Around the crags. What fine clear sounds!
Oh, list!

ECHOES, *unseen*
 Echoes we: listen!
 We cannot stay:
 As dew-stars glisten
 Then fade away —
 Child of Ocean! 170

ASIA
Hark! Spirits speak. The liquid re-
 sponses
Of their aërial tongues yet sound.

PANTHEA
 I hear.

ECHOES
 Oh, follow, follow,
 As our voice recedeth
 Through the caverns hollow,
 Where the forest spreadeth;
 (*More distant*)
 Oh, follow, follow!
 Through the caverns hollow,
 As the song floats thou pursue,
 Where the wild bee never flew, 180
 Through the noontide darkness deep,
 By the odor-breathing sleep
 Of faint night-flowers, and the waves
 At the fountain-lighted caves,
 While our music, wild and sweet,
 Mocks thy gently falling feet,
 Child of Ocean!

ASIA
Shall we pursue the sound? It grows
 more faint
And distant.

PANTHEA
 List! the strain floats nearer now.

ECHOES
 In the world unknown 190
 Sleeps a voice unspoken;
 By thy step alone
 Can its rest be broken;
 Child of Ocean!

ASIA
How the notes sink upon the ebbing wind!

ECHOES
 Oh, follow, follow!
 Through the caverns hollow,
 As the song floats thou pursue,
 By the woodland noontide dew;
 By the forests, lakes, and fountains, 200
 Through the many-folded mountains;
 To the rents, and gulfs, and chasms,
 Where the Earth reposed from spasms,
 On the day when He and thou
 Parted, to commingle now;
 Child of Ocean!

ASIA

Come, sweet Panthea, link thy hand in
 mine,
And follow, ere the voices fade away.

SCENE II. — *A Forest intermingled with Rocks
and Caverns.* ASIA *and* PANTHEA *pass into
it. Two young Fauns are sitting on a Rock,
listening.*

SEMICHORUS I OF SPIRITS

The path through which that lovely twain
 Have passed, by cedar, pine, and yew,
 And each dark tree that ever grew,
 Is curtained out from Heaven's wide
 blue;
Nor sun, nor moon, nor wind, nor rain,
 Can pierce its interwoven bowers,
 Nor aught, save where some cloud of
 dew,
Drifted along the earth-creeping breeze
Between the trunks of the hoar trees, 9
 Hangs each a pearl in the pale flowers
 Of the green laurel blown anew,
And bends, and then fades silently,
One frail and fair anemone;
Or when some star of many a one
That climbs and wanders through steep
 night,
Has found the cleft through which alone
Beams fall from high those depths upon, —
Ere it is borne away, away,
By the swift Heavens that cannot stay,
It scatters drops of golden light, 20
Like lines of rain that ne'er unite;
And the gloom divine is all around;
And underneath is the mossy ground.

SEMICHORUS II

There the voluptuous nightingales,
 Are awake through all the broad noon-
 day:
When one with bliss or sadness fails,
 And through the windless ivy-boughs,
 Sick with sweet love, droops dying away
On its mate's music-panting bosom;
Another from the swinging blossom, 30
 Watching to catch the languid close
 Of the last strain, then lifts on high
 The wings of the weak melody,
Till some new strain of feeling bear
 The song, and all the woods are mute;
When there is heard through the dim air
 The rush of wings, and rising there,
 Like many a lake-surrounded flute,

Sounds overflow the listener's brain
So sweet, that joy is almost pain. 40

SEMICHORUS I

There those enchanted eddies play
 Of echoes, music-tongued, which draw,
 By Demogorgon's mighty law,
 With melting rapture, or sweet awe,
All spirits on that secret way,
 As inland boats are driven to Ocean
Down streams made strong with mountain-
 thaw;
And first there comes a gentle sound
To those in talk or slumber bound,
 And wakes the destined; soft emo-
 tion 50
Attracts, impels them; those who saw
Say from the breathing earth behind
There steams a plume-uplifting wind
Which drives them on their path, while
 they
Believe their own swift wings and feet
The sweet desires within obey;
And so they float upon their way,
 Until, still sweet, but loud and strong,
 The storm of sound is driven along,
 Sucked up and hurrying; as they fleet 60
Behind, its gathering billows meet
And to the fatal mountain bear
Like clouds amid the yielding air.

FIRST FAUN

Canst thou imagine where those spirits
 live
Which make such delicate music in the
 woods ?
We haunt within the least frequented caves
And closest coverts, and we know these
 wilds,
Yet never meet them, though we hear
 them oft:
Where may they hide themselves ?

SECOND FAUN

 'T is hard to tell;
I have heard those more skilled in spirits
 say, 70
The bubbles, which the enchantment of the
 sun
Sucks from the pale faint water-flowers
 that pave
The oozy bottom of clear lakes and pools,
Are the pavilions where such dwell and
 float
Under the green and golden atmosphere

Which noontide kindles through the woven
 leaves;
And when these burst, and the thin fiery
 air,
The which they breathed within those lu-
 cent domes,
Ascends to flow like meteors through the
 night,
They ride on them, and rein their headlong
 speed, 80
And bow their burning crests, and glide in
 fire
Under the waters of the earth again.

FIRST FAUN

If such live thus, have others other lives,
Under pink blossoms or within the bells
Of meadow flowers or folded violets deep,
Or on their dying odors, when they die,
Or in the sunlight of the spherèd dew ?

SECOND FAUN

Ay, many more which we may well divine.
But should we stay to speak, noontide
 would come,
And thwart Silenus find his goats un-
 drawn, 90
And grudge to sing those wise and lovely
 songs
Of Fate, and Chance, and God, and Chaos
 old,
And Love and the chained Titan's woful
 doom,
And how he shall be loosed, and make the
 earth
One brotherhood; delightful strains which
 cheer
Our solitary twilights, and which charm
To silence the unenvying nightingales.

SCENE III. — *A Pinnacle of Rock among
 Mountains.* ASIA *and* PANTHEA.

PANTHEA

Hither the sound has borne us — to the
 realm
Of Demogorgon, and the mighty portal,
Like a volcano's meteor-breathing chasm,
Whence the oracular vapor is hurled up
Which lonely men drink wandering in their
 youth,
And call truth, virtue, love, genius, or joy,
That maddening wine of life, whose dregs
 they drain

To deep intoxication; and uplift,
Like Mænads who cry loud, Evoe ! Evoe!
The voice which is contagion to the
 world. 10

ASIA

Fit throne for such a Power! Magnifi-
 cent !
How glorious art thou, Earth ! and if thou
 be
The shadow of some spirit lovelier still,
Though evil stain its work, and it should
 be
Like its creation, weak yet beautiful,
I could fall down and worship that and
 thee.
Even now my heart adoreth. Wonderful !
Look, sister, ere the vapor dim thy brain:
Beneath is a wide plain of billowy mist,
As a lake, paving in the morning sky, 20
With azure waves which burst in silver
 light,
Some Indian vale. Behold it, rolling on
Under the curdling winds, and islanding
The peak whereon we stand, midway,
 around,
Encinctured by the dark and blooming
 forests,
Dim twilight-lawns, and stream-illumined
 caves,
And wind-enchanted shapes of wandering
 mist;
And far on high the keen sky-cleaving
 mountains
From icy spires of sunlike radiance fling 29
The dawn, as lifted Ocean's dazzling spray,
From some Atlantic islet scattered up,
Spangles the wind with lamp-like water-
 drops.
The vale is girdled with their walls, a
 howl
Of cataracts from their thaw-cloven ra-
 vines
Satiates the listening wind, continuous, vast,
Awful as silence. Hark ! the rushing
 snow !
The sun-awakened avalanche ! whose mass,
Thrice sifted by the storm, had gathered
 there
Flake after flake, in heaven-defying minds
As thought by thought is piled, till some
 great truth 40
Is loosened, and the nations echo round,
Shaken to their roots, as do the mountains
 now.

PANTHEA

Look how the gusty sea of mist is breaking
In crimson foam, even at our feet ! it rises
As Ocean at the enchantment of the moon
Round foodless men wrecked on some oozy
 isle.

ASIA

The fragments of the cloud are scattered
 up;
The wind that lifts them disentwines my
 hair;
Its billows now sweep o'er mine eyes; my
 brain 49
Grows dizzy; I see shapes within the mist.

PANTHEA

A countenance with beckoning smiles;
 there burns
An azure fire within its golden locks !
Another and another: hark ! they speak !

SONG OF SPIRITS

To the deep, to the deep,
 Down, down !
Through the shade of sleep,
Through the cloudy strife
Of Death and of Life;
Through the veil and the bar
Of things which seem and are, 60
Even to the steps of the remotest throne,
 Down, down !

While the sound whirls around,
 Down, down !
As the fawn draws the hound,
As the lightning the vapor,
As a weak moth the taper;
Death, despair; love, sorrow;
Time, both; to-day, to-morrow;
As steel obeys the spirit of the stone, 70
 Down, down !

Through the gray, void abysm,
 Down, down !
Where the air is no prism,
And the moon and stars are not,
And the cavern-crags wear not
The radiance of Heaven,
Nor the gloom to Earth given,
Where there is one pervading, one alone,
 Down, down ! 80

In the depth of the deep
 Down, down !

Like veiled lightning asleep,
Like the spark nursed in embers,
The last look Love remembers,
Like a diamond, which shines
On the dark wealth of mines,
A spell is treasured but for thee alone.
 Down, down !

We have bound thee, we guide thee; 90
 Down, down !
With the bright form beside thee;
 Resist not the weakness,
Such strength is in meekness
That the Eternal, the Immortal,
Must unloose through life's portal
The snake-like Doom coiled underneath
 his throne
 By that alone.

SCENE IV. — *The Cave of* DEMOGORGON.
 ASIA *and* PANTHEA.

PANTHEA

What veilèd form sits on that ebon throne ?

ASIA

The veil has fallen.

PANTHEA

 I see a mighty darkness
Filling the seat of power, and rays of gloom
Dart round, as light from the meridian sun,
Ungazed upon and shapeless; neither limb,
Nor form, nor outline; yet we feel it is
A living Spirit.

DEMOGORGON

 Ask what thou wouldst know.

ASIA

What canst thou tell ?

DEMOGORGON

 All things thou dar'st demand.

ASIA

Who made the living world ?

DEMOGORGON

 God.

ASIA

 Who made all
That it contains ? thought, passion, reason,
 will, 10
Imagination ?

DEMOGORGON

God : Almighty God.

ASIA

Who made that sense which, when the
 winds of spring
In rarest visitation, or the voice
Of one belovèd heard in youth alone,
Fills the faint eyes with falling tears which
 dim
The radiant looks of unbewailing flowers,
And leaves this peopled earth a solitude
When it returns no more ?

DEMOGORGON

Merciful God.

ASIA

And who made terror, madness, crime, re-
 morse,
Which from the links of the great chain of
 things 20
To every thought within the mind of man
Sway and drag heavily, and each one reels
Under the load towards the pit of death ;
Abandoned hope, and love that turns to
 hate;
And self-contempt, bitterer to drink than
 blood;
Pain, whose unheeded and familiar speech
Is howling, and keen shrieks, day after
 day;
And Hell, or the sharp fear of Hell ?

DEMOGORGON

He reigns.

ASIA

Utter his name ; a world pining in pain
Asks but his name; curses shall drag him
 down. 30

DEMOGORGON

He reigns.

ASIA

I feel, I know it: who ?

DEMOGORGON

He reigns.

ASIA

Who reigns ? There was the Heaven and
 Earth at first,

And Light and Love; then Saturn, from
 whose throne
Time fell, an envious shadow; such the
 state
Of the earth's primal spirits beneath his
 sway,
As the calm joy of flowers and living
 leaves
Before the wind or sun has withered them
And semivital worms ; but he refused
The birthright of their being, knowledge,
 power,
The skill which wields the elements, the
 thought 40
Which pierces this dim universe like light,
Self-empire, and the majesty of love;
For thirst of which they fainted. Then
 Prometheus
Gave wisdom, which is strength, to Jupiter,
And with this law alone, ' Let man be
 free,'
Clothed him with the dominion of wide
 Heaven.
To know nor faith, nor love, nor law, to be
Omnipotent but friendless, is to reign;
And Jove now reigned; for on the race of
 man
First famine, and then toil, and then dis-
 ease, 50
Strife, wounds, and ghastly death unseen
 before,
Fell; and the unseasonable seasons drove,
With alternating shafts of frost and fire,
Their shelterless, pale tribes to mountain
 caves;
And in their desert hearts fierce wants he
 sent,
And mad disquietudes, and shadows idle
Of unreal good, which levied mutual war,
So ruining the lair wherein they raged.
Prometheus saw, and waked the legioned
 hopes 59
Which sleep within folded Elysian flowers,
Nepenthe, Moly, Amaranth, fadeless
 blooms,
That they might hide with thin and rain-
 bow wings
The shape of Death; and Love he sent to
 bind
The disunited tendrils of that vine
Which bears the wine of life, the human
 heart;
And he tamed fire which, like some beast
 of prey,
Most terrible, but lovely, played beneath

The frown of man; and tortured to his
 will
Iron and gold, the slaves and signs of
 power,
And gems and poisons, and all subtlest
 forms 70
Hidden beneath the mountains and the
 waves.
He gave man speech, and speech created
 thought,
Which is the measure of the universe;
And Science struck the thrones of earth
 and heaven,
Which shook, but fell not; and the har-
 monious mind
Poured itself forth in all-prophetic song;
And music lifted up the listening spirit
Until it walked, exempt from mortal care,
Godlike, o'er the clear billows of sweet
 sound;
And human hands first mimicked and then
 mocked, 80
With moulded limbs more lovely than its
 own,
The human form, till marble grew divine;
And mothers, gazing, drank the love men
 see
Reflected in their race, behold, and perish.
He told the hidden power of herbs and
 springs,
And Disease drank and slept. Death grew
 like sleep.
He taught the implicated orbits woven
Of the wide-wandering stars; and how the
 sun
Changes his lair, and by what secret spell
The pale moon is transformed, when her
 broad eye 90
Gazes not on the interlunar sea.
He taught to rule, as life directs the limbs,
The tempest-wingèd chariots of the Ocean,
And the Celt knew the Indian. Cities then
Were built, and through their snow-like
 columns flowed
The warm winds, and the azure ether shone,
And the blue sea and shadowy hills were
 seen.
Such, the alleviations of his state,
Prometheus gave to man, for which he
 hangs
Withering in destined pain; but who rains
 down 100
Evil, the immedicable plague, which, while
Man looks on his creation like a god
And sees that it is glorious, drives him on,

The wreck of his own will, the scorn of
 earth,
The outcast, the abandoned, the alone ?
Not Jove: while yet his frown shook heaven
 ay, when
His adversary from adamantine chains
Cursed him, he trembled like a slave. De-
 clare
Who is his master ? Is he too a slave ?

DEMOGORGON

All spirits are enslaved which serve things
 evil: 110
Thou knowest if Jupiter be such or no.

ASIA

Whom called'st thou God ?

DEMOGORGON

 I spoke but as ye speak,
For Jove is the supreme of living things.

ASIA

Who is the master of the slave ?

DEMOGORGON

 If the abysm
Could vomit forth its secrets — but a voice
Is wanting, the deep truth is imageless;
For what would it avail to bid thee gaze
On the revolving world ? What to bid
 speak
Fate, Time, Occasion, Chance and Change ?
 To these
All things are subject but eternal Love. 120

ASIA

So much I asked before, and my heart gave
The response thou hast given; and of such
 truths
Each to itself must be the oracle.
One more demand; and do thou answer me
As my own soul would answer, did it know
That which I ask. Prometheus shall arise
Henceforth the sun of this rejoicing world:
When shall the destined hour arrive ?

DEMOGORGON

 Behold !

ASIA

The rocks are cloven, and through the pur-
 ple night
I see cars drawn by rainbow - wingèd
 steeds 130

Which trample the dim winds; in each there
　　stands
A wild-eyed charioteer urging their flight.
Some look behind, as fiends pursued them
　　there,
And yet I see no shapes but the keen stars;
Others, with burning eyes, lean forth, and
　　drink
With eager lips the wind of their own
　　speed,
As if the thing they loved fled on before,
And now, even now, they clasped it.　Their
　　bright locks
Stream like a comet's flashing hair; they
　　all　　　　　　　　　　　　　139
Sweep onward.

DEMOGORGON

　　　　These are the immortal Hours,
Of whom thou didst demand.　One waits
　　for thee.

ASIA

A Spirit with a dreadful countenance
Checks its dark chariot by the craggy gulf.
Unlike thy brethren, ghastly Charioteer,
Who art thou?　Whither wouldst thou
　　bear me?　Speak!

SPIRIT

I am the Shadow of a destiny
More dread than is my aspect; ere yon
　　planet
Has set, the darkness which ascends with
　　me
Shall wrap in lasting night heaven's kingless
　　throne.　　　　　　　　　　　149

ASIA

What meanest thou?

PANTHEA

　　　　That terrible Shadow floats
Up from its throne, as may the lurid smoke
Of earthquake-ruined cities o'er the sea.
Lo! it ascends the car; the coursers fly
Terrified; watch its path among the stars
Blackening the night!

ASIA

Thus I am answered: strange!

PANTHEA

See, near the verge, another chariot stays;
An ivory shell inlaid with crimson fire,

Which comes and goes within its sculptured
　　rim
Of delicate strange tracery; the young
　　Spirit
That guides it has the dove-like eyes of
　　hope;　　　　　　　　　　　160
How its soft smiles attract the soul! as
　　light
Lures wingèd insects through the lampless
　　air.

SPIRIT

My coursers are fed with the lightning,
　　They drink of the whirlwind's stream,
And when the red morning is bright'ning
　　They bathe in the fresh sunbeam.
　　They have strength for their swiftness I
　　　　deem;
Then ascend with me, daughter of Ocean.

I desire — and their speed makes night
　　kindle;
　　I fear — they outstrip the typhoon;　170
Ere the cloud piled on Atlas can dwindle
　　We encircle the earth and the moon.
　　We shall rest from long labors at noon;
Then ascend with me, daughter of Ocean.

SCENE V. — *The Car pauses within a Cloud on
　　the Top of a snowy Mountain.*　ASIA, PAN-
　　THEA, *and the* SPIRIT OF THE HOUR.

SPIRIT

On the brink of the night and the morning
　　My coursers are wont to respire;
But the Earth has just whispered a warn-
　　ing
　　That their flight must be swifter than
　　　　fire;
　　They shall drink the hot speed of desire!

ASIA

Thou breathest on their nostrils, but my
　　breath
Would give them swifter speed.

SPIRIT

　　　　　　　Alas! it could not.

PANTHEA

O Spirit! pause, and tell whence is the
　　light
Which fills the cloud? the sun is yet un-
　　risen.　　　　　　　　　　　　9

SPIRIT

The sun will rise not until noon. Apollo
Is held in heaven by wonder; and the light
Which fills this vapor, as the aërial hue
Of fountain-gazing roses fills the water,
Flows from thy mighty sister.

PANTHEA

Yes, I feel —

ASIA

What is it with thee, sister? Thou art
pale.

PANTHEA

How thou art changed! I dare not look
on thee;
I feel but see thee not. I scarce endure
The radiance of thy beauty. Some good
change
Is working in the elements, which suffer
Thy presence thus unveiled. The Nereids
tell 20
That on the day when the clear hyaline
Was cloven at thy uprise, and thou didst
stand
Within a veinèd shell, which floated on
Over the calm floor of the crystal sea,
Among the Ægean isles, and by the shores
Which bear thy name, — love, like the at-
mosphere
Of the sun's fire filling the living world,
Burst from thee, and illumined earth and
heaven
And the deep ocean and the sunless caves
And all that dwells within them; till grief
cast 30
Eclipse upon the soul from which it came.
Such art thou now; nor is it I alone,
Thy sister, thy companion, thine own chosen
one,
But the whole world which seeks thy sym-
pathy.
Hearest thou not sounds i' the air which
speak the love
Of all articulate beings? Feelest thou not
The inanimate winds enamoured of thee?
List! [Music.

ASIA

Thy words are sweeter than aught else but
his
Whose echoes they are; yet all love is
sweet,
Given or returned. Common as light is
love, 40

And its familiar voice wearies not ever.
Like the wide heaven, the all-sustaining air,
It makes the reptile equal to the God;
They who inspire it most are fortunate,
As I am now; but those who feel it most
Are happier still, after long sufferings,
As I shall soon become.

PANTHEA

List! Spirits speak.

VOICE *in the air, singing*

Life of Life, thy lips enkindle
 With their love the breath between them;
And thy smiles before they dwindle 50
 Make the cold air fire; then screen them
In those looks, where whoso gazes
Faints, entangled in their mazes.

Child of Light! thy limbs are burning
 Through the vest which seems to hide
 them;
As the radiant lines of morning
 Through the clouds, ere they divide
 them;
And this atmosphere divinest
Shrouds thee wheresoe'er thou shinest.

Fair are others; none beholds thee, 60
 But thy voice sounds low and tender
Like the fairest, for it folds thee
 From the sight, that liquid splendor,
And all feel, yet see thee never,
As I feel now, lost forever!

Lamp of Earth! where'er thou movest
 Its dim shapes are clad with brightness,
And the souls of whom thou lovest
 Walk upon the winds with lightness,
Till they fail, as I am failing, 70
Dizzy, lost, yet unbewailing!

ASIA

My soul is an enchanted boat,
 Which, like a sleeping swan, doth float
Upon the silver waves of thy sweet sing-
 ing;
 And thine doth like an angel sit
 Beside a helm conducting it,
Whilst all the winds with melody are ring-
 ing.
 It seems to float ever, forever,
 Upon that many-winding river,
Between mountains, woods, abysses, 80
A paradise of wildernesses!

Till, like one in slumber bound,
Borne to the ocean, I float down, around,
Into a sea profound of ever-spreading
 sound.

Meanwhile thy spirit lifts its pinions
 In music's most serene dominions;
Catching the winds that fan that happy
 heaven.
 And we sail on, away, afar,
 Without a course, without a star,
 But, by the instinct of sweet music
 driven; 90
Till through Elysian garden islets
 By thee most beautiful of pilots,
Where never mortal pinnace glided,
 The boat of my desire is guided;
Realms where the air we breathe is love,
Which in the winds on the waves doth
 move,
Harmonizing this earth with what we feel
 above.

We have passed Age's icy caves,
 And Manhood's dark and tossing waves,
And Youth's smooth ocean, smiling to
 betray; 100
 Beyond the glassy gulfs we flee
 Of shadow-peopled Infancy,
Through Death and Birth, to a diviner day;
 A paradise of vaulted bowers
 Lit by downward-gazing flowers,
 And watery paths that wind between
Wildernesses calm and green,
Peopled by shapes too bright to see,
And rest, having beheld; somewhat like
 thee;
Which walk upon the sea, and chant melo-
 diously! 110

ACT III

SCENE I. — *Heaven.* JUPITER *on his Throne ;*
THETIS *and the other Deities assembled.*

JUPITER

YE congregated powers of heaven, who
 share
The glory and the strength of him ye
 serve,
Rejoice ! henceforth I am omnipotent.
All else had been subdued to me ; alone
The soul of man, like unextinguished fire,
Yet burns towards heaven with fierce re-
 proach, and doubt,

And lamentation, and reluctant prayer,
Hurling up insurrection, which might
 make
Our antique empire insecure, though built
On eldest faith, and hell's coeval, fear; 10
And though my curses through the pendu-
 lous air,
Like snow on herbless peaks, fall flake by
 flake,
And cling to it; though under my wrath's
 night
It climb the crags of life, step after step,
Which wound it, as ice wounds unsandalled
 feet,
It yet remains supreme o'er misery,
Aspiring, unrepressed, yet soon to fall;
Even now have I begotten a strange won-
 der,
That fatal child, the terror of the earth,
Who waits but till the destined hour ar-
 rive, 20
Bearing from Demogorgon's vacant throne
The dreadful might of ever-living limbs
Which clothed that awful spirit unbeheld,
To redescend, and trample out the spark.

Pour forth heaven's wine, Idæan Gany-
 mede,
And let it fill the dædal cups like fire,
And from the flower-inwoven soil divine,
Ye all-triumphant harmonies, arise,
As dew from earth under the twilight
 stars.
Drink ! be the nectar circling through your
 veins 30
The soul of joy, ye ever-living Gods,
Till exultation burst in one wide voice
Like music from Elysian winds.
 And thou
Ascend beside me, veilèd in the light
Of the desire which makes thee one with
 me,
Thetis, bright image of eternity !
When thou didst cry, 'Insufferable might !
God ! spare me ! I sustain not the quick
 flames,
The penetrating presence; all my being,
Like him whom the Numidian seps did
 thaw 40
Into a dew with poison, is dissolved,
Sinking through its foundations,' — even
 then
Two mighty spirits, mingling, made a
 third
Mightier than either, which, unbodied now,

Between us floats, felt, although unbeheld,
Waiting the incarnation, which ascends,
(Hear ye the thunder of the fiery wheels
Griding the winds?) from Demogorgon's
 throne.
Victory! victory! Feel'st thou not, O
 world,
The earthquake of his chariot thundering
 up 50
Olympus?

> [*The Car of the* HOUR *arrives.* DEMO-
> GORGON *descends and moves towards the
> Throne of* JUPITER.

Awful shape, what art thou? Speak!

DEMOGORGON

Eternity. Demand no direr name.
Descend, and follow me down the abyss.
I am thy child, as thou wert Saturn's
 child;
Mightier than thee; and we must dwell to-
 gether
Henceforth in darkness. Lift thy light-
 nings not.
The tyranny of heaven none may retain,
Or reassume, or hold, succeeding thee;
Yet if thou wilt, as 't is the destiny
Of trodden worms to writhe till they are
 dead, 60
Put forth thy might.

JUPITER

 Detested prodigy!
Even thus beneath the deep Titanian
 prisons
I trample thee! Thou lingerest?
 Mercy! mercy!
No pity, no release, no respite! Oh,
That thou wouldst make mine enemy my
 judge,
Even where he hangs, seared by my long
 revenge,
On Caucasus! he would not doom me
 thus.
Gentle, and just, and dreadless, is he not
The monarch of the world? What then
 art thou? 69
No refuge! no appeal!
 Sink with me then,
We two will sink on the wide waves of
 ruin,
Even as a vulture and a snake outspent
Drop, twisted in inextricable fight,
Into a shoreless sea! Let hell unlock

Its mounded oceans of tempestuous fire,
And whelm on them into the bottomless
 void
This desolated world, and thee, and me,
The conqueror and the conquered, and the
 wreck
Of that for which they combated!
 Ai, Ai!
The elements obey me not. I sink 80
Dizzily down, ever, forever, down.
And, like a cloud, mine enemy above
Darkens my fall with victory! Ai, Ai!

SCENE II. — *The Mouth of a great River in the
Island Atlantis.* OCEAN *is discovered reclin-
ing near the shore;* APOLLO *stands beside
him.*

OCEAN

He fell, thou sayest, beneath his conquer-
 or's frown?

APOLLO

Ay, when the strife was ended which made
 dim
The orb I rule, and shook the solid stars,
The terrors of his eye illumined heaven
With sanguine light, through the thick
 ragged skirts
Of the victorious darkness, as he fell;
Like the last glare of day's red agony,
Which, from a rent among the fiery clouds,
Burns far along the tempest-wrinkled deep.

OCEAN

He sunk to the abyss? to the dark
 void? 10

APOLLO

An eagle so caught in some bursting cloud
On Caucasus, his thunder-baffled wings
Entangled in the whirlwind, and his eyes,
Which gazed on the undazzling sun, now
 blinded
By the white lightning, while the ponder-
 ous hail
Beats on his struggling form, which sinks
 at length
Prone, and the aërial ice clings over it.

OCEAN

Henceforth the fields of Heaven-reflecting
 sea
Which are my realm, will heave, unstained
 with blood,

Beneath the uplifting winds, like plains of
 corn 20
Swayed by the summer air; my streams
 will flow
Round many-peopled continents, and round
Fortunate isles; and from their glassy
 thrones
Blue Proteus and his humid nymphs shall
 mark
The shadow of fair ships, as mortals see
The floating bark of the light-laden moon
With that white star, its sightless pilot's
 crest,
Borne down the rapid sunset's ebbing sea ;
Tracking their path no more by blood and
 groans,
And desolation, and the mingled voice 30
Of slavery and command; but by the light
Of wave-reflected flowers, and floating
 odors,
And music soft, and mild, free, gentle
 voices,
That sweetest music, such as spirits love.

APOLLO

And I shall gaze not on the deeds which
 make
My mind obscure with sorrow, as eclipse
Darkens the sphere I guide. But list, I hear
The small, clear, silver lute of the young
 Spirit
That sits i' the morning star.

OCEAN

 Thou must away ;
Thy steeds will pause at even, till when
 farewell. 40
The loud deep calls me home even now to
 feed it
With azure calm out of the emerald urns
Which stand forever full beside my throne.
Behold the Nereids under the green sea,
Their wavering limbs borne on the wind-
 like stream,
Their white arms lifted o'er their stream-
 ing hair,
With garlands pied and starry sea-flower
 crowns,
Hastening to grace their mighty sister's joy.
 [*A sound of waves is heard.*
It is the unpastured sea hungering for calm.
Peace, monster; I come now. Farewell.

APOLLO

 Farewell. 50

SCENE III. — *Caucasus.* PROMETHEUS, HER-
CULES, IONE, *the* EARTH, SPIRITS, ASIA, *and*
PANTHEA, *borne in the Car with the* SPIRIT
OF THE HOUR. HERCULES *unbinds* PRO-
METHEUS, *who descends.*

HERCULES

Most glorious among spirits ! thus doth
 strength
To wisdom, courage, and long-suffering
 love,
And thee, who art the form they animate,
Minister like a slave.

PROMETHEUS

 Thy gentle words
Are sweeter even than freedom long de-
 sired
And long delayed.

 Asia, thou light of life,
Shadow of beauty unbeheld; and ye,
Fair sister nymphs, who made long years
 of pain
Sweet to remember, through your love and
 care;
Henceforth we will not part. There is a
 cave, 10
All overgrown with trailing odorous plants,
Which curtain out the day with leaves and
 flowers,
And paved with veinèd emerald; and a
 fountain
Leaps in the midst with an awakening
 sound.
From its curved roof the mountain's frozen
 tears,
Like snow, or silver, or long diamond spires,
Hang downward, raining forth a doubtful
 light;
And there is heard the ever-moving air
Whispering without from tree to tree, and
 birds,
And bees; and all around are mossy
 seats, 20
And the rough walls are clothed with long
 soft grass;
A simple dwelling, which shall be our
 own ;
Where we will sit and talk of time and
 change,
As the world ebbs and flows, ourselves un-
 changed.
What can hide man from mutability ?
And if ye sigh, then I will smile; and thou,

Ione, shalt chant fragments of sea-music,
Until I weep, when ye shall smile away
The tears she brought, which yet were
 sweet to shed.
We will entangle buds and flowers and
 beams 30
Which twinkle on the fountain's brim, and
 make
Strange combinations out of common
 things,
Like human babes in their brief innocence;
And we will search, with looks and words
 of love,
For hidden thoughts, each lovelier than the
 last,
Our unexhausted spirits; and, like lutes
Touched by the skill of the enamoured wind,
Weave harmonies divine, yet ever new,
From difference sweet where discord can-
 not be;
And hither come, sped on the charmèd
 winds, 40
Which meet from all the points of heaven
 — as bees
From every flower aërial Enna feeds
At their known island-homes in Himera —
The echoes of the human world, which
 tell
Of the low voice of love, almost unheard,
And dove-eyed pity's murmured pain, and
 music,
Itself the echo of the heart, and all
That tempers or improves man's life, now
 free;
And lovely apparitions, — dim at first,
Then radiant, as the mind arising bright 50
From the embrace of beauty (whence the
 forms
Of which these are the phantoms) casts on
 them
The gathered rays which are reality —
Shall visit us, the progeny immortal
Of Painting, Sculpture, and rapt Poesy,
And arts, though unimagined, yet to be;
The wandering voices and the shadows
 these
Of all that man becomes, the mediators
Of that best worship, love, by him and us
Given and returned; swift shapes and
 sounds, which grow 60
More fair and soft as man grows wise and
 kind,
And, veil by veil, evil and error fall.
Such virtue has the cave and place around.

[*Turning to the* SPIRIT OF THE HOUR.

For thee, fair Spirit, one toil remains.
 Ione,
Give her that curvèd shell, which Proteus
 old
Made Asia's nuptial boon, breathing within
 it
A voice to be accomplished, and which thou
Didst hide in grass under the hollow rock.

IONE

Thou most desired Hour, more loved and
 lovely
Than all thy sisters, this is the mystic
 shell. 70
See the pale azure fading into silver
Lining it with a soft yet glowing light.
Looks it not like lulled music sleeping
 there ?

SPIRIT

It seems in truth the fairest shell of Ocean:
Its sound must be at once both sweet and
 strange.

PROMETHEUS

Go, borne over the cities of mankind
On whirlwind-footed coursers; once again
Outspeed the sun around the orbèd world;
And as thy chariot cleaves the kindling air,
Thou breathe into the many-folded shell,
Loosening its mighty music; it shall be 81
As thunder mingled with clear echoes; then
Return; and thou shalt dwell beside our
 cave.

And thou, O Mother Earth ! —

THE EARTH

 I hear, I feel;
Thy lips are on me, and thy touch runs
 down
Even to the adamantine central gloom
Along these marble nerves; 't is life, 't is
 joy,
And, through my withered, old, and icy
 frame
The warmth of an immortal youth shoots
 down
Circling. Henceforth the many children
 fair 90
Folded in my sustaining arms; all plants,
And creeping forms, and insects rainbow-
 winged,
And birds, and beasts, and fish, and human
 shapes,

Which drew disease and pain from my
 wan bosom,
Draining the poison of despair, shall take
And interchange sweet nutriment; to me
Shall they become like sister-antelopes
By one fair dam, snow-white, and swift as
 wind,
Nursed among lilies near a brimming
 stream.
The dew-mists of my sunless sleep shall
 float 100
Under the stars like balm; night-folded
 flowers
Shall suck unwithering hues in their repose;
And men and beasts in happy dreams shall
 gather
Strength for the coming day, and all its
 joy;
And death shall be the last embrace of her
Who takes the life she gave, even as a mo-
 ther,
Folding her child, says, 'Leave me not
 again.'

ASIA

Oh, mother ! wherefore speak the name of
 death ?
Cease they to love, and move, and breathe,
 and speak,
Who die ?

THE EARTH

 It would avail not to reply; 110
Thou art immortal and this tongue is known
But to the uncommunicating dead.
Death is the veil which those who live call
 life;
They sleep, and it is lifted; and meanwhile
In mild variety the seasons mild
With rainbow-skirted showers, and odorous
 winds,
And long blue meteors cleansing the dull
 night,
And the life-kindling shafts of the keen
 sun's
All-piercing bow, and the dew-mingled rain
Of the calm moonbeams, a soft influence
 mild, 120
Shall clothe the forests and the fields, ay,
 even
The crag-built deserts of the barren deep,
With ever-living leaves, and fruits, and
 flowers.
And thou ! there is a cavern where my
 spirit

Was panted forth in anguish whilst thy
 pain
Made my heart mad, and those who did
 inhale it
Became mad too, and built a temple there,
And spoke, and were oracular, and lured
The erring nations round to mutual war,
And faithless faith, such as Jove kept with
 thee; 130
Which breath now rises as amongst tall
 weeds
A violet's exhalation, and it fills
With a serener light and crimson air
Intense, yet soft, the rocks and woods
 around;
It feeds the quick growth of the serpent
 vine,
And the dark linkèd ivy tangling wild,
And budding, blown, or odor-faded blooms
Which star the winds with points of col-
 ored light
As they rain through them, and bright
 golden globes
Of fruit suspended in their own green hea-
 ven, 140
And through their veinèd leaves and amber
 stems
The flowers whose purple and translucid
 bowls
Stand ever mantling with aërial dew,
The drink of spirits; and it circles round,
Like the soft waving wings of noonday
 dreams,
Inspiring calm and happy thoughts, like
 mine,
Now thou art thus restored. This cave is
 thine.
Arise ! Appear !

 [*A* SPIRIT *rises in the likeness of a winged
 child.*

 This is my torch-bearer;
Who let his lamp out in old time with gazing
On eyes from which he kindled it anew 150
With love, which is as fire, sweet daughter
 mine,
For such is that within thine own. Run,
 wayward,
And guide this company beyond the peak
Of Bacchic Nysa, Mænad-haunted moun-
 tain,
And beyond Indus and its tribute rivers,
Trampling the torrent streams and glassy
 lakes
With feet unwet, unwearied, undelaying,
And up the green ravine, across the vale,

Beside the windless and crystalline pool,
Where ever lies, on unerasing waves, 160
The image of a temple, built above,
Distinct with column, arch, and architrave,
And palm-like capital, and overwrought,
And populous most with living imagery,
Praxitelean shapes, whose marble smiles
Fill the hushed air with everlasting love.
It is deserted now, but once it bore
Thy name, Prometheus; there the emulous
 youths
Bore to thy honor through the divine
 gloom
The lamp which was thine emblem; even
 as those 170
Who bear the untransmitted torch of hope
Into the grave, across the night of life,
As thou hast borne it most triumphantly
To this far goal of Time. Depart, fare-
 well !
Beside that temple is the destined cave.

SCENE IV. — *A Forest. In the background a
 Cave.* PROMETHEUS, ASIA, PANTHEA, IONE,
 and the SPIRIT OF THE EARTH.

IONE

Sister, it is not earthly; how it glides
Under the leaves ! how on its head there
 burns
A light, like a green star, whose emerald
 beams
Are twined with its fair hair ! how, as it
 moves,
The splendor drops in flakes upon the
 grass !
Knowest thou it ?

PANTHEA
 It is the delicate spirit
That guides the earth through heaven.
 From afar
The populous constellations call that light
The loveliest of the planets; and sometimes
It floats along the spray of the salt sea, 10
Or makes its chariot of a foggy cloud,
Or walks through fields or cities while men
 sleep,
Or o'er the mountain tops, or down the
 rivers,
Or through the green waste wilderness, as
 now,
Wondering at all it sees. Before Jove
 reigned
It loved our sister Asia, and it came

Each leisure hour to drink the liquid light
Out of her eyes, for which it said it thirsted
As one bit by a dipsas, and with her
It made its childish confidence, and told
 her 20
All it had known or seen, for it saw much,
Yet idly reasoned what it saw; and called
 her,
For whence it sprung it knew not, nor
 do I,
Mother, dear mother.

THE SPIRIT OF THE EARTH, *running to* ASIA
 Mother, dearest mother !
May I then talk with thee as I was wont ?
May I then hide my eyes in thy soft arms,
After thy looks have made them tired of
 joy ?
May I then play beside thee the long
 noons,
When work is none in the bright silent
 air ? 29

ASIA

I love thee, gentlest being, and henceforth
Can cherish thee unenvied. Speak, I
 pray;
Thy simple talk once solaced, now de-
 lights.

SPIRIT OF THE EARTH

Mother, I am grown wiser, though a child
Cannot be wise like thee, within this day;
And happier too; happier and wiser both.
Thou knowest that toads, and snakes, and
 loathly worms,
And venomous and malicious beasts, and
 boughs
That bore ill berries in the woods, were
 ever
An hindrance to my walks o'er the green
 world;
And that, among the haunts of human-
 kind, 40
Hard-featured men, or with proud, angry
 looks,
Or cold, staid gait, or false and hollow
 smiles,
Or the dull sneer of self-loved ignorance,
Or other such foul masks, with which ill
 thoughts
Hide that fair being whom we spirits call
 man;
And women too, ugliest of all things evil,
(Though fair, even in a world where thou
 art fair,

When good and kind, free and sincere like
 thee)
When false or frowning made me sick at
 heart
To pass them, though they slept, and I un-
 seen. 50
Well, my path lately lay through a great
 city
Into the woody hills surrounding it;
A sentinel was sleeping at the gate;
When there was heard a sound, so loud, it
 shook
The towers amid the moonlight, yet more
 sweet
Than any voice but thine, sweetest of all;
A long, long sound, as it would never end;
And all the inhabitants leapt suddenly
Out of their rest, and gathered in the
 streets,
Looking in wonder up to Heaven, while
 yet 60
The music pealed along. I hid myself
Within a fountain in the public square,
Where I lay like the reflex of the moon
Seen in a wave under green leaves; and
 soon
Those ugly human shapes and visages
Of which I spoke as having wrought me
 pain,
Passed floating through the air, and fading
 still
Into the winds that scattered them; and
 those
From whom they passed seemed mild and
 lovely forms
After some foul disguise had fallen, and
 all 70
Were somewhat changed, and after brief
 surprise
And greetings of delighted wonder, all
Went to their sleep again; and when the
 dawn
Came, wouldst thou think that toads, and
 snakes, and efts,
Could e'er be beautiful ? yet so they were,
And that with little change of shape or
 hue;
All things had put their evil nature off;
I cannot tell my joy, when o'er a lake,
Upon a drooping bough with nightshade
 twined,
I saw two azure halcyons clinging down-
 ward 80
And thinning one bright bunch of amber
 berries,

With quick long beaks, and in the deep
 there lay
Those lovely forms imaged as in a sky;
So with my thoughts full of these happy
 changes,
We meet again, the happiest change of all.

ASIA

And never will we part, till thy chaste
 sister,
Who guides the frozen and inconstant
 moon,
Will look on thy more warm and equal
 light
Till her heart thaw like flakes of April
 snow, 89
And love thee.

SPIRIT OF THE EARTH

 What ! as Asia loves Prometheus ?

ASIA

Peace, wanton ! thou art yet not old
 enough.
Think ye by gazing on each other's eyes
To multiply your lovely selves, and fill
With spherèd fires the interlunar air ?

SPIRIT OF THE EARTH

Nay, mother, while my sister trims her
 lamp
'T is hard I should go darkling.

ASIA

 Listen; look !

The SPIRIT OF THE HOUR *enters*

PROMETHEUS

We feel what thou hast heard and seen;
 yet speak.

SPIRIT OF THE HOUR

Soon as the sound had ceased whose thunder
 filled
The abysses of the sky and the wide earth,
There was a change; the impalpable thin
 air 100
And the all-circling sunlight were trans-
 formed,
As if the sense of love, dissolved in them,
Had folded itself round the spherèd world.
My vision then grew clear, and I could see
Into the mysteries of the universe.
Dizzy as with delight I floated down;

Winnowing the lightsome air with languid
 plumes,
My coursers sought their birthplace in the
 sun,
Where they henceforth will live exempt
 from toil,
Pasturing flowers of vegetable fire, 110
And where my moonlike car will stand
 within
A temple, gazed upon by Phidian forms
Of thee, and Asia, and the Earth, and me,
And you, fair nymphs, looking the love we
 feel, —
In memory of the tidings it has borne, —
Beneath a dome fretted with graven
 flowers,
Poised on twelve columns of resplendent
 stone,
And open to the bright and liquid sky.
Yoked to it by an amphisbenic snake
The likeness of those wingèd steeds will
 mock 120
The flight from which they find repose.
 Alas,
Whither has wandered now my partial
 tongue
When all remains untold which ye would
 hear ?
As I have said, I floated to the earth;
It was, as it is still, the pain of bliss
To move, to breathe, to be. I wandering
 went
Among the haunts and dwellings of man-
 kind,
And first was disappointed not to see
Such mighty change as I had felt within
Expressed in outward things; but soon I
 looked, 130
And behold, thrones were kingless, and men
 walked
One with the other even as spirits do —
None fawned, none trampled; hate, dis-
 dain, or fear,
Self-love or self-contempt, on human brows
No more inscribed, as o'er the gate of hell,
'All hope abandon, ye who enter here.'
None frowned, none trembled, none with
 eager fear
Gazed on another's eye of cold command,
Until the subject of a tyrant's will 139
Became, worse fate, the abject of his own,
Which spurred him, like an outspent horse,
 to death.
None wrought his lips in truth-entangling
 lines

Which smiled the lie his tongue disdained
 to speak.
None, with firm sneer, trod out in his own
 heart
The sparks of love and hope till there re-
 mained
Those bitter ashes, a soul self-consumed,
And the wretch crept a vampire among
 men,
Infecting all with his own hideous ill.
None talked that common, false, cold, hol-
 low talk
Which makes the heart deny the *yes* it
 breathes, 150
Yet question that unmeant hypocrisy
With such a self-mistrust as has no name.
And women, too, frank, beautiful, and kind,
As the free heaven which rains fresh light
 and dew
On the wide earth, passed; gentle, radiant
 forms,
From custom's evil taint exempt and pure;
Speaking the wisdom once they could not
 think,
Looking emotions once they feared to feel,
And changed to all which once they dared
 not be,
Yet being now, made earth like heaven;
 nor pride, 160
Nor jealousy, nor envy, nor ill shame,
The bitterest of those drops of treasured
 gall,
Spoiled the sweet taste of the nepenthe,
 love.

Thrones, altars, judgment-seats, and pris-
 ons, wherein,
And beside which, by wretched men were
 borne
Sceptres, tiaras, swords, and chains, and
 tomes
Of reasoned wrong, glozed on by ignorance,
Were like those monstrous and barbaric
 shapes,
The ghosts of a no-more-remembered fame
Which from their unworn obelisks, look
 forth 170
In triumph o'er the palaces and tombs
Of those who were their conquerors; mould-
 ering round,
Those imaged to the pride of kings and
 priests
A dark yet mighty faith, a power as wide
As is the world it wasted, and are now
But an astonishment; even so the tools

And emblems of its last captivity,
Amid the dwellings of the peopled earth,
Stand, not o'erthrown, but unregarded now.
And those foul shapes, — abhorred by god
 and man, 180
Which, under many a name and many a
 form
Strange, savage, ghastly, dark, and ex-
 ecrable,
Were Jupiter, the tyrant of the world,
And which the nations, panic-stricken,
 served
With blood, and hearts broken by long
 hope, and love
Dragged to his altars soiled and garland-
 less,
And slain among men's unreclaiming tears,
Flattering the thing they feared, which fear
 was hate, —
Frown, mouldering fast, o'er their aban-
 doned shrines.
The painted veil, by those who were, called
 life, 190
Which mimicked, as with colors idly spread,
All men believed and hoped, is torn aside;
The loathsome mask has fallen, the man
 remains
Sceptreless, free, uncircumscribed, but man
Equal, unclassed, tribeless, and nationless,
Exempt from awe, worship, degree, the
 king
Over himself; just, gentle, wise; but man
Passionless — no, yet free from guilt or pain,
Which were, for his will made or suffered
 them;
Nor yet exempt, though ruling them like
 slaves, 200
From chance, and death, and mutability,
The clogs of that which else might over-
 soar
The loftiest star of unascended heaven,
Pinnacled dim in the intense inane.

ACT IV

SCENE — *A part of the Forest near the Cave
of* PROMETHEUS. PANTHEA *and* IONE *are
sleeping: they awaken gradually during the
first Song.*

VOICE OF UNSEEN SPIRITS

THE pale stars are gone !
For the sun, their swift shepherd
To their folds them compelling,
In the depths of the dawn,

Hastes, in meteor-eclipsing array, and they
 flee
 Beyond his blue dwelling,
 As fawns flee the leopard,
 But where are ye ?

*A Train of dark Forms and Shadows passes by
 confusedly, singing.*

 Here, oh, here !
 We bear the bier 10
Of the father of many a cancelled year !
 Spectres we
 Of the dead Hours be;
We bear Time to his tomb in eternity.

 Strew, oh, strew
 Hair, not yew !
Wet the dusty pall with tears, not dew !
 Be the faded flowers
 Of Death's bare bowers
Spread on the corpse of the King of
 Hours ! 20

 Haste, oh, haste !
 As shades are chased,
Trembling, by day, from heaven's blue
 waste,
 We melt away,
 Like dissolving spray,
From the children of a diviner day,
 With the lullaby
 Of winds that die
On the bosom of their own harmony !

IONE

What dark forms were they ? 30

PANTHEA

The past Hours weak and gray,
With the spoil which their toil
 Raked together
From the conquest but One could foil.

IONE

Have they passed ?

PANTHEA

 They have passed;
They outspeeded the blast,
While 't is said, they are fled !

IONE

Whither, oh, whither ?

PANTHEA

To the dark, to the past, to the dead.

VOICE OF UNSEEN SPIRITS

Bright clouds float in heaven, 40
Dew-stars gleam on earth,
Waves assemble on ocean,
They are gathered and driven
By the storm of delight, by the panic of
 glee !
They shake with emotion,
They dance in their mirth.
 But where are ye ?

The pine boughs are singing
Old songs with new gladness,
The billows and fountains 50
Fresh music are flinging,
Like the notes of a spirit from land and
 from sea;
The storms mock the mountains
With the thunder of gladness,
 But where are ye ?

IONE

What charioteers are these ?

PANTHEA

 Where are their chariots ?

SEMICHORUS OF HOURS

The voice of the Spirits of Air and of
 Earth
 Has drawn back the figured curtain of
 sleep,
Which covered our being and darkened
 our birth 59
 In the deep.

A VOICE
 In the deep ?

SEMICHORUS II
 Oh ! below the deep.

SEMICHORUS I

An hundred ages we had been kept
 Cradled in visions of hate and care,
And each one who waked as his brother
 slept
Found the truth —

SEMICHORUS II
Worse than his visions were !

SEMICHORUS I
We have heard the lute of Hope in sleep;

We have known the voice of Love in
 dreams ;
We have felt the wand of Power, and
 leap —

SEMICHORUS II
As the billows leap in the morning beams !

CHORUS

Weave the dance on the floor of the breeze,
 Pierce with song heaven's silent light, 70
Enchant the day that too swiftly flees,
 To check its flight ere the cave of night.

Once the hungry Hours were hounds
 Which chased the day like a bleeding
 deer,
And it limped and stumbled with many
 wounds
 Through the nightly dells of the desert
 year.

But now, oh, weave the mystic measure
 Of music, and dance, and shapes of light,
Let the Hours, and the Spirits of might
 and pleasure, 79
 Like the clouds and sunbeams, unite —

A VOICE
 Unite !

PANTHEA
See, where the Spirits of the human mind,
Wrapped in sweet sounds, as in bright veils,
 approach.

CHORUS OF SPIRITS
 We join the throng
 Of the dance and the song,
By the whirlwind of gladness borne along;
 As the flying-fish leap
 From the Indian deep
And mix with the sea-birds half-asleep.

CHORUS OF HOURS
Whence come ye, so wild and so fleet, 89
For sandals of lightning are on your feet,
And your wings are soft and swift as
 thought,
And your eyes are as love which is veiled
 not ?

CHORUS OF SPIRITS
 We come from the mind
 Of humankind,

Which was late so dusk, and obscene, and
 blind ;
 Now 't is an ocean
 Of clear emotion,
A heaven of serene and mighty motion.

 From that deep abyss
 Of wonder and bliss, 100
Whose caverns are crystal palaces;
 From those skyey towers
 Where Thought's crowned powers
Sit watching your dance, ye happy Hours !

 From the dim recesses
 Of woven caresses,
Where lovers catch ye by your loose tresses;
 From the azure isles,
 Where sweet Wisdom smiles, 109
Delaying your ships with her siren wiles.

 From the temples high
 Of Man's ear and eye,
Roofed over Sculpture and Poesy;
 From the murmurings
 Of the unsealed springs,
Where Science bedews his dædal wings.

 Years after years,
 Through blood, and tears,
And a thick hell of hatreds, and hopes, and
 fears,
 We waded and flew, 120
 And the islets were few
Where the bud-blighted flowers of happi-
 ness grew.

 Our feet now, every palm,
 Are sandalled with calm,
And the dew of our wings is a rain of
 balm;
 And, beyond our eyes,
 The human love lies,
Which makes all it gazes on Paradise.

CHORUS OF SPIRITS AND HOURS

Then weave the web of the mystic mea-
 sure;
 From the depths of the sky and the ends
 of the earth, 130
Come, swift Spirits of might and of plea-
 sure,
 Fill the dance and the music of mirth,
As the waves of a thousand streams rush
 by
To an ocean of splendor and harmony !

CHORUS OF SPIRITS

 Our spoil is won,
 Our task is done,
We are free to dive, or soar, or run;
 Beyond and around,
 Or within the bound 139
Which clips the world with darkness round.

 We 'll pass the eyes
 Of the starry skies
Into the hoar deep to colonize;
 Death, Chaos and Night,
 From the sound of our flight,
Shall flee, like mist from a tempest's might.

 And Earth, Air and Light,
 And the Spirit of Might,
Which drives round the stars in their fiery
 flight;
 And Love, Thought and Breath, 150
 The powers that quell Death,
Wherever we soar shall assemble beneath.

 And our singing shall build
 In the void's loose field
A world for the Spirit of Wisdom to wield;
 We will take our plan
 From the new world of man,
And our work shall be called the Prome-
 thean.

CHORUS OF HOURS

 Break the dance, and scatter the song;
 Let some depart, and some remain;160

SEMICHORUS I

We, beyond heaven, are driven along;

SEMICHORUS II

Us the enchantments of earth retain;

SEMICHORUS I

Ceaseless, and rapid, and fierce, and free,
With the Spirits which build a new earth
 and sea,
And a heaven where yet heaven could never
 be;

SEMICHORUS II

Solemn, and slow, and serene, and bright,
Leading the Day, and outspeeding the
 Night,
With the powers of a world of perfect
 light;

SEMICHORUS I

We whirl, singing loud, round the gather-
ing sphere,
Till the trees, and the beasts, and the clouds
appear 170
From its chaos made calm by love, not
fear;

SEMICHORUS II

We encircle the ocean and mountains of
earth,
And the happy forms of its death and birth
Change to the music of our sweet mirth.

CHORUS OF HOURS AND SPIRITS

Break the dance, and scatter the song;
Let some depart, and some remain;
Wherever we fly we lead along
In leashes, like star-beams, soft yet strong,
The clouds that are heavy with love's
sweet rain. 179

PANTHEA

Ha! they are gone!

IONE

Yet feel you no delight
From the past sweetness?

PANTHEA

As the bare green hill,
When some soft cloud vanishes into rain,
Laughs with a thousand drops of sunny
water
To the unpavilioned sky!

IONE

Even whilst we speak
New notes arise. What is that awful
sound?

PANTHEA

'T is the deep music of the rolling world,
Kindling within the strings of the waved
air
Æolian modulations.

IONE

Listen too,
How every pause is filled with under-notes,
Clear, silver, icy, keen awakening tones,
Which pierce the sense, and live within the
soul, 191
As the sharp stars pierce winter's crystal
air
And gaze upon themselves within the sea.

PANTHEA

But see where, through two openings in
the forest
Which hanging branches overcanopy,
And where two runnels of a rivulet,
Between the close moss violet-inwoven,
Have made their path of melody, like sis-
ters
Who part with sighs that they may meet
in smiles,
Turning their dear disunion to an isle 200
Of lovely grief, a wood of sweet sad
thoughts;
Two visions of strange radiance float upon
The ocean-like enchantment of strong
sound,
Which flows intenser, keener, deeper yet,
Under the ground and through the wind-
less air.

IONE

I see a chariot like that thinnest boat
In which the mother of the months is borne
By ebbing night into her western cave,
When she upsprings from interlunar
dreams; 209
O'er which is curved an orb-like canopy
Of gentle darkness, and the hills and woods,
Distinctly seen through that dusk airy veil,
Regard like shapes in an enchanter's glass;
Its wheels are solid clouds, azure and gold,
Such as the genii of the thunder-storm
Pile on the floor of the illumined sea
When the sun rushes under it; they roll
And move and grow as with an inward
wind;
Within it sits a wingèd infant — white
Its countenance, like the whiteness of bright
snow, 220
Its plumes are as feathers of sunny frost,
Its limbs gleam white, through the wind-
flowing folds
Of its white robe, woof of ethereal pearl,
Its hair is white, the brightness of white
light
Scattered in strings; yet its two eyes are
heavens
Of liquid darkness, which the Deity
Within seems pouring, as a storm is poured
From jagged clouds, out of their arrowy
lashes,
Tempering the cold and radiant air around
With fire that is not brightness; in its hand
It sways a quivering moonbeam, from whose
point 231

A guiding power directs the chariot's prow
Over its wheelèd clouds, which as they roll
Over the grass, and flowers, and waves,
 wake sounds,
Sweet as a singing rain of silver dew.

PANTHEA

And from the other opening in the wood
Rushes, with loud and whirlwind harmony,
A sphere, which is as many thousand
 spheres;
Solid as crystal, yet through all its mass
Flow, as through empty space, music and
 light; 240
Ten thousand orbs involving and involved,
Purple and azure, white, green and golden,
Sphere within sphere; and every space
 between
Peopled with unimaginable shapes,
Such as ghosts dream dwell in the lampless
 deep;
Yet each inter-transpicuous; and they whirl
Over each other with a thousand motions,
Upon a thousand sightless axles spinning,
And with the force of self-destroying swift-
 ness,
Intensely, slowly, solemnly, roll on, 250
Kindling with mingled sounds, and many
 tones,
Intelligible words and music wild.
With mighty whirl the multitudinous orb
Grinds the bright brook into an azure mist
Of elemental subtlety, like light;
And the wild odor of the forest flowers,
The music of the living grass and air,
The emerald light of leaf-entangled beams,
Round its intense yet self-conflicting speed
Seem kneaded into one aërial mass 260
Which drowns the sense. Within the orb
 itself,
Pillowed upon its alabaster arms,
Like to a child o'erwearied with sweet toil,
On its own folded wings and wavy hair
The Spirit of the Earth is laid asleep,
And you can see its little lips are moving,
Amid the changing light of their own smiles,
Like one who talks of what he loves in
 dream.

IONE

'T is only mocking the orb's harmony.

PANTHEA

And from a star upon its forehead shoot, 270
Like swords of azure fire or golden spears

With tyrant-quelling myrtle overtwined,
Embleming heaven and earth united now,
Vast beams like spokes of some invisible
 wheel
Which whirl as the orb whirls, swifter than
 thought,
Filling the abyss with sun-like lightnings,
And perpendicular now, and now transverse,
Pierce the dark soil, and as they pierce and
 pass
Make bare the secrets of the earth's deep
 heart;
Infinite mine of adamant and gold, 280
Valueless stones, and unimagined gems,
And caverns on crystalline columns poised
With vegetable silver overspread;
Wells of unfathomed fire, and water-springs
Whence the great sea even as a child is fed,
Whose vapors clothe earth's monarch
 mountain-tops
With kingly, ermine snow. The beams
 flash on
And make appear the melancholy ruins
Of cancelled cycles; anchors, beaks of
 ships;
Planks turned to marble; quivers, helms,
 and spears, 290
And gorgon-headed targes, and the wheels
Of scythèd chariots, and the emblazonry
Of trophies, standards, and armorial beasts,
Round which death laughed, sepulchred
 emblems
Of dead destruction, ruin within ruin !
The wrecks beside of many a city vast,
Whose population which the earth grew
 over
Was mortal, but not human; see, they lie,
Their monstrous works, and uncouth skele-
 tons,
Their statues, homes and fanes; prodigious
 shapes 300
Huddled in gray annihilation, split,
Jammed in the hard, black deep; and over
 these,
The anatomies of unknown wingèd things,
And fishes which were isles of living scale,
And serpents, bony chains, twisted around
The iron crags, or within heaps of dust
To which the tortuous strength of their last
 pangs
Had crushed the iron crags; and over these
The jagged alligator, and the might 309
Of earth-convulsing behemoth, which once
Were monarch beasts, and on the slimy
 shores,

And weed-overgrown continents of earth,
Increased and multiplied like summer
 worms
On an abandoned corpse, till the blue globe
Wrapped deluge round it like a cloke, and
 they
Yelled, gasped, and were abolished; or
 some God,
Whose throne was in a comet, passed, and
 cried,
Be not! and like my words they were no
 more.

THE EARTH

The joy, the triumph, the delight, the mad-
 ness!
The boundless, overflowing, bursting glad-
 ness, 320
The vaporous exultation not to be confined!
Ha! ha! the animation of delight
Which wraps me, like an atmosphere of
 light,
And bears me as a cloud is borne by its
 own wind.

THE MOON

Brother mine, calm wanderer,
Happy globe of land and air,
Some Spirit is darted like a beam from
 thee,
Which penetrates my frozen frame,
And passes with the warmth of flame,
With love, and odor, and deep melody 330
 Through me, through me!

THE EARTH

Ha! ha! the caverns of my hollow moun-
 tains,
My cloven fire-crags, sound-exulting
 fountains,
Laugh with a vast and inextinguishable
 laughter.
The oceans, and the deserts, and the
 abysses,
And the deep air's unmeasured wilder-
 nesses,
Answer from all their clouds and billows,
 echoing after.

They cry aloud as I do. Sceptred curse,
Who all our green and azure universe
Threatenedst to muffle round with black
 destruction, sending 340
A solid cloud to rain hot thunder-stones
And splinter and knead down my chil-
 dren's bones,

All I bring forth, to one void mass batter-
 ing and blending,

Until each crag-like tower, and storied
 column,
Palace, and obelisk, and temple solemn,
My imperial mountains crowned with cloud,
 and snow, and fire,
My sea-like forests, every blade and
 blossom
Which finds a grave or cradle in my
 bosom,
Were stamped by thy strong hate into a
 lifeless mire:

How art thou sunk, withdrawn, covered,
 drunk up 350
By thirsty nothing, as the brackish cup
Drained by a desert-troop, a little drop for
 all;
And from beneath, around, within, above,
Filling thy void annihilation, love
Bursts in like light on caves cloven by the
 thunder-ball!

THE MOON

The snow upon my lifeless mountains
Is loosened into living fountains,
My solid oceans flow, and sing and shine;
A spirit from my heart bursts forth,
It clothes with unexpected birth 360
My cold bare bosom. Oh, it must be thine
 On mine, on mine!

Gazing on thee I feel, I know,
Green stalks burst forth, and bright
 flowers grow,
And living shapes upon my bosom move;
Music is in the sea and air,
Wingèd clouds soar here and there
Dark with the rain new buds are dream-
 ing of:
 'T is love, all love!

THE EARTH

It interpenetrates my granite mass, 370
Through tangled roots and trodden clay
 doth pass
Into the utmost leaves and delicatest flow-
 ers;
Upon the winds, among the clouds 't is
 spread,
It wakes a life in the forgotten dead, —
They breathe a spirit up from their obscur-
 est bowers;

And like a storm bursting its cloudy
prison
With thunder, and with whirlwind, has
arisen
Out of the lampless caves of unimagined
being;
With earthquake shock and swiftness
making shiver
Thought's stagnant chaos, unremoved
forever, 380
Till hate, and fear, and pain, light-van-
quished shadows, fleeing,

Leave Man, who was a many-sided mir-
ror
Which could distort to many a shape of
error
This true fair world of things, a sea re-
flecting love;
Which over all his kind, as the sun's hea-
ven
Gliding o'er ocean, smooth, serene, and
even,
Darting from starry depths radiance and
life doth move:

Leave Man even as a leprous child is
left,
Who follows a sick beast to some warm
cleft
Of rocks, through which the might of heal-
ing springs is poured; 390
Then when it wanders home with rosy
smile,
Unconscious, and its mother fears awhile
It is a spirit, then weeps on her child re-
stored:

Man, oh, not men ! a chain of linkèd
thought,
Of love and might to be divided not,
Compelling the elements with adamantine
stress;
As the sun rules even with a tyrant's
gaze
The unquiet republic of the maze
Of planets, struggling fierce towards hea-
ven's free wilderness:

Man, one harmonious soul of many a
soul, 400
Whose nature is its own divine control,
Where all things flow to all, as rivers to the
sea;
Familiar acts are beautiful through love;

Labor, and pain, and grief, in life's green
grove
Sport like tame beasts; none knew how
gentle they could be !

His will, with all mean passions, bad
delights,
And selfish cares, its trembling satellites,
A spirit ill to guide, but mighty to obey,
Is as a tempest-wingèd ship, whose helm
Love rules, through waves which dare
not overwhelm, 410
Forcing life's wildest shores to own its sov-
ereign sway.

All things confess his strength. Through
the cold mass
Of marble and of color his dreams
pass —
Bright threads whence mothers weave the
robes their children wear;
Language is a perpetual Orphic song,
Which rules with dædal harmony a
throng
Of thoughts and forms, which else senseless
and shapeless were.

The lightning is his slave; heaven's ut-
most deep
Gives up her stars, and like a flock of
sheep
They pass before his eye, are numbered,
and roll on ! 420
The tempest is his steed, he strides the
air;
And the abyss shouts from her depth
laid bare,
' Heaven, hast thou secrets ? Man unveils
me; I have none.'

THE MOON

The shadow of white death has passed
From my path in heaven at last,
A clinging shroud of solid frost and sleep;
And through my newly woven bowers,
Wander happy paramours,
Less mighty, but as mild as those who
keep
Thy vales more deep. 430

THE EARTH

As the dissolving warmth of dawn may
fold
A half unfrozen dew-globe, green, and
gold,

And crystalline, till it becomes a wingèd
 mist,
 And wanders up the vault of the blue
 day,
 Outlives the noon, and on the sun's last
 ray
Hangs o'er the sea, a fleece of fire and
 amethyst.

THE MOON

 Thou art folded, thou art lying
 In the light which is undying
 Of thine own joy, and heaven's smile
 divine;
 All suns and constellations shower 440
 On thee a light, a life, a power,
 Which doth array thy sphere; thou pour-
 est thine
 On mine, on mine !

THE EARTH

 I spin beneath my pyramid of night
 Which points into the heavens, dreaming
 delight,
Murmuring victorious joy in my enchanted
 sleep;
 As a youth lulled in love-dreams faintly
 sighing,
 Under the shadow of his beauty lying,
Which round his rest a watch of light and
 warmth doth keep.

THE MOON

 As in the soft and sweet eclipse, 450
 When soul meets soul on lovers' lips,
 High hearts are calm, and brightest eyes
 are dull;
 So when thy shadow falls on me,
 Then am I mute and still, by thee
Covered; of thy love, Orb most beautiful,
 Full, oh, too full !

 Thou art speeding round the sun,
 Brightest world of many a one;
 Green and azure sphere which shinest
 With a light which is divinest 460
 Among all the lamps of Heaven
 To whom life and light is given;
 I, thy crystal paramour,
 Borne beside thee by a power
 Like the polar Paradise,
 Magnet-like, of lovers' eyes;
 I, a most enamoured maiden,
 Whose weak brain is overladen

 With the pleasure of her love,
 Maniac-like around thee move, 470
 Gazing, an insatiate bride,
 On thy form from every side,
 Like a Mænad round the cup
 Which Agave lifted up
 In the weird Cadmean forest.
 Brother, wheresoe'er thou soarest
 I must hurry, whirl and follow
 Through the heavens wide and hollow,
 Sheltered by the warm embrace
 Of thy soul from hungry space, 480
 Drinking from thy sense and sight
 Beauty, majesty and might,
 As a lover or a chameleon
 Grows like what it looks upon,
 As a violet's gentle eye
 Gazes on the azure sky
Until its hue grows like what it beholds,
 As a gray and watery mist
 Glows like solid amethyst
Athwart the western mountain it en-
 folds, 490
 When the sunset sleeps
 Upon its snow.

THE EARTH

 And the weak day weeps
 That it should be so.
O gentle Moon, the voice of thy delight
Falls on me like thy clear and tender light
Soothing the seaman borne the summer
 night
 Through isles forever calm;
O gentle Moon, thy crystal accents pierce
The caverns of my pride's deep universe, 500
Charming the tiger joy, whose tramplings
 fierce
 Made wounds which need thy balm.

PANTHEA

I rise as from a bath of sparkling water,
A bath of azure light, among dark rocks,
Out of the stream of sound.

IONE

 Ah me ! sweet sister,
The stream of sound has ebbed away from
 us,
And you pretend to rise out of its wave,
Because your words fall like the clear soft
 dew
Shaken from a bathing wood-nymph's limbs
 and hair.

PANTHEA

Peace, peace ! a mighty Power, which is as
 darkness, 510
Is rising out of Earth, and from the sky
Is showered like night, and from within
 the air
Bursts, like eclipse which had been gathered
 up
Into the pores of sunlight; the bright
 visions,
Wherein the singing Spirits rode and shone,
Gleam like pale meteors through a watery
 night.

IONE

There is a sense of words upon mine ear.

PANTHEA

An universal sound like words: Oh, list !

DEMOGORGON

Thou, Earth, calm empire of a happy soul,
 Sphere of divinest shapes and harmo-
 nies, 520
Beautiful orb ! gathering as thou dost roll
 The love which paves thy path along the
 skies:

THE EARTH

I hear: I am as a drop of dew that dies.

DEMOGORGON

Thou, Moon, which gazest on the nightly
 Earth
 With wonder, as it gazes upon thee;
Whilst each to men, and beasts, and the
 swift birth
Of birds, is beauty, love, calm, harmony:

THE MOON

I hear: I am a leaf shaken by thee.

DEMOGORGON

Ye kings of suns and stars, Dæmons and
 Gods,
 Ethereal Dominations, who possess 530
Elysian, windless, fortunate abodes
 Beyond Heaven's constellated wilder-
 ness:

A VOICE (*from above*)

Our great Republic hears: we are blessed,
 and bless.

DEMOGORGON

Ye happy dead, whom beams of brightest
 verse

Are clouds to hide, not colors to portray,
Whether your nature is that universe
 Which once ye saw and suffered —

A VOICE FROM BENEATH

 Or, as they
Whom we have left, we change and pass
 away.

DEMOGORGON

Ye elemental Genii, who have homes
 From man's high mind even to the cen-
 tral stone 540
Of sullen lead; from Heaven's star-fretted
 domes
 To the dull weed some sea-worm battens
 on:

A CONFUSED VOICE

We hear: thy words waken Oblivion.

DEMOGORGON

Spirits, whose homes are flesh; ye beasts
 and birds,
 Ye worms and fish; ye living leaves and
 buds;
Lightning and wind; and ye untamable
 herds,
 Meteors and mists, which throng air's
 solitudes:

A VOICE

Thy voice to us is wind among still woods.

DEMOGORGON

Man, who wert once a despot and a slave,
 A dupe and a deceiver, a decay, 550
A traveller from the cradle to the grave
 Through the dim night of this immortal
 day:

ALL

Speak: thy strong words may never pass
 away.

DEMOGORGON

This is the day which down the void abysm
At the Earth-born's spell yawns for Hea-
 ven's despotism,
 And Conquest is dragged captive through
 the deep;
Love, from its awful throne of patient
 power
In the wise heart, from the last giddy hour
 Of dread endurance, from the slippery,
 steep,

And narrow verge of crag-like agony,
 springs 560
And folds over the world its healing wings.

Gentleness, Virtue, Wisdom, and Endur-
 ance —
These are the seals of that most firm assur-
 ance
 Which bars the pit over Destruction's
 strength;
And if, with infirm hand, Eternity,
Mother of many acts and hours, should
 free
 The serpent that would clasp her with
 his length,

These are the spells by which to reassume
An empire o'er the disentangled doom. 569

To suffer woes which Hope thinks infinite;
To forgive wrongs darker than death or
 night;
 To defy Power, which seems omnipotent;
To love, and bear; to hope till Hope creates
From its own wreck the thing it contem-
 plates;
 Neither to change, nor falter, nor repent;
This, like thy glory, Titan, is to be
Good, great and joyous, beautiful and free;
This is alone Life, Joy, Empire, and Vic-
 tory !

THE MASK OF ANARCHY

WRITTEN ON THE OCCASION OF THE MASSACRE AT MANCHESTER

The Mask of Anarchy was composed in the fall of 1819, soon after the Manchester riot of that summer. The Manchester or ' Peterloo Massacre,' as it was called, was occasioned by an attempt to hold a mass meeting on August 9, 1819, at St. Peter's Field, Manchester, in behalf of parliamentary reform. It was declared illegal and forbidden by the magistrates, and was in consequence postponed. It was held August 16, and attended by several thousands. The chief constable was ordered to arrest the ringleaders, and in particular the chairman, Henry Hunt. an agitator unconnected with Leigh Hunt. He asked military aid, and went accompanied by forty cavalrymen; on the failure of the officer and his escort to penetrate the crowd which surrounded them, orders were given three hundred hussars to disperse the people; in the charge six persons were killed, twenty or thirty received sabre wounds, and fifty or more were injured in other ways. Eldon was Lord High Chancellor, Sidmouth, Home Secretary, and Castlereagh, Foreign Secretary; the government supported the authorities and publicly approved their conduct. News of these events reached Shelley while still residing at the Villa Valsovano, near Leghorn, and employed in

revising *The Cenci*, and ' roused in him,' says Mrs. Shelley, ' violent emotions of indignation and compassion.' The nature of these emotions is shown in the letter he wrote to Ollier, from whom he heard of the affair: ' The same day that your letter came, came the news of the Manchester work, and the torrent of my indignation has not yet done boiling in my veins. I wait anxiously to hear how the country will express its sense of this bloody, murderous oppression of its destroyers. "Something must be done. What, yet I know not."' In a similar vein he addressed Peacock, who had forwarded newspaper accounts: ' Many thanks for your attention in sending the papers which contain the terrible and important news of Manchester. These are, as it were, the distant thunders of the terrible storm which is approaching. The tyrants here, as in the French Revolution, have first shed blood. May their execrable lessons not be learned with equal docility! I still think there will be no coming to close quarters until financial affairs bring the oppressors and the oppressed together. Pray let me have the *earliest* political news which you consider of importance at this crisis.'

Shelley sent the poem to Leigh Hunt to be published in *The Examiner*, but it did not appear. He wrote to Hunt on the subject in November.

' You do not tell me whether you have received my lines on the Manchester affair. They are of the exoteric species, and are meant, not for the *Indicator*, but the *Examiner*. . . . The great thing to do is to hold the balance between popular impatience and tyrannical obstinacy; to inculcate with fervor both the right of resistance and the duty of forbearance. You know my principles incite me to take all the good I can get in politics, forever aspiring to something more. I am one of those whom nothing will fully satisfy, but who are ready to be partially satisfied by all that is practicable. We shall see.'

The poem was at last issued, under Hunt's editorship, in 1832. He assigns, in his preface, as the reason for his failure to publish it when it was written, his own belief that ' the public at large had not become sufficiently discerning to do justice to the sincerity and kindheartedness of his spirit, that walked in the flaming robe of verse.'

I

As I lay asleep in Italy,
There came a voice from over the sea,
And with great power it forth led me
To walk in the visions of Poesy.

II

I met Murder on the way —
He had a mask like Castlereagh;
Very smooth he looked, yet grim;
Seven bloodhounds followed him.

III

All were fat; and well they might
Be in admirable plight,
For one by one, and two by two,
He tossed them human hearts to chew,
Which from his wide cloak he drew.

IV

Next came Fraud, and he had on,
Like Eldon, an ermined gown;
His big tears, for he wept well,
Turned to mill-stones as they fell;

V

And the little children, who
Round his feet played to and fro,
Thinking every tear a gem,
Had their brains knocked out by them.

VI

Clothed with the Bible as with light,
And the shadows of the night,
Like Sidmouth, next Hypocrisy
On a crocodile rode by.

VII

And many more Destructions played
In this ghastly masquerade,
All disguised, even to the eyes,
Like bishops, lawyers, peers or spies.

VIII

Last came Anarchy; he rode
On a white horse splashed with blood;
He was pale even to the lips,
Like Death in the Apocalypse.

IX

And he wore a kingly crown;
In his grasp a sceptre shone;
On his brow this mark I saw —
' I AM GOD, AND KING, AND LAW !'

X

With a pace stately and fast,
Over English land he passed,
Trampling to a mire of blood
The adoring multitude.

XI

And a mighty troop around
With their trampling shook the ground,
Waving each a bloody sword
For the service of their Lord.

XII

And, with glorious triumph, they
Rode through England, proud and gay,
Drunk as with intoxication
Of the wine of desolation.

XIII

O'er fields and towns, from sea to sea,
Passed that Pageant swift and free,
Tearing up, and trampling down,
Till they came to London town.

XIV

And each dweller, panic-stricken,
Felt his heart with terror sicken,
Hearing the tempestuous cry
Of the triumph of Anarchy.

XV

For with pomp to meet him came,
Clothed in arms like blood and flame,
The hired murderers who did sing,
'Thou art God, and Law, and King.

XVI

'We have waited, weak and lone,
For thy coming, Mighty One !
Our purses are empty, our swords are
 cold,
Give us glory, and blood, and gold.'

XVII

Lawyers and priests, a motley crowd,
To the earth their pale brows bowed;
Like a bad prayer not over loud,
Whispering — ' Thou art Law and God !'

XVIII

Then all cried with one accord,
' Thou art King, and God, and Lord;
Anarchy, to thee we bow,
Be thy name made holy now !'

XIX

And Anarchy, the Skeleton,
Bowed and grinned to every one,
As well as if his education
Had cost ten millions to the nation.

XX

For he knew the palaces
Of our kings were rightly his;
His the sceptre, crown, and globe,
And the gold-inwoven robe.

XXI

So he sent his slaves before
To seize upon the Bank and Tower,
And was proceeding with intent
To meet his pensioned parliament,

XXII

When one fled past, a maniac maid,
And her name was Hope, she said;
But she looked more like Despair,
And she cried out in the air:

XXIII

' My father Time is weak and gray
With waiting for a better day;
See how idiot-like he stands,
Fumbling with his palsied hands !

XXIV

' He has had child after child,
And the dust of death is piled
Over every one but me.
Misery ! oh, misery !'

XXV

Then she lay down in the street,
Right before the horses' feet,
Expecting with a patient eye
Murder, Fraud, and Anarchy;

XXVI

When between her and her foes
A mist, a light, an image rose, —
Small at first, and weak, and frail,
Like the vapor of a vale;

XXVII

Till as clouds grow on the blast,
Like tower-crowned giants striding fast,
And glare with lightnings as they fly,
And speak in thunder to the sky,

XXVIII

It grew — a Shape arrayed in mail
Brighter than the viper's scale,
And upborne on wings whose grain
Was as the light of sunny rain.

XXIX

On its helm, seen far away,
A planet, like the Morning's, lay;
And those plumes its light rained through,
Like a shower of crimson dew.

XXX

With step as soft as wind it passed
O'er the heads of men — so fast
That they knew the presence there,
And looked — but all was empty air.

XXXI

As flowers beneath May's footstep waken,
As stars from Night's loose hair are
 shaken,
As waves arise when loud winds call,
Thoughts sprung where'er that step did fall.

XXXII

And the prostrate multitude
Looked — and ankle-deep in blood,
Hope, that maiden most serene,
Was walking with a quiet mien;

XXXIII

And Anarchy, the ghastly birth,
Lay dead earth upon the earth;
The Horse of Death, tameless as wind
Fled, and with his hoofs did grind
To dust the murderers thronged behind.

XXXIV

A rushing light of clouds and splendor,
A sense, awakening and yet tender,
Was heard and felt — and at its close
These words of joy and fear arose,

XXXV

As if their own indignant earth,
Which gave the sons of England birth,
Had felt their blood upon her brow,
And shuddering with a mother's throe

XXXVI

Had turned every drop of blood,
By which her face had been bedewed,
To an accent unwithstood,
As if her heart cried out aloud:

XXXVII

' Men of England, heirs of glory,
Heroes of unwritten story,
Nurslings of one mighty Mother,
Hopes of her, and one another:

XXXVIII

' Rise like lions after slumber,
In unvanquishable number;
Shake your chains to earth like dew
Which in sleep had fallen on you —
Ye are many, they are few.

XXXIX

' What is Freedom ? — Ye can tell
That which Slavery is too well,
For its very name has grown
To an echo of your own.

XL

' 'T is to work, and have such pay
As just keeps life from day to day
In your limbs, as in a cell,
For the tyrants' use to dwell,

XLI

' So that ye for them are made
Loom, and plough, and sword, and spade ◄━
With or without your own will bent
To their defence and nourishment.

XLII

' 'T is to see your children weak
With their mothers pine and peak,
When the winter winds are bleak —
They are dying whilst I speak.

XLIII

' 'T is to hunger for such diet,
As the rich man in his riot
Casts to the fat dogs that lie
Surfeiting beneath his eye.

XLIV

' 'T is to let the Ghost of Gold
Take from toil a thousand-fold
More than e'er its substance could
In the tyrannies of old ;

XLV

' Paper coin — that forgery
Of the title deeds which ye
Hold to something of the worth
Of the inheritance of Earth.

XLVI

' 'T is to be a slave in soul,
And to hold no strong control
Over your own will, but be
All that others make of ye.

XLVII

'And at length when ye complain
With a murmur weak and vain,
'T is to see the Tyrant's crew
Ride over your wives and you —
Blood is on the grass like dew !

XLVIII

'Then it is to feel revenge,
Fiercely thirsting to exchange
Blood for blood — and wrong for wrong :
Do not thus when ye are strong !

XLIX

'Birds find rest in narrow nest,
When weary of their wingèd quest,
Beasts find fare in woody lair,
When storm and snow are in the air.

L

'Horses, oxen, have a home,
When from daily toil they come ;
Household dogs, when the wind roars,
Find a home within warm doors.

LI

'Asses, swine, have litter spread,
And with fitting food are fed ;
All things have a home but one —
Thou, O Englishman, hast none !

LII

'This is Slavery; savage men,
Or wild beasts within a den,
Would endure not as ye do —
But such ills they never knew.

LIII

'What art thou, Freedom ? Oh, could
 slaves
Answer from their living graves
This demand, tyrants would flee
Like a dream's dim imagery.

LIV

'Thou art not, as impostors say,
A shadow soon to pass away
A superstition and a name
Echoing from the cave of Fame.

LV

'For the laborer thou art bread
And a comely table spread,
From his daily labor come
In a neat and happy home.

LVI

'Thou art clothes, and fire, and food,
For the trampled multitude;
No — in countries that are free
Such starvation cannot be
As in England now we see.

LVII

'To the rich thou art a check;
When his foot is on the neck
Of his victim, thou dost make
That he treads upon a snake.

LVIII

'Thou art Justice — ne'er for gold
May thy righteous laws be sold,
As laws are in England; thou
Shield'st alike both high and low.

LIX

'Thou art Wisdom — freemen never
Dream that God will damn forever
All who think those things untrue
Of which priests make such ado.

LX

'Thou art Peace — never by thee
Would blood and treasure wasted be,
As tyrants wasted them, when all
Leagued to quench thy flame in Gaul.

LXI

'What if English toil and blood
Was poured forth, even as a flood ?
It availed, O Liberty !
To dim, but not extinguish thee.

LXII

'Thou art Love — the rich have kissed
Thy feet, and, like him following Christ,
Give their substance to the free
And through the rough world follow thee;

LXIII

'Or turn their wealth to arms, and make
War for thy belovèd sake
On wealth and war and fraud, whence
 they
Drew the power which is their prey.

LXIV

'Science, Poetry and Thought
Are thy lamps; they make the lot
Of the dwellers in a cot
Such they curse their maker not.

LXV

'Spirit, Patience, Gentleness,
All that can adorn and bless,
Art thou — let deeds, not words, express
Thine exceeding loveliness.

LXVI

'Let a great Assembly be
Of the fearless and the free
On some spot of English ground,
Where the plains stretch wide around.

LXVII

'Let the blue sky overhead,
The green earth on which ye tread,
All that must eternal be,
Witness the solemnity.

LXVIII

'From the corners uttermost
Of the bounds of English coast;
From every hut, village and town,
Where those, who live and suffer, moan
For others' misery or their own;

LXIX

'From the workhouse and the prison,
Where pale as corpses newly risen,
Women, children, young and old,
Groan for pain, and weep for cold;

LXX

'From the haunts of daily life,
Where is waged the daily strife
With common wants and common cares,
Which sows the human heart with tares;

LXXI

'Lastly, from the palaces
Where the murmur of distress
Echoes, like the distant sound
Of a wind alive, around

LXXII

'Those prison-halls of wealth and fashion,
Where some few feel such compassion
For those who groan, and toil, and wail,
As must make their brethren pale; —

LXXIII

'Ye who suffer woes untold,
Or to feel or to behold
Your lost country bought and sold
With a price of blood and gold:

LXXIV

'Let a vast assembly be,
And with great solemnity
Declare with measured words that ye
Are, as God has made ye, free !

LXXV

'Be your strong and simple words
Keen to wound as sharpened swords;
And wide as targes let them be,
With their shade to cover ye.

LXXVI

'Let the tyrants pour around
With a quick and startling sound,
Like the loosening of a sea,
Troops of armed emblazonry.

LXXVII

'Let the charged artillery drive
Till the dead air seems alive
With the clash of clanging wheels
And the tramp of horses' heels.

LXXVIII

'Let the fixèd bayonet
Gleam with sharp desire to wet
Its bright point in English blood,
Looking keen as one for food.

LXXIX

'Let the horsemen's scimitars
Wheel and flash, like sphereless stars
Thirsting to eclipse their burning
In a sea of death and mourning.

LXXX

'Stand ye calm and resolute,
Like a forest close and mute,
With folded arms, and looks which are
Weapons of unvanquished war.

LXXXI

'And let Panic, who outspeeds
The career of armèd steeds,
Pass, a disregarded shade,
Through your phalanx undismayed.

LXXXII

'Let the laws of your own land,
Good or ill, between ye stand,
Hand to hand, and foot to foot,
Arbiters of the dispute: —

LXXXIII

'The old laws of England — they
Whose reverend heads with age are gray,
Children of a wiser day;
And whose solemn voice must be
Thine own echo — Liberty !

LXXXIV

'On those who first should violate
Such sacred heralds in their state
Rest the blood that must ensue;
And it will not rest on you.

LXXXV

'And if then the tyrants dare,
Let them ride among you there,
Slash, and stab, and maim, and hew;
What they like, that let them do.

LXXXVI

'With folded arms and steady eyes,
And little fear, and less surprise,
Look upon them as they slay,
Till their rage has died away.

LXXXVII

'Then they will return with shame
To the place from which they came;
And the blood thus shed will speak
In hot blushes on their cheek.

LXXXVIII

'Every woman in the land
Will point at them as they stand;
They will hardly dare to greet
Their acquaintance in the street.

LXXXIX

'And the bold true warriors,
Who have hugged Danger in wars,
Will turn to those who would be free,
Ashamed of such base company.

XC

'And that slaughter to the Nation
Shall steam up like inspiration,
Eloquent, oracular;
A volcano heard afar.

XCI

'And these words shall then become
Like oppression's thundered doom,
Ringing through each heart and brain,
Heard again — again — again !

XCII

'Rise like lions after slumber
In unvanquishable number !
Shake your chains to earth, like dew
Which in sleep had fallen on you —
Ye are many, they are few ! '

PETER BELL THE THIRD

BY MICHING MALLECHO, ESQ.

Is it a party in a parlor,
Crammed just as they on earth were crammed,
Some sipping punch — some sipping tea ;
But, as you by their faces see,
All silent, and all —— damned !
Peter Bell, by W. WORDSWORTH.

Ophelia.— What means this, my lord ?
Hamlet. — Marry, this is Miching Mallecho ; it means mischief.
SHAKESPEARE.

Peter Bell the Third was suggested by some reviews, in *The Examiner*, of Wordsworth's *Peter Bell* and of John Hamilton Reynolds's satire on Wordsworth of the same title. They amused Shelley, and he wrote the present poem in that vein of fun which seldom appeared in his verse, though it was a characteristic trait of his private life. 'I think *Peter* not bad in his way,' wrote Shelley to Ollier, 'but perhaps no one will believe in anything in the shape of a joke from me.' Shelley's satire is

meant pleasantly enough, as his admiration for Wordsworth's poetic powers is evident in many ways, and he was careful to change the name *Emma* to *Betty*, having inadvertently used the former, — ' Emma, I recollect, is the real name of the sister of a great poet who might be mistaken for *Peter.*' Mrs. Shelley in her note states the case frankly and fairly :

'A critique on Wordsworth's *Peter Bell* reached us at Leghorn, which amused Shelley exceedingly and suggested this poem. I need

scarcely observe that nothing personal to the Author of *Peter Bell* is intended in this poem. No man ever admired Wordsworth's poetry more; — he read it perpetually, and taught others to appreciate its beauties. This poem is, like all others written by Shelley, ideal. He conceived the idealism of a poet — a man of lofty and creative genius — quitting the glorious calling of discovering and announcing the beautiful and good, to support and propagate ignorant prejudices and pernicious errors; imparting to the unenlightened, not that ardor for truth and spirit of toleration which Shelley looked on as the sources of the moral improvement and happiness of mankind; but false and injurious opinions, that evil was good, and that ignorance and force were the best allies of purity and virtue. His idea was that a man gifted even as transcendently as the Author of *Peter Bell*, with the highest qualities of genius, must, if he fostered such errors, be infected with dulness. This poem was written, as a warning — not as a narration of the reality. He was unacquainted personally with Wordsworth or with Coleridge (to whom he alludes in the fifth part of the poem), and therefore, I repeat, his poem is purely ideal; — it contains something of criticism on the compositions of these great poets, but nothing injurious to the men themselves.

' No poem contains more of Shelley's peculiar views, with regard to the errors into which many of the wisest have fallen, and of the pernicious effects of certain opinions on society. Much of it is beautifully written — and though, like the burlesque drama of Swellfoot, it must be looked on as a plaything, it has so much merit and poetry — so much of *himself* in it, that it cannot fail to interest greatly, and by right belongs to the world for whose instruction and benefit it was written.'

Shelley's own account of the burlesque is given in a letter to Hunt:

' Now, I only send you a *very heroic* poem, which I wish you to give to Ollier, and desire him to print and publish immediately, you being kind enough to take upon yourself the correction of the press — not, however, with my name; and you must tell Ollier that the author is to be kept a secret, and that I confide in him for this object as I would confide in a physician or lawyer, or any other man whose professional situation renders the betraying of what is entrusted a dishonor. My motive in this is solely not to prejudge myself in the present moment, as I have only expended a few days in this party squib, and, of course, taken little pains. The verses and language I have let come as they would, and I am about to publish more serious things this winter; afterwards. that is next year, if the thing should be remembered

so long, I have no objection to the author being known, but *not now*. I should like well enough that it should both go to press and be printed very quickly; as more serious things are on the eve of engaging both the public attention and mine.'

The poem was written at Florence, in the latter part of October, 1819, and sent forward to Hunt at once for publication. It did not appear, however, until twenty years after, when it was included in Mrs. Shelley's second edition of the collected poems, 1839.

DEDICATION

TO THOMAS BROWN, ESQ., THE YOUNGER, H. F.

DEAR TOM, — Allow me to request you to introduce Mr. Peter Bell to the respectable family of the Fudges. Although he may fall short of those very considerable personages in the more active properties which characterize the Rat and the Apostate, I suspect that even you, their historian, will confess that he surpasses them in the more peculiarly legitimate qualification of intolerable dulness.

You know Mr. Examiner Hunt; well — it was he who presented me to two of the Mr. Bells. My intimacy with the younger Mr. Bell naturally sprung from this introduction to his brothers. And in presenting him to you I have the satisfaction of being able to assure you that he is considerably the dullest of the three.

There is this particular advantage in an acquaintance with any one of the Peter Bells that, if you know one Peter Bell, you know three Peter Bells; they are not one, but three; not three, but one. An awful mystery, which, after having caused torrents of blood and having been hymned by groans enough to deafen the music of the spheres, is at length illustrated to the satisfaction of all parties in the theological world by the nature of Mr. Peter Bell.

Peter is a polyhedric Peter, or a Peter with many sides. He changes colors like a chameleon and his coat like a snake. He is a Proteus of a Peter. He was at first sublime, pathetic, impressive, profound; then dull; then prosy and dull; and now dull — oh, so very dull! it is an ultra-legitimate dulness.

You will perceive that it is not necessary to consider Hell and the Devil as supernatural machinery. The whole scene of my epic is in ' this world which is ' — so Peter informed us before his conversion to *White Obi* —

> The world of all of us, *and where*
> *We find our happiness, or not at all.*

Let me observe that I have spent six or seven days in composing this sublime piece;

the orb of my moon-like genius has made the fourth part of its revolution round the dull earth which you inhabit, driving you mad, while it has retained its calmness and its splendor, and I have been fitting this its last phase 'to occupy a permanent station in the literature of my country.'

Your works, indeed, dear Tom, sell better; but mine are far superior. The public is no judge; posterity sets all to rights.

Allow me to observe that so much has been written of Peter Bell that the present history can be considered only, like the Iliad, as a continuation of that series of cyclic poems which have already been candidates for bestowing immortality upon, at the same time that they receive it from, his character and adventures. In this point of view I have violated no rule of syntax in beginning my composition with a conjunction; the full stop, which closes the poem continued by me, being, like the full stops at the end of the Iliad and Odyssey, a full stop of a very qualified import.

Hoping that the immortality which you have given to the Fudges, you will receive from them; and in the firm expectation that when London shall be an habitation of bitterns, when St. Paul's and Westminster Abbey shall stand, shapeless and nameless ruins, in the midst of an unpeopled marsh; when the piers of Waterloo Bridge shall become the nuclei of islets of reeds and osiers, and cast the jagged shadows of their broken arches on the solitary stream, some transatlantic commentator will be weighing in the scales of some new and now unimagined system of criticism the respective merits of the Bells and the Fudges and their historians,

I remain, dear Tom,
Yours sincerely,
December 1, 1819. MICHING MALLECHO.

P. S. — Pray excuse the date of place; so soon as the profits of the publication come in, I mean to hire lodgings in a more respectable street.

PROLOGUE

PETER BELLS, one, two and three,
O'er the wide world wandering be.
First, the antenatal Peter,
Wrapped in weeds of the same metre,
The so long predestined raiment,
Clothed in which to walk his way meant
The second Peter; whose ambition
Is to link the proposition,
As the mean of two extremes,
(This was learned from Aldrich's themes),
Shielding from the guilt of schism
The orthodoxal syllogism;
The First Peter — he who was
Like the shadow in the glass
Of the second, yet unripe,
His substantial antitype.
Then came Peter Bell the Second,
Who henceforward must be reckoned
The body of a double soul,
And that portion of the whole
Without which the rest would seem
Ends of a disjointed dream.
And the Third is he who has
O'er the grave been forced to pass
To the other side, which is —
Go and try else — just like this.
Peter Bell the First was Peter
Smugger, milder, softer, neater,
Like the soul before it is
Born from *that* world into *this.*
The next Peter Bell was he,

Predevote, like you and me,
To good or evil, as may come;
His was the severer doom, —
For he was an evil Cotter,
And a polygamic Potter.
And the last is Peter Bell,
Damned since our first parents fell,
Damned eternally to Hell —
Surely he deserves it well!

PART THE FIRST

DEATH

I

AND Peter Bell, when he had been
 With fresh-imported Hell-fire warmed,
Grew serious — from his dress and mien
'T was very plainly to be seen
 Peter was quite reformed.

II

His eyes turned up, his mouth turned
 down;
 His accent caught a nasal twang;
He oiled his hair; there might be heard
The grace of God in every word
 Which Peter said or sang.

III

But Peter now grew old, and had
 An ill no doctor could unravel;

His torments almost drove him mad;
 Some said it was a fever bad;
 Some swore it was the gravel.

IV

His holy friends then came about,
 And with long preaching and persuasion
Convinced the patient that without
The smallest shadow of a doubt
 He was predestined to damnation.

V

They said — ' Thy name is Peter Bell;
 Thy skin is of a brimstone hue;
Alive or dead — ay, sick or well —
The one God made to rhyme with hell;
 The other, I think, rhymes with you.'

VI

Then Peter set up such a yell !
 The nurse, who with some water gruel
Was climbing up the stairs, as well
As her old legs could climb them — fell,
 And broke them both — the fall was
 cruel.

VII

The Parson from the casement leapt
 Into the lake of Windermere;
And many an eel — though no adept
In God's right reason for it — kept
 Gnawing his kidneys half a year.

VIII

And all the rest rushed through the door,
 And tumbled over one another,
And broke their skulls. — Upon the floor
Meanwhile sat Peter Bell, and swore,
 And cursed his father and his mother;

IX

And raved of God, and sin, and death,
 Blaspheming like an infidel;
And said that with his clenchèd teeth
He'd seize the earth from underneath
 And drag it with him down to hell.

X

As he was speaking came a spasm
 And wrenched his gnashing teeth asun-
 der;
Like one who sees a strange phantasm
He lay, — there was a silent chasm
 Betwixt his upper jaw and under.

XI

And yellow death lay on his face;
 And a fixed smile that was not human
Told, as I understand the case,
That he was gone to the wrong place.
 I heard all this from the old woman.

XII

Then there came down from Langdale
 Pike
 A cloud, with lightning, wind and hail;
It swept over the mountains like
An ocean, — and I heard it strike
 The woods and crags of Grasmere vale.

XIII

And I saw the black storm come
 Nearer, minute after minute;
Its thunder made the cataracts dumb;
With hiss, and clash, and hollow hum,
 It neared as if the Devil was in it.

XIV

The Devil *was* in it; he had bought
 Peter for half-a-crown; and when
The storm which bore him vanished,
 nought
That in the house that storm had caught
 Was ever seen again.

XV

The gaping neighbors came next day;
 They found all vanished from the shore;
The Bible, whence he used to pray,
Half scorched under a hen-coop lay;
 Smashed glass — and nothing more !

PART THE SECOND

THE DEVIL

I

The Devil, I safely can aver,
 Has neither hoof, nor tail, nor sting;
Nor is he, as some sages swear,
A spirit, neither here nor there,
 In nothing — yet in everything.

II

He is — what we are; for sometimes
 The Devil is a gentleman;
At others a bard bartering rhymes
For sack; a statesman spinning crimes;
 A swindler, living as he can;

III

A thief, who cometh in the night,
 With whole boots and net pantaloons,
Like some one whom it were not right
To mention, — or the luckless wight,
 From whom he steals nine silver spoons.

IV

But in this case he did appear
 Like a slop-merchant from Wapping,
And with smug face and eye severe
On every side did perk and peer
 Till he saw Peter dead or napping.

V

He had on an upper Benjamin
 (For he was of the driving schism)
In the which he wrapped his skin
From the storm he travelled in,
 For fear of rheumatism.

VI

He called the ghost out of the corse, —
 It was exceedingly like Peter,
Only its voice was hollow and hoarse;
It had a queerish look, of course;
 Its dress too was a little neater.

VII

The Devil knew not his name and lot;
 Peter knew not that he was Bell ;
Each had an upper stream of thought,
Which made all seem as it was not,
 Fitting itself to all things well.

VIII

Peter thought he had parents dear,
 Brothers, sisters, cousins, cronies,
In the fens of Lincolnshire;
He perhaps had found them there
 Had he gone and boldly shown his

IX

Solemn phiz in his own village,
 Where he thought oft when a boy
He 'd clomb the orchard walls to pillage
The produce of his neighbor's tillage,
 With marvellous pride and joy.

X

And the Devil thought he had,
 'Mid the misery and confusion
Of an unjust war, just made
A fortune by the gainful trade
Of giving soldiers rations bad —
 The world is full of strange delusion;

XI

That he had a mansion planned
 In a square like Grosvenor-square,
That he was aping fashion, and
That he now came to Westmoreland
 To see what was romantic there.

XII

And all this, though quite ideal,
 Ready at a breath to vanish,
Was a state not more unreal
Than the peace he could not feel,
 Or the care he could not banish.

XIII

After a little conversation,
 The Devil told Peter, if he chose,
He 'd bring him to the world of fashion
By giving him a situation
 In his own service — and new clothes.

XIV

And Peter bowed, quite pleased and proud,
 And after waiting some few days
For a new livery — dirty yellow
Turned up with black — the wretched fellow
 Was bowled to Hell in the Devil's chaise.

PART THE THIRD

HELL

I

HELL is a city much like London —
 A populous and a smoky city;
There are all sorts of people undone,
And there is little or no fun done;
 Small justice shown, and still less pity.

II

There is a Castles, and a Canning,
 A Cobbett, and a Castlereagh;
All sorts of caitiff corpses planning
All sorts of cozening for trepanning
 Corpses less corrupt than they.

III

There is a ——, who has lost
 His wits, or sold them, none knows which;

He walks about a double ghost,
And, though as thin as Fraud almost,
 Ever grows more grim and rich.

IV

There is a Chancery Court; a King;
 A manufacturing mob; a set
Of thieves who by themselves are sent
Similar thieves to represent;
 An army; and a public debt.

V

Which last is a scheme of paper money,
 And means — being interpreted —
' Bees, keep your wax — give us the honey,
And we will plant, while skies are sunny,
 Flowers, which in winter serve instead.'

VI

There is great talk of revolution —
 And a great chance of despotism —
German soldiers — camps — confusion —
Tumults — lotteries — rage — delusion —
 Gin — suicide — and methodism;

VII

Taxes too, on wine and bread,
 And meat, and beer, and tea, and cheese,
From which those patriots pure are fed,
Who gorge before they reel to bed,
 The tenfold essence of all these.

VIII

There are mincing women, mewing
 (Like cats, who *amant misere*)
Of their own virtue, and pursuing
Their gentler sisters to that ruin
 Without which — what were chastity ?

IX

Lawyers — judges — old hobnobbers
 Are there — bailiffs — chancellors —
Bishops — great and little robbers —
Rhymesters — pamphleteers — stock-job-
 bers —
 Men of glory in the wars;

X

Things whose trade is, over ladies
 To lean, and flirt, and stare, and sim-
 per,
Till all that is divine in woman
Grows cruel, courteous, smooth, inhuman,
 Crucified 'twixt a smile and whimper;

XI

Thrusting, toiling, wailing, moiling,
 Frowning, preaching — such a riot !
Each with never-ceasing labor,
Whilst he thinks he cheats his neighbor,
 Cheating his own heart of quiet.

XII

And all these meet at levees;
 Dinners convivial and political;
Suppers of epic poets; teas,
Where small talk dies in agonies;
 Breakfasts professional and critical;

XIII

Lunches and snacks so aldermanic
 That one would furnish forth ten din-
 ners,
Where reigns a Cretan-tongued panic,
Lest news Russ, Dutch, or Alemannic
 Should make some losers, and some
 winners;

XIV

At conversazioni — balls —
 Conventicles — and drawing-rooms —
Courts of law — committees — calls
Of a morning — clubs — book-stalls —
 Churches — masquerades — and tombs.

XV

And this is Hell — and in this smother
 Are all damnable and damned;
Each one, damning, damns the other;
They are damned by one another,
 By none other are they damned.

XVI

'T is a lie to say, ' God damns ! '
 Where was Heaven's Attorney-General
When they first gave out such flams ?
Let there be an end of shams;
 They are mines of poisonous mineral.

XVII

Statesmen damn themselves to be
 Cursed; and lawyers damn their souls
To the auction of a fee;
Churchmen damn themselves to see
 God's sweet love in burning coals.

XVIII

The rich are damned, beyond all cure,
 To taunt, and starve, and trample on

The weak and wretched; and the poor
Damn their broken hearts to endure
 Stripe on stripe, with groan on groan.

XIX

Sometimes the poor are damned indeed
 To take, not means for being blessed,
But Cobbett's snuff, revenge; that weed
From which the worms that it doth feed
 Squeeze less than they before pos-
 sessed.

XX

And some few, like we know who,
 Damned — but God alone knows why —
To believe their minds are given
To make this ugly Hell a Heaven;
 In which faith they live and die.

XXI

Thus, as in a town, plague-stricken,
 Each man, be he sound or no,
Must indifferently sicken;
As when day begins to thicken,
 None knows a pigeon from a crow;

XXII

So good and bad, sane and mad,
 The oppressor and the oppressed;
Those who weep to see what others
Smile to inflict upon their brothers;
 Lovers, haters, worst and best;

XXIII

All are damned — they breathe an air,
 Thick, infected, joy-dispelling;
Each pursues what seems most fair,
Mining, like moles, through mind, and
 there
Scoop palace-caverns vast, where Care
 In throned state is ever dwelling.

PART THE · FOURTH

SIN

I

Lo, Peter in Hell's Grosvenor-square,
 A footman in the Devil's service !
And the misjudging world would swear
That every man in service there
 To virtue would prefer vice.

II

But Peter, though now damned, was not
 What Peter was before damnation.
Men oftentimes prepare a lot
Which, ere it finds them, is not what
 Suits with their genuine station.

III

All things that Peter saw and felt
 Had a peculiar aspect to him ;
And when they came within the belt
Of his own nature, seemed to melt,
 Like cloud to cloud, into him.

IV

And so the outward world uniting
 To that within him, he became
Considerably uninviting
To those, who meditation slighting,
 Were moulded in a different frame.

V

And he scorned them, and they scorned
 him;
 And he scorned all they did; and they
Did all that men of their own trim
Are wont to do to please their whim —
 Drinking, lying, swearing, play.

VI

Such were his fellow-servants; thus
 His virtue, like our own, was built
Too much on that indignant fuss
Hypocrite Pride stirs up in us
 To bully one another's guilt.

VII

He had a mind which was somehow
 At once circumference and centre
Of all he might or feel or know;
Nothing went ever out, although
 Something did ever enter.

VIII

He had as much imagination
 As a pint-pot; — he never could
Fancy another situation,
From which to dart his contemplation,
 Than that wherein he stood.

IX

Yet his was individual mind,
 And new-created all he saw
In a new manner, and refined

Those new creations, and combined
 Them, by a master-spirit's law

X

Thus — though unimaginative —
 An apprehension clear, intense,
Of his mind's work, had made alive
The things it wrought on; I believe
 Wakening a sort of thought in sense.

XI

But from the first 't was Peter's drift
 To be a kind of moral eunuch;
He touched the hem of Nature's shift,
Felt faint — and never dared uplift
 The closest, all-concealing tunic.

XII

She laughed the while, with an arch
 smile,
 And kissed him with a sister's kiss,
And said — ' My best Diogenes,
I love you well — but, if you please,
 Tempt not again my deepest bliss.

XIII

' 'T is you are cold — for I, not coy,
 Yield love for love, frank, warm and
 true;
And Burns, a Scottish peasant boy —
His errors prove it — knew my joy
 More, learnèd friend, than you.

XIV

' *Bocca bacciata non perde ventura*
 Anzi rinnuova come fa la luna : —
So thought Boccaccio, whose sweet words
 might cure a
Male prude, like you, from what you now
 endure, a
 Low-tide in soul, like a stagnant laguna.'

XV

Then Peter rubbed his eyes severe,
 And smoothed his spacious forehead
 down,
With his broad palm; 'twixt love and
 fear,
He looked, as he no doubt felt, queer,
 And in his dream sate down.

XVI

The Devil was no uncommon creature;
 A leaden-witted thief — just huddled
Out of the dross and scum of nature;

A toad-like lump of limb and feature,
 With mind, and heart, and fancy mud-
 dled.

XVII

He was that heavy, dull, cold thing,
 The spirit of evil well may be;
A drone too base to have a sting;
Who gluts, and grimes his lazy wing,
 And calls lust luxury.

XVIII

Now he was quite the kind of wight
 Round whom collect, at a fixed era,
Venison, turtle, hock, and claret, —
Good cheer — and those who come to share
 it —
 And best East Indian madeira !

XIX

It was his fancy to invite
 Men of science, wit, and learning,
Who came to lend each other light;
He proudly thought that his gold's might
 Had set those spirits burning.

XX

And men of learning, science, wit,
 Considered him as you and I
Think of some rotten tree, and sit
Lounging and dining under it,
 Exposed to the wide sky.

XXI

And all the while, with loose fat smile,
 The willing wretch sat winking there,
Believing 't was his power that made
That jovial scene — and that all paid
 Homage to his unnoticed chair;

XXII

Though to be sure this place was Hell;
 He was the Devil — and all they —
What though the claret circled well,
And wit, like ocean, rose and fell ? —
 Were damned eternally.

PART THE FIFTH

GRACE

I

AMONG the guests who often stayed
 Till the Devil's petits-soupers,

A man there came, fair as a maid,
And Peter noted what he said,
 Standing behind his master's chair.

II

He was a mighty poet — and
A subtle-souled psychologist;
All things he seemed to understand,
Of old or new — of sea or land —
 But his own mind — which was a mist.

III

This was a man who might have turned
 Hell into Heaven — and so in gladness
A Heaven unto himself have earned;
But he in shadows undiscerned
 Trusted, — and damned himself to madness.

IV

He spoke of poetry, and how
 'Divine it was — a light — a love —
A spirit which like wind doth blow
As it listeth, to and fro;
 A dew rained down from God above;

V

'A power which comes and goes like dream,
 And which none can ever trace —
Heaven's light on earth — Truth's brightest beam.'
And when he ceased there lay the gleam
 Of those words upon his face.

VI

Now Peter, when he heard such talk,
 Would, heedless of a broken pate,
Stand like a man asleep, or balk
Some wishing guest of knife or fork,
 Or drop and break his master's plate.

VII

At night he oft would start and wake
 Like a lover, and began
In a wild measure songs to make
On moor, and glen, and rocky lake,
 And on the heart of man, —

VIII

And on the universal sky,
 And the wide earth's bosom green,
And the sweet, strange mystery
Of what beyond these things may lie,
 And yet remain unseen.

IX

For in his thought he visited
 The spots in which, ere dead and damned,
He his wayward life had led;
Yet knew not whence the thoughts were fed,
 Which thus his fancy crammed.

X

And these obscure remembrances
 Stirred such harmony in Peter,
That whensoever he should please,
He could speak of rocks and trees
 In poetic metre.

XI

For though it was without a sense
 Of memory, yet he remembered well
Many a ditch and quick-set fence;
Of lakes he had intelligence;
 He knew something of heath and fell.

XII

He had also dim recollections
 Of pedlers tramping on their rounds;
Milk-pans and pails; and odd collections
Of saws and proverbs; and reflections
 Old parsons make in burying-grounds.

XIII

But Peter's verse was clear, and came
 Announcing from the frozen hearth
Of a cold age, that none might tame
The soul of that diviner flame
 It augured to the Earth;

XIV

Like gentle rains, on the dry plains,
 Making that green which late was gray,
Or like the sudden moon, that stains
Some gloomy chamber's window panes
 With a broad light like day.

XV

For language was in Peter's hand
 Like clay while he was yet a potter;
And he made songs for all the land,
Sweet, both to feel and understand,
 As pipkins late to mountain cotter.

XVI

And Mr. ——, the bookseller,
 Gave twenty pounds for some; — then scorning

A footman's yellow coat to wear,
Peter, too proud of heart, I fear,
 Instantly gave the Devil warning.

XVII

Whereat the Devil took offence,
 And swore in his soul a great oath
 then,
' That for his damned impertinence,
He 'd bring him to a proper sense
 Of what was due to gentlemen ! '

PART THE SIXTH

DAMNATION

I

' O THAT mine enemy had written
 A book ! ' — cried Job ; a fearful curse,
If to the Arab, as the Briton,
 'T was galling to be critic-bitten ;
 The Devil to Peter wished no worse.

II

When Peter's next new book found vent,
 The Devil to all the first Reviews
A copy of it slyly sent,
With five-pound note as compliment,
 And this short notice — ' Pray abuse.'

III

Then *seriatim*, month and quarter,
 Appeared such mad tirades. One said, —
' Peter seduced Mrs. Foy's daughter,
Then drowned the mother in Ullswater
 The last thing as he went to bed.'

IV

Another — ' Let him shave his head !
 Where 's Dr. Willis ? — Or is he jok-
 ing ?
What does the rascal mean or hope,
No longer imitating Pope,
 In that barbarian Shakespeare poking ? '

V

One more, ' Is incest not enough,
 And must there be adultery too ?
Grace after meat ? Miscreant and Liar !
Thief ! Blackguard ! Scoundrel ! Fool !
 Hell-fire
 Is twenty times too good for you.

VI

' By that last book of yours WE think
 You 've double damned yourself to
 scorn ;
We warned you whilst yet on the brink
You stood. From your black name will
 shrink
 The babe that is unborn.'

VII

All these Reviews the Devil made
 Up in a parcel. which he had
Safely to Peter's house conveyed.
For carriage, tenpence Peter paid —
 Untied them — read them — went half-
 mad.

VIII

' What ! ' cried he, ' this is my reward
 For nights of thought, and days of
 toil ?
Do poets, but to be abhorred
By men of whom they never heard,
 Consume their spirits' oil ?

IX

' What have I done to them ? — and
 who
 Is Mrs. Foy ? 'T is very cruel
To speak of me and Betty so !
Adultery ! God defend me ! Oh !
 I 've half a mind to fight a duel.

X

' Or,' cried he, a grave look collecting,
 ' Is it my genius, like the moon,
Sets those who stand her face inspecting,
That face within their brain reflecting,
 Like a crazed bell-chime, out of tune ?'

XI

For Peter did not know the town,
 But thought, as country readers do,
For half a guinea or a crown
He bought oblivion or renown
 From God's own voice in a Review.

XII

All Peter did on this occasion
 Was writing some sad stuff in prose.
It is a dangerous invasion
When poets criticise ; their station
 Is to delight, not pose.

XIII

The Devil then sent to Leipsic fair,
 For Born's translation of Kant's book;
A world of words, tail foremost, where
Right, wrong, false, true, and foul, and
 fair
 As in a lottery-wheel are shook;

XIV

Five thousand crammed octavo pages
 Of German psychologics, — he
Who his *furor verborum* assuages
Thereon deserves just seven months' wages
 More than will e'er be due to me.

XV

I looked on them nine several days,
 And then I saw that they were bad;
A friend, too, spoke in their dispraise, —
He never read them; with amaze
 I found Sir William Drummond had.

XVI

When the book came, the Devil sent
 It to P. Verbovale, Esquire,
With a brief note of compliment,
By that night's Carlisle mail. It went,
 And set his soul on fire —

XVII

Fire, which *ex luce præbens fumum*,
 Made him beyond the bottom see
Of truth's clear well — when I and you,
 Ma'am,
Go, as we shall do, *subter humum*,
 We may know more than he.

XVIII

Now Peter ran to seed in soul
 Into a walking paradox;
For he was neither part nor whole,
Nor good, nor bad, nor knave nor fool, —
 Among the woods and rocks.

XIX

Furious he rode, where late he ran,
 Lashing and spurring his tame hobby;
Turned to a formal puritan,
A solemn and unsexual man, —
 He half believed *White Obi.*

XX

This steed in vision he would ride,
 High trotting over nine-inch bridges,

With Flibbertigibbet, imp of pride,
Mocking and mowing by his side —
A mad-brained goblin for a guide —
 Over cornfields, gates and hedges.

XXI

After these ghastly rides, he came
 Home to his heart, and found from
 thence
Much stolen of its accustomed flame;
His thoughts grew weak, drowsy, and lame
 Of their intelligence.

XXII

To Peter's view, all seemed one hue;
 He was no whig, he was no tory;
No Deist and no Christian he;
He got so subtle that to be
 Nothing was all his glory.

XXIII

One single point in his belief
 From his organization sprung,
The heart-enrooted faith, the chief
Ear in his doctrines' blighted sheaf,
 That ' happiness is wrong.'

XXIV

So thought Calvin and Dominic;
 So think their fierce successors, who
Even now would neither stint nor stick
Our flesh from off our bones to pick,
 If they might ' do their do.'

XXV

His morals thus were undermined;
 The old Peter — the hard, old Potter
Was born anew within his mind;
He grew dull, harsh, sly, unrefined,
 As when he tramped beside the Otter.

XXVI

In the death hues of agony
 Lambently flashing from a fish,
Now Peter felt amused to see
Shades like a rainbow's rise and flee,
 Mixed with a certain hungry wish.

XXVII

So in his Country's dying face
 He looked — and lovely as she lay,
Seeking in vain his last embrace,
Wailing her own abandoned case,
 With hardened sneer he turned away;

XXVIII

And coolly to his own soul said, —
 'Do you not think that we might make
A poem on her when she 's dead;
Or, no — a thought is in my head —
 Her shroud for a new sheet I 'll take;

XXIX

'My wife wants one. Let who will bury
 This mangled corpse ! And I and you,
My dearest Soul, will then make merry,
As the Prince Regent did with Sherry, —
 Ay — and at last desert me too.'

XXX

And so his soul would not be gay,
 But moaned within him; like a fawn
Moaning within a cave, it lay
Wounded and wasting, day by day,
 Till all its life of life was gone.

XXXI

As troubled skies stain waters clear,
 The storm in Peter's heart and mind
Now made his verses dark and queer;
They were the ghosts of what they were,
 Shaking dim grave clothes in the wind.

XXXII

For he now raved enormous folly,
 Of Baptisms, Sunday-schools, and
 Graves;
'T would make George Colman melancholy
To have heard him, like a male Molly,
 Chanting those stupid staves.

XXXIII

Yet the Reviews, who heaped abuse
 On Peter while he wrote for freedom,
So soon as in his song they spy
The folly which soothes tyranny,
 Praise him, for those who feed 'em.

XXXIV

'He was a man, too great to scan;
 A planet lost in truth's keen rays;
His virtue, awful and prodigious;
He was the most sublime, religious,
 Pure-minded Poet of these days.'

XXXV

As soon as he read that, cried Peter,
 'Eureka ! I have found the way
To make a better thing of metre
Than e'er was made by living creature
 Up to this blessèd day.'

XXXVI

Then Peter wrote odes to the Devil,
 In one of which he meekly said:
'May Carnage and Slaughter,
Thy niece and thy daughter,
May Rapine and Famine,
Thy gorge ever cramming,
 Glut thee with living and dead !

XXXVII

'May death and damnation,
 And consternation,
Flit up from hell with pure intent !
 Slash them at Manchester,
 Glasgow, Leeds and Chester;
Drench all with blood from Avon to Trent.

XXXVIII

'Let thy body-guard yeomen
 Hew down babes and women
And laugh with bold triumph till Heaven
 be rent !
 When Moloch in Jewry
 Munched children with fury,
It was thou, Devil, dining with pure in-
 tent.'

PART THE SEVENTH

DOUBLE DAMNATION

I

The Devil now knew his proper cue.
 Soon as he read the ode, he drove
To his friend Lord MacMurderchouse's,
A man of interest in both houses,
 And said: — 'For money or for love,

II

'Pray find some cure or sinecure;
 To feed from the superfluous taxes,
A friend of ours — a poet; fewer
Have fluttered tamer to the lure
 Than he.' His lordship stands and racks
 his

III

Stupid brains, while one might count
 As many beads as he had boroughs, —

At length replies, from his mean front,
Like one who rubs out an account,
 Smoothing away the unmeaning fur-
 rows:

IV

'It happens fortunately, dear Sir,
 I can. I hope I need require
No pledge from you that he will stir
In our affairs; — like Oliver,
 That he 'll be worthy of his hire.'

V

These words exchanged, the news sent off
 To Peter, home the Devil hied, —
Took to his bed; he had no cough,
No doctor, — meat and drink enough, —
 Yet that same night he died.

VI

The Devil's corpse was leaded down;
 His decent heirs enjoyed his pelf;
Mourning-coaches, many a one,
Followed his hearse along the town; —
 Where was the Devil himself?

VII

When Peter heard of his promotion,
 His eyes grew like two stars for bliss;
There was a bow of sleek devotion,
Engendering in his back; each motion
 Seemed a Lord's shoe to kiss.

VIII

He hired a house, bought plate, and made
 A genteel drive up to his door,
With sifted gravel neatly laid,
As if defying all who said,
 Peter was ever poor.

IX

But a disease soon struck into
 The very life and soul of Peter;
He walked about — slept — had the hue
Of health upon his cheeks — and few
 Dug better — none a heartier eater.

X

And yet a strange and horrid curse
 Clung upon Peter, night and day;
Month after month the thing grew worse,
And deadlier than in this my verse
 I can find strength to say.

XI

Peter was dull — he was at first
 Dull — oh, so dull — so very dull!
Whether he talked, wrote, or rehearsed —
Still with this dulness was he cursed —
 Dull — beyond all conception — dull.

XII

No one could read his books — no mortal,
 But a few natural friends, would hear
 him;
The parson came not near his portal;
His state was like that of the immortal
 Described by Swift — no man could bear
 him.

XIII

His sister, wife, and children yawned,
 With a long, slow, and drear ennui,
All human patience far beyond;
Their hopes of Heaven each would have
 pawned
 Anywhere else to be.

XIV

But in his verse, and in his prose,
 The essence of his dulness was
Concentred and compressed so close,
'T would have made Guatimozin doze
 On his red gridiron of brass.

XV

A printer's boy, folding those pages,
 Fell slumbrously upon one side,
Like those famed seven who slept three
 ages;
To wakeful frenzy's vigil rages,
 As opiates, were the same applied.

XVI

Even the Reviewers who were hired
 To do the work of his reviewing,
With adamantine nerves, grew tired;
Gaping and torpid they retired
 To dream of what they should be do-
 ing.

XVII

And worse and worse the drowsy curse
 Yawned in him, till it grew a pest —
A wide contagious atmosphere
Creeping like cold through all things
 near,
 A power to infect and to infest.

XVIII

His servant-maids and dogs grew dull;
 His kitten, late a sportive elf;
The woods and lakes, so beautiful,
Of dim stupidity were full;
 All grew dull as Peter's self.

XIX

The earth under his feet — the springs
 Which lived within it a quick life,
The air, the winds of many wings
That fan it with new murmurings,
 Were dead to their harmonious strife.

XX

The birds and beasts within the wood,
 The insects, and each creeping thing,
Were now a silent multitude;
Love's work was left unwrought — no
 brood
 Near Peter's house took wing.

XXI

And every neighboring cottager
 Stupidly yawned upon the other;

No jackass brayed; no little cur
Cocked up his ears; no man would stir
 To save a dying mother.

XXII

Yet all from that charmed district went
 But some half-idiot and half-knave,
Who rather than pay any rent
Would live with marvellous content
 Over his father's grave.

XXIII

No bailiff dared within that space,
 For fear of the dull charm to enter;
A man would bear upon his face,
For fifteen months in any case,
 The yawn of such a venture.

XXIV

Seven miles above — below — around —
 This pest of dulness holds its sway;
A ghastly life without a sound;
To Peter's soul the spell is bound —
 How should it ever pass away ?

EPIPSYCHIDION

VERSES ADDRESSED TO THE NOBLE AND UNFORTUNATE LADY

EMILIA V———

NOW IMPRISONED IN THE CONVENT OF ———

L' anima amante si slancia fuori del creato, e si crea nell' infinito un mondo tutto per essa, diverso assai da questo oscuro e pauroso baratro.

 HER OWN WORDS.

The noble and unfortunate lady, Emilia V———, who inspired *Epipsychidion* was Teresa Emilia Viviani, eldest daughter of Count Viviani, a nobleman of Pisa. She had been placed by her family in the neighboring Convent of St. Anna, and there Shelley met her at the be-ginning of December, 1820, and interested himself in her fortunes. The episode, which is too long for narration in a note, is best described in Mrs. Marshall's *Life of Mary Wollstonecraft Shelley*. Its personal incidents are unimportant, since they do not enter into the

substance of the poem, which is 'an idealized history' of Shelley's spirit. The lady, to whom the verses are addressed, soon lost the enchantment which Shelley's imagination and sympathy had woven about her, and she ceased to interest him except as an object of compassion.

Shelley was fully aware of the mystical nature of the poem, which shows the most spiritual elements of his genius at their point of highest intensity of passion. He wrote to Gisborne : 'The *Epipsychidion* is a mystery ; as to real flesh and blood, you know that I do not deal in those articles ; you might as well go to a gin-shop for a leg of mutton, as expect anything human or earthly from me ;' and again, 'The *Epipsychidion* I cannot look at ; the person whom it celebrates was a cloud instead of a Juno, and poor Ixion starts from the centaur that was the offspring of his own embrace. If you are curious, however, to hear what I am and have been, it will tell you something thereof. It is an idealized history of my life and feelings. I think one is always in love with something or other; the error, and I confess it is not easy for spirits cased in flesh and blood to avoid it, consists in seeking in a mortal image the likeness of what is, perhaps, eternal.'

In sending it for publication to Ollier, he says : 'I send you . . . and a longer piece, entitled *Epipsychidion*. . . . The longer poem, I desire, should not be considered as my own ; indeed, in a certain sense, it is a production of a portion of me already dead ; and in this sense the advertisement is no fiction. It is to be published simply for the esoteric few ; and I make its author a secret, to avoid the malignity of those who turn sweet food into poison, transforming all they touch into the corruption of their own natures. My wish with respect to it is that it should be printed immediately in the simplest form, and merely one hundred copies : those who are capable of judging and feeling rightly with respect to a composition of so abstruse a nature, certainly do not arrive at that number — among those, at least, who would ever be excited to read an obscure and anonymous production ; and it would give me no pleasure that the vulgar should read it. If you have any book-selling reason against publishing so small a number as a hundred, merely, distribute copies among those to whom you think the poetry would afford any pleasure,

and send me, as soon as you can, a copy by the post.'

The poem was composed at Pisa during the first weeks of 1821, and an edition of one hundred copies was published at London the following summer. The title means, as Dr. Stopford Brooke points out, 'this soul out of my soul.'

ADVERTISEMENT

THE writer of the following lines died at Florence, as he was preparing for a voyage to one of the wildest of the Sporades, which he had bought and where he had fitted up the ruins of an old building, and where it was his hope to have realized a scheme of life, suited perhaps to that happier and better world of which he is now an inhabitant, but hardly practicable in this. His life was singular ; less on account of the romantic vicissitudes which diversified it than the ideal tinge which it received from his own character and feelings. The present Poem, like the *Vita Nuova* of Dante, is sufficiently intelligible to a certain class of readers without a matter-of-fact history of the circumstances to which it relates ; and to a certain other class it must ever remain incomprehensible from a defect of a common organ of perception for the ideas of which it treats. Not but that, *gran vergogna sarebbe a colui, che rimasse cosa sotto veste di figura o di colore rettorico : e domandato non sapesse denudare le sue parole da cotal veste, in guisa che avessero verace intendimento.*

The present poem appears to have been intended by the writer as the dedication to some longer one. The stanza on the opposite page [below] is almost a literal translation from Dante's famous Canzone

Voi, ch' intendendo, il terzo ciel movete, etc.

The presumptuous application of the concluding lines to his own composition will raise a smile at the expense of my unfortunate friend : be it a smile not of contempt, but pity.

My Song, I fear that thou wilt find but few
Who fitly shall conceive thy reasoning,
Of such hard matter dost thou entertain ;
Whence, if by misadventure chance should bring
Thee to base company (as chance may do)
Quite unaware of what thou dost contain,
I prithee, comfort thy sweet self again,
My last delight ! tell them that they are dull,
And bid them own that thou art beautiful.

SWEET Spirit ! sister of that orphan one,
Whose empire is the name thou weepest on,
In my heart's temple I suspend to thee
These votive wreaths of withered memory.

Poor captive bird ! who from thy narrow cage
Pourest such music that it might assuage
The rugged hearts of those who prisoned thee,

Were they not deaf to all sweet melody, —
This song shall be thy rose; its petals pale
Are dead, indeed, my adored nightingale !
But soft and fragrant is the faded blos-
 som,
And it has no thorn left to wound thy
 bosom. 12

High, spirit-wingèd Heart ! who dost
 forever
Beat thine unfeeling bars with vain en-
 deavor,
Till those bright plumes of thought, in
 which arrayed
It over-soared this low and worldly shade,
Lie shattered; and thy panting wounded
 breast
Stains with dear blood its unmaternal nest !
I weep vain tears; blood would less bitter
 be,
Yet poured forth gladlier, could it profit
 thee. 20

Seraph of Heaven ! too gentle to be
 human,
Veiling beneath that radiant form of Wo-
 man
All that is insupportable in thee
Of light, and love, and immortality !
Sweet Benediction in the eternal Curse !
Veiled glory of this lampless Universe !
Thou Moon beyond the clouds ! thou living
 Form
Among the Dead ! thou Star above the
 Storm !
Thou Wonder, and thou Beauty, and thou
 Terror !
Thou Harmony of Nature's art ! thou Mir-
 ror 30
In whom, as in the splendor of the Sun,
All shapes look glorious which thou gazest
 on !
Ay, even the dim words which obscure thee
 now
Flash, lightning-like, with unaccustomed
 glow;
I pray thee that thou blot from this sad
 song
All of its much mortality and wrong,
With those clear drops, which start like
 sacred dew
From the twin lights thy sweet soul dark-
 ens through,
Weeping, till sorrow becomes ecstasy —
Then smile on it, so that it may not die. 40

I never thought before my death to see
Youth's vision thus made perfect. Emily,
I love thee; though the world by no thin
 name
Will hide that love from its unvalued
 shame.
Would we two had been twins of the same
 mother !
Or that the name my heart lent to another
Could be a sister's bond for her and thee,
Blending two beams of one eternity !
Yet were one lawful and the other true,
These names, though dear, could paint not,
 as is due, 50
How beyond refuge I am thine. Ah me !
I am not thine — I am a part of *thee*.

Sweet Lamp ! my moth-like Muse has
 burned its wings;
Or, like a dying swan who soars and sings,
Young Love should teach Time, in his own
 gray style,
All that thou art. Art thou not void of
 guile,
A lovely soul formed to be blessed and
 bless ?
A well of sealed and secret happiness,
Whose waters like blithe light and music
 are,
Vanquishing dissonance and gloom ? a
 star 60
Which moves not in the moving Heavens,
 alone ?
A smile amid dark frowns ? a gentle tone
Amid rude voices ? a belovèd light ?
A solitude, a refuge, a delight ?
A lute, which those whom love has taught to
 play
Make music on, to soothe the roughest day
And lull fond grief asleep ? a buried trea-
 sure ?
A cradle of young thoughts of wingless
 pleasure ?
A violet-shrouded grave of woe ? — I mea-
 sure
The world of fancies, seeking one like thee,
And find — alas ! mine own infirmity. 71

She met me, Stranger, upon life's rough
 way,
And lured me towards sweet death; as
 Night by Day,
Winter by Spring, or Sorrow by swift
 Hope,
Led into light, life, peace. An antelope,

In the suspended impulse of its lightness,
Were less ethereally light; the brightness
Of her divinest presence trembles through
Her limbs, as underneath a cloud of dew 79
Embodied in the windless heaven of June,
Amid the splendor-wingèd stars, the Moon
Burns, inextinguishably beautiful;
And from her lips, as from a hyacinth full
Of honey-dew, a liquid murmur drops,
Killing the sense with passion, sweet as
 stops
Of planetary music heard in trance.
In her mild lights the starry spirits dance,
The sunbeams of those wells which ever
 leap
Under the lightnings of the soul — too
 deep
For the brief fathom-line of thought or
 sense. 90
The glory of her being, issuing thence,
Stains the dead, blank, cold air with a warm
 shade
Of unentangled intermixture, made
By Love, of light and motion; one intense
Diffusion, one serene Omnipresence,
Whose flowing outlines mingle in their
 flowing,
Around her cheeks and utmost fingers glow-
 ing,
With the unintermitted blood, which there
Quivers (as in a fleece of snow-like air
The crimson pulse of living morning
 quiver) 100
Continuously prolonged, and ending never
Till they are lost, and in that Beauty furled
Which penetrates, and clasps and fills the
 world;
Scarce visible from extreme loveliness.
Warm fragrance seems to fall from her
 light dress,
And her loose hair; and where some heavy
 tress
The air of her own speed has disentwined,
The sweetness seems to satiate the faint
 wind;
And in the soul a wild odor is felt,
Beyond the sense, like fiery dews that
 melt
Into the bosom of a frozen bud. 111
See where she stands! a mortal shape in-
 dued
With love and life and light and deity,
And motion which may change but cannot
 die;
An image of some bright Eternity;

A shadow of some golden dream; a Splen-
 dor
Leaving the third sphere pilotless; a ten-
 der
Reflection of the eternal Moon of Love,
Under whose motions life's dull billows
 move;
A metaphor of Spring and Youth and
 Morning; 120
A vision like incarnate April, warning,
With smiles and tears, Frost the Anatomy
Into his summer grave.

 Ah! woe is me!
What have I dared? where am I lifted?
 how
Shall I descend, and perish not? I know
That Love makes all things equal; I have
 heard
By mine own heart this joyous truth
 averred:
The spirit of the worm beneath the sod,
In love and worship, blends itself with God.

Spouse! Sister! Angel! Pilot of the
 Fate 130
Whose course has been so starless! Oh,
 too late
Belovèd! Oh, too soon adored, by me!
For in the fields of immortality
My spirit should at first have worshipped
 thine,
A divine presence in a place divine;
Or should have moved beside it on this
 earth,
A shadow of that substance, from its
 birth;
But not as now. I love thee; yes, I feel
That on the fountain of my heart a seal
Is set, to keep its waters pure and bright
For thee, since in those *tears* thou hast de-
 light. 141
We — are we not formed, as notes of music
 are,
For one another, though dissimilar;
Such difference without discord as can
 make
Those sweetest sounds, in which all spirits
 shake
As trembling leaves in a continuous air?

Thy wisdom speaks in me, and bids me
 dare
Beacon the rocks on which high hearts are
 wrecked.

I never was attached to that great sect,
Whose doctrine is, that each one should
 select 150
Out of the crowd a mistress or a friend,
And all the rest, though fair and wise,
 commend
To cold oblivion, though 't is in the code
Of modern morals, and the beaten road
Which those poor slaves with weary foot-
 steps tread
Who travel to their home among the dead
By the broad highway of the world, and so
With one chained friend, perhaps a jealous
 foe,
The dreariest and the longest journey go.

 True Love in this differs from gold and
 clay, 160
That to divide is not to take away.
Love is like understanding that grows
 bright
Gazing on many truths; 't is like thy light,
Imagination ! which, from earth and sky,
And from the depths of human fantasy,
As from a thousand prisms and mirrors,
 fills
The Universe with glorious beams, and
 kills
Error, the worm, with many a sun-like
 arrow
Of its reverberated lightning. Narrow
The heart that loves, the brain that con-
 templates, 170
The life that wears, the spirit that creates
One object, and one form, and builds
 thereby
A sepulchre for its eternity.

 Mind from its object differs most in this;
Evil from good; misery from happiness;
The baser from the nobler; the impure
And frail, from what is clear and must
 endure:
If you divide suffering and dross, you
 may
Diminish till it is consumed away;
If you divide pleasure and love and thought,
Each part exceeds the whole; and we know
 not 181
How much, while any yet remains unshared,
Of pleasure may be gained, of sorrow
 spared.
This truth is that deep well, whence sages
 draw
The unenvied light of hope; the eternal law

By which those live, to whom this world of
 life
Is as a garden ravaged, and whose strife
Tills for the promise of a later birth
The wilderness of this Elysian earth. 189

 There was a Being whom my spirit oft
Met on its visioned wanderings, far aloft,
In the clear golden prime of my youth's
 dawn,
Upon the fairy isles of sunny lawn,
Amid the enchanted mountains, and the
 caves
Of divine sleep, and on the air-like waves
Of wonder-level dream, whose tremulous
 floor
Paved her light steps. On an imagined
 shore,
Under the gray beak of some promontory
She met me, robed in such exceeding glory
That I beheld her not. In solitudes 200
Her voice came to me through the whis-
 pering woods,
And from the fountains and the odors deep
Of flowers, which, like lips murmuring in
 their sleep
Of the sweet kisses which had lulled them
 there,
Breathed but of *her* to the enamoured air;
And from the breezes whether low or loud,
And from the rain of every passing cloud,
And from the singing of the summer-birds,
And from all sounds, all silence. In the
 words
Of antique verse and high romance, in
 form, 210
Sound, color, in whatever checks that Storm
Which with the shattered present chokes
 the past,
And in that best philosophy, whose taste
Makes this cold common hell, our life, a
 doom
As glorious as a fiery martyrdom —
Her Spirit was the harmony of truth.

 Then from the caverns of my dreamy
 youth
I sprang, as one sandalled with plumes of
 fire,
And towards the lodestar of my one desire
I flitted, like a dizzy moth, whose flight 220
Is as a dead leaf's in the owlet light,
When it would seek in Hesper's setting
 sphere
A radiant death, a fiery sepulchre,

As if it were a lamp of earthly flame.
But She, whom prayers or tears then could
not tame,
Passed, like a god throned on a wingèd
planet,
Whose burning plumes to tenfold swiftness
fan it,
Into the dreary cone of our life's shade;
And as a man with mighty loss dismayed,
I would have followed, though the grave
between 230
Yawned like a gulf whose spectres are un-
seen;
When a voice said: — 'O Thou of hearts
the weakest,
The phantom is beside thee whom thou
seekest.'
Then I — 'Where?' the world's echo an-
swered 'Where?'
And in that silence, and in my despair,
I questioned every tongueless wind that
flew
Over my tower of mourning, if it knew
Whither 't was fled, this soul out of my
soul;
And murmured names and spells which
have control
Over the sightless tyrants of our fate; 240
But neither prayer nor verse could dissipate
The night which closed on her; nor uncreate
That world within this Chaos, mine and
me,
Of which she was the veiled Divinity, —
The world I say of thoughts that wor-
shipped her;
And therefore I went forth, with hope and
fear
And every gentle passion sick to death,
Feeding my course with expectation's
breath,
Into the wintry forest of our life;
And struggling through its error with vain
strife, 250
And stumbling in my weakness and my
haste,
And half bewildered by new forms, I
passed
Seeking among those untaught foresters
If I could find one form resembling hers,
In which she might have masked herself
from me.
There, — One whose voice was venomed
melody
Sate by a well, under blue night-shade
bowers;

The breath of her false mouth was like
faint flowers;
Her touch was as electric poison, — flame
Out of her looks into my vitals came, 260
And from her living cheeks and bosom flew
A killing air, which pierced like honey-dew
Into the core of my green heart, and lay
Upon its leaves; until, as hair grown gray
O'er a young brow, they hid its unblown
prime
With ruins of unseasonable time.

In many mortal forms I rashly sought
The shadow of that idol of my thought.
And some were fair — but beauty dies
away;
Others were wise — but honeyed words
betray; 270
And one was true — oh! why not true to
me?
Then, as a hunted deer that could not flee,
I turned upon my thoughts, and stood at
bay,
Wounded and weak and panting; the cold
day
Trembled, for pity of my strife and pain,
When, like a noonday dawn, there shone
again
Deliverance. One stood on my path who
seemed
As like the glorious shape, which I had
dreamed,
As is the Moon, whose changes ever run
Into themselves, to the eternal Sun; 280
The cold chaste Moon, the Queen of Hea-
ven's bright isles,
Who makes all beautiful on which she
smiles;
That wandering shrine of soft yet icy flame,
Which ever is transformed, yet still the
same,
And warms not but illumines. Young and
fair
As the descended Spirit of that sphere,
She hid me, as the Moon may hide the
night
From its own darkness, until all was bright
Between the Heaven and Earth of my
calm mind,
And, as a cloud charioted by the wind, 290
She led me to a cave in that wild place,
And sate beside me, with her downward
face
Illumining my slumbers, like the Moon
Waxing and waning o'er Endymion.

And I was laid asleep, spirit and limb,
And all my being became bright or dim
As the Moon's image in a summer sea,
According as she smiled or frowned on me;
And there I lay, within a chaste cold bed.
Alas, I then was nor alive nor dead; 300
For at her silver voice came Death and Life,
Unmindful each of their accustomed strife,
Masked like twin babes, a sister and a brother,
The wandering hopes of one abandoned mother,
And through the cavern without wings they flew,
And cried, ' Away ! he is not of our crew.'
I wept, and though it be a dream, I weep.

What storms then shook the ocean of my sleep,
Blotting that Moon, whose pale and waning lips 309
Then shrank as in the sickness of eclipse;
And how my soul was as a lampless sea,
And who was then its Tempest: and when She,
The Planet of that hour, was quenched, what frost
Crept o'er those waters, till from coast to coast
The moving billows of my being fell
Into a death of ice, immovable;
And then what earthquakes made it gape and split,
The white Moon smiling all the while on it ; —
These words conceal; if not, each word would be
The key of stanchless tears. Weep not for me ! 320

At length, into the obscure forest came
The Vision I had sought through grief and shame.
Athwart that wintry wilderness of thorns
Flashed from her motion splendor like the Morn's,
And from her presence life was radiated
Through the gray earth and branches bare and dead;
So that her way was paved and roofed above
With flowers as soft as thoughts of budding love;
And music from her respiration spread

Like light, — all other sounds were penetrated 330
By the small, still, sweet spirit of that sound,
So that the savage winds hung mute around;
And odors warm and fresh fell from her hair
Dissolving the dull cold in the frore air.
Soft as an Incarnation of the Sun,
When light is changed to love, this glorious One
Floated into the cavern where I lay,
And called my Spirit, and the dreaming clay
Was lifted by the thing that dreamed below 339
As smoke by fire, and in her beauty's glow
I stood, and felt the dawn of my long night
Was penetrating me with living light;
I knew it was the Vision veiled from me
So many years — that it was Emily.

Twin Spheres of light who rule this passive Earth,
This world of love, this me ; and into birth
Awaken all its fruits and flowers, and dart
Magnetic might into its central heart;
And lift its billows and its mists, and guide
By everlasting laws each wind and tide 350
To its fit cloud, and its appointed cave;
And lull its storms, each in the craggy grave
Which was its cradle, luring to faint bowers
The armies of the rainbow-wingèd showers;
And, as those married lights, which from the towers
Of Heaven look forth and fold the wandering globe
In liquid sleep and splendor, as a robe;
And all their many-mingled influence blend,
If equal, yet unlike, to one sweet end; —
So ye, bright regents, with alternate sway,
Govern my sphere of being, night and day !
Thou, not disdaining even a borrowed might; 362
Thou, not eclipsing a remoter light;
And, through the shadow of the seasons three,
From Spring to Autumn's sere maturity,
Light it into the Winter of the tomb,
Where it may ripen to a brighter bloom.
Thou too, O Comet, beautiful and fierce,
Who drew the heart of this frail Universe

Towards thine own; till, wrecked in that
 convulsion, 370
Alternating attraction and repulsion,
Thine went astray, and that was rent in
 twain;
Oh, float into our azure heaven again !
Be there love's folding-star at thy return;
The living Sun will feed thee from its urn
Of golden fire; the Moon will veil her horn
In thy last smiles; adoring Even and Morn
Will worship thee with incense of calm
 breath
And lights and shadows, as the star of
 Death
And Birth is worshipped by those sisters
 wild 380
Called Hope and Fear — upon the heart
 are piled
Their offerings, — of this sacrifice divine
A World shall be the altar.

 Lady mine,
Scorn not these flowers of thought, the
 fading birth,
Which from its heart of hearts that plant
 puts forth,
Whose fruit, made perfect by thy sunny
 eyes,
Will be as of the trees of Paradise.

 The day is come, and thou wilt fly with
 me.
To whatsoe'er of dull mortality
Is mine remain a vestal sister still; 390
To the intense, the deep, the imperishable,
Not mine, but me, henceforth be thou
 united
Even as a bride, delighting and delighted.
The hour is come — the destined Star has
 risen
Which shall descend upon a vacant prison.
The walls are high, the gates are strong,
 thick set
The sentinels — but true love never yet
Was thus constrained; it overleaps all
 fence;
Like lightning, with invisible violence
Piercing its continents; like Heaven's free
 breath, 400
Which he who grasps can hold not; liker
 Death,
Who rides upon a thought, and makes his
 way
Through temple, tower, and palace, and the
 array

Of arms; more strength has Love than he
 or they;
For it can burst his charnel, and make free
The limbs in chains, the heart in agony,
The soul in dust and chaos.

 Emily,
A ship is floating in the harbor now,
A wind is hovering o'er the mountain's
 brow;
There is a path on the sea's azure floor —
No keel has ever ploughed that path be-
 fore; 411
The halcyons brood around the foamless
 isles;
The treacherous Ocean has forsworn its
 wiles;
The merry mariners are bold and free :
Say, my heart's sister, wilt thou sail with
 me ?
Our bark is as an albatross, whose nest
Is a far Eden of the purple East;
And we between her wings will sit, while
 Night,
And Day, and Storm, and Calm, pursue
 their flight,
Our ministers, along the boundless Sea, 420
Treading each other's heels, unheededly.
It is an isle under Ionian skies,
Beautiful as a wreck of Paradise,
And, for the harbors are not safe and good,
This land would have remained a solitude
But for some pastoral people native there,
Who from the Elysian, clear, and golden
 air
Draw the last spirit of the age of gold,
Simple and spirited, innocent and bold.
The blue Ægean girds this chosen home 430
With ever-changing sound and light and
 foam
Kissing the sifted sands and caverns hoar;
And all the winds wandering along the
 shore
Undulate with the undulating tide;
There are thick woods where sylvan forms
 abide,
And many a fountain, rivulet, and pond,
As clear as elemental diamond,
Or serene morning air; and far beyond,
The mossy tracks made by the goats and
 deer
(Which the rough shepherd treads but once
 a year) 440
Pierce into glades, caverns, and bowers,
 and halls

Built round with ivy, which the waterfalls
Illumining, with sound that never fails
Accompany the noonday nightingales;
And all the place is peopled with sweet airs;
The light clear element which the isle
 wears
Is heavy with the scent of lemon-flowers,
Which floats like mist laden with unseen
 showers,
And falls upon the eyelids like faint sleep;
And from the moss violets and jonquils
 peep, 450
And dart their arrowy odor through the
 brain
Till you might faint with that delicious pain.
And every motion, odor, beam, and tone,
With that deep music is in unison,
Which is a soul within the soul; they seem
Like echoes of an antenatal dream.
It is an isle 'twixt Heaven, Air, Earth, and
 Sea,
Cradled and hung in clear tranquillity;
Bright as that wandering Eden, Lucifer,
Washed by the soft blue Oceans of young
 air. 460
It is a favored place. Famine or Blight,
Pestilence, War, and Earthquake, never
 light
Upon its mountain-peaks; blind vultures,
 they
Sail onward far upon their fatal way;
The wingèd storms, chanting their thunder-
 psalm
To other lands, leave azure chasms of calm
Over this isle, or weep themselves in dew,
From which its fields and woods ever renew
Their green and golden immortality.
And from the sea there rise, and from the
 sky 470
There fall, clear exhalations, soft and
 bright,
Veil after veil, each hiding some delight,
Which Sun or Moon or zephyr draw aside,
Till the isle's beauty, like a naked bride
Glowing at once with love and loveliness,
Blushes and trembles at its own excess;
Yet, like a buried lamp, a Soul no less
Burns in the heart of this delicious isle,
An atom of the Eternal, whose own smile
Unfolds itself, and may be felt, not seen, 480
O'er the gray rocks, blue waves, and forests
 green,
Filling their bare and void interstices.
But the chief marvel of the wilderness
Is a lone dwelling, built by whom or how

None of the rustic island-people know;
'Tis not a tower of strength, though with
 its height
It overtops the woods; but, for delight,
Some wise and tender Ocean-King, ere
 crime
Had been invented, in the world's young
 prime,
Reared it, a wonder of that simple time, 490
And envy of the isles, a pleasure-house
Made sacred to his sister and his spouse.
It scarce seems now a wreck of human art,
But, as it were, Titanic, in the heart
Of Earth having assumed its form, then
 grown
Out of the mountains, from the living stone,
Lifting itself in caverns light and high;
For all the antique and learned imagery
Has been erased, and in the place of it
The ivy and the wild vine interknit 500
The volumes of their many-twining stems;
Parasite flowers illume with dewy gems
The lampless halls, and, when they fade,
 the sky
Peeps through their winter-woof of tracery
With moonlight patches, or star-atoms keen,
Or fragments of the day's intense serene,
Working mosaic on their Parian floors.
And, day and night, aloof, from the high
 towers
And terraces, the Earth and Ocean seem
To sleep in one another's arms, and dream
Of waves, flowers, clouds, woods, rocks,
 and all that we 511
Read in their smiles, and call reality.

 This isle and house are mine, and I have
 vowed
Thee to be lady of the solitude.
And I have fitted up some chambers there
Looking towards the golden Eastern air,
And level with the living winds, which flow
Like waves above the living waves below.
I have sent books and music there, and all
Those instruments with which high spirits
 call 520
The future from its cradle, and the past
Out of its grave, and make the present last
In thoughts and joys which sleep, but can-
 not die,
Folded within their own eternity.
Our simple life wants little, and true taste
Hires not the pale drudge Luxury to waste
The scene it would adorn, and therefore still
Nature with all her children haunts the hill

The ring-dove, in the embowering ivy, yet
Keeps up her love-lament, and the owls flit
Round the evening tower, and the young
 stars glance 531
Between the quick bats in their twilight
 dance;
The spotted deer bask in the fresh moon-
 light
Before our gate, and the slow silent night
Is measured by the pants of their calm
 sleep.
Be this our home in life, and when years
 heap
Their withered hours, like leaves, on our
 decay,
Let us become the overhanging day,
The living soul of this Elysian isle, 539
Conscious, inseparable, one. Meanwhile
We two will rise, and sit, and walk together
Under the roof of blue Ionian weather,
And wander in the meadows, or ascend
The mossy mountains, where the blue hea-
 vens bend
With lightest winds, to touch their para-
 mour;
Or linger, where the pebble-paven shore,
Under the quick faint kisses of the sea
Trembles and sparkles as with ecstasy, —
Possessing and possessed by all that is 549
Within that calm circumference of bliss,
And by each other, till to love and live
Be one; or, at the noontide hour, arrive
Where some old cavern hoar seems yet to
 keep
The moonlight of the expired night asleep,
Through which the awakened day can never
 peep;
A veil for our seclusion, close as Night's,
Where secure sleep may kill thine innocent
 lights;
Sleep, the fresh dew of languid love, the rain
Whose drops quench kisses till they burn
 again. 559
And we will talk, until thought's melody
Become too sweet for utterance, and it die
In words, to live again in looks, which dart
With thrilling tone into the voiceless heart,
Harmonizing silence without a sound.
Our breath shall intermix, our bosoms
 bound,
And our veins beat together; and our lips,
With other eloquence than words, eclipse
The soul that burns between them; and the
 wells
Which boil under our being's inmost cells,

The fountains of our deepest life, shall be
Confused in passion's golden purity, 571
As mountain-springs under the morning
 Sun.
We shall become the same, we shall be one
Spirit within two frames, oh! wherefore
 two?
One passion in twin-hearts, which grows
 and grew,
Till like two meteors of expanding flame
Those spheres instinct with it become the
 same,
Touch, mingle, are transfigured; ever still
Burning, yet ever inconsumable;
In one another's substance finding food, 580
Like flames too pure and light and unim-
 bued
To nourish their bright lives with baser
 prey,
Which point to Heaven and cannot pass
 away;
One hope within two wills, one will beneath
Two overshadowing minds, one life, one
 death,
One Heaven, one Hell, one immortality,
And one annihilation. Woe is me!
The wingèd words on which my soul would
 pierce
Into the height of love's rare Universe,
Are chains of lead around its flight of fire.
I pant, I sink, I tremble, I expire! 591

———

Weak Verses, go, kneel at your Sover-
 eign's feet,
And say: — 'We are the masters of thy
 slave;
What wouldest thou with us and ours and
 thine?'
Then call your sisters from Oblivion's cave,
All singing loud: 'Love's very pain is
 sweet,
But its reward is in the world divine,
Which, if not here, it builds beyond the
 grave.'
So shall ye live when I am there. Then
 haste
Over the hearts of men, until ye meet 600
Marina, Vanna, Primus, and the rest,
And bid them love each other and be
 blessed;
And leave the troop which errs, and which
 reproves,
And come and be my guest, — for I am
 Love's.

ADONAIS

AN ELEGY ON THE DEATH OF JOHN KEATS

'Αστὴρ πρὶν μὲν ἔλαμπες ἐνὶ ζώοισιν ἑῶος.
Νῦν δὲ θανὼν, λάμπεις ἕσπερος ἐν φθιμένοις.

PLATO.

Adonais, perhaps the most widely read of the longer poems of Shelley, owes something of its charm to the fact noted by Mrs. Shelley that much in it 'seems now more applicable to Shelley himself than to the young and gifted poet whom he mourned.' The elegy has contributed much to the feeling that links these two poets in one memory, though in life they were rather pleasant than intimate friends. Keats died at Rome, February 23, 1821; and Shelley composed the poem between the late days of May and June 11, or at the latest, June 16; it was printed at Pisa, under his own care, by July 13, and copies sent to London for issue there by his publisher. During the period of composition he felt that he was succeeding, and wrote of it as 'a highly wrought *piece of art*, and perhaps better, in point of composition, than anything I have written;' and after its completion, he says, 'The *Adonais*, in spite of its mysticism, is the least imperfect of my compositions, and, as the image of my regret and honor for poor Keats, I wish it to be so.' He continued to indulge hopes of its success, as in the case of *The Cenci*, though on a different plane, and wrote to Ollier, 'I am especially curious to hear the fate of *Adonais*. I confess I should be surprised if *that* poem were born to an immortality of oblivion;' and, shortly after this, to Hunt, — 'Pray tell me what effect was produced by *Adonais*. My faculties are shaken to atoms, and torpid. I can write nothing; and if *Adonais* had no success and excited no interest, what incentive can I have to write?' A month or two later he writes to Gisborne, still strong in his faith in the poem, — 'I know what to think of *Adonais*, but what to think of those who confound it with the many bad poems of the day, I know not. ... It is absurd in any Review to criticise *Adonais*, and still more to pretend that the verses are bad.' His friends praised it, except Byron, who kept silence, perhaps, Shelley says, because he was mentioned in it. Shelley's letter to Severn has a peculiar interest : —

'I send you the Elegy on poor Keats — and I wish it were better worth your acceptance. You will see, by the preface, that it was written before I could obtain any particular account of his last moments ; all that I still know, was communicated to me by a friend who had derived his information from Colonel Finch ; I have ventured to express, as I felt, the respect and admiration which *your* conduct towards him demands.

'In spite of his transcendent genius, Keats never was, nor ever will be, a popular poet; and the total neglect and obscurity in which the astonishing remnants of his mind still lie, was hardly to be dissipated by a writer, who, however he may differ from Keats in more important qualities, at least resembles him in that accidental one, a want of popularity.

'I have little hope, therefore, that the poem I send you will excite any attention, nor do I feel assured that a critical notice of his writings would find a single reader. But for these considerations, it had been my intention to have collected the remnants of his compositions, and to have published them with a Life and Criticism. Has he left any poems or writings of whatsoever kind, and in whose possession are they ? Perhaps you would oblige me by information on this point.'

PREFACE

Φάρμακον ἦλθε, Βίων, ποτὶ σὸν στόμα, φάρμακον εἶδες.
Τοιούτοις χείλεσσι ποτέδραμε, κοὐκ ἐγλυκάνθη ;
Τίς δὲ βροτὸς τοσσοῦτον ἀνάμερος, ἢ κεράσαι τοι
*Ἡ δοῦναι χατέοντι τὸ φάρμακον ἔκφυγεν ἄδαν ;

MOSCHUS, EPITAPH. BION.

It is my intention to subjoin to the London edition of this poem a criticism upon the claims of its lamented object to be classed among the writers of the highest genius who have adorned our age. My known repugnance to the narrow principles of taste on which several of his earlier compositions were modelled prove, at least, that I am an impartial judge. I consider the fragment of Hyperion as second to nothing that was ever produced by a writer of the same years.

John Keats died at Rome of a consumption, in his twenty-fourth year, on the —— of —— 1821 ; and was buried in the romantic and lonely cemetery of the Protestants in that city, under the pyramid which is the tomb of Cestius and the massy walls and towers, now mouldering and desolate, which formed the circuit of ancient Rome. The cemetery is an

open space among the ruins, covered in winter with violets and daisies. It might make one in love with death to think that one should be buried in so sweet a place.

The genius of the lamented person to whose memory I have dedicated these unworthy verses was not less delicate and fragile than it was beautiful; and where cankerworms abound what wonder if its young flower was blighted in the bud? The savage criticism on his *Endymion*, which appeared in the *Quarterly Review*, produced the most violent effect on his susceptible mind; the agitation thus originated ended in the rupture of a blood-vessel in the lungs; a rapid consumption ensued, and the succeeding acknowledgments from more candid critics of the true greatness of his powers were ineffectual to heal the wound thus wantonly inflicted.

It may be well said that these wretched men know not what they do. They scatter their insults and their slanders without heed as to whether the poisoned shaft lights on a heart made callous by many blows, or one like Keats's composed of more penetrable stuff. One of their associates is, to my knowledge, a most base and unprincipled calumniator. As to *Endymion*, was it a poem, whatever might be its defects, to be treated contemptuously by those who had celebrated with various degrees of complacency and panegyric *Paris* and *Woman* and a *Syrian Tale*, and Mrs. Lefanu and Mr. Barrett and Mr. Howard Payne and a long list of the illustrious obscure? Are these the men who in their venal good nature presumed to draw a parallel between the Rev. Mr. Milman and Lord Byron? What gnat did they

strain at here after having swallowed all those camels? Against what woman taken in adultery dares the foremost of these literary prostitutes to cast his opprobrious stone? Miserable man! you, one of the meanest, have wantonly defaced one of the noblest specimens of the workmanship of God. Nor shall it be your excuse that, murderer as you are, you have spoken daggers but used none.

The circumstances of the closing scene of poor Keats's life were not made known to me until the *Elegy* was ready for the press. I am given to understand that the wound which his sensitive spirit had received from the criticism of *Endymion* was exasperated by the bitter sense of unrequited benefits; the poor fellow seems to have been hooted from the stage of life no less by those on whom he had wasted the promise of his genius than those on whom he had lavished his fortune and his care. He was accompanied to Rome and attended in his last illness by Mr. Severn, a young artist of the highest promise, who, I have been informed, ' almost risked his own life, and sacrificed every prospect to unwearied attendance upon his dying friend.' Had I known these circumstances before the completion of my poem, I should have been tempted to add my feeble tribute of applause to the more solid recompense which the virtuous man finds in the recollection of his own motives. Mr. Severn can dispense with a reward from ' such stuff as dreams are made of.' His conduct is a golden augury of the success of his future career — may the unextinguished Spirit of his illustrious friend animate the creations of his pencil, and plead against Oblivion for his name!

I

I WEEP for Adonais — he is dead!
Oh, weep for Adonais! though our tears
Thaw not the frost which binds so dear a
 head!
And thou, sad Hour, selected from all
 years
To mourn our loss, rouse thy obscure
 compeers,
And teach them thine own sorrow! Say:
 ' With me
Died Adonais; till the Future dares
Forget the Past, his fate and fame shall be
An echo and a light unto eternity!'

II

Where wert thou, mighty Mother, when
 he lay,
When thy Son lay, pierced by the shaft
 which flies

In darkness? where was lorn Urania
When Adonais died? With veilèd eyes,
'Mid listening Echoes, in her Paradise
She sate, while one, with soft enamoured
 breath,
Rekindled all the fading melodies,
With which, like flowers that mock the
 corse beneath,
He had adorned and hid the coming bulk
 of death.

III

Oh, weep for Adonais — he is dead!
Wake, melancholy Mother, wake and
 weep!
Yet wherefore? Quench within their
 burning bed
Thy fiery tears, and let thy loud heart
 keep
Like his a mute and uncomplaining
 sleep;

For he is gone where all things wise and
fair
Descend. Oh, dream not that the amor-
ous Deep
Will yet restore him to the vital air;
Death feeds on his mute voice, and laughs
at our despair.

IV

Most musical of mourners, weep again !
Lament anew, Urania ! — He died,
Who was the sire of an immortal strain,
Blind, old, and lonely, when his country's
pride
The priest, the slave, and the liberticide
Trampled and mocked with many a
loathèd rite
Of lust and blood; he went, unterrified,
Into the gulf of death; but his clear
Sprite
Yet reigns o'er earth, the third among the
sons of light.

V

Most musical of mourners, weep anew !
Not all to that bright station dared to
climb;
And happier they their happiness who
knew,
Whose tapers yet burn through that
night of time
In which suns perished; others more
sublime,
Struck by the envious wrath of man or
God,
Have sunk, extinct in their refulgent
prime;
And some yet live, treading the thorny
road,
Which leads, through toil and hate, to
Fame's serene abode.

VI

But now, thy youngest, dearest one has
perished,
The nursling of thy widowhood, who
grew,
Like a pale flower by some sad maiden
cherished
And fed with true-love tears instead of
dew;
Most musical of mourners, weep anew !
Thy extreme hope, the loveliest and the
last,

The bloom, whose petals, nipped before
they blew,
Died on the promise of the fruit, is waste;
The broken lily lies — the storm is over-
past.

VII

To that high Capital, where kingly Death
Keeps his pale court in beauty and decay,
He came; and bought, with price of pur-
est breath,
A grave among the eternal. — Come
away !
Haste, while the vault of blue Italian day
Is yet his fitting charnel-roof ! while
still
He lies, as if in dewy sleep he lay;
Awake him not ! surely he takes his fill
Of deep and liquid rest, forgetful of all ill.

VIII

He will awake no more, oh, never more !
Within the twilight chamber spreads
apace
The shadow of white Death, and at the
door
Invisible Corruption waits to trace
His extreme way to her dim dwelling-
place;
The eternal Hunger sits, but pity and
awe
Soothe her pale rage, nor dares she to
deface
So fair a prey, till darkness and the law
Of change shall o'er his sleep the mortal
curtain draw.

IX

Oh, weep for Adonais ! — The quick
Dreams,
The passion-wingèd ministers of thought,
Who were his flocks, whom near the liv-
ing streams
Of his young spirit he fed, and whom he
taught
The love which was its music, wander
not, —
Wander no more, from kindling brain to
brain,
But droop there, whence they sprung;
and mourn their lot
Round the cold heart, where, after their
sweet pain,
They ne'er will gather strength, or find a
home again.

X

And one with trembling hand clasps his
 cold head,
And fans him with her moonlight wings,
 and cries,
'Our love, our hope, our sorrow, is not
 dead;
See, on the silken fringe of his faint eyes,
Like dew upon a sleeping flower, there
 lies
A tear some Dream has loosened from
 his brain.'
Lost Angel of a ruined Paradise !
She knew not 't was her own; as with no
 stain
She faded, like a cloud which had outwept
 its rain.

XI

One from a lucid urn of starry dew
Washed his light limbs, as if embalming
 them;
Another clipped her profuse locks, and
 threw
The wreath upon him, like an anadem,
Which frozen tears instead of pearls be-
 gem;
Another in her wilful grief would break
Her bow and wingèd reeds, as if to stem
A greater loss with one which was more
 weak;
And dull the barbèd fire against his frozen
 cheek.

XII

Another Splendor on his mouth alit,
That mouth whence it was wont to draw
 the breath
Which gave it strength to pierce the
 guarded wit,
And pass into the panting heart beneath
With lightning and with music; the
 damp death
Quenched its caress upon his icy lips;
And, as a dying meteor stains a wreath
Of moonlight vapor, which the cold night
 clips,
It flushed through his pale limbs, and
 passed to its eclipse.

XIII

And others came — Desires and Adora-
 tions,
Wingèd Persuasions and veiled Desti-
 nies,

Splendors, and Glooms, and glimmering
 Incarnations
Of hopes and fears, and twilight Fanta-
 sies;
And Sorrow, with her family of Sighs,
And Pleasure, blind with tears, led by
 the gleam
Of her own dying smile instead of eyes,
Came in slow pomp; — the moving pomp
 might seem
Like pageantry of mist on an autumnal
 stream.

XIV

All he had loved, and moulded into
 thought
From shape, and hue, and odor, and sweet
 sound,
Lamented Adonais. Morning sought
Her eastern watch tower, and her hair
 unbound,
Wet with the tears which should adorn
 the ground,
Dimmed the aërial eyes that kindle day;
Afar the melancholy thunder moaned,
Pale Ocean in unquiet slumber lay,
And the wild winds flew round, sobbing in
 their dismay.

XV

Lost Echo sits amid the voiceless moun-
 tains,
And feeds her grief with his remem-
 bered lay,
And will no more reply to winds or
 fountains,
Or amorous birds perched on the young
 green spray,
Or herdsman's horn, or bell at closing
 day;
Since she can mimic not his lips, more
 dear
Than those for whose disdain she pined
 away
Into a shadow of all sounds: — a drear
Murmur, between their songs, is all the
 woodmen hear.

XVI

Grief made the young Spring wild, and
 she threw down
Her kindling buds, as if she Autumn
 were,
Or they dead leaves; since her delight is
 flown,

For whom should she have waked the
 sullen year ?
To Phœbus was not Hyacinth so dear,
Nor to himself Narcissus, as to both
Thou, Adonais; wan they stand and sere
Amid the faint companions of their youth,
With dew all turned to tears; odor, to
 sighing ruth.

XVII

Thy spirit's sister, the lorn nightingale,
Mourns not her mate with such melo-
 dious pain;
Not so the eagle, who like thee could scale
Heaven, and could nourish in the sun's
 domain
Her mighty youth with morning, doth
 complain,
Soaring and screaming round her empty
 nest,
As Albion wails for thee: the curse of
 Cain
Light on his head who pierced thy inno-
 cent breast,
And scared the angel soul that was its
 earthly guest !

XVIII

Ah woe is me ! Winter is come and gone,
But grief returns with the revolving
 year;
The airs and streams renew their joyous
 tone;
The ants, the bees, the swallows, reap-
 pear;
Fresh leaves and flowers deck the dead
 Seasons' bier;
The amorous birds now pair in every
 brake,
And build their mossy homes in field and
 brere;
And the green lizard and the golden
 snake,
Like unimprisoned flames, out of their
 trance awake.

XIX

Through wood and stream and field and
 hill and Ocean,
A quickening life from the Earth's heart
 has burst,
As it has ever done, with change and
 motion,
From the great morning of the world
 when first

God dawned on Chaos; in its stream im-
 mersed,
The lamps of Heaven flash with a softer
 light;
All baser things pant with life's sacred
 thirst,
Diffuse themselves, and spend in love's
 delight
The beauty and the joy of their renewèd
 might.

XX

The leprous corpse, touched by this spirit
 tender.
Exhales itself in flowers of gentle breath;
Like incarnations of the stars, when
 splendor
Is changed to fragrance, they illumine
 death
And mock the merry worm that wakes
 beneath.
Nought we know dies. Shall that alone
 which knows
Be as a sword consumed before the
 sheath
By sightless lightning ? the intense atom
 glows
A moment, then is quenched in a most cold
 repose.

XXI

Alas ! that all we loved of him should be,
But for our grief, as if it had not been,
And grief itself be mortal ! Woe is me !
Whence are we, and why are we ? of
 what scene
The actors or spectators ? Great and
 mean
Meet massed in death, who lends what
 life must borrow.
As long as skies are blue and fields are
 green,
Evening must usher night, night urge
 the morrow,
Month follow month with woe, and year
 wake year to sorrow.

XXII

He will awake no more, oh, never more !
'Wake thou,' cried Misery, 'childless
 Mother, rise
Out of thy sleep, and slake, in thy heart's
 core,
A wound more fierce than his with tears
 and sighs.'

And all the Dreams that watched Ura-
nia's eyes,
And all the Echoes whom their sister's
song
Had held in holy silence, cried, ' Arise ! '
Swift as a Thought by the snake Mem-
ory stung,
From her ambrosial rest the fading Splen-
dor sprung.

XXIII

She rose like an autumnal Night, that
springs
Out of the East, and follows wild and
drear
The golden Day, which, on eternal wings,
Even as a ghost abandoning a bier,
Had left the Earth a corpse; — sorrow
and fear
So struck, so roused, so rapt Urania;
So saddened round her like an atmo-
sphere
Of stormy mist; so swept her on her way
Even to the mournful place where Adonais
lay.

XXIV

Out of her secret Paradise she sped,
Through camps and cities rough with
stone, and steel,
And human hearts which, to her airy
tread
Yielding not, wounded the invisible
Palms of her tender feet where'er they
fell;
And barbèd tongues, and thoughts more
sharp than they,
Rent the soft Form they never could
repel,
Whose sacred blood, like the young tears
of May,
Paved with eternal flowers that undeserving
way.

XXV

In the death-chamber for a moment
Death,
Shamed by the presence of that living
Might,
Blushed to annihilation, and the breath
Revisited those lips, and life's pale light
Flashed through those limbs, so late her
dear delight.
' Leave me not wild and drear and com-
fortless,

As silent lightning leaves the starless
night !
Leave me not ! ' cried Urania; her dis-
tress
Roused Death; Death rose and smiled, and
met her vain caress.

XXVI

' Stay yet awhile ! speak to me once again;
Kiss me, so long but as a kiss may live;
And in my heartless breast and burning
brain
That word, that kiss, shall all thoughts
else survive,
With food of saddest memory kept
alive,
Now thou art dead, as if it were a part
Of thee, my Adonais ! I would give
All that I am to be as thou now art !
But I am chained to Time, and cannot
thence depart !

XXVII

' O gentle child, beautiful as thou wert,
Why didst thou leave the trodden paths
of men
Too soon, and with weak hands though
mighty heart
Dare the unpastured dragon in his den ?
Defenceless as thou wert, oh, where was
then
Wisdom the mirrored shield, or scorn
the spear ?
Or hadst thou waited the full cycle, when
Thy spirit should have filled its crescent
sphere,
The monsters of life's waste had fled from
thee like deer.

XXVIII

' The herded wolves, bold only to pursue;
The obscene ravens, clamorous o'er the
dead;
The vultures, to the conqueror's banner
true,
Who feed where Desolation first has
fed,
And whose wings rain contagion; — how
they fled,
When, like Apollo, from his golden bow
The Pythian of the age one arrow sped
And smiled ! — The spoilers tempt no
second blow,
They fawn on the proud feet that spurn
them lying low.

XXIX

'The sun comes forth, and many reptiles
spawn;
He sets, and each ephemeral insect then
Is gathered into death without a dawn,
And the immortal stars awake again;
So is it in the world of living men:
A godlike mind soars forth, in its de-
light
Making earth bare and veiling heaven,
and when
It sinks, the swarms that dimmed or
shared its light
Leave to its kindred lamps the spirit's aw-
ful night.'

XXX

Thus ceased she; and the mountain
shepherds came,
Their garlands sere, their magic mantles
rent;
The Pilgrim of Eternity, whose fame
Over his living head like Heaven is bent,
An early but enduring monument,
Came, veiling all the lightnings of his
song
In sorrow; from her wilds Ierne sent
The sweetest lyrist of her saddest wrong,
And love taught grief to fall like music
from his tongue.

XXXI

'Midst others of less note, came one frail
Form,
A phantom among men; companionless
As the last cloud of an expiring storm
Whose thunder is its knell; he, as I guess,
Had gazed on Nature's naked loveliness,
Actæon-like, and now he fled astray
With feeble steps o'er the world's wil-
derness,
And his own thoughts, along that rugged
way,
Pursued, like raging hounds, their father
and their prey.

XXXII

A pard-like Spirit beautiful and swift —
A love in desolation masked; — a Power
Girt round with weakness; — it can
scarce uplift
The weight of the superincumbent hour;
It is a dying lamp, a falling shower,
A breaking billow; — even whilst we
speak

Is it not broken? On the withering
flower
The killing sun smiles brightly; on a
cheek
The life can burn in blood, even while the
heart may break.

XXXIII

His head was bound with pansies over-
blown,
And faded violets, white, and pied, and
blue;
And a light spear topped with a cypress
cone,
Round whose rude shaft dark ivy-tresses
grew
Yet dripping with the forest's noonday
dew,
Vibrated, as the ever-beating heart
Shook the weak hand that grasped it; of that crew
He came the last, neglected and apart;
A herd-abandoned deer struck by the
hunter's dart.

XXXIV

All stood aloof, and at his partial moan
Smiled through their tears; well knew
that gentle band
Who in another's fate now wept his own,
As in the accents of an unknown land
He sung new sorrow; sad Urania scanned
The Stranger's mien, and murmured:
'Who art thou?'
He answered not, but with a sudden hand
Made bare his branded and ensanguined
brow,
Which was like Cain's or Christ's — oh!
that it should be so!

XXXV

What softer voice is hushed over the
dead?
Athwart what brow is that dark mantle
thrown?
What form leans sadly o'er the white
death-bed,
In mockery of monumental stone,
The heavy heart heaving without a moan?
If it be He, who, gentlest of the wise,
Taught, soothed, loved, honored the de-
parted one,
Let me not vex with inharmonious sighs
The silence of that heart's accepted sacri-
fice.

XXXVI

Our Adonais has drunk poison — oh,
What deaf and viperous murderer could
 crown
Life's early cup with such a draught of
 woe ?
The nameless worm would now itself
 disown;
It felt, yet could escape the magic tone
Whose prelude held all envy, hate and
 wrong,
But what was howling in one breast
 alone,
Silent with expectation of the song,
Whose master's hand is cold, whose silver
 lyre unstrung.

XXXVII

Live thou, whose infamy is not thy
 fame !
Live ! fear no heavier chastisement from
 me,
Thou noteless blot on a remembered
 name !
But be thyself, and know thyself to
 be !
And ever at thy season be thou free
To spill the venom when thy fangs o'er-
 flow;
Remorse and Self-contempt shall cling
 to thee;
Hot Shame shall burn upon thy secret
 brow,
And like a beaten hound tremble thou shalt
 — as now.

XXXVIII

Nor let us weep that our delight is
 fled
Far from these carrion kites that scream
 below;
He wakes or sleeps with the enduring
 dead;
Thou canst not soar where he is sitting
 now.
Dust to the dust ! but the pure spirit
 shall flow
Back to the burning fountain whence it
 came,
A portion of the Eternal, which must
 glow
Through time and change, unquenchably
 the same,
Whilst thy cold embers choke the sordid
 hearth of shame.

XXXIX

Peace, peace ! he is not dead, he doth
 not sleep —
He hath awakened from the dream of
 life —
'T is we, who, lost in stormy visions, keep
With phantoms an unprofitable strife,
And in mad trance strike with our spir-
 it's knife
Invulnerable nothings. *We* decay
Like corpses in a charnel; fear and grief
Convulse us and consume us day by
 day,
And cold hopes swarm like worms within
 our living clay.

XL

He has outsoared the shadow of our
 night;
Envy and calumny and hate and pain,
And that unrest which men miscall de-
 light,
Can touch him not and torture not again;
From the contagion of the world's slow
 stain
He is secure, and now can never mourn
A heart grown cold, a head grown gray
 in vain;
Nor, when the spirit's self has ceased to
 burn,
With sparkless ashes load an unlamented
 urn.

XLI

He lives, he wakes — 't is Death is dead,
 not he;
Mourn not for Adonais. — Thou young
 Dawn,
Turn all thy dew to splendor, for from
 thee
The spirit thou lamentest is not gone;
Ye caverns and ye forests, cease to moan !
Cease, ye faint flowers and fountains, and
 thou Air,
Which like a mourning veil thy scarf
 hadst thrown
O'er the abandoned Earth, now leave it
 bare
Even to the joyous stars which smile on its
 despair !

XLII

He is made one with Nature: there is
 heard
His voice in all her music, from the moan

Of thunder to the song of night's sweet
bird;
He is a presence to be felt and known
In darkness and in light, from herb and
stone,
Spreading itself where'er that Power
may move
Which has withdrawn his being to its own;
Which wields the world with never-wea-
ried love,
Sustains it from beneath, and kindles it
above.

XLIII

He is a portion of the loveliness
Which once he made more lovely; he
doth bear
His part, while the one Spirit's plastic
stress
Sweeps through the dull dense world,
compelling there
All new successions to the forms they
wear,
Torturing the unwilling dross that checks
its flight
To its own likeness, as each mass may
bear,
And bursting in its beauty and its might
From trees and beasts and men into the
Heaven's light.

XLIV

The splendors of the firmament of time
May be eclipsed, but are extinguished
not;
Like stars to their appointed height they
climb,
And death is a low mist which cannot
blot
The brightness it may veil. When lofty
thought
Lifts a young heart above its mortal
lair,
And love and life contend in it for what
Shall be its earthly doom, the dead live
there
And move like winds of light on dark and
stormy air.

XLV

The inheritors of unfulfilled renown
Rose from their thrones, built beyond
mortal thought,
Far in the Unapparent. Chatterton
Rose pale, — his solemn agony had not

Yet faded from him; Sidney, as he fought
And as he fell and as he lived and loved
Sublimely mild, a Spirit without spot,
Arose; and Lucan, by his death ap-
proved;
Oblivion as they rose shrank like a thing
reproved.

XLVI

And many more, whose names on earth
are dark
But whose transmitted effluence cannot
die
So long as fire outlives the parent spark,
Rose, robed in dazzling immortality.
'Thou art become as one of us,' they
cry;
'It was for thee yon kingless sphere has
long
Swung blind in unascended majesty,
Silent alone amid an Heaven of song.
Assume thy wingèd throne, thou Vesper of
our throng!'

XLVII

Who mourns for Adonais? Oh, come
forth,
Fond wretch! and know thyself and him
aright.
Clasp with thy panting soul the pendu-
lous Earth;
As from a centre, dart thy spirit's light
Beyond all worlds, until its spacious
might
Satiate the void circumference; then
shrink
Even to a point within our day and night;
And keep thy heart light lest it make
thee sink
When hope has kindled hope, and lured
thee to the brink.

XLVIII

Or go to Rome, which is the sepulchre,
Oh, not of him, but of our joy; 't is
nought
That ages, empires, and religions, there
Lie buried in the ravage they have
wrought;
For such as he can lend, — they borrow
not
Glory from those who made the world
their prey;
And he is gathered to the kings of
thought

Who waged contention with their time's
decay,
And of the past are all that cannot pass
away.

XLIX

Go thou to Rome, — at once the Para-
dise,
The grave, the city, and the wilderness;
And where its wrecks like shattered
mountains rise,
And flowering weeds and fragrant copses
dress
The bones of Desolation's nakedness,
Pass, till the Spirit of the spot shall
lead
Thy footsteps to a slope of green access,
Where, like an infant's smile, over the
dead
A light of laughing flowers along the grass
is spread;

L

And gray walls moulder round, on which
dull Time
Feeds, like slow fire upon a hoary brand;
And one keen pyramid with wedge sub-
lime,
Pavilioning the dust of him who planned
This refuge for his memory, doth stand
Like flame transformed to marble; and
beneath,
A field is spread, on which a newer band
Have pitched in Heaven's smile their
camp of death,
Welcoming him we lose with scarce extin-
guished breath.

LI

Here pause: these graves are all too
young as yet
To have outgrown the sorrow which con-
signed
Its charge to each; and if the seal is
set,
Here, on one fountain of a mourning
mind,
Break it not thou ! too surely shalt thou
find
Thine own well full, if thou returnest
home,
Of tears and gall. From the world's
bitter wind
Seek shelter in the shadow of the tomb.
What Adonais is, why fear we to become ?

LII

The One remains, the many change and
pass;
Heaven's light forever shines, Earth's
shadows fly;
Life, like a dome of many-colored glass,
Stains the white radiance of Eternity,
Until Death tramples it to fragments. —
Die,
If thou wouldst be with that which thou
dost seek !
Follow where all is fled ! — Rome's
azure sky,
Flowers, ruins, statues, music, words, are
weak
The glory they transfuse with fitting truth
to speak.

LIII

Why linger, why turn back, why shrink,
my Heart ?
Thy hopes are gone before; from all
things here
They have departed; thou shouldst now
depart !
A light is passed from the revolving
year,
And man, and woman; and what still is
dear
Attracts to crush, repels to make thee
wither.
The soft sky smiles, — the low wind
whispers near;
'T is Adonais calls ! oh, hasten thither,
No more let Life divide what Death can
join together.

LIV

That Light whose smile kindles the Uni-
verse,
That Beauty in which all things work
and move,
That Benediction which the eclipsing
Curse
Of birth can quench not, that sustaining
Love
Which through the web of being blindly
wove
By man and beast and earth and air and
sea,
Burns bright or dim, as each are mirrors
of
The fire for which all thirst, now beams
on me,
Consuming the last clouds of cold mortality.

LV

The breath whose might I have invoked
 in song
Descends on me; my spirit's bark is
 driven
Far from the shore, far from the trem-
 bling throng
Whose sails were never to the tempest
 given;

The massy earth and spherèd skies are
 riven !
I am borne darkly, fearfully, afar;
Whilst, burning through the inmost veil
 of Heaven,
The soul of Adonais, like a star,
Beacons from the abode where the Eternal
 are.

HELLAS

A LYRICAL DRAMA

ΜΑΝΤΙΣ 'ΕΙΜ' 'ΕΣΘΛΩΝ 'ΑΓΩΝΩΝ
ŒDIP. COLON.

Hellas, the last of Shelley's political poems, was written at Pisa in the fall of 1821, and published the next spring at London by Ollier, who made some omissions in the notes and preface with Shelley's permission. Edward Williams suggested the title, and was much interested in the poem as it grew. Shelley describes it, during its composition, as ' a sort of imitation of the *Persæ* of Æschylus, full of lyrical poetry. I try to be what I might have been, but am not successful; ' and in mentioning to Gisborne the accuracy of the proof-reading he says, — ' Am I to thank you for the revision of the press ? or who acted as midwife to this last of my orphans, introducing it to oblivion, and me to my accustomed failure ? May the cause it celebrates be more fortunate than either ! Tell me how you like *Hellas*, and give me your opinion freely. It was written without much care, and in one of those few moments of enthusiasm which now seldom visit me, and which make me pay dear for their visits.'

Mrs. Shelley's note gives an excellent account of the circumstances amid which it was written, and of its spirit :

' The south of Europe was in a state of great political excitement at the beginning of the year 1821. The Spanish Revolution had been a signal to Italy — secret societies were formed — and when Naples rose to declare the Constitution, the call was responded to from Brundusium to the foot of the Alps. To crush these attempts to obtain liberty, early in 1821, the Austrians poured their armies into the Peninsula : at first their coming rather seemed to add energy and resolution to a people long enslaved. The Piedmontese asserted their freedom; Genoa threw off the yoke of the King of Sardinia ; and, as if in playful imitation, the people of the little state of Massa and Carrara gave the *congé* to their sovereign and set up a republic.

' Tuscany alone was perfectly tranquil. It was said that the Austrian minister presented a list of sixty Carbonari to the grand-duke, urging their imprisonment; and the grand-duke replied, " I do not know whether these sixty men are Carbonari, but I know if I imprison them, I shall directly have sixty thousand start up." But though the Tuscans had no desire to disturb the paternal government, beneath whose shelter they slumbered, they regarded the progress of the various Italian revolutions with intense interest, and hatred for the Austrian was warm in every bosom. But they had slender hopes ; they knew that the Neapolitans would offer no fit resistance to the regular German troops, and that the overthrow of the Constitution in Naples would act as a decisive blow against all struggles for liberty in Italy.

' We have seen the rise and progress of reform. But the Holy Alliance was alive and active in those days, and few could dream of the peaceful triumph of liberty. It seemed then that the armed assertion of freedom in the south of Europe was the only hope of the liberals, as, if it prevailed, the nations of the north would imitate the example. Happily the reverse has proved the fact. The countries accustomed to the exercise of the privileges of freemen, to a limited extent, have extended, and are extending these limits. Freedom and knowledge have now a chance of proceeding hand in hand ; and if it continue thus, we may hope for the durability of both. Then, as I have said, in 1821, Shelley, as well as every other lover of liberty, looked upon the struggles in Spain and Italy as decisive of the destinies of the world, probably for centuries to come. The interest he took in the progress

of affairs was intense. When Genoa declared itself free, his hopes were at their highest. Day after day, he read the bulletins of the Austrian army, and sought eagerly to gather tokens of its defeat. He heard of the revolt of Genoa with emotions of transport. His whole heart and soul were in the triumph of their cause. We were living at Pisa at that time; and several well-informed Italians, at the head of whom we may place the celebrated Vaccá, were accustomed to seek for sympathy in their hopes from Shelley: they did not find such for the despair they too generally experienced, founded on contempt for their southern countrymen.

'While the fate of the progress of the Austrian armies then invading Naples was yet in suspense, the news of another revolution filled him with exultation. We had formed the acquaintance at Pisa of several Constantinopolitan Greeks, of the family of Prince Caradja, formerly Hospodar of Wallachia, who, hearing that the bowstring, the accustomed finale of his viceroyalty, was on the road to him, escaped with his treasures, and took up his abode in Tuscany. Among these was the gentleman to whom the drama of *Hellas* is dedicated. Prince Mavrocordato was warmed by those aspirations for the independence of his country, which filled the hearts of many of his countrymen. He often intimated the possibility of an insurrection in Greece; but we had no idea of its being so near at hand, when, on the 1st of April, 1821, he called on Shelley; bringing the proclamation of his cousin, Prince Ipsilanti, and, radiant with exultation and delight, declared that henceforth Greece would be free.

'Shelley had hymned the dawn of liberty in Spain and Naples, in two odes, dictated by the warmest enthusiasm; — he felt himself naturally impelled to decorate with poetry the uprise of the descendants of that people, whose works he regarded with deep admiration; and to adopt the vaticinatory character in prophesying their success. *Hellas* was written in a moment of enthusiasm. It is curious to remark how well he overcomes the difficulty of forming a drama out of such scant materials. His prophecies, indeed, came true in their general, not their particular purport. He did not foresee the death of Lord Londonderry, which was to be the epoch of a change in English politics, particularly as regarded foreign affairs; nor that the navy of his country would fight for instead of against the Greeks: and by the battle of Navarino secure their enfranchisement from the Turks. Almost against reason, as it appeared to him, he resolved to believe that Greece would prove triumphant: and in this spirit, auguring ultimate good, yet grieving over the vicissitudes to be endured in the interval, he composed his drama. . . .

'*Hellas* was among the last of his compositions, and is among the most beautiful. The choruses are singularly imaginative, and melodious in their versification. There are some stanzas that beautifully exemplify Shelley's peculiar style. . . .

'The conclusion of the last chorus is among the most beautiful of his lyrics; the imagery is distinct and majestic; the prophecy, such as poets love to dwell upon, the regeneration of mankind — and that regeneration reflecting back splendor on the foregone time, from which it inherits so much of intellectual wealth, and memory of past virtuous deeds, as must render the possession of happiness and peace of tenfold value.'

To

HIS EXCELLENCY

PRINCE ALEXANDER MAVROCORDATO

LATE SECRETARY FOR FOREIGN AFFAIRS
TO THE HOSPODAR OF WALLACHIA

THE DRAMA OF HELLAS

IS INSCRIBED

AS AN IMPERFECT TOKEN

OF THE ADMIRATION, SYMPATHY, AND FRIENDSHIP

OF

THE AUTHOR.

PISA, *November* 1, 1821.

PREFACE

THE poem of *Hellas*, written at the suggestion of the events of the moment, is a mere improvise, and derives its interest (should it be found to possess any) solely from the intense sympathy which the Author feels with the cause he would celebrate.

The subject in its present state is insusceptible of being treated otherwise than lyrically, and if I have called this poem a drama from the circumstance of its being composed in dialogue, the license is not greater than that which has been assumed by other poets who have called their productions epics, only because they have been divided into twelve or twenty-four books.

The *Persæ* of Æschylus afforded me the first model of my conception, although the decision of the glorious contest now waging in Greece being yet suspended forbids a catastrophe parallel to the return of Xerxes and the desolation of the Persians. I have, therefore, contented myself with exhibiting a series of lyric pictures and with having wrought upon

the curtain of futurity, which falls upon the unfinished scene, such figures of indistinct and visionary delineation as suggest the final triumph of the Greek cause as a portion of the cause of civilization and social improvement.

The drama (if drama it must be called) is, however, so inartificial that I doubt whether, if recited on the Thespian wagon to an Athenian village at the Dionysiaca, it would have obtained the prize of the goat. I shall bear with equanimity any punishment greater than the loss of such a reward which the Aristarchi of the hour may think fit to inflict.

The only *goat-song* which I have yet attempted has, I confess, in spite of the unfavorable nature of the subject, received a greater and a more valuable portion of applause than I expected or than it deserved.

Common fame is the only authority which I can allege for the details which form the basis of the poem, and I must trespass upon the forgiveness of my readers for the display of newspaper erudition to which I have been reduced. Undoubtedly, until the conclusion of the war, it will be impossible to obtain an account of it sufficiently authentic for historical materials; but poets have their privilege, and it is unquestionable that actions of the most exalted courage have been performed by the Greeks — that they have gained more than one naval victory, and that their defeat in Wallachia was signalized by circumstances of heroism more glorious even than victory.

The apathy of the rulers of the civilized world to the astonishing circumstance of the descendants of that nation to which they owe their civilization — rising as it were from the ashes of their ruin — is something perfectly inexplicable to a mere spectator of the shows of this mortal scene. We are all Greeks. Our laws, our literature, our religion, our arts, have their root in Greece. But for Greece, Rome, the instructor, the conqueror, or the metropolis of our ancestors, would have spread no illumination with her arms, and we might still have been savages and idolaters; or, what is worse, might have arrived at such a stagnant and miserable state of social institution as China and Japan possess.

The human form and the human mind attained to a perfection in Greece which has impressed its image on those faultless productions whose very fragments are the despair of modern art, and has propagated impulses which cannot cease, through a thousand channels of manifest or imperceptible operation, to ennoble and delight mankind until the extinction of the race.

The modern Greek is the descendant of those glorious beings whom the imagination almost refuses to figure to itself as belonging to our kind, and he inherits much of their sensibility, their rapidity of conception, their enthusiasm and their courage. If in many instances he is degraded by moral and political slavery to the practice of the basest vices it engenders — and that below the level of ordinary degradation — let us reflect that the corruption of the best produces the worst, and that habits which subsist only in relation to a peculiar state of social institution may be expected to cease so soon as that relation is dissolved. In fact, the Greeks, since the admirable novel of *Anastasius* could have been a faithful picture of their manners, have undergone most important changes; the flower of their youth returning to their country from the universities of Italy, Germany and France have communicated to their fellow-citizens the latest results of that social perfection of which their ancestors were the original source. The university of Chios contained before the breaking out of the revolution eight hundred students, and among them several Germans and Americans. The munificence and energy of many of the Greek princes and merchants, directed to the renovation of their country with a spirit and a wisdom which has few examples, is above all praise.

The English permit their own oppressors to act according to their natural sympathy with the Turkish tyrant, and to brand upon their name the indelible blot of an alliance with the enemies of domestic happiness, of Christianity and civilization.

Russia desires to possess, not to liberate Greece; and is contented to see the Turks, its natural enemies, and the Greeks, its intended slaves, enfeeble each other until one or both fall into its net. The wise and generous policy of England would have consisted in establishing the independence of Greece and in maintaining it both against Russia and the Turk; — but when was the oppressor generous or just?

Should the English people ever become free, they will reflect upon the part which those who presume to represent their will have played in the great drama of the revival of liberty, with feelings which it would become them to anticipate. This is the age of the war of the oppressed against the oppressors, and every one of those ringleaders of the privileged gangs of murderers and swindlers, called sovereigns, look to each other for aid against the common enemy, and suspend their mutual jealousies in the presence of a mightier fear. Of this holy alliance all the despots of the earth are virtual members. But a new race has arisen throughout Europe, nursed in the abhorrence of the opinions which are its chains, and she will continue to produce fresh generations to accom-

plish that destiny which tyrants foresee and dread.

The Spanish Peninsula is already free. France is tranquil in the enjoyment of a partial exemption from the abuses which its unnatural and feeble government are vainly attempting to revive. The seed of blood and misery has been sown in Italy, and a more vigorous race is arising to go forth to the harvest. The world waits only the news of a revolution of Germany to see the tyrants who have pinna-

cled themselves on its supineness precipitated into the ruin from which they shall never arise. Well do these destroyers of mankind know their enemy, when they impute the insurrection in Greece to the same spirit before which they tremble throughout the rest of Europe, and that enemy well knows the power and the cunning of its opponents and watches the moment of their approaching weakness and inevitable division to wrest the bloody sceptres from their grasp.

HELLAS

DRAMATIS PERSONÆ

The Prologue : —
 Herald of Eternity.
 Christ.
 Satan.
 Mahomet.
 Chorus.

The Drama : —
 Mahmud.
 Hassan.
 Daood.
 Ahasuerus, a Jew.
 Phantom of Mahomet the Second.
 Chorus of Greek Captive Women.
 Messengers, Slaves and Attendants.

 Scene. Constantinople.
 Time. Sunset.

PROLOGUE : A FRAGMENT

HERALD OF ETERNITY

It is the day when all the sons of God
Wait in the roofless senate-house, whose floor
Is Chaos, and the immovable abyss
Frozen by His steadfast word to hyaline
.
The shadow of God, and delegate
Of that before whose breath the universe
Is as a print of dew.

 Hierarchs and kings
Who from your thrones pinnacled on the past
Sway the reluctant present, ye who sit
Pavilioned on the radiance or the gloom 10
Of mortal thought, which like an exhalation
Steaming from earth conceals the of
 heaven
Which gave it birth, assemble here
Before your Father's throne; the swift decree
Yet hovers, and the fiery incarnation

Is yet withheld, clothèd in which it shall
 annul
The fairest of those wandering isles that gem
The sapphire space of interstellar air,
That green and azure sphere, that earth
 enwrapped 20
Less in the beauty of its tender light
Than in an atmosphere of living spirit
Which interpenetrating all the . . .
 it rolls from realm to realm
And age to age, and in its ebb and flow
Impels the generations
To their appointed place,
Whilst the high Arbiter
Beholds the strife, and at the appointed time
Sends his decrees veiled in eternal . . . 30

Within the circuit of this pendant orb
There lies an antique region, on which fell
The dews of thought in the world's golden dawn
Earliest and most benign, and from it sprung
Temples and cities and immortal forms
And harmonies of wisdom and of song,
And thoughts, and deeds worthy of thoughts so fair.
And when the sun of its dominion failed,
And when the winter of its glory came,
The winds that stripped it bare blew on, and swept 40
That dew into the utmost wildernesses
In wandering clouds of sunny rain that thawed
The unmaternal bosom of the North.
Haste, sons of God, for ye beheld,
Reluctant, or consenting, or astonished,
The stern decrees go forth, which heaped on Greece
Ruin and degradation and despair.
A fourth now waits : assemble, sons of God,

To speed, or to prevent, or to suspend,
If, as ye dream, such power be not with-
 held, 50
The unaccomplished destiny.

.

CHORUS

The curtain of the Universe
 Is rent and shattered,
The splendor-wingèd worlds disperse
 Like wild doves scattered.

 Space is roofless and bare,
And in the midst a cloudy shrine,
 Dark amid thrones of light.
In the blue glow of hyaline
Golden worlds revolve and shine. 60
 In flight
From every point of the Infinite,
Like a thousand dawns on a single night,
The splendors rise and spread;
And through thunder and darkness dread
Light and music are radiated,
And, in their pavilioned chariots led
By living wings high overhead,
 The giant Powers move, 69
Gloomy or bright as the thrones they fill.

.

 A chaos of light and motion
 Upon that glassy ocean.

.

 The senate of the Gods is met,
 Each in his rank and station set;
 There is silence in the spaces —
 Lo! Satan, Christ, and Mahomet
 Start from their places!

CHRIST

 Almighty Father!
Low-kneeling at the feet of Destiny

.

There are two fountains in which spirits
 weep 80
When mortals err, Discord and Slavery
 named,
And with their bitter dew two Destinies
Filled each their irrevocable urns; the third,
Fiercest and mightiest, mingled both, and
 added
Chaos and Death, and slow Oblivion's lymph,
And hate and terror, and the poisoned rain

.

The Aurora of the nations. By this brow
Whose pores wept tears of blood, by these
 wide wounds,

By this imperial crown of agony,
By infamy and solitude and death, 90
For this I underwent, and by the pain
Of pity for those who would for me
The unremembered joy of a revenge,
For this I felt — by Plato's sacred light,
Of which my spirit was a burning morrow —
By Greece and all she cannot cease to be,
Her quenchless words, sparks of immortal
 truth,
Stars of all night — her harmonies and
 forms,
Echoes and shadows of what Love adores
In thee, I do compel thee, send forth
 Fate, 100
Thy irrevocable child: let her descend
A seraph-wingèd victory [arrayed]
In tempest of the omnipotence of God
Which sweeps through all things.
From hollow leagues, from Tyranny which
 arms
Adverse miscreeds and emulous anarchies
To stamp, as on a wingèd serpent's seed,
Upon the name of Freedom; from the
 storm
Of faction, which like earthquake shakes
 and sickens
The solid heart of enterprise; from all 110
By which the holiest dreams of highest
 spirits
Are stars beneath the dawn . . .

 She shall arise
Victorious as the world arose from Chaos!
And as the Heavens and the Earth arrayed
Their presence in the beauty and the light
Of thy first smile, O Father, as they gather
The spirit of thy love which paves for them
Their path o'er the abyss, till every sphere
Shall be one living Spirit, so shall Greece —

SATAN

Be as all things beneath the empyrean 120
Mine! Art thou eyeless like old Destiny,
Thou mockery-king, crowned with a wreath
 of thorns?
Whose sceptre is a reed, the broken reed
Which pierces thee! whose throne a chair
 of scorn;
For seest thou not beneath this crystal floor
The innumerable worlds of golden light
Which are my empire, and the least of
 them
 which thou wouldst redeem from me?
Know'st thou not them my portion?

Or wouldst rekindle the strife ? 130
Which our great Father then did arbitrate
When he assigned to his competing sons
Each his apportioned realm ?
 Thou Destiny,
Thou who art mailed in the omnipotence
Of Him who sends thee forth, whate'er
 thy task,
Speed, spare not to accomplish, and be mine
Thy trophies, whether Greece again become
The fountain in the desert whence the
 earth
Shall drink of freedom, which shall give it
 strength
To suffer, or a gulf of hollow death 140
To swallow all delight, all life, all hope.
Go, thou Vicegerent of my will, no less
Than of the Father's; but lest thou shouldst
 faint,
The wingèd hounds, Famine and Pestilence,
Shall wait on thee, the hundred-forkèd
 snake,
Insatiate Superstition, still shall
The earth behind thy steps, and War shall
 hover
Above, and Fraud shall gape below, and
 Change
Shall flit before thee on her dragon wings,
Convulsing and consuming, and I add 150
Three vials of the tears which demons weep
When virtuous spirits through the gate of
 Death
Pass triumphing over the thorns of life,
Sceptres and crowns, mitres and swords and
 snares,
Trampling in scorn, like Him and Socrates.
The first is Anarchy; when Power and
 Pleasure,
Glory and science and security,
On Freedom hang like fruit on the green
 tree,
Then pour it forth, and men shall gather
 ashes.
The second Tyranny —

CHRIST
 Obdurate spirit !
Thou seest but the Past in the To-come. 161
Pride is thy error and thy punishment.
Boast not thine empire, dream not that thy
 worlds
Are more than furnace-sparks or rainbow-
 drops
Before the Power that wields and kindles
 them.

True greatness asks not space, true excel-
 lence
Lives in the Spirit of all things that live,
Which lends it to the worlds thou callest
 thine.

.

MAHOMET

.
 Haste thou and fill the waning crescent
With beams as keen as those which pierced
 the shadow 170
Of Christian night rolled back upon the
 West
When the orient moon of Islam rode in
 triumph
From Tmolus to the Acroceraunian snow.

.
 Wake, thou Word
Of God, and from the throne of Destiny
Even to the utmost limit of thy way
May Triumph

.
 Be thou a curse on them whose creed
Divides and multiplies the most high God.

HELLAS

SCENE — *A Terrace, on the Seraglio.* MAHMUD
*(sleeping) ; an Indian Slave sitting beside his
Couch.*

CHORUS OF GREEK CAPTIVE WOMEN
We strew these opiate flowers
 On thy restless pillow;
They were stripped from orient bowers,
 By the Indian billow.
 Be thy sleep
 Calm and deep,
Like theirs who fell — not ours who weep !

INDIAN
Away, unlovely dreams !
 Away, false shapes of sleep !
Be his, as Heaven seems, 10
 Clear, and bright, and deep !
Soft as love, and calm as death,
Sweet as a summer night without a breath.

CHORUS
Sleep, sleep ! our song is laden
 With the soul of slumber;
It was sung by a Samian maiden,

Whose lover was of the number
Who now keep
That calm sleep
Whence none may wake, where none shall
weep. 20

INDIAN

I touch thy temples pale!
I breathe my soul on thee!
And could my prayers avail,
All my joy should be
Dead, and I would live to weep,
So thou mightst win one hour of quiet
sleep.

CHORUS

Breathe low, low,
The spell of the mighty mistress now!
When Conscience lulls her sated snake,
And Tyrants sleep, let Freedom wake. 30
Breathe low — low,
The words, which, like secret fire, shall
flow
Through the veins of the frozen earth —
low, low!

SEMICHORUS I

Life may change, but it may fly not;
Hope may vanish, but can die not;
Truth be veiled, but still it burneth;
Love repulsed, — but it returneth.

SEMICHORUS II

Yet were life a charnel, where
Hope lay coffined with Despair;
Yet were truth a sacred lie. 40
Love were lust —

SEMICHORUS I

 If Liberty
Lent not life its soul of light,
Hope its iris of delight,
Truth its prophet's robe to wear,
Love its power to give and bear.

CHORUS

In the great morning of the world,
The spirit of God with might unfurled
The flag of Freedom over Chaos,
 And all its banded anarchs fled,
Like vultures frighted from Imaus 50
 Before an earthquake's tread.
So from Time's tempestuous dawn
Freedom's splendor burst and shone;
Thermopylæ and Marathon

Caught, like mountains beacon-lighted,
 The springing Fire; the wingèd
 glory
On Philippi half-alighted,
 Like an eagle on a promontory.
Its unwearied wings could fan
The quenchless ashes of Milan. 60
From age to age, from man to man
 It lived; and lit from land to land
 Florence, Albion, Switzerland.

Then night fell; and, as from night,
Reassuming fiery flight,
From the West swift Freedom came,
 Against the course of heaven and
 doom,
A second sun arrayed in flame,
 To burn, to kindle, to illume.
From far Atlantis its young beams 70
Chased the shadows and the dreams.
France, with all her sanguine steams,
Hid, but quenched it not; again
Through clouds its shafts of glory rain
From utmost Germany to Spain.

As an eagle fed with morning
Scorns the embattled tempest's warning,
 When she seeks her aerie hanging
 In the mountain-cedar's hair,
And her brood expect the clanging 80
 Of her wings through the wild air,
Sick with famine; — Freedom so
To what of Greece remaineth now
Returns; her hoary ruins glow
 Like orient mountains lost in day;
 Beneath the safety of her wings
Her renovated nurslings play,
 And in the naked lightnings
Of truth they purge their dazzled eyes.
Let Freedom leave, where'er she flies, 90
A desert, or a paradise;
 Let the beautiful and the brave
 Share her glory, or a grave.

SEMICHORUS I

With the gifts of gladness
 Greece did thy cradle strew;

SEMICHORUS II

With the tears of sadness
 Greece did thy shroud bedew;

SEMICHORUS I

With an orphan's affection
 She followed thy bier through time;

SEMICHORUS II

And at thy resurrection 100
Reappeareth, like thou, sublime !

SEMICHORUS I

If Heaven should resume thee,
To Heaven shall her spirit ascend;

SEMICHORUS II

If Hell should entomb thee,
To Hell shall her high hearts bend.

SEMICHORUS I

If Annihilation —

SEMICHORUS II

Dust let her glories be;
And a name and a nation
Be forgotten, Freedom, with thee !

INDIAN

His brow grows darker — breathe not —
move not ! 110
He starts — he shudders; ye that love not,
With your panting loud and fast
Have awakened him at last.

MAHMUD (*starting from his sleep*)

Man the Seraglio-guard ! make fast the
gate.
What ! from a cannonade of three short
hours ?
'T is false ! that breach towards the Bos-
phorus
Cannot be practicable yet — who stirs ?
Stand to the match, that, when the foe pre-
vails,
One spark may mix in reconciling ruin
The conqueror and the conquered ! Heave
the tower 120
Into the gap — wrench off the roof.

Enter HASSAN

Ha ! what !
The truth of day lightens upon my dream,
And I am Mahmud still.

HASSAN

Your Sublime Highness
Is strangely moved.

MAHMUD

The times do cast strange shadows
On those who watch and who must rule
their course,

Lest they, being first in peril as in glory,
Be whelmed in the fierce ebb: — and these
are of them.
Thrice has a gloomy vision hunted me
As thus from sleep into the troubled day;
It shakes me as the tempest shakes the
sea, 130
Leaving no figure upon memory's glass.
Would that — no matter. Thou didst say
thou knewest
A Jew, whose spirit is a chronicle
Of strange and secret and forgotten things.
I bade thee summon him; 't is said his tribe
Dream, and are wise interpreters of dreams.

HASSAN

The Jew of whom I spake is old, so old
He seems to have outlived a world's decay;
The hoary mountains and the wrinkled
ocean
Seem younger still than he; his hair and
beard 140
Are whiter than the tempest-sifted snow;
His cold pale limbs and pulseless arteries
Are like the fibres of a cloud instinct
With light, and to the soul that quickens
them
Are as the atoms of the mountain-drift
To the winter wind; but from his eye
looks forth
A life of unconsumèd thought which pierces
The present, and the past, and the to-
come.
Some say that this is he whom the great
prophet
Jesus, the son of Joseph, for his mockery,
Mocked with the curse of immortality. 151
Some feign that he is Enoch; others dream
He was pre-adamite, and has survived
Cycles of generation and of ruin.
The sage, in truth, by dreadful abstinence,
And conquering penance of the mutinous
flesh,
Deep contemplation, and unwearied study,
In years outstretched beyond the date of
man,
May have attained to sovereignty and sci-
ence
Over those strong and secret things and
thoughts 160
Which others fear and know not.

MAHMUD

I would talk
With this old Jew.

HASSAN

Thy will is even now
Made known to him, where he dwells in a
sea-cavern
'Mid the Demonesi, less accessible
Than thou or God ! He who would ques-
tion him
Must sail alone at sunset, where the stream
Of Ocean sleeps around those foamless
isles,
When the young moon is westering as now,
And evening airs wander upon the wave;
And when the pines of that bee-pasturing
isle, 170
Green Erebinthus, quench the fiery shadow
Of its gilt prow within the sapphire water,
Then must the lonely helmsman cry aloud,
Ahasuerus ! and the caverns round
Will answer, Ahasuerus ! If his prayer
Be granted, a faint meteor will arise,
Lighting him over Marmora, and a wind
Will rush out of the sighing pine forest,
And with the wind a storm of harmony
Unutterably sweet, and pilot him 180
Through the soft twilight to the Bos-
phorus:
Thence, at the hour and place and circum-
stance
Fit for the matter of their conference,
The Jew appears. Few dare, and few who
dare
Win the desired communion — but that
shout
Bodes —
 [A shout within.

MAHMUD

Evil, doubtless; like all human sounds.
Let me converse with spirits.

HASSAN

 That shout again.

MAHMUD

This Jew whom thou hast summoned —

HASSAN

 Will be here —

MAHMUD

When the omnipotent hour, to which are
yoked
He, I, and all things, shall compel —
 enough. 190

Silence those mutineers — that drunken
crew
That crowd about the pilot in the storm.
Ay ! strike the foremost shorter by a head !
They weary me, and I have need of rest.
Kings are like stars — they rise and set,
they have
The worship of the world, but no repose.
 [Exeunt severally.

CHORUS

Worlds on worlds are rolling ever
 From creation to decay,
Like the bubbles on a river,
 Sparkling, bursting, borne away. 200
But they are still immortal
Who, through birth's orient portal
And death's dark chasm hurrying to and
 fro,
 Clothe their unceasing flight
 In the brief dust and light
Gathered around their chariots as they
 go;
 New shapes they still may weave,
 New gods, new laws receive,
Bright or dim are they, as the robes they
 last
On Death's bare ribs had cast. 210

A power from the unknown God,
 A Promethean conqueror, came ;
Like a triumphal path he trod
 The thorns of death and shame.
 A mortal shape to him
 Was like the vapor dim
Which the orient planet animates with
 light;
 Hell, Sin and Slavery came,
 Like bloodhounds mild and tame,
Nor preyed until their lord had taken
 flight; 220
 The moon of Mahomet
 Arose, and it shall set;
While blazoned as on heaven's immortal
 noon
The cross leads generations on.

Swift as the radiant shapes of sleep
 From one, whose dreams are Paradise,
Fly, when the fond wretch wakes to
 weep,
 And day peers forth with her blank
 eyes;
 So fleet, so faint, so fair,
 The Powers of earth and air 230

Fled from the folding star of Bethlehem;
 Apollo, Pan, and Love,
 And even Olympian Jove,
Grew weak, for killing Truth had glared
 on them;
 Our hills and seas and streams,
 Dispeopled of their dreams,
Their waters turned to blood, their dew to
 tears,
 Wailed for the golden years.

Enter MAHMUD, HASSAN, DAOOD, *and others*

MAHMUD

More gold ? our ancestors bought gold with
 victory, 239
And shall I sell it for defeat ?

DAOOD
 The Janizars
Clamor for pay.

MAHMUD
 Go, bid them pay themselves
With Christian blood ! Are there no Gre-
 cian virgins
Whose shrieks and spasms and tears they
 may enjoy ?
No infidel children to impale on spears ?
No hoary priests after that Patriarch
Who bent the curse against his country's
 heart,
Which clove his own at last ? Go ! bid
 them kill;
Blood is the seed of gold.

DAOOD
 It has been sown,
And yet the harvest to the sickle-men 249
Is as a grain to each.

MAHMUD
 Then take this signet.
Unlock the seventh chamber, in which lie
The treasures of victorious Solyman,
An empire's spoil stored for a day of ruin.
O spirit of my sires, is it not come ?
The prey-birds and the wolves are gorged
 and sleep;
But these, who spread their feast on the
 red earth,
Hunger for gold, which fills not. — See
 them fed;
Then lead them to the rivers of fresh death.
 [*Exit* DAOOD.

Oh, miserable dawn, after a night
More glorious than the day which it
 usurped ! 260
O faith in God ! O power on earth ! O
 word
Of the great Prophet, whose o'ershadowing
 wings
Darkened the thrones and idols of the
 West,
Now bright ! — for thy sake cursèd be the
 hour,
Even as a father by an evil child,
When the orient moon of Islam rolled in
 triumph
From Caucasus to white Ceraunia !
Ruin above, and anarchy below;
Terror without, and treachery within;
The chalice of destruction full, and all 270
Thirsting to drink; and who among us
 dares
To dash it from his lips ? and where is
 Hope ?

HASSAN

The lamp of our dominion still rides high;
One God is God — Mahomet is his Pro-
 phet.
Four hundred thousand Moslems, from the
 limits
Of utmost Asia, irresistibly
Throng, like full clouds at the Sirocco's cry,
But not like them to weep their strength
 in tears;
They bear destroying lightning, and their
 step
Wakes earthquake, to consume and over-
 whelm, 280
And reign in ruin. Phrygian Olympus,
Tmolus, and Latmos, and Mycale, roughen
With horrent arms; and lofty ships, even
 now,
Like vapors anchored to a mountain's edge,
Freighted with fire and whirlwind, wait at
 Scala
The convoy of the ever-veering wind.
Samos is drunk with blood; the Greek has
 paid
Brief victory with swift loss and long de-
 spair.
The false Moldavian serfs fled fast and far
When the fierce shout of Allah-illa-Allah
Rose like the war-cry of the northern
 wind, 291
Which kills the sluggish clouds, and leaves
 a flock

Of wild swans struggling with the naked
 storm.
So were the lost Greeks on the Danube's
 day !
If night is mute, yet the returning sun
Kindles the voices of the morning birds;
Nor at thy bidding less exultingly
Than birds rejoicing in the golden day
The Anarchies of Africa unleash
Their tempest-wingèd cities of the sea, 300
To speak in thunder to the rebel world.
Like sulphurous clouds half-shattered by
 the storm,
They sweep the pale Ægean, while the
 Queen
Of Ocean, bound upon her island throne,
Far in the West, sits mourning that her
 sons,
Who frown on Freedom, spare a smile for
 thee.
Russia still hovers, as an eagle might
Within a cloud, near which a kite and
 crane
Hang tangled in inextricable fight,
To stoop upon the victor; for she fears 310
The name of Freedom, even as she hates
 thine.
But recreant Austria loves thee as the
 Grave
Loves Pestilence, and her slow dogs of war,
Fleshed with the chase, come up from
 Italy,
And howl upon their limits; for they see
The panther, Freedom, fled to her old
 cover,
Amid seas and mountains, and a mightier
 brood
Crouch round. What Anarch wears a
 crown or mitre,
Or bears the sword, or grasps the key of
 gold,
Whose friends are not thy friends, whose
 foes thy foes ? 320
Our arsenals and our armories are full;
Our forts defy assault; ten thousand can-
 non
Lie ranged upon the beach, and hour by
 hour
Their earth-convulsing wheels affright the
 city;
The galloping of fiery steeds makes pale
The Christian merchant; and the yellow
 Jew
Hides his hoard deeper in the faithless
 earth.

Like clouds, and like the shadows of the
 clouds,
Over the hills of Anatolia,
Swift in wide troops the Tartar chivalry 330
Sweep; the far-flashing of their starry
 lances
Reverberates the dying light of day.
We have one God, one King, one Hope,
 one Law;
But many-headed Insurrection stands
Divided in itself, and soon must fall.

MAHMUD

Proud words, when deeds come short, are
 seasonable.
Look, Hassan, on yon crescent moon, em-
 blazoned
Upon that shattered flag of fiery cloud
Which leads the rear of the departing
 day,
Wan emblem of an empire fading now 340
See how it trembles in the blood-red air,
And like a mighty lamp whose oil is spent,
Shrinks on the horizon's edge, while, from
 above,
One star with insolent and victorious light,
Hovers above its fall, and with keen beams
Like arrows through a fainting antelope,
Strikes its weak form to death.

HASSAN
 Even as that moon
Renews itself —

MAHMUD
 Shall we be not renewed!
Far other bark than ours were needed now
To stem the torrent of descending time; 350
The spirit that lifts the slave before his
 lord
Stalks through the capitals of armèd kings,
And spreads his ensign in the wilderness;
Exults in chains; and, when the rebel
 falls,
Cries like the blood of Abel from the dust;
And the inheritors of the earth, like beasts
When earthquake is unleashed, with idiot
 fear
Cower in their kingly dens — as I do now.
What were Defeat, when Victory must
 appall ?
Or Danger, when Security looks pale ? 360
How said the messenger, who from the fort
Islanded in the Danube saw the battle
Of Bucharest ? that —

HASSAN

 Ibrahim's scimitar
Drew with its gleam swift victory from
 heaven
To burn before him in the night of battle —
A light and a destruction.

MAHMUD

 Ay ! the day
Was ours; but how ?

HASSAN

 The light Wallachians,
The Arnaut, Servian, and Albanian allies,
Fled from the glance of our artillery
Almost before the thunder-stone alit; 370
One half the Grecian army made a bridge
Of safe and slow retreat with Moslem
 dead;
The other —

MAHMUD

Speak — tremble not.

HASSAN

 Islanded
By victor myriads formed in hollow square
With rough and steadfast front, and thrice
 flung back
The deluge of our foaming cavalry;
Thrice their keen wedge of battle pierced
 our lines.
Our baffled army trembled like one man
Before a host, and gave them space; but
 soon
From the surrounding hills the batteries
 blazed, 380
Kneading them down with fire and iron
 rain.
Yet none approached; till, like a field of
 corn
Under the hook of the swart sickle-man,
The band, entrenched in mounds of Turk-
 ish dead,
Grew weak and few. Then said the Pacha,
 ' Slaves,
Render yourselves — they have abandoned
 you —
What hope of refuge, or retreat, or aid ?
We grant your lives.' — ' Grant that which
 is thine own ! '
Cried one, and fell upon his sword and
 died !
Another — ' God, and man, and hope aban-
 don me; 390

But I to them and to myself remain
Constant;' he bowed his head and his
 heart burst.
A third exclaimed, ' There is a refuge,
 tyrant,
Where thou darest not pursue; and canst
 not harm,
Shouldst thou pursue; there we shall meet
 again.'
Then held his breath, and, after a brief
 spasm,
The indignant spirit cast its mortal garment
Among the slain — dead earth upon the
 earth !
So these survivors, each by different ways,
Some strange, all sudden, none dishonor-
 able, 400
Met in triumphant death; and, when our
 army
Closed in, while yet wonder, and awe, and
 shame
Held back the base hyenas of the battle
That feed upon the dead and fly the living,
One rose out of the chaos of the slain;
And if it were a corpse which some dread
 spirit
Of the old saviors of the land we rule
Had lifted in its anger, wandering by;
Or if there burned within the dying man
Unquenchable disdain of death, and faith
Creating what it feigned, — I cannot tell;
But he cried, ' Phantoms of the free, we
 come ! 412
Armies of the Eternal, ye who strike
To dust the citadels of sanguine kings,
And shake the souls throned on their stony
 hearts,
And thaw their frost-work diadems like
 dew;
O ye who float around this clime, and weave
The garment of the glory which it wears,
Whose fame, though earth betray the dust
 it clasped,
Lies sepulchred in monumental thought; 420
Progenitors of all that yet is great,
Ascribe to your bright senate, oh, accept
In your high ministrations, us, your sons —
Us first, and the more glorious yet to
 come !
And ye, weak conquerors ! giants, who look
 pale
When the crushed worm rebels beneath
 your tread —
The vultures, and the dogs, your pensioners
 tame,

Are overgorged; but, like oppressors, still
They crave the relic of Destruction's feast.
The exhalations and the thirsty winds 430
Are sick with blood; the dew is foul with
 death;
Heaven's light is quenched in slaughter;
 thus where'er
Upon your camps, cities, or towers, or
 fleets,
The obscene birds the reeking remnants
 cast
Of these dead limbs, — upon your streams
 and mountains,
Upon your fields, your gardens, and your
 housetops, —
Where'er the winds shall creep, or the
 clouds fly,
Or the dews fall, or the angry sun look
 down
With poisoned light — Famine, and Pesti-
 lence, 439
And Panic, shall wage war upon our side !
Nature from all her boundaries is moved
Against ye; Time has found ye light as
 foam.
The Earth rebels; and Good and Evil stake
Their empire o'er the unborn world of men
On this one cast; but ere the die be thrown,
The renovated genius of our race,
Proud umpire of the impious game, de-
 scends,
A seraph-wingèd Victory, bestriding
The tempest of the Omnipotence of God,
Which sweeps all things to their appointed
 doom, 450
And you to oblivion ! ' — More he would
 have said,
But —

MAHMUD

Died — as thou shouldst ere thy lips had
 painted
Their ruin in the hues of our success.
A rebel's crime, gilt with a rebel's tongue !
Your heart is Greek, Hassan.

HASSAN

It may be so:
A spirit not my own wrenched me within,
And I have spoken words I fear and hate;
Yet would I die for —

MAHMUD

Live ! oh, live ! outlive
Me and this sinking empire. But the
 fleet —

HASSAN

Alas !

MAHMUD

The fleet which, like a flock of clouds
Chased by the wind, flies the insurgent
 banner ! 461
Our wingèd castles from their merchant
 ships !
Our myriads before their weak pirate
 bands !
Our arms before their chains ! our years of
 empire
Before their centuries of servile fear !
Death is awake ! Repulse is on the wa-
 ters;
They own no more the thunder-bearing
 banner
Of Mahmud, but, like hounds of a base
 breed,
Gorge from a stranger's hand, and rend
 their master.

HASSAN

Latmos, and Ampelos, and Phanæ, saw 470
The wreck —

MAHMUD

The caves of the Icarian isles
Told each to the other in loud mockery,
And with the tongue as of a thousand
 echoes,
First of the sea-convulsing fight — and
 then —
Thou darest to speak — senseless are the
 mountains;
Interpret thou their voice !

HASSAN

My presence bore
A part in that day's shame. The Grecian
 fleet
Bore down at daybreak from the north, and
 hung
As multitudinous on the ocean line
As cranes upon the cloudless Thracian
 wind. 480
Our squadron, convoying ten thousand
 men,
Was stretching towards Nauplia when the
 battle
Was kindled.
First through the hail of our artillery
The agile Hydriote barks with press of sail
Dashed; ship to ship, cannon to cannon,
 man

To man, were grappled in the embrace of
 war,
Inextricable but by death or victory.
The tempest of the raging fight convulsed
To its crystalline depths that stainless sea,
And shook heaven's roof of golden morn-
 ing clouds 491
Poised on an hundred azure mountain isles.
In the brief trances of the artillery
One cry from the destroyed and the de-
 stroyer
Rose, and a cloud of desolation wrapped
The unforeseen event, till the north wind
Sprung from the sea, lifting the heavy veil
Of battle-smoke — then victory — victory !
For, as we thought, three frigates from
 Algiers
Bore down from Naxos to our aid, but soon
The abhorrèd cross glimmered behind, be-
 fore, 501
Among, around us; and that fatal sign
Dried with its beams the strength in Mos-
 lem hearts,
As the sun drinks the dew. — What more ?
 We fled !
Our noonday path over the sanguine foam
Was beaconed — and the glare struck the
 sun pale —
By our consuming transports; the fierce
 light
Made all the shadows of our sails blood-
 red,
And every countenance blank. Some ships
 lay feeding
The ravening fire even to the water's level:
Some were blown up; some, settling heav-
 ily, 511
Sunk; and the shrieks of our companions
 died
Upon the wind that bore us fast and far,
Even after they were dead. Nine thousand
 perished !
We met the vultures legioned in the air,
Stemming the torrent of the tainted wind;
They, screaming from their cloudy moun-
 tain peaks,
Stooped through the sulphurous battle-
 smoke, and perched
Each on the weltering carcass that we
 loved,
Like its ill angel or its damnèd soul, 520
Riding upon the bosom of the sea.
We saw the dog-fish hastening to their
 feast.
Joy waked the voiceless people of the sea,

And ravening Famine left his ocean-cave
To dwell with War, with us, and with De-
 spair.
We met night three hours to the west of
 Patmos,
And with night, tempest —

MAHMUD

Cease !

Enter a Messenger

MESSENGER
 Your Sublime Highness,
That Christian hound, the Muscovite am-
 bassador,
Has left the city. If the rebel fleet
Had anchored in the port, had victory 530
Crowned the Greek legions in the Hippo-
 drome,
Panic were tamer. Obedience and Mutiny,
Like giants in contention planet-struck,
Stand gazing on each other. There is peace
In Stamboul.

MAHMUD
 Is the grave not calmer still ?
Its ruins shall be mine.

HASSAN
 Fear not the Russian;
The tiger leagues not with the stag at bay
Against the hunter. Cunning, base, and
 cruel,
He crouches, watching till the spoil be won,
And must be paid for his reserve in blood.
After the war is fought, yield the sleek
 Russian 541
That which thou canst not keep, his de-
 served portion
Of blood, which shall not flow through
 streets and fields,
Rivers and seas, like that which we may
 win,
But stagnate in the veins of Christian
 slaves !

Enter Second Messenger

SECOND MESSENGER
Nauplia, Tripolizza, Mothon, Athens,
Navarin, Artas, Monembasia,
Corinth and Thebes, are carried by as-
 sault;
And every Islamite who made his dogs
Fat with the flesh of Galilean slaves 550

Passed at the edge of the sword; the lust
 of blood,
Which made our warriors drunk, is
 quenched in death;
But like a fiery plague breaks out anew
In deeds which make the Christian cause
 look pale
In its own light. The garrison of Patras
Has store but for ten days, nor is there
 hope
But from the Briton; at once slave and
 tyrant,
His wishes still are weaker than his fears,
Or he would sell what faith may yet re-
 main
From the oaths broke in Genoa and in
 Norway; 560
And if you buy him not, your treasury
Is empty even of promises — his own coin.
The freedman of a western poet chief
Holds Attica with seven thousand rebels,
And has beat back the Pacha of Negropont;
The aged Ali sits in Yanina,
A crownless metaphor of empire;
His name, that shadow of his withered
 might,
Holds our besieging army like a spell
In prey to famine, pest, and mutiny; 570
He, bastioned in his citadel, looks forth
Joyless upon the sapphire lake that mirrors
The ruins of the city where he reigned,
Childless and sceptreless. The Greek has
 reaped
The costly harvest his own blood matured,
Not the sower, Ali — who has bought a
 truce
From Ypsilanti, with ten camel-loads
Of Indian gold.

Enter a Third Messenger

MAHMUD
What more?

THIRD MESSENGER
 The Christian tribes
Of Lebanon and the Syrian wilderness
Are in revolt; Damascus, Hems, Aleppo, 580
Tremble; the Arab menaces Medina;
The Æthiop has entrenched himself in Sen-
 naar,
And keeps the Egyptian rebel well em-
 ployed,
Who denies homage, claims investiture
As price of tardy aid. Persia demands

The cities on the Tigris, and the Georgians
Refuse their living tribute. Crete and
 Cyprus,
Like mountain-twins that from each other's
 veins
Catch the volcano fire and earthquake
 spasm,
Shake in the general fever. Through the
 city, 590
Like birds before a storm, the Santons
 shriek,
And prophesyings horrible and new
Are heard among the crowd; that sea of
 men
Sleeps on the wrecks it made, breathless
 and still.
A Dervise, learnèd in the Koran, preaches
That it is written how the sins of Islam
Must raise up a destroyer even now.
The Greeks expect a Saviour from the west,
Who shall not come, men say, in clouds
 and glory,
But in the Omnipresence of that Spirit 600
In which all live and are. Ominous signs
Are blazoned broadly on the noonday sky;
One saw a red cross stamped upon the
 sun;
It has rained blood; and monstrous births
 declare
The secret wrath of Nature and her Lord.
The army encamped upon the Cydaris
Was roused last night by the alarm of bat-
 tle,
And saw two hosts conflicting in the air, —
The shadows doubtless of the unborn time
Cast on the mirror of the night. While
 yet 610
The fight hung balanced, there arose a
 storm
Which swept the phantoms from among
 the stars.
At the third watch the Spirit of the Plague
Was heard abroad flapping among the
 tents;
Those who relieved watch found the senti-
 nels dead.
The last news from the camp is that a
 thousand
Have sickened, and —

Enter a Fourth Messenger

MAHMUD
 And thou, pale ghost, dim shadow
Of some untimely rumor, speak !

FOURTH MESSENGER

 One comes
Fainting with toil, covered with foam and
 blood;
He stood, he says, on Chelonites' 620
Promontory, which o'erlooks the isles that
 groan
Under the Briton's frown, and all their wa-
 ters
Then trembling in the splendor of the
 moon;
When, as the wandering clouds unveiled or
 hid
Her boundless light, he saw two adverse
 fleets
Stalk through the night in the horizon's
 glimmer,
Mingling fierce thunders and sulphureous
 gleams,
And smoke which strangled every infant
 wind
That soothed the silver clouds through the
 deep air.
At length the battle slept, but the Sirocco
Awoke, and drove his flock of thunder-
 clouds 631
Over the sea-horizon, blotting out
All objects — save that in the faint moon-
 glimpse
He saw, or dreamed he saw, the Turkish
 admiral
And two the loftiest of our ships of war
With the bright image of that Queen of
 Heaven,
Who hid, perhaps, her face for grief, re-
 versed;
And the abhorrèd cross —

Enter an Attendant

ATTENDANT

 Your Sublime Highness,
The Jew, who —

MAHMUD

 Could not come more seasonably.
Bid him attend. I 'll hear no more ! too
 long 640
We gaze on danger through the mist of
 fear,
And multiply upon our shattered hopes
The images of ruin. Come what will !
To-morrow and to-morrow are as lamps
Set in our path to light us to the edge
Through rough and smooth; nor can we
 suffer aught
Which he inflicts not in whose hand we are.
 [Exeunt.

SEMICHORUS I

Would I were the wingèd cloud
Of a tempest swift and loud !
 I would scorn 650
 The smile of morn,
And the wave where the moonrise is born !
 I would leave
 The spirits of eve
A shroud for the corpse of the day to weave
 From other threads than mine !
Bask in the deep blue noon divine
 Who would, not I.

SEMICHORUS II

 Whither to fly ?

SEMICHORUS I

Where the rocks that gird the Ægean 660
Echo to the battle pæan
 Of the free,
 I would flee,
A tempestuous herald of victory !
 My golden rain
 For the Grecian slain
Should mingle in tears with the bloody
 main;
 And my solemn thunder-knell
Should ring to the world the passing-bell
 Of tyranny ! 670

SEMICHORUS II

 Ah king ! wilt thou chain
 The rack and the rain ?
Wilt thou fetter the lightning and hurri-
 cane ?
 The storms are free,
 But we ——

CHORUS

O Slavery ! thou frost of the world's prime,
 Killing its flowers and leaving its thorns
 bare !
Thy touch has stamped these limbs with
 crime,
 These brows thy branding garland bear;
 But the free heart, the impassive soul,
 Scorn thy control ! 68-

SEMICHORUS I

Let there be light ! said Liberty;
And like sunrise from the sea

Athens arose ! — Around her born,
Shone like mountains in the morn
Glorious states; — and are they now
Ashes, wrecks, oblivion ?

SEMICHORUS II

Go
Where Thermæ and Asopus swallowed
 Persia, as the sand does foam;
Deluge upon deluge followed, 690
 Discord, Macedon, and Rome;
And, lastly, thou !

SEMICHORUS I

Temples and towers,
 Citadels and marts, and they
Who live and die there, have been ours,
 And may be thine, and must decay;
But Greece and her foundations are
Built below the tide of war,
Based on the crystalline sea
Of thought and its eternity;
Her citizens, imperial spirits, 700
 Rule the present from the past;
On all this world of men inherits
 Their seal is set.

SEMICHORUS II

Hear ye the blast,
Whose Orphic thunder thrilling calls
From ruin her Titanian walls ?
Whose spirit shakes the sapless bones
Of Slavery ? Argos, Corinth, Crete,
Hear, and from their mountain thrones
 The dæmons and the nymphs repeat
The harmony.

SEMICHORUS I

I hear, I hear ! 710

SEMICHORUS II

The world's eyeless charioteer,
 Destiny, is hurrying by !
What faith is crushed, what empire
 bleeds
Beneath her earthquake-footed steeds ?
What eagle-wingèd Victory sits
At her right hand ? what Shadow flits
Before ? what Splendor rolls behind ?
 Ruin and Renovation cry,
 Who but we ?

SEMICHORUS I

I hear, I hear !
The hiss as of a rushing wind, 720

The roar as of an ocean foaming,
The thunder as of earthquake coming
 I hear, I hear !
The crash as of an empire falling,
The shrieks as of a people calling
Mercy ! Mercy ! — How they thrill !
Then a shout of ' Kill, kill, kill ! '
And then a small still voice, thus —

SEMICHORUS II

For
Revenge and Wrong bring forth their kind;
 The foul cubs like their parents are; 730
Their den is in the guilty mind,
 And Conscience feeds them with despair;

SEMICHORUS I

In sacred Athens, near the fane
 Of Wisdom, Pity's altar stood;
Serve not the unknown God in vain,
But pay that broken shrine again
 Love for hate, and tears for blood.

Enter MAHMUD *and* AHASUERUS

MAHMUD

Thou art a man, thou sayest, even as we.

AHASUERUS

No more !

MAHMUD

But raised above thy fellow-men
By thought, as I by power.

AHASUERUS

Thou sayest so.

MAHMUD

Thou art an adept in the difficult lore 741
Of Greek and Frank philosophy; thou
 numberest
The flowers, and thou measurest the stars;
Thou severest element from element;
Thy spirit is present in the past, and sees
The birth of this old world through all its
 cycles
Of desolation and of loveliness,
And when man was not, and how man be-
 came
The monarch and the slave of this low
 sphere,
And all its narrow circles — it is much. 750
I honor thee, and would be what thou art
Were I not what I am; but the unborn
 hour,

Cradled in fear and hope, conflicting storms,
Who shall unveil? Nor thou, nor I, nor
 any
Mighty or wise. I apprehended not
What thou hast taught me, but I now per-
 ceive
That thou art no interpreter of dreams;
Thou dost not own that art, device, or God,
Can make the future present — let it come!
Moreover thou disdainest us and ours! 760
Thou art as God, whom thou contemplatest.

AHASUERUS

Disdain thee? — not the worm beneath
 thy feet!
The Fathomless has care for meaner things
Than thou canst dream, and has made
 pride for those
Who would be what they may not, or would
 seem
That which they are not. Sultan! talk no
 more
Of thee and me, the future and the past;
But look on that which cannot change —
 the One,
The unborn and the undying. Earth and
 Ocean,
Space, and the isles of life or light that
 gem 770
The sapphire floods of interstellar air,
This firmament pavilioned upon chaos,
With all its cressets of immortal fire,
Whose outwall, bastioned impregnably
Against the escape of boldest thoughts,
 repels them
As Calpe the Atlantic clouds — this Whole
Of suns, and worlds, and men, and beasts,
 and flowers,
With all the silent or tempestuous workings
By which they have been, are, or cease to
 be,
Is but a vision; all that it inherits 780
Are motes of a sick eye, bubbles, and
 dreams;
Thought is its cradle and its grave, nor less
The future and the past are idle shadows
Of thought's eternal flight — they have no
 being;
Nought is but that which feels itself to be.

MAHMUD

What meanest thou? thy words stream
 like a tempest
Of dazzling mist within my brain — they
 shake

The earth on which I stand, and hang like
 night
On Heaven above me. What can they
 avail?
They cast on all things, surest, brightest,
 best, — 790
Doubt, insecurity, astonishment.

AHASUERUS

Mistake me not! All is contained in each.
Dodona's forest to an acorn's cup
Is that which has been or will be, to that
Which is — the absent to the present.
 Thought
Alone, and its quick elements, Will, Pas-
 sion,
Reason, Imagination, cannot die;
They are what that which they regard ap-
 pears,
The stuff whence mutability can weave
All that it hath dominion o'er — worlds,
 worms, 800
Empires, and superstitions. What has
 thought
To do with time, or place, or circumstance?
Wouldst thou behold the future? — ask
 and have!
Knock and it shall be opened — look, and
 lo!
The coming age is shadowed on the past
As on a glass.

MAHMUD

 Wild, wilder thoughts convulse
My spirit. Did not Mahomet the Second
Win Stamboul?

AHASUERUS

 Thou wouldst ask that giant spirit
The written fortunes of thy house and
 faith.
Thou wouldst cite one out of the grave to
 tell 810
How what was born in blood must die.

MAHMUD

 Thy words
Have power on me! I see —

AHASUERUS

 What hearest thou?

MAHMUD

A far whisper —
 Terrible silence.

AHASUERUS

What succeeds?

MAHMUD

The sound
As of the assault of an imperial city,
The hiss of inextinguishable fire,
The roar of giant cannon; the earth-quak-
ing
Fall of vast bastions and precipitous towers,
The shock of crags shot from strange en-
ginery,
The clash of wheels, and clang of armèd
hoofs 820
And crash of brazen mail, as of the wreck
Of adamantine mountains; the mad blast
Of trumpets, and the neigh of raging
steeds,
And shrieks of women whose thrill jars
the blood,
And one sweet laugh, most horrible to
hear,
As of a joyous infant waked, and playing
With its dead mother's breast; and now
more loud
The mingled battle-cry — ha! hear I not
Ἐν τούτῳ νίκη. Allah-illah-Allah!

AHASUERUS

The sulphurous mist is raised — thou
seest —

MAHMUD

A chasm,
As of two mountains, in the wall of Stam-
boul; 831
And in that ghastly breach the Islamites,
Like giants on the ruins of a world,
Stand in the light of sunrise. In the dust
Glimmers a kingless diadem, and one
Of regal port has cast himself beneath
The stream of war. Another proudly clad
In golden arms spurs a Tartarian barb
Into the gap, and with his iron mace
Directs the torrent of that tide of men, 840
And seems — he is — Mahomet!

AHASUERUS

What thou seest
Is but the ghost of thy forgotten dream;
A dream itself, yet less, perhaps, than that
Thou call'st reality. Thou mayst behold
How cities, on which empire sleeps en-
throned,
Bow their towered crests to mutability.

Poised by the flood, e'en on the height thou
holdest,
Thou mayst now learn how the full tide of
power
Ebbs to its depths. Inheritor of glory
Conceived in darkness, born in blood, and
nourished 850
With tears and toil, thou seest the mortal
throes
Of that whose birth was but the same.
The Past
Now stands before thee like an Incarnation
Of the To-come; yet wouldst thou commune
with
That portion of thyself which was ere thou
Didst start for this brief race whose crown
is death,
Dissolve with that strong faith and fervent
passion,
Which called it from the uncreated deep,
Yon cloud of war with its tempestuous
phantoms
Of raging death; and draw with mighty
will 860
The imperial shade hither.
 [Exit AHASUERUS.

MAHMUD

Approach!

PHANTOM

I come
Thence whither thou must go! The grave
is fitter
To take the living than give up the dead;
Yet has thy faith prevailed, and I am here.
The heavy fragments of the power which
fell
When I arose, like shapeless crags and
clouds,
Hang round my throne on the abyss, and
voices
Of strange lament soothe my supreme re-
pose,
Wailing for glory never to return.
A later empire nods in its decay; 870
The autumn of a greener faith is come;
And wolfish change, like winter, howls to
strip
The foliage in which Fame, the eagle,
built
Her aerie, while Dominion whelped below.
The storm is in its branches, and the frost
Is on its leaves, and the blank deep expects
Oblivion on oblivion, spoil on spoil,

Ruin on ruin. Thou art slow, my son;
The Anarchs of the world of darkness keep
A throne for thee, round which thine em-
　　pire lies　　　　　　　　　　　880
Boundless and mute; and for thy subjects
　　thou,
Like us, shalt rule the ghosts of murdered
　　life,
The phantoms of the powers who rule thee
　　now —
Mutinous passions and conflicting fears,
And hopes that sate themselves on dust and
　　die,
Stripped of their mortal strength, as thou
　　of thine.
Islam must fall, but we will reign together
Over its ruins in the world of death;
And if the trunk be dry, yet shall the seed
Unfold itself even in the shape of that　890
Which gathers birth in its decay. Woe!
　　Woe!
To the weak people tangled in the grasp
Of its last spasms!

MAHMUD

　　　　　　　Spirit, woe to all;
Woe to the wronged and the avenger!
　　Woe
To the destroyer, woe to the destroyed!
Woe to the dupe, and woe to the deceiver!
Woe to the oppressed, and woe to the op-
　　pressor!
Woe both to those that suffer and inflict;
Those who are born, and those who die!
　　But say,
Imperial shadow of the thing I am,　　900
When, how, by whom, Destruction must
　　accomplish
Her consummation?

PHANTOM

　　　　　　　Ask the cold pale Hour,
Rich in reversion of impending death,
When *he* shall fall upon whose ripe gray
　　hairs
Sit Care, and Sorrow, and Infirmity —
The weight which Crime, whose wings are
　　plumed with years,
Leaves in his flight from ravaged heart to
　　heart
Over the heads of men, under which bur-
　　den
They bow themselves unto the grave.
　　Fond wretch!
He leans upon his crutch, and talks of years

To come, and how in hours of youth re-
　　newed　　　　　　　　　　　911
He will renew lost joys, and —

VOICE (*without*)

　　　　　　　　Victory! victory!
　　　　　　　[*The Phantom vanishes.*

MAHMUD

What sound of the importunate earth has
　　broken
My mighty trance?

VOICE (*without*)

　　　　　　　　Victory! victory!

MAHMUD

Weak lightning before darkness! poor
　　faint smile
Of dying Islam! Voice which art the re-
　　sponse
Of hollow weakness! Do I wake and
　　live?
Were there such things? or may the un-
　　quiet brain,
Vexed by the wise mad talk of the old
　　Jew,
Have shaped itself these shadows of its
　　fear?　　　　　　　　　　　920
It matters not! — for nought we see or
　　dream,
Possess, or lose, or grasp at, can be worth
More than it gives or teaches. Come what
　　may,
The future must become the past, and I
As they were, to whom once this present
　　hour,
This gloomy crag of time to which I cling,
Seemed an Elysian isle of peace and joy
Never to be attained. — I must rebuke
This drunkenness of triumph ere it die,
And dying, bring despair. Victory! poor
　　slaves!　　　　　　　　　　930
　　　　　　　[*Exit* MAHMUD.

VOICE (*without*)

Shout in the jubilee of death! the Greeks
Are as a brood of lions in the net
Round which the kingly hunters of the
　　earth
Stand smiling. Anarchs, ye whose daily
　　food
Are curses, groans, and gold, the fruit of
　　death,
From Thule to the girdle of the world,

Come, feast ! the board groans with the
 flesh of men;
The cup is foaming with a nation's blood;
Famine and Thirst await ! eat, drink, and
 die !

SEMICHORUS I

Victorious Wrong, with vulture scream,
Salutes the risen sun, pursues the flying
 day ! 941
I saw her ghastly as a tyrant's dream,
Perch on the trembling pyramid of night,
Beneath which earth and all her realms
 pavilioned lay
In visions of the dawning undelight.
 Who shall impede her flight ?
 Who rob her of her prey ?

VOICE (*without*)

Victory, victory ! Russia's famished eagles
Dare not to prey beneath the crescent's
 light.
Impale the remnant of the Greeks ! de-
 spoil ! 950
Violate ! make their flesh cheaper than
 dust !

SEMICHORUS II

Thou voice which art
 The herald of the ill in splendor hid !
 Thou echo of the hollow heart
Of monarchy, bear me to thine abode
When desolation flashes o'er a world de-
 stroyed.
 Oh, bear me to those isles of jagged cloud
 Which float like mountains on the
 earthquake, mid 958
 The momentary oceans of the lightning;
 Or to some toppling promontory proud
 Of solid tempest, whose black pyramid,
 Riven, overhangs the founts intensely
 brightning
Of those dawn-tinted deluges of fire
Before their waves expire,
When heaven and earth are light, and only
 light
 In the thunder-night !

VOICE (*without*)

Victory, victory ! Austria, Russia, England,
And that tame serpent, that poor shadow,
 France,
Cry peace, and that means death when
 monarchs speak.
Ho, there ! bring torches, sharpen those
 red stakes ! 970

These chains are light, fitter for slaves and
 poisoners
Than Greeks. Kill, plunder, burn ! let
 none remain.

SEMICHORUS I

Alas for Liberty !
If numbers, wealth, or unfulfilling years,
 Or fate, can quell the free !
 Alas for Virtue ! when
Torments, or contumely, or the sneers
 Of erring judging men
Can break the heart where it abides !
Alas ! if Love, whose smile makes this ob-
 scure world splendid, 980
Can change, with its false times and tides,
 Like hope and terror —
 Alas for Love !
And Truth, who wanderest lone and unbe-
 friended,
If thou canst veil thy lie-consuming mir-
 ror
Before the dazzled eyes of Error,
Alas for thee ! Image of the Above !

SEMICHORUS II

Repulse, with plumes from conquest torn,
Led the ten thousand from the limits of
 the morn
 Through many an hostile Anarchy ! 990
At length they wept aloud and cried, 'the
 sea ! the sea !'
 Through exile, persecution, and despair,
 Rome was, and young Atlantis shall
 become,
 The wonder, or the terror, or the tomb,
Of all whose step wakes Power lulled in
 her savage lair.
 But Greece was as a hermit child,
 Whose fairest thoughts and limbs were
 built
 To woman's growth by dreams so mild
 She knew not pain or guilt;
And now, O Victory, blush ! and Empire,
 tremble, 1000
 When ye desert the free !
 If Greece must be
A wreck, yet shall its fragments reassem-
 ble,
And build themselves again impregnably
 In a diviner clime,
To Amphionic music, on some Cape sub-
 lime
Which frowns above the idle foam of
 time.

SEMICHORUS I

Let the tyrants rule the desert they have
 made;
 Let the free possess the paradise they
 claim;
Be the fortune of our fierce oppressors
 weighed 1010
 With our ruin, our resistance, and our
 name !

SEMICHORUS II

Our dead shall be the seed of their decay,
 Our survivors be the shadows of their
 pride,
Our adversity a dream to pass away, —
 Their dishonor a remembrance to abide !

VOICE (*without*)

Victory ! Victory ! the bought Briton sends
The keys of ocean to the Islamite.
Now shall the blazon of the cross be veiled,
And British skill, directing Othman might,
Thunder-strike rebel victory. Oh, keep
 holy 1020
This jubilee of unrevengèd blood !
Kill, crush, despoil ! Let not a Greek es-
 cape !

SEMICHORUS I

Darkness has dawned in the East
 On the noon of time;
The death birds descend to their feast,
 From the hungry clime.
Let Freedom and Peace flee far
 To a sunnier strand,
And follow Love's folding star
 To the Evening land ! 1030

SEMICHORUS II

The young moon has fed
 Her exhausted horn
With the sunset's fire;
 The weak day is dead,
 But the night is not born;
And, like loveliness panting with wild de
 sire,
While it trembles with fear and delight,
Hesperus flies from awakening night,
And pants in its beauty and speed with light
Fast-flashing, soft and bright. 1040
Thou beacon of love ! thou lamp of the free !
 Guide us far, far away,
To climes where now, veiled by the ardor
 of day,
 Thou art hidden

From waves on which weary Noon
Faints in her summer swoon,
Between kingless continents, sinless as
 Eden,
Around mountains and islands inviola-
 bly
Pranked on the sapphire sea.

SEMICHORUS I

Through the sunset of hope, 1050
Like the shapes of a dream,
What Paradise islands of glory gleam !
 Beneath Heaven's cope,
 Their shadows more clear float by;
The sound of their oceans, the light of
 their sky,
The music and fragrance their solitudes
 breathe,
Burst like morning on dream, or like Hea-
 ven on death,
 Through the walls of our prison;
 And Greece, which was dead, is arisen !

CHORUS

The world's great age begins anew, 1060
 The golden years return,
The earth doth like a snake renew
 Her winter weeds outworn;
Heaven smiles, and faiths and empires
 gleam,
Like wrecks of a dissolving dream.

A brighter Hellas rears its mountains
 From waves serener far;
A new Peneus rolls his fountains
 Against the morning-star.
Where fairer Tempes bloom, there sleep
Young Cyclads on a sunnier deep. 1071

A loftier Argo cleaves the main,
 Fraught with a later prize;
Another Orpheus sings again,
 And loves, and weeps, and dies.
A new Ulysses leaves once more
Calypso for his native shore.

Oh, write no more the tale of Troy,
 If earth Death's scroll must be !
Nor mix with Laian rage the joy 1080
 Which dawns upon the free;
Although a subtler Sphinx renew
Riddles of death Thebes never knew.

Another Athens shall arise,
 And to remoter time

Bequeath, like sunset to the skies,
 The splendor of its prime;
And leave, if nought so bright may live,
 All earth can take or Heaven can give.

Saturn and Love their long repose 1090
 Shall burst, more bright and good
Than all who fell, than One who rose,
 Than many unsubdued;

Not gold, not blood, their altar dowers,
But votive tears and symbol flowers.

Oh, cease ! must hate and death return ?
 Cease ! must men kill and die ?
Cease ! drain not to its dregs the urn
 Of bitter prophecy.
The world is weary of the past, 1100
Oh, might it die or rest at last !

MISCELLANEOUS POEMS

EARLY POEMS

1813–1815

The *Miscellaneous Poems*, with some exceptions, were published either by Shelley, in his successive volumes, or by Mrs. Shelley, in *Posthumous Poems*, 1824, and the two editions of 1839. A few first appeared elsewhere and were included in the collected editions by Mrs. Shelley, and still others have from time to time found their way to the public. The original issue of each poem is here stated in the introductory note, and its history so far as known is given. By far the greater portion of Shelley's shorter poems is personal, and many of them are addressed to his friends and companions or those who made up the domestic circle in his wanderings; even those which are most entirely poems of nature are, with few exceptions, charged with his moods, and governed by passing circumstances; as a whole, therefore, they require, for full understanding, intimacy with the events of his private life, and the reader must be referred to the *Life* of the poet for such a narrative as could not be condensed intelligibly into brief introductory notes, with respect both to persons and facts. Mrs. Shelley's biographical notes, however, have been largely used to preface the poems of each year because of their extraordinary truth to the feeling and atmosphere of Shelley's Italian life. The few political poems are sufficiently

explained by reference to current events; in most of these Shelley owes the manner to Coleridge's example.

Tradition has established *Queen Mab* at the head of Shelley's mature work, and in accordance with it all poems earlier than *Queen Mab* are included under *Juvenilia*. A more just sense would have given this honor to *Alastor*, and have relegated the poems of 1815 to the period of immaturity, to which with all the events relating to them they together with *Queen Mab* belong. It is, however, not deemed wise to attempt to disturb the traditionary arrangement at so late a time.

The Early Poems mainly relate to Shelley's domestic history. A few only show his political interest. Mrs. Shelley describes the summer of 1815 as one of rest, but it was exceptional, as these years were the most troubled of his life. Her record begins with 1815.

'He never spent a season more tranquilly than the summer of 1815. He had just recovered from a severe pulmonary attack; the weather was warm and pleasant. He lived near Windsor Forest, and his life was spent under its shades, or on the water; meditating subjects for verse. Hitherto, he had chiefly aimed at extending his political doctrines; and attempted so to do by appeals, in prose essays, to the people, exhorting them to claim their rights; but he had now begun to feel that the time for action was not ripe in England, and that the pen was the only instrument wherewith to prepare the way for better things.'

EVENING

TO HARRIET

Composed at Bracknell, July 31, 1813, for the birthday (August 1) of Harriet, his first wife, on the completion of her eighteenth year. Published by Dowden, *Life of Shelley*, 1887.

O THOU bright Sun ! beneath the dark blue line
 Of western distance that sublime descendest,
 And, gleaming lovelier as thy beams decline,
 Thy million hues to every vapor lendest,

And, over cobweb lawn and grove and
 stream
 Sheddest the liquid magic of thy light,
 Till calm Earth, with the parting splen-
 dor bright,
 Shows like the vision of a beauteous
 dream;
What gazer now with astronomic eye
 Could coldly count the spots within thy
 sphere ?
Such were thy lover, Harriet, could he fly
The thoughts of all that makes his passion
 dear,
 And, turning senseless from thy warm
 caress,
 Pick flaws in our close-woven happiness.

TO IANTHE

Elizabeth Ianthe, Shelley's first child, was
born June, 1813. Published by Dowden, *Life
of Shelley*, 1887.

I LOVE thee, Baby ! for thine own sweet
 sake;
 Those azure eyes, that faintly dimpled
 cheek,
 Thy tender frame, so eloquently weak,
 Love in the sternest heart of hate might
 wake;
But more when o'er thy fitful slumber
 bending
 Thy mother folds thee to her wakeful
 heart,
 Whilst love and pity, in her glances
 blending,
 All that thy passive eyes can feel im-
 part;
More, when some feeble lineaments of her,
 Who bore thy weight beneath her spot-
 less bosom,
 As with deep love I read thy face, re-
 cur, —
More dear art thou, O fair and fragile
 blossom;
 Dearest when most thy tender traits ex-
 press
 The image of thy mother's loveliness.

STANZA

WRITTEN AT BRACKNELL

The stanza apparently refers to Mrs. Boin-
ville, from whose house Shelley writes to Hogg,

March 16, 1814 : ' I have written nothing but
one stanza, which has no meaning, and that I
have only written in thought. This is the
vision of a delirious and distempered dream,
which passes away at the cold clear light of
morning. Its surpassing excellence and ex-
quisite perfections have no more reality than
the color of an autumnal sunset.' Published
by Hogg, *Life of Shelley*. 1858.

THY dewy looks sink in my breast;
 Thy gentle words stir poison there;
Thou hast disturbed the only rest
 That was the portion of despair !
Subdued to Duty's hard control,
 I could have borne my wayward lot:
The chains that bind this ruined soul
 Had cankered then — but crushed it not.

TO ——

ΔΑΚΡΥΣΙ ΔΙΟΙΣΩ ΠΟΤΜΟΝ ᾿ΑΠΟΤΜΟΝ.

Mrs. Shelley states that Coleridge is the per-
son addressed : ' The poem beginning " Oh,
there are spirits in the air " was addressed in
idea to Coleridge, whom he never knew ; and
at whose character he could only guess imper-
fectly, through his writings and accounts he
heard of him from some who knew him well.
He regarded his change of opinions as rather
an act of will than conviction, and believed
that in his inner heart he would be haunted by
what Shelley considered the better and holier
aspirations of his youth.' Dowden questions
' whether it was not rather addressed in a de-
spondent mood by Shelley to his own spirit.'
This suggestion was first advanced by Bertram
Dobell, in his reprint of *Alastor*, and supported
by the assent of Rossetti there given ; that it
is correct is reasonably certain. Published
with *Alastor*, 1816.

OH, there are spirits of the air,
 And genii of the evening breeze,
And gentle ghosts, with eyes as fair
 As star-beams among twilight trees !
Such lovely ministers to meet
Oft hast thou turned from men thy lonely
 feet.

With mountain winds, and babbling
 springs,
 And moonlight seas, that are the voice
Of these inexplicable things,
 Thou didst hold commune, and rejoice
When they did answer thee; but they
Cast, like a worthless boon, thy love away.

And thou hast sought in starry eyes
　　Beams that were never meant for
　　　thine,
Another's wealth; — tame sacrifice
　　To a fond faith ! still dost thou pine ?
Still dost thou hope that greeting hands,
Voice, looks or lips, may answer thy de-
　　　mands ?

Ah, wherefore didst thou build thine hope
　　On the false earth's inconstancy ?
Did thine own mind afford no scope
　　Of love, or moving thoughts to thee,
That natural scenes or human smiles
Could steal the power to wind thee in their
　　　wiles ?

Yes, all the faithless smiles are fled
　　Whose falsehood left thee broken-
　　　hearted;
The glory of the moon is dead;
　　Night's ghost and dreams have now
　　　departed;
Thine own soul still is true to thee,
But changed to a foul fiend through misery.

This fiend, whose ghastly presence ever
　　Beside thee like thy shadow hangs,
Dream not to chase; — the mad endeavor
　　Would scourge thee to severer pangs.
Be as thou art. Thy settled fate,
Dark as it is, all change would aggravate.

TO ——

This poem is placed conjecturally by Mrs.
Shelley with the poems of 1817; but Dowden
suggests that it was addressed to Mary Godwin
in June, 1814. Harriet answers as well or
better to the situation described. Published
by Mrs. Shelley, 2d ed., 1839.

YET look on me — take not thine eyes
　　away,
　　Which feed upon the love within mine
　　　own,
Which is indeed but the reflected ray
　　Of thine own beauty from my spirit
　　　thrown.
　　Yet speak to me — thy voice is as the
　　　tone
Of my heart's echo, and I think I hear
　　That thou yet lovest me; yet thou alone
Like one before a mirror, without care

Of aught but thine own features, imaged
　　there;
And yet I wear out life in watching thee;
　　A toil so sweet at times, and thou indeed
Art kind when I am sick, and pity me.

STANZAS. APRIL, 1814

Described by Dowden as ' a fragment of
transmuted biography ; ' he ascribes Shelley's
mood to his bidding farewell to the Boinvilles
on his return to his own home. The incident
that occasioned the verses has not been re-
corded. It was composed at Bracknell, and
published with *Alastor*, 1816.

AWAY ! the moor is dark beneath the moon,
　　Rapid clouds have drunk the last pale
　　　beam of even.
Away ! the gathering winds will call the
　　darkness soon,
　　And profoundest midnight shroud the
　　　serene lights of heaven.
Pause not ! the time is past ! every voice
　　cries, Away !
　　Tempt not with one last tear thy friend's
　　　ungentle mood;
Thy lover's eye, so glazed and cold, dares
　　not entreat thy stay;
　　Duty and dereliction guide thee back to
　　　solitude.

Away, away ! to thy sad and silent home;
　　Pour bitter tears on its desolated hearth;
Watch the dim shades as like ghosts they
　　go and come,
　　And complicate strange webs of melan-
　　　choly mirth.
The leaves of wasted autumn woods shall
　　float around thine head;
　　The blooms of dewy spring shall gleam
　　　beneath thy feet;
But thy soul or this world must fade in the
　　frost that binds the dead,
　　Ere midnight's frown and morning's
　　　smile, ere thou and peace, may meet.

The cloud-shadows of midnight possess
　　their own repose,
　　For the weary winds are silent, or the
　　　moon is in the deep;
Some respite to its turbulence unresting
　　ocean knows;
　　Whatever moves, or toils, or grieves,
　　　hath its appointed sleep.

Thou in the grave shalt rest — yet till the
 phantoms flee,
Which that house and heath and garden
 made dear to thee erewhile,
Thy remembrance, and repentance, and
 deep musings are not free
From the music of two voices, and the
 light of one sweet smile.

TO HARRIET

Dowden, who published the poem in *Life of
Shelley*, 1887, describes it as ' the first of a few
[five] short pieces added in Harriet's hand-
writing to the MS. collection of poems pre-
pared for publication in the early days of the
preceding year.' It was composed in May,
1814.

THY look of love has power to calm
 The stormiest passion of my soul;
Thy gentle words are drops of balm
 In life's too bitter bowl;
No grief is mine, but that alone
These choicest blessings I have known.

Harriet ! if all who long to live
 In the warm sunshine of thine eye,
That price beyond all pain must give, —
 Beneath thy scorn to die;
Then hear thy chosen own too late
His heart most worthy of thy hate.

Be thou, then, one among mankind
 Whose heart is harder not for state,
Thou only virtuous, gentle, kind,
 Amid a world of hate;
And by a slight endurance seal
A fellow-being's lasting weal.

For pale with anguish is his cheek,
 His breath comes fast, his eyes are dim,
Thy name is struggling ere he speak,
 Weak is each trembling limb;
In mercy let him not endure
The misery of a fatal cure.

Oh, trust for once no erring guide !
 Bid the remorseless feeling flee;
'T is malice, 't is revenge, 't is pride,
 'T is anything but thee;
Oh, deign a nobler pride to prove,
And pity if thou canst not love.

TO MARY WOLLSTONECRAFT GODWIN

Composed in June, 1814, and published by
Mrs. Shelley, *Posthumous Poems*, 1824.

I

MINE eyes were dim with tears unshed;
 Yes, I was firm — thus wert not thou;
My baffled looks did fear yet dread
 To meet thy looks — I could not know
How anxiously they sought to shine
With soothing pity upon mine.

II

To sit and curb the soul's mute rage
 Which preys upon itself alone;
To curse the life which is the cage
 Of fettered grief that dares not groan,
Hiding from many a careless eye
The scornèd load of agony;

III

Whilst thou alone, then not regarded,
 The thou alone should be, —
To spend years thus, and be rewarded,
 As thou, sweet love, requited me
When none were near — Oh, I did wake
From torture for that moment's sake.

IV

Upon my heart thy accents sweet
 Of peace and pity fell like dew
On flowers half dead; thy lips did meet
 Mine tremblingly; thy dark eyes threw
Their soft persuasion on my brain,
Charming away its dream of pain.

V

We are not happy, sweet ! our state
 Is strange and full of doubt and fear;
More need of words that ills abate; —
 Reserve or censure come not near
Our sacred friendship, lest there be
No solace left for thee and me.

VI

Gentle and good and mild thou art,
 Nor can I live if thou appear
Aught but thyself, or turn thine heart
 Away from me, or stoop to wear
The mask of scorn, although it be
To hide the love thou feel'st for me.

MUTABILITY

Published with *Alastor*, 1816.

WE are as clouds that veil the midnight
 moon;
 How restlessly they speed, and gleam,
 and quiver,
Streaking the darkness radiantly! — yet
 soon
 Night closes round, and they are lost
 forever:

Or like forgotten lyres whose dissonant
 strings
 Give various response to each varying
 blast,
To whose frail frame no second motion
 brings
 One mood or modulation like the last.

We rest — a dream has power to poison
 sleep;
 We rise — one wandering thought pol-
 lutes the day;
We feel, conceive or reason, laugh or weep;
 Embrace fond woe, or cast our cares
 away:

It is the same! — for, be it joy or sorrow,
 The path of its departure still is free;
Man's yesterday may ne'er be like his
 morrow;
 Nought may endure but Mutability.

ON DEATH

Published with *Alastor*, 1816. An earlier
version is among the Esdaile MSS. in the collec-
tion Shelley intended to issue with *Queen Mab*
in 1813, and the poem is the only one preserved
by him out of that collection.

There is no work, nor device, nor knowledge, nor
wisdom, in the grave, whither thou goest. — ECCLESI-
ASTES.

THE pale, the cold, and the moony smile
 Which the meteor beam of a starless
 night
Sheds on a lonely and sea-girt isle,
 Ere the dawning of morn's undoubted
 light,
Is the flame of life so fickle and wan
That flits round our steps till their strength
 is gone.

O man! hold thee on in courage of soul
 Through the stormy shades of thy
 worldly way,
And the billows of cloud that around thee
 roll
 Shall sleep in the light of a wondrous
 day,
Where hell and heaven shall leave thee
 free
To the universe of destiny.

This world is the nurse of all we know,
 This world is the mother of all we feel;
And the coming of death is a fearful blow
 To a brain unencompassed with nerves of
 steel,
When all that we know, or feel, or see,
Shall pass like an unreal mystery.

The secret things of the grave are there,
 Where all but this frame must surely be,
Though the fine-wrought eye and the won-
 drous ear
 No longer will live to hear or to see
All that is great and all that is strange
In the boundless realm of unending
 change.

Who telleth a tale of unspeaking death?
 Who lifteth the veil of what is to come?
Who painteth the shadows that are beneath
 The wide-winding caves of the peopled
 tomb?
Or uniteth the hopes of what shall be
With the fears and the love for that which
 we see?

A SUMMER EVENING CHURCH-
YARD

LECHLADE, GLOUCESTERSHIRE

Composed September, 1815, while on a voy-
age up the Thames with Peacock. Published
with *Alastor*, 1816.

THE wind has swept from the wide atmo-
 sphere
 Each vapor that obscured the sunset's
 ray;
And pallid Evening twines its beaming
 hair
 In duskier braids around the languid
 eyes of Day.

Silence and Twilight, unbeloved of men,
Creep hand in hand from yon obscurest
glen.

They breathe their spells toward the de-
parting day,
Encompassing the earth, air, stars and
sea;
Light, sound and motion own the potent
sway,
Responding to the charm with its own
mystery.
The winds are still, or the dry church-
tower grass
Knows not their gentle motions as they
pass.

Thou too, aërial Pile, whose pinnacles
Point from one shrine like pyramids of
fire,
Obeyest in silence their sweet solemn
spells,
Clothing in hues of heaven thy dim and
distant spire,
Around whose lessening and invisible
height
Gather among the stars the clouds of
night.

The dead are sleeping in their sepulchres;
And, mouldering as they sleep, a thrill-
ing sound,
Half sense, half thought, among the dark-
ness stirs,
Breathed from their wormy beds all liv-
ing things around;
And mingling with the still night and
mute sky
Its awful hush is felt inaudibly.

Thus solemnized and softened, death is
mild
And terrorless as this serenest night;
Here could I hope, like some inquiring child
Sporting on graves, that death did hide
from human sight
Sweet secrets, or beside its breathless sleep
That loveliest dreams perpetual watch did
keep.

TO WORDSWORTH

This poem reflects the contemporary feeling
of the radicals toward Wordsworth's conserva-
tive politics. Published with *Alastor*, 1816.

Poet of Nature, thou hast wept to know
That things depart which never may re-
turn;
Childhood and youth, friendship and
love's first glow,
Have fled like sweet dreams, leaving thee
to mourn.
These common woes I feel. One loss is
mine,
Which thou too feel'st, yet I alone de-
plore;
Thou wert as a lone star whose light did
shine
On some frail bark in winter's midnight
roar;
Thou hast like to a rock-built refuge
stood
Above the blind and battling multitude;
In honored poverty thy voice did weave
Songs consecrate to truth and liberty; —
Deserting these, thou leavest me to
grieve,
Thus having been, that thou shouldst
cease to be.

FEELINGS OF A REPUBLICAN ON THE FALL OF BONAPARTE

Published with *Alastor*, 1816.

I hated thee, fallen tyrant! I did groan
To think that a most unambitious slave,
Like thou, shouldst dance and revel on
the grave
Of Liberty. Thou mightst have built
thy throne
Where it had stood even now: thou didst
prefer
A frail and bloody pomp which time has
swept
In fragments towards oblivion. Massa-
cre,
For this I prayed, would on thy sleep
have crept,
Treason and Slavery, Rapine, Fear, and
Lust,
And stifled thee, their minister. I know
Too late, since thou and France are in
the dust,
That Virtue owns a more eternal foe
Than Force or Fraud: old Custom,
Legal Crime,
And bloody Faith, the foulest birth of
time.

LINES

This poem apparently refers to the death of
Harriet, in November, 1816, and was published
by Hunt in *The Literary Pocket-Book*, 1823.

THE cold earth slept below;
 Above the cold sky shone;
 And all around,
 With a chilling sound,
From caves of ice and fields of snow
The breath of night like death did flow
 Beneath the sinking moon.

The wintry hedge was black;
 The green grass was not seen;
 The birds did rest
 On the bare thorn's breast,
Whose roots, beside the pathway track,
Had bound their folds o'er many a crack
 Which the frost had made between.

Thine eyes glowed in the glare
 Of the moon's dying light;
 As a fen-fire's beam
 On a sluggish stream
Gleams dimly — so the moon shone there,
And it yellowed the strings of thy tangled
 hair,
 That shook in the wind of night.

The moon made thy lips pale, belovèd;
 The wind made thy bosom chill;
 The night did shed
 On thy dear head
Its frozen dew, and thou didst lie
Where the bitter breath of the naked sky
 Might visit thee at will.

POEMS WRITTEN IN 1816

THE SUNSET

This poem seems to contain elements of
memory as well as of imagination. It was
composed at Bishopsgate in the spring, and
published in part by Hunt, *The Literary
Pocket-Book*, 1823, and entire by Mrs. Shelley, *Posthumous Poems*, 1824.

THERE late was One within whose subtle
 being,
As light and wind within some delicate
 cloud

That fades amid the blue noon's burning
 sky,
Genius and death contended. None may
 know
The sweetness of the joy which made his
 breath
Fail, like the trances of the summer air,
When, with the lady of his love, who then
First knew the unreserve of mingled being,
He walked along the pathway of a field,
Which to the east a hoar wood shadowed
 o'er, 10
But to the west was open to the sky.
There now the sun had sunk; but lines of
 gold
Hung on the ashen clouds, and on the
 points
Of the far level grass and nodding flowers,
And the old dandelion's hoary beard,
And, mingled with the shades of twilight,
 lay
On the brown massy woods; and in the
 east
The broad and burning moon lingeringly
 rose
Between the black trunks of the crowded
 trees,
While the faint stars were gathering over-
 head. 20
'Is it not strange, Isabel,' said the youth,
'I never saw the sun? We will walk here
To-morrow; thou shalt look on it with me.'

That night the youth and lady mingled lay
In love and sleep; but when the morning
 came
The lady found her lover dead and cold.
Let none believe that God in mercy gave
That stroke. The lady died not, nor grew
 wild, 28
But year by year lived on; in truth I think
Her gentleness and patience and sad smiles,
And that she did not die, but lived to tend
Her aged father, were a kind of madness,
If madness 't is to be unlike the world.
For but to see her were to read the tale
Woven by some subtlest bard to make
 hard hearts
Dissolve away in wisdom-working grief.
Her eyes were black and lustreless and wan,
Her eyelashes were worn away with tears,
Her lips and cheeks were like things dead
 — so pale;
Her hands were thin, and through their
 wandering veins 40

And weak articulations might be seen
Day's ruddy light. The tomb of thy dead
 self
Which one vexed ghost inhabits, night and
 day,
Is all, lost child, that now remains of
 thee !

'Inheritor of more than earth can give,
Passionless calm and silence unreproved, —
Whether the dead find, oh, not sleep, but
 rest,
And are the uncomplaining things they
 seem,
Or live, or drop in the deep sea of Love;
Oh, that, like thine, mine epitaph were —
 Peace !' 50
This was the only moan she ever made.

HYMN TO INTELLECTUAL BEAUTY

Composed in Switzerland, where Shelley
spent the summer, and conceived, Mrs. Shelley
says, during his voyage round the Lake of Ge-
neva with Lord Byron. It was published by
Hunt, *The Examiner*, 1817.

I

THE awful shadow of some unseen Power
 Floats though unseen among us, visit-
 ing
 This various world with as inconstant
 wing
As summer winds that creep from flower
 to flower;
Like moonbeams that behind some piny
 mountain shower,
 It visits with inconstant glance
 Each human heart and countenance;
Like hues and harmonies of evening,
 Like clouds in starlight widely spread,
 Like memory of music fled,
 Like aught that for its grace may
 be
Dear, and yet dearer for its mystery.

II

Spirit of Beauty, that dost consecrate
 With thine own hues all thou dost
 shine upon
 Of human thought or form, where art
 thou gone ?
Why dost thou pass away, and leave our
 state,

This dim vast vale of tears, vacant and
 desolate ? —
 Ask why the sunlight not forever
 Weaves rainbows o'er yon mountain
 river;
Why aught should fail and fade that
 once is shown;
 Why fear and dream and death and
 birth
 Cast on the daylight of this earth
 Such gloom; why man has such a
 scope
For love and hate, despondency and
 hope.

III

No voice from some sublimer world hath
 ever
 To sage or poet these responses given;
 Therefore the names of Demon, Ghost
 and Heaven,
Remain the records of their vain en-
 deavor —
Frail spells, whose uttered charm might
 not avail to sever,
 From all we hear and all we see,
 Doubt, chance and mutability.
Thy light alone, like mist o'er mountains
 driven,
 Or music by the night wind sent
 Through strings of some still instru-
 ment,
 Or moonlight on a midnight stream,
Gives grace and truth to life's unquiet
 dream.

IV

Love, Hope and Self-esteem, like clouds,
 depart,
 And come, for some uncertain mo-
 ments lent.
 Man were immortal and omnipotent,
Didst thou, unknown and awful as thou
 art,
Keep with thy glorious train firm state
 within his heart.
 Thou messenger of sympathies
 That wax and wane in lovers' eyes !
Thou, that to human thought art nourish-
 ment,
 Like darkness to a dying flame,
 Depart not as thy shadow came !
 Depart not, lest the grave should
 be,
Like life and fear, a dark reality !

V

While yet a boy I sought for ghosts, and
 sped
 Through many a listening chamber,
 cave and ruin,
 And starlight wood, with fearful steps
 pursuing
Hopes of high talk with the departed
 dead;
I called on poisonous names with which our
 youth is fed.
 I was not heard — I saw them not —
 When, musing deeply on the lot
Of life, at that sweet time when winds
 are wooing
 All vital things that wake to bring
 News of birds and blossoming, —
 Sudden thy shadow fell on me;
I shrieked, and clasped my hands in
 ecstasy!

VI

I vowed that I would dedicate my
 powers
 To thee and thine — have I not kept
 the vow?
 With beating heart and streaming
 eyes, even now
I call the phantoms of a thousand hours
Each from his voiceless grave: they have
 in visioned bowers
 Of studious zeal or love's delight
 Outwatched with me the envious
 night —
 They know that never joy illumed my
 brow
 Unlinked with hope that thou wouldst
 free
 This world from its dark slavery, —
 That thou, O awful Loveliness,
Wouldst give whate'er these words can-
 not express.

VII

The day becomes more solemn and
 serene
 When noon is past; there is a harmony
 In autumn, and a lustre in its sky,
 Which through the summer is not heard
 or seen,
As if it could not be, as if it had not been!
 Thus let thy power, which like the
 truth
 Of nature on my passive youth
 Descended, to my onward life supply

Its calm, — to one who worships thee,
And every form containing thee,
 Whom, Spirit fair, thy spells did bind
To fear himself, and love all humankind.

MONT BLANC

LINES WRITTEN IN THE VALE OF CHA-
MOUNI

'The poem,' Shelley writes, in his Preface to
History of a Six Weeks Tour, 1817, where it
appeared, 'was composed under the immediate
impression of the deep and powerful feelings
excited by the objects which it attempts to de-
scribe; and, as an undisciplined overflowing of
the soul, rests its claim to approbation on an
attempt to imitate the untamable wildness and
inaccessible solemnity from which those feel-
ings sprang.'
 The, 'objects' referred to, Mrs. Shelley
notes, were Mont Blanc and 'its surrounding
peaks and valleys, as he lingered on the Bridge
of Arve on his way through the Valley of
Chamouni.'

I

THE everlasting universe of things
Flows through the mind, and rolls its rapid
 waves,
Now dark, now glittering, now reflecting
 gloom,
Now lending splendor, where from secret
 springs
The source of human thought its tribute
 brings
Of waters, — with a sound but half its own,
Such as a feeble brook will oft assume
In the wild woods, among the mountains
 lone,
Where waterfalls around it leap forever,
Where woods and winds contend, and a
 vast river 10
Over its rocks ceaselessly bursts and raves.

II

Thus thou, Ravine of Arve — dark, deep
 Ravine —
Thou many-colored, many-voicèd vale,
Over whose pines, and crags, and caverns
 sail
Fast cloud-shadows, and sunbeams! awful
 scene,
Where Power in likeness of the Arve comes
 down
From the ice-gulfs that gird his secret throne,

Bursting through these dark mountains like
 the flame
Of lightning through the tempest! thou
 dost lie, —
Thy giant brood of pines around thee cling-
 ing, 20
Children of elder time, in whose devotion
The chainless winds still come and ever
 came
To drink their odors, and their mighty
 swinging
To hear — an old and solemn harmony;
Thine earthly rainbows stretched across the
 sweep
Of the ethereal waterfall, whose veil
Robes some unsculptured image; the
 strange sleep
Which when the voices of the desert fail
Wraps all in its own deep eternity;
Thy caverns echoing to the Arve's commo-
 tion — 30
A loud, lone sound no other sound can
 tame.
Thou art pervaded with that ceaseless mo-
 tion,
Thou art the path of that unresting sound,
Dizzy Ravine! and when I gaze on thee,
I seem as in a trance sublime and strange
To muse on my own separate fantasy,
My own, my human mind, which passively
Now renders and receives fast influencings,
Holding an unremitting interchange
With the clear universe of things around;
One legion of wild thoughts, whose wan-
 dering wings 41
Now float above thy darkness, and now
 rest,
Where that or thou art no unbidden guest,
In the still cave of the witch Poesy,
Seeking among the shadows that pass by —
Ghosts of all things that are — some shade
 of thee,
Some phantom, some faint image; till the
 breast
From which they fled recalls them, thou
 art there!

III

Some say that gleams of a remoter world
Visit the soul in sleep, — that death is
 slumber, 50
And that its shapes the busy thoughts out-
 number
Of those who wake and live. I look on
 high;

Has some unknown Omnipotence unfurled
The veil of life and death? or do I lie
In dream, and does the mightier world of
 sleep
Spread far around and inaccessibly
Its circles? for the very spirit fails,
Driven like a homeless cloud from steep to
 steep
That vanishes among the viewless gales!
Far, far above, piercing the infinite sky, 60
Mont Blanc appears, — still, snowy and
 serene —
Its subject mountains their unearthly forms
Pile around it, ice and rock; broad vales
 between
Of frozen floods, unfathomable deeps,
Blue as the overhanging heaven, that spread
And wind among the accumulated steeps;
A desert peopled by the storms alone,
Save when the eagle brings some hunter's
 bone,
And the wolf tracks her there. How hid-
 eously
Its shapes are heaped around! rude, bare
 and high, 70
Ghastly, and scarred, and riven. — Is this
 the scene
Where the old Earthquake-dæmon taught
 her young
Ruin? Were these their toys? or did a
 sea
Of fire envelop once this silent snow?
None can reply — all seems eternal now.
The wilderness has a mysterious tongue
Which teaches awful doubt, or faith so
 mild,
So solemn, so serene, that man may be
But for such faith with Nature reconciled;
Thou hast a voice, great Mountain, to re-
 peal 80
Large codes of fraud and woe; not under-
 stood
By all, but which the wise, and great, and
 good,
Interpret, or make felt, or deeply feel.

IV

The fields, the lakes, the forests and the
 streams,
Ocean, and all the living things that dwell
Within the dædal earth, lightning, and
 rain,
Earthquake, and fiery flood, and hurricane,
The torpor of the year when feeble dreams
Visit the hidden buds or dreamless sleep

Holds every future leaf and flower, the
 bound 90
With which from that detested trance they
 leap,
The works and ways of man, their death
 and birth,
And that of him and all that his may be, —
All things that move and breathe with toil
 and sound
Are born and die, revolve, subside and
 swell;
Power dwells apart in its tranquillity,
Remote, serene, and inaccessible; —
And *this*, the naked countenance of earth
On which I gaze, even these primeval
 mountains,
Teach the adverting mind. The glaciers
 creep, 100
Like snakes that watch their prey, from
 their far fountains,
Slow rolling on; there many a precipice
Frost and the Sun in scorn of mortal power
Have piled — dome, pyramid and pinnacle,
A city of death, distinct with many a tower
And wall impregnable of beaming ice;
Yet not a city, but a flood of ruin
Is there, that from the boundaries of the
 sky
Rolls its perpetual stream; vast pines are
 strewing
Its destined path, or in the mangled soil
Branchless and shattered stand; the rocks,
 drawn down 111
From yon remotest waste, have overthrown
The limits of the dead and living world,
Never to be reclaimed. The dwelling-place
Of insects, beasts and birds, becomes its
 spoil,
Their food and their retreat forever gone;
So much of life and joy is lost. The race
Of man flies far in dread; his work and
 dwelling

Vanish, like smoke before the tempest's
 stream,
And their place is not known. Below,
 vast caves 120
Shine in the rushing torrents' restless
 gleam,
Which from those secret chasms in tumult
 welling
Meet in the Vale; and one majestic River,
The breath and blood of distant lands, for-
 ever
Rolls its loud waters to the ocean waves,
Breathes its swift vapors to the circling air.

V

Mont Blanc yet gleams on high: the power
 is there,
The still and solemn power of many sights
And many sounds, and much of life and
 death.
In the calm darkness of the moonless
 nights, 130
In the lone glare of day, the snows descend
Upon that Mountain; none beholds them
 there,
Nor when the flakes burn in the sinking sun,
Or the star-beams dart through them;
 winds contend
Silently there, and heap the snow, with
 breath
Rapid and strong, but silently ! Its home
The voiceless lightning in these solitudes
Keeps innocently, and like vapor broods
Over the snow. The secret strength of
 things,
Which governs thought, and to the infinite
 dome 140
Of heaven is as a law, inhabits thee !
And what were thou, and earth, and stars,
 and sea,
If to the human mind's imaginings
Silence and solitude were vacancy ?

POEMS WRITTEN IN 1817

Mrs. Shelley, in her note on the poems of
this year, summarizes Shelley's life at the time :
'The very illness that oppressed, and the as-
pect of death which had approached so near
Shelley, appears to have kindled to yet keener
life the spirit of poetry in his heart. The rest-
less thoughts kept awake by pain clothed
themselves in verse. Much was composed dur-
ing this year. *The Revolt of Islam*, written
and printed, was a great effort — *Rosalind and*

Helen was begun — and the fragments and
poems I can trace to the same period, show
how full of passion and reflection were his sol-
itary hours.

.

'His readings this year were chiefly Greek.
Besides the Hymns of Homer and the Iliad,
he read the Dramas of Æschylus and Sopho-
cles, the Symposium of Plato, and Arrian's
Historia Indica. In Latin, Apuleius alone is

named. In English, the Bible was his constant study ; he read a great portion of it aloud in the evening. Among these evening readings, I find also mentioned the Faëry Queen ; and other modern works, the production of his contemporaries, Coleridge, Wordsworth, Moore, and Byron.

' His life was now spent more in thought than action — he had lost the eager spirit which believed it could achieve what it projected for the benefit of mankind. And yet in the converse of daily life Shelley was far from being a melancholy man. He was eloquent when philosophy, or politics, or taste were the subjects of conversation. He was playful — and indulged in the wild spirit that mocked itself and others — not in bitterness, but in sport. The Author of *Nightmare Abbey* [Peacock] seized on some points of his character and some habits

of his life when he painted *Scythrop*. He was not addicted to " port or madeira," but in youth he had read of " Illuminati and Eleutherarchs," and believed that he possessed the power of operating an immediate change in the minds of men and the state of society. These wild dreams had faded ; sorrow and adversity had struck home ; but he struggled with despondency as he did with physical pain. There are few who remember him sailing paper boats, and watching the navigation of his tiny craft with eagerness — or repeating with wild energy *The Ancient Mariner*, and Southey's *Old Woman of Berkeley* — but those who do, will recollect that it was in such, and in the creations of his own fancy, when that was most daring and ideal, that he sheltered himself from the storms and disappointments, the pain and sorrow, that beset his life.'

MARIANNE'S DREAM

The dream here put into verse was told Shelley by Mrs. Hunt, the ' Marianne ' of the poem. It was composed at Marlow, and published by Hunt, *The Literary Pocket-Book*, 1819.

I

A PALE dream came to a Lady fair,
 And said, ' A boon, a boon, I pray !
I know the secrets of the air;
 And things are lost in the glare of day,
Which I can make the sleeping see,
If they will put their trust in me.

II

' And thou shalt know of things unknown,
 If thou wilt let me rest between
The veiny lids whose fringe is thrown
 Over thine eyes so dark and sheen.'
And half in hope and half in fright
The Lady closed her eyes so bright.

III

At first all deadly shapes were driven
 Tumultuously across her sleep,
And o'er the vast cope of bending heaven
 All ghastly-visaged clouds did sweep;
And the Lady ever looked to spy
If the golden sun shone forth on high.

IV

And, as towards the east she turned,
 She saw aloft in the morning air,
Which now with hues of sunrise burned,
 A great black Anchor rising there;

And, wherever the Lady turned her eyes,
It hung before her in the skies.

V

The sky was blue as the summer sea,
 The depths were cloudless overhead,
The air was calm as it could be,
 There was no sight or sound of dread,
But that black Anchor floating still
Over the piny eastern hill.

VI

The Lady grew sick with a weight of
 fear
 To see that Anchor ever hanging,
And veiled her eyes; she then did hear
 The sound as of a dim low clanging,
And looked abroad if she might know
Was it aught else, or but the flow
Of the blood in her own veins, to and
 fro.

VII

There was a mist in the sunless air,
 Which shook as it were with an earthquake's shock,
But the very weeds that blossomed there
 Were moveless, and each mighty rock
Stood on its basis steadfastly;
The Anchor was seen no more on high.

VIII

But piled around, with summits hid
 In lines of cloud at intervals,
Stood many a mountain pyramid,
 Among whose everlasting walls

Two mighty cities shone, and ever
Through the red mist their domes did
 quiver.

IX

On two dread mountains, from whose
 crest
 Might seem the eagle for her brood
Would ne'er have hung her dizzy nest,
 Those tower-encircled cities stood.
A vision strange such towers to see,
Sculptured and wrought so gorgeously,
Where human art could never be.

X

And columns framed of marble white,
 And giant fanes, dome over dome
Piled, and triumphant gates, all bright
 With workmanship, which could not come
From touch of mortal instrument,
Shot o'er the vales, or lustre lent
From its own shapes magnificent.

XI

But still the Lady heard that clang
 Filling the wide air far away;
And still the mist whose light did hang
 Among the mountains shook alway;
So that the Lady's heart beat fast,
As, half in joy and half aghast,
On those high domes her look she cast.

XII

Sudden from out that city sprung
 A light that made the earth grow red;
Two flames that each with quivering
 tongue
 Licked its high domes, and overhead
Among those mighty towers and fanes
Dropped fire, as a volcano rains
Its sulphurous ruin on the plains.

XIII

And hark ! a rush, as if the deep
 Had burst its bonds; she looked behind,
And saw over the western steep
 A raging flood descend, and wind
Through that wide vale; she felt no fear,
But said within herself, ' 'T is clear
These towers are Nature's own, and she
To save them has sent forth the sea.'

XIV

And now those raging billows came
 Where that fair Lady sate, and she

Was borne towards the showering flame
 By the wild waves heaped tumultuously;
And, on a little plank, the flow
Of the whirlpool bore her to and fro.

XV

The flames were fiercely vomited
 From every tower and every dome,
And dreary light did widely shed
 O'er that vast flood's suspended foam,
Beneath the smoke which hung its night
On the stained cope of heaven's light.

XVI

The plank whereon that Lady sate
 Was driven through the chasms, about
 and about,
Between the peaks so desolate
 Of the drowning mountains, in and out,
As the thistle-beard on a whirlwind sails —
While the flood was filling those hollow
 vales.

XVII

At last her plank an eddy crossed,
 And bore her to the city's wall,
Which now the flood had reached almost;
 It might the stoutest heart appall
To hear the fire roar and hiss
Through the domes of those mighty
 palaces.

XVIII

The eddy whirled her round and round
 Before a gorgeous gate, which stood
Piercing the clouds of smoke which bound
 Its aëry arch with light like blood;
She looked on that gate of marble clear
With wonder that extinguished fear;

XIX

For it was filled with sculptures rarest,
 Of forms most beautiful and strange,
Like nothing human, but the fairest
 Of wingèd shapes, whose legions range
Throughout the sleep of those that are,
Like this same Lady, good and fair.

XX

And as she looked, still lovelier grew
 Those marble forms; — the sculptor sure
Was a strong spirit, and the hue
 Of his own mind did there endure,
After the touch, whose power had braided
Such grace, was in some sad change faded.

XXI

She looked, — the flames were dim, the
 flood
 Grew tranquil as a woodland river
Winding through hills in solitude;
 Those marble shapes then seemed to
 quiver,
And their fair limbs to float in motion,
Like weeds unfolding in the ocean;

XXII

And their lips moved; one seemed to
 speak,
 When suddenly the mountains cracked,
And through the chasm the flood did
 break
With an earth-uplifting cataract;
The statues gave a joyous scream,
And on its wings the pale thin dream
Lifted the Lady from the stream.

XXIII

The dizzy flight of that phantom pale
 Waked the fair Lady from her sleep,
And she arose, while from the veil
 Of her dark eyes the dream did creep;
And she walked about as one who knew
That sleep has sights as clear and true
As any waking eyes can view.

TO CONSTANTIA

SINGING

This poem was addressed to Miss Clairmont,
and the name *Constantia* was probably due to
Shelley's admiration for the character of *Con-
stantia Dudley*, in Charles Brockden Brown's
Ormond. It was published by Mrs. Shelley,
Posthumous Poems, 1824.

I

Thus to be lost and thus to sink and die,
 Perchance were death indeed ! — Con-
 stantia, turn !
In thy dark eyes a power like light doth
 lie,
 Even though the sounds which were thy
 voice, which burn
Between thy lips, are laid to sleep;
 Within thy breath, and on thy hair, like
 odor it is yet,
And from thy touch like fire doth leap.
 Even while I write, my burning cheeks
 are wet —

Alas, that the torn heart can bleed, but
 not forget !

II

A breathless awe, like the swift change
 Unseen but felt in youthful slumbers,
Wild, sweet, but uncommunicably strange,
 Thou breathest now in fast ascending
 numbers.
The cope of heaven seems rent and cloven
 By the enchantment of thy strain;
And on my shoulders wings are woven
 To follow its sublime career
Beyond the mighty moons that wane
 Upon the verge of Nature's utmost
 sphere,
 Till the world's shadowy walls are passed
 and disappear.

III

Her voice is hovering o'er my soul — it
 lingers
 O'ershadowing it with soft and lulling
 wings;
The blood and life within those snowy
 fingers
 Teach witchcraft to the instrumental
 strings.
My brain is wild, my breath comes
 quick —
 The blood is listening in my frame,
And thronging shadows, fast and thick,
 Fall on my overflowing eyes;
My heart is quivering like a flame;
 As morning dew, that in the sunbeam
 dies,
 I am dissolved in these consuming
 ecstasies.

IV

I have no life, Constantia, now, but thee,
 Whilst, like the world-surrounding air,
 thy song
Flows on, and fills all things with mel-
 ody.
 Now is thy voice a tempest swift and
 strong,
On which, like one in trance upborne,
 Secure o'er rocks and waves I sweep,
Rejoicing like a cloud of morn;
 Now 't is the breath of summer night,
Which, when the starry waters sleep,
Round western isles, with incense-blossoms
 bright,
Lingering, suspends my soul in its voluptu-
 ous flight.

TO THE LORD CHANCELLOR

The decree which deprived Shelley of the custody of his children was pronounced in August. Mrs. Shelley writes: 'His heart, attuned to every kindly affection, was full of burning love for his offspring. No words can express the anguish he felt when his elder children were torn from him. In his first resentment against the Chancellor, on the passing of the decree, he had written a curse, in which there breathes, besides haughty indignation, all the tenderness of a father's love, which could imagine and fondly dwell upon its loss and the consequences.' It was published by Mrs. Shelley, in her first collected edition, 1839.

I

THY country's curse is on thee, darkest crest
 Of that foul, knotted, many-headed worm
Which rends our Mother's bosom! —
 Priestly Pest!
 Masked Resurrection of a buried Form!

II

Thy country's curse is on thee! Justice sold,
 Truth trampled, Nature's landmarks overthrown,
And heaps of fraud-accumulated gold,
 Plead, loud as thunder, at Destruction's throne.

III

And, whilst that sure slow Angel, which aye stands
 Watching the beck of Mutability,
Delays to execute her high commands,
 And, though a nation weeps, spares thine and thee,

IV

Oh, let a father's curse be on thy soul,
 And let a daughter's hope be on thy tomb;
Be both, on thy gray head, a leaden cowl
 To weigh thee down to thine approaching doom!

V

I curse thee! By a parent's outraged love,
 By hopes long cherished and too lately lost, —

By gentle feelings thou couldst never prove,
 By griefs which thy stern nature never crossed;

VI

By those infantine smiles of happy light,
 Which were a fire within a stranger's hearth,
Quenched even when kindled, — in untimely night,
 Hiding the promise of a lovely birth;

VII

By those unpractised accents of young speech,
 Which he who is a father thought to frame
To gentlest lore, such as the wisest teach —
 Thou strike the lyre of mind! — oh, grief and shame!

VIII

By all the happy see in children's growth,
 That undeveloped flower of budding years —
Sweetness and sadness interwoven both,
 Source of the sweetest hopes and saddest fears —

IX

By all the days under an hireling's care,
 Of dull constraint and bitter heaviness, —
Oh, wretched ye if ever any were, —
 Sadder than orphans, yet not fatherless!

X

By the false cant which on their innocent lips
 Must hang like poison on an opening bloom,
By the dark creeds which cover with eclipse
 Their pathway from the cradle to the tomb —

XI

By thy most impious Hell, and all its terror;
 By all the grief, the madness, and the guilt
Of thine impostures, which must be their error —
 That sand on which thy crumbling Power is built —

XII

By thy complicity with lust and hate —
 Thy thirst for tears — thy hunger after
 gold —
The ready frauds which ever on thee
 wait —
 The servile arts in which thou hast grown
 old —

XIII

By thy most killing sneer, and by thy
 smile —
 By all the arts and snares of thy black
 den,
And — for thou canst outweep the croco-
 dile —
 By thy false tears — those millstones
 braining men —

XIV

By all the hate which checks a father's
 love —
 By all the scorn which kills a father's
 care —
By those most impious hands which dared
 remove
 Nature's high bounds — by thee — and
 by despair —

XV

Yes, the despair which bids a father
 groan,
 And cry, 'My children are no longer
 mine —
The blood within those veins may be mine
 own,
 But, Tyrant, their polluted souls are
 thine;' —

XVI

I curse thee, though I hate thee not. — O
 slave !
 If thou couldst quench the earth-consum-
 ing Hell
Of which thou art a demon, on thy grave
 This curse should be a blessing. Fare
 thee well !

TO WILLIAM SHELLEY

William Shelley was born at Bishopsgate,
January 24, 1816, baptized at St.-Giles-in-the-
Fields, March 9, 1818, died at Rome, June 7,
1819. Mrs. Shelley notes : 'At one time, while
the question was still pending, the Chancellor
had said some words that seemed to intimate
that Shelley should not be permitted the care
of any of his children, and for a moment he
feared that our infant son would be torn from
us. He did not hesitate to resolve, if such
were menaced, to abandon country, fortune,
everything, and to escape with his child ; and
I find some unfinished stanzas addressed to this
son, whom afterwards we lost at Rome, written
under the idea that we might suddenly be
forced to cross the sea, so to preserve him.
This poem, as well as the one previously
quoted, were not written to exhibit the pangs
of distress to the public ; they were the sponta-
neous outbursts of a man who brooded over his
wrongs and woes, and was impelled to shed the
grace of his genius over the uncontrollable
emotions of his heart.' The poem was pub-
lished by Mrs. Shelley, in part, in her first col-
lected edition, 1839, and entire, in the second, of
the same year.

I

THE billows on the beach are leaping
 around it,
 The bark is weak and frail,
The sea looks black, and the clouds that
 bound it
 Darkly strew the gale.
Come with me, thou delightful child,
Come with me — though the wave is wild,
And the winds are loose, we must not stay,
Or the slaves of the law may rend thee
 away.

II

They have taken thy brother and sister
 dear,
 They have made them unfit for thee;
They have withered the smile and dried
 the tear
 Which should have been sacred to me.
To a blighting faith and a cause of crime
They have bound them slaves in youthly
 prime,
And they will curse my name and thee
Because we are fearless and free.

III

Come thou, belovèd as thou art;
 Another sleepeth still
Near thy sweet mother's anxious heart,
 Which thou with joy shalt fill, —
With fairest smiles of wonder thrown
On that which is indeed our own,
And which in distant lands will be
The dearest playmate unto thee.

IV

Fear not the tyrants will rule forever,
 Or the priests of the evil faith;
They stand on the brink of that raging
 river
 Whose waves they have tainted with
 death.
It is fed from the depth of a thousand
 dells,
Around them it foams and rages and swells;
And their swords and their sceptres I float-
 ing see,
Like wrecks on the surge of eternity.

V

Rest, rest, and shriek not, thou gentle
 child !
 The rocking of the boat thou fearest,
And the cold spray and the clamor wild ? —
 There sit between us two, thou dear-
 est —
Me and thy mother — well we know
The storm at which thou tremblest so,
With all its dark and hungry graves,
Less cruel than the savage slaves
Who hunt us o'er these sheltering waves.

VI

This hour will in thy memory
 Be a dream of days forgotten long;
We soon shall dwell by the azure sea
Of serene and golden Italy,
Or Greece, the Mother of the free;
 And I will teach thine infant tongue
To call upon those heroes old
In their own language, and will mould
Thy growing spirit in the flame
Of Grecian lore, that by such name
A patriot's birthright thou mayst claim !

ON FANNY GODWIN

Fanny Godwin, half-sister of Mary, com-
mitted suicide by taking laudanum, at an inn in
Swansea, October 9, 1816. Shelley had re-
cently seen her in London. The poem was
published by Mrs. Shelley in her first col-
lected edition, 1839.

HER voice did quiver as we parted,
 Yet knew I not that heart was broken
From which it came, and I departed
 Heeding not the words then spoken.
 Misery — O Misery,
 This world is all too wide for thee.

LINES

Composed November 5, and published by
Mrs. Shelley, *Posthumous Poems*, 1824.

I

THAT time is dead forever, child,
Drowned, frozen, dead forever !
 We look on the past,
 And stare aghast
At the spectres wailing, pale and ghast,
Of hopes which thou and I beguiled
 To death on life's dark river.

II

The stream we gazed on then, rolled by;
Its waves are unreturning;
 But we yet stand
 In a lone land,
Like tombs to mark the memory
Of hopes and fears, which fade and flee
 In the light of life's dim morning.

DEATH

Published by Mrs. Shelley, *Posthumous
Poems*, 1824.

THEY die — the dead return not. Misery
 Sits near an open grave and calls them
 over,
A Youth with hoary hair and haggard eye.
 They are the names of kindred, friend
 and lover,
Which he so feebly calls; they all are
 gone —
Fond wretch, all dead ! those vacant names
 alone,
 This most familiar scene, my pain,
 These tombs, — alone remain.

Misery, my sweetest friend, oh, weep no
 more !
 Thou wilt not be consoled — I wonder
 not !
For I have seen thee from thy dwelling's
 door
 Watch the calm sunset with them, and
 this spot
Was even as bright and calm, but transi-
 tory, —
And now thy hopes are gone, thy hair is
 hoary;
 This most familiar scene, my pain,
 These tombs, — alone remain.

SONNET. — OZYMANDIAS

Published by Hunt, *The Examiner*, 1818.

I MET a traveller from an antique land
Who said: 'Two vast and trunkless legs of
 stone
Stand in the desert. Near them, on the
 sand,
Half sunk, a shattered visage lies, whose
 frown,
And wrinkled lip, and sneer of cold com-
 mand,
Tell that its sculptor well those passions
 read
Which yet survive, stamped on these life-
 less things,
The hand that mocked them and the heart
 that fed.
And on the pedestal these words appear —
" My name is Ozymandias, king of kings:
Look on my works, ye Mighty, and de-
 spair ! "
Nothing beside remains. Round the de-
 cay
Of that colossal wreck, boundless and bare
The lone and level sands stretch far away.'

LINES TO A CRITIC

Published by Hunt, *The Liberal*, 1823.

I

HONEY from silkworms who can gather,
 Or silk from the yellow bee ?
The grass may grow in winter weather
 As soon as hate in me.

II

Hate men who cant, and men who pray,
 And men who rail like thee;
An equal passion to repay
 They are not coy like me.

III

Or seek some slave of power and gold,
 To be thy dear heart's mate;
Thy love will move that bigot cold
 Sooner than me thy hate.

IV

A passion like the one I prove
 Cannot divided be;
I hate thy want of truth and love —
 How should I then hate thee ?

POEMS WRITTEN IN 1818

Mrs. Shelley describes the scenes and char-
acter of this first year in Italy at length : ' I
Capuccini was a villa built on the site of a
Capuchin convent, demolished when the French
suppressed religious houses; it was situated on
the very overhanging brow of a low hill at the
foot of a range of higher ones. The house
was cheerful and pleasant; a vine-trellised
walk, a *pergola*, as it is called in Italian, led
from the hall door to a summer-house at the
end of the garden, which Shelley made his
study, and in which he began the *Prometheus;*
and here also, as he mentions in a letter, he
wrote *Julian and Maddalo ;* a slight ravine,
with a road in its depth, divided the garden
from the hill, on which stood the ruins of the
ancient castle of Este, whose dark massive wall
gave forth an echo, and from whose ruined
crevices, owls and bats flitted forth at night,
as the crescent moon sunk behind the black
and heavy battlements. We looked from the
garden over the wide plain of Lombardy,
bounded to the west by the far Apennines,
while to the east, the horizon was lost in misty
distance. After the picturesque but limited
view of mountain, ravine, and chestnut wood

at the baths of Lucca, there was something
infinitely gratifying to the eye in the wide
range of prospect commanded by our new
abode.
' Our first misfortune, of the kind from which
we soon suffered even more severely, happened
here. Our little girl, an infant in whose small
features I fancied that I traced great resem-
blance to her father, showed symptoms of suf-
fering from the heat of the climate. Teething
increased her illness and danger. We were at
Este, and when we became alarmed, hastened
to Venice for the best advice. When we ar-
rived at Fusina, we found that we had for-
gotten our passport, and the soldiers on duty
attempted to prevent our crossing the laguna ;
but they could not resist Shelley's impetuosity
at such a moment. We had scarcely arrived
at Venice, before life fled from the little suf-
ferer, and we returned to Este to weep her
loss.
' After a few weeks spent in this retreat,
which were interspersed by visits to Venice,
we proceeded southward. We often hear of
persons disappointed by a first visit to Italy.
This was not Shelley's case — the aspect of its

nature, its sunny sky, its majestic storms; of the luxuriant vegetation of the country, and the noble marble-built cities, enchanted him. The sight of the works of art was full [of] enjoyment and wonder; he had not studied pictures or statues before; he now did so with the eye of taste, that referred not to the rules of schools, but to those of nature and truth. The first entrance to Rome opened to him a scene of remains of antique grandeur that far surpassed his expectations; and the unspeakable beauty of Naples and its environs added to the impression he received of the transcendent and glorious beauty of Italy. As I have said, he wrote long letters during the first year of our residence in this country, and these, when published, will be the best testimonials of his appreciation of the harmonious and beautiful in art and nature, and his delicate taste in discerning and describing them.

'Our winter was spent at Naples. Here he wrote the fragments of *Marenghi* and *The Woodman and the Nightingale*, which he afterwards threw aside. At this time Shelley suffered greatly in health. He put himself under the care of a medical man, who promised great things, and made him endure severe bodily pain, without any good results. Constant and poignant physical suffering exhausted him; and though he preserved the appearance of cheerfulness, and often greatly enjoyed our wanderings in the environs of Naples, and our excursions on its sunny sea, yet many hours were passed when his thoughts, shadowed by illness, became gloomy, and then he escaped to solitude, and in verses, which he hid from fear of wounding me, poured forth morbid but too natural bursts of discontent and sadness. One looks back with unspeakable regret and gnawing remorse to such periods; fancying that had one been more alive to the nature of his feelings, and more attentive to soothe them, such would not have existed — and yet enjoying, as he appeared to do, every sight or influence of earth or sky, it was difficult to imagine that any melancholy he showed was aught but the effect of the constant pain to which he was a martyr.

'We lived in utter solitude — and such is often not the nurse of cheerfulness; for then, at least with those who have been exposed to adversity, the mind broods over its sorrows too intently; while the society of the enlightened, the witty, and the wise, enables us to forget ourselves by making us the sharers of the thoughts of others, which is a portion of the philosophy of happiness. Shelley never liked society in numbers, it harassed and wearied him; but neither did he like loneliness, and usually when alone sheltered himself against memory and reflection, in a book. But with one or two whom he loved, he gave way to wild and joyous spirits, or in more serious conversation expounded his opinions with vivacity and eloquence.'

SONNET: TO THE NILE

This is the sonnet composed in competition with Hunt and Keats, on the same subject February 4. It was published in the *St. James Magazine*, 1876.

MONTH after month the gathered rains descend
 Drenching yon secret Æthiopian dells;
 And from the desert's ice-girt pinnacles,
 Where Frost and Heat in strange embraces blend
On Atlas, fields of moist snow half depend;
 Girt there with blasts and meteors, Tempest dwells
 By Nile's aërial urn, with rapid spells
 Urging those waters to their mighty end.
O'er Egypt's land of Memory floods are level,
 And they are thine, O Nile! — and well thou knowest
That soul-sustaining airs and blasts of evil,
 And fruits and poisons, spring where'er thou flowest.
 Beware, O Man! for knowledge must to thee
 Like the great flood to Egypt ever be.

PASSAGE OF THE APENNINES

Composed May 4, and published by Mrs. Shelley, *Posthumous Poems*, 1824.

LISTEN, listen, Mary mine,
To the whisper of the Apennine,
It bursts on the roof like the thunder's roar,
Or like the sea on a northern shore,
Heard in its raging ebb and flow
By the captives pent in the cave below.
The Apennine in the light of day
Is a mighty mountain dim and gray,
Which between the earth and sky doth lay;

But when night comes, a chaos dread
On the dim starlight then is spread,
And the Apennine walks abroad with the
 storm.

THE PAST

Published by Mrs. Shelley, *Posthumous Poems*, 1824.

WILT thou forget the happy hours
Which we buried in Love's sweet bow-
 ers,
Heaping over their corpses cold
Blossoms and leaves instead of mould ?
 Blossoms which were the joys that fell,
 And leaves, the hopes that yet re-
 main.

Forget the dead, the past ? Oh, yet
There are ghosts that may take revenge
 for it;
Memories that make the heart a tomb,
Regrets which glide through the spirit's
 gloom,
 And with ghastly whispers tell
 That joy, once lost, is pain.

ON A FADED VIOLET

Sent by Shelley, in a letter, to Miss Sophia Stacey, March 7, 1820: ' I promised you what I cannot perform : a song on singing : — there are only two subjects remaining. I have a few old stanzas on one which, though simple and rude, look as if they were dictated by the heart. — And so — if you tell no one *whose* they are, you are welcome to them. Pardon these dull verses from one who is dull — but who is not the less, ever yours, P. B. S.' It was published by Hunt, *The Literary Pocket-Book*, 1821.

I

THE odor from the flower is gone,
 Which like thy kisses breathed on me;
The color from the flower is flown,
 Which glowed of thee, and only thee !

II

A shrivelled, lifeless, vacant form,
 It lies on my abandoned breast,
And mocks the heart, which yet is warm,
 With cold and silent rest.

III

I weep — my tears revive it not;
 I sigh — it breathes no more on me;
Its mute and uncomplaining lot
 Is such as mine should be.

LINES WRITTEN AMONG THE EUGANEAN HILLS

Composed at Este, in October, and possibly revised at Naples the following month. The passage on Byron was inserted after the poem had gone to the printer. It was published with *Rosalind and Helen*, 1819, and in the Preface Shelley says it ' was written after a day's excursion among those lovely mountains which surround what was once the retreat, and where is now the sepulchre, of Petrarch. If any one is inclined to condemn the insertion of the introductory lines, which image forth the sudden relief of a state of deep despondency by the radiant visions disclosed by the sudden burst of an Italian sunrise in autumn, on the highest peak of those delightful mountains, I can only offer as my excuse, that they were not erased at the request of a dear friend, with whom added years of intercourse only add to my apprehension of its value, and who would have had more right than any one to complain, that she has not been able to extinguish in me the very power of delineating sadness.'

MANY a green isle needs must be
In the deep, wide sea of misery,
Or the mariner, worn and wan,
Never thus could voyage on
Day and night, and night and day,
Drifting on his dreary way,
With the solid darkness black
Closing round his vessel's track;
Whilst above, the sunless sky,
Big with clouds, hangs heavily, 10
And behind, the tempest fleet
Hurries on with lightning feet,
Riving sail, and cord, and plank,
Till the ship has almost drank
Death from the o'er-brimming deep,
And sinks down, down — like that sleep
When the dreamer seems to be
Weltering through eternity;
And the dim low line before
Of a dark and distant shore 20
Still recedes, as ever still,
Longing with divided will
But no power to seek or shun,
He is ever drifted on

O'er the unreposing wave
To the haven of the grave.
What, if there no friends will greet ?
What, if there no heart will meet
His with love's impatient beat ?
Wander wheresoe'er he may, 30
Can he dream before that day
To find refuge from distress
In friendship's smile, in love's caress ?
Then 't will wreak him little woe
Whether such there be or no.
Senseless is the breast, and cold,
Which relenting love would fold;
Bloodless are the veins, and chill,
Which the pulse of pain did fill;
Every little living nerve 40
That from bitter words did swerve
Round the tortured lips and brow,
Are like sapless leaflets now
Frozen upon December's bough.

On the beach of a northern sea
Which tempests shake eternally,
As once the wretch there lay to sleep,
Lies a solitary heap,
One white skull and seven dry bones,
On the margin of the stones, 50
Where a few gray rushes stand,
Boundaries of the sea and land:
Nor is heard one voice of wail
But the sea-mews, as they sail
O'er the billows of the gale;
Or the whirlwind up and down
Howling, like a slaughtered town
When a king in glory rides
Through the pomp of fratricides.
Those unburied bones around 60
There is many a mournful sound;
There is no lament for him,
Like a sunless vapor, dim,
Who once clothed with life and thought
What now moves nor murmurs not.

Ay, many flowering islands lie
In the waters of wide Agony.
To such a one this morn was led
My bark, by soft winds piloted.
Mid the mountains Euganean 70
I stood listening to the pæan
With which the legioned rooks did hail
The sun's uprise majestical;
Gathering round with wings all hoar,
Through the dewy mist they soar
Like gray shades, till the eastern heaven
Bursts, and then, as clouds of even,

Flecked with fire and azure, lie
In the unfathomable sky,
So their plumes of purple grain, 80
Starred with drops of golden rain,
Gleam above the sunlight woods,
As in silent multitudes
On the morning's fitful gale
Through the broken mist they sail,
And the vapors cloven and gleaming
Follow down the dark steep streaming,
Till all is bright, and clear, and still,
Round the solitary hill.

Beneath is spread like a green sea 90
The waveless plain of Lombardy,
Bounded by the vaporous air,
Islanded by cities fair.
Underneath day's azure eyes,
Ocean's nursling, Venice lies,
A peopled labyrinth of walls,
Amphitrite's destined halls,
Which her hoary sire now paves
With his blue and beaming waves.
Lo ! the sun upsprings behind, 100
Broad, red, radiant, half-reclined
On the level quivering line
Of the waters crystalline;
And before that chasm of light,
As within a furnace bright,
Column, tower, and dome and spire,
Shine like obelisks of fire,
Pointing with inconstant motion
From the altar of dark ocean
To the sapphire-tinted skies; 110
As the flames of sacrifice
From the marble shrines did rise
As to pierce the dome of gold
Where Apollo spoke of old.

Sun-girt City ! thou hast been
Ocean's child, and then his queen;
Now is come a darker day,
And thou soon must be his prey,
If the power that raised thee here
Hallow so thy watery bier. 120
A less drear ruin then than now,
With thy conquest-branded brow
Stooping to the slave of slaves
From thy throne among the waves,
Wilt thou be, when the sea-mew
Flies, as once before it flew,
O'er thine isles depopulate,
And all is in its ancient state,
Save where many a palace-gate
With green sea-flowers overgrown 130

Like a rock of ocean's own,
Topples o'er the abandoned sea
As the tides change sullenly.
The fisher on his watery way,
Wandering at the close of day,
Will spread his sail and seize his oar
Till he pass the gloomy shore,
Lest thy dead should, from their sleep
Bursting o'er the starlight deep,
Lead a rapid masque of death 140
O'er the waters of his path.

Those who alone thy towers behold
Quivering through aërial gold,
As I now behold them here,
Would imagine not they were
Sepulchres, where human forms,
Like pollution-nourished worms,
To the corpse of greatness cling,
Murdered, and now mouldering.
But if Freedom should awake 150
In her omnipotence, and shake
From the Celtic Anarch's hold
All the keys of dungeons cold,
Where a hundred cities lie
Chained like thee, ingloriously,
Thou and all thy sister band
Might adorn this sunny land,
Twining memories of old time
With new virtues more sublime.
If not, perish thou and they!— 160
Clouds which stain truth's rising day
By her sun consumed away—
Earth can spare ye; while like flowers,
In the waste of years and hours,
From your dust new nations spring
With more kindly blossoming.

Perish! let there only be
Floating o'er thy heartless sea,
As the garment of thy sky
Clothes the world immortally, 170
One remembrance, more sublime
Than the tattered pall of time,
Which scarce hides thy visage wan;—
That a tempest-cleaving Swan
Of the songs of Albion,
Driven from his ancestral streams
By the might of evil dreams,
Found a nest in thee; and Ocean
Welcomed him with such emotion
That its joy grew his, and sprung 180
From his lips like music flung
O'er a mighty thunder-fit,

Chastening terror. What though yet
Poesy's unfailing River,
Which through Albion winds forever
Lashing with melodious wave
Many a sacred poet's grave,
Mourn its latest nursling fled?
What though thou with all thy dead
Scarce can for this fame repay 190
Aught thine own? oh, rather say
Though thy sins and slaveries foul
Overcloud a sun-like soul?
As the ghost of Homer clings
Round Scamander's wasting springs;
As divinest Shakespeare's might
Fills Avon and the world with light
Like omniscient power which he
Imaged 'mid mortality;
As the love from Petrarch's urn 200
Yet amid yon hills doth burn,
A quenchless lamp, by which the heart,
Sees things unearthly;—so thou art,
Mighty spirit! so shall be
The City that did refuge thee!

Lo, the sun floats up the sky,
Like thought-wingèd Liberty,
Till the universal light
Seems to level plain and height.
From the sea a mist has spread, 210
And the beams of morn lie dead
On the towers of Venice now,
Like its glory long ago.
By the skirts of that gray cloud
Many-domèd Padua proud
Stands, a peopled solitude,
Mid the harvest-shining plain,
Where the peasant heaps his grain
In the garner of his foe,
And the milk-white oxen slow 220
With the purple vintage strain,
Heaped upon the creaking wain,
That the brutal Celt may swill
Drunken sleep with savage will;
And the sickle to the sword
Lies unchanged, though many a lord,
Like a weed whose shade is poison,
Overgrows this region's foison,
Sheaves of whom are ripe to come
To destruction's harvest-home. 230
Men must reap the things they sow,
Force from force must ever flow,
Or worse; but 't is a bitter woe
That love or reason cannot change
The despot's rage, the slave's revenge.

Padua, thou within whose walls
Those mute guests at festivals,
Son and Mother, Death and Sin,
Played at dice for Ezzelin,
Till Death cried, 'I win, I win!' 240
And Sin cursed to lose the wager,
But Death promised, to assuage her,
That he would petition for
Her to be made Vice-Emperor,
When the destined years were o'er,
Over all between the Po
And the eastern Alpine snow,
Under the mighty Austrian.
Sin smiled so as Sin only can,
And since that time, ay, long before, 250
Both have ruled from shore to shore —
That incestuous pair, who follow
Tyrants as the sun the swallow,
As Repentance follows Crime,
And as changes follow Time.

In thine halls the lamp of learning,
Padua, now no more is burning;
Like a meteor whose wild way
Is lost over the grave of day,
It gleams betrayed and to betray. 260
Once remotest nations came
To adore that sacred flame,
When it lit not many a hearth
On this cold and gloomy earth;
Now new fires from antique light
Spring beneath the wide world's might;
But their spark lies dead in thee,
Trampled out by tyranny.
As the Norway woodman quells,
In the depth of piny dells, 270
One light flame among the brakes,
While the boundless forest shakes,
And its mighty trunks are torn
By the fire thus lowly born; —
The spark beneath his feet is dead,
He starts to see the flames it fed
Howling through the darkened sky
With myriad tongues victoriously,
And sinks down in fear; — so thou,
O Tyranny! beholdest now 280
Light around thee, and thou hearest
The loud flames ascend, and fearest.
Grovel on the earth! ay, hide
In the dust thy purple pride!

Noon descends around me now.
'T is the noon of autumn's glow,
When a soft and purple mist,
Like a vaporous amethyst,

Or an air-dissolvèd star
Mingling light and fragrance, far 290
From the curved horizon's bound
To the point of heaven's profound
Fills the overflowing sky.
And the plains that silent lie
Underneath; the leaves unsodden
Where the infant frost has trodden
With his morning-wingèd feet,
Whose bright print is gleaming yet;
And the red and golden vines,
Piercing with their trellised lines 300
The rough, dark-skirted wilderness;
The dun and bladed grass no less,
Pointing from this hoary tower
In the windless air; the flower
Glimmering at my feet; the line
Of the olive-sandalled Apennine
In the south dimly islanded;
And the Alps, whose snows are spread
High between the clouds and sun;
And of living things each one; 310
And my spirit, which so long
Darkened this swift stream of song, —
Interpenetrated lie
By the glory of the sky:
Be it love, light, harmony,
Odor, or the soul of all
Which from heaven like dew doth fall,
Or the mind which feeds this verse
Peopling the lone universe.

Noon descends, and after noon 320
Autumn's evening meets me soon,
Leading the infantine moon
And that one star, which to her
Almost seems to minister
Half the crimson light she brings
From the sunset's radiant springs;
And the soft dreams of the morn
(Which like wingèd winds had borne
To that silent isle, which lies
Mid remembered agonies, 330
The frail bark of this lone being)
Pass, to other sufferers fleeing,
And its ancient pilot, Pain,
Sits beside the helm again.

Other flowering isles must be
In the sea of life and agony;
Other spirits float and flee
O'er that gulf: even now, perhaps,
On some rock the wild wave wraps,
With folding wings they waiting sit 340
For my bark, to pilot it

To some calm and blooming cove,
Where for me, and those I love,
May a windless bower be built,
Far from passion, pain, and guilt,
In a dell mid lawny hills,
Which the wild sea-murmur fills,
And soft sunshine, and the sound
Of old forests echoing round,
And the light and smell divine 350
Of all flowers that breathe and shine.
We may live so happy there,
That the spirits of the air,
Envying us, may even entice
To our healing paradise
The polluting multitude;
But their rage would be subdued
By that clime divine and calm,
And the winds whose wings rain balm
On the uplifted soul, and leaves 360
Under which the bright sea heaves;
While each breathless interval
In their whisperings musical
The inspired soul supplies
With its own deep melodies,
And the love which heals all strife,
Circling, like the breath of life,
All things in that sweet abode
With its own mild brotherhood.
They, not it, would change; and soon 370
Every sprite beneath the moon
Would repent its envy vain,
And the earth grow young again.

INVOCATION TO MISERY

Published by Medwin, *The Athenæum*, 1832.
He wove about it a mystery of a lady who
followed Shelley to Naples and there died in
hopeless love for him. The tale has never been
substantiated, but his various biographers take
note of it, in connection with his depression at
Naples. The poem itself is purely ideal, and
such as he might have written at any time.

I

Come, be happy! — sit near me,
Shadow-vested Misery;
Coy, unwilling, silent bride,
Mourning in thy robe of pride,
Desolation — deified!

II

Come, be happy! — sit near me.
Sad as I may seem to thee,

I am happier far than thou,
Lady, whose imperial brow
Is endiademed with woe.

III

Misery! we have known each other,
Like a sister and a brother
Living in the same lone home,
Many years — we must live some
Hours or ages yet to come.

IV

'T is an evil lot, and yet
Let us make the best of it;
If love can live when pleasure dies,
We two will love, till in our eyes
This heart's Hell seem Paradise.

V

Come, be happy! — lie thee down
On the fresh grass newly mown,
Where the grasshopper doth sing
Merrily — one joyous thing
In a world of sorrowing.

VI

There our tent shall be the willow,
And mine arm shall be thy pillow;
Sounds and odors, sorrowful
Because they once were sweet, shall
 lull
Us to slumber, deep and dull.

VII

Ha! thy frozen pulses flutter
With a love thou darest not utter.
Thou art murmuring — thou art weep-
 ing —
Is thine icy bosom leaping
While my burning heart lies sleeping?

VIII

Kiss me; — oh! thy lips are cold;
Round my neck thine arms enfold —
They are soft, but chill and dead;
And thy tears upon my head
Burn like points of frozen lead.

IX

Hasten to the bridal bed —
Underneath the grave 't is spread:
In darkness may our love be hid,
Oblivion be our coverlid —
We may rest, and none forbid.

X

Clasp me, till our hearts be grown
Like two shadows into one;
Till this dreadful transport may
Like a vapor fade away
In the sleep that lasts alway.

XI

We may dream, in that long sleep,
That we are not those who weep;
E'en as Pleasure dreams of thee,
Life-deserting Misery,
Thou mayst dream of her with me.

XII

Let us laugh, and make our mirth,
At the shadows of the earth,
As dogs bay the moonlight clouds,
Which, like spectres wrapped in shrouds,
Pass o'er night in multitudes.

XIII

All the wide world beside us
Show like multitudinous
Puppets passing from a scene;
What but mockery can they mean,
Where I am — where thou hast been ?

STANZAS

WRITTEN IN DEJECTION, NEAR NAPLES

This poem, in the same mood as the preceding, was composed in December, and published by Mrs. Shelley, *Posthumous Poems*, 1824.

I

THE sun is warm, the sky is clear,
 The waves are dancing fast and bright;
Blue isles and snowy mountains wear
 The purple noon's transparent might;
 The breath of the moist earth is light
Around its unexpanded buds;
 Like many a voice of one delight,
 The winds, the birds, the ocean floods,
The City's voice itself is soft like Solitude's.

II

I see the Deep's untrampled floor
 With green and purple sea-weeds strown;
I see the waves upon the shore,
 Like light dissolved in star-showers, thrown;

I sit upon the sands alone —
 The lightning of the noontide ocean
 Is flashing round me, and a tone
 Arises from its measured motion,
How sweet ! did any heart now share in my emotion.

III

Alas ! I have nor hope nor health,
 Nor peace within nor calm around,
Nor that content surpassing wealth
 The sage in meditation found,
 And walked with inward glory crowned —
Nor fame, nor power, nor love, nor leisure.
 Others I see whom these surround —
Smiling they live, and call life pleasure; —
To me that cup has been dealt in another measure.

IV

Yet now despair itself is mild,
 Even as the winds and waters are;
I could lie down like a tired child,
 And weep away the life of care
Which I have borne and yet must bear,
 Till death like sleep might steal on me,
 And I might feel in the warm air
My cheek grow cold, and hear the sea
Breathe o'er my dying brain its last monotony.

V

Some might lament that I were cold,
 As I when this sweet day is gone,
Which my lost heart, too soon grown old,
 Insults with this untimely moan;
 They might lament — for I am one
Whom men love not, — and yet regret,
 Unlike this day, which, when the sun
Shall on its stainless glory set,
Will linger, though enjoyed, like joy in memory yet.

SONNET

Published by Mrs. Shelley, *Posthumous Poems*, 1824.

LIFT not the painted veil which those who live
Call Life; though unreal shapes be pictured there,

And it but mimic all we would believe
With colors idly spread, — behind, lurk
 Fear
And Hope, twin Destinies, who ever weave
Their shadows o'er the chasm sightless and
 drear.
I knew one who had lifted it — he sought,
For his lost heart was tender, things to
 love,

But found them not, alas ! nor was there
 aught
The world contains the which he could ap-
 prove.
Through the unheeding many he did move,
A splendor among shadows, a bright blot
Upon this gloomy scene, a Spirit that strove
For truth, and like the Preacher found it
 not.

POEMS WRITTEN IN 1819

This was the year of the composition of *Prometheus Unbound, The Cenci, The Mask of Anarchy,* and *Peter Bell The Third.* Its his-tory has already been given with sufficient fulness under these titles, from Mrs. Shelley's notes.

LINES

WRITTEN DURING THE CASTLEREAGH ADMINISTRATION

Published by Medwin, *The Athenæum,* 1832.

I

CORPSES are cold in the tomb —
Stones on the pavement are dumb —
Abortions are dead in the womb,
And their mothers look pale, like the death-
 white shore
 Of Albion, free no more.

II

Her sons are as stones in the way —
They are masses of senseless clay —
They are trodden and move not
 away —
The abortion with which *she* travaileth
 Is Liberty, smitten to death

III

Then trample and dance, thou Op-
 pressor !
For thy victim is no redresser —
Thou art sole lord and possessor
Of her corpses, and clods, and abortions
 — they pave
 Thy path to the grave.

IV

Hearest thou the festival din
Of Death and Destruction and Sin,
And Wealth crying, Havoc ! within ?
'T is the Bacchanal triumph that makes
 truth dumb, —
 Thine Epithalamium.

V

Ay, marry thy ghastly wife !
Let Fear and Disquiet and Strife
Spread thy couch in the chamber of
 Life;
Marry Ruin, thou Tyrant ! and Hell be thy
 guide
 To the bed of the bride !

SONG

TO THE MEN OF ENGLAND

This poem, like all the group, is to be ascribed to Shelley's renewed political excitement ow-ing to the Manchester Massacre. It was pub-lished by Mrs. Shelley, in her first collected edition, 1839.

I

MEN of England, wherefore plough
For the lords who lay ye low ?
Wherefore weave with toil and care
The rich robes your tyrants wear ?

II

Wherefore feed, and clothe, and save,
From the cradle to the grave,
Those ungrateful drones who would
Drain your sweat — nay, drink your
 blood ?

III

Wherefore, Bees of England, forge
Many a weapon, chain, and scourge,
That these stingless drones may spoil
The forced produce of your toil ?

IV

Have ye leisure, comfort, calm,
Shelter, food, love's gentle balm?
Or what is it ye buy so dear
With your pain and with your fear?

V

The seed ye sow, another reaps;
The wealth ye find, another keeps;
The robes ye weave, another wears;
The arms ye forge, another bears.

VI

Sow seed, — but let no tyrant reap;
Find wealth, — let no impostor heap;
Weave robes, — let not the idle wear;
Forge arms, — in your defence to bear.

VII

Shrink to your cellars, holes, and cells;
In halls ye deck, another dwells.
Why shake the chains ye wrought? Ye see
The steel ye tempered glance on ye.

VIII

With plough and spade, and hoe and
 loom,
Trace your grave, and build your tomb,
And weave your winding-sheet, till fair
England be your sepulchre.

TO SIDMOUTH AND CASTLE-REAGH

Published by Medwin, *The Athenæum*, 1832.

I

As from an ancestral oak
 Two empty ravens sound their clarion,
Yell by yell, and croak by croak,
When they scent the noonday smoke
 Of fresh human carrion: —

II

As two gibbering night-birds flit
 From their bowers of deadly yew
Through the night to frighten it,
When the moon is in a fit,
 And the stars are none, or few: —

III

As a shark and dog-fish wait,
 Under an Atlantic isle,

For the negro-ship, whose freight
Is the theme of their debate,
 Wrinkling their red gills the while —

IV

Are ye, two vultures sick for battle,
 Two scorpions under one wet stone,
Two bloodless wolves whose dry throats
 rattle,
Two crows perched on the murrained cat-
 tle,
 Two vipers tangled into one.

ENGLAND IN 1819

This sonnet was sent by Shelley to Hunt, November 23, 1819, — 'I don't expect you to publish it, but you may show it to whom you please.' It was published by Mrs. Shelley, in her first collected edition, 1839.

An old, mad, blind, despised and dying
 king;
Princes, the dregs of their dull race, who
 flow
Through public scorn — mud from a muddy
 spring;
Rulers, who neither see, nor feel, nor know,
But leech-like to their fainting country
 cling,
Till they drop, blind in blood, without a
 blow;
A people starved and stabbed in the un-
 tilled field;
An army which liberticide and prey
Makes as a two-edged sword to all who
 wield;
Golden and sanguine laws which tempt and
 slay;
Religion Christless, Godless — a book
 sealed;
A Senate — Time's worst statute unrepealed,
Are graves from which a glorious Phantom
 may
Burst to illumine our tempestuous day.

NATIONAL ANTHEM

Published by Mrs. Shelley in her second collected edition, 1839.

I

God prosper, speed, and save,
God raise from England's grave
 Her murdered Queen!

Pave with swift victory
The steps of Liberty,
 Whom Britons own to be
 Immortal Queen.

II

See, she comes throned on high,
On swift Eternity,
 God save the Queen!
Millions on millions wait
Firm, rapid, and elate,
On her majestic state!
 God save the Queen!

III

She is thine own pure soul
Moulding the mighty whole, —
 God save the Queen!
She is thine own deep love
Rained down from heaven above, —
Wherever she rest or move,
 God save our Queen!

IV

Wilder her enemies
In their own dark disguise, —
 God save our Queen!
All earthly things that dare
Her sacred name to bear,
Strip them, as kings are, bare;
 God save the Queen!

V

Be her eternal throne
Built in our hearts alone, —
 God save the Queen!
Let the oppressor hold
Canopied seats of gold;
She sits enthroned of old
 O'er our hearts Queen.

VI

Lips touched by seraphim
Breathe out the choral hymn, —
 God save the Queen!
Sweet as if angels sang,
Loud as that trumpet's clang,
Wakening the world's dead gang, —
 God save the Queen!

ODE TO HEAVEN

Composed as early as December, and published with *Prometheus Unbound*, 1820. Mrs.

Shelley writes as follows: 'Shelley was a disciple of the immaterial philosophy of Berkeley. This theory gave unity and grandeur to his ideas, while it opened a wide field for his imagination. The creation, such as it was perceived by his mind — a unit in immensity, was slight and narrow compared with the interminable forms of thought that might exist beyond, to be perceived perhaps hereafter by his own mind; all of which are perceptible to other minds that fill the universe, not of space in the material sense, but of infinity in the immaterial one. Such ideas are, in some degree, developed in his poem entitled *Heaven:* and when he makes one of the interlocutors exclaim,

> "Peace! the abyss is wreathed in scorn
> Of thy presumption, atom-born"

he expresses his despair of being able to conceive, far less express, all of variety, majesty, and beauty, which is veiled from our imperfect senses in the unknown realm, the mystery of which his poetic vision sought in vain to penetrate.'

CHORUS OF SPIRITS

FIRST SPIRIT

PALACE-ROOF of cloudless nights!
Paradise of golden lights!
 Deep, immeasurable, vast,
Which art now, and which wert then,
Of the present and the past,
Of the eternal where and when,
 Presence-chamber, temple, home,
 Ever-canopying dome
Of acts and ages yet to come!

Glorious shapes have life in thee,
Earth, and all earth's company;
 Living globes which ever throng
Thy deep chasms and wildernesses;
 And green worlds that glide along;
And swift stars with flashing tresses;
 And icy moons most cold and bright,
 And mighty suns beyond the night,
 Atoms of intensest light.

Even thy name is as a god,
Heaven! for thou art the abode
 Of that power which is the glass
Wherein man his nature sees.
Generations as they pass
Worship thee with bended knees.
 Their unremaining gods and they
 Like a river roll away;
 Thou remainest such alway.

SECOND SPIRIT

Thou art but the mind's first chamber,
Round which its young fancies clamber,
 Like weak insects in a cave,
Lighted up by stalactites;
 But the portal of the grave,
Where a world of new delights
 Will make thy best glories seem
 But a dim and noonday gleam
 From the shadow of a dream !

THIRD SPIRIT

Peace ! the abyss is wreathed with scorn
At your presumption, atom-born !
 What is heaven ? and what are ye
Who its brief expanse inherit ?
 What are suns and spheres which flee
With the instinct of that Spirit
 Of which ye are but a part ?
 Drops which Nature's mighty heart
Drives through thinnest veins. Depart !

What is heaven ? a globe of dew,
Filling in the morning new
 Some eyed flower whose young leaves
 waken
On an unimagined world;
 Constellated suns unshaken,
Orbits measureless, are furled
 In that frail and fading sphere,
 With ten millions gathered there,
 To tremble, gleam, and disappear.

AN EXHORTATION

Shelley writes to Mrs. Gisborne, May 8,
1820, concerning this poem : ' As an excuse for
mine and Mary's incurable stupidity, I send
a little thing about poets, which is itself a
kind of excuse for Wordsworth.' It was pub-
lished with *Prometheus Unbound*, 1820.

CHAMELEONS feed on light and air;
 Poets' food is love and fame;
If in this wide world of care
 Poets could but find the same
With as little toil as they,
 Would they ever change their hue
 As the light chameleons do,
Suiting it to every ray
 Twenty times a day ?

Poets are on this cold earth,
 As chameleons might be,

Hidden from their early birth
 In a cave beneath the sea.
Where light is, chameleons change;
 Where love is not, poets do;
 Fame is love disguised; if few
Find either, never think it strange
 That poets range.

Yet dare not stain with wealth or power
 A poet's free and heavenly mind.
If bright chameleons should devour
 Any food but beams and wind,
They would grow as earthly soon
 As their brother lizards are.
Children of a sunnier star,
Spirits from beyond the moon,
 Oh, refuse the boon !

ODE TO THE WEST WIND

Shelley describes in a note the circumstances
under which this ode was composed : ' This
poem was conceived and chiefly written in a
wood that skirts the Arno, near Florence, and
on a day when that tempestuous wind, whose
temperature is at once mild and animating,
was collecting the vapors which pour down the
autumnal rains. They began, as I foresaw, at
sunset with a violent tempest of hail and rain,
attended by that magnificent thunder and light-
ning peculiar to the Cisalpine regions.
 ' The phenomenon alluded to at the conclu-
sion of the third stanza is well known to nat-
uralists. The vegetation at the bottom of the
sea, of rivers, and of lakes, sympathizes with
that of the land in the change of seasons, and
is consequently influenced by the winds which
announce it.' It was published with *Prome-
theus Unbound*, 1820.

I

O WILD West Wind, thou breath of Au-
 tumn's being,
Thou, from whose unseen presence the
 leaves dead
Are driven, like ghosts from an enchanter
 fleeing,

Yellow, and black, and pale, and hectic red,
Pestilence-stricken multitudes : O thou,
Who chariotest to their dark wintry bed

The wingèd seeds, where they lie cold and
 low,
Each like a corpse within its grave, until
Thine azure sister of the Spring shall blow

Her clarion o'er the dreaming earth, and
 fill
(Driving sweet buds like flocks to feed in
 air)
With living hues and odors plain and hill :

Wild Spirit, which art moving everywhere ;
Destroyer and preserver; hear, oh, hear !

II

Thou on whose stream, mid the steep sky's
 commotion,
Loose clouds like earth's decaying leaves
 are shed,
Shook from the tangled boughs of Heaven
 and Ocean,

Angels of rain and lightning: there are
 spread
On the blue surface of thine airy surge,
Like the bright hair uplifted from the
 head

Of some fierce Mænad, even from the dim
 verge
Of the horizon to the zenith's height,
The locks of the approaching storm. Thou
 dirge

Of the dying year, to which this closing
 night
Will be the dome of a vast sepulchre,
Vaulted with all thy congregated might

Of vapors, from whose solid atmosphere
Black rain, and fire, and hail will burst:
 oh, hear !

III

Thou who didst waken from his summer
 dreams
The blue Mediterranean, where he lay,
Lulled by the coil of his crystalline
 streams,

Beside a pumice isle in Baiæ's bay,
And saw in sleep old palaces and towers
Quivering within the wave's intenser day,

All overgrown with azure moss and flow-
 ers
So sweet the sense faints picturing them !
 thou
For whose path the Atlantic's level pow-
 ers

Cleave themselves into chasms, while far
 below
The sea-blooms and the oozy woods which
 wear
The sapless foliage of the ocean know

Thy voice, and suddenly grow gray with
 fear,
And tremble and despoil themselves : oh,
 hear !

IV

If I were a dead leaf thou mightest bear;
If I were a swift cloud to fly with thee;
A wave to pant beneath thy power, and
 share

The impulse of thy strength, only less free
Than thou, O uncontrollable ! If even
I were as in my boyhood, and could be

The comrade of thy wanderings over
 heaven,
As then, when to outstrip thy skyey speed
Scarce seemed a vision; I would ne'er have
 striven

As thus with thee in prayer in my sore need.
Oh, lift me as a wave, a leaf, a cloud !
I fall upon the thorns of life ! I bleed !

A heavy weight of hours has chained and
 bowed
One too like thee: tameless, and swift, and
 proud.

V

Make me thy lyre, even as the forest is :
What if my leaves are falling like its own !
The tumult of thy mighty harmonies

Will take from both a deep, autumnal tone,
Sweet though in sadness. Be thou, Spirit
 fierce,
My spirit ! Be thou me, impetuous one !

Drive my dead thoughts over the universe
Like withered leaves to quicken a new
 birth !
And, by the incantation of this verse,

Scatter, as from an unextinguished hearth
Ashes and sparks, my words among man-
 kind !
Be through my lips to unawakened earth

The trumpet of a prophecy ! O Wind,
If Winter comes, can Spring be far be-
 hind ?

AN ODE

WRITTEN OCTOBER, 1819, BEFORE THE
SPANIARDS HAD RECOVERED THEIR
LIBERTY

Published with *Prometheus Unbound*, 1820.
Mrs. Shelley's note exhibits the state of Shel-
ley's mind in his efforts to arouse and agitate
among the people : ' Shelley loved the people,
and respected them as often more virtuous, as
always more suffering, and, therefore, more de-
serving of sympathy, than the great. He be-
lieved that a clash between the two classes of
society was inevitable, and he eagerly ranged
himself on the people's side. He had an idea
of publishing a series of poems adapted ex-
pressly to commemorate their circumstances
and wrongs — he wrote a few, but in those
days of prosecution for libel they could not be
printed. They are not among the best of his
productions, a writer being always shackled
when he endeavors to write down to the com-
prehension of those who could not understand
or feel a highly imaginative style ; but they
show his earnestness, and with what heartfelt
compassion he went home to the direct point
of injury — that oppression is detestable, as
being the parent of starvation, nakedness, and
ignorance. Besides these outpourings of com-
passion and indignation, he had meant to adorn
the cause he loved with loftier poetry of glory
and triumph — such is the scope of the *Ode to
the Assertors of Liberty.* He sketched also a new
version of our national anthem, as addressed to
Liberty.'

ARISE, arise, arise !
There is blood on the earth that denies
 ye bread !
 Be your wounds like eyes
To weep for the dead, the dead, the dead.
What other grief were it just to pay ?
Your sons, your wives, your brethren, were
 they !
Who said they were slain on the battle-
 day ?

Awaken, awaken, awaken !
The slave and the tyrant are twin-born
 foes.
 Be the cold chains shaken
To the dust where your kindred repose,
 repose.

Their bones in the grave will start and
 move
When they hear the voices of those they
 love
Most loud in the holy combat above.

Wave, wave high the banner,
When Freedom is riding to conquest by!
 Though the slaves that fan her
 Be Famine and Toil, giving sigh for
 sigh.
And ye who attend her imperial car,
Lift not your hands in the banded war
But in her defence whose children ye are.

Glory, glory, glory,
To those who have greatly suffered and
 done !
 Never name in story
Was greater than that which ye shall
 have won.
Conquerors have conquered their foes alone,
Whose revenge, pride, and power, they
 have overthrown.
Ride ye, more victorious, over your own.

Bind, bind every brow
With crownals of violet, ivy, and pine !
 Hide the blood-stains now
 With hues which sweet nature has made
 divine —
Green strength, azure hope, and eternity;
But let not the pansy among them be —
Ye were injured, and that means memory.

ON THE MEDUSA OF LEO-NARDO DA VINCI

IN THE FLORENTINE GALLERY

Composed at Florence, in the latter part of
the year, and published by Mrs. Shelley, *Post-
humous Poems,* 1824.

I

IT lieth, gazing on the midnight sky,
 Upon the cloudy mountain peak supine;
Below, far lands are seen tremblingly;
 Its horror and its beauty are divine.
Upon its lips and eyelids seems to lie
 Loveliness like a shadow, from which
 shine,
Fiery and lurid, struggling underneath,
The agonies of anguish and of death.

II

Yet it is less the horror than the grace
　Which turns the gazer's spirit into stone,
Whereon the lineaments of that dead face
　Are graven, till the characters be grown
Into itself, and thought no more can trace;
　'T is the melodious hue of beauty thrown
Athwart the darkness and the glare of
　　pain,
Which humanize and harmonize the strain.

III

And from its head as from one body grow,
　As　　　grass out of a watery rock,
Hairs which are vipers, and they curl and
　　flow
　And their long tangles in each other
　　lock,
And with unending involutions show
　Their mailèd radiance, as it were to
　　mock
The torture and the death within, and saw
The solid air with many a ragged jaw.

IV

And, from a stone beside, a poisonous eft
　Peeps idly into those Gorgonian eyes;
Whilst in the air a ghastly bat, bereft
　Of sense, has flitted with a mad surprise
Out of the cave this hideous light had
　　cleft,
　And he comes hastening like a moth that
　　hies
After a taper; and the midnight sky
Flares, a light more dread than obscurity.

V

'T is the tempestuous loveliness of terror;
　For from the serpents gleams a brazen
　　glare
Kindled by that inextricable error,
　Which makes a thrilling vapor of the air
Become a　　　and ever-shifting mirror
　Of all the beauty and the terror there —
A woman's countenance, with serpent
　　locks,
Gazing in death on heaven from those wet
　rocks.

THE INDIAN SERENADE

This poem, erroneously said to have been
composed for Mrs. Williams and ' adapted to
the celebrated Persian air sung by the Knautch

girls, *Tazee be tazee no be no*,' was given to Miss
Sophia Stacey in 1819. Several versions of it
exist. Browning's account of deciphering one
of them is interesting : he writes to Hunt, Octo-
ber 6, 1857 : ' Is it not strange that I should
have transcribed for the first time last night
the *Indian Serenade* that, together with some
verses of *Metastasio*, accompanied that book ?
[the volume of Keats found in Shelley's pocket
and burned with his body] — that I should
have been reserved to tell the present posses-
sor of them, to whom they were given by Cap-
tain Roberts, *what* the poem was, and *that it
had been published ?* It is preserved religiously ;
but the characters are all but illegible, and I
needed a good magnifying-glass to be quite
sure of such of them as remain. The end is
that I have rescued three or four variations in
the reading of that divine little poem — as one
reads it, at least, in the *Posthumous Poems*.'
It was published by Hunt, *The Liberal*, 1822.

I

I ARISE from dreams of thee
In the first sweet sleep of night,
When the winds are breathing low,
And the stars are shining bright;
I arise from dreams of thee,
And a spirit in my feet
Hath led me — who knows how ?
To thy chamber window, sweet !

II

The wandering airs, they faint
On the dark, the silent stream;
The champak odors fail
Like sweet thoughts in a dream;
The nightingale's complaint,
It dies upon her heart,
As I must die on thine,
Oh, belovèd as thou art !

III

Oh, lift me from the grass !
I die ! I faint ! I fail !
Let thy love in kisses rain
On my lips and eyelids pale.
My cheek is cold and white, alas !
My heart beats loud and fast,
Oh ! press it close to thine again,
Where it will break at last.

TO SOPHIA

Mrs. Shelley describes the lady to whom
these lines are addressed, in a letter to Mrs.

Gisborne, December 1, 1819: 'There are some
ladies come to this house who knew Shelley's
family: the younger one was *entousiasmée* to
see him. . . . The younger lady was a ward
of one of Shelley's uncles. She is lively and
unaffected. She sings well for an English
débutante and, if she would learn the scales,
would sing exceedingly well, for she has a
sweet voice.' Miss Sophia Stacey was a ward
of Mr. Parker, of Bath, an uncle by marriage
of Shelley. The poem was published by Ros-
setti, 1870.

I

Thou art fair, and few are fairer
 Of the nymphs of earth or ocean;
They are robes that fit the wearer —
 Those soft limbs of thine, whose mo-
 tion
Ever falls and shifts and glances
As the life within them dances.

II

Thy deep eyes, a double Planet,
 Gaze the wisest into madness
With soft clear fire; the winds that fan
 it
Are those thoughts of tender gladness
Which, like zephyrs on the billow,
Make thy gentle soul their pillow.

III

If, whatever face thou paintest
 In those eyes, grows pale with pleasure,
If the fainting soul is faintest
 When it hears thy harp's wild measure,

Wonder not that when thou speakest
Of the weak my heart is weakest.

IV

As dew beneath the wind of morning,
 As the sea which whirlwinds waken,
As the birds at thunder's warning,
 As aught mute yet deeply shaken,
As one who feels an unseen spirit, —
Is my heart when thine is near it.

LOVE'S PHILOSOPHY

Published by Hunt, *The Indicator*, 1819.

I

The fountains mingle with the river,
 And the rivers with the ocean;
The winds of heaven mix forever
 With a sweet emotion;
Nothing in the world is single;
 All things by a law divine
In one another's being mingle:
 Why not I with thine?

II

See the mountains kiss high heaven,
 And the waves clasp one another;
No sister flower would be forgiven
 If it disdained its brother;
And the sunlight clasps the earth,
 And the moonbeams kiss the sea:
What are all these kissings worth,
 If thou kiss not me?

POEMS WRITTEN IN 1820

Mrs. Shelley gives in brief passages the ac-
count of the various removals of this year, and
of Shelley's general state: 'There was some-
thing in Florence that disagreed excessively
with his health, and he suffered far more pain
than usual; so much so that we left it sooner
than we intended, and removed to Pisa, where
we had some friends, and, above all, where we
could consult the celebrated Vaccà, as to the
cause of Shelley's sufferings. He, like every
other medical man, could only guess at that,
and gave little hope of immediate relief; he
enjoined him to abstain from all physicians
and medicine, and to leave his complaint to
nature. As he had vainly consulted medical
men of the highest repute in England, he was
easily persuaded to adopt this advice. Pain
and ill-health followed him to the end, but the

residence at Pisa agreed with him better than
any other, and there in consequence we re-
mained. . . .
 'We spent the summer at the baths of San
Giuliano, four miles from Pisa. These baths
were of great use to Shelley in soothing his
nervous irritability. We made several excur-
sions in the neighborhood. The country around
is fertile, and diversified and rendered pictur-
esque by ranges of near hills and more distant
mountains. The peasantry are a handsome,
intelligent race, and there was a gladsome sunny
heaven spread over us, that rendered home and
every scene we visited cheerful and bright. . . .
 'We then removed to Pisa, and took up our
abode there for the winter. The extreme
mildness of the climate suited Shelley, and his
solitude was enlivened by an intercourse with

several intimate friends. Chance cast us, strangely enough, on this quiet, half-unpeopled town; but its very peace suited Shelley, — its river, the near mountains, and not distant sea, added to its attractions, and were the objects of many delightful excursions. We feared the south of Italy, and a hotter climate, on account of our child ; our former bereavement inspiring us with terror. We seemed to take root here, and moved little afterwards; often, indeed, entertaining projects for visiting other parts of Italy, but still delaying. But for our fears on account of our child, I believe we should have wandered over the world, both being passionately fond of travelling. But human life, besides its great unalterable necessities, is ruled by a thousand Liliputian ties, that shackle at the time, although it is difficult to account afterwards for their influence over our destiny.'

THE SENSITIVE PLANT

Composed at Pisa, as early as March, and published with *Prometheus Unbound*, 1820. Shelley afterward identified Mrs. Williams as ' the exact antitype of the lady I described in *The Sensitive Plant*, though this must have been *a pure anticipated cognition*, as it was written a year before I knew her.'

PART FIRST

A SENSITIVE Plant in a garden grew,
And the young winds fed it with silver dew,
And it opened its fan-like leaves to the light,
And closed them beneath the kisses of Night.

And the Spring arose on the garden fair,
Like the Spirit of Love felt everywhere;
And each flower and herb on Earth's dark breast
Rose from the dreams of its wintry rest.

But none ever trembled and panted with bliss
In the garden, the field, or the wilderness,
Like a doe in the noontide with love's sweet want,⁣ 11
As the companionless Sensitive Plant.

The snowdrop, and then the violet,
Arose from the ground with warm rain wet,
And their breath was mixed with fresh odor, sent
From the turf, like the voice and the instrument.

Then the pied wind-flowers and the tulip tall,
And narcissi, the fairest among them all,

Who gaze on their eyes in the stream's recess
Till they die of their own dear loveliness; 20

And the Naiad-like lily of the vale,
Whom youth makes so fair, and passion so pale,
That the light of its tremulous bells is seen
Through their pavilions of tender green;

And the hyacinth purple, and white, and blue,
Which flung from its bells a sweet peal anew
Of music so delicate, soft, and intense,
It was felt like an odor within the sense;

And the rose like a nymph to the bath addressed,
Which unveiled the depth of her glowing breast, 30
Till, fold after fold, to the fainting air
The soul of her beauty and love lay bare;

And the wand-like lily, which lifted up,
As a Mænad, its moonlight-colored cup,
Till the fiery star, which is its eye,
Gazed through clear dew on the tender sky;

And the jessamine faint, and the sweet tube-rose,
The sweetest flower for scent that blows ;
And all rare blossoms from every clime
Grew in that garden in perfect prime. 40

And on the stream whose inconstant bosom
Was pranked, under boughs of embowering blossom,
With golden and green light, slanting through
Their heaven of many a tangled hue,

Broad water-lilies lay tremulously,
And starry river-buds glimmered by,
And around them the soft stream did glide
 and dance
With a motion of sweet sound and radi-
 ance.

And the sinuous paths of lawn and of moss,
Which led through the garden along and
 across, 50
Some open at once to the sun and the
 breeze,
Some lost among bowers of blossoming
 trees, —

Were all paved with daisies and delicate
 bells,
As fair as the fabulous asphodels,
And flowrets which, drooping as day
 drooped too,
Fell into pavilions white, purple, and blue,
To roof the glowworm from the evening
 dew.

And from this undefiled Paradise
The flowers (as an infant's awakening eyes
Smile on its mother, whose singing sweet 60
Can first lull, and at last must awaken it)

When Heaven's blithe winds had unfolded
 them
As mine-lamps enkindle a hidden gem,
Shone smiling to Heaven, and every one
Shared joy in the light of the gentle sun;

For each one was interpenetrated
With the light and the odor its neighbor
 shed,
Like young lovers whom youth and love
 make dear,
Wrapped and filled by their mutual atmo-
 sphere.

But the Sensitive Plant, which could give
 small fruit 70
Of the love which it felt from the leaf to
 the root,
Received more than all, it loved more than
 ever,
Where none wanted but it, could belong to
 the giver;

For the Sensitive Plant has no bright
 flower;
Radiance and odor are not its dower;

It loves, even like Love, its deep heart is
 full,
It desires what it has not, the beautiful !

The light winds which from unsustaining
 wings
Shed the music of many murmurings;
The beams which dart from many a star 80
Of the flowers whose hues they bear afar;

The plumèd insects swift and free,
Like golden boats on a sunny sea,
Laden with light and odor, which pass
Over the gleam of the living grass;

The unseen clouds of the dew, which lie
Like fire in the flowers till the sun rides
 high,
Then wander like spirits among the
 spheres,
Each cloud faint with the fragance it
 bears;

The quivering vapors of dim noontide, 90
Which like a sea o'er the warm earth
 glide,
In which every sound, and odor, and beam,
Move, as reeds in a single stream; —

Each and all like ministering angels were
For the Sensitive Plant sweet joy to bear,
Whilst the lagging hours of the day went
 by
Like windless clouds o'er a tender sky.

And when evening descended from heaven
 above,
And the Earth was all rest, and the air was
 all love,
And delight, though less bright, was far
 more deep, 100
And the day's veil fell from the world of
 sleep,

And the beasts, and the birds, and the in-
 sects were drowned
In an ocean of dreams without a sound,
Whose waves never mark, though they
 ever impress
The light sand which paves it, conscious-
 ness;

(Only overhead the sweet nightingale
Ever sang more sweet as the day might
 fail,

And snatches of its Elysian chant
Were mixed with the dreams of the Sensi-
tive Plant); —

The Sensitive Plant was the earliest 110
Upgathered into the bosom of rest;
A sweet child weary of its delight,
The feeblest and yet the favorite,
Cradled within the embrace of night.

PART SECOND

There was a Power in this sweet place,
An Eve in this Eden; a ruling grace
Which to the flowers, did they waken or
dream,
Was as God is to the starry scheme.

A Lady, the wonder of her kind,
Whose form was upborne by a lovely mind
Which, dilating, had moulded her mien
and motion
Like ·a sea-flower unfolded beneath the
ocean,

Tended the garden from morn to even;
And the meteors of that sublunar heaven,
Like the lamps of the air when Night walks
forth, 11
Laughed round her footsteps up from the
Earth !

She had no companion of mortal race,
But her tremulous breath and her flushing
face
Told, whilst the morn kissed the sleep from
her eyes,
That her dreams were less slumber than
Paradise :

As if some bright Spirit for her sweet
sake
Had deserted heaven while the stars were
awake,
As if yet around her he lingering were,
Though the veil of daylight concealed him
from her. 20

Her step seemed to pity the grass it
pressed;
You might hear, by the heaving of her
breast,
That the coming and going of the wind
Brought pleasure there and left passion
behind.

And wherever her airy footstep trod,
Her trailing hair from the grassy sod
Erased its light vestige, with shadowy
sweep,
Like a sunny storm o'er the dark green
deep.

I doubt not the flowers of that garden
sweet
Rejoiced in the sound of her gentle feet; 30
I doubt not they felt the spirit that came
From her glowing fingers through all their
frame.

She sprinkled bright water from the stream
On those that were faint with the sunny
beam;
And out of the cups of the heavy flowers
She emptied the rain of the thunder
showers.

She lifted their heads with her tender
hands,
And sustained them with rods and osier-
bands;
If the flowers had been her own infants,
she
Could never have nursed them more ten-
derly. 40

And all killing insects and gnawing worms,
And things of obscene and unlovely forms,
She bore in a basket of Indian woof,
Into the rough woods far aloof, —

In a basket, of grasses and wild flowers
full,
The freshest her gentle hands could pull
For the poor banished insects, whose in-
tent,
Although they did ill, was innocent.

But the bee, and the beam-like ephemeris
Whose path is the lightning's, and soft
moths that kiss 50
The sweet lips of the flowers, and harm not,
did she
Make her attendant angels be.

And many an antenatal tomb,
Where butterflies dream of the life to
come,
She left clinging round the smooth and
dark
Edge of the odorous cedar bark.

This fairest creature from earliest spring
Thus moved through the garden minister-
 ing
All the sweet season of summer tide,
And ere the first leaf looked brown — she
 died ! 60

PART THIRD

Three days the flowers of the garden fair,
Like stars when the moon is awakened,
 were,
Or the waves of Baiæ, ere luminous
She floats up through the smoke of Vesu-
 vius.

And on the fourth, the Sensitive Plant
Felt the sound of the funeral chant,
And the steps of the bearers, heavy and
 slow,
And the sobs of the mourners, deep and
 low;

The weary sound and the heavy breath,
And the silent motions of passing death, 10
And the smell, cold, oppressive, and dank,
Sent through the pores of the coffin plank.

The dark grass, and the flowers among the
 grass,
Were bright with tears as the crowd did
 pass;
From their sighs the wind caught a mourn-
 ful tone,
And sate in the pines, and gave groan for
 groan.

The garden, once fair, became cold and
 foul,
Like the corpse of her who had been its
 soul
Which at first was lovely as if in sleep,
Then slowly changed, till it grew a heap 20
To make men tremble who never weep.

Swift summer into the autumn flowed,
And frost in the mist of the morning rode,
Though the noonday sun looked clear and
 bright,
Mocking the spoil of the secret night.

The rose leaves, like flakes of crimson
 snow,
Paved the turf and the moss below.

The lilies were drooping, and white, and
 wan,
Like the head and the skin of a dying man.

And Indian plants, of scent and hue 30
The sweetest that ever were fed on dew,
Leaf by leaf, day after day,
Were massed into the common clay.

And the leaves, brown, yellow, and gray,
 and red,
And white with the whiteness of what is
 dead,
Like troops of ghosts on the dry wind
 passed;
Their whistling noise made the birds aghast.

And the gusty winds waked the wingèd
 seeds
Out of their birthplace of ugly weeds,
Till they clung round many a sweet flower's
 stem,
Which rotted into the earth with them. 40

The water-blooms under the rivulet
Fell from the stalks on which they were
 set;
And the eddies drove them here and there,
As the winds did those of the upper air.

Then the rain came down, and the broken
 stalks
Were bent and tangled across the walks;
And the leafless network of parasite bow-
 ers
Massed into ruin, and all sweet flowers.

Between the time of the wind and the
 snow 50
All loathliest weeds began to grow,
Whose coarse leaves were splashed with
 many a speck,
Like the water-snake's belly and the toad's
 back.

And thistles, and nettles, and darnels rank,
And the dock, and henbane, and hemlock
 dank,
Stretched out its long and hollow shank,
And stifled the air till the dead wind stank.

And plants, at whose names the verse feels
 loath,
Filled the place with a monstrous under-
 growth,

Prickly, and pulpous, and blistering, and
 blue, 60
Livid, and starred with a lurid dew.

And agarics and fungi, with mildew and
 mould,
Started like mist from the wet ground
 cold;
Pale, fleshy, as if the decaying dead
With a spirit of growth had been animated !

Spawn, weeds, and filth, a leprous scum,
Made the running rivulet thick and dumb,
And at its outlet flags huge as stakes
Dammed it up with roots knotted like wa-
 ter-snakes.

And hour by hour, when the air was still, 70
The vapors arose which have strength to
 kill;
At morn they were seen, at noon they were
 felt,
At night they were darkness no star could
 melt.

And unctuous meteors from spray to spray
Crept and flitted in broad noonday
Unseen; every branch on which they alit
By a venomous blight was burned and
 bit.

The Sensitive Plant, like one forbid,
Wept, and the tears within each lid 79
Of its folded leaves, which together grew,
Were changed to a blight of frozen glue.

For the leaves soon fell, and the branches
 soon
By the heavy axe of the blast were hewn;
The sap shrank to the root through every
 pore,
As blood to a heart that will beat no more.

For Winter came; the wind was his whip;
One choppy finger was on his lip;
He had torn the cataracts from the hills
And they clanked at his girdle like mana-
 cles;

His breath was a chain which without a
 sound 90
The earth, and the air, and the water bound;
He came, fiercely driven, in his chariot-
 throne,
By the tenfold blasts of the Arctic zone.

Then the weeds which were forms of living
 death
Fled from the frost to the earth beneath.
Their decay and sudden flight from frost
Was but like the vanishing of a ghost !

And under the roots of the Sensitive Plant
The moles and the dormice died for want;
The birds dropped stiff from the frozen air
And were caught in the branches naked
 and bare. 101

First there came down a thawing rain,
And its dull drops froze on the boughs
 again;
Then there steamed up a freezing dew
Which to the drops of the thaw-rain grew;

And a northern whirlwind, wandering
 about
Like a wolf that had smelt a dead child
 out,
Shook the boughs thus laden and heavy and
 stiff,
And snapped them off with his rigid griff.

When Winter had gone and Spring came
 back, 110
The Sensitive Plant was a leafless wreck;
But the mandrakes, and toadstools, and
 docks, and darnels,
Rose like the dead from their ruined char-
 nels.

CONCLUSION

Whether the Sensitive Plant, or that
Which within its boughs like a spirit sat,
Ere its outward form had known decay,
Now felt this change, I cannot say.

Whether that lady's gentle mind,
No longer with the form combined
Which scattered love, as stars do light, 120
Found sadness where it left delight,

I dare not guess; but in this life
Of error, ignorance and strife,
Where nothing is, but all things seem,
And we the shadows of the dream,

It is a modest creed, and yet
Pleasant, if one considers it,
To own that death itself must be,
Like all the rest, a mockery.

That garden sweet, that lady fair, 130
And all sweet shapes and odors there,
In truth have never passed away :
'T is we, 't is ours, are changed; not they.

For love, and beauty, and delight,
There is no death nor change : their might
Exceeds our organs, which endure
No light, being themselves obscure.

A VISION OF THE SEA

Composed at Pisa as early as April, and published with *Prometheus Unbound*, 1820.

'T is the terror of tempest. The rags of
 the sail
Are flickering in ribbons within the fierce
 gale;
From the stark night of vapors the dim rain
 is driven,
And, when lightning is loosed, like a deluge
 from heaven,
She sees the black trunks of the water-
 spouts spin
And bend, as if heaven was ruining in,
Which they seemed to sustain with their
 terrible mass
As if ocean had sunk from beneath them;
 they pass
To their graves in the deep with an earth-
 quake of sound,
And the waves and the thunders, made
 silent around, 10
Leave the wind to its echo. The vessel,
 now tossed
Through the low trailing rack of the tem-
 pest, is lost
In the skirts of the thundercloud; now
 down the sweep
Of the wind-cloven wave to the chasm of
 the deep
It sinks, and the walls of the watery vale
Whose depths of dread calm are unmoved
 by the gale,
Dim mirrors of ruin, hang gleaming about;
While the surf, like a chaos of stars, like
 a rout
Of death-flames, like whirlpools of fire-
 flowing iron,
With splendor and terror the black ship
 environ, 20
Or, like sulphur-flakes hurled from a mine
 of pale fire,
In fountains spout o'er it. In many a spire

The pyramid-billows, with white points of
 brine,
In the cope of the lightning inconstantly
 shine,
As piercing the sky from the floor of the
 sea.
The great ship seems splitting ! it cracks
 as a tree,
While an earthquake is splintering its root,
 ere the blast
Of the whirlwind that stripped it of
 branches has passed.
The intense thunder-balls which are rain-
 ing from heaven
Have shattered its mast, and it stands black
 and riven. 30
The chinks suck destruction. The heavy
 dead hulk
On the living sea rolls an inanimate bulk,
Like a corpse on the clay which is hunger-
 ing to fold
Its corruption around it. Meanwhile, from
 the hold,
One deck is burst up by the waters be-
 low,
And it splits like the ice when the thaw-
 breezes blow
O'er the lakes of the desert ! Who sit on
 the other ?
Is that all the crew that lie burying each
 other,
Like the dead in a breach, round the fore-
 mast ? Are those
Twin tigers who burst, when the waters
 arose, 40
In the agony of terror, their chains in the
 hold, —
(What now makes them tame is what then
 made them bold)
Who crouch, side by side, and have driven,
 like a crank,
The deep grip of their claws through the
 vibrating plank, —
Are these all ? Nine weeks the tall vessel
 had lain
On the windless expanse of the watery
 plain,
Where the death-darting sun cast no shadow
 at noon,
And there seemed to be fire in the beams
 of the moon,
Till a lead-colored fog gathered up from
 the deep,
Whose breath was quick pestilence; then,
 the cold sleep 50

Crept, like blight through the ears of a
 thick field of corn,
O'er the populous vessel. And even and
 morn,
With their hammocks for coffins, the sea-
 men aghast
Like dead men the dead limbs of their
 comrades cast
Down the deep, which closed on them above
 and around,
And the sharks and the dogfish their grave-
 clothes unbound,
And were glutted like Jews with this
 manna rained down
From God on their wilderness. One after
 one
The mariners died; on the eve of this day,
When the tempest was gathering in cloudy
 array, 60
But seven remained. Six the thunder has
 smitten,
And they lie black as mummies on which
 Time has written
His scorn of the embalmer; the seventh,
 from the deck
An oak-splinter pierced through his breast
 and his back,
And hung out to the tempest, a wreck on
 the wreck.
No more? At the helm sits a woman
 more fair
Than heaven when, unbinding its star-
 braided hair,
It sinks with the sun on the earth and the
 sea.
She clasps a bright child on her upgathered
 knee;
It laughs at the lightning, it mocks the
 mixed thunder 70
Of the air and the sea; with desire and
 with wonder
It is beckoning the tigers to rise and come
 near;
It would play with those eyes where the
 radiance of fear
Is outshining the meteors; its bosom beats
 high,
The heart-fire of pleasure has kindled its eye,
Whilst its mother's is lustreless: 'Smile
 not, my child,
But sleep deeply and sweetly, and so be
 beguiled
Of the pang that awaits us, whatever that be,
So dreadful since thou must divide it with
 me !

Dream, sleep ! This pale bosom, thy cra-
 dle and bed, 80
Will it rock thee not, infant ? 'T is beat-
 ing with dread !
Alas ! what is life, what is death, what are
 we,
That when the ship sinks we no longer
 may be ?
What ! to see thee no more, and to feel
 thee no more ?
To be after life what we have been before ?
Not to touch those sweet hands, not to look
 on those eyes,
Those lips, and that hair, all that smiling
 disguise
Thou yet wearest, sweet spirit, which I,
 day by day,
Have so long called my child, but which
 now fades away
Like a rainbow, and I the fallen shower ?'
 Lo ! the ship 90
Is settling, it topples, the leeward ports dip;
The tigers leap up when they feel the slow
 brine
Crawling inch by inch on them; hair, ears,
 limbs, and eyne
Stand rigid with horror; a loud, long,
 hoarse cry
Bursts at once from their vitals tremen-
 dously,
And 't is borne down the mountainous vale
 of the wave,
Rebounding, like thunder, from crag to
 cave,
Mixed with the clash of the lashing rain,
Hurried on by the might of the hurricane.
The hurricane came from the west, and
 passed on 100
By the path of the gate of the eastern sun,
Transversely dividing the stream of the
 storm;
As an arrowy serpent, pursuing the form
Of an elephant, bursts through the brakes
 of the waste.
Black as a cormorant the screaming blast,
Between ocean and heaven, like an ocean,
 passed,
Till it came to the clouds on the verge of
 the world
Which, based on the sea and to heaven up-
 curled,
Like columns and walls did surround and
 sustain
The dome of the tempest; it rent them in
 twain, 110

As a flood rends its barriers of mountain-
ous crag;
And the dense clouds in many a ruin and
rag,
Like the stones of a temple ere earthquake
has passed,
Like the dust of its fall, on the whirlwind
are cast;
They are scattered like foam on the tor-
rent; and where
The wind has burst out through the chasm,
from the air
Of clear morning the beams of the sunrise
flow in,
Unimpeded, keen, golden, and crystalline,
Banded armies of light and of air; at one
gate
They encounter, but interpenetrate. 120
And that breach in the tempest is widening
away,
And the caverns of cloud are torn up by
the day,
And the fierce winds are sinking with weary
wings,
Lulled by the motion and murmurings
And the long glassy heave of the rocking
sea,
And overhead glorious, but dreadful to
see,
The wrecks of the tempest, like vapors of
gold,
Are consuming in sunrise. The heaped
waves behold
The deep calm of blue heaven dilating
above,
And, like passions made still by the pre-
sence of Love, 130
Beneath the clear surface reflecting it slide
Tremulous with soft influence; extending
its tide
From the Andes to Atlas, round mountain
and isle,
Round sea-birds and wrecks, paved with
heaven's azure smile,
The wide world of waters is vibrating.
Where
Is the ship? On the verge of the wave
where it lay
One tiger is mingled in ghastly affray
With a sea-snake. The foam and the
smoke of the battle
Stain the clear air with sunbows. The jar,
and the rattle 139
Of solid bones crushed by the infinite stress
Of the snake's adamantine voluminousness;

And the hum of the hot blood that spouts
and rains
Where the gripe of the tiger has wounded
the veins,
Swollen with rage, strength, and effort; the
whirl and the splash
As of some hideous engine whose brazen
teeth smash
The thin winds and soft waves into thun-
der; the screams
And hissings, crawl fast o'er the smooth
ocean-streams,
Each sound like a centipede. Near this
commotion
A blue shark is hanging within the blue
ocean,
The fin-wingèd tomb of the victor. The
other 150
Is winning his way from the fate of his
brother,
To his own with the speed of despair. Lo!
a boat
Advances; twelve rowers with the impulse
of thought
Urge on the keen keel, — the brine foams.
At the stern
Three marksmen stand levelling. Hot
bullets burn
In the breast of the tiger, which yet bears
him on
To his refuge and ruin. One fragment
alone —
'T is dwindling and sinking, 't is now almost
gone —
Of the wreck of the vessel peers out of the
sea.
With her left hand she grasps it impetu-
ously, 160
With her right hand she sustains her fair
infant. Death, Fear,
Love, Beauty, are mixed in the atmo-
sphere,
Which trembles and burns with the fervor
of dread
Around her wild eyes, her bright hand,
and her head,
Like a meteor of light o'er the waters! her
child
Is yet smiling, and playing, and murmur-
ing; so smiled
The false deep ere the storm. Like a sis-
ter and brother
The child and the ocean still smile on each
other,
Whilst ——

THE CLOUD

Published with *Prometheus Unbound*, 1820.

I BRING fresh showers for the thirsting
 flowers,
 From the seas and the streams;
I bear light shade for the leaves when laid
 In their noonday dreams.
From my wings are shaken the dews that
 waken
 The sweet buds every one,
When rocked to rest on their mother's
 breast,
 As she dances about the sun.
I wield the flail of the lashing hail,
 And whiten the green plains under, 10
And then again I dissolve it in rain,
 And laugh as I pass in thunder.

I sift the snow on the mountains below,
 And their great pines groan aghast;
And all the night 't is my pillow white,
 While I sleep in the arms of the blast.
Sublime on the towers of my skyey bow-
 ers,
 Lightning my pilot sits;
In a cavern under is fettered the thunder,
 It struggles and howls at fits; 20
Over earth and ocean with gentle motion,
 This pilot is guiding me,
Lured by the love of the genii that move
 In the depths of the purple sea;
Over the rills, and the crags, and the hills,
 Over the lakes and the plains,
Wherever he dream, under mountain or
 stream,
 The Spirit he loves remains;
And I all the while bask in heaven's blue
 smile,
 Whilst he is dissolving in rains. 30

The sanguine sunrise, with his meteor eyes,
 And his burning plumes outspread,
Leaps on the back of my sailing rack,
 When the morning star shines dead;
As on the jag of a mountain crag,
 Which an earthquake rocks and swings,
An eagle alit one moment may sit
 In the light of its golden wings.
And when sunset may breathe, from the
 lit sea beneath,
 Its ardors of rest and of love, 40
And the crimson pall of eve may fall
 From the depth of heaven above,

With wings folded I rest, on mine airy
 nest,
 As still as a brooding dove.

That orbèd maiden, with white fire laden,
 Whom mortals call the Moon,
Glides glimmering o'er my fleece-like floor,
 By the midnight breezes strewn;
And wherever the beat of her unseen feet,
 Which only the angels hear, 50
May have broken the woof of my tent's
 thin roof,
 The stars peep behind her and peer;
And I laugh to see them whirl and flee,
 Like a swarm of golden bees,
When I widen the rent in my wind-built
 tent,
 Till the calm rivers, lakes, and seas,
Like strips of the sky fallen through me
 on high,
 Are each paved with the moon and
 these.

I bind the sun's throne with a burning zone,
 And the moon's with a girdle of pearl;
The volcanoes are dim, and the stars reel
 and swim, 61
 When the whirlwinds my banner unfurl.
From cape to cape, with a bridge-like
 shape,
 Over a torrent sea,
Sunbeam-proof, I hang like a roof, —
 The mountains its columns be.
The triumphal arch, through which I
 march,
 With hurricane, fire, and snow,
When the powers of the air are chained to
 my chair,
 Is the million-colored bow; 70
The sphere-fire above its soft colors wove,
 While the moist earth was laughing
 below.

I am the daughter of earth and water,
 And the nursling of the sky;
I pass through the pores of the ocean and
 shores;
 I change, but I cannot die.
For after the rain, when with never a stain
 The pavilion of heaven is bare,
And the winds and sunbeams with their
 convex gleams
 Build up the blue dome of air, 80
I silently laugh at my own cenotaph,
 And out of the caverns of rain,

Like a child from the womb, like a ghost
 from the tomb,
I arise and unbuild it again.

TO A SKYLARK

Composed at Leghorn, and published with
Prometheus Unbound, 1820. The occasion is
described by Mrs. Shelley : ' In the spring we
spent a week or two near Leghorn, borrowing
the house of some friends, who were absent on
a journey to England. It was on a beautiful
summer evening while wandering among the
lanes, whose myrtle hedges were the bowers
of the fireflies, that we heard the carolling of
the skylark, which inspired one of the most
beautiful of his poems.'

HAIL to thee, blithe Spirit !
 Bird thou never wert,
That from Heaven, or near it,
 Pourest thy full heart
In profuse strains of unpremeditated art.

 Higher still and higher
 From the earth thou springest
 Like a cloud of fire;
 The blue deep thou wingest,
And singing still dost soar, and soaring
 ever singest. 10

 In the golden lightning
 Of the sunken sun,
 O'er which clouds are bright'ning,
 Thou dost float and run;
Like an unbodied joy whose race is just
 begun.

 The pale purple even
 Melts around thy flight;
 Like a star of heaven
 In the broad daylight
Thou art unseen, — but yet I hear thy shrill
 delight, 20

 Keen as are the arrows
 Of that silver sphere,
 Whose intense lamp narrows
 In the white dawn clear
Until we hardly see — we feel that it is
 there;

 All the earth and air
 With thy voice is loud,

 As when Night is bare
 From one lonely cloud
The moon rains out her beams, and Heaven
 is overflowed. 30

 What thou art we know not;
 What is most like thee ?
 From rainbow clouds there flow
 not
 Drops so bright to see
As from thy presence showers a rain of
 melody.

 Like a Poet hidden
 In the light of thought,
 Singing hymns unbidden
 Till the world is wrought
To sympathy with hopes and fears it heeded
 not : 40

 Like a high-born maiden
 In a palace tower,
 Soothing her love-laden
 Soul in secret hour
With music sweet as love, — which over=
 flows her bower :

 Like a glowworm golden
 In a dell of dew,
 Scattering unbeholden
 Its aërial hue
Among the flowers and grass which screen
 it from the view : 50

 Like a rose embowered
 In its own green leaves,
 By warm winds deflowered,
 Till the scent it gives
Makes faint with too much sweet those
 heavy wingèd thieves.

 Sound of vernal showers
 On the twinkling grass,
 Rain-awakened flowers,
 All that ever was
Joyous and clear and fresh, thy music doth
 surpass. 60

 Teach us, Sprite or Bird,
 What sweet thoughts are thine;
 I have never heard
 Praise of love or wine
That panted forth a flood of rapture so
 divine.

Chorus Hymeneal,
 Or triumphal chant,
Matched with thine, would be all
 But an empty vaunt,
A thing wherein we feel there is some
hidden want. 70

What objects are the fountains
 Of thy happy strain ?
What fields or waves or mountains ?
 What shapes of sky or plain ?
What love of thine own kind ? what igno-
rance of pain ?

With thy clear keen joyance
 Languor cannot be;
Shadow of annoyance
 Never came near thee;
Thou lovest — but ne'er knew love's sad
satiety. 80

Waking or asleep
 Thou of death must deem
Things more true and deep
 Than we mortals dream —
Or how could thy notes flow in such a crys-
tal stream ?

We look before and after,
 And pine for what is not;
Our sincerest laughter
 With some pain is fraught;
Our sweetest songs are those that tell of
saddest thought. 90

Yet if we could scorn
 Hate and pride and fear;
If we were things born
 Not to shed a tear,
I know not how thy joy we ever should
come near.

Better than all measures
 Of delightful sound,
Better than all treasures
 That in books are found,
Thy skill to poet were, thou scorner of the
ground ! 100

Teach me half the gladness
 That thy brain must know,
Such harmonious madness
 From my lips would flow
The world should listen then — as I am
listening now.

ODE TO LIBERTY

Published with *Prometheus Unbound*, 1820.
Shelley sent it to Peacock with permission to
insert asterisks in stanzas fifteen and sixteen
in case his publisher objected to the expressions
there used.

 Yet Freedom, yet, thy banner torn but flying
Streams like a thunder-storm against the wind.
 BYRON.

I

A GLORIOUS people vibrated again
 The lightning of the Nations; Liberty,
From heart to heart, from tower to tower,
 o'er Spain,
 Scattering contagious fire into the sky,
Gleamed. My soul spurned the chains of
 its dismay,
 And in the rapid plumes of song
 Clothed itself, sublime and strong;
As a young eagle soars the morning clouds
 among,
 Hovering in verse o'er its accustomed
 prey;
 Till from its station in the Heaven of
 fame
 The Spirit's whirlwind rapt it, and the ray
 Of the remotest sphere of living flame
Which paves the void was from behind it
 flung,
 As foam from a ship's swiftness, when
 there came
 A voice out of the deep: I will record the
 same.

II

The Sun and the serenest Moon sprang
 forth;
 The burning stars of the abyss were
 hurled
Into the depths of heaven. The dædal
 earth,
 That island in the ocean of the world,
Hung in its cloud of all-sustaining air;
 But this divinest universe
 Was yet a chaos and a curse,
For thou wert not; but power from worst
 producing worse,
 The spirit of the beasts was kindled there,
 And of the birds, and of the watery
 forms,
 And there was war among them, and
 despair
 Within them, raging without truce or
 terms.

The bosom of their violated nurse
 Groaned, for beasts warred on beasts,
 and worms on worms,
And men on men; each heart was as a hell
 of storms.

III

Man, the imperial shape, then multiplied
 His generations under the pavilion
Of the Sun's throne; palace and pyramid,
 Temple and prison, to many a swarming
 million
Were as to mountain wolves their ragged
 caves.
 This human living multitude
 Was savage, cunning, blind, and rude,
For thou wert not; but o'er the populous
 solitude,
 Like one fierce cloud over a waste of
 waves,
 Hung Tyranny; beneath, sate deified
The sister-pest, congregator of slaves;
 Into the shadow of her pinions wide
Anarchs and priests who feed on gold and
 blood
 Till with the stain their inmost souls are
 dyed,
 Drove the astonished herds of men from
 every side.

IV

The nodding promontories, and blue isles,
 And cloud-like mountains, and dividuous
 waves
Of Greece, basked glorious in the open
 smiles
 Of favoring heaven; from their en-
 chanted caves
Prophetic echoes flung dim melody.
 On the unapprehensive wild
 The vine, the corn, the olive mild,
Grew savage yet, to human use unrecon-
 ciled;
 And, like unfolded flowers beneath the sea,
 Like the man's thought dark in the in-
 fant's brain,
 Like aught that is which wraps what is
 to be,
 Art's deathless dreams lay veiled by
 many a vein
Of Parian stone; and, yet a speechless child,
 Verse murmured, and Philosophy did
 strain
 Her lidless eyes for thee; when o'er the
 Ægean main

V

Athens arose; a city such as vision
 Builds from the purple crags and silver
 towers
Of battlemented cloud, as in derision
 Of kingliest masonry: the ocean floors
Pave it; the evening sky pavilions it;
 Its portals are inhabited
 By thunder-zonèd winds, each head
Within its cloudy wings with sun-fire gar-
 landed, —
 A divine work! Athens, diviner yet,
 Gleamed with its crest of columns, on
 the will
 Of man, as on a mount of diamond,
 set;
 For thou wert, and thine all-creative
 skill
Peopled, with forms that mock the eternal
 dead
 In marble immortality, that hill
 Which was thine earliest throne and lat-
 est oracle.

VI

Within the surface of Time's fleeting river
 Its wrinkled image lies, as then it lay
Immovably unquiet, and forever
 It trembles, but it cannot pass away!
The voices of thy bards and sages thunder
 With an earth-awakening blast
 Through the caverns of the past;
Religion veils her eyes; Oppression shrinks
 aghast.
 A wingèd sound of joy, and love, and
 wonder,
 Which soars where Expectation never
 flew,
 Rending the veil of space and time asun-
 der!
 One ocean feeds the clouds, and
 streams, and dew;
One sun illumines heaven; one spirit vast
 With life and love makes chaos ever new,
 As Athens doth the world with thy de-
 light renew.

VII

Then Rome was, and from thy deep bosom
 fairest,
 Like a wolf-cub from a Cadmean Mænad,
She drew the milk of greatness, though thy
 dearest
 From that Elysian food was yet un-
 weanèd;

And many a deed of terrible uprightness
By thy sweet love was sanctified;
And in thy smile, and by thy side,
Saintly Camillus lived, and firm Atilius died.
But when tears stained thy robe of vestal
whiteness,
And gold profaned thy Capitolian
throne,
Thou didst desert, with spirit-wingèd
lightness,
The senate of the tyrants: they sunk
prone
Slaves of one tyrant. Palatinus sighed
Faint echoes of Ionian song; that tone
Thou didst delay to hear, lamenting to
disown.

VIII

From what Hyrcanian glen or frozen hill,
Or piny promontory of the Arctic main,
Or utmost islet inaccessible,
Didst thou lament the ruin of thy reign,
Teaching the woods and waves, and desert
rocks,
And every Naiad's ice-cold urn,
To talk in echoes sad and stern,
Of that sublimest lore which man had dared
unlearn?
For neither didst thou watch the wizard
flocks
Of the Scald's dreams, nor haunt the
Druid's sleep.
What if the tears rained through thy
shattered locks
Were quickly dried? for thou didst
groan, not weep,
When from its sea of death, to kill and
burn,
The Galilean serpent forth did creep,
And made thy world an undistinguishable
heap.

IX

A thousand years the Earth cried, Where
art thou?
And then the shadow of thy coming
fell
On Saxon Alfred's olive-cinctured brow;
And many a warrior-peopled citadel,
Like rocks which fire lifts out of the flat
deep,
Arose in sacred Italy,
Frowning o'er the tempestuous sea
Of kings, and priests, and slaves, in tower-
crowned majesty;

That multitudinous anarchy did sweep
And burst around their walls, like idle
foam,
Whilst from the human spirit's deepest
deep,
Strange melody with love and awe
struck dumb
Dissonant arms; and Art, which cannot die,
With divine wand traced on our earthly
home
Fit imagery to pave heaven's everlasting
dome.

X

Thou huntress swifter than the Moon!
thou terror
Of the world's wolves! thou bearer of
the quiver,
Whose sun-like shafts pierce tempest-
wingèd Error,
As light may pierce the clouds when they
dissever
In the calm regions of the orient day!
Luther caught thy wakening glance;
Like lightning, from his leaden lance
Reflected, it dissolved the visions of the
trance
In which, as in a tomb, the nations lay;
And England's prophets hailed thee
as their queen,
In songs whose music cannot pass away,
Though it must flow forever; not un-
seen
Before the spirit-sighted countenance
Of Milton didst thou pass, from the sad
scene
Beyond whose night he saw, with a de-
jected mien.

XI

The eager hours and unreluctant years
As on a dawn-illumined mountain stood,
Trampling to silence their loud hopes and
fears,
Darkening each other with their multi-
tude,
And cried aloud, Liberty! Indignation
Answered Pity from her cave;
Death grew pale within the grave,
And Desolation howled to the destroyer,
Save!
When, like heaven's sun girt by the ex-
halation
Of its own glorious light, thou didst
arise,

Chasing thy foes from nation unto nation
 Like shadows: as if day had cloven
 the skies
At dreaming midnight o'er the western
 wave,
 Men started, staggering with a glad sur-
 prise,
Under the lightnings of thine unfamiliar
 eyes.

XII

Thou heaven of earth! what spells could
 pall thee then,
 In ominous eclipse? a thousand years,
Bred from the slime of deep oppression's
 den,
 Dyed all thy liquid light with blood and
 tears,
Till thy sweet stars could weep the stain
 away;
 How like Bacchanals of blood
 Round France, the ghastly vintage,
 stood
Destruction's sceptred slaves, and Folly's
 mitred brood!
 When one, like them, but mightier far
 than they,
 The Anarch of thine own bewildered
 powers,
 Rose; armies mingled in obscure array,
 Like clouds with clouds, darkening the
 sacred bowers
Of serene heaven. He, by the past pur-
 sued,
 Rests with those dead but unforgotten
 hours,
 Whose ghosts scare victor kings in their
 ancestral towers.

XIII

England yet sleeps: was she not called of
 old?
 Spain calls her now, as with its thrilling
 thunder
Vesuvius wakens Ætna, and the cold
 Snow-crags by its reply are cloven in
 sunder;
O'er the lit waves every Æolian isle
 From Pithecusa to Pelorus
 Howls, and leaps, and glares in
 chorus;
They cry, Be dim, ye lamps of heaven
 suspended o'er us!
 Her chains are threads of gold, she need
 but smile

And they dissolve; but Spain's were
 links of steel,
Till bit to dust by virtue's keenest file.
 Twins of a single destiny! appeal
To the eternal years enthroned before us
 In the dim West; impress us from a seal,
 All ye have thought and done! Time
 cannot dare conceal.

XIV

Tomb of Arminius! render up thy dead
 Till, like a standard from a watch-tower's
 staff,
His soul may stream over the tyrant's head;
 Thy victory shall be his epitaph,
Wild Bacchanal of truth's mysterious wine,
 King-deluded Germany,
 His dead spirit lives in thee.
Why do we fear or hope? thou art already
 free!
 And thou, lost Paradise of this divine
 And glorious world! thou flowery
 wilderness!
 Thou island of eternity! thou shrine
 Where desolation clothed with loveli-
 ness
Worships the thing thou wert! O Italy,
 Gather thy blood into thy heart; repress
 The beasts who make their dens thy
 sacred palaces.

XV

Oh, that the free would stamp the impious
 name
 Of King into the dust! or write it there,
So that this blot upon the page of fame
 Were as a serpent's path, which the light
 air
Erases, and the flat sands close behind!
 Ye the oracle have heard.
 Lift the victory-flashing sword,
And cut the snaky knots of this foul gor-
 dian word,
 Which, weak itself as stubble, yet can
 bind
 Into a mass, irrefragably firm,
 The axes and the rods which awe man-
 kind;
 The sound has poison in it, 't is the
 sperm
Of what makes life foul, cankerous, and
 abhorred;
 Disdain not thou, at thine appointed term,
 To set thine armèd heel on this reluctant
 worm.

XVI

Oh, that the wise from their bright minds
 would kindle
 Such lamps within the dome of this dim
 world,
That the pale name of Priest might shrink
 and dwindle
 Into the hell from which it first was
 hurled,
A scoff of impious pride from fiends im-
 pure;
 Till human thoughts might kneel
 alone,
 Each before the judgment-throne
Of its own aweless soul, or of the power
 unknown!
 Oh, that the words which make the
 thoughts obscure
 From which they spring, as clouds of
 glimmering dew
 From a white lake blot heaven's blue
 portraiture,
 Were stripped of their thin masks and
 various hue
And frowns and smiles and splendors not
 their own,
 Till in the nakedness of false and true
 They stand before their Lord, each to re-
 ceive its due.

XVII

He who taught man to vanquish whatsoever
 Can be between the cradle and the grave
Crowned him the King of Life. Oh, vain
 endeavor!
 If on his own high will, a willing slave,
He has enthroned the oppression and the
 oppressor.
 What if earth can clothe and feed
 Amplest millions at their need,
And power in thought be as the tree within
 the seed?
 Oh, what if Art, an ardent intercessor,
 Driving on fiery wings to Nature's
 throne,
 Checks the great mother stooping to ca-
 ress her
 And cries: "Give me, thy child, domin-
 ion
Over all height and depth?' if Life can
 breed
 New wants, and wealth from those who
 toil and groan
 Rend of thy gifts and hers a thousand-
 fold for one.

XVIII

Come thou, but lead out of the inmost
 cave
 Of man's deep spirit, as the morning-
 star
Beckons the sun from the Eoan wave,
 Wisdom. I hear the pennons of her
 car
Self-moving, like cloud charioted by flame;
 Comes she not, and come ye not,
 Rulers of eternal thought,
To judge with solemn truth life's ill-appor-
 tioned lot?
 Blind Love, and equal Justice, and the
 Fame
 Of what has been, the Hope of what
 will be?
 O Liberty! if such could be thy name
 Wert thou disjoined from these, or
 they from thee —
If thine or theirs were treasures to be
 bought
 By blood or tears, have not the wise and
 free
 Wept tears, and blood like tears? — The
 solemn harmony

XIX

Paused, and the Spirit of that mighty sing-
 ing
 To its abyss was suddenly withdrawn;
Then as a wild swan, when sublimely wing-
 ing
 Its path athwart the thunder-smoke of
 dawn,
Sinks headlong through the aërial golden
 light
 On the heavy sounding plain,
 When the bolt has pierced its
 brain;
 As summer clouds dissolve unburdened of
 their rain;
 As a far taper fades with fading
 night,
 As a brief insect dies with dying
 day, —
 My song, its pinions disarrayed of might,
 Drooped; o'er it closed the echoes far
 away
Of the great voice which did its flight sus-
 tain,
 As waves which lately paved his watery
 way
 Hiss round a drowner's head in their
 tempestuous play.

TO ——

Published by **Mrs.** Shelley, *Posthumous Poems*, 1824.

I FEAR thy kisses, gentle maiden,
Thou needest not fear mine;
My spirit is too deeply laden
Ever to burden thine.

I fear thy mien, thy tones, thy motion,
Thou needest not fear mine;
Innocent is the heart's devotion
With which I worship thine.

ARETHUSA

Composed at Pisa, and published by Mrs. Shelley, *Posthumous Poems*, 1824.

I

ARETHUSA arose
From her couch of snows
In the Acroceraunian mountains,
From cloud and from crag,
With many a jag,
Shepherding her bright fountains.
She leapt down the rocks,
With her rainbow locks
Streaming among the streams;
Her steps paved with green
The downward ravine
Which slopes to the western gleams;
And gliding and springing,
She went, ever singing,
In murmurs as soft as sleep;
The Earth seemed to love her,
And Heaven smiled above her,
As she lingered towards the deep.

II

Then Alpheus bold,
On his glacier cold,
With his trident the mountains strook;
And opened a chasm
In the rocks — with the spasm
All Erymanthus shook.
And the black south wind
It unsealed behind
The urns of the silent snow,
And earthquake and thunder
Did rend in sunder
The bars of the springs below.

The beard and the hair
Of the River-god were
Seen through the torrent's sweep,
As he followed the light
Of the fleet nymph's flight
To the brink of the Dorian deep.

III

'Oh, save me! Oh, guide me,
And bid the deep hide me,
For he grasps me now by the hair!'
The loud Ocean heard,
To its blue depth stirred,
And divided at her prayer;
And under the water
The Earth's white daughter
Fled like a sunny beam;
Behind her descended
Her billows, unblended
With the brackish Dorian stream.
Like a gloomy stain
On the emerald main
Alpheus rushed behind,
As an eagle pursuing
A dove to its ruin
Down the streams of the cloudy wind.

IV

Under the bowers
Where the Ocean Powers
Sit on their pearlèd thrones;
Through the coral woods
Of the weltering floods,
Over heaps of unvalued stones;
Through the dim beams
Which amid the streams
Weave a network of colored light;
And under the caves,
Where the shadowy waves
Are as green as the forest's night;
Outspeeding the shark,
And the swordfish dark,
Under the ocean foam,
And up through the rifts
Of the mountain clifts
They passed to their Dorian home.

V

And now from their fountains
In Enna's mountains,
Down one vale where the morning basks,
Like friends once parted
Grown single-hearted,
They ply their watery tasks.

At sunrise they leap
From their cradles steep
In the cave of the shelving hill;
At noontide they flow
Through the woods below
And the meadows of asphodel;
And at night they sleep
In the rocking deep
Beneath the Ortygian shore,
Like spirits that lie
In the azure sky
When they love but live no more.

SONG OF PROSERPINE

WHILE GATHERING FLOWERS ON THE
PLAIN OF ENNA

Published by Mrs. Shelley, in her first col-
lected edition, 1839.

SACRED Goddess, Mother Earth,
Thou from whose immortal bosom
Gods, and men, and beasts have birth,
Leaf and blade, and bud and blossom,
Breathe thine influence most divine
On thine own child, Proserpine.

If with mists of evening dew
Thou dost nourish these young flowers
Till they grow, in scent and hue,
Fairest children of the hours,
Breathe thine influence most divine
On thine own child, Proserpine.

HYMN OF APOLLO

This and the following poem were com-
posed for insertion in a projected drama of
Williams, *Midas*. It was published by Mrs.
Shelley, *Posthumous Poems*, 1824.

I

THE sleepless Hours who watch me as I
lie,
Curtained with star-inwoven tapestries
From the broad moonlight of the sky,
Fanning the busy dreams from my dim
eyes,
Waken me when their Mother, the gray
Dawn,
Tells them that dreams and that the moon
is gone.

II

Then I arise, and climbing Heaven's blue
dome,
I walk over the mountains and the waves,
Leaving my robe upon the ocean foam;
My footsteps pave the clouds with fire;
the caves
Are filled with my bright presence, and the
air
Leaves the green earth to my embraces
bare.

III

The sunbeams are my shafts, with which I
kill
Deceit, that loves the night and fears the
day;
All men who do or even imagine ill
Fly me, and from the glory of my ray
Good minds and open actions take new
might,
Until diminished by the reign of night.

IV

I feed the clouds, the rainbows and the
flowers
With their ethereal colors; the moon's
globe
And the pure stars in their eternal bowers
Are cinctured with my power as with a
robe;
Whatever lamps on Earth or Heaven may
shine
Are portions of one power, which is mine.

V

I stand at noon upon the peak of Heaven,
Then with unwilling steps I wander
down
Into the clouds of the Atlantic even;
For grief that I depart they weep and
frown.
What look is more delightful than the
smile
With which I soothe them from the western
isle?

VI

I am the eye with which the Universe
Beholds itself, and knows itself divine;
All harmony of instrument or verse,
All prophecy, all medicine are mine,
All light of Art or Nature; — to my song
Victory and praise in its own right be-
long.

HYMN OF PAN

Published by Mrs. Shelley, *Posthumous Poems*, 1824.

I

FROM the forests and highlands
 We come, we come;
From the river-girt islands,
 Where loud waves are dumb
 Listening to my sweet pipings.
The wind in the reeds and the rushes,
 The bees on the bells of thyme,
The birds on the myrtle bushes,
 The cicale above in the lime,
And the lizards below in the grass,
Were as silent as ever old Tmolus was,
 Listening my sweet pipings.

II

Liquid Peneus was flowing,
 And all dark Tempe lay
In Pelion's shadow, outgrowing
 The light of the dying day,
 Speeded by my sweet pipings.
The Sileni, and Sylvans, and Fauns,
 And the Nymphs of the woods and waves,
To the edge of the moist river-lawns,
 And the brink of the dewy caves,
And all that did then attend and follow,
Were silent with love, as you now, Apollo,
 With envy of my sweet pipings.

III

I sang of the dancing stars,
 I sang of the dædal Earth,
And of Heaven — and the giant wars,
 And Love, and Death, and Birth; —
 And then I changed my pipings,
Singing how down the vale of Mænalus
I pursued a maiden and clasped a reed.
Gods and men, we are all deluded thus !
It breaks in our bosom and then we bleed.
All wept, as I think both ye now would
If envy or age had not frozen your blood,
 At the sorrow of my sweet pipings.

THE QUESTION

Published by Hunt, *The Literary Pocket-Book*, 1822.

I

I DREAMED that, as I wandered by the way,
 Bare winter suddenly was changed to
 spring,
And gentle odors led my steps astray,
 Mixed with a sound of waters murmuring
Along a shelving bank of turf, which lay
 Under a copse, and hardly dared to fling
Its green arms round the bosom of the
 stream,
But kissed it and then fled, as thou might-
 est in dream.

II

There grew pied wind-flowers and violets,
 Daisies, those pearled Arcturi of the
 earth,
The constellated flower that never sets;
 Faint oxlips; tender bluebells, at whose
 birth
The sod scarce heaved; and that tall flower
 that wets —
 (Like a child, half in tenderness and
 mirth)
Its mother's face with heaven - collected
 tears,
When the low wind, its playmate's voice,
 it hears.

III

And in the warm hedge grew lush eglan-
 tine,
 Green cowbind and the moonlight-colored
 May,
And cherry blossoms, and white cups,
 whose wine
 Was the bright dew yet drained not by
 the day,
And wild roses, and ivy serpentine,
 With its dark buds and leaves, wander-
 ing astray;
And flowers azure, black, and streaked
 with gold,
Fairer than any wakened eyes behold.

IV

And nearer to the river's trembling edge
 There grew broad flag-flowers, purple
 pranked with white;
And starry river buds among the sedge;
 And floating water-lilies, broad and
 bright,
Which lit the oak that overhung the hedge
 With moonlight beams of their own
 watery light;
And bulrushes and reeds, of such deep
 green
As soothed the dazzled eye with sober
 sheen.

V

Methought that of these visionary flowers
 I made a nosegay, bound in such a way
That the same hues, which in their natural
 bowers
Were mingled or opposed, the like array
Kept these imprisoned children of the
 Hours
Within my hand, — and then, elate and
 gay,
I hastened to the spot whence I had come,
That I might there present it ! — Oh, to
 whom ?

THE TWO SPIRITS
AN ALLEGORY

Published by Mrs. Shelley, *Posthumous
Poems*, 1824.

FIRST SPIRIT

O THOU, who plumed with strong desire
 Wouldst float above the earth, beware !
A Shadow tracks thy flight of fire —
 Night is coming !
Bright are the regions of the air,
 And among the winds and beams
It were delight to wander there —
 Night is coming !

SECOND SPIRIT

The deathless stars are bright above;
 If I would cross the shade of night,
Within my heart is the lamp of love,
 And that is day !
And the moon will smile with gentle light
 On my golden plumes where'er they
 move;
The meteors will linger round my flight,
 And make night day.

FIRST SPIRIT

But if the whirlwinds of darkness waken
 Hail, and lightning, and stormy rain ?
See, the bounds of the air are shaken —
 Night is coming !
The red swift clouds of the hurricane
 Yon declining sun have overtaken;
The clash of the hail sweeps over the
 plain —
 Night is coming !

SECOND SPIRIT

I see the light, and I hear the sound;
 I 'll sail on the flood of the tempest dark,
With the calm within and the light around
 Which makes night day;
And thou, when the gloom is deep and
 stark,
 Look from thy dull earth, slumber-
 bound;
My moon-like flight thou then mayst mark
 On high, far away.

———

Some say there is a precipice
 Where one vast pine is frozen to ruin
O'er piles of snow and chasms of ice
 Mid Alpine mountains;
And that the languid storm pursuing
 That wingèd shape forever flies
Round those hoar branches, aye renewing
 Its aëry fountains.

Some say when nights are dry and clear,
 And the death-dews sleep on the mo-
 rass,
Sweet whispers are heard by the travel-
 ler,
 Which make night day;
And a silver shape like his early love doth
 pass,
 Upborne by her wild and glittering hair,
And, when he awakes on the fragrant
 grass,
 He finds night day.

LETTER TO MARIA GISBORNE

This letter was written from the house of
Mrs. Gisborne, where Shelley had turned the
workshop of her son, Mr. Reveley, an engineer,
into a study. 'Mrs. Gisborne,' writes Mrs.
Shelley, 'had been a friend of my father in her
younger days. She was a lady of great accom-
plishments, and charming from her frank and
affectionate nature. She had the most intense
love of knowledge, a delicate and trembling
sensibility, and preserved freshness of mind
after a life of considerable adversity. As a
favorite friend of my father we had sought her
with eagerness, and the most open and cordial
friendship was established between us.' Shel-
ley also describes her : 'Mrs. Gisborne is a suffi-
ciently amiable and very accomplished woman ;
[she is δημοκρατικη and αθεη — how far she
may be φιλανθρωπη I don't know, for] she is
the antipodes of enthusiasm.'
 The poem was published by Mrs. Shelley,
Posthumous Poems, 1824.

LEGHORN, *July* 1. 1820.

THE spider spreads her webs whether she be
In poet's tower, cellar, or barn, or tree;
The silkworm in the dark green mulberry
 leaves
His winding sheet and cradle ever weaves;
So I, a thing whom moralists call worm,
Sit spinning still round this decaying form,
From the fine threads of rare and subtle
 thought —
No net of words in garish colors wrought
To catch the idle buzzers of the day —
But a soft cell, where when that fades away
Memory may clothe in wings my living
 name 11
And feed it with the asphodels of fame,
Which in those hearts which must remem-
 ber me
Grow, making love an immortality.

Whoever should behold me now, I wist,
Would think I were a mighty mechanist,
Bent with sublime Archimedean art
To breathe a soul into the iron heart
Of some machine portentous, or strange gin,
Which by the force of figured spells might
 win 20
Its way over the sea, and sport therein;
For round the walls are hung dread engines,
 such
As Vulcan never wrought for Jove to
 clutch
Ixion or the Titan, — or the quick
Wit of that man of God, St. Dominic,
To convince Atheist, Turk or Heretic,
Or those in philanthropic council met,
Who thought to pay some interest for the
 debt
They owed to Jesus Christ for their salva-
 tion,
By giving a faint foretaste of damnation 30
To Shakespeare, Sidney, Spenser and the
 rest
Who made our land an island of the blest,
When lamp-like Spain, who now relumes
 her fire
On Freedom's hearth, grew dim with Em-
 pire: —
With thumbscrews, wheels, with tooth and
 spike and jag,
Which fishers found under the utmost crag
Of Cornwall and the storm-encompassed
 isles,
Where to the sky the rude sea rarely
 smiles

Unless in treacherous wrath, as on the
 morn
When the exulting elements in scorn, 40
Satiated with destroyed destruction, lay
Sleeping in beauty on their mangled prey,
As panthers sleep; — and other strange
 and dread
Magical forms the brick floor overspread —
Proteus transformed to metal did not make
More figures, or more strange; nor did he
 take
Such shapes of unintelligible brass,
Or heap himself in such a horrid mass
Of tin and iron, not to be understood,
And forms of unimaginable wood 50
To puzzle Tubal Cain and all his brood;
Great screws, and cones, and wheels, and
 groovèd blocks, —
The elements of what will stand the shocks
Of wave and wind and time. Upon the
 table
More knacks and quips there be than I am
 able
To catalogize in this verse of mine : —
A pretty bowl of wood — not full of wine,
But quicksilver; that dew which the gnomes
 drink
When at their subterranean toil they swink,
Pledging the demons of the earthquake,
 who 60
Reply to them in lava — cry halloo !
And call out to the cities o'er their head, —
Roofs, towers and shrines, the dying and
 the dead,
Crash through the chinks of earth — and
 then all quaff
Another rouse, and hold their sides and
 laugh.
This quicksilver no gnome has drunk —
 within
The walnut bowl it lies, veinèd and thin,
In color like the wake of light that stains
The Tuscan deep, when from the moist
 moon rains
The inmost shower of its white fire — the
 breeze 70
Is still — blue heaven smiles over the pale
 seas.
And in this bowl of quicksilver — for I
Yield to the impulse of an infancy
Outlasting manhood — I have made to float
A rude idealism of a paper boat, —
A hollow screw with cogs — Henry will
 know
The thing I mean and laugh at me, if so

He fears not I should do more mischief.
 Next
Lie bills and calculations much perplexed,
With steamboats, frigates, and machinery
 quaint 80
Traced over them in blue and yellow paint.
Then comes a range of mathematical
Instruments, for plans nautical and stati-
 cal;
A heap of rosin, a queer broken glass
With ink in it; a china cup that was
What it will never be again, I think,
A thing from which sweet lips were wont
 to drink
The liquor doctors rail at — and which I
Will quaff in spite of them — and when we
 die
We 'll toss up who died first of drinking tea,
And cry out, · heads or tails ? ' where'er we
 be. 91
Near that a dusty paint box, some odd
 hooks,
A half-burnt match, an ivory block, three
 books,
Where conic sections, spherics, logarithms,
To great Laplace from Saunderson and
 Sims,
Lie heaped in their harmonious disarray
Of figures, — disentangle them who may.
Baron de Tott's Memoirs beside them lie,
And some odd volumes of old chemistry.
Near those a most inexplicable thing, 100
With lead in the middle — I 'm conjectur-
 ing
How to make Henry understand; but no —
I 'll leave, as Spenser says, with many mo,
This secret in the pregnant womb of time,
Too vast a matter for so weak a rhyme.

 And here like some weird Archimage
 sit I,
Plotting dark spells, and devilish enginery,
The self-impelling steam-wheels of the
 mind
Which pump up oaths from clergymen,
 and grind
The gentle spirit of our meek reviews 110
Into a powdery foam of salt abuse,
Ruffling the ocean of their self-content;
I sit — and smile or sigh as is my bent,
But not for them; Libeccio rushes round
With an inconstant and an idle sound —
I heed him more than them; the thunder-
 smoke
Is gathering on the mountains, like a cloak

Folded athwart their shoulders broad and
 bare;
The ripe corn under the undulating air
Undulates like an ocean; and the vines 120
Are trembling wide in all their trellised
 lines.
The murmur of the awakening sea doth
 fill
The empty pauses of the blast; the hill
Looks hoary through the white electric
 rain,
And from the glens beyond, in sullen strain,
The interrupted thunder howls; above
One chasm of heaven smiles, like the eye
 of Love
On the unquiet world; — while such things
 are,
How could one worth your friendship heed
 the war
Of worms ? the shriek of the world's car-
 rion jays, 130
Their censure, or their wonder, or their
 praise ?

 You are not here ! the quaint witch
 Memory sees
In vacant chairs your absent images,
And points where once you sat, and now
 should be
But are not. I demand if ever we
Shall meet as then we met; and she re-
 plies,
Veiling in awe her second-sighted eyes;
' I know the past alone — but summon
 home
My sister Hope, — she speaks of all to
 come.'
But I, an old diviner, who knew well 140
Every false verse of that sweet oracle,
Turned to the sad enchantress once again,
And sought a respite from my gentle pain,
In citing every passage o'er and o'er
Of our communion — how on the seashore
We watched the ocean and the sky to-
 gether,
Under the roof of blue Italian weather;
How I ran home through last year's thun-
 der-storm,
And felt the transverse lightning linger
 warm 149
Upon my cheek; and how we often made
Feasts for each other, where good-will out-
 weighed
The frugal luxury of our country cheer,
As well it might, were it less firm and clear

Than ours must ever be; and how we
 spun
A shroud of talk to hide us from the sun
Of this familiar life which seems to be
But is not — or is but quaint mockery
Of all we would believe — and sadly blame
The jarring and inexplicable frame 159
Of this wrong world; and then anatomize
The purposes and thoughts of men whose
 eyes
Were closed in distant years; or widely
 guess
The issue of the earth's great business,
When we shall be as we no longer are, —
Like babbling gossips safe, who hear the
 war
Of winds, and sigh, but tremble not; — or
 how
You listened to some interrupted flow
Of visionary rhyme, — in joy and pain
Struck from the inmost fountains of my
 brain, 169
With little skill perhaps; or how we sought
Those deepest wells of passion or of thought
Wrought by wise poets in the waste of
 years,
Staining their sacred waters with our
 tears, —
Quenching a thirst ever to be renewed.
Or how I, wisest lady! then indued
The language of a land which now is
 free,
And, winged with thoughts of truth and
 majesty,
Flits round the tyrant's sceptre like a cloud,
And bursts the peopled prisons, and cries
 aloud,
'My name is Legion!' — that majestic
 tongue 180
Which Calderon over the desert flung
Of ages and of nations, — and which found
An echo in our hearts, — and with the
 sound
Startled oblivion; — thou wert then to me
As is a nurse — when inarticulately
A child would talk as its grown parents do.
If living winds the rapid clouds pursue,
If hawks chase doves through the ethereal
 way,
Huntsmen the innocent deer, and beasts
 their prey,
Why should not we rouse with the spirit's
 blast 190
Out of the forest of the pathless past
These recollected pleasures?

You are now
In London, that great sea, whose ebb and
 flow
At once is deaf and loud, and on the shore
Vomits its wrecks, and still howls on for
 more.
Yet in its depth what treasures! You will
 see
That which was Godwin, — greater none
 than he
Though fallen — and fallen on evil times
 — to stand
Among the spirits of our age and land,
Before the dread tribunal of *to come* 200
The foremost, — while Rebuke cowers pale
 and dumb.
You will see Coleridge — he who sits ob-
 scure
In the exceeding lustre and the pure
Intense irradiation of a mind,
Which, with its own internal lightning
 blind,
Flags wearily through darkness and de-
 spair —
A cloud-encircled meteor of the air,
A hooded eagle among blinking owls.
You will see Hunt — one of those happy
 souls
Which are the salt of the earth, and with-
 out whom 210
This world would smell like what it is — a
 tomb;
Who is what others seem; his room no
 doubt
Is still adorned by many a cast from Shout,
With graceful flowers tastefully placed
 about,
And coronals of bay from ribbons hung,
And brighter wreaths in neat disorder
 flung, —
The gifts of the most learned among some
 dozens
Of female friends, sisters-in-law and cous-
 ins.
And there is he with his eternal puns,
Which beat the dullest brain for smiles,
 like duns 220
Thundering for money at a poet's door;
Alas! it is no use to say, 'I 'm poor!'
Or oft in graver mood, when he will
 look
Things wiser than were ever read in book,
Except in Shakespeare's wisest tender-
 ness. —
You will see Hogg, — and I cannot express

His virtues, — though I know that they
 are great,
Because he locks, then barricades the gate
Within which they inhabit; of his wit
And wisdom you 'll cry out when you are
 bit. 230
He is a pearl within an oyster shell,
One of the richest of the deep. And there
Is English Peacock, with his mountain fair,
Turned into a Flamingo, — that shy bird
That gleams i' the Indian air; — have you
 not heard
When a man marries, dies, or turns Hindoo,
His best friends hear no more of him ? —
 but you
Will see him, and will like him too, I hope,
With the milk-white Snowdonian Antelope
Matched with this camelopard; his fine
 wit 240
Makes such a wound, the knife is lost in
 it;
A strain too learnèd for a shallow age,
Too wise for selfish bigots; let his page
Which charms the chosen spirits of the
 time,
Fold itself up for the serener clime
Of years to come, and find its recompense
In that just expectation. Wit and sense,
Virtue and human knowledge; all that
 might
Make this dull world a business of de-
 light, —
Are all combined in Horace Smith. And
 these, 250
With some exceptions, which I need not
 tease
Your patience by descanting on, are all
You and I know in London.

 I recall
My thoughts, and bid you look upon the
 night.
As water does a sponge, so the moonlight
Fills the void, hollow, universal air.
What see you ? — unpavilioned heaven is
 fair
Whether the moon, into her chamber gone,
Leaves midnight to the golden stars, or wan
Climbs with diminished beams the azure
 steep; 260
Or whether clouds sail o'er the inverse
 deep,
Piloted by the many-wandering blast,
And the rare stars rush through them dim
 and fast: —

All this is beautiful in every land.
But what see you beside ? — a shabby stand
Of Hackney coaches — a brick house or
 wall
Fencing some lonely court, white with the
 scrawl
Of our unhappy politics; or worse —
A wretched woman reeling by, whose curse
Mixed with the watchman's, partner of her
 trade, 270
You must accept in place of serenade, —
Or yellow-haired Pollonia murmuring
To Henry, some unutterable thing.
I see a chaos of green leaves and fruit
Built round dark caverns, even to the root
Of the living stems that feed them — in
 whose bowers
There sleep in their dark dew the folded
 flowers;
Beyond, the surface of the unsickled corn
Trembles not in the slumbering air, and
 borne 279
In circles quaint and ever changing dance,
Like wingèd stars, the fireflies flash and
 glance,
Pale in the open moonshine, but each one
Under the dark trees seems a little sun,
A meteor tamed, a fixed star gone astray
From the silver regions of the milky way;
Afar the Contadino's song is heard,
Rude, but made sweet by distance — and a
 bird
Which cannot be the Nightingale, and yet
I know none else that sings so sweet as
 it
At this late hour; — and then all is still. —
Now Italy or London, which you will ! 291

 Next winter you must pass with me; I 'll
 have
My house by that time turned into a grave
Of dead despondence and low-thoughted
 care,
And all the dreams which our tormentors
 are;
Oh ! that Hunt, Hogg, Peacock and Smith
 were there,
With every thing belonging to them fair ! —
We will have books, Spanish, Italian,
 Greek;
And ask one week to make another week
As like his father, as I 'm unlike mine, 300
Which is not his fault, as you may divine.
Though we eat little flesh and drink no
 wine,

Yet let's be merry: we'll have tea and
 toast;
Custards for supper, and an endless host
Of syllabubs and jellies and mince-pies,
And other such lady-like luxuries, —
Feasting on which we will philosophize !
And we'll have fires out of the Grand
 Duke's wood,
To thaw the six weeks' winter in our blood.
And then we'll talk; — what shall we talk
 about ? 310
Oh ! there are themes enough for many a
 bout
Of thought-entangled descant; — as to
 nerves —
With cones and parallelograms and curves
I've sworn to strangle them if once they
 dare
To bother me — when you are with me
 there.
And they shall never more sip laudanum,
From Helicon or Himeros; — well, come,
And in despite of God and of the devil,
We'll make our friendly philosophic revel
Outlast the leafless time; till buds and
 flowers 320
Warn the obscure inevitable hours
Sweet meeting by sad parting to renew; —
'To-morrow to fresh woods and pastures
 new.'

ODE TO NAPLES

The revolutionary uprisings of this year af-
fected Shelley as powerfully as the Manchester
Riot of 1819, and this poem is the fruit of that
fleeting renascence of political hope so often
illustrated in his verse. He composed it at the
Baths of San Giuliano, August 17–25, and it
was published by Mrs. Shelley, *Posthumous
Poems*, 1824. Shelley added a note to the
poem, as follows : ' The author has connected
many recollections of his visit to Pompeii
and Baiæ with the enthusiasm excited by the
intelligence of the proclamation of a Constitu-
tional Government at Naples. This has given
a tinge of picturesque and descriptive imagery
to the introductory Epodes which depicture
these scenes, and some of the majestic feelings
permanently connected with the scene of the
animating event.'

EPODE I α

I STOOD within the city disinterred;
 And heard the autumnal leaves like
 light footfalls

Of spirits passing through the streets; and
 heard
 The Mountain's slumberous voice at
 intervals
 Thrill through those roofless halls;
The oracular thunder penetrating shook
 The listening soul in my suspended
 blood;
I felt that Earth out of her deep heart
 spoke —
 I felt, but heard not. Through white
 columns glowed
 The isle-sustaining Ocean-flood, 10
A plane of light between two Heavens of
 azure:
 Around me gleamed many a bright sep-
 ulchre
Of whose pure beauty, Time, as if his plea-
 sure
 Were to spare Death, had never made
 erasure;
 But every living lineament was clear
 As in the sculptor's thought; and
 there
The wreaths of stony myrtle, ivy and
 pine,
 Like winter leaves o'ergrown by moulded
 snow,
 Seemed only not to move and grow
 Because the crystal silence of the air 20
 Weighed on their life; even as the Power
 divine,
 Which then lulled all things, brooded
 upon mine.

EPODE II α

 Then gentle winds arose,
 With many a mingled close
Of wild Æolian sound and mountain odor
 keen;
 And where the Baian ocean
 Welters with air-like motion,
Within, above, around its bowers of starry
 green,
 Moving the sea-flowers in those purple
 caves, 29
 Even as the ever stormless atmosphere
 Floats o'er the Elysian realm,
It bore me, like an angel, o'er the waves
 Of sunlight, whose swift pinnace of
 dewy air
 No storm can overwhelm.
 I sailed where ever flows
 Under the calm Serene
 A spirit of deep emotion

From the unknown graves
Of the dead kings of Melody.
Shadowy Aornus darkened o'er the helm 40
The horizontal ether; heaven stripped
bare
Its depths over Elysium, where the prow
Made the invisible water white as snow;
From that Typhæan mount, Inarimé,
 There streamed a sunbright vapor, like
 the standard
 Of some ethereal host;
 Whilst from all the coast,
 Louder and louder, gathering round,
 there wandered
Over the oracular woods and divine sea
Prophesyings which grew articulate — 50
They seize me — I must speak them — be
 they fate !

<center>STROPHE a 1</center>

Naples, thou Heart of men, which ever
 pantest
 Naked, beneath the lidless eye of hea-
 ven !
Elysian City, which to calm enchantest
 The mutinous air and sea ! they round
 thee, even
 As sleep round Love, are driven !
Metropolis of a ruined Paradise
 Long lost, late won, and yet but half re-
 gained !
Bright Altar of the bloodless sacrifice,
 Which armèd Victory offers up un-
 stained 60
 To Love, the flower-enchained !
Thou which wert once, and then didst cease
 to be,
Now art, and henceforth ever shalt be,
 free,
 If Hope, and Truth, and Justice can
 avail, —
 Hail, hail, all hail !

<center>STROPHE β 2</center>

Thou youngest giant birth,
 Which from the groaning earth
Leap'st, clothed in armor of impenetrable
 scale !
 Last of the intercessors
 Who 'gainst the Crowned Trans-
 gressors 70
Pleadest before God's love ! Arrayed in
 Wisdom's mail,
 Wave thy lightning lance in mirth,
 Nor let thy high heart fail,

Though from their hundred gates the
 leagued Oppressors,
 With hurried legions move !
 Hail, hail, all hail !

<center>ANTISTROPHE a 1</center>

What though Cimmerian anarchs dare blas-
 pheme
 Freedom and thee ? thy shield is as a
 mirror
To make their blind slaves see, and with
 fierce gleam
 To turn his hungry sword upon the
 wearer; 80
 A new Actæon's error
Shall theirs have been — devoured by their
 own hounds !'
Be thou like the imperial Basilisk,
Killing thy foe with unapparent wounds !
 Gaze on oppression, till, at that dread
 risk
 Aghast, she pass from the Earth's
 disk;
Fear not, but gaze — for freemen mightier
 grow,
And slaves more feeble, gazing on their
 foe.
If Hope, and Truth, and Justice may
 avail,
Thou shalt be great. — All hail ! 90

<center>ANTISTROPHE β 2</center>

 From Freedom's form divine,
 From Nature's inmost shrine,
Strip every impious gaud, rend Error veil
 by veil;
 O'er Ruin desolate,
 O'er Falsehood's fallen state,
Sit thou sublime, unawed; be the Destroyer
 pale !
 And equal laws be thine,
 And wingèd words let sail,
Freighted with truth even from the throne
 of God;
 That wealth, surviving fate, 100
 Be thine. — All hail !

<center>ANTISTROPHE a γ</center>

Didst thou not start to hear Spain's thrill-
 ing pæan
 From land to land reëchoed solemnly,
Till silence became music ? From the
 Ææan
 To the cold Alps, eternal Italy
 Starts to hear thine ! The Sea

Which paves the desert streets of Venice
 laughs
 In light and music ; widowed Genoa
 wan
By moonlight spells ancestral epitaphs,
 Murmuring, Where is Doria ? Fair Milan,
 Within whose veins long ran 111
The viper's palsying venom, lifts her heel
To bruise his head. The signal and the
 seal
 (If Hope, and Truth, and Justice can
 avail)
 Art thou of all these hopes. — O hail !

ANTISTROPHE β γ

 Florence ! beneath the sun,
 Of cities fairest one,
Blushes within her bower for Freedom's
 expectation
 From eyes of quenchless hope
 Rome tears the priestly cope, 120
As ruling once by power, so now by ad-
 miration,—
 An athlete stripped to run
 From a remoter station
For the high prize lost on Philippi's
 shore : —
 As then Hope, Truth, and Justice did
 avail,
 So now may Fraud and Wrong ! O
 hail !

EPODE I β

Hear ye the march as of the Earth-born
 Forms
 Arrayed against the ever-living Gods ?
The crash and darkness of a thousand
 storms
 Bursting their inaccessible abodes 130
 Of crags and thunder-clouds ?
See ye the banners blazoned to the day,
 Inwrought with emblems of barbaric
 pride ?
Dissonant threats kill Silence far away,
 The serene Heaven which wraps our
 Eden wide
 With iron light is dyed,
The Anarchs of the North lead forth their
 legions
 Like Chaos o'er creation, uncreat-
 ing ;
An hundred tribes nourished on strange re-
 ligions
And lawless slaveries, — down the aërial
 regions 140

Of the white Alps, desolating,
 Famished wolves that bide no wait-
 ing,
Blotting the glowing footsteps of old glory,
Trampling our columned cities into dust,
 Their dull and savage lust
 On Beauty's corse to sickness satiat-
 ing —
They come ! The fields they tread look
 black and hoary
With fire — from their red feet the streams
 run gory !

EPODE II β

 Great Spirit, deepest Love !
 Which rulest and dost move 150
All things which live and are, within the
 Italian shore ;
 Who spreadest heaven around it,
 Whose woods, rocks, waves, sur-
 round it ;
Who sittest in thy star, o'er Ocean's west-
 ern floor ;
 Spirit of beauty ! at whose soft com-
 mand
The sunbeams and the showers distil its
 foison
 From the Earth's bosom chill ;
 Oh, bid those beams be each a blinding
 brand
Of lightning ! bid those showers be dews of
 poison !
 Bid the Earth's plenty kill ! 160
 Bid thy bright Heaven above,
 Whilst light and darkness bound it,
 Be their tomb who planned
 To make it ours and thine !
Or with thine harmonizing ardors fill
And raise thy sons, as o'er the prone hori-
 zon
Thy lamp feeds every twilight wave with
 fire !
Be man's high hope and unextinct de-
 sire
The instrument to work thy will divine !
 Then clouds from sunbeams, antelopes
 from leopards, 170
 And frowns and fears from Thee,
 Would not more swiftly flee,
 Than Celtic wolves from the Ausonian
 shepherds. —
 Whatever, Spirit, from thy starry
 shrine
 Thou yieldest or withholdest, oh, let be
 This city of thy worship, ever free !

AUTUMN

A DIRGE

Published by Mrs. Shelley, *Posthumous Poems*, 1824.

THE warm sun is failing, the bleak wind is
 wailing,
The bare boughs are sighing, the pale
 flowers are dying,
 And the year
On the earth, her death-bed, in a shroud of
 leaves dead,
 Is lying.
 Come, Months, come away,
 From November to May,
 In your saddest array;
 Follow the bier
 Of the dead cold year,
And like dim shadows watch by her sepul-
 chre.

The chill rain is falling, the nipped worm
 is crawling,
The rivers are swelling, the thunder is
 knelling
 For the year;
The blithe swallows are flown, and the liz-
 ards each gone
 To his dwelling;
 Come, Months, come away,
 Put on white, black, and gray;
 Let your light sisters play —
 Ye, follow the bier
 Of the dead cold year,
And make her grave green with tear on
 tear.

DEATH

Published by Mrs. Shelley, *Posthumous Poems*, 1824.

I

DEATH is here, and death is there,
Death is busy everywhere,
All around, within, beneath,
Above, is death — and we are death.

II

Death has set his mark and seal
On all we are and all we feel,
On all we know and all we fear,

III

First our pleasures die — and then
Our hopes, and then our fears — and when
These are dead, the debt is due,
Dust claims dust — and we die too.

IV

All things that we love and cherish,
Like ourselves, must fade and perish;
Such is our rude mortal lot —
Love itself would, did they not.

LIBERTY

Published by Mrs. Shelley, *Posthumous Poems*, 1824.

I

THE fiery mountains answer each other,
Their thunderings are echoed from zone to
 zone;
The tempestuous oceans awake one another,
And the ice-rocks are shaken round Win-
 ter's throne,
 When the clarion of the Typhoon is
 blown.

II

From a single cloud the lightning flashes,
Whilst a thousand isles are illumined
 around;
Earthquake is trampling one city to ashes,
An hundred are shuddering and tottering;
 the sound
 Is bellowing underground.

III

But keener thy gaze than the lightning's
 glare,
And swifter thy step than the earthquake's
 tramp;
Thou deafenest the rage of the ocean; thy
 stare
Makes blind the volcanoes; the sun's
 bright lamp
 To thine is a fen-fire damp.

IV

From billow and mountain and exhalation
The sunlight is darted through vapor and
 blast;
From spirit to spirit, from nation to nation,
From city to hamlet, thy dawning is cast, —
And tyrants and slaves are like shadows of
 night
 In the van of the morning light.

SUMMER AND WINTER

Published by Mrs. Shelley, *The Keepsake*,
1829.

It was a bright and cheerful afternoon
Towards the end of the sunny month of
 June,
When the north wind congregates in crowds
The floating mountains of the silver clouds
From the horizon — and the stainless sky
Opens beyond them like eternity.
All things rejoiced beneath the sun; the
 weeds,
The river, and the cornfields, and the
 reeds;
The willow leaves that glanced in the light
 breeze,
And the firm foliage of the larger trees.

It was a winter such as when birds die
In the deep forests; and the fishes lie
Stiffened in the translucent ice, which
 makes
Even the mud and slime of the warm lakes
A wrinkled clod as hard as brick; and
 when
Among their children comfortable men
Gather about great fires, and yet feel
 cold:
Alas, then, for the homeless beggar old !

THE TOWER OF FAMINE

Published by Mrs. Shelley, *The Keepsake*,
1829.

Amid the desolation of a city,
Which was the cradle and is now the grave
Of an extinguished people, — so that pity

Weeps o'er the shipwrecks of oblivion's
 wave,
There stands the Tower of Famine. It is
 built
Upon some prison-homes, whose dwellers
 rave

For bread, and gold, and blood; pain, linked
 to guilt,
Agitates the light flame of their hours,
Until its vital oil is spent or spilt.

There stands the pile, a tower amid the
 towers

And sacred domes, — each marble-ribbèd
 roof,
The brazen-gated temples and the bowers

Of solitary wealth; the tempest-proof
Pavilions of the dark Italian air
Are by its presence dimmed — they stand
 aloof,

And are withdrawn — so that the world is
 bare;
As if a spectre, wrapped in shapeless ter-
 ror,
Amid a company of ladies fair

Should glide and glow, till it became a
 mirror
Of all their beauty, — and their hair and
 hue,
The life of their sweet eyes, with all its
 error,
Should be absorbed, till they to marble
 grew.

AN ALLEGORY

Published by Mrs. Shelley, *Posthumous
Poems*, 1824.

I

A PORTAL as of shadowy adamant
 Stands yawning on the highway of the
 life
Which we all tread, a cavern huge and
 gaunt;
 Around it rages an unceasing strife
Of shadows, like the restless clouds that
 haunt
The gap of some cleft mountain, lifted
 high
Into the whirlwinds of the upper sky.

II

And many pass it by with careless tread,
 Not knowing that a shadowy . . .
Tracks every traveler even to where the
 dead
 Wait peacefully for their companion
 new;
But others, by more curious humor led,
 Pause to examine; these are very few,
And they learn little there, except to know
That shadows follow them where'er they
 go.

THE WORLD'S WANDERERS

Published by Mrs. Shelley, *Posthumous Poems*, 1824.

I

TELL me, thou star, whose wings of light
Speed thee in thy fiery flight,
In what cavern of the night
 Will thy pinions close now ?

II

Tell me, moon, thou pale and gray
Pilgrim of heaven's homeless way,
In what depth of night or day
 Seekest thou repose now ?

III

Weary wind, who wanderest
Like the world's rejected guest,
Hast thou still some secret nest
 On the tree or billow ?

SONNET

Published by Hunt, *The Literary Pocket-Book*, 1824.

YE hasten to the grave ! What seek ye
 there,
Ye restless thoughts and busy purposes
Of the idle brain, which the world's livery
 wear ?
O thou quick heart, which pantest to pos-
 sess
All that pale expectation feigneth fair !
Thou vainly curious mind which wouldest
 guess
Whence thou didst come, and whither thou
 must go,
And all that never yet was known would
 know, —
Oh, whither hasten ye, that thus ye
 press
With such swift feet life's green and plea-
 sant path,
Seeking alike from happiness and woe
A refuge in the cavern of gray death ?
O heart, and mind, and thoughts ! what
 thing do you
Hope to inherit in the grave below ?

LINES TO A REVIEWER

Published by Hunt, *The Literary Pocket-Book*, 1823.

ALAS ! good friend, what profit can you see
In hating such a hateless thing as me ?
There is no sport in hate when all the rage
Is on one side. In vain would you assuage
Your frowns upon an unresisting smile,
In which not even contempt lurks to beguile
Your heart by some faint sympathy of hate.
Oh, conquer what you cannot satiate !
For to your passion I am far more coy
Than ever yet was coldest maid or boy
In winter noon. Of your antipathy
If I am the Narcissus, you are free
To pine into a sound with hating me.

TIME LONG PAST

Published by Rossetti, 1870.

I

LIKE the ghost of a dear friend dead
 Is Time long past.
A tone which is now forever fled,
A hope which is now forever past,
A love so sweet it could not last,
 Was Time long past.

II

There were sweet dreams in the night
 Of Time long past.
And, was it sadness or delight,
Each day a shadow onward cast
Which made us wish it yet might last —
 That Time long past.

III

There is regret, almost remorse,
 For Time long past.
'T is like a child's belovèd corse
A father watches, till at last
Beauty is like remembrance cast
 From Time long past.

BUONA NOTTE

Published by Medwin, *The Angler in Wales*, 1834.

Medwin writes in his *Life of Shelley*: ' I often asked Shelley if he had never attempted to write, like Matthias, in Italian, and he

showed me a sort of serenade which I give as a curiosity,—but proving that he had not made a profound study of the language, which, like Spanish, he had acquired without a grammar, —trusting to his fine ear and memory, rather than to rules.'

I

' BUONA notte, buona notte !' — Come mai
 La notte sarà buona senza te ?
Non dirmi buona notte, — chè tu sai,
 La notte sà star buona da per sè.

II

Solinga, scura, cupa, senza speme,
 La notte quando Lilla m'abbandona;
Pei cuori chi si batton insieme
 Ogni notte, senza dirla, sarà buona.

III

Come male buona notte si suona
 Con sospiri e parole interrotte ! —
Il modo di aver la notte buona
 E mai non di dir la buona notte.

GOOD-NIGHT

Published by Hunt, *The Literary Pocket Book*, 1822.

I

GOOD-NIGHT ? ah, no ! the hour is ill
 Which severs those it should unite;
Let us remain together still,
 Then it will be *good night.*

II

How can I call the lone night good,
 Though thy sweet wishes wing its flight ?
Be it not said, thought, understood,
 Then it will be *good night.*

III

To hearts which near each other move
 From evening close to morning light,
The night is good; because, my love,
 They never *say* good-night.

POEMS WRITTEN IN 1821

Mrs. Shelley gives, as usual, the general scene and atmosphere of the year, which was spent at Pisa or the Baths of San Giuliano: ' We were not, as our wont had been, alone — friends had gathered round us. Nearly all are dead; and when memory recurs to the past, she wanders among tombs: the genius with all his blighting errors and mighty powers ; the companion of Shelley's ocean-wanderings, and the sharer of his fate, than whom no man ever existed more gentle, generous, and fearless ; and others, who found in Shelley's society, and in his great knowledge and warm sympathy, delight, instruction and solace, have joined him beyond the grave. . . .

' Shelley's favorite taste was boating ; when living near the Thames, or by the lake of Geneva, much of his life was spent on the water. On the shore of every lake, or stream, or sea, near which he dwelt, he had a boat moored. He had latterly enjoyed this pleasure again. There are no pleasure-boats on the Arno, and the shallowness of its waters, except in winter time, when the stream is too turbid and impetuous for boating, rendered it difficult to get any skiff light enough to float. Shelley, however, overcame the difficulty; he, together with a friend, contrived a boat such as the huntsmen carry about with them in the Maremma, to cross the sluggish but deep streams that intersect the forests, a boat of laths and pitched canvas ; it held three persons, and he was often seen on the Arno in it, to the horror of the Italians, who remonstrated on the danger, and could not understand how any one could take pleasure in an exercise that risked life. " Ma va per la vita !" they exclaimed. I little thought how true their words would prove. He once ventured with a friend [Williams], on the glassy sea of a calm day, down the Arno and round the coast, to Leghorn, which by keeping close in shore was very practicable. They returned to Pisa by the canal, when, missing the direct cut, they got entangled among weeds, and the boat upset ; a wetting was all the harm done except that the intense cold of his drenched clothes made Shelley faint. Once I went down with him to the mouth of the Arno, where the stream, then high and swift, met the tideless sea and disturbed its sluggish waters ; it was a waste and dreary scene ; the desert sand stretched into a point surrounded by waves that broke idly though perpetually around ; it was a scene very similar to Lido, of which he had said, —

 ' " I love all waste
And solitary places, where we taste
The pleasure of believing what we see
Is boundless, as we wish our souls to be;
And such was this wide ocean, and this shore
More barren than its billows."

'Our little boat was of greater use, unaccompanied by any danger, when we removed to the baths. Some friends [the Williamses] lived at the village of Pugnano, four miles off, and we went to and fro to see them, in our boat, by the canal, which, fed by the Serchio, was, though an artificial, a full and picturesque stream, making its way under verdant banks, sheltered by trees that dipped their boughs into the murmuring waters. By day, multitudes of ephemera darted to and fro on the surface; at night, the fireflies came out among the shrubs on the banks; the cicale at noonday kept up their hum; the aziola cooed in the quiet evening. It was a pleasant summer, bright in all but Shelley's health and inconstant spirits; yet he enjoyed himself greatly, and became more and more attached to the part of the country where chance appeared to cast us. Sometimes he projected taking a farm, situated on the height of one of the near hills, surrounded by chestnut and pine woods, and overlooking a wide extent of country; or of settling still further in the maritime Apennines, at Massa. Several of his slighter and unfinished poems were inspired by these scenes, and by the companions around us. It is the nature of that poetry, however, which overflows from the soul, oftener to express sorrow and regret than joy; for it is when oppressed by the weight of life, and away from those he loves that the poet has recourse to the solace of expression in verse.

'Still Shelley's passion was the ocean; and he wished that our summers, instead of being passed among the hills near Pisa, should be spent on the shores of the sea. It was very difficult to find a spot. We shrank from Naples from a fear that the heats would disagree with Percy; Leghorn had lost its only attraction, since our friends who had resided there were returned to England; and Monte Nero being the resort of many English, we did not wish to find ourselves in the midst of a colony of chance travellers. No one then thought it possible to reside at Viareggio, which latterly has become a summer resort. The low lands and bad air of Maremma stretch the whole length of the western shores of the Mediterranean, till broken by the rocks and hills of Spezia. It was a vague idea; but Shelley suggested an excursion to Spezia, to see whether it would be feasible to spend a summer there. The beauty of the bay enchanted him — we saw no house to suit us — but the notion took root, and many circumstances, enchained as by fatality, occurred to urge him to execute it.'

DIRGE FOR THE YEAR

Composed January 1, and published by Mrs. Shelley, *Posthumous Poems*, 1824.

I

ORPHAN hours, the year is dead,
Come and sigh, come and weep!
Merry hours, smile instead,
For the year is but asleep.
See, it smiles as it is sleeping,
Mocking your untimely weeping.

II

As an earthquake rocks a corse
In its coffin in the clay,
So White Winter, that rough nurse,
Rocks the death-cold year to-day;
Solemn hours! wail aloud
For your mother in her shroud.

III

As the wild air stirs and sways
The tree-swung cradle of a child,
So the breath of these rude days
Rocks the year: — be calm and mild,
Trembling hours; she will arise
With new love within her eyes.

IV

January gray is here,
Like a sexton by her grave;
February bears the bier,
March with grief doth howl and rave,
And April weeps — but, O ye hours!
Follow with May's fairest flowers.

TIME

Published by Mrs. Shelley, *Posthumous Poems*, 1824.

UNFATHOMABLE Sea! whose waves are years,
Ocean of Time, whose waters of deep woe
Are brackish with the salt of human tears!
Thou shoreless flood, which in thy ebb and flow
Claspest the limits of mortality,
And sick of prey, yet howling on for more,
Vomitest thy wrecks on its inhospitable shore;
Treacherous in calm, and terrible in storm,
Who shall put forth on thee,
Unfathomable Sea?

FROM THE ARABIC

AN IMITATION

Published by Mrs. Shelley, *Posthumous Poems*, 1824.

I

My faint spirit was sitting in the light
 Of thy looks, my love;
It panted for thee like the hind at noon
 For the brooks, my love.
Thy barb, whose hoofs outspeed the tempest's flight,
 Bore thee far from me;
My heart, for my weak feet were weary soon,
 Did companion thee.

II

Ah ! fleeter far than fleetest storm or steed,
 Or the death they bear,
The heart which tender thought clothes like a dove
 With the wings of care;
In the battle, in the darkness, in the need,
 Shall mine cling to thee,
Nor claim one smile for all the comfort, love,
 It may bring to thee.

SONG

Published by Mrs. Shelley, *Posthumous Poems*, 1824.

I

Rarely, rarely, comest thou,
 Spirit of Delight !
Wherefore hast thou left me now
 Many a day and night ?
Many a weary night and day
'T is since thou art fled away.

II

How shall ever one like me
 Win thee back again ?
With the joyous and the free
 Thou wilt scoff at pain.
Spirit false ! thou hast forgot
All but those who need thee not.

III

As a lizard with the shade
 Of a trembling leaf.

Thou with sorrow art dismayed;
 Even the sighs of grief
Reproach thee, that thou art not near,
And reproach thou wilt not hear.

IV

Let me set my mournful ditty
 To a merry measure;
Thou wilt never come for pity,
 Thou wilt come for pleasure;
Pity then will cut away
Those cruel wings, and thou wilt stay.

V

I love all that thou lovest,
 Spirit of Delight !
The fresh Earth in new leaves dressed,
 And the starry night;
Autumn evening, and the morn
When the golden mists are born.

VI

I love snow, and all the forms
 Of the radiant frost;
I love waves, and winds, and storms,
 Everything almost
Which is Nature's, and may be
Untainted by man's misery.

VII

I love tranquil solitude,
 And such society
As is quiet, wise, and good;
 Between thee and me
What difference ? but thou dost possess
The things I seek, not love them less.

VIII

I love Love — though he has wings,
 And like light can flee,
But above all other things,
 Spirit, I love thee.
Thou art love and life ! Oh, come,
Make once more my heart thy home.

TO NIGHT

Published by Mrs. Shelley, *Posthumous Poems*, 1824.

I

Swiftly walk o'er the western wave,
 Spirit of Night !
Out of the misty eastern cave,
Where all the long and lone daylight

Thou wovest dreams of joy and fear,
Which make thee terrible and dear, —
 Swift be thy flight !

II

Wrap thy form in a mantle gray,
 Star-inwrought !
Blind with thine hair the eyes of Day;
Kiss her until she be wearied out;
Then wander o'er city, and sea, and land,
Touching all with thine opiate wand —
 Come, long-sought !

III

When I arose and saw the dawn,
 I sighed for thee;
When light rode high, and the dew was
 gone,
And noon lay heavy on flower and tree,
And the weary Day turned to his rest,
Lingering like an unloved guest,
 I sighed for thee.

IV

Thy brother Death came, and cried,
 Wouldst thou me ?
Thy sweet child Sleep, the filmy-eyed,
Murmured like a noontide bee,
Shall I nestle near thy side ?
Wouldst thou me ? — and I replied,
 No, not thee !

V

Death will come when thou art dead,
 Soon, too soon;
Sleep will come when thou art fled;
Of neither would I ask the boon
I ask of thee, belovèd Night, —
Swift be thine approaching flight,
 Come soon, soon !

TO ——

*Published by Mrs. Shelley, Posthumous
Poems, 1824.*

Music, when soft voices die,
Vibrates in the memory;
Odors, when sweet violets sicken,
Live within the sense they quicken.

Rose leaves, when the rose is dead,
Are heaped for the belovèd's bed;
And so thy thoughts, when thou art gone,
Love itself shall slumber on.

TO ——

*Published by Mrs. Shelley, Posthumous
Poems, 1824.*

I

When passion's trance is overpast,
If tenderness and truth could last,
Or live, whilst all wild feelings keep
Some mortal slumber, dark and deep,
I should not weep, I should not weep !

II

It were enough to feel, to see
Thy soft eyes gazing tenderly,
And dream the rest — and burn and be
The secret food of fires unseen,
Couldst thou but be as thou hast been.

III

After the slumber of the year
The woodland violets reappear;
All things revive in field or grove,
And sky and sea, but two, which move
And form all others, life and love.

MUTABILITY

*Published by Mrs. Shelley, Posthumous
Poems, 1824.*

I

The flower that smiles to-day
 To-morrow dies;
All that we wish to stay,
 Tempts and then flies.
What is this world's delight?
Lightning that mocks the night,
 Brief even as bright.

II

Virtue, how frail it is !
 Friendship how rare !
Love, how it sells poor bliss
 For proud despair !
But we, though soon they fall,
Survive their joy and all
 Which ours we call.

III

Whilst skies are blue and bright,
 Whilst flowers are gay,
Whilst eyes that change ere night
 Make glad the day,

Whilst yet the calm hours creep,
Dream thou — and from thy sleep
Then wake to weep.

LINES

Published by Mrs. Shelley, *Posthumous
Poems*, 1824.

I

FAR, far away, O ye
Halcyons of Memory,
Seek some far calmer nest
Than this abandoned breast !
No news of your false spring
To my heart's winter bring;
Once having gone, in vain
 Ye come again.

II

Vultures, who build your bowers
High in the Future's towers,
Withered hopes on hopes are spread !
Dying joys, choked by the dead,
Will serve your beaks for prey
 Many a day.

THE FUGITIVES

Published by Mrs. Shelley, *Posthumous
Poems*, 1824.

I

THE waters are flashing,
The white hail is dashing,
The lightnings are glancing,
The hoar-spray is dancing —
 Away !

The whirlwind is rolling,
The thunder is tolling,
The forest is swinging,
The minster bells ringing —
 Come away !

The Earth is like Ocean,
Wreck-strewn and in motion;
Bird, beast, man and worm
Have crept out of the storm —
 Come away !

II

' Our boat has one sail,
And the helmsman is pale;

A bold pilot I trow,
Who should follow us now,' —
 Shouted he;

And she cried, ' Ply the oar;
Put off gayly from shore ! ' —
As she spoke, bolts of death
Mixed with hail specked their path
 O'er the sea.

And from isle, tower and rock,
The blue beacon cloud broke
And though dumb in the blast,
The red cannon flashed fast
 From the lee.

III

And fear'st thou, and fear'st thou ?
And see'st thou, and hear'st thou ?
And drive we not free
O'er the terrible sea,
 I and thou ? '

One boat-cloak did cover
The loved and the lover;
Their blood beats one measure,
They murmur proud pleasure
 Soft and low;

While around the lashed Ocean,
Like mountains in motion,
Is withdrawn and uplifted,
Sunk, shattered and shifted
 To and fro.

IV

In the court of the fortress
Beside the pale portress,
Like a bloodhound well beaten
The bridegroom stands, eaten
 By shame;

On the topmost watch-turret,
As a death-boding spirit,
Stands the gray tyrant father;
To his voice the mad weather
 Seems tame;

And with curses as wild
As e'er clung to child,
He devotes to the blast
The best, loveliest, and last
 Of his name !

LINES

WRITTEN ON HEARING THE NEWS OF THE
DEATH OF NAPOLEON

Published with *Hellas*, 1821.

WHAT ! alive and so bold, O Earth ?
 Art thou not over-bold ?
 What ! leapest thou forth as of old
In the light of thy morning mirth,
The last of the flock of the starry fold ?
Ha ! leapest thou forth as of old ?
Are not the limbs still when the ghost is fled,
And canst thou move, Napoleon being dead ?

How ! is not thy quick heart cold ?
 What spark is alive on thy hearth?
 How ! is not *his* death-knell knolled ?
And livest *thou* still, Mother Earth ?
Thou wert warming thy fingers old
 O'er the embers covered and cold
Of that most fiery spirit, when it fled;
What, Mother, do you laugh now he is dead?

' Who has known me of old,' replied
 Earth,
 ' Or who has my story told?
 It is thou who art over-bold.'
And the lightning of scorn laughed forth
As she sang, ' To my bosom I fold
All my sons when their knell is knolled,
And so with living motion all are fed,
And the quick spring like weeds out of the
 dead.

' Still alive and still bold,' shouted Earth,
 ' I grow bolder, and still more bold.
 The dead fill me ten thousand-fold
Fuller of speed, and splendor, and mirth.
I was cloudy, and sullen, and cold,
 Like a frozen chaos uprolled,
Till by the spirit of the mighty dead
My heart grew warm. I feed on whom I fed.

' Ay, alive and still bold,' muttered Earth,
 ' Napoleon's fierce spirit rolled,
 In terror, and blood, and gold,
A torrent of ruin to death from his birth.
Leave the millions who follow to mould
 The metal before it be cold;
And weave into his shame, which like the
 dead
Shrouds me, the hopes that from his glory
 fled.'

SONNET

POLITICAL GREATNESS

Published by Mrs. Shelley, *Posthumous
Poems*, 1824.

NOR happiness, nor majesty, nor fame,
Nor peace, nor strength, nor skill in arms
 or arts,
Shepherd those herds whom tyranny makes
 tame;
Verse echoes not one beating of their hearts,
History is but the shadow of their shame,
Art veils her glass, or from the pageant
 starts
As to oblivion their blind millions fleet,
Staining that Heaven with obscene imagery
Of their own likeness. What are numbers
 knit
By force or custom? Man who man would be
Must rule the empire of himself; in it
Must be supreme, establishing his throne
On vanquished will, quelling the anarchy
Of hopes and fears, being himself alone.

A BRIDAL SONG

The poem was composed for insertion in a
projected play of Williams, *The Promise, or a
Year, a Month, and a Day.* Published by
Mrs. Shelley, *Posthumous Poems*, 1824.

I

THE golden gates of sleep unbar
 Where strength and beauty, met to-
 gether,
Kindle their image like a star
 In a sea of glassy weather !
Night, with all thy stars look down;
 Darkness, weep thy holiest dew;
Never smiled the inconstant moon
 On a pair so true.
Let eyes not see their own delight;—
Haste, swift hour, and thy flight
 Oft renew.

II

Fairies, sprites, and angels, keep her !
 Holy stars, permit no wrong !
And return to wake the sleeper,
 Dawn, — ere it be long.
O joy ! O fear ! what will be done
 In the absence of the sun!
 Come along !

EPITHALAMIUM

Published by Medwin, *Life of Shelley*, 1847.

NIGHT, with all thine eyes look down !
 Darkness, shed its holiest dew !
When ever smiled the inconstant moon
 On a pair so true ?
Hence, coy hour ! and quench thy light,
Lest eyes see their own delight!
Hence, swift hour ! and thy loved flight
 Oft renew.

BOYS

O joy ! O fear ! what may be done
In the absence of the sun ?
 Come along !

The golden gates of sleep unbar !
 When strength and beauty meet together,
Kindles their image like a star
 In a sea of glassy weather.
Hence, coy hour ! and quench thy light,
Lest eyes see their own delight !
Hence, swift hour ! and thy loved flight
 Oft renew.

GIRLS

O joy ! O fear ! what may be done
In the absence of the sun ?

 Come along !
Fairies ! sprites ! and angels keep her !
 Holiest powers, permit no wrong !
And return, to wake the sleeper,
 Dawn, ere it be long.
Hence, swift hour ! and quench thy light,
Lest eyes see their own delight !
Hence, coy hour ! and thy loved flight
 Oft renew.

BOYS AND GIRLS

O joy ! O fear ! what will be done
In the absence of the sun ?
 Come along !

ANOTHER VERSION

Published by Rossetti, 1870.

BOYS SING

NIGHT ! with all thine eyes look down !
 Darkness ! weep thy holiest dew !
Never smiled the inconstant moon
 On a pair so true.

Haste, coy hour ! and quench all light,
Lest eyes see their own delight !
Haste, swift hour ! and thy loved flight
 Oft renew !

GIRLS SING

Fairies, sprites, and angels, keep her !
 Holy stars ! permit no wrong !
And return to wake the sleeper,
 Dawn, ere it be long !
O joy ! O fear ! there is not one
Of us can guess what may be done
 In the absence of the sun : —
 Come along !

BOYS

Oh, linger long, thou envious eastern lamp
 In the damp
 Caves of the deep !

GIRLS

Nay, return, Vesper ! urge thy lazy car !
 Swift unbar
 The gates of Sleep !

CHORUS

The golden gate of Sleep unbar,
 When Strength and Beauty, met together,
Kindle their image, like a star
 In a sea of glassy weather.
May the purple mist of love
Round them rise, and with them move,
Nourishing each tender gem
Which, like flowers, will burst from them.
As the fruit is to the tree
May their children ever be !

EVENING

PONTE AL MARE, PISA

Published by Mrs. Shelley, *Posthumous Poems*, 1824.

I

THE sun is set; the swallows are asleep;
 The bats are flitting fast in the gray air ;
The slow soft toads out of damp corners creep,
 And evening's breath, wandering here and there
Over the quivering surface of the stream,
Wakes not one ripple from its summer dream.

II

There is no dew on the dry grass to-night,
 Nor damp within the shadow of the
 trees;
The wind is intermitting, dry, and light;
 And in the inconstant motion of the
 breeze
The dust and straws are driven up and
 down,
And whirled about the pavement of the
 town.

III

Within the surface of the fleeting river
 The wrinkled image of the city lay,
Immovably unquiet, and forever
 It trembles, but it never fades away;
Go to the
You, being changed, will find it then as
 now.

IV

The chasm in which the sun has sunk is
 shut
 By darkest barriers of enormous cloud,
Like mountain over mountain huddled —
 but
 Growing and moving upwards in a
 crowd,
And over it a space of watery blue,
Which the keen evening star is shining
 through.

THE AZIOLA

Published by Mrs. Shelley, *The Keepsake*,
1829.

I

' Do you not hear the Aziola cry ?
 Methinks she must be nigh,'
 Said Mary, as we sate
In dusk, ere stars were lit, or candles
 brought;
 And I, who thought
This Aziola was some tedious woman,
 Asked, ' Who is Aziola ? ' How elate
I felt to know that it was nothing human,
 No mockery of myself to fear or hate !
 And Mary saw my soul,
And laughed, and said, ' Disquiet yourself
 not,
'T is nothing but a little downy owl.'

II

Sad Aziola ! many an eventide
 Thy music I had heard
By wood and stream, meadow and moun-
 tain-side,
 And fields and marshes wide, —
Such as nor voice, nor lute, nor wind, nor
 bird,
 The soul ever stirred;
Unlike and far sweeter than them all.
Sad Aziola ! from that moment I
 Loved thee and thy sad cry.

TO ——

Published by Mrs. Shelley, *Posthumous
Poems*, 1824.

I

ONE word is too often profaned
 For me to profane it,
One feeling too falsely disdained
 For thee to disdain it;
One hope is too like despair
 For prudence to smother,
And pity from thee more dear
 Than that from another.

II

I can give not what men call love,
 But wilt thou accept not
The worship the heart lifts above
 And the Heavens reject not, —
The desire of the moth for the star,
 Of the night for the morrow,
The devotion to something afar
 From the sphere of our sorrow ?

REMEMBRANCE

Shelley sent these lines enclosed in a letter
to Mrs. Williams : ' Dear Jane, — If this mel-
ancholy old song suits any of your tunes, or
any that humor of the moment may dictate,
you are welcome to it. Do not say it is mine
to any one, even if you think so ; indeed, it is
from the torn leaf of a book out of date. How
are you to-day, and how is Williams ? Tell
him that I dreamed of nothing but sailing
and fishing up coral. Your ever affectionate
P. B. S.' It was published by Mrs. Shelley,
Posthumous Poems, 1824.

I

Swifter far than summer's flight,
Swifter far than youth's delight,
Swifter far than happy night,
 Art thou come and gone.
As the wood when leaves are shed,
As the night when sleep is fled,
As the heart when joy is dead,
 I am left lone, alone.

II

The swallow summer comes again,
The owlet night resumes his reign,
But the wild swan youth is fain
 To fly with thee, false as thou.
My heart each day desires the morrow;
Sleep itself is turned to sorrow;
Vainly would my winter borrow
 Sunny leaves from any bough.

III

Lilies for a bridal bed,
Roses for a matron's head,
Violets for a maiden dead —
 Pansies let *my* flowers be;
On the living grave I bear,
Scatter them without a tear —
Let no friend, however dear,
 Waste one hope, one fear for me.

TO EDWARD WILLIAMS

Published by Ascham, 1834.

I

The serpent is shut out from paradise.
 The wounded deer must seek the herb
 no more
 In which its heart-cure lies;
 The widowed dove must cease to haunt
 a bower,
Like that from which its mate with
 feignèd sighs
 Fled in the April hour.
I, too, must seldom seek again
Near happy friends a mitigated pain.

II

Of hatred I am proud, — with scorn content;
 Indifference, that once hurt me, now is
 grown
 Itself indifferent;
But, not to speak of love, pity alone

Can break a spirit already more than
 bent.
 The miserable one
 Turns the mind's poison into food, —
Its medicine is tears, — its evil good.

III

Therefore if now I see you seldomer,
 Dear friends, dear *friend !* know that I
 only fly
 Your looks, because they stir
 Griefs that should sleep, and hopes that
 cannot die.
The very comfort that they minister
 I scarce can bear; yet I,
 So deeply is the arrow gone,
Should quickly perish if it were withdrawn.

IV

When I return to my cold home, you ask
 Why I am not as I have ever been.
 You spoil me for the task
 Of acting a forced part in life's dull
 scene,
Of wearing on my brow the idle mask
 Of author, great or mean,
 In the world's carnival. I sought
Peace thus, and but in you I found it not.

V

Full half an hour, to-day, I tried my lot
 With various flowers, and every one still
 said,
 ' She loves me — loves me not.'
 And if this meant a vision long since
 fled —
If it meant fortune, fame, or peace of
 thought —
 If it meant, — but I dread
 To speak what you may know too well:
Still there was truth in the sad oracle.

VI

The crane o'er seas and forests seeks her
 home;
 No bird so wild but has its quiet nest,
 When it no more would roam;
 The sleepless billows on the ocean's
 breast
Break like a bursting heart, and die in
 foam,
 And thus at length find rest:

Doubtless there is a place of peace
Where *my* weak heart and all its throbs
will cease.

VII

I asked her, yesterday, if she believed
That I had resolution. One who *had*
Would ne'er have thus relieved
His heart with words, — but what his
judgment bade
Would do, and leave the scorner unre-
lieved.
These verses are too sad
To send to you, but that I know,
Happy yourself, you feel another's woe.

TO-MORROW

Published by Mrs. Shelley, *Posthumous
Poems*, 1824.

WHERE art thou, belovèd To-morrow?
When young and old, and strong and
weak,
Rich and poor, through joy and sorrow,
Thy sweet smiles we ever seek, —
In thy place — ah! well-a-day!
We find the thing we fled — To-day.

LINES

Published by Rossetti, 1870.

IF I walk in Autumn's even
While the dead leaves pass,
If I look on Spring's soft heaven, —
Something is not there which was.
Winter's wondrous frost and snow,
Summer's clouds, where are they now?

A LAMENT

Published by Mrs. Shelley, *Posthumous
Poems*, 1824.

I

O WORLD! O life! O time!
On whose last steps I climb,
Trembling at that where I had stood
before;
When will return the glory of your prime?
No more — oh, never more!

II

Out of the day and night
A joy has taken flight;
Fresh spring, and summer, and winter
hoar,
Move my faint heart with grief, but with
delight
No more — oh, never more!

POEMS WRITTEN IN 1822

The last months of Shelley's life were passed at Pisa and Lerici. The incidents, and the general character of the household with its group of friends, are minutely recorded in Mrs. Shelley's long note, in Trelawny's *Records*, and in nearly all biographies of later date. A brief narrative is inadequate to tell the story.

LINES

Published by Mrs. Shelley, *Posthumous
Poems*, 1824.

I

WHEN the lamp is shattered,
The light in the dust lies dead;
When the cloud is scattered,
The rainbow's glory is shed;
When the lute is broken,
Sweet tones are remembered not;
When the lips have spoken,
Loved accents are soon forgot.

II

As music and splendor
Survive not the lamp and the lute,
The heart's echoes render
No song when the spirit is mute: —
No song but sad dirges,
Like the wind through a ruined cell,
Or the mournful surges
That ring the dead seaman's knell.

III

When hearts have once mingled,
Love first leaves the well-built nest;

The weak one is singled
To endure what it once possessed.
O Love ! who bewailest
The frailty of all things here,
 Why choose you the frailest
For your cradle, your home, and your
 bier ?

IV

Its passions will rock thee,
As the storms rock the ravens on high;
 Bright reason will mock thee,
Like the sun from a wintry sky.
 From thy nest every rafter
Will rot, and thine eagle home
 Leave thee naked to laughter,
When leaves fall and cold winds come.

THE MAGNETIC LADY TO HER PATIENT

Shelley wrote on this poem, ' For Jane and
Williams only to see.' Medwin, who published
it, *The Athenæum*, 1832, gives an account of
the experiments out of which it grew, in his
Shelley Papers: ' Shelley was a martyr to a
most painful complaint, which constantly men-
aced to terminate fatally ; and was subject to
violent paroxysms which, to his irritable nerves,
were each a separate death. I had seen mag-
netism practised in India and at Paris, and at
his earnest request consented to try its efficacy.
Mesmer himself could not have hoped for more
complete success. The imposition of my hand
on his forehead instantaneously put a stop to
the spasm, and threw him into a magnetic
sleep, which for want of a better word is called
somnambulism. Mrs. Shelley and another lady
[Mrs. Williams] were present. The experi-
ment was repeated more than once. During
his trances I put some questions to him. He
always pitched his voice in the same tone as
mine. I enquired about his complaint, and its
cure — the usual magnetic enquiries. His
reply was, " What would cure me would kill
me " . . . [Shelley answered in Italian.] He
improvised also verses in Italian, in which lan-
guage he was never known to write poetry.'
Medwin adds, in his *Life of Shelley :* ' After
my departure from Pisa he was magnetized by
a lady, which gave rise to the beautiful stanzas
entitled *The Magnetic Lady to her Patient*, and
during which operation he made the same re-
ply to an enquiry as to his disease and its cure
as he had done to me, — " What would cure
me would kill me." . . . Mrs. Shelley also
magnetized him, but soon discontinued the
practice, from finding that he got up in his
sleep, and went one night to the window (for-
tunately barred), having taken to his old habit
of sleep-walking, which I mentioned, in his
boyhood and also in London.'

I

' SLEEP, sleep on ! forget thy pain;
 My hand is on thy brow,
My spirit on thy brain;
My pity on thy heart, poor friend;
 And from my fingers flow
The powers of life, and like a sign,
 Seal thee from thine hour of woe;
And brood on thee, but may not blend
 With thine.

II

' Sleep, sleep on ! I love thee not;
 But when I think that he
Who made and makes my lot
As full of flowers, as thine of weeds,
 Might have been lost like thee;
And that a hand which was not mine
 Might then have charmed his agony
As I another's — my heart bleeds
 For thine.

III

' Sleep, sleep, and with the slumber of
 The dead and the unborn
Forget thy life and love;
Forget that thou must wake forever;
 Forget the world's dull scorn;
Forget lost health, and the divine
 Feelings which died in youth's brief
 morn;
And forget me, for I can never
 Be thine.

IV

' Like a cloud big with a May shower,
 My soul weeps healing rain
On thee, thou withered flower;
It breathes mute music on thy sleep;
 Its odor calms thy brain !
Its light within thy gloomy breast
 Spreads like a second youth again.
By mine thy being is to its deep
 Possessed.

V

' The spell is done. How feel you now ?'
 ' Better — quite well,' replied
The sleeper, — ' What would do

You good when suffering and awake?
 What cure your head and side?'
'What would cure, that would kill me,
 Jane;
 And as I must on earth abide
Awhile, yet tempt me not to break
 My chain.'

TO JANE

THE INVITATION

Williams, in his Journal, February 2, describes such an excursion: 'Fine warm day. Jane accompanies Mary and S. to the sea-shore through the Cascine. They return about three.' The poem was published by Mrs. Shelley, in an earlier form, in *Posthumous Poems*, 1824, and, as here given, in her second collected edition, 1839.

BEST and brightest, come away!
Fairer far than this fair Day,
Which, like thee to those in sorrow,
Comes to bid a sweet good-morrow
To the rough Year just awake
In its cradle on the brake.
The brightest hour of unborn Spring
Through the winter wandering,
Found it seems the halcyon Morn,
To hoar February born. 10
Bending from Heaven, in azure mirth,
It kissed the forehead of the Earth,
And smiled upon the silent sea,
And bade the frozen streams be free,
And waked to music all their fountains,
And breathed upon the frozen mountains,
And like a prophetess of May
Strewed flowers upon the barren way,
Making the wintry world appear
Like one on whom thou smilest, dear. 20

Away, away, from men and towns,
To the wild wood and the downs;
To the silent wilderness
Where the soul need not repress
Its music, lest it should not find
An echo in another's mind,
While the touch of Nature's art
Harmonizes heart to heart.
I leave this notice on my door
For each accustomed visitor:— 30
'I am gone into the fields
To take what this sweet hour yields.
Reflection, you may come to-morrow,
Sit by the fireside with Sorrow.

You with the unpaid bill, Despair,—
You, tiresome verse-reciter, Care,—
I will pay you in the grave,—
Death will listen to your stave.
Expectation too, be off!
To-day is for itself enough. 40
Hope, in pity mock not Woe
With smiles, nor follow where I go;
Long having lived on thy sweet food,
At length I find one moment's good
After long pain—with all your love,
This you never told me of.'

Radiant Sister of the Day,
Awake! arise! and come away!
To the wild woods and the plains,
And the pools where winter rains 50
Image all their roof of leaves,
Where the pine its garland weaves
Of sapless green, and ivy dun,
Round stems that never kiss the sun;
Where the lawns and pastures be
And the sand-hills of the sea;
Where the melting hoar-frost wets
The daisy-star that never sets,
And wind-flowers and violets,
Which yet join not scent to hue, 60
Crown the pale year weak and new:
When the night is left behind
In the deep east, dun and blind,
And the blue noon is over us,
And the multitudinous
Billows murmur at our feet,
Where the earth and ocean meet,
And all things seem only one,
In the universal sun.

THE RECOLLECTION

Shelley sent the lines to Mrs. Williams—'not to be opened unless you are alone or with Williams.'

I

Now the last day of many days,
 All beautiful and bright as thou,
 The loveliest and the last, is dead,—
Rise, Memory, and write its praise!
 Up,—to thy wonted work! come, trace
 The epitaph of glory fled,
For now the Earth has changed its face,
 A frown is on the Heaven's brow.

II

We wandered to the Pine Forest
 That skirts the Ocean's foam,

The lightest wind was in its nest,
 The tempest in its home.
The whispering waves were half asleep,
 The clouds were gone to play,
And on the bosom of the deep
 The smile of Heaven lay;
It seemed as if the hour were one
 Sent from beyond the skies,
Which scattered from above the sun
 A light of Paradise.

III

We paused amid the pines that stood
 The giants of the waste,
Tortured by storms to shapes as rude
 As serpents interlaced,
And soothed by every azure breath,
 That under heaven is blown,
To harmonies and hues beneath,
 As tender as its own;
Now all the treetops lay asleep,
 Like green waves on the sea,
As still as in the silent deep
 The ocean woods may be.

IV

How calm it was ! — the silence there
 By such a chain was bound
That even the busy woodpecker
 Made stiller by her sound
The inviolable quietness;
 The breath of peace we drew
With its soft motion made not less
 The calm that round us grew.
There seemed, from the remotest seat
 Of the white mountain waste
To the soft flower beneath our feet,
 A magic circle traced,
A spirit interfused around,
 A thrilling silent life, —
To momentary peace it bound
 Our mortal nature's strife;
And still I felt the centre of
 The magic circle there
Was one fair form that filled with love
 The lifeless atmosphere.

V

We paused beside the pools that lie
 Under the forest bough, —
Each seemed as 't were a little sky
 Gulfed in a world below;
A firmament of purple light,
 Which in the dark earth lay,

More boundless than the depth of night,
 And purer than the day, —
In which the lovely forests grew,
 As in the upper air,
More perfect both in shape and hue
 Than any spreading there,
There lay the glade and neighboring lawn,
 And through the dark green wood
The white sun twinkling like the dawn
 Out of a speckled cloud.
Sweet views which in our world above
 Can never well be seen,
Were imaged by the water's love
 Of that fair forest green.
And all was interfused beneath
 With an Elysian glow,
An atmosphere without a breath,
 A softer day below.
Like one beloved the scene had lent
 To the dark water's breast,
Its every leaf and lineament
 With more than truth expressed;
Until an envious wind crept by,
 Like an unwelcome thought,
Which from the mind's too faithful eye
 Blots one dear image out.
Though thou art ever fair and kind,
 The forests ever green,
Less oft is peace in Shelley's mind,
 Than calm in waters seen.

WITH A GUITAR: TO JANE

Shelley originally intended to give a harp to Mrs. Williams, and wrote to Horace Smith with regard to its purchase. The suggestion for the poem is found by Dr. Garnett in the fact that 'the front portion of the guitar is made of Swiss pine.' He continues : 'It is now clear how the poem took shape in Shelley's mind. The actual thought of the imprisonment of the Spirit of Music in the material of the instrument suggested Ariel's penance in the cloven pine ; the identification of himself with Ariel and of Jane Williams with Miranda was the easiest of feats to his brilliant imagination ; and hence an allegory of unequalled grace and charm, which could never have existed if the instrument had not been partly made of pine wood. The back, it should be added, is of mahogany, the finger board of ebony, and minor portions, chiefly ornamental, of some wood not identified. It was made by Ferdinando Bottari of Pisa in 1816. Having been religiously preserved since Shelley's death, it is in as perfect condition as when made. The

strings, it is said, are better than those that are produced now.

'This guitar is also in a measure the subject of another of Shelley's most beautiful lyrics, "The keen stars were twinkling." In a letter dated June 18, 1822, speaking of his cruises "in the evening wind under the summer moon," he adds, "Jane brings her guitar." There is probably no other relic of a great poet so intimately associated with the arts of poetry and music, or ever will be, unless Milton's organ should turn up at a broker's or some excavating explorer should bring to light the lyre of Sappho.'

The guitar was given to the Bodleian Library by E. W. Silsbee, of Salem, Mass., who bought it of the grandson of Mrs. Williams on condition that it should be so disposed of. The composition of the poem is described by Trelawny : 'The strong light streamed through the opening of the trees. One of the pines, undermined by the water, had fallen into it. Under its lee, and nearly hidden, sat the Poet, gazing on the dark mirror beneath, so lost in his bardish reverie that he did not hear my approach. . . . The day I found Shelley in the pine-forest he was writing verses on a guitar. I picked up a fragment, but could only make out the first two lines. . . . It was a frightful scrawl ; words smeared out with his finger, and one upon the other, over and over in tiers, and all run together " in most admired disorder ; " it might have been taken for a sketch of a marsh overrun with bulrushes, and the blots for wild ducks ; such a dashed-off daub as self-conceited artists mistake for a manifestation of genius.' The poem was published by Medwin, in two parts, *The Athenæum*, 1832, and *Fraser's*, 1833.

ARIEL to Miranda : — Take
This slave of Music, for the sake
Of him who is the slave of thee ;
And teach it all the harmony
In which thou canst, and only thou,
Make the delighted spirit glow,
Till joy denies itself again,
And, too intense, is turned to pain.
For by permission and command
Of thine own Prince Ferdinand, 10
Poor Ariel sends this silent token
Of more than ever can be spoken ;
Your guardian spirit, Ariel, who
From life to life must still pursue
Your happiness, — for thus alone
Can Ariel ever find his own.
From Prospero's enchanted cell,
As the mighty verses tell,

To the throne of Naples he
Lit you o'er the trackless sea, 20
Flitting on, your prow before,
Like a living meteor.
When you die, the silent Moon,
In her interlunar swoon,
Is not sadder in her cell
Than deserted Ariel.
When you live again on earth,
Like an unseen star of birth
Ariel guides you o'er the sea
Of life from your nativity. 30
Many changes have been run
Since Ferdinand and you begun
Your course of love, and Ariel still
Has tracked your steps and served your
 will ;
Now in humbler, happier lot,
This is all remembered not ;
And now, alas ! the poor sprite is
Imprisoned, for some fault of his,
In a body like a grave.
From you, he only dares to crave, 40
For his service and his sorrow,
A smile to-day, a song to-morrow.

The artist who this idol wrought
To echo all harmonious thought,
Felled a tree, while on the steep
The woods were in their winter sleep,
Rocked in that repose divine
On the wind-swept Apennine ;
And dreaming, some of Autumn past,
And some of Spring approaching fast, 50
And some of April buds and showers,
And some of songs in July bowers,
And all of love ; and so this tree —
Oh, that such our death may be ! —
Died in sleep, and felt no pain,
To live in happier form again :
From which, beneath Heaven's fairest
 star,
The artist wrought this loved guitar,
And taught it justly to reply,
To all who question skilfully, 60
In language gentle as thine own ;
Whispering in enamoured tone
Sweet oracles of woods and dells,
And summer winds in sylvan cells ;
For it had learned all harmonies
Of the plains and of the skies,
Of the forests and the mountains,
And the many-voicèd fountains ;
The clearest echoes of the hills,
The softest notes of falling rills, 70

The melodies of birds and bees,
The murmuring of summer seas,
And pattering rain, and breathing dew,
And airs of evening; and it knew
That seldom-heard mysterious sound,
Which, driven on its diurnal round,
As it floats through boundless day,
Our world enkindles on its way.
All this it knows, but will not tell
To those who cannot question well 80
The spirit that inhabits it;
It talks according to the wit
Of its companions; and no more
Is heard than has been felt before
By those who tempt it to betray
These secrets of an elder day.
But, sweetly as its answers will
Flatter hands of perfect skill,
It keeps its highest, holiest tone
For our belovèd Jane alone. 90

TO JANE

Shelley sent the lines to Mrs. Williams with a note. 'I sat down to write some words for an ariette which might be profane ; but it was in vain to struggle with the ruling spirit who compelled me to speak of things sacred to yours and to Wilhelm Meister's indulgence. I commit them to your secrecy and your mercy, and will try to do better another time.'

The poem was published in part by Medwin, *The Athenæum*, 1832, and complete by Mrs. Shelley in her second collected edition, 1839.

I

THE keen stars were twinkling,
And the fair moon was rising among them,
 Dear Jane.
The guitar was tinkling,
But the notes were not sweet till you sung
 them
 Again.

II

As the moon's soft splendor
O'er the faint cold starlight of heaven
 Is thrown,
So your voice most tender
To the strings without soul had then given
 Its own.

III

The stars will awaken,
Though the moon sleep a full hour later
 To-night;
No leaf will be shaken

Whilst the dews of your melody scatter
 Delight.

IV

Though the sound overpowers,
Sing again, with your dear voice revealing
 A tone
Of some world far from ours,
Where music and moonlight and feeling
 Are one.

EPITAPH

Published by Mrs. Shelley, *Posthumous Poems*, 1824.

THESE are two friends whose lives were undivided;
So let their memory be, now they have glided
Under the grave; let not their bones be parted,
For their two hearts in life were single-hearted.

THE ISLE

Published by Mrs. Shelley, *Posthumous Poems*, 1824.

THERE was a little lawny islet
By anemone and violet,
 Like mosaic, paven;
And its roof was flowers and leaves
Which the summer's breath enweaves,
Where nor sun nor showers nor breeze
Pierce the pines and tallest trees,
 Each a gem engraven; —
Girt by many an azure wave
With which the clouds and mountains pave
 A lake's blue chasm.

A DIRGE

Published by Mrs. Shelley, *Posthumous Poems*, 1824.

ROUGH wind, that moanest loud
 Grief too sad for song;
 Wild wind, when sullen cloud
Knells all the night long;
Sad storm, whose tears are vain,
Bare woods whose branches strain,
Deep caves and dreary main, —
 Wail, for the world's wrong.

LINES WRITTEN IN THE BAY OF LERICI

Published by Garnett, *Macmillan's*, 1862.

She left me at the silent time
When the moon had ceased to climb
The azure path of Heaven's steep,
And like an albatross asleep,
Balanced on her wings of light,
Hovered in the purple night,
Ere she sought her ocean nest
In the chambers of the West.
She left me, and I stayed alone
Thinking over every tone 10
Which, though silent to the ear,
The enchanted heart could hear,
Like notes which die when born, but still
Haunt the echoes of the hill;
And feeling ever — oh, too much ! —
The soft vibration of her touch,
As if her gentle hand, even now,
Lightly trembled on my brow;
And thus, although she absent were,
Memory gave me all of her 20
That even Fancy dares to claim: —
Her presence had made weak and tame
All passions, and I lived alone
In the time which is our own;
The past and future were forgot,
As they had been, and would be, not.
But soon, the guardian angel gone,
The dæmon reassumed his throne
In my faint heart. I dare not speak
My thoughts, but thus disturbed and
 weak
I sat and saw the vessels glide 30
Over the ocean bright and wide,
Like spirit-wingèd chariots sent
O'er some serenest element
For ministrations strange and far;
As if to some Elysian star
They sailed for drink to medicine
Such sweet and bitter pain as mine.
And the wind that winged their flight
From the land came fresh and light, 40
And the scent of wingèd flowers,
And the coolness of the hours
Of dew, and sweet warmth left by day,
Were scattered o'er the twinkling bay.
And the fisher with his lamp
And spear about the low rocks damp
Crept, and struck the fish which came
To worship the delusive flame.
Too happy they, whose pleasure sought
Extinguishes all sense and thought 50
Of the regret that pleasure leaves,
Destroying life alone, not peace !

FRAGMENTS

Under FRAGMENTS are included, with a few exceptions, incomplete poems, sketches and cancelled passages, and those more inchoate passages which have been recovered from Shelley's notebooks. The exceptions are the *Prologue to Hellas*, which has been put with that drama, *A Vision of the Sea*, published by Shelley with the poems accompanying *Prometheus Unbound*, and five pieces, *To Mary Wollstonecraft Godwin*, 1814, *Death, An Allegory, On the Medusa of Leonardo da Vinci*, and *Evening, Pisa*, which, though lacking a word or a line, are in effect complete. The order of the FRAGMENTS is not strictly chronological in the first division, and is altogether arbitrary in the second. The dates assigned are those generally accepted, but, as a rule, they are conjectural and approximate only, not exact. The text is derived from the editions of Mrs. Shelley, the studies of Dr. Garnett in the Boscombe MSS., published by him mainly in *Relics of Shelley*, 1862, or by Rossetti, 1870, and Rossetti's own studies both in the same and other MSS. of which the results were given in his edition. A few pieces, originally published elsewhere, were also gathered by Rossetti and Forman in their editions, and Forman was enabled to add something more from independent MSS. The date and original publication of each piece are briefly indicated under each poem.

I

THE DÆMON OF THE WORLD

Nec tantum prodere vati,
Quantum scire licet. Venit ætas omnis in unam
Congeriem, miserumque premunt tot sæcula pectus.
LUCAN, PHARS. v. 176-178.

Shelley in his preface to *Alastor*, where this poem was published, says : ' The Fragment entitled *The Dæmon of the World* is a detached part of a poem which the author does not intend for publication. The metre in which it is composed is that of *Samson Agonistes* and the Italian pastoral drama, and may be considered as the natural measure into which poetical conceptions, expressed in harmonious language, necessarily fall.' The poem is part of a revision of *Queen Mab*.

I

How wonderful is Death,
Death and his brother Sleep !
One, pale as yonder wan and hornèd moon,
　　With lips of lurid blue;
The other, glowing like the vital morn
　　When throned on ocean's wave
　　It breathes over the world;
Yet both so passing strange and wonder-
　　ful !

Hath then the iron-sceptred Skeleton,
Whose reign is in the tainted sepulchres, 10
To the hell dogs that couch beneath his
　　throne
Cast that fair prey ?　Must that divinest
　　form,
Which love and admiration cannot view
Without a beating heart, whose azure veins
Steal like dark streams along a field of
　　snow,
Whose outline is as fair as marble clothed
In light of some sublimest mind, decay ?
　　Nor putrefaction's breath
Leave aught of this pure spectacle
　　But loathsomeness and ruin ?　　　20
　　Spare aught but a dark theme,
On which the lightest heart might moral-
　　ize ?
Or is it but that downy-wingèd slumbers
Have charmed their nurse, coy Silence, near
　　her lids
　　To watch their own repose ?
　　Will they, when morning's beam
　　Flows through those wells of light,
Seek far from noise and day some western
　　cave,
Where woods and streams with soft and
　　pausing winds
　　A lulling murmur weave ? —　　　30

Ianthe doth not sleep
　　The dreamless sleep of death;
Nor in her moonlight chamber silently
Doth Henry hear her regular pulses throb,
　　Or mark her delicate cheek
With interchange of hues mock the broad
　　moon,
　　Outwatching weary night,
　　Without assured reward.
　　Her dewy eyes are closed;
On their translucent lids, whose texture
　　fine　　　40
Scarce hides the dark blue orbs that burn
　　below

With unapparent fire,
　　The baby Sleep is pillowed;
　　Her golden tresses shade
　　The bosom's stainless pride,
Twining like tendrils of the parasite
　　Around a marble column.

Hark ! whence that rushing sound ?
'T is like a　wondrous strain that
　　sweeps
　　Around a lonely ruin　　　50
When west winds sigh and evening waves
　　respond
　　In whispers from the shore:
'T is wilder than the unmeasured notes
Which from the unseen lyres of dells and
　　groves
The genii of the breezes sweep.

Floating on waves of music and of light
The chariot of the Dæmon of the World
　　Descends in silent power.
Its shape reposed within; slight as some
　　cloud
That catches but the palest tinge of day 60
　　When evening yields to night;
Bright as that fibrous woof when stars
　　endue
　　Its transitory robe.
Four shapeless shadows bright and beauti-
　　ful
Draw that strange car of glory; reins of
　　light
Check their unearthly speed; they stop and
　　fold
　　Their wings of braided air.
The Dæmon, leaning from the ethereal car,
Gazed on the slumbering maid.
Human eye hath ne'er beheld　　　70
A shape so wild, so bright, so beautiful,
As that which o'er the maiden's charmèd
　　sleep,
　　Waving a starry wand,
　　Hung like a mist of light.
Such sounds as breathed around like odor-
　　ous winds
　　Of wakening spring arose,
Filling the chamber and the moonlight sky.

' Maiden, the world's supremest spirit
　　Beneath the shadow of her wings
Folds all thy memory doth inherit　　　80
　　From ruin of divinest things, —
　　Feelings that lure thee to betray,
　　And light of thoughts that pass away

' For thou hast earned a mighty boon;
　The truths, which wisest poets see
Dimly, thy mind may make its own,
　　Rewarding its own majesty,
　　Entranced in some diviner mood
　Of self-oblivious solitude.

' Custom and Faith and Power thou spurn-
　　　est; 90
　From hate and awe thy heart is free;
Ardent and pure as day thou burnest,
　　For dark and cold mortality
　　A living light, to cheer it long,
　The watch-fires of the world among.

' Therefore from Nature's inner shrine,
　Where gods and fiends in worship bend,
Majestic spirit, be it thine
　　The flame to seize, the veil to rend,
　　Where the vast snake Eternity 100
　In charmèd sleep doth ever lie.

' All that inspires thy voice of love,
　Or speaks in thy unclosing eyes,
Or through thy frame doth burn or move,
　　Or think or feel, awake, arise !
　　Spirit, leave for mine and me
　Earth's unsubstantial mimicry ! '

It ceased, and from the mute and move-
　　　less frame
　　A radiant spirit arose,
All beautiful in naked purity. 110
Robed in its human hues it did ascend,
Disparting as it went the silver clouds
It moved towards the car, and took its seat
　Beside the Dæmon shape.

Obedient to the sweep of aëry song,
　The mighty ministers
Unfurled their prismy wings.
The magic car moved on.
The night was fair — innumerable stars
Studded heaven's dark blue vault; 120
　The eastern wave grew pale
　With the first smile of morn.

　The magic car moved on.
From the swift sweep of wings
The atmosphere in flaming sparkles flew;
　And where the burning wheels
Eddied above the mountain's loftiest peak
　Was traced a line of lightning.
Now far above a rock, the utmost verge
　Of the wide earth, it flew, — 130

The rival of the Andes, whose dark brow
　Frowned o'er the silver sea.

Far, far below the chariot's stormy path,
　Calm as a slumbering babe,
　Tremendous ocean lay.
Its broad and silent mirror gave to view
　The pale and waning stars,
　The chariot's fiery track,
　And the gray light of morn
　Tingeing those fleecy clouds 140
That cradled in their folds the infant
　　　dawn.
　The chariot seemed to fly
Through the abyss of an immense concave,
Radiant with million constellations, tinged
　With shades of infinite color,
　And semicircled with a belt
　Flashing incessant meteors.

　As they approached their goal,
The wingèd shadows seemed to gather
　　　speed.
The sea no longer was distinguished; earth
Appeared a vast and shadowy sphere, sus-
　　　pended 151
　In the black concave of heaven
　With the sun's cloudless orb,
　Whose rays of rapid light
Parted around the chariot's swifter course,
And fell like ocean's feathery spray
　Dashed from the boiling surge
　Before a vessel's prow.

　The magic car moved on.
Earth's distant orb appeared 160
The smallest light that twinkles in the
　　　heavens,
　Whilst round the chariot's way
Innumerable systems widely rolled,
　And countless spheres diffused
　　An ever-varying glory.
It was a sight of wonder ! Some were
　　　horned,
And like the moon's argentine crescent
　　　hung
In the dark dome of heaven; some did shed
A clear mild beam like Hesperus, while the
　　　sea
Yet glows with fading sunlight; others
　　　dashed 170
Athwart the night with trains of bickering
　　　fire,
Like spherèd worlds to death and ruin
　　　driven ;

Some shone like stars, and as the chariot
 passed
 Bedimmed all other light.

 Spirit of Nature ! here,
 In this interminable wilderness
 Of worlds, at whose involved immensity
 Even soaring fancy staggers,
 Here is thy fitting temple !
 Yet not the lightest leaf 180
 That quivers to the passing breeze
 Is less instinct with thee;
 Yet not the meanest worm,
 That lurks in graves and fattens on the
 dead,
 Less shares thy eternal breath.
 Spirit of Nature ! thou,
 Imperishable as this glorious scene,
 Here is thy fitting temple !

 If solitude hath ever led thy steps
 To the shore of the immeasurable sea, 190
 And thou hast lingered there
 Until the sun's broad orb
 Seemed resting on the fiery line of ocean,
 Thou must have marked the braided webs
 of gold
 That without motion hang
 Over the sinking sphere;
 Thou must have marked the billowy moun-
 tain clouds,
 Edged with intolerable radiancy,
 Towering like rocks of jet
 Above the burning deep; 200
 And yet there is a moment,
 When the sun's highest point
 Peers like a star o'er ocean's western edge,
 When those far clouds of feathery purple
 gleam
 Like fairy lands girt by some heavenly
 sea;
 Then has thy rapt imagination soared
 Where in the midst of all existing things
 The temple of the mightiest Dæmon stands.

 Yet not the golden islands
 That gleam amid yon flood of purple light,
 Nor the feathery curtains 211
 That canopy the sun's resplendent couch,
 Nor the burnished ocean waves
 Paving that gorgeous dome,
 So fair, so wonderful a sight
 As the eternal temple could afford.
 The elements of all that human thought
 Can frame of lovely or sublime did join

To rear the fabric of the fane, nor aught
Of earth may image forth its majesty. 220
Yet likest evening's vault that faëry hall;
As heaven low resting on the wave it
 spread
 Its floors of flashing light,
 Its vast and azure dome;
And on the verge of that obscure abyss,
Where crystal battlements o'erhang the
 gulf
Of the dark world, ten thousand spheres
 diffuse
Their lustre through its adamantine gates.

 The magic car no longer moved.
 The Dæmon and the Spirit 230
 Entered the eternal gates.
 Those clouds of aëry gold,
 That slept in glittering billows
 Beneath the azure canopy,
With the ethereal footsteps trembled not;
 While slight and odorous mists
Floated to strains of thrilling melody
Through the vast columns and the pearly
 shrines.

 The Dæmon and the Spirit
Approached the overhanging battlement.
Below lay stretched the boundless uni-
 verse ! 241
 There, far as the remotest line
That limits swift imagination's flight,
Unending orbs mingled in mazy motion,
 Immutably fulfilling
 Eternal Nature's law.
 Above, below, around,
 The circling systems formed
 A wilderness of harmony —
 Each with undeviating aim 250
In eloquent silence through the depths of
 space
 Pursued its wondrous way.

Awhile the Spirit paused in ecstasy.
Yet soon she saw, as the vast spheres swept
 by,
Strange things within their belted orbs
 appear.
Like animated frenzies, dimly moved
Shadows, and skeletons, and fiendly shapes,
Thronging round human graves, and o'er
 the dead
Sculpturing records for each memory
In verse, such as malignant gods pro-
 nounce, 260

Blasting the hopes of men, when heaven
and hell
Confounded burst in ruin o'er the world;
And they did build vast trophies, instru-
ments
Of murder, human bones, barbaric gold,
Skins torn from living men, and towers of
skulls
With sightless holes gazing on blinder
heaven,
Mitres, and crowns, and brazen chariots
stained
With blood, and scrolls of mystic wicked-
ness,
The sanguine codes of venerable crime.
The likeness of a thronèd king came by,
When these had passed, bearing upon his
brow 271
A threefold crown; his countenance was
calm,
His eye severe and cold; but his right hand
Was charged with bloody coin, and he did
gnaw
By fits, with secret smiles, a human heart
Concealed beneath his robe; and motley
shapes,
A multitudinous throng, around him knelt,
With bosoms bare, and bowed heads, and
false looks
Of true submission, as the sphere rolled by,
Brooking no eye to witness their foul
shame, 280
Which human hearts must feel, while hu-
man tongues
Tremble to speak ; they did rage horribly,
Breathing in self-contempt fierce blas-
phemies
Against the Dæmon of the World, and
high
Hurling their armèd hands where the pure
Spirit,
Serene and inaccessibly secure,
Stood on an isolated pinnacle,
The flood of ages combating below,
The depth of the unbounded universe
Above, and all around 290
Necessity's unchanging harmony.

THE DÆMON OF THE WORLD

This second part of the poem was published
by Forman, 1876, from a printed copy of
Queen Mab, on which Shelley had made MS.
revisions, with a view to republication under
the new title.

II

O HAPPY Earth ! reality of Heaven !
To which those restless powers that cease-
lessly
Throng through the human universe
aspire !
Thou consummation of all mortal hope !
Thou glorious prize of blindly-working
will,
Whose rays, diffused throughout all space
and time,
Verge to one point and blend forever there !
Of purest spirits thou pure dwelling-place,
Where care and sorrow, impotence and
crime,
Languor, disease, and ignorance dare not
come ! 10
O happy Earth, reality of Heaven !

Genius has seen thee in her passionate
dreams,
And dim forebodings of thy loveliness
Haunting the human heart have there en-
twined
Those rooted hopes, that the proud Power
of Evil
Shall not forever on this fairest world
Shake pestilence and war, or that his slaves
With blasphemy for prayer, and human
blood
For sacrifice, before his shrine forever
In adoration bend, or Erebus 20
With all its banded fiends shall not uprise
To overwhelm in envy and revenge
The dauntless and the good, who dare to
hurl
Defiance at his throne, girt though it be
With Death's omnipotence. Thou hast be-
held
His empire, o'er the present and the past;
It was a desolate sight — now gaze on mine,
Futurity. Thou hoary giant Time,
Render thou up thy half-devoured babes,
And from the cradles of eternity, 30
Where millions lie lulled to their portioned
sleep
By the deep murmuring stream of passing
things,
Tear thou that gloomy shroud ! Spirit, be-
hold
Thy glorious destiny !

 The Spirit saw
The vast frame of the renovated world
Smile in the lap of Chaos, and the sense

Of hope through her fine texture did suffuse
Such varying glow, as summer evening
 casts
On undulating clouds and deepening lakes.
Like the vague sighings of a wind at even,
That wakes the wavelets of the slumbering
 sea 41
And dies on the creation of its breath,
And sinks and rises, fails and swells by fits,
Was the sweet stream of thought that with
 mild motion
Flowed o'er the Spirit's human sympathies.
The mighty tide of thought had paused
 awhile,
Which from the Dæmon now like Ocean's
 stream
Again began to pour. —
 To me is given
The wonders of the human world to keep —
Space, matter, time and mind — let the
 sight 50
Renew and strengthen all thy failing hope.
All things are recreated, and the flame
Of consentaneous love inspires all life;
The fertile bosom of the earth gives suck
To myriads, who still grow beneath her care,
Rewarding her with their pure perfectness;
The balmy breathings of the wind inhale
Her virtues, and diffuse them all abroad;
Health floats amid the gentle atmosphere,
Glows in the fruits, and mantles on the
 stream; 60
No storms deform the beaming brow of
 heaven,
Nor scatter in the freshness of its pride
The foliage of the undecaying trees;
But fruits are ever ripe, flowers ever fair,
And Autumn proudly bears her matron
 grace,
Kindling a flush on the fair cheek of Spring,
Whose virgin bloom beneath the ruddy
 fruit
Reflects its tint and blushes into love.

The habitable earth is full of bliss;
Those wastes of frozen billows that were
 hurled 70
By everlasting snowstorms round the poles,
Where matter dared nor vegetate nor live,
But ceaseless frost round the vast solitude
Bound its broad zone of stillness, are un-
 loosed;
And fragrant zephyrs there from spicy isles
Ruffle the placid ocean-deep, that rolls
Its broad, bright surges to the sloping sand,

Whose roar is wakened into echoings sweet
To murmur through the heaven-breathing
 groves
And melodize with man's blest nature there.

The vast tract of the parched and sandy
 waste 81
Now teems with countless rills and shady
 woods,
Cornfields and pastures and white cottages;
And where the startled wilderness did hear
A savage conqueror stained in kindred blood
Hymning his victory, or the milder snake
Crushing the bones of some frail antelope
Within his brazen folds, the dewy lawn,
Offering sweet incense to the sunrise, smiles
To see a babe before his mother's door 90
Share with the green and golden basilisk,
That comes to lick his feet, his morning's
 meal.

Those trackless deeps, where many a
 weary sail
Has seen above the illimitable plain
Morning on night, and night on morning
 rise,
Whilst still no land to greet the wanderer
 spread
Its shadowy mountains on the sun-bright
 sea,
Where the loud roarings of the tempest-
 waves
So long have mingled with the gusty wind
In melancholy loneliness, and swept 100
The desert of those ocean solitudes,
But vocal to the sea-bird's harrowing shriek,
The bellowing monster, and the rushing
 storm,
Now to the sweet and many - mingling
 sounds
Of kindliest human impulses respond;
Those lonely realms bright garden-isles
 begem,
With lightsome clouds and shining seas
 between,
And fertile valleys, resonant with bliss,
Whilst green woods overcanopy the wave,
Which like a toil-worn laborer leaps to
 shore 110
To meet the kisses of the flowerets there.

Man chief perceives the change; his
 being notes
The gradual renovation, and defines
Each movement of its progress on his mind.

Man, where the gloom of the long polar
 night
Lowered o'er the snow-clad rocks and
 frozen soil,
Where scarce the hardest herb that braves
 the frost
Basked in the moonlight's ineffectual glow,
Shrank with the plants, and darkened with
 the night;
Nor where the tropics bound the realms of
 day 120
With a broad belt of mingling cloud and
 flame,
Where blue mists through the unmoving
 atmosphere
Scattered the seeds of pestilence, and fed
Unnatural vegetation, where the land
Teemed with all earthquake, tempest and
 disease,
Was man a nobler being; slavery
Had crushed him to his country's blood-
 stained dust.

Even where the milder zone afforded man
A seeming shelter, yet contagion there, 129
Blighting his being with unnumbered ills,
Spread like a quenchless fire; nor truth
 availed
Till late to arrest its progress, or create
That peace which first in bloodless victory
 waved
Her snowy standard o'er this favored
 clime;
There man was long the train-bearer of
 slaves,
The mimic of surrounding misery,
The jackal of ambition's lion-rage,
The bloodhound of religion's hungry zeal.

Here now the human being stands adorn-
 ing
This loveliest earth with taintless body and
 mind; 140
Blest from his birth with all bland im-
 pulses,
Which gently in his noble bosom wake
All kindly passions and all pure desires.
Him, still from hope to hope the bliss pur-
 suing
Which from the exhaustless lore of human
 weal
Draws on the virtuous mind, the thoughts
 that rise
In time-destroying infiniteness gift
With self-enshrined eternity, that mocks

The unprevailing hoariness of age;
And man, once fleeting o'er the transient
 scene 150
Swift as an unremembered vision, stands
Immortal upon earth; no longer now
He slays the beast that sports around his
 dwelling,
And horribly devours its mangled flesh,
Or drinks its vital blood, which like a
 stream
Of poison through his fevered veins did
 flow
Feeding a plague that secretly consumed
His feeble frame, and kindling in his mind
Hatred, despair, and fear and vain belief,
The germs of misery, death, disease, and
 crime. 160
No longer now the wingèd habitants,
That in the woods their sweet lives sing
 away,
Flee from the form of man; but gather
 round,
And prune their sunny feathers on the
 hands
Which little children stretch in friendly
 sport
Towards these dreadless partners of their
 play.
All things are void of terror; man has lost
His desolating privilege, and stands
An equal amidst equals; happiness
And science dawn though late upon the
 earth; 170
Peace cheers the mind, health renovates the
 frame;
Disease and pleasure cease to mingle here,
Reason and passion cease to combat there;
Whilst mind unfettered o'er the earth ex-
 tends
Its all-subduing energies, and wields
The sceptre of a vast dominion there.

Mild is the slow necessity of death.
The tranquil spirit fails beneath its grasp,
Without a groan, almost without a fear,
Resigned in peace to the necessity, 180
Calm as a voyager to some distant land,
And full of wonder, full of hope as he.
The deadly germs of languor and disease
Waste in the human frame, and Nature
 gifts
With choicest boons her human worship-
 pers.
How vigorous now the athletic form of
 age!

How clear its open and unwrinkled brow!
Where neither avarice, cunning, pride, or
 care,
Had stamped the zeal of gray deformity
On all the mingling lineaments of time. 190
How lovely the intrepid front of youth!
How sweet the smiles of taintless infancy.

Within the massy prison's mouldering
 courts
Fearless and free the ruddy children play,
Weaving gay chaplets for their innocent
 brows
With the green ivy and the red wall-flower,
That mock the dungeon's unavailing gloom;
The ponderous chains, and gratings of
 strong iron,
There rust amid the accumulated ruins
Now mingling slowly with their native
 earth; 200
There the broad beam of day, which feebly
 once
Lighted the cheek of lean captivity
With a pale and sickly glare, now freely
 shines
On the pure smiles of infant playfulness;
No more the shuddering voice of hoarse
 despair
Peals through the echoing vaults, but
 soothing notes
Of ivy-fingered winds and gladsome birds
And merriment are resonant around.

The fanes of Fear and Falsehood hear no
 more
The voice that once waked multitudes to
 war 210
Thundering through all their aisles, but
 now respond
To the death dirge of the melancholy wind.
It were a sight of awfulness to see
The works of faith and slavery, so vast,
So sumptuous, yet withal so perishing,
Even as the corpse that rests beneath their
 wall!
A thousand mourners deck the pomp of
 death
To-day, the breathing marble glows above
To decorate its memory, and tongues
Are busy of its life; to-morrow, worms 220
In silence and in darkness seize their
 prey.
These ruins soon leave not a wreck behind;
Their elements, wide scattered o'er the
 globe,

To happier shapes are moulded, and be-
 come
Ministrant to all blissful impulses;
Thus human things are perfected, and
 earth,
Even as a child beneath its mother's love,
Is strengthened in all excellence, and
 grows
Fairer and nobler with each passing year.

Now Time his dusky pennons o'er the
 scene 230
Closes in steadfast darkness, and the past
Fades from our charmèd sight. My task
 is done;
Thy lore is learned. Earth's wonders are
 thine own,
With all the fear and all the hope they
 bring.
My spells are past; the present now recurs.
Ah me! a pathless wilderness remains
Yet unsubdued by man's reclaiming hand.

Yet, human Spirit, bravely hold thy
 course.
Let virtue teach thee firmly to pursue 239
The gradual paths of an aspiring change.
For birth and life and death, and that
 strange state
Before the naked powers, that through the
 world
Wander like winds, have found a human
 home;
All tend to perfect happiness, and urge
The restless wheels of being on their way,
Whose flashing spokes, instinct with infinite
 life,
Bicker and burn to gain their destined
 goal;
For birth but wakes the universal mind,
Whose mighty streams might else in silence
 flow
Through the vast world, to individual sense
Of outward shows, whose unexperienced
 shape 251
New modes of passion to its frame may
 lend;
Life is its state of action, and the store
Of all events is aggregated there
That variegate the eternal universe;
Death is a gate of dreariness and gloom,
That leads to azure isles and beaming
 skies
And happy regions of eternal hope.
Therefore, O Spirit! fearlessly bear on.

Though storms may break the primrose on
 its stalk, 260
Though frosts may blight the freshness of
 its bloom,
Yet spring's awakening breath will woo
 the earth
To feed with kindliest dews its favorite
 flower,
That blooms in mossy banks and darksome
 glens,
Lighting the green wood with its sunny
 smile.

Fear not then, Spirit, death's disrobing
 hand,
So welcome when the tyrant is awake,
So welcome when the bigot's hell-torch
 flares;
'T is but the voyage of a darksome hour,
The transient gulf-dream of a startling
 sleep. 270
For what thou art shall perish utterly,
But what is thine may never cease to be;
Death is no foe to virtue; earth has seen
Love's brightest roses on the scaffold
 bloom,
Mingling with freedom's fadeless laurels
 there,
And presaging the truth of visioned bliss.
Are there not hopes within thee, which this
 scene
Of linked and gradual being has confirmed?
Hopes that not vainly thou, and living fires
Of mind, as radiant and as pure as thou
Have shone upon the paths of men — re-
 turn 281
Surpassing Spirit, to that world, where thou
Art destined an eternal war to wage
With tyranny and falsehood, and uproot
The germs of misery from the human heart.
Thine is the hand whose piety would soothe
The thorny pillow of unhappy crime,
Whose impotence an easy pardon gains,
Watching its wanderings as a friend's
 disease;
Thine is the brow whose mildness would
 defy 290
Its fiercest rage, and brave its sternest will,
When fenced by power and master of the
 world.
Thou art sincere and good; of resolute
 mind,
Free from heart-withering custom's cold
 control,
Of passion lofty, pure and unsubdued.

Earth's pride and meanness could not van-
 quish thee,
And therefore art thou worthy of the boon
Which thou hast now received; virtue shall
 keep
Thy footsteps in the path that thou hast
 trod, 299
And many days of beaming hope shall bless
Thy spotless life of sweet and sacred love.
Go, happy one, and give that bosom joy
 Whose sleepless spirit waits to catch
 Light, life and rapture from thy smile.

The Dæmon called its wingèd ministers.
Speechless with bliss the Spirit mounts the
 car,
That rolled beside the crystal battlement,
Bending her beamy eyes in thankfulness.
 The burning wheels inflame
The steep descent of Heaven's untrodden
 way. 310
 Fast and far the chariot flew.
 The mighty globes that rolled
Around the gate of the Eternal Fane
Lessened by slow degrees, and soon ap-
 peared
Such tiny twinklers as the planet orbs,
That, ministering on the solar power,
With borrowed light, pursued their nar-
 rower way.
 Earth floated then below.
 The chariot paused a moment;
 The Spirit then descended; 320
 And from the earth departing
 The shadows with swift wings
Speeded like thought upon the light of
 Heaven.

The Body and the Soul united then;
A gentle start convulsed Ianthe's frame;
Her veiny eyelids quietly unclosed;
Moveless awhile the dark blue orbs re-
 mained.
She looked around in wonder and beheld
Henry, who kneeled in silence by her couch,
Watching her sleep with looks of speech-
 less love, 330
 And the bright beaming stars
 That through the casement shone.

PRINCE ATHANASE

Shelley writes in a note: 'The Author was
pursuing a fuller development of the ideal
character of Athanase, when it struck him that

in an attempt at extreme refinement and analysis, his conceptions might be betrayed into the assuming a morbid character. The reader will judge whether he is a loser or gainer by the difference.'

Mrs. Shelley adds : ' The idea Shelley had formed of Prince Athanase was a good deal modelled on *Alastor.* In the first sketch of the poem, he named it *Pandemos and Urania.* Athanase seeks through the world the One whom he may love. He meets, in the ship in which he is embarked, a lady who appears to him to embody his ideal of love and beauty. But she proves to be Pandemos, or the earthly and unworthy Venus ; who, after disappointing his cherished dreams and hopes, deserts him. Athanase, crushed by sorrow, pines and dies. "On his deathbed, the lady who can really reply to his soul comes and kisses his lips." (*The Deathbed of Athanase.*) The poet describes her [ii. 155–160]. This slender note is all we have to aid our imagination in shaping out the form of the poem, such as its author imagined.' Date, 1817. Published, Mrs. Shelley, 1824.

PART I

THERE was a youth, who, as with toil and travel,
Had grown quite weak and gray before his time;
Nor any could the restless griefs unravel

Which burned within him, withering up his prime
And goading him, like fiends, from land to land.
Not his the load of any secret crime,

For nought of ill his heart could understand,
But pity and wild sorrow for the same;
Not his the thirst for glory or command,

Baffled with blast of hope-consuming shame; 10
Nor evil joys, which fire the vulgar breast
And quench in speedy smoke its feeble flame,

Had left within his soul their dark unrest;
Nor what religion fables of the grave
Feared he, — Philosophy's accepted guest.

For none than he a purer heart could have,
Or that loved good more for itself alone;
Of nought in heaven or earth was he the slave.

What sorrow strange, and shadowy, and unknown,
Sent him, a hopeless wanderer, through mankind ? — 20
If with a human sadness he did groan,

He had a gentle yet aspiring mind;
Just, innocent, with varied learning fed;
And such a glorious consolation find

In others' joy, when all their own is dead.
He loved, and labored for his kind in grief,
And yet, unlike all others, it is said,

That from such toil he never found relief.
Although a child of fortune and of power,
Of an ancestral name the orphan chief, 30

His soul had wedded wisdom, and her dower
Is love and justice, clothed in which he sate
Apart from men, as in a lonely tower,

Pitying the tumult of their dark estate.
Yet even in youth did he not e'er abuse
The strength of wealth or thought to consecrate

Those false opinions which the harsh rich use
To blind the world they famish for their pride;
Nor did he hold from any man his dues,

But, like a steward in honest dealings tried
With those who toiled and wept, the poor and wise, 41
His riches and his cares he did divide.

Fearless he was, and scorning all disguise;
What he dared do or think, though men might start,
He spoke with mild yet unaverted eyes;

Liberal he was of soul, and frank of heart,
And to his many friends — all loved him well —
Whate'er he knew or felt he would impart,

If words he found those inmost thoughts to tell;
If not, he smiled or wept; and his weak foes 50
He neither spurned nor hated, though with fell

And mortal hate their thousand voices
 rose, —
They passed like aimless arrows from his
 ear;
Nor did his heart or mind its portal close

To those, or them, or any whom life's
 sphere
May comprehend within its wide array.
What sadness made that vernal spirit
 sere ? —

He knew not. Though his life, day after
 day,
Was failing like an unreplenished stream,
Though in his eyes a cloud and burden lay,

Through which his soul, like Vesper's se-
 rene beam 61
Piercing the chasms of ever rising clouds,
Shone, softly burning; though his lips did
 seem

Like reeds which quiver in impetuous
 floods;
And through his sleep, and o'er each wak-
 ing hour,
Thoughts after thoughts, unresting multi-
 tudes,

Were driven within him by some secret
 power,
Which bade them blaze, and live, and roll
 afar,
Like lights and sounds from haunted tower
 to tower

O'er castled mountains borne, when tem-
 pest's war 70
Is levied by the night-contending winds
And the pale dalesmen watch with eager
 ear; —

Though such were in his spirit, as the
 fiends
Which wake and feed on ever living
 woe, —
What was this grief, which ne'er in other
 minds

A mirror found, he knew not — none could
 know;
But on whoe'er might question him he
 turned
The light of his frank eyes, as if to show

He knew not of the grief within that
 burned,
But asked forbearance with a mournful
 look; 80
Or spoke in words from which none ever
 learned

The cause of his disquietude; or shook
With spasms of silent passion; or turned
 pale:
So that his friends soon rarely undertook

To stir his secret pain without avail;
For all who knew and loved him then per-
 ceived
That there was drawn an adamantine veil

Between his heart and mind, — both unre-
 lieved
Wrought in his brain and bosom separate
 strife.
Some said that he was mad; others be-
 lieved 90

That memories of an antenatal life
Made this, where now he dwelt, a penal
 hell;
And others said that such mysterious grief

From God's displeasure, like a darkness,
 fell
On souls like his which owned no higher law
Than love; love calm, steadfast, invincible

By mortal fear or supernatural awe;
And others, — ' 'T is the shadow of a
 dream
Which the veiled eye of memory never saw,

'But through the soul's abyss, like some
 dark stream 100
Through shattered mines and caverns
 underground,
Rolls, shaking its foundations; and no
 beam

'Of joy may rise but it is quenched and
 drowned
In the dim whirlpools of this dream ob-
 scure;
Soon its exhausted waters will have found

' A lair of rest beneath thy spirit pure,
O Athanase ! — in one so good and great,
Evil or tumult cannot long endure.' 108

So spake they — idly of another's state
Babbling vain words and fond philosophy;
This was their consolation; such debate

Men held with one another; nor did he,
Like one who labors with a human woe,
Decline this talk; as if its theme might be

Another, not himself, he to and fro
Questioned and canvassed it with subtlest wit,
And none but those who loved him best could know

That which he knew not, how it galled and bit
His weary mind, this converse vain and cold; 119
For like an eyeless nightmare grief did sit

Upon his being; a snake which fold by fold
Pressed out the life of life, a clinging fiend
Which clenched him if he stirred with deadlier hold; —
And so his grief remained — let it remain — untold.

PART II

Prince Athanase had one belovèd friend,
An old, old man, with hair of silver white,
And lips where heavenly smiles would hang and blend

With his wise words, and eyes whose arrowy light
Shone like the reflex of a thousand minds.
He was the last whom superstition's blight

Had spared in Greece — the blight that cramps and blinds —
And in his olive bower at Œnoe
Had sate from earliest youth. Like one who finds

A fertile island in the barren sea, 10
One mariner who has survived his mates
Many a drear month in a great ship — so he

With soul-sustaining songs, and sweet debates
Of ancient lore there fed his lonely being.
'The mind becomes that which it contemplates,' —

And thus Zonoras, by forever seeing
Their bright creations, grew like wisest men;
And when he heard the crash of nations fleeing

A bloodier power than ruled thy ruins then,
O sacred Hellas! many weary years 20
He wandered, till the path of Laian's glen

Was grass-grown, and the unremembered tears
Were dry in Laian for their honored chief,
Who fell in Byzant, pierced by Moslem spears;

And as the lady looked with faithful grief
From her high lattice o'er the rugged path,
Where she once saw that horseman toil, with brief,

And blighting hope, who with the news of death
Struck body and soul as with a mortal blight,
She saw beneath the chestnuts, far beneath, 30

An old man toiling up, a weary wight;
And soon within her hospitable hall
She saw his white hairs glittering in the light

Of the wood-fire, and round his shoulders fall;
And his wan visage and his withered mien
Yet calm and gentle and majestical.

And Athanase, her child, who must have been
Then three years old, sate opposite and gazed
In patient silence.

.

Such was Zonoras; and as daylight finds
One amaranth glittering on the path of frost, 41
When autumn nights have nipped all weaker kinds,

Thus through his age, dark, cold, and tempest-tossed,
Shone truth upon Zonoras; and he filled
From fountains pure, nigh overgrown and lost,

The spirit of Prince Athanase, a child,
With soul-sustaining songs of ancient lore
And philosophic wisdom, clear and mild.

And sweet and subtle talk they ever-
more,
The pupil and the master, shared; until, 50
Sharing that undiminishable store,

The youth, as shadows on a grassy hill
Outrun the winds that chase them, soon
outran
His teacher, and did teach with native
skill

Strange truths and new to that experienced
man;
Still they were friends, as few have ever
been
Who mark the extremes of life's discord-
ant span.

So in the caverns of the forest green,
Or by the rocks of echoing ocean hoar,
Zonoras and Prince Athanase were seen 60

By summer woodmen; and when winter's
roar
Sounded o'er earth and sea its blast of
war,
The Balearic fisher, driven from shore,

Hanging upon the peakèd wave afar,
Then saw their lamp from Laian's turret
gleam,
Piercing the stormy darkness like a star

Which pours beyond the sea one steadfast
beam,
Whilst all the constellations of the sky
Seemed reeling through the storm. They
did but seem —

For, lo! the wintry clouds are all gone
by, 70
And bright Arcturus through yon pines is
glowing,
And far o'er southern waves, immovably

Belted Orion hangs — warm light is flow-
ing
From the young moon into the sunset's
chasm.
'O summer eve with power divine, be-
stowing

' On thine own bird the sweet enthusiasm
Which overflows in notes of liquid glad-
ness,
Filling the sky like light! How many a
spasm

'Of fevered brains, oppressed with grief
and madness,
Were lulled by thee, delightful nightin-
gale! 80
And these soft waves, murmuring a gentle
sadness,

' And the far sighings of yon piny dale
Made vocal by some wind we feel not
here, —
I bear alone what nothing may avail

' To lighten — a strange load!' — No hu-
man ear
Heard this lament; but o'er the visage
wan
Of Athanase a ruffling atmosphere

Of dark emotion, a swift shadow, ran,
Like wind upon some forest-bosomed lake,
Glassy and dark. And that divine old
man 90

Beheld his mystic friend's whole being
shake,
Even where its inmost depths were gloom-
iest;
And with a calm and measured voice he
spake,

And with a soft and equal pressure,
pressed
That cold, lean hand: — 'Dost thou re-
member yet,
When the curved moon, then lingering in
the west,

' Paused in yon waves her mighty horns to
wet,
How in those beams we walked, half rest-
ing on the sea?
'T is just one year — sure thou dost not
forget —

' Then Plato's words of light in thee and
me 100
Lingered like moonlight in the moonless
east;
For we had just then read — thy memory

'Is faithful now — the story of the feast;
And Agathon and Diotima seemed
From death and dark forgetfulness re-
 leased.'

.

'Twas at the season when the Earth up-
 springs
From slumber, as a spherèd angel's child,
Shadowing its eyes with green and golden
 wings,

Stands up before its mother bright and
 mild,
Of whose soft voice the air expectant
 seems — 110
So stood before the sun, which shone and
 smiled

To see it rise thus joyous from its dreams,
The fresh and radiant Earth. The hoary
 grove
Waxed green, and flowers burst forth like
 starry beams;

The grass in the warm sun did start and
 move,
And sea-buds burst beneath the waves se-
 rene.
How many a one, though none be near to
 love,

Loves then the shade of his own soul, half
 seen
In any mirror, or the spring's young min-
 ions,
The wingèd leaves amid the copses green !

How many a spirit then puts on the pin-
 ions 121
Of fancy, and outstrips the lagging blast,
And his own steps, and over wide domin-
 ions

Sweeps in his dream-drawn chariot, far
 and fast,
More fleet than storms — the wide world
 shrinks below,
When winter and despondency are passed !

'Twas at this season that Prince Athanase
Passed the white Alps; those eagle-baffling
 mountains
Slept in their shrouds of snow; beside the
 ways

The waterfalls were voiceless, for their
 fountains 130
Were changed to mines of sunless crystal
 now;
Or, by the curdling winds, like brazen
 wings

Which clanged along the mountain's mar-
 ble brow,
Warped into adamantine fretwork, hung,
And filled with frozen light the chasm be-
 low.

.

Thou art the wine whose drunkenness is
 all
We can desire, O Love ! and happy
 souls,
Ere from thy vine the leaves of autumn
 fall,

Catch thee, and feed from their o'erflow-
 ing bowls
Thousands who thirst for thy ambrosial
 dew ! 140
Thou art the radiance which where ocean
 rolls

Investest it; and when the heavens are
 blue
Thou fillest them; and when the earth is
 fair
The shadow of thy moving wings imbue

Its deserts and its mountains, till they
 wear
Beauty like some bright robe; thou ever
 soarest
Among the towers of men, and as soft air

In spring, which moves the unawakened
 forest,
Clothing with leaves its branches bare and
 bleak,
Thou floatest among men, and aye im-
 plorest 150

That which from thee they should implore;
 the weak
Alone kneel to thee, offering up the
 hearts
The strong have broken; yet where shall
 any seek

A garment whom thou clothest not ?

. °

Her hair was brown, her spherèd eyes were
 brown,
And in their dark and liquid moisture
 swam,
Like the dim orb of the eclipsèd moon;

Yet when the spirit flashed beneath, there
 came
The light from them, as when tears of de-
 light 159
Double the western planet's serene flame.

THE WOODMAN AND THE NIGHTINGALE

Date, 1818. Published in part by Mrs. Shel-
ley, 1824, and the remainder by Garnett, 1862.

A woodman, whose rough heart was out
 of tune
(I think such hearts yet never came to
 good),
Hated to hear, under the stars or moon,

One nightingale in an interfluous wood
Satiate the hungry dark with melody; —
And as a vale is watered by a flood,

Or as the moonlight fills the open sky
Struggling with darkness, as a tuberose
Peoples some Indian dell with scents which
 lie

Like clouds above the flower from which
 they rose, 10
The singing of that happy nightingale
In this sweet forest, from the golden close

Of evening till the star of dawn may fail,
Was interfused upon the silentness.
The folded roses and the violets pale

Heard her within their slumbers, the abyss
Of heaven with all its planets; the dull ear
Of the night-cradled earth; the loneliness

Of the circumfluous waters; every sphere
And every flower and beam and cloud and
 wave, 20
And every wind of the mute atmosphere,

And every beast stretched in its rugged
 cave,
And every bird lulled on its mossy bough,
And every silver moth fresh from the grave

Which is its cradle; — ever from below
Aspiring like one who loves too fair, too
 far,
To be consumed within the purest glow

Of one serene and unapproachèd star,
As if it were a lamp of earthly light,
Unconscious as some human lovers are 30

Itself how low, how high beyond all height
The heaven where it would perish ! — and
 every form
That worshipped in the temple of the
 night

Was awed into delight, and by the charm
Girt as with an interminable zone,
Whilst that sweet bird, whose music was a
 storm

Of sound, shook forth the dull oblivion
Out of their dreams; harmony became love
In every soul but one.

.

And so this man returned with axe and
 saw 40
At evening close from killing the tall treen,
The soul of whom by nature's gentle law

Was each a wood-nymph, and kept ever
 green
The pavement and the roof of the wild
 copse,
Checkering the sunlight of the blue serene

With jagged leaves, and from the forest
 tops
Singing the winds to sleep, or weeping oft
Fast showers of aërial water drops

Into their mother's bosom, sweet and soft,
Nature's pure tears which have no bitter-
 ness; — 50
Around the cradles of the birds aloft

They spread themselves into the loveliness
Of fan-like leaves, and over pallid flow-
 ers
Hang like moist clouds; or, where high
 branches kiss,

Make a green space among the silent bow-
 ers,
Like a vast fane in a metropolis,
Surrounded by the columns and the towers

All overwrought with branch-like traceries
In which there is religion — and the mute
Persuasion of unkindled melodies, 60

Odors and gleams and murmurs, which the
 lute
Of the blind pilot-spirit of the blast
Stirs as it sails, now grave and now acute,

Wakening the leaves and waves ere it has
 passed
To such brief unison as on the brain
One tone, which never can recur, has cast,

One accent never to return again.

· · · · · · · ·

The world is full of Woodmen who expel
Love's gentle Dryads from the haunt of life,
And vex the nightingales in every dell. 70

OTHO

Date, 1817. Published, in part, by Mrs.
Shelley, 1839, first edition, and the remainder
by Garnett, 1862. Mrs. Shelley states that the
poem was suggested by Tacitus.

I

THOU wert not, Cassius, and thou couldst
 not be,
 Last of the Romans, though thy memory
 claim
From Brutus his own glory, and on thee
 Rests the full splendor of his sacred
 fame;
Nor he who dared make the foul tyrant
 quail
 Amid his cowering senate with thy name,
Though thou and he were great; it will
 avail
To thine own fame that Otho's should not
 fail.

II

'T will wrong thee not — thou wouldst, if
 thou couldst feel,
 Abjure such envious fame — great Otho
 died
Like thee — he sanctified his country's
 steel,
 At once the tyrant and tyrannicide,
In his own blood. A deed it was to bring
 Tears from all men — though full of
 gentle pride,

Such pride as from impetuous love may
 spring,
That will not be refused its offering.

III

Dark is the realm of grief: but human
 things
 Those may not know who cannot weep
 for them.

· · · · · · · ·

TASSO

Date, 1818. Published by Garnett, 1862,
and the SONG by Mrs. Shelley, 1824. Shelley
writes to Peacock regarding the drama: 'I
have devoted this summer, and indeed the next
year, to the composition of a tragedy on the
subject of Tasso's madness; which, I find upon
inspection, is, if properly treated, admirably
dramatic and poetical. But you will say I
have no dramatic talent. Very true, in a cer-
tain sense; but I have taken the resolution to
see what kind of tragedy a person without
dramatic talent could write. It shall be better
morality than *Fazio*, and better poetry than
Bertram, at least.'

MADDALO, *a Courtier*. PIGNA, *a Minister*.
MALPIGLIO, *a Poet*. ALBANO, *an Usher*.

MADDALO

No access to the Duke! You have not
 said
That the Count Maddalo would speak with
 him?

PIGNA

Did you inform his Grace that Signor
 Pigna
Waits with state papers for his signature?

MALPIGLIO

The Lady Leonora cannot know
That I have written a sonnet to her fame,
In which I Venus and Adonis.
You should not take my gold and serve me
 not.

ALBANO

In truth I told her, and she smiled and said,
' If I am Venus, thou, coy Poesy,
Art the Adonis whom I love, and he
The Erymanthian boar that wounded him.'
Oh, trust to me, Signor Malpiglio,
Those nods and smiles were favors worth
 the zechin.

MALPIGLIO

The words are twisted in some double
 sense
That I reach not; the smiles fell not on
 me.

PIGNA

How are the Duke and Duchess occupied ?

ALBANO

Buried in some strange talk. The Duke
 was leaning,
His finger on his brow, his lips unclosed.
The Princess sate within the window-seat,
And so her face was hid; but on her knee
Her hands were clasped, veinèd, and pale
 as snow,
And quivering — young Tasso, too, was
 there.

MADDALO

Thou seest on whom from thine own wor-
 shipped heaven
Thou drawest down smiles — they did not
 rain on thee.

MALPIGLIO

Would they were parching lightnings for
 his sake
On whom they fell !

.

SONG

I

I loved — alas ! our life is love;
But when we cease to breathe and move
I do suppose love ceases too.
I thought, but not as now I do,
Keen thoughts and bright of linkèd lore,
Of all that men had thought before,
And all that nature shows, and more.

II

And still I love and still I think,
But strangely, for my heart can drink
The dregs of such despair, and live,
And love;
And if I think, my thoughts come fast,
I mix the present with the past,
And each seems uglier than the last.

III

Sometimes I see before me flee
A silver spirit's form, like thee,

O Leonora, and I sit
 still watching it,
Till by the grated casement's ledge
It fades, with such a sigh, as sedge
Breathes o'er the breezy streamlet's edge.

MARENGHI

Date, 1818. Published in part by Mrs. Shel-
ley, 1824, and the remainder by Rossetti, 1870.
Mrs. Shelley gives as the source Sismondi, *His-
toire des Républiques Italiennes.*

I

LET those who pine in pride or in revenge,
 Or think that ill for ill should be repaid,
Or barter wrong for wrong, until the ex-
 change
 Ruins the merchants of such thriftless
 trade,
Visit the tower of Vado, and unlearn
Such bitter faith beside Marenghi's urn.

II

A massy tower yet overhangs the town,
 A scattered group of ruined dwellings
 now.

.

III

Another scene ere wise Etruria knew
 Its second ruin through internal strife,
And tyrants through the breach of discord
 threw
 The chain which binds and kills. As
 death to life,
As winter to fair flowers (though some be
 poison)
So Monarchy succeeds to Freedom's foison.

IV

In Pisa's church a cup of sculptured gold
 Was brimming with the blood of feuds
 forsworn
At sacrament; more holy ne'er of old
 Etrurians mingled with the shades forlorn
Of moon-illumined forests.

.

V

And reconciling factions wet their lips
 With that dread wine, and swear to keep
 each spirit
Undarkened by their country's last eclipse.

.

VI

Was Florence the liberticide ? that band
 Of free and glorious brothers who had
 planted,
Like a green isle 'mid Æthiopian sand,
 A nation amid slaveries, disenchanted
Of many impious faiths — wise, just — do
 they,
Does Florence, gorge the sated tyrants'
 prey ?

VII

O foster-nurse of man's abandoned glory,
 Since Athens, its great mother, sunk in
 splendor;
Thou shadowest forth that mighty shape in
 story,
 As ocean its wrecked fanes, severe yet
 tender.
The light-invested angel Poesy
Was drawn from the dim world to welcome
 thee.

VIII

And thou in painting didst transcribe all
 taught
 By loftiest meditations; marble knew
The sculptor's fearless soul, and as he
 wrought,
 The grace of his own power and freedom
 grew.
And more than all, heroic, just, sublime,
Thou wert among the false — was this thy
 crime ?

IX

Yes; and on Pisa's marble walls the twine
 Of direst weeds hangs garlanded; the
 snake
Inhabits its wrecked palaces; — in thine
 A beast of subtler venom now doth make
Its lair, and sits amid their glories over-
 thrown,
And thus thy victim's fate is as thine own.

X

The sweetest flowers are ever frail and rare,
 And love and freedom blossom but to
 wither;
And good and ill like vines entangled are,
 So that their grapes may oft be plucked
 together.
Divide the vintage ere thou drink, then
 make
Thy heart rejoice for dead Marenghi's sake.

XI

No record of his crime remains in story,
 But if the morning bright as evening
 shone,
It was some high and holy deed, by glory
 Pursued into forgetfulness, which won
From the blind crowd he made secure and
 free
The patriot's meed, toil, death, and infamy.

XII

For when by sound of trumpet was declared
 A price upon his life, and there was
 set
A penalty of blood on all who shared
 So much of water with him as might
 wet
His lips, which speech divided not, he
 went
Alone, as you may guess, to banishment.

XIII

Amid the mountains, like a hunted beast,
 He hid himself, and hunger, toil, and
 cold,
Month after month endured; it was a feast
 Whene'er he found those globes of deep-
 red gold
Which in the woods the strawberry-tree
 doth bear,
Suspended in their emerald atmosphere

XIV

And in the roofless huts of vast morasses,
 Deserted by the fever-stricken serf,
All overgrown with reeds and long rank
 grasses,
 And hillocks heaped of moss-inwoven
 turf,
And where the huge and speckled aloe
 made,
Rooted in stones, a broad and pointed
 shade,

XV

He housed himself. There is a point of
 strand
 Near Vado's tower and town; and on
 one side
The treacherous marsh divides it from the
 land,
 Shadowed by pine and ilex forests wide,
And on the other creeps eternally,
Through muddy weeds, the shallow sullen
 sea.

XVI

Here the earth's breath is pestilence, and
 few
 But things whose nature is at war with
 life —
Snakes and ill worms — endure its mortal
 dew.
 The trophies of the clime's victorious
 strife —
White bones, and locks of dun and yellow
 hair,
And ringèd horns which buffaloes did
 wear —

.

XVII

And at the utmost point stood there
 The relics of a weed-inwoven cot,
Thatched with broad flags. An outlawed
 murderer
 Had lived seven days there; the pursuit
 was hot
When he was cold. The birds that were
 his grave
Fell dead upon their feast in Vado's wave.

XVIII

There must have lived within Marenghi's
 heart
 That fire, more warm and bright than
 life or hope,
(Which to the martyr makes his dun-
 geon . . .
 More joyous than the heaven's majestic
 cope
To his oppressor), warring with decay, —
Or he could ne'er have lived years, day by
 day.

XIX

Nor was his state so lone as you might
 think.
 He had tamed every newt and snake and
 toad,
And every seagull which sailed down to
 drink
 Those ere the death-mist went
 abroad.
And each one, with peculiar talk and play,
Wiled, not untaught, his silent time away.

XX

And the marsh-meteors, like tame beasts,
 at night
 Came licking with blue tongues his
 veinèd feet;

And he would watch them, as, like spirits
 bright,
 In many entangled figures quaint and
 sweet
To some enchanted music they would
 dance —
Until they vanished at the first moon-
 glance.

XXI

He mocked the stars by grouping on each
 weed
 The summer dewdrops in the golden
 dawn;
And, ere the hoarfrost vanished, he could
 read
 Its pictured footprints, as on spots of lawn
Its delicate brief touch in silence weaves
The likeness of the wood's remembered
 leaves.

XXII

And many a fresh Spring morn would he
 awaken,
 While yet the unrisen sun made glow,
 like iron
Quivering in crimson fire, the peaks un-
 shaken
 Of mountains and blue isles which did
 environ
With air-clad crags that plain of land and
 sea, —
And feel liberty.

XXIII

And in the moonless nights, when the dim
 ocean
 Heaved underneath the heaven, . . .
Starting from dreams . . .
 Communed with the immeasurable
 world;
And felt his life beyond his limbs dilated,
Till his mind grew like that it contem-
 plated.

XXIV

His food was the wild fig and strawberry;
 The milky pine-nuts which the autumnal
 blast
Shakes into the tall grass; and such small fry
 As from the sea by winter-storms are
 cast;
And the coarse bulbs of iris flowers he
 found
Knotted in clumps under the spongy ground.

XXV

And so were kindled powers and thoughts
 which made
 His solitude less dark. When memory
 came
(For years gone by leave each a deepening
 shade),
 His spirit basked in its internal flame, —
As, when the black storm hurries round at
 night
The fisher basks beside his red firelight.

XXVI

Yet human hopes and cares and faiths and
 errors,
 Like billows unawakened by the wind,
Slept in Marenghi still; but that all ter-
 rors,
 Weakness, and doubt, had withered in
 his mind.
His couch

.

XXVII

And, when he saw beneath the sunset's
 planet
 A black ship walk over the crimson
 ocean, —
Its pennons streaming on the blasts that
 fan it,
 Its sails and ropes all tense and without
 motion,
Like the dark ghost of the unburied even
Striding across the orange-colored hea-
 ven, —

XXVIII

The thought of his own kind who made the
 soul
 Which sped that wingèd shape through
 night and day, —
The thought of his own country . . .

.

LINES WRITTEN FOR JULIAN AND MADDALO

Published by Garnett, 1862, who conjectures
the title.

WHAT think you the dead are ?
 Why, dust and clay,
What should they be ?
 'T is the last hour of day.

Look on the west, how beautiful it is
Vaulted with radiant vapors ! The deep
 bliss
Of that unutterable light has made
The edges of that cloud fade
Into a hue, like some harmonious thought,
Wasting itself on that which it had
 wrought,
Till it dies and between
The light hues of the tender, pure, serene,
And infinite tranquillity of heaven.
Ay, beautiful ! but when our . . .

.

Perhaps the only comfort which remains
Is the unheeded clanking of my chains,
The which I make, and call it melody.

LINES WRITTEN FOR PROMETHEUS UNBOUND

Published by Mrs. Shelley, 1839, first edition.

As a violet's gentle eye
 Gazes on the azure sky,
Until its hue grows like what it beholds;
 As a gray and empty mist
 Lies like solid amethyst
Over the western mountain it enfolds,
 When the sunset sleeps
 Upon its snow,
 As a strain of sweetest sound
 Wraps itself the wind around,
Until the voiceless wind be music too;
 As aught dark, vain and dull,
 Basking in what is beautiful,
 Is full of light and love.

LINES WRITTEN FOR MONT BLANC

Published by Garnett, 1862.

THERE is a voice, not understood by all,
Sent from these desert-caves. It is the roar
Of the rent ice-cliff which the sunbeams call,
Plunging into the vale — it is the blast
Descending on the pines—the torrents pour.

LINES WRITTEN FOR THE INDIAN SERENADE

Published by Rossetti, 1870, who conjectures
the title.

O PILLOW cold and wet with tears !
Thou breathest sleep no more !

LINES WRITTEN FOR THE ODE TO LIBERTY

Published by Garnett, 1862.

WITHIN a cavern of man's trackless spirit
Is throned an Image, so intensely fair
That the adventurous thoughts that wander
 near it
 Worship, and as they kneel tremble and
 wear
The splendor of its presence, and the light
 Penetrates their dreamlike frame
Till they become charged with the strength
 of flame.

STANZA WRITTEN FOR THE ODE WRITTEN OCTOBER, 1819

Published by Rossetti, *The Times.*

GATHER, oh, gather,
Foeman and friend in love and peace !
Waves sleep together
When the blasts that called them to
 battle cease.
For fangless Power, grown tame and mild,
Is at play with Freedom's fearless child —
The dove and the serpent reconciled !

LINES CONNECTED WITH EPIPSYCHIDION

Published in part by Mrs. Shelley, 1839, second edition, and the remainder by Garnett, 1862. From these lines, and also from other fragments, it is to be inferred that a poem, substantially *Epipsychidion*, was in Shelley's mind before his meeting with Emilia Viviani, and that she was less the inspiration of it than the occasion of the form it took.

HERE, my dear friend, is a new book for
 you;
I have already dedicated two
To other friends, one female and one
 male, —
What you are is a thing that I must veil;
What can this be to those who praise or
 rail ?
I never was attached to that great sect
Whose doctrine is that each one should se-
 lect
Out of the world a mistress or a friend,
And all the rest, though fair and wise,
 commend 9

To cold oblivion — though 't is in the code
Of modern morals, and the beaten road
Which those poor slaves with weary foot-
 steps tread
Who travel to their home among the dead
By the broad highway of the world — and so
With one sad friend, and many a jealous
 foe,
The dreariest and the longest journey go.

Free love has this, different from gold
 and clay,
That to divide is not to take away.
Like ocean, which the general north wind
 breaks
Into ten thousand waves, and each one
 makes 20
A mirror of the moon — like some great
 glass,
Which did distort whatever form might
 pass,
Dashed into fragments by a playful child,
Which then reflects its eyes and forehead
 mild;
Giving for one, which it could ne'er ex-
 press,
A thousand images of loveliness.

If I were one whom the loud world held
 wise,
I should disdain to quote authorities
In commendation of this kind of love.
Why there is first the God in heaven
 above, 30
Who wrote a book called Nature — 't is to
 be
Reviewed, I hear, in the next Quarterly;
And Socrates, the Jesus Christ of Greece,
And Jesus Christ himself did never cease
To urge all living things to love each
 other,
And to forgive their mutual faults, and
 smother
The Devil of disunion in their souls.

I love you ! — Listen, O embodied Ray
Of the great Brightness; I must pass away
While you remain, and these light words
 must be 40
Tokens by which you may remember me.
Start not — the thing you are is unbe-
 trayed,
If you are human, and if but the shade
Of some sublimer Spirit.

.

And as to friend or mistress, 't is a form;
Perhaps I wish you were one Some de-
 clare
You a familiar spirit, as you are;
Others with a more inhuman
Hint that, though not my wife, you are a
 woman —
What is the color of your eyes and hair ? 50
Why, if you were a lady, it were fair
The world should know — but, as I am
 afraid,
The Quarterly would bait you if betrayed;
And if, as it will be sport to see them
 stumble
Over all sorts of scandals, hear them
 mumble
Their litany of curses — some guess right,
And others swear you 're a Hermaphro-
 dite;
Like that sweet marble monster of both
 sexes,
With looks so sweet and gentle that it
 vexes
The very soul that the soul is gone 60
Which lifted from her limbs the veil of
 stone.

.

It is a sweet thing, friendship, a dear
 balm,
A happy and auspicious bird of calm,
Which rides o'er life's ever tumultuous
 Ocean;
A God that broods o'er chaos in commo-
 tion;
A flower which fresh as Lapland roses are,
Lifts its bold head into the world's frore
 air,
And blooms most radiantly when others
 die,
Health, hope, and youth, and brief pros-
 perity; 69
And with the light and odor of its bloom,
Shining within the dungeon and the tomb;
Whose coming is as light and music are
'Mid dissonance and gloom — a star
Which moves not 'mid the moving heavens
 alone —
A smile among dark frowns — a gentle
 tone
Among rude voices, a belovèd light,
A solitude, a refuge, a delight.
If I had but a friend ! Why, I have
 three
Even by my own confession; there may be

Some more, for what I know, for 't is my
 mind 80
To call my friends all who are wise and
 kind, —
And these, Heaven knows, at best are very
 few;
But none can ever be more dear than you.
Why should they be ? My muse has lost
 her wings,
Or like a dying swan who soars and sings,
I should describe you in heroic style,
But as it is, are you not void of guile ?
A lovely soul, formed to be blessed and
 bless;
A well of sealed and secret happiness;
A lute which those whom Love has taught
 to play 90
Make music on to cheer the roughest day,
And enchant sadness till it sleeps ?

.

To the oblivion whither I and thou,
All loving and all lovely, hasten now
With steps, ah, too unequal ! may we meet
In one Elysium or one winding sheet !
If any should be curious to discover
Whether to you I am a friend or lover,
Let them read Shakespeare's sonnets, tak-
 ing thence
A whetstone for their dull intelligence 100
That tears and will not cut, or let them
 guess
How Diotima, the wise prophetess,
Instructed the instructor, and why he
Rebuked the infant spirit of melody
On Agathon's sweet lips, which as he spoke
Was as the lovely star when morn has
 broke
The roof of darkness, in the golden dawn,
Half-hidden, and yet beautiful.

 I 'll pawn
My hopes of Heaven — you know what
 they are worth —
That the presumptuous pedagogues of
 Earth, 110
If they could tell the riddle offered here
Would scorn to be, or, being, to appear
What now they seem and are — but let
 them chide,
They have few pleasures in the world beside;
Perhaps we should be dull were we not
 chidden;
Paradise fruits are sweetest when forbidden.
Folly can season Wisdom, Hatred Love.

.

Farewell, if it can be to say farewell
To those who —

.
I will not, as most dedicators do, 120
Assure myself and all the world and you,
That you are faultless — would to God they
 were
Who taunt me with your love ! I then
 should wear
These heavy chains of life with a light
 spirit,
And would to God I were, or even as near
 it
As you, dear heart. Alas ! what are we ?
 Clouds
Driven by the wind in warring multi-
 tudes,
Which rain into the bosom of the earth,
And rise again, and in our death and birth,
And through our restless life, take as from
 heaven 130
Hues which are not our own, but which are
 given,
And then withdrawn, and with inconstant
 glance
Flash from the spirit to the countenance.
There is a Power, a Love, a Joy, a God,
Which makes in mortal hearts its brief
 abode,
A Pythian exhalation, which inspires
Love, only love — a wind which o'er the
 wires
Of the soul's giant harp —
There is a mood which language faints be-
 neath;
You feel it striding, as Almighty Death 140
His bloodless steed.

.
And what is that most brief and bright de-
 light
Which rushes through the touch and
 through the sight,
And stands before the spirit's inmost throne,
A naked Seraph ? None hath ever known.
Its birth is darkness, and its growth desire;
Untamable and fleet and fierce as fire,
Not to be touched but to be felt alone,
It fills the world with glory — and is gone.

.
It floats with rainbow pinions o'er the
 stream 150
Of life, which flows, like a dream
Into the light of morning, to the grave
As to an ocean.

.

What is that joy which serene infancy
Perceives not, as the hours content them
 by,
Each in a chain of blossoms, yet enjoys
The shapes of this new world, in giant toys
Wrought by the busy ever new ?
Remembrance borrows Fancy's glass, to
 show
These forms more sincere 160
Than now they are, than then, perhaps,
 they were.
When everything familiar seemed to be
Wonderful, and the immortality
Of this great world, which all things must
 inherit,
Was felt as one with the awakening spirit,
Unconscious of itself, and of the strange
Distinctions which in its proceeding change
It feels and knows, and mourns as if each
 were
A desolation.

.
Were it not a sweet refuge, Emily, 170
For all those exiles from the dull insane
Who vex this pleasant world with pride
 and pain,
For all that band of sister-spirits known
To one another by a voiceless tone ?

LINES WRITTEN FOR ADONAIS

 Published by Garnett, 1862, who furnishes the
following note : 'Several cancelled passages of
the *Adonais* have been met with in Shelley's
notebooks. He appears to have originally
framed his conception on a larger scale than he
eventually found practicable. The passage in
which the contemporary minstrels are intro-
duced, as mourning for Adonais, would have
been considerably extended, and the character-
istics of each delineated at some length. It
must, however, have occurred to him that the
parenthesis would be too long, and would tend
to distract the reader's attention from the main
subject. Nothing, therefore, of the original
draft was allowed to subsist but the four in-
comparable stanzas descriptive of himself. A
fifth was cancelled, which ran as follows [first
fragment]. Several stanzas relating to Byron
and Moore are too imperfect for publication.
The following refers to the latter [second frag-
ment]. Leigh Hunt was thus described [third
fragment]. · The following lines were also
written for the *Adonais* [remaining frag-
ments].' Forman conjectures that Coleridge
is described in the last fragment.

AND ever as he went he swept a lyre
Of unaccustomed shape, and strings
Now like the of impetuous fire,
Which shakes the forest with its mur-
 murings,
Now like the rush of the aërial wings
Of the enamoured wind among the treen,
Whispering unimaginable things,
And dying on the streams of dew serene,
Which feed the unmown meads with ever-
 during green.

.

And the green Paradise which western
 waves
Embosom in their ever wailing sweep,
Talking of freedom to their tongueless
 caves,
Or to the spirits which within them
 keep
A record of the wrongs which, though
 they sleep,
Die not, but dream of retribution, heard
His hymns, and echoing them from steep
 to steep,
Kept —

.

And then came one of sweet and earnest
 looks,
Whose soft smiles to his dark and night-
 like eyes
Were as the clear and ever living brooks
Are to the obscure fountains whence they
 rise,
Showing how pure they are: a Paradise
Of happy truth upon his forehead low
Lay, making wisdom lovely, in the guise
Of earth-awakening morn upon the brow
Of star-deserted heaven, while ocean
 gleams below.

His song, though very sweet, was low and
 faint,
A simple strain —

.

 A mighty Phantasm, half concealed
In darkness of his own exceeding light,
Which clothed his awful presence unre-
 vealed,
Charioted on the night
Of thunder-smoke, whose skirts were chrys-
 olite.

And like a sudden meteor, which outstrips
The splendor-wingèd chariot of the sun,
 eclipse

The armies of the golden stars, each one
Pavilioned in its tent of light — all strewn
Over the chasms of blue night —

LINES WRITTEN FOR HELLAS

Published by Garnett, 1862, who conjectures
the title.

I

FAIREST of the Destinies,
Disarray thy dazzling eyes:
Keener far thy lightnings are
 Than the wingèd [bolts] thou bear-
 est,
 And the smile thou wearest
Wraps thee as a star
 Is wrapped in light.

II

Could Arethuse to her forsaken urn
From Alpheus and the bitter Doris run,
 Or could the morning shafts of purest
 light
Again into the quivers of the Sun
 Be gathered — could one thought from
 its wild flight
Return into the temple of the brain
 Without a change, without a stain, —
 Could aught that is, ever again
 Be what it once has ceased to be,
 Greece might again be free !

III

A star has fallen upon the earth
'Mid the benighted nations,
 A quenchless atom of immortal light,
 A living spark of Night,
A cresset shaken from the constellations.
Swifter than the thunder fell
To the heart of Earth, the well
Where its pulses flow and beat,
And unextinct in that cold source
Burns, and on course
Guides the sphere which is its prison,
Like an angelic spirit pent
In a form of mortal birth,
Till, as a spirit half arisen
Shatters its charnel, it has rent,
In the rapture of its mirth,
The thin and painted garment of the
 Earth,
 Ruining its chaos — a fierce breath
Consuming all its forms of living death.

THE PINE FOREST OF THE CASCINE NEAR PISA

FIRST DRAFT OF 'TO JANE: THE INVI-
TATION, THE RECOLLECTION'

Date 1821. Published by Mrs. Shelley, 1824.

DEAREST, best and brightest,
 Come away,
To the woods and to the fields !
Dearer than this fairest day
Which, like thee to those in sorrow,
Comes to bid a sweet good-morrow
To the rough Year just awake
In its cradle in the brake.

The eldest of the hours of Spring,
Into the winter wandering, 10
Looks upon the leafless wood;
And the banks all bare and rude
Found, it seems, this halcyon Morn
In February's bosom born,
Bending from Heaven, in azure mirth,
Kissed the cold forehead of the Earth,
And smiled upon the silent sea,
And bade the frozen streams be free;
And waked to music all the fountains,
And breathed upon the rigid mountains, 20
And made the wintry world appear
Like one on whom thou smilest, dear.
Radiant Sister of the Day,
Awake ! arise ! and come away !
To the wild woods and the plains,
To the pools where winter rains
Image all the roof of leaves,
Where the pine its garland weaves
Sapless, gray, and ivy dun
Round stems that never kiss the sun — 30
To the sandhills of the sea,
Where the earliest violets be.

Now the last day of many days,
All beautiful and bright as thou,
The loveliest and the last, is dead,
Rise, Memory, and write its praise !
And do thy wonted work and trace
The epitaph of glory fled;
For now the Earth has changed its face,
A frown is on the Heaven's brow. 40

We wandered to the Pine Forest
 That skirts the Ocean's foam,
The lightest wind was in its nest,
 The tempest in its home.

The whispering waves were half asleep,
 The clouds were gone to play,
And on the woods, and on the deep,
 The smile of Heaven lay.

It seemed as if the day were one
 Sent from beyond the skies, 50
Which shed to earth above the sun
 A light of Paradise.

We paused amid the pines that stood
 The giants of the waste,
Tortured by storms to shapes as rude
 With stems like serpents interlaced

How calm it was — the silence there
 By such a chain was bound
That even the busy woodpecker
 Made stiller by her sound 60

The inviolable quietness;
 The breath of peace we drew
With its soft motion made not less
 The calm that round us grew.

It seemed that from the remotest seat
 Of the white mountain's waste,
To the bright flower beneath our feet,
 A magic circle traced; —

A spirit interfused around,
 A thinking silent life, 70
To momentary peace it bound
 Our mortal nature's strife; —

And still it seemed the centre of
 The magic circle there,
Was one whose being filled with love
 The breathless atmosphere.

Were not the crocuses that grew
 Under that ilex-tree
As beautiful in scent and hue
 As ever fed the bee ? 80

We stood beside the pools that lie
 Under the forest bough,
And each seemed like a sky
 Gulfed in a world below;

A purple firmament of light,
 Which in the dark earth lay,
More boundless than the depth of night,
 And clearer than the day —

In which the massy forests grew
 As in the upper air, 90
More perfect both in shape and hue
 Than any waving there.

Like one beloved the scene had lent
 To the dark water's breast
Its every leaf and lineament
 With that clear truth expressed;

There lay far glades and neighboring lawn,
 And through the dark green crowd
The white sun twinkling like the dawn
 Under a speckled cloud. 100

Sweet views, which in our world above
 Can never well be seen,
Were imaged by the water's love
 Of that fair forest green.

And all was interfused beneath
 Within an Elysium air
An atmosphere without a breath,
 A silence sleeping there.

Until a wandering wind crept by,
 Like an unwelcome thought, 110
Which from my mind's too faithful eye
 Blots thy bright image out.

For thou art good and dear and kind,
 The forest ever green,
But less of peace in S———'s mind,
 Than calm in waters seen.

ORPHEUS

Date, 1820. Published by Garnett, 1862, and revised and enlarged by Rossetti, 1870. Garnett adds the following note: 'No trace of this poem appears in Shelley's notebooks; it exists only in a transcript by Mrs. Shelley, who has written, in playful allusion to her toils as an amanuensis, "*Aspetto fin che il diluvio cala, ed allora cerco di posare argine alle sue parole.*" "I await the descent of the flood, and then I endeavor to embank the words." From this circumstance, as well as from the internal evidence of the piece, I should conjecture that it was an attempt at improvisation. Shelley had several times heard Sgricci, the renowned *improvvisatore*, in the winter of 1820, and this may have inspired him with the idea of attempting a similar feat. Assuredly this poem, though containing many felicitous passages, hardly attains his usual standard, either of thought or expression. It *may* be a translation from the Italian.'

A

Not far from hence. From yonder pointed hill,
Crowned with a ring of oaks, you may behold
A dark and barren field, through which there flows,
Sluggish and black, a deep but narrow stream,
Which the wind ripples not, and the fair moon
Gazes in vain, and finds no mirror there.
Follow the herbless banks of that strange brook
Until you pause beside a darksome pond,
The fountain of this rivulet, whose gush
Cannot be seen, hid by a rayless night 10
That lives beneath the overhanging rock
That shades the pool — an endless spring of gloom,
Upon whose edge hovers the tender light,
Trembling to mingle with its paramour, —
But, as Syrinx fled Pan, so night flies day,
Or, with most sullen and regardless hate,
Refuses stern her heaven-born embrace.
On one side of this jagged and shapeless hill
There is a cave, from which there eddies up
A pale mist, like aërial gossamer, 20
Whose breath destroys all life; awhile it veils
The rock; then, scattered by the wind, it flies
Along the stream, or lingers on the clefts,
Killing the sleepy worms, if aught bide there.
Upon the beetling edge of that dark rock
There stands a group of cypresses; not such
As, with a graceful spire and stirring life,
Pierce the pure heaven of your native vale,
Whose branches the air plays among, but not
Disturbs, fearing to spoil their solemn grace; 29
But blasted and all wearily they stand,
One to another clinging; their weak boughs
Sigh as the wind buffets them, and they shake
Beneath its blasts — a weather-beaten crew!

CHORUS

What wondrous sound is that, mournful and faint,

But more melodious than the murmuring
 wind
Which through the columns of a temple
 glides?

 A

It is the wandering voice of Orpheus' lyre,
Borne by the winds, who sigh that their
 rude king
Hurries them fast from these air-feeding
 notes; 40
But in their speed they bear along with
 them
The waning sound, scattering it like dew
Upon the startled sense.

 CHORUS
 Does he still sing?
Methought he rashly cast away his harp
When he had lost Eurydice.

 A
 Ah no!
Awhile he paused. — As a poor hunted
 stag
A moment shudders on the fearful brink
Of a swift stream — the cruel hounds press
 on
With deafening yell, the arrows glance and
 wound, —
He plunges in: so Orpheus, seized and
 torn 50
By the sharp fangs of an insatiate grief,
Mænad-like waved his lyre in the bright
 air,
And wildly shrieked, 'Where she is, it is
 dark!'
And then he struck from forth the strings
 a sound
Of deep and fearful melody. Alas!
In times long past, when fair Eurydice
With her bright eyes sat listening by his
 side,
He gently sang of high and heavenly
 themes.
As in a brook, fretted with little waves,
By the light airs of spring, each riplet
 makes 60
A many-sided mirror for the sun,
While it flows musically through green
 banks,
Ceaseless and pauseless, ever clear and
 fresh,
So flowed his song, reflecting the deep joy
And tender love that fed those sweetest
 notes,

The heavenly offspring of ambrosial food.
But that is past. Returning from drear
 Hell,
He chose a lonely seat of unhewn stone,
Blackened with lichens, on a herbless plain.
Then from the deep and overflowing spring
Of his eternal, ever-moving grief 71
There rose to Heaven a sound of angry
 song.
'T is as a mighty cataract that parts
Two sister rocks with waters swift and
 strong,
And casts itself with horrid roar and din
Adown a steep; from a perennial source
It ever flows and falls, and breaks the air
With loud and fierce, but most harmonious
 roar,
And as it falls casts up a vaporous spray 79
Which the sun clothes in hues of Iris light.
Thus the tempestuous torrent of his grief
Is clothed in sweetest sounds and varying
 words
Of poesy. Unlike all human works
It never slackens, and through every
 change
Wisdom and beauty and the power divine
Of mighty poesy together dwell,
Mingling in sweet accord. As I have seen
A fierce south blast tear through the dark-
 ened sky,
Driving along a rack of wingèd clouds, 89
Which may not pause, but ever hurry on,
As their wild shepherd wills them, while
 the stars,
Twinkling and dim, peep from between the
 plumes.
Anon the sky is cleared, and the high dome
Of serene Heaven, starred with fiery flow-
 ers,
Shuts in the shaken earth; or the still
 moon
Swiftly, yet gracefully, begins her walk,
Rising all bright behind the eastern hills.
I talk of moon, and wind, and stars, and
 not
Of song; but, would I echo his high song,
Nature must lend me words ne'er used be-
 fore, 100
Or I must borrow from her perfect works,
To picture forth his perfect attributes.
He does no longer sit upon his throne
Of rock upon a desert herbless plain,
For the evergreen and knotted ilexes,
And cypresses that seldom wave their
 boughs,

And sea-green olives with their grateful
 fruit,
And elms dragging along the twisted vines,
Which drop their berries as they follow
 fast,
And blackthorn bushes with their infant
 race 110
Of blushing rose blooms; beeches, to lovers
 dear,
And weeping willow trees; all swift or slow,
As their huge boughs or lighter dress per-
 mit,
Have circled in his throne; and Earth her-
 self
Has sent from her maternal breast a growth
Of starlike flowers and herbs of odors
 sweet,
To pave the temple that his poesy
Has framed, while near his feet grim lions
 couch,
And kids, fearless from love, creep near
 his lair.
Even the blind worms seem to feel the
 sound. 120
The birds are silent, hanging down their
 heads,
Perched on the lowest branches of the
 trees;
Not even the nightingale intrudes a note
In rivalry, but all entranced she listens.

FIORDISPINA

Date, 1820. Published in part by Mrs.
Shelley, 1824, and the remainder by Garnett,
1862, who adds a note : ' *Fiordispina* and the
piece which I have ventured to entitle *To His
Genius* (using the latter word in the sense of
δαίμων) may be regarded as preliminary,
though unconscious studies, for this crowning
work [*Epipsychidion*]. This is indicated by
the general similarity among the three, as
well as by the fact that very many lines now
found in *Epipsychidion* have been transferred
to it from the others. Most of these have been
omitted from the poem as now published ; but
some instances will be observed in the second,
which was probably the earlier in point of date.
Fiordispina seems to have been written during
the first days of Shelley's acquaintance with
Emilia Viviani, who is also the *Ginevra* of the
poem thus entitled.'

THE season was the childhood of sweet
 June,
Whose sunny hours from morning until
 noon

Went creeping through the day with silent
 feet,
Each with its load of pleasure, slow yet
 sweet;
Like the long years of blest Eternity
Never to be developed. Joy to thee,
Fiordispina, and thy Cosimo,
For thou the wonders of the depth canst
 know
Of this unfathomable flood of hours,
Sparkling beneath the heaven which em-
 bowers — 10
.
They were two cousins, almost like two
 twins,
Except that from the catalogue of sins
Nature had rased their love — which could
 not be
But by dissevering their nativity.
And so they grew together like two flowers
Upon one stem, which the same beams and
 showers
Lull or awaken in their purple prime,
Which the same hand will gather, the same
 clime
Shake with decay. This fair day smiles to
 see
All those who love — and who e'er loved
 like thee, 20
Fiordispina ? Scarcely Cosimo,
Within whose bosom and whose brain now
 glow
The ardors of a vision which obscure
The very idol of its portraiture.
He faints, dissolved into a sea of love;
But thou art as a planet sphered above ;
But thou art Love itself — ruling the
 motion
Of his subjected spirit; such emotion
Must end in sin or sorrow, if sweet May
Had not brought forth this morn, your wed-
 ding-day. 30

' Lie there; sleep awhile in your own dew,
Ye faint-eyed children of the Hours,'
Fiordispina said, and threw the flowers
Which she had from the breathing —

.
A table near of polished porphyry.
They seemed to wear a beauty from the
 eye
That looked on them, a fragrance from the
 touch
Whose warmth checked their life; a
 light such

As sleepers wear, lulled by the voice they
 love,
 which did reprove 40
The childish pity that she felt for them,
And a remorse that from their stem
She had divided such fair shapes made
A feeling in the which was a shade
Of gentle beauty on the flowers; there lay
All gems that make the earth's dark bosom
 gay.
 rods of myrtle-buds and lemon-blooms,
And that leaf tinted lightly which assumes
The livery of unremembered snow —
Violets whose eyes have drunk — 50

Fiordispina and her nurse are now
Upon the steps of the high portico;
Under the withered arm of Media
She flings her glowing arm

 step by step and stair by stair,
That withered woman, gray and white and
 brown —
More like a trunk by lichens overgrown
Than anything which once could have been
 human.
And ever as she goes the palsied woman

'How slow and painfully you seem to
 walk, 60
Poor Media! you tire yourself with talk.'
 'And well it may,
Fiordispina, dearest — well-a-day!
You are hastening to a marriage-bed;
I to the grave!'— 'And if my love were
 dead,
Unless my heart deceives me, I would lie
Beside him in my shroud as willingly
As now in the gay night-dress Lilla
 wrought.'
'Fie, child! Let that unseasonable thought
Not be remembered till it snows in June; 70
Such fancies are a music out of tune
With the sweet dance your heart must keep
 to-night.
What! would you take all beauty and de-
 light
Back to the Paradise from which you
 sprung,
And leave to grosser mortals? —
And say, sweet lamb, would you not learn
 the sweet
And subtle mystery by which spirits meet?
Who knows whether the loving game is
 played,

When, once of mortal [venture] disarrayed,
The naked soul goes wandering here and
 there 80
Through the wide deserts of Elysian air?
The violet dies not till it '—

THE BIRTH OF PLEASURE

Date, 1819. Published by Garnett, 1862.

AT the creation of the Earth
Pleasure, that divinest birth,
From the soil of Heaven did rise,
Wrapped in sweet wild melodies —
Like an exhalation wreathing
To the sound of air low-breathing
Through Æolian pines, which make
A shade and shelter to the lake
Whence it rises soft and slow;
Her life-breathing [limbs] did flow
In the harmony divine
Of an ever-lengthening line
Which enwrapped her perfect form
With a beauty clear and warm.

LOVE, HOPE, DESIRE, AND FEAR

Date, 1821. Published by Garnett, 1862.

AND many there were hurt by that strong
 boy;
 His name, they said, was Pleasure.
And near him stood, glorious beyond mea-
 sure,
Four Ladies who possess all empery
 In earth and air and sea;
Nothing that lives from their award is
 free.
 Their names will I declare to thee, —
 Love, Hope, Desire, and Fear;
 And they the regents are
Of the four elements that frame the
 heart, — 10
And each diversely exercised her art
 By force or circumstance or sleight
 To prove her dreadful might
 Upon that poor domain.
Desire presented her [false] glass, and then
 The spirit dwelling there
Was spellbound to embrace what seemed
 so fair
 Within that magic mirror;
 And, dazed by that bright error,

It would have scorned the [shafts] of the
avenger, 20
And death, and penitence, and danger,
Had not then silent Fear
Touched with her palsying spear, —
So that, as if a frozen torrent,
The blood was curdled in its current;
It dared not speak, even in look or motion,
But chained within itself its proud devo-
tion.
Between Desire and Fear thou wert
A wretched thing, poor Heart!
Sad was his life who bore thee in his breast,
Wild bird for that weak nest. 31
Till Love even from fierce Desire it bought,
And from the very wound of tender thought
Drew solace, and the pity of sweet eyes
Gave strength to bear those gentle agonies,
Surmount the loss, the terror, and the
sorrow.
Then Hope approached, she who can
borrow
For poor to-day from rich to-morrow;
And Fear withdrew, as night when day
Descends upon the orient ray; 40
And after long and vain endurance
The poor heart woke to her assurance.

At one birth these four were born
With the world's forgotten morn,
And from Pleasure still they hold
All it circles, as of old.
When, as summer lures the swallow,
Pleasure lures the heart to follow —
O weak heart of little wit —
The fair hand that wounded it, 50
Seeking, like a panting hare,
Refuge in the lynx's lair, —
Love, Desire, Hope, and Fear,
Ever will be near.

A SATIRE ON SATIRE

Date, 1820. Published by Dowden, *Corre-
spondence of Robert Southey and Caroline
Bowles*, 1880. Shelley writes to Hunt: 'I
began once a satire on satire, which I meant
to be very severe; it was full of *small knives*,
in the use of which practice would have soon
made me very expert.'

IF gibbets, axes, confiscations, chains,
And racks of subtle torture, if the pains
Of shame, of fiery Hell's tempestuous wave,
Seen through the caverns of the shadowy
grave,

Hurling the damned into the murky air
While the meek blest sit smiling; if Despair
And Hate, the rapid bloodhounds with
which Terror
Hunts through the world the homeless
steps of Error,
Are the true secrets of the commonweal
To make men wise and just; . . . 10
And not the sophisms of revenge and fear,
Bloodier than is revenge . . .
Then send the priests to every hearth and
home
To preach the burning wrath which is to
come,
In words like flakes of sulphur, such as
thaw
The frozen tears . . .
If Satire's scourge could wake the slum-
bering hounds
Of Conscience, or erase the deeper wounds,
The leprous scars of callous infamy;
If it could make the present not to be, 20
Or charm the dark past never to have been,
Or turn regret to hope; who that has seen
What Southey is and was, would not ex-
claim,
Lash on! be the keen verse dipped
in flame;
Follow his flight with wingèd words, and
urge
The strokes of the inexorable scourge
Until the heart be naked, till his soul
See the contagion's spots foul;
And from the mirror of Truth's sunlike
shield,
From which his Parthian arrow . . . 30
Flash on his sight the spectres of the past,
Until his mind's eye paint thereon —
Let scorn like yawn below,
And rain on him like flakes of fiery snow.
This cannot be, it ought not, evil still —
Suffering makes suffering, ill must follow
ill.
Rough words beget sad thoughts, and,
beside,
Men take a sullen and a stupid pride
In being all they hate in others' shame,
By a perverse antipathy of fame. 40
'T is not worth while to prove, as I could,
how
From the sweet fountains of our Nature
flow
These bitter waters; I will only say,
If any friend would take Southey some
day,

And tell him, in a country walk alone,
Softening harsh words with friendship's
 gentle tone,
How incorrect his public conduct is,
And what men think of it, 't were not
 amiss.
Far better than to make innocent ink —

GINEVRA

Date, 1821. Published by Mrs. Shelley,
1824, who gives the source of the story as
L'Osservatore Fiorentino.

WILD, pale, and wonder-stricken, even
 as one
Who staggers forth into the air and sun
From the dark chamber of a mortal fever,
Bewildered, and incapable, and ever
Fancying strange comments in her dizzy
 brain
Of usual shapes, till the familiar train
Of objects and of persons passed like things
Strange as a dreamer's mad imaginings,
Ginevra from the nuptial altar went;
The vows to which her lips had sworn as-
 sent 10
Rung in her brain still with a jarring din,
Deafening the lost intelligence within.

And so she moved under the bridal veil,
Which made the paleness of her cheek
 more pale,
And deepened the faint crimson of her
 mouth,
And darkened her dark locks, as moonlight
 doth, —
And of the gold and jewels glittering there
She scarce felt conscious, but the weary
 glare
Lay like a chaos of unwelcome light,
Vexing the sense with gorgeous undelight.
A moonbeam in the shadow of a cloud 21
Was less heavenly fair — her face was
 bowed,
And as she passed, the diamonds in her hair
Were mirrored in the polished marble stair
Which led from the cathedral to the street;
And even as she went her light fair feet
Erased these images.

The bride-maidens who round her
 thronging came,
Some with a sense of self-rebuke and
 shame,

Envying the unenviable; and others 30
Making the joy which should have been
 another's
Their own by gentle sympathy; and some
Sighing to think of a unhappy home;
Some few admiring what can ever lure
Maidens to leave the heaven serene and
 pure
Of parents' smiles for life's great cheat; a
 thing
Bitter to taste, sweet in imagining.

But they are all dispersed — and lo ! she
 stands
Looking in idle grief on her white hands,
Alone within the garden now her own; 40
And through the sunny air, with jangling
 tone,
The music of the merry marriage-bells,
Killing the azure silence, sinks and
 swells; —
Absorbed like one within a dream who
 dreams
That he is dreaming, until slumber seems
A mockery of itself — when suddenly
Antonio stood before her, pale as she.
With agony, with sorrow, and with pride,
He lifted his wan eyes upon the bride,
And said — 'Is this thy faith ?' and then
 as one 50
Whose sleeping face is stricken by the
 sun
With light like a harsh voice, which bids
 him rise
And look upon his day of life with eyes
Which weep in vain that they can dream
 no more,
Ginevra saw her lover, and forbore
To shriek or faint, and checked the stifling
 blood
Rushing upon her heart, and unsubdued
Said — 'Friend, if earthly violence or ill,
Suspicion, doubt, or the tyrannic will
Of parents, chance, or custom, time, or
 change, 60
Or circumstance, or terror, or revenge,
Or wildered looks, or words, or evil speech,
With all their stings and venom, can im-
 peach
Our love, — we love not. If the grave,
 which hides
The victim from the tyrant, and divides
The cheek that whitens from the eyes that
 dart
Imperious inquisition to the heart

That is another's, could dissever ours,
We love not.' — ' What ! do not the silent
 hours
Beckon thee to Gherardi's bridal bed ? 70
Is not that ring ' — a pledge, he would have
 said,
Of broken vows, but she with patient look
The golden circle from her finger took,
And said — ' Accept this token of my faith,
The pledge of vows to be absolved by
 death;
And I am dead or shall be soon — my
 knell
Will mix its music with that merry bell;
Does it not sound as if they sweetly said,
" We toll a corpse out of the marriage-
 bed " ?
The flowers upon my bridal chamber
 strewn 80
Will serve unfaded for my bier — so soon
That even the dying violet will not die
Before Ginevra.' The strong fantasy
Had made her accents weaker and more
 weak,
And quenched the crimson life upon her
 cheek,
And glazed her eyes, and spread an atmo-
 sphere
Round her, which chilled the burning noon
 with fear,
Making her but an image of the thought,
Which, like a prophet or a shadow, brought
News of the terrors of the coming time. 90
Like an accuser branded with the crime
He would have cast on a belovèd friend,
Whose dying eyes reproach not to the end
The pale betrayer — he then with vain re-
 pentance
Would share, he cannot now avert, the
 sentence —
Antonio stood and would have spoken,
 when
The compound voice of women and of
 men
Was heard approaching; he retired, while
 she
Was led amid the admiring company
Back to the palace, — and her maidens
 soon 100
Changed her attire for the afternoon,
And left her at her own request to keep
An hour of quiet and rest. Like one
 asleep
With open eyes and folded hands she lay,
Pale in the light of the declining day.

Meanwhile the day sinks fast, the sun is
 set,
And in the lighted hall the guests are met;
The beautiful looked lovelier in the light
Of love, and admiration, and delight,
Reflected from a thousand hearts and
 eyes 110
Kindling a momentary Paradise.
This crowd is safer than the silent wood,
Where love's own doubts disturb the soli-
 tude;
On frozen hearts the fiery rain of wine
Falls, and the dew of music more divine
Tempers the deep emotions of the time
To spirits cradled in a sunny clime.
How many meet, who never yet have
 met,
To part too soon, but never to forget ?
How many saw the beauty, power, and
 wit 120
Of looks and words which ne'er enchanted
 yet !
But life's familiar veil was now withdrawn.
As the world leaps before an earthquake's
 dawn,
And unprophetic of the coming hours
The matin winds from the expanded flow-
 ers
Scatter their hoarded incense, and awaken
The earth, until the dewy sleep is shaken
From every living heart which it possesses,
Through seas and winds, cities and wilder-
 nesses,
As if the future and the past were all 130
Treasured i' the instant; so Gherardi's hall
Laughed in the mirth of its lord's festi-
 val, —
Till some one asked, ' Where is the Bride ? '
 And then
A bridesmaid went, and ere she came again
A silence fell upon the guests — a pause
Of expectation, as when beauty awes
All hearts with its approach, though unbe-
 held;
Then wonder, and then fear that wonder
 quelled; —
For whispers passed from mouth to ear
 which drew
The color from the hearer's cheeks, and
 flew 140
Louder and swifter round the company;
And then Gherardi entered with an eye
Of ostentatious trouble, and a crowd
Surrounded him, and some were weeping
 loud.

They found Ginevra dead ! if it be death
To lie without motion, or pulse, or breath,
With waxen cheeks, and limbs cold, stiff,
 and white,
And open eyes, whose fixed and glassy
 light
Mocked at the speculation they had owned;
If it be death, when there is felt around 150
A smell of clay, a pale and icy glare,
And silence, and a sense that lifts the hair
From the scalp to the ankles, as it were
Corruption from the spirit passing forth,
And giving all it shrouded to the earth,
And leaving as swift lightning in its flight
Ashes, and smoke, and darkness: in our
 night
Of thought we know thus much of death,
 — no more
Than the unborn dream of our life before
Their barks are wrecked on its inhospitable
 shore. 160

The marriage feast and its solemnity
Was turned to funeral pomp; the company,
With heavy hearts and looks, broke up;
 nor they
Who loved the dead went weeping on their
 way
Alone, but sorrow mixed with sad surprise
Loosened the strings of pity in all eyes,
On which that form, whose fate they weep
 in vain,
Will never, thought they, kindle smiles
 again.
The lamps which, half-extinguished in their
 haste
Gleamed few and faint o'er the abandoned
 feast, 170
Showed as it were within the vaulted room
A cloud of sorrow hanging, as if gloom
Had passed out of men's minds into the
 air.
Some few yet stood around Gherardi there,
Friends and relations of the dead, — and
 he,
A loveless man, accepted torpidly
The consolation that he wanted not;
Awe in the place of grief within him
 wrought.
Their whispers made the solemn silence
 seem
More still — some wept, 180
Some melted into tears without a sob,
And some with hearts that might be heard
 to throb

Leaned on the table, and at intervals
Shuddered to hear through the deserted
 halls
And corridors the thrilling shrieks which
 came
Upon the breeze of night, that shook the
 flame
Of every torch and taper, as it swept
From out the chamber where the women
 kept; —
Their tears fell on the dear companion
 cold
Of pleasures now departed; then was
 knolled 190
The bell of death, and soon the priests ar-
 rived,
And finding death their penitent had
 shrived,
Returned like ravens from a corpse whereon
A vulture has just feasted to the bone.
And then the mourning-women came. —

THE DIRGE

Old winter was gone
In his weakness back to the mountains
 hoar,
 And the spring came down
From the planet that hovers upon the shore
 Where the sea of sunlight encroaches 200
On the limits of wintry night; —
If the land, and the air, and the sea,
 Rejoice not when spring approaches,
We did not rejoice in thee,
 Ginevra !

She is still, she is cold
 On the bridal couch.
One step to the white death-bed,
 And one to the bier,
And one to the charnel — and one, oh
 where ? 210
 The dark arrow fled
 In the noon.

Ere the sun through heaven once more has
 rolled,
 The rats in her heart
 Will have made their nest,
And the worms be alive in her golden hair;
While the spirit that guides the sun
Sits throned in his flaming chair,
 She shall sleep.

THE BOAT ON THE SERCHIO

Date, 1821. Published in part by Mrs. Shelley, 1824, and the remainder by Rossetti, 1870. Medwin furnishes the note: 'I have heard Shelley often speak with rapture of the excursions they [Shelley and Williams] made together. The canal fed by the Serchio, of the clearest water, is so rapid that they were obliged to tow the boat up against the current; but the swift descent, through green banks enamelled with flowers and overhung with trees that mirrored themselves on its glassy surface, gave him a wonderful delight. He has left a record of these trips in a poem entitled *The Boat on the Serchio*, and calls Williams and himself *Melchior* and *Lionel*.'

OUR boat is asleep on Serchio's stream,
Its sails are folded like thoughts in a
 dream,
The helm sways idly, hither and thither;
 Dominic, the boatman, has brought the
 mast,
 And the oars, and the sails; but 't is
 sleeping fast
Like a beast, unconscious of its tether.

The stars burned out in the pale blue air,
And the thin white moon lay withering
 there;
To tower, and cavern, and rift, and tree,
The owl and the bat fled drowsily. 10
Day had kindled the dewy woods,
 And the rocks above and the stream be-
 low,
And the vapors in their multitudes,
 And the Apennine's shroud of summer
 snow,
And clothed with light of aëry gold
The mists in their eastern caves uprolled.

Day had awakened all things that be, —
The lark and the thrush and the swallow
 free,
 And the milkmaid's song and mower's
 scythe, 19
And the matin-bell and the mountain bee.
Fire-flies were quenched on the dewy corn;
 Glow-worms went out on the river's
 brim,
 Like lamps which a student forgets to
 trim;
The beetle forgot to wind his horn;
 The crickets were still in the meadow
 and hill;

Like a flock of rooks at a farmer's gun,
Night's dreams and terrors, every one,
Fled from the brains which are their prey
From the lamp's death to the morning ray.

All rose to do the task He set to each, 30
 Who shaped us to his ends and not our
 own;
The million rose to learn, and one to teach
 What none yet ever knew or can be
 known.
 And many rose
 Whose woe was such that fear became
 desire;
Melchior and Lionel were not among those;
They from the throng of men had stepped
 aside,
And made their home under the green
 hillside.
It was that hill, whose intervening brow
 Screens Lucca from the Pisan's envious
 eye, 40
Which the circumfluous plain waving be-
 low,
 Like a wide lake of green fertility,
With streams and fields and marshes bare,
 Divides from the far Apennines, which
 lie
Islanded in the immeasurable air.

'What think you, as she lies in her green
 cove,
Our little sleeping boat is dreaming of?
If morning dreams are true, why I should
 guess
That she was dreaming of our idleness,
And of the miles of watery way 50
We should have led her by this time of
 day.'
 'Never mind,' said Lionel,
'Give care to the winds, they can bear it
 well
About yon poplar tops; and see!
The white clouds are driving merrily,
And the stars we miss this morn will light
More willingly our return to-night.
How it whistles, "Dominic's long black
 hair!
List, my dear fellow, the breeze blows fair;
 Hear how it sings into the air." 60
 — of us and of our lazy motions,'
Impatiently said Melchior,
'If I can guess a boat's emotions;
 And how we ought, two hours before,
To have been the devil knows where.'

And then, in such transalpine Tuscan
As would have killed a Della-Cruscan,

.

So, Lionel according to his art
 Weaving his idle words, Melchior said:
'She dreams that we are not yet out of
 bed; 70
We'll put a soul into her, and a heart
Which like a dove chased by a dove shall
 beat.'

.

 'Ay, heave the ballast overboard,
And stow the eatables in the aft locker.'
'Would not this keg be best a little low-
 ered?'
'No, now all's right.' 'Those bottles of
 warm tea —
(Give me some straw) — must be stowed
 tenderly;
Such as we used, in summer after six,
To cram in great-coat pockets, and to
 mix
Hard eggs and radishes and rolls at Eton, 80
And, couched on stolen hay in those green
 harbors
Farmers called gaps, and we schoolboys
 called arbors,
Would feast till eight.'

.

 With a bottle in one hand,
As if his very soul were at a stand,
Lionel stood, when Melchior brought him
 steady, —
'Sit at the helm — fasten this sheet — all
 ready!'

The chain is loosed, the sails are spread,
 The living breath is fresh behind,
As with dews and sunrise fed 90
 Comes the laughing morning wind.
The sails are full, the boat makes head
Against the Serchio's torrent fierce,
Then flags with intermitting course,
 And hangs upon the wave, and stems
 The tempest of the
Which fervid from its mountain source
Shallow, smooth, and strong, doth come, —
Swift as fire, tempestuously
It sweeps into the affrighted sea; 100
 In morning's smile its eddies coil,
 Its billows sparkle, toss, and boil,
 Torturing all its quiet light
 Into columns fierce and bright.

 The Serchio, twisting forth
Between the marble barriers which it clove
 At Ripafratta, leads through the dread
 chasm
The wave that died the death which lovers
 love,
 Living in what it sought; as if this spasm
Had not yet passed, the toppling mountains
 cling, 110
 But the clear stream in full enthusiasm
Pours itself on the plain, then wandering,
 Down one clear path of effluence crystal-
 line
Sends its superfluous waves, that they may
 fling
 At Arno's feet tribute of corn and wine;
Then, through the pestilential deserts wild
 Of tangled marsh and woods of stunted
 pine,
It rushes to the Ocean.

THE ZUCCA

Date, January, 1822. Published by Mrs.
Shelley, 1824.

I

SUMMER was dead and Autumn was expir-
 ing,
 And infant Winter laughed upon the land
All cloudlessly and cold; when I, desiring
 More in this world than any understand,
Wept o'er the beauty, which, like sea re-
 tiring,
 Had left the earth bare as the wave-worn
 sand
Of my lorn heart, and o'er the grass and
 flowers
Pale for the falsehood of the flattering hours.

II

Summer was dead, but I yet lived to weep
 The instability of all but weeping;
And on the earth lulled in her winter sleep
 I woke, and envied her as she was sleep-
 ing.
Too happy Earth! over thy face shall creep
 The wakening vernal airs, until thou,
 leaping
From unremembered dreams shalt see
No death divide thy immortality.

III

I loved — oh, no, I mean not one of ye,
 Or any earthly one, though ye are dear

As human heart to human heart may be;
 I loved I know not what — but this low
 sphere,
And all that it contains, contains not thee,
 Thou, whom, seen nowhere, I feel every-
 where.
From heaven and earth, and all that in
 them are
Veiled art thou like a star.

IV

By Heaven and Earth, from all whose
 shapes thou flowest,
 Neither to be contained, delayed, nor
 hidden;
Making divine the loftiest and the lowest,
 When for a moment thou art not for-
 bidden
To live within the life which thou bestow-
 est;
 And leaving noblest things vacant and
 chidden,
Cold as a corpse after the spirit's flight,
Blank as the sun after the birth of night.

V

In winds, and trees, and streams, and all
 things common,
 In music, and the sweet unconscious
 tone
Of animals, and voices which are human,
 Meant to express some feelings of their
 own;
In the soft motions and rare smile of wo-
 man,
 In flowers and leaves, and in the grass
 fresh shown
Or dying in the autumn, — I the most
Adore thee present, or lament thee lost.

VI

And thus I went lamenting, when I saw
 A plant upon the river's margin lie,
Like one who loved beyond his nature's
 law,
 And in despair had cast him down to
 die;
Its leaves which had outlived the frost, the
 thaw
 Had blighted, like a heart which hatred's
 eye
Can blast not, but which pity kills; the
 dew
Lay on its spotted leaves like tears too
 true.

VII

The Heavens had wept upon it, but the
 Earth
 Had crushed it on her unmaternal breast.
.

VIII

I bore it to my chamber and I planted
 It in a vase full of the lightest mould;
The winter beams which out of Heaven
 slanted
 Fell through the window panes, disrobed
 of cold,
Upon its leaves and flowers; the star which
 panted
 In evening for the Day, whose car has
 rolled
Over the horizon's wave, with looks of light
Smiled on it from the threshold of the
 night.

IX

The mitigated influences of air
 And light revived the plant, and from it
 grew
Strong leaves and tendrils, and its flowers
 fair,
 Full as a cup with the vine's burning dew,
O'erflowed with golden colors; an atmo-
 sphere
 Of vital warmth enfolded it anew,
And every impulse sent to every part
The unbeheld pulsations of its heart.

X

Well might the plant grow beautiful and
 strong,
 Even if the air and sun had smiled not
 on it;
For one wept o'er it all the winter long
 Tears pure as Heaven's rain, which fell
 upon it
Hour after hour; for sounds of softest
 song,
 Mixed with the stringèd melodies that
 won it
To leave the gentle lips on which it slept,
Had loosed the heart of him who sat and
 wept.

XI

Had loosed his heart, and shook the leaves
 and flowers
 On which he wept, the while the savage
 storm

Waked by the darkest of December's hours
 Was raving round the chamber hushed
 and warm;
The birds were shivering in their leafless
 bowers,
 The fish were frozen in the pools, the
 form
Of every summer plant was dead
Whilst this

LINES

Date, 1822. Published by Garnett, 1862.

I

WE meet not as we parted,
 We feel more than all may see;
My bosom is heavy-hearted,
 And thine full of doubt for me.
 One moment has bound the free.

II

That moment is gone forever,
 Like lightning that flashed and died,
Like a snowflake upon the river,
 Like a sunbeam upon the tide,
 Which the dark shadows hide.

III

That moment from time was singled
 As the first of a life of pain;
The cup of its joy was mingled —
 Delusion too sweet though vain!
 Too sweet to be mine again.

IV

Sweet lips, could my heart have hidden
 That its life was crushed by you,
Ye would not have then forbidden
 The death which a heart so true
 Sought in your briny dew.

V

Methinks too little cost
 For a moment so found, so lost!

CHARLES THE FIRST

Shelley had the subject of Charles the First
in mind for a tragedy as early as 1818, and de-
sired Mrs. Shelley to attempt it. He had be-
gun to think of it for himself in the summer of
1820 and wrote to Medwin: 'What think you
of my boldness? I mean to write a play, in
the spirit of human nature, without prejudice

or passion, entitled *Charles the First*. So van-
ity intoxicates people; but let those few who
praise my verses, and in whose approbation I
take so much delight, answer for the sin.'

Later, he wrote to Ollier: 'I doubt about
Charles the First; but, if I do write it, it shall
be the birth of severe and high feelings. You
are very welcome to it, on the terms you men-
tion, and, when once I see and feel that I can
write it, it is already written. My thoughts
aspire to a production of a far higher char-
acter; but the execution of it will require
some years. I write what I write chiefly to
enquire, by the reception which my writings
meet with, how far I am fit for so great a task,
or not.'

By the summer of 1821 he had done some
shaping-out thought on it, and in September
wrote again to Ollier: '*Charles the First* is
conceived, but not born. Unless I am sure of
making something good, the play will not
be written. Pride, that ruined Satan, will kill
Charles the First, for his midwife would be
only *less than him whom thunder has made
greater*. I am full of great plans; and if I
should tell you them, I should add to the list
of these riddles.'

He began seriously upon it about January 1,
1822, and wrote to Ollier it would be ready by
spring, saying that it 'promises to be good, as
tragedies go,' and that it 'is not colored by
the party-spirit of the author;' to Hunt he
confided his hope that it would 'hold a higher
rank than *The Cenci* as a work of art.' He
apparently soon discontinued the work, and in
answer to Hunt wrote, in March: 'So you
think I can make nothing of Charles the First.
Tanto peggio. Indeed, I have written nothing
for this last two months: a slight circumstance
gave a new train to my ideas, and shattered
the fragile edifice when half built. What
motives have I to write? I *had* motives, and
I thank the God of my own heart they were
totally different from those of the other apes of
humanity who make mouths in the glass of the
time. But what are *those* motives now? The
only inspiration of an ordinary kind I could de-
scend to acknowledge would be the earning
£100 for you; and that it seems I cannot.' In
the same strain he wrote in April to Gisborne:
'I have done some of *Charles the First*; but al-
though the poetry succeeded very well, I can-
not seize on the conception of the subject as a
whole, and seldom now touch the canvas;' and
again, in June: 'I write little now. It is im-
possible to compose except under the strong
excitement of an assurance of finding sympathy
in what you write. Imagine Demosthenes re-
citing a Philippic to the waves of the Atlantic.
Lord Byron is in this respect fortunate. He
touched the chord to which a million hearts

responded, and the coarse music which he produced to please them, disciplined him to the perfection to which he now approaches. I do not go on with *Charles the First.* I feel too little certainty of the future, and too little satisfaction with regard to the past to undertake any subject seriously and deeply. I stand, as it were, upon a precipice, which I have ascended with great, and cannot descend without greater peril, and I am content if the heaven above me is calm for the passing moment.'

Medwin adds some details: 'I must now speak of his *Charles the First.* He had designed to write a tragedy on this ungrateful subject as far back as 1818, and had begun it at the end of the following year, when he asked me to obtain for him that well-known pamphlet, which was in my father's library — *Killing no Murder.* He was, however, *in limine,* diverted at that time to more attractive subjects, and now resumed his abandoned labors, of which he has left a very unsatisfactory, though valuable, *bozzo.* The task seemed to him an irksome one. His progress was slow; one day he expunged what he had written the day before. He occasionally showed and read to me his MS., which was lined and interlined and interworded, so as to render it almost illegible. The scenes were disconnected, and intended to be interwoven in the tissue of the drama. He did not thus compose *The Cenci.* He seemed tangled in an inextricable web of difficulties, as to the treatment of his subject; and it was clear that he had formed no definite plan in his own mind, how to connect the links of the complicated yarn of events that led to that frightful catastrophe, or to justify it. . . . Shelley meant to have made the last of King's fools, Archy, a more than subordinate among his *dramatis personæ,* as Calderon had done in his *Cisma de l'Inglaterra,* a fool *sui generis,* who talks in fable, "weaving a world of mirth out of the wreck of all around." . . . Other causes, besides doubt as to the manner of treating the subject, operated to impede its progress. The ever-growing fastidiousness of his taste had, I have often thought, begun to cramp his genius. The opinion of the world, too, at times shook his confidence in himself. I have often been shown the scenes of this tragedy in which he was engaged; like the MSS. of Tasso's *Gerusalemme Liberata,* in the library at Ferrara, his were larded with word on word, till they were scarcely decipherable.'

Mrs. Shelley writes: 'Whether the subject proved more difficult than he anticipated, or whether in fact he could not bend his mind away from the broodings and wanderings of thought divested from human interest, which

he best loved, I cannot tell; but he proceeded slowly, and threw it aside for one of the most mystical of his poems, *The Triumph of Life,* on which he was employed at the last.'

The fragment was published in part by Mrs. Shelley, 1824, and the remainder by Rossetti, 1870.

CHARLES THE FIRST

DRAMATIS PERSONÆ

KING CHARLES I.	JUXON.
QUEEN HENRIETTA.	ST. JOHN.
LAUD, Archbishop of Canterbury.	ARCHY, the Court Fool.
	HAMPDEN.
WENTWORTH, Earl of Strafford.	PYM.
	CROMWELL.
LORD COTTINGTON.	CROMWELL'S DAUGHTER.
LORD WESTON.	SIR HARRY VANE the younger.
LORD COVENTRY.	
WILLIAMS, Bishop of Lincoln.	LEIGHTON.
Secretary LYTTELTON.	BASTWICK.
	PRYNNE.

Gentlemen of the Inns of Court, Citizens, Pursuivants, Marshalsmen, Law Students, Judges, Clerk.

SCENE I. — *The Masque of the Inns of Court.*

A PURSUIVANT

PLACE for the Marshal of the Masque!

FIRST CITIZEN

What thinkest thou of this quaint masque which turns,
Like morning from the shadow of the night,
The night to day, and London to a place
Of peace and joy?

SECOND CITIZEN

 And Hell to Heaven.
Eight years are gone,
And they seem hours, since in this populous street
I trod on grass made green by summer's rain;
For the red plague kept state within that palace
Where now that vanity reigns. In nine years more 10
The roots will be refreshed with civil blood;
And thank the mercy of insulted Heaven
That sin and wrongs wound, as an orphan's cry,
The patience of the great Avenger's ear.

A YOUTH

Yet, father, 't is a happy sight to see,
Beautiful, innocent, and unforbidden

By God or man. 'T is like the bright pro-
cession
Of skyey visions in a solemn dream
From which men wake as from a paradise,
And draw new strength to tread the thorns
of life. 20
If God be good, wherefore should this be
evil ?
And if this be not evil, dost thou not draw
Unseasonable poison from the flowers
Which bloom so rarely in this barren
world ?
Oh, kill these bitter thoughts which make
the present
Dark as the future ! —

.

When Avarice and Tyranny, vigilant Fear
And open-eyed Conspiracy, lie sleeping
As on Hell's threshold; and all gentle
thoughts
Waken to worship Him who giveth joys 30
With his own gift.

SECOND CITIZEN

How young art thou in this old age of
time !
How green in this gray world ! Canst thou
discern
The signs of seasons, yet perceive no hint
Of change in that stage-scene in which
thou art
Not a spectator but an actor ? or
Art thou a puppet moved by [enginery ?]
The day that dawns in fire will die in
storms,
Even though the noon be calm. My
travel 's done, —
Before the whirlwind wakes I shall have
found 40
My inn of lasting rest; but thou must
still
Be journeying on in this inclement air.
Wrap thy old cloak about thy back;
Nor leave the broad and plain and beaten
road,
Although no flowers smile on the trodden
dust,
For the violet paths of pleasure. This
Charles the First
Rose like the equinoctial sun, . . .
By vapors, through whose threatening omi-
nous veil
Darting his altered influence he has gained
This height of noon — from which he must
decline 50

Amid the darkness of conflicting storms,
To dank extinction and to latest night . . .
There goes
The apostate Strafford; he whose titles . . .
whispered aphorisms
From Machiavel and Bacon; and, if Judas
Had been as brazen and as bold as he . . .

FIRST CITIZEN
 That
Is the Archbishop.

SECOND CITIZEN
 Rather say the Pope:
London will be soon his Rome. He walks
As if he trod upon the heads of men. 61
He looks elate, drunken with blood and
gold.
Beside him moves the Babylonian woman
Invisibly, and with her as with his shadow,
Mitred adulterer ! he is joined in sin,
Which turns Heaven's milk of mercy to
revenge.

THIRD CITIZEN (*lifting up his eyes*)
Good Lord ! rain it down upon him ! . . .
Amid her ladies walks the papist queen,
As if her nice feet scorned our English
earth.
The Canaanitish Jezebel ! I would be 70
A dog if I might tear her with my teeth !
There 's old Sir Henry Vane, the Earl of
Pembroke,
Lord Essex, and Lord Keeper Coventry,
And others who made base their English
breed
By vile participation of their honors
With papists, atheists, tyrants, and apos-
tates.
When lawyers masque 't is time for honest
men
To strip the vizor from their purposes.
A seasonable time for masquers this !
When Englishmen and Protestants should
sit 80
dust on their dishonored heads,
To avert the wrath of Him whose scourge
is felt
For the great sins which have drawn down
from Heaven
and foreign overthrow.
The remnant of the martyred saints in
Rochefort
Have been abandoned by their faithless
allies

To that idolatrous and adulterous torturer
Lewis of France, — the Palatinate is
 lost. . . .

Enter LEIGHTON (*who has been branded in the
face*) *and* BASTWICK

Canst thou be — art thou . . . ?

LEIGHTON

 I *was* Leighton: what
I *am* thou seest. And yet turn thine eyes,
And with thy memory look on thy friend's
 mind, 91
Which is unchanged, and where is written
 deep
The sentence of my judge.

THIRD CITIZEN

 Are these the marks with which
Laud thinks to improve the image of his
 Maker
Stamped on the face of man? Curses
 upon him,
The impious tyrant !

SECOND CITIZEN

 It is said besides
That lewd and papist drunkards may pro-
 fane
The Sabbath with their
And has permitted that most heathenish
 custom
Of dancing round a pole dressed up with
 wreaths 100
On May-day.
A man who thus twice crucifies his God
May well his brother. In my mind,
 friend,
The root of all this ill is prelacy.
I would cut up the root.

THIRD CITIZEN

 And by what means ?

SECOND CITIZEN

Smiting each Bishop under the fifth rib.

THIRD CITIZEN

You seem to know the vulnerable place
Of these same crocodiles.

SECOND CITIZEN

 I learned it in
Egyptian bondages, sir. Your worm of
 Nile

Betrays not with its flattering tears like
 they; 110
For, when they cannot kill, they whine and
 weep.
Nor is it half so greedy of men's bodies
As they of soul and all; nor does it wallow
In slime as they in simony and lies
And close lusts of the flesh.

A MARSHALSMAN

 Give place, give place !
You torch-bearers, advance to the great
 gate,
And then attend the Marshal of the Masque
Into the royal presence.

A LAW STUDENT

 What thinkest thou
Of this quaint show of ours, my agèd
 friend ?
Even now we see the redness of the torches
Inflame the night to the eastward, and the
 clarions 121
[Gasp ?] to us on the wind's wave. It
 comes !
And their sounds, floating hither round the
 pageant,
Rouse up the astonished air.

FIRST CITIZEN

I will not think but that our country's
 wounds
May yet be healed. The king is just and
 gracious,
Though wicked counsels now pervert his
 will.
These once cast off —

SECOND CITIZEN

 As adders cast their skins
And keep their venom, so kings often
 change;
Counsels and counsellors hang on one
 another, 130
Hiding the loathsome . . .
Like the base patchwork of a leper's rags.

THE YOUTH

Oh, still those dissonant thoughts ! — List
 how the music
Grows on the enchanted air ! And see, the
 torches
Restlessly flashing, and the crowd divided
Like waves before an admiral's prow !

A MARSHALSMAN
 Give place
To the Marshal of the Masque !

A PURSUIVANT
 Room for the King !

THE YOUTH

How glorious ! See those thronging char-
iots
Rolling, like painted clouds before the wind,
Behind their solemn steeds: how some are
shaped 140
Like curved sea-shells dyed by the azure
depths
Of Indian seas; some like the new-born
moon;
And some like cars in which the Romans
climbed
(Canopied by Victory's eagle-wings out-
spread)
The Capitolian ! See how gloriously
The mettled horses in the torchlight stir
Their gallant riders, while they check their
pride,
Like shapes of some diviner element
Than English air, and beings nobler than
The envious and admiring multitude. 150

SECOND CITIZEN

Ay, there they are —
Nobles, and sons of nobles, patentees,
Monopolists, and stewards of this poor
farm,
On whose lean sheep sit the prophetic
crows.
Here is the pomp that strips the houseless
orphan,
Here is the pride that breaks the desolate
heart.
These are the lilies glorious as Solomon,
Who toil not, neither do they spin — unless
It be the webs they catch poor rogues
withal.
Here is the surfeit which to them who
earn 160
The niggard wages of the earth scarce
leaves
The tithe that will support them till they
crawl
Back to her cold, hard bosom. Here is
health
Followed by grim disease, glory by shame,
Waste by lame famine, wealth by squalid
want,

And England's sin by England's punish-
ment.
And, as the effect pursues the cause fore-
gone,
Lo, giving substance to my words, behold
At once the sign and the thing signified —
A troop of cripples, beggars, and lean out-
casts, 170
Horsed upon stumbling jades, carted with
dung,
Dragged for a day from cellars and low
cabins
And rotten hiding-holes, to point the moral
Of this presentment, and bring up the rear
Of painted pomp with misery !

THE YOUTH
 'T is but
The anti-masque, and serves as discords do
In sweetest music. Who would love May
flowers
If they succeeded not to Winter's flaw;
Or day unchanged by night; or joy itself
Without the touch of sorrow ?

SECOND CITIZEN
 I and thou . . .

A MARSHALSMAN
Place, give place ! 181

SCENE II. — *A Chamber in Whitehall.*

Enter the KING, QUEEN, LAUD, LORD
STRAFFORD, LORD COTTINGTON, *and other
Lords ;* ARCHY ; *also* ST. JOHN, *with some
Gentlemen of the Inns of Court.*

KING

Thanks, gentlemen. I heartily accept
This token of your service; your gay
masque
Was performed gallantly. And it shows
well
When subjects twine such flowers of [ob-
servance ?]
With the sharp thorns that deck the Eng-
lish crown.
A gentle heart enjoys what it confers,
Even as it suffers that which it inflicts,
Though Justice guides the stroke.
Accept my hearty thanks.

QUEEN
 And, gentlemen,
Call your poor Queen your debtor. Your
quaint pageant 10

Rose on me like the figures of past years,
Treading their still path back to infancy,
More beautiful and mild as they draw
 nearer
The quiet cradle. I could have almost wept
To think I was in Paris, where these shows
Are well devised — such as I was ere yet
My young heart shared a portion of the
 burden,
The careful weight, of this great monarchy.
There, gentlemen, between the sovereign's
 pleasure
And that which it regards, no clamor lifts
Its proud interposition. 21
In Paris ribald censurers dare not move
Their poisonous tongues against these sin-
 less sports;
And *his* smile
Warms those who bask in it, as ours would
 do
If . . . Take my heart's thanks; add them,
 gentlemen,
To those good words which, were he King
 of France,
My royal lord would turn to golden deeds.

ST. JOHN

Madam, the love of Englishmen can make
The lightest favor of their lawful king 30
Outweigh a despot's. We humbly take our
 leaves,
Enriched by smiles which France can never
 buy.

[*Exeunt* ST. JOHN *and the Gentlemen of the
 Inns of Court.*

KING

My Lord Archbishop.
Mark you what spirit sits in St. John's
 eyes?
Methinks it is too saucy for this presence.

ARCHY

Yes, pray your Grace look : for, like an
unsophisticated [eye] sees everything upside
down, you who are wise will discern the
shadow of an idiot in lawn sleeves and a
rochet setting springes to catch woodcocks
in haymaking time. Poor Archy, whose
owl-eyes are tempered to the error of his
age, and because he is a fool, and by spe-
cial ordinance of God forbidden ever to see
himself as he is, sees now in that deep eye
a blindfold devil sitting on the ball, and
weighing words out between king and sub-

jects. One scale is full of promises, and
the other full of protestations; and then
another devil creeps behind the first out
of the dark windings [of a] pregnant law-
yer's brain, and takes the bandage from
the other's eyes, and throws a sword into
the left-hand scale, for all the world like
my Lord Essex's there.

STRAFFORD

A rod in pickle for the Fool's back !

ARCHY

Ay, and some are now smiling whose
tears will make the brine; for Fool sees . . .

STRAFFORD

Insolent ! You shall have your coat
turned and be whipped out of the palace
for this.

ARCHY

When all the fools are whipped, and all
the protestant writers, while the knaves
are whipping the fools ever since a thief
was set to catch a thief. If all turncoats
were whipped out of palaces, poor Archy
would be disgraced in good company. Let
the knaves whip the fools, and all the fools
laugh at it. [Let the] wise and godly slit
each other's noses and ears (having no need
of any sense of discernment in their craft);
and the knaves, to marshal them, join in a
procession to Bedlam, to entreat the mad-
men to omit their sublime Platonic contem-
plations, and manage the state of England.
Let all the honest men who lie penned up
at the prisons or the pillories, in custody
of the pursuivants of the High-Commission
Court, marshal them.

Enter Secretary LYTTELTON, *with papers*

KING (*looking over the papers*)
 These stiff Scots 80
His Grace of Canterbury must take order
To force under the Church's yoke. — You,
 Wentworth,
Shall be myself in Ireland, and shall add
Your wisdom, gentleness, and energy,
To what in me were wanting. — My Lord
 Weston,
Look that those merchants draw not with-
 out loss
Their bullion from the Tower; and, on the
 payment

Of ship-money, take fullest compensation
For violation of our royal forests,
Whose limits, from neglect, have been o'er-
 grown 90
With cottages and cornfields. The utter-
 most
Farthing exact from those who claim ex-
 emption
From knighthood; that which once was a
 reward
Shall thus be made a punishment, that sub-
 jects
May know how majesty can wear at will
The rugged mood. — My Lord of Coven-
 try,
Lay my command upon the Courts below
That bail be not accepted for the prisoners
Under the warrant of the Star Chamber.
The people shall not find the stubbornness
Of Parliament a cheap or easy method 101
Of dealing with their rightful sovereign;
And doubt not this, my Lord of Coventry,
We will find time and place for fit re-
 buke. —
My Lord of Canterbury.

ARCHY

 The fool is here.

LAUD

I crave permission of your Majesty
To order that this insolent fellow be
Chastised; he mocks the sacred character,
Scoffs at the state, and —

KING

 What, my Archy ?
He mocks and mimics all he sees and hears,
Yet with a quaint and graceful license.
 Prithee 111
For this once do not as Prynne would, were
 he
Primate of England. With your Grace's
 leave,
He lives in his own world; and, like a
 parrot
Hung in his gilded prison from the win-
 dow
Of a queen's bower over the public way,
Blasphemes with a bird's mind; his words,
 like arrows
Which know no aim beyond the archer's
 wit,
Strike sometimes what eludes philosophy.
 (To ARCHY)

Go, sirrah, and repent of your offence 120
Ten minutes in the rain; be it your pen-
 ance
To bring news how the world goes there. —
 Poor Archy !
 [Exit ARCHY.
He weaves about himself a world of mirth
Out of the wreck of ours.

LAUD

I take with patience, as my Master did,
All scoffs permitted from above.

KING

 My lord,
Pray overlook these papers. Archy's
 words
Had wings, but these have talons.

QUEEN

 And the lion
That wears them must be tamed. My
 dearest lord, 129
I see the new-born courage in thine eye
Armed to strike dead the spirit of the time,
Which spurs to rage the many-headed
 beast.
Do thou persist; for, faint but in resolve,
And it were better thou hadst still re-
 mained
The slave of thine own slaves, who tear
 like curs
The fugitive, and flee from the pursuer;
And Opportunity, that empty wolf,
Flies at his throat who falls. Subdue thy
 actions
Even to the disposition of thy purpose, 139
And be that tempered as the Ebro's steel;
And banish weak-eyed Mercy to the weak,
Whence she will greet thee with a gift of
 peace,
And not betray thee with a traitor's kiss,
As when she keeps the company of rebels,
Who think that she is Fear. This do, lest
 we
Should fall as from a glorious pinnacle
In a bright dream, and wake, as from a
 dream,
Out of our worshipped state.

KING

 Belovèd friend,
God is my witness that this weight of
 power,
Which he sets me my earthly task to wield

Under his law, is my delight and pride　151
Only because thou lovest that and me.
For a king bears the office of a God
To all the under world; and to his God
Alone he must deliver up his trust,
Unshorn of its permitted attributes.
[It seems] now as the baser elements
Had mutinied against the golden sun
That kindles them to harmony, and quells
Their self-destroying rapine.　The wild
　　million　160
Strike at the eye that guides them; like as
　　humors
Of the distempered body that conspire
Against the spirit of life throned in the
　　heart, —
And thus become the prey of one another,
And last of death. . . .

STRAFFORD

That which would be ambition in a subject
Is duty in a sovereign; for on him,
As on a keystone, hangs the arch of life,
Whose safety is its strength.　Degree and
　　form,
And all that makes the age of reasoning
　　man　170
More memorable than a beast's, depend on
　　this —
That Right should fence itself inviolably
With power; in which respect the state of
　　England
From usurpation by the insolent commons
Cries for reform.
Get treason, and spare treasure.　Fee with
　　coin
The loudest murmurers; feed with jealous-
　　ies
Opposing factions, — be thyself of none;
And borrow gold of many, for those who
　　lend
Will serve thee till thou payest them; and
　　thus　180
Keep the fierce spirit of the hour at bay,
Till time, and its coming generations
Of nights and days unborn, bring some one
　　chance,

.

Or war or pestilence or Nature's self,
By some distemperature or terrible sign,
Be as an arbiter betwixt themselves.
　　　　Nor let your Majesty
Doubt here the peril of the unseen event.
How did your brother kings, coheritors
In your high interest in the subject earth,

Rise past such troubles to that height of
　　power　191
Where now they sit, and awfully serene
Smile on the trembling world?　Such
　　popular storms
Philip the Second of Spain, this Lewis of
　　France,
And late the German head of many bodies,
And every petty lord of Italy,
Quelled or by arts or arms.　Is England,
　　poorer
Or feebler? or art thou who wield'st her
　　power
Tamer than they? or shall this island be —
[Girdled] by its inviolable waters —　200
To the world present and the world to come
Sole pattern of extinguished monarchy?
Not if thou dost as I would have thee do.

KING

Your words shall be my deeds;
You speak the image of my thought.　My
　　friend
(If kings can have a friend, I call thee
　　so),
Beyond the large commission which [be-
　　longs?]
Under the great seal of the realm, take
　　this:
And, for some obvious reasons, let there be
No seal on it, except my kingly word　210
And honor as I am a gentleman.
Be — as thou art within my heart and
　　mind —
Another self, here and in Ireland:
Do what thou judgest well, take amplest
　　license,
And stick not even at questionable means.
Hear me, Wentworth.　My word is as a
　　wall
Between thee and this world thine enemy —
That hates thee, for thou lovest me.

STRAFFORD

　　　　　　　　I own
No friend but thee, no enemies but thine;
Thy lightest thought is my eternal law.　220
How weak, how short, is life to pay —

KING

　　　　　　　Peace, peace!
Thou ow'st me nothing yet. —
　　　　　　(To LAUD)
　　　　　　My lord, what say
Those papers?

LAUD

Your Majesty has ever interposed,
In lenity towards your native soil,
Between the heavy vengeance of the
Church
And Scotland. Mark the consequence of
warning
This brood of northern vipers in your
bosom.
The rabble, instructed no doubt
By Loudon, Lindsay, Hume, and false
Argyll, 230
(For the waves never menace heaven until
Scourged by the wind's invisible tyranny)
Have in the very temple of the Lord
Done outrage to his chosen ministers.
They scorn the liturgy of the Holy Church,
Refuse to obey her canons, and deny
The apostolic power with which the Spirit
Has filled its elect vessels, even from him
Who held the keys with power to loose
and bind
To him who now pleads in this royal pre-
sence. — 240
Let ampler powers and new instructions be
Sent to the High Commissioners in Scot-
land.
To death, imprisonment, and confiscation,
Add torture, add the ruin of the kindred
Of the offender, add the brand of infamy,
Add mutilation: and if this suffice not,
Unleash the sword and fire, that in their
thirst
They may lick up that scum of schismatics.
I laugh at those weak rebels who, desiring
What we possess, still prate of Christian
peace; 250
As if those dreadful arbitrating messengers
Which play the part of God 'twixt right
and wrong,
Should be let loose against the innocent
sleep
Of templed cities and the smiling fields,
For some poor argument of policy
Which touches our own profit or our pride,
(Where it indeed were Christian charity
To turn the cheek even to the smiter's
hand);
And, when our great Redeemer, when our
God,
When he who gave, accepted, and retained,
Himself in propitiation of our sins, 261
Is scorned in his immediate ministry,
With hazard of the inestimable loss
Of all the truth and discipline which is

Salvation to the extremest generation
Of men innumerable, they talk of peace!
Such peace as Canaan found, let Scotland
now!
For, by that Christ who came to bring a
sword,
Not peace, upon the earth, and gave com-
mand
To his disciples at the passover 270
That each should sell his robe and buy a
sword, —
Once strip that minister of naked wrath,
And it shall never sleep in peace again
Till Scotland bend or break.

KING

My Lord Archbishop,
Do what thou wilt and what thou canst in
this.
Thy earthly even as thy heavenly King
Gives thee large power in his unquiet
realm.
But we want money, and my mind mis-
gives me
That for so great an enterprise, as yet,
We are unfurnished.

STRAFFORD

Yet it may not long
Rest on our wills.

COTTINGTON

The expenses 281
Of gathering ship-money, and of distraining
For every petty rate (for we encounter
A desperate opposition inch by inch
In every warehouse and on every farm),
Have swallowed up the gross sum of the
imposts;
So that, though felt as a most grievous
scourge
Upon the land, they stand us in small stead
As touches the receipt.

STRAFFORD

'Tis a conclusion
Most arithmetical: and thence you infer
Perhaps the assembling of a parliament.
Now, if a man should call his dearest
enemies 292
To sit in licensed judgment on his life,
His Majesty might wisely take that course.
(Aside to COTTINGTON)
It is enough to expect from these lean im-
posts

That they perform the office of a scourge,
Without more profit.

(*Aloud*)
 Fines and confiscations,
And a forced loan from the refractory
 city,
Will fill our coffers; and the golden love
Of loyal gentlemen and noble friends 300
For the worshipped father of our common
 country,
With contributions from the Catholics,
Will make Rebellion pale in our excess.
Be these the expedients until time and
 wisdom
Shall frame a settled state of government.

LAUD

And weak expedients they ! Have we not
 drained
All, till the which seemed
A mine exhaustless ?

STRAFFORD

 And the love which *is*,
If loyal hearts could turn their blood to
 gold. 309

LAUD

Both now grow barren; and I speak it not
As loving parliaments, which, as they have
 been
In the right hand of bold, bad, mighty
 kings
The scourges of the bleeding Church, I
 hate.
Methinks they scarcely can deserve our
 fear.

STRAFFORD

Oh, my dear liege, take back the wealth
 thou gavest;
With that, take all I held, but as in trust
For thee, of mine inheritance; leave me but
This unprovided body for thy service,
And a mind dedicated to no care
Except thy safety; but assemble not 320
A parliament. Hundreds will bring, like
 me,
Their fortunes, as they would their blood,
 before —

KING

No ! thou who judgest them art but one.
 Alas !
We should be too much out of love with
 heaven,

Did this vile world show many such as
 thee,
Thou perfect just and honorable man !
Never shall it be said that Charles of Eng-
 land
Stripped those ᴜe loved for fear of those
 he scorns;
Nor will he so much misbecome his throne
As to impoverish those who most adorn
And best defend it. That you urge, dear
 Strafford, 331
Inclines me rather —

QUEEN

 To a parliament ?
Is this thy firmness ? and thou wilt preside
Over a knot of censurers, ˎ
To the unswearing of thy best resolves,
And choose the worst, when the worst
 comes too soon ?
Plight not the worst before the worst must
 come.
Oh, wilt thou smile whilst our ribald foes,
Dressed in their own usurped authority,
Sharpen their tongues on Henrietta's fame ?
It is enough ! Thou lovest me no more !
 (*Weeps*)

KING

Oh, Henrietta !

 (*They talk apart*)

COTTINGTON [*to* LAUD]
 Money we have none;
And all the expedients of my Lord of
 Strafford 343
Will scarcely meet the arrears.

LAUD

 Without delay
An army must be sent into the north;
Followed by a Commission of the Church,
With amplest power to quench in fire and
 blood,
And tears and terror, and the pity of hell,
The intenser wrath of Heresy. God will
 give
Victory; and victory over Scotland give 350
The lion England tamed into our hands.
That will lend power, and power bring gold

COTTINGTON

 Meanwhile
We must begin first where your Grace
 leaves off.
Gold must give power, or —

LAUD
 I am not averse
From the assembling of a parliament.
Strong actions and smooth words might
 teach them soon
The lesson to obey. And are they not
A bubble fashioned by the monarch's mouth,
The birth of one light breath? If they
 serve no purpose, 360
A word dissolves them.

STRAFFORD
 The engine of parliaments
Might be deferred until I can bring over
The Irish regiments; they will serve to
 assure
The issue of the war against the Scots.
And, this game won — which if lost, all is
 lost —
Gather these chosen leaders of the rebels,
And call them, if you will, a parliament.

KING
Oh, be our feet still tardy to shed blood,
Guilty though it may be ! I would still
 spare 369
The stubborn country of my birth, and ward
From countenances which I loved in youth
The wrathful Church's lacerating hand.
 (*To* LAUD)
Have you o'erlooked the other articles ?

Reënter ARCHY

LAUD
Hazlerig, Hampden, Pym, young Harry
 Vane,
Cromwell, and other rebels of less note,
Intend to sail with the next favoring wind
For the Plantations.

ARCHY
 Where they think to found
A commonwealth like Gonzalo's in the play,
Gynæcocœnic and pantisocratic.

KING
What 's that, sirrah ?

ARCHY
 New devil's politics.
Hell is the pattern of all commonwealths;
Lucifer was the first republican. 382
Will you hear Merlin's prophecy, how three
 [posts ?]

'In one brainless skull, when the white-
 thorn is full,
Shall sail round the world, and come back
 again:
Shall sail round the world in a brainless
 skull,
And come back again when the moon is at
 full: ' —
When, in spite of the Church,
They will hear homilies of whatever length
Or form they please. 390

[COTTINGTON ?]
So please your Majesty to sign this order
For their detention.

ARCHY
 If your Majesty were tormented night
and day by fever, gout, rheumatism, and
stone, and asthma, etc., and you found these
diseases had secretly entered into a con-
spiracy to abandon you, should you think it
necessary to lay an embargo on the port by
which they meant to dispeople your un-
quiet kingdom of man ?

KING
If fear were made for kings, the Fool
 mocks wisely ; 401
But in this case — (*writing*) Here, my lord,
 take the warrant,
And see it duly executed forthwith. —
That imp of malice and mockery shall be
 punished.
 [*Exeunt all but* KING, QUEEN, *and* ARCHY.

ARCHY
 Ay, I am the physician of whom Plato
prophesied, who was to be accused by the
confectioner before a jury of children, who
found him guilty without waiting for the
summing-up, and hanged him without bene-
fit of clergy. Thus Baby Charles, and the
Twelfth-night Queen of Hearts, and the
overgrown schoolboy Cottington, and that
little urchin Laud — who would reduce a
verdict of 'guilty, death,' by famine, if it
were impregnable by composition — all im-
panelled against poor Archy for presenting
them bitter physic the last day of the holi-
days.

QUEEN
Is the rain over, sirrah ?

KING

When it rains
And the sun shines, 't will rain again to-
 morrow; 420
And therefore never smile till you 've done
 crying.

ARCHY

But 't is all over now; like the April
anger of woman, the gentle sky has wept
itself serene.

QUEEN

What news abroad? how looks the world
this morning?

ARCHY

Gloriously as a grave covered with virgin
flowers. There 's a rainbow in the sky.
Let your Majesty look at it, for 429

 ' A rainbow in the morning
 Is the shepherd's warning; '

and the flocks of which you are the pastor
are scattered among the mountain-tops,
where every drop of water is a flake of
snow, and the breath of May pierces like a
January blast.

KING

The sheep have mistaken the wolf for
their shepherd, my poor boy; and the shep-
herd, the wolves for the watchdogs. 439

QUEEN

But the rainbow was a good sign, Archy;
it says that the waters of the deluge are
gone, and can return no more.

ARCHY

Ay, the salt-water one; but that of tears
and blood must yet come down, and that of
fire follow, if there be any truth in lies. —
The rainbow hung over the city with all its
shops, . . . and churches, from north to
south, like a bridge of congregated light-
ning pieced by the masonry of heaven —
like a balance in which the angel that dis-
tributes the coming hour was weighing that
heavy one whose poise is now felt in the
lightest hearts, before it bows the proudest
heads under the meanest feet.

QUEEN

Who taught you this trash, sirrah?

ARCHY

A torn leaf out of an old book trampled
in the dirt. — But for the rainbow. It
moved as the sun moved, and . . . until
the top of the Tower . . . of a cloud
through its left-hand tip, and Lambeth
Palace look as dark as a rock before the
other. Methought I saw a crown figured
upon one tip, and a mitre on the other. So,
as I had heard treasures were found where
the rainbow quenches its points upon the
earth, I set off, and at the Tower —— But
I shall not tell your Majesty what I found
close to the closet-window on which the
rainbow had glimmered.

KING

Speak: I will make my Fool my conscience.

ARCHY

Then conscience is a fool. — I saw there
a cat caught in a rat-trap. I heard the
rats squeak behind the wainscots; it seemed
to me that the very mice were consulting
on the manner of her death.

QUEEN

Archy is shrewd and bitter.

ARCHY

Like the season,
so blow the winds. — But at the other end
of the rainbow, where the gray rain was
tempered along the grass and leaves by a
tender interfusion of violet and gold in the
meadows beyond Lambeth, what think you
that I found instead of a mitre?

KING

Vane's wits perhaps.

ARCHY

Something as vain. I saw
a gross vapor hovering in a stinking ditch
over the carcass of a dead ass, some rotten
rags, and broken dishes — the wrecks of
what once administered to the stuffing-out
and the ornament of a worm of worms.
His Grace of Canterbury expects to enter
the New Jerusalem some Palm Sunday in
triumph on the ghost of this ass.

QUEEN

Enough, enough! Go desire Lady Jane
She place my lute, together with the music

Mari received last week from Italy,
In my boudoir, and —

[Exit ARCHY.

KING

I 'll go in.

QUEEN

My belovèd lord,
Have you not noted that the Fool of late
Has lost his careless mirth, and that his
 words
Sound like the echoes of our saddest fears ?
What can it mean ? I should be loath to
 think 500
Some factious slave had tutored him.

KING

Oh, no !
He is but Occasion's pupil. Partly 't is
That our minds piece the vacant intervals
Of his wild words with their own fashion-
 ing;
As in the imagery of summer clouds,
Or coals of the winter fire, idlers find
The perfect shadows of their teeming
 thoughts;
And, partly, that the terrors of the time
Are sown by wandering Rumor in all
 spirits,
And in the lightest and the least may best
Be seen the current of the coming wind. 511

QUEEN

Your brain is overwrought with these deep
 thoughts.
Come, I will sing to you; let us go try
These airs from Italy; and, as we pass
The gallery, we 'll decide where that Cor-
 reggio
Shall hang — the Virgin Mother
With her child, born the King of heaven
 and earth,
Whose reign is men's salvation. And you
 shall see
A cradled miniature of yourself asleep, 519
Stamped on the heart by never-erring love;
Liker than any Vandyke ever made,
A pattern to the unborn age of thee,
Over whose sweet beauty I have wept for
 joy
A thousand times, and now should weep
 for sorrow,
Did I not think that after we were dead
Our fortunes would spring high in him,
 and that

The cares we waste upon our heavy crown
Would make it light and glorious as a
 wreath
Of heaven's beams for his dear innocent
 brow.

KING

Dear Henrietta ! 530

SCENE III. — *The Star Chamber.* LAUD,
 JUXON, STRAFFORD, *and others, as Judges.*
 PRYNNE, *as a Prisoner, and then* BASTWICK.

LAUD

Bring forth the prisoner Bastwick; let the
 clerk
Recite his sentence.

CLERK

'That he pay five thousand
Pounds to the king, lose both his ears, be
 branded
With red-hot iron on the cheek and fore-
 head,
And be imprisoned within Lancaster Castle
During the pleasure of the Court.'

LAUD

Prisoner,
If you have aught to say wherefore this
 sentence
Should not be put into effect, now speak.

JUXON

If you have aught to plead in mitigation,
Speak.

BASTWICK

Thus, my lords. If, like the prelates, I
Were an invader of the royal power, 11
A public scorner of the word of God,
Profane, idolatrous, popish, superstitious,
Impious in heart and in tyrannic act,
Void of wit, honesty and temperance;
If Satan were my lord, as theirs, — our
 God
Pattern of all I should avoid to do;
Were I an enemy of my God and King
And of good men, as ye are; — I should
 merit
Your fearful state and gilt prosperity, 20
Which, when ye wake from the last sleep,
 shall turn
To cowls and robes of everlasting fire.
But, as I am, I bid ye grudge me not
The only earthly favor ye can yield,

Or I think worth acceptance at your
 hands, —
Scorn, mutilation and imprisonment.
 Even as my Master did,
Until Heaven's kingdom shall descend on
 earth,
Or earth be like a shadow in the light
Of Heaven absorbed. Some few tumultu-
 ous years 30
Will pass, and leave no wreck of what op-
 poses
His will whose will is power.

LAUD

Officer, take the prisoner from the bar,
And be his tongue slit for his insolence.

BASTWICK

While this hand holds a pen —

LAUD

 Be his hands —

JUXON

 Stop!
Forbear, my lord! The tongue, which
 now can speak
No terror, would interpret, being dumb,
Heaven's thunder to our harm; . . .
And hands, which now write only their own
 shame
With bleeding stumps might sign our blood
 away. 40

LAUD

Much more such 'mercy' among men
 would be,
Did all the ministers of Heaven's revenge
Flinch thus from earthly retribution. I
Could suffer what I would inflict.
 [*Exit* BASTWICK *guarded.*
 Bring up
The Lord Bishop of Lincoln. —
 (*To* STRAFFORD)
 Know you not
That, in distraining for ten thousand pounds
Upon his books and furniture at Lincoln,
Were found these scandalous and seditious
 letters 48
Sent from one Osbaldistone, who is fled?
I speak it not as touching this poor person;
But of the office which should make it holy,
Were it as vile as it was ever spotless.
Mark too, my lord, that this expression
 strikes
His Majesty, if I misinterpret not.

Enter BISHOP WILLIAMS *guarded*

STRAFFORD

'T were politic and just that Williams taste
The bitter fruit of his connection with
The schismatics. But you, my Lord Arch-
 bishop,
Who owed your first promotion to his favor,
Who grew beneath his smile —

LAUD

 Would therefore beg
The office of his judge from this High
 Court, — 60
That it shall seem, even as it is, that I,
In my assumption of this sacred robe,
Have put aside all worldly preference,
All sense of all distinction of all persons,
All thoughts but of the service of the
 Church. —
Bishop of Lincoln!

WILLIAMS

 Peace, proud hierarch!
I know my sentence, and I own it just.
Thou wilt repay me less than I deserve
In stretching to the utmost

.

SCENE IV. — HAMPDEN, PYM, CROMWELL, *his
 Daughter, and young* SIR HARRY VANE.

HAMPDEN

England, farewell! Thou, who hast been
 my cradle,
Shalt never be my dungeon or my grave!
I held what I inherited in thee
As pawn for that inheritance of freedom
Which thou hast sold for thy despoiler's
 smile.
How can I call thee England, or my coun-
 try? —
Does the wind hold?

VANE

 The vanes sit steady
Upon the Abbey towers. The silver light-
 nings
Of the evening star, spite of the city's
 smoke,
Tell that the north wind reigns in the upper
 air. 10
Mark too that fleet of fleecy-wingèd clouds
Sailing athwart St. Margaret's.

HAMPDEN

Hail, fleet herald
Of tempest! that rude pilot who shall
 guide
Hearts free as his, to realms as pure as
 thee,
Beyond the shot of tyranny,
Beyond the webs of that swoln spider . . .
Beyond the curses, calumnies, and [lies?]
Of atheist priests! And thou
Fair star, whose beam lies on the wide At-
 lantic, 19
Athwart its zones of tempest and of calm,
Bright as the path to a belovèd home,
Oh, light us to the isles of the evening
 land!
Like floating Edens cradled in the glimmer
Of sunset, through the distant mist of years
Touched by departing hope, they gleam!
 lone regions,
Where power's poor dupes and victims yet
 have never
Propitiated the savage fear of kings
With purest blood of noblest hearts; whose
 dew
Is yet unstained with tears of those who
 wake
To weep each day the wrongs on which it
 dawns; 30
Whose sacred silent air owns yet no echo
Of formal blasphemies; nor impious rites
Wrest man's free worship, from the God
 who loves,
To the poor worm who envies us his love!
Receive, thou young of Paradise,
These exiles from the old and sinful world!

.

This glorious clime, this firmament, whose
 lights
Dart mitigated influence through their
 veil
Of pale blue atmosphere; whose tears keep
 green
The pavement of this moist all-feeding
 earth; 40
This vaporous horizon, whose dim round
Is bastioned by the circumfluous sea,
Repelling invasion from the sacred
 towers, —
Presses upon me like a dungeon's grate,
A low dark roof, a damp and narrow wall.
The boundless universe
Becomes a cell too narrow for the soul
That owns no master; while the loathliest
 ward

Of this wide prison, England, is a nest
Of cradling peace built on the mountain
 tops, — 50
To which the eagle spirits of the free,
Which range through heaven and earth,
 and scorn the storm
Of time, and gaze upon the light of truth,
Return to brood on thoughts that cannot
 die
And cannot be repelled.
Like eaglets floating in the heaven of time,
They soar above their quarry, and shall
 stoop
Through palaces and temples thunder-
 proof.

SCENE V

ARCHY

I'll go live under the ivy that overgrows
the terrace, and count the tears shed on its
old [roots?] as the [wind?] plays the song
of

'A widow bird sate mourning
 Upon a wintry bough.'

(*Sings*)

Heigho! the lark and the owl!
 One flies the morning, and one lulls
 the night;
Only the nightingale, poor fond soul,
 Sings like the fool through darkness
 and light.

'A widow bird sate mourning for her
 love 10
 Upon a wintry bough;
The frozen wind crept on above,
 The freezing stream below.

'There was no leaf upon the forest bare,
 No flower upon the ground,
And little motion in the air
 Except the mill-wheel's sound.'

FRAGMENTS OF AN UNFIN-
ISHED DRAMA

Date 1821–22. Published in part by Mrs.
Shelley, 1824, and the remainder by Garnett,
1862, and Rossetti, 1870. Mrs. Shelley writes:
'The following fragments are part of a drama,
undertaken for the amusement of the individ-
uals who composed our intimate society, but

left unfinished. I have preserved a sketch of the story, so far as it had been shadowed out in the poet's mind.' It is possibly connected with the project of a play on Trelawny's career. Garnett gives a note on the portion which he called *The Magic Plant*. 'A close scrutiny, however, of one of Shelley's MS. books has revealed the existence of much more of this piece than has hitherto been suspected to exist. By far the larger portion of this, forming an episode complete in itself, is here made public, under the title of *The Magic Plant*. . . . The little drama of which this charming sport of fancy forms a portion was written at Pisa during the late winter or early spring of 1822. The episode of *The Magic Plant* was obviously suggested by the pleasure Shelley received from the plants grown indoors in his Pisan dwelling, which he says in a letter written in January, 1822, " turn the sunny winter into spring." See also the poem of *The Zucca*, composed about the same time.'

[An Enchantress, living in one of the islands of the Indian Archipelago, saves the life of a Pirate, a man of savage but noble nature. She becomes enamoured of him; and he, inconstant to his mortal love, for a while returns her passion : but at length, recalling the memory of her whom he left, and who laments his loss, he escapes from the enchanted island, and returns to his lady. His mode of life makes him again go to sea, and the Enchantress seizes the opportunity to bring him, by a spirit-brewed tempest, back to her island.]

SCENE — *Before the Cavern of the Indian Enchantress. The* ENCHANTRESS *comes forth.*

ENCHANTRESS

HE came like a dream in the dawn of life,
 He fled like a shadow before its noon;
He is gone, and my peace is turned to strife,
 And I wander and wane like the weary moon.
 O sweet Echo, wake,
 And for my sake
Make answer the while my heart shall break !

But my heart has a music which Echo's lips,
 Though tender and true, yet can answer not,
And the shadow that moves in the soul's eclipse 10
 Can return not the kiss by his now forgot;

Sweet lips ! he who hath
 On my desolate path
Cast the darkness of absence, worse than death !

(*The* ENCHANTRESS *makes her spell : she is answered by a Spirit*)

SPIRIT

Within the silent centre of the earth
My mansion is; where I have lived insphered
From the beginning, and around my sleep
Have woven all the wondrous imagery
Of this dim spot, which mortals call the world;
Infinite depths of unknown elements 20
Massed into one impenetrable mask;
Sheets of immeasurable fire, and veins
Of gold and stone, and adamantine iron.
And as a veil in which I walk through Heaven
I have wrought mountains, seas, and waves, and clouds,
And lastly light, whose interfusion dawns
In the dark space of interstellar air.

.

[A good Spirit, who watches over the Pirate's fate, leads, in a mysterious manner, the lady of his love to the Enchanted Isle. She is accompanied by a youth, who loves the lady, but whose passion she returns only with a sisterly affection. The ensuing scene takes place between them on their arrival at the Isle.]

INDIAN YOUTH *and* LADY

INDIAN

And, if my grief should still be dearer to me
Than all the pleasures in the world beside,
Why would you lighten it ? —

LADY

 I offer only
That which I seek, some human sympathy
In this mysterious island.

INDIAN

 Oh, my friend,
My sister, my belovèd ! — What do I say ?
My brain is dizzy, and I scarce know whether
I speak to thee or her.

LADY

 Peace, perturbèd heart !
I am to thee only as thou to mine,

The passing wind which heals the brow at
 noon,
And may strike cold into the breast at night,
Yet cannot linger where it soothes the most,
Or long soothe could it linger.

 INDIAN

 But you said
You also loved ?

 LADY

 Loved ! Oh, I love. Methinks
This word of love is fit for all the world, 42
And that for gentle hearts another name
Would speak of gentler thoughts than the
 world owns.
I have loved.

 INDIAN

 And thou lovest not ? if so
Young as thou art thou canst afford to weep.

 LADY

Oh, would that I could claim exemption
From all the bitterness of that sweet name.
I loved, I love, and when I love no more
Let joys and grief perish, and leave de-
 spair 50
To ring the knell of youth. He stood be-
 side me,
The embodied vision of the brightest dream,
Which like a dawn heralds the day of life;
The shadow of his presence made my world
A paradise. All familiar things he touched,
All common words he spoke, became to me
Like forms and sounds of a diviner world.
He was as is the sun in his fierce youth,
As terrible and lovely as a tempest; 59
He came, and went, and left me what I am.
Alas ! Why must I think how oft we two
Have sate together near the river springs,
Under the green pavilion which the willow
Spreads on the floor of the unbroken foun-
 tain,
Strewn, by the nurslings that linger there,
Over that islet paved with flowers and
 moss, —
While the musk-rose leaves, like flakes of
 crimson snow,
Showered on us, and the dove mourned in
 the pine,
Sad prophetess of sorrows not her own ? 69
The crane returned to her unfrozen haunt,
And the false cuckoo bade the spray good
 morn;
And on a wintry bough the widowed bird,

Hid in the deepest night of ivy-leaves,
Renewed the vigils of a sleepless sorrow.
I, left like her, and leaving one like her,
Alike abandoned and abandoning
(Oh ! unlike her in this !) the gentlest
 youth,
Whose love had made my sorrows dear to
 him,
Even as my sorrow made his love to me !

 INDIAN

One curse of Nature stamps in the same
 mould 80
The features of the wretched; and they are
As like as violet to violet,
When memory, the ghost, their odors keeps
Mid the cold relics of abandoned joy. —
Proceed.

 LADY

 He was a simple innocent boy.
I loved him well, but not as he desired;
Yet even thus he was content to be: —
A short content, for I was . . .

 INDIAN (*aside*)

 God of heaven !
From such an islet, such a river-spring . . . !
I dare not ask her if there stood upon it 90
A pleasure-dome, surmounted by a cres-
 cent,
With steps to the blue water. (*Aloud*) It
 may be
That Nature masks in life several copies
Of the same lot, so that the sufferers
May feel another's sorrow as their own
And find in friendship what they lost in
 love.
That cannot be: yet it is strange that we,
From the same scene, by the same path to
 this
Realm of abandonment . . . But speak !
 your breath —
Your breath is like soft music, your words
 are 100
The echoes of a voice which on my heart
Sleeps like a melody of early days.
But as you said —

 LADY

 He was so awful, yet
So beautiful in mystery and terror,
Calming me as the loveliness of heaven
Soothes the unquiet sea: — and yet not so,
For he seemed stormy, and would often
 seem

A quenchless sun masked in portentous
 clouds;
For such his thoughts, and even his actions
 were; 109
But he was not of them, nor they of him,
But as they hid his splendor from the
 earth.
Some said he was a man of blood and peril,
And steeped in bitter infamy to the lips.
More need was there I should be innocent,
More need that I should be most true and
 kind,
And much more need that there should be
 found one
To share remorse, and scorn and solitude,
And all the ills that wait on those who do
The tasks of ruin in the world of life.
He fled, and I have followed him.

<center>INDIAN</center>

 Such a one
Is he who was the winter of my peace. 121
But, fairest stranger, when didst thou de-
 part
From the far hills where rise the springs of
 India ?
How didst thou pass the intervening sea ?

<center>LADY</center>

If I be sure I am not dreaming now,
I should not doubt to say it was a dream.
Methought a star came down from heaven,
And rested mid the plants of India,
Which I had given a shelter from the frost
Within my chamber. There the meteor
 lay, 130
Panting forth light among the leaves and
 flowers,
As if it lived, and was outworn with speed;
Or that it loved, and passion made the
 pulse
Of its bright life throb like an anxious
 heart,
Till it diffused itself, and all the chamber
And walls seemed melted into emerald fire
That burned not ; in the midst of which
 appeared
A spirit like a child, and laughed aloud
A thrilling peal of such sweet merriment
As made the blood tingle in my warm
 feet; 140
Then bent over a vase, and murmuring
Low, unintelligible melodies,
Placed something in the mould like melon-
 seeds,

And slowy faded, and in place of it
A soft hand issued from the veil of fire,
Holding a cup like a magnolia flower,
And poured upon the earth within the vase
The element with which it overflowed,
Brighter than morning light and purer
 than
The water of the springs of Himalah. 150

<center>INDIAN</center>

You waked not ?

<center>LADY</center>

 Not until my dream became
Like a child's legend on the tideless sand,
Which the first foam erases half, and half
Leaves legible. At length I rose, and went,
Visiting my flowers from pot to pot, and
 thought
To set new cuttings in the empty urns,
And when I came to that beside the lat-
 tice,
I saw two little dark-green leaves
Lifting the light mould at their birth, and
 then 159
I half-remembered my forgotten dream.
And day by day, green as a gourd in June,
The plant grew fresh and thick, yet no one
 knew
What plant it was; its stem and tendrils
 seemed
Like emerald snakes, mottled and dia-
 monded
With azure mail and streaks of woven
 silver;
And all the sheaths that folded the dark
 buds
Rose like the crest of cobra-di-capel,
Until the golden eye of the bright flower
Through the dark lashes of those veinèd
 lids,
Disencumbered of their silent sleep, 170
Gazed like a star into the morning light.
Its leaves were delicate, you almost saw
The pulses
With which the purple velvet flower was
 fed
To overflow, and, like a poet's heart
Changing bright fancy to sweet sentiment,
Changed half the light to fragrance. It
 soon fell,
And to a green and dewy embryo-fruit
Left all its treasured beauty. Day by day
I nursed the plant, and on the double flute
Played to it on the sunny winter days 181

Soft melodies, as sweet as April rain
On silent leaves, and sang those words in
 which
Passion makes Echo taunt the sleeping
 strings;
And I would send tales of forgotten love
Late into the lone night, and sing wild songs
Of maids deserted in the olden time,
And weep like a soft cloud in April's bosom
Upon the sleeping eyelids of the plant,
So that perhaps it dreamed that Spring was
 come, 190
And crept abroad into the moonlight air,
And loosened all its limbs, as, noon by noon,
The sun averted less his oblique beam.

<div align="center">INDIAN</div>

And the plant died not in the frost ?

<div align="center">LADY</div>

 It grew;
And went out of the lattice which I left
Half open for it, trailing its quaint spires
Along the garden and across the lawn,
And down the slope of moss and through
 the tufts
Of wild-flower roots, and stumps of trees
 o'ergrown 199
With simple lichens, and old hoary stones,
On to the margin of the glassy pool,
Even to a nook of unblown violets
And lilies-of-the-valley yet unborn,
Under a pine with ivy overgrown.
And there its fruit lay like a sleeping lizard
Under the shadows; but when Spring in-
 deed
Came to unswathe her infants, and the
 lilies
Peeped from their bright green masks to
 wonder at
This shape of autumn couched in their re-
 cess,
Then it dilated, and it grew until 210
One half lay floating on the fountain wave,
Whose pulse, elapsed in unlike sympathies,
Kept time
Among the snowy water-lily buds.
Its shape was such as summer melody
Of the south wind in spicy vales might
 give
To some light cloud bound from the golden
 dawn
To fairy isles of evening, and it seemed
In hue and form that it had been a mirror
Of all the hues and forms around it and

Upon it pictured by the sunny beams 221
Which, from the bright vibrations of the
 pool,
Were thrown upon the rafters and the roof
Of boughs and leaves, and on the pillared
 stems
Of the dark sylvan temple, and reflections
Of every infant flower and star of moss
And veined leaf in the azure odorous air.
And thus it lay in the Elysian calm
Of its own beauty, floating on the line
Which, like a film in purest space, divided
The heaven beneath the water from the
 heaven 231
Above the clouds; and every day I went
Watching its growth and wondering;
And as the day grew hot, methought I saw
A glassy vapor dancing on the pool,
And on it little quaint and filmy shapes,
With dizzy motion, wheel and rise and fall,
Like clouds of gnats with perfect linea-
 ments.

.

O friend, sleep was a veil uplift from
 heaven —
As if heaven dawned upon the world of
 dream — 240
When darkness rose on the extinguished
 day
Out of the eastern wilderness.

<div align="center">INDIAN</div>

 I too
Have found a moment's paradise in sleep
Half compensate a hell of waking sorrow.

THE TRIUMPH OF LIFE

The circumstances of this poem are described
by Mrs. Shelley in words that should always
accompany the verse because of the clearness
with which they render the scene of Shelley's
last composition : ' In the wild but beautiful
Bay of Spezzia the winds and waves which he
loved became his playmates. His days were
chiefly spent on the water ; the management
of his boat, its alterations and improvements,
were his principal occupations. At night,
when the unclouded moon shone on the calm
sea, he often went alone in his little shallop to
the rocky caves that bordered it, and sitting
beneath their shelter wrote *The Triumph of
Life*, the last of his productions. The beauty
but strangeness of this lonely place, the refined
pleasure which he felt in the companionship of
a few selected friends, our entire sequestration

from the rest of the world, all contributed to render this period of his life one of continued enjoyment. I am convinced that the two months we passed there were the happiest he had ever known. . . .

'At first the fatal boat had not arrived, and was expected with great impatience. On Monday, May 12th, it came. Williams records the long wished for fact in his journal: "Cloudy and threatening weather. M. Maglian called, and after dinner and while walking with him on the terrace, we discovered a strange sail coming round the point of Porto Venere, which proved at length to be Shelley's boat. She had left Genoa on Thursday last, but had been driven back by the prevailing bad winds. A Mr. Heslop and two English seamen brought her round, and they speak most highly of her performances. She does indeed excite my surprise and admiration. Shelley and I walked to Lerici, and made a stretch off the land to try her; and I find she fetches whatever she looks at. In short, we have now a perfect plaything for the summer." — It was thus that short-sighted mortals welcomed death, he having disguised his grim form in a pleasing mask! The time of the friends was now spent on the sea; the weather became fine, and our whole party often passed the evenings on the water, when the wind promised pleasant sailing. Shelley and Williams made longer excursions; they sailed several times to Massa; they had engaged one of the seamen who brought her round, a boy, by name Charles Vivian; and they had not the slightest apprehension of danger. When the weather was unfavorable, they employed themselves with alterations in the rigging, and by building a boat of canvas and reeds, as light as possible, to have on board the other, for the convenience of landing in waters too shallow for the larger vessel. When Shelley was on board, he had his papers with him; and much of the *Triumph of Life* was written as he sailed or weltered on that sea which was soon to engulf him.'

The fragment was published by Mrs. Shelley, 1824; she describes it as 'in so unfinished a state that I arranged it in its present form with the greatest difficulty.'

SWIFT as a spirit hastening to his task
Of glory and of good, the Sun sprang forth
Rejoicing in his splendor, and the mask

Of darkness fell from the awakened Earth;
The smokeless altars of the mountain snows
Flamed above crimson clouds, and at the birth

Of light the Ocean's orison arose,
To which the birds tempered their matin lay.
All flowers in field or forest, which unclose

Their trembling eyelids to the kiss of day,
Swinging their censers in the element, 11
With orient incense lit by the new ray

Burned slow and inconsumably, and sent
Their odorous sighs up to the smiling air;
And, in succession due, did continent,

Isle, ocean, and all things that in them wear
The form and character of mortal mould,
Rise, as the Sun their father rose, to bear

Their portion of the toil which he of old
Took as his own and then imposed on them. 20
But I, whom thoughts which must remain untold

Had kept as wakeful as the stars that gem
The cone of night, now they were laid asleep
Stretched my faint limbs beneath the hoary stem

Which an old chestnut flung athwart the steep
Of a green Apennine. Before me fled
The night; behind me rose the day; the deep

Was at my feet, and Heaven above my head; —
When a strange trance over my fancy grew
Which was not slumber, for the shade it spread 30

Was so transparent that the scene came through,
As clear as when a veil of light is drawn
O'er evening hills they glimmer; and I knew

That I had felt the freshness of that dawn
Bathe in the same cold dew my brow and hair,
And sate as thus upon that slope of lawn

Under the self-same bough, and heard as there

The birds, the fountains and the ocean hold
Sweet talk in music through the enamoured
 air. 39
And then a vision on my brain was rolled.

As in that trance of wondrous thought I lay,
This was the tenor of my waking dream.
Methought I sate beside a public way

Thick strewn with summer dust; and a
 great stream
Of people there was hurrying to and fro,
Numerous as gnats upon the evening
 gleam, —

All hastening onward, yet none seemed to
 know
Whither he went, or whence he came, or
 why
He made one of the multitude, and so

Was borne amid the crowd, as through the
 sky 50
One of the million leaves of summer's bier.
Old age and youth, manhood and infancy,

Mixed in one mighty torrent did appear;
Some flying from the thing they feared,
 and some
Seeking the object of another's fear;

And others, as with steps towards the tomb,
Pored on the trodden worms that crawled
 beneath;
And others mournfully within the gloom

Of their own shadow walked, and called it
 death;
And some fled from it as it were a ghost,
Half fainting in the affliction of vain
 breath; 61

But more, with motions which each other
 crossed,
Pursued or shunned the shadows the clouds
 threw
Or birds within the noonday ether lost,

Upon that path where flowers never
 grew, —
And, weary with vain toil and faint for
 thirst,
Heard not the fountains whose melodious
 dew

Out of their mossy cells forever burst,
Nor felt the breeze which from the forest
 told
Of grassy paths and wood-lawns inter-
 spersed 70

With overarching elms, and caverns cold,
And violet banks where sweet dreams
 brood; but they
Pursued their serious folly as of old.

And, as I gazed, methought that in the way
The throng grew wilder, as the woods of
 June
When the south wind shakes the extin-
 guished day;

And a cold glare, intenser than the noon
But icy cold, obscured with blinding light
The sun, as he the stars. Like the young
 moon —

When on the sunlit limits of the night 80
Her white shell trembles amid crimson air,
And whilst the sleeping tempest gathers
 might —

Doth, as the herald of its coming, bear
The ghost of its dead mother, whose dim
 form
Bends in dark ether from her infant's
 chair; —

So came a chariot on the silent storm
Of its own rushing splendor; and a Shape
So sate within, as one whom years deform,

Beneath a dusky hood and double cape,
Crouching within the shadow of a tomb; 90
And o'er what seemed the head a cloud-
 like crape

Was bent, a dun and faint ethereal gloom
Tempering the light. Upon the chariot-
 beam
A Janus-visaged Shadow did assume

The guidance of that wonder-wingèd team;
The shapes which drew it in thick lightnings
Were lost — I heard alone on the air's soft
 stream

The music of their ever-moving wings.
All the four faces of that charioteer 99
Had their eyes banded; little profit brings

Speed in the van and blindness in the rear,
Nor then avail the beams that quench the
 sun, —
Or that with banded eyes could pierce the
 sphere

Of all that is, has been or will be done;
So ill was the car guided — but it passed
With solemn speed majestically on.

The crowd gave way, and I arose aghast,
Or seemed to rise, so mighty was the
 trance,
And saw, like clouds upon the thunder
 blast,

The million with fierce song and maniac
 dance 110
Raging around. Such seemed the jubilee
As when to greet some conqueror's ad-
 vance

Imperial Rome poured forth her living sea
From senate-house, and forum, and theatre,
When upon the free

Had bound a yoke, which soon they stooped
 to bear.
Nor wanted here the just similitude
Of a triumphal pageant, for, where'er

The chariot rolled, a captive multitude
Was driven; — all those who had grown
 old in power 120
Or misery; all who had their age subdued

By action or by suffering, and whose hour
Was drained to its last sand in weal or woe,
So that the trunk survived both fruit and
 flower;

All those whose fame or infamy must grow
Till the great winter lay the form and
 name
Of this green earth with them forever low;

All but the sacred few who could not tame
Their spirits to the conquerors, but, as soon
As they had touched the world with living
 flame, 130

Fled back like eagles to their native
 noon, —
Or those who put aside the diadem
Of earthly thrones or gems . . .

Were there, of Athens or Jerusalem,
Were neither mid the mighty captives
 seen,
Nor mid the ribald crowd that followed
 them,

Nor those who went before fierce and ob-
 scene.
The wild dance maddens in the van; and
 those
Who lead it, fleet as shadows on the green,

Outspeed the chariot, and without repose
Mix with each other in tempestuous mea-
 sure 141
To savage music, wilder as it grows.

They, tortured by their agonizing pleasure,
Convulsed and on the rapid whirlwinds
 spun
Of that fierce spirit whose unholy leisure

Was soothed by mischief since the world
 begun,
Throw back their heads and loose their
 streaming hair;
And, in their dance round her who dims
 the sun,

Maidens and youths fling their wild arms
 in air
As their feet twinkle; they recede, and
 now, 150
Bending within each other's atmosphere,

Kindle invisibly, and, as they glow,
Like moths by light attracted and repelled,
Oft to their bright destruction come and
 go:

Till, like two clouds into one vale im-
 pelled
That shake the mountains when their light-
 nings mingle
And die in rain, the fiery band which held

Their natures, snaps, while the shock still
 may tingle; —
One falls and then another in the path
Senseless, nor is the desolation single, 160

Yet ere I can say *where*, the chariot hath
Passed over them — nor other trace I
 find
But as of foam after the ocean's wrath

Is spent upon the desert shore. Behind,
Old men and women foully disarrayed
Shake their gray hairs in the insulting
 wind

And follow in the dance, with limbs de-
 cayed,
Seeking to reach the light which leaves
 them still
Farther behind and deeper in the shade.

But not the less with impotence of will 170
They wheel, though ghastly shadows inter-
 pose
Round them and round each other, and
 fulfil

Their work, and in the dust from whence
 they rose
Sink, and corruption veils them as they
 lie,
And past in these performs what in
 those.

Struck to the heart by this sad pageantry,
Half to myself I said — 'And what is
 this ?
Whose shape is that within the car ? And
 why ' —

I would have added — 'is all here
 amiss ? ' —
But a voice answered — ' Life ! ' — I
 turned, and knew 180
(O Heaven, have mercy on such wretched-
 ness !)

That what I thought was an old root which
 grew
To strange distortion of the hillside
Was indeed one of those deluded crew;

And that the grass, which methought hung
 so wide
And white, was but his thin discolored
 hair;
And that the holes he vainly sought to hide

Were or had been eyes: — 'If thou canst,
 forbear
To join the dance, which I had well for-
 borne ! '
Said the grim Feature (of my thought
 aware). 190

' I will unfold that which to this deep scorn
Led me and my companions, and relate
The progress of the pageant since the
 morn.

' If thirst of knowledge shall not then abate,
Follow it thou even to the night; but I
Am weary.' — Then like one who with the
 weight

Of his own words is staggered, wearily
He paused ; and ere he could resume, I
 cried:
' First, who art thou ? ' — ' Before thy mem-
 ory,

' I feared, loved, hated, suffered, did, and
 died, 200
And if the spark with which Heaven lit my
 spirit
Had been with purer nutriment supplied,

' Corruption would not now thus much in-
 herit
Of what was once Rousseau, — nor this
 disguise
Stain that which ought to have disdained
 to wear it;

' If I have been extinguished, yet there rise
A thousand beacons from the spark I
 bore ' —
' And who are those chained to the car ? '
 ' The wise,

' The great, the unforgotten, — they who
 wore
Mitres and helms and crowns, or wreaths
 of light, 210
Signs of thought's empire over thought;
 their lore

' Taught them not this, to know themselves;
 their might
Could not repress the mystery within,
And, for the morn of truth they feigned,
 deep night

' Caught them ere evening.' ' Who is he
 with chin
Upon his breast, and hands crossed on his
 chain ? '
' The child of a fierce hour; he sought to
 win

'The world, and lost all that it did contain
Of greatness, in its hope destroyed; and
more
Of fame and peace than virtue's self can
gain 220

'Without the opportunity which bore
Him on its eagle pinions to the peak
From which a thousand climbers have be-
fore

'Fallen, as Napoleon fell.' — I felt my
cheek
Alter, to see the shadow pass away,
Whose grasp had left the giant world so
weak

That every pigmy kicked it as it lay;
And much I grieved to think how power
and will
In opposition rule our mortal day,

And why God made irreconcilable 230
Good and the means of good; and for de-
spair
I half disdained mine eyes' desire to fill

With the spent vision of the times that
were
And scarce have ceased to be. 'Dost thou
behold,'
Said my guide, 'those spoilers spoiled, Vol-
taire,

'Frederick, and Paul, Catherine, and Leo-
pold,
And hoary anarchs, demagogues, and
sage —
 names which the world thinks
always old, 238

'For in the battle Life and they did wage,
She remained conqueror. I was overcome
By my own heart alone, which neither
age,

'Nor tears, nor infamy, nor now the tomb,
Could temper to its object.' — 'Let them
pass,'
I cried, 'the world and its mysterious
doom

'Is not so much more glorious than it was
That I desire to worship those who drew
New figures on its false and fragile glass

'As the old faded.' — 'Figures ever new
Rise on the bubble, paint them as you
may;
We have but thrown, as those before us
threw, 250

'Our shadows on it as it passed away.
But mark how chained to the triumphal
chair
The mighty phantoms of an elder day;

'All that is mortal of great Plato there
Expiates the joy and woe his Master knew
not;
The star that ruled his doom was far too
fair,

'And life, where long that flower of Hea-
ven grew not,
Conquered that heart by love, which gold,
or pain,
Or age, or sloth, or slavery, could subdue
not.

'And near him walk the twain, 260
The tutor and his pupil, whom Dominion
Followed as tame as vulture in a chain.

'The world was darkened beneath either
pinion
Of him whom from the flock of conquerors
Fame singled out for her thunder-bearing
minion;

'The other long outlived both woes and
wars,
Throned in the thoughts of men, and still
had kept
The jealous key of truth's eternal doors,

'If Bacon's eagle spirit had not leapt
Like lightning out of darkness — he com-
pelled 270
The Proteus shape of Nature, as it slept,

'To wake, and lead him to the caves that
held
The treasure of the secrets of its reign.
See the great bards of elder time, who
quelled

'The passions which they sung, as by their
strain
May well be known: their living melody
Tempers its own contagion to the vein

'Of those who are infected with it. I
Have suffered what I wrote, or viler
 pain ! 279
And so my words have seeds of misery —

.

'Even as the deeds of others, not as theirs.'
And then he pointed to a company,

'Midst whom I quickly recognized the
 heirs
Of Cæsar's crime, from him to Constan-
 tine;
The anarch chiefs, whose force and mur-
 derous snares

Had founded many a sceptre-bearing line,
And spread the plague of gold and blood
 abroad;
And Gregory and John, and men divine,

Who rose like shadows between man and
 God,
Till that eclipse, still hanging over heaven,
Was worshipped, by the world o'er which
 they strode, 291

For the true sun it quenched. 'Their
 power was given
But to destroy,' replied the leader: — 'I
Am one of those who have created, even

'If it be but a world of agony.'
'Whence camest thou ? and whither goest
 thou ?
How did thy course begin ?' I said, 'and
 why ?

'Mine eyes are sick of this perpetual
 flow
Of people, and my heart sick of one sad
 thought —
Speak !' — 'Whence I am, I partly seem
 to know, 300

'And how and by what paths I have been
 brought
To this dread pass, methinks even thou
 mayst guess.
Why this should be, my mind can compass
 not;

'Whither the conqueror hurries me, still
 less.
But follow thou, and from spectator turn
Actor or victim in this wretchedness;

'And what thou wouldst be taught I then
 may learn
From thee. Now listen: — In the April
 prime,
When all the forest tips began to burn

'With kindling green, touched by the
 azure clime 310
Of the young season, I was laid asleep
Under a mountain, which from unknown
 time

'Had yawned into a cavern, high and deep;
And from it came a gentle rivulet,
Whose water, like clear air, in its calm
 sweep

'Bent the soft grass, and kept forever
 wet
The stems of the sweet flowers, and filled
 the grove
With sounds which whoso hears must needs
 forget

'All pleasure and all pain, all hate and
 love,
Which they had known before that hour of
 rest. 320
A sleeping mother then would dream not of

'Her only child who died upon the breast
At eventide; a king would mourn no more
The crown of which his brows were dispos-
 sessed

'When the sun lingered o'er his ocean floor
To gild his rival's new prosperity;
Thou wouldst forget thus vainly to deplore

'Ills, which, if ills, can find no cure from
 thee,
The thought of which no other sleep will
 quell,
Nor other music blot from memory, — 330

'So sweet and deep is the oblivious spell;
And whether life had been before that
 sleep
The heaven which I imagine, or a hell

'Like this harsh world in which I wake to
 weep,
I know not. I arose, and for a space
The scene of woods and waters seemed to
 keep,

'Though it was now broad day, a gentle
 trace
Of light diviner than the common sun
Sheds on the common earth, and all the
 place

'Was filled with magic sounds woven into
 one 340
Oblivious melody, confusing sense
Amid the gliding waves and shadows dun;

'And, as I looked, the bright omnipre-
 sence
Of morning through the orient cavern
 flowed,
And the sun's image radiantly intense

'Burned on the waters of the well that
 glowed
Like gold, and threaded all the forest's
 maze
With winding paths of emerald fire. There
 stood

'Amid the sun, as he amid the blaze
Of his own glory, on the vibrating 350
Floor of the fountain, paved with flashing
 rays,

'A Shape all light, which with one hand
 did fling
Dew on the earth, as if she were the dawn,
And the invisible rain did ever sing

'A silver music on the mossy lawn;
And still before me on the dusky grass,
Iris her many-colored scarf had drawn:

'In her right hand she bore a crystal glass,
Mantling with bright nepenthe; the fierce
 splendor
Fell from her as she moved under the
 mass 360

'Of the deep cavern, and, with palms so
 tender
Their tread broke not the mirror of its
 billow,
Glided along the river, and did bend her

'Head under the dark boughs, till like a
 willow,
Her fair hair swept the bosom of the stream
That whispered with delight to be its pil-
 low.

'As one enamoured is upborne in dream
O'er lily-paven lakes mid silver mist,
To wondrous music, so this Shape might
 seem

'Partly to tread the waves with feet which
 kissed 370
The dancing foam; partly to glide along
The air which roughened the moist ame-
 thyst,

'Or the faint morning beams that fell
 among
The trees, or the soft shadows of the trees;
And her feet, ever to the ceaseless song

'Of leaves and winds and waves and birds
 and bees
And falling drops, moved in a measure new,
Yet sweet, as on the summer evening
 breeze

'Up from the lake a shape of golden dew
Between two rocks, athwart the rising
 moon, 380
Dances i' the wind, where never eagle flew;

'And still her feet, no less than the sweet
 tune
To which they moved, seemed as they
 moved to blot
The thoughts of him who gazed on them;
 and soon

'All that was seemed as if it had been not;
And all the gazer's mind was strewn be-
 neath
Her feet like embers; and she, thought by
 thought,

'Trampled its sparks into the dust of death,
As Day upon the threshold of the east
Treads out the lamps of night, until the
 breath 390

'Of darkness reillumine even the least
Of heaven's living eyes; like day she came,
Making the night a dream; and ere she
 ceased

'To move, as one between desire and
 shame
Suspended, I said — "If, as it doth seem,
Thou comest from the realm without a
 name,

' "Into this valley of perpetual dream,
Show whence I came, and where I am, and
 why —
Pass not away upon the passing stream."

' " Arise and quench thy thirst," was her
 reply. 400
And, as a shut lily stricken by the wand
Of dewy morning's vital alchemy,

' I rose; and, bending at her sweet com-
 mand,
Touched with faint lips the cup she raised,
And suddenly my brain became as sand

' Where the first wave had more than half
 erased
The track of deer on desert Labrador,
Whilst the wolf, from which they fled
 amazed,

' Leaves his stamp visibly upon the shore
Until the second bursts; — so on my sight
Burst a new Vision, never seen before, 411

' And the fair Shape waned in the coming
 light,
As veil by veil the silent splendor drops
From Lucifer, amid the chrysolite

' Of sunrise, ere it tinge the mountain tops;
And as the presence of that fairest planet,
Although unseen, is felt by one who hopes

' That his day's path may end, as he be-
 gan it,
In that star's smile whose light is like the
 scent 419
Of a jonquil when evening breezes fan it,

' Or the soft note in which his dear lament
The Brescian shepherd breathes, or the
 caress
That turned his weary slumber to con-
 tent, —

' So knew I in that light's severe excess
The presence of that Shape which on the
 stream
Moved, as I moved along the wilderness,

' More dimly than a day-appearing dream,
The ghost of a forgotten form of sleep,
A light of heaven whose half-extinguished
 beam

' Through the sick day, in which we wake
 to weep, 430
Glimmers, forever sought, forever lost;
So did that Shape its obscure tenor keep

' Beside my path, as silent as a ghost.
But the new Vision, and the cold bright car,
With solemn speed and stunning music,
 crossed

' The forest; and, as if from some dread
 war
Triumphantly returning, the loud million
Fiercely extolled the fortune of her star.

' A moving arch of victory, the vermilion
And green and azure plumes of Iris had 440
Built high over her wind-wingèd pavilion;

' And underneath ethereal glory clad
The wilderness; and far before her flew
The tempest of the splendor, which for-
 bade

' Shadow to fall from leaf and stone. The
 crew
Seemed in that light, like atomies to dance
Within a sunbeam. Some upon the new

' Embroidery of flowers, that did enhance
The grassy vesture of the desert, played,
Forgetful of the chariot's swift advance; 450

' Others stood gazing, till within the shade
Of the great mountain its light left them
 dim;
Others outspeeded it; and others made

' Circles around it, like the clouds that swim
Round the high moon in a bright sea of air;
And more did follow, with exulting hymn,

' The chariot and the captives fettered there;
But all like bubbles on an eddying flood
Fell into the same track at last, and were

' Borne onward. I among the multitude
Was swept. Me sweetest flowers delayed
 not long; 461
Me not the shadow nor the solitude;

' Me not that falling stream's Lethean
 song;
Me not the phantom of that early Form
Which moved upon its motion; but among

'The thickest billows of that living storm
I plunged, and bared my bosom to the
 clime
Of that cold light, whose airs too soon de-
 form.

'Before the chariot had begun to climb
The opposing steep of that mysterious dell,
Behold a wonder worthy of the rhyme 471

'Of him who from the lowest depths of hell,
Through every paradise and through all
 glory,
Love led serene, and who returned to tell

'The words of hate and awe, — the won-
 drous story
How all things are transfigured except
 Love;
For deaf as is a sea which wrath makes
 hoary,

'The world can hear not the sweet notes
 that move
The sphere whose light is melody to
 lovers, —
A wonder worthy of his rhyme. The grove

'Grew dense with shadows to the inmost
 covers; 481
The earth was gray with phantoms; and
 the air
Was peopled with dim forms, as when there
 hovers

'A flock of vampire-bats before the glare
Of the tropic sun, bringing, ere evening,
Strange night upon some Indian isle.
 Thus were

'Phantoms diffused around; and some did
 fling
Shadows of shadows, yet unlike themselves,
Behind them; some like eaglets on the
 wing

'Were lost in the white day; others like
 elves 490
Danced in a thousand unimagined shapes
Upon the sunny streams and grassy shelves;

'And others sate chattering like restless
 apes
On vulgar hands, . . .
Some made a cradle of the ermined capes

'Of kingly mantles; some across the tiar
Of pontiffs sate like vultures; others played
Under the crown which girt with empire

'A baby's or an idiot's brow, and made
Their nests in it. The old anatomies 500
Sate hatching their bare broods under the
 shade

'Of demon wings, and laughed from their
 dead eyes
To reassume the delegated power,
Arrayed in which those worms did mon-
 archize

'Who made this earth their charnel.
 Others more
Humble, like falcons, sate upon the fist
Of common men, and round their heads
 did soar;

'Or like small gnats and flies, as thick as
 mist
On evening marshes, thronged about the
 brow 509
Of lawyers, statesmen, priest and theorist;

'And others, like discolored flakes of
 snow,
On fairest bosoms and the sunniest hair,
Fell, and were melted by the youthful
 glow

'Which they extinguished; and, like tears,
 they were
A veil to those from whose faint lids they
 rained
In drops of sorrow. I became aware

'Of whence those forms proceeded which
 thus stained
The track in which we moved. After
 brief space,
From every form the beauty slowly waned;

'From every firmest limb and fairest face
The strength and freshness fell like dust,
 and left 521
The action and the shape without the grace

'Of life. The marble brow of youth was
 cleft
With care; and in those eyes where once
 hope shone,
Desire, like a lioness bereft

'Of her last cub, glared ere it died; each
 one
Of that great crowd sent forth incessantly
These shadows, numerous as the dead
 leaves blown

'In autumn evening from a poplar tree. 529
Each like himself and like each other were
At first; but some, distorted, seemed to be

'Obscure clouds, moulded by the casual
 air;
And of this stuff the car's creative ray
Wrought all the busy phantoms that were
 there,

'As the sun shapes the clouds. Thus on
 the way
Mask after mask fell from the countenance
And form of all; and, long before the day

'Was old, the joy, which waked like
 heaven's glance
The sleepers in the oblivious valley, died;
And some grew weary of the ghastly dance,

'And fell, as I have fallen, by the way-
 side; — 541
Those soonest from whose forms most
 shadows passed,
And least of strength and beauty did abide.'

'Then, what is life? I cried.' —

John Keats

SELECTED POEMS

JOHN KEATS

JOHN KEATS was born in 1795, the son of a livery stable manager in Moorfields, England. He spent the early portion of his short life studying medicine, first as an apothecary's apprentice, then as a pupil at Guy's Hospital. He received his apothecary license in 1816, but, under the encouragement of Leigh Hunt, Keats decided to leave the profession and turn his full attention to poetry.

In March of 1817 Keats published his first collection of poetry, and in the spring of the next year he published *Endymion*. The extreme criticism both works received from *Blackwood's*, an innovative monthly periodical that had been supportive of Wordsworth and Shelley, had a deeply adverse effect on Keats.

In 1818, Keats travelled extensively in Great Britain. He later moved to Hampstead, where he fell in love with Fanny Brawne. Although ill and plagued by financial troubles, Keats had an inordinately fruitful year beginning in September 1818. During this period, he wrote most of his best work, including "The Eve of St. Agnes," "Ode to Psyche," "Ode to a Nightingale," "Ode on a Grecian Urn," and "The Fall of Hyperion."

In 1820, Keats published the collection *Lamia, Isabella, The Eve of St. Agnes, and Other Poems* to considerable critical praise. Keats died in 1821 of tuberculosis during a visit to Rome.

EARLY POEMS

In this group are included the contents of the volume *Poems by John Keats*, published in March, 1817, as well as certain poems composed before the publication of *Endymion*. The order followed is as nearly chronological as the evidence permits.

IMITATION OF SPENSER

Lord Houghton states, on the authority of the notes of Charles Armitage Brown, given to him in Florence in 1832, that this was the earliest known composition of Keats, and that it was written during his residence in Edmonton at the end of his eighteenth year, which would make the date in the autumn of 1813. The poem was included in the 1817 volume, which bore on its title-page this motto: —

> What more felicity can fall to creature
> Than to enjoy delight with liberty?
> *Fate of the Butterfly.* — SPENSER.

.

Now Morning from her orient chamber came,
And her first footsteps touch'd a verdant hill;
Crowning its lawny crest with amber flame,
Silv'ring the untainted gushes of its rill;
Which, pure from mossy beds, did down distil,
And after parting beds of simple flowers,
By many streams a little lake did fill,
Which round its marge reflected woven bowers,
And, in its middle space, a sky that never lowers.

There the kingfisher saw his plumage bright,
Vying with fish of brilliant dye below;
Whose silken fins' and golden scales' light
Cast upward, through the waves, a ruby glow:
There saw the swan his neck of arched snow,
And oar'd himself along with majesty;
Sparkled his jetty eyes; his feet did show
Beneath the waves like Afric's ebony,
And on his back a fay reclin'd voluptuously.

Ah! could I tell the wonders of an isle
That in that fairest lake had placed been,
I could e'en Dido of her grief beguile;
Or rob from aged Lear his bitter teen:
For sure so fair a place was never seen,
Of all that ever charm'd romantic eye:
It seem'd an emerald in the silver sheen
Of the bright waters; or as when on high,
Through clouds of fleecy white, laughs the cœrulean sky.

And all around it dipp'd luxuriously
Slopings of verdure through the glossy tide,
Which, as it were in gentle amity,
Rippled delighted up the flowery side;
As if to glean the ruddy tears, it tried,
Which fell profusely from the rose-tree stem!
Haply it was the workings of its pride,
In strife to throw upon the shore a gem
Outvying all the buds in Flora's diadem.

.

ON DEATH

Assigned by George Keats to the year 1814, and first printed in Forman's edition, 1883.

Can death be sleep, when life is but a dream,
And scenes of bliss pass as a phantom by?

757

The transient pleasures as a vision seem,
 And yet we think the greatest pain's to
 die.

How strange it is that man on earth should
 roam,
 And lead a life of woe, but not forsake
His rugged path; nor dare he view alone
 His future doom, which is but to awake.

TO CHATTERTON

First printed in *Life, Letters, and Literary
Remains*, but undated. Keats's admiration of
Chatterton was early and constant.

O CHATTERTON! how very sad thy fate!
 Dear child of sorrow — son of misery!
 How soon the film of death obscur'd that
 eye,
Whence Genius mildly flash'd, and high
 debate.
How soon that voice, majestic and elate,
 Melted in dying numbers! Oh! how
 nigh
 Was night to thy fair morning. Thou
 didst die
A half-blown flow'ret which cold blasts
 amate.
But this is past: thou art among the stars
 Of highest Heaven: to the rolling spheres
Thou sweetly singest: nought thy hymning
 mars,
 Above the ingrate world and human
 fears.
On earth the good man base detraction
 bars
 From thy fair name, and waters it with
 tears.

TO BYRON

The date of December, 1814, is given to this
sonnet by Lord Houghton in *Life, Letters, and
Literary Remains*, where it was first published.

BYRON! how sweetly sad thy melody!
 Attuning still the soul to tenderness,

As if soft Pity, with unusual stress,
Had touch'd her plaintive lute, and thou,
 being by,
Hadst caught the tones, nor suffer'd them
 to die.
O'ershadowing sorrow doth not make
 thee less
Delightful: thou thy griefs dost dress
With a bright halo, shining beamily,
As when a cloud the golden moon doth veil,
 Its sides are ting'd with a resplendent
 glow,
Through the dark robe oft amber rays pre-
 vail,
 And like fair veins in sable marble flow;
Still warble, dying swan! still tell the tale,
 The enchanting tale, the tale of pleasing
 woe.

'WOMAN! WHEN I BEHOLD THEE FLIPPANT, VAIN'

In the 1817 volume, where this poem was
first published, with no title, it is placed at
the end of a group of poems which are thus
advertised on the leaf containing the dedica-
tion: 'The Short Pieces in the middle of the
Book as well as some of the Sonnets, were
written at an earlier period than the rest of
the Poems.' In the absence of any documen-
tary evidence, it seems reasonable to place it
near the 'Imitation of Spenser' rather than
near 'Calidore.'

WOMAN! when I behold thee flippant, vain,
 Inconstant, childish, proud, and full of
 fancies;
 Without that modest softening that en-
 hances
The downcast eye, repentant of the pain
That its mild light creates to heal again:
 E'en then, elate, my spirit leaps and
 prances,
 E'en then my soul with exultation dances
For that to love, so long, I've dormant
 lain:
 But when I see thee meek, and kind, and
 tender,

Heavens! how desperately do I adore
Thy winning graces; — to be thy defender
I hotly burn — to be a Calidore —
A very Red Cross Knight — a stout Le-
 ander —
Might I be lov'd by thee like these of
 yore.

Light feet, dark violet eyes, and parted
 hair;
 Soft dimpled hands, white neck, and
 creamy breast,
 Are things on which the dazzled senses
 rest
Till the fond, fixèd eyes forget they stare.
From such fine pictures, Heavens! I cannot
 dare
 To turn my admiration, though unpos-
 sess'd
 They be of what is worthy, — though not
 drest
In lovely modesty, and virtues rare.
Yet these I leave as thoughtless as a lark;
 These lures I straight forget, — e'en ere
 I dine,
Or thrice my palate moisten: but when I
 mark
 Such charms with mild intelligences
 shine,
My ear is open like a greedy shark,
 To catch the tunings of a voice divine.

Ah! who can e'er forget so fair a being?
 Who can forget her half-retiring sweets?
 God! she is like a milk-white lamb that
 bleats
For man's protection. Surely the All-see-
 ing,
Who joys to see us with his gifts agree-
 ing,
 Will never give him pinions, who intreats
 Such innocence to ruin, — who vilely
 cheats
A dove-like bosom. In truth there is no
 freeing
One's thoughts from such a beauty; when
 I hear
 A lay that once I saw her hand awake,

Her form seems floating palpable, and near:
 Had I e'er seen her from an arbour take
A dewy flower, oft would that hand appear,
 And o'er my eyes the trembling moisture
 shake.

TO SOME LADIES

This and the poem following were included
in the 1817 volume. George Keats says fur-
ther that it was 'written on receiving a copy
of Tom Moore's "Golden Chain" and a most
beautiful Dome shaped shell from a Lady.'
The exact title of Moore's poem is 'The
Wreath and the Chain,' and it will be readily
seen how expressly imitative these lines are of
Moore's verse in general. The poems are not
dated, but they are the first in a group stated
by Keats to have been 'written at an earlier
period than the rest of the Poems;' it is safe to
assume that they belong very near the begin-
ning of Keats's poetical career. It is quite
likely that they were included in the volume a
few years later on personal grounds.

WHAT though, while the wonders of nature
 exploring,
 I cannot your light, mazy footsteps at-
 tend;
Nor listen to accents, that almost adoring,
 Bless Cynthia's face, the enthusiast's
 friend:

Yet over the steep, whence the mountain-
 stream rushes,
 With you, kindest friends, in idea I rove;
Mark the clear tumbling crystal, its pas-
 sionate gushes,
 Its spray that the wild flower kindly
 bedews.

Why linger you so, the wild labyrinth
 strolling?
 Why breathless, unable your bliss to de-
 clare?
Ah! you list to the nightingale's tender
 condoling,
 Responsive to sylphs, in the moon-beamy
 air.

'T is morn, and the flowers with dew are
 yet drooping,
 I see you are treading the verge of the
 sea:
And now ! ah, I see it — you just now are
 stooping
 To pick up the keepsake intended for me.

If a cherub, on pinions of silver descending,
 Had brought me a gem from the fret-
 work of Heaven;
And smiles, with his star-cheering voice
 sweetly blending,
 The blessings of Tighe had melodiously
 given;

It had not created a warmer emotion
 Than the present, fair nymphs, I was
 blest with from you;
Than the shell, from the bright golden
 sands of the ocean,
 Which the emerald waves at your feet
 gladly threw.

For, indeed, 't is a sweet and peculiar plea-
 sure,
 (And blissful is he who such happiness
 finds,)
To possess but a span of the hour of leisure,
 In elegant, pure, and aerial minds.

ON RECEIVING A CURIOUS
SHELL AND A COPY OF
VERSES FROM THE SAME
LADIES

Hast thou from the caves of Golconda, a
 gem
 Pure as the ice-drop that froze on the
 mountain ?
Bright as the humming-bird's green diadem,
 When it flutters in sunbeams that shine
 through a fountain ?

Hast thou a goblet for dark sparkling wine ?
 That goblet right heavy, and massy, and
 gold ?

And splendidly mark'd with the story di-
 vine
 Of Armida the fair, and Rinaldo the
 bold ?

Hast thou a steed with a mane richly flow-
 ing ?
 Hast thou a sword that thine enemy's
 smart is ?
Hast thou a trumpet rich melodies blowing ?
 And wear'st thou the shield of the fam'd
 Britomartis ?

What is it that hangs from thy shoulder,
 so brave,
 Embroider'd with many a spring peering
 flower ?
Is it a scarf that thy fair lady gave ?
 And hastest thou now to that fair lady's
 bower ?

Ah ! courteous Sir Knight, with large joy
 thou art crown'd;
 Full many the glories that brighten thy
 youth !
I will tell thee my blisses, which richly
 abound
 In magical powers to bless and to soothe.

On this scroll thou seest written in charac-
 ters fair
 A sun-beaming tale of a wreath, and a
 chain:
And, warrior, it nurtures the property rare
 Of charming my mind from the trammels
 of pain.

This canopy mark: 't is the work of a fay;
 Beneath its rich shade did King Oberon
 languish,
When lovely Titania was far, far away,
 And cruelly left him to sorrow and an-
 guish.

There, oft would he bring from his soft-
 sighing lute
 Wild strains to which, spell-bound, the
 nightingales listen'd !

The wondering spirits of Heaven were mute,
And tears 'mong the dewdrops of morning oft glisten'd.

In this little dome, all those melodies strange,
Soft, plaintive, and melting, for ever will sigh;
Nor e'er will the notes from their tenderness change,
Nor e'er will the music of Oberon die.

So when I am in a voluptuous vein,
I pillow my head on the sweets of the rose,
And list to the tale of the wreath and the chain,
Till its echoes depart; then I sink to repose.

Adieu, valiant Eric! with joy thou art crown'd,
Full many the glories that brighten thy youth;
I too have my blisses, which richly abound
In magical powers to bless, and to soothe.

WRITTEN ON THE DAY THAT MR. LEIGH HUNT LEFT PRISON

Either the 2d or 3d of February, 1815. Charles Cowden Clarke, to whom Keats showed the sonnet, writes in his recollections: 'This I feel to be the first proof I had received of his having committed himself in verse; and how clearly do I recollect the conscious look and hesitation with which he offered it! There are some momentary glances by beloved friends that fade only with life.' The sonnet was printed in the 1817 volume.

WHAT though, for showing truth to flatter'd state,
Kind Hunt was shut in prison, yet has he,
In his immortal spirit, been as free

As the sky-searching lark, and as elate.
Minion of grandeur! think you he did wait?
Think you he nought but prison-walls did see,
Till, so unwilling, thou unturn'dst the key?
Ah, no! far happier, nobler was his fate!
In Spenser's halls he stray'd, and bowers fair,
Culling enchanted flowers; and he flew
With daring Milton through the fields of air:
To regions of his own his genius true
Took happy flights. Who shall his fame impair
When thou art dead, and all thy wretched crew?

TO HOPE

Keats dates this poem in the volume of 1817, February, 1815.

WHEN by my solitary hearth I sit,
And hateful thoughts enwrap my soul in gloom;
When no fair dreams before my 'mind's eye' flit,
And the bare heath of life presents no bloom;
Sweet Hope, ethereal balm upon me shed,
And wave thy silver pinions o'er my head.

Whene'er I wander, at the fall of night,
Where woven boughs shut out the moon's bright ray,
Should sad Despondency my musings fright,
And frown, to drive fair Cheerfulness away,
Peep with the moonbeams through the leafy roof,
And keep that fiend Despondence far aloof.

Should Disappointment, parent of Despair,
 Strive for her son to seize my careless
 heart;
When, like a cloud, he sits upon the air,
 Preparing on his spell-bound prey to
 dart:
 Chase him away, sweet Hope, with
 visage bright,
 And fright him as the morning fright-
 ens night !

Whene'er the fate of those I hold most dear
 Tells to my fearful breast a tale of sorrow,
O bright-eyed Hope, my morbid fancy
 cheer;
 Let me awhile thy sweetest comforts
 borrow:
 Thy heaven-born radiance around me
 shed,
 And wave thy silver pinions o'er my
 head !

Should e'er unhappy love my bosom pain,
 From cruel parents, or relentless fair,
O let me think it is not quite in vain
 To sigh out sonnets to the midnight air !
 Sweet Hope, ethereal balm upon me
 shed,
 And wave thy silver pinions o'er my
 head.

In the long vista of the years to roll,
 Let me not see our country's honour fade:
O let me see our land retain her soul,
 Her pride, her freedom; and not free-
 dom's shade.
 From thy bright eyes unusual bright-
 ness shed —
 Beneath thy pinions canopy my head !

Let me not see the patriot's high bequest,
 Great liberty ! how great in plain attire !
With the base purple of a court oppress'd,
 Bowing her head, and ready to expire:
 But let me see thee stoop from Hea-
 ven on wings
 That fill the skies with silver glitter-
 ings !

And as, in sparkling majesty, a star
 Gilds the bright summit of some gloomy
 cloud;
Brightening the half veil'd face of heaven
 afar:
 So, when dark thoughts my boding spirit
 shroud,
 Sweet Hope, celestial influence round
 me shed,
 Waving thy silver pinions o'er my head.

ODE TO APOLLO

The *Ode* and the *Hymn* which follows were
first printed by Lord Houghton in *Life, Letters
and Literary Remains ;* the former is there
dated February, 1815.

IN thy western halls of gold
 When thou sittest in thy state,
Bards, that erst sublimely told
 Heroic deeds, and sang of fate,
With fervour seize their adamantine
 lyres,
Whose chords are solid rays, and twinkle
 radiant fires.

Here Homer with his nervous arms
 Strikes the twanging harp of war,
And even the western splendour warms,
 While the trumpets sound afar:
But, what creates the most intense sur-
 prise,
His soul looks out through renovated eyes.

Then, through thy Temple wide, melodi-
 ous swells
 The sweet majestic tone of Maro's lyre:
The soul delighted on each accent
 dwells, —
 Enraptur'd dwells, — not daring to re-
 spire,
The while he tells of grief around a funeral
 pyre.

'T is awful silence then again;
 Expectant stand the spheres;
 Breathless the laurell'd peers,

Nor move, till ends the lofty strain,
Nor move till Milton's tuneful thunders
cease,
And leave once more the ravish'd heavens
in peace.

Thou biddest Shakspeare wave his hand,
And quickly forward spring
The Passions — a terrific band —
And each vibrates the string
That with its tyrant temper best accords,
While from their Master's lips pour forth
the inspiring words.

A silver trumpet Spenser blows,
And, as its martial notes to silence flee,
From a virgin chorus flows
A hymn in praise of spotless Chastity.
'T is still! Wild warblings from the
Æolian lyre
Enchantment softly breathe, and trem-
blingly expire.

Next thy Tasso's ardent numbers
Float along the pleasèd air,
Calling youth from idle slumbers,
Rousing them from Pleasure's lair: —
Then o'er the strings his fingers gently
move,
And melt the soul to pity and to love.

But when *Thou* joinest with the Nine,
And all the powers of song combine,
We listen here on earth:
The dying tones that fill the air,
And charm the ear of evening fair,
From thee, Great God of Bards, receive
their heavenly birth.

HYMN TO APOLLO

GOD of the golden bow,
And of the golden lyre,
And of the golden hair,
And of the golden fire,
Charioteer
Of the patient year,

Where — where slept thine ire,
When like a blank idiot I put on thy wreath,
Thy laurel, thy glory,
The light of thy story,
Or was I a worm — too low crawling, for
death ?
O Delphic Apollo !

The Thunderer grasp'd and grasp'd,
The Thunderer frown'd and frown'd;
The eagle's feathery mane
For wrath became stiffen'd — the sound
Of breeding thunder
Went drowsily under,
Muttering to be unbound.
O why didst thou pity, and for a worm
Why touch thy soft lute
Till the thunder was mute,
Why was not I crush'd — such a pitiful
germ ?
O Delphic Apollo !

The Pleiades were up,
Watching the silent air;
The seeds and roots in the Earth
Were swelling for summer fare;
The Ocean, its neighbour,
Was at its old labour,
When, who — who did dare
To tie, like a madman, thy plant round his
brow,
And grin and look proudly,
And blaspheme so loudly,
And live for that honour, to stoop to thee
now ?
O Delphic Apollo !

TO A YOUNG LADY WHO SENT ME A LAUREL CROWN

First printed by Lord Houghton in the *Life,
Letters and Literary Remains*, but undated.

FRESH morning gusts have blown away all
fear
From my glad bosom, — now from gloom-
iness
I mount for ever — not an atom less

Than the proud laurel shall content my
 bier.
No! by the eternal stars! or why sit here
 In the Sun's eye, and 'gainst my temples
 press
Apollo's very leaves, woven to bless
By thy white fingers and thy spirit clear.
Lo! who dares say, 'Do this?' Who dares
 call down
 My will from its high purpose? Who
 say, 'Stand,'
Or 'Go?' This mighty moment I would
 frown
 On abject Cæsars — not the stoutest
 band
Of mailèd heroes should tear off my crown:
 Yet would I kneel and kiss thy gentle
 hand!

SONNET

Published in the 1817 volume. Lord Hough-
ton states that this sonnet 'was the means of
introducing Keats to Mr. Leigh Hunt's society.
Mr. Cowden Clarke had brought some of his
young friend's verses and read them aloud.
Mr. Horace Smith, who happened to be there,
was struck with the last six lines, especially
the penultimate, saying "what a well condensed
expression!" and Keats was shortly after in-
troduced to the literary circle.' This would
appear to fix the date as not later than the
summer of 1815.

How many bards gild the lapses of time!
 A few of them have ever been the food
Of my delighted fancy, — I could brood
Over their beauties, earthly, or sublime:
And often, when I sit me down to rhyme,
 These will in throngs before my mind
 intrude.
But no confusion, no disturbance rude
Do they occasion; 'tis a pleasing chime.
So the unnumber'd sounds that evening
 store;
 The songs of birds — the whispering of
 the leaves —
 The voice of waters — the great bell
 that heaves

With solemn sound, — and thousand others
 more,
That distance of recognizance bereaves,
Make pleasing music, and not wild uproar.

SONNET

According to Charles Cowden Clarke, this
sonnet was written upon Keats first visiting
Hunt in the Vale of Health. It was published
in the 1817 volume.

KEEN, fitful gusts are whisp'ring here and
 there
 Among the bushes, half leafless and dry,
 The stars look very cold about the sky,
And I have many miles on foot to fare.
Yet feel I little of the cool bleak air,
 Or of the dead leaves rustling drearily,
 Or of those silver lamps that burn on
 high,
Or of the distance from home's pleasant
 lair:
For I am brimful of the friendliness
 That in a little cottage I have found;
Of fair-hair'd Milton's eloquent distress,
 And all his love for gentle Lycid drown'd;
Of lovely Laura in her light green dress,
 And faithful Petrarch gloriously crown'd.

SPENSERIAN STANZA

WRITTEN AT THE CLOSE OF CANTO II. BOOK V. OF 'THE FAERIE QUEENE'

Given by Lord Houghton in *Life, Letters and
Literary Remains*, who comments as follows:
'His sympathies were very much on the side
of the revolutionary Giant, who "undertook for
to repair" the "realms and nations run awry,"
and to suppress "tyrants that make men sub-
ject to their law," "and lordings curbe that
commons over-aw," while he grudged the le-
gitimate victory, as he rejected the conserva-
tive philosophy, of the "righteous Artegall"
and his comrade, the fierce defender of privi-
lege and order. And he expressed in this
ex post facto prophecy, his conviction of the

ultimate triumph of freedom and equality by the power of transmitted knowledge.' No date is assigned, and the verse may as well be placed in the early period of Keats's acquaintance with Spenser and friendship with Leigh Hunt.

In after-time, a sage of mickle lore
Yclep'd Typographus, the Giant took,
And did refit his limbs as heretofore,
And made him read in many a learned book,
And into many a lively legend look;
Thereby in goodly themes so training him,
That all his brutishness he quite forsook,
When, meeting Artegall and Talus grim,
The one he struck stone-blind, the other's eyes wox dim.

ON LEAVING SOME FRIENDS AT AN EARLY HOUR

Written, as Clarke intimates, in connection with Keats's visits to Leigh Hunt in the Vale of Health. Published in the 1817 volume.

Give me a golden pen, and let me lean
On heap'd-up flowers, in regions clear and far;
Bring me a tablet whiter than a star,
Or hand of hymning angel, when 't is seen
The silver strings of heavenly harp atween:
And let there glide by many a pearly car,
Pink robes, and wavy hair, and diamond jar,
And half-discover'd wings, and glances keen.
The while let music wander round my ears,
And as it reaches each delicious ending,
Let me write down a line of glorious tone,
And full of many wonders of the spheres:
For what a height my spirit is contending!
'T is not content so soon to be alone.

ON FIRST LOOKING INTO CHAPMAN'S HOMER

It was Charles Cowden Clarke who was with Keats when the friends made the acquaintance of this translation of Homer by the Elizabethan poet. The two young men had sat up nearly all one night in the summer of 1815 in Clarke's lodging, reading from a folio volume of the book which they had borrowed. Keats left for his own lodgings at dawn, and when Clarke came down to breakfast the next morning, he found this sonnet which Keats had sent him.

Much have I travell'd in the realms of gold,
And many goodly states and kingdoms seen;
Round many western islands have I been
Which bards in fealty to Apollo hold.
Oft of one wide expanse had I been told
That deep-brow'd Homer ruled as his demesne:
Yet did I never breathe its pure serene
Till I heard Chapman speak out loud and bold:
Then felt I like some watcher of the skies
When a new planet swims into his ken;
Or like stout Cortez when with eagle eyes
He stared at the Pacific — and all his men
Look'd at each other with a wild surmise —
Silent, upon a peak in Darien.

EPISTLE TO GEORGE FELTON MATHEW

Mathew, who was of Keats's age, was his companion when he first went to London. The two had common tastes in literature and read together, and Mathew also made essays in writing, so that Keats, who was living much in Elizabethan literature at the time, might easily transfer in imagination some of the great deeds of partnership to himself and his friend. It is worth while to note Mathew's own recollection, thirty years later, of the contrast of him-

self with Keats: 'Keats and I, though about
the same age, and both inclined to literature,
were in many respects as different as two in-
dividuals could be. He enjoyed good health —
a fine flow of animal spirits — was fond of
company — could amuse himself admirably
with the frivolities of life — and had great
confidence in himself. I, on the other hand,
was languid and melancholy — fond of repose
— thoughtful beyond my years — and diffi-
dent to the last degree.' The epistle is dated
November, 1815, in the volume of 1817, where
it is the first of a group of three epistles with
the motto from Browne's *Britannia's Pas-
torals*:

> Among the rest a shepherd (though but young
> Yet hartned to his pipe) with all the skill
> His few yeeres could, began to fit his quill.

SWEET are the pleasures that to verse
 belong,
And doubly sweet a brotherhood in song;
Nor can remembrance, Mathew ! bring to
 view
A fate more pleasing, a delight more true
Than that in which the brother Poets joy'd,
Who, with combinèd powers, their wit em-
 ploy'd
To raise a trophy to the drama's muses.
The thought of this great partnership dif-
 fuses
Over the genius-loving heart, a feeling
Of all that 's high, and great, and good,
 and healing. 10

Too partial friend ! fain would I follow
 thee
Past each horizon of fine poesy;
Fain would I echo back each pleasant note
As o'er Sicilian seas, clear anthems float
'Mong the light skimming gondolas far
 parted,
Just when the sun his farewell beam has
 darted:
But 't is impossible; far different cares
Beckon me sternly from soft 'Lydian airs,'
And hold my faculties so long in thrall,
That I am oft in doubt whether at all 20
I shall again see Phœbus in the morning:
Or flush'd Aurora in the roseate dawning !

Or a white Naiad in a rippling stream;
Or a rapt seraph in a moonlight beam;
Or again witness what with thee I 've seen,
The dew by fairy feet swept from the
 green,
After a night of some quaint jubilee
Which every elf and fay had come to see:
When bright processions took their airy
 march
Beneath the curvèd moon's triumphal
 arch. 30

But might I now each passing moment
 give
To the coy Muse, with me she would not
 live
In this dark city, nor would condescend
'Mid contradictions her delights to lend.
Should e'er the fine-eyed maid to me be
 kind,
Ah ! surely it must be whene'er I find
Some flowery spot, sequester'd, wild, ro-
 mantic,
That often must have seen a poet fran-
 tic;
Where oaks, that erst the Druid knew, are
 growing,
And flowers, the glory of one day, are
 blowing; 40
Where the dark-leav'd laburnum's droop-
 ing clusters
Reflect athwart the stream their yellow
 lustres,
And intertwined the cassia's arms unite,
With its own drooping buds, but very white.
Where on one side are covert branches
 hung,
'Mong which the nightingales have always
 sung
In leafy quiet: where to pry, aloof
Atween the pillars of the sylvan roof,
Would be to find where violet beds were
 nestling,
And where the bee with cowslip bells was
 wrestling. 50
There must be too a ruin dark and gloomy,
To say 'Joy not too much in all that 's
 bloomy.'

Yet this is vain — O Mathew, lend thy
aid
To find a place where I may greet the
maid —
Where we may soft humanity put on,
And sit, and rhyme, and think on Chatter-
ton;
And that warm-hearted Shakspeare sent to
meet him
Four laurell'd spirits, heavenward to en-
treat him.
With reverence would we speak of all the
sages
Who have left streaks of light athwart
their ages: 60
And thou shouldst moralize on Milton's
blindness,
And mourn the fearful dearth of human
kindness
To those who strove with the bright golden
wing
Of genius, to flap away each sting
Thrown by the pitiless world. We next
could tell
Of those who in the cause of freedom fell;
Of our own Alfred, of Helvetian Tell;
Of him whose name to every heart's a
solace,
High-minded and unbending William
Wallace.
While to the rugged north our musing
turns, 70
We well might drop a tear for him and
Burns.

Felton! without incitements such as these,
How vain for me the niggard Muse to
tease:
For thee, she will thy every dwelling grace,
And make ' a sunshine in a shady place: '
For thou wast once a flow'ret blooming
wild,
Close to the source, bright, pure, and unde-
fil'd,
Whence gush the streams of song: in
happy hour
Came chaste Diana from her shady bower,
Just as the sun was from the east uprising;

And, as for him some gift she was devising,
Beheld thee, pluck'd thee, cast thee in the
stream 82
To meet her glorious brother's greeting
beam.
I marvel much that thou hast never told
How, from a flower, into a fish of gold
Apollo chang'd thee: how thou next didst
seem
A black-ey'd swan upon the widening
stream;
And when thou first didst in that mirror
trace
The placid features of a human face;
That thou hast never told thy travels
strange, 90
And all the wonders of the mazy range
O'er pebbly crystal, and o'er golden sands;
Kissing thy daily food from Naiads' pearly
hands.

TO ——

A valentine written in 1816 by Keats for his
brother George to send to the lady Georgiana
Wylie, whom he afterward married, was later
expanded into the following lines. It was in-
cluded in the 1817 volume.

HADST thou liv'd in days of old,
O what wonders had been told
Of thy lively countenance,
And thy humid eyes that dance
In the midst of their own brightness;
In the very fane of lightness;
Over which thine eyebrows, leaning,
Picture out each lovely meaning:
In a dainty bend they lie,
Like to streaks across the sky, 10
Or the feathers from a crow,
Fallen on a bed of snow.
Of thy dark hair, that extends
Into many graceful bends:
As the leaves of Hellebore
Turn to whence they sprung before.
And behind each ample curl

Peeps the richness of a pearl.
Downward too flows many a tress
With a glossy waviness; 20
Full, and round like globes that rise
From the censer to the skies
Through sunny air. Add too, the sweet-
 ness
Of thy honied voice; the neatness
Of thine ankle lightly turn'd:
With those beauties scarce discern'd,
Kept with such sweet privacy,
That they seldom meet the eye
Of the little Loves that fly
Round about with eager pry; 30
Saving when, with freshening lave,
Thou dipp'st them in the taintless wave;
Like twin water-lilies, born
In the coolness of the morn.
O, if thou hadst breathèd then,
Now the Muses had been ten.
Couldst thou wish for lineage higher
Than twin-sister of Thalia?
At least for ever, evermore
Will I call the Graces four. 40

Hadst thou liv'd when chivalry
Lifted up her lance on high,
Tell me what thou wouldst have been?
Ah! I see the silver sheen
Of thy broider'd, floating vest
Cov'ring half thine ivory breast:
Which, O Heavens! I should see,
But that cruel Destiny
Has plac'd a golden cuirass there;
Keeping secret what is fair. 50
Like sunbeams in a cloudlet nested
Thy locks in knightly casque are rested:
O'er which bend four milky plumes
Like the gentle lily's blooms
Springing from a costly vase.
See with what a stately pace
Comes thine alabaster steed;
Servant of heroic deed!
O'er his loins his trappings glow
Like the northern lights on snow. 60
Mount his back! thy sword unsheath!
Sign of the enchanter's death;
Bane of every wicked spell;

Silencer of dragon's yell.
Alas! thou this wilt never do:
Thou art an enchantress too,
And wilt surely never spill
Blood of those whose eyes can kill.

SONNET

Lord Houghton gives the date of 1816. It
appears in the Aldine edition of 1876.

As from the darkening gloom a silver dove
 Upsoars, and darts into the eastern light,
 On pinions that nought moves but pure
 delight,
So fled thy soul into the realms above,
Regions of peace and everlasting love;
 Where happy spirits, crown'd with cir-
 clets bright
 Of starry beam, and gloriously bedight,
Taste the high joy none but the blest can
 prove.
There thou or joinest the immortal quire
 In melodies that even heaven fair
Fill with superior bliss, or, at desire,
 Of the omnipotent Father, cleav'st the
 air
On holy message sent — What pleasure's
 higher?
 Wherefore does any grief our joy impair?

SONNET TO SOLITUDE

Published in *The Examiner*, 5 May, 1816, and
the first piece printed by Keats. It was re-
issued in the 1817 volume.

O SOLITUDE! if I must with thee dwell,
 Let it not be among the jumbled heap
 Of murky buildings: climb with me the
 steep, —
Nature's observatory, — whence the dell,
In flowery slopes, its river's crystal swell,
 May seem a span; let me thy vigils keep
 'Mongst boughs pavilion'd, where the
 deer's swift leap
Startles the wild bee from the foxglove
 bell.

But though I'll gladly trace these scenes
 with thee,
 Yet the sweet converse of an innocent
 mind,
 Whose words are images of thoughts re-
 fin'd,
Is my soul's pleasure; and it sure must be
 Almost the highest bliss of human-kind,
When to thy haunts two kindred spirits flee.

SONNET

George Keats has a memorandum on this
sonnet, 'written in the Fields, June, 1816.'
Published in the 1817 volume.

To one who has been long in city pent,
 'T is very sweet to look into the fair
 And open face of heaven, — to breathe
 a prayer
Full in the smile of the blue firmament.
Who is more happy, when, with heart's
 content,
 Fatigued he sinks into some pleasant lair
 Of wavy grass, and reads a debonair
And gentle tale of love and languishment?
Returning home at evening, with an ear
 Catching the notes of Philomel, — an eye
 Watching the sailing cloudlet's bright ca-
 reer,
 He mourns that day so soon has glided
 by:
E'en like the passage of an angel's tear
 That falls through the clear ether si-
 lently.

TO A FRIEND WHO SENT ME
SOME ROSES

The friend was Charles J. Wells, author of
the dramatic poem *Joseph and his Brethren*,
which was published in 1824, when it died al-
most at once and was recalled to life by a few
words printed by D. G. Rossetti in 1863, and has
since been reprinted for the curious. In Tom
Keats's copy book the sonnet is dated 29 June,
1816. It is included in the volume of 1817.

As late I rambled in the happy fields,
 What time the skylark shakes the tremu-
 lous dew
 From his lush clover covert; — when anew
Adventurous knights take up their dinted
 shields:
I saw the sweetest flower wild nature yields,
 A fresh-blown musk-rose; 't was the first
 that threw
 Its sweets upon the summer: graceful it
 grew
As is the wand that Queen Titania wields.
And, as I feasted on its fragrancy,
 I thought the garden-rose it far excell'd:
But when, O Wells! thy roses came to me,
 My sense with their deliciousness was
 spell'd:
Soft voices had they, that with tender plea
 Whisper'd of peace, and truth, and
 friendliness unquell'd.

SONNET

First printed by Lord Houghton in the *Life,
Letters and Literary Remains*, with the date
1816.

OH! how I love, on a fair summer's eve,
 When streams of light pour down the
 golden west,
 And on the balmy zephyrs tranquil rest
The silver clouds, far — far away to leave
All meaner thoughts, and take a sweet re-
 prieve
 From little cares; to find, with easy quest,
 A fragrant wild, with Nature's beauty
 drest,
And there into delight my soul deceive.
There warm my breast with patriotic lore,
 Musing on Milton's fate — on Sydney's
 bier —
 Till their stern forms before my mind
 arise:
Perhaps on wings of Poesy upsoar,
 Full often dropping a delicious tear,
 When some melodious sorrow spells
 mine eyes.

'I STOOD TIPTOE UPON A LITTLE HILL'

'Places of nestling green, for poets made.'
LEIGH HUNT, *The Story of Rimini.*

Leigh Hunt, in *Lord Byron and Some of His Contemporaries*, says that 'this poem was suggested to Keats by a delightful summer's day as he stood beside the gate that leads from the Battery on Hampstead Heath into a field by Caen Wood ; ' but it is not needful for one to put himself into the same geographical position. It is more to the point to remember that when Keats wrote the lines which here follow he was living in the Vale of Health in Hampstead, happy in the association of Hunt and kindred spirits, and trembling with the consciousness of his own poetic power. He had not yet essayed a long flight, as in *Endymion ;* but these lines indeed were written as a prelude to a poem which he was devising, which should narrate the loves of Diana, and it will be seen how, with circling flight, he draws nearer and nearer to his theme ; but after all, his song ends with a half agitated and passionate speculation over his own poetic birth. The date of the poem, which is the first after the dedication, in the 1817 volume, was presumably in the summer of 1816, for Keats appears to have written promptly under the stimulus of momentary experience.

I STOOD tiptoe upon a little hill,
The air was cooling, and so very still
That the sweet buds which with a modest pride
Pull droopingly, in slanting curve aside,
Their scantly-leav'd and finely tapering stems,
Had not yet lost those starry diadems
Caught from the early sobbing of the morn.
The clouds were pure and white as flocks new shorn,
And fresh from the clear brook; sweetly they slept
On the blue fields of heaven, and then there crept 10
A little noiseless noise among the leaves,
Born of the very sigh that silence heaves;
For not the faintest motion could be seen

Of all the shades that slanted o'er the green.
There was wide wandering for the greediest eye
To peer about upon variety;
Far round the horizon's crystal air to skim,
And trace the dwindled edgings of its brim;
To picture out the quaint and curious bending
Of a fresh woodland alley never-ending: 20
Or by the bowery clefts, and leafy shelves,
Guess where the jaunty streams refresh themselves.
I gazed awhile, and felt as light and free
As though the fanning wings of Mercury
Had play'd upon my heels: I was light-hearted,
And many pleasures to my vision started;
So I straightway began to pluck a posy
Of luxuries bright, milky, soft, and rosy.

A bush of May flowers with the bees about them;
Ah, sure no tasteful nook could be without them ! 30
And let a lush laburnum oversweep them,
And let long grass grow round the roots to keep them
Moist, cool, and green; and shade the violets,
That they may bind the moss in leafy nets.

A filbert-hedge with wild-briar over-twin'd,
And clumps of woodbine taking the soft wind
Upon their summer thrones; there too should be
The frequent chequer of a youngling tree,
That with a score of light green brethren shoots
From the quaint mossiness of aged roots: 40
Round which is heard a spring-head of clear waters
Babbling so wildly of its lovely daughters,
The spreading blue-bells: it may haply mourn
That such fair clusters should be rudely torn

From their fresh beds, and scattered
thoughtlessly
By infant hands, left on the path to die.

Open afresh your round of starry folds,
Ye ardent marigolds !
Dry up the moisture from your golden lids,
For great Apollo bids 50
That in these days your praises should be
sung
On many harps, which he has lately strung;
And when again your dewiness he kisses,
Tell him, I have you in my world of blisses:
So haply when I rove in some far vale,
His mighty voice may come upon the gale.

Here are sweet peas, on tiptoe for a
flight:
With wings of gentle flush o'er delicate
white,
And taper fingers catching at all things,
To bind them all about with tiny rings. 60

Linger awhile upon some bending planks
That lean against a streamlet's rushy banks,
And watch intently Nature's gentle doings:
They will be found softer than ring-dove's
cooings.
How silent comes the water round that bend;
Not the minutest whisper does it send
To the o'erhanging sallows: blades of grass
Slowly across the chequer'd shadows pass.
Why, you might read two sonnets, ere they
reach
To where the hurrying freshnesses aye
preach 70
A natural sermon o'er their pebbly beds;
Where swarms of minnows show their little
heads,
Staying their wavy bodies 'gainst the
streams,
To taste the luxury of sunny beams
Temper'd with coolness. How they ever
wrestle
With their own sweet delight, and ever
nestle
Their silver bellies on the pebbly sand.
If you but scantily hold out the hand,

That very instant not one will remain;
But turn your eye, and they are there again.
The ripples seem right glad to reach those
cresses, 81
And cool themselves among the em'rald
tresses;
The while they cool themselves, they fresh-
ness give,
And moisture, that the bowery green may
live:
So keeping up an interchange of favours,
Like good men in the truth of their be-
haviours.
Sometimes goldfinches one by one will drop
From low-hung branches; little space they
stop;
But sip, and twitter, and their feathers
sleek;
Then off at once, as in a wanton freak: 90
Or perhaps, to show their black, and golden
wings,
Pausing upon their yellow flutterings.
Were I in such a place, I sure should pray
That nought less sweet, might call my
thoughts away,
Than the soft rustle of a maiden's gown
Fanning away the dandelion's down;
Than the light music of her nimble toes
Patting against the sorrel as she goes.
How she would start, and blush, thus to be
caught
Playing in all her innocence of thought. 100
O let me lead her gently o'er the brook,
Watch her half-smiling lips, and downward
look;
O let me for one moment touch her wrist;
Let me one moment to her breathing list;
And as she leaves me, may she often turn
Her fair eyes looking through her locks au-
burne.
What next ? A tuft of evening primroses,
O'er which the mind may hover till it dozes;
O'er which it well might take a pleasant
sleep,
But that 't is ever startled by the leap 110
Of buds into ripe flowers; or by the flitting
Of diverse moths, that aye their rest are
quitting;

Or by the moon lifting her silver rim
Above a cloud, and with a gradual swim
Coming into the blue with all her light.
O Maker of sweet poets, dear delight
Of this fair world, and all its gentle livers;
Spangler of clouds, halo of crystal rivers,
Mingler with leaves, and dew and tumbling
 streams,
Closer of lovely eyes to lovely dreams, 120
Lover of loneliness, and wandering,
Of upcast eye, and tender pondering !
Thee must I praise above all other glo-
 ries
That smile us on to tell delightful stories.
For what has made the sage or poet write
But the fair paradise of Nature's light ?
In the calm grandeur of a sober line,
We see the waving of the mountain pine;
And when a tale is beautifully staid,
We feel the safety of a hawthorn glade: 130
When it is moving on luxurious wings,
The soul is lost in pleasant smotherings:
Fair dewy roses brush against our faces,
And flowering laurels spring from diamond
 vases;
O'erhead we see the jasmine and sweet-
 briar,
And bloomy grapes laughing from green
 attire;
While at our feet, the voice of crystal
 bubbles
Charms us at once away from all our trou-
 bles:
So that we feel uplifted from the world,
Walking upon the white clouds wreath'd
 and curl'd. 140
So felt he, who first told, how Psyche
 went
On the smooth wind to realms of wonder-
 ment;
What Psyche felt, and Love, when their
 full lips
First touch'd; what amorous and fondling
 nips
They gave each other's cheeks; with all
 their sighs,
And how they kist each other's tremulous
 eyes:

The silver lamp, — the ravishment, — the
 wonder —
The darkness, — loneliness, — the fearful
 thunder;
Their woes gone by, and both to heaven up-
 flown, 149
To bow for gratitude before Jove's throne.
So did he feel, who pull'd the boughs
 aside,
That we might look into a forest wide,
To catch a glimpse of Fauns, and Dryades
Coming with softest rustle through the
 trees;
And garlands woven of flowers wild, and
 sweet,
Upheld on ivory wrists, or sporting feet:
Telling us how fair, trembling Syrinx fled
Arcadian Pan, with such a fearful dread.
Poor Nymph, — poor Pan, — how he did
 weep to find
Nought but a lovely sighing of the wind 160
Along the reedy stream; a half-heard strain,
Full of sweet desolation — balmy pain.

 What first inspired a bard of old to sing
Narcissus pining o'er the untainted spring ?
In some delicious ramble, he had found
A little space, with boughs all woven round;
And in the midst of all, a clearer pool
Than e'er reflected in its pleasant cool,
The blue sky here, and there, serenely peep-
 ing
Through tendril wreaths fantastically creep-
 ing. 170
And on the bank a lonely flower he spied,
A meek and forlorn flower, with naught of
 pride,
Drooping its beauty o'er the watery clear-
 ness,
To woo its own sad image into nearness:
Deaf to light Zephyrus it would not move;
But still would seem to droop, to pine, to
 love.
So while the Poet stood in this sweet spot,
Some fainter gleamings o'er his fancy
 shot;
Nor was it long ere he had told the tale
Of young Narcissus, and sad Echo's bale. 180

Where had he been, from whose warm
　　head outflew
That sweetest of all songs, that ever new,
That aye refreshing, pure deliciousness,
Coming ever to bless
The wanderer by moonlight ? to him
　　bringing
Shapes from the invisible world, unearthly
　　singing
From out the middle air, from flowery
　　nests,
And from the pillowy silkiness that rests
Full in the speculation of the stars. 189
Ah ! surely he had burst our mortal bars;
Into some wond'rous region he had gone,
To search for thee, divine Endymion !

He was a Poet, sure a lover too,
Who stood on Latmus' top, what time
　　there blew
Soft breezes from the myrtle vale below;
And brought in faintness solemn, sweet,
　　and slow
A hymn from Dian's temple; while up-
　　swelling,
The incense went to her own starry dwell-
　　ing.
But though her face was clear as infant's
　　eyes, 199
Though she stood smiling o'er the sacrifice,
The Poet wept at her so piteous fate,
Wept that such beauty should be deso-
　　late:
So in fine wrath some golden sounds he won,
And gave meek Cynthia her Endymion.

Queen of the wide air; thou most lovely
　　queen
Of all the brightness that mine eyes have
　　seen !
As thou exceedest all things in thy shine,
So every tale, does this sweet tale of thine.
O for three words of honey, that I might
Tell but one wonder of thy bridal night ! 210

Where distant ships do seem to show
　　their keels,
Phœbus awhile delay'd his mighty wheels,

And turn'd to smile upon thy bashful eyes,
Ere he his unseen pomp would solem-
　　nize.
The evening weather was so bright, and
　　clear,
That men of health were of unusual cheer;
Stepping like Homer at the trumpet's
　　call,
Or young Apollo on the pedestal:
And lovely women were as fair and warm,
As Venus looking sideways in alarm. 220
The breezes were ethereal, and pure,
And crept through half closed lattices to
　　cure
The languid sick; it cool'd their fever'd
　　sleep,
And soothed them into slumbers full and
　　deep.
Soon they awoke clear-eyed: nor burnt
　　with thirsting,
Nor with hot fingers, nor with temples
　　bursting:
And springing up, they met the wond'ring
　　sight
Of their dear friends, nigh foolish with
　　delight;
Who feel their arms, and breasts, and kiss
　　and stare,
And on their placid foreheads part the
　　hair. 230
Young men and maidens at each other
　　gaz'd,
With hands held back, and motionless,
　　amaz'd
To see the brightness in each other's eyes;
And so they stood, fill'd with a sweet sur-
　　prise,
Until their tongues were loos'd in poesy.
Therefore no lover did of anguish die∙
But the soft numbers, in that moment
　　spoken,
Made silken ties, that never may be broken.
Cynthia ! I cannot tell the greater blisses
That follow'd thine, and thy dear shep-
　　herd's kisses: 240
Was there a Poet born ? — But now no
　　more,
My wand'ring spirit must no further soar.

SLEEP AND POETRY

The last poem in the 1817 volume. Charles
Cowden Clarke relates that 'it was in the
library of Hunt's cottage, where an extempore
bed had been put up for Keats on the sofa, that
he composed the framework and many lines
of this poem, the last sixty or seventy being
an inventory of the art garniture of the room.'
It may be assigned to the summer of 1816.

> As I lay in my bed slepe full unmete
> Was unto me, but why that I ne might
> Rest I ne wist, for there in' as erthly wight
> (As I suppose) had more of hertis ese
> Than I, for I n' ad sicknesse nor disese.
> CHAUCER.

WHAT is more gentle than a wind in sum-
mer ?
What is more soothing than the pretty
hummer
That stays one moment in an open flower,
And buzzes cheerily from bower to bower ?
What is more tranquil than a musk-rose
blowing
In a green island, far from all men's know-
ing ?
More healthful than the leafiness of dales ?
More secret than a nest of nightingales ?
More serene than Cordelia's countenance ?
More full of visions than a high romance ?
What, but thee, Sleep ? Soft closer of our
eyes ! 11
Low murmurer of tender lullabies !
Light hoverer around our happy pillows !
Wreather of poppy buds, and weeping
willows !
Silent entangler of a beauty's tresses !
Most happy listener ! when the morning
blesses
Thee for enlivening all the cheerful eyes
That glance so brightly at the new sun-
rise.

But what is higher beyond thought than
thee ?
Fresher than berries of a mountain-tree ?
More strange, more beautiful, more smooth,
more regal, 21

Than wings of swans, than doves, than dim-
seen eagle ?
What is it ? And to what shall I compare
it ?
It has a glory, and nought else can share it:
The thought thereof is awful, sweet, and
holy,
Chasing away all worldliness and folly:
Coming sometimes like fearful claps of
thunder,
Or the low rumblings earth's regions un-
der;
And sometimes like a gentle whispering 29
Of all the secrets of some wond'rous thing
That breathes about us in the vacant air;
So that we look around with prying stare,
Perhaps to see shapes of light, aerial lim-
ning;
And catch soft floatings from a faint-heard
hymning;
To see the laurel wreath, on high suspended,
That is to crown our name when life is
ended.
Sometimes it gives a glory to the voice,
And from the heart up-springs, rejoice !
rejoice !
Sounds which will reach the Framer of all
things,
And die away in ardent mutterings. 40

No one who once the glorious sun has
seen,
And all the clouds, and felt his bosom clean
For his great Maker's presence, but must
know
What 't is I mean, and feel his being glow:
Therefore no insult will I give his spirit,
By telling what he sees from native merit.

O Poesy ! for thee I hold my pen,
That am not yet a glorious denizen
Of thy wide heaven — should I rather kneel
Upon some mountain-top until I feel 50
A growing splendour round about me hung,
And echo back the voice of thine own
tongue ?
O Poesy ! for thee I grasp my pen,
That am not yet a glorious denizen

Of thy wide heaven; yet, to my ardent
 prayer,
Yield from thy sanctuary some clear air,
Smoothed for intoxication by the breath
Of flowering bays, that I may die a death
Of luxury, and my young spirit follow
The morning sunbeams to the great Apollo
Like a fresh sacrifice; or, if I can bear 61
The o'erwhelming sweets, 't will bring to
 me the fair
Visions of all places: a bowery nook
Will be elysium — an eternal book
Whence I may copy many a lovely saying
About the leaves, and flowers — about the
 playing
Of nymphs in woods, and fountains; and
 the shade
Keeping a silence round a sleeping maid;
And many a verse from so strange influence
That we must ever wonder how, and whence
It came. Also imaginings will hover 71
Round my fire-side, and haply there dis-
 cover
Vistas of solemn beauty, where I 'd wander
In happy silence, like the clear Meander
Through its lone vales; and where I found
 a spot
Of awfuller shade, or an enchanted grot,
Or a green hill o'erspread with chequer'd
 dress
Of flowers, and fearful from its loveliness,
Write on my tablets all that was permitted,
All that was for our human senses fitted.
Then the events of this wide world I 'd
 seize 81
Like a strong giant, and my spirit tease
Till at its shoulders it should proudly see
Wings to find out an immortality.

Stop and consider ! life is but a day;
A fragile dewdrop on its perilous way
From a tree's summit; a poor Indian's sleep
While his boat hastens to the monstrous
 steep
Of Montmorenci. Why so sad a moan ?
Life is the rose's hope while yet unblown;
The reading of an ever-changing tale; 91
The light uplifting of a maiden's veil;

A pigeon tumbling in clear summer air;
A laughing school-boy, without grief or
 care,
Riding the springy branches of an elm.

 O for ten years, that I may overwhelm
Myself in poesy; so I may do the deed
That my own soul has to itself decreed.
Then I will pass the countries that I see
In long perspective, and continually 100
Taste their pure fountains. First the realm
 I 'll pass
Of Flora, and old Pan: sleep in the grass,
Feed upon apples red, and strawberries,
And choose each pleasure that my fancy
 sees;
Catch the white-handed nymphs in shady
 places,
To woo sweet kisses from averted faces, —
Play with their fingers, touch their shoul-
 ders white
Into a pretty shrinking with a bite
As hard as lips can make it: till agreed, 110
And one will teach a tame dove how it best
May fan the cool air gently o'er my rest;
Another, bending o'er her nimble tread,
Will set a green robe floating round her
 head,
And still will dance with ever-varied ease,
Smiling upon the flowers and the trees:
Another will entice me on, and on
Through almond blossoms and rich cinna-
 mon;
Till in the bosom of a leafy world
We rest in silence, like two gems upcurl'd
In the recesses of a pearly shell. 121

 And can I ever bid these joys farewell ?
Yes, I must pass them for a nobler life,
Where I may find the agonies, the strife
Of human hearts: for lo ! I see afar,
O'er-sailing the blue cragginess, a car
And steeds with streamy manes — the
 charioteer
Looks out upon the winds with glorious fear:
And now the numerous tramplings quiver
 lightly

Along a huge cloud's ridge; and now with
 sprightly 130
Wheel downward come they into fresher
 skies,
Tipt round with silver from the sun's bright
 eyes.
Still downward with capacious whirl they
 glide;
And now I see them on a green-hill's side
In breezy rest among the nodding stalks.
The charioteer with wond'rous gesture
 talks
To the trees and mountains; and there soon
 appear
Shapes of delight, of mystery, and fear,
Passing along before a dusky space
Made by some mighty oaks: as they would
 chase 140
Some ever-fleeting music, on they sweep.
Lo! how they murmur, laugh, and smile,
 and weep:
Some with upholden hand and mouth severe;
Some with their faces muffled to the ear
Between their arms; some, clear in youth-
 ful bloom,
Go glad and smilingly athwart the gloom;
Some looking back, and some with upward
 gaze;
Yes, thousands in a thousand different ways
Flit onward — now a lovely wreath of girls
Dancing their sleek hair into tangled curls;
And now broad wings. Most awfully in-
 tent 151
The driver of those steeds is forward bent,
And seems to listen: O that I might know
All that he writes with such a hurrying
 glow.

The visions all are fled — the car is fled
Into the light of heaven, and in their stead
A sense of real things comes doubly strong,
And, like a muddy stream, would bear
 along
My soul to nothingness: but I will strive
Against all doubtings, and will keep alive
The thought of that same chariot, and the
 strange 161
Journey it went.

 Is there so small a range
In the present strength of manhood, that
 the high
Imagination cannot freely fly
As she was wont of old? prepare her
 steeds,
Paw up against the light, and do strange
 deeds
Upon the clouds? Has she not shewn us
 all?
From the clear space of ether, to the small
Breath of new buds unfolding? From the
 meaning
Of Jove's large eyebrow, to the tender
 greening 170
Of April meadows? here her altar shone,
E'en in this isle; and who could paragon
The fervid choir that lifted up a noise
Of harmony, to where it aye will poise
Its mighty self of convoluting sound,
Huge as a planet, and like that roll round,
Eternally around a dizzy void?
Ay, in those days the Muses were nigh
 cloy'd
With honours; nor had any other care
Than to sing out and soothe their wavy
 hair. 180

 Could all this be forgotten? Yes, a
 schism
Nurtured by foppery and barbarism,
Made great Apollo blush for this his land.
Men were thought wise who could not un-
 derstand
His glories: with a puling infant's force
They sway'd about upon a rocking-horse,
And thought it Pegasus. Ah, dismal-soul'd!
The winds of heaven blew, the ocean
 roll'd
Its gathering waves — ye felt it not. The
 blue
Bared its eternal bosom, and the dew 190
Of summer nights collected still to make
The morning precious: beauty was awake!
Why were ye not awake? But ye were
 dead
To things ye knew not of, — were closely
 wed

To musty laws lined out with wretched
 rule
And compass vile: so that ye taught a
 school
Of dolts to smooth, inlay, and clip, and
 fit,
Till, like the certain wands of Jacob's wit,
Their verses tallied. Easy was the task:
A thousand handicraftsmen wore the mask
Of Poesy. Ill-fated, impious race ! 201
That blasphem'd the bright Lyrist to his
 face,
And did not know it, — no, they went about,
Holding a poor, decrepid standard out,
Mark'd with most flimsy mottoes, and in
 large
The name of one Boileau !

 O ye whose charge
It is to hover round our pleasant hills !
Whose congregated majesty so fills
My boundly reverence, that I cannot trace
Your hallowed names, in this unholy place,
So near those common folk; did not their
 shames 211
Affright you ? Did our old lamenting
 Thames
Delight you ? did ye never cluster round
Delicious Avon, with a mournful sound,
And weep ? Or did ye wholly bid adieu
To regions where no more the laurel grew ?
Or did ye stay to give a welcoming
To some lone spirits who could proudly
 sing
Their youth away, and die ? 'T was even
 so: 219
But let me think away those times of woe:
Now 't is a fairer season; ye have breathed
Rich benedictions o'er us; ye have wreathed
Fresh garlands: for sweet music has been
 heard
In many places; — some has been upstirr'd
From out its crystal dwelling in a lake,
By a swan's ebon bill; from a thick brake,
Nested and quiet in a valley mild,
Bubbles a pipe; fine sounds are floating
 wild
About the earth: happy are ye and glad.

These things are, doubtless; yet in truth
 we 've had 230
Strange thunders from the potency of song;
Mingled indeed with what is sweet and
 strong
From majesty: but in clear truth the themes
Are ugly clubs, the Poets Polyphemes
Disturbing the grand sea. A drainless
 shower
Of light is Poesy; 't is the supreme of
 power;
'T is might half slumb'ring on its own right
 arm.
The very archings of her eyelids charm
A thousand willing agents to obey,
And still she governs with the mildest sway:
But strength alone though of the Muses
 born 241
Is like a fallen angel: trees uptorn,
Darkness, and worms, and shrouds, and
 sepulchres
Delight it; for it feeds upon the burrs
And thorns of life; forgetting the great
 end
Of Poesy, that it should be a friend
To soothe the cares, and lift the thoughts
 of man.

 Yet I rejoice: a myrtle fairer than 248
E'er grew in Paphos, from the bitter weeds
Lifts its sweet head into the air, and feeds
A silent space with ever sprouting green.
All tenderest birds there find a pleasant
 screen,
Creep through the shade with jaunty flut-
 tering,
Nibble the little cuppèd flowers and sing.
Then let us clear away the choking thorns
From round its gentle stem; let the young
 fawns,
Yeanèd in after-times, when we are flown,
Find a fresh sward beneath it, overgrown
With simple flowers: let there nothing be
More boisterous than a lover's bended knee;
Nought more ungentle than the placid look
Of one who leans upon a closèd book; 262
Nought more untranquil than the grassy
 slopes

Between two hills. All hail, delightful
 hopes !
As she was wont, th' imagination
Into most lovely labyrinths will be gone,
And they shall be accounted poet kings
Who simply tell the most heart-easing
 things.
O may these joys be ripe before I die.

Will not some say that I presumptu-
 ously 270
Have spoken ? that from hastening disgrace
'T were better far to hide my foolish face ?
That whining boyhood should with rever-
 ence bow
Ere the dread thunderbolt could reach ?
 How !
If I do hide myself, it sure shall be
In the very fane, the light of Poesy :
If I do fall, at least I will be laid
Beneath the silence of a poplar shade ;
And over me the grass shall be smooth
 shaven ;
And there shall be a kind memorial
 graven. 280
But off, Despondence ! miserable bane !
They should not know thee, who athirst to
 gain
A noble end, are thirsty every hour.
What though I am not wealthy in the dower
Of spanning wisdom ; though I do not know
The shiftings of the mighty winds that
 blow
Hither and thither all the changing
 thoughts
Of man : though no great minist'ring rea-
 son sorts
Out the dark mysteries of human souls
To clear conceiving : yet there ever
 rolls 290
A vast idea before me, and I glean
Therefrom my liberty ; thence too I 've
 seen
The end and aim of Poesy. 'T is clear
As anything most true ; as that the year
Is made of the four seasons — manifest
As a large cross, some old cathedral's
 crest,

Lifted to the white clouds. Therefore
 should I
Be but the essence of deformity,
A coward, did my very eyelids wink
At speaking out what I have dared to
 think. 300
Ah ! rather let me like a madman run
Over some precipice ; let the hot sun
Melt my Dædalian wings, and drive me
 down
Convuls'd and headlong ! Stay ! an in-
 ward frown
Of conscience bids me be more calm awhile.
An ocean dim, sprinkled with many an
 isle,
Spreads awfully before me. How much
 toil !
How many days ! what desperate turmoil !
Ere I can have explored its widenesses.
Ah, what a task ! upon my bended
 knees, 310
I could unsay those — no, impossible !
Impossible !

For sweet relief I 'll dwell
On humbler thoughts, and let this strange
 assay
Begun in gentleness die so away.
E'en now all tumult from my bosom fades :
I turn full-hearted to the friendly aids
That smooth the path of honour ; brother-
 hood,
And friendliness the nurse of mutual good.
The hearty grasp that sends a pleasant
 sonnet
Into the brain ere one can think upon it ; 320
The silence when some rhymes are coming
 out ;
And when they 're come, the very pleasant
 rout:
The message certain to be done to-morrow.
'T is perhaps as well that it should be to
 borrow
Some precious book from out its snug
 retreat,
To cluster round it when we next shall
 meet.
Scarce can I scribble on ; for lovely airs

Are fluttering round the room like doves in
 pairs ;
Many delights of that glad day recalling,
When first my senses caught their tender
 falling. 330
And with these airs come forms of elegance
Stooping their shoulders o'er a horse's
 prance,
Careless, and grand — fingers soft and
 round
Parting luxuriant curls ; — and the swift
 bound
Of Bacchus from his chariot, when his eye
Made Ariadne's cheek look blushingly.
Thus I remember all the pleasant flow
Of words at opening a portfolio.

 Things such as these are ever harbingers
To trains of peaceful images : the stirs 340
Of a swan's neck unseen among the rushes :
A linnet starting all about the bushes :
A butterfly, with golden wings broad
 parted,
Nestling a rose, convuls'd as though it
 smarted
With over pleasure — many, many more,
Might I indulge at large in all my store
Of luxuries : yet I must not forget
Sleep, quiet with his poppy coronet :
For what there may be worthy in these
 rhymes
I partly owe to him : and thus, the
 chimes 350
Of friendly voices had just given place
To as sweet a silence, when I 'gan retrace
The pleasant day, upon a couch at ease.
It was a poet's house who keeps the keys
Of pleasure's temple. Round about were
 hung
The glorious features of the bards who
 sung
In other ages — cold and sacred busts
Smiled at each other. Happy he who trusts
To clear Futurity his darling fame !
Then there were fauns and satyrs taking
 aim 360
At swelling apples with a frisky leap
And reaching fingers, 'mid a luscious heap

Of vine leaves. Then there rose to view a
 fane
Of liny marble, and thereto a train
Of nymphs approaching fairly o'er the
 sward :
One, loveliest, holding her white hand
 toward
The dazzling sunrise : two sisters sweet
Bending their graceful figures till they meet
Over the trippings of a little child :
And some are hearing, eagerly, the wild 370
Thrilling liquidity of dewy piping.
See, in another picture, nymphs are wiping
Cherishingly Diana's timorous limbs ; —
A fold of lawny mantle dabbling swims
At the bath's edge, and keeps a gentle
 motion
With the subsiding crystal : as when ocean
Heaves calmly its broad swelling smooth-
 iness o'er
Its rocky marge, and balances once more
The patient weeds ; that now unshent by
 foam
Feel all about their undulating home. 380

Sappho's meek head was there half smiling
 down
At nothing ; just as though the earnest
 frown
Of over-thinking had that moment gone
From off her brow, and left her all alone.

 Great Alfred's too, with anxious, pitying
 eyes,
As if he always listened to the sighs
Of the goaded world ; and Kosciusko's,
 worn
By horrid suffrance — mightily forlorn.

 Petrarch, outstepping from the shady
 green,
Starts at the sight of Laura ; nor can
 wean 390
His eyes from her sweet face. Most happy
 they !
For over them was seen a free display
Of outspread wings, and from between them
 shone

The face of Poesy : from off her throne
She overlook'd things that I scarce could
 tell.
The very sense of where I was might well
Keep Sleep aloof : but more than that there
 came
Thought after thought to nourish up the
 flame
Within my breast ; so that the morning
 light
Surprised me even from a sleepless
 night ; 400
And up I rose refresh'd, and glad, and gay,
Resolving to begin that very day
These lines ; and howsoever they be done,
I leave them as a father does his son.

EPISTLE TO MY BROTHER GEORGE

Written according to George Keats at Margate, August, 1816, and included in the 1817 volume.

FULL many a dreary hour have I past,
My brain bewilder'd, and my mind o'ercast
With heaviness; in seasons when I.'ve
 thought
No spherey strains by me could e'er be
 caught
From the blue dome, though I to dimness
 gaze
On the far depth where sheeted lightning
 plays;
Or, on the wavy grass outstretch'd supinely,
Pry 'mong the stars, to strive to think divinely:
That I should never hear Apollo's song,
Though feathery clouds were floating all
 along 10
The purple west, and, two bright streaks
 between,
The golden lyre itself were dimly seen:
That the still murmur of the honey bee
Would never teach a rural song to me:
That the bright glance from beauty's eyelids slanting
Would never make a lay of mine enchanting,

Or warm my breast with ardour to unfold
Some tale of love and arms in time of old.

But there are times, when those that love
 the bay,
Fly from all sorrowing far, far away; 20
A sudden glow comes on them, nought
 they see
In water, earth, or air, but poesy.
It has been said, dear George, and true I
 hold it,
(For knightly Spenser to Libertas told it,)
That when a Poet is in such a trance,
In air he sees white coursers paw and
 prance,
Bestridden of gay knights, in gay apparel,
Who at each other tilt in playful quarrel;
And what we, ignorantly, sheet-lightning
 call,
Is the swift opening of their wide portal, 30
When the bright warder blows his trumpet
 clear,
Whose tones reach nought on earth but
 Poet's ear.
When these enchanted portals open wide,
And through the light the horsemen swiftly
 glide,
The Poet's eye can reach those golden halls,
And view the glory of their festivals:
Their ladies fair, that in the distance seem
Fit for the silv'ring of a seraph's dream;
Their rich brimm'd goblets, that incessant
 run
Like the bright spots that move about the
 sun; 40
And, when upheld, the wine from each
 bright jar
Pours with the lustre of a falling star.
Yet further off are dimly seen their bowers,
Of which no mortal eye can reach the flowers;
And 't is right just, for well Apollo knows
'T would make the Poet quarrel with the
 rose.
All that's reveal'd from that far seat of
 blisses,
Is, the clear fountains' interchanging kisses,
As gracefully descending, light and thin,

Like silver streaks across a dolphin's fin, 50
When he upswimmeth from the coral caves,
And sports with half his tail above the
 waves.

These wonders strange he sees, and many
 more,
Whose head is pregnant with poetic lore.
Should he upon an evening ramble fare
With forehead to the soothing breezes bare,
Would he naught see but the dark, silent
 blue,
With all its diamonds trembling through
 and through ?
Or the coy moon, when in the waviness 59
Of whitest clouds she does her beauty dress,
And staidly paces higher up, and higher,
Like a sweet nun in holiday attire ?
Ah, yes ! much more would start into his
 sight —
The revelries, and mysteries of night:
And should I ever see them, I will tell you
Such tales as needs must with amazement
 spell you.

These are the living pleasures of the
 bard:
But richer far posterity's award.
What does he murmur with his latest breath,
While his proud eye looks through the film
 of death ? 70
'What though I leave this dull and earthly
 mould,
Yet shall my spirit lofty converse hold
With after times. — The patriot shall feel
My stern alarum, and unsheath his steel;
Or in the senate thunder out my numbers,
To startle princes from their easy slumbers.
The sage will mingle with each moral theme
My happy thoughts sententious; he will
 teem
With lofty periods when my verses fire
 him,
And then I 'll stoop from heaven to inspire
 him. 80
Lays have I left of such a dear delight
That maids will sing them on their bridal
 night.

Gay villagers, upon a morn of May,
When they have tired their gentle limbs
 with play,
And form'd a snowy circle on the grass,
And plac'd in midst of all that lovely lass
Who chosen is their queen, — with her fine
 head
Crownèd with flowers purple, white, and
 red:
For there the lily, and the musk-rose, sigh-
 ing, 89
Are emblems true of hapless lovers dying:
Between her breasts, that never yet felt
 trouble,
A bunch of violets full blown, and double,
Serenely sleep: — she from a casket takes
A little book, — and then a joy awakes
About each youthful heart, — with stifled
 cries,
And rubbing of white hands, and sparkling
 eyes:
For she 's to read a tale of hopes and fears;
One that I foster'd in my youthful years:
The pearls, that on each glist'ning circlet
 sleep,
Gush ever and anon with silent creep, 100
Lured by the innocent dimples. To sweet
 rest
Shall the dear babe, upon its mother's
 breast,
Be lull'd with songs of mine. Fair world,
 adieu !
Thy dales and hills are fading from my
 view:
Swiftly I mount, upon wide-spreading
 pinions,
Far from the narrow bounds of thy do-
 minions.
Full joy I feel, while thus I cleave the air,
That my soft verse will charm thy daugh-
 ters fair,
And warm thy sons ! ' Ah, my dear friend
 and brother, 109
Could I, at once, my mad ambition smother,
For tasting joys like these, sure I should be
Happier, and dearer to society.
At times, 't is true, I 've felt relief from
 pain

When some bright thought has darted
 through my brain:
Through all that day I 've felt a greater
 pleasure
Than if I 'd brought to light a hidden trea-
 sure.
As to my sonnets, though none else should
 heed them,
I feel delighted, still, that you should read
 them.
Of late, too, I have had much calm enjoy-
 ment,
Stretch'd on the grass at my best lov'd em-
 ployment 120
Of scribbling lines for you. These things
 I thought
While, in my face, the freshest breeze I
 caught.
E'en now I 'm pillow'd on a bed of flowers
That crowns a lofty cliff, which proudly
 towers
Above the ocean waves. The stalks and
 blades
Chequer my tablet with their quivering
 shades.
On one side is a field of drooping oats,
Through which the poppies show their
 scarlet coats; 128
So pert and useless, that they bring to mind
The scarlet coats that pester human-kind.
And on the other side, outspread, is seen
Ocean's blue mantle, streak'd with purple,
 and green;
Now 't is I see a canvass'd ship, and now
Mark the bright silver curling round her
 prow.
I see the lark down-dropping to his nest,
And the broad-winged sea-gull never at rest;
For when no more he spreads his feathers
 free,
His breast is dancing on the restless sea.
Now I direct my eyes into the west,
Which at this moment is in sunbeams
 drest: 140
Why westward turn ? 'T was but to say
 adieu !
'T was but to kiss my hand, dear George,
 to you !

TO MY BROTHER GEORGE

The first in the group of sonnets in the 1817
volume. A transcript by George Keats bears
the date ' Margate, August, 1816.'

MANY the wonders I this day have seen:
 The sun, when first he kist away the tears
 That fill'd the eyes of morn; — the lau-
 rell'd peers
Who from the feathery gold of evening
 lean; —
The ocean with its vastness, its blue green,
 Its ships, its rocks, its caves, its hopes,
 its fears, —
 Its voice mysterious, which whoso hears
Must think on what will be, and what has
 been.
E'en now, dear George, while this for you I
 write,
 Cynthia is from her silken curtains peep-
 ing
So scantly, that it seems her bridal night,
 And she her half-discover'd revels keep-
 ing.
But what, without the social thought of
 thee,
Would be the wonders of the sky and sea ?

TO ——

There is no clue to the identity of the per-
son addressed and no date is affixed. It was
published in the 1817 volume, and there follows
the one addressed to his brother George.

HAD I a man's fair form, then might my
 sighs
 Be echoed swiftly through that ivory
 shell
 Thine ear, and find thy gentle heart; so
 well
Would passion arm me for the enterprise:
But ah ! I am no knight whose foeman dies;
 No cuirass glistens on my bosom's swell;
 I am no happy shepherd of the dell
Whose lips have trembled with a maiden's
 eyes.

Yet must I dote upon thee, — call thee
 sweet,
 Sweeter by far than Hybla's honied roses
 When steep'd in dew rich to intoxica-
 tion.
Ah! I will taste that dew, for me 't is meet,
 And when the moon her pallid face dis-
 closes,
 I 'll gather some by spells, and incan-
 tation.

SPECIMEN OF AN INDUCTION
TO A POEM

 This poem was published in the 1817 volume
where it immediately precedes *Calidore.* Leigh
Hunt, when reviewing the volume on its ap-
pearance, speaks of the two poems as connected,
and in Tom Keats's copybook they are written
continuously. The same copy contains a memo-
randum 'marked by Leigh Hunt — 1816.'

Lo! I must tell a tale of chivalry;
For large white plumes are dancing in mine
 eye.
Not like the formal crest of latter days:
But bending in a thousand graceful ways;
So graceful, that it seems no mortal hand,
Or e'en the touch of Archimago's wand,
Could charm them into such an attitude.
We must think rather, that in playful mood,
Some mountain breeze had turned its chief
 delight,
To show this wonder of its gentle might. 10
Lo! I must tell a tale of chivalry;
For while I muse, the lance points slant-
 ingly
Athwart the morning air; some lady sweet,
Who cannot feel for cold her tender feet,
From the worn top of some old battlement
Hails it with tears, her stout defender sent:
And from her own pure self no joy dissem-
 bling,
Wraps round her ample robe with happy
 trembling.
Sometimes, when the good Knight his rest
 would take,
It is reflected, clearly, in a lake, 20

With the young ashen boughs, 'gainst
 which it rests,
And th' half-seen mossiness of linnets'
 nests.
Ah! shall I ever tell its cruelty,
When the fire flashes from a warrior's eye,
And his tremendous hand is grasping it,
And his dark brow for very wrath is knit?
Or when his spirit, with more calm intent,
Leaps to the honours of a tournament,
And makes the gazers round about the
 ring
Stare at the grandeur of the balancing? 30
No, no! this is far off: — then how shall I
Revive the dying tones of minstrelsy,
Which linger yet about long gothic arches,
In dark green ivy, and among wild larches?
How sing the splendour of the revelries,
When butts of wine are drunk off to the
 lees?
And that bright lance, against the fretted
 wall,
Beneath the shade of stately banneral,
Is slung with shining cuirass, sword, and
 shield?
Where ye may see a spur in bloody field. 40
Light-footed damsels move with gentle
 paces
Round the wide hall, and show their happy
 faces;
Or stand in courtly talk by fives and sevens:
Like those fair stars that twinkle in the
 heavens.
Yet must I tell a tale of chivalry:
Or wherefore comes that knight so proudly
 by?
Wherefore more proudly does the gentle
 knight,
Rein in the swelling of his ample might?

Spenser! thy brows are archèd, open, kind,
And come like a clear sunrise to my
 mind; 50
And always does my heart with pleasure
 dance,
When I think on thy noble countenance:
Where never yet was ought more earthly
 seen

Than the pure freshness of thy laurels
 green.
Therefore, great bard, I not so fearfully
Call on thy gentle spirit to hover nigh
My daring steps : or if thy tender care,
Thus startled unaware,
Be jealous that the foot of other wight
Should madly follow that bright path of
 light 60
Trac'd by thy lov'd Libertas; he will
 speak,
And tell thee that my prayer is very meek;
That I will follow with due reverence,
And start with awe at mine own strange
 pretence.
Him thou wilt hear; so I will rest in hope
To see wide plains, fair trees, and lawny
 slope:
The morn, the eve, the light, the shade, the
 flowers;
Clear streams, smooth lakes, and overlook-
 ing towers.

CALIDORE

A FRAGMENT

YOUNG Calidore is paddling o'er the lake ;
His healthful spirit eager and awake
To feel the beauty of a silent eve,
Which seem'd full loth this happy world to
 leave;
The light dwelt o'er the scene so linger-
 ingly.
He bares his forehead to the cool blue sky,
And smiles at the far clearness all around,
Until his heart is well nigh over wound,
And turns for calmness to the pleasant
 green
Of easy slopes, and shadowy trees that
 lean 10
So elegantly o'er the waters' brim
And show their blossoms trim.
Scarce can his clear and nimble eyesight
 follow
The freaks and dartings of the black-wing'd
 swallow,
Delighting much, to see it half at rest,

Dip so refreshingly its wings, and breast
'Gainst the smooth surface, and to mark
 anon,
The widening circles into nothing gone.

And now the sharp keel of his little boat
Comes up with ripple, and with easy
 float, 20
And glides into a bed of water-lilies:
Broad-leav'd are they, and their white can-
 opies
Are upward turn'd to catch the heavens'
 dew.
Near to a little island's point they grew;
Whence Calidore might have the goodliest
 view
Of this sweet spot of earth. The bowery
 shore
Went off in gentle windings to the hoar
And light blue mountains : but no breath-
 ing man
With a warm heart, and eye prepared to scan
Nature's clear beauty, could pass lightly
 by 30
Objects that look'd out so invitingly
On either side. These, gentle Calidore
Greeted, as he had known them long before.

The sidelong view of swelling leafiness,
Which the glad setting sun in gold doth
 dress;
Whence, ever and anon, the jay outsprings,
And scales upon the beauty of its wings.

The lonely turret, shatter'd, and outworn,
Stands venerably proud; too proud to
 mourn
Its long lost grandeur : fir-trees grow
 around, 40
Aye dropping their hard fruit upon the
 ground.

The little chapel, with the cross above,
Upholding wreaths of ivy; the white dove,
That on the windows spreads his feathers
 light,
And seems from purple clouds to wing its
 flight.

Green tufted islands casting their soft
 shades
Across the lake; sequester'd leafy glades,
That through the dimness of their twilight
 show
Large dock-leaves, spiral foxgloves, or the
 glow
Of the wild cat's-eyes, or the silvery stems
Of delicate birch-trees, or long grass which
 hems 51
A little brook. The youth had long been
 viewing
These pleasant things, and heaven was
 bedewing
The mountain flowers, when his glad senses
 caught
A trumpet's silver voice. Ah! it was
 fraught
With many joys for him : the warder's ken
Had found white coursers prancing in the
 glen:
Friends very dear to him he soon will see;
So pushes off his boat most eagerly,
And soon upon the lake he skims along, 60
Deaf to the nightingale's first under-song;
Nor minds he the white swans that dream
 so sweetly:
His spirit flies before him so completely.

And now he turns a jutting point of land,
Whence may be seen the castle gloomy, and
 grand:
Nor will a bee buzz round two swelling
 peaches,
Before the point of his light shallop reaches
Those marble steps that through the water
 dip:
Now over them he goes with hasty trip,
And scarcely stays to ope the folding
 doors: 70
Anon he leaps along the oaken floors
Of halls and corridors.

Delicious sounds! those little bright-eyed
 things
That float about the air on azure wings,
Had been less heartfelt by him than the
 clang

Of clattering hoofs; into the court he
 sprang,
Just as two noble steeds, and palfreys twain,
Were slanting out their necks with loosen'd
 rein;
While from beneath the threat'ning port-
 cullis
They brought their happy burthens. What
 a kiss, 80
What gentle squeeze he gave each lady's
 hand !
How tremblingly their delicate ankles
 spann'd !
Into how sweet a trance his soul was gone,
While whisperings of affection
Made him delay to let their tender feet
Come to the earth; with an incline so sweet
From their low palfreys o'er his neck they
 bent:
And whether there were tears of languish-
 ment,
Or that the evening dew had pearl'd their
 tresses,
He feels a moisture on his cheek, and
 blesses 90
With lips that tremble, and with glistening
 eye,
All the soft luxury
That nestled in his arms. A dimpled hand,
Fair as some wonder out of fairy land,
Hung from his shoulder like the drooping
 flowers
Of whitest Cassia, fresh from summer
 showers:
And this he fondled with his happy cheek,
As if for joy he would no further seek;
When the kind voice of good Sir Clerimond
Came to his ear, like something from be-
 yond 100
His present being: so he gently drew
His warm arms, thrilling now with pulses
 new,
From their sweet thrall, and forward gently
 bending,
Thank'd Heaven that his joy was never
 ending;
While 'gainst his forehead he devoutly
 press'd

A hand Heaven made to succour the dis-
 tress'd;
A hand that from the world's bleak promon-
 tory
Had lifted Calidore for deeds of glory.

 Amid the pages, and the torches' glare,
There stood a knight, patting the flowing
 hair 110
Of his proud horse's mane: he was withal
A man of elegance, and stature tall:
So that the waving of his plumes would be
High as the berries of a wild ash-tree,
Or as the wingèd cap of Mercury.
His armour was so dexterously wrought
In shape, that sure no living man had
 thought
It hard, and heavy steel: but that indeed
It was some glorious form, some splendid
 weed,
In which a spirit new come from the
 skies 120
Might live, and show itself to human eyes.
'T is the far-fam'd, the brave Sir Gondi-
 bert,
Said the good man to Calidore alert;
While the young warrior with a step of
 grace
Came up, — a courtly smile upon his face,
And mailèd hand held out, ready to greet
The large-eyed wonder, and ambitious heat
Of the aspiring boy; who as he led
Those smiling ladies, often turned his head
To admire the visor arched so gracefully 130
Over a knightly brow; while they went by
The lamps that from the high-roof'd hall
 were pendent,
And gave the steel a shining quite tran-
 scendent.

 Soon in a pleasant chamber they are
 seated ;
The sweet-lipp'd ladies have already
 greeted
All the green leaves that round the window
 clamber,
To show their purple stars, and bells of
 amber.

Sir Gondibert has doff'd his shining steel,
Gladdening in the free, and airy feel
Of a light mantle; and while Clerimond 140
Is looking round about him with a fond
And placid eye, young Calidore is burning
To hear of knightly deeds, and gallant
 spurning
Of all unworthiness; and how the strong of
 arm
Kept off dismay, and terror, and alarm
From lovely woman: while brimful of this,
He gave each damsel's hand so warm a kiss,
And had such manly ardour in his eye,
That each at other look'd half-staringly;
And then their features started into
 smiles, 150
Sweet as blue heavens o'er enchanted isles.

Softly the breezes from the forest came,
Softly they blew aside the taper's flame;
Clear was the song from Philomel's far
 bower;
Grateful the incense from the lime-tree
 flower;
Mysterious, wild, the far heard trumpet's
 tone;
Lovely the moon in ether, all alone:
Sweet too the converse of these happy mor-
 tals,
As that of busy spirits when the portals
Are closing in the west; or that soft hum-
 ming 160
We hear around when Hesperus is coming.
Sweet be their sleep. . . .

EPISTLE TO CHARLES
COWDEN CLARKE

 This epistle printed in the 1817 volume is
there dated September, 1816, when Clarke was
in his twenty-ninth year. He was by eight
years Keats's senior, and he lived till his nineti-
eth year.

OFT have you seen a swan superbly frown-
 ing,
And with proud breast his own white
 shadow crowning;

He slants his neck beneath the waters
 bright
So silently, it seems a beam of light
Come from the galaxy: anon he sports, —
With outspread wings the Naiad Zephyr
 courts,
Or ruffles all the surface of the lake
In striving from its crystal face to take
Some diamond water-drops, and them to
 treasure
In milky nest, and sip them off at lei-
 sure. 10
But not a moment can he there insure them,
Nor to such downy rest can he allure them;
For down they rush as though they would
 be free,
And drop like hours into eternity.
Just like that bird am I in loss of time,
Whene'er I venture on the stream of rhyme;
With shatter'd boat, oar snapt, and canvas
 rent,
I slowly sail, scarce knowing my intent;
Still scooping up the water with my fingers,
In which a trembling diamond never
 lingers. 20

 By this, friend Charles, you may full
 plainly see
Why I have never penn'd a line to thee:
Because my thoughts were never free, and
 clear,
And little fit to please a classic ear;
Because my wine was of too poor a savour
For one whose palate gladdens in the fla-
 vour
Of sparkling Helicon: — small good it were
To take him to a desert rude, and bare,
Who had on Baiæ's shore reclin'd at ease,
While Tasso's page was floating in a
 breeze 30
That gave soft music from Armida's
 bowers,
Mingled with fragrance from her rarest
 flowers:
Small good to one who had by Mulla's
 stream
Fondled the maidens with the breasts of
 cream;

Who had beheld Belphœbe in a brook,
And lovely Una in a leafy nook,
And Archimago leaning o'er his book:
Who had of all that's sweet tasted, and
 seen,
From silv'ry ripple, up to beauty's queen;
From the sequester'd haunts of gay Tita-
 nia, 40
To the blue dwelling of divine Urania:
One, who of late had ta'en sweet forest
 walks
With him who elegantly chats and talks —
The wrong'd Libertas, — who has told you
 stories
Of laurel chaplets, and Apollo's glories;
Of troops chivalrous prancing through a
 city,
And tearful ladies made for love, and pity:
With many else which I have never known.
Thus have I thought; and days on days
 have flown
Slowly, or rapidly — unwilling still 50
For you to try my dull, unlearned quill.
Nor should I now, but that I 've known you
 long;
That you first taught me all the sweets of
 song:
The grand, the sweet, the terse, the free,
 the fine:
What swell'd with pathos, and what right
 divine:
Spenserian vowels that elope with ease,
And float along like birds o'er summer
 seas:
Miltonian storms, and more, Miltonian ten-
 derness:
Michael in arms, and more, meek Eve's fair
 slenderness.
Who read for me the sonnet swelling
 loudly 60
Up to its climax, and then dying proudly?
Who found for me the grandeur of the
 ode,
Growing, like Atlas, stronger from its load?
Who let me taste that more than cordial
 dram,
The sharp, the rapier-pointed epigram?
Show'd me that epic was of all the king,

Round, vast, and spanning all, like Saturn's
 ring ?
You too upheld the veil from Clio's beauty,
And pointed out the patriot's stern duty;
The might of Alfred, and the shaft of
 Tell; 70
The hand of Brutus, that so grandly fell
Upon a tyrant's head. Ah! had I never
 seen,
Or known your kindness, what might I
 have been ?
What my enjoyments in my youthful years,
Bereft of all that now my life endears ?
And can I e'er these benefits forget ?
And can I e'er repay the friendly debt ?
No, doubly no; — yet should these rhym-
 ings please,
I shall roll on the grass with twofold ease;
For I have long time been my fancy feed-
 ing 80
With hopes that you would one day think
 the reading
Of my rough verses not an hour misspent;
Should it e'er be so, what a rich content !
Some weeks have pass'd since last I saw
 the spires
In lucent Thames reflected: — warm de-
 sires
To see the sun o'er-peep the eastern dim-
 ness
And morning shadows streaking into slim-
 ness,
Across the lawny fields, and pebbly water;
To mark the time as they grow broad, and
 shorter;
To feel the air that plays about the hills, 90
And sips its freshness from the little rills;
To see high, golden corn wave in the light
When Cynthia smiles upon a summer's
 night,
And peers among the cloudlet's jet and
 white,
As though she were reclining in a bed
Of bean blossoms, in heaven freshly shed.
No sooner had I stepp'd into these plea-
 sures,
Than I began to think of rhymes and mea-
 sures;

The air that floated by me seem'd to say
' Write ! thou wilt never have a better
 day.' 100
And so I did. When many lines I'd
 written,
Though with their grace I was not over-
 smitten,
Yet, as my hand was warm, I thought I'd
 better
Trust to my feelings, and write you a letter.
Such an attempt required an inspiration
Of a peculiar sort, — a consummation; —
Which, had I felt, these scribblings might
 have been
Verses from which the soul would never
 wean;
But many days have past since last my
 heart 109
Was warm'd luxuriously by divine Mozart;
By Arne delighted, or by Handel mad-
 den'd; .
Or by the song of Erin pierc'd and sad-
 den'd:
What time you were before the music
 sitting,
And the rich notes to each sensation fitting.
Since I have walk'd with you through shady
 lanes
That freshly terminate in open plains,
And revell'd in a chat that ceasèd not
When at night-fall among your books we
 got:
No, nor when supper came, nor after that, —
Nor when reluctantly I took my hat; 120
No, nor till cordially you shook my hand
Mid-way between our homes: — your ac-
 cents bland
Still sounded in my ears, when I no more
Could hear your footsteps touch the grav'ly
 floor.
Sometimes I lost them, and then found
 again;
You changed the foot-path for the grassy
 plain.
In those still moments I have wish'd you
 joys
That well you know to honour: — ' Life's
 very toys

With him,' said I, ' will take a pleasant
 charm;
It cannot be that ought will work him
 harm.' 130
These thoughts now come o'er me with all
 their might: —
Again I shake your hand, — friend Charles,
 good night.

TO MY BROTHERS

Though the poem is thus headed in the 1817
volume, where it is dated November 18, 1816,
it might as properly have the heading given it
in Tom Keats's copybook: ' Written to his
Brother Tom on his Birthday,' with the same
date.

SMALL, busy flames play through the fresh-
 laid coals,
 And their faint cracklings o'er our si-
 lence creep
 Like whispers of the household gods that
 keep
A gentle empire o'er fraternal souls.
And while, for rhymes, I search around the
 poles,
 Your eyes are fix'd, as in poetic sleep,
 Upon the lore so voluble and deep,
That aye at fall of night our care condoles.
This is your birth-day, Tom, and I rejoice
That thus it passes smoothly, quietly:
Many such eves of gently whisp'ring noise
 May we together pass, and calmly try
What are this world's true joys, — ere the
 great Voice,
 From its fair face, shall bid our spirits fly.

ADDRESSED TO BENJAMIN
ROBERT HAYDON

The first of these two sonnets was sent by
Keats with this brief note: ' November 20,
1816. My dear Sir — Last evening wrought
me up, and I cannot forbear sending you the
following.' In his prompt acknowledgment
Haydon suggested the omission of the last four
words in the penultimate line, and proposed
sending the sonnet to Wordsworth. Keats re-
plied on the same day as his first note : ' Your
letter has filled me with a proud pleasure, and
shall be kept by me as a stimulus to exertion —
I begin to fix my eye upon one horizon. My
feelings entirely fall in with yours in regard to
the Ellipsis, and I glory in it. The Idea of
your sending it to Wordsworth put me out of
breath. You know with what Reverence I
would send my Well-wishes to him.' The pre-
sentation copy of the 1817 volume bears the
inscription ' To W. Wordsworth with the Au-
thor's sincere Reverence.' Both sonnets were
printed, but in the reverse order in the 1817
volume, and the ellipsis was preserved.

I

GREAT spirits now on earth are sojourning;
 He of the cloud, the cataract, the lake,
 Who on Helvellyn's summit, wide awake,
Catches his freshness from Archangel's
 wing:
He of the rose, the violet, the spring,
 The social smile, the chain for Freedom's
 sake:
 And lo ! — whose steadfastness would
 never take
A meaner sound than Raphael's whispering.
And other spirits there are standing apart
 Upon the forehead of the age to come;
These, these will give the world another
 heart,
 And other pulses. Hear ye not the hum
Of mighty workings in the human mart ?
Listen awhile ye nations, and be dumb.

II

HIGHMINDEDNESS, a jealousy for good,
 A loving-kindness for the great man's
 fame,
 Dwells here and there with people of no
 name,
In noisome alley, and in pathless wood:
And where we think the truth least under-
 stood,
 Oft may be found a ' singleness of aim,'
 That ought to frighten into hooded shame
A money-mong'ring, pitiable brood.
How glorious this affection for the cause
 Of steadfast genius, toiling gallantly !

What when a stout unbending champion
 awes
 Envy, and Malice to their native sty?
Unnumber'd souls breathe out a still ap-
 plause,
 Proud to behold him in his country's eye.

TO KOSCIUSKO

First published in *The Examiner*, where it
is dated 'Dec., 1816.' It is included in the
1817 volume.

GOOD Kosciusko, thy great name alone
 Is a full harvest whence to reap high
 feeling;
 It comes upon us like the glorious pealing
Of the wide spheres — an everlasting tone.
And now it tells me, that in worlds unknown,
 The names of heroes, burst from clouds
 concealing,
 Are changed to harmonies, for ever
 stealing
Through cloudless blue, and round each
 silver throne.
It tells me too, that on a happy day,
 When some good spirit walks upon the
 earth,
 Thy name with Alfred's, and the great
 of yore,
 Gently commingling, gives tremendous
 birth
To a loud hymn, that sounds far, far away
 To where the great God lives for ever-
 more.

TO G. A. W.

Georgiana Augusta Wylie, who afterward
married George Keats. For other verses ad-
dressed to this lady see pp. 11, 240, 243.
 This sonnet in Tom Keats's copybook is
dated December, 1816; it was published in the
1817 volume.

NYMPH of the downward smile and side-
 long glance,
 In what diviner moments of the day
 Art thou most lovely? When gone far
 astray

Into the labyrinths of sweet utterance?
Or when serenely wand'ring in a trance
 Of sober thought? Or when starting
 away,
 With careless robe, to meet the morning
 ray,
Thou spar'st the flowers in thy mazy dance?
Haply 't is when thy ruby lips part sweetly,
 And so remain, because thou listenest:
·But thou to please wert nurtured so com-
 pletely
 That I can never tell what mood is best.
I shall as soon pronounce which Grace more
 neatly
 Trips it before Apollo than the rest.

STANZAS

There is no date given to this poem by Lord
Houghton, who published it in the 1848 edi-
tion, and no reference occurs to it in the *Letters*.
It was probably an early careless poem, very
likely a set of album verses.

IN a drear-nighted December,
 Too happy, happy tree,
Thy branches ne'er remember
 Their green felicity:
 The north cannot undo them,
 With a sleety whistle through them;
 Nor frozen thawings glue them
 From budding at the prime.

In a drear-nighted December,
 Too happy, happy brook,
Thy bubblings ne'er remember
 Apollo's summer look;
 But with a sweet forgetting,
 They stay their crystal fretting,
 Never, never petting
 About the frozen time.

Ah! would 't were so with many
 A gentle girl and boy!
But were there ever any
 Writh'd not at passèd joy?
 To know the change and feel it,
 When there is none to heal it,

Nor numbèd sense to steal it,
Was never said in rhyme.

WRITTEN IN DISGUST OF VULGAR SUPERSTITION

In Tom Keats's copybook this sonnet is dated 'Sunday evening, Dec. 24, 1816.' Lord Houghton gives it in the Aldine edition, and heads it 'Written on a Summer Evening.' Possibly the seventh line may be adduced as evidence of the wintry season.

THE church bells toll a melancholy round,
 Calling the people to some other prayers,
 Some other gloominess, more dreadful cares,
More hearkening to the sermon's horrid sound.
Surely the mind of man is closely bound
 In some black spell; seeing that each one tears
 Himself from fireside joys, and Lydian airs,
And converse high of those with glory crown'd.
Still, still they toll, and I should feel a damp, —
A chill as from a tomb, did I not know
That they are dying like an outburnt lamp;
 That 't is their sighing, wailing ere they go
Into oblivion; — that fresh flowers will grow,
And many glories of immortal stamp.

SONNET

Published in the 1817 volume, but there is no evidence as to its exact date. It is the latest in order of the sonnets, immediately preceding *Sleep and Poetry.*

HAPPY is England! I could be content
 To see no other verdure than its own;
 To feel no other breezes than are blown
Through its tall woods with high romances blent:

Yet do I sometimes feel a languishment
For skies Italian, and an inward groan
To sit upon an Alp as on a throne,
And half forget what world or worldling meant.
Happy is England, sweet her artless daughters;
 Enough their simple loveliness for me,
 Enough their whitest arms in silence clinging:
 Yet do I often warmly burn to see
 Beauties of deeper glance, and hear their singing,
And float with them about the summer waters.

ON THE GRASSHOPPER AND CRICKET

Written December 30, 1816, on a challenge from Leigh Hunt, who printed both his and Keats's sonnets in his paper, *The Examiner.* Keats included the sonnet in his 1817 volume. Leigh Hunt's sonnet will be found in the NOTES AND ILLUSTRATIONS.

THE poetry of earth is never dead:
 When all the birds are faint with the hot sun,
 And hide in cooling trees, a voice will run
From hedge to hedge about the new-mown mead;
That is the Grasshopper's — he takes the lead
 In summer luxury, — he has never done
 With his delights; for when tired out with fun,
He rests at ease beneath some pleasant weed.
The poetry of earth is ceasing never:
 On a lone winter evening, when the frost
 Has wrought a silence, from the stove there shrills
The Cricket's song, in warmth increasing ever,
 And seems to one, in drowsiness half lost,
 The Grasshopper's among some grassy hills.

SONNET

Printed in The Examiner, *February 23, 1817,
and dated by Lord Houghton, when reprinting
it, ' January, 1817.'*

AFTER dark vapours have oppress'd our
 plains
 For a long dreary season, comes a day
 Born of the gentle South, and clears
 away
From the sick heavens all unseemly stains.
The anxious month, relieved its pains,
 Takes as a long-lost right the feel of
 May;
 The eyelids with the passing coolness
 play,
Like rose leaves with the drip of summer
 rains.
And calmest thoughts come round us; as,
 of leaves
 Budding, — fruit ripening in stillness, —
 Autumn suns
Smiling at eve upon the quiet sheaves, —
Sweet Sappho's cheek, — a sleeping infant's
 breath, —
 The gradual sand that through an hour-
 glass runs, —
A woodland rivulet, — a Poet's death.

WRITTEN ON THE BLANK SPACE AT THE END OF CHAUCER'S TALE OF 'THE FLOURE AND THE LEFE'

Written in February, 1817, and published in
The Examiner, *March 16, 1817. There is a
pleasant story that Charles Cowden Clarke had
fallen asleep over the book, and woke to find
this epilogue.*

THIS pleasant tale is like a little copse:
 The honied lines so freshly interlace,
 To keep the reader in so sweet a place,
So that he here and there full-hearted
 stops;
And oftentimes he feels the dewy drops
 Come cool and suddenly against his face,

And, by the wandering melody, may trace
Which way the tender-legged linnet hops.
Oh! what a power has white simplicity !
 What mighty power has this gentle story !
 I, that do ever feel athirst for glory,
Could at this moment be content to lie
 Meekly upon the grass, as those whose
 sobbings
 Were heard of none beside the mournful
 robins.

ON SEEING THE ELGIN MARBLES

*This and the following sonnet were printed
in* The Examiner, *March 9, 1817, and reprinted
in* Life, Letters and Literary Remains.

MY spirit is too weak — mortality
 Weighs heavily on me like unwilling
 sleep,
 And each imagin'd pinnacle and steep
Of godlike hardship tells me I must die
Like a sick Eagle looking at the sky.
 Yet 't is a gentle luxury to weep
 That I have not the cloudy winds to
 keep,
Fresh for the opening of the morning's eye.
Such dim-conceivèd glories of the brain
 Bring round the heart an indescribable
 feud;
So do these wonders a most dizzy pain,
 That mingles Grecian grandeur with the
 rude
Wasting of old Time — with a billowy
 main —
 A sun — a shadow of a magnitude.

TO HAYDON

(WITH THE PRECEDING SONNET)

HAYDON ! forgive me that I cannot speak
 Definitively of these mighty things;
 Forgive me, that I have not Eagle's
 wings —
That ' what I want I know not where to
 seek:

And think that I would not be over meek,
 In rolling out upfollow'd thunderings,
 Even to the steep of Heliconian springs,
Were I of ample strength for such a
 freak —
Think too, that all those numbers should
 be thine;
 Whose else ? In this who touch thy
 vesture's hem ?
For when men star'd at what was most
 divine
 With browless idiotism — o'erwise
 phlegm —
Thou hadst beheld the Hesperean shine
 Of their star in the East, and gone to
 worship them.

TO LEIGH HUNT, ESQ.

This stood as dedication to the 1817 volume,
which was published in the month of March.
Charles Cowden Clarke makes the statement:
'On the evening when the last proof sheet was
brought from the printer, it was accompanied
by the information that if a " dedication to the
book was intended, it must be sent forthwith."
Whereupon he withdrew to a side table, and in
the buzz of a mixed conversation (for there
were several friends in the room) he composed
and brought to Charles Ollier, the publisher,
the dedication sonnet to Leigh Hunt.'

GLORY and loveliness have pass'd away;
 For if we wander out in early morn,
 No wreathèd incense do we see upborne
Into the east, to meet the smiling day:
No crowd of nymphs soft-voic'd and young,
 and gay,
 In woven baskets bringing ears of corn,
 Roses, and pinks, and violets, to adorn
The shrine of Flora in her early May.
But there are left delights as high as these,
 And I shall ever bless my destiny,
That in a time, when under pleasant trees
 Pan is no longer sought, I feel a free,
A leafy luxury, seeing I could please
 With these poor offerings, a man like
 thee.

ON THE SEA

Sent in a letter to Reynolds, dated April 17,
1817. 'From want of regular rest,' Keats
says, 'I have been rather *narvus*, and the pas-
sage in *Lear* — " Do you not hear the sea ? " —
has haunted me intensely.' He then copies the
sonnet, which was published in *The Champion*,
August 17 of the same year. The letter was
written from Carisbrooke. He had been sent
away from London by his brothers a month
before, shortly after the appearance of his first
volume of *Poems*, and his letters show the
nervous, restless condition into which he had
been driven by that venture.

IT keeps eternal whisperings around
 Desolate shores, and with its mighty
 swell
 Gluts twice ten thousand caverns, till the
 spell
Of Hecate leaves them their old shadowy
 sound.
Often 't is in such gentle temper found,
 That scarcely will the very smallest shell
 Be mov'd for days from where it some-
 time fell,
When last the winds of Heaven were
 unbound.
O ye ! who have your eyeballs vex'd and
 tir'd,
 Feast them upon the wideness of the Sea;
 O ye ! whose ears are dinn'd with up-
 roar rude,
 Or fed too much with cloying melody,—
 Sit ye near some old cavern's mouth,
 and brood
Until ye start, as if the sea-nymphs quired !

LINES

First published, with the date 1817, in *Life,
Letters and Literary Remains*. It is barely
possible that this is the 'song' to which Keats
refers in a letter to Benjamin Bailey, dated
November 22, 1817, when he says : 'I am cer-
tain of nothing but the holiness of the Heart's
affections, and the truth of Imagination. What
the Imagination seizes as Beauty must be truth

— whether it existed before or not — for I have the same idea of all our passions as of Love : they are all, in their sublime, creative of essential Beauty. In a word, you may know my favourite speculation by my first Book, and the little Song I sent in my last, which is a representation from the fancy of the probable mode of operating in these matters.'

UNFELT, unheard, unseen,
　I 've left my little queen,
Her languid arms in silver slumber lying:
　Ah ! through their nestling touch,
　Who — who could tell how much
There is for madness — cruel, or comply-
　ing ?

Those faery lids how sleek !
　Those lips how moist ! — they speak,
In ripest quiet, shadows of sweet sounds:
　Into my fancy's ear
　Melting a burden dear,
How 'Love doth know no fulness, and no
　bounds.'

True ! — tender monitors !
　I bend unto your laws:
This sweetest day for dalliance was born !
　So, without more ado,
　I 'll feel my heaven anew,
For all the blushing of the hasty morn.

ON ——

Published with the date 1817 by Lord Houghton in *Life, Letters and Literary Remains*, but slightly varied in form when reprinted in the Aldine edition.

THINK not of it, sweet one, so; —
　Give it not a tear;
Sigh thou mayst, and bid it go
　Any — any where.

Do not look so sad, sweet one, —
　Sad and fadingly;
Shed one drop, then it is gone,
　Oh ! 't was born to die !

Still so pale ? then dearest weep;
　Weep, I 'll count the tears,
For each will I invent a bliss
　For thee in after years.

Brighter has it left thine eyes
　Than a sunny rill;
And thy whispering melodies
　Are more tender still.

Yet — as all things mourn awhile
　At fleeting blisses;
E'en let us too; but be our dirge
　A dirge of kisses.

ON A PICTURE OF LEANDER

This sonnet was printed in 1829 in *The Gem, a Literary Annual*, edited by Thomas Hood. It is not dated, but may fairly be assigned to this time.

COME hither, all sweet maidens soberly,
　Down-looking aye, and with a chasten'd
　　light
Hid in the fringes of your eyelids white,
And meekly let your fair hands joined be,
As if so gentle that ye could not see,
　Untouch'd, a victim of your beauty bright,
　Sinking away to his young spirit's night,
Sinking bewilder'd 'mid the dreary sea:
'T is young Leander toiling to his death;
　Nigh swooning, he doth purse his weary
　　lips
　　For Hero's cheek, and smiles against
　　　her smile.
　O horrid dream ! see how his body dips
　　Dead-heavy; arms and shoulders gleam
　　　awhile:
He 's gone; up bubbles all his amorous
　breath !

ON LEIGH HUNT'S POEM, 'THE STORY OF RIMINI'

Dated 1817 in the *Life, Letters and Literary Remains*, and placed next after the preceding.

Who loves to peer up at the morning sun,
 With half-shut eyes and comfortable
 cheek,
Let him, with this sweet tale, full often
 seek
For meadows where the little rivers run;
Who loves to linger with that brightest one
 Of Heaven — Hesperus — let him lowly
 speak
 These numbers to the night, and star-
 light meek,
Or moon, if that her hunting be begun.
He who knows these delights, and too is
 prone
To moralize upon a smile or tear,
Will find at once a region of his own,
 A bower for his spirit, and will steer
To alleys, where the fir-tree drops its cone,
 Where robins hop, and fallen leaves are
 sear.

SONNET

First published in *Life, Letters and Literary
Remains*, but dated 1817 in a manuscript copy
owned by Sir Charles Dilke. Keats sends it
as his 'last sonnet' in a letter to Reynolds
written on the last day of January, 1818.

When I have fears that I may cease to
 be
 Before my pen has glean'd my teeming
 brain,
Before high pilèd books, in charactry,
 Hold like rich garners the full-ripen'd
 grain;
When I behold, upon the night's starr'd
 face,
 Huge cloudy symbols of a high romance,
And think that I may never live to trace
 Their shadows, with the magic hand of
 chance;
And when I feel, fair creature of an hour !
 That I shall never look upon thee more,
Never have relish in the faery power
 Of unreflecting love; — then on the shore
Of the wide world I stand alone, and think
Till Love and Fame to nothingness do sink.

ON SEEING A LOCK OF MILTON'S HAIR

'I was at Hunt's the other day,' writes
Keats to Bailey, January 23, 1818, 'and he
surprised me with a real authenticated lock of
Milton's Hair. I know you would like what I
wrote thereon, so here it is — *as they say of a
sheep in a Nursery Book*.' 'This I did,' he
adds, after copying the lines, 'at Hunt's at
his request — perhaps I should have done
something better alone and at home.' Lord
Houghton printed the verse in *Life, Letters
and Literary Remains*.

Chief of organic numbers !
 Old Scholar of the Spheres !
Thy spirit never slumbers,
 But rolls about our ears,
For ever and for ever !
 O what a mad endeavour
 Worketh he,
Who to thy sacred and ennobled hearse
Would offer a burnt sacrifice of verse
 And melody.

How heavenward thou soundest,
 Live Temple of sweet noise,
And Discord unconfoundest,
 Giving Delight new joys,
And Pleasure nobler pinions !
 O, where are thy dominions ?
 Lend thine ear
To a young Delian oath, — ay, by thy soul,
By all that from thy mortal lips did roll,
And by the kernel of thine earthly love,
Beauty, in things on earth, and things above,
 I swear !
 When every childish fashion
 Has vanish'd from my rhyme,
 Will I, grey-gone in passion,
 Leave to an after-time,
 Hymning and harmony
Of thee, and of thy works, and of thy
 life;
But vain is now the burning and the strife.
Pangs are in vain, until I grow high-rife
 With old Philosophy,
And mad with glimpses of futurity !

For many years my offering must be hush'd;
 When I do speak, I'll think upon this
 hour,
Because I feel my forehead hot and flush'd.
 Even at the simplest vassal of thy
 power, —
 A lock of thy bright hair —
 Sudden it came,
And I was startled, when I caught thy name
 Coupled so unaware;
Yet, at the moment, temperate was my
 blood.
I thought I had beheld it from the flood.

ON SITTING DOWN TO READ 'KING LEAR' ONCE AGAIN

In a letter to his brothers, dated January 23, 1818, Keats says: 'I think a little change has taken place in my intellect lately — I cannot bear to be uninterested or unemployed, I, who for so long a time have been addicted to passiveness. Nothing is finer for the purposes of great productions than a very gradual ripening of the intellectual powers. As an instance of this — observe — I sat down yesterday to read King Lear once again : the thing appeared to demand the prologue of a sonnet, I wrote it, and began to read — (I know you would like to see it). So you see,' he goes on after copying the sonnet, 'I am getting at it with a sort of determination and strength, though verily I do not feel it at this moment.' The sonnet was printed in *Life, Letters and Literary Remains.*

O GOLDEN-TONGUED Romance, with se-
 rene lute !
 Fair plumèd Syren, Queen of far away !
 Leave melodizing on this wintry day,
Shut up thine olden pages, and be mute:
Adieu ! for once again the fierce dispute,
 Betwixt damnation and impassion'd clay,
 Must I burn through; once more humbly
 assay
The bitter sweet of this Shakespearean
 fruit:
Chief Poet ! and ye clouds of Albion,
 Begetters of our deep eternal theme !

When through the old oak forest I am gone,
 Let me not wander in a barren dream,
But when I am consumèd in the Fire,
Give me new Phœnix-wings to fly at my
 desire.

LINES ON THE MERMAID TAVERN

In sending his *Robin Hood* verses to Reynolds (see next poem), Keats added the following, but from the tenor of his letter, it would appear that they had been written earlier and were sent at Reynolds's request. The poem was published by Keats in his *Lamia, Isabella, The Eve of St. Agnes, and other Poems,* 1820. The friends were then in full tide of sympathy with the Elizabethans, and would have been very much at home with Shakespeare, Jonson, and Marlowe at the Mermaid.

SOULS of Poets dead and gone,
What Elysium have ye known,
Happy field or mossy cavern,
Choicer than the Mermaid Tavern ?
Have ye tippled drink more fine
Than mine host's Canary wine ?
Or are fruits of Paradise
Sweeter than these dainty pies
Of venison ? O generous food !
Drest as though bold Robin Hood 10
Would, with his maid Marian,
Sup and bowse from horn and can.

 I have heard that on a day
Mine host's sign-board flew away,
Nobody knew whither, till
An astrologer's old quill
To a sheepskin gave the story,
Said he saw you in your glory,
Underneath a new-old sign
Sipping beverage divine, 20
And pledging with contented smack
The Mermaid in the Zodiac.

 Souls of Poets dead and gone,
What Elysium have ye known,
Happy field or mossy cavern,
Choicer than the Mermaid Tavern ?

ROBIN HOOD

TO A FRIEND

The friend was J. H. Reynolds, who had sent Keats two sonnets which he had written on Robin Hood. Keats's letter, dated February 3, 1818, is full of energetic pleasantry on the poetry which ' has a palpable design upon us,' and concludes: ' Let us have the old Poets and Robin Hood. Your letter and its sonnets gave me more pleasure than will the Fourth Book of *Childe Harold*, and the whole of anybody's life and opinions. In return for your Dish of Filberts, I have gathered a few Catkins. I hope they 'll look pretty.' Keats included the poem in his *Lamia, Isabella, The Eve of St. Agnes and other Poems*, 1820, with some trifling changes of text.

No ! those days are gone away,
And their hours are old and gray,
And their minutes buried all
Under the down-trodden pall
Of the leaves of many years:
Many times have Winter's shears,
Frozen North, and chilling East,
Sounded tempests to the feast
Of the forest's whispering fleeces,
Since men knew nor rent nor leases. 10

No, the bugle sounds no more,
And the twanging bow no more;
Silent is the ivory shrill
Past the heath and up the hill;
There is no mid-forest laugh,
Where lone Echo gives the half
To some wight, amaz'd to hear
Jesting, deep in forest drear.

On the fairest time of June
You may go, with sun or moon, 20
Or the seven stars to light you,
Or the polar ray to right you;
But you never may behold
Little John, or Robin bold;
Never one, of all the clan,
Thrumming on an empty can
Some old hunting ditty, while
He doth his green way beguile

To fair hostess Merriment,
Down beside the pasture Trent; 30
For he left the merry tale,
Messenger for spicy ale.

Gone, the merry morris din;
Gone, the song of Gamelyn;
Gone, the tough-belted outlaw
Idling in the ' grenè shawe;'
All are gone away and past !
And if Robin should be cast
Sudden from his turfèd grave,
And if Marian should have 40
Once again her forest days,
She would weep, and he would craze:
He would swear, for all his oaks,
Fall'n beneath the dock-yard strokes,
Have rotted on the briny seas;
She would weep that her wild bees
Sang not to her — Strange ! that honey
Can't be got without hard money !

So it is; yet let us sing
Honour to the old bow-string ! 50
Honour to the bugle horn !
Honour to the woods unshorn !
Honour to the Lincoln green !
Honour to the archer keen !
Honour to tight little John,
And the horse he rode upon !
Honour to bold Robin Hood,
Sleeping in the underwood !
Honour to Maid Marian,
And to all the Sherwood clan ! 60
Though their days have hurried by,
Let us two a burden try.

TO THE NILE

Composed February 4, 1818, in company with Shelley and Hunt, who each wrote a sonnet on the same theme. It was first published by Lord Houghton in the *Life, Letters and Literary Remains*.

Son of the old moon-mountains African !
 Chief of the Pyramid and Crocodile !
 We call thee fruitful, and that very while

A desert fills our seeing's inward span;
Nurse of swart nations since the world
 began,
 Art thou so fruitful? or dost thou be-
 guile
 Such men to honour thee, who, worn with
 toil,
Rest for a space 'twixt Cairo and De-
 can?
O may dark fancies err! They surely
 do;
 'T is ignorance that makes a barren waste
Of all beyond itself. Thou dost bedew
 Green rushes like our rivers, and dost
 taste
The pleasant sun-rise. Green isles hast
 thou too,
 And to the sea as happily dost haste.

TO SPENSER

Printed in *Life, Letters and Literary Re-
mains*, and undated. Afterward, when Lord
Houghton printed it in the Aldine edition of
1876, he noted that he had seen a transcript
given by Keats to Mrs. Longmore, a sister of
Reynolds, dated by the recipient, February 5,
1818. But Lord Houghton is confident that
the sonnet was written much earlier.

SPENSER! a jealous honourer of thine,
 A forester deep in thy midmost trees,
Did last eve ask my promise to refine
 Some English that might strive thine ear
 to please.
 But Elfin Poet, 't is impossible
For an inhabitant of wintry earth
 To rise like Phœbus with a golden quill
Fire-wing'd and make a morning in his
 mirth.
It is impossible to escape from toil
O' the sudden and receive thy spiriting:
 The flower must drink the nature of the
 soil
Before it can put forth its blossoming:
 Be with me in the summer days, and I
 Will for thine honour and his pleasure
 try.

SONG

WRITTEN ON A BLANK PAGE IN BEAU-
MONT AND FLETCHER'S WORKS, BE-
TWEEN 'CUPID'S REVENGE' AND
'THE TWO NOBLE KINSMEN'

First published in *Life, Letters and Literary
Remains*, and undated.

SPIRIT here that reignest!
Spirit here that painest!
Spirit here that burnest!
Spirit here that mournest!
 Spirit, I bow
 My forehead low,
Enshaded with thy pinions.
 Spirit, I look
 All passion-struck
Into thy pale dominions.

Spirit here that laughest!
Spirit here that quaffest!
Spirit here that dancest!
Noble soul that prancest!
 Spirit, with thee
 I join in the glee
A-nudging the elbow of Momus.
 Spirit, I flush
 With a Bacchanal blush
Just fresh from the Banquet of
 Comus.

FRAGMENT

Under the flag
Of each his faction, they to battle bring
Their embryo atoms.
 MILTON.

Published in *Life, Letters and Literary Re-
mains*, without date.

WELCOME joy, and welcome sorrow,
 Lethe's weed and Hermes' feather;
Come to-day, and come to-morrow,
 I do love you both together!
 I love to mark sad faces in fair weather;
And hear a merry laugh amid the thunder;

Fair and foul I love together.
Meadows sweet where flames are under,
And a giggle at a wonder;
Visage sage at pantomime;
Funeral, and steeple-chime;
Infant playing with a skull;
Morning fair, and shipwreck'd hull;
Nightshade with the woodbine kissing;
Serpents in red roses hissing;
Cleopatra regal-dress'd
With the aspic at her breast;
Dancing music, music sad,
Both together, sane and mad;
Muses bright, and muses pale;
Sombre Saturn, Momus hale;—
Laugh and sigh, and laugh again;
Oh, the sweetness of the pain !
Muses bright and muses pale,
Bare your faces of the veil;
Let me see; and let me write
Of the day, and of the night—
Both together : — let me slake
All my thirst for sweet heart-ache !
Let my bower be of yew,
Interwreath'd with myrtles new;
Pines and lime-trees full in bloom,
And my couch a low grass-tomb.

WHAT THE THRUSH SAID

In a long letter to Reynolds, dated February 19, 1818, Keats writes earnestly of the sources of inspiration to a poet, and especially of the need of a receptive attitude : ' Let us open our leaves like a flower, and be passive and receptive ; budding patiently under the eye of Apollo and taking hints from every noble insect that favours us with a visit.—Sap will be given us for meat, and dew for drink. I was led into these thoughts, my dear Reynolds, by the beauty of the morning operating on a sense of Idleness. I have not read any Book —the Morning said I was right—I had no idea but of the Morning, and the Thrush said I was right, seeming to say,' and then follows the poem. It was first printed in *Life, Letters and Literary Remains.*

O THOU whose face hath felt the Winter's wind,
Whose eye has seen the snow-clouds hung in mist,
And the black elm tops 'mong the freezing stars,
To thee the spring will be a harvest-time.
O thou, whose only book has been the light
Of supreme darkness which thou feddest on
Night after night when Phœbus was away,
To thee the Spring shall be a triple morn.
O fret not after knowledge — I have none,
And yet my song comes native with the warmth.
O fret not after knowledge — I have none,
And yet the Evening listens. He who saddens
At thought of idleness cannot be idle,
And he 's awake who thinks himself asleep.

WRITTEN IN ANSWER TO A SONNET ENDING THUS:—

' Dark eyes are dearer far
Than those that mock the hyacinthine bell '
BY J. H. REYNOLDS.

Dated by Lord Houghton ' February, 1818,' in *Life, Letters and Literary Remains,* where it was first printed.

BLUE ! 'T is the life of heaven, — the domain
Of Cynthia, — the wide palace of the sun, —
The tent of Hesperus, and all his train, —
The bosomer of clouds, gold, gray, and dun.
Blue ! 'T is the life of waters — ocean
And all its vassal streams, pools numberless,
May rage, and foam, and fret, but never can
Subside, if not to dark blue nativeness.
Blue ! Gentle cousin of the forest-green,
Married to green in all the sweetest flowers, —
Forget-me-not, — the blue bell, — and, that queen

Of secrecy, the violet: what strange
 powers
Hast thou, as a mere shadow! But how
 great,
When in an Eye thou art, alive with fate!

TO JOHN HAMILTON
REYNOLDS

Undated, but placed by Lord Houghton di-
rectly after the preceding in *Life, Letters and
Literary Remains.*

O THAT a week could be an age, and we
 Felt parting and warm meeting every
 week;
Then one poor year a thousand years would
 be,
 The flush of welcome ever on the cheek:
So could we live long life in little space,
 So time itself would be annihilate,
So a day's journey in oblivious haze
 To serve our joys would lengthen and
 dilate.
O to arrive each Monday morn from Ind!
 To land each Tuesday from the rich Le-
 vant!
In little time a host of joys to bind,
 And keep our souls in one eternal pant!

This morn, my friend, and yester-evening
 taught
Me how to harbor such a happy thought.

THE HUMAN SEASONS

This sonnet was sent by Keats in a letter to
Benjamin Bailey, from Teignmouth, March 13,
1818, and was printed the next year in Leigh
Hunt's *Literary Pocket-Book*, but Keats did
not include the verses in his 1820 volume.

FOUR Seasons fill the measure of the year;
 There are four seasons in the mind of
 man:
He has his lusty Spring, when fancy clear
 Takes in all beauty with an easy span:
He has his Summer, when luxuriously
 Spring's honied cud of youthful thought
 he loves
To ruminate, and by such dreaming high
 Is nearest unto heaven: quiet coves
His soul has in its Autumn, when his wings
 He furleth close; contented so to look
On mists in idleness — to let fair things
 Pass by unheeded as a threshold brook.
He has his Winter too of pale misfeature,
 Or else he would forego his mortal na-
 ture.

ENDYMION

KEATS began this poem in the spring of 1817 and finished it and saw it through the press in just about a year. It is interesting to follow in his correspondence the growth of the poem. The subject in general had been in his mind at least since the summer of 1816, when he wrote *I stood tiptoe upon a little hill*, and the poem *Sleep and Poetry* hints also at the occupation of his mind, though through all the earlier and partly imitative period of his poetical growth he was drawn almost equally by the romance to which Spenser and Leigh Hunt introduced him, and the classic themes which his early studies, Chapman and the Elgin marbles, all conspired to make real. In April, 1817, he writes as one absorbed in the delights of poetry and stimulated by it to production. 'I find,' he writes to Reynolds from Carisbrooke, April 18, 'I cannot exist without Poetry — half the day will not do — the whole of it — I began with a little, but habit has made me a Leviathan. I had become all in a Tremble from not having written anything of late — the Sonnet overleaf [*On the Sea*] did me good. I slept the better last night for it — this morning, however, I am nearly as bad again. Just now I opened Spenser, and the first lines I saw were these —

"The noble heart that harbours virtuous thought,
And is with child of glorious great intent,
Can never rest until it forth have brought
Th' eternal brood of glory excellent."

. . . I shall forthwith begin my *Endymion*, which I hope I shall have got some way with by the time you come, when we will read our verses in a delightful place I have set my heart upon, near the Castle.'

He reported progress to his friends from time to time during the summer: the poem was his great occupation, and he had the alternate exhilaration and depression which such an undertaking naturally would produce in a temperament as sensitive as his; indeed, one is not surprised to find him near the end of September expressing himself to Haydon as tired of the poem, and looking forward to a Romance to which he meant to devote himself the next summer, for so did his mind swing back and forth, though in truth romance was always uppermost, whether expressed in terms of Grecian mythology or mediævalism. But the main significance of *Endymion*, as one traces the growth of Keats's mind, is in the strong impulse which possessed him to try his wings in a great flight. In a letter to Bailey, October 8, 1817, he quotes from his own letter to George Keats 'in the spring,' and thus at the very time of his setting forth on his great venture, the following notable passage : —

'As to what you say about my being a Poet, I can return no answer but by saying that the high idea I have of poetical fame makes me think I see it towering too high above me. At any rate I have no right to talk until *Endymion* is finished — it will be a test, a trial of my Powers of Imagination, and chiefly of my invention, which is a rare thing indeed — by which I must make 4000 lines of one bare circumstance, and fill them with Poetry: and when I consider that this is a great task, and that when done it will take me but a dozen paces towards the temple of fame — it makes me say: God forbid that I should be without such a task ! I have heard Hunt say, and I may be asked — "Why endeavour after a long Poem ? " To which I would answer, Do not the lovers of poetry like to have a little region to wander in, where

they may pick and choose, and in which the images are so numerous that many are forgotten and found new in a second reading: which may be food for a week's stroll in summer ? Do not they like this better than what they can read through before Mrs. Williams comes down stairs ? a morning work at most.

'Besides, a long poem is a test of invention, which I take to be the polar star of Poetry, as Fancy is the sails, and Imagination the rudder. Did our great Poets ever write short Pieces ? I mean in the shape of Tales — this same invention seems indeed of late years to have been forgotten as a poetical excellence — But enough of this; I put on no laurels till I shall have finished *Endymion.*'

Keats was drawing near the end of his task when he wrote to Bailey November 22: 'At present I am just arrived at Dorking — to change the scene, change the air

and give me a spur to wind up my Poem, of which there are wanting 500 lines.' And at the end of the first draft is written 'Barford Bridge [near Dorking] November 28, 1817.' Early in January, 1818, Keats gave the first book to Taylor, who 'seemed,' he says, 'more than satisfied with it,' and to Keats's surprise proposed issuing it in quarto if Haydon would make a drawing for a frontispiece. Haydon, when asked, was more eager to paint a picture from some scene in the book, but proposed now to make a finished chalk sketch of Keats's head to be engraved for a frontispiece; for some unmentioned reason, this plan was not carried out.

Keats was copying out the poem for the printer, giving it in book by book and reading the proofs until April, when it was ready save the Preface. This with dedication and title-page he had sent to his Publishers March 21. They were as follows:

ENDYMION

A ROMANCE

By JOHN KEATS

'The stretched metre of an antique song.'
Shakspeare's Sonnets.

INSCRIBED,
WITH EVERY FEELING OF PRIDE AND REGRET
AND WITH 'A BOWED MIND'
TO THE MEMORY OF
THE MOST ENGLISH OF POETS EXCEPT SHAKSPEARE,
THOMAS CHATTERTON

PREFACE

IN a great nation, the work of an individual is of so little importance; his pleadings and excuses are so uninteresting; his 'way of life' such a nothing, that a Preface seems a sort of impertinent bow to strangers who care nothing about it.

A Preface, however, should be down in so many words; and such a one that by an

eye-glance over the type the Reader may catch an idea of an Author's modesty, and non-opinion of himself — which I sincerely hope may be seen in the few lines I have to write, notwithstanding many proverbs of many ages old which men find a great pleasure in receiving as gospel.

About a twelvemonth since, I published a little book of verses ; it was read by some dozen of my friends who lik'd it; and some

dozen whom I was unacquainted with, who did not.

Now, when a dozen human beings are at words with another dozen, it becomes a matter of anxiety to side with one's friends — more especially when excited thereto by a great love of Poetry. I fought under disadvantages. Before I began I had no inward feel of being able to finish; and as I proceeded my steps were all uncertain. So this Poem must rather be considered as an endeavour than as a thing accomplished; a poor prologue to what, if I live, I humbly hope to do. In duty to the Public I should have kept it back for a year or two, knowing it to be so faulty; but I really cannot do so, — by repetition my favourite passages sound vapid in my ears, and I would rather redeem myself with a new Poem should this one be found of any interest.

I have to apologize to the lovers of simplicity for touching the spell of loneliness that hung about Endymion; if any of my lines plead for me with such people I shall be proud.

It has been too much the fashion of late to consider men bigoted and addicted to every word that may chance to escape their lips; now I here declare that I have not any particular affection for any particular phrase, word, or letter in the whole affair. I have written to please myself, and in hopes to please others, and for a love of fame; if I neither please myself, nor others, nor get fame, of what consequence is Phraseology.

I would fain escape the bickerings that all works not exactly in chime bring upon their begetters — but this is not fair to expect, there must be conversation of some sort and to object shows a man's consequence. In case of a London drizzle or a Scotch mist, the following quotation from Marston may perhaps 'stead me as an umbrella for an hour or so: 'let it be the curtesy of my peruser rather to pity my self-hindering labours than to malice me.'

One word more — for we cannot help seeing our own affairs in every point of view — should any one call my dedication to Chatterton affected I answer as followeth: 'Were I dead, sir, I should like a book dedicated to me.'

TEIGNMOUTH,
March 19th, 1818.

This Preface was shown either before or after it was in type to Reynolds and other friends, and Reynolds objected to it in terms which may be inferred from the following letter which Keats wrote him April 9, 1818, and which is so striking a reflection of his mind, when contemplating his finished work, that it should be read in connection with the poem: —

'Since you all agree that the thing is bad, it must be so — though I am not aware there is anything like Hunt in it (and if there is, it is my natural way, and I have something in common with Hunt). Look it over again, and examine into the motives, the seeds, from which any one sentence sprung — I have not the slightest feel of humility toward the public — or to anything in existence, — but the eternal Being, the Principle of Beauty, and the Memory of Great Men. When I am writing for myself for the mere sake of the moment's enjoyment, perhaps nature has its course with me — but a Preface is written to the Public; a thing I cannot help looking upon as an Enemy, and which I cannot address without feelings of Hostility. If I write a Preface in a supple or subdued style, it will not be in character with me as a public speaker — I would be subdued before my friends, and thank them for subduing me — but among Multitudes of Men — I have no feel of stooping; I hate the idea of humility to them.

'I never wrote one single line of Poetry with the least Shadow of public thought.

'Forgive me for vexing you and making a Trojan horse of such a Trifle, both with respect to the matter in question, and myself — but it eases me to tell you — I could

not live without the love of my friends — I would jump down Ætna for any great Public good — but I hate a mawkish Popularity. I cannot be subdued before them; my Glory would be to daunt and dazzle the thousand jabberers about pictures and books. I see swarms of Porcupines with their quills erect "like lime-twigs set to catch my wingèd book," and I would fright them away with a torch. You will say my Preface is not much of a Torch. It would have been too insulting "to begin from Jove," and I could not set a golden head upon a thing of clay. If there is any fault in the Preface it is not affectation, but an undersong of disrespect to the Public. If I write another Preface, it must be without a thought of those people — I will think about it. If it should not reach you in four or five days, tell Taylor to publish it without a Preface, and let the Dedication simply stand "Inscribed to the Memory of Thomas Chatterton."' The next day he wrote to his friend, inclosing a new draft: 'I am anxious you should find this Preface tolerable. If there is an affectation in it 't is natural to me. Do let the Printer's Devil cook it, and let me be as "the casing air." You are too good in this matter — were I in your state, I am certain I should have no thought but of discontent and illness — I might though be taught Patience: I had an idea of giving no Preface; however, don't you think this had better go? O, let it — one should not be too timid — of committing faults.'

The Dedication stood as Keats proposed, and the new Preface, which is as follows:

PREFACE

KNOWING within myself the manner in which this Poem has been produced, it is not without a feeling of regret that I make it public.

What manner I mean, will be quite clear to the reader, who must soon perceive great inexperience, immaturity, and every error denoting a feverish attempt, rather than a deed accomplished. The two first books, and indeed the two last, I feel sensible are not of such completion as to warrant their passing the press; nor should they if I thought a year's castigation would do them any good; — it will not: the foundations are too sandy. It is just that this youngster should die away: a sad thought for me, if I had not some hope that while it is dwindling I may be plotting, and fitting myself for verses fit to live.

This may be speaking too presumptuously, and may deserve a punishment: but no feeling man will be forward to inflict it: he will leave me alone, with the conviction that there is not a fiercer hell than the failure in a great object. This is not written with the least atom of purpose to forestall criticisms of course, but from the desire I have to conciliate men who are competent to look, and who do look with a zealous eye, to the honour of English literature.

The imagination of a boy is healthy, and the mature imagination of a man is healthy; but there is a space of life between, in which the soul is in a ferment, the character undecided, the way of life uncertain, the ambition thick-sighted: thence proceeds mawkishness, and all the thousand bitters which those men I speak of must necessarily taste in going over the following pages.

I hope I have not in too late a day touched the beautiful mythology of Greece, and dulled its brightness: for I wish to try once more, before I bid it farewel.

TEIGNMOUTH,
April 10, 1818.

BOOK I

A THING of beauty is a joy for ever:
Its loveliness increases; it will never
Pass into nothingness; but still will keep
A bower quiet for us, and a sleep
Full of sweet dreams, and health, and quiet
 breathing.
Therefore, on every morrow, are we wreath-
 ing
A flowery band to bind us to the earth,
Spite of despondence, of the inhuman dearth
Of noble natures, of the gloomy days,
Of all the unhealthy and o'er-darken'd
 ways 10
Made for our searching: yes, in spite of
 all,
Some shape of beauty moves away the pall
From our dark spirits. Such the sun, the
 moon,
Trees old and young, sprouting a shady
 boon
For simple sheep; and such are daffodils
With the green world they live in; and clear
 rills
That for themselves a cooling covert make
'Gainst the hot season; the mid-forest brake,
Rich with a sprinkling of fair musk-rose
 blooms: 19
And such too is the grandeur of the dooms
We have imagined for the mighty dead;
All lovely tales that we have heard or read:
An endless fountain of immortal drink,
Pouring unto us from the heaven's brink.

Nor do we merely feel these essences
For one short hour; no, even as the trees
That whisper round a temple become soon
Dear as the temple's self, so does the moon,
The passion poesy, glories infinite, 29
Haunt us till they become a cheering light
Unto our souls, and bound to us so fast,
That, whether there be shine, or gloom o'er-
 cast,
They alway must be with us, or we die.

Therefore 't is with full happiness that I
Will trace the story of Endymion.

The very music of the name has gone
Into my being, and each pleasant scene
Is growing fresh before me as the green
Of our own valleys: so I will begin
Now while I cannot hear the city's din; 40
Now while the early budders are just new,
And run in mazes of the youngest hue
About old forests; while the willow trails
Its delicate amber; and the dairy pails
Bring home increase of milk. And, as the
 year
Grows lush in juicy stalks, I'll smoothly
 steer
My little boat, for many quiet hours,
With streams that deepen freshly into bow-
 ers.
Many and many a verse I hope to write,
Before the daisies, vermeil rimm'd and
 white, 50
Hide in deep herbage; and ere yet the bees
Hum about globes of clover and sweet peas,
I must be near the middle of my story.
O may no wintry season, bare, and hoary,
See it half-finish'd: but let Autumn bold,
With universal tinge of sober gold,
Be all about me when I make an end.
And now at once, adventuresome, I send
My herald thought into a wilderness:
There let its trumpet blow, and quickly
 dress 60
My uncertain path with green, that I may
 speed
Easily onward, thorough flowers and weed.

Upon the sides of Latmos was outspread
A mighty forest; for the moist earth fed
So plenteously all weed-hidden roots
Into o'erhanging boughs, and precious
 fruits.
And it had gloomy shades, sequestered
 deep,
Where no man went; and if from shepherd's
 keep
A lamb stray'd far a-down those inmost
 glens,
Never again saw he the happy pens 70
Whither his brethren, bleating with con-
 tent,

Over the hills at every nightfall went.
Among the shepherds, 't was believed ever,
That not one fleecy lamb which thus did
 sever
From the white flock, but pass'd unworrièd
By angry wolf, or pard with prying head,
Until it came to some unfooted plains
Where fed the herds of Pan: aye great his
 gains
Who thus one lamb did lose. Paths there
 were many,
Winding through palmy fern, and rushes
 fenny, 80
And ivy banks; all leading pleasantly
To a wide lawn, whence one could only see
Stems thronging all around between the
 swell
Of turf and slanting branches: who could
 tell
The freshness of the space of heaven
 above,
Edged round with dark tree-tops ? through
 which a dove
Would often beat its wings, and often too
A little cloud would move across the blue.

Full in the middle of this pleasantness
There stood a marble altar, with a tress 90
Of flowers budded newly; and the dew
Had taken fairy phantasies to strew
Daisies upon the sacred sward last eve,
And so the dawned light in pomp receive.
For 't was the morn: Apollo's upward fire
Made every eastern cloud a silvery pyre
Of brightness so unsullied, that therein
A melancholy spirit well might win
Oblivion, and melt out his essence fine
Into the winds: rain-scented eglantine 100
Gave temperate sweets to that well-wooing
 sun;
The lark was lost in him; cold springs had
 run
To warm their chilliest bubbles in the grass;
Man's voice was on the mountains; and the
 mass
Of nature's lives and wonders pulsed ten-
 fold,
To feel this sun-rise and its glories old.

Now while the silent workings of the
 dawn
Were busiest, into that self-same lawn
All suddenly, with joyful cries, there sped
A troop of little children garlanded; 110
Who gathering round the altar seem'd to pry
Earnestly round as wishing to espy
Some folk of holiday: nor had they waited
For many moments, ere their ears were
 sated
With a faint breath of music, which ev'n
 then
Fill'd out its voice, and died away again.
Within a little space again it gave
Its airy swellings, with a gentle wave,
To light-hung leaves, in smoothest echoes
 breaking
Through copse - clad valleys, — ere their
 death, o'ertaking 120
The surgy murmurs of the lonely sea.

And now, as deep into the wood as we
Might mark a lynx's eye, there glimmer'd
 light
Fair faces and a rush of garments white,
Plainer and plainer showing, till at last
Into the widest alley they all past,
Making directly for the woodland altar.
O kindly muse ! let not my weak tongue
 faulter
In telling of this goodly company,
Of their old piety, and of their glee: 130
But let a portion of ethereal dew
Fall on my head, and presently unmew
My soul; that I may dare, in wayfaring,
To stammer where old Chaucer used to
 sing.

Leading the way, young damsels danced
 along,
Bearing the burden of a shepherd song;
Each having a white wicker, overbrimm'd
With April's tender younglings: next, well
 trimm'd,
A crowd of shepherds with as sunburnt
 looks
As may be read of in Arcadian books; 140
Such as sat listening round Apollo's pipe,

When the great deity, for earth too ripe,
Let his divinity o'erflowing die
In music, through the vales of Thessaly:
Some idly trail'd their sheep-hooks on the
ground,
And some kept up a shrilly mellow sound
With ebon-tipped flutes: close after these,
Now coming from beneath the forest trees,
A venerable priest full soberly,
Begirt with minist'ring looks: alway his
eye 150
Steadfast upon the matted turf he kept,
And after him his sacred vestments swept.
From his right hand there swung a vase,
milk-white,
Of mingled wine, out-sparkling generous
light;
And in his left he held a basket full
Of all sweet herbs that searching eye could
cull:
Wild thyme, and valley-lilies whiter still
Than Leda's love, and cresses from the rill.
His aged head, crowned with beechen
wreath,
Seem'd like a poll of ivy in the teeth 160
Of winter hoar. Then came another
crowd
Of shepherds, lifting in due time aloud
Their share of the ditty. After them ap-
pear'd,
Up-follow'd by a multitude that rear'd
Their voices to the clouds, a fair-wrought
car,
Easily rolling so as scarce to mar
The freedom of three steeds of dapple
brown:
Who stood therein did seem of great re-
nown
Among the throng. His youth was fully
blown,
Showing like Ganymede to manhood grown;
And, for those simple times, his garments
were 171
A chieftain king's ; beneath his breast, half
bare,
Was hung a silver bugle, and between
His nervy knees there lay a boar-spear
keen.

A smile was on his countenance ; he seem'd
To common lookers-on, like one who
dream'd
Of idleness in groves Elysian:
But there were some who feelingly could
scan
A lurking trouble in his nether lip,
And see that oftentimes the reins would slip
Through his forgotten hands: then would
they sigh, 181
And think of yellow leaves, of owlets' cry,
Of logs piled solemnly. — Ah, well-a-day,
Why should our young Endymion pine
away !

Soon the assembly, in a circle ranged,
Stood silent round the shrine: each look
was changed
To sudden veneration: women meek
Beckon'd their sons to silence; while each
cheek
Of virgin bloom paled gently for slight fear.
Endymion too, without a forest peer, 190
Stood, wan, and pale, and with an awed
face,
Among his brothers of the mountain chase.
In midst of all, the venerable priest
Eyed them with joy from greatest to the
least,
And, after lifting up his aged hands,
Thus spake he: ' Men of Latmos ! shepherd
bands !
Whose care it is to guard a thousand flocks:
Whether descended from beneath the rocks
That overtop your mountains; whether
come
From valleys where the pipe is never
dumb; 200
Or from your swelling downs, where sweet
air stirs
Blue harebells lightly, and where prickly
furze
Buds lavish gold; or ye, whose precious
charge
Nibble their fill at ocean's very marge,
Whose mellow reeds are touch'd with
sounds forlorn
By the dim echoes of old Triton's horn:

Mothers and wives ! who day by day pre-
pare
The scrip, with needments, for the moun-
tain air;
And all ye gentle girls who foster up
Udderless lambs, and in a little cup 210
Will put choice honey for a favour'd youth:
Yea, every one attend ! for in good truth
Our vows are wanting to our great god
Pan.
Are not our lowing heifers sleeker than
Night-swollen mushrooms ? Are not our
wide plains
Speckled with countless fleeces ? Have
not rains
Green'd over April's lap ? No howling sad
Sickens our fearful ewes; and we have had
Great bounty from Endymion our lord.
The earth is glad: the merry lark has
pour'd 220
His early song against yon breezy sky,
That spreads so clear o'er our solemnity.'

Thus ending, on the shrine he heap'd a
spire
Of teeming sweets, enkindling sacred fire;
Anon he stain'd the thick and spongy sod
With wine, in honour of the shepherd-god.
Now while the earth was drinking it, and
while
Bay leaves were crackling in the fragrant
pile,
And gummy frankincense was sparkling
bright
'Neath smothering parsley, and a hazy
light 230
Spread grayly eastward, thus a chorus
sang:

'O thou, whose mighty palace roof doth
hang
From jagged trunks, and overshadoweth
Eternal whispers, glooms, the birth, life,
death
Of unseen flowers in heavy peacefulness;
Who lov'st to see the hamadryads dress
Their ruffled locks where meeting hazels
darken;

And through whole solemn hours dost sit,
and hearken
The dreary melody of bedded reeds —
In desolate places, where dank moisture
breeds 240
The pipy hemlock to strange overgrowth;
Bethinking thee, how melancholy loth
Thou wast to lose fair Syrinx — do thou
now,
By thy love's milky brow !
By all the trembling mazes that she ran,
Hear us, great Pan !

'O thou, for whose soul-soothing quiet,
turtles
Passion their voices cooingly 'mong myrtles,
What time thou wanderest at eventide
Through sunny meadows, that outskirt the
side 250
Of thine enmossed realms: O thou, to whom
Broad-leaved fig-trees even now foredoom
Their ripen'd fruitage; yellow-girted bees
Their golden honeycombs; our village leas
Their fairest blossom'd beans and poppied
corn;
The chuckling linnet its five young unborn,
To sing for thee; low-creeping strawberries
Their summer coolness; pent-up butterflies
Their freckled wings; yea, the fresh-bud-
ding year
All its completions — be quickly near, 260
By every wind that nods the mountain pine,
O forester divine !

'Thou, to whom every faun and satyr
flies
For willing service; whether to surprise
The squatted hare while in half-sleeping
fit;
Or upward ragged precipices flit
To save poor lambkins from the eagle's
maw;
Or by mysterious enticement draw
Bewilder'd shepherds to their path again;
Or to tread breathless round the frothy
main, 270
And gather up all fancifullest shells
For thee to tumble into Naiads' cells,

And, being hidden, laugh at their out-peep-
ing;
Or to delight thee with fantastic leaping,
The while they pelt each other on the
crown
With silvery oak-apples, and fir-cones
brown —
By all the echoes that about thee ring,
Hear us, O satyr king !

'O Hearkener to the loud-clapping
shears,
While ever and anon to his shorn peers 280
A ram goes bleating: Winder of the horn,
When snouted wild-boars routing tender
corn
Anger our huntsman: Breather round our
farms,
To keep off mildews, and all weather
harms:
Strange ministrant of undescribed sounds,
That come a-swooning over hollow grounds,
And wither drearily on barren moors:
Dread opener of the mysterious doors
Leading to universal knowledge — see,
Great son of Dryope, 290
The many that are come to pay their vows
With leaves about their brows !

'Be still the unimaginable lodge
For solitary thinkings; such as dodge
Conception to the very bourne of heaven,
Then leave the naked brain: be still the
leaven,
That spreading in this dull and clodded
earth
Gives it a touch ethereal — a new birth:
Be still a symbol of immensity;
A firmament reflected in a sea; 300
An element filling the space between;
An unknown — but no more: we humbly
screen
With uplift hands our foreheads, lowly
bending,
And giving out a shout most heaven-rend-
ing,
Conjure thee to receive our humble Pæan,
Upon thy Mount Lycean !'

Even while they brought the burden to a
close,
A shout from the whole multitude arose,
That linger'd in the air like dying rolls
Of abrupt thunder, when Ionian shoals 310
Of dolphins bob their noses through the
brine.
Meantime, on shady levels, mossy fine,
Young companies nimbly began dancing
To the swift treble pipe, and humming
string.
Aye, those fair living forms swam heavenly
To tunes forgotten — out of memory:
Fair creatures ! whose young children's
children bred
Thermopylæ its heroes — not yet dead,
But in old marbles ever beautiful.
High genitors, unconscious did they cull 320
Time's sweet first-fruits — they danced to
weariness,
And then in quiet circles did they press
The hillock turf, and caught the latter end
Of some strange history, potent to send
A young mind from its bodily tenement.
Or they might watch the quoit-pitchers,
intent
On either side; pitying the sad death
Of Hyacinthus, when the cruel breath
Of Zephyr slew him, — Zephyr penitent,
Who now, ere Phœbus mounts the firma-
ment, 330
Fondles the flower amid the sobbing rain.
The archers too, upon a wider plain,
Beside the feathery whizzing of the shaft,
And the dull twanging bowstring, and the
raft
Branch down sweeping from a tall ash top,
Call'd up a thousand thoughts to envelope
Those who would watch. Perhaps, the
trembling knee
And frantic gape of lonely Niobe,
Poor, lonely Niobe ! when her lovely young
Were dead and gone, and her caressing
tongue 340
Lay a lost thing upon her paly lip,
And very, very deadliness did nip
Her motherly cheeks. Aroused from this
sad mood

By one, who at a distance loud halloo'd,
Uplifting his strong bow into the air,
Many might after brighter visions stare:
After the Argonauts, in blind amaze
Tossing about on Neptune's restless ways,
Until, from the horizon's vaulted side,
There shot a golden splendour far and
 wide, 350
Spangling those million poutings of the
 brine
With quivering ore: 't was even an awful
 shine
From the exaltation of Apollo's bow;
A heavenly beacon in their dreary woe.
Who thus were ripe for high contemplating,
Might turn their steps towards the sober
 ring
Where sat Endymion and the aged priest
'Mong shepherds gone in eld, whose looks
 increased
The silvery setting of their mortal star.
There they discoursed upon the fragile
 bar 360
That keeps us from our homes ethereal;
And what our duties there: to nightly call
Vesper, the beauty-crest of summer wea-
 ther;
To summon all the downiest clouds together
For the sun's purple couch; to emulate
In minist'ring the potent rule of fate
With speed of fire-tail'd exhalations;
To tint her pallid cheek with bloom, who
 cons
Sweet poesy by moonlight: besides these,
A world of other unguess'd offices. 370
Anon they wander'd, by divine converse,
Into Elysium; vying to rehearse
Each one his own anticipated bliss.
One felt heart-certain that he could not
 miss
His quick-gone love, among fair blossom'd
 boughs,
Where every zephyr-sigh pouts, and endows
Her lips with music for the welcoming.
Another wish'd, 'mid that eternal spring,
To meet his rosy child, with feathery sails,
Sweeping, eye-earnestly, through almond
 vales: 380

Who, suddenly, should stoop through the
 smooth wind,
And with the balmiest leaves his temples
 bind;
And, ever after, through those regions be
His messenger, his little Mercury.
Some were athirst in soul to see again
Their fellow-huntsmen o'er the wide cham-
 paign
In times long past; to sit with them, and
 talk
Of all the chances in their earthly walk;
Comparing, joyfully, their plenteous stores
Of happiness, to when upon the moors, 390
Benighted, close they huddled from the
 cold,
And shared their famish'd scrips. Thus
 all out-told
Their fond imaginations, — saving him
Whose eyelids curtain'd up their jewels
 dim,
Endymion: yet hourly had he striven
To hide the cankering venom, that had
 riven
His fainting recollections. Now indeed
His senses had swoon'd off: he did not heed
The sudden silence, or the whispers low,
Or the old eyes dissolving at his woe, 400
Or anxious calls, or close of trembling
 palms,
Or maiden's sigh, that grief itself embalms:
But in the self-same fixed trance he kept,
Like one who on the earth had never stept.
Aye, even as dead-still as a marble man,
Frozen in that old tale Arabian.

Who whispers him so pantingly and
 close ?
Peona, his sweet sister: of all those,
His friends, the dearest. Hushing signs
 she made,
And breathed a sister's sorrow to per-
 suade 410
A yielding up, a cradling on her care.
Her eloquence did breathe away the curse:
She led him, like some midnight spirit nurse
Of happy changes in emphatic dreams,
Along a path between two little streams, —

Guarding his forehead, with her round
 elbow,
From low-grown branches, and his foot-
 steps slow
From stumbling over stumps and hillocks
 small;
Until they came to where these streamlets
 fall,
With mingled bubblings and a gentle
 rush, 420
Into a river, clear, brimful, and flush
With crystal mocking of the trees and
 sky.
A little shallop, floating there hard by,
Pointed its beak over the fringed bank;
And soon it lightly dipt, and rose, and sank,
And dipt again, with the young couple's
 weight, —
Peona guiding, through the water straight,
Towards a bowery island opposite;
Which gaining presently, she steered light
Into a shady, fresh, and ripply cove, 430
Where nested was an arbour, overwove
By many a summer's silent fingering;
To whose cool bosom she was used to bring
Her playmates, with their needle broid-
 ery,
And minstrel memories of times gone by.

So she was gently glad to see him laid
Under her favourite bower's quiet shade,
On her own couch, new made of flower
 leaves,
Dried carefully on the cooler side of sheaves
When last the sun his autumn tresses
 shook, 440
And the tann'd harvesters rich armfuls
 took.
Soon was he quieted to slumbrous rest:
But, ere it crept upon him, he had prest
Peona's busy hand against his lips,
And still, a-sleeping, held her finger-tips
In tender pressure. And as a willow keeps
A patient watch over the stream that creeps
Windingly by it, so the quiet maid
Held her in peace: so that a whispering
 blade
Of grass, a wailful gnat, a bee bustling 450

Down in the bluebells, or a wren light
 rustling
Among sere leaves and twigs, might all be
 heard.

 O magic sleep! O comfortable bird,
That broodest o'er the troubled sea of the
 mind
Till it is hush'd and smooth! O unconfined
Restraint! imprison'd liberty! great key
To golden palaces, strange minstrelsy,
Fountains grotesque, new trees, bespangled
 caves,
Echoing grottoes, full of tumbling waves
And moonlight; aye, to all the mazy
 world 460
Of silvery enchantment! — who, upfurl'd
Beneath thy drowsy wing a triple hour,
But renovates and lives? — Thus, in the
 bower,
Endymion was calm'd to life again.
Opening his eyelids with a healthier brain,
He said: 'I feel this thine endearing love
All through my bosom: thou art as a dove
Trembling its closed eyes and sleeked
 wings
About me; and the pearliest dew not brings
Such morning incense from the fields of
 May, 470
As do those brighter drops that twinkling
 stray
From those kind eyes, — the very home and
 haunt
Of sisterly affection. Can I want
Aught else, aught nearer heaven, than such
 tears?
Yet dry them up, in bidding hence all fears
That, any longer, I will pass my days
Alone and sad. No, I will once more raise
My voice upon the mountain-heights; once
 more
Make my horn parley from their foreheads
 hoar:
Again my trooping hounds their tongues
 shall loll 480
Around the breathed boar: again I 'll poll
The fair-grown yew-tree, for a chosen bow:
And, when the pleasant sun is getting low,

Again I'll linger in a sloping mead
To hear the speckled thrushes, and see feed
Our idle sheep. So be thou cheered, sweet!
And, if thy lute is here, softly intreat
My soul to keep in its resolved course.'

Hereat Peona, in their silver source,
Shut her pure sorrow-drops with glad ex-
 claim, 490
And took a lute, from which there pulsing
 came
A lively prelude, fashioning the way
In which her voice should wander. 'T was
 a lay
More subtle cadenced, more forest wild
Than Dryope's lone lulling of her child;
And nothing since has floated in the air
So mournful strange. Surely some influ-
 ence rare
Went, spiritual, through the damsel's hand;
For still, with Delphic emphasis, she spann'd
The quick invisible strings, even though
 she saw 500
Endymion's spirit melt away and thaw
Before the deep intoxication.
But soon she came, with sudden burst, upon
Her self-possession — swung the lute aside,
And earnestly said: ' Brother, 't is vain to
 hide
That thou dost know of things mysterious,
Immortal, starry; such alone could thus
Weigh down thy nature. Hast thou sinn'd
 in aught
Offensive to the heavenly powers? Caught
A Paphian dove upon a message sent? 510
Thy deathful bow against some deer-herd
 bent,
Sacred to Dian? Haply, thou hast seen
Her naked limbs among the alders green;
And that, alas! is death. No, I can trace
Something more high perplexing in thy
 face!'

Endymion look'd at her, and press'd her
 hand,
And said, ' Art thou so pale, who wast so
 bland
And merry in our meadows? How is this?

Tell me thine ailment: tell me all amiss! —
Ah! thou hast been unhappy at the change
Wrought suddenly in me. What indeed
 more strange? 521
Or more complete to overwhelm surmise?
Ambition is no sluggard: 't is no prize,
That toiling years would put within my
 grasp,
That I have sigh'd for: with so deadly gasp
No man e'er panted for a mortal love.
So all have set my heavier grief above
These things which happen. Rightly have
 they done:
I, who still saw the horizontal sun
Heave his broad shoulder o'er the edge of
 the world, 530
Out-facing Lucifer, and then had hurl'd
My spear aloft, as signal for the chase —
I, who, for very sport of heart, would
 race
With my own steed from Araby; pluck
 down
A vulture from his towery perching; frown
A lion into growling, loth retire —
To lose, at once, all my toil-breeding fire,
And sink thus low! but I will ease my
 breast
Of secret grief, here in this bowery nest.

 ' This river does not see the naked sky,
Till it begins to progress silverly 541
Around the western border of the wood,
Whence, from a certain spot, its winding
 flood
Seems at the distance like a crescent moon:
And in that nook, the very pride of June,
Had I been used to pass my weary eves;
The rather for the sun unwilling leaves
So dear a picture of his sovereign power,
And I could witness his most kingly hour,
When he doth tighten up the golden reins,
And paces leisurely down amber plains 551
His snorting four. Now when his chariot
 last
Its beams against the zodiac-lion cast,
There blossom'd suddenly a magic bed
Of sacred ditamy, and poppies red:
At which I wondered greatly, knowing well

That but one night had wrought this flow-
ery spell;
And, sitting down close by, began to muse
What it might mean. Perhaps, thought I,
Morpheus,
In passing here, his owlet pinions shook;
Or, it may be, ere matron Night uptook 561
Her ebon urn, young Mercury, by stealth,
Had dipt his rod in it: such garland wealth
Came not by common growth. Thus on I
thought,
Until my head was dizzy and distraught.
Moreover, through the dancing poppies
stole
A breeze, most softly lulling to my soul;
And shaping visions all about my sight
Of colours, wings, and bursts of spangly
light;
The which became more strange, and
strange, and dim, 570
And then were gulf'd in a tumultuous swim:
And then I fell asleep. Ah, can I tell
The enchantment that afterwards befell?
Yet it was but a dream: yet such a dream
That never tongue, although it overteem
With mellow utterance, like a cavern
spring,
Could figure out and to conception bring
All I beheld and felt. Methought I lay
Watching the zenith, where the milky way
Among the stars in virgin splendour pours;
And travelling my eye, until the doors 581
Of heaven appear'd to open for my flight,
I became loth and fearful to alight
From such high soaring by a downward
glance :
So kept me steadfast in that airy trance,
Spreading imaginary pinions wide.
When, presently, the stars began to glide,
And faint away, before my eager view:
At which I sigh'd that I could not pursue,
And dropt my vision to the horizon's verge;
And lo! from opening clouds, I saw
emerge 591
The loveliest moon, that ever silver'd o'er
A shell for Neptune's goblet ; she did
soar
So passionately bright, my dazzled soul

Commingling with her argent spheres did
roll
Through clear and cloudy, even when she
went
At last into a dark and vapoury tent —
Whereat, methought, the lidless-eyed train
Of planets all were in the blue again.
To commune with those orbs, once more I
raised 600
My sight right upward: but it was quite
dazed
By a bright something, sailing down apace,
Making me quickly veil my eyes and face:
Again I look'd, and, O ye deities,
Who from Olympus watch our destinies !
Whence that completed form of all com-
pleteness ?
Whence came that high perfection of all
sweetness ?
Speak, stubborn earth, and tell me where,
O where
Hast thou a symbol of her golden hair ?
Not oat-sheaves drooping in the western
sun; 610
Not — thy soft hand, fair sister ! let me
shun
Such follying before thee — yet she had,
Indeed, locks bright enough to make me
mad;
And they were simply gordian'd up and
braided,
Leaving, in naked comeliness, unshaded,
Her pearl round ears, white neck, and
orbed brow ;
The which were blended in, I know not
how,
With such a paradise of lips and eyes,
Blush-tinted cheeks, half smiles, and faint-
est sighs,
That, when I think thereon, my spirit
clings 620
And plays about its fancy, till the stings
Of human neighbourhood envenom all.
Unto what awful power shall I call ?
To what high fane ? — Ah ! see her hover-
ing feet,
More bluely vein'd, more soft, more whitely
sweet

Than those of sea-born Venus, when she
rose
From out her cradle shell. The wind out-
blows
Her scarf into a fluttering pavilion ;
'T is blue, and over-spangled with a million
Of little eyes, as though thou wert to shed,
Over the darkest, lushest bluebell bed, 631
Handfuls of daisies.' — 'Endymion, how
strange !
Dream within dream !' — ' She took an
airy range,
And then, towards me, like a very maid,
Came blushing, waning, willing, and afraid,
And press'd me by the hand: Ah ! 't was
too much;
Methought I fainted at the charmed touch,
Yet held my recollection, even as one
Who dives three fathoms where the waters
run
Gurgling in beds of coral: for anon, 640
I felt upmounted in that region
Where falling stars dart their artillery forth,
And eagles struggle with the buffeting
north
That balances the heavy meteor-stone; —
Felt too, I was not fearful, nor alone,
But lapp'd and lull'd along the dangerous
sky.
Soon, as it seem'd, we left our journeying
high,
And straightway into frightful eddies
swoop'd;
Such as ay muster where gray time has
scoop'd
Huge dens and caverns in a mountain's
side: 650
There hollow sounds aroused me, and I
sigh'd
To faint once more by looking on my bliss —
I was distracted; madly did I kiss
The wooing arms which held me, and did
give
My eyes at once to death : but 't was to live,
To take in draughts of life from the gold
fount
Of kind and passionate looks; to count,
and count

The moments, by some greedy help that
seem'd
A second self, that each might be redeem'd
And plunder'd of its load of blessed-
ness. 660
Ah, desperate mortal ! I ev'n dared to press
Her very cheek against my crowned lip,
And, at that moment, felt my body dip
Into a warmer air: a moment more,
Our feet were soft in flowers. There was
store
Of newest joys upon that alp. Sometimes
A scent of violets, and blossoming limes,
Loiter'd around us; then of honey cells,
Made delicate from all white-flower bells;
And once, above the edges of our nest, 670
An arch face peep'd, — an Oread as I
guess'd.

 ' Why did I dream that sleep o'erpower'd
me
In midst of all this heaven ? Why not see,
Far off, the shadows of his pinions dark,
And stare them from me ? But no, like a
spark
That needs must die, although its little
beam
Reflects upon a diamond, my sweet dream
Fell into nothing — into stupid sleep.
And so it was, until a gentle creep,
A careful moving caught my waking
ears, 680
And up I started: Ah ! my sighs, my tears,
My clenched hands; — for lo ! the poppies
hung
Dew-dabbled on their stalks, the ouzel sung
A heavy ditty, and the sullen day
Had chidden herald Hesperus away,
With leaden looks: the solitary breeze
Bluster'd, and slept, and its wild self did
tease
With wayward melancholy; and I thought,
Mark me, Peona ! that sometimes it brought
Faint fare-thee-wells, and sigh-shrilled
adieus ! — 690
Away I wander'd — all the pleasant hues
Of heaven and earth had faded: deepest
shades

Were deepest dungeons; heaths and sunny
 glades
Were full of pestilent light; our taintless
 rills
Seem'd sooty, and o'erspread with upturn'd
 gills
Of dying fish; the vermeil rose had blown
In frightful scarlet, and its thorns outgrown
Like spiked aloe. If an innocent bird
Before my heedless footsteps stirr'd, and
 stirr'd
In little journeys, I beheld in it 700
A disguised demon, missioned to knit
My soul with under darkness; to entice
My stumblings down some monstrous pre-
 cipice:
Therefore I eager follow'd, and did curse
The disappointment. Time, that aged
 nurse,
Rock'd me to patience. Now, thank gentle
 heaven !
These things, with all their comfortings,
 are given
To my down-sunken hours, and with thee,
Sweet sister, help to stem the ebbing sea
Of weary life.'

 Thus ended he, and both
Sat silent: for the maid was very loth 711
To answer; feeling well that breathed
 words
Would all be lost, unheard, and vain as
 swords
Against the enchased crocodile, or leaps
Of grasshoppers against the sun. She
 weeps,
And wonders; struggles to devise some
 blame;
To put on such a look as would say, *Shame
On this poor weakness !* but, for all her
 strife,
She could as soon have crush'd away the
 life
From a sick dove. At length, to break the
 pause, 720
She said with trembling chance: 'Is this
 the cause ?
This all ? Yet it is strange, and sad, alas !

That one who through this middle earth
 should pass
Most like a sojourning demi-god, and leave
His name upon the harp-string, should
 achieve
No higher bard than simple maidenhood,
Singing alone, and fearfully, — how the
 blood
Left his young cheek; and how he used to
 stray
He knew not where; and how he would
 say, *nay,*
If any said 't was love: and yet 't was
 love; 730
What could it be but love ? How a ring-
 dove
Let fall a sprig of yew-tree in his path;
And how he died: and then, that love doth
 scathe
The gentle heart, as northern blasts do
 roses;
And then the ballad of his sad life closes
With sighs, and an alas ! — Endymion !
Be rather in the trumpet's mouth, — anon
Among the winds at large — that all may
 hearken !
Although, before the crystal heavens
 darken,
I watch and dote upon the silver lakes 740
Pictured in western cloudiness, that takes
The semblance of gold rocks and bright
 gold sands,
Islands, and creeks, and amber-fretted
 strands
With horses prancing o'er them, palaces
And towers of amethyst, — would I so tease
My pleasant days, because I could not
 mount
Into those regions ? The Morphean fount
Of that fine element that visions, dreams,
And fitful whims of sleep are made of,
 streams
Into its airy channels with so subtle, 750
So thin a breathing, not the spider's shuttle,
Circled a million times within the space
Of a swallow's nest-door, could delay a
 trace,
A tinting of its quality: how light

Must dreams themselves be; seeing they 're
 more slight
Than the mere nothing that engenders
 them !
Then wherefore sully the entrusted gem
Of high and noble life with thoughts so
 sick ?
Why pierce high-fronted honour to the
 quick
For nothing but a dream ? ' Hereat the
 youth 760
Look'd up: a conflicting of shame and ruth
Was in his plaited brow: yet his eyelids
Widen'd a little, as when Zephyr bids
A little breeze to creep between the fans
Of careless butterflies: amid his pains
He seem'd to taste a drop of manna-dew,
Full palatable; and a colour grew
Upon his cheek, while thus he lifeful spake.

'Peona! ever have I long'd to slake
My thirst for the world's praises: nothing
 base, 770
No merely slumberous phantasm, could
 unlace
The stubborn canvas for my voyage pre-
 pared —
Though now 't is tatter'd; leaving my bark
 bared
And sullenly drifting: yet my higher hope
Is of too wide, too rainbow-large a scope,
To fret at myriads of earthly wrecks.
Wherein lies happiness ? In that which
 becks
Our ready minds to fellowship divine,
A fellowship with essence; till we shine,
Full alchemized, and free of space. Be-
 hold 780
The clear religion of heaven ! Fold
A rose leaf round thy finger's taperness,
And soothe thy lips: hist, when the airy
 stress
Of music's kiss impregnates the free winds,
And with a sympathetic touch unbinds
Æolian magic from their lucid wombs:
Then old songs waken from enclouded
 tombs;
Old ditties sigh above their father's grave;

Ghosts of melodious prophesyings rave
Round every spot where trod Apollo's
 foot; 790
Bronze clarions awake, and faintly bruit,
Where long ago a giant battle was;
And, from the turf, a lullaby doth pass
In every place where infant Orpheus slept.
Feel we these things ? — that moment have
 we stept
Into a sort of oneness, and our state
Is like a floating spirit's. But there are
Richer entanglements, enthralments far
More self-destroying, leading, by degrees,
To the chief intensity: the crown of these
Is made of love and friendship, and sits
 high 801
Upon the forehead of humanity.
All its more ponderous and bulky worth
Is friendship, whence there ever issues forth
A steady splendour; but at the tip-top,
There hangs by unseen film, an orbed drop
Of light, and that is love: its influence
Thrown in our eyes genders a novel sense,
At which we start and fret: till in the end,
Melting into its radiance, we blend, 810
Mingle, and so become a part of it, —
Nor with aught else can our souls interknit
So wingedly: when we combine therewith,
Life's self is nourish'd by its proper pith,
And we are nurtured like a pelican brood.
Aye, so delicious is the unsating food,
That men, who might have tower'd in the
 van
Of all the congregated world, to fan
And winnow from the coming step of time
All chaff of custom, wipe away all slime 820
Left by men-slugs and human serpentry,
Have been content to let occasion die,
Whilst they did sleep in love's Elysium.
And, truly, I would rather be struck dumb,
Than speak against this ardent listless-
 ness:
For I have ever thought that it might bless
The world with benefits unknowingly;
As does the nightingale, up-perched high,
And cloister'd among cool and bunched
 leaves — 829
She sings but to her love, nor e'er conceives

How tiptoe Night holds back her dark-
gray hood.
Just so may love, although 't is understood
The mere commingling of passionate breath,
Produce more than our searching witness-
eth:
What I know not: but who, of men, can
tell
That flowers would bloom, or that green
fruit would swell
To melting pulp, that fish would have
bright mail,
The earth its dower of river, wood, and
vale,
The meadows runnels, runnels pebble-
stones, 839
The seed its harvest, or the lute its tones,
Tones ravishment, or ravishment its sweet,
If human souls did never kiss and greet?

' Now, if this earthly love has power to
make
Men's being mortal, immortal; to shake
Ambition from their memories, and brim
Their measure of content; what merest
whim,
Seems all this poor endeavour after fame,
To one, who keeps within his steadfast
aim
A love immortal, an immortal too.
Look not so wilder'd; for these things are
true 850
And never can be born of atomies
That buzz about our slumbers, like brain-
flies,
Leaving us fancy-sick. No, no, I 'm sure,
My restless spirit never could endure
To brood so long upon one luxury,
Unless it did, though fearfully, espy
A hope beyond the shadow of a dream.
My sayings will the less obscured seem
When I have told thee how my waking
sight
Has made me scruple whether that same
night 860
Was pass'd in dreaming. Hearken, sweet
Peona !
Beyond the matron-temple of Latona,

Which we should see but for these dark-
ening boughs,
Lies a deep hollow, from whose ragged
brows
Bushes and trees do lean all round athwart,
And meet so nearly, that with wings out-
raught,
And spreaded tail, a vulture could not glide
Past them, but he must brush on every
side.
Some moulder'd steps lead into this cool
cell,
Far as the slabbed margin of a well, 870
Whose patient level peeps its crystal eye
Right upward, through the bushes, to the
sky.
Oft have I brought thee flowers, on their
stalks set
Like vestal primroses, but dark velvet
Edges them round, and they have golden
pits:
'T was there I got them, from the gaps and
slits
In a mossy stone, that sometimes was my
seat,
When all above was faint with mid-day
heat.
And there in strife no burning thoughts to
heed,
I 'd bubble up the water through a reed;
So reaching back to boyhood: make me
ships 881
Of moulted feathers, touchwood, alder
chips,
With leaves stuck in them; and the Nep-
tune be
Of their petty ocean. Oftener, heavily,
When lovelorn hours had left me less a
child,
I sat contemplating the figures wild
Of o'er-head clouds melting the mirror
through.
Upon a day, while thus I watch'd, by flew
A cloudy Cupid, with his bow and quiver;
So plainly character'd, no breeze would
shiver 890
The happy chance: so happy, I was fain
To follow it upon the open plain,

And, therefore, was just going; when, be-
 hold !
A wonder, fair as any I have told —
The same bright face I tasted in my sleep,
Smiling in the clear well. My heart did
 leap
Through the cool depth. — It moved as if
 to flee —
I started up, when lo ! refreshfully,
There came upon my face, in plenteous
 showers,
Dew-drops, and dewy buds, and leaves, and
 flowers, 900
Wrapping all objects from my smother'd
 sight,
Bathing my spirit in a new delight.
Aye, such a breathless honey-feel of bliss
Alone preserved me from the drear abyss
Of death, for the fair form had gone again.
Pleasure is oft a visitant; but pain
Clings cruelly to us, like the gnawing sloth
On the deer's tender haunches: late, and
 loth,
'T is scared away by slow returning plea-
 sure.
How sickening, how dark the dreadful lei-
 sure 910
Of weary days, made deeper exquisite,
By a foreknowledge of unslumbrous night !
Like sorrow came upon me, heavier still,
Than when I wander'd from the poppy
 hill:
And a whole age of lingering moments
 crept
Sluggishly by, ere more contentment swept
Away at once the deadly yellow spleen.
Yes, thrice have I this fair enchantment
 seen;
Once more been tortured with renewed life.
When last the wintry gusts gave over
 strife 920
With the conquering sun of spring, and
 left the skies
Warm and serene, but yet with moisten'd
 eyes
In pity of the shatter'd infant buds, —
That time thou didst adorn, with amber
 studs,

My hunting cap, because I laugh'd and
 smiled,
Chatted with thee, and many days exiled
All torment from my breast; — 't was even
 then,
Straying about, yet coop'd up in the den
Of helpless discontent, — hurling my lance
From place to place, and following at
 chance, 930
At last, by hap, through some young trees
 it struck,
And, plashing among bedded pebbles, stuck
In the middle of a brook, — whose silver
 ramble
Down twenty little falls through reeds and
 bramble,
Tracing along, it brought me to a cave,
Whence it ran brightly forth, and white
 did lave
The nether sides of mossy stones and
 rock, —
'Mong which it gurgled blithe adieus, to
 mock
Its own sweet grief at parting. Overhead,
Hung a lush screen of drooping weeds, and
 spread 940
Thick, as to curtain up some wood-nymph's
 home.
" Ah ! impious mortal, whither do I roam ! "
Said I, low-voiced: " Ah, whither ! 'T is the
 grot
Of Proserpine, when Hell, obscure and hot,
Doth her resign; and where her tender
 hands
She dabbles, on the cool and sluicy sands:
Or 't is the cell of Echo, where she sits,
And babbles thorough silence, till her wits
Are gone in tender madness, and anon,
Faints into sleep, with many a dying tone
Of sadness. O that she would take my
 vows, 951
And breathe them sighingly among the
 boughs,
To sue her gentle ears for whose fair head,
Daily, I pluck sweet flowerets from their
 bed,
And weave them dyingly — send honey-
 whispers

Round every leaf, that all those gentle
 lispers
May sigh my love unto her pitying !
O charitable Echo ! hear, and sing
This ditty to her ! — tell her " — So I stay'd
My foolish tongue, and listening, half
 afraid, 960
Stood stupefied with my own empty folly,
And blushing for the freaks of melancholy.
Salt tears were coming, when I heard my
 name
Most fondly lipp'd, and then these accents
 came:
" Endymion ! the cave is secreter
Than the isle of Delos. Echo hence shall
 stir
No sighs but sigh-warm kisses, or light
 noise
Of thy combing hand, the while it travel-
 ling cloys
And trembles through my labyrinthine
 hair."
At that oppress'd, I hurried in. — Ah !
 where 970
Are those swift moments ? Whither are
 they fled ?
I 'll smile no more, Peona; nor will wed
Sorrow, the way to death; but patiently
Bear up against it: so farewell, sad sigh;
And come instead demurest meditation,
To occupy me wholly, and to fashion
My pilgrimage for the world's dusky brink.
No more will I count over, link by link,
My chain of grief: no longer strive to find
A half-forgetfulness in mountain wind 980
Blustering about my ears: aye, thou shalt
 see,
Dearest of sisters, what my life shall be;
What a calm round of hours shall make
 my days.
There is a paly flame of hope that plays
Where'er I look: but yet, I 'll say 't is
 naught —
And here I bid it die. Have not I caught,
Already, a more healthy countenance ?
By this the sun is setting; we may chance
Meet some of our near-dwellers with my
 car.'

This said, he rose, faint-smiling like a
 star 990
Through autumn mists, and took Peona's
 hand:
They stept into the boat, and launch'd from
 land.

BOOK II

O SOVEREIGN power of love ! O grief ! O
 balm !
All records, saving thine, come cool, and
 calm,
And shadowy, through the mist of passed
 years:
For others, good or bad, hatred and
 tears
Have become indolent; but touching thine,
One sigh doth echo, one poor sob doth
 pine,
One kiss brings honey-dew from buried
 days.
The woes of Troy, towers smothering o'er
 their blaze,
Stiff - holden shields, far - piercing spears,
 keen blades,
Struggling, and blood, and shrieks — all
 dimly fades 10
Into some backward corner of the brain;
Yet, in our very souls, we feel amain
The close of Troïlus and Cressid sweet.
Hence, pageant history ! hence, gilded
 cheat !
Swart planet in the universe of deeds !
Wide sea, that one continuous murmur
 breeds
Along the pebbled shore of memory !
Many old rotten - timber'd boats there
 be
Upon thy vaporous bosom, magnified
To goodly vessels; many a sail of pride, 20
And golden-keel'd, is left unlaunch'd and
 dry.
But wherefore this ? What care, though
 owl did fly
About the great Athenian admiral's mast ?
What care, though striding Alexander past

The Indus with his Macedonian numbers ?
Though old Ulysses tortured from his
 slumbers
The glutted Cyclops, what care ? — Juliet
 leaning
Amid her window - flowers, — sighing, —
 weaning
Tenderly her fancy from its maiden snow,
Doth more avail than these: the silver
 flow 30
Of Hero's tears, the swoon of Imogen,
Fair Pastorella in the bandit's den,
Are things to brood on with more ardency
Than the death-day of empires. Fearfully
Must such conviction come upon his head,
Who, thus far, discontent, has dared to
 tread,
Without one muse's smile, or kind behest,
The path of love and poesy. But rest,
In chafing restlessness, is yet more drear
Than to be crush'd, in striving to uprear 40
Love's standard on the battlements of song.
So once more days and nights aid me along,
Like legion'd soldiers.

 Brain-sick shepherd-prince,
What promise hast thou faithful guarded
 since
The day of sacrifice ? Or, have new sor-
 rows
Come with the constant dawn upon thy
 morrows ?
Alas ! 't is his old grief. For many days,
Has he been wandering in uncertain ways:
Through wilderness, and woods of mossed
 oaks;
Counting his woe-worn minutes, by the
 strokes 50
Of the lone wood-cutter ; and listening
 still,
Hour after hour, to each lush-leaved rill.
Now he is sitting by a shady spring,
And elbow-deep with feverous fingering
Stems the upbursting cold: a wild rose tree
Pavilions him in bloom, and he doth see
A bud which snares his fancy: lo ! but now
He plucks it, dips its stalk in the water:
 how !

It swells, it buds, it flowers beneath his
 sight;
And, in the middle, there is softly pight 60
A golden butterfly; upon whose wings
There must be surely character'd strange
 things,
For with wide eye he wonders, and smiles
 oft.

 Lightly this little herald flew aloft,
Follow'd by glad Endymion's clasped
 hands:
Onward it flies. From languor's sullen
 bands
His limbs are loosed, and eager, on he hies
Dazzled to trace it in the sunny skies.
It seem'd he flew, the way so easy was;
And like a new-born spirit did he pass 70
Through the green evening quiet in the sun,
O'er many a heath, through many a wood-
 land dun,
Through buried paths, where sleepy twi-
 light dreams
The summer time away. One track un-
 seams
A wooded cleft, and, far away, the blue
Of ocean fades upon him; then, anew,
He sinks adown a solitary glen,
Where there was never sound of mortal
 men,
Saving, perhaps, some snow-light cadences
Melting to silence, when upon the breeze 80
Some holy bark let forth an anthem sweet,
To cheer itself to Delphi. Still his feet
Went swift beneath the merry - winged
 guide,
Until it reach'd a splashing fountain's side
That, near a cavern's mouth, for ever
 pour'd
Unto the temperate air: then high it soar'd,
And, downward, suddenly began to dip,
As if, athirst with so much toil, 't would
 sip
The crystal spout-head: so it did, with
 touch
Most delicate, as though afraid to smutch, 90
Even with mealy gold, the waters clear.
But, at that very touch, to disappear

So fairy-quick, was strange ! Bewildered,
Endymion sought around, and shook each
 bed
Of covert flowers in vain; and then he flung
Himself along the grass. What gentle
 tongue,
What whisperer, disturb'd his gloomy rest ?
It was a nymph uprisen to the breast
In the fountain's pebbly margin, and she
 stood
'Mong lilies, like the youngest of the
 brood. 100
To him her dripping hand she softly kist,
And anxiously began to plait and twist
Her ringlets round her fingers, saying:
 'Youth !
Too long, alas, hast thou starved on the
 ruth,
The bitterness of love: too long indeed,
Seeing thou art so gentle. Could I weed
Thy soul of care, by heavens, I would offer
All the bright riches of my crystal coffer
To Amphitrite; all my clear-eyed fish,
Golden, or rainbow-sided, or purplish, 110
Vermilion - tail'd, or finn'd with silvery
 gauze;
Yea, or my veined pebble-floor, that draws
A virgin light to the deep; my grotto-sands,
Tawny and gold, oozed slowly from far
 lands
By my diligent springs: my level lilies,
 shells,
My charming rod, my potent river spells;
Yes, every thing, even to the pearly cup
Meander gave me, — for I bubbled up
To fainting creatures in a desert wild.
But woe is me, I am but as a child 120
To gladden thee; and all I dare to say,
Is, that I pity thee; that on this day
I 've been thy guide; that thou must wander
 far
In other regions, past the scanty bar
To mortal steps, before thou canst be ta'en
From every wasting sigh, from every pain,
Into the gentle bosom of thy love.
Why it is thus, one knows in heaven above:
But, a poor Naiad, I guess not. Farewell !
I have a ditty for my hollow cell.' 130

Hereat she vanish'd from Endymion's
 gaze,
Who brooded o'er the water in amaze:
The dashing fount pour'd on, and where
 its pool
Lay, half asleep, in grass and rushes cool,
Quick waterflies and gnats were sporting
 still,
And fish were dimpling, as if good nor ill
Had fallen out that hour. The wanderer,
Holding his forehead, to keep off the burr
Of smothering fancies, patiently sat down;
And, while beneath the evening's sleepy
 frown 140
Glowworms began to trim their starry
 lamps,
Thus breathed he to himself: ' Whoso en-
 camps
To take a fancied city of delight,
O what a wretch is he ! and when 't is his,
After long toil and travelling, to miss
The kernel of his hopes, how more than
 vile :
Yet, for him there 's refreshment even in
 toil :
Another city doth he set about,
Free from the smallest pebble - bead of
 doubt 149
That he will seize on trickling honey-combs:
Alas, he finds them dry; and then he foams,
And onward to another city speeds.
But this is human life: the war, the deeds,
The disappointment, the anxiety,
Imagination's struggles, far and nigh,
All human; bearing in themselves this good,
That they are still the air, the subtle food,
To make us feel existence, and to show
How quiet death is. Where soil is, men
 grow, 159
Whether to weeds or flowers; but for me,
There is no depth to strike in: I can see
Naught earthly worth my compassing; so
 stand
Upon a misty, jutting head of land —
Alone ? No, no; and by the Orphean lute,
When mad Eurydice is listening to 't,
I 'd rather stand upon this misty peak,
With not a thing to sigh for, or to seek,

But the soft shadow of my thrice seen love,
Than be — I care not what. O meekest
 dove
Of heaven! O Cynthia, ten-times bright
 and fair! 170
From thy blue throne, now filling all the
 air,
Glance but one little beam of temper'd
 light
Into my bosom, that the dreadful might
And tyranny of love be somewhat scared!
Yet do not so, sweet queen ; one torment
 spared,
Would give a pang to jealous misery,
Worse than the torment's self: but rather
 tie
Large wings upon my shoulders, and point
 out
My love's far dwelling. Though the play-
 ful rout 179
Of Cupids shun thee, too divine art thou,
Too keen in beauty, for thy silver prow
Not to have dipp'd in love's most gentle
 stream.
O be propitious, nor severely deem
My madness impious; for, by all the stars
That tend thy bidding, I do think the bars
That kept my spirit in are burst — that I
Am sailing with thee through the dizzy
 sky!
How beautiful thou art! The world how
 deep!
How tremulous-dazzlingly the wheels sweep
Around their axle! Then these gleaming
 reins, 190
How lithe! When this thy chariot attains
Its airy goal, haply some bower veils
Those twilight eyes? Those eyes! — my
 spirit fails —
Dear goddess, help! or the wide gaping
 air
Will gulf me — help!' — At this, with
 madden'd stare,
And lifted hands, and trembling lips, he
 stood;
Like old Deucalion mountain'd o'er the
 flood,
Or blind Orion hungry for the morn.

And, but from the deep cavern there was
 borne
A voice, he had been froze to senseless
 stone; 200
Nor sigh of his, nor plaint, nor passion'd
 moan
Had more been heard. Thus swell'd it
 forth: 'Descend,
Young mountaineer! descend where alleys
 bend
Into the sparry hollows of the world!
Oft hast thou seen bolts of the thunder
 hurl'd
As from thy threshold; day by day hast
 been
A little lower than the chilly sheen
Of icy pinnacles, and dipp'dst thine arms
Into the deadening ether that still charms
Their marble being: now, as deep pro-
 found
As those are high, descend! He ne'er is
 crown'd 211
With immortality, who fears to follow
Where airy voices lead: so through the
 hollow,
The silent mysteries of earth, descend!'

 He heard but the last words, nor could
 contend
One moment in reflection: for he fled
Into the fearful deep, to hide his head
From the clear moon, the trees, and com-
 ing madness.

 'T was far too strange, and wonderful
 for sadness;
Sharpening, by degrees, his appetite 220
To dive into the deepest. Dark, nor light,
The region; nor bright, nor sombre wholly,
But mingled up; a gleaming melancholy;
A dusky empire and its diadems;
One faint eternal eventide of gems.
Aye, millions sparkled on a vein of gold,
Along whose track the prince quick foot-
 steps told,
With all its lines abrupt and angular:
Out-shooting sometimes, like a meteor-star,
Through a vast antre; then the metal woof,

Like Vulcan's rainbow, with some mon-
 strous roof 231
Curves hugely: now, far in the deep abyss,
It seems an angry lightning, and doth hiss
Fancy into belief: anon it leads
Through winding passages, where sameness
 breeds
Vexing conceptions of some sudden change;
Whether to silver grots, or giant range
Of sapphire columns, or fantastic bridge
Athwart a flood of crystal. On a ridge
Now fareth he, that o'er the vast beneath
Towers like an ocean-cliff, and whence he
 seeth 241
A hundred waterfalls, whose voices come
But as the murmuring surge. Chilly and
 numb
His bosom grew, when first he, far away,
Descried an orbed diamond, set to fray
Old Darkness from his throne: 't was like
 the sun
Uprisen o'er chaos: and with such a stun
Came the amazement, that, absorb'd in it,
He saw not fiercer wonders — past the
 wit
Of any spirit to tell, but one of those 250
Who, when this planet's sphering time doth
 close
Will be its high remembrancers: who they ?
The mighty ones who have made eternal
 day
For Greece and England. While astonish-
 ment
With deep-drawn sighs was quieting, he
 went
Into a marble gallery, passing through
A mimic temple, so complete and true
In sacred custom, that he well nigh fear'd
To search it inwards; whence far off ap-
 pear'd,
Through a long pillar'd vista, a fair shrine,
And, just beyond, on light tiptoe divine, 261
A quiver'd Dian. Stepping awfully,
The youth approach'd; oft turning his
 veil'd eye
Down sidelong aisles, and into niches old:
And when, more near against the marble
 cold

He had touch'd his forehead, he began to
 thread
All courts and passages, where silence dead,
Roused by his whispering footsteps, mur-
 mur'd faint:
And long he traversed to and fro, to ac-
 quaint
Himself with every mystery, and awe; 270
Till, weary, he sat down before the maw
Of a wide outlet, fathomless and dim,
To wild uncertainty and shadows grim.
There, when new wonders ceased to float
 before,
And thoughts of self came on, how crude
 and sore
The journey homeward to habitual self !
A mad pursuing of the fog-born elf,
Whose flitting lantern, through rude nettle-
 brier,
Cheats us into a swamp, into a fire,
Into the bosom of a hated thing. 280

What misery most drowningly doth sing
In lone Endymion's ear, now he has raught
The goal of consciousness ? Ah, 't is the
 thought,
The deadly feel of solitude: for lo !
He cannot see the heavens, nor the flow
Of rivers, nor hill-flowers running wild
In pink and purple chequer, nor, up-piled,
The cloudy rack slow journeying in the
 west,
Like herded elephants; nor felt, nor prest
Cool grass, nor tasted the fresh slumberous
 air; 290
But far from such companionship to wear
An unknown time, surcharged with grief,
 away,
Was now his lot. And must he patient stay,
Tracing fantastic figures with his spear ?
'No !' exclaim'd he, 'why should I tarry
 here ? '
No ! loudly echoed times innumerable.
At which he straightway started, and 'gan
 tell
His paces back into the temple's chief;
Warming and glowing strong in the belief
Of help from Dian: so that when again 300

He caught her airy form, thus did he plain,
Moving more near the while: ' O Haunter chaste
Of river sides, and woods, and heathy waste,
Where with thy silver bow and arrows keen
Art thou now forested ? O woodland Queen,
What smoothest air thy smoother forehead woos ?
Where dost thou listen to the wide halloos
Of thy disparted nymphs ? Through what dark tree
Glimmers thy crescent ? Wheresoe'er it be,
'T is in the breath of heaven: thou dost taste 310
Freedom as none can taste it, nor dost waste
Thy loveliness in dismal elements;
But, finding in our green earth sweet contents,
There livest blissfully. Ah, if to thee
It feels Elysian, how rich to me,
An exiled mortal, sounds its pleasant name !
Within my breast there lives a choking flame —
O let me cool 't the zephyr-boughs among !
A homeward fever parches up my tongue —
O let me slake it at the running springs ! 320
Upon my ear a noisy nothing rings —
O let me once more hear the linnet's note !
Before mine eyes thick films and shadows float —
O let me 'noint them with the heaven's light !
Dost thou now lave thy feet and ankles white ?
O think how sweet to me the freshening sluice !
Dost thou now please thy thirst with berry-juice ?
O think how this dry palate would rejoice !
If in soft slumber thou dost hear my voice,
O think how I should love a bed of flowers ! — 330
Young goddess ! let me see my native bowers !
Deliver me from this rapacious deep ! '

Thus ending loudly, as he would o'er-leap
His destiny, alert he stood: but when
Obstinate silence came heavily again,
Feeling about for its old couch of space
And airy cradle, lowly bow'd his face,
Desponding, o'er the marble floor's cold thrill.
But 't was not long; for, sweeter than the rill
To its old channel, or a swollen tide 340
To margin sallows, were the leaves he spied,
And flowers, and wreaths, and ready myrtle crowns
Upheaping through the slab: refreshment drowns
Itself, and strives its own delights to hide —
Nor in one spot alone; the floral pride
In a long whispering birth enchanted grew
Before his footsteps; as when heaved anew
Old ocean rolls a lengthened wave to the shore,
Down whose green back the short-lived foam, all hoar,
Bursts gradual, with a wayward indolence. 350

Increasing still in heart, and pleasant sense,
Upon his fairy journey on he hastes;
So anxious for the end, he scarcely wastes
One moment with his hand among the sweets:
Onward he goes — he stops — his bosom beats
As plainly in his ear, as the faint charm
Of which the throbs were born. This still alarm,
This sleepy music, forced him walk tip-toe:
For it came more softly than the east could blow
Arion's magic to the Atlantic isles; 360
Or than the west, made jealous by the smiles
Of thronèd Apollo, could breathe back the lyre
To seas Ionian and Tyrian.

O did he ever live, that lonely man,
Who loved — and music slew not ? 'T is
the pest
Of love, that fairest joys give most unrest;
That things of delicate and tenderest worth
Are swallow'd all, and made a seared
dearth,
By one consuming flame: it doth immerse
And suffocate true blessings in a curse. 370
Half-happy, by comparison of bliss,
Is miserable. 'T was even so with this
Dew-dropping melody, in the Carian's
ear ;
First heaven, then hell, and then forgotten
clear,
Vanish'd in elemental passion.

And down some swart abysm he had
gone,
Had not a heavenly guide benignant led
To where thick myrtle branches, 'gainst
his head
Brushing, awakened: then the sounds again
Went noiseless as a passing noontide
rain 380
Over a bower, where little space he stood;
For as the sunset peeps into a wood,
So saw he panting light, and towards it
went
Through winding alleys; and lo, wonder-
ment !
Upon soft verdure saw, one here, one there,
Cupids a-slumbering on their pinions fair.

After a thousand mazes overgone,
At last, with sudden step, he came upon
A chamber, myrtle-wall'd, embower'd high,
Full of light, incense, tender minstrelsy, 390
And more of beautiful and strange beside:
For on a silken couch of rosy pride,
In midst of all, there lay a sleeping youth
Of fondest beauty; fonder, in fair sooth,
Than sighs could fathom, or contentment
reach:
And coverlids gold-tinted like the peach,
Or ripe October's faded marigolds,
Fell sleek about him in a thousand folds —
Not hiding up an Apollonian curve

Of neck and shoulder, nor the tenting
swerve 400
Of knee from knee, nor ankles pointing
light;
But rather, giving them to the fill'd sight
Officiously. Sideway his face reposed
On one white arm, and tenderly unclosed,
By tenderest pressure, a faint damask
mouth
To slumbery pout; just as the morning
south
Disparts a dew-lipp'd rose. Above his
head,
Four lily stalks did their white honours
wed
To make a coronal; and round him grew
All tendrils green, of every bloom and
hue, 410
Together intertwined and trammell'd fresh:
The vine of glossy sprout; the ivy mesh,
Shading its Ethiop berries; and woodbine,
Of velvet-leaves and bugle-blooms divine;
Convolvulus in streaked vases flush;
The creeper, mellowing for an autumn
blush;
And virgin's bower, trailing airily;
With others of the sisterhood. Hard by,
Stood serene Cupids watching silently.
One, kneeling to a lyre, touch'd the
strings, 420
Muffling to death the pathos with his wings;
And, ever and anon, uprose to look
At the youth's slumber; while another took
A willow bough, distilling odorous dew,
And shook it on his hair; another flew
In through the woven roof, and fluttering-
wise
Rain'd violets upon his sleeping eyes.

At these enchantments, and yet many
more,
The breathless Latmian wonder'd o'er and
o'er;
Until impatient in embarrassment, 430
He forthright pass'd, and lightly treading
went
To that same feather'd lyrist, who straight-
way,

Smiling, thus whisper'd: 'Though from
　　upper day
Thou art a wanderer, and thy presence
　　here
Might seem unholy, be of happy cheer!
For 't is the nicest touch of human honour,
When some ethereal and high-favouring
　　donor
Presents immortal bowers to mortal sense;
As now 't is done to thee, Endymion. Hence
Was I in no wise startled. So recline　440
Upon these living flowers. Here is wine,
Alive with sparkles — never, I aver,
Since Ariadne was a vintager,
So cool a purple: taste these juicy pears,
Sent me by sad Vertumnus, when his fears
Were high about Pomona: here is cream,
Deepening to richness from a snowy gleam;
Sweeter than that nurse Amalthea skimm'd
For the boy Jupiter: and here, undimm'd
By any touch, a bunch of blooming plums
Ready to melt between an infant's gums:
And here is manna pick'd from Syrian
　　trees,　452
In starlight, by the three Hesperides.
Feast on, and meanwhile I will let thee
　　know
Of all these things around us.' He did
　　so,
Still brooding o'er the cadence of his lyre;
And thus: 'I need not any hearing tire
By telling how the sea-born goddess pined
For a mortal youth, and how she strove to
　　bind
Him all in all unto her doating self.　460
Who would not be so prison'd? but, fond
　　elf,
He was content to let her amorous plea
Faint through his careless arms; content to
　　see
An unseized heaven dying at his feet;
Content, O fool! to make a cold retreat,
When on the pleasant grass such love, love-
　　lorn,
Lay sorrowing; when every tear was born
Of diverse passion; when her lips and eyes
Were closed in sullen moisture, and quick
　　sighs

Came vex'd and pettish through her nos-
　　trils small.　470
Hush! no exclaim — yet, justly might'st
　　thou call
Curses upon his head. — I was half glad,
But my poor mistress went distract and
　　mad,
When the boar tusk'd him: so away she flew
To Jove's high throne, and by her plainings
　　drew
Immortal tear-drops down the thunderer's
　　beard;
Whereon, it was decreed he should be
　　rear'd
Each summer-time to life. Lo! this is he,
That same Adonis, safe in the privacy
Of this still region all his winter-sleep.　480
Aye, sleep; for when our love-sick queen
　　did weep
Over his waned corse, the tremulous
　　shower
Heal'd up the wound, and, with a balmy
　　power,
Medicined death to a lengthened drowsi-
　　ness:
The which she fills with visions, and doth
　　dress
In all this quiet luxury; and hath set
Us young immortals, without any let,
To watch his slumber through. 'T is well
　　nigh pass'd,
Even to a moment's filling up, and fast
She scuds with summer breezes, to pant
　　through　490
The first long kiss, warm firstling, to renew
Embower'd sports in Cytherea's isle.
Look! how those winged listeners all this
　　while
Stand anxious: see! behold!' — This cla-
　　mant word
Broke through the careful silence; for
　　they heard
A rustling noise of leaves, and out there
　　flutter'd
Pigeons and doves: Adonis something
　　mutter'd,
The while one hand, that erst upon his
　　thigh

Lay dormant, moved convulsed and gradu-
ally
Up to his forehead. Then there was a
hum 500
Of sudden voices, echoing, ' Come ! come !
Arise ! awake ! Clear summer has forth
walk'd
Unto the clover-sward, and she has talk'd
Full soothingly to every nested finch:
Rise, Cupids ! or we 'll give the bluebell
pinch
To your dimpled arms. Once more sweet
life begin !'
At this, from every side they hurried in,
Rubbing their sleepy eyes with lazy wrists,
And doubling overhead their little fists
In backward yawns. But all were soon
alive: 510
For, as delicious wine doth, sparkling, dive
In nectar'd clouds and curls through water
fair,
So from the arbour roof down swell'd an air
Odorous and enlivening; making all
To laugh, and play, and sing, and loudly call
For their sweet queen: when lo ! the
wreathed green
Disparted, and far upward could be seen
Blue heaven, and a silver car, air-borne,
Whose silent wheels, fresh wet from clouds
of morn,
Spun off a drizzling dew, — which falling
chill 520
On soft Adonis' shoulders, made him still
Nestle and turn uneasily about.
Soon were the white doves plain, with necks
stretch'd out,
And silken traces lighten'd in descent;
And soon, returning from love's banish-
ment,
Queen Venus leaning downward open-
arm'd:
Her shadow fell upon his breast, and
charm'd
A tumult to his heart, and a new life
Into his eyes. Ah, miserable strife,
But for her comforting ! unhappy sight, 530
But meeting her blue orbs ! Who, who
can write

Of these first minutes ? The unchariest
muse
To embracements warm as theirs makes
coy excuse.

O it has ruffled every spirit there,
Saving Love's self, who stands superb to
share
The general gladness: awfully he stands;
A sovereign quell is in his waving hands;
No sight can bear the lightning of his bow;
His quiver is mysterious, none can know
What themselves think of it; from forth
his eyes 540
There darts strange light of varied hues
and dyes:
A scowl is sometimes on his brow, but who
Look full upon it feel anon the blue
Of his fair eyes run liquid through their
souls.
Endymion feels it, and no more controls
The burning prayer within him; so, bent
low,
He had begun a plaining of his woe.
But Venus, bending forward, said: ' My
child,
Favour this gentle youth; his days are wild
With love — he — but alas ! too well I see
Thou know'st the deepness of his misery.
Ah, smile not so, my son: I tell thee true,
That when through heavy hours I used to
rue 553
The endless sleep of this new-born Adon',
This stranger ay I pitied. For upon
A dreary morning once I fled away
Into the breezy clouds, to weep and pray
For this my love: for vexing Mars had
teased
Me even to tears: thence, when a little
eased,
Down-looking, vacant, through a hazy wood,
I saw this youth as he despairing stood: 561
Those same dark curls blown vagrant in
the wind;
Those same full fringed lids a constant
blind
Over his sullen eyes: I saw him throw
Himself on wither'd leaves, even as though

Death had come sudden; for no jot he
 moved,
Yet mutter'd wildly. I could hear he loved
Some fair immortal, and that his embrace
Had zoned her through the night. There
 is no trace
Of this in heaven: I have mark'd each
 cheek, 570
And find it is the vainest thing to seek;
And that of all things 't is kept secretest.
Endymion ! one day thou wilt be blest:
So still obey the guiding hand that fends
Thee safely through these wonders for
 sweet ends.
'T is a concealment needful in extreme;
And if I guess'd not so, the sunny beam
Thou shouldst mount up with me. Now
 adieu !
Here must we leave thee.' — At these
 words upflew
The impatient doves, uprose the floating
 car, 580
Up went the hum celestial. High afar
The Latmian saw them minish into naught;
And, when all were clear vanish'd, still he
 caught
A vivid lightning from that dreadful bow.
When all was darken'd, with Ætnean throe
The earth closed — gave a solitary moan —
And left him once again in twilight lone.

He did not rave, he did not stare aghast,
For all those visions were o'ergone, and
 past,
And he in loneliness: he felt assured 590
Of happy times, when all he had endured
Would seem a feather to the mighty prize.
So, with unusual gladness, on he hies
Through caves, and palaces of mottled
 ore,
Gold dome, and crystal wall, and turquois
 floor,
Black polish'd porticos of awful shade,
And, at the last, a diamond balustrade,
Leading afar past wild magnificence,
Spiral through ruggedest loopholes, and
 thence
Stretching across a void, then guiding o'er

Enormous chasms, where, all foam and
 roar, 601
Streams subterranean tease their granite
 beds;
Then heighten'd just above the silvery heads
Of a thousand fountains, so that he could
 dash
The waters with his spear; but at the
 splash,
Done heedlessly, those spouting columns
 rose
Sudden a poplar's height, and 'gan to en-
 close
His diamond path with fretwork, streaming
 round
Alive, and dazzling cool, and with a sound,
Haply, like dolphin tumults, when sweet
 shells 610
Welcome the float of Thetis. Long he
 dwells
On this delight; for, every minute's space,
The streams with changed magic interlace:
Sometimes like delicatest lattices,
Cover'd with crystal vines; then weeping
 trees,
Moving about as in a gentle wind,
Which, in a wink, to watery gauze refined,
Pour'd into shapes of curtain'd canopies,
Spangled, and rich with liquid broideries
Of flowers, peacocks, swans, and naiads
 fair. 620
Swifter than lightning went these wonders
 rare;
And then the water, into stubborn streams
Collecting, mimick'd the wrought oaken
 beams,
Pillars, and frieze, and high fantastic roof,
Of those dusk places in times far aloof
Cathedrals call'd. He bade a loth fare-
 well
To these founts Protean, passing gulf, and
 dell,
And torrent, and ten thousand jutting
 shapes,
Half seen through deepest gloom, and
 griesly gapes,
Blackening on every side, and overhead 630
A vaulted dome like Heaven's, far bespread

With starlight gems: aye, all so huge and
 strange,
The solitary felt a hurried change
Working within him into something
 dreary, —
Vex'd like a morning eagle, lost, and weary,
And purblind amid foggy, midnight wolds.
But he revives at once: for who beholds
New sudden things, nor casts his mental
 slough?
Forth from a rugged arch, in the dusk be-
 low, 639
Came mother Cybele! alone — alone —
In sombre chariot; dark foldings thrown
About her majesty, and front death-pale,
With turrets crown'd. Four maned lions
 hale
The sluggish wheels; solemn their toothed
 maws,
Their surly eyes brow-hidden, heavy paws
Uplifted drowsily, and nervy tails
Cowering their tawny brushes. Silent sails
This shadowy queen athwart, and faints
 away
In another gloomy arch.

 Wherefore delay,
Young traveller, in such a mournful place?
Art thou wayworn, or canst not further
 trace 651
The diamond path? And does it indeed
 end
Abrupt in middle air? Yet earthward
 bend
Thy forehead, and to Jupiter cloud-borne
Call ardently! He was indeed wayworn;
Abrupt, in middle air, his way was lost;
To cloud-borne Jove he bowed, and there
 crost
Towards him a large eagle, 'twixt whose
 wings,
Without one impious word, himself he
 flings,
Committed to the darkness and the gloom:
Down, down, uncertain to what pleasant
 doom, 661
Swift as a fathoming plummet down he
 fell

Through unknown things; till exhaled as-
 phodel,
And rose, with spicy fannings interbreathed,
Came swelling forth where little caves were
 wreathed
So thick with leaves and mosses, that they
 seem'd
Large honeycombs of green, and freshly
 teem'd
With airs delicious. In the greenest nook
The eagle landed him, and farewell took.

 It was a jasmine bower, all bestrown 670
With golden moss. His every sense had
 grown
Ethereal for pleasure; 'bove his head
Flew a delight half-graspable; his tread
Was Hesperean; to his capable ears
Silence was music from the holy spheres;
A dewy luxury was in his eyes;
The little flowers felt his pleasant sighs
And stirr'd them faintly. Verdant cave
 and cell
He wander'd through, oft wondering at
 such swell
Of sudden exaltation: but, 'Alas!' 680
Said he, 'will all this gush of feeling pass
Away in solitude? And must they wane,
Like melodies upon a sandy plain,
Without an echo? Then shall I be left
So sad, so melancholy, so bereft!
Yet still I feel immortal! O my love,
My breath of life, where art thou? High
 above,
Dancing before the morning gates of
 heaven?
Or keeping watch among those starry seven,
Old Atlas' children? Art a maid of the
 waters, 690
One of shell-winding Triton's bright-hair'd
 daughters?
Or art, impossible! a nymph of Dian's,
Weaving a coronal of tender scions
For very idleness? Where'er thou art,
Methinks it now is at my will to start
Into thine arms; to scare Aurora's train,
And snatch thee from the morning; o'er
 the main

To scud like a wild bird, and take thee off
From thy sea-foamy cradle; or to doff
Thy shepherd vest, and woo thee 'mid
 fresh leaves. 700
No, no, too eagerly my soul deceives
Its powerless self: I know this cannot be.
O let me then by some sweet dreaming
 flee
To her entrancements: hither sleep awhile!
Hither most gentle sleep! and soothing foil
For some few hours the coming solitude.'

 Thus spake he, and that moment felt
 endued
With power to dream deliciously; so wound
Through a dim passage, searching till he
 found
The smoothest mossy bed and deepest,
 where 710
He threw himself, and just into the air
Stretching his indolent arms, he took, O
 bliss!
A naked waist: 'Fair Cupid, whence is
 this?'
A well-known voice sigh'd, 'Sweetest,
 here am I!'
At which soft ravishment, with doting cry
They trembled to each other. — Helicon!
O fountain'd hill! Old Homer's Helicon!
That thou wouldst spout a little streamlet
 o'er
These sorry pages; then the verse would
 soar
And sing above this gentle pair, like lark
Over his nested young: but all is dark 721
Around thine aged top, and thy clear fount
Exhales in mists to heaven. Aye, the count
Of mighty Poets is made up; the scroll
Is folded by the Muses; the bright roll
Is in Apollo's hand: our dazed eyes
Have seen a new tinge in the western skies:
The world has done its duty. Yet, oh yet,
Although the sun of poesy is set,
These lovers did embrace, and we must
 weep 730
That there is no old power left to steep
A quill immortal in their joyous tears.
Long time in silence did their anxious fears

Question that thus it was; long time they
 lay
Fondling and kissing every doubt away;
Long time ere soft caressing sobs began
To mellow into words, and then there ran
Two bubbling springs of talk from their
 sweet lips.
'O known Unknown! from whom my be-
 ing sips 739
Such darling essence, wherefore may I not
Be ever in these arms? in this sweet spot
Pillow my chin for ever? ever press
These toying hands and kiss their smooth
 excess?
Why not for ever and for ever feel
That breath about my eyes? Ah, thou wilt
 steal
Away from me again, indeed, indeed —
Thou wilt be gone away, and wilt not heed
My lonely madness. Speak, delicious fair
Is — is it to be so? No! Who will dare
To pluck thee from me? And, of thine
 own will, 750
Full well I feel thou wouldst not leave me.
 Still
Let me entwine thee surer, surer — now
How can we part? Elysium! Who art
 thou?
Who, that thou canst not be for ever here,
Or lift me with thee to some starry sphere?
Enchantress! tell me by this soft embrace,
By the most soft completion of thy face,
Those lips, O slippery blisses, twinkling
 eyes,
And by these tenderest, milky sovereign-
 ties —
These tenderest, and by the nectar-wine,
The passion' ———— 'O doved Ida the di-
 vine! 761
Endymion! dearest! Ah, unhappy me!
His soul will 'scape us — O felicity!
How he does love me! His poor temples
 beat
To the very tune of love — how sweet,
 sweet, sweet.
Revive, dear youth, or I shall faint and
 die;
Revive, or these soft hours will hurry by

In tranced dullness; speak, and let that
 spell
Affright this lethargy! I cannot quell
Its heavy pressure, and will press at least
My lips to thine, that they may richly
 feast 771
Until we taste the life of love again.
What! dost thou move? dost kiss? O
 bliss! O pain!
I love thee, youth, more than I can con-
 ceive;
And so long absence from thee doth be-
 reave
My soul of any rest: yet must I hence:
Yet, can I not to starry eminence
Uplift thee; nor for very shame can own
Myself to thee. Ah, dearest, do not groan
Or thou wilt force me from this secrecy, 780
And I must blush in heaven. O that I
Had done it already; that the dreadful
 smiles
At my lost brightness, my impassion'd
 wiles,
Had waned from Olympus' solemn height,
And from all serious Gods; that our de-
 light
Was quite forgotten, save of us alone!
And wherefore so ashamed? 'T is but to
 atone
For endless pleasure, by some coward
 blushes:
Yet must I be a coward! — Honour rushes
Too palpable before me — the sad look 790
Of Jove — Minerva's start — no bosom
 shook
With awe of purity — no Cupid pinion
In reverence veiled — my crystalline do-
 minion
Half lost, and all old hymns made nul-
 lity!
But what is this to love? O I could fly
With thee into the ken of heavenly pow-
 ers,
So thou wouldst thus, for many sequent
 hours,
Press me so sweetly. Now I swear at
 once
That I am wise, that Pallas is a dunce —

Perhaps her love like mine is but un-
 known — 800
O I do think that I have been alone
In chastity: yes, Pallas has been sighing,
While every eve saw me my hair uptying
With fingers cool as aspen leaves. Sweet
 love,
I was as vague as solitary dove,
Nor knew that nests were built. Now a
 soft kiss —
Aye, by that kiss, I vow an endless bliss,
An immortality of passion 's thine:
Ere long I will exalt thee to the shine
Of heaven ambrosial; and we will shade 810
Ourselves whole summers by a river glade;
And I will tell thee stories of the sky,
And breathe thee whispers of its minstrelsy.
My happy love will overwing all bounds!
O let me melt into thee; let the sounds
Of our close voices marry at their birth;
Let us entwine hoveringly — O dearth
Of human words! roughness of mortal
 speech!
Lispings empyrean will I sometime teach
Thine honey'd tongue — lute-breathings,
 which I gasp 820
To have thee understand, now while I
 clasp
Thee thus, and weep for fondness — I am
 pain'd,
Endymion: woe! woe! is grief contain'd
In the very deeps of pleasure, my sole
 life?' —
Hereat, with many sobs, her gentle strife
Melted into a languor. He return'd
Entranced vows and tears.

 Ye who have yearn'd
With too much passion, will here stay and
 pity,
For the mere sake of truth; as 't is a ditty
Not of these days, but long ago 't was told
By a cavern wind unto a forest old; 831
And then the forest told it in a dream
To a sleeping lake, whose cool and level
 gleam
A poet caught as he was journeying
To Phœbus' shrine; and in it he did fling

His weary limbs, bathing an hour's space,
And after, straight in that inspired place
He sang the story up into the air,
Giving it universal freedom. There
Has it been ever sounding for those ears 840
Whose tips are glowing hot. The legend cheers
Yon sentinel stars; and he who listens to it
Must surely be self - doom'd or he will rue it:
For quenchless burnings come upon the heart,
Made fiercer by a fear lest any part
Should be engulfed in the eddying wind.
As much as here is penn'd doth always find
A resting-place, thus much comes clear and plain;
Anon the strange voice is upon the wane —
And 't is but echoed from departing sound,
That the fair visitant at last unwound 851
Her gentle limbs, and left the youth asleep. —
Thus the tradition of the gusty deep.

 Now turn we to our former chroniclers. —
Endymion awoke, that grief of hers
Sweet paining on his ear: he sickly guess'd
How lone he was once more, and sadly press'd
His empty arms together, hung his head,
And most forlorn upon that widow'd bed
Sat silently. Love's madness he had known: 860
Often with more than tortured lion's groan
Moanings had burst from him; but now that rage
Had pass'd away: no longer did he wage
A rough-voiced war against the dooming stars.
No, he had felt too much for such harsh jars:
The lyre of his soul Æolian tuned
Forgot all violence, and but communed
With melancholy thought : O he had swoon'd

Drunken from pleasure's nipple; and his love
Henceforth was dove-like. — Loth was he to move 870
From the imprinted couch, and when he did,
'T was with slow, languid paces, and face hid
In muffling hands. So temper'd, out he stray'd
Half seeing visions that might have dismay'd
Alecto's serpents; ravishments more keen
Than Hermes' pipe, when anxious he did lean
Over eclipsing eyes: and at the last
It was a sounding grotto, vaulted, vast,
O'erstudded with a thousand, thousand pearls,
And crimson-mouthed shells with stubborn curls, 880
Of every shape and size, even to the bulk
In which whales harbour close, to brood and sulk
Against an endless storm. Moreover too,
Fish-semblances, of green and azure hue,
Ready to snort their streams. In this cool wonder
Endymion sat down, and 'gan to ponder
On all his life: his youth, up to the day
When 'mid acclaim, and feasts, and garlands gay,
He stept upon his shepherd throne: the look
Of his white palace in wild forest nook, 890
And all the revels he had lorded there:
Each tender maiden whom he once thought fair,
With every friend and fellow-woodlander —
Pass'd like a dream before him. Then the spur
Of the old bards to mighty deeds: his plans
To nurse the golden age 'mong shepherd clans:
That wondrous night: the great Pan-festival:
His sister's sorrow; and his wanderings all,
Until into the earth's deep maw he rush'd:
Then all its buried magic, till it flush'd 900

High with excessive love. 'And now,' thought he,
'How long must I remain in jeopardy
Of blank amazements that amaze no more?
Now I have tasted her sweet soul to the core,
All other depths are shallow: essences,
Once spiritual, are like muddy lees,
Meant but to fertilize my earthly root,
And make my branches lift a golden fruit
Into the bloom of heaven: other light,
Though it be quick and sharp enough to blight 910
The Olympian eagle's vision, is dark,
Dark as the parentage of chaos. Hark!
My silent thoughts are echoing from these shells;
Or they are but the ghosts, the dying swells
Of noises far away? — list!' — Hereupon
He kept an anxious ear. The humming tone
Came louder, and behold, there as he lay,
On either side outgush'd, with misty spray,
A copious spring; and both together dash'd
Swift, mad, fantastic round the rocks, and lash'd 920
Among the conchs and shells of the lofty grot,
Leaving a trickling dew. At last they shot
Down from the ceiling's height, pouring a noise
As of some breathless racers whose hopes poise
Upon the last few steps, and with spent force
Along the ground they took a winding course.
Endymion follow'd — for it seem'd that one
Ever pursued, the other strove to shun —
Follow'd their languid mazes, till well nigh
He had left thinking of the mystery, — 930
And was now rapt in tender hoverings
Over the vanish'd bliss. Ah! what is it sings
His dream away? What melodies are these?

They sound as through the whispering of trees,
Not native in such barren vaults. Give ear!

'O Arethusa, peerless nymph! why fear
Such tenderness as mine? Great Dian, why,
Why didst thou hear her prayer? O that I
Were rippling round her dainty fairness now, 939
Circling about her waist, and striving how
To entice her to a dive! then stealing in
Between her luscious lips and eyelids thin.
O that her shining hair was in the sun,
And I distilling from it thence to run
In amorous rillets down her shrinking form!
To linger on her lily shoulders, warm
Between her kissing breasts, and every charm
Touch raptured! — see how painfully I flow:
Fair maid, be pitiful to my great woe.
Stay, stay thy weary course, and let me lead, 950
A happy wooer, to the flowery mead
Where all that beauty snared me.' —
'Cruel god,
Desist! or my offended mistress' nod
Will stagnate all thy fountains: — tease me not
With siren words — Ah, have I really got
Such power to madden thee? And is it true —
Away, away, or I shall dearly rue
My very thoughts: in mercy then away,
Kindest Alpheus, for should I obey 959
My own dear will, 't would be a deadly bane.'
'O, Oread-Queen! would that thou hadst a pain
Like this of mine, then would I fearless turn
And be a criminal.' 'Alas, I burn,
I shudder — gentle river, get thee hence.
Alpheus! thou enchanter! every sense
Of mine was once made perfect in these woods.

Fresh breezes, bowery lawns, and innocent
 floods,
Ripe fruits, and lonely couch, contentment
 gave;
But ever since I heedlessly did lave
In thy deceitful stream, a panting glow 970
Grew strong within me: wherefore serve
 me so,
And call it love ?　Alas !　't was cruelty.
Not once more did I close my happy eye
Amid the thrush's song.　Away ! avaunt !
O 't was a cruel thing.' — ' Now thou dost
 taunt
So softly, Arethusa, that I think
If thou wast playing on my shady brink,
Thou wouldst bathe once again.　Innocent
 maid !
Stifle thine heart no more; — nor be afraid
Of angry powers: there are deities 980
Will shade us with their wings.　Those
 fitful sighs
'T is almost death to hear: O let me pour
A dewy balm upon them ! — fear no more,
Sweet Arethusa !　Dian's self must feel
Sometimes these very pangs.　Dear maiden,
 steal
Blushing into my soul, and let us fly
These dreary caverns for the open sky.
I will delight thee all my winding course,
From the green sea up to my hidden source
About Arcadian forests; and will show 990
The channels where my coolest waters flow
Through mossy rocks; where 'mid exuber-
 ant green,
I roam in pleasant darkness, more unseen
Than Saturn in his exile; where I brim
Round flowery islands, and take thence a
 skim
Of mealy sweets, which myriads of bees
Buzz from their honey'd wings: and thou
 shouldst please
Thyself to choose the richest, where we
 might
Be incense-pillow'd every summer night.
Doff all sad fears, thou white deliciousness,
And let us be thus comforted; unless 1001
Thou couldst rejoice to see my hopeless
 stream

Hurry distracted from Sol's temperate
 beam,
And pour to death along some hungry
 sands.' —
' What can I do, Alpheus ?　Dian stands
Severe before me: persecuting fate !
Unhappy Arethusa ! thou wast late
A huntress free in ' — At this, sudden
 fell
Those two sad streams adown a fearful
 dell.
The Latmian listen'd, but he heard no
 more, 1010
'Save echo, faint repeating o'er and o'er
The name of Arethusa.　On the verge
Of that dark gulf he wept, and said: ' I
 urge
Thee, gentle Goddess of my pilgrimage,
By our eternal hopes, to soothe, to assuage,
If thou art powerful, these lovers' pains;
And make them happy in some happy
 plains.'

He turn'd — there was a whelming sound
 — he stept,
There was a cooler light; and so he kept
Towards it by a sandy path, and lo ! 1020
More suddenly than doth a moment go,
The visions of the earth were gone and
 fled —
He saw the giant sea above his head.

BOOK III

THERE are who lord it o'er their fellow-
 men
With most prevailing tinsel: who unpen
Their baaing vanities, to browse away
The comfortable green and juicy hay
From human pastures; or, O torturing
 fact !
Who, through an idiot blink, will see un-
 pack'd
Fire-branded foxes to sear up and singe
Our gold and ripe-ear'd hopes.　With not
 one tinge
Of sanctuary splendour, not a sight

Able to face an owl's, they still are dight
By the blear-eyed nations in empurpled
 vests, 11
And crowns, and turbans. With unladen
 breasts,
Save of blown self-applause, they proudly
 mount
To their spirit's perch, their being's high
 account,
Their tiptop nothings, their dull skies, their
 thrones —
Amid the fierce intoxicating tones
Of trumpets, shoutings, and belabour'd
 drums,
And sudden cannon. Ah! how all this
 hums,
In wakeful ears, like uproar past and
 gone —
Like thunder-clouds that spake to Baby-
 lon, 20
And set those old Chaldeans to their
 tasks. —
Are then regalities all gilded masks?
No, there are throned seats unscalable
But by a patient wing, a constant spell,
Or by ethereal things that, unconfined,
Can make a ladder of the eternal wind,
And poise about in cloudy thunder-tents
To watch the abysm-birth of elements.
Aye, 'bove the withering of old-lipp'd Fate
A thousand Powers keep religious state, 30
In water, fiery realm, and airy bourne;
And, silent as a consecrated urn,
Hold spherey sessions for a season due.
Yet few of these far majesties, ah, few!
Have bared their operations to this globe —
Few, who with gorgeous pageantry enrobe
Our piece of heaven — whose benevolence
Shakes hand with our own Ceres; every
 sense
Filling with spiritual sweets to plenitude,
As bees gorge full their cells. And, by
 the feud 40
'Twixt Nothing and Creation, I here swear,
Eterne Apollo! that thy Sister fair
Is of all these the gentlier-mightiest.
When thy gold breath is misting in the
 west,

She unobserved steals unto her throne,
And there she sits most meek and most
 alone;
As if she had not pomp subservient;
As if thine eye, high Poet! was not bent
Towards her with the Muses in thine heart;
As if the minist'ring stars kept not apart,
Waiting for silver-footed messages. 51
O Moon! the oldest shades 'mong oldest
 trees
Feel palpitations when thou lookest in:
O Moon! old boughs lisp forth a holier din
The while they feel thine airy fellowship.
Thou dost bless everywhere, with silver lip
Kissing dead things to life. The sleeping
 kine,
Couch'd in thy brightness, dream of fields
 divine:
Innumerable mountains rise, and rise,
Ambitious for the hallowing of thine eyes;
And yet thy benediction passeth not 61
One obscure hiding-place, one little spot
Where pleasure may be sent: the nested
 wren
Has thy fair face within its tranquil ken,
And from beneath a sheltering ivy leaf
Takes glimpses of thee; thou art a relief
To the poor patient oyster, where it sleeps
Within its pearly house. — The mighty
 deeps,
The monstrous sea is thine — the myriad
 sea!
O Moon! far-spooming Ocean bows to
 thee, 70
And Tellus feels his forehead's cumbrous
 load.

 Cynthia! where art thou now? What
 far abode
Of green or silvery bower doth enshrine
Such utmost beauty? Alas, thou dost pine
For one as sorrowful: thy cheek is pale
For one whose cheek is pale: thou dost be-
 wail
His tears, who weeps for thee. Where dost
 thou sigh?
Ah! surely that light peeps from Vesper's
 eye,

Or what a thing is love ! 'T is She, but lo!
How changed, how full of ache, how gone
 in woe ! 80
She dies at the thinnest cloud; her loveli-
 ness
Is wan on Neptune's blue: yet there 's a
 stress
Of love-spangles, just off yon cape of trees,
Dancing upon the waves, as if to please
The curly foam with amorous influence.
O, not so idle: for down-glancing thence,
She fathoms eddies, and runs wild about
O'erwhelming water-courses; scaring out
The thorny sharks from hiding-holes, and
 fright'ning
Their savage eyes with unaccustom'd light-
 ning. 90
Where will the splendour be content to
 reach ?
O love ! how potent hast thou been to
 teach
Strange journeyings ! Wherever beauty
 dwells,
In gulf or aerie, mountains or deep dells,
In light, in gloom, in star or blazing sun,
Thou pointest out the way, and straight 't is
 won.
Amid his toil thou gavest Leander breath;
Thou leddest Orpheus through the gleams
 of death;
Thou madest Pluto bear thin element;
And now, O winged Chieftain ! thou hast
 sent 100
A moonbeam to the deep, deep water-
 world,
To find Endymion.

 On gold sand impearl'd
With lily shells, and pebbles milky white,
Poor Cynthia greeted him, and soothed her
 light
Against his pallid face: he felt the charm
To breathlessness, and suddenly a warm
Of his heart's blood: 't was very sweet; he
 stay'd
His wandering steps, and half-entranced
 laid
His head upon a tuft of straggling weeds,

To taste the gentle moon, and freshening
 beads, 110
Lash'd from the crystal roof by fishes'
 tails.
And so he kept, until the rosy veils
Mantling the east, by Aurora's peering
 hand
Were lifted from the water's breast, and
 fann'd
Into sweet air; and sober'd morning came
Meekly through billows: — when like taper-
 flame
Left sudden by a dallying breath of air,
He rose in silence, and once more 'gan fare
Along his fated way.

 Far had he roam'd,
With nothing save the hollow vast, that
 foam'd 120
Above, around, and at his feet; save things
More dead than Morpheus' imaginings:
Old rusted anchors, helmets, breastplates
 large
Of gone sea-warriors; brazen beaks and
 targe;
Rudders that for a hundred years had lost
The sway of human hand; gold vase em-
 boss'd
With long-forgotten story, and wherein
No reveller had ever dipp'd a chin
But those of Saturn's vintage; mouldering
 scrolls,
Writ in the tongue of heaven, by those
 souls 130
Who first were on the earth; and sculptures
 rude
In ponderous stone, developing the mood
Of ancient Nox; — then skeletons of man,
Of beast, behemoth, and leviathan,
And elephant, and eagle, and huge jaw
Of nameless monster. A cold leaden awe
These secrets struck into him; and unless
Dian had chased away that heaviness,
He might have died: but now, with cheered
 feel,
He onward kept; wooing these thoughts to
 steal 140
About the labyrinth in his soul of love.

'What is there in thee, Moon! that
 thou shouldst move
My heart so potently? When yet a child
I oft have dried my tears when thou hast
 smiled.
Thou seem'dst my sister: hand in hand we
 went
From eve to morn across the firmament.
No apples would I gather from the tree,
Till thou hadst cool'd their cheeks de-
 liciously:
No tumbling water ever spake romance,
But when my eyes with thine thereon could
 dance: 150
No woods were green enough, no bower
 divine,
Until thou liftedst up thine eyelids fine:
In sowing-time ne'er would I dibble take,
Or drop a seed, till thou wast wide awake;
And, in the summer tide of blossoming,
No one but thee hath heard me blithely sing
And mesh my dewy flowers all the night.
No melody was like a passing spright
If it went not to solemnize thy reign.
Yes, in my boyhood, every joy and pain 160
By thee were fashion'd to the self-same end;
And as I grew in years, still didst thou
 blend
With all my ardours; thou wast the deep
 glen;
Thou wast the mountain-top — the sage's
 pen —
The poet's harp — the voice of friends —
 the sun;
Thou wast the river — thou wast glory
 won;
Thou wast my clarion's blast — thou wast
 my steed —
My goblet full of wine — my topmost
 deed: —
Thou wast the charm of women, lovely
 Moon!
O what a wild and harmonized tune 170
My spirit struck from all the beautiful!
On some bright essence could I lean, and
 lull
Myself to immortality: I prest
Nature's soft pillow in a wakeful rest.

But gentle Orb! there came a nearer bliss —
My strange love came — Felicity's abyss!
She came, and thou didst fade, and fade
 away —
Yet not entirely; no, thy starry sway
Has been an under-passion to this hour.
Now I begin to feel thine orby power 180
Is coming fresh upon me: O be kind,
Keep back thine influence, and do not blind
My sovereign vision. — Dearest love, for-
 give
That I can think away from thee and live! —
Pardon me, airy planet, that I prize
One thought beyond thine argent luxuries!
How far beyond!' At this a surprised
 start
Frosted the springing verdure of his heart;
For as he lifted up his eyes to swear
How his own goddess was past all things
 fair, 190
He saw far in the concave green of the sea
An old man sitting calm and peacefully.
Upon a weeded rock this old man sat,
And his white hair was awful, and a mat
Of weeds were cold beneath his cold thin
 feet;
And, ample as the largest winding-sheet,
A cloak of blue wrapp'd up his aged bones,
O'erwrought with symbols by the deepest
 groans
Of ambitious magic: every ocean-form
Was woven in with black distinctness;
 storm, 200
And calm, and whispering, and hideous roar
Quicksand, and whirlpool, and deserted
 shore
Were emblem'd in the woof; with every
 shape
That skims, or dives, or sleeps, 'twixt cape
 and cape.
The gulphing whale was like a dot in the
 spell,
Yet look upon it, and 't would size and
 swell
To its huge self; and the minutest fish
Would pass the very hardest gazer's wish,
And show his little eye's anatomy.
Then there was pictured the regality 210

Of Neptune; and the sea-nymphs round
 his state,
In beauteous vassalage, look up and wait.
Beside this old man lay a pearly wand,
And in his lap a book, the which he conn'd
So steadfastly, that the new denizen
Had time to keep him in amazed ken,
To mark these shadowings, and stand in
 awe.

 The old man raised his hoary head and
 saw
The wilder'd stranger — seeming not to
 see,
His features were so lifeless. Suddenly 220
He woke as from a trance; his snow-white
 brows
Went arching up, and like two magic
 ploughs
Furrow'd deep wrinkles in his forehead
 large,
Which kept as fixedly as rocky marge,
Till round his wither'd lips had gone a
 smile.
Then up he rose, like one whose tedious toil
Had watch'd for years in forlorn hermitage,
Who had not from mid-life to utmost age
Eased in one accent his o'erburden'd soul,
Even to the trees. He rose: he grasp'd
 his stole, 230
With convulsed clenches waving it abroad,
And in a voice of solemn joy, that awed
Echo into oblivion, he said: —

 'Thou art the man! Now shall I lay
 my head
In peace upon my watery pillow: now
Sleep will come smoothly to my weary
 brow.
O Jove! I shall be young again, be young!
O shell-borne Neptune, I am pierced and
 stung
With new-born life! What shall I do?
 Where go,
When I have cast this serpent-skin of
 woe? — 240
I'll swim to the sirens, and one moment
 listen

Their melodies, and see their long hair
 glisten;
Anon upon that giant's arm I'll be,
That writhes about the roots of Sicily:
To northern seas I'll in a twinkling sail,
And mount upon the snortings of a whale
To some black cloud; thence down I'll
 madly sweep
On forked lightning, to the deepest deep,
Where through some sucking pool I will
 be hurl'd
With rapture to the other side of the
 world! 250
O, I am full of gladness! Sisters three,
I bow full-hearted to your old decree!
Yes, every god be thank'd, and power be-
 nign,
For I no more shall wither, droop, and pine.
Thou art the man!' Endymion started
 back
Dismay'd; and, like a wretch from whom
 the rack
Tortures hot breath, and speech of agony,
Mutter'd: 'What lonely death am I to die
In this cold region? Will he let me freeze,
And float my brittle limbs o'er polar seas?
Or will he touch me with his searing hand,
And leave a black memorial on the sand?
Or tear me piecemeal with a bony saw, 263
And keep me as a chosen food to draw
His magian fish through hated fire and
 flame?
O misery of hell! resistless, tame,
Am I to be burnt up? No, I will shout,
Until the gods through heaven's blue look
 out! —
O Tartarus! but some few days agone
Her soft arms were entwining me, and on
Her voice I hung like fruit among green
 leaves: 271
Her lips were all my own, and — ah, ripe
 sheaves
Of happiness! ye on the stubble droop,
But never may be garner'd. I must stoop
My head, and kiss death's foot. Love!
 love, farewell!
Is there no hope from thee? This horrid
 spell

Would melt at thy sweet breath. — By
 Dian's hind
Feeding from her white fingers, on the
 wind
I see thy streaming hair ! and now, by
 Pan,
I care not for this old mysterious man !' 280

He spake, and walking to that aged form,
Look'd high defiance. Lo ! his heart 'gan
 warm
With pity, for the gray-hair'd creature
 wept.
Had he then wrong'd a heart where sorrow
 kept ?
Had he, though blindly contumelious,
 brought
Rheum to kind eyes, a sting to human
 thought,
Convulsion to a mouth of many years ?
He had in truth; and he was ripe for tears.
The penitent shower fell, as down he knelt
Before that care-worn sage, who trembling
 felt 290
About his large dark locks, and faltering
 spake:

'Arise, good youth, for sacred Phœbus'
 sake !
I know thine inmost bosom, and I feel
A very brother's yearning for thee steal
Into mine own: for why ? thou openest
The prison gates that have so long opprest
My weary watching. Though thou know'st
 it not,
Thou art commission'd to this fated spot
For great enfranchisement. O weep no
 more !
I am a friend to love, to loves of yore: 300
Aye, hadst thou never loved an unknown
 power,
I had been grieving at this joyous hour.
But even now most miserable old,
I saw thee, and my blood no longer cold
Gave mighty pulses: in this tottering case
Grew a new heart, which at this moment
 plays
As dancingly as thine. Be not afraid,

For thou shalt hear this secret all display'd,
Now as we speed towards our joyous task.'

So saying, this young soul in age's
 mask 310
Went forward with the Carian side by side:
Resuming quickly thus; while ocean's tide
Hung swollen at their backs, and jewell'd
 sands
Took silently their foot-prints.

 'My soul stands
Now past the midway from mortality,
And so I can prepare without a sigh
To tell thee briefly all my joy and pain.
I was a fisher once, upon this main,
And my boat danced in every creek and bay;
Rough billows were my home by night and
 day, — 320
The sea-gulls not more constant; for I had
No housing from the storm and tempests
 mad,
But hollow rocks, — and they were palaces
Of silent happiness, of slumberous ease:
Long years of misery have told me so.
Aye, thus it was one thousand years ago.
One thousand years ! — Is it then possible
To look so plainly through them ? to dispel
A thousand years with backward glance
 sublime ?
To breathe away as 't were all scummy
 slime 330
From off a crystal pool, to see its deep,
And one's own image from the bottom
 peep ?
Yes: now I am no longer wretched thrall,
My long captivity and moanings all
Are but a slime, a thin-pervading scum,
The which I breathe away, and thronging
 come
Like things of yesterday my youthful plea-
 sures:

'I touch'd no lute, I sang not, trod no
 measures :
I was a lonely youth on desert shores.
My sports were lonely, 'mid continuous
 roars, 340

And craggy isles, and sea-mew's plaintive
cry
Plaining discrepant between sea and sky.
Dolphins were still my playmates; shapes
unseen
Would let me feel their scales of gold and
green,
Nor be my desolation; and, full oft,
When a dread waterspout had rear'd aloft
Its hungry hugeness, seeming ready ripe
To burst with hoarsest thunderings, and
wipe
My life away like a vast sponge of fate, 349
Some friendly monster, pitying my sad
state,
Has dived to its foundations, gulf'd it down,
And left me tossing safely. But the crown
Of all my life was utmost quietude:
More did I love to lie in cavern rude,
Keeping in wait whole days for Neptune's
voice,
And if it came at last, hark, and rejoice !
There blush'd no summer eve but I would
steer
My skiff along green shelving coasts, to hear
The shepherd's pipe come clear from aery
steep,
Mingled with ceaseless bleatings of his
sheep: 360
And never was a day of summer shine,
But I beheld its birth upon the brine:
For I would watch all night to see unfold
Heaven's gates, and Æthon snort his morn-
ing gold
Wide o'er the swelling streams: and con-
stantly
At brim of day-tide, on some grassy lea,
My nets would be spread out, and I at rest.
The poor folk of the sea-country I blest
With daily boon of fish most delicate:
They knew not whence this bounty, and
elate 370
Would strew sweet flowers on a sterile
beach.

' Why was I not contented ? Wherefore
reach
At things which, but for thee, O Latmian !

Had been my dreary death ? Fool ! I began
To feel distemper'd longings: to desire
The utmost privilege that ocean's sire
Could grant in benediction: to be free
Of all his kingdom. Long in misery
I wasted, ere in one extremist fit 379
I plunged for life or death. To interknit
One's senses with so dense a breathing stuff
Might seem a work of pain; so not enough
Can I admire how crystal-smooth it felt,
And buoyant round my limbs. At first I
dwelt
Whole days and days in sheer astonishment;
Forgetful utterly of self-intent;
Moving but with the mighty ebb and flow.
Then, like a new-fledged bird that first doth
show
His spreaded feathers to the morrow chill,
I tried in fear the pinions of my will. 390
'T was freedom ! and at once I visited
The ceaseless wonders of this ocean-bed.
No need to tell thee of them, for I see
That thou hast been a witness — it must be
For these I know thou canst not feel a
drouth,
By the melancholy corners of that mouth.
So I will in my story straightway pass
To more immediate matter. Woe, alas !
That love should be my bane ! Ah, Scylla
fair !
Why did poor Glaucus ever — ever dare 400
To sue thee to his heart ? Kind stranger-
youth !
I loved her to the very white of truth,
And she would not conceive it. Timid
thing !
She fled me swift as sea-bird on the wing,
Round every isle, and point, and promon-
tory,
From where large Hercules wound up his
story
Far as Egyptian Nile. My passion grew
The more, the more I saw her dainty hue
Gleam delicately through the azure clear:
Until 't was too fierce agony to bear; 410
And in that agony, across my grief
It flash'd, that Circe might find some re-
lief —

Cruel enchantress! So above the water
I rear'd my head, and look'd for Phœbus'
 daughter.
Æœa's isle was wondering at the moon: —
It seem'd to whirl around me, and a swoon
Left me dead-drifting to that fatal power.

 ' When I awoke, 't was in a twilight
 bower;
Just when the light of morn, with hum of
 bees,
Stole through its verdurous matting of
 fresh trees. 420
How sweet, and sweeter! for I heard a
 lyre,
And over it a sighing voice expire.
It ceased — I caught light footsteps; and
 anon
The fairest face that morn e'er look'd upon
Push'd through a screen of roses. Starry
 Jove!
With tears, and smiles, and honey-words
 she wove
A net whose thraldom was more bliss than
 all
The range of flower'd Elysium. Thus did
 fall
The dew of her rich speech: "Ah! art
 awake?
O let me hear thee speak, for Cupid's
 sake! 430
I am so oppress'd with joy! Why, I have
 shed
An urn of tears, as though thou wert cold
 dead;
And now I find thee living, I will pour
From these devoted eyes their silver store,
Until exhausted of the latest drop,
So it will pleasure thee, and force thee
 stop
Here, that I too may live: but if beyond
Such cool and sorrowful offerings, thou art
 fond
Of soothing warmth, of dalliance supreme;
If thou art ripe to taste a long love-dream;
If smiles, if dimples, tongues for ardour
 mute, 441
Hang in thy vision like a tempting fruit,

O let me pluck it for thee!" Thus she
 link'd
Her charming syllables, till indistinct
Their music came to my o'er-sweeten'd
 soul;
And then she hover'd over me, and stole
So near, that if no nearer it had been
This furrow'd visage thou hadst never seen.

 ' Young man of Latmos! thus particu-
 lar
Am I, that thou may'st plainly see how
 far 450
This fierce temptation went: and thou
 may'st not
Exclaim, How, then, was Scylla quite for-
 got?

 ' Who could resist? Who in this uni-
 verse?
She did so breathe ambrosia; so immerse
My fine existence in a golden clime.
She took me like a child of suckling time,
And cradled me in roses. Thus con-
 demn'd,
The current of my former life was stemm'd,
And to this arbitrary queen of sense
I bow'd a tranced vassal: nor would thence
Have moved, even though Amphion's harp
 had woo'd 461
Me back to Scylla o'er the billows rude.
For as Apollo each eve doth devise
A new apparelling for western skies;
So every eve, nay, every spendthrift hour
Shed balmy consciousness within that
 bower.
And I was free of haunts umbrageous;
Could wander in the mazy forest-house
Of squirrels, foxes shy, and antler'd deer,
And birds from coverts innermost and
 drear 470
Warbling for very joy mellifluous sor-
 row —
To me new-born delights!

 ' Now let me borrow,
For moments few, a temperament as stern
As Pluto's sceptre, that my words not burn

These uttering lips, while I in calm speech
 tell
How specious heaven was changed to real
 hell.

 ' One morn she left me sleeping: half
 awake
I sought for her smooth arms and lips, to
 slake
My greedy thirst with nectarous camel-
 draughts;
But she was gone. Whereat the barbed
 shafts 480
Of disappointment stuck in me so sore,
That out I ran and search'd the forest o'er.
Wandering about in pine and cedar gloom
Damp awe assail'd me; for there 'gan to
 boom
A sound of moan, an agony of sound,
Sepulchral from the distance all around.
Then came a conquering earth-thunder, and
 rumbled
That fierce complain to silence: while I
 stumbled
Down a precipitous path, as if impell'd.
I came to a dark valley. — Groanings
 swell'd 490
Poisonous about my ears, and louder grew,
The nearer I approach'd a flame's gaunt
 blue,
That glared before me through a thorny
 brake.
This fire, like the eye of gordian snake,
Bewitch'd me towards; and I soon was
 near
A sight too fearful for the feel of fear:
In thicket hid I cursed the haggard scene —
The banquet of my arms, my arbour queen,
Seated upon an uptorn forest root;
And all around her shapes, wizard and
 brute, 500
Laughing, and wailing, grovelling, serpent-
 ing,
Showing tooth, tusk, and venom-bag, and
 sting !
O such deformities ! old Charon's self,
Should he give up awhile his penny pelf,
And take a dream 'mong rushes Stygian,

It could not be so fantasied. Fierce, wan,
And tyrannizing was the lady's look,
As over them a gnarled staff she shook.
Ofttimes upon the sudden she laugh'd out,
And from a basket emptied to the rout 510
Clusters of grapes, the which they raven'd
 quick
And roar'd for more; with many a hungry
 lick
About their shaggy jaws. Avenging, slow,
Anon she took a branch of mistletoe,
And emptied on 't a black dull-gurgling
 phial:
Groan'd one and all, as if some piercing
 trial
Was sharpening for their pitiable bones.
She lifted up the charm: appealing groans
From their poor breasts went sueing to her
 ear
In vain; remorseless as an infant's bier 520
She whisk'd against their eyes the sooty
 oil.
Whereat was heard a noise of painful toil,
Increasing gradual to a tempest rage,
Shrieks, yells, and groans of torture-pil-
 grimage;
Until their grieved bodies 'gan to bloat
And puff from the tail's end to stifled
 throat:
Then was appalling silence: then a sight
More wildering than all that hoarse af-
 fright;
For the whole herd, as by a whirlwind
 writhen,
Went through the dismal air like one huge
 Python 530
Antagonizing Boreas, — and so vanish'd.
Yet there was not a breath of wind: she
 banish'd
These phantoms with a nod. Lo ! from the
 dark
Came waggish fauns, and nymphs, and
 satyrs stark,
With dancing and loud revelry, — and went
Swifter than centaurs after rapine bent. —
Sighing an elephant appear'd and bow'd
Before the fierce witch, speaking thus aloud
In human accent: " Potent goddess ! chief

Of pains resistless ! make my being brief,
Or let me from this heavy prison fly: 541
Or give me to the air, or let me die !
I sue not for my happy crown again;
I sue not for my phalanx on the plain;
I sue not for my lone, my widow'd wife:
I sue not for my ruddy drops of life,
My children fair, my lovely girls and boys !
I will forget them; I will pass these joys;
Ask nought so heavenward, so too — too
 high:
Only I pray, as fairest boon, to die, 550
Or be deliver'd from this cumbrous flesh,
From this gross, detestable, filthy mesh,
And merely given to the cold bleak air.
Have mercy, Goddess ! Circe, feel my
 prayer !''

'That curst magician's name fell icy numb
Upon my wild conjecturing: truth had
 come
Naked and sabre-like against my heart.
I saw a fury whetting a death-dart;
And my slain spirit, overwrought with
 fright,
Fainted away in that dark lair of night. 560
Think, my deliverer, how desolate
My waking must have been ! disgust, and
 hate,
And terrors manifold divided me
A spoil amongst them. I prepared to flee
Into the dungeon core of that wild wood:
I fled three days — when lo ! before me
 stood
Glaring the angry witch. O Dis, even now,
A clammy dew is beading on my brow,
At mere remembering her pale laugh, and
 curse.
"Ha ! ha ! Sir Dainty ! there must be a
 nurse 570
Made of rose-leaves and thistle-down, ex-
 press,
To cradle thee my sweet, and lull thee:
 yes,
I am too flinty-hard for thy nice touch:
My tenderest squeeze is but a giant's clutch.
So, fairy-thing, it shall have lullabies
Unheard of yet; and it shall still its cries

Upon some breast more lily-feminine.
Oh, no — it shall not pine, and pine, and
 pine
More than one pretty, trifling thousand
 years;
And then 't were pity, but fate's gentle
 shears 580
Cut short its immortality. Sea-flirt !
Young dove of the waters ! truly I 'll not
 hurt
One hair of thine: see how I weep and sigh,
That our heart-broken parting is so nigh.
And must we part ? Ah, yes, it must be so.
Yet ere thou leavest me in utter woe,
Let me sob over thee my last adieus,
And speak a blessing: Mark me ! thou hast
 thews
Immortal, for thou art of heavenly race:
But such a love is mine, that here I chase
Eternally away from thee all bloom 591
Of youth, and destine thee towards a tomb.
Hence shalt thou quickly to the watery
 vast;
And there, ere many days be overpast,
Disabled age shall seize thee; and even
 then
Thou shalt not go the way of aged men;
But live and wither, cripple and still breathe
Ten hundred years: which gone, I then be-
 queath
Thy fragile bones to unknown burial.
Adieu, sweet love, adieu ! " — As shot stars
 fall, 600
She fled ere I could groan for mercy.
 Stung
And poisoned was my spirit: despair sung
A war-song of defiance 'gainst all hell.
A hand was at my shoulder to compel
My sullen steps; another 'fore my eyes
Moved on with pointed finger. In this
 guise
Enforced, at the last by ocean's foam
I found me; by my fresh, my native home.
Its tempering coolness, to my life akin,
Came salutary as I waded in; 610
And, with a blind voluptuous rage, I gave
Battle to the swollen billow-ridge, and
 drave

Large froth before me, while there yet
 remain'd
Hale strength, nor from my bones all mar-
 row drain'd.

 'Young lover, I must weep — such hell-
 ish spite
With dry cheek who can tell? While
 thus my might
Proving upon this element, dismay'd,
Upon a dead thing's face my hand I laid;
I look'd — 't was Scylla! Cursed, cursed
 Circe!
O vulture-witch, hast never heard of mercy?
Could not thy harshest vengeance be con-
 tent, 621
But thou must nip this tender innocent
Because I loved her? — Cold, O cold in-
 deed
Were her fair limbs, and like a common
 weed
The sea-swell took her hair. Dead as she
 was
I clung about her waist, nor ceased to pass
Fleet as an arrow through unfathom'd
 brine,
Until there shone a fabric crystalline,
Ribb'd and inlaid with coral, pebble, and
 pearl.
Headlong I darted; at one eager swirl 630
Gain'd its bright portal, enter'd, and be-
 hold!
'T was vast, and desolate, and icy-cold;
And all around — But wherefore this to
 thee
Who in few minutes more thyself shalt
 see? —
I left poor Scylla in a niche and fled.
My fever'd parchings up, my scathing
 dread
Met palsy half way: soon these limbs be-
 came
Gaunt, wither'd, sapless, feeble, cramp'd,
 and lame.

 'Now let me pass a cruel, cruel space,
Without one hope, without one faintest
 trace 640

Of mitigation, or redeeming bubble
Of colour'd phantasy: for I fear 't would
 trouble
Thy brain to loss of reason: and next tell
How a restoring chance came down to quell
One half of the witch in me.

 'On a day,
Sitting upon a rock above the spray,
I saw grow up from the horizon's brink
A gallant vessel: soon she seem'd to sink
Away from me again, as though her course
Had been resumed in spite of hindering
 force — 650
So vanish'd: and not long, before arose
Dark clouds, and muttering of winds mo-
 rose.
Old Æolus would stifle his mad spleen,
But could not; therefore, all the billows
 green
Toss'd up the silver spume against the
 clouds.
The tempest came: I saw that vessel's
 shrouds
In perilous bustle; while upon the deck
Stood trembling creatures. I beheld the
 wreck;
The final gulfing; the poor struggling souls;
I heard their cries amid loud thunder-
 rolls. 660
O they had all been saved but crazed eld
Annull'd my vigorous cravings; and thus
 quell'd
And curb'd, think on 't, O Latmian! did I
 sit
Writhing with pity, and a cursing fit
Against that hell-born Circe. The crew
 had gone,
By one and one, to pale oblivion;
And I was gazing on the surges prone,
With many a scalding tear, and many a
 groan,
When at my feet emerged an old man's
 hand,
Grasping this scroll, and this same slender
 wand. 670
I knelt with pain — reach'd out my hand
 — had grasp'd

These treasures — touch'd the knuckles —
 they unclasp'd —
I caught a finger: but the downward weight
O'erpower'd me — it sank. Then 'gan
 abate
The storm, and through chill aguish gloom
 outburst
The comfortable sun. I was athirst
To search the book, and in the warming
 air
Parted its dripping leaves with eager care.
Strange matters did it treat of, and drew
 on
My soul page after page, till well nigh
 won 680
Into forgetfulness; when, stupefied,
I read these words, and read again, and
 tried
My eyes against the heavens, and read
 again.
O what a load of misery and pain
Each Atlas-line bore off ! — a shine of hope
Came gold around me, cheering me to
 cope
Strenuous with hellish tyranny. Attend !
For thou hast brought their promise to an
 end.'

In the wide sea there lives a forlorn wretch,
Doom'd with enfeebled carcase to outstretch 690
His loath'd existence through ten centuries,
And then to die alone. Who can devise
A total opposition ? No one. So
One million times ocean must ebb and flow,
And he oppressed. Yet he shall not die,
These things accomplish'd : — If he utterly
Scans all the depths of magic, and expounds
The meanings of all motions, shapes, and
 sounds ;
If he explores all forms and substances
Straight homeward to their symbol-essences ;
He shall not die. Moreover, and in chief, 701
He must pursue this task of joy and grief
Most piously ; — all lovers tempest-tost,
And in the savage overwhelming lost,
He shall deposit side by side, until
Time's creeping shall the dreary space fulfil :
Which done, and all these labours ripened,

A youth, by heavenly power loved and led,
Shall stand before him ; whom he shall direct
How to consummate all. The youth elect 710
Must do the thing, or both will be de-
 stroy'd. —

'Then,' cried the young Endymion, over-
 joy'd,
'We are twin brothers in this destiny !
Say, I entreat thee, what achievement high
Is, in this restless world, for me reserved.
What ! if from thee my wandering feet
 had swerved,
Had we both perish'd ? ' — ' Look ! ' the
 sage replied,
' Dost thou not mark a gleaming through
 the tide,
Of divers brilliances ? 't is the edifice
I told thee of, where lovely Scylla lies; 720
And where I have enshrined piously
All lovers, whom fell storms have doom'd
 to die
Throughout my bondage.' Thus discours-
 ing, on
They went till unobscured the porches
 shone;
Which hurryingly they gain'd, and enter'd
 straight.
Sure never since king Neptune held his
 state
Was seen such wonder underneath the
 stars.
Turn to some level plain where haughty
 Mars
Has legion'd all his battle; and behold
How every soldier, with firm foot, doth
 hold 730
His even breast: see, many steeled squares,
And rigid ranks of iron — whence who
 dares
One step ? Imagine further, line by line,
These warrior thousands on the field su-
 pine : —
So in that crystal place, in silent rows,
Poor lovers lay at rest from joys and
 woes. —
The stranger from the mountains, breath-
 less, traced

Such thousands of shut eyes in order
 placed;
Such ranges of white feet, and patient lips
All ruddy, — for here death no blossom
 nips. 740
He mark'd their brows and foreheads; saw
 their hair
Put sleekly on one side with nicest care;
And each one's gentle wrists, with rever-
 ence,
Put cross-wise to its heart.

 ' Let us commence,'
Whisper'd the guide, stuttering with joy,
 ' even now.'
He spake, and, trembling like an aspen-
 bough,
Began to tear his scroll in pieces small,
Uttering the while some mumblings fu-
 neral.
He tore it into pieces small as snow
That drifts unfeather'd when bleak north-
 erns blow; 750
And having done it, took his dark blue
 cloak
And bound it round Endymion: then struck
His wand against the empty air times
 nine. —
' What more there is to do, young man, is
 thine:
But first a little patience; first undo
This tangled thread, and wind it to a clue.
Ah, gentle ! 't is as weak as spider's skein;
And shouldst thou break it — What, is it
 done so clean ?
A power overshadows thee ! Oh, brave !
The spite of hell is tumbling to its grave.
Here is a shell; 't is pearly blank to me, 761
Nor mark'd with any sign or charactery —
Canst thou read aught ? O read for pity's
 sake !
Olympus ! we are safe ! Now, Carian,
 break
This wand against yon lyre on the pedes-
 tal.'

 'T was done: and straight with sudden
 swell and fall

Sweet music breathed her soul away, and
 sigh'd
A lullaby to silence. — ' Youth ! now strew
These minced leaves on me, and passing
 through
Those files of dead, scatter the same
 around, 770
And thou wilt see the issue.' — 'Mid the
 sound
Of flutes and viols, ravishing his heart,
Endymion from Glaucus stood apart,
And scatter'd in his face some fragments
 light.
How lightning-swift the change ! a youth-
 ful wight
Smiling beneath a coral diadem,
Out-sparkling sudden like an upturn'd gem,
Appear'd, and, stepping to a beauteous
 corse,
Kneel'd down beside it, and with tenderest
 force
Press'd its cold hand, and wept, — and
 Scylla sigh'd ! 780
Endymion, with quick hand, the charm ap-
 plied —
The nymph arose: he left them to their joy,
And onward went upon his high employ,
Showering those powerful fragments on
 the dead.
And, as he pass'd, each lifted up its head,
As doth a flower at Apollo's touch.
Death felt it to his inwards: 't was too
 much:
Death fell a-weeping in his charnel-house.
The Latmian persevered along, and thus
All were reanimated. There arose 790
A noise of harmony, pulses and throes
Of gladness in the air — while many, who
Had died in mutual arms devout and true,
Sprang to each other madly; and the rest
Felt a high certainty of being blest.
They gazed upon Endymion. Enchant-
 ment
Grew drunken, and would have its head
 and bent.
Delicious symphonies, like airy flowers,
Budded, and swell'd, and, full-blown, shed
 full showers

Of light, soft, unseen leaves of sounds
 divine. 800
The two deliverers tasted a pure wine
Of happiness, from fairy press oozed out.
Speechless they eyed each other, and about
The fair assembly wandered to and fro,
Distracted with the richest overflow
Of joy that ever pour'd from heaven.

 —— ' Away ! '
Shouted the new born god; 'Follow, and
 pay
Our piety to Neptunus supreme ! ' —
Then Scylla, blushing sweetly from her
 dream,
They led on first, bent to her meek sur-
 prise, 810
Through portal columns of a giant size
Into the vaulted, boundless emerald.
Joyous all follow'd, as the leader call'd,
Down marble steps; pouring as easily
As hour-glass sand — and fast, as you
 might see
Swallows obeying the south summer's call,
Or swans upon a gentle waterfall.

 Thus went that beautiful multitude, nor
 far,
Ere from among some rocks of glittering
 spar, 819
Just within ken, they saw descending thick
Another multitude. Whereat more quick
Moved either host. On a wide sand they
 met,
And of those numbers every eye was wet;
For each their old love found. A mur-
 muring rose,
Like what was never heard in all the
 throes
Of wind and waters: 't is past human wit
To tell; 't is dizziness to think of it.

 This mighty consummation made, the
 host
Moved on for many a league; and gain'd
 and lost
Huge sea-marks; vanward swelling in
 array, 830

And from the rear diminishing away, —
Till a faint dawn surprised them. Glaucus
 cried,
' Behold ! behold, the palace of his pride !
God Neptune's palaces.' With noise in-
 creased,
They shoulder'd on towards that brighten-
 ing east.
At every onward step proud domes arose
In prospect, — diamond gleams and golden
 glows
Of amber 'gainst their faces levelling.
Joyous, and many as the leaves in spring,
Still onward; still the splendour gradual
 swell'd. 840
Rich opal domes were seen, on high upheld
By jasper pillars, letting through their
 shafts
A blush of coral. Copious wonder-draughts
Each gazer drank; and deeper drank more
 near:
For what poor mortals fragment up, as
 mere
As marble was there lavish, to the vast
Of one fair palace, that far, far surpass'd,
Even for common bulk, those olden three,
Memphis, and Babylon, and Nineveh.

 As large, as bright, as colour'd as the
 bow 850
Of Iris, when unfading it doth show
Beyond a silvery shower, was the arch
Through which this Paphian army took its
 march,
Into the outer courts of Neptune's state :
Whence could be seen, direct, a golden
 gate,
To which the leaders sped; but not half
 raught
Ere it burst open swift as fairy thought,
And made those dazzled thousands veil
 their eyes
Like callow eagles at the first sunrise.
Soon with an eagle nativeness their gaze 860
Ripe from hue-golden swoons took all the
 blaze,
And then, behold ! large Neptune on his
 throne

Of emerald deep: yet not exalt alone;
At his right hand stood winged Love, and on
His left sat smiling Beauty's paragon.

Far as the mariner on highest mast
Can see all round upon the calmed vast,
So wide was Neptune's hall: and as the blue
Doth vault the waters, so the waters drew
Their doming curtains, high, magnificent, 870
Awed from the throne aloof; — and when
 storm rent
Disclosed the thunder-gloomings in Jove's
 air;
But soothed as now, flash'd sudden every-
 where,
Noiseless, sub-marine cloudlets, glittering
Death to a human eye: for there did spring
From natural west, and east, and south, and
 north,
A light as of four sunsets, blazing forth
A gold-green zenith 'bove the Sea-God's
 head.
Of lucid depth the floor, and far outspread
As breezeless lake, on which the slim
 canoe 880
Of feather'd Indian darts about, as through
The delicatest air: air verily,
But for the portraiture of clouds and sky:
This palace floor breath-air, — but for the
 amaze
Of deep-seen wonders motionless, — and
 blaze
Of the dome pomp, reflected in extremes,
Globing a golden sphere.

 They stood in dreams
Till Triton blew his horn. The palace rang;
The Nereids danced; the Sirens faintly
 sang;
And the great Sea-King bow'd his dripping
 head. 890
Then Love took wing, and from his pinions
 shed
On all the multitude a nectarous dew.
The ooze-born Goddess beckoned and drew
Fair Scylla and her guides to conference;
And when they reach'd the throned emi-
 nence

She kiss'd the sea-nymph's cheek, — who
 sat her down
A-toying with the doves. Then, — ' Mighty
 crown
And sceptre of this kingdom !' Venus
 said,
' Thy vows were on a time to Nais paid:
Behold !' — Two copious tear-drops instant
 fell 900
From the God's large eyes; he smiled de-
 lectable,
And over Glaucus held his blessing hands. —
' Endymion ! Ah ! still wandering in the
 bands
Of love ? Now this is cruel. Since the
 hour
I met thee in earth's bosom, all my power
Have I put forth to serve thee. What, not
 yet
Escaped from dull mortality's harsh net ?
A little patience, youth ! 't will not be long,
Or I am skilless quite: an idle tongue,
A humid eye, and steps luxurious, 910
Where these are new and strange, are
 ominous.
Aye, I have seen these signs in one of
 heaven,
When others were all blind; and were I
 given
To utter secrets, haply I might say
Some pleasant words: — but Love will have
 his day.
So wait awhile expectant. Pr'ythee soon,
Even in the passing of thine honey-moon,
Visit thou my Cytherea: thou wilt find
Cupid well-natured, my Adonis kind;
And pray persuade with thee — Ah, I have
 done, 920
All blisses be upon thee, my sweet son !' —
Thus the fair goddess: while Endymion
Knelt to receive those accents halcyon.

Meantime a glorious revelry began
Before the Water-Monarch. Nectar ran
In courteous fountains to all cups out-
 reach'd;
And plunder'd vines, teeming exhaustless,
 pleach'd

New growth about each shell and pendent lyre;
The which, in disentangling for their fire,
Pull'd down fresh foliage and coverture 930
For dainty toying. Cupid, empire-sure,
Flutter'd and laugh'd, and oft-times through the throng
Made a delighted way. Then dance, and song,
And garlanding, grew wild; and pleasure reign'd.
In harmless tendril they each other chain'd,
And strove who should be smother'd deepest in
Fresh crush of leaves.

 O 'tis a very sin
For one so weak to venture his poor verse
In such a place as this. O do not curse, 939
High Muses! let him hurry to the ending.

 All suddenly were silent. A soft blending
Of dulcet instruments came charmingly;
And then a hymn.

 'King of the stormy sea!
Brother of Jove, and co-inheritor
Of elements! Eternally before
Thee the waves awful bow. Fast, stubborn rock,
At thy fear'd trident shrinking, doth unlock
Its deep foundations, hissing into foam.
All mountain-rivers, lost in the wide home
Of thy capacious bosom, ever flow. 950
Thou frownest, and old Æolus thy foe
Skulks to his cavern, 'mid the gruff complaint
Of all his rebel tempests. Dark clouds faint
When, from thy diadem, a silver gleam
Slants over blue dominion. Thy bright team
Gulfs in the morning light, and scuds along
To bring thee nearer to that golden song
Apollo singeth, while his chariot
Waits at the doors of heaven. Thou art not

For scenes like this: an empire stern hast thou; 960
And it hath furrow'd that large front: yet now,
As newly come of heaven, dost thou sit
To blend and interknit
Subdued majesty with this glad time.
O shell-borne King sublime!
We lay our hearts before thee evermore —
We sing, and we adore!

 'Breathe softly, flutes;
Be tender of your strings, ye soothing lutes;
Nor be the trumpet heard! O vain, O vain; 970
Not flowers budding in an April rain,
Nor breath of sleeping dove, nor river's flow, —
No, nor the Æolian twang of Love's own bow,
Can mingle music fit for the soft ear
Of goddess Cytherea!
Yet deign, white Queen of Beauty, thy fair eyes
On our soul's sacrifice.

 'Bright-winged Child!
Who has another care when thou hast smiled?
Unfortunates on earth, we see at last 980
All death-shadows, and glooms that overcast
Our spirits, fann'd away by thy light pinions.
O sweetest essence! sweetest of all minions!
God of warm pulses, and dishevell'd hair,
And panting bosoms bare!
Dear unseen light in darkness! eclipser
Of light in light! delicious poisoner!
Thy venom'd goblet will we quaff until
We fill — we fill! 989
And by thy Mother's lips —— '

 Was heard no more
For clamour, when the golden palace door
Open'd again, and from without, in shone

A new magnificence. On oozy throne
Smooth-moving came Oceanus the old,
To take a latest glimpse at his sheepfold,
Before he went into his quiet cave
To muse for ever — Then a lucid wave,
Scoop'd from its trembling sisters of mid-sea,
Afloat, and pillowing up the majesty
Of Doris, and the Ægean seer, her spouse —
Next, on a dolphin, clad in laurel boughs,
Theban Amphion leaning on his lute: 1002
His fingers went across it — All were mute
To gaze on Amphitrite, queen of pearls,
And Thetis pearly too. —

 The palace whirls
Around giddy Endymion; seeing he
Was there far strayed from mortality.
He could not bear it — shut his eyes in vain;
Imagination gave a dizzier pain.
' O I shall die ! sweet Venus, be my stay !
Where is my lovely mistress ? Well-away ! 1011
I die — I hear her voice — I feel my wing — '
At Neptune's feet he sank. A sudden ring
Of Nereids were about him, in kind strife
To usher back his spirit into life:
But still he slept. At last they interwove
Their cradling arms, and purposed to convey
Towards a crystal bower far away.

 Lo ! while slow carried through the pity-
 ing crowd,
To his inward senses these words spake
 aloud; 1020
Written in starlight on the dark above:
' *Dearest Endymion ! my entire love !*
How have I dwelt in fear of fate ; 't is
 done —
Immortal bliss for me too hast thou won.
Arise then ! for the hen-dove shall not
 hatch
Her ready eggs, before I'll kissing snatch
Thee into endless heaven. Awake ! awake !'

 The youth at once arose: a placid lake
Came quiet to his eyes; and forest green,
Cooler than all the wonders he had seen,
Lull'd with its simple song his fluttering
 breast. 1031
How happy once again in grassy nest !

BOOK IV

Muse of my native land ! loftiest Muse !
O first-born on the mountains ! by the
 hues
Of heaven on the spiritual air begot:
Long didst thou sit alone in northern grot,
While yet our England was a wolfish den;
Before our forests heard the talk of men;
Before the first of Druids was a child; —
Long didst thou sit amid our regions wild,
Rapt in a deep prophetic solitude.
There came an eastern voice of solemn
 mood: — 10
Yet wast thou patient. Then sang forth
 the Nine,
Apollo's garland: — yet didst thou divine
Such home-bred glory, that they cried in
 vain,
' Come hither, Sister of the Island !' Plain
Spake fair Ausonia; and once more she
 spake
A higher summons: — still didst thou be-take
Thee to thy native hopes. O thou hast
 won
A full accomplishment ! The thing is
 done,
Which undone, these our latter days had
 risen
On barren souls. Great Muse, thou know'st
 what prison 20
Of flesh and bone, curbs, and confines, and
 frets
Our spirits' wings: despondency besets
Our pillows; and the fresh to-morrow morn
Seems to give forth its light in very scorn
Of our dull, uninspired, snail-paced lives.
Long have I said, how happy he who
 shrives

To thee! But then I thought on poets
 gone,
And could not pray: — nor can I now — so
 on
I move to the end in lowliness of heart. —

 'Ah, woe is me! that I should fondly
 part 30
From my dear native land! Ah, foolish
 maid!
Glad was the hour, when, with thee, myri-
 ads bade
Adieu to Ganges and their pleasant fields!
To one so friendless the clear freshet
 yields
A bitter coolness; the ripe grape is sour:
Yet I would have, great gods! but one
 short hour
Of native air — let me but die at home.'

Endymion to heaven's airy dome
Was offering up a hecatomb of vows,
When these words reach'd him. Where-
 upon he bows 40
His head through thorny-green entangle-
 ment
Of underwood, and to the sound is bent,
Anxious as hind towards her hidden fawn.

 'Is no one near to help me? No fair
 dawn
Of life from charitable voice? No sweet
 saying
To set my dull and sadden'd spirit playing?
No hand to toy with mine? No lips so
 sweet
That I may worship them? No eyelids
 meet
To twinkle on my bosom? No one dies
Before me, till from these enslaving eyes 50
Redemption sparkles! — I am sad and
 lost.'

Thou, Carian lord, hadst better have been
 tost
Into a whirlpool. Vanish into air,
Warm mountaineer! for canst thou only
 bear

A woman's sigh alone and in distress?
See not her charms! Is Phœbe passion-
 less?
Phœbe is fairer far — O gaze no more: —
Yet if thou wilt behold all beauty's store,
Behold her panting in the forest grass!
Do not those curls of glossy jet surpass 60
For tenderness the arms so idly lain
Amongst them? Feelest not a kindred
 pain,
To see such lovely eyes in swimming search
After some warm delight, that seems to
 perch
Dovelike in the dim cell lying beyond
Their upper lids? — Hist!

 'O for Hermes' wand,
To touch this flower into human shape!
That woodland Hyacinthus could escape
From his green prison, and here kneeling
 down
Call me his queen, his second life's fair
 crown! 70
Ah me, how I could love! — My soul doth
 melt
For the unhappy youth — Love! I have
 felt
So faint a kindness, such a meek surrender
To what my own full thoughts had made
 too tender,
That but for tears my life had fled away!
Ye deaf and senseless minutes of the day,
And thou, old forest, hold ye this for true,
There is no lightning, no authentic dew
But in the eye of love: there 's not a sound,
Melodious howsoever, can confound 80
The heavens and earth in one to such a
 death
As doth the voice of love: there 's not a
 breath
Will mingle kindly with the meadow air,
Till it has panted round, and stolen a share
Of passion from the heart!' —

 Upon a bough
He leant, wretched. He surely cannot now
Thirst for another love: O impious,
That he can even dream upon it thus! —

Thought he, 'Why am I not as are the
 dead,
Since to a woe like this I have been led 90
Through the dark earth, and through the
 wondrous sea?
Goddess! I love thee not the less: from
 thee
By Juno's smile I turn not — no, no, no —
While the great waters are at ebb and
 flow. —
I have a triple soul! O fond pretence —
For both, for both my love is so immense,
I feel my heart is cut for them in twain.'

And so he groan'd, as one by beauty
 slain.
The lady's heart beat quick, and he could
 see
Her gentle bosom heave tumultuously. 100
He sprang from his green covert: there
 she lay,
Sweet as a musk-rose upon new-made hay;
With all her limbs on tremble, and her
 eyes
Shut softly up alive. To speak he tries:
'Fair damsel, pity me! forgive that I
Thus violate thy bower's sanctity!
O pardon me, for I am full of grief —
Grief born of thee, young angel! fairest
 thief!
Who stolen hast away the wings where-
 with
I was to top the heavens. Dear maid, sith
Thou art my executioner, and I feel 111
Loving and hatred, misery and weal,
Will in a few short hours be nothing to me,
And all my story that much passion slew
 me;
Do smile upon the evening of my days;
And, for my tortured brain begins to craze,
Be thou my nurse; and let me understand
How dying I shall kiss that lily hand. —
Dost weep for me? Then should I be con-
 tent.
Scowl on, ye fates! until the firmament 120
Outblackens Erebus, and the full-cavern'd
 earth
Crumbles into itself. By the cloud-girth

Of Jove, those tears have given me a thirst
To meet oblivion.' — As her heart would
 burst
The maiden sobb'd awhile, and then re-
 plied:
'Why must such desolation betide
As that thou speakest of? Are not these
 green nooks
Empty of all misfortune? Do the brooks
Utter a gorgon voice? Does yonder
 thrush,
Schooling its half-fledged little ones to
 brush 130
About the dewy forest, whisper tales? —
Speak not of grief, young stranger, or cold
 snails
Will slime the rose to-night. Though if
 thou wilt,
Methinks 't would be a guilt — a very
 guilt —
Not to companion thee, and sigh away
The light — the dusk — the dark — till
 break of day!'
'Dear lady,' said Endymion, ''t is past:
I love thee! and my days can never last.
That I may pass in patience still speak:
Let me have music dying, and I seek 140
No more delight — I bid adieu to all.
Didst thou not after other climates call,
And murmur about Indian streams?' —
 Then she,
Sitting beneath the midmost forest tree,
For pity sang this roundelay ——

 'O Sorrow,
 Why dost borrow
The natural hue of health, from vermeil
 lips? —
 To give maiden blushes
 To the white rose bushes? 150
Or is 't thy dewy hand the daisy tips?

 'O Sorrow,
 Why dost borrow
The lustrous passion from a falcon-eye? —
 To give the glowworm light?
 Or, on a moonless night,
To tinge, on siren shores, the salt sea-spry?

'O Sorrow,
　Why dost borrow
The mellow ditties from a mourning
　　tongue? —　　　　　　　　　160
　　To give at evening pale
　　Unto the nightingale,
That thou mayst listen the cold dews
　　among?

'O Sorrow,
　Why dost borrow
Heart's lightness from the merriment of
　　May? —
　　A lover would not tread
　　A cowslip on the head,
Though he should dance from eve till peep
　　of day —
　　Nor any drooping flower　　　170
　　Held sacred for thy bower,
Wherever he may sport himself and play.

'To Sorrow,
　I bade good morrow,
And thought to leave her far away behind;
　　But cheerly, cheerly,
　　She loves me dearly;
She is so constant to me, and so kind:
　　I would deceive her,
　　And so leave her,　　　　　180
But ah! she is so constant and so kind.

'Beneath my palm-trees, by the river side,
I sat a-weeping: in the whole world wide
There was no one to ask me why I wept, —
　　And so I kept
Brimming the water-lily cups with tears
　　Cold as my fears.

'Beneath my palm-trees, by the river side,
I sat a-weeping: what enamour'd bride,
Cheated by shadowy wooer from the clouds,
　　But hides and shrouds　　　191
Beneath dark palm-trees by a river side?

'And as I sat, over the light blue hills
There came a noise of revellers: the rills
Into the wide stream came of purple hue —
　　'T was Bacchus and his crew!

The earnest trumpet spake, and silver
　　thrills
From kissing cymbals made a merry din —
　　'T was Bacchus and his kin!
Like to a moving vintage down they came,
Crown'd with green leaves, and faces all
　　on flame;　　　　　　　　201
All madly dancing through the pleasant
　　valley,
　　To scare thee, Melancholy!
O then, O then, thou wast a simple name!
And I forgot thee, as the berried holly
By shepherds is forgotten, when, in June,
Tall chestnuts keep away the sun and
　　moon: —
　　I rush'd into the folly!

'Within his car, aloft, young Bacchus stood,
Trifling his ivy-dart, in dancing mood,　210
　　With sidelong laughing;
And little rills of crimson wine imbrued
His plump white arms, and shoulders,
　　enough white
　　For Venus' pearly bite;
And near him rode Silenus on his ass,
Pelted with flowers as he on did pass
　　Tipsily quaffing.

'Whence came ye, merry Damsels! whence
　　came ye!
So many, and so many, and such glee?
Why have ye left your bowers desolate, 220
　　Your lutes, and gentler fate? —
"We follow Bacchus! Bacchus on the wing,
　　A conquering!
Bacchus, young Bacchus! good or ill be-
　　tide,
We dance before him thorough kingdoms
　　wide: —
Come hither, lady fair, and joined be
　　To our wild minstrelsy!"

'Whence came ye, jolly Satyrs! whence
　　came ye,
So many, and so many, and such glee?
Why have ye left your forest haunts, why
　　left　　　　　　　　　　230
　　Your nuts in oak-tree cleft? —

" For wine, for wine we left our kernel tree;
For wine we left our heath, and yellow
 brooms,
 And cold mushrooms;
For wine we follow Bacchus through the
 earth;
Great god of breathless cups and chirping
 mirth ! —
Come hither, lady fair, and joined be
 To our mad minstrelsy ! "

' Over wide streams and mountains great
 we went,
And, save when Bacchus kept his ivy tent,
Onward the tiger and the leopard pants, 241
 With Asian elephants:
Onward these myriads — with song and
 dance,
With zebras striped, and sleek Arabians'
 prance,
Web-footed alligators, crocodiles,
Bearing upon their scaly backs, in files,
Plump infant laughers mimicking the coil
Of seamen, and stout galley-rowers' toil:
With toying oars and silken sails they glide,
 Nor care for wind and tide. 250

' Mounted on panthers' furs and lions'
 manes,
From rear to van they scour about the
 plains;
A three days' journey in a moment done:
And always, at the rising of the sun,
About the wilds they hunt with spear and
 horn,
 On spleenful unicorn.

' I saw Osirian Egypt kneel adown
 Before the vine-wreath crown !
I saw parch'd Abyssinia rouse and sing
 To the silver cymbals' ring ! 260
I saw the whelming vintage hotly pierce
 Old Tartary the fierce !
The Kings of Inde their jewel-sceptres vail,
And from their treasures scatter pearled
 hail;
Great Brahma from his mystic heaven
 groans,

And all his priesthood moans;
Before young Bacchus' eye-wink turning
 pale. —
Into these regions came I following him,
Sick-hearted, weary — so I took a whim
To stray away into these forests drear 270
 Alone, without a peer:
And I have told thee all thou mayest hear.

 ' Young Stranger !
 I 've been a ranger
In search of pleasure throughout every
 clime:
 Alas, 't is not for me !
 Bewitch'd I sure must be,
To lose in grieving all my maiden prime.

 ' Come then, Sorrow !
 Sweetest Sorrow ! 280
Like an own babe I nurse thee on my
 breast:
 I thought to leave thee
 And deceive thee,
But now of all the world I love thee best.

 ' There is not one,
 No, no, not one
But thee to comfort a poor lonely maid;
 Thou art her mother,
 And her brother,
Her playmate, and her wooer in the
 shade.' 290

O what a sigh she gave in finishing,
And look, quite dead to every worldly
 thing !
Endymion could not speak, but gazed on
 her:
And listened to the wind that now did stir
About the crisped oaks full drearily,
Yet with as sweet a softness as might be
Remember'd from its velvet summer song.
At last he said: ' Poor lady, how thus long
Have I been able to endure that voice ? 299
Fair Melody ! kind Siren ! I 've no choice;
I must be thy sad servant evermore:
I cannot choose but kneel here and adore.
Alas, I must not think — by Phœbe, no !

Let me not think, soft Angel! shall it be
 so?
Say, beautifullest, shall I never think?
O thou couldst foster me beyond the brink
Of recollection! make my watchful care
Close up its bloodshot eyes, nor see de-
 spair!
Do gently murder half my soul, and I
Shall feel the other half so utterly!— 310
I'm giddy at that cheek so fair and smooth;
O let it blush so ever! let it soothe
My madness! let it mantle rosy-warm
With the tinge of love, panting in safe
 alarm.—
This cannot be thy hand, and yet it is;
And this is sure thine other softling—this
Thine own fair bosom, and I am so near!
Wilt fall asleep? O let me sip that tear!
And whisper one sweet word that I may
 know
This is this world—sweet dewy blossom!'
 — *Woe!* 320
*Woe! woe to that Endymion! Where is
 he?—*

Even these words went echoing dismally
Through the wide forest—a most fearful
 tone,
Like one repenting in his latest moan;
And while it died away a shade pass'd by,
As of a thundercloud. When arrows fly
Through the thick branches, poor ring-
 doves sleek forth
Their timid necks and tremble; so these
 both 328
Leant to each other trembling, and sat so
Waiting for some destruction—when lo!
Foot-feather'd Mercury appear'd sublime
Beyond the tall tree tops; and in less time
Than shoots the slanted hail-storm, down
 he dropt
Towards the ground; but rested not, nor
 stopt
One moment from his home: only the
 sward
He with his wand light touch'd, and hea-
 venward
Swifter than sight was gone—even be-
 fore

The teeming earth a sudden witness bore
Of his swift magic. Diving swans appear
Above the crystal circlings white and
 clear; 340
And catch the cheated eye in wild surprise,
How they can dive in sight and unseen
 rise—
So from the turf outsprang two steeds jet-
 black,
Each with large dark blue wings upon his
 back.
The youth of Caria placed the lovely dame
On one, and felt himself in spleen to tame
The other's fierceness. Through the air
 they flew,
High as the eagles. Like two drops of
 dew
Exhaled to Phœbus' lips, away they are
 gone, 349
Far from the earth away—unseen, alone,
Among cool clouds and winds, but that the
 free,
The buoyant life of song can floating be
Above their heads, and follow them untired.
Muse of my native land, am I inspired?
This is the giddy air, and I must spread
Wide pinions to keep here; nor do I dread
Or height, or depth, or width, or any
 chance
Precipitous: I have beneath my glance
Those towering horses and their mournful
 freight. 359
Could I thus sail, and see, and thus await
Fearless for power of thought, without
 thine aid?—
 There is a sleepy dusk, an odorous shade
From some approaching wonder, and be-
 hold
Those winged steeds, with snorting nostrils
 bold
Snuff at its faint extreme, and seem to
 tire,
Dying to embers from their native fire!

 There curl'd a purple mist around them;
 soon,
It seem'd as when around the pale new
 moon

Sad Zephyr droops the clouds like weeping
 willow:
'T was Sleep slow journeying with head on
 pillow 370
For the first time, since he came nigh dead-
 born
From the old womb of night, his cave for-
 lorn
Had he left more forlorn; for the first
 time,
He felt aloof the day and morning's
 prime —
Because into his depth Cimmerian
There came a dream, showing how a young
 man,
Ere a lean bat could plump its wintery
 skin,
Would at high Jove's empyreal footstool
 win
An immortality, and how espouse
Jove's daughter, and be reckon'd of his
 house. 380
Now was he slumbering towards heaven's
 gate,
That he might at the threshold one hour
 wait
To hear the marriage melodies, and then
Sink downward to his dusky cave again.
His litter of smooth semilucent mist,
Diversely tinged with rose and amethyst,
Puzzled those eyes that for the centre
 sought;
And scarcely for one moment could be
 caught
His sluggish form reposing motionless.
Those two on winged steeds, with all the
 stress 390
Of vision search'd for him, as one would
 look
Athwart the sallows of a river nook
To catch a glance at silver-throated eels, —
Or from old Skiddaw's top, when fog con-
 ceals
His rugged forehead in a mantle pale,
With an eye-guess towards some pleasant
 vale
Descry a favourite hamlet faint and far.

These raven horses, though they foster'd
 are
Of earth's splenetic fire, dully drop
Their full-vein'd ears, nostrils blood wide,
 and stop; 400
Upon the spiritless mist have they out-
 spread
Their ample feathers, are in slumber
 dead, —
And on those pinions, level in mid air,
Endymion sleepeth and the lady fair.
Slowly they sail, slowly as icy isle
Upon a calm sea drifting: and meanwhile
The mournful wanderer dreams. Behold !
 he walks
On heaven's pavement; brotherly he talks
To divine powers: from his hand full fain
Juno's proud birds are pecking pearly
 grain: 410
He tries the nerve of Phœbus' golden bow,
And asketh where the golden apples grow:
Upon his arm he braces Pallas' shield,
And strives in vain to unsettle and wield
A Jovian thunderbolt: arch Hebe brings
A full-brimm'd goblet, dances lightly, sings
And tantalizes long; at last he drinks,
And lost in pleasure, at her feet he sinks,
Touching with dazzled lips her starlight
 hand.
He blows a bugle, — an ethereal band 420
Are visible above: the Seasons four, —
Green-kirtled Spring, flush Summer, golden
 store
In Autumn's sickle, Winter frosty hoar,
Join dance with shadowy Hours; while still
 the blast,
In swells unmitigated, still doth last
To sway their floating morris. 'Whose is
 this ?
Whose bugle ? ' he inquires: they smile —
 'O Dis !
Why is this mortal here ? Dost thou not
 know
Its mistress' lips ? Not thou ? — 'T is
 Dian's: lo ! 429
She rises crescented !' He looks, 't is she,
His very goddess: good-bye earth, and sea,

And air, and pains, and care, and suffering;
Good-bye to all but love! Then doth he
 spring
Towards her, and awakes — and, strange,
 o'erhead,
Of those same fragrant exhalations bred,
Beheld awake his very dream: the gods
Stood smiling; merry Hebe laughs and
 nods;
And Phœbe bends towards him crescented.
O state perplexing! On the pinion bed,
Too well awake, he feels the panting side 440
Of his delicious lady. He who died
For soaring too audacious in the sun,
When that same treacherous wax began to
 run,
Felt not more tongue-tied than Endymion.
His heart leapt up as to its rightful throne,
To that fair - shadow'd passion pulsed its
 way —
Ah, what perplexity! Ah, well a day!
So fond, so beauteous was his bed-fellow,
He could not help but kiss her: then he
 grew
Awhile forgetful of all beauty save 450
Young Phœbe's, golden-hair'd; and so 'gan
 crave
Forgiveness: yet he turn'd once more to look
At the sweet sleeper, — all his soul was
 shook, —
She press'd his hand in slumber; so once
 more
He could not help but kiss her and adore.
At this the shadow wept, melting away.
The Latmian started up: 'Bright goddess,
 stay!
Search my most hidden breast! By truth's
 own tongue,
I have no dædale heart; why is it wrung 459
To desperation? Is there nought for me,
Upon the bourne of bliss, but misery?'

These words awoke the stranger of dark
 tresses:
Her dawning love - look rapt Endymion
 blesses
With 'haviour soft. Sleep yawn'd from
 underneath.

'Thou swan of Ganges, let us no more
 breathe
This murky phantasm! thou contented
 seem'st
Pillow'd in lovely idleness, nor dream'st
What horrors may discomfort thee and
 me.
Ah, shouldst thou die from my heart-
 treachery! — 469
Yet did she merely weep — her gentle soul
Hath no revenge in it: as it is whole
In tenderness, would I were whole in love!
Can I prize thee, fair maid, all price above,
Even when I feel as true as innocence?
I do, I do. — What is this soul then?
 Whence
Came it? It does not seem my own, and I
Have no self-passion or identity.
Some fearful end must be: where, where
 is it?
By Nemesis, I see my spirit flit 479
Alone about the dark — Forgive me, sweet:
Shall we away?' He roused the steeds;
 they beat
Their wings chivalrous into the clear air,
Leaving old Sleep within his vapoury lair.

The good-night blush of eve was waning
 slow,
And Vesper, risen star, began to throe
In the dusk heavens silvery, when they
Thus sprang direct towards the Galaxy.
Nor did speed hinder converse soft and
 strange —
Eternal oaths and vows they interchange,
In such wise, in such temper, so aloof 490
Up in the winds, beneath a starry roof,
So witless of their doom, that verily
'T is well nigh past man's search their hearts
 to see;
Whether they wept, or laugh'd, or grieved
 or toy'd —
Most like with joy gone mad, with sorrow
 cloy'd.

Full facing their swift flight, from ebon
 streak,
The moon put forth a little diamond peak,

No bigger than an unobserved star,
Or tiny point of fairy scimetar;
Bright signal that she only stoop'd to tie 500
Her silver sandals, ere deliciously
She bow'd into the heavens her timid head.
Slowly she rose, as though she would have
 fled,
While to his lady meek the Carian turn'd,
To mark if her dark eyes had yet discern'd
This beauty in its birth — Despair ! despair !
He saw her body fading gaunt and spare
In the cold moonshine. Straight he seized
 her wrist;
It melted from his grasp; her hand he
 kiss'd,
And, horror ! kiss'd his own — he was
 · alone. 510
Her steed a little higher soar'd, and then
Dropt hawk-wise to the earth.

 There lies a den,
Beyond the seeming confines of the space
Made for the soul to wander in and trace
Its own existence, of remotest glooms.
Dark regions are around it, where the
 tombs
Of buried griefs the spirit sees, but scarce
One hour doth linger weeping, for the
 pierce
Of new-born woe it feels more inly smart:
And in these regions many a venom'd
 dart 520
At random flies; they are the proper home
Of every ill: the man is yet to come
Who hath not journey'd in this native hell.
But few have ever felt how calm and well
Sleep may be had in that deep den of all.
There anguish does not sting, nor pleasure
 pall;
Woe-hurricanes beat ever at the gate,
Yet all is still within and desolate.
Beset with painful gusts, within ye hear 529
No sound so loud as when on curtain'd bier
The death-watch tick is stifled. Enter none
Who strive therefore: on the sudden it is
 won.
Just when the sufferer begins to burn,
Then it is free to him; and from an urn,

Still fed by melting ice, he takes a
 draught —
Young Semele such richness never quaff'd
In her maternal longing. Happy gloom !
Dark Paradise ! where pale becomes the
 bloom
Of health by due; where silence dreariest
Is most articulate; where hopes infest; 540
Where those eyes are the brightest far that
 keep
Their lids shut longest in a dreamless sleep.
O happy spirit-home ! O wondrous soul !
Pregnant with such a den to save the whole
In thine own depth. Hail, gentle Carian !
For, never since thy griefs and woes began,
Hast thou felt so content: a grievous feud
Hath led thee to this Cave of Quietude.
Aye, his lull'd soul was there, although up-
 borne
With dangerous speed: and so he did not
 mourn 550
Because he knew not whither he was going.
So happy was he, not the aerial blowing
Of trumpets at clear parley from the east
Could rouse from that fine relish, that high
 feast.
They stung the feather'd horse; with fierce
 alarm
He flapp'd towards the sound. Alas, no
 charm
Could lift Endymion's head, or he had
 view'd
A skyey mask, a pinion'd multitude, —
And silvery was its passing: voices sweet
Warbling the while as if to lull and greet
The wanderer in his path. Thus warbled
 they, 561
While past the vision went in bright array.

 ' Who, who from Dian's feast would be
 away ?
For all the golden bowers of the day
Are empty left ? Who, who away would
 be
From Cynthia's wedding and festivity ?
Not Hesperus: lo ! upon his silver wings
He leans away for highest heaven and sings,
Snapping his lucid fingers merrily ! —

Ah, Zephyrus! art here, and Flora too! 570
Ye tender bibbers of the rain and dew,
Young playmates of the rose and daffodil,
Be careful, ere ye enter in, to fill
 Your baskets high
With fennel green, and balm, and golden
 pines,
Savory, latter-mint, and columbines,
Cool parsley, basil sweet, and sunny thyme;
Yea, every flower and leaf of every clime,
All gather'd in the dewy morning: hie
 Away! fly, fly! — 580
Crystalline brother of the belt of heaven,
Aquarius! to whom king Jove has given
Two liquid pulse streams 'stead of feath-
 er'd wings,
Two fanlike fountains, — thine illuminings
 For Dian play:
Dissolve the frozen purity of air;
Let thy white shoulders silvery and bare
Show cold through watery pinions; make
 more bright
The Star-Queen's crescent on her marriage
 night:
 Haste, haste away! — 590
Castor has tamed the planet Lion, see!
And of the Bear has Pollux mastery:
A third is in the race! who is the third,
Speeding away swift as the eagle bird?
 The ramping Centaur!
The Lion's mane 's on end: the Bear how
 fierce!
The Centaur's arrow ready seems to pierce
Some enemy: far forth his bow is bent
Into the blue of heaven. He 'll be shent,
 Pale unrelentor, 600
When he shall hear the wedding lutes
 a-playing. —
Andromeda! sweet woman! why delaying
So timidly among the stars: come hither!
Join this bright throng, and nimbly follow
 whither
 They all are going.
Danae's Son, before Jove newly bow'd,
Has wept for thee, calling to Jove aloud.
Thee, gentle lady, did he disenthrall:
Ye shall for ever live and love, for all
 Thy tears are flowing. — 610
By Daphne's fright, behold Apollo!' —

 More
Endymion heard not: down his steed him
 bore,
Prone to the green head of a misty hill.

His first touch of the earth went nigh to
 kill.
'Alas!' said he, ' were I but always borne
Through dangerous winds, had but my
 footsteps worn
A path in hell, for ever would I bless
Horrors which nourish an uneasiness
For my own sullen conquering: to him
Who lives beyond earth's boundary, grief
 is dim, 620
Sorrow is but a shadow: now I see
The grass; I feel the solid ground — Ah,
 me!
It is thy voice — divinest! Where? —
 who? who
Left thee so quiet on this bed of dew?
Behold upon this happy earth we are;
Let us ay love each other; let us fare
On forest-fruits, and never, never go
Among the abodes of mortals here below,
Or be by phantoms duped. O destiny!
Into a labyrinth now my soul would fly, 630
But with thy beauty will I deaden it.
Where didst thou melt to? By thee will
 I sit
For ever: let our fate stop here — a kid
I on this spot will offer: Pan will bid
Us live in peace, in love and peace among
His forest wildernesses. I have clung
To nothing, loved a nothing, nothing seen
Or felt but a great dream! Oh, I have
 been
Presumptuous against love, against the
 sky,
Against all elements, against the tie 640
Of mortals each to each, against the blooms
Of flowers, rush of rivers, and the tombs
Of heroes gone! Against his proper glory
Has my own soul conspired: so my story
Will I to children utter, and repent.
There never lived a mortal man, who bent
His appetite beyond his natural sphere,
But starved and died. My sweetest Indian,
 here,

Here will I kneel, for thou redeemed hast
My life from too thin breathing: gone and
 past 650
Are cloudy phantasms. Caverns lone,
 farewell !
And air of visions, and the monstrous swell
Of visionary seas ! No, never more
Shall airy voices cheat me to the shore
Of tangled wonder, breathless and aghast.
Adieu, my daintiest Dream ! although so
 vast
My love is still for thee. The hour may
 come
When we shall meet in pure elysium.
On earth I may not love thee; and there-
 fore
Doves will I offer up, and sweetest store 660
All through the teeming year : so thou wilt
 shine
On me, and on this damsel fair of mine,
And bless our simple lives. My Indian
 bliss !
My river-lily bud ! one human kiss !
One sigh of real breath — one gentle
 squeeze,
Warm as a dove's nest among summer
 trees,
And warm with dew at ooze from living
 blood !
Whither didst melt ? Ah, what of that ! —
 all good
We 'll talk about — no more of dreaming.
 — Now,
Where shall our dwelling be ? Under the
 brow 670
Of some steep mossy hill, where ivy dun
Would hide us up, although spring leaves
 were none;
And where dark yew trees, as we rustle
 through
Will drop their scarlet berry cups of dew ?
O thou wouldst joy to live in such a place;
Dusk for our loves, yet light enough to
 grace
Those gentle limbs on mossy bed reclined:
For by one step the blue sky shouldst thou
 find,
And by another, in deep dell below,

See, through the trees, a little river go 680
All in its mid-day gold and glimmering.
Honey from out the gnarled hive I 'll bring,
And apples, wan with sweetness, gather
 thee, —
Cresses that grow where no man may them
 see,
And sorrel untorn by the dew-claw'd stag:
Pipes will I fashion of the syrinx flag,
That thou mayst always know whither I
 roam,
When it shall please thee in our quiet
 home
To listen and think of love. Still let me
 speak;
Still let me dive into the joy I seek, — 690
For yet the past doth prison me. The
 rill,
Thou haply mayst delight in, will I fill
With fairy fishes from the mountain tarn,
And thou shalt feed them from the squir-
 rel's barn.
Its bottom will I strew with amber shells,
And pebbles blue from deep enchanted
 wells.
Its sides I 'll plant with dew-sweet eglan-
 tine,
And honeysuckles full of clear bee-wine.
I will entice this crystal rill to trace
Love's silver name upon the meadow's
 face. 700
I 'll kneel to Vesta, for a flame of fire;
And to god Phœbus, for a golden lyre;
To Empress Dian, for a hunting-spear;
To Vesper, for a taper silver-clear,
That I may see thy beauty through the
 night;
To Flora, and a nightingale shall light
Tame on thy finger; to the River-gods,
And they shall bring thee taper fishing-
 rods
Of gold, and lines of Naiads' long bright
 tress.
Heaven shield thee for thine utter loveli-
 ness ! 710
Thy mossy footstool shall the altar be
'Fore which I 'll bend, bending, dear love,
 to thee:

Those lips shall be my Delphos, and shall
 speak
Laws to my footsteps, colour to my cheek,
Trembling or steadfastness to this same
 voice,
And of three sweetest pleasurings the
 choice:
And that affectionate light, those diamond
 things,
Those eyes, those passions, those supreme
 pearl springs,
Shall be my grief, or twinkle me to plea-
 sure.
Say, is not bliss within our perfect seiz-
 ure ? 720
O that I could not doubt ! '

 The mountaineer
Thus strove by fancies vain and crude to
 clear
His brier'd path to some tranquillity.
It gave bright gladness to his lady's eye,
And yet the tears she wept were tears of
 sorrow;
Answering thus, just as the golden mor-
 row
Beam'd upward from the valleys of the
 east:
' O that the flutter of his heart had ceased,
Or the sweet name of love had pass'd
 away.
Young feather'd tyrant ! by a swift de-
 cay 730
Wilt thou devote this body to the earth:
And I do think that at my very birth
I lisp'd thy blooming titles inwardly;
For at the first, first dawn and thought of
 thee,
With uplift hands I blest the stars of hea-
 ven.
Art thou not cruel ? Ever have I striven
To think thee kind, but ah, it will not do !
When yet a child, I heard that kisses drew
Favour from thee, and so I gave and gave
To the void air, bidding them find out
 love: 740
But when I came to feel how far above
All fancy, pride, and fickle maidenhood,

All earthly pleasure, all imagined good,
Was the warm tremble of a devout kiss, —
Even then, that moment, at the thought of
 this,
Fainting I fell into a bed of flowers,
And languish'd there three days. Ye
 milder powers,
Am I not cruelly wrong'd ? Believe, be-
 lieve
Me, dear Endymion, were I to weave
With my own fancies garlands of sweet
 life, 750
Thou shouldst be one of all. Ah, bitter
 strife !
I may not be thy love: I am forbidden —
Indeed I am — thwarted, affrighted, chid-
 den,
By things I tremble at, and gorgon wrath.
Twice hast thou ask'd whither I went:
 henceforth
Ask me no more ! I may not utter it,
Nor may I be thy love. We might com-
 mit
Ourselves at once to vengeance; we might
 die;
We might embrace and die: voluptuous
 thought !
Enlarge not to my hunger, or I 'm caught
In trammels of perverse deliciousness. 761
No, no, that shall not be: thee will I bless,
And bid a long adieu.'

 The Carian
No word return'd: both lovelorn, silent,
 wan,
Into the valleys green together went.
Far wandering, they were perforce con-
 tent
To sit beneath a fair lone beechen tree;
Nor at each other gazed, but heavily
Pored on its hazel cirque of shedded leaves.

Endymion ! unhappy ! it nigh grieves 770
Me to behold thee thus in last extreme:
Enskied ere this, but truly that I deem
Truth the best music in a first-born song.
Thy lute-voiced brother will I sing ere
 long,

And thou shalt aid — hast thou not aided
 me ?
Yes, moonlight Emperor ! felicity
Has been thy meed for many thousand
 years;
Yet often have I, on the brink of tears,
Mourn'd as if yet thou wert a forester; —
Forgetting the old tale.

 He did not stir
His eyes from the dead leaves, or one small
 pulse 781
Of joy he might have felt. The spirit culls
Unfaded amaranth, when wild it strays
Through the old garden-ground of boyish
 days.
A little onward ran the very stream
By which he took his first soft poppy
 dream;
And on the very bark 'gainst which he
 leant
A crescent he had carved, and round it
 spent
His skill in little stars. The teeming tree
Had swollen and green'd the pious charac-
 tery, 790
But not ta'en out. Why, there was not a
 slope
Up which he had not fear'd the antelope;
And not a tree, beneath whose rooty shade
He had not with his tamed leopards play'd;
Nor could an arrow light, or javelin,
Fly in the air where his had never been —
And yet he knew it not.

 O treachery !
Why does his lady smile, pleasing her eye
With all his sorrowing ? He sees her not.
But who so stares on him ? His sister
 sure ! 800
Peona of the woods ! — Can she endure —
Impossible — how dearly they embrace !
His lady smiles; delight is in her face;
It is no treachery.

 ' Dear brother mine !
Endymion, weep not so ! Why shouldst
 thou pine

When all great Latmos so exalt will be ?
Thank the great gods, and look not bit-
 terly;
And speak not one pale word, and sigh no
 more.
Sure I will not believe thou hast such store
Of grief, to last thee to my kiss again. 810
Thou surely canst not bear a mind in pain,
Come hand in hand with one so beauti-
 ful.
Be happy both of you ! for I will pull
The flowers of autumn for your coronals.
Pan's holy priest for young Endymion calls;
And when he is restored, thou, fairest
 dame,
Shalt be our queen. Now, is it not a shame
To see ye thus, — not very, very sad ?
Perhaps ye are too happy to be glad:
O feel as if it were a common day; 820
Free-voiced as one who never was away.
No tongue shall ask, Whence come ye ? but
 ye shall
Be gods of your own rest imperial.
Not even I, for one whole month, will pry
Into the hours that have pass'd us by,
Since in my arbour I did sing to thee.
O Hermes ! on this very night will be
A hymning up to Cynthia, queen of light;
For the soothsayers old saw yesternight
Good visions in the air, — whence will be-
 fall, 830
As say these sages, health perpetual
To shepherds and their flocks; and further-
 more,
In Dian's face they read the gentle lore:
Therefore for her these vesper-carols are.
Our friends will all be there from nigh and
 far.
Many upon thy death have ditties made;
And many, even now, their foreheads shade
With cypress, on a day of sacrifice.
New singing for our maids shalt thou devise,
And pluck the sorrow from our huntsmen's
 brows. 840
Tell me, my lady-queen, how to espouse
This wayward brother to his rightful joys!
His eyes are on thee bent, as thou didst
 poise

His fate most goddess-like. Help me, I
 pray,
To lure — Endymion, dear brother, say
What ails thee ? ' He could bear no more,
 and so
Bent his soul fiercely like a spiritual bow,
And twang'd it inwardly, and calmly said:
' I would have thee my only friend, sweet
 maid !
My only visitor ! not ignorant though, 850
That those deceptions which for pleasure
 go
'Mong men, are pleasures real as real may
 be:
But there are higher ones I may not see,
If impiously an earthly realm I take.
Since I saw thee, I have been wide awake
Night after night, and day by day, until
Of the empyrean I have drunk my fill.
Let it content thee, Sister, seeing me
More happy than betides mortality.
A hermit young, I 'll live in mossy cave, 860
Where thou alone shalt come to me, and
 lave
Thy spirit in the wonders I shall tell.
Through me the shepherd realm shall pro-
 sper well;
For to thy tongue will I all health confide.
And, for my sake, let this young maid abide
With thee as a dear sister. Thou alone,
Peona, mayst return to me. I own
This may sound strangely: but when, dear-
 est girl,
Thou seest it for my happiness, no pearl
Will trespass down those cheeks. Compan-
 ion fair ! 870
Wilt be content to dwell with her, to share
This sister's love with me ? ' Like one re-
 sign'd
And bent by circumstance, and thereby
 blind
In self-commitment, thus that meek un-
 known:
' Aye, but a buzzing by my ears has flown,
Of jubilee to Dian: — truth I heard !
Well then, I see there is no little bird,
Tender soever, but is Jove's own care.
Long have I sought for rest, and, unaware,

Behold I find it ! so exalted too ! 880
So after my own heart ! I knew, I knew
There was a place untenanted in it;
In that same void white Chastity shall sit,
And monitor me nightly to lone slumber.
With sanest lips I vow me to the number
Of Dian's sisterhood; and, kind lady,
With thy good help, this very night shall
 see
My future days to her fane consecrate.'

As feels a dreamer what doth most cre-
 ate
His own particular fright, so these three
 felt: 890
Or like one who, in after ages, knelt
To Lucifer or Baal, when he 'd pine
After a little sleep: or when in mine
Far under-ground, a sleeper meets his
 friends
Who know him not. Each diligently bends
Towards common thoughts and things for
 very fear;
Striving their ghastly malady to cheer,
By thinking it a thing of yes and no,
That housewives talk of. But the spirit-
 blow
Was struck, and all were dreamers. At
 the last 900
Endymion said: ' Are not our fates all
 cast ?
Why stand we here ? Adieu, ye tender
 pair !
Adieu ! ' Whereat those maidens, with
 wild stare,
Walk'd dizzily away. Pained and hot
His eyes went after them, until they got
Near to a cypress grove, whose deadly
 maw,
In one swift moment, would what then he
 saw
Engulf for ever. ' Stay,' he cried, ' ah,
 stay !
Turn, damsels ! hist ! one word I have to
 say:
Sweet Indian, I would see thee once again.
It is a thing I dote on: so I 'd fain, 911
Peona, ye should hand in hand repair,

Into those holy groves that silent are
Behind great Dian's temple. I 'll be yon,
At Vesper's earliest twinkle — they are
 gone —
But once, once, once again — ' At this he
 press'd
His hands against his face, and then did
 rest
His head upon a mossy hillock green,
And so remain'd as he a corpse had been
All the long day; save when he scantly
 lifted 920
His eyes abroad, to see how shadows shifted
With the slow move of time, — sluggish
 and weary
Until the poplar tops, in journey dreary,
Had reach'd the river's brim. Then up he
 rose,
And, slowly as that very river flows,
Walk'd towards the temple grove with this
 lament:
'Why such a golden eve? The breeze is
 sent
Careful and soft, that not a leaf may fall
Before the serene father of them all
Bows down his summer head below the
 west. 930
Now am I of breath, speech, and speed
 possest,
But at the setting I must bid adieu
To her for the last time. Night will·strew
On the damp grass myriads of lingering
 leaves,
And with them shall I die; nor much it
 grieves
To die, when summer dies on the cold
 sward.
Why, I have been a butterfly, a lord
Of flowers, garlands, love-knots, silly po-
 sies,
Groves, meadows, melodies, and arbour-
 roses; 939
My kingdom 's at its death, and just it is
That I should die with it: so in all this
We miscall grief, bale, sorrow, heart-break,
 woe,
What is there to plain of? By Titan's foe
I am but rightly served.' So saying, he

Tripp'd lightly on, in sort of deathful glee;
Laughing at the clear stream and setting
 sun,
As though they jests had been: nor had he
 done
His laugh at nature's holy countenance,
Until that grove appear'd, as if perchance,
And then his tongue with sober seemlihed
Gave utterance as he enter'd: 'Ha !' I
 said, 951
'King of the butterflies; but by this gloom,
And by old Rhadamanthus' tongue of doom,
This dusk religion, pomp of solitude,
And the Promethean clay by thief endued,
By old Saturnus' forelock, by his head
Shook with eternal palsy, I did wed
Myself to things of light from infancy;
And thus to be cast out, thus lorn to die,
Is sure enough to make a mortal man 960
Grow impious.' So he inwardly began
On things for which no wording can be
 found;
Deeper and deeper sinking, until drown'd
Beyond the reach of music: for the choir
Of Cynthia he heard not, though rough
 brier
Nor muffling thicket interposed to dull
The vesper hymn, far swollen, soft and full,
Through the dark pillars of those sylvan
 aisles.
He saw not the two maidens, nor their
 smiles,
Wan as primroses gather'd at midnight 970
By chilly-finger'd spring. 'Unhappy wight !
Endymion !' said Peona, 'we are here !
What wouldst thou ere we all are laid on
 bier ?'
Then he embraced her, and his lady's hand
Press'd, saying: 'Sister, I would have com-
 mand,
If it were heaven's will, on our sad fate.'
At which that dark-eyed stranger stood
 elate
And said, in a new voice, but sweet as love,
To Endymion's amaze: 'By Cupid's dove,
And so thou shalt ! and by the lily truth
Of my own breast thou shalt, beloved
 youth !'
 981

And as she spake, into her face there
 came
Light, as reflected from a silver flame:
Her long black hair swell'd ampler, in dis-
 play
Full golden; in her eyes a brighter day
Dawn'd blue, and full of love. Aye, he
 beheld
Phœbe, his passion! joyous she upheld
Her lucid bow, continuing thus: " Drear,
 drear
Has our delaying been; but foolish fear
Withheld me first; and then decrees of
 fate; 990
And then 't was fit that from this mortal
 state

Thou shouldst, my love, by some unlook'd-
 for change
Be spiritualized. Peona, we shall range
These forests, and to thee they safe shall be
As was thy cradle; hither shalt thou flee
To meet us many a time.' Next Cynthia
 bright
Peona kiss'd, and bless'd with fair good
 night:
Her brother kiss'd her too, and knelt adown
Before his goddess, in a blissful swoon. 999
She gave her fair hands to him, and behold,
Before three swiftest kisses he had told,
They vanish'd far away! — Peona went
Home through the gloomy wood in won-
 derment.

The most pregnant year of Keats's genius was that which dates roughly from the spring of 1818 to the spring of 1819, as one may readily see who scans the titles of the poems included in this division. The group here given, beginning with *Isabella* and closing with *Lamia*, includes, besides those poems and *The Eve of St. Agnes*, the great Odes, *Fancy*, and some of the notable Sonnets. The division, besides being a convenient one, seems almost logical and not merely chronological.

ISABELLA, OR THE POT OF BASIL

A STORY FROM BOCCACCIO

Keats and Reynolds projected a volume of metrical tales translated from or based on Boccaccio. Apparently, Keats began *Isabella*, which was to be one of his contributions, some time before he went to Teignmouth, where he finished *Endymion*. At any rate, from that place April 27, 1818, he wrote to Reynolds, who was then quite ill: ' I have written for my folio Shakespeare, in which there are the first few stanzas of my *Pot of Basil*. I have the rest here finished, and will copy the whole out fairly shortly, and George will bring it you — The compliment is paid by us to Boccace, whether we publish or no: so there is content in this world — *mine* is short — you must be deliberate about yours ; you must not think of it till many months after you are quite well : then put your passion to it, and I shall be bound up with you in the shadows of Mind, as we are in our matters of human life.' Keats did not wait for Reynolds, but published his *Isabella* in the volume entitled *Lamia, Isabella, The Eve of St. Agnes, and other Poems* issued in the summer of 1820.

I

FAIR Isabel, poor simple Isabel !
 Lorenzo, a young palmer in Love's eye !
They could not in the self-same mansion dwell
 Without some stir of heart, some mal-
 ady;

They could not sit at meals but feel how well
 It soothed each to be the other by;
They could not, sure, beneath the same roof sleep
But to each other dream, and nightly weep.

II

With every morn their love grew tenderer,
 With every eve deeper and tenderer still;
He might not in house, field, or garden stir,
 But her full shape would all his seeing fill;
And his continual voice was pleasanter
 To her, than noise of trees or hidden rill;
Her lute-string gave an echo of his name,
She spoilt her half-done broidery with the same.

III

He knew whose gentle hand was at the latch,
 Before the door had given her to his eyes;
And from her chamber-window he would catch
 Her beauty farther than the falcon spies;
And constant as her vespers would he watch,
 Because her face was turn'd to the same skies;
And with sick longing all the night out-wear,
To hear her morning-step upon the stair.

IV

A whole long month of May in this sad
 plight
Made their cheeks paler by the break of
 June:
'To-morrow will I bow to my delight,
 To-morrow will I ask my lady's boon.' —
'O may I never see another night,
 Lorenzo, if thy lips breathe not love's
 tune.' —
So spake they to their pillows; but, alas,
Honeyless days and days did he let pass;

V

Until sweet Isabella's untouch'd cheek
 Fell sick within the rose's just domain,
Fell thin as a young mother's, who doth
 seek
 By every lull to cool her infant's pain:
'How ill she is!' said he, 'I may not
 speak,
 And yet I will, and tell my love all plain:
If looks speak love-laws, I will drink her
 tears,
And at the least 't will startle off her
 cares.'

VI

So said he one fair morning, and all day
 His heart beat awfully against his side;
And to his heart he inwardly did pray
 For power to speak; but still the ruddy
 tide
Stifled his voice, and pulsed resolve away —
 Fever'd his high conceit of such a bride,
Yet brought him to the meekness of a
 child:
Alas! when passion is both meek and wild!

VII

So once more he had waked and anguished
 A dreary night of love and misery,
If Isabel's quick eye had not been wed
 To every symbol on his forehead high;
She saw it waxing very pale and dead,
 And straight all flush'd; so, lisped ten-
 derly,

'Lorenzo!' — here she ceased her timid
 quest,
But in her tone and look he read the rest.

VIII

'O Isabella, I can half perceive
 That I may speak my grief into thine ear;
If thou didst ever any thing believe,
 Believe how I love thee, believe how
 near
My soul is to its doom: I would not grieve
 Thy hand by unwelcome pressing, would
 not fear
Thine eyes by gazing; but I cannot live
Another night, and not my passion shrive.

IX

'Love! thou art leading me from wintry
 cold,
 Lady! thou leadest me to summer clime,
And I must taste the blossoms that unfold
 In its ripe warmth this gracious morning
 time.'
So said, his erewhile timid lips grew bold,
 And poesied with hers in dewy rhyme:
Great bliss was with them, and great hap-
 piness
Grew, like a lusty flower in June's caress.

X

Parting they seem'd to tread upon the air,
 Twin roses by the zephyr blown apart
Only to meet again more close, and share
 The inward fragrance of each other's
 heart.
She, to her chamber gone, a ditty fair
 Sang, of delicious love and honey'd dart;
He with light steps went up a western hill,
And bade the sun farewell, and joy'd his
 fill.

XI

All close they met again, before the dusk
 Had taken from the stars its pleasant
 veil,
All close they met, all eves, before the dusk
 Had taken from the stars its pleasant
 veil,

Close in a bower of hyacinth and musk,
 Unknown of any, free from whispering
 tale.
Ah ! better had it been for ever so,
Than idle ears should pleasure in their
 woe.

XII

Were they unhappy then ? — It cannot
 be —
 Too many tears for lovers have been
 shed,
Too many sighs give we to them in fee,
 Too much of pity after they are dead,
Too many doleful stories do we see,
 Whose matter in bright gold were best
 be read;
Except in such a page where Theseus'
 spouse
Over the pathless waves towards him bows.

XIII

But, for the general award of love,
 The little sweet doth kill much bitter-
 ness;
Though Dido silent is in under-grove,
 And Isabella's was a great distress,
Though young Lorenzo in warm Indian
 clove
 Was not embalm'd, this truth is not the
 less —
Even bees, the little almsmen of spring-
 bowers,
Know there is richest juice in poison-
 flowers.

XIV

With her two brothers this fair lady dwelt,
 Enriched from ancestral merchandise,
And for them many a weary hand did swelt
In torched mines and noisy factories,
And many once proud-quiver'd loins did
 melt
 In blood from stinging whip; — with
 hollow eyes
Many all day in dazzling river stood,
To take the rich-ored driftings of the flood.

XV

For them the Ceylon diver held his breath,
 And went all naked to the hungry shark;
For them his ears gush'd blood; for them
 in death
 The seal on the cold ice with piteous
 bark
Lay full of darts; for them alone did
 seethe
 A thousand men in troubles wide and
 dark:
Half-ignorant, they turn'd an easy wheel,
That set sharp racks at work, to pinch and
 peel.

XVI

Why were they proud ? Because their
 marble founts
 Gush'd with more pride than do a
 wretch's tears ? —
Why were they proud ? Because fair
 orange-mounts
 Were of more soft ascent than lazar
 stairs ? —
Why were they proud ? Because red-
 lined accounts
 Were richer than the songs of Grecian
 years ? —
Why were they proud ? again we ask
 aloud,
Why in the name of Glory were they
 proud ?

XVII

Yet were these Florentines as self-retired
 In hungry pride and gainful cowardice,
As two close Hebrews in that land inspired,
 Paled in and vineyarded from beggar-
 spies;
The hawks of ship-mast forests — the un-
 tired
 And pannier'd mules for ducats and old
 lies —
Quick cat's-paws on the generous stray-
 away, —
Great wits in Spanish, Tuscan, and Malay.

XVIII

How was it these same ledger-men could
 spy
 Fair Isabella in her downy nest?
How could they find out in Lorenzo's eye
 A straying from his toil? Hot Egypt's
 pest
Into their vision covetous and sly!
 How could these money-bags see east
 and west? —
Yet so they did — and every dealer fair
Must see behind, as doth the hunted hare.

XIX

O eloquent and famed Boccaccio!
 Of thee we now should ask forgiving
 boon,
And of thy spicy myrtles as they blow,
 And of thy roses amorous of the moon,
And of thy lilies, that do paler grow
 Now they can no more hear thy ghittern's
 tune,
For venturing syllables that ill beseem
The quiet glooms of such a piteous theme.

XX

Grant thou a pardon here, and then the tale
 Shall move on soberly, as it is meet;
There is no other crime, no mad assail
 To make old prose in modern rhyme
 more sweet:
But it is done — succeed the verse or fail —
 To honour thee, and thy gone spirit
 greet;
To stead thee as a verse in English tongue,
An echo of thee in the north-wind sung.

XXI

These brethren having found by many
 signs
 What love Lorenzo for their sister had,
And how she loved him too, each unconfines
 His bitter thoughts to other, well-nigh
 mad
That he, the servant of their trade designs,
 Should in their sister's love be blithe and
 glad,
When 't was their plan to coax her by de-
 grees
To some high noble and his olive-trees.

XXII

And many a jealous conference had they,
 And many times they bit their lips alone,
Before they fix'd upon a surest way
 To make the youngster for his crime
 atone;
And at the last, these men of cruel clay
 Cut Mercy with a sharp knife to the bone;
For they resolved in some forest dim
To kill Lorenzo, and there bury him.

XXIII

So on a pleasant morning, as he leant
 Into the sunrise, o'er the balustrade
Of the garden-terrace, towards him they
 bent
 Their footing through the dews; and to
 him said,
'You seem there in the quiet of content,
 Lorenzo, and we are most loth to invade
Calm speculation; but if you are wise,
Bestride your steed while cold is in the skies.

XXIV

'To-day we purpose, aye, this hour we
 mount
 To spur three leagues towards the Apen-
 nine;
Come down, we pray thee, ere the hot sun
 count
 His dewy rosary on the eglantine.'
Lorenzo, courteously as he was wont,
 Bow'd a fair greeting to these serpents'
 whine;
And went in haste, to get in readiness,
With belt, and spur, and bracing hunts-
 man's dress.

XXV

And as he to the court-yard pass'd along,
 Each third step did he pause, and lis-
 ten'd oft
If he could hear his lady's matin-song,
 Or the light whisper of her footstep soft;

And as he thus over his passion hung,
 He heard a laugh full musical aloft;
When, looking up, he saw her features
 bright
Smile through an in-door lattice, all delight.

XXVI

'Love, Isabel!' said he, 'I was in pain
 Lest I should miss to bid thee a good
 morrow:
Ah! what if I should lose thee, when so
 fain
 I am to stifle all the heavy sorrow
Of a poor three hours' absence? but we 'll
 gain
 Out of the amorous dark what day doth
 borrow.
Good bye! I 'll soon be back.' — 'Good
 bye!' said she: —
And as he went she chanted merrily.

XXVII

So the two brothers and their murder'd
 man
 Rode past fair Florence, to where Arno's
 stream
Gurgles through straighten'd banks, and
 still doth fan
 Itself with dancing bulrush, and the
 bream
Keeps head against the freshets. Sick and
 wan
 The brothers' faces in the ford did seem,
Lorenzo's flush with love. — They pass'd the
 water
Into a forest quiet for the slaughter.

XXVIII

There was Lorenzo slain and buried in,
 There in that forest did his great love
 cease;
Ah! when a soul doth thus its freedom
 win,
 It aches in loneliness — is ill at peace
As the break-covert bloodhounds of such
 sin:
 They dipp'd their swords in the water,
 and did tease

Their horses homeward, with convulsed
 spur,
Each richer by his being a murderer.

XXIX

They told their sister how, with sudden
 speed,
 Lorenzo had ta'en ship for foreign lands,
Because of some great urgency and need
 In their affairs, requiring trusty hands.
Poor Girl! put on thy stifling widow's weed,
 And 'scape at once from Hope's accursed
 bands;
To-day thou wilt not see him, nor to-morrow,
And the next day will be a day of sorrow.

XXX

She weeps alone for pleasures not to be;
 Sorely she wept until the night came on,
And then, instead of love, O misery!
 She brooded o'er the luxury alone:
His image in the dusk she seem'd to see,
 And to the silence made a gentle moan,
Spreading her perfect arms upon the air,
And on her couch low murmuring,
 'Where? O where?'

XXXI

But Selfishness, Love's cousin, held not long
 Its fiery vigil in her single breast;
She fretted for the golden hour, and hung
 Upon the time with feverish unrest —
Not long — for soon into her heart a throng
 Of higher occupants, a richer zest,
Came tragic; passion not to be subdued,
And sorrow for her love in travels rude.

XXXII

In the mid days of autumn, on their eves
 The breath of Winter comes from far
 away,
And the sick west continually bereaves
 Of some gold tinge, and plays a rounde-
 lay
Of death among the bushes and the leaves,
 To make all bare before he dares to stray
From his north cavern. So sweet Isabel
By gradual decay from beauty fell,

XXXIII

Because Lorenzo came not. Oftentimes
 She ask'd her brothers, with an eye all
 pale,
Striving to be itself, what dungeon climes
 Could keep him off so long ? They spake
 a tale
Time after time, to quiet her. Their
 crimes
 Came on them, like a smoke from Hin-
 nom's vale;
And every night in dreams they groan'd
 aloud,
To see their sister in her snowy shroud.

XXXIV

And she had died in drowsy ignorance,
 But for a thing more deadly dark than
 all;
It came like a fierce potion, drunk by
 chance,
 Which saves a sick man from the feath-
 er'd pall
For some few gasping moments; like a
 lance,
Waking an Indian from his cloudy hall
With cruel pierce, and bringing him again
Sense of the gnawing fire at heart and
 brain.

XXXV

It was a vision. — In the drowsy gloom,
 The dull of midnight, at her couch's foot
Lorenzo stood, and wept: the forest tomb
 Had marr'd his glossy hair which once
 could shoot
Lustre into the sun, and put cold doom
 Upon his lips, and taken the soft lute
From his lorn voice, and past his loamed
 ears
Had made a miry channel for his tears.

XXXVI

Strange sound it was, when the pale shadow
 spake;
 For there was striving, in its piteous
 tongue,

To speak as when on earth it was awake,
 And Isabella on its music hung:
Languor there was in it, and tremulous
 shake,
 As in a palsied Druid's harp unstrung;
And through it moan'd a ghostly under-
 song,
Like hoarse night-gusts sepulchral briars
 among.

XXXVII

Its eyes, though wild, were still all dewy
 bright
 With love, and kept all phantom fear
 aloof
From the poor girl by magic of their light,
 The while it did unthread the horrid
 woof
Of the late darken'd time, — the murder-
 ous spite
 Of pride and avarice, — the dark pine
 roof
In the forest, — and the sodden turfed
 dell,
Where, without any word, from stabs he
 fell.

XXXVIII

Saying moreover, ' Isabel, my sweet !
 Red whortleberries droop above my
 head,
And a large flint-stone weighs upon my
 feet;
 Around me beeches and high chestnuts
 shed
Their leaves and prickly nuts; a sheepfold
 bleat
Comes from beyond the river to my bed:
Go, shed one tear upon my heather-bloom,
And it shall comfort me within the tomb.

XXXIX

' I am a shadow now, alas ! alas !
 Upon the skirts of human nature dwell-
 ing
Alone: I chant alone the holy mass,
 While little sounds of life are round me
 knelling,

And glossy bees at noon do fieldward pass,
　And many a chapel bell the hour is telling,
Paining me through: those sounds grow
　　strange to me,
And thou art distant in Humanity.

XL

' I know what was, I feel full well what is,
　And I should rage, if spirits could go
　　mad;
Though I forget the taste of earthly bliss,
　That paleness warms my grave, as
　　though I had
A Seraph chosen from the bright abyss
　To be my spouse: thy paleness makes
　　me glad;
Thy beauty grows upon me, and I feel
A greater love through all my essence
　　steal.'

XLI

The Spirit mourn'd ' Adieu !' — dissolved,
　　and left
　The atom darkness in a slow turmoil;
As when of healthful midnight sleep bereft,
　Thinking on rugged hours and fruitless
　　toil,
We put our eyes into a pillowy cleft,
　And see the spangly gloom froth up and
　　boil:
It made sad Isabella's eyelids ache,
And in the dawn she started up awake

XLII

' Ha ! ha !' said she, ' I knew not this hard
　　life,
　I thought the worst was simple misery;
I thought some Fate with pleasure or with
　　strife
　Portion'd us — happy days, or else to
　　die;
But there is crime — a brother's bloody
　　knife !
　Sweet Spirit, thou hast school'd my infancy:
I'll visit thee for this, and kiss thine eyes,
And greet thee morn and even in the skies.'

XLIII

When the full morning came, she had devised
　How she might secret to the forest hie;
How she might find the clay, so dearly
　　prized,
　And sing to it one latest lullaby;
How her short absence might be unsurmised,
　While she the inmost of the dream would
　　try.
Resolved, she took with her an aged nurse,
And went into that dismal forest-hearse.

XLIV

See, as they creep along the river side,
　How she doth whisper to that aged
　　Dame,
And, after looking round the champaign
　　wide,
　Shows her a knife. — ' What feverous
　　hectic flame
Burns in thee, child ? — what good can
　　thee betide,
　That thou shouldst smile again ?' —
　　The evening came,
And they had found Lorenzo's earthy bed;
The flint was there, the berries at his head.

XLV

Who hath not loiter'd in a green churchyard,
　And let his spirit, like a demon-mole,
Work through the clayey soil and gravel
　　hard,
　To see skull, coffin'd bones, and funeral
　　stole;
Pitying each form that hungry Death hath
　　marr'd,
　And filling it once more with human soul ?
Ah ! this is holiday to what was felt
When Isabella by Lorenzo knelt.

XLVI

She gazed into the fresh-thrown mould, as
　　though
　One glance did fully all its secrets tell;

Clearly she saw, as other eyes would know
 Pale limbs at bottom of a crystal well;
Upon the murderous spot she seem'd to
 grow,
 Like to a native lily of the dell:
Then with her knife, all sudden, she began
To dig more fervently than misers can.

XLVII

Soon she turn'd up a soiled glove, whereon
 Her silk had play'd in purple phanta-
 sies:
She kiss'd it with a lip more chill than
 stone,
 And put it in her bosom, where it dries
And freezes utterly unto the bone
 Those dainties made to still an infant's
 cries;
Then 'gan she work again; nor stay'd her
 care,
But to throw back at times her veiling hair.

XLVIII

That old nurse stood beside her wonder-
 ing,
 Until her heart felt pity to the core
At sight of such a dismal labouring,
 And so she kneeled, with her locks all
 hoar,
And put her lean hands to the horrid
 thing:
 Three hours they labour'd at this travail
 sore:
At last they felt the kernel of the grave,
And Isabella did not stamp and rave.

XLIX

Ah! wherefore all this wormy circum-
 stance?
 Why linger at the yawning tomb so
 long?
O for the gentleness of old Romance,
 The simple plaining of a minstrel's song!
Fair reader, at the old tale take a glance,
 For here, in truth, it doth not well be-
 long
To speak:— O turn thee to the very tale,
And taste the music of that vision pale.

L

With duller steel than the Perséan sword
 They cut away no formless monster's
 head,
But one, whose gentleness did well accord
 With death, as life. The ancient harps
 have said,
Love never dies, but lives, immortal Lord:
 If Love impersonate was ever dead,
Pale Isabella kiss'd it, and low moan'd.
'T was love; cold,— dead indeed, but not
 dethron'd.

LI

In anxious secrecy they took it home,
 And then the prize was all for Isabel:
She calm'd its wild hair with a golden
 comb,
 And all around each eye's sepulchral cell
Pointed each fringed lash; the smeared
 loam
 With tears, as chilly as a dripping well,
She drench'd away: and still she comb'd,
 and kept
Sighing all day — and still she kiss'd and
 wept.

LII

Then in a silken scarf, — sweet with the
 dews
 Of precious flowers pluck'd in Araby,
And divine liquids come with odorous ooze
 Through the cold serpent-pipe refresh-
 fully, —
She wrapp'd it up; and for its tomb did
 choose
 A garden-pot, wherein she laid it by,
And cover'd it with mould, and o'er it set
Sweet Basil, which her tears kept ever wet.

LIII

And she forgot the stars, the moon, and
 sun,
 And she forgot the blue above the trees,
And she forgot the dells where waters
 run,
 And she forgot the chilly autumn breeze;

She had no knowledge when the day was
　　done,
　　And the new morn she saw not: but in
　　　peace
Hung over her sweet Basil evermore,
And moisten'd it with tears unto the core.

LIV

And so she ever fed it with thin tears,
　　Whence thick, and green, and beautiful
　　　it grew,
So that it smelt more balmy than its peers
　　Of Basil-tufts in Florence; for it drew
Nurture besides, and life, from human
　　fears,
　　From the fast mouldering head there
　　　shut from view:
So that the jewel, safely casketed,
Came forth, and in perfumed leafits spread.

LV

O Melancholy, linger here awhile !
　　O Music, Music, breathe despondingly !
O Echo, Echo, from some sombre isle,
　　Unknown, Lethean, sigh to us — O sigh !
Spirits in grief, lift up your heads, and
　　smile;
　　Lift up your heads, sweet Spirits, heavily,
And make a pale light in your cypress
　　glooms,
Tinting with silver wan your marble tombs.

LVI

Moan hither, all ye syllables of woe,
　　From the deep throat of sad Melpomene !
Through bronzed lyre in tragic order go,
　　And touch the strings into a mystery;
Sound mournfully upon the winds and low;
　　For simple Isabel is soon to be
Among the dead: She withers, like a palm
Cut by an Indian for its juicy balm.

LVII

O leave the palm to wither by itself;
　　Let not quick Winter chill its dying
　　　hour ! —
It may not be — those Baälites of pelf,
　　Her brethren, noted the continual shower

From her dead eyes; and many a curious
　　elf,
　　Among her kindred, wonder'd that such
　　　dower
Of youth and beauty should be thrown aside
By one mark'd out to be a Noble's bride.

LVIII

And, furthermore, her brethren wonder'd
　　much
　　Why she sat drooping by the Basil green,
And why it flourish'd, as by magic touch;
　　Greatly they wonder'd what the thing
　　　might mean:
They could not surely give belief, that such
　　A very nothing would have power to
　　　wean
Her from her own fair youth, and pleasures
　　gay,
And even remembrance of her love's delay.

LIX

Therefore they watch'd a time when they
　　might sift
　　This hidden whim; and long they watch'd
　　　in vain;
For seldom did she go to chapel-shrift,
　　And seldom felt she any hunger-pain:
And when she left, she hurried back, as
　　swift
As bird on wing to breast its eggs again:
And, patient as a hen-bird, sat her there
Beside her Basil, weeping through her hair.

LX

Yet they contrived to steal the Basil-pot,
　　And to examine it in secret place:
The thing was vile with green and livid
　　spot,
And yet they knew it was Lorenzo's face:
The guerdon of their murder they had got,
　　And so left Florence in a moment's space,
Never to turn again. — Away they went,
With blood upon their heads, to banishment.

LXI

O Melancholy, turn thine eyes away !
　　O Music, Music, breathe despondingly !

O Echo, Echo, on some other day,
 From isles Lethean, sigh to us — O
 sigh !
Spirits of grief, sing not your ' Well-a-
 way ! '
For Isabel, sweet Isabel, will die;
Will die a death too lone and incomplete,
Now they have ta'en away her Basil sweet.

LXII

Piteous she look'd on dead and senseless
 things,
 Asking for her lost Basil amorously:
And with melodious chuckle in the strings
 Of her lorn voice, she oftentimes would
 cry
After the Pilgrim in his wanderings,
 To ask him where her Basil was; and why
'T was hid from her: ' For cruel 't is,' said
 she,
' To steal my Basil-pot away from me.'

LXIII

And so she pined, and so she died forlorn,
 Imploring for her Basil to the last.
No heart was there in Florence but did
 mourn
 In pity of her love, so overcast.
And a sad ditty of this story born
 From mouth to mouth through all the
 country pass'd :
Still is the burthen sung — ' O cruelty,
To steal my Basil-pot away from me ! '

TO HOMER

The date 1818 was affixed to this by Lord
Houghton in *Life, Letters and Literary Re-
mains*, where it was first published, and is found
also where it occurs in the Dilke manuscripts.
In a letter to Reynolds, dated April 27, 1818,
Keats writes eagerly of his desire to study
Greek.

STANDING aloof in giant ignorance,
 Of thee I hear and of the Cyclades,
As one who sits ashore and longs perchance
 To visit dolphin-coral in deep seas.

So thou wast blind ! — but then the veil
 was rent,
 For Jove uncurtain'd Heaven to let thee
 live,
And Neptune made for thee a spumy tent,
 And Pan made sing for thee his forest-
 hive;
Ay on the shores of darkness there is
 light,
 And precipices show untrodden green;
There is a budding morrow in midnight;
 There is a triple sight in blindness
 keen:
Such seeing hadst thou, as it once befell
To Dian, Queen of Earth, and Heaven,
 and Hell.

FRAGMENT OF AN ODE TO MAIA

Copied in a letter to Reynolds, dated May 3,
1818, in which Keats says : ' With respect to
the affections and Poetry you must know by a
sympathy my thoughts that way, and I dare
say these few lines will be but a ratification : I
wrote them on May day — and intend to finish
the ode all in good time ; ' a purpose appar-
ently never accomplished.

MOTHER of Hermes ! and still youthful
 Maia !
 May I sing to thee
As thou wast hymned on the shores of
 Baiae ?
 Or may I woo thee
In earlier Sicilian ? or thy smiles
Seek as they once were sought, in Grecian
 isles,
By bards who died content on pleasant
 sward,
 Leaving great verse unto a little clan ?
O, give me their old vigour, and unheard
 Save of the quiet Primrose, and the span
 Of heaven and few ears,
Rounded by thee, my song should die away
 Content as theirs,
Rich in the simple worship of a day.

SONG

First published in *Life, Letters and Literary Remains*, and there dated 1818.

I

HUSH, hush ! tread softly ! hush, hush, my
 dear !
 All the house is asleep, but we know very
 well
That the jealous, the jealous old bald-pate
 may hear,
 Tho' you 've padded his night-cap — O
 sweet Isabel !
 Tho' your feet are more light than a
 Faery's feet,
 Who dances on bubbles where brook-
 lets meet, —
Hush, hush ! soft tiptoe ! hush, hush, my
 dear !
For less than a nothing the jealous can
 hear.

II

No leaf doth tremble, no ripple is there
 On the river, — all 's still, and the night's
 sleepy eye
Closes up, and forgets all its Lethean
 care,
 Charm'd to death by the drone of the
 humming May-fly;
 And the Moon, whether prudish or
 complaisant,
 Has fled to her bower, well knowing I
 want
No light in the dusk, no torch in the gloom,
But my Isabel's eyes, and her lips pulp'd
 with bloom.

III

Lift the latch ! ah gently ! ah tenderly —
 sweet !
 We are dead if that latchet gives one
 little clink !
Well done — now those lips, and a flowery
 seat —
 The old man may sleep, and the planets
 may wink;

The shut rose shall dream of our loves
 and awake
Full-blown, and such warmth for the
 morning take,
The stock-dove shall hatch her soft brace
 and shall coo,
While I kiss to the melody, aching all
 through.

VERSES WRITTEN DURING A TOUR IN SCOTLAND

Keats saw his brother George and wife set sail from Liverpool at the end of June, 1818, and then set forth with his friend Charles Armitage Brown on a walking tour through Wordsworth's country and into Scotland. The verses included in this section were all sent in letters, chiefly to his brother Tom. He did not include any in the volume which he published in 1820, and they first saw the light when Lord Houghton included them in the *Life, Letters and Literary Remains*.

I

ON VISITING THE TOMB OF BURNS

Written at Dumfries on the evening of July 1, 1818. ' Burns's tomb,' writes Keats, ' is in the Churchyard corner, not very much to my taste, though on a scale large enough to show they wanted to honour him. This Sonnet I have written in a strange mood, half asleep. I know not how it is, the Clouds, the Sky, the Houses, all seem anti-Grecian and anti-Charlemagnish.'

THE Town, the churchyard, and the setting
 sun,
 The Clouds, the trees, the rounded hills
 all seem,
 Though beautiful, cold — strange — as
 in a dream,
I dreamed long ago, now new begun.
The short-lived, paly Summer is but won
 From Winter's ague, for one hour's
 gleam;
 Though sapphire-warm, their Stars do
 never beam:

All is cold Beauty; pain is never done:
For who has mind to relish, Minos-wise,
 The Real of Beauty, free from that dead
 hue
 Sickly imagination and sick pride
Cast wan upon it ! Burns ! with honour
 due
 I oft have honour'd thee. Great
 shadow, hide
Thy face; I sin against thy native skies.

II

TO AILSA ROCK

The tourists crossed to Ireland for a short trip, and after returning to Scotland, made their way into Ayrshire, entering it a little beyond Cairn. Their walk led them into a long wooded glen. 'At the end,' writes Keats, July 10, 1818, 'we had a gradual ascent and got among the tops of the mountains whence in a little time I descried in the Sea Ailsa Rock, 940 feet high — it was 15 Miles distant and seemed close upon us. The effect of Ailsa with the peculiar perspective of the Sea in connection with the ground we stood on, and the misty rain then falling gave me a complete Idea of a deluge. Ailsa struck me very suddenly — really I was a little alarmed.'

HEARKEN, thou craggy ocean pyramid !
 Give answer from thy voice, the sea-
 fowls' screams !
 When were thy shoulders mantled in
 huge streams ?
When, from the sun, was thy broad fore-
 head hid ?
How long is 't since the mighty power bid
 Thee heave to airy sleep from fathom
 dreams ?
 Sleep in the lap of thunder or sunbeams,
Or when gray clouds are thy cold coverlid.
Thou answer'st not; for thou art dead
 asleep;
 Thy life is but two dead eternities —
The last in air, the former in the deep;
 First with the whales, last with the eagle-
 skies —

Drown'd wast thou till an earthquake made
 thee steep,
Another cannot wake thy giant size.

III

WRITTEN IN THE COTTAGE WHERE BURNS WAS BORN

From Kingswell's, July 13, 1818, Keats wrote of his experience in visiting Burns's birthplace : ' The approach to it [Ayr] is extremely fine — quite outwent my expectations — richly meadowed, wooded, heathed and rivuleted — with a grand Sea view terminated by the black Mountains of the isle of Annan. As soon as I saw them so nearby I said to myself, " How is it they did not beckon Burns to some grand attempt at Epic ? " The bonny Doon is the sweetest river I ever saw — overhung with fine trees as far as we could see — We stood some time on the Brig across it, over which Tam o' Shanter fled — we took a pinch of snuff on the Keystone — then we proceeded to the " auld Kirk Alloway." As we were looking at it a Farmer pointed the spots where Mungo's Mither hang'd hersel' and " drunken Charlie brake 's neck's bane." Then we proceeded to the Cottage he was born in — there was a board to that effect by the door side — it had the same effect as the same sort of memorial at Stratford on Avon. We drank some Toddy to Burns's memory with an old Man who knew Burns — damn him and damn his anecdotes — he was a great bore — it was impossible for a Southron to understand above 5 words in a hundred. — There was something good in his description of Burns's melancholy the last time he saw him. I was determined to write a sonnet in the Cottage — I did — but it was so bad I cannot venture it here.' He wrote in the same strain to Reynolds, saying, ' I wrote a sonnet for the mere sake of writing some lines under the Roof — they are so bad I cannot transcribe them. . . . I cannot write about scenery and visitings — Fancy is indeed less than a present palpable reality, but it is greater than remembrance. . . . One song of Burns's is of more worth to you than all I could think for a whole year in his native country.'

THIS mortal body of a thousand days
 Now fills, O Burns, a space in thine own
 room,
Where thou didst dream alone on budded
 bays,
 Happy and thoughtless of thy day of
 doom !
My pulse is warm with thine old Barley-
 bree,
 My head is light with pledging a great
 soul,
My eyes are wandering, and I cannot see,
 Fancy is dead and drunken at its goal;
Yet can I stamp my foot upon thy floor,
 Yet can I ope thy window-sash to find
The meadow thou hast tramped o'er and
 o'er, —
 Yet can I think of thee till thought is
 blind, —
Yet can I gulp a bumper to thy name, —
O smile among the shades, for this is fame !

IV

AT FINGAL'S CAVE

The verses which follow were first printed in *Life, Letters and Literary Remains*. They occur in a letter to Tom Keats from Oban, July 26, 1818, and were preceded by this description : ' I am puzzled how to give you an Idea of Staffa. It can only be represented by a first-rate drawing. One may compare the surface of the Island to a roof — this roof is supported by grand pillars of basalt standing together as thick as honeycombs. The finest thing is Fingal's cave — it is entirely a hollowing out of Basalt Pillars. Suppose now the Giants who rebelled against Jove had taken a whole Mass of black Columns and bound them together like bunches of matches — and then with immense axes had made a cavern in the body of these columns — Of course the roof and floor must be composed of the broken ends of the Columns — such is Fingal's cave, except that the Sea has done the work of excavations, and is continually dashing there — so that we walk along the sides of the cave on the pillars which are left as if for convenient stairs. The roof is arched somewhat gothic-wise, and the length of some of the entire side-pillars is fifty feet. About the island you might seat an army of men each on a pillar. The length of the Cave is 120 feet, and from its extremity the view into the sea, through the large arch at the entrance — the colour of the column is a sort of black with a lurking gloom of purple therein. For solemnity and grandeur it far surpasses the finest Cathedral. At the extremity of the Cave there is a small perforation into another Cave, at which the waters meeting and buffeting each other there is sometimes produced a report as of a cannon heard as far as Iona, which must be 12 miles. As we approached in the boat, there was such a fine swell of the sea that the pillars appeared rising immediately out of the crystal. But it is impossible to describe it.'

NOT Aladdin magian
Ever such a work began;
Not the wizard of the Dee
Ever such a dream could see;
Not St. John, in Patmos' isle,
In the passion of his toil,
When he saw the churches seven,
Golden aisled, built up in heaven,
Gazed at such a rugged wonder,
As I stood its roofing under.
Lo ! I saw one sleeping there,
On the marble cold and bare;
While the surges wash'd his feet,
And his garments white did beat
Drench'd about the sombre rocks;
On his neck his well-grown locks,
Lifted dry above the main,
Were upon the curl again.
' What is this ? and what art thou ? '
Whisper'd I, and touch'd his brow;
' What art thou ? and what is this ? '
Whisper'd I, and strove to kiss
The spirit's hand, to wake his eyes;
Up he started in a trice:
' I am Lycidas,' said he,
' Famed in funeral minstrelsy ! '
This was architectured thus
By the great Oceanus ! —
Here his mighty waters play

Hollow organs all the day;
Here, by turns, his dolphins all,
Finny palmers, great and small,
Come to pay devotion due, —
Each a mouth of pearls must strew !
Many a mortal of these days
Dares to pass our sacred ways;
Dares to touch, audaciously,
This cathedral of the sea !
I have been the pontiff-priest,
Where the waters never rest,
Where a fledgy sea-bird choir
Soars for ever ! Holy fire
I have hid from mortal man;
Proteus is my Sacristan !
But the dulled eye of mortal
Hath pass'd beyond the rocky portal;
So for ever will I leave
Such a taint, and soon unweave
All the magic of the place.'
So saying, with a Spirit's glance
He dived !

V

WRITTEN UPON THE TOP OF BEN NEVIS

Enclosed in a letter to Tom Keats from
Letter Findlay, August 3, 1818.

READ me a lesson, Muse, and speak it loud
 Upon the top of Nevis, blind in mist !
I look into the chasms, and a shroud
 Vaporous doth hide them, — just so
 much I wist
Mankind do know of hell; I look o'erhead,
 And there is sullen mist, — even so much
Mankind can tell of heaven; mist is spread
 Before the earth, beneath me, — even
 such,
Even so vague is man's sight of himself !
 Here are the craggy stones beneath my
 feet, —
Thus much I know that, a poor witless elf,
 I tread on them, — that all my eye doth
 meet
Is mist and crag, not only on this height,
But in the world of thought and mental
 might !

TRANSLATION FROM A SONNET OF RONSARD

Published in *Life, Letters and Literary Remains* in a letter to Reynolds, of which the probable date is September 22, 1818; in a letter to Charles Wentworth Dilke September 21, 1818, Keats quotes the last line with the remark : 'You have passed your Romance, and I never gave in to it, or else I think this line a feast for one of your Lovers.' The text of the sonnet will be found in the Appendix.

NATURE withheld Cassandra in the skies,
 For more adornment, a full thousand
 years;
She took their cream of Beauty's fairest
 dyes,
 And shaped and tinted her above all
 Peers:
Meanwhile Love kept her dearly with his
 wings,
 And underneath their shadow fill'd her
 eyes
With such a richness that the cloudy Kings
Of high Olympus utter'd slavish sighs.
When from the Heavens I saw her first
 descend,
 My heart took fire, and only burning
 pains,
They were my pleasures — they my Life's
 sad end;
 Love pour'd her beauty into my warm
 veins.

.

TO A LADY SEEN FOR A FEW MOMENTS AT VAUXHALL

First published in *Hood's Magazine* for April 1844, and afterward included in *Life, Letters and Literary Remains*. No date is given, and the poem is placed here from a fancied association with the lady whom Keats saw at Hastings and who started the train of thought in his letter to his brother and sister, October 25, 1818.

TIME's sea hath been five years at its slow
 ebb,
 Long hours have to and fro let creep the
 sand,
Since I was tangled in thy beauty's web,
 And snared by the ungloving of thine
 hand.
And yet I never look on midnight sky,
 But I behold thine eyes' well-memoried
 light;
I cannot look upon the rose's dye,
 But to thy cheek my soul doth take its
 flight ;
I cannot look on any budding flower,
 But my fond ear, in fancy at thy lips
And hearkening for a love-sound, doth de-
 vour
 Its sweets in the wrong sense: — Thou
 dost eclipse
Every delight with sweet remembering,
And grief unto my darling joys dost bring.

FANCY

Keats enclosed these lines, as lately written,
in a letter to George and Georgiana Keats,
January 2, 1819. He included the poem in the
1820 volume. Mr. John Knowles Paine has
published a cantata for soprano solo, chorus,
and orchestra, entitled *The Realm of Fancy*,
using these lines for his book.

EVER let the Fancy roam,
Pleasure never is at home:
At a touch sweet Pleasure melteth,
Like to bubbles when rain pelteth;
Then let winged Fancy wander
Through the thought still spread beyond
 her:
Open wide the mind's cage-door,
She 'll dart forth, and cloudward soar.
O sweet Fancy ! let her loose;
Summer's joys are spoilt by use, 10
And the enjoying of the Spring
Fades as does its blossoming;
Autumn's red-lipp'd fruitage too,
Blushing through the mist and dew,
Cloys with tasting : What do then ?

Sit thee by the ingle, when
The sear faggot blazes bright,
Spirit of a winter's night;
When the soundless earth is muffled,
And the caked snow is shuffled 20
From the ploughboy's heavy shoon;
When the Night doth meet the Noon
In a dark conspiracy
To banish Even from her sky.
Sit thee there, and send abroad,
With a mind self-overawed,
Fancy, high-commission'd: — send her !
She has vassals to attend her:
She will bring, in spite of frost,
Beauties that the earth hath lost; 30
She will bring thee, all together,
All delights of summer weather;
All the buds and bells of May,
From dewy sward or thorny spray;
All the heaped Autumn's wealth,
With a still, mysterious stealth:
She will mix these pleasures up
Like three fit wines in a cup,
And thou shalt quaff it: — thou shalt hear
Distant harvest-carols clear; 40
Rustle of the reaped corn;
Sweet birds antheming the morn:
And, in the same moment — hark !
'T is the early April lark,
Or the rooks, with busy caw,
Foraging for sticks and straw.
Thou shalt, at one glance, behold
The daisy and the marigold;
White-plumed lilies, and the first
Hedge-grown primrose that hath burst ; 50
Shaded hyacinth, alway
Sapphire queen of the mid-May;
And every leaf, and every flower
Pearled with the self-same shower.
Thou shalt see the field-mouse peep
Meagre from its celled sleep;
And the snake all winter-thin
Cast on sunny bank its skin;
Freckled nest-eggs thou shalt see
Hatching in the hawthorn-tree, 60
When the hen-bird's wing doth rest
Quiet on her mossy nest;

Then the hurry and alarm
When the bee-hive casts its swarm;
Acorns ripe down-pattering
While the autumn breezes sing.

Oh, sweet Fancy! let her loose;
Every thing is spoilt by use;
Where 's the cheek that doth not fade,
Too much gazed at? Where 's the maid 70
Whose lip mature is ever new?
Where 's the eye, however blue,
Doth not weary? Where 's the face
One would meet in every place?
Where 's the voice, however soft,
One would hear so very oft?
At a touch sweet Pleasure melteth
Like to bubbles when rain pelteth.
Let, then, winged Fancy find
Thee a mistress to thy mind: 80
Dulcet-eyed as Ceres' daughter
Ere the God of Torment taught her
How to frown and how to chide;
With a waist and with a side
White as Hebe's, when her zone
Slipt its golden clasp, and down
Fell her kirtle to her feet,
While she held the goblet sweet,
And Jove grew languid. — Break the mesh
Of the Fancy's silken leash; 90
Quickly break her prison-string,
And such joys as these she 'll bring. —
Let the winged Fancy roam,
Pleasure never is at home.

ODE

Written on the blank page before Beaumont
and Fletcher's tragi-comedy, *The Fair Maid of
the Inn*, and addressed thus to these bards in
particular. Sent in a letter to George and Geor-
giana Keats, January 2, 1819. It is included
in the 1820 volume.

BARDS of Passion and of Mirth,
Ye have left your souls on earth!
Have ye souls in heaven too,
Double-lived in regions new?
Yes, and those of heaven commune

With the spheres of sun and moon;
With the noise of fountains wond'rous
And the parle of voices thund'rous;
With the whisper of heaven's trees
And one another, in soft ease 10
Seated on Elysian lawns
Browsed by none but Dian's fawns;
Underneath large blue-bells tented,
Where the daisies are rose-scented,
And the rose herself has got
Perfume which on earth is not;
Where the nightingale doth sing
Not a senseless, tranced thing,
But divine melodious truth;
Philosophic numbers smooth; 20
Tales and golden histories
Of heaven and its mysteries.

Thus ye live on high, and then
On the earth ye live again;
And the souls ye left behind you
Teach us, here, the way to find you,
Where your other souls are joying,
Never slumber'd, never cloying.
Here, your earth-born souls still speak
To mortals, of their little week; 30
Of their sorrows and delights;
Of their passions and their spites;
Of their glory and their shame;
What doth strengthen and what maim.
Thus ye teach us, every day,
Wisdom, though fled far away.

Bards of Passion and of Mirth,
Ye have left your souls on earth!
Ye have souls in heaven too,
Double-lived in regions new! 40

SONG

'There is just room, I see, in this page to
copy a little thing I wrote off to some Music
as it was playing.' Keats to George and
Georgiana Keats, January 2, 1819.

I HAD a dove and the sweet dove died;
 And I have thought it died of grieving:

O, what could it grieve for ? Its feet
 were tied,
 With a silken thread of my own hand's
 weaving;
Sweet little red feet ! why should you
 die —
Why should you leave me, sweet bird !
 why ?
You lived alone in the forest-tree,
Why, pretty thing ! would you not live
 with me ?
I kiss'd you oft and gave you white peas;
Why not live sweetly, as in the green
 trees ?

ODE ON MELANCHOLY

Published in *Lamia, Isabella, the Eve of St.
Agnes and other Poems,* 1820. There is no
date affixed to it, but if it takes its color at
all from Keats's own experience, it might not
be amiss to refer it to the early part of 1819,
when he had come under the influence of his
passion for Fanny Brawne. In a letter to
Haydon, written between January 7 and 14,
1819, Keats says : ' I have been writing a little
now and then lately : but nothing to speak of
— being discontented and as it were moulting.
Yet I do not think I shall ever come to the
rope or the pistol. For after a day or two's
melancholy, although I smoke more and more
my own insufficiency — I see by little and lit-
tle more of what is to be done, and how it is
to be done, should I ever be able to do it.'
Lord Houghton, in the Aldine edition of
1876, makes the following prefatory note :
' A singular instance of Keats's delicate per-
ception occurred in the composition of this
Ode. In the original manuscript he had in-
tended to represent the vulgar conception of
Melancholy with gloom and horror, in contrast
with the emotion that incites to —

> " glut thy sorrow on a morning rose
> Or on the rainbow of the salt sand-wave,
> Or on the wealth of globed peonies ; "

and which essentially

> " lives in Beauty — Beauty that must die,
> And Joy, whose hand is ever at his lips
> Bidding adieu."

The first stanza, therefore, was the following :
as grim a passage as Blake or Fuseli could
have dreamed and painted : —

> " Though you should build a bark of dead men's bones,
> And rear a platform gibbet for a mast,
> Stitch shrouds together for a sail, with groans
> To fill it out, blood-stained and aghast ;
> Although your rudder be a dragon's tail
> Long sever'd, yet still hard with agony,
> Your cordage large uprootings from the skull
> Of bald Medusa, certes you would fail
> To find the Melancholy — whether she
> Dreameth in any isle of Lethe dull."

But no sooner was this written, than the poet
became conscious that the coarseness of the
contrast would destroy the general effect of
luxurious tenderness which it was the object
of the poem to produce, and he confined the
gross notion of Melancholy to less violent im-
ages, and let the ode at once begin, — '

No, no ! go not to Lethe, neither twist
 Wolf's-bane, tight-rooted, for its poison-
 ous wine;
Nor suffer thy pale forehead to be kiss'd
 By nightshade, ruby grape of Proserpine;
Make not your rosary of yew-berries,
 Nor let the beetle, nor the death-moth
 be
 Your mournful Psyche, nor the downy
 owl
A partner in your sorrow's mysteries;
 For shade to shade will come too drows-
 ily,
 And drown the wakeful anguish of the
 soul.

But when the melancholy fit shall fall
 Sudden from heaven like a weeping
 cloud,
That fosters the droop-headed flowers all,
 And hides the green hill in an April
 shroud;
Then glut thy sorrow on a morning rose,
 Or on the rainbow of the salt sand-wave,
 Or on the wealth of globed peonies;
Or if thy mistress some rich anger shows,
 Emprison her soft hand, and let her rave,
 And feed deep, deep upon her peerless
 eyes.

She dwells with Beauty — Beauty that
 must die;
 And Joy, whose hand is ever at his
 lips
Bidding adieu; and aching Pleasure nigh,
 Turning to poison while the bee-mouth
 sips:
Aye, in the very temple of Delight
 Veil'd Melancholy has her sovran shrine,
 Though seen of none save him whose
 strenuous tongue
 Can burst Joy's grape against his palate
 fine;
His soul shall taste the sadness of her
 might,
 And be among her cloudy trophies
 hung.

THE EVE OF ST. AGNES

Begun early in 1819. In a letter to George
and Georgiana Keats, dated February 14, 1819,
Keats says: 'I was nearly a fortnight at Mr.
John Snook's and a few days at old Mr. Dilke's
(Chichester in Hampshire). Nothing worth
speaking of happened at either place. I took
down some thin paper and wrote on it a little
poem called St. Agnes's Eve.' The poem
underwent a great deal of revision, and was not
in final form before September; it was pub-
lished in the 1820 volume.

I

St. Agnes' Eve — Ah, bitter chill it
 was !
The owl, for all his feathers, was a-cold;
The hare limp'd trembling through the
 frozen grass,
And silent was the flock in woolly fold:
Numb were the Beadsman's fingers, while
 he told
His rosary, and while his frosted breath,
Like pious incense from a censer old,
Seem'd taking flight for heaven, without
 a death,
Past the sweet Virgin's picture, while his
 prayer he saith.

II

His prayer he saith, this patient, holy
 man;
Then takes his lamp, and riseth from his
 knees,
And back returneth, meagre, barefoot,
 wan,
Along the chapel aisle by slow degrees:
The sculptured dead, on each side, seem
 to freeze,
Emprison'd in black, purgatorial rails:
Knights, ladies, praying in dumb orat'ries,
He passeth by; and his weak spirit fails
To think how they may ache in icy hoods
 and mails.

III

Northward he turneth through a little
 door,
 And scarce three steps, ere Music's
 golden tongue
Flatter'd to tears this aged man and
 poor;
But no — already had his death-bell rung;
The joys of all his life were said and
 sung:
His was harsh penance on St. Agnes'
 Eve:
Another way he went, and soon among
Rough ashes sat he for his soul's re-
 prieve,
And all night kept awake, for sinners' sake
 to grieve.

IV

That ancient Beadsman heard the pre-
 lude soft;
And so it chanced, for many a door was
 wide,
From hurry to and fro. Soon, up aloft,
The silver, snarling trumpets 'gan to
 chide:
The level chambers, ready with their
 pride,
Were glowing to receive a thousand
 guests:
The carved angels, ever eager-eyed,

Stared, where upon their heads the cornice rests,
With hair blown back, and wings put crosswise on their breasts.

V

At length burst in the argent revelry,
With plume, tiara, and all rich array,
Numerous as shadows haunting fairily
The brain, new-stuff'd, in youth, with triumphs gay
Of old romance. These let us wish away,
And turn, sole-thoughted, to one Lady there,
Whose heart had brooded, all that wintry day,
On love, and wing'd St. Agnes' saintly care,
As she had heard old dames full many times declare.

VI

They told her how, upon St. Agnes' Eve,
Young virgins might have visions of delight,
And soft adorings from their loves receive
Upon the honey'd middle of the night,
If ceremonies due they did aright;
As, supperless to bed they must retire,
And couch supine their beauties, lily white;
Nor look behind, nor sideways, but require
Of Heaven with upward eyes for all that they desire.

VII

Full of this whim was thoughtful Madeline:
The music, yearning like a God in pain,
She scarcely heard: her maiden eyes divine,
Fix'd on the floor, saw many a sweeping train
Pass by — she heeded not at all: in vain
Came many a tiptoe, amorous cavalier,

And back retired; not cool'd by high disdain,
But she saw not: her heart was otherwhere:
She sigh'd for Agnes' dreams, the sweetest of the year.

VIII

She danced along with vague, regardless eyes,
Anxious her lips, her breathing quick and short:
The hallow'd hour was near at hand: she sighs
Amid the timbrels, and the throng'd resort
Of whisperers in anger, or in sport;
'Mid looks of love, defiance, hate, and scorn,
Hoodwink'd with faery fancy; all amort,
Save to St. Agnes and her lambs unshorn,
And all the bliss to be before to-morrow morn.

IX

So, purposing each moment to retire,
She linger'd still. Meantime, across the moors,
Had come young Porphyro, with heart on fire
For Madeline. Beside the portal doors,
Buttress'd from moonlight, stands he, and implores
All saints to give him sight of Madeline,
But for one moment in the tedious hours,
That he might gaze and worship all unseen;
Perchance speak, kneel, touch, kiss — in sooth such things have been.

X

He ventures in: let no buzz'd whisper tell:
All eyes be muffled, or a hundred swords
Will storm his heart, Love's fev'rous citadel:
For him, those chambers held barbarian hordes,

Hyena foemen, and hot-blooded lords,
Whose very dogs would execrations howl
Against his lineage: not one breast af-
fords
Him any mercy, in that mansion foul,
Save one old beldame, weak in body and in
soul.

XI

Ah, happy chance! the aged creature
came,
Shuffling along with ivory-headed wand,
To where he stood, hid from the torch's
flame,
Behind a broad hall-pillar, far beyond
The sound of merriment and chorus
bland:
He startled her; but soon she knew his
face,
And grasp'd his fingers in her palsied
hand,
Saying, 'Mercy, Porphyro! hie thee
from this place;
They are all here to-night, the whole
bloodthirsty race!

XII

Get hence! get hence! there's dwarf-
ish Hildebrand;
He had a fever late, and in the fit
He cursed thee and thine, both house and
land:
Then there's that old Lord Maurice, not
a whit
More tame for his gray hairs — Alas me!
flit!
Flit like a ghost away.' — 'Ah, Gossip
dear,
We're safe enough; here in this arm-
chair sit,
And tell me how' — 'Good Saints! not
here, not here;
Follow me, child, or else these stones will
be thy bier.'

XIII

He follow'd through a lowly arched way,
Brushing the cobwebs with his lofty
plume;

And as she mutter'd 'Well-a — well-a-
day!'
He found him in a little moonlight room,
Pale, latticed, chill, and silent as a tomb.
'Now tell me where is Madeline,' said
he,
'O tell me, Angela, by the holy loom
Which none but secret sisterhood may
see,
When they St. Agnes' wool are weaving
piously.'

XIV

'St. Agnes! Ah! it is St. Agnes' Eve —
Yet men will murder upon holy days:
Thou must hold water in a witch's sieve,
And be liege-lord of all the Elves and
Fays,
To venture so: it fills me with amaze
To see thee, Porphyro! — St. Agnes'
Eve!
God's help! my lady fair the conjuror
plays
This very night: good angels her de-
ceive!
But let me laugh awhile, I've mickle time
to grieve.'

XV

Feebly she laugheth in the languid moon,
While Porphyro upon her face doth look,
Like puzzled urchin on an aged crone
Who keepeth closed a wond'rous riddle-
book,
As spectacled she sits in chimney nook.
But soon his eyes grew brilliant, when she
told
His lady's purpose; and he scarce could
brook
Tears, at the thought of those enchant-
ments cold,
And Madeline asleep in lap of legends old.

XVI

Sudden a thought came like a full-blown
rose,
Flushing his brow, and in his pained
heart

Made purple riot: then doth he propose
A stratagem, that makes the beldame
 start:
‘ A cruel man and impious thou art:
Sweet lady, let her pray, and sleep, and
 dream
Alone with her good angels, far apart
From wicked men like thee. Go, go ! I
 deem
Thou canst not surely be the same that thou
 didst seem.’

XVII

‘ I will not harm her, by all saints I
 swear,’
Quoth Porphyro: ‘ O may I ne’er find
 grace
When my weak voice shall whisper its
 last prayer,
If one of her soft ringlets I displace,
Or look with ruffian passion in her face:
Good Angela, believe me by these tears;
Or I will, even in a moment’s space,
Awake, with horrid shout, my foemen’s
 ears,
And beard them, though they be more
 fang’d than wolves and bears.’

XVIII

‘ Ah ! why wilt thou affright a feeble
 soul ?
A poor, weak, palsy-stricken, church-yard
 thing,
Whose passing-bell may ere the midnight
 toll ;
Whose prayers for thee, each morn and
 evening,
Were never miss’d.’ Thus plaining, doth
 she bring
A gentler speech from burning Porphyro;
So woful, and of such deep sorrowing,
That Angela gives promise she will do
Whatever he shall wish, betide her weal or
 woe.

XIX

Which was, to lead him, in close secrecy,
Even to Madeline’s chamber, and there
 hide

Him in a closet, of such privacy
That he might see her beauty unespied,
And win perhaps that night a peerless
 bride,
While legion’d fairies paced the coverlet,
And pale enchantment held her sleepy-
 eyed.
Never on such a night have lovers met,
Since Merlin paid his Demon all the mon-
 strous debt.

XX

‘ It shall be as thou wishest,’ said the
 Dame:
‘ All cates and dainties shall be stored
 there
Quickly on this feast-night: by the tam-
 bour frame
Her own lute thou wilt see: no time to
 spare,
For I am slow and feeble, and scarce
 dare
On such a catering trust my dizzy head.
Wait here, my child, with patience;
 kneel in prayer
The while: Ah ! thou must needs the
 lady wed,
Or may I never leave my grave among
 the dead.’

XXI

So saying she hobbled off with busy fear.
The lover’s endless minutes slowly pass’d;
The Dame return’d, and whisper’d in
 his ear
To follow her; with aged eyes aghast
From fright of dim espial. Safe at last,
Through many a dusky gallery, they gain
The maiden’s chamber, silken, hush’d
 and chaste;
Where Porphyro took covert, pleased
 amain.
His poor guide hurried back with agues in
 her brain.

XXII

Her falt’ring hand upon the balustrade,
Old Angela was feeling for the stair,

When Madeline, St. Agnes' charmed
 maid,
Rose, like a mission'd spirit, unaware:
With silver taper's light, and pious care,
She turn'd, and down the aged gossip led
To a safe level matting. Now prepare,
Young Porphyro, for gazing on that bed;
She comes, she comes again, like ring-dove
 fray'd and fled.

XXIII

Out went the taper as she hurried in;
Its little smoke, in pallid moonshine,
 died:
She closed the door, she panted, all akin
To spirits of the air, and visions wide:
No uttered syllable, or, woe betide !
But to her heart, her heart was voluble,
Paining with eloquence her balmy side;
As though a tongueless nightingale
 should swell
Her throat in vain, and die, heart-stifled in
 her dell.

XXIV

A casement high and triple arch'd there
 was,
All garlanded with carven imag'ries
Of fruits, and flowers, and bunches of
 knot-grass,
And diamonded with panes of quaint de-
 vice,
Innumerable of stains and splendid
 dyes,
As are the tiger-moth's deep-damask'd
 wings;
And in the midst, 'mong thousand herald-
 ries,
And twilight saints, and dim emblazon-
 ings,
A shielded scutcheon blush'd with blood of
 queens and kings.

XXV

Full on this casement shone the wintry
 moon,
And threw warm gules on Madeline's
 fair breast,

As down she knelt for heaven's grace
 and boon;
Rose-bloom fell on her hands, together
 prest,
And on her silver cross soft amethyst,
And on her hair a glory, like a saint:
She seem'd a splendid angel, newly drest,
Save wings, for heaven: — Porphyro grew
 faint;
She knelt, so pure a thing, so free from
 mortal taint.

XXVI

Anon his heart revives: her vespers
 done,
Of all its wreathed pearls her hair she
 frees;
Unclasps her warmed jewels one by
 one;
Loosens her fragrant bodice; by degrees
Her rich attire creeps rustling to her
 knees:
Half-hidden, like a mermaid in sea-weed,
Pensive awhile she dreams awake, and
 sees,
In fancy, fair St. Agnes in her bed,
But dares not look behind, or all the charm
 is fled.

XXVII

Soon, trembling in her soft and chilly
 nest,
In sort of wakeful swoon, perplex'd she
 lay,
Until the poppied warmth of sleep op-
 press'd
Her soothed limbs, and soul fatigued
 away;
Flown, like a thought, until the morrow-
 day;
Blissfully haven'd both from joy and
 pain;
Clasp'd like a missal where swart Pay-
 nims pray;
Blinded alike from sunshine and from
 rain,
As though a rose should shut, and be a bud
 again.

XXVIII

Stol'n to this paradise, and so entranced,
Porphyro gazed upon her empty dress,
And listen'd to her breathing, if it
chanced
To wake into a slumberous tenderness;
Which when he heard, that minute did
he bless,
And breathed himself: then from the
closet crept,
Noiseless as fear in a wide wilderness,
And over the hush'd carpet, silent,
stept,
And 'tween the curtains peep'd, where, lo!
— how fast she slept.

XXIX

Then by the bed-side, where the faded
moon
Made a dim, silver twilight, soft he set
A table, and, half anguish'd, threw
thereon
A cloth of woven crimson, gold, and
jet: —
O for some drowsy Morphean amulet!
The boisterous, midnight, festive clarion,
The kettle-drum, and far-heard clarionet,
Affray his ears, though, but in dying
tone: —
The hall-door shuts again, and all the noise
is gone.

XXX

And still she slept an azure-lidded sleep,
In blanched linen, smooth, and laven-
der'd,
While he from forth the closet brought
a heap
Of candied apple, quince, and plum, and
gourd;
With jellies soother than the creamy
curd,
And lucent syrops, tinct with cinnamon;
Manna and dates, in argosy transferr'd
From Fez; and spiced dainties, every
one,
From silken Samarcand to cedar'd Leba-
non.

XXXI

These delicates he heap'd with glowing
hand
On golden dishes and in baskets bright
Of wreathed silver: sumptuous they
stand
In the retired quiet of the night,
Filling the chilly room with perfume
light. —
'And now, my love, my seraph fair,
awake!
Thou art my heaven, and I thine ere-
mite:
Open thine eyes, for meek St. Agnes'
sake,
Or I shall drowse beside thee, so my soul
doth ache.'

XXXII

Thus whispering, his warm, unnerved
arm
Sank in her pillow. Shaded was her
dream
By the dusk curtains: — 't was a mid-
night charm
Impossible to melt as iced stream:
The lustrous salvers in the moonlight
gleam;
Broad golden fringe upon the carpet
lies:
It seem'd he never, never could redeem
From such a steadfast spell his lady's
eyes;
So mused awhile, entoil'd in woofed phan-
tasies.

XXXIII

Awakening up, he took her hollow
lute, —
Tumultuous, — and, in chords that ten-
derest be,
He play'd an ancient ditty, long since
mute,
In Provence call'd 'La belle dame sans
mercy:'
Close to her ear touching the melody; —
Wherewith disturb'd, she utter'd a soft
moan:

He ceased — she panted quick — and
 suddenly
Her blue affrayed eyes wide open shone:
Upon his knees he sank, pale as smooth-
 sculptured stone.

XXXIV

Her eyes were open, but she still beheld,
Now wide awake, the vision of her sleep:
There was a painful change, that nigh
 expell'd
The blisses of her dream so pure and
 deep
At which fair Madeline began to weep,
And moan forth witless words with
 many a sigh;
While still her gaze on Porphyro would
 keep;
Who knelt, with joined hands and piteous
 eye,
Fearing to move or speak, she look'd so
 dreamingly.

XXXV

' Ah, Porphyro!' said she, ' but even now
Thy voice was at sweet tremble in mine
 ear,
Made tuneable with every sweetest vow;
And those sad eyes were spiritual and
 clear:
How changed thou art! how pallid, chill,
 and drear!
Give me that voice again, my Porphyro,
Those looks immortal, those complain-
 ings dear!
Oh leave me not in this eternal woe,
For if thou diest, my Love, I know not
 where to go.'

XXXVI

Beyond a mortal man impassion'd far
At these voluptuous accents, he arose,
Ethereal, flush'd, and like a throbbing
 star
Seen mid the sapphire heaven's deep re-
 pose;
Into her dream he melted, as the rose
Blendeth its odour with the violet, —

Solution sweet: meantime the frost-wind
 blows
Like Love's alarum pattering the sharp
 sleet
Against the window-panes; St. Agnes' moon
 hath set.

XXXVII

'T is dark: quick pattereth the flaw-
 blown sleet:
' This is no dream, my bride, my Made-
 line!'
'T is dark: the iced gusts still rave and
 beat:
' No dream, alas! alas! and woe is mine!
Porphyro will leave me here to fade and
 pine. —
Cruel! what traitor could thee hither
 bring?
I curse not, for my heart is lost in thine,
Though thou forsakest a deceived
 thing; —
A dove forlorn and lost with sick unpruned
 wing.'

XXXVIII

' My Madeline! sweet dreamer! lovely
 bride!
Say, may I be for aye thy vassal blest?
Thy beauty's shield, heart-shaped and
 vermeil dyed?
Ah, silver shrine, here will I take my
 rest
After so many hours of toil and quest,
A famish'd pilgrim, — saved by miracle.
Though I have found, I will not rob thy
 nest
Saving of thy sweet self; if thou think'st
 well
To trust, fair Madeline, to no rude infidel.

XXXIX

' Hark! 't is an elfin storm from faery
 land,
Of haggard seeming, but a boon indeed:
Arise — arise! the morning is at hand: —
The bloated wassailers will never heed: —
Let us away, my love, with happy speed;

There are no ears to hear, or eyes to
 see, —
Drown'd all in Rhenish and the sleepy
 mead:
Awake ! arise ! my love, and fearless be,
For o'er the southern moors I have a home
 for thee.'

XL

She hurried at his words, beset with
 fears,
For there were sleeping dragons all
 around,
At glaring watch, perhaps, with ready
 spears —
Down the wide stairs a darkling way they
 found. —
In all the house was heard no human
 sound.
A chain-droop'd lamp was flickering by
 each door;
The arras, rich with horseman, hawk,
 and hound,
Flutter'd in the besieging wind's up-
 roar;
And the long carpets rose along the gusty
 floor.

XLI

They glide, like phantoms, into the wide
 hall;
Like phantoms to the iron porch they
 glide,
Where lay the Porter, in uneasy sprawl,
With a huge empty flagon by his side:
The wakeful bloodhound rose, and shook
 his hide,
But his sagacious eye an inmate owns:
By one, and one, the bolts full easy
 slide: —
The chains lie silent on the footworn
 stones; —
The key turns, and the door upon its hinges
 groans.

XLII

And they are gone: aye, ages long ago
These lovers fled away into the storm.

That night the Baron dreamt of many a
 woe,
And all his warrior-guests, with shade
 and form
Of witch, and demon, and large coffin-
 worm,
Were long be-nightmared. Angela the
 old
Died palsy-twitch'd, with meagre face
 deform;
The Beadsman, after thousand aves told,
For aye unsought-for slept among his ashes
 cold.

ODE ON A GRECIAN URN

Lemprière's classical dictionary made Keats
acquainted with the names and attributes of the
inhabitants of the heavens in the ancient world,
and the Shakesperean Chapman introduced
him to Homer, but his acquaintance with the
subtlest spirit of Greece was by a more direct
means. Keats did not read Greek, and he had
no scholar's knowledge of Greek art, but he
had the poetic divination which scholars some-
times fail to possess, and when he strolled into
the British Museum and saw the Elgin marbles,
the greatest remains in continuous series of per-
haps the greatest of Greek sculptures, he saw
them as an artist of kindred spirit with their
makers. He saw them also with the complex
emotion of a modern, and read into them his
own thoughts. The result is most surely read
in his longer poem of *Hyperion*, but the spirit
evoked found its finest expression in this ode.

The ode appears to have been composed in
the spring of 1819 and first published in Janu-
ary, 1820, in *Annals of the Fine Arts*. There are
then about four years in time between the son-
net, 'On first looking into Chapman's Homer,'
and this ode ; if the former suggests a Balboa,
this suggests a Magellan who has traversed the
Pacific. It is not needful to find any single
piece of ancient sculpture as a model for the
poem, although there is at Holland House,
where Keats might have seen it, an urn with
just such a scene of pastoral sacrifice as is de-
scribed in the fourth stanza. The ode was
included by Keats in *Lamia, Isabella, The Eve
of St. Agnes and other Poems*.

I

Thou still unravish'd bride of quietness,
 Thou foster-child of Silence and slow
 Time,
Sylvan historian, who canst thus express
 A flowery tale more sweetly than our
 rhyme:
What leaf-fringed legend haunts about thy
 shape
 Of deities or mortals, or of both,
 In Tempe or the dales of Arcady?
 What men or gods are these? what
 maidens loth?
What mad pursuit? What struggle to es-
 cape?
 What pipes and timbrels? What wild
 ecstasy? 10

II

Heard melodies are sweet, but those un-
 heard
 Are sweeter; therefore, ye soft pipes,
 play on;
Not to the sensual ear, but, more endear'd
 Pipe to the spirit ditties of no tone:
Fair youth, beneath the trees, thou canst
 not leave
 Thy song, nor ever can those trees be
 bare;
 Bold Lover, never, never canst thou
 kiss,
Though winning near the goal — yet, do
 not grieve;
 She cannot fade, though thou hast not
 thy bliss, 19
 For ever wilt thou love, and she be fair!

III

Ah, happy, happy boughs! that cannot
 shed
 Your leaves, nor ever bid the Spring
 adieu;
And, happy melodist, unwearied,
 For ever piping songs for ever new;
More happy love! more happy, happy
 love!
 For ever warm and still to be enjoy'd,
 For ever panting, and for ever young;

All breathing human passion far above,
 That leaves a heart high-sorrowful and
 cloy'd,
 A burning forehead, and a parching
 tongue. 30

IV

Who are these coming to the sacrifice?
 To what green altar, O mysterious priest,
Lead'st thou that heifer lowing at the skies,
 And all her silken flanks with garlands
 drest?
What little town by river or sea shore,
 Or mountain-built with peaceful citadel,
 Is emptied of this folk, this pious
 morn?
And, little town, thy streets for evermore
 Will silent be; and not a soul to tell
 Why thou art desolate, can e'er re-
 turn. 40

V

O Attic shape! Fair attitude! with brede
 Of marble men and maidens overwrought,
With forest branches and the trodden weed;
 Thou, silent form, dost tease us out of
 thought
As doth eternity: Cold Pastoral!
 When old age shall this generation waste,
 Thou shalt remain, in midst of other
 woe
 Than ours, a friend to man, to whom
 thou say'st,
'Beauty is truth, truth beauty,' — that is
 all
 Ye know on earth, and all ye need to
 know. 50

ODE ON INDOLENCE

' They toil not, neither do they spin.'

Published in *Life, Letters and Literary Re-
mains*. In a letter to George and Georgiana
Keats, dated March 19, 1819, Keats uses lan-
guage which shows this poem to have been
just then in his mind: ' This morning I am in a
sort of temper, indolent and supremely careless

— I long after a stanza or two of Thomson's Castle of Indolence — my passions are all asleep, from my having slumbered till nearly eleven, and weakened the animal fibre all over me, to a delightful sensation, about three degrees on this side of faintness. If I had teeth of pearl and the breath of lilies I should call it languor, but as I am I must call it laziness. In this state of effeminacy the fibres of the brain are relaxed in common with the rest of the body, and to such a happy degree that pleasure has no show of enticement and pain no unbearable power. Neither Poetry, nor Ambition, nor Love have any alertness of countenance as they pass by me; they seem rather like figures on a Greek vase — a man and two women whom no one but myself could distinguish in their disguisement. This is the only happiness, and is a rare instance of the advantage of the body overpowering the Mind.'

I

ONE morn before me were three figures seen,
 With bowed necks, and joined hands, side-faced;
And one behind the other stepp'd serene,
 In placid sandals, and in white robes graced;
They pass'd, like figures on a marble urn,
 When shifted round to see the other side;
 They came again; as when the urn once more
Is shifted round, the first seen shades return;
 And they were strange to me, as may betide
 With vases, to one deep in Phidian lore.

II

How is it, Shadows! that I knew ye not?
How came ye muffled in so hush a mask?
Was it a silent deep-disguised plot
 To steal away, and leave without a task
My idle days? Ripe was the drowsy hour;

The blissful cloud of summer-indolence
 Benumb'd my eyes; my pulse grew less and less;
Pain had no sting, and pleasure's wreath no flower:
 O, why did ye not melt, and leave my sense
 Unhaunted quite of all but — nothingness?

III

A third time pass'd they by, and, passing, turn'd
 Each one the face a moment whiles to me;
Then faded, and to follow them I burn'd
 And ached for wings, because I knew the three;
The first was a fair Maid, and Love her name;
 The second was Ambition, pale of cheek,
 And ever watchful with fatigued eye;
The last, whom I love more, the more of blame
 Is heap'd upon her, maiden most unmeek, —
 I knew to be my demon Poesy.

IV

They faded, and, forsooth! I wanted wings:
 O folly! What is Love? and where is it?
And for that poor Ambition! it springs
 From a man's little heart's short fever-fit;
For Poesy! — no, — she has not a joy, —
 At least for me, — so sweet as drowsy noons,
 And evenings steep'd in honied indolence;
O, for an age so shelter'd from annoy,
 That I may never know how change the moons,
 Or hear the voice of busy commonsense!

V

And once more came they by; — alas!
 wherefore?
My sleep had been embroider'd with dim
 dreams;
My soul had been a lawn besprinkled
 o'er
 With flowers, and stirring shades, and
 baffled beams:
The morn was clouded, but no shower fell,
 Tho' in her lids hung the sweet tears of
 May;
 The open casement press'd a new-
 leaved vine,
 Let in the budding warmth and throstle's
 lay;
O Shadows! 't was a time to bid farewell!
 Upon your skirts had fallen no tears
 of mine.

VI

So, ye three Ghosts, adieu! Ye cannot
 raise
 My head cool - bedded in the flowery
 grass;
For I would not be dieted with praise,
 A pet-lamb in a sentimental farce!
Fade softly from my eyes and be once
 more
 In masque-like figures on the dreamy
 urn;
 Farewell! I yet have visions for the
 night,
And for the day faint visions there is store;
 Vanish, ye Phantoms! from my idle
 spright,
 Into the clouds, and nevermore return!

SONNET

Published in *Life, Letters and Literary Re-
mains*. In a letter to his brother George and
wife, Keats writes March 19, 1819: 'I am
ever afraid that your anxiety for me will lead
you to fear for the violence of my tempera-
ment continually smothered down: for that
reason I did not intend to have sent you the
following sonnet — but look over the two last
pages [of his letter] and ask yourselves whether
I have not that in me which will bear the buf-
fets of the world. It will be the best comment
on my sonnet; it will show you that it was
written with no Agony but that of ignorance;
with no thirst of anything but Knowledge
when pushed to the point, though the first
steps to it were through my human passions, —
they went away and I wrote with my Mind
— and perhaps I must confess a little bit of my
heart.'

WHY did I laugh to-night? No voice will
 tell;
 No God, no Demon of severe response,
Deigns to reply from Heaven or from Hell:
 Then to my human heart I turn at once.
Heart! Thou and I are here sad and alone;
 I say, why did I laugh? O mortal pain!
O Darkness! Darkness! ever must I moan,
 To question Heaven and Hell and Heart
 in vain.
Why did I laugh? I know this Being's
 lease,
 My fancy to its utmost blisses spreads;
Yet would I on this very midnight cease,
 And the world's gaudy ensigns see in
 shreds;
Verse, Fame, and Beauty are intense
 indeed,
But Death intenser — Death is Life's high
 meed.

ODE TO FANNY

First published in *Life, Letters and Literary
Remains*, and there undated.

PHYSICIAN Nature! let my spirit blood!
 O ease my heart of verse and let me rest;
Throw me upon thy Tripod, till the flood
 Of stifling numbers ebbs from my full
 breast.
 A theme! a theme! great Nature!
 give a theme;
 Let me begin my dream.
I come — I see thee, as thou standest there;
Beckon me not into the wintry air.

Ah! dearest love, sweet home of all my
 fears,
 And hopes, and joys, and panting mis-
 eries, —
To-night, if I may guess, thy beauty wears
 A smile of such delight,
 As brilliant and as bright,
 As when with ravished, aching, vassal
 eyes,
 Lost in soft amaze,
 I gaze, I gaze!

Who now, with greedy looks, eats up my
 feast?
What stare outfaces now my silver moon!
Ah! keep that hand unravished at the least;
 Let, let the amorous burn —
 But, pr'ythee, do not turn
 The current of your heart from me so
 soon.
 O! save, in charity,
 The quickest pulse for me.

Save it for me, sweet love! though music
 breathe
 Voluptuous visions into the warm air,
Though swimming through the dance's dan-
 gerous wreath;
 Be like an April day,
 Smiling and cold and gay,
 A temperate lily, temperate as fair;
 Then, Heaven! there will be
 A warmer June for me.

Why, this — you'll say, my Fanny! is not
 true:
 Put your soft hand upon your snowy side,
Where the heart beats: confess — 't is
 nothing new —
 Must not a woman be
 A feather on the sea,
 Sway'd to and fro by every wind and
 tide?
 Of as uncertain speed
 As blow-ball from the mead?

I know it — and to know it is despair
 To one who loves you as I love, sweet
 Fanny!

Whose heart goes fluttering for you every-
 where,
 Nor, when away you roam,
 Dare keep its wretched home:
Love, love alone, has pains severe and
 many:
 Then, loveliest! keep me free
 From torturing jealousy.

Ah! if you prize my subdued soul above
 The poor, the fading, brief pride of an
 hour;
Let none profane my Holy See of love,
 Or with a rude hand break
 The sacramental cake:
Let none else touch the just new-budded
 flower;
 If not — may my eyes close,
 Love! on their last repose.

A DREAM, AFTER READING DANTE'S EPISODE OF PAOLO AND FRANCESCA

To George and Georgiana Keats, April 18 or
19, 1819, Keats writes: 'The fifth canto of
Dante pleases me more and more — it is that
one in which he meets with Paolo and Fran-
cesca. I had passed many days in rather a
low state of mind, and in the midst of them I
dreamt of being in that region of Hell. The
dream was one of the most delightful enjoy-
ments I ever had in my life. I floated about
the whirling atmosphere, as it is described, with
a beautiful figure, to whose lips mine were
joined as it seemed for an age — and in the
midst of all this cold and darkness I was warm
— even flowery tree-tops sprung up, and we
rested on them, sometimes with the lightness
of a cloud, till the wind blew us away again.
I tried a sonnet upon it — there are fourteen
lines, but nothing of what I felt in it — O that
I could dream it every night.' Keats after-
wards printed the sonnet in *The Indicator* for
June 28, 1820.

As Hermes once took to his feathers light,
 When lulled Argus, baffled, swoon'd and
 slept
So on a Delphic reed, my idle spright

So play'd, so charm'd, so conquer'd, so
 bereft
The dragon-world of all its hundred eyes;
 And, seeing it asleep, so fled away —
Not to pure Ida with its snow-cold skies,
 Nor unto Tempe where Jove grieved a
 day;
But to that second circle of sad hell,
 Where 'mid the gust, the whirlwind, and
 the flaw
Of rain and hail-stones, lovers need not tell
 Their sorrows. Pale were the sweet lips
 I saw,
Pale were the lips I kiss'd, and fair the form
I floated with, about that melancholy storm.

LA BELLE DAME SANS MERCI

Sent in a letter to George and Georgiana
Keats, April 28, 1819, and printed by Leigh
Hunt in *The Indicator*, May 10, 1820. Hunt
says the poem was suggested by that title at
the head of a translation from Alan Chartier
at the end of Chaucer's works.

I

AH, what can ail thee, wretched wight,
 Alone and palely loitering?
The sedge is wither'd from the lake,
 And no birds sing.

II

Ah, what can ail thee, wretched wight,
 So haggard and so woe-begone?
The squirrel's granary is full,
 And the harvest's done.

III

I see a lily on thy brow,
 With anguish moist and fever dew;
And on thy cheek a fading rose
 Fast withereth too.

IV

I met a lady in the meads,
 Full beautiful — a faery's child;
Her hair was long, her foot was light,
 And her eyes were wild.

V

I set her on my pacing steed,
 And nothing else saw all day long,
For sideways would she lean, and sing
 A faery's song.

VI

I made a garland for her head,
 And bracelets too, and fragrant zone;
She look'd at me as she did love,
 And made sweet moan.

VII

She found me roots of relish sweet,
 And honey wild, and manna dew;
And sure in language strange she said —
 'I love thee true.'

VIII

She took me to her elfin grot,
 And there she gazed, and sighed deep,
And there I shut her wild wild eyes
 So kiss'd to sleep.

IX

And there we slumber'd on the moss,
 And there I dream'd — Ah! woe betide!
The latest dream I ever dream'd
 On the cold hill side.

X

I saw pale kings, and princes too,
 Pale warriors, death-pale were they all;
They cried — 'La Belle Dame sans Merci
 Hath thee in thrall!'

XI

I saw their starved lips in the gloam,
 With horrid warning gaped wide,
And I awoke, and found me here
 On the cold hill side.

XII

And this is why I sojourn here,
 Alone and palely loitering,
Though the sedge is wither'd from the
 lake,
 And no birds sing.

CHORUS OF FAIRIES

Inclosed in a letter to George and Georgiana
Keats, April 28, 1819, and printed in *Life,
Letters and Literary Remains.*

FIRE, AIR, EARTH, AND WATER
SALAMANDER, ZEPHYR, DUSKETHA, AND
BREAMA

SALAMANDER

Happy, happy glowing fire !

ZEPHYR

Fragrant air ! delicious light !

DUSKETHA

Let me to my glooms retire !

BREAMA

I to green-weed rivers bright !

SALAMANDER

Happy, happy glowing fire !
Dazzling bowers of soft retire,
Ever let my nourish'd wing,
Like a bat's, still wandering,
Faintly fan your fiery spaces,
Spirit sole in deadly places. 10
In unhaunted roar and blaze,
Open eyes that never daze,
Let me see the myriad shapes
Of men, and beasts, and fish, and apes,
Portray'd in many a fiery den,
And wrought by spumy bitumen.
On the deep intenser roof,
Arched every way, aloof,
Let me breathe upon my skies,
And anger their live tapestries; 20
Free from cold, and every care,
Of chilly rain, and shivering air.

ZEPHYR

Spright of Fire ! away ! away !
Or your very roundelay
Will sear my plumage newly budded
From its quilled sheath, and studded
With the self-same dews that fell
On the May-grown Asphodel.
Spright of Fire — away ! away !

BREAMA

Spright of Fire — away ! away ! 30
Zephyr, blue-eyed Faery, turn,
And see my cool sedge-shaded urn,
Where it rests its mossy brim
'Mid water-mint and cresses dim;
And the flowers, in sweet troubles,
Lift their eyes above the bubbles,
Like our Queen, when she would please
To sleep, and Oberon will tease.
Love me, blue-eyed Faery ! true,
Soothly I am sick for you. 40

ZEPHYR

Gentle Breama ! by the first
Violet young nature nurst,
I will bathe myself with thee,
So you sometime follow me
To my home, far, far, in west,
Far beyond the search and quest
Of the golden-browed sun.
Come with me, o'er tops of trees,
To my fragrant palaces,
Where they ever floating are 50
Beneath the cherish of a star
Call'd Vesper, who with silver veil
Ever hides his brilliance pale,
Ever gently-drowsed doth keep
Twilight for the Fays to sleep.
Fear not that your watery hair
Will thirst in drouthy ringlets there;
Clouds of stored summer rains
Thou shalt taste, before the stains
Of the mountain soil they take, 60
And too unlucent for thee make.
I love thee, crystal Faery, true !
Sooth I am as sick for you !

SALAMANDER

Out, ye aguish Faeries, out !
Chilly lovers, what a rout
Keep ye with your frozen breath,
Colder than the mortal death.
Adder-eyed Dusketha, speak,
Shall we leave them, and go seek
In the earth's wide entrails old 70
Couches warm as theirs is cold ?
O for a fiery gloom and thee,

Dusketha, so enchantingly
Freckle-wing'd and lizard-sided !

DUSKETHA

By thee, Spright, will I be guided !
I care not for cold or heat;
Frost and flame, or sparks, or sleet,
To my essence are the same; —
But I honour more the flame.
Spright of fire, I follow thee 80
Wheresoever it may be;
To the torrid spouts and fountains,
Underneath earth-quaked mountains;
Or, at thy supreme desire,
Touch the very pulse of fire
With my bare unlidded eyes.

SALAMANDER

Sweet Dusketha ! paradise !
Off, ye icy Spirits, fly !
Frosty creatures of the sky !

DUSKETHA

Breathe upon them, fiery Spright ! 90

ZEPHYR, BREAMA (*to each other*)

Away ! away to our delight !

SALAMANDER

Go, feed on icicles, while we
Bedded in tongued flames will be.

DUSKETHA

Lead me to these fev'rous glooms,
Spright of Fire !

BREAMA

 Me to the blooms,
Blue eyed Zephyr of those flowers
Far in the west where the May-cloud lowers:
 And the beams of still Vesper, where
 winds are all whist,
 Are shed thro' the rain and the milder
 mist,
And twilight your floating bowers. 100

FAERY SONGS

These two songs are given in *Life, Letters
and Literary Remains*, but without date. It

seems not inapt to place them near the *Song of
Four Fairies*.

I

SHED no tear ! O shed no tear !
The flower will bloom another year.
Weep no more ! O weep no more !
Young buds sleep in the root's white core.
Dry your eyes ! O dry your eyes,
For I was taught in Paradise
To ease my breast of melodies —
 Shed no tear.

Overhead ! look overhead
'Mong the blossoms white and red —
Look up, look up — I flutter now
On this flush pomegranate bough.
See me ! 't is this silvery bill
Ever cures the good man's ill.
Shed no tear ! O shed no tear !
The flower will bloom another year.
Adieu, Adieu — I fly, adieu,
I vanish in the heaven's blue —
 Adieu, Adieu !

II

Ah ! woe is me ! poor silver-wing !
 That I must chant thy lady's dirge,
And death to this fair haunt of spring,
 Of melody, and streams of flowery
 verge, —
 Poor silver-wing ! ah ! woe is me !
 That I must see
These blossoms snow upon thy lady's pall !
 Go, pretty page ! and in her ear
 Whisper that the hour is near !
 Softly tell her not to fear
Such calm favonian burial !
 Go, pretty page ! and soothly tell, —
 The blossoms hang by a melting spell,
And fall they must, ere a star wink thrice
 Upon her closed eyes,
That now in vain are weeping their last
 tears,
 At sweet life leaving, and those arbours
 green, —
Rich dowry from the Spirit of the
 Spheres, —
 Alas ! poor Queen !

ON FAME

'You cannot eat your cake and have it too.' — *Proverb.*

Sent with the next two to George and Georgiana Keats, April 30, 1819, and printed in *Life, Letters and Literary Remains.*

How fever'd is that man, who cannot look
　　Upon his mortal days with temperate
　　　　blood,
Who vexes all the leaves of his life's book,
　　And robs his fair name of its maiden-
　　　　hood:
It is as if the rose should pluck herself,
　　Or the ripe plum finger its misty bloom;
As if a Naiad, like a meddling elf,
　　Should darken her pure grot with muddy
　　　　gloom.
But the rose leaves herself upon the brier,
　　For winds to kiss and grateful bees to
　　　　feed,
And the ripe plum still wears its dim at-
　　　　tire,
　　　The undisturbed lake has crystal space:
　　Why then should man, teasing the
　　　　world for grace,
　　Spoil his salvation for a fierce miscreed ?

ANOTHER ON FAME

FAME, like a wayward girl, will still be coy
　　To those who woo her with too slavish
　　　　knees,
But makes surrender to some thoughtless
　　　　boy,
　　And dotes the more upon a heart at ease;
She is a Gipsy, — will not speak to those
　　Who have not learnt to be content with-
　　　　out her;
A Jilt, whose ear was never whisper'd
　　　　close,
　　Who *t*hinks they scandal her who talk
　　　　about her;
A very Gipsy is she, Nilus-born,
　　Sister-in-law to jealous Potiphar;
Ye lovesick Bards ! repay her scorn for
　　　　scorn;

Ye Artists lovelorn ! madmen that ye
　　are !
Make your best bow to her and bid adieu,
Then, if she likes it, she will follow you.

TO SLEEP

O SOFT embalmer of the still midnight,
　　Shutting, with careful fingers and benign,
Our gloom-pleased eyes, embower'd from
　　　　the light,
　　Enshaded in forgetfulness divine:
O soothest Sleep ! if so it please thee,
　　　　close,
　　In midst of this thine hymn, my willing
　　　　eyes,
Or wait the amen, ere thy poppy throws
　　Around my bed its dewy charities;
　　Then save me, or the passed day will
　　　　shine
Upon my pillow, breeding many woes;
　　Save me from curious conscience, that
　　　　still lords
Its strength for darkness, burrowing like a
　　　　mole;
　　Turn the key deftly in the oiled wards,
And seal the hushed casket of my soul.

ODE TO PSYCHE

' The following poem — the last I have writ-
ten — is the first and only one with which I have
taken even moderate pains. I have, for the
most part, dashed off my lines in a hurry. This
I have done leisurely — I think it reads the more
richly for it, and will I hope encourage me to
write other things in even a more peaceable
and healthy spirit. You must recollect that
Psyche was not embodied as a goddess before
the time of Apuleius the Platonist, who lived
after the Augustan age, and consequently the
Goddess was never worshipped or sacrificed to
with any of the ancient fervour — and perhaps
never thought of in the old religion — I am
more orthodox than to let a heathen Goddess
be so neglected.' Keats to his Brother and
Sister, April 30, 1819. He afterward included
the poem in his volume, *Lamia, Isabella, The
Eve of St. Agnes and other Poems,* 1820.

I

O Goddess! hear these tuneless numbers, wrung
 By sweet enforcement and remembrance dear,
And pardon that thy secrets should be sung
 Even into thine own soft-conched ear:
Surely I dreamt to-day, or did I see
 The winged Psyche with awaken'd eyes?
I wander'd in a forest thoughtlessly,
 And, on the sudden, fainting with surprise,
Saw two fair creatures, couched side by side
 In deepest grass, beneath the whisp'ring roof 10
 Of leaves and trembled blossoms, where there ran
 A brooklet, scarce espied:

II

'Mid hush'd, cool-rooted flowers fragrant-eyed,
 Blue, silver-white, and budded Tyrian,
They lay calm-breathing on the bedded grass;
 Their arms embraced, and their pinions too;
 Their lips touch'd not, but had not bade adieu,
As if disjoined by soft-handed slumber,
And ready still past kisses to outnumber
 At tender eye-dawn of aurorean love: 20
 The winged boy I knew;
 But who wast thou, O happy, happy dove?
 His Psyche true!

III

O latest-born and loveliest vision far
 Of all Olympus' faded hierarchy!
Fairer than Phœbe's sapphire-region'd star,
 Or Vesper, amorous glow-worm of the sky;
Fairer than these, though temple thou hast none,
 Nor altar heap'd with flowers;
Nor virgin-choir to make delicious moan
 Upon the midnight hours; 31

No voice, no lute, no pipe, no incense sweet
 From chain-swung censer teeming;
No shrine, no grove, no oracle, no heat
 Of pale-mouth'd prophet dreaming.

IV

O brightest! though too late for antique vows,
 Too, too late for the fond believing lyre,
When holy were the haunted forest boughs,
 Holy the air, the water, and the fire;
Yet even in these days so far retired 40
 From happy pieties, thy lucent fans,
 Fluttering among the faint Olympians,
I see, and sing, by my own eyes inspired.
So let me be thy choir, and make a moan
 Upon the midnight hours;
Thy voice, thy lute, thy pipe, thy incense sweet
 From swinged censer teeming;
Thy shrine, thy grove, thy oracle, thy heat
 Of pale-mouth'd prophet dreaming.

V

Yes, I will be thy priest, and build a fane
 In some untrodden region of my mind,
Where branched thoughts, new-grown with pleasant pain, 52
 Instead of pines shall murmur in the wind:
Far, far around shall those dark-cluster'd trees
 Fledge the wild-ridged mountains steep by steep;
And there by zephyrs, streams, and birds, and bees,
 The moss-lain Dryads shall be lulled to sleep;
And in the midst of this wide quietness
A rosy sanctuary will I dress
With the wreath'd trellis of a working brain, 60
 With buds, and bells, and stars without a name,
With all the gardener Fancy e'er could feign,
 Who breeding flowers, will never breed the same:

And there shall be for thee all soft delight
 That shadowy thought can win,
A bright torch, and a casement ope at
 night,
 To let the warm Love in !

SONNET

In copying his ' Ode to Psyche,' Keats added
the flourish ' Here endethe ye Ode to Psyche,'
and went on ' Incipit altera soneta.' ' I have
been endeavouring,' he writes, 'to discover a
better Sonnet Stanza than we have. The legiti-
mate does not suit the language over well from
the pouncing rhymes — the other kind appears
too elegiac — and the couplet at the end of it
has seldom a pleasing effect — I do not pre-
tend to have succeeded — it will explain itself.'
The sonnet was printed in *Life, Letters and Lit-
erary Remains.*

IF by dull rhymes our English must be
 chain'd,
 And, like Andromeda, the Sonnet sweet
Fetter'd, in spite of pained loveliness;
 Let us find out, if we must be constrain'd,
 Sandals more interwoven and complete
To fit the naked foot of poesy;
 Let us inspect the lyre, and weigh the
 stress
Of every chord, and see what may be
 gain'd
 By ear industrious, and attention meet;
Misers of sound and syllable, no less
Than Midas of his coinage, let us be
 Jealous of dead leaves in the bay-wreath
 crown:
So, if we may not let the Muse be free,
 She will be bound with garlands of her
 own.

ODE TO A NIGHTINGALE

First published in the July, 1819, *Annals of
the Fine Arts* and included in the 1820 volume.
It was composed in May, 1819. In the Aldine
edition of 1876 Lord Houghton prefixes this
note: ' In the spring of 1819 a nightingale
built her nest next Mr. Bevan's house. Keats

took great pleasure in her song, and one morn-
ing took his chair from the breakfast table to
the grass plot under a plum tree, where he
remained between two and three hours. He
then reached the house with some scraps of
paper in his hand, which he soon put together
in the form of this Ode.' Haydon in a letter
to Miss Mitford says: ' The death of his bro-
ther [in December, 1818] wounded him deeply,
and it appeared to me from that hour he began
to droop. He wrote his exquisite ' Ode to the
Nightingale ' at this time, and as we were one
evening walking in the Kilburn meadows he
repeated it to me, before he put it to paper, in
a low, tremulous undertone which affected me
extremely.' It may well be that Tom Keats
was in the poet's mind when he wrote line 26.

I

MY heart aches, and a drowsy numbness
 pains
 My sense, as though of hemlock I had
 drunk,
Or emptied some dull opiate to the drains
 One minute past, and Lethe-wards had
 sunk:
'T is not through envy of thy happy lot,
 But being too happy in thine happiness, —
 That thou, light-winged Dryad of the
 trees,
 In some melodious plot
 Of beechen green, and shadows number-
 less,
 Singest of summer in full-throated
 ease. *10*

II

O for a draught of vintage ! that hath been
 Cool'd a long age in the deep-delved
 earth,
Tasting of Flora and the country-green,
 Dance, and Provençal song, and sun-
 burnt mirth !
O for a beaker full of the warm South,
 Full of the true, the blushful Hippo-
 crene,
 With beaded bubbles winking at the
 brim,
 And purple-stained mouth ;

That I might drink, and leave the world
 unseen,
 And with thee fade away into the for-
 est dim: 20

III

Fade far away, dissolve, and quite forget
 What thou among the leaves hast never
 known,
The weariness, the fever, and the fret
 Here, where men sit and hear each other
 groan;
Where palsy shakes a few, sad, last gray
 hairs,
 Where youth grows pale, and spectre-
 thin, and dies;
 Where but to think is to be full of
 sorrow
 And leaden-eyed despairs,
 Where Beauty cannot keep her lustrous
 eyes,
 Or new Love pine at them beyond to-
 morrow. 30

IV

Away! away! for I will fly to thee,
 Not charioted by Bacchus and his pards,
But on the viewless wings of Poesy,
 Though the dull brain perplexes and re-
 tards:
Already with thee! tender is the night,
 And haply the Queen-Moon is on her
 throne,
 Cluster'd around by all her starry
 Fays;
 But here there is no light,
 Save what from heaven is with the breezes
 blown
 Through verdurous glooms and wind-
 ing mossy ways. 40

V

I cannot see what flowers are at my feet,
 Nor what soft incense hangs upon the
 boughs,
But, in embalmed darkness, guess each
 sweet

Wherewith the seasonable month en-
 dows
The grass, the thicket, and the fruit-tree
 wild;
 White hawthorn, and the pastoral eglan-
 tine;
 Fast fading violets cover'd up in
 leaves;
 And mid-May's eldest child,
 The coming musk-rose, full of dewy
 wine,
 The murmurous haunt of flies on sum-
 mer eves. 50

VI

Darkling I listen; and, for many a time
 I have been half in love with easeful
 Death,
Call'd him soft names in many a mused
 rhyme,
 To take into the air my quiet breath;
Now more than ever seems it rich to die,
 To cease upon the midnight with no
 pain,
 While thou art pouring forth thy soul
 abroad
 In such an ecstasy!
 Still wouldst thou sing, and I have ears
 in vain —
 To thy high requiem become a sod. 60

VII

Thou wast not born for death, immortal
 Bird!
No hungry generations tread thee down;
The voice I hear this passing night was
 heard
 In ancient days by emperor and clown:
Perhaps the self-same song that found a
 path
 Through the sad heart of Ruth, when,
 sick for home,
 She stood in tears amid the alien corn;
 The same that oft-times hath
 Charm'd magic casements, opening on
 the foam
 Of perilous seas, in faery lands for-
 lorn. 70

VIII

Forlorn ! the very word is like a bell
　To toll me back from thee to my sole
　　self !
Adieu ! the fancy cannot cheat so well
　As she is famed to do, deceiving elf.
Adieu ! adieu ! thy plaintive anthem fades
　Past the near meadows, over the still
　　stream,
　　Up the hill-side; and now 't is buried
　　　deep
　　　In the next valley-glades:
Was it a vision, or a waking dream ?
　　Fled is that music: — do I wake or
　　　sleep ?　　　　　　　　　　　80

LAMIA

In the early summer of 1819 Keats felt the
pressure of want of money and determined to
go into the country, where he could live cheaply,
and devote himself to writing. He went ac-
cordingly to Shanklin, Isle of Wight, and wrote
thence to Reynolds, July 12, 'I have finished
the Act [the first of *Otho the Great*], and in the
interval of beginning the 2nd have proceeded
pretty well with *Lamia*, finishing the first part
which consists of about 400 lines. I have
great hope of success [in this enterprise of
maintenance], because I make use of my judg-
ment more deliberately than I have yet done.'
He continued to work at *Lamia* in connection
with the tragedy, completing it in August at
Winchester. It formed the leading poem in the
volume *Lamia, Isabella, the Eve of St. Agnes
and other Poems*, published in 1820. Keats's
own judgment of it is in his words: 'I am cer-
tain there is that sort of fire in it which must
take hold of people in some way — give them
either pleasant or unpleasant association.' He
found the germ of the story in Burton's *Anat-
omy of Melancholy*, where it is credited to Phi-
lostratus.

PART I

UPON a time, before the faery broods
Drove Nymph and Satyr from the pros-
　　perous woods,

Before King Oberon's bright diadem,
Sceptre, and mantle, clasp'd with dewy gem,
Frighted away the Dryads and the Fauns
From rushes green, and brakes, and cow-
　　slipp'd lawns,
The ever-smitten Hermes empty left
His golden throne, bent warm on amorous
　　theft;
From high Olympus had he stolen light,
On this side of Jove's clouds, to escape the
　　sight　　　　　　　　　　　10
Of his great summoner, and made retreat
Into a forest on the shores of Crete.
For somewhere in that sacred island dwelt
A nymph, to whom all hoofed Satyrs knelt;
At whose white feet the languid Tritons
　　poured
Pearls, while on land they wither'd and
　　adored.
Fast by the springs where she to bathe was
　　wont,
And in those meads where sometimes she
　　might haunt,
Were strewn rich gifts, unknown to any
　　Muse,
Though Fancy's casket were unlock'd to
　　choose.　　　　　　　　　　　20
Ah, what a world of love was at her feet !
So Hermes thought, and a celestial heat
Burnt from his winged heels to either ear,
That from a whiteness, as the lily clear,
Blush'd into roses 'mid his golden hair,
Fallen in jealous curls about his shoulders
　　bare.

From vale to vale, from wood to wood,
　　he flew,
Breathing upon the flowers his passion new,
And wound with many a river to its head,
To find where this sweet nymph prepared
　　her secret bed:　　　　　　　30
In vain; the sweet nymph might nowhere
　　be found,
And so he rested, on the lonely ground,
Pensive, and full of painful jealousies
Of the Wood-Gods, and even the very trees.
There as he stood, he heard a mournful
　　voice,

Such as once heard, in gentle heart, de-
stroys
All pain but pity: thus the lone voice spake:
'When from this wreathed tomb shall I
awake!
When move in a sweet body fit for life,
And love, and pleasure, and the ruddy
strife 40
Of hearts and lips! Ah, miserable me!'
The God, dove-footed, glided silently
Round bush and tree, soft-brushing, in his
speed,
The taller grasses and full-flowering weed,
Until he found a palpitating snake,
Bright, and cirque-couchant in a dusky
brake.

She was a gordian shape of dazzling hue,
Vermilion - spotted, golden, green, and
blue;
Striped like a zebra, freckled like a pard,
Eyed like a peacock, and all crimson barr'd;
And full of silver moons, that, as she
breathed, 51
Dissolved, or brighter shone, or inter-
wreathed
Their lustres with the gloomier tapes-
tries —
So rainbow-sided, touch'd with miseries,
She seem'd, at once, some penanced lady
elf,
Some demon's mistress, or the demon's
self.
Upon her crest she wore a wannish fire
Sprinkled with stars, like Ariadne's tiar:
Her head was serpent, but ah, bitter-sweet!
She had a woman's mouth with all its
pearls complete: 60
And for her eyes — what could such eyes
do there
But weep, and weep, that they were born
so fair?
As Proserpine still weeps for her Sicilian
air.
Her throat was serpent, but the words she
spake
Came, as through bubbling honey, for
Love's sake,

And thus; while Hermes on his pinions lay,
Like a stoop'd falcon ere he takes his prey:

'Fair Hermes! crown'd with feathers,
fluttering light,
I had a splendid dream of thee last night:
I saw thee sitting, on a throne of gold, 70
Among the Gods, upon Olympus old,
The only sad one; for thou didst not hear
The soft, lute - finger'd Muses chanting
clear,
Nor even Apollo when he sang alone,
Deaf to his throbbing throat's long, long
melodious moan.
I dreamt I saw thee, robed in purple flakes,
Break amorous through the clouds, as
morning breaks,
And, swiftly as a bright Phœbean dart,
Strike for the Cretan isle; and here thou
art!
Too gentle Hermes, hast thou found the
maid?' 80
Whereat the star of Lethe not delay'd
His rosy eloquence, and thus inquired:
'Thou smooth-lipp'd serpent, surely high-
inspired!
Thou beauteous wreath, with melancholy
eyes,
Possess whatever bliss thou canst devise,
Telling me only where my nymph is fled, —
Where she doth breathe!' 'Bright planet,
thou hast said,'
Return'd the snake, 'but seal with oaths,
fair God!'
'I swear,' said Hermes, 'by my serpent rod,
And by thine eyes, and by thy starry
crown!' 90
Light flew his earnest words, among the
blossoms blown.
Then thus again the brilliance feminine:
'Too frail of heart! for this lost nymph of
thine,
Free as the air, invisibly, she strays
About these thornless wilds; her pleasant
days
She tastes unseen; unseen her nimble
feet
Leave traces in the grass and flowers sweet;

From weary tendrils, and bow'd branches
 green,
She plucks the fruit unseen, she bathes un-
 seen:
And by my power is her beauty veil'd 100
To keep it unaffronted, unassail'd
By the love-glances of unlovely eyes,
Of Satyrs, Fauns, and blear'd Silenus' sighs.
Pale grew her immortality, for woe
Of all these lovers, and she grieved so
I took compassion on her, bade her steep
Her hair in weïrd syrops, that would keep
Her loveliness invisible, yet free
To wander as she loves, in liberty.
Thou shalt behold her, Hermes, thou alone,
If thou wilt, as thou swearest, grant my
 boon !' 111
Then, once again, the charmed God began
An oath, and through the serpent's ears it
 ran
Warm, tremulous, devout, psalterian.
Ravish'd she lifted her Circean head,
Blush'd a live damask, and swift-lisping
 said,
' I was a woman, let me have once more
A woman's shape, and charming as before.
I love a youth of Corinth — O the bliss !
Give me my woman's form, and place me
 where he is. 120
Stoop, Hermes, let me breathe upon thy
 brow,
And thou shalt see thy sweet nymph even
 now.'
The God on half-shut feathers sank serene,
She breathed upon his eyes, and swift was
 seen
Of both the guarded nymph near-smiling
 on the green.
It was no dream; or say a dream it was,
Real are the dreams of Gods, and smoothly
 pass
Their pleasures in a long immortal dream.
One warm, flush'd moment, hovering, it
 might seem
Dash'd by the wood-nymph's beauty, so he
 burn'd; 130
Then, lighting on the printless verdure,
 turn'd

To the swoon'd serpent, and with languid
 arm,
Delicate, put to proof the lithe Caducean
 charm.
So done, upon the nymph his eyes he bent
Full of adoring tears and blandishment,
And towards her stept: she, like a moon in
 wane,
Faded before him, cower'd, nor could re-
 strain
Her fearful sobs, self-folding like a flower
That faints into itself at evening hour:
But the God fostering her chilled hand, 140
She felt the warmth, her eyelids open'd
 bland,
And, like new flowers at morning song of
 bees,
Bloom'd, and gave up her honey to the
 lees.
Into the green-recessed woods they flew;
Nor grew they pale, as mortal lovers do.

 Left to herself, the serpent now began
To change; her elfin blood in madness ran,
Her mouth foam'd, and the grass, there-
 with besprent,
Wither'd at dew so sweet and virulent;
Her eyes in torture fix'd, and anguish
 drear, 150
Hot, glazed, and wide, with lid-lashes all
 sear,
Flash'd phosphor and sharp sparks, without
 one cooling tear.
The colours all inflamed throughout her
 train,
She writhed about, convulsed with scarlet
 pain:
A deep volcanian yellow took the place
Of all her milder-mooned body's grace;
And, as the lava ravishes the mead,
Spoilt all her silver mail, and golden brede:
Made gloom of all her frecklings, streaks
 and bars,
Eclipsed her crescents, and lick'd up her
 stars: 160
So that, in moments few, she was undrest
Of all her sapphires, greens, and amethyst,
And rubious-argent: of all these bereft,

Nothing but pain and ugliness were left.
Still shone her crown; that vanish'd, also she
Melted and disappear'd as suddenly;
And in the air, her new voice luting soft,
Cried, 'Lycius! gentle Lycius!'—Borne aloft
With the bright mists about the mountains hoar
These words dissolved: Crete's forests heard no more. 170

Whither fled Lamia, now a lady bright,
A full-born beauty new and exquisite?
She fled into that valley they pass o'er
Who go to Corinth from Cenchreas' shore:
And rested at the foot of those wild hills,
The rugged founts of the Peræan rills,
And of that other ridge whose barren back
Stretches, with all its mist and cloudy rack,
South-westward to Cleone. There she stood 179
About a young bird's flutter from a wood,
Fair, on a sloping green of mossy tread,
By a clear pool, wherein she passioned
To see herself escaped from so sore ills,
While her robes flaunted with the daffo-dils.

Ah, happy Lycius!—for she was a maid
More beautiful than ever twisted braid,
Or sigh'd, or blush'd, or on spring-flowered lea
Spread a green kirtle to the minstrelsy:
A virgin purest lipp'd, yet in the lore
Of love deep learned to the red heart's core: 190
Not one hour old, yet of sciential brain
To unperplex bliss from its neighbour pain;
Define their pettish limits, and estrange
Their points of contact, and swift counter-change;
Intrigue with the specious chaos, and dis-part
Its most ambiguous atoms with sure art;
As though in Cupid's college she had spent

Sweet days a lovely graduate, still unshent,
And kept his rosy terms in idle languish-ment.

Why this fair creature chose so fairily
By the wayside to linger, we shall see; 201
But first 't is fit to tell how she could muse
And dream, when in the serpent prison-house,
Of all she list, strange or magnificent:
How, ever, where she will'd, her spirit went;
Whether to faint Elysium, or where
Down through tress-lifting waves the Ne-reids fair
Wind into Thetis' bower by many a pearly stair;
Or where God Bacchus drains his cups divine,
Stretch'd out, at ease, beneath a glutinous pine; 210
Or where in Pluto's gardens palatine
Mulciber's columns gleam in far piazzian line.
And sometimes into cities she would send
Her dream, with feast and rioting to blend;
And once, while among mortals dreaming thus,
She saw the young Corinthian Lycius
Charioting foremost in the envious race,
Like a young Jove with calm uneager face,
And fell into a swooning love of him. 219
Now on the moth-time of that evening dim
He would return that way, as well she knew,
To Corinth from the shore; for freshly blew
The eastern soft wind, and his galley now
Grated the quay-stones with her brazen prow
In port Cenchreas, from Egina isle
Fresh anchor'd; whither he had been awhile
To sacrifice to Jove, whose temple there
Waits with high marble doors for blood and incense rare.
Jove heard his vows, and better'd his de-sire;

For by some freakful chance he made re-
 tire 230
From his companions, and set forth to
 walk,
Perhaps grown wearied of their Corinth
 talk:
Over the solitary hills he fared,
Thoughtless at first, but ere eve's star ap-
 pear'd
His phantasy was lost, where reason fades,
In the calm'd twilight of Platonic shades.
Lamia beheld him coming, near, more
 near —
Close to her passing, in indifference drear,
His silent sandals swept the mossy green;
So neighbour'd to him, and yet so unseen 240
She stood: he pass'd, shut up in mysteries,
His mind wrapp'd like his mantle, while
 her eyes
Follow'd his steps, and her neck regal
 white
Turn'd — syllabling thus, 'Ah, Lycius
 bright!
And will you leave me on the hills alone ?
Lycius, look back! and be some pity shown.'
He did; not with cold wonder fearingly,
But Orpheus-like at an Eurydice;
For so delicious were the words she sung,
It seem'd he had loved them a whole sum-
 mer long: 250
And soon his eyes had drunk her beauty
 up,
Leaving no drop in the bewildering cup,
And still the cup was full, — while he,
 afraid
Lest she should vanish ere his lips had paid
Due adoration, thus began to adore;
Her soft look growing coy, she saw his
 chain so sure:
'Leave thee alone! Look back! Ah, God-
 dess, see
Whether my eyes can ever turn from thee !
For pity do not this sad heart belie —
Even as thou vanishest so I shall die. 260
Stay ! though a Naiad of the rivers, stay !
To thy far wishes will thy streams obey:
Stay ! though the greenest woods be thy
 domain,

Alone they can drink up the morning rain:
Though a descended Pleiad, will not one
Of thine harmonious sisters keep in tune
Thy spheres, and as thy silver proxy shine ?
So sweetly to these ravish'd ears of mine
Came thy sweet greeting, that if thou
 shouldst fade,
Thy memory will waste me to a shade: —
For pity do not melt !' — 'If I should
 stay,' 271
Said Lamia, 'here, upon this floor of clay,
And pain my steps upon these flowers too
 rough,
What canst thou say or do of charm enough
To dull the nice remembrance of my home ?
Thou canst not ask me with thee here to
 roam
Over these hills and vales, where no joy
 is, —
Empty of immortality and bliss !
Thou art a scholar, Lycius, and must know
That finer spirits cannot breathe below 280
In human climes, and live: Alas ! poor
 youth,
What taste of purer air hast thou to soothe
My essence ? What serener palaces,
Where I may all my many senses please,
And by mysterious sleights a hundred thirsts
 appease ?
It cannot be — Adieu !' So said, she rose
Tiptoe with white arms spread. He, sick
 to lose
The amorous promise of her lone complain,
Swoon'd murmuring of love, and pale with
 pain.
The cruel lady, without any show 290
Of sorrow for her tender favourite's woe,
But rather, if her eyes could brighter be,
With brighter eyes and slow amenity,
Put her new lips to his, and gave afresh
The life she had so tangled in her mesh:
And as he from one trance was wakening
Into another, she began to sing,
Happy in beauty, life, and love, and every
 thing,
A song of love, too sweet for earthly lyres,
While, like held breath, the stars drew in
 their panting fires. 300

And then she whisper'd in such trembling
tone,
As those who, safe together met alone
For the first time through many anguish'd
days,
Use other speech than looks; bidding him
raise
His drooping head, and clear his soul of
doubt,
For that she was a woman, and without
Any more subtle fluid in her veins
Than throbbing blood, and that the self-
same pains
Inhabited her frail-strung heart as his.
And next she wonder'd how his eyes could
miss 310
Her face so long in Corinth, where, she
said,
She dwelt but half retired, and there had
led
Days happy as the gold coin could invent
Without the aid of love; yet in content
Till she saw him, as once she pass'd him by,
Where 'gainst a column he leant thought-
fully
At Venus' temple porch, 'mid baskets
heap'd
Of amorous herbs and flowers, newly reap'd
Late on that eve, as 't was the night before
The Adonian feast; whereof she saw no
more, 320
But wept alone those days, for why should
she adore ?
Lycius from death awoke into amaze,
To see her still, and singing so sweet lays;
Then from amaze into delight he fell
To hear her whisper woman's lore so well;
And every word she spake enticed him on
To unperplex'd delight and pleasure known.
Let the mad poets say whate'er they please
Of the sweets of Fairies, Peris, Goddesses,
There is not such a treat among them
all, 330
Haunters of cavern, lake, and waterfall,
As a real woman, lineal indeed
From Pyrrha's pebbles or old Adam's seed.
Thus gentle Lamia judged, and judged
aright,

That Lycius could not love in half a fright,
So threw the goddess off, and won his heart
More pleasantly by playing woman's part,
With no more awe than what her beauty
gave,
That, while it smote, still guaranteed to
save.
Lycius to all made eloquent reply, 340
Marrying to every word a twin-born sigh:
And last, pointing to Corinth, ask'd her
sweet,
If 't was too far that night for her soft
feet.
The way was short, for Lamia's eagerness
Made, by a spell, the triple league decrease
To a few paces; not at all surmised
By blinded Lycius, so in her comprised:
They pass'd the city gates, he knew not how,
So noiseless, and he never thought to know.

As men talk in a dream, so Corinth all, 350
Throughout her palaces imperial,
And all her populous streets and temples
lewd,
Mutter'd, like tempest in the distance
brew'd,
To the wide-spreaded night above her
towers.
Men, women, rich and poor, in the cool
hours,
Shuffled their sandals o'er the pavement
white,
Companion'd or alone; while many a light
Flared, here and there, from wealthy festi-
vals,
And threw their moving shadows on the
walls,
Or found them cluster'd in the corniced
shade 360
Of some arch'd temple door, or dusky
colonnade.

Muffling his face, of greeting friends in
fear,
Her fingers he press'd hard, as one came
near
With curl'd gray beard, sharp eyes, and
smooth bald crown,

Slow-stepp'd, and robed in philosophic
 gown:
Lycius shrank closer, as they met and
 past,
Into his mantle, adding wings to haste,
While hurried Lamia trembled: ' Ah,' said
 he,
' Why do you shudder, love, so ruefully ?
Why does your tender palm dissolve in
 dew ? '— 370
' I 'm wearied,' said fair Lamia: ' tell me
 who
Is that old man ? I cannot bring to mind
His features: — Lycius ! wherefore did you
 blind
Yourself from his quick eyes ? ' Lycius
 replied,
' 'T is Apollonius sage, my trusty guide
And good instructor; but to-night he seems
The ghost of folly haunting my sweet
 dreams.'

 While yet he spake they had arrived
 before
A pillar'd porch, with lofty portal door,
Where hung a silver lamp, whose phosphor
 glow 380
Reflected in the slabbed steps below,
Mild as a star in water; for so new
And so unsullied was the marble hue,
So through the crystal polish, liquid fine,
Ran the dark veins, that none but feet
 divine
Could e'er have touch'd there. Sounds
 Æolian
Breathed from the hinges, as the ample
 span
Of the wide doors disclosed a place un-
 known
Some time to any, but those two alone,
And a few Persian mutes, who that same
 year 390
Were seen about the markets: none knew
 where
They could inhabit; the most curious
Were foil'd, who watch'd to trace them to
 their house:
And but the flitter-winged verse must tell,

For truth's sake, what woe afterwards
 befell,
'T would humour many a heart to leave
 them thus,
Shut from the busy world of more incredu-
 lous.

PART II

LOVE in a hut, with water and a crust,
Is — Love, forgive us ! — cinders, ashes,
 dust;
Love in a palace is perhaps at last
More grievous torment than a hermit's
 fast: —
That is a doubtful tale from faery land,
Hard for the non-elect to understand.
Had Lycius lived to hand his story down,
He might have given the moral a fresh
 frown,
Or clench'd it quite: but too short was
 their bliss
To breed distrust and hate, that make the
 soft voice hiss. 10
Besides, there, nightly, with terrific glare,
Love, jealous grown of so complete a pair,
Hover'd and buzz'd his wings, with fearful
 roar,
Above the lintel of their chamber door,
And down the passage cast a glow upon
 the floor.

 For all this came a ruin: side by side
They were enthroned, in the even tide,
Upon a couch, near to a curtaining
Whose airy texture, from a golden string,
Floated into the room, and let appear 20
Unveil'd the summer heaven, blue and
 clear,
Betwixt two marble shafts: — there they
 reposed,
Where use had made it sweet, with eyelids
 closed,
Saving a tithe which love still open kept,
That they might see each other while they
 almost slept;
When from the slope side of a suburb
 hill,

Deafening the swallow's twitter, came a
 thrill
Of trumpets — Lycius started — the sounds
 fled,
But left a thought, a buzzing in his head.
For the first time, since first he harbour'd
 in 30
That purple-lined palace of sweet sin,
His spirit pass'd beyond its golden bourn
Into the noisy world almost forsworn.
The lady, ever watchful, penetrant,
Saw this with pain, so arguing a want
Of something more, more than her empery
Of joys; and she began to moan and sigh
Because he mused beyond her, knowing well
That but a moment's thought is passion's
 passing bell.
' Why do you sigh, fair creature ? ' whis-
 per'd he: 40
' Why do you think ? ' return'd she ten-
 derly:
' You have deserted me; — where am I
 now ?
Not in your heart while care weighs on
 your brow:
No, no, you have dismiss'd me; and I go
From your breast houseless: aye, it must be
 so.'
He answer'd, bending to her open eyes,
Where he was mirror'd small in paradise,
' My silver planet, both of eve and morn !
Why will you plead yourself so sad forlorn,
While I am striving how to fill my heart 50
With deeper crimson, and a double smart ?
How to entangle, trammel up and snare
Your soul in mine, and labyrinth you
 there,
Like the hid scent in an unbudded rose ?
Aye, a sweet kiss — you see your mighty
 woes.
My thoughts ! shall I unveil them ? Lis-
 ten then !
What mortal hath a prize, that other men
May be confounded and abash'd withal,
But lets it sometimes pace abroad majes-
 tical,
And triumph, as in thee I should rejoice 60
Amid the hoarse alarm of Corinth's voice.

Let my foes choke, and my friends shout
 afar,
While through the thronged streets your
 bridal car
Wheels round its dazzling spokes.' — The
 lady's cheek
Trembled; she nothing said, but, pale and
 meek,
Arose and knelt before him, wept a rain
Of sorrows at his words ; at last with
 pain
Beseeching him, the while his hand she
 wrung,
To change his purpose. He thereat was
 stung,
Perverse, with stronger fancy to reclaim 70
Her wild and timid nature to his aim;
Besides, for all his love, in self despite,
Against his better self, he took delight
Luxurious in her sorrows, soft and new.
His passion, cruel grown, took on a hue
Fierce and sanguineous as 't was possible
In one whose brow had no dark veins to
 swell.
Fine was the mitigated fury, like
Apollo's presence when in act to strike
The serpent — Ha ! the serpent ! certes,
 she 80
Was none. She burnt, she loved the
 tyranny,
And, all subdued, consented to the hour
When to the bridal he should lead his par-
 amour.
Whispering in midnight silence, said the
 youth,
' Sure some sweet name thou hast, though,
 by my truth,
I have not ask'd it, ever thinking thee
Not mortal, but of heavenly progeny,
As still I do. Hast any mortal name,
Fit appellation for this dazzling frame ?
Or friends or kinsfolk on the citied earth,
To share our marriage feast and nuptial
 mirth ? ' 91
' I have no friends,' said Lamia, ' no, not
 one;
My presence in wide Corinth hardly known:
My parents' bones are in their dusty urns

Sepulchred, where no kindled incense
　　burns,
Seeing all their luckless race are dead,
　　save me,
And I neglect the holy rite for thee.
Even as you list invite your many guests;
But if, as now it seems, your vision rests
With any pleasure on me, do not bid　　100
Old Apollonius — from him keep me hid.'
Lycius, perplex'd at words so blind and
　　blank,
Made close inquiry; from whose touch she
　　shrank,
Feigning a sleep; and he to the dull shade
Of deep sleep in a moment was betray'd.

It was the custom then to bring away
The bride from home at blushing shut of
　　day,
Veil'd, in a chariot, heralded along
By strewn flowers, torches, and a marriage
　　song,
With other pageants: but this fair un-
　　known　　110
Had not a friend.　So being left alone,
(Lycius was gone to summon all his kin,)
And knowing surely she could never win
His foolish heart from its mad pompous-
　　ness,
She set herself, high-thoughted, how to
　　dress
The misery in fit magnificence.
She did so, but 't is doubtful how and
　　whence
Came, and who were her subtle servitors.
About the halls, and to and from the doors,
There was a noise of wings, till in short
　　space　　120
The glowing banquet - room shone with
　　wide-arched grace.
A haunting music, sole perhaps and lone
Supportress of the faery-roof, made moan
Throughout, as fearful the whole charm
　　might fade.
Fresh carved cedar, mimicking a glade
Of palm and plantain, met from either side,
High in the midst, in honour of the bride:
Two palms and then two plantains, and so on,

From either side their stems branch'd one
　　to one
All down the aisled place; and beneath all
There ran a stream of lamps straight on
　　from wall to wall.　　131
So canopied, lay an untasted feast
Teeming with odours.　Lamia, regal drest,
Silently paced about, and as she went,
In pale contented sort of discontent,
Mission'd her viewless servants to enrich
The fretted splendour of each nook and
　　niche.
Between the tree-stems, marbled plain at
　　first,
Came jasper panels; then, anon, there burst
Forth creeping imagery of slighter trees, 140
And with the larger wove in small intrica-
　　cies.
Approving all, she faded at self-will,
And shut the chamber up, close, hush'd
　　and still,
Complete and ready for the revels rude,
When dreadful guests would come to spoil
　　her solitude.

　　The day appear'd, and all the gossip
　　rout.
O senseless Lycius!　Madman! wherefore
　　flout
The silent-blessing fate, warm cloister'd
　　hours,
And show to common eyes these secret
　　bowers?
The herd approach'd; each guest, with busy
　　brain,　　150
Arriving at the portal, gazed amain,
And enter'd marvelling: for they knew the
　　street,
Remember'd it from childhood all complete
Without a gap, yet ne'er before had seen
That royal porch, that high-built fair de-
　　mesne;
So in they hurried all, mazed, curious and
　　keen:
Save one, who look'd thereon with eye se-
　　vere,
And with calm-planted steps walk'd in aus-
　　tere:

'T was Apollonius: something too he
 laugh'd,
As though some knotty problem, that had
 daft 160
His patient thought, had now begun to
 thaw,
And solve and melt: — 't was just as he
 foresaw.

He met within the murmurous vestibule
His young disciple. ' 'T is no common rule,
Lycius,' said he, 'for uninvited guest
To force himself upon you, and infest
With an unbidden presence the bright
 throng
Of younger friends; yet must I do this
 wrong,
And you forgive me.' Lycius blush'd, and
 led
The old man through the inner doors broad-
 spread; 170
With reconciling words and courteous mien
Turning into sweet milk the sophist's
 spleen.

Of wealthy lustre was the banquet-room,
Fill'd with pervading brilliance and per-
 fume:
Before each lucid panel fuming stood
A censer fed with myrrh and spiced wood,
Each by a sacred tripod held aloft,
Whose slender feet wide-swerved upon the
 soft
Wool - woofed carpets: fifty wreaths of
 smoke
From fifty censers their light voyage took
To the high roof, still mimick'd as they
 rose 181
Along the mirror'd walls by twin-clouds
 odorous.
Twelve sphered tables, by silk seats in-
 spher'd,
High as the level of a man's breast rear'd
On libbard's paws, upheld the heavy gold
Of cups and goblets, and the store thrice told
Of Ceres' horn, and, in huge vessels, wine
Came from the gloomy tun with merry
 shine.

Thus loaded with a feast the tables stood,
Each shrining in the midst the image of a
 God. 190

When in an antechamber every guest
Had felt the cold full sponge to pleasure
 press'd,
By ministering slaves, upon his hands and
 feet,
And fragrant oils with ceremony meet
Pour'd on his hair, they all moved to the
 feast
In white robes, and themselves in order
 placed
Around the silken couches, wondering
Whence all this mighty cost and blaze of
 wealth could spring.

Soft went the music the soft air along,
While fluent Greek a vowel'd under-song
Kept up among the guests, discoursing
 low 201
At first, for scarcely was the wine at flow;
But when the happy vintage touch'd their
 brains,
Louder they talk, and louder come the
 strains
Of powerful instruments: — the gorgeous
 dyes,
The space, the splendour of the draperies,
The roof of awful richness, nectarous cheer,
Beautiful slaves, and Lamia's self, appear,
Now, when the wine has done its rosy
 deed,
And every soul from human trammels
 freed, 210
No more so strange; for merry wine, sweet
 wine,
Will make Elysian shades not too fair, too
 divine.
Soon was God Bacchus at meridian height;
Flush'd were their cheeks, and bright eyes
 double bright:
Garlands of every green, and every scent
From vales deflower'd, or forest - trees
 branch-rent,
In baskets of bright osier'd gold were
 brought

High as the handles heap'd, to suit the
 thought
Of every guest: that each, as he did please,
Might fancy-fit his brows, silk-pillow'd at
 his ease. 220

 What wreath for Lamia? What for Ly-
 cius?
What for the sage, old Apollonius?
Upon her aching forehead be there hung
The leaves of willow and of adder's tongue;
And for the youth, quick, let us strip for
 him
The thyrsus, that his watching eyes may
 swim
Into forgetfulness; and, for the sage,
Let spear-grass and the spiteful thistle
 wage
War on his temples. Do not all charms fly
At the mere touch of cold philosophy? 230
There was an awful rainbow once in
 heaven:
We know her woof, her texture; she is
 given
In the dull catalogue of common things.
Philosophy will clip an Angel's wings,
Conquer all mysteries by rule and line,
Empty the haunted air, and gnomed mine —
Unweave a rainbow, as it erewhile made
The tender-person'd Lamia melt into a
 shade.

 By her glad Lycius sitting, in chief place,
Scarce saw in all the room another face, 240
Till, checking his love trance, a cup he
 took
Full brimm'd, and opposite sent forth a
 look
'Cross the broad table, to beseech a glance
From his old teacher's wrinkled counte-
 nance,
And pledge him. The bald-head philoso-
 pher
Had fix'd his eye, without a twinkle or
 stir,
Full on the alarmed beauty of the bride,
Brow-beating her fair form, and troubling
 her sweet pride.

Lycius then press'd her hand, with devout
 touch,
As pale it lay upon the rosy couch: 250
'T was icy, and the cold ran through his
 veins;
Then sudden it grew hot, and all the pains
Of an unnatural heat shot to his heart.
'Lamia, what means this? Wherefore dost
 thou start?
Know'st thou that man?' Poor Lamia an-
 swer'd not.
He gazed into her eyes, and not a jot
Own'd they the lovelorn piteous appeal:
More, more he gazed: his human senses
 reel:
Some hungry spell that loveliness absorbs:
There was no recognition in those orbs. 260
'Lamia!' he cried — and no soft-toned
 reply.
The many heard, and the loud revelry
Grew hush: the stately music no more
 breathes;
The myrtle sicken'd in a thousand wreaths.
By faint degrees, voice, lute, and pleasure
 ceased;
A deadly silence step by step increased,
Until it seem'd a horrid presence there,
And not a man but felt the terror in his
 hair.
'Lamia!' he shriek'd; and nothing but
 the shriek
With its sad echo did the silence break. 270
'Begone, foul dream!' he cried, gazing
 again
In the bride's face, where now no azure
 vein
Wander'd on fair-spaced temples; no soft
 bloom
Misted the cheek; no passion to illume
The deep-recessed vision: — all was blight;
Lamia, no longer fair, there sat a deadly
 white.
'Shut, shut those juggling eyes, thou ruth-
 less man!
Turn them aside, wretch! or the righteous
 ban
Of all the Gods, whose dreadful images
Here represent their shadowy presences,

May pierce them on the sudden with the
thorn 281
Of painful blindness ; leaving thee for-
lorn,
In trembling dotage to the feeblest fright
Of conscience, for their long - offended
might,
For all thine impious proud-heart sophis-
tries,
Unlawful magic, and enticing lies.
Corinthians ! look upon that gray-beard
wretch !
Mark how, possess'd, his lashless eyelids
stretch
Around his demon eyes ! Corinthians, see !
My sweet bride withers at their potency.' 290
' Fool ! ' said the sophist, in an under-tone
Gruff with contempt; which a death-nigh-
ing moan
From Lycius answer'd, as heart-struck and
lost,
He sank supine beside the aching ghost.
' Fool ! Fool ! ' repeated he, while his eyes
still

Relented not, nor moved; ' from every ill
Of life have I preserved thee to this day,
And shall I see thee made a serpent's
prey ? '
Then Lamia breathed death breath; the
sophist's eye,
Like a sharp spear, went through her ut-
terly, 300
Keen, cruel, perceant, stinging: she, as
well
As her weak hand could any meaning tell,
Motion'd him to be silent; vainly so,
He look'd and look'd again a level — No !
' A serpent ! ' echoed he; no sooner said,
Than with a frightful scream she vanished:
And Lycius' arms were empty of delight,
As were his limbs of life, from that same
night.
On the high couch he lay ! — his friends
came round —
Supported him — no pulse or breath they
found, 310
And, in its marriage robe, the heavy body
wound.

TRAGEDIES

OTHO THE GREAT

A TRAGEDY IN FIVE ACTS

When Keats went to the Isle of Wight in the early summer of 1819, it was with the determination to make his literary powers yield him a support, and the theatre, which he knew well, offered the surest means, in his judgment, for an immediate return. There was, indeed, something of a literary revival of the drama at this time, and Keats had often discussed with his friends the merits of plays then before the public, and especially the character of Kean's acting. They were rather skeptical of Keats's ability to produce a successful play, and their doubts had some good basis, if we may judge from the account which Charles Armitage Brown gives of Keats's mode of composition. Lord Houghton quotes the following from a manuscript by Brown, who was Keats's companion at Shanklin: 'At Shanklin he undertook a difficult task: I engaged to furnish him with the title, characters and dramatic conduct of a tragedy, and he was to enwrap it in poetry. The progress of this work was curious, for while I sat opposite to him, he caught my description of each scene entire, with the characters to be brought forward, the events, and everything connected with it. Thus he went on, scene after scene, never knowing nor enquiring into the scene which was to follow, until four acts were completed. It was then he required to know at once all the events that were to occupy the fifth act; I explained them to him, but, after a patient hearing and some thought, he insisted that many incidents in it were too humorous, or, as he termed them, too melodramatic. He wrote the fifth act in accordance with his own views, and so contented was I with his poetry that at the time, and for a long time after, I thought he was in the right.'

Keats himself says little of the tragedy, except as a piece of work solely designed for pro-fit. 'Brown and I,' he writes to John Taylor, his publisher, 'have together been engaged (this I should wish to remain secret) on a Tragedy which I have just finished and from which we hope to share moderate profits. . . . I feel every confidence that, if I choose, I may be a popular writer. That I will never be; but for all that I will get a livelihood.' He wrote shortly after to the same friend: 'Brown likes the tragedy very much. But he is not a fit judge of it, as I have only acted as midwife to his plot; and of course he will be fond of his child.' The money to be got from the tragedy was uppermost in his mind when he wrote to his brother George, who shared his pecuniary difficulties: 'We are certainly in a very low estate — I say we, for I am in such a situation, that were it not for the assistance of Brown and Taylor, I must be as badly off as a man can be. I could not raise any sum by the promise of any poem, no, not by the mortgage of my intellect. We must wait a little while. I really have hopes of success. I have finished a tragedy, which if it succeeds will enable me to sell what I may have in manuscript to a good advantage. I have passed my time in reading, writing, and fretting — the last I intend to give up, and stick to the other two. They are the only chances of benefit to us. . . . Take matters as coolly as you can; and confidently expecting help from England, act as if no help were nigh. Mine, I am sure, is a tolerable tragedy; it would have been a bank to me, if just as I had finished it, I had not heard of Kean's resolution to go to America. That was the worst news I could have had. There is no actor can do the principal character besides Kean. At Covent Garden there is a great chance of its being damn'd. Were it to succeed even there it would lift me out of the mire; I mean the mire of a bad reputation which is continually rising against me. My name with the literary fashionables is vulgar. I am a weaver-boy to them. A tragedy would

lift me out of this mess, and mess it is as far as regards our pockets.'

Keats continued to pin his faith on Kean. 'The report seems now,' he writes to the same, September 27, 'more in favour of Kean's stopping in England. If he should I have confident hopes of our tragedy. If he invokes the hot-blooded character of Ludolph, — and he is the only actor that can do it, — he will add to

his own fame and improve my fortune.' Keats waited with slowly ebbing hopes. Elliston read it, but wished to put it off till another season. 'Perhaps,' Keats writes in December, 'we may give it another furbish, and try it at Covent Garden. 'T would do one's heart good to see Macready in Ludolph.' But the play never was acted at either Drury Lane or Covent Garden.

OTHO THE GREAT

DRAMATIS PERSONÆ

OTHO THE GREAT, *Emperor of Germany.*
LUDOLPH, *his Son.*
CONRAD, *Duke of Franconia.*
ALBERT, *a Knight, favoured by Otho.*
SIGIFRED, *an Officer, friend of Ludolph.*
THEODORE, } *Officers.*
GONFRED, }
ETHELBERT, *an Abbot.*
GERSA, *Prince of Hungary.*
An Hungarian Captain.
Physician.
Page.
Nobles, Knights, Attendants, and Soldiers.
ERMINIA, *Niece of Otho.*
AURANTHE, *Conrad's Sister.*
Ladies and Attendants.
SCENE. — *The Castle of Friedburg, its vicinity, and the Hungarian Camp.*
TIME. — *One Day.*

ACT I

SCENE I. — *An Apartment in the Castle*

Enter CONRAD.

Conrad. So, I am safe emerged from these broils!
Amid the wreck of thousands I am whole;
For every crime I have a laurel-wreath,
For every lie a lordship. Nor yet has
My ship of fortune furl'd her silken sails, —
Let her glide on! This danger'd neck is saved,
By dexterous policy, from the rebel's axe;
And of my ducal palace not one stone
Is bruised by the Hungarian petards.
Toil hard, ye slaves, and from the miser-earth 10
Bring forth once more my bullion, treasured deep,

With all my jewel'd salvers, silver and gold,
And precious goblets that make rich the wine.
But why do I stand babbling to myself?
Where is Auranthe? I have news for her
Shall —

Enter AURANTHE.

Auranthe. Conrad! what tidings? Good, if I may guess
From your alert eyes and high-lifted brows.
What tidings of the battle? Albert? Ludolph? Otho?
Conrad. You guess aright. And, sister, slurring o'er
Our by-gone quarrels, I confess my heart
Is beating with a child's anxiety, 21
To make our golden fortune known to you.
Auranthe. So serious?
Conrad. Yes, so serious, that before
I utter even the shadow of a hint
Concerning what will make that sin-worn cheek
Blush joyous blood through every lineament,
You must make here a solemn vow to me.
Auranthe. I pr'ythee, Conrad, do not overact
The hypocrite. What vow would you impose?
Conrad. Trust me for once. That you may be assured 30
'T is not confiding to a broken reed,
A poor court-bankrupt, outwitted and lost,

Revolve these facts in your acutest mood,
In such a mood as now you listen to me: —
A few days since, I was an open rebel, —
Against the Emperor, had suborn'd his
 son, —
Drawn off his nobles to revolt, — and
 shown
Contented fools causes for discontent,
Fresh hatched in my ambition's eagle-nest;
So thrived I as a rebel, — and, behold ! 40
Now I am Otho's favourite, his dear friend,
His right hand, his brave Conrad.

Auranthe. I confess
You have intrigued with these unsteady
 times
To admiration; but to be a favourite —

Conrad. I saw my moment. The Hun-
 garians,
Collected silently in holes and corners,
Appear'd, a sudden host, in the open day.
I should have perish'd in our empire's
 wreck,
But, calling interest loyalty, swore faith
To most believing Otho; and so help'd 50
His blood-stain'd ensigns to the victory
In yesterday's hard fight, that it has turn'd
The edge of his sharp wrath to eager kind-
 ness.

Auranthe. So far yourself. But what is
 this to me
More than that I am glad ? I gratulate
 you.

Conrad. Yes, sister, but it does regard
 you greatly,
Nearly, momentously, — aye, painfully !
Make me this vow —

Auranthe. Concerning whom or what ?

Conrad. Albert !

Auranthe. I would inquire somewhat of
 him:
You had a letter from me touching him ? 60
No treason 'gainst his head in deed or
 word !
Surely you spared him at my earnest
 prayer ?
Give me the letter — it should not ex-
 ist !

Conrad. At one pernicious charge of the
 enemy,
I, for a moment-whiles, was prisoner ta'en
And rifled, — stuff ! the horses' hoofs have
 minced it !

Auranthe. He is alive ?

Conrad. He is ! but here make oath
To alienate him from your scheming brain,
Divorce him from your solitary thoughts,
And cloud him in such utter banishment, 70
That when his person meets again your
 eye,
Your vision shall quite lose its memory,
And wander past him as through vacancy.

Auranthe. I 'll not be perjured.

Conrad. No, nor great, nor mighty;
You would not wear a crown, or rule a
 kingdom.
To you it is indifferent.

Auranthe. What means this ?

Conrad. You 'll not be perjured ! Go to
 Albert then,
That camp-mushroom — dishonour of our
 house.
Go, page his dusty heels upon a march,
Furbish his jingling baldric while he sleeps,
And share his mouldy ration in a siege. 81
Yet stay, — perhaps a charm may call you
 back,
And make the widening circlets of your
 eyes
Sparkle with healthy fevers. — The Em-
 peror
Hath given consent that you should marry
 Ludolph !

Auranthe. Can it be, brother ? For a
 golden crown
With a queen's awful lips I doubly thank
 you !
This is to wake in Paradise ! Farewell
Thou clod of yesterday — 't was not my-
 self !
Not till this moment did I ever feel 90
My spirit's faculties ! I 'll flatter you
For this, and be you ever proud of it;
Thou, Jove-like, struck'dst thy forehead,
And from the teeming marrow of thy brain

I spring complete Minerva! but the
 prince —
His highness Ludolph — where is he?
 Conrad. I know not:
When, lackying my counsel at a beck,
The rebel lords, on bended knees, received
The Emperor's pardon, Ludolph kept aloof,
Sole, in a stiff, fool-hardy, sulky pride; 100
Yet, for all this, I never saw a father
In such a sickly longing for his son.
We shall soon see him, for the Emperor
He will be here this morning.
 Auranthe. That I heard
Among the midnight rumours from the
 camp.
 Conrad. You give up Albert to me?
 Auranthe. Harm him not!
E'en for his highness Ludolph's sceptry
 hand,
I would not Albert suffer any wrong.
 Conrad. Have I not laboured, plotted — ?
 Auranthe. See you spare him:
Nor be pathetic, my kind benefactor! 110
On all the many bounties of your hand, —
'T was for yourself you laboured — not for
 me!
Do you not count, when I am queen, to
 take
Advantage of your chance discoveries
Of my poor secrets, and so hold a rod
Over my life?
 Conrad. Let not this slave — this vil-
 lain —
Be cause of feud between us. See! he
 comes!
Look, woman, look, your Albert is quite
 safe!
In haste it seems. Now shall I be in the
 way,
And wish'd with silent curses in my grave,
Or side by side with' whelmed mariners. 121

Enter ALBERT.

 Albert. Fair on your graces fall this
 early morrow!
So it is like to do without my prayers,
For your right noble names, like favourite
 tunes,

Have fallen full frequent from our Em-
 peror's lips,
High commented with smiles.
 Auranthe. Noble Albert!
 Conrad (*aside*). Noble!
 Auranthe. Such salutation argues a glad
 heart
In our prosperity. We thank you, sir.
 Albert. Lady!
O, would to Heaven your poor servant
Could do you better service than mere
 words! 130
But I have other greeting than mine own,
From no less man than Otho, who has sent
This ring as pledge of dearest amity;
'T is chosen I hear from Hymen's jewelry,
And you will prize it, lady, I doubt not,
Beyond all pleasures past, and all to come.
To you great duke —
 Conrad. To me! What of me, ha?
 Albert. What pleased your grace to say?
 Conrad. Your message, sir!
 Albert. You mean not this to me?
 Conrad. Sister, this way;
For there shall be no 'gentle Alberts' now,
 [*Aside.*
No 'sweet Auranthes!' 141
 [*Exeunt* CONRAD *and* AURANTHE.
 Albert (*solus*). The duke is out of temper;
 if he knows
More than a brother of his sister ought,
I should not quarrel with his peevishness.
Auranthe — Heaven preserve her always
 fair! —
Is in the heady, proud, ambitious vein;
I bicker not with her, — bid her farewell!
She has taken flight from me, then let her
 soar, —
He is a fool who stands at pining gaze!
But for poor Ludolph, he is food for sor-
 row: 150
No leveling bluster of my licensed thoughts,
No military swagger of my mind,
Can smother from myself the wrong I've
 done him, —
Without design indeed, — yet it is so, —
And opiate for the conscience have I none!
 [*Exit.*

SCENE II. — *The Court-yard of the Castle*

Martial Music. Enter, from the outer gate, OTHO, *Nobles, Knights, and Attendants. The Soldiers halt at the gate, with Banners in sight.*

Otho. Where is my noble Herald?

Enter CONRAD, *from the Castle, attended by two Knights and Servants.* ALBERT *following.*

 Well, hast told
Auranthe our intent imperial?
Lest our rent banners, too o' the sudden
 shown,
Should fright her silken casements, and
 dismay
Her household to our lack of entertain-
 ment.
A victory!
 Conrad. God save illustrious Otho!
 Otho. Aye, Conrad, it will pluck out all
 gray hairs;
It is the best physician for the spleen;
The courtliest inviter to a feast;
The subtlest excuser of small faults; 10
And a nice judge in the age and smack of
 wine.

Enter from the Castle, AURANTHE, *followed by Pages, holding up her robes, and a train of Women. She kneels.*

Hail my sweet hostess! I do thank the
 stars,
Or my good soldiers, or their ladies' eyes,
That, after such a merry battle fought,
I can, all safe in body and in soul,
Kiss your fair hand and lady fortune's too.
My ring! now, on my life, it doth rejoice
These lips to feel 't on this soft ivory!
Keep it, my brightest daughter; it may
 prove
The little prologue to a line of kings. 20
I strove against thee and my hot-blood son,
Dull blockhead that I was to be so blind,
But now my sight is clear; forgive me,
 lady.

Auranthe. My lord, I was a vassal to
 your frown,
And now your favour makes me but more
 humble;
In wintry winds the simple snow is safe,
But fadeth at the greeting of the sun:
Unto thine anger I might well have spoken,
Taking on me a woman's privilege,
But this so sudden kindness makes me
 dumb. 30
 Otho. What need of this? Enough, if
 you will be
A potent tutoress to my wayward boy.
And teach him, what it seems his nurse
 could not,
To say, for once, I thank you! Sigifred!
 Albert. He has not yet returned, my
 gracious liege.
 Otho. What then! No tidings of my
 friendly Arab?
 Conrad. None, mighty Otho.
 [*To one of his Knights who goes out.*
 Send forth instantly
An hundred horsemen from my honoured
 gates,
To scour the plains and search the cot-
 tages.
Cry a reward, to him who shall first bring
News of that vanished Arabian, 41
A full-heap'd helmet of the purest gold.
 Otho. More thanks, good Conrad; for,
 except my son's,
There is no face I rather would behold
Than that same quick-eyed pagan's. By
 the saints,
This coming night of banquets must not
 light
Her dazzling torches; nor the music
 breathe
Smooth, without clashing cymbal, tones of
 peace
And in-door melodies; nor the ruddy wine
Ebb spouting to the lees; if I pledge not, 50
In my first cup, that Arab!
 Albert. Mighty Monarch,
I wonder not this stranger's victor-deeds
So hang upon your spirit. Twice in the
 fight

It was my chance to meet his olive brow,
Triumphant in the enemy's shatter'd
 rhomb;
And, to say truth, in any Christian arm
I never saw such prowess.
 Otho. Did you ever?
O, 't is a noble boy ! — tut ! — what do I
 say ?
I mean a triple Saladin, whose eyes,
When in the glorious scuffle they met
 mine, 60
Seem'd to say — ' Sleep, old man, in safety
 sleep;
I am the victory !'
 Conrad. Pity he 's not here.
 Otho. And my son too, pity he is not
 here.
Lady Auranthe, I would not make you
 blush,
But can you give a guess where Ludolph
 is ?
Know you not of him ?
 Auranthe. Indeed, my liege, no secret —
 Otho. Nay, nay, without more words,
 dost know of him ?
 Auranthe. I would I were so over-fortu-
 nate,
Both for his sake and mine, and to make
 glad
A father's ears with tidings of his son. 70
 Otho. I see 't is like to be a tedious day.
Were Theodore and Gonfred and the rest
Sent forth with my commands ?
 Albert. Aye, my lord.
 Otho. And no news ! No news ! 'Faith !
 · 't is very strange
He thus avoids us. Lady, is 't not strange ?
Will he be truant to you too ? It is a
 shame.
 Conrad. Will 't please your highness en-
 ter, and accept,
The unworthy welcome of your servant's
 house ?
Leaving your cares to one whose diligence
May in few hours make pleasures of them
 all. 80
 Otho. Not so tedious, Conrad. No, no,
 no, —

I must see Ludolph or the — What 's that
 shout ?
 Voices without. Huzza ! huzza ! Long live
 the Emperor !
 Other voices. Fall back ! Away there !
 Otho. Say what noise is that ?

ALBERT *advancing from the back of the
Stage, whither he had hastened on hearing
the cheers of the soldiery.*

 Albert. It is young Gersa, the Hungarian
 prince,
Pick'd like a red stag from the fallow herd
Of prisoners. Poor prince, forlorn he steps,
Slow, and demure, and proud in his de-
 spair.
If I may judge by his so tragic bearing, 89
His eye not downcast, and his folded arm,
He doth this moment wish himself asleep
Among his fallen captains on yon plains.

 Enter GERSA, *in chains, and guarded.*

 Otho. Well said, Sir Albert.
 Gersa. Not a word of greeting,
No welcome to a princely visitor,
Most mighty Otho ? Will not my great
 host
Vouchsafe a syllable, before he bids
His gentlemen conduct me with all care
To some securest lodging — cold perhaps !
 Otho. What mood is this ? Hath fortune
 touch'd thy brain ?
 Gersa. O kings and princes of this fev'-
 rous world, 100
What abject things, what mockeries must
 ye be,
What nerveless minions of safe palaces !
When here, a monarch, whose proud foot
 is used
To fallen princes' necks, as to his stirrup,
Must needs exclaim that I am mad for-
 sooth,
Because I cannot flatter with bent knees
My conqueror !
 Otho. Gersa, I think you wrong me:
I think I have a better fame abroad.
 Gersa. I pr'ythee mock me not with gen-
 tle speech, 109

But, as a favour, bid me from thy presence;
Let me no longer be the wondering food
Of all these eyes; pr'ythee command me
 hence !
 Otho. Do not mistake me, Gersa. That
 you may not,
Come, fair Auranthe, try if your soft hands
Can manage those hard rivets to set free
So brave a prince and soldier.
 Auranthe (sets him free). Welcome task !
 Gersa. I am wound up in deep astonish-
 ment !
Thank you, fair lady. Otho ! emperor !
You rob me of myself; my dignity
Is now your infant; I am a weak child. 120
 Otho. Give me your hand, and let this
 kindly grasp
Live in our memories.
 Gersa. In mine it will.
I blush to think of my unchasten'd tongue;
But I was haunted by the monstrous ghost
Of all our slain battalions. Sire, reflect,
And pardon you will grant, that, at this
 hour,
The bruised remnants of our stricken camp
Are huddling undistinguish'd my dear
 friends,
With common thousands, into shallow
 graves.
 Otho. Enough, most noble Gersa. You
 are free 130
To cheer the brave remainder of your host
By your own healing presence, and that
 too,
Not as their leader merely, but their king;
For, as I hear, the wily enemy,
Who eased the crownet from your infant
 brows,
Bloody Taraxa, is among the dead.
 Gersa. Then I retire, so generous Otho
 please,
Bearing with me a weight of benefits
Too heavy to be borne.
 Otho. It is not so;
Still understand me, King of Hungary, 140
Nor judge my open purposes awry.
Though I did hold you high in my esteem
For your self's sake, I do not personate

The stage-play emperor to entrap applause,
To set the silly sort o' the world agape,
And make the politic smile; no, I have
 heard
How in the Council you condemn'd this
 war,
Urging the perfidy of broken faith, —
For that I am your friend.
 Gersa. If ever, sire,
You are my enemy, I dare here swear 150
'T will not be Gersa's fault. Otho, fare-
 well !
 Otho. Will you return, Prince, to our
 banqueting ?
 Gersa. As to my father's board I will
 return.
 Otho. Conrad, with all due ceremony,
 give
The prince a regal escort to his camp;
Albert, go thou and bear him company.
Gersa, farewell !
 Gersa. All happiness attend you !
 Otho. Return with what good speed you
 may; for soon
We must consult upon our terms of peace.
 [*Exeunt* GERSA *and* ALBERT *with others.*
And thus a marble column do I build 160
To prop my empire's dome. Conrad, in
 thee
I have another steadfast one, to uphold
The portals of my state; and, for my own
Pre-eminence and safety, I will strive
To keep thy strength upon its pedestal.
For, without thee, this day I might have
 been
A show-monster about the streets of Prague,
In chains, as just now stood that noble
 prince:
And then to me no mercy had been shown,
For when the conquer'd lion is once dun-
 geon'd, 170
Who lets him forth again ? or dares to
 give
An old lion sugar-cakes of mild reprieve ?
Not to thine ear alone I make confession,
But to all here, as, by experience,
I know how the great basement of all
 power

Is frankness, and a true tongue to the
 world;
And how intriguing secrecy is proof
Of fear and weakness, and a hollow state.
Conrad, I owe thee much.
 Conrad. To kiss that hand,
My emperor, is ample recompense, 180
For a mere act of duty.
 Otho. Thou art wrong;
For what can any man on earth do more?
We will make trial of your house's wel-
 come,
My bright Auranthe!
 Conrad. How is Friedburg honoured!

Enter ETHELBERT *and six Monks.*

 Ethelbert. The benison of heaven on your
 head,
Imperial Otho!
 Otho. Who stays me? Speak! Quick!
 Ethelbert. Pause but one moment, mighty
 conqueror!
Upon the threshold of this house of joy.
 Otho. Pray, do not prose, good Ethelbert,
 but speak
What is your purpose.
 Ethelbert. The restoration of some cap-
 tive maids, 190
Devoted to Heaven's pious ministries,
Who, driven forth from their religious
 cells,
And kept in thraldom by our enemy,
When late this province was a lawless spoil,
Still weep amid the wild Hungarian camp,
Though hemm'd around by thy victorious
 arms.
 Otho. Demand the holy sisterhood in our
 name
From Gersa's tents. Farewell, old Ethel-
 bert.
 Ethelbert. The saints will bless you for
 this pious care.
 Otho. Daughter, your hand; Ludolph's
 would fit it best. 200
 Conrad. Ho! let the music sound!
[*Music.* ETHELBERT *raises his hands, as in
 benediction of* OTHO. *Exeunt severally.
 The scene closes on them.*

SCENE III. — *The Country, with the
 Castle in the distance*

Enter LUDOLPH *and* SIGIFRED.

 Ludolph. You have my secret; let it not
 be breathed.
 Sigifred. Still give me leave to wonder
 that the Prince
Ludolph and the swift Arab are the same;
Still to rejoice that 't was a German
 arm
Death doing in a turban'd masquerade.
 Ludolph. The emperor must not know it,
 Sigifred.
 Sigifred. I pr'ythee, why? What hap-
 pier hour of time
Could thy pleased star point down upon
 from heaven
With silver index, bidding thee make
 peace?
 Ludolph. Still it must not be known, good
 Sigifred; 10
The star may point oblique.
 Sigifred. If Otho knew
His son to be that unknown Mussulman,
After whose spurring heels he sent me
 forth,
With one of his well-pleased Olympian
 oaths,
The charters of man's greatness, at this
 hour
He would be watching round the castle
 walls,
And, like an anxious warder, strain his
 sight
For the first glimpse of such a son re-
 turn'd —
Ludolph, that blast of the Hungarians,
That Saracenic meteor of the fight, 20
That silent fury, whose fell scimitar
Kept danger all aloof from Otho's head,
And left him space for wonder.
 Ludolph. Say no more.
Not as a swordsman would I pardon claim,
But as a son. The bronzed centurion,
Long toil'd in foreign wars, and whose high
 deeds
Are shaded in a forest of tall spears,

Known only to his troop, hath greater plea
Of favour with my sire than I can have.

 Sigifred. My lord, forgive me that I can-
not see 30
How this proud temper with clear reason
 squares.
What made you then, with such an anxious
 love,
Hover around that life, whose bitter days
You vext with bad revolt? Was 't opium,
Or the mad-fumed wine? Nay, do not
 frown,
I rather would grieve with you than up-
 braid.

 Ludolph. I do believe you. No, 't was not
to make
A father his son's debtor, or to heal
His deep heart-sickness for a rebel child.
'T was done in memory of my boyish days,
Poor cancel for his kindness to my youth, 41
For all his calming of my childish griefs,
And all his smiles upon my merriment.
No, not a thousand foughten fields could
 sponge
Those days paternal from my memory,
Though now upon my head he heaps dis-
 grace.

 Sigifred. My prince, you think too
 harshly —

 Ludolph. Can I so?
Hath he not gall'd my spirit to the quick?
And with a sullen rigour obstinate 49
Pour'd out a phial of wrath upon my faults?
Hunted me as the Tartar does the boar,
Driven me to the very edge o' the world,
And almost put a price upon my head?

 Sigifred. Remember how he spared the
rebel lords.

 Ludolph. Yes, yes, I know he hath a no-
ble nature
That cannot trample on the fallen. But
 his
Is not the only proud heart in his realm.
He hath wrong'd me, and I have done him
 wrong;
He hath loved me, and I have shown him
 kindness;
We should be almost equal.

 Sigifred. Yet, for all this,
I would you had appear'd among those
 lords, 61
And ta'en his favour.

 Ludolph. Ha! till now I thought
My friend had held poor Ludolph's honour
 dear.
What! would you have me sue before his
 throne
And kiss the courtier's missal, its silk
 steps?
Or hug the golden housings of his steed,
Amid a camp, whose steeled swarms I
 dared
But yesterday? And, at the trumpet
 sound,
Bow like some unknown mercenary's flag
And lick the soiled grass? No, no, my
 friend, 70
I would not, I, be pardon'd in the heap,
And bless indemnity with all that scum, —
Those men I mean, who on my shoulders
 propp'd
Their weak rebellion, winning me with
 lies,
And pitying forsooth my many wrongs;
Poor self-deceived wretches, who must
 think
Each one himself a king in embryo,
Because some dozen vassals cried — my
 lord!
Cowards, who never knew their little hearts,
Till flurried danger held the mirror up, 80
And then they own'd themselves without a
 blush,
Curling, like spaniels, round my father's
 feet.
Such things deserted me and are forgiven,
While I, less guilty, am an outcast still,
And will be, for I love such fair disgrace.

 Sigifred. I know the clear truth; so
 would Otho see,
For he is just and noble. Fain would I
Be pleader for you —

 Ludolph. He 'll hear none of it;
You know his temper, hot, proud, obstinate;
Endanger not yourself so uselessly. 90
I will encounter his thwart spleen myself,

To-day, at the Duke Conrad's, where he
 keeps
His crowded state after the victory,
There will I be, a most unwelcome guest,
And parley with him, as a son should do,
Who doubly loathes a father's tyranny;
Tell him how feeble is that tyranny;
How the relationship of father and son
Is no more valid than a silken leash
Where lions tug adverse, if love grow not
From interchanged love through many
 years. 101
Aye, and those turreted Franconian walls,
Like to a jealous casket, hold my pearl —
My fair Auranthe ! Yes, I will be there.
 Sigifred. Be not so rash; wait till his
 wrath shall pass,
Until his royal spirit softly ebbs
Self-influenced; then, in his morning dreams
He will forgive thee, and awake in grief
To have not thy good morrow.
 Ludolph. Yes, to-day
I must be there, while her young pulses
 beat 110
Among the new-plumed minions of the
 war.
Have you seen her of late ? No ? Au-
 ranthe,
Franconia's fair sister, 't is I mean.
She should be paler for my troublous
 days —
And there it is — my father's iron lips
Have sworn divorcement 'twixt me and my
 right.
 Sigifred (aside). Auranthe ! I had hoped
 this whim had pass'd.
 Ludolph. And, Sigifred, with all his love
 of justice,
When will he take that grandchild in his
 arms,
That, by my love I swear, shall soon be
 his ? 120
This reconcilement is impossible,
For see — but who are these ?
 Sigifred. They are messengers
From our great emperor; to you, I doubt
 not,
For couriers are abroad to seek you out.

Enter THEODORE *and* GONFRED.

 Theodore. Seeing so many vigilant eyes
 explore
The province to invite your highness back
To your high dignities, we are too happy.
 Gonfred. We have eloquence to colour
 justly
The emperor's anxious wishes.
 Ludolph. Go. I follow you.
 [*Exeunt* THEODORE *and* GONFRED.
I play the prude: it is but venturing —
Why should he be so earnest ? Come, my
 friend, 131
Let us to Friedburg castle.

ACT II

SCENE I. — *An antechamber in the Castle*

Enter LUDOLPH *and* SIGIFRED.

 Ludolph. No more advices, no more cau-
 tioning;
I leave it all to fate — to any thing !
I cannot square my conduct to time, place,
Or circumstance; to me 't is all a mist !
 Sigifred. I say no more.
 Ludolph. It seems I am to wait
Here in the anteroom; — that may be a
 trifle.
You see now how I dance attendance here,
Without that tyrant temper, you so blame,
Snapping the rein. You have medicined
 me
With good advices; and I here remain, 10
In this most honourable anteroom,
Your patient scholar.
 Sigifred. Do not wrong me, Prince.
By Heavens, I 'd rather kiss Duke Conrad's
 slipper,
When in the morning he doth yawn with
 pride,
Than see you humbled but a half-degree !
Truth is, the Emperor would fain dismiss
The Nobles ere he sees you.

Enter GONFRED *from the Council-room.*

 Ludolph. Well, sir ! what ?

Gonfred. Great honour to the Prince!
The Emperor,
Hearing that his brave son had reappeared,
Instant dismiss'd the Council from his
　sight,　　　　　　　　　　　　　　20
As Jove fans off the clouds. Even now
　they pass.　　　　　　　　　[*Exit.*

*Enter the Nobles from the Council-room.
They cross the Stage, bowing with respect
to* LUDOLPH, *he frowning on them.* CON-
RAD *follows.* Exeunt Nobles.

Ludolph. Not the discoloured poisons of
　a fen,
Which he, who breathes, feels warning of
　his death,
Could taste so nauseous to the bodily sense,
As these prodigious sycophants disgust
The soul's fine palate.
Conrad.　　　　　Princely Ludolph, hail!
Welcome, thou younger sceptre to the
　realm!
Strength to thy virgin crownet's golden
　buds,
That they, against the winter of thy sire,
May burst, and swell, and flourish round
　thy brows,　　　　　　　　　30
Maturing to a weighty diadem!
Yet be that hour far off; and may he live,
Who waits for thee, as the chapp'd earth
　for rain.
Set my life's star! I have lived long
　enough,
Since under my glad roof, propitiously,
Father and son each other re-possess.
Ludolph. Fine wording, Duke! but words
　could never yet
Forestall the fates; have you not learnt that
　yet?
Let me look well: your features are the
　same;
Your gait the same; your hair of the same
　shade;　　　　　　　　　　　40
As one I knew some passed weeks ago,
Who sung far different notes into mine
　ears.
I have mine own particular comments on 't;
You have your own, perhaps.

Conrad.　　　　　　My gracious Prince,
All men may err. In truth I was deceived
In your great father's nature, as you were.
Had I known that of him I have since
　known,
And what you soon will learn, I would have
　turn'd
My sword to my own throat, rather than
　held
Its threatening edge against a good King's
　quiet:　　　　　　　　　　　50
Or with one word fever'd you, gentle
　Prince,
Who seem'd to me, as rugged times then
　went,
Indeed too much oppress'd. May I be
　bold
To tell the Emperor you will haste to him?
Ludolph. Your Dukedom's privilege will
　grant so much.
　　　　　　　　　　　[*Exit* CONRAD.
He's very close to Otho, a tight leech!
Your hand — I go! Ha! here the thunder
　comes
Sullen against the wind! If in two angry
　brows
My safety lies, then Sigifred, I'm safe.

Enter OTHO *and* CONRAD.

Otho. Will you make Titan play the
　lackey-page　　　　　　　　60
To chattering pigmies? I would have you
　know
That such neglect of our high Majesty
Annuls all feel of kindred. What is son, —
Or friend — or brother — or all ties of
　blood, —
When the whole kingdom, centred in our-
　self,
Is rudely slighted? Who am I to wait?
By Peter's chair! I have upon my tongue
A word to fright the proudest spirit
　here! —
Death! — and slow tortures to the hardy
　fool,
Who dares take such large charter from
　our smiles!　　　　　　　　70
Conrad, we would be private! Sigifred!

Off ! And none pass this way on pain of
 death !
 [*Exeunt* CONRAD *and* SIGIFRED.
 Ludolph. This was but half expected, my
 good sire,
Yet I am grieved at it, to the full height,
As though my hopes of favour had been
 whole.
 Otho. How you indulge yourself ! What
 can you hope for ?
 Ludolph. Nothing, my liege, I have to
 hope for nothing.
I come to greet you as a loving son,
And then depart, if I may be so free,
Seeing that blood of yours in my warm
 veins 80
Has not yet mitigated into milk.
 Otho. What would you, sir ?
 Ludolph. A lenient banishment;
So please you let me unmolested pass
This Conrad's gates, to the wide air again.
I want no more. A rebel wants no more.
 Otho. And shall I let a rebel loose again
To muster kites and eagles 'gainst my
 head ?
No, obstinate boy, you shall be kept caged
 up,
Served with harsh food, with scum for
 Sunday-drink.
 Ludolph. Indeed !
 Otho. And chains too heavy for your life:
I 'll choose a jailer, whose swart monstrous
 face 90
Shall be a hell to look upon, and she —
 Ludolph. Ha !
 Otho. Shall be your fair Auranthe.
 Ludolph. Amaze ! Amaze !
 Otho. To-day you marry her.
 Ludolph. This is a sharp jest !
 Otho. No. None at all. When have I
 said a lie ?
 Ludolph. If I sleep not, I am a waking
 wretch.
 Otho. Not a word more. Let me em-
 brace my child.
 Ludolph. I dare not. 'T would pollute
 so good a father !
O heavy crime! that your son's blinded eyes

Could not see all his parent's love aright,
As now I see it. Be not kind to me — 101
Punish me not with favour.
 Otho. Are you sure,
Ludolph, you have no saving plea in store ?
 Ludolph. My father, none !
 Otho. Then you astonish me.
 Ludolph. No, I have no plea. Disobedi-
 ence,
Rebellion, obstinacy, blasphemy,
Are all my counsellors. If they can make
My crooked deeds show good and plausible,
Then grant me loving pardon, but not else,
Good Gods ! not else, in any way, my liege !
 Otho. You are a most perplexing, noble
 boy. 111
 Ludolph. You not less a perplexing noble
 father.
 Otho. Well, you shall have free passport
 through the gates.
Farewell !
 Ludolph. Farewell ! and by these tears
 believe,
And still remember, I repent in pain
All my misdeeds !
 Otho. Ludolph, I will ! I will !
But, Ludolph, ere you go, I would inquire
If you, in all your wandering, ever met
A certain Arab haunting in these parts.
 Ludolph. No, my good lord, I cannot say
 I did. 120
 Otho. Make not your father blind before
 his time;
Nor let these arms paternal hunger more
For an embrace, to dull the appetite
Of my great love for thee, my supreme
 child !
Come close, and let me breathe into thine
 ear.
I knew you through disguise. You are the
 Arab !
You can't deny it. [*Embracing him.*
 Ludolph. Happiest of days !
 Otho. We 'll make it so.
 Ludolph. 'Stead of one fatted calf
Ten hecatombs shall bellow out their last,
Smote 'twixt the horns by the death-stun-
 ning mace 130

Of Mars, and all the soldiery shall feast
Nobly as Nimrod's masons, when the
 towers
Of Nineveh new kiss'd the parted clouds !
 Otho. Large as a God speak out, where
 all is thine.
 Ludolph. Ay, father, but the fire in my
 sad breast
Is quench'd with inward tears ! I must
 rejoice
For you, whose wings so shadow over me
In tender victory, but for myself
I still must mourn. The fair Auranthe
 mine ! 139
Too great a boon ! I pr'ythee let me ask
What more than I know of could so have
 changed
Your purpose touching her.
 Otho. At a word, this:
In no deed did you give me more offence
Than your rejection of Erminia.
To my appalling, I saw too good proof
Of your keen-eyed suspicion, — she is
 naught !
 Ludolph. You are convinced ?
 Otho. Ay, spite of her sweet looks.
O, that my brother's daughter should so fall !
Her fame has pass'd into the grosser lips
Of soldiers in their cups.
 Ludolph. 'T is very sad.
 Otho. No more of her. Auranthe — Lu-
 dolph, come ! 151
This marriage be the bond of endless peace !
 [Exeunt.

SCENE II. — *The entrance of* GERSA'S
 Tent in the Hungarian Camp

Enter ERMINIA.

 Erminia. Where ! where ! where shall I
 finu a messenger ?
A trusty soul ? A good man in the camp ?
Shall I go myself ? Monstrous wicked-
 ness !
O cursed Conrad ! devilish Auranthe !
Here is proof palpable as the bright sun !
O for a voice to reach the Emperor's ears !
 [Shouts in the camp.

Enter an HUNGARIAN CAPTAIN.

 Captain. Fair prisoner, you hear those
 joyous shouts ?
The king — aye, now our king, — but still
 your slave,
Young Gersa, from a short captivity
Has just return'd. He bids me say, bright
 dame, 10
That even the homage of his ranged chiefs
Cures not his keen impatience to behold
Such beauty once again. What ails you,
 lady ?
 Erminia. Say, is not that a German, yon-
 der ? There !
 Captain. Methinks by his stout bearing
 he should be —
Yes — it is Albert; a brave German knight,
And much in the Emperor's favour.
 Erminia. I would fain
Inquire of friends and kinsfolk; how they
 fared
In these rough times. Brave soldier, as
 you pass
To royal Gersa with my humble thanks, 20
Will you send yonder knight to me ?
 Captain. I will. *[Exit.*
 Erminia. Yes, he was ever known to be
 a man
Frank, open, generous; Albert I may trust.
O proof ! proof ! proof ! Albert's an
 honest man;
Not Ethelbert the monk, if he were here,
Would I hold more trustworthy. Now !

Enter ALBERT.

 Albert. Good Gods !
Lady Erminia ! are you prisoner
In this beleaguer'd camp ? Or are you
 here
Of your own will ? You pleased to send
 for me.
By Venus, 't is a pity I knew not 30
Your plight before, and, by her Son, I
 swear
To do you every service you can ask.
What would the fairest — ?
 Erminia. Albert, will you swear ?
 Albert. I have. Well ?

Erminia. Albert, you have fame to lose.
If men, in court and camp, lie not outright,
You should be, from a thousand, chosen
 forth
To do an honest deed. Shall I confide — ?
 Albert. Aye, any thing to me, fair crea-
 ture. Do ;
Dictate my task. Sweet woman, —
 Erminia. Truce with that.
You understand me not ; and, in your
 speech, 40
I see how far the slander is abroad.
Without proof could you think me inno-
 cent ?
 Albert. Lady, I should rejoice to know
 you so.
 Erminia. If you have any pity for a
 maid,
Suffering a daily death from evil tongues;
Any compassion for that Emperor's niece,
Who, for your bright sword and clear hon-
 esty,
Lifted you from the crowd of common men
Into the lap of honour; — save me, knight !
 Albert. How ? Make it clear; if it be
 possible, 50
I by the banner of Saint Maurice swear
To right you.
 Erminia. Possible ! — Easy. O my
 heart !
This letter 's not so soil'd but you may
 read it; —
Possible ! There — that letter ! Read —
 read it. [*Gives him a letter.*

ALBERT (*reading*).

' To the Duke Conrad. — Forget the
threat you made at parting, and I will for-
get to send the Emperor letters and papers
of yours I have become possessed of. His
life is no trifle to me; his death you shall
find none to yourself.' (*Speaks to himself.*)
'T is me — my life that 's pleaded for !
(*Reads.*) ' He, for his own sake, will be
dumb as the grave. Erminia has my shame
fix'd upon her, sure as a wen. We are
safe.

' AURANTHE.'

A she-devil ! A dragon ! I her imp !
Fire of Hell ! Auranthe — lewd demon !
Where got you this ? Where ? When ?
 Erminia. I found it in the tent, among
 some spoils
Which, being noble, fell to Gersa's lot. 70
Come in, and see.
 [*They go in and return.*
 Albert. Villainy ! Villainy !
Conrad's sword, his corslet, and his helm,
And his letter. Caitiff, he shall feel —
 Erminia. I see you are thunderstruck.
 Haste, haste away !
 Albert. O, I am tortured by this villainy.
 Erminia. You needs must be. Carry it
 swift to Otho;
Tell him, moreover, I am prisoner
Here in this camp, where all the sisterhood,
Forced from their quiet cells, are parcel'd
 out
For slaves among these Huns. Away !
 Away ! 80
 Albert. I am gone.
 Erminia. Swift be your steed ! Within
 this hour
The Emperor will see it.
 Albert. Ere I sleep:
That I can swear. [*Hurries out.*
 Gersa (*without*). Brave captains ! thanks.
 Enough
Of loyal homage now !

Enter GERSA.

 Erminia. Hail, royal Hun !
 Gersa. What means this, fair one ? Why
 in such alarm ?
Who was it hurried by me so distract ?
It seem'd you were in deep discourse to-
 gether;
Your doctrine has not been so harsh to
 him
As to my poor deserts. Come, come, be
 plain.
I am no jealous fool to kill you both, 90
Or, for such trifles, rob th' adorned world
Of such a beauteous vestal.
 Erminia. I grieve, my Lord,
To hear you condescend to ribald-phrase.

Gersa. This is too much ! Hearken, my lady pure !

Erminia. Silence ! and hear the magic of a name —

Erminia ! I am she, — the Emperor's niece !

Praised be the Heavens, I now dare own myself !

Gersa. Erminia ! Indeed ! I 've heard of her.

Pr'ythee, fair lady, what chance brought you here ? 99

Erminia. Ask your own soldiers.

Gersa. And you dare own your name.

For loveliness you may — and for the rest

My vein is not censorious.

Erminia. Alas ! poor me !

'T is false indeed.

Gersa. Indeed you are too fair:

The swan, soft leaning on her fledgy breast,

When to the stream she launches, looks not back

With such a tender grace; nor are her wings

So white as your soul is, if that but be

Twin picture to your face, Erminia !

To-day, for the first day, I am a king, 109

Yet would I give my unworn crown away

To know you spotless.

Erminia. Trust me one day more,

Generously, without more certain guarantee,

Than this poor face you deign to praise so much;

After that, say and do whate'er you please.

If I have any knowledge of you, sir,

I think, nay I am sure, you will grieve much

To hear my story. O be gentle to me,

For I am sick and faint with many wrongs,

Tired out, and weary-worn with contumelies. 119

Gersa. Poor lady !

Enter ETHELBERT.

Erminia. Gentle Prince, 't is false indeed.

Good morrow, holy father ! I have had

Your prayers, though I look'd for you in vain.

Ethelbert. Blessings upon you, daughter ! Sure you look

Too cheerful for these foul pernicious days.

Young man, you heard this virgin say 't was false, —

'T is false, I say. What ! can you not employ

Your temper elsewhere, 'mong those burly tents,

But you must taunt this dove, for she hath lost

The Eagle Otho to beat off assault ?

Fie ! Fie ! But I will be her guard myself, 130

I' the Emperor's name. I here demand

Herself, and all her sisterhood. She false !

Gersa. Peace ! peace, old man ! I cannot think she is.

Ethelbert. Whom I have known from her first infancy,

Baptized her in the bosom of the Church,

Watch'd her, as anxious husbandmen the grain,

From the first shoot till the unripe mid-May,

Then to the tender ear of her June days,

Which, lifting sweet abroad its timid green,

Is blighted by the touch of calumny; 140

You cannot credit such a monstrous tale.

Gersa. I cannot. Take her. Fair Erminia,

I follow you to Friedburg, — is 't not so ?

Erminia. Ay, so we purpose.

Ethelbert. Daughter, do you so ?

How 's this ? I marvel ! Yet you look not mad.

Erminia. I have good news to tell you, Ethelbert.

Gersa. Ho ! ho, there ! Guards !

Your blessing, father ! Sweet Erminia,

Believe me, I am well nigh sure —

Erminia. Farewell

Short time will show. [*Enter Chiefs.*

Yes, father Ethelbert,

I have news precious as we pass along. 151

Ethelbert. Dear daughter, you shall guide me.

Erminia. To no ill.

Gersa. Command an escort to the Fried-
 burg lines. [*Exeunt Chiefs.*
Pray let me lead. Fair lady, forget not
Gersa, how he believed you innocent.
I follow you to Friedburg with all speed.
 [*Exeunt.*

ACT III

SCENE I. — *The Country*

Enter ALBERT.

Albert. O that the earth were empty, as
 when Cain
Had no perplexity to hide his head !
Or that the sword of some brave enemy
Had put a sudden stop to my hot breath,
And hurl'd me down the illimitable gulf
Of times past, unremember'd ! Better so
Than thus fast-limed in a cursed snare,
The white limbs of a wanton. This the end
Of an aspiring life ! My boyhood past
In feud with wolves and bears, when no
 eye saw 10
The solitary warfare, fought for love
Of honour 'mid the growling wilderness.
My sturdier youth, maturing to the sword,
Won by the syren-trumpets, and the ring
Of shields upon the pavement, when bright
 mail'd
Henry the Fowler pass'd the streets of
 Prague.
Was 't to this end I louted and became
The menial of Mars, and held a spear
Sway'd by command, as corn is by the
 wind ?
Is it for this, I now am lifted up 20
By Europe's throned Emperor, to see
My honour be my executioner, —
My love of fame, my prided honesty
Put to the torture for confessional ?
Then the damn'd crime of blurting to the
 world
A woman's secret ! — Though a fiend she
 be,
Too tender of my ignominious life;
But then to wrong the generous Emperor
In such a searching point, were to give up

My soul for foot-ball at Hell's holiday ! 30
I must confess, — and cut my throat, — to-
 day ?
To-morrow ? Ho ! some wine !

Enter SIGIFRED.

Sigifred. A fine humour —
Albert. Who goes there ? Count Sigi-
 fred ? Ha ! ha !
Sigifred. What, man, do you mistake the
 hollow sky
For a throng'd tavern, — and these stubbed
 trees
For old serge hangings, — me, your humble
 friend,
For a poor waiter ? Why, man, how you
 stare !
What gipsies have you been carousing
 with ?
No, no more wine; methinks you 've had
 enough. 39
 Albert. You well may laugh and banter.
 What a fool
An injury may make of a staid man !
You shall know all anon.
 Sigifred. Some tavern brawl ?
 Albert. 'T was with some people out of
 common reach;
Revenge is difficult.
 Sigifred. I am your friend;
We meet again to-day, and can confer
Upon it. For the present I 'm in haste.
 Albert. Whither ?
 Sigifred. To fetch King Gersa to the
 feast.
The Emperor on this marriage is so hot,
Pray Heaven it end not in apoplexy !
The very porters, as I pass'd the doors, 50
Heard his loud laugh, and answer'd in full
 choir.
I marvel, Albert, you delay so long
From these bright revelries; go, show your-
 self,
You may be made a duke.
 Albert. Ay, very like:
Pray, what day has his Highness fix'd
 upon ?
 Sigifred. For what ?

Albert. The marriage. What else can I
　　mean ?

Sigifred. To-day. O, I forgot, you could
　　not know;
The news is scarce a minute old with me.

Albert. Married to-day ! To-day ! You
　　did not say so ?

Sigifred. Now, while I speak to you,
　　their comely heads　　　　　　60
Are bow'd before the mitre.

Albert.　　　　　　O ! monstrous !

Sigifred. What is this ?

Albert.　　　Nothing, Sigifred. Farewell !
We 'll meet upon our subject. Farewell,
　　count !　　　　　　　　　　[*Exit.*

Sigifred. Is this clear-headed Albert ?
　　He brain-turn'd !
'T is as portentous as a meteor.　[*Exit.*

SCENE II. — *An Apartment in the Castle*

Enter as from the Marriage, OTHO, LU-
DOLPH, AURANTHE, CONRAD, *Nobles,*
Knights, Ladies, etc.　Music.

Otho. Now Ludolph ! Now, Auranthe !
　　Daughter fair !
What can I find to grace your nuptial
　　day
More than my love, and these wide realms
　　in fee ?

Ludolph. I have too much.

Auranthe.　　　And I, my liege, by far.

Ludolph. Auranthe ! I have ! O, my
　　bride, my love !
Not all the gaze upon us can restrain
My eyes, too long poor exiles from thy
　　face,
From adoration, and my foolish tongue
From uttering soft responses to the love
I see in thy mute beauty beaming forth ! 10
Fair creature, bless me with a single word !
All mine !

Auranthe.　Spare, spare me, my Lord; I
　　swoon else.

Ludolph. Soft beauty ! by to-morrow I
　　should die,
Wert thou not mine.

　　　　　　　　　　　[*They talk apart.*

1st Lady.　How deep she has bewitch'd
　　him !

1st Knight. Ask you for her recipe for
　　love philtres.

2d Lady. They hold the Emperor in ad-
　　miration.

Otho. If ever king was happy, that am I !
What are the cities 'yond the Alps to
　　me,
The provinces about the Danube's mouth,
The promise of fair sail beyond the Rhone;
Or routing out of Hyperborean hordes, 21
To these fair children, stars of a new age ?
Unless perchance I might rejoice to win
This little ball of earth, and chuck it them
To play with !

Auranthe. Nay, my Lord, I do not know.

Ludolph. Let me not famish.

Otho (to Conrad).　　Good Franconia,
You heard what oath I sware, as the sun
　　rose,
That unless Heaven would send me back
　　my son,
My Arab, — no soft music should enrich
The cool wine, kiss'd off with a soldier's
　　smack;　　　　　　　　　　30
Now all my empire, barter'd for one feast,
Seems poverty.

Conrad.　　Upon the neighbour-plain
The heralds have prepared a royal lists;
Your knights, found war-proof in the bloody
　　field,
Speed to the game.

Otho.　　Well, Ludolph, what say you ?

Ludolph. My lord !

Otho.　　　　A tourney ?

Conrad.　　Or, if 't please you best —

Ludolph. I want no more !

1st Lady.　　　He soars !

2d Lady.　　　　Past all reason.

Ludolph. Though heaven's choir
Should in a vast circumference descend 39
And sing for my delight, I 'd stop my ears !
Though bright Apollo's car stood burning
　　here,
And he put out an arm to bid me mount,
His touch an immortality, not I !
This earth, this palace, this room, Auranthe !

Otho. This is a little painful; just too
 much.
Conrad, if he flames longer in this wise,
I shall believe in wizard-woven loves
And old romances; but I 'll break the spell.
Ludolph!
 Conrad. He 'll be calm, anon.
 Ludolph. You call'd!
Yes, yes, yes, I offend. You must forgive
 me: 50
Not being quite recover'd from the stun
Of your large bounties. A tourney, is it
 not?
 [A senet heard faintly.
 Conrad. The trumpets reach us.
 Ethelbert (without). On your peril, sirs,
Detain us!
 1st Voice (without). Let not the abbot
 pass.
 2d Voice (without). No,
On your lives!
 1st Voice (without). Holy father, you
 must not.
 Ethelbert (without). Otho!
 Otho. Who calls on Otho?
 Ethelbert (without). Ethelbert!
 Otho. Let him come in.

Enter ETHELBERT *leading in* ERMINIA.
 Thou cursed abbot, why
Hast brought pollution to our holy rites?
Hast thou no fear of hangman, or the fag-
 got?
 Ludolph. What portent — what strange
 prodigy is this? 60
 Conrad. Away!
 Ethelbert. You, Duke?
 Erminia. Albert has surely fail'd me!
Look at the Emperor's brow upon me
 bent!
 Ethelbert. A sad delay!
 Conrad. Away, thou guilty thing!
 Ethelbert. You again, Duke? Justice,
 most noble Otho!
You — go to your sister there and plot
 again,
A quick plot, swift as thought to save your
 heads;

For lo! the toils are spread around your
 den,
The world is all agape to see dragg'd forth
Two ugly monsters.
 Ludolph. What means he, my lord?
 Conrad. I cannot guess.
 Ethelbert. Best ask your lady sister,
Whether the riddle puzzles her beyond 71
The power of utterance.
 Conrad. Foul barbarian, cease;
The Princess faints!
 Ludolph. Stab him! O, sweetest wife!
 [Attendants bear off AURANTHE.
 Erminia. Alas!
 Ethelbert. Your wife!
 Ludolph. Ay, Satan! does that yerk ye?
 Ethelbert. Wife! so soon!
 Ludolph. Ay, wife! Oh, impudence!
Thou bitter mischief! Venomous bad
 priest!
How dar'st thou lift those beetle brows at
 me?
Me — the prince Ludolph, in this presence
 here, 78
Upon my marriage day, and scandalize
My joys with such opprobrious surprise?
Wife! Why dost linger on that syllable,
As if it were some demon's name pro-
 nounced
To summon harmful lightning, and make
 yawn
The sleepy thunder? Hast no sense of
 fear?
No ounce of man in thy mortality?
Tremble! for, at my nod, the sharpen'd axe
Will make thy bold tongue quiver to the
 roots,
Those gray lids wink, and thou not know
 it, monk!
 Ethelbert. O, poor deceived Prince! I
 pity thee! 89
Great Otho! I claim justice —
 Ludolph. Thou shalt have 't!
Thine arms from forth a pulpit of hot fire
Shall sprawl distracted! O that that dull
 cowl
Were some most sensitive portion of thy
 life,

That I might give it to my hounds to tear !
Thy girdle some fine zealous-pained nerve
To girth my saddle ! And those devil's
 beads
Each one a life, that I might, every day,
Crush one with Vulcan's hammer !
 Otho. Peace, my son ;
You far outstrip my spleen in this affair.
Let us be calm, and hear the abbot's plea
For this intrusion.
 Ludolph. I am silent, sire.
 Otho. Conrad, see all depart not wanted
 here. 102
 [*Exeunt Knights, Ladies, etc.*
Ludolph, be calm. Ethelbert, peace awhile.
This mystery demands an audience
Of a just judge, and that will Otho be.
 Ludolph. Why has he time to breathe
 another word ?
 Otho. Ludolph, old Ethelbert, be sure,
 comes not
To beard us for no cause ; he 's not the
 man
To cry himself up an ambassador
Without credentials.
 Ludolph. I 'll chain up myself.
 Otho. Old abbot, stand here forth. Lady
 Erminia, 111
Sit. And now, abbot ! what have you to
 say ?
Our ear is open. First we here denounce
Hard penalties against thee, if 't be found
The cause for which you have disturb'd us
 here,
Making our bright hours muddy, be a thing
Of little moment.
 Ethelbert. See this innocent !
Otho ! thou father of the people call'd,
Is her life nothing ? Her fair honour no-
 thing ?
Her tears from matins until even-song 120
Nothing ? Her burst heart nothing ? Em-
 peror !
Is this your gentle niece — the simplest
 flower
Of the world's herbal — this fair lily
 blanch'd
Still with the dews of piety, this meek lady

Here sitting like an angel newly-shent,
Who veils its snowy wings and grows all
 pale, —
Is she nothing ?
 Otho. What more to the purpose, abbot ?
 Ludolph. Whither is he winding ?
 Conrad. No clue yet !
 Ethelbert. You have heard, my Liege, and
 so, no doubt, all here, 129
Foul, poisonous, malignant whisperings ;
Nay open speech, rude mockery grown
 common,
Against the spotless nature and clear fame
Of the princess Erminia, your niece.
I have intruded here thus suddenly,
Because I hold those base weeds, with tight
 hand,
Which now disfigure her fair growing stem,
Waiting but for your sign to pull them up
By the dark roots, and leave her palpable,
To all men's sight, a lady innocent.
The ignominy of that whisper'd tale 140
About a midnight gallant, seen to climb
A window to her chamber neighbour'd
 near,
I will from her turn off, and put the load
On the right shoulders ; on that wretch's
 head,
Who, by close stratagems, did save her-
 self,
Chiefly by shifting to this lady's room
A rope-ladder for false witness.
 Ludolph. Most atrocious !
 Otho. Ethelbert, proceed.
 Ethelbert. With sad lips I shall :
For, in the healing of one wound, I fear
To make a greater. His young highness
 here 150
To-day was married.
 Ludolph. Good.
 Ethelbert. Would it were good !
Yet why do I delay to spread abroad
The names of those two vipers, from whose
 jaw
A deadly breath went forth to taint and
 blast
This guileless lady ?
 Otho. Abbot, speak their names.

Ethelbert. A minute first. It cannot be — but may
I ask, great judge, if you to-day have put
A letter by unread ?
 Otho. Does 't end in this ?
 Conrad. Out with their names !
 Ethelbert. Bold sinner, say you so ?
 Ludolph. Out, hideous monk !
 Otho. Confess, or by the wheel —
 Ethelbert. My evidence cannot be far
 away; 161
And, though it never come, be on my head
The crime of passing an attaint upon
The slanderers of this virgin.
 Ludolph. Speak aloud !
 Ethelbert. Auranthe, and her brother
 there.
 Conrad. Amaze !
 Ludolph. Throw them from the win-
 dows !
 Otho. Do what you will !
 Ludolph. What shall I do with them ?
Something of quick dispatch, for should she
 hear,
My soft Auranthe, her sweet mercy would
Prevail against my fury. Damned priest !
What swift death wilt thou die ? As to the
 lady, 171
I touch her not.
 Ethelbert. Illustrious Otho, stay !
An ample store of misery thou hast,
Choke not the granary of thy noble mind
With more bad bitter grain, too difficult
A cud for the repentance of a man
Gray-growing. To thee only I appeal,
Not to thy noble son, whose yeasting youth
Will clear itself, and crystal turn again.
A young man's heart, by Heaven's bless-
 ing, is 180
A wide world, where a thousand new-born
 hopes
Empurple fresh the melancholy blood :
But an old man's is narrow, tenantless
Of hopes, and stuff 'd with many memories,
Which, being pleasant, ease the heavy
 pulse —
Painful, clog up and stagnate. Weigh this
 matter

Even as a miser balances his coin;
And, in the name of mercy, give command
That your knight Albert be brought here
 before you. 189
He will expound this riddle; he will show
A noon-day proof of bad Auranthe's guilt.
 Otho. Let Albert straight be summon'd.
 [*Exit one of the Nobles.*
 Ludolph. Impossible !
I cannot doubt — I will not — no — to
 doubt
Is to be ashes ! — wither'd up to death !
 Otho. My gentle Ludolph, harbour not a
 fear;
You do yourself much wrong.
 Ludolph. O, wretched dolt !
Now, when my foot is almost on thy neck,
Wilt thou infuriate me? Proof ! Thou fool !
Why wilt thou tease impossibility 199
With such a thick-skull'd persevering suit ?
Fanatic obstinacy ! Prodigy !
Monster of folly ! Ghost of a turn'd
 brain !
You puzzle me, — you haunt me, — when I
 dream
Of you my brain will split ! Bold sor-
 cerer !
Juggler ! May I come near you ? On my
 soul
I know not whether to pity, curse, or
 laugh.

 Enter ALBERT, *and the Nobleman.*

Here, Albert, this old phantom wants a
 proof !
Give him his proof ! A camel's load of
 proofs !
 Otho. Albert, I speak to you as a man
Whose words once utter'd pass like current
 gold; 210
And therefore fit to calmly put a close
To this brief tempest. Do you stand pos-
 sess'd
Of any proof against the honourableness
Of Lady Auranthe, our new-spoused daugh-
 ter ?
 Albert. You chill me with astonishment.
 How 's this ?

My liege, what proof should I have 'gainst
 a fame
Impossible of slur ?

 [OTHO *rises.*

Erminia. O wickedness !
Ethelbert. Deluded monarch, 't is a cruel
 lie. 218
Otho. Peace, rebel-priest !
Conrad. Insult beyond credence !
Erminia. Almost a dream !
Ludolph. We have awaked from !
A foolish dream that from my brow hath
 wrung
A wrathful dew. O folly ! why did I
So act the lion with this silly gnat ?
Let them depart. Lady Erminia !
I ever grieved for you, as who did not ?
But now you have, with such a brazen
 front,
So most maliciously, so madly striven
To dazzle the soft moon, when tenderest
 clouds
Should be unloop'd around to curtain her;
I leave you to the desert of the world 230
Almost with pleasure. Let them be set
 free
For me ! I take no personal revenge
More than against a nightmare, which a
 man
Forgets in the new dawn. [*Exit* LUDOLPH.
 Otho. Still in extremes ! No, they must
 not be loose.
 Ethelbert. Albert, I must suspect thee of
 a crime
So fiendish —
 Otho. Fear'st thou not my fury, monk ?
Conrad, be they in your safe custody
Till we determine some fit punishment. 240
It is so mad a deed, I must reflect
And question them in private; for per-
 haps,
By patient scrutiny, we may discover
Whether they merit death, or should be
 placed
In care of the physicians.
 [*Exeunt* OTHO *and Nobles,* ALBERT
 following.

Conrad. My guards, ho !
Erminia. Albert, wilt thou follow there ?
Wilt thou creep dastardly behind his back,
And shrink away from a weak woman's
 eye ?
Turn, thou court - Janus ! thou forgett'st
 thyself;
Here is the duke, waiting with open
 arms,
 Enter Guards.
To thank thee; here congratulate each
 other; 250
Wring hands; embrace; and swear how
 lucky 't was
That I, by happy chance, hit the right
 man
Of all the world to trust in.
 Albert. Trust ! to me !
 Conrad (*aside*). He is the sole one in this
 mystery.
 Erminia. Well, I give up, and save my
 prayers for Heaven !
You, who could do this deed, would ne'er
 relent,
Though, at my words, the hollow prison-
 vaults
Would groan for pity.
 Conrad. Manacle them both !
 Ethelbert. I know it — it must be — I
 see it all ! 259
Albert, thou art the minion !
 Erminia. Ah ! too plain —
 Conrad. Silence ! Gag up their mouths !
 I cannot bear
More of this brawling. That the Emperor
Had placed you in some other custody !
Bring them away.
 [*Exeunt all but* ALBERT.
 Albert. Though my name perish from
 the book of honour,
Almost before the recent ink is dry,
And be no more remember'd after death,
Than any drummer's in the muster-roll;
Yet shall I season high my sudden fall 269
With triumph o'er that evil-witted duke !
He shall feel what it is to have the hand
Of a man drowning, on his hateful throat.

Enter GERSA *and* SIGIFRED.

Gersa. What discord is at ferment in this house ?

Sigifred. We are without conjecture; not a soul
We met could answer any certainty.

Gersa. Young Ludolph, like a fiery ar-
row, shot
By us.

Sigifred. The Emperor, with cross'd arms, in thought.

Gersa. In one room music, in another sadness,
Perplexity every where !

Albert. A trifle more !
Follow ; your presences will much avail 280
To tune our jarred spirits. I 'll explain.
 [*Exeunt.*

ACT IV

SCENE I. — AURANTHE'S *Apartment*

AURANTHE *and* CONRAD *discovered.*

Conrad. Well, well, I know what ugly jeopardy
We are caged in; you need not pester that
Into my ears. Pr'ythee, let me be spared
A foolish tongue, that I may bethink me
Of remedies with some deliberation.
You cannot doubt but 't is in Albert's power
To crush or save us ?

Auranthe. No, I cannot doubt.
He has, assure yourself, by some strange means,
My secret; which I ever hid from him, 9
Knowing his mawkish honesty.

Conrad. Cursed slave !

Auranthe. Ay, I could almost curse him now myself.
Wretched impediment ! Evil genius !
A glue upon my wings, that cannot spread,
When they should span the provinces ! A snake,
A scorpion, sprawling on the first gold step,
Conducting to the throne, high canopied.

Conrad. You would not hear my counsel, when his life
Might have been trodden out, all sure and hush'd;
Now the dull animal forsooth must be
Intreated, managed ! When can you con-
trive 20
The interview he demands ?

Auranthe. As speedily
It must be done as my bribed woman can
Unseen conduct him to me; but I fear
'T will be impossible, while the broad day
Comes through the panes with persecuting glare.
Methinks, if 't now were night I could in-
trigue
With darkness, bring the stars to second me,
And settle all this trouble.

Conrad. Nonsense ! Child !
See him immediately; why not now ?

Auranthe. Do you forget that even the senseless door-posts 30
Are on the watch and gape through all the house ?
How many whisperers there are about,
Hungry for evidence to ruin me:
Men I have spurn'd, and women I have taunted ?
Besides, the foolish prince sends, minute whiles,
His pages — so they tell me — to inquire
After my health, intreating, if I please,
To see me.

Conrad. Well, suppose this Albert here;
What is your power with him ?

Auranthe. He should be
My echo, my taught parrot ! but I fear 40
He will be cur enough to bark at me;
Have his own say; read me some silly creed
'Bout shame and pity.

Conrad. What will you do then ?

Auranthe. What I shall do, I know not; what I would
Cannot be done; for see, this chamber-
floor
Will not yield to the pick-axe and the spade, —
Here is no quiet depth of hollow ground.

Conrad. Sister, you have grown sensible
　　　and wise,
Seconding, ere I speak it, what is now, 49
I hope, resolved between us.
Auranthe. 　　　　　　　Say, what is 't ?
Conrad. You need not be his sexton too;
　　　a man
May carry that with him shall make him
　　　die
Elsewhere, — give that to him; pretend
　　　the while
You will to-morrow succumb to his wishes,
Be what they may, and send him from the
　　　Castle
On some fool's errand: let his latest groan
Frighten the wolves !
Auranthe. 　　　　Alas ! he must not die !
Conrad. Would you were both hearsed
　　　up in stifling lead !
Detested —
Auranthe. Conrad, hold ! I would not
　　　bear 　　　　　　　　　　　　　59
The little thunder of your fretful tongue,
Tho' I alone were taken in these toils,
And you could free me; but remember,
　　　sir,
You live alone in my security:
So keep your wits at work, for your own
　　　sake,
Not mine, and be more mannerly.
Conrad. 　　　　　　　Thou wasp !
If my domains were emptied of these folk,
And I had thee to starve —
Auranthe. 　　　　　　O, marvellous !
But Conrad, now be gone; the Host is
　　　look'd for;
Cringe to the Emperor, entertain the Lords,
And, do ye mind, above all things, pro-
　　　claim 　　　　　　　　　　　　70
My sickness, with a brother's sadden'd eye,
Condoling with Prince Ludolph. In fit
　　　time
Return to me.
Conrad. I leave you to your thoughts.
　　　　　　　　　　　　　　　[*Exit.*
Auranthe (*sola*). Down, down, proud
　　　temper ! down, Auranthe's pride !
Why do I anger him when I should kneel ?

Conrad ! Albert ! help ! help ! What can
　　　I do ?
O wretched woman ! lost, wreck'd, swal-
　　　low'd up,
Accursed, blasted ! O, thou golden Crown,
Orbing along the serene firmament 　　79
Of a wide empire, like a glowing moon;
And thou, bright sceptre ! lustrous in my
　　　eyes, —
There — as the fabled fair Hesperian tree,
Bearing a fruit more precious ! graceful
　　　thing,
Delicate, godlike, magic ! must I leave
Thee to melt in the visionary air,
Ere, by one grasp, this common hand is
　　　made
Imperial ? I do not know the time
When I have wept for sorrow; but me-
　　　thinks 　　　　　　　　　　　88
I could now sit upon the ground, and shed
Tears, tears of misery ! O, the heavy day !
How shall I bear my life till Albert comes ?
Ludolph ! Erminia ! Proofs ! O heavy
　　　day !
Bring me some mourning weeds, that I
　　　may 'tire
Myself, as fits one wailing her own death:
Cut off these curls, and brand this lily
　　　hand,
And throw these jewels from my loathing
　　　sight, —
Fetch me a missal, and a string of beads, —
A cup of bitter'd water, and a crust, —
I will confess, O holy Abbot ! — How ! 　99
What is this ? Auranthe ! thou fool, dolt,
Whimpering idiot ! up ! up ! and quell !
I am safe ! Coward ! why am I in fear ?
Albert ! he cannot stickle, chew the cud
In such a fine extreme, — impossible !
Who knocks ?
　　　[*Goes to the door, listens, and opens it.*

Enter ALBERT.

Albert, I have been waiting for you here
With such an aching heart, such swooning
　　　throbs
On my poor brain, such cruel — cruel sor-
　　　row,

That I should claim your pity ! Art not
 well ? 109
 Albert. Yes, lady, well.
 Auranthe. You look not so, alas !
But pale, as if you brought some heavy
 news.
 Albert. You know full well what makes
 me look so pale.
 Auranthe. No ! Do I ? Surely I am
 still to learn
Some horror; all I know, this present, is
I am near hustled to a dangerous gulf,
Which you can save me from, — and there-
 fore safe,
So trusting in thy love; that should not
 make
Thee pale, my Albert.
 Albert. It doth make me freeze.
 Auranthe. Why should it, love ?
 Albert. You should not ask me that,
But make your own heart monitor, and save
Me the great pain of telling. You must
 know. 121
 Auranthe. Something has vext you, Al-
 bert. There are times
When simplest things put on a sombre
 cast;
A melancholy mood will haunt a man,
Until most easy matters take the shape
Of unachievable tasks; small rivulets
Then seem impassable.
 Albert. Do not cheat yourself
With hope that gloss of words, or suppliant
 action,
Or tears, or ravings, or self-threaten'd
 death, 129
Can alter my resolve.
 Auranthe. You make me tremble;
Not so much at your threats, as at your
 voice,
Untuned, and harsh, and barren of all love.
 Albert. You suffocate me ! Stop this
 devil's parley,
And listen to me; know me once for all.
 Auranthe. I thought I did. Alas ! I
 am deceived.
 Albert. No, you are not deceived. You
 took me for

A man detesting all inhuman crime;
And therefore kept from me your demon's
 plot
Against Erminia. Silent ? Be so still;
For ever ! Speak no more; but hear my
 words, 140
Thy fate. Your safety I have bought to-
 day
By blazoning a lie, which in the dawn
I 'll expiate with truth.
 Auranthe. O cruel traitor !
 Albert. For I would not set eyes upon
 thy shame;
I would not see thee dragg'd to death by
 the hair,
Penanced, and taunted on a scaffolding !
To-night, upon the skirts of the blind wood
That blackens northward of these horrid
 towers,
I wait for you with horses. Choose your
 fate. 149
Farewell !
 Auranthe. Albert, you jest; I 'm sure
 you must.
You, an ambitious Soldier ! I, a Queen,
One who could say, — here, rule these Pro-
 vinces !
Take tribute from those cities for thyself !
Empty these armouries, these treasuries,
Muster thy warlike thousands at a nod !
Go ! Conquer Italy !
 Albert. Auranthe, you have made
The whole world chaff to me. Your doom
 is fix'd.
 Auranthe. Out, villain ! dastard !
 Albert. Look there to the door !
Who is it ?
 Auranthe. Conrad, traitor !
 Albert. Let him in.

Enter CONRAD.

Do not affect amazement, hypocrite, 160
At seeing me in this chamber.
 Conrad. Auranthe ?
 Albert. Talk not with eyes, but speak
 your curses out
Against me, who would sooner crush and
 grind

A brace of toads, than league with them
 t' oppress
An innocent lady, gull an Emperor,
More generous to me than autumn sun
To ripening harvests.
 Auranthe. No more insult, sir !
 Albert. Ay, clutch your scabbard; but,
 for prudence sake,
Draw not the sword; 't would make an up-
 roar, Duke,
You would not hear the end of. At night-
 fall 170
Your lady sister, if I guess aright,
Will leave this busy castle. You had best
Take farewell too of worldly vanities.
 Conrad. Vassal !
 Albert. To-morrow, when the Emperor
 sends
For loving Conrad, see you fawn on him.
Good even !
 Auranthe. You 'll be seen !
 Albert. See the coast clear then.
 Auranthe (as he goes). Remorseless Al-
 bert ! Cruel, cruel wretch !
 [*She lets him out.*
 Conrad. So, we must lick the dust ?
 Auranthe. I follow him.
 Conrad. How ? Where ? The plan of
 your escape ?
 Auranthe. He waits
For me with horses by the forest-side, 180
Northward.
 Conrad. Good, good ! he dies. You go,
 say you ?
 Auranthe. Perforce.
 Conrad. Be speedy, darkness! Till that
 comes,
Fiends keep you company ! [*Exit.*
 Auranthe. And you ! And you !
And all men ! Vanish !
 [*Retires to an inner apartment.*

SCENE II. — *An Apartment in the Castle*

 Enter LUDOLPH *and a Page.*

 Page. Still very sick, my lord; but now
 I went,
Knowing my duty to so good a Prince;

And there her women, in a mournful throng,
Stood in the passage whispering; if any
Moved, 't was with careful steps, and hush'd
 as death:
They bade me stop.
 Ludolph. Good fellow, once again
Make soft inquiry; pr'ythee, be not stay'd
By any hindrance, but with gentlest force
Break through her weeping servants, till
 thou com'st
E'en to her chamber door, and there, fair
 boy — 10
If with thy mother's milk thou hast suck'd
 in
Any divine eloquence — woo her ears
With plaints for me, more tender than the
 voice
Of dying Echo, echoed.
 Page. Kindest master !
To know thee sad thus, will unloose my
 tongue
In mournful syllables. Let but my words
 reach
Her ears, and she shall take them coupled
 with
Moans from my heart, and sighs not coun-
 terfeit.
May I speed better ! [*Exit Page.*
 Ludolph (solus). Auranthe ! My Life !
Long have I loved thee, yet till now not
 loved: 20
Remembering, as I do, hard-hearted times
When I had heard e'en of thy death per-
 haps,
And thoughtless, suffer'd thee to pass alone
Into Elysium ! — now I follow thee
A substance or a shadow, wheresoe'er
Thou leadest me, — whether thy white feet
 press,
With pleasant weight, the amorous-aching
 earth,
Or thro' the air thou pioneerest me,
A shade ! Yet sadly I predestinate !
O unbenignest Love, why wilt thou let 30
Darkness steal out upon the sleepy world
So wearily; as if night's chariot-wheels
Were clogg'd in some thick cloud ? O,
 changeful Love,

Let not her steeds with drowsy-footed pace
Pass the high stars, before sweet embas-
 sage
Comes from the pillow'd beauty of that
 fair
Completion of all delicate Nature's wit !
Pout her faint lips anew with rubious
 health;
And, with thine infant fingers, lift the
 fringe
Of her sick eyelids; that those eyes may
 glow 40
With wooing light upon me, ere the Morn
Peers with disrelish, gray, barren, and
 cold !

 Enter GERSA *and Courtiers.*

Otho calls me his Lion — should I blush
To be so tamed ? so —
 Gersa. Do me the courtesy,
Gentlemen, to pass on.
 1st Knight. We are your servants.
 [*Exeunt Courtiers.*
 Ludolph. It seems then, Sir, you have
 found out the man
You would confer with; — me ?
 Gersa. If I break not
Too much upon your thoughtful mood, I
 will
Claim a brief while your patience.
 Ludolph. For what cause
Soe'er, I shall be honour'd.
 Gersa. I not less.
 Ludolph. What may it be ? No trifle
 can take place 51
Of such deliberate prologue, serious 'hav-
 iour.
But, be it what it may, I cannot fail
To listen with no common interest;
For though so new your presence is to
 me,
I have a soldier's friendship for your fame.
Please you explain.
 Gersa. As thus: — for, pardon me,
I cannot in plain terms grossly assault
A noble nature; and would faintly sketch
What your quick apprehension will fill up;
So finely I esteem you.

 Ludolph. I attend. 61
 Gersa. Your generous father, most illus-
 trious Otho,
Sits in the banquet-room among his chiefs;
His wine is bitter, for you are not there;
His eyes are fix'd still on the open doors,
And ev'ry passer in he frowns upon,
Seeing no Ludolph comes.
 Ludolph. I do neglect —
 Gersa. And for your absence may I guess
 the cause ?
 Ludolph. Stay there ! No — guess ?
 More princely you must be 69
Than to make guesses at me. 'T is enough.
I 'm sorry I can hear no more.
 Gersa. And I
As grieved to force it on you so abrupt;
Yet, one day, you must know a grief, whose
 sting
Will sharpen more the longer 't is con-
 ceal'd.
 Ludolph. Say it at once, sir ! dead —
 dead — is she dead ?
 Gersa. Mine is a cruel task: she is not
 dead,
And would, for your sake, she were inno-
 cent —
 Ludolph. Thou liest ! Thou amazest me
 beyond
All scope of thought, convulsest my heart's
 blood 79
To deadly churning ! Gersa, you are young,
As I am; let me observe you, face to face:
Not gray-brow'd like the poisonous Ethel-
 bert,
No rheumed eyes, no furrowing of age,
No wrinkles, where all vices nestle in
Like crannied vermin — no ! but fresh and
 young,
And hopeful featured. Ha ! by Heaven
 you weep
Tears, human tears ! Do you repent you
 then
Of a cursed torturer's office ? Why shouldst
 join —
Tell me, the league of devils ? Confess —
 confess —
The Lie !

Gersa. Lie ! — but begone all ceremo-
nious points 90
Of honour battailous ! I could not turn
My wrath against thee for the orbed world.
 Ludolph. Your wrath, weak boy ? Trem-
ble at mine, unless
Retraction follow close upon the heels
Of that late stounding insult ! Why has
my sword
Not done already a sheer judgment on
thee ?
Despair, or eat thy words ! Why, thou
wast nigh
Whimpering away my reason ! Hark ye,
Sir,
It is no secret, that Erminia,
Erminia, Sir, was hidden in your tent; 100
O bless'd asylum ! Comfortable home !
Begone ! I pity thee; thou art a gull,
Erminia's last new puppet !
 Gersa. Furious fire !
Thou mak'st me boil as hot as thou canst
flame !
And in thy teeth I give thee back the lie !
Thou liest ! Thou, Auranthe's fool ! A
wittol —
 Ludolph. Look ! look at this bright
sword:
There is no part of it, to the very hilt,
But shall indulge itself about thine heart !
Draw ! but remember thou must cower thy
plumes, 110
As yesterday the Arab made thee stoop —
 Gersa. Patience ! Not here; I would
not spill thy blood
Here, underneath this roof where Otho
breathes, —
Thy father, — almost mine.
 Ludolph. O faltering coward !

Re-enter PAGE.

Stay, stay; here is one I have half a word
with.
Well — What ails thee, child ?
 Page. My lord !
 Ludolph. Good fellow !
 Page. They are fled !
 Ludolph. They ! Who ?

 Page. When anxiously
I hasten'd back, your grieving messenger,
I found the stairs all dark, the lamps ex-
tinct,
And not a foot or whisper to be heard. 120
I thought her dead, and on the lowest step
Sat listening; when presently came by
Two muffled up, — one sighing heavily,
The other cursing low, whose voice I knew
For the Duke Conrad's. Close I follow'd
them
Thro' the dark ways they chose to the open
air;
And, as I follow'd, heard my lady speak.
 Ludolph. Thy life answers the truth !
 Page. The chamber's empty !
 Ludolph. As I will be of mercy ! So, at
last, 129
This nail is in my temples !
 Gersa. Be calm in this.
 Ludolph. I am.
 Gersa. And Albert too has disappear'd;
Ere I met you, I sought him every where;
You would not hearken.
 Ludolph. Which way went they, boy ?
 Gersa. I 'll hunt with you.
 Ludolph. No, no, no. My senses are
Still whole. I have survived. My arm is
strong —
My appetite sharp — for revenge ! I 'll no
sharer
In my feast; my injury is all my own,
And so is my revenge, my lawful chat-
tels !
Terrier, ferret them out ! Burn — burn
the witch !
Trace me their footsteps ! Away ! 140
 [*Exeunt.*

ACT V

SCENE I. — *A part of the Forest*

Enter CONRAD *and* AURANTHE.

Auranthe. Go no further; not a step
more. Thou art
A master-plague in the midst of miseries.
Go, — I fear thee ! I tremble every limb,

Who never shook before. There's moody
 death
In thy resolved looks ! Yes, I could kneel
To pray thee far away ! Conrad, go !
 go ! —
There ! yonder underneath the boughs I see
Our horses !
 Conrad. Ay, and the man.
 Auranthe. Yes, he is there.
Go, go, — no blood ! no blood ! — go, gen-
 tle Conrad !
 Conrad. Farewell !
 Auranthe. Farewell ! For this Heaven
 pardon you ! 10
 [*Exit* AURANTHE.
 Conrad. If he survive one hour, then
 may I die
In unimagined tortures, or breathe through
A long life in the foulest sink o' the world !
He dies ! 'T is well she do not advertise
The caitiff of the cold steel at his back.
 [*Exit* CONRAD.

 Enter LUDOLPH *and Page.*

 Ludolph. Miss'd the way, boy ? Say not
 that on your peril !
 Page. Indeed, indeed I cannot trace
 them further.
 Ludolph. Must I stop here ? Here soli-
 tary die ?
Stifled beneath the thick oppressive shade
Of these dull boughs, — this oven of dark
 thickets, — 20
Silent, — without revenge ? — pshaw ! —
 bitter end, —
A bitter death, — a suffocating death, —
A gnawing — silent — deadly, quiet death !
Escaped ? — fled ? — vanish'd ? melted into
 air ?
She 's gone ! I cannot clutch her ! no re-
 venge !
A muffled death, ensnared in horrid silence !
Suck'd to my grave amid a dreamy calm !
O, where is that illustrious noise of war,
To smother up this sound of labouring
 breath, 29
This rustle of the trees !
 [AURANTHE *shrieks at a distance.*

 Page. My lord, a noise !
This way — hark !
 Ludolph. Yes, yes ! A hope ! A music !
A glorious clamour ! How I live again !
 [*Exeunt.*

SCENE II. — *Another part of the Forest*

 Enter ALBERT (*wounded*).

 Albert. O ! for enough life to support me
 on
To Otho's feet !

 Enter LUDOLPH.

 Ludolph. Thrice villanous, stay there !
Tell me where that detested woman is,
Or this is through thee !
 Albert. My good Prince, with me
The sword has done its worst; not without
 worst
Done to another, — Conrad has it home —
I see you know it all —
 Ludolph. Where is his sister ?

 Enter AURANTHE.

 Auranthe. Albert !
 Ludolph. Ha ! There ! there ! — He is
 the paramour ! —
There — hug him — dying ! O, thou inno-
 cence,
Shrine him and comfort him at his last
 gasp, 10
Kiss down his eyelids ! Was he not thy
 love ?
Wilt thou forsake him at his latest hour ?
Keep fearful and aloof from his last gaze,
His most uneasy moments, when cold death
Stands with the door ajar to let him in ?
 Albert. O that that door with hollow slam
 would close
Upon me sudden, for I cannot meet,
In all the unknown chambers of the dead,
Such horrors —
 Ludolph. Auranthe ! what can he mean ?
What horrors ? Is it not a joyous time ?
Am I not married to a paragon 21
'Of personal beauty and untainted soul ?'
A blushing fair-eyed purity ? A sylph,

Whose snowy timid hand has never sinn'd
Beyond a flower pluck'd, white as itself ?
Albert, you do insult my bride — your mis-
　　tress —
To talk of horrors on our wedding-night !
　　Albert. Alas ! poor Prince, I would you
　　　　knew my heart !
'T is not so guilty —
　　Ludolph.　　　Hear, he pleads not guilty !
You are not ? or, if so, what matters it ?
You have escaped me, free as the dusk
　　air,　　　　　　　　　　　　　　31
Hid in the forest, safe from my revenge;
I cannot catch you !　You should laugh at
　　me,
Poor cheated Ludolph !　Make the forest
　　hiss
With jeers at me !　You tremble; faint at
　　once,
You will come to again.　O cockatrice,
I have you !　Whither wander those fair
　　eyes
To entice the Devil to your help, that he
May change you to a spider, so to crawl
Into some cranny to escape my wrath ?　40
　　Albert. Sometimes the counsel of a dy-
　　　　ing man
Doth operate quietly when his breath is
　　gone:
Disjoin those hands — part — part — do
　　not destroy
Each other — forget her ! — Our miseries
Are equal shared, and mercy is —
　　Ludolph.　　　　　　A boon
When one can compass it.　Auranthe, try
Your oratory; your breath is not so hitch'd.
Ay, stare for help !
　　　　　　　　[ALBERT *groans and dies.*
　　　　　There goes a spotted soul
Howling in vain along the hollow night !
Hear him !　He calls you — sweet Auran-
　　the, come !　　　　　　　　　50
　　Auranthe. Kill me !
　　Ludolph. No !　What, upon our mar-
　　　　riage-night !
The earth would shudder at so foul a deed !
A fair bride !　A sweet bride !　An inno-
　　cent bride !

No ! we must revel it, as 't is in use
In times of delicate brilliant ceremony:
Come, let me lead you to our halls again !
Nay, linger not ; make no resistance,
　　sweet; —
Will you ?　Ah, wretch, thou canst not, for
　　I have
The strength of twenty lions 'gainst a
　　lamb !
Now — one adieu for Albert ! — Come
　　away !　　　　　　　　　60
　　　　　　　　　　　　　　[*Exeunt.*

SCENE III. — *An inner Court of the
　　　　　Castle*

Enter SIGIFRED, GONFRED, *and* THEODORE,
　　　　　meeting.

　　1st Knight. Was ever such a night ?
　　Sigifred.　　　　What horrors more ?
Things unbelieved one hour, so strange
　　they are,
The next hour stamps with credit.
　　1st Knight.　　　Your last news ?
　　Gonfred. After the Page's story of the
　　　　death
Of Albert and Duke Conrad ?
　　Sigifred.　　　　　And the return
Of Ludolph with the Princess.
　　Gonfred.　　　　No more, save
Prince Gersa's freeing Abbot Ethelbert,
And the sweet lady, fair Erminia,
From prison.
　　1st Knight. Where are they now ?　Hast
　　　　yet heard ?
　　Gonfred. With the sad Emperor they
　　　　are closeted;　　　　　　　10
I saw the three pass slowly up the stairs,
The lady weeping, the old Abbot cowl'd.
　　Sigifred. What next ?
　　1st Knight.　　　I ache to think on 't.
　　Gonfred.　　　　　　'T is with fate.
　　1st Knight. One while these proud towers
　　　　are hush'd as death.
　　Gonfred. The next our poor Prince fills
　　　　the arched rooms
With ghastly ravings.
　　Sigifred.　　　I do fear his brain.

Gonfred. I will see more. Bear you so
 stout a heart ?
 [*Exeunt into the Castle.*

SCENE IV. — *A Cabinet, opening towards
 a terrace*

OTHO, ERMINIA, ETHELBERT, *and a Phy-
 sician, discovered.*

 Otho. O, my poor boy ! My son ! My
 son ! My Ludolph !
Have ye no comfort for me, ye physicians
Of the weak body and soul ?
 Ethelbert. 'T is not in medicine,
Either of heaven or earth, to cure, unless
Fit time be chosen to administer.
 Otho. A kind forbearance, holy Abbot.
 Come,
Erminia; here, sit by me, gentle girl;
Give me thy hand; hast thou forgiven me ?
 Erminia. Would I were with the saints
 to pray for you !
 Otho. Why will ye keep me from my
 darling child ? 10
 Physician. Forgive me, but he must not
 see thy face.
 Otho. Is then a father's countenance a
 Gorgon ?
Hath it not comfort in it ? Would it not
Console my poor boy, cheer him, help his
 spirits ?
Let me embrace him; let me speak to him;
I will ! Who hinders me ? Who 's Em-
 peror ?
 Physician. You may not, Sire; 't would
 overwhelm him quite,
He is so full of grief and passionate wrath;
Too heavy a sigh would kill him, or do
 worse.
He must be saved by fine contrivances; 20
And, most especially, we must keep clear
Out of his sight a father whom he loves;
His heart is full, it can contain no more,
And do its ruddy office.
 Ethelbert. Sage advice;
We must endeavour how to ease and slacken
The tight-wound energies of his despair,
Not make them tenser.

 Otho. Enough ! I hear, I hear;
Yet you were about to advise more, — I
 listen.
 Ethelbert. This learned doctor will agree
 with me,
That not in the smallest point should he be
 thwarted, 30
Or gainsaid by one word; his very mo-
 tions,
Nods, becks, and hints, should be obey'd
 with care,
Even on the moment; so his troubled mind
May cure itself.
 Physician. There are no other means.
 Otho. Open the door; let 's hear if all is
 quiet.
 Physician. Beseech you, Sire, forbear.
 Erminia. Do, do.
 Otho. I command !
Open it straight; — hush ! — quiet ! — my
 lost boy !
My miserable child !
 Ludolph (*indistinctly without*). Fill, fill
 my goblet, — here 's a health !
 Erminia. O, close the door !
 Otho. Let, let me hear his voice; this
 cannot last: 39
And fain would I catch up his dying words,
Though my own knell they be ! This can-
 not last !
O let me catch his voice — for lo ! I hear
This silence whisper me that he is dead !
It is so ! Gersa ?

 Enter GERSA.

 Physician. Say, how fares the prince ?
 Gersa. More calm; his features are less
 wild and flush'd;
Once he complain'd of weariness.
 Physician. Indeed !
'T is good, — 't is good; let him but fall
 asleep,
That saves him.
 Otho. Gersa, watch him like a child;
Ward him from harm, — and bring me
 better news !
 Physician. Humour him to the height.
 I fear to go; 50

For should he catch a glimpse of my dull
　　garb,
It might affright him, fill him with suspi-
　　cion
That we believe him sick, which must not
　　be.
Gersa. I will invent what soothing means
　　I can.
　　　　　　　　　　　　　　[*Exit* GERSA.
Physician. This should cheer up your
　　Highness; weariness
Is a good symptom, and most favourable;
It gives me pleasant hopes. Please you,
　　walk forth
Upon the terrace; the refreshing air
Will blow one half of your sad doubts
　　away.　　　　　　　　　[*Exeunt.*

SCENE V. — *A Banqueting Hall, bril-
liantly illuminated, and set forth with
all costly magnificence, with supper-
tables laden with services of gold and
silver. A door in the back scene, guarded
by two Soldiers. Lords, Ladies, Knights,
Gentlemen, etc., whispering sadly, and
ranging themselves ; part entering and
part discovered.*

1st Knight. Grievously are we tantalized,
　　one and all;
Sway'd here and there, commanded to and
　　fro,
As though we were the shadows of a sleep,
And link'd to a dreaming fancy. What do
　　we here ?
Gonfred. I am no seer; you know we
　　must obey
The prince from A to Z, though it should
　　be
To set the place in flames. I pray, hast
　　heard
Where the most wicked Princess is ?
1st Knight.　　　　　　　There, sir,
In the next room; have you remark'd those
　　two　　　　　　　　　　　　　　　9
Stout soldiers posted at the door ?
Gonfred.　　　　　　　For what ?
　　　　　　　　　　　[*They whisper.*
1st Lady. How ghast a train !

2d Lady. Sure this should be some splen-
　　did burial.
1st Lady. What fearful whispering ! See,
　　see, — Gersa there !

　　　　　　Enter GERSA.

Gersa. Put on your brightest looks;
　　smile if you can;
Behave as all were happy; keep your eyes
From the least watch upon him; if he
　　speaks
To any one, answer collectedly,
Without surprise, his questions, howe'er
　　strange.
Do this to the utmost — though, alas ! with
　　me
The remedy grows hopeless ! Here he
　　comes, —　　　　　　　　　　　　20
Observe what I have said — show no sur-
　　prise.

Enter LUDOLPH, *followed by* SIGIFRED *and
Page.*

Ludolph. A splendid company ! rare
　　beauties here !
I should have Orphean lips, and Plato's
　　fancy,
Amphion's utterance, toned with his lyre,
Or the deep key of Jove's sonorous mouth,
To give fit salutation. Methought I heard,
As I came in, some whispers — what of
　　that ?
'Tis natural men should whisper; at the
　　kiss
Of Psyche given by Love, there was a
　　buzz
Among the gods ! — and silence is as natu-
　　ral.　　　　　　　　　　　　　　30
These draperies are fine, and, being a
　　mortal,
I should desire no better; yet, in truth,
There must be some superior costliness,
Some wider-domed high magnificence !
I would have, as a mortal I may not,
Hangings of heaven's clouds, purple and
　　gold,
Slung from the spheres; gauzes of silver
　　mist,

Loop'd up with cords of twisted wreathed
 light,
And tassel'd round with weeping meteors !
These pendent lamps and chandeliers are
 bright 40
As earthly fires from dull dross can be
 cleansed;
Yet could my eyes drink up intenser beams
Undazzled — this is darkness — when I
 close
These lids, I see far fiercer brilliances, —
Skies full of splendid moons, and shooting
 stars,
And spouting exhalations, diamond fires,
And panting fountains quivering with deep
 glows !
Yes — this is dark — is it not dark ?
 Sigifred. My Lord,
'T is late; the lights of festival are ever 49
Quench'd in the morn.
 Ludolph. 'T is not to-morrow then ?
 Sigifred. 'T is early dawn.
 Gersa. Indeed full time we slept;
Say you so, Prince ?
 Ludolph. I say I quarrel'd with you;
We did not tilt each other — that 's a
 blessing, —
Good gods ! no innocent blood upon my
 head !
 Sigifred. Retire, Gersa !
 Ludolph. There should be three more
 here:
For two of them, they stay away perhaps,
Being gloomy-minded, haters of fair rev-
 els, —
They know their own thoughts best.
 As for the third,
Deep blue eyes, semi-shaded in white lids,
Finish'd with lashes fine for more soft
 shade, 60
Completed by her twin-arch'd ebon-brows;
White temples, of exactest elegance,
Of even mould, felicitous and smooth;
Cheeks fashion'd tenderly on either side,
So perfect, so divine, that our poor eyes
Are dazzled with the sweet proportioning,
And wonder that 't is so — the magic
 chance !

Her nostrils, small, fragrant, fairy-delicate;
Her lips — I swear no human bones e'er
 wore
So taking a disguise; — you shall behold
 her ! 70
We 'll have her presently; ay, you shall see
 her,
And wonder at her, friends, she is so fair;
She is the world's chief jewel, and, by
 heaven,
She 's mine by right of marriage ! — she is
 mine !
Patience, good people, in fit time I send
A summoner, — she will obey my call,
Being a wife most mild and dutiful.
First I would hear what music is prepared
To herald and receive her; let me hear !
 Sigifred. Bid the musicians soothe him
 tenderly. 80
 [*A soft strain of Music.*
 Ludolph. Ye have none better ? No, I
 am content;
'T is a rich sobbing melody, with reliefs
Full and majestic; it is well enough,
And will be sweeter, when you see her pace
Sweeping into this presence, glistened o'er
With emptied caskets, and her train upheld
By ladies, habited in robes of lawn,
Sprinkled with golden crescents, others
 bright
In silks, with spangles shower'd, and bow'd
 to 89
By Duchesses and pearled Margravines !
Sad, that the fairest creature of the earth —
I pray you mind me not — 't is sad, I say,
That the extremest beauty of the world
Should so entrench herself away from me,
Behind a barrier of engender'd guilt !
 2d Lady. Ah ! what a moan !
 1st Knight. Most piteous indeed !
 Ludolph. She shall be brought before this
 company,
And then — then —
 1st Lady. He muses.
 Gersa. O, Fortune, where will this
 end ?
 Sigifred. I guess his purpose ! Indeed
 he must not have

That pestilence brought in, — that cannot
 be, 100
There we must stop him.
 Gersa. I am lost ! Hush, hush !
He is about to rave again.
 Ludolph. A barrier of guilt ! I was the
 fool,
She was the cheater ! Who 's the cheater
 now,
And who the fool ? The entrapp'd, the
 caged fool,
The bird-limed raven ? She shall croak to
 death
Secure ! Methinks I have her in my fist,
To crush her with my heel ! Wait, wait !
 I marvel
My father keeps away. Good friend — ah !
 Sigifred !
Do bring him to me, — and Erminia 110
I fain would see before I sleep — and Eth-
 elbert,
That he may bless me, as I know he will,
Though I have cursed him.
 Sigifred. Rather suffer me
To lead you to them.
 Ludolph. No, excuse me, — no !
The day is not quite done. Go, bring them
 hither. [*Exit* Sigifred.
Certes, a father's smile should, like sun
 light,
Slant on my sheafed harvest of ripe bliss.
Besides, I thirst to pledge my lovely bride
In a deep goblet: let me see — what wine ?
The strong Iberian juice, or mellow Greek ?
Or pale Calabrian ? Or the Tuscan grape ?
Or of old Ætna's pulpy wine-presses, 122
Black stain'd with the fat vintage, as it
 were
The purple slaughter-house, where Bac-
 chus' self
Prick'd his own swollen veins ? Where is
 my page ?
 Page. Here, here !
 Ludolph. Be ready to obey me; anon
 thou shalt
Bear a soft message for me; for the hour
Draws near when I must make a winding
 up

Of bridal mysteries — a fine-spun ven-
 geance !
Carve it on my tomb, that, when I rest
 beneath, 130
Men shall confess this Prince was gull'd
 and cheated,
But from the ashes of disgrace he rose
More than a fiery phœnix, and did burn
His ignominy up in purging fires !
Did I not send, Sir, but a moment past,
For my Father ?
 Gersa. You did.
 Ludolph. Perhaps 't would be
Much better he came not.
 Gersa. He enters now !

Enter Otho, Erminia, Ethelbert, Sigi-
 fred, *and Physician.*

 Ludolph. O thou good man, against whose
 sacred head
I was a mad conspirator, chiefly too, 139
For the sake of my fair newly wedded wife,
Now to be punish'd, do not look so sad !
Those charitable eyes will thaw my heart,
Those tears will wash away a just resolve,
A verdict ten times sworn ! Awake —
 awake —
Put on a judge's brow, and use a tongue
Made iron-stern by habit ! Thou shalt see
A deed to be applauded, 'scribed in gold !
Join a loud voice to mine, and so denounce
What I alone will execute
 Otho. Dear son,
What is it ? By your father's love, I sue
That it be nothing merciless !
 Ludolph. To that demon ?
Not so ! No ! She is in temple-stall 152
Being garnish'd for the sacrifice, and I,
The Priest of Justice, will immolate her
Upon the altar of wrath ! She stings me
 through ! —
Even as the worm doth feed upon the nut,
So she, a scorpion, preys upon my brain !
I feel her gnawing here ! Let her but
 vanish,
Then, father, I will lead your legions forth,
Compact in steeled squares, and speared
 files, 160

And bid our trumpets speak a fell rebuke
To nations drows'd in peace!

Otho. To-morrow, son,
Be your word law; forget to-day—

Ludolph. I will
When I have finish'd it! Now,—now,
 I 'm pight,
Tight-footed for the deed!

Erminia. Alas! Alas!

Ludolph. What angel's voice is that?
 Erminia!
Ah! gentlest creature, whose sweet inno-
 cence
Was almost murder'd; I am penitent;
Wilt thou forgive me? And thou, holy
 man,
Good Ethelbert, shall I die in peace with
 you? 170

Erminia. Die, my lord!

Ludolph. I feel it possible.

Otho. Physician?

Physician. I fear me he is past my skill.

Otho. Not so!

Ludolph. I see it—I see it—I have
 been wandering!
Half mad—not right here—I forget my
 purpose.
Bestir—bestir—Auranthe! Ha! ha! ha!
Youngster! Page! go bid them drag her
 to me!
Obey! This shall finish it!
 [*Draws a dagger.*

Otho. Oh, my son! my son!

Sigifred. This must not be—stop there!

Ludolph. Am I obey'd?
A little talk with her—no harm—haste!
 haste! [*Exit Page.*
Set her before me—never fear I can strike.

Several Voices. My Lord! My Lord!

Gersa. Good Prince!

Ludolph. Why do ye trouble me? out
 —out—away! 182
There she is! take that! and that! no, no—
That 's not well done.—Where is she?

*The doors open. Enter Page. Several wo-
men are seen grouped about* AURANTHE *in
the inner-room.*

Page. Alas! My Lord, my Lord! they
 cannot move her!
Her arms are stiff,—her fingers clench'd
 and cold!

Ludolph. She 's dead!
 [*Staggers and falls into their arms.*

Ethelbert. Take away the dagger.

Gersa. Softly; so!

Otho. Thank God for that!

Sigifred. It could not harm him now.

Gersa. No!—brief be his anguish!

Ludolph. She 's gone! I am content—
 Nobles, good night! 190
We are all weary—faint—set ope the
 doors—
I will to bed!—To-morrow—
 [*Dies.*

 The Curtain falls.

KING STEPHEN

A DRAMATIC FRAGMENT

Lord Houghton, when reprinting this piece in the Aldine edition of 1876, appends the following note from the MSS. of Charles Armitage Brown: ' As soon as Keats had finished *Otho the Great* I pointed out to him a subject for an English historical tragedy in the reign of Stephen, beginning with his defeat by the Empress Maud and ending with the death of his son Eustace. He was struck with the variety of events and characters which must necessarily be introduced, and I offered to give, as before, their dramatic conduct. " The play must open," I began, " with the field of battle, when Stephen's forces are retreating." — " Stop," he cried, " I have been too long in leading strings; I will do all this myself." He immediately set about it, and wrote two or three scenes.'

ACT I

SCENE I. — *Field of Battle*

Alarum. Enter King STEPHEN, *Knights, and Soldiers.*

Stephen. If shame can on a soldier's vein-
swoll'n front
Spread deeper crimson than the battle's
toil,
Blush in your casing helmets ! for see, see !
Yonder my chivalry, my pride of war,
Wrench'd with an iron hand from firm
array,
Are routed loose about the plashy meads,
Of honour forfeit. O, that my known
voice
Could reach your dastard ears, and fright
you more !
Fly, cowards, fly ! Glocester is at your
backs !
Throw your slack bridles o'er the flurried
manes,
Ply well the rowell with faint trembling
heels, 10
Scampering to death at last !
1st Knight. The enemy
Bears his flaunt standard close upon their
rear.

2d Knight. Sure of a bloody prey, seeing
the fens
Will swamp them girth-deep.
Stephen. Over head and ears,
No matter ! 'T is a gallant enemy;
How like a comet he goes streaming on.
But we must plague him in the flank, —
hey, friends ?
We are well breathed, — follow !

Enter Earl BALDWIN *and Soldiers, as
defeated.*

Stephen. De Redvers !
What is the monstrous bugbear that can
fright 20
Baldwin ?
Baldwin. No scare-crow, but the fortu-
nate star
Of boisterous Chester, whose fell truncheon
now
Points level to the goal of victory.
This way he comes, and if you would main-
tain
Your person unaffronted by vile odds,
Take horse, my Lord.
Stephen. And which way spur for life ?
Now I thank Heaven I am in the toils,
That soldiers may bear witness how my
arm

948

Can burst the meshes. Not the eagle more
Loves to beat up against a tyrannous blast,
Than I to meet the torrent of my foes. 31
This is a brag, — be 't so, — but if I fall,
Carve it upon my 'scutcheon'd sepulchre.
On, fellow soldiers! Earl of Redvers,
 back!
Not twenty Earls of Chester shall brow-
 beat
The diadem. [*Exeunt. Alarum.*

SCENE II. — *Another part of the Field*

*Trumpets sounding a Victory. Enter
GLOCESTER, Knights, and Forces.*

Glocester. Now may we lift our bruised
 visors up,
And take the flattering freshness of the
 air,
While the wide din of battle dies away
Into times past, yet to be echoed sure
In the silent pages of our chroniclers.
 1*st Knight.* Will Stephen's death be
 mark'd there, my good Lord,
Or that we gave him lodging in yon towers?
Glocester. Fain would I know the great
 usurper's fate.

Enter two Captains severally.

1*st Captain.* My Lord!
2*d Captain.* Most noble Earl!
1*st Captain.* The King —
2*d Captain.* The Empress greets —
Glocester. What of the King?
1*st Captain.* He sole and lone maintains
A hopeless bustle 'mid our swarming arms,
And with a nimble savageness attacks, 13
Escapes, makes fiercer onset, then anew
Eludes death, giving death to most that
 dare
Trespass within the circuit of his sword!
He must by this have fallen. Baldwin is
 taken;
And for the Duke of Bretagne, like a stag
He flies, for the Welsh beagles to hunt
 down.
God save the Empress!

Glocester. Now our dreaded Queen:
What message from her Highness?
 2*d Captain.* Royal Maud
From the throng'd towers of Lincoln hath
 look'd down, 22
Like Pallas from the walls of Ilion,
And seen her enemies havock'd at her feet.
She greets most noble Glocester from her
 heart,
Entreating him, his captains, and brave
 knights,
To grace a banquet. The high city gates
Are envious which shall see your triumph
 pass;
The streets are full of music.

Enter 2d Knight.

Glocester. Whence come you?
2*d Knight.* From Stephen, my good
 Prince, — Stephen! Stephen! 30
Glocester. Why do you make such echo-
 ing of his name?
2*d Knight.* Because I think, my lord, he
 is no man,
But a fierce demon, 'nointed safe from
 wounds,
And misbaptized with a Christian name.
 Glocester. A mighty soldier! — Does he
 still hold out?
 2*d Knight.* He shames our victory. His
 valour still
Keeps elbow-room amid our eager swords,
And holds our bladed falchions all aloof —
His gleaming battle-axe being slaughter-
 sick,
Smote on the morion of a Flemish knight,
Broke short in his hand; upon the which
 he flung 41
The heft away with such a vengeful force,
It paunch'd the Earl of Chester's horse,
 who then
Spleen-hearted came in full career at him.
 Glocester. Did no one take him at a van-
 tage then?
 2*d Knight.* Three then with tiger leap
 upon him flew,
Whom, with his sword swift-drawn and
 nimbly held,

He stung away again, and stood to breathe,
Smiling. Anon upon him rush'd once more
A throng of foes, and in this renew'd strife,
My sword met his and snapp'd off at the
 hilt. 51
 Glocester. Come, lead me to this man —
 and let us move
In silence, not insulting his sad doom
With clamorous trumpets. To the Em-
 press bear
My salutation as befits the time.
 [*Exeunt* GLOCESTER *and Forces.*

SCENE III. — *The Field of Battle*

Enter STEPHEN *unarmed.*

 Stephen. Another sword! And what if
 I could seize
One from Bellona's gleaming armoury,
Or choose the fairest of her sheafed spears!
Where are my enemies? Here, close at
 hand,
Here come the testy brood. O, for a
 sword!
I'm faint — a biting sword! A noble
 sword!
A hedge-stake — or a ponderous stone to
 hurl
With brawny vengeance, like the labourer
 Cain.
Come on! Farewell my kingdom, and all
 hail
Thou superb, plumed, and helmeted re-
 nown, 10
All hail — I would not truck this brilliant
 day
To rule in Pylos with a Nestor's beard —
Come on!

Enter DE KAIMS *and Knights, etc.*

 De Kaims. Is 't madness or a hunger
 after death
That makes thee thus unarm'd throw
 taunts at us? —
Yield, Stephen, or my sword's point dips in
The gloomy current of a traitor's heart.
 Stephen. Do it, De Kaims, I will not
 budge an inch.

 De Kaims. Yes, of thy madness thou
 shalt take the meed.
 Stephen. Darest thou?
 De Kaims. How dare, against a man dis-
 arm'd?
 Stephen. What weapons has the lion but
 himself? 20
Come not near me, De Kaims, for by the
 price
Of all the glory I have won this day,
Being a king, I will not yield alive
To any but the second man of the realm,
Robert of Glocester.
 De Kaims. Thou shalt vail to me.
 Stephen. Shall I, when I have sworn
 against it, sir?
Thou think'st it brave to take a breathing
 king,
That, on a court-day bow'd to haughty
 Maud,
The awed presence-chamber may be bold
To whisper, there's the man who took
 alive 30
Stephen — me — prisoner. Certes, De
 Kaims,
The ambition is a noble one.
 De Kaims. 'T is true,
And, Stephen, I must compass it.
 Stephen. No, no,
Do not tempt me to throttle you on the
 gorge,
Or with my gauntlet crush your hollow
 breast,
Just when your knighthood is grown ripe
 and full
For lordship.
 A Soldier. Is an honest yeoman's spear
Of no use at a need? Take that.
 Stephen. Ah, dastard!
 De Kaims. What, you are vulnerable!
 my prisoner!
 Stephen. No, not yet. I disclaim it, and
 demand 40
Death as a sovereign right unto a king
Who 'sdains to yield to any but his peer,
If not in title, yet in noble deeds,
The Earl of Glocester. Stab to the hilt,
 De Kaims,

For I will never by mean hands be led
From this so famous field. Do you hear !
 Be quick !
Trumpets. Enter the Earl of CHESTER *and*
 Knights.

SCENE IV.—*A Presence Chamber. Queen*
 MAUD *in a Chair of State, the Earls*
 of GLOCESTER *and* CHESTER, *Lords,*
 Attendants

 Maud. Glocester, no more: I will behold
 that Boulogne:
Set him before me. Not for the poor sake
Of regal pomp and a vain-glorious hour,
As thou with wary speech, yet near enough,
Hast hinted.
 Glocester. Faithful counsel have I given;
If wary, for your Highness' benefit.
 Maud. The Heavens forbid that I should
not do so,
For by thy valour have I won this realm,
Which by thy wisdom I will ever keep.
To sage advisers let me ever bend 10
A meek attentive ear, so that they treat
Of the wide kingdom's rule and govern-
 ment,
Not trenching on our actions personal.
Advised, not school'd, I would be; and
 henceforth
Spoken to in clear, plain, and open terms,
Not side-ways sermon'd at.
 Glocester. Then in plain terms,
Once more for the fallen king —
 Maud. Your pardon, Brother,
I would no more of that; for, as I said,
'T is not for worldly pomp I wish to see
The rebel, but as dooming judge to give 20
A sentence something worthy of his guilt.
 Glocester. If 't must be so, I 'll bring him
 to your presence.
 [*Exit* GLOCESTER.
 Maud. A meaner summoner might do as
 well —
My Lord of Chester, is 't true what I
 hear
Of Stephen of Boulogne, our prisoner,
That he, as a fit penance for his crimes,

Eats wholesome, sweet, and palatable food
Off Glocester's golden dishes — drinks pure
 wine,
Lodges soft ?
 Chester. More than that, my gracious
 Queen,
Has anger'd me. The noble Earl, me-
 thinks, 30
Full soldier as he is, and without peer
In counsel, dreams too much among his
 books.
It may read well, but sure 't is out of date
To play the Alexander with Darius.
 Maud. Truth ! I think so. By Heavens
 it shall not last !
 Chester. It would amaze your Highness
 now to mark
How Glocester overstrains his courtesy
To that crime-loving rebel, that Boulogne —
 Maud. That ingrate !
 Chester. For whose vast ingratitude
To our late sovereign lord, your noble sire,
The generous Earl condoles in his mishaps,
And with a sort of lackeying friendliness,
Talks off the mighty frowning from his
 brow, 43
Woos him to hold a duet in a smile,
Or, if it please him, play an hour at chess —
 Maud. A perjured slave !
 Chester. And for his perjury,
Glocester has fit rewards — nay, I believe,
He sets his bustling household's wits at
 work
For flatteries to ease this Stephen's hours,
And make a heaven of his purgatory; 50
Adorning bondage with the pleasant gloss
Of feasts and music, and all idle shows
Of indoor pageantry; while syren whispers,
Predestined for his ear, 'scape as half-
 check'd
From lips the courtliest and the rubiest,
Of all the realm, admiring of his deeds.
 Maud. A frost upon his summer !
 Chester. A queen's nod
Can make his June December. Here he
 comes.

.

THE EVE OF ST. MARK

A FRAGMENT

In a letter to George and Georgiana Keats, dated February 14, 1819, Keats says that he means to send them in the next packet 'The Pot of Basil,' 'St. Agnes' Eve,' and 'if I should have finished it a little thing called "The Eve of St. Mark."' He does not refer to the poem again directly, until writing from Winchester to the same, September 20, when he says: 'The great beauty of poetry is that it makes everything in every place interesting. The palatine Vienna and the abbotine Winchester are equally interesting. Some time since I began a poem called "The Eve of St. Mark," quite in the spirit of town quietude. I think I will give you the sensation of walking about an old country town in a coolish evening. I know not whether I shall ever finish it. I will give it as far as I have gone.' The poem appears never to have been finished, and was published in this fragmentary form in *Life, Letters and Literary Remains.*

Mr. Forman gives an interesting extract from a letter written him by Mr. Rossetti, which throws a possible light on the origin of the poem. He had been reading Keats's letters to Fanny Brawne, and writes : ' I should think it very conceivable — nay, I will say *to myself* highly probable and almost certain, — that the " Poem which I have in my head " referred to by Keats at page 106 was none other than the fragmentary "Eve of St. Mark." By the light of the extract, . . . I judge that the heroine — remorseful after trifling with a sick and now absent lover — might make her way to the minster-porch to learn his fate by the spell, and perhaps see his figure enter but not return.' The extract from Keats's letter is as follows : ' If my health would bear it, I could write a Poem which I have in my head, which would be a consolation for people in such a situation as mine. I would show some one in Love as I am, with a person living in such Liberty as you do.'

Upon a Sabbath-day it fell;
Twice holy was the Sabbath-bell,
That call'd the folk to evening prayer;
The city streets were clean and fair
From wholesome drench of April rains;
And, on the western window panes,
The chilly sunset faintly told
Of unmatured green valleys cold,
Of the green thorny bloomless hedge,
Of rivers new with spring-tide sedge, 10
Of primroses by shelter'd rills,
And daisies on the aguish hills.
Twice holy was the Sabbath-bell:
The silent streets were crowded well
With staid and pious companies,
Warm from their fireside orat'ries;
And moving, with demurest air,
To even-song, and vesper prayer.

Each arched porch, and entry low,
Was fill'd with patient folk and slow, 20
With whispers hush, and shuffling feet,
While play'd the organ loud and sweet.

The bells had ceased, the prayers begun,
And Bertha had not yet half done
A curious volume, patch'd and torn,
That all day long, from earliest morn,
Had taken captive her two eyes,
Among its golden broideries;
Perplex'd her with a thousand things, —
The stars of Heaven, and angels' wings, 30
Martyrs in a fiery blaze,
Azure saints and silver rays,
Moses' breastplate, and the seven
Candlesticks John saw in Heaven,
The winged Lion of Saint Mark,

And the Covenantal Ark,
With its many mysteries,
Cherubim and golden mice.

Bertha was a maiden fair,
Dwelling in th' old Minster-square; 40
From her fireside she could see,
Sidelong, its rich antiquity,
Far as the Bishop's garden-wall;
Where sycamores and elm-trees tall,
Full-leaved, the forest had outstript,
By no sharp north-wind ever nipt,
So shelter'd by the mighty pile.
Bertha arose, and read awhile,
With forehead 'gainst the window-pane.
Again she tried, and then again, 50
Until the dusk eve left her dark
Upon the legend of St. Mark.
From plaited lawn-frill, fine and thin,
She lifted up her soft warm chin,
With aching neck and swimming eyes,
And dazed with saintly imag'ries.

All was gloom, and silent all,
Save now and then the still foot-fall
Of one returning homewards late,
Past the echoing minster-gate. 60
The clamorous daws, that all the day
Above tree-tops and towers play,
Pair by pair had gone to rest,
Each in its ancient belfry-nest,
Where asleep they fall betimes,
To music and the drowsy chimes.

All was silent, all was gloom,
Abroad and in the homely room:
Down she sat, poor cheated soul!
And struck a lamp from the dismal coal; 70
Lean'd forward, with bright drooping hair
And slant book, full against the glare.
Her shadow, in uneasy guise,
Hover'd about, a giant size,
On ceiling-beam and old oak chair,
The parrot's cage, and panel-square;

And the warm angled winter-screen,
On which were many monsters seen,
Call'd doves of Siam, Lima mice,
And legless birds of Paradise, 80
Macaw, and tender Avadavat,
And silken-furr'd Angora cat.
Untired she read, her shadow still
Glower'd about, as it would fill
The room with wildest forms and shades,
As though some ghostly queen of spades
Had come to mock behind her back,
And dance, and ruffle her garments black.
Untired she read the legend page,
Of holy Mark, from youth to age, 90
On land, on sea, in pagan chains,
Rejoicing for his many pains.
Sometimes the learned eremite,
With golden star, or dagger bright,
Referr'd to pious poesies
Written in smallest crow-quill size
Beneath the text; and thus the rhyme
Was parcell'd out from time to time:
—— ' Als writith he of swevenis,
Men han beforne they wake in bliss, 100
Whanne that hir friendes thinke him bound
In crimped shroude farre under grounde;
And how a litling child mote be
A saint er its nativitie,
Gif that the modre (God her blesse!)
Kepen in solitarinesse,
And kissen devoute the holy croce,
Of Goddes love, and Sathan's force, —
He writith; and thinges many mo
Of swiche thinges I may not show. 110
Bot I must tellen verilie
Somdel of Saintè Cicilie,
And chieflie what he auctorethe
Of Saintè Markis life and dethe:'

At length her constant eyelids come
Upon the fervent martyrdom;
Then lastly to his holy shrine,
Exalt amid the tapers' shine
At Venice, —

HYPERION

A FRAGMENT

The first mention of *Hyperion* in Keats's letters occurs in that written on Christmas day, 1818, to his brother and sister in America, in which he says: 'I think you knew before you left England that my next subject would be "the fall of Hyperion." I went on a little with it last night, but it will take some time to get into the vein again. I will not give you any extracts because I wish the whole to make an impression.' He speaks of it a week later as 'scarce begun.' Again, February 14, 1819, he writes to the same: 'I have not gone on with *Hyperion* — for to tell the truth I have not been in great cue for writing lately — I must wait for the spring to rouse me up a little.' In August he told Bailey that he had been writing parts of *Hyperion*, but it is quite plain that he did little continuous work on it, but was drawn off by his tales and tragedy. From Winchester, September 22, 1819, he writes to Reynolds : ' I have given up *Hyperion* — there were too many Miltonic inversions in it — Miltonic verse cannot be written but in an artful, or, rather, artist's humour. I wish to give myself up to other sensations. English ought to be kept up. It may be interesting to you to pick out some lines from *Hyperion*, and put a mark × to the false beauty proceeding from art, and one ‖ to the true voice of feeling. Upon my soul 't was imagination — I cannot make the distinction — every now and then there is a Miltonic intonation — but I cannot make the division properly.' From the silence regarding the poem in his after letters, it would appear that he left it at this stage.

That Keats designed a large epic in *Hyperion*, which was to be in ten books, is plain, but it is also tolerably clear that he abandoned his purpose, for he did not actually forbid the publication of the fragment, though it is doubtful if the whole reason for his action is given in the *Publishers' Advertisement* to the 1820 volume, containing the poem. 'If any apology be thought necessary,' it is there said, ' for the appearance of the unfinished poem of *Hyperion*, the publishers beg to state that they alone are responsible, as it was printed at their particular request, and contrary to the wish of the author. The poem was intended to have been of equal length with *Endymion*, but the reception given to that work discouraged the author from proceeding.'

Keats's friend Woodhouse, in his interleaved and annotated copy of *Endymion*, says of *Hyperion*: 'The poem if completed would have treated of the dethronement of Hyperion, the former God of the Sun, by Apollo, — and incidentally of those of Oceanus by Neptune, of Saturn by Jupiter. etc., and of the war of the Giants for Saturn's reëstablishment, with other events, of which we have but very dark hints in the mythological poets of Greece and Rome.'

It is not impossible that besides the inertia produced by diminution of physical powers, another reason existed for Keats's failure to complete his poem. In the two full books which we have, he had stated so fully and explicitly the underlying thought in his interpretation of the myth that his interest in any delineation of a hopeless struggle might well have been unequal to the task. The speeches successively of Oceanus and Clymene which so enraged Enceladus were the masculine and feminine confessions that as their own supremacy over the antecedent chaos had been due to the law which made order expel disorder, so the supremacy of the new race of gods over them was due to the still further law

'That first in beauty should be first in might.'

Nay, more, the vision they have is not of a restoration of the old order, but of the defeat of the new by some still more distant evolution.

' Another race may drive
Our conquerors to mourn as we do now.'

BOOK I

DEEP in the shady sadness of a vale
Far sunken from the healthy breath of
 morn,
Far from the fiery noon, and eve's one
 star,
Sat gray-hair'd Saturn, quiet as a stone,
Still as the silence round about his lair;
Forest on forest hung about his head
Like cloud on cloud. No stir of air was
 there,
Not so much life as on a summer's day
Robs not one light seed from the feather'd
 grass,
But where the dead leaf fell, there did it
 rest. 10
A stream went voiceless by, still deadened
 more
By reason of his fallen divinity
Spreading a shade: the Naiad 'mid her
 reeds
Press'd her cold finger closer to her lips.

Along the margin-sand large foot-marks
 went,
No further than to where his feet had
 stray'd,
And slept there since. Upon the sodden
 ground
His old right hand lay nerveless, listless,
 dead,
Unsceptred; and his realmless eyes were
 closed ;
While his bow'd head seem'd list'ning to
 the Earth, 20
His ancient mother, for some comfort yet.

It seem'd no force could wake him from
 his place;
But there came one, who with a kindred
 hand
Touch'd his wide shoulders, after bending
 low
With reverence, though to one who knew
 it not.
She was a Goddess of the infant world;
By her in stature the tall Amazon

Had stood a pigmy's height: she would
 have ta'en
Achilles by the hair and bent his neck;
Or with a finger stay'd Ixion's wheel. 30
Her face was large as that of Memphian
 sphinx,
Pedestal'd haply in a palace-court,
When sages look'd to Egypt for their lore.
But oh ! how unlike marble was that face;
How beautiful, if sorrow had not made
Sorrow more beautiful than Beauty's self.
There was a listening fear in her regard,
As if calamity had but begun;
As if the vanward clouds of evil days 39
Had spent their malice, and the sullen rear
Was with its stored thunder labouring up.
One hand she press'd upon that aching
 spot
Where beats the human heart, as if just
 there,
Though an immortal, she felt cruel pain:
The other upon Saturn's bended neck
She laid, and to the level of his ear
Leaning with parted lips, some words she
 spake
In solemn tenour and deep organ tone:
Some mourning words, which in our feeble
 tongue
Would come in these like accents; O how
 frail 50
To that large utterance of the early Gods !
' Saturn, look up ! — though wherefore,
 poor old King ?
I have no comfort for thee, no not one:
I cannot say, " O wherefore sleepest thou ? "
For heaven is parted from thee, and the
 earth
Knows thee not, thus afflicted, for a God;
And ocean too, with all its solemn noise,
Has from thy sceptre pass'd; and all the
 air
Is emptied of thine hoary majesty.
Thy thunder, conscious of the new com-
 mand, 60
Rumbles reluctant o'er our fallen house;
And thy sharp lightning in unpractised
 hands
Scorches and burns our once serene domain.

O aching time! O moments big as years!
All as ye pass swell out the monstrous
 truth,
And press it so upon our weary griefs
That unbelief has not a space to breathe.
Saturn, sleep on:— O thoughtless, why
 did I
Thus violate thy slumbrous solitude?
Why should I ope thy melancholy eyes? 70
Saturn, sleep on! while at thy feet I
 weep.'

As when, upon a tranced summer-night,
Those green-robed senators of mighty
 woods,
Tall oaks, branch-charmed by the earnest
 stars,
Dream, and so dream all night without a
 stir,
Save from one gradual solitary gust
Which comes upon the silence, and dies off,
As if the ebbing air had but one wave:
So came these words and went; the while
 in tears
She touch'd her fair large forehead to the
 ground, 80
Just where her falling hair might be out-
 spread
A soft and silken mat for Saturn's feet.
One moon, with alteration slow, had shed
Her silver seasons four upon the night,
And still these two were postured motion-
 less,
Like natural sculpture in cathedral cavern;
The frozen God still couchant on the earth,
And the sad Goddess weeping at his feet:
Until at length old Saturn lifted up 89
His faded eyes, and saw his kingdom gone,
And all the gloom and sorrow of the place,
And that fair kneeling Goddess; and then
 spake,
As with a palsied tongue, and while his
 beard
Shook horrid with such aspen-malady:
' O tender spouse of gold Hyperion,
Thea, I feel thee ere I see thy face;
Look up, and let me see our doom in it;
Look up, and tell me if this feeble shape

Is Saturn's; tell me, if thou hear'st the
 voice
Of Saturn; tell me, if this wrinkling brow,
Naked and bare of its great diadem, 101
Peers like the front of Saturn. Who had
 power
To make me desolate? whence came the
 strength?
How was it nurtured to such bursting forth,
While Fate seem'd strangled in my nervous
 grasp?
But it is so; and I am smother'd up,
And buried from all godlike exercise
Of influence benign on planets pale,
Of admonitions to the winds and seas, 109
Of peaceful sway above man's harvesting,
And all those acts which Deity supreme
Doth ease its heart of love in.— I am gone
Away from my own bosom: I have left
My strong identity, my real self,
Somewhere between the throne, and where
 I sit
Here on this spot of earth. Search, Thea,
 search!
Open thine eyes eterne, and sphere them
 round
Upon all space: space starr'd, and lorn of
 light;
Space region'd with life-air, and barren
 void;
Spaces of fire, and all the yawn of hell. 120
Search, Thea, search! and tell me if thou
 seest
A certain shape or shadow, making way
With wings or chariot fierce to repossess
A heaven he lost erewhile: it must — it
 must
Be of ripe progress — Saturn must be King.
Yes, there must be a golden victory;
There must be Gods thrown down, and
 trumpets blown
Of triumph calm, and hymns of festival
Upon the gold clouds metropolitan,
Voices of soft proclaim, and silver stir 130
Of strings in hollow shells; and there shall
 be
Beautiful things made new, for the sur-
 prise

Of the sky-children; I will give command:
Thea! Thea! Thea! where is Saturn?'

This passion lifted him upon his feet,
And made his hands to struggle in the air,
His Druid locks to shake and ooze with
 sweat,
His eyes to fever out, his voice to cease.
He stood, and heard not Thea's sobbing
 deep; 139
A little time, and then again he snatch'd
Utterance thus: — 'But cannot I create?
Cannot I form? Cannot I fashion forth
Another world, another universe,
To overbear and crumble this to nought?
Where is another chaos? Where?' — That
 word
Found way unto Olympus, and made quake
The rebel three. — Thea was startled up,
And in her bearing was a sort of hope,
As thus she quick-voiced spake, yet full of
 awe.

'This cheers our fallen house: come to
 our friends, 150
O Saturn! come away, and give them
 heart;
I know the covert, for thence came I
 hither.'
Thus brief; then with beseeching eyes she
 went
With backward footing through the shade
 a space:
He follow'd, and she turn'd to lead the
 way
Through aged boughs, that yielded like the
 mist
Which eagles cleave upmounting from
 their nest.

Meanwhile in other realms big tears
 were shed,
More sorrow like to this, and such like
 woe,
Too huge for mortal tongue or pen of
 scribe: 160
The Titans fierce, self-hid, or prison-
 bound,

Groan'd for the old allegiance once more,
And listen'd in sharp pain for Saturn's
 voice.
But one of the whole mammoth-brood still
 kept
His sov'reignty, and rule, and majesty;
Blazing Hyperion on his orbed fire
Still sat, still snuff'd the incense, teeming
 up
From man to the sun's God; yet unsecure:
For as among us mortals omens drear
Fright and perplex, so also shudder'd he,
Not at dog's howl, or gloom-bird's hated
 screech, 171
Or the familiar visiting of one
Upon the first toll of his passing-bell,
Or prophesyings of the midnight lamp;
But horrors, portion'd to a giant nerve,
Oft made Hyperion ache. His palace
 bright
Bastion'd with pyramids of glowing gold,
And touch'd with shade of bronzed obe-
 lisks,
Glared a blood-red through all its thousand
 courts,
Arches, and domes, and fiery galleries; 180
And all its curtains of Aurorian clouds
Flush'd angerly: while sometimes eagles'
 wings,
Unseen before by Gods or wondering men,
Darken'd the place; and neighing steeds
 were heard,
Not heard before by Gods or wondering
 men.
Also, when he would taste the spicy
 wreaths
Of incense, breathed aloft from sacred hills,
Instead of sweets, his ample palate took
Savour of poisonous brass and metal sick:
And so, when harbour'd in the sleepy west,
After the full completion of fair day, 191
For rest divine upon exalted couch
And slumber in the arms of melody,
He paced away the pleasant hours of ease
With stride colossal, on from hall to hall;
While far within each aisle and deep re-
 cess,
His winged minions in close clusters stood,

Amazed and full of fear; like anxious men
Who on wide plains gather in panting
 troops,
When earthquakes jar their battlements
 and towers. 200
Even now, while Saturn, roused from icy
 trance,
Went step for step with Thea through the
 woods,
Hyperion, leaving twilight in the rear,
Came slope upon the threshold of the west;
Then, as was wont, his palace-door flew ope
In smoothest silence, save what solemn
 tubes,
Blown by the serious Zephyrs, gave of
 sweet
And wandering sounds, slow-breathed melo-
 dies;
And like a rose in vermeil tint and shape,
In fragrance soft, and coolness to the eye, 210
That inlet to severe magnificence
Stood full blown, for the God to enter in.

He enter'd, but he enter'd full of wrath;
His flaming robes stream'd out beyond his
 heels,
And gave a roar, as if of earthly fire,
That scared away the meek ethereal Hours
And made their dove-wings tremble. On
 he flared,
From stately nave to nave, from vault to
 vault,
Through bowers of fragrant and enwreathed
 light,
And diamond - paved lustrous long ar-
 cades, 220
Until he reach'd the great main cupola;
There standing fierce beneath, he stampt
 his foot,
And from the basements deep to the high
 towers
Jarr'd his own golden region; and before
The quavering thunder thereupon had
 ceased,
His voice leapt out, despite of godlike
 curb,
To this result: 'O dreams of day and
 night !

O monstrous forms ! O effigies of pain !
O spectres busy in a cold, cold gloom !
O lank-ear'd Phantoms of black-weeded
 pools ! 230
Why do I know ye ? why have I seen ye ?
 why
Is my eternal essence thus distraught
To see and to behold these horrors new ?
Saturn is fallen, am I too to fall ?
Am I to leave this haven of my rest,
This cradle of my glory, this soft clime,
This calm luxuriance of blissful light,
These crystalline pavilions, and pure fanes,
Of all my lucent empire ? It is left
Deserted, void, nor any haunt of mine. 240
The blaze, the splendour, and the symme-
 try,
I cannot see — but darkness, death and
 darkness.
Even here, into my centre of repose,
The shady visions come to domineer,
Insult, and blind, and stifle up my pomp. —
Fall ! — No, by Tellus and her briny robes !
Over the fiery frontier of my realms
I will advance a terrible right arm
Shall scare that infant thunderer, rebel
 Jove,
And bid old Saturn take his throne again.'
He spake, and ceased, the while a heavier
 threat 251
Held struggle with his throat, but came
 not forth;
For as in theatres of crowded men
Hubbub increases more they call out
 'Hush !'
So at Hyperion's words the Phantoms pale
Bestirr'd themselves, thrice horrible and
 cold;
And from the mirror'd level where he stood
A mist arose, as from a scummy marsh.
At this, through all his bulk an agony
Crept gradual, from the feet unto the
 crown, 260
Like a lithe serpent vast and muscular
Making slow way, with head and neck con-
 vulsed
From over-strained might. Released, he
 fled

To the eastern gates, and full six dewy
 hours
Before the dawn in season due should
 blush,
He breathed fierce breath against the sleepy
 portals,
Clear'd them of heavy vapours, burst them
 wide
Suddenly on the ocean's chilly streams.
The planet orb of fire, whereon he rode
Each day from east to west the heavens
 through, 270
Spun round in sable curtaining of clouds;
Not therefore veiled quite, blindfold, and
 hid,
But ever and anon the glancing spheres,
Circles, and arcs, and broad-belting colure,
Glow'd through, and wrought upon the
 muffling dark
Sweet-shaped lightnings from the nadir
 deep
Up to the zenith, — hieroglyphics old,
Which sages and keen-eyed astrologers
Then living on the earth, with labouring
 thought
Won from the gaze of many centuries: 280
Now lost, save what we find on remnants
 huge
Of stone, or marble swart; their import
 gone,
Their wisdom long since fled. — Two wings
 this orb
Possess'd for glory, two fair argent wings,
Ever exalted at the God's approach:
And now, from forth the gloom their
 plumes immense
Rose, one by one, till all outspreaded were;
While still tho dazzling globe maintain'd
 eclipse,
Awaiting for Hyperion's command.
Fain would he have commanded, fain took
 throne 290
And bid the day begin, if but for change.
He might not: — No, though a primeval
 God:
The sacred seasons might not be disturb'd.
Therefore the operations of the dawn
Stay'd in their birth, even as here 't is told.

Those silver wings expanded sisterly,
Eager to sail their orb; the porches wide
Open'd upon the dusk demesnes of night;
And the bright Titan, phrenzied with new
 woes, 299
Unused to bend, by hard compulsion bent
His spirit to the sorrow of the time;
And all along a dismal rack of clouds,
Upon the boundaries of day and night,
He stretch'd himself in grief and radiance
 faint.
There as he lay, the Heaven with its stars
Look'd down on him with pity, and the
 voice
Of Cœlus, from the universal space,
Thus whisper'd low and solemn in his ear:
' O brightest of my children dear, earth-born
And sky-engendered, Son of Mysteries 310
All unrevealed even to the powers
Which met at thy creating; at whose joys
And palpitations sweet, and pleasures soft,
I, Cœlus, wonder, how they came and
 whence;
And at the fruits thereof what shapes they
 be,
Distinct, and visible; symbols divine,
Manifestations of that beauteous life
Diffused unseen throughout eternal space:
Of these new-form'd art thou, oh brightest
 child !
Of these, thy brethren and the God-
 desses ! 320
There is sad feud among ye, and rebellion
Of son against his sire. I saw him fall,
I saw my first-born tumbled from his
 throne !
To me his arms were spread, to me his
 voice
Found way from forth the thunders round
 his head !
Pale wox I, and in vapours hid my face.
Art thou, too, near such doom ? vague fear
 there is:
For I have seen my sons most unlike Gods.
Divine ye were created, and divine
In sad demeanour, solemn, undisturb'd, 330
Unruffled, like high Gods, ye lived and
 ruled:

Now I behold in you fear, hope, and
 wrath;
Actions of rage and passion; even as
I see them, on the mortal world beneath,
In men who die. — This is the grief, O
 Son !
Sad sign of ruin, sudden dismay, and fall !
Yet do thou strive; as thou art capable,
As thou canst move about, an evident
 God;
And canst oppose to each malignant hour
Ethereal presence: — I am but a voice; 340
My life is but the life of winds and tides,
No more than winds and tides can I
 avail: —
But thou canst. — Be thou therefore in the
 van
Of circumstance; yea, seize the arrow's
 barb
Before the tense string murmur. — To the
 earth !
For there thou wilt find Saturn, and his
 woes.
Meantime I will keep watch on thy bright
 sun,
And of thy seasons be a careful nurse.' —
Ere half this region-whisper had come
 down,
Hyperion arose, and on the stars 350
Lifted his curved lids, and kept them wide
Until it ceased; and still he kept them
 wide:
And still they were the same bright, pa-
 tient stars.
Then with a slow incline of his broad
 breast,
Like to a diver in the pearly seas,
Forward he stoop'd over the airy shore,
And plunged all noiseless into the deep
 night.

BOOK II

Just at the self-same beat of Time's wide
 wings
Hyperion slid into the rustled air,
And Saturn gain'd with Thea that sad
 place

Where Cybele and the bruised Titans
 mourn'd.
It was a den where no insulting light
Could glimmer on their tears; where their
 own groans
They felt, but heard not, for the solid roar
Of thunderous waterfalls and torrents
 hoarse,
Pouring a constant bulk, uncertain where.
Crag jutting forth to crag, and rocks that
 seem'd 10
Ever as if just rising from a sleep,
Forehead to forehead held their monstrous
 horns;
And thus in thousand hugest phantasies
Made a fit roofing to this nest of woe.
Instead of thrones, hard flint they sat upon,
Couches of rugged stone, and slaty ridge
Stubborn'd with iron. All were not assem-
 bled:
Some chain'd in torture, and some wander-
 ing.
Cœus, and Gyges, and Briareüs,
Typhon, and Dolor, and Porphyrion, 20
With many more, the brawniest in assault,
Were pent in regions of laborious breath;
Dungeon'd in opaque element to keep
Their clenched teeth still clench'd, and all
 their limbs
Lock'd up like veins of metal, crampt and
 screw'd;
Without a motion, save of their big hearts
Heaving in pain, and horribly convulsed
With sanguine, feverous, boiling gurge of
 pulse.
Mnemosyne was straying in the world;
Far from her moon had Phœbe wandered; 30
And many else were free to roam abroad,
But for the main, here found they covert
 drear.
Scarce images of life, one here, one there,
Lay vast and edgeways; like a dismal
 cirque .
Of Druid stones, upon a forlorn moor,
When the chill rain begins at shut of eve,
In dull November, and their chancel vault,
The Heaven itself, is blinded throughout
 night.

Each one kept shroud, nor to his neighbour gave
Or word, or look, or action of despair. 40
Creüs was one; his ponderous iron mace
Lay by him, and a shatter'd rib of rock
Told of his rage, ere he thus sank and pined.
Iapetus another; in his grasp,
A serpent's plashy neck; its barbed tongue
Squeezed from the gorge, and all its uncurl'd length
Dead; and because the creature could not spit
Its poison in the eyes of conquering Jove.
Next Cottus: prone he lay, chin uppermost,
As though in pain: for still upon the flint 50
He ground severe his skull, with open mouth
And eyes at horrid working. Nearest him
Asia, born of most enormous Caf,
Who cost her mother Tellus keener pangs,
Though feminine, than any of her sons:
More thought than woe was in her dusky face,
For she was prophesying of her glory;
And in her wide imagination stood
Palm-shaded temples, and high rival fanes,
By Oxus or in Ganges' sacred isles. 60
Even as Hope upon her anchor leans,
So leant she, not so fair, upon a tusk
Shed from the broadest of her elephants.
Above her, on a crag's uneasy shelve,
Upon his elbow raised, all prostrate else,
Shadow'd Enceladus; once tame and mild
As grazing ox unworried in the meads;
Now tiger-passion'd, lion-thoughted, wroth,
He meditated, plotted, and even now
Was hurling mountains in that second war, 70
Not long delay'd, that scared the younger Gods
To hide themselves in forms of beast and bird.
Not far hence Atlas; and beside him prone
Phorcus, the sire of Gorgons. Neighbour'd close
Oceanus, and Tethys, in whose lap
Sobb'd Clymene among her tangled hair.

In midst of all lay Themis, at the feet
Of Ops the queen all clouded round from sight;
No shape distinguishable, more than when
Thick night confounds the pine-tops with the clouds: 80
And many else whose names may not be told.
For when the Muse's wings are air-ward spread,
Who shall delay her flight ? And she must chant
Of Saturn, and his guide, who now had climb'd
With damp and slippery footing from a depth
More horrid still. Above a sombre cliff
Their heads appear'd, and up their stature grew
Till on the level height their steps found ease:
Then Thea spread abroad her trembling arms
Upon the precincts of this nest of pain, 90
And sidelong fix'd her eye on Saturn's face:
There saw she direst strife; the supreme God
At war with all the frailty of grief,
Of rage, of fear, anxiety, revenge,
Remorse, spleen, hope, but most of all despair.
Against these plagues he strove in vain: for Fate
Had pour'd a mortal oil upon his head,
A disanointing poison: so that Thea,
Affrighted, kept her still, and let him pass
First onwards in, among the fallen tribe. 100

As with us mortal men, the laden heart
Is persecuted more, and fever'd more,
When it is nighing to the mournful house
Where other hearts are sick of the same bruise;
So Saturn, as he walk'd into the midst,
Felt faint, and would have sunk among the rest,
But that he met Enceladus's eye,

Whose mightiness, and awe of him, at once
Came like an inspiration; and he shouted,
' Titans, behold your God ! ' at which some groan'd; 110
Some started on their feet; some also shouted;
Some wept, some wail'd — all bow'd with reverence;
And Ops, uplifting her black folded veil,
Show'd her pale cheeks, and all her forehead wan,
Her eyebrows thin and jet, and hollow eyes.
There is a roaring in the bleak-grown pines
When Winter lifts his voice; there is a noise
Among immortals when a God gives sign,
With hushing finger, how he means to load
His tongue with the full weight of utterless thought, 120
With thunder, and with music, and with pomp:
Such noise is like the roar of bleak-grown pines;
Which, when it ceases in this mountain'd world,
No other sound succeeds; but ceasing here,
Among these fallen, Saturn's voice therefrom
Grew up like organ, that begins anew
Its strain, when other harmonies, stopt short,
Leave the dinn'd air vibrating silverly.
Thus grew it up: — ' Not in my own sad breast,
Which is its own great judge and searcher out, 130
Can I find reason why ye should be thus:
Not in the legends of the first of days,
Studied from that old spirit-leaved book
Which starry Uranus with finger bright
Saved from the shores of darkness, when the waves
Low - ebb'd still hid it up in shallow gloom; —

And the which book ye know I ever kept
For my firm-based footstool: — Ah, infirm !
Not there, nor in sign, symbol, or portent
Of element, earth, water, air, and fire, —
At war, at peace, or inter-quarrelling 141
One against one, or two, or three, or all
Each several one against the other three,
As fire with air loud warring when rainfloods
Drown both, and press them both against earth's face,
Where, finding sulphur, a quadruple wrath
Unhinges the poor world; — not in that strife,
Wherefrom I take strange lore, and read it deep,
Can I find reason why ye should be thus:
No, nowhere can unriddle, though I search,
And pore on Nature's universal scroll 151
Even to swooning, why ye, Divinities,
The first-born of all shaped and palpable Gods,
Should cower beneath what, in comparison,
Is untremendous might. Yet ye are here,
O'erwhelm'd, and spurn'd, and batter'd, ye are here !
O Titans, shall I say " Arise ! " — Ye groan:
Shall I say " Crouch ! " — Ye groan. What can I then ?
O Heaven wide ! O unseen parent dear !
What can I ? Tell me, all ye brethren Gods, 160
How we can war, how engine our great wrath !
O speak your counsel now, for Saturn's ear
Is all a-hunger'd. Thou, Oceanus,
Ponderest high and deep; and in thy face
I see, astonied, that severe content
Which comes of thought and musing: give us help ! '

So ended Saturn; and the God of the Sea,
Sophist and sage, from no Athenian grove,
But cogitation in his watery shades,
Arose, with locks not oozy, and began, 170

In murmurs, which his first-endeavouring
 tongue
Caught infant-like from the far-foamed
 sands.
'O ye, whom wrath consumes! who, pas-
 sion-stung,
Writhe at defeat, and nurse your agonies!
Shut up your senses, stifle up your ears,
My voice is not a bellows unto ire.
Yet listen, ye who will, whilst I bring
 proof
How ye, perforce, must be content to stoop;
And in the proof much comfort will I give,
If ye will take that comfort in its truth. 180
We fall by course of Nature's law, not
 force
Of thunder, or of Jove. Great Saturn, thou
Hast sifted well the atom-universe;
But for this reason, that thou art the King,
And only blind from sheer supremacy,
One avenue was shaded from thine eyes,
Through which I wander'd to eternal truth.
And first, as thou wast not the first of pow-
 ers,
So art thou not the last; it cannot be;
Thou art not the beginning nor the end. 190
From chaos and parental darkness came
Light, the first fruits of that intestine
 broil,
That sullen ferment, which for wondrous
 ends
Was ripening in itself. The ripe hour
 came,
And with it light, and light engendering
Upon its own producer, forthwith touch'd
The whole enormous matter into life.
Upon that very hour, our parentage,
The Heavens and the Earth, were manifest:
Then thou first-born, and we the giant-
 race, 200
Found ourselves ruling new and beauteous
 realms.
Now comes the pain of truth, to whom 't is
 pain;
O folly! for to bear all naked truths,
And to envisage circumstance, all calm,
That is the top of sovereignty. Mark
 well!

As Heaven and Earth are fairer, fairer far
Than Chaos and blank Darkness, though
 once chiefs;
And as we show beyond that Heaven and
 Earth
In form and shape compact and beautiful,
In will, in action free, companionship, 210
And thousand other signs of purer life;
So on our heels a fresh perfection treads,
A power more strong in beauty, born of us
And fated to excel us, as we pass
In glory that old Darkness: nor are we
Thereby more conquer'd, than by us the
 rule
Of shapeless Chaos. Say, doth the dull
 soil
Quarrel with the proud forests it hath fed,
And feedeth still, more comely than itself?
Can it deny the chiefdom of green groves?
Or shall the tree be envious of the dove 221
Because it cooeth, and hath snowy wings
To wander wherewithal and find its joys?
We are such forest-trees, and our fair
 boughs
Have bred forth, not pale solitary doves,
But eagles golden-feather'd, who do tower
Above us in their beauty, and must reign
In right thereof; for 't is the eternal law
That first in beauty should be first in
 might: 229
Yea, by that law, another race may drive
Our conquerors to mourn as we do now.
Have ye beheld the young God of the Seas,
My dispossessor? Have ye seen his face?
Have ye beheld his chariot, foam'd along
By noble winged creatures he hath made?
I saw him on the calmed waters scud,
With such a glow of beauty in his eyes,
That it enforced me to bid sad farewell
To all my empire; farewell sad I took,
And hither came, to see how dolorous fate
Had wrought upon ye; and how I might
 best 241
Give consolation in this woe extreme.
Receive the truth, and let it be your balm.'

Whether through poz'd conviction, or
 disdain,

They guarded silence, when Oceanus
Left murmuring, what deepest thought can tell?
But so it was, none answer'd for a space,
Save one whom none regarded, Clymene:
And yet she answer'd not, only complain'd,
With hectic lips, and eyes up - looking mild, 250
Thus wording timidly among the fierce:
' O Father, I am here the simplest voice,
And all my knowledge is that joy is gone,
And this thing woe crept in among our hearts,
There to remain for ever, as I fear:
I would not bode of evil, if I thought
So weak a creature could turn off the help
Which by just right should come of mighty Gods;
Yet let me tell my sorrow, let me tell
Of wh..t I heard, and how it made me weep, 260
And know that we had parted from all hope.
I stood upon a shore, a pleasant shore,
Where a sweet clime was breathed from a land
Of fragrance, quietness, and trees, and flowers.
Full of calm joy it was, as I of grief;
Too full of joy and soft delicious warmth;
So that I felt a movement in my heart
To chide, and to reproach that solitude
With songs of misery, music of our woes;
And sat me down, and took a mouthed shell 270
And murmur'd into it, and made melody —
O melody no more ! for while I sang,
And with poor skill let pass into the breeze
The dull shell's echo, from a bowery strand
Just opposite, an island of the sea,
There came enchantment with the shifting wind,
That did both drown and keep alive my ears.
I threw my shell away upon the sand,
And a wave fill'd it, as my sense was fill'd
With that new blissful golden melody. 280
A living death was in each gush of sounds,

Each family of rapturous hurried notes,
That fell, one after one, yet all at once,
Like pearl beads dropping sudden from their string:
And then another, then another strain,
Each like a dove leaving its olive perch,
With music wing'd instead of silent plumes,
To hover round my head, and make me sick
Of joy and grief at once. Grief overcame,
And I was stopping up my frantic ears, 290
When, past all hindrance of my trembling hands,
A voice came sweeter, sweeter than all tune,
And still it cried, "Apollo ! young Apollo !
The morning-bright Apollo ! young Apollo ! "
I fled, it follow'd me, and cried, "Apollo ! "
O Father, and O Brethren, had ye felt
Those pains of mine; O Saturn, hadst thou felt,
Ye would not call this too indulged tongue
Presumptuous, in thus venturing to be heard.'

So far her voice flow'd on, like timorous brook 300
That, lingering along a pebbled coast,
Doth fear to meet the sea: but sea it met,
And shudder'd; for the overwhelming voice
Of huge Enceladus swallow'd it in wrath:
The ponderous syllables, like sullen waves
In the half-glutted hollows of reef-rocks,
Came booming thus, while still upon his arm
He lean'd; not rising, from supreme contempt.
' Or shall we listen to the over-wise,
Or to the over-foolish giant, Gods ? 310
Not thunderbolt on thunderbolt, till all
That rebel Jove's whole armoury were spent,
Not world on world upon these shoulders piled,
Could agonize me more than baby-words
In midst of this dethronement horrible.

Speak! roar! shout! yell! ye sleepy Ti-
 tans all.
Do ye forget the blows, the buffets vile?
Are ye not smitten by a youngling arm?
Dost thou forget, sham Monarch of the
 Waves,
Thy scalding in the seas? What! have I
 roused 320
Your spleens with so few simple words as
 these?
O joy! for now I see ye are not lost:
O joy! for now I see a thousand eyes
Wide-glaring for revenge.' — As this he
 said,
He lifted up his stature vast, and stood,
Still without intermission speaking thus:
'Now ye are flames, I 'll tell you how to
 burn,
And purge the ether of our enemies;
How to feed fierce the crooked stings of fire,
And singe away the swollen clouds of
 Jove, 330
Stifling that puny essence in its tent.
O let him feel the evil he hath done;
For though I scorn Oceanus's lore,
Much pain have I for more than loss of
 realms:
The days of peace and slumberous calm
 are fled;
Those days, all innocent of scathing war,
When all the fair Existences of heaven
Came open-eyed to guess what we would
 speak: —
That was before our brows were taught to
 frown,
Before our lips knew else but solemn
 sounds; 340
That was before we knew the winged
 thing,
Victory, might be lost, or might be won,
And be ye mindful that Hyperion,
Our brightest brother, still is undis-
 graced —
Hyperion, lo! his radiance is here!'

All eyes were on Enceladus's face,
And they beheld, while still Hyperion's
 name

Flew from his lips up to the vaulted rocks,
A pallid gleam across his features stern:
Not savage, for he saw full many a God
Wroth as himself. He look'd upon them
 all, 351
And in each face he saw a gleam of light,
But splendider in Saturn's, whose hoar
 locks
Shone like the bubbling foam about a keel
When the prow sweeps into a midnight
 cove.
In pale and silver silence they remain'd,
Till suddenly a splendour, like the morn,
Pervaded all the beetling gloomy steeps,
All the sad spaces of oblivion,
And every gulf, and every chasm old, 360
And every height, and every sullen depth,
Voiceless, or hoarse with loud tormented
 streams:
And all the everlasting cataracts,
And all the headlong torrents far and near,
Mantled before in darkness and huge
 shade,
Now saw the light and made it terrible.
It was Hyperion: — a granite peak
His bright feet touch'd, and there he stay'd
 to view
The misery his brilliance had betray'd
To the most hateful seeing of itself. 370
Golden his hair of short Numidian curl,
Regal his shape majestic, a vast shade
In midst of his own brightness, like the
 bulk
Of Memnon's image at the set of sun
To one who travels from the dusking
 East:
Sighs, too, as mournful as that Memnon's
 harp,
He utter'd, while his hands contemplative
He press'd together, and in silence stood.
Despondence seized again the fallen Gods
At sight of the dejected King of Day, 380
And many hid their faces from the light:
But fierce Enceladus sent forth his eyes
Among the brotherhood; and, at their
 glare,
Uprose Iäpetus, and Creüs too,
And Phorcus, sea-born, and together strode

To where he tower'd on his eminence.
There those four shouted forth old Saturn's
 name;
Hyperion from the peak loud answered
 ' Saturn ! '
Saturn sat near the Mother of the Gods,
In whose face was no joy, though all the
 Gods 390
Gave from their hollow throats the name
 of ' Saturn ! '

BOOK III

Thus in alternate uproar and sad peace,
Amazed were those Titans utterly.
O leave them, Muse ! O leave them to
 their woes;
For thou art weak to sing such tumults
 dire:
A solitary sorrow best befits
Thy lips, and antheming a lonely grief.
Leave them, O Muse ! for thou anon wilt
 find
Many a fallen old Divinity
Wandering in vain about bewildered shores.
Meantime touch piously the Delphic harp,
And not a wind of heaven but will
 breathe 11
In aid soft warble from the Dorian flute;
For lo ! 't is for the Father of all verse.
Flush every thing that hath a vermeil hue,
Let the rose glow intense and warm the air,
And let the clouds of even and of morn
Float in voluptuous fleeces o'er the hills;
Let the red wine within the goblet boil,
Cold as a bubbling well; let faint-lipp'd
 shells,
On sands or in great deeps, vermilion turn
Through all their labyrinths; and let the
 maid 21
Blush keenly, as with some warm kiss sur-
 prised.
Chief isle of the embowered Cyclades,
Rejoice, O Delos, with thine olives green,
And poplars, and lawn-shading palms, and
 beech,
In which the Zephyr breathes the loudest
 song,
And hazels thick, dark-stemm'd beneath
 the shade:
Apollo is once more the golden theme !
Where was he, when the Giant of the Sun
Stood bright, amid the sorrow of his peers ?
Together had he left his mother fair 31
And his twin-sister sleeping in their bower,
And in the morning twilight wandered
 forth
Beside the osiers of a rivulet,
Full ankle-deep in lilies of the vale.
The nightingale had ceased, and a few
 stars
Were lingering in the heavens, while the
 thrush
Began calm-throated. Throughout all the
 isle
There was no covert, no retired cave
Unhaunted by the murmurous noise of
 waves, 40
Though scarcely heard in many a green re-
 cess.
He listen'd, and he wept, and his bright
 tears
Went trickling down the golden bow he
 held.
Thus with half-shut suffused eyes he stood,
While from beneath some cumbrous boughs
 hard by
With solemn step an awful Goddess came,
And there was purport in her looks for
 him,
Which he with eager guess began to read
Perplex'd, the while melodiously he said:
' How cam'st thou over the unfooted sea ?
Or hath that antique mien and robed
 form 51
Moved in these vales invisible till now ?
Sure I have heard those vestments sweep-
 ing o'er
The fallen leaves, when I have sat alone
In cool mid-forest. Surely I have traced
The rustle of those ample skirts about
These grassy solitudes, and seen the flow-
 ers
Lift up their heads, and still the whisper
 pass'd.
Goddess ! I have beheld those eyes before,

And their eternal calm, and all that face,
Or I have dream'd.' — 'Yes,' said the su-
 preme shape, 61
'Thou hast dream'd of me; and awaking
 up
Didst find a lyre all golden by thy side,
Whose strings touch'd by thy fingers, all
 the vast
Unwearied ear of the whole universe
Listen'd in pain and pleasure at the birth
Of such new tuneful wonder. Is 't not
 strange
That thou shouldst weep, so gifted? Tell
 me, youth,
What sorrow thou canst feel; for I am sad
When thou dost shed a tear: explain thy
 griefs 70
To one who in this lonely isle hath been
The watcher of thy sleep and hours of life,
From the young day when first thy infant
 hand
Pluck'd witless the weak flowers, till thine
 arm
Could bend that bow heroic to all times.
Show thy heart's secret to an ancient
 Power
Who hath forsaken old and sacred thrones
For prophecies of thee, and for the sake
Of loveliness new-born.' — Apollo then,
With sudden scrutiny and gloomless eyes,
Thus answer'd, while his white melodious
 throat 81
Throbb'd with the syllables: — 'Mnemo-
 syne!
Thy name is on my tongue, I know not
 how;
Why should I tell thee what thou so well
 seest?
Why should I strive to show what from
 thy lips
Would come no mystery? For me, dark,
 dark,
And painful vile oblivion seals my eyes:
I strive to search wherefore I am so sad,
Until a melancholy numbs my limbs;
And then upon the grass I sit, and moan, 90
Like one who once had wings. — O why
 should I

Feel cursed and thwarted, when the liege-
 less air
Yields to my step aspirant? why should I
Spurn the green turf as hateful to my
 feet?
Goddess benign, point forth some unknown
 thing:
Are there not other regions than this isle?
What are the stars? There is the sun, the
 sun!
And the most patient brilliance of the
 moon!
And stars by thousands! Point me out
 the way
To any one particular beauteous star, 100
And I will flit into it with my lyre,
And make its silvery splendour pant with
 bliss.
I have heard the cloudy thunder: Where
 is power?
Whose hand, whose essence, what divinity
Makes this alarum in the elements,
While I here idle listen on the shores
In fearless yet in aching ignorance?
O tell me, lonely Goddess, by thy harp,
That waileth every morn and eventide,
Tell me why thus I rave, about these
 groves! 110
Mute thou remainest — Mute! yet I can
 read
A wondrous lesson in thy silent face:
Knowledge enormous makes a God of me.
Names, deeds, gray legends, dire events,
 rebellions,
Majesties, sovran voices, agonies,
Creations and destroyings, all at once
Pour into the wide hollows of my brain,
And deify me, as if some blithe wine
Or bright elixir peerless I had drunk, 119
And so become immortal.' — Thus the God,
While his enkindled eyes, with level glance
Beneath his white soft temples, steadfast
 kept
Trembling with light upon Mnemosyne.
Soon wild commotions shook him, and made
 flush
All the immortal fairness of his limbs:
Most like the struggle at the gate of death;

Or liker still to one who should take leave
Of pale immortal death, and with a pang
As hot as death's is chill, with fierce con-
 vulse
Die into life: so young Apollo anguish'd: 130
His very hair, his golden tresses famed
Kept undulation round his eager neck.

During the pain Mnemosyne upheld
Her arms as one who prophesied. — At
 length
Apollo shriek'd; — and lo ! from all his
 limbs
Celestial
.

TO AUTUMN

In a letter to Reynolds, written from Winchester, September 22, 1819, Keats jots down these sentences: ' How beautiful the season is now — How fine the air. A temperate sharpness about it. Really, without joking, chaste weather — Dian skies — I never liked stubblefields so much as now — Aye, better than the chilly green of the spring. Somehow, a stubble-field looks warm in the same way that some pictures look warm. This struck me so much in my Sunday's walk that I composed upon it.' These autumn days in Winchester were the last of happy health for Keats. The poem was included in the 1820 volume.

I

SEASON of mists and mellow fruitfulness,
 Close bosom-friend of the maturing sun;
Conspiring with him how to load and bless
 With fruit the vines that round the
 thatch-eaves run;
To bend with apples the moss'd cottage-
 trees,
 And fill all fruit with ripeness to the
 core;
 To swell the gourd, and plump the
 hazel shells
 With a sweet kernel; to set budding
 more,
And still more, later flowers for the bees,
Until they think warm days will never
 cease,
 For Summer has o'er-brimm'd their
 clammy cells.

II

Who hath not seen thee oft amid thy store?
 Sometimes whoever seeks abroad may
 find
Thee sitting careless on a granary floor,
 Thy hair soft-lifted by the winnowing
 wind;
Or on a half-reap'd furrow sound asleep,
 Drowsed with the fume of poppies, while
 thy hook
 Spares the next swath and all its
 twined flowers:
And sometimes like a gleaner thou dost keep
 Steady thy laden head across a brook;
 Or by a cider-press, with patient look,
 Thou watchest the last oozings, hours
 by hours.

III

Where are the songs of Spring? Ay,
 where are they?
 Think not of them, thou hast thy music
 too, —
While barred clouds bloom the soft-dying
 day,
 And touch the stubble-plains with rosy
 hue;
Then in a wailful choir the small gnats
 mourn
 Among the river sallows, borne aloft
 Or sinking as the light wind lives or
 dies;
And full-grown lambs loud bleat from
 hilly bourn;
 Hedge-crickets sing; and now with treble
 soft
The redbreast whistles from a garden-
 croft,
 And gathering swallows twitter in the
 skies.

VERSES TO FANNY BRAWNE

Although these are not the only poems which owe their origin to Keats's consuming passion, they are grouped here because, apparently written in the same period, they stand as a painful witness to the ebbing tide of Keats's life.

SONNET

The date 1819 is appended to this sonnet in *Life, Letters and Literary Remains.* Mr. Forman connects it with a letter written to Fanny Brawne, October 11, 1819.

THE day is gone, and all its sweets are gone !
 Sweet voice, sweet lips, soft hand, and softer breast,
Warm breath, light whisper, tender semitone,
 Bright eyes, accomplish'd shape, and lang'rous waist !
Faded the flower and all its budded charms,
 Faded the sight of beauty from my eyes,
Faded the shape of beauty from my arms,
 Faded the voice, warmth, whiteness, paradise !
Vanish'd unseasonably at shut of eve,
 When the dusk holiday — or holinight —
Of fragrant-curtain'd love begins to weave
 The woof of darkness thick, for hid delight:
But, as I 've read love's missal through today,
He 'll let me sleep, seeing I fast and pray.

LINES TO FANNY

First published in *Life, Letters and Literary Remains,* and there dated October, 1819; their exact date seems to be indicated by a passage in a letter to Fanny Brawne, written October 13, 1819, intimating some work, and breaking out into : ' I cannot proceed with any degree of content. I must write you a line or two and see if that will assist in dismissing you from my mind for ever so short a time.'

WHAT can I do to drive away
Remembrance from my eyes ? for they have seen,
Aye, an hour ago, my brilliant Queen !
Touch has a memory. O say, love, say,
What can I do to kill it and be free
In my old liberty ?
When every fair one that I saw was fair,
Enough to catch me in but half a snare,
Not keep me there:
When, howe'er poor or particolour'd things,
My muse had wings,
And ever ready was to take her course
Whither I bent her force,
Unintellectual, yet divine to me; —
Divine, I say ! — What sea-bird o'er the sea
Is a philosopher the while he goes
Winging along where the great water throes ?

How shall I do
To get anew
Those moulted feathers, and so mount once more
Above, above
The reach of fluttering Love,
And make him cower lowly while I soar ?
Shall I gulp wine ? No, that is vulgarism,
A heresy and schism,
Foisted into the canon law of love; —
No, — wine is only sweet to happy men;
More dismal cares
Seize on me unawares, —
Where shall I learn to get my peace again ?
To banish thoughts of that most hateful land,

Dungeoner of my friends, that wicked
 strand
Where they were wreck'd and live a
 wrecked life;
That monstrous region, whose dull rivers
 pour,
Ever from their sordid urns unto the shore,
Unown'd of any weedy-haired gods;
Whose winds, all zephyrless, hold scour-
 ging rods,
Iced in the great lakes, to afflict mankind;
Whose rank-grown forests, frosted, black,
 and blind,
Would fright a Dryad; whose harsh herb-
 aged meads
Make lean and lank the starved ox while
 he feeds;
There bad flowers have no scent, birds no
 sweet song,
And great unerring Nature once seems
 wrong.

O, for some sunny spell
To dissipate the shadows of this hell !
Say they are gone, — with the new dawn-
 ing light
Steps forth my lady bright !
O, let me once more rest
My soul upon that dazzling breast !
Let once again these aching arms be placed,
The tender gaolers of thy waist !
And let me feel that warm breath here and
 there

To spread a rapture in my very hair, —
O, the sweetness of the pain !
Give me those lips again !
Enough ! Enough ! it is enough for me
To dream of thee !

TO FANNY

With the date 1819 in *Life, Letters and Lit-
erary Remains.*

I CRY your mercy — pity — love — aye,
 love !
 Merciful love that tantalizes not,
One-thoughted, never-wandering, guileless
 love,
 Unmask'd, and being seen — without a
 blot !
O ! let me have thee whole, — all — all —
 be mine !
 That shape, that fairness, that sweet mi-
 nor zest
Of love, your kiss, — those hands, those
 eyes divine,
 That warm, white, lucent, million-plea-
 sured breast, —
Yourself — your soul — in pity give me
 all,
 Withhold no atom's atom, or I die,
Or living on perhaps, your wretched thrall,
 Forget, in the mist of idle misery,
Life's purposes — the palate of my mind
Losing its gust, and my ambition blind !

THE CAP AND BELLS

OR, THE JEALOUSIES

A Faery Tale. Unfinished

In a letter to John Taylor, his publisher, written from Hampstead, November 17, 1819, Keats, who was then in his most restless mood, writes impulsively: 'I have come to a determination not to publish anything I have now ready written; but, for all that, to publish a poem before long, and that I hope to make a fine one. As the marvellous is the most enticing, and the surest guarantee of harmonious numbers, I have been endeavouring to persuade myself to untether Fancy, and to let her manage for herself. I and myself cannot agree about this at all. Wonders are no wonders to me. I am more at home amongst men and women. I would rather read Chaucer than Ariosto. The little dramatic skill I may as yet have, however badly it might show in a drama, would, I think, be sufficient for a poem. I wish to diffuse the colouring of "St. Agnes' Eve" throughout a poem in which character and sentiment would be the figures to such drapery. Two or three such poems, if God should spare me, written in the course of the next six years, would be a famous Gradus ad Parnassum altissimum — I mean they would nerve me up to the writing of a few fine plays — my greatest ambition, when I do feel ambitious. I am sorry to say that is very seldom.'

Lord Houghton quotes from Keats's friend, Charles Armitage Brown: 'This Poem was written subject to future amendments and omissions; it was begun without a plot, and without any presented laws for the supernatural machinery.' Keats apparently designed publishing the poem with the signature 'Lucy Vaughan Lloyd,' and it can only be taken as one of his feverish attempts at using his intellectual powers for self-maintenance, when he was discouraged at the prospect of commercial success with his genuine poetry. Hunt published some of the stanzas in *The Indicator* August 23, 1820, as written by 'a very good poetess Lucy V—— L——' and Lord Houghton included the whole in *Life, Letters and Literary Remains.*

I

In midmost Ind, beside Hydaspes cool,
There stood, or hover'd, tremulous in the
 air,
A faery city, 'neath the potent rule
Of Emperor Elfinan; famed ev'rywhere
For love of mortal women, maidens fair,
Whose lips were solid, whose soft hands
 were made
Of a fit mould and beauty, ripe and rare,
To pamper his slight wooing, warm yet
 staid:
He loved girls smooth as shades, but hated
 a mere shade.

II

This was a crime forbidden by the law;
And all the priesthood of his city wept,
For ruin and dismay they well foresaw,
If impious prince no bound or limit kept,
And faery Zendervester overstept;
They wept, he sinn'd, and still he would
 sin on,
They dreamt of sin, and he sinn'd while
 they slept;
In vain the pulpit thunder'd at the
 throne,
Caricature was vain, and vain the tart lampoon.

III

Which seeing, his high court of parliament
Laid a remonstrance at his Highness'
 feet,
Praying his royal senses to content
Themselves with what in faery land was
 sweet,
Befitting best that shade with shade
 should meet:
Whereat, to calm their fears, he pro-
 mised soon
From mortal tempters all to make re-
 treat —
Ay, even on the first of the new moon,
An immaterial wife to espouse as heaven's
 boon.

IV

Meantime he sent a fluttering embassy
To Pigmio, of Imaus sovereign,
To half beg, and half demand, respect-
 fully,
The hand of his fair daughter Bella-
 naine;
An audience had, and speeching done,
 they gain
Their point, and bring the weeping bride
 away;
Whom, with but one attendant, safely
 lain
Upon their wings, they bore in bright
 array,
While little harps were touch'd by many a
 lyric fay.

V

As in old pictures tender cherubim
A child's soul thro' the sapphired canvas
 bear,
So, thro' a real heaven, on they swim
With the sweet princess on her plumaged
 lair,
Speed giving to the winds her lustrous
 hair;
And so she journey'd, sleeping or awake,
Save when, for healthful exercise and
 air,

She chose to 'promener à l'aile,' or take
A pigeon's somerset, for sport or change's
 sake.

VI

' Dear Princess, do not whisper me so
 loud,'
Quoth Corallina, nurse and confidant,
' Do not you see there, lurking in a cloud,
Close at your back, that sly old Crafti-
 cant ?
He hears a whisper plainer than a rant:
Dry up your tears, and do not look so
 blue;
He 's Elfinan's great state-spy militant,
He 's running, lying, flying footman,
 too —
Dear mistress, let him have no handle
 against you !

VII

' Show him a mouse's tail, and he will
 guess,
With metaphysic swiftness, at the mouse;
Show him a garden, and with speed no
 less,
He 'll surmise sagely of a dwelling-
 house,
And plot, in the same minute, how to
 chouse
The owner out of it; show him a — '
 ' Peace !
Peace ! nor contrive thy mistress' ire to
 rouse !'
Return'd the princess, ' my tongue shall
 not cease
Till from this hated match I get a free
 release.

VIII

' Ah, beauteous mortal !' ' Hush !' quoth
 Coralline,
' Really you must not talk of him indeed.'
' You hush !' replied the mistress, with
 a shine
Of anger in her eyes, enough to breed
In stouter hearts than nurse's fear and
 dread:

'T was not the glance itself made nursey
 flinch,
But of its threat she took the utmost
 heed;
Not liking in her heart an hour-long
 pinch,
Or a sharp needle run into her back an
 inch.

IX

So she was silenced, and fair Bellanaine,
Writhing her little body with ennui,
Continued to lament and to complain,
That Fate, cross-purposing, should let
 her be
Ravish'd away far from her dear coun-
 tree;
That all her feelings should be set at
 nought,
In trumping up this match so hastily,
With lowland blood; and lowland blood
 she thought
Poison, as every stanch true-born Imaian
 ought.

X

Sorely she grieved, and wetted three or
 four
White Provence rose-leaves with her
 faery tears,
But not for this cause; — alas! she had
 more
Bad reasons for her sorrow, as appears
In the famed memoirs of a thousand
 years,
Written by Crafticant, and published
By Parpaglion and Co., (those sly com-
 peers
Who raked up ev'ry fact against the
 dead,)
In Scarab Street, Panthea, at the Jubal's
 Head.

XI

Where, after a long hypercritic howl
Against the vicious manners of the
 age,

He goes on to expose, with heart and
 soul,
What vice in this or that year was the
 rage,
Backbiting all the world in every page;
With special strictures on the horrid
 crime,
(Section'd and subsection'd with learn-
 ing sage,)
Of faeries stooping on their wings sub-
 lime
To kiss a mortal's lips, when such were in
 their prime.

XII

Turn to the copious index, you will find
Somewhere in the column, headed let-
 ter B,
The name of Bellanaine, if you 're not
 blind;
Then pray refer to the text, and you
 will see
An article made up of calumny
Against this highland princess, rating
 her
For giving way, so over fashionably,
To this new-fangled vice, which seems a
 burr
Stuck in his moral throat, no coughing e'er
 could stir.

XIII

There he says plainly that she loved a
 man!
That she around him flutter'd, flirted,
 toy'd,
Before her marriage with great Elfi-
 nan;
That after marriage too, she never joy'd
In husband's company, but still employ'd
Her wits to 'scape away to Angle-land;
Where lived the youth, who worried and
 annoy'd
Her tender heart, and its warm ardours
 fann'd
To such a dreadful blaze, her side would
 scorch her hand.

XIV

But let us leave this idle tittle-tattle
To waiting - maids, and bed - room co-
 teries,
Nor till fit time against her fame wage
 battle.
Poor Elfinan is very ill at ease,
Let us resume his subject if you please:
For it may comfort and console him
 much,
To rhyme and syllable his miseries;
Poor Elfinan ! whose cruel fate was
 such,
He sat and cursed a bride he knew he
 could not touch.

XV

Soon as (according to his promises)
The bridal embassy had taken wing,
And vanish'd, bird-like, o'er the suburb
 trees,
The emperor, empierced with the sharp
 sting
Of love, retired, vex'd and murmuring
Like any drone shut from the fair bee-
 queen,
Into his cabinet, and there did fling
His limbs upon the sofa, full of spleen,
And damn'd his House of Commons, in
 complete chagrin.

XVI

' I 'll trounce some of the members,' cried
 the Prince,
' I 'll put a mark against some rebel
 names,
I 'll make the Opposition-benches wince,
I 'll show them very soon, to all their
 shames,
What 't is to smother up a Prince's
 flames;
That ministers should join in it, I own,
Surprises me ! — they too at these high
 games !
Am I an Emperor ? Do I wear a crown ?
Imperial Elfinan, go hang thyself or drown !

XVII

' I 'll trounce 'em ! — there 's the square-
 cut chancellor,
His son shall never touch that bishopric;
And for the nephew of old Palfior,
I 'll show him that his speeches made me
 sick,
And give the colonelcy to Phalaric;
The tiptoe marquis, moral and gallant,
Shall lodge in shabby taverns upon tick;
And for the Speaker's second cousin's
 aunt,
She sha'n't be maid of honour, — by heaven
 that she sha'n't !

XVIII

' I 'll shirk the Duke of A.; I 'll cut his
 brother;
I 'll give no garter to his eldest son;
I won't speak to his sister or his mother !
The Viscount B. shall live at cut-and-
 run;
But how in the world can I contrive to
 stun
That fellow's voice, which plagues me
 worse than any,
That stubborn fool, that impudent state-
 dun,
Who sets down ev'ry sovereign as a
 zany, —
That vulgar commoner, Esquire Bianco-
 pany ?

XIX

' Monstrous affair ! Pshaw ! pah ! what
 ugly minx
Will they fetch from Imaus for my
 bride ?
Alas ! my wearied heart within me
 sinks,
To think that I must be so near allied
To a cold dullard fay, — ah, woe betide !
Ah, fairest of all human loveliness !
Sweet Bertha ! what crime can it be to
 glide
About the fragrant plaitings of thy dress,
Or kiss thine eye, or count thy locks, tress
 after tress ? '

XX

So said, one minute's while his eyes re-
 main'd
Half lidded, piteous, languid, innocent;
But, in a wink, their splendour they re-
 gain'd,
Sparkling revenge with amorous fury
 blent.
Love thwarted in bad temper oft has
 vent:
He rose, he stampt his foot, he rang the
 bell,
And order'd some death-warrants to be
 sent
For signature: — somewhere the tem-
 pest fell,
As many a poor fellow does not live to
 tell.

XXI

' At the same time, Eban,' — (this was
 his page,
A fay of colour, slave from top to toe,
Sent as a present, while yet under age,
From the Viceroy of Zanguebar, — wise,
 slow,
His speech, his only words were ' yes '
 and ' no,'
But swift of look, and foot, and wing
 was he,) —
' At the same time, Eban, this instant
 go
To Hum the soothsayer, whose name I
 see
Among the fresh arrivals in our empery.

XXII

' Bring Hum to me ! But stay — here
 take my ring,
The pledge of favour, that he not sus-
 pect
Any foul play, or awkward murdering,
Tho' I have bowstrung many of his sect;
Throw in a hint, that if he should neg-
 lect
One hour, the next shall see him in my
 grasp,
And the next after that shall see him
 neck'd,

Or swallow'd by my hunger-starved
 asp, —
And mention ('t is as well) the torture of
 the wasp.'

XXIII

These orders given, the Prince, in half a
 pet,
Let o'er the silk his propping elbow
 slide,
Caught up his little legs, and, in a fret,
Fell on the sofa on his royal side.
The slave retreated backwards, humble-
 eyed,
And with a slave-like silence closed the
 door,
And to old Hum thro' street and alley
 hied;
He ' knew the city,' as we say, of yore,
And for short cuts and turns, was nobody
 knew more.

XXIV

It was the time when wholesale dealers
 close
Their shutters with a moody sense of
 wealth,
But retail dealers, diligent, let loose
The gas (objected to on score of health),
Convey'd in little solder'd pipes by
 stealth,
And make it flare in many a brilliant
 form,
That all the powers of darkness it re-
 pell'th,
Which to the oil-trade doth great scaith
 and harm,
And supersedeth quite the use of the glow-
 worm.

XXV

Eban, untempted by the pastry-cooks,
(Of pastry he got store within the pal-
 ace,)
With hasty steps, wrapp'd cloak, and
 solemn looks,
Incognito upon his errand sallies,
His smelling-bottle ready for the allies;

He pass'd the hurdy-gurdies with dis-
dain,
Vowing he'd have them sent on board
the galleys;
Just as he made his vow, it 'gan to rain,
Therefore he call'd a coach, and bade it
drive amain.

XXVI

'I'll pull the string,' said he, and further
said,
'Polluted Jarvey! Ah, thou filthy hack!
Whose springs of life are all dried up
and dead,
Whose linsey-woolsey lining hangs all
slack,
Whose rug is straw, whose wholeness is
a crack ;
And evermore thy steps go clatter-clit-
ter;
Whose glass once up can never be got
back,
Who prov'st, with jolting arguments and
bitter,
That 't is of modern use to travel in a
litter.

XXVII

'Thou inconvenience! thou hungry crop
For all corn! thou snail-creeper to and
fro,
Who while thou goest ever seem'st to
stop,
And fiddle-faddle standest while you go;
I' the morning, freighted with a weight
of woe,
Unto some lazar-house thou journeyest,
And in the evening tak'st a double row
Of dowdies, for some dance or party
drest,
Besides the goods meanwhile thou movest
east and west.

XXVIII

'By thy ungallant bearing and sad mien,
An inch appears the utmost thou couldst
budge:
Yet at the slightest nod, or hint, or sign,
Round to the curb-stone patient dost
thou trudge,
School'd in a beckon, learned in a nudge,
A dull-eyed Argus watching for a fare;
Quiet and plodding thou dost bear no
grudge
To whisking tilburies, or phaetons rare,
Curricles, or mail-coaches, swift beyond
compare.'

XXIX

Philosophizing thus, he pull'd the check,
And bade the coachman wheel to such a
street,
Who turning much his body, more his
neck,
Louted full low, and hoarsely did him
greet:
'Certes, Monsieur were best take to his
feet,
Seeing his servant can no farther drive
For press of coaches, that to-night here
meet,
Many as bees about a straw-capp'd hive,
When first for April honey into faint flow-
ers they dive.'

XXX

Eban then paid his fare, and tiptoe went
To Hum's hotel; and, as he on did pass
With head inclined, each dusky linea-
ment
Show'd in the pearl-paved street as in a
glass;
His purple vest, that ever peeping was
Rich from the fluttering crimson of his
cloak,
His silvery trowsers, and his silken sash
Tied in a burnish'd knot, their semblance
took
Upon the mirror'd walls, wherever he
might look.

XXXI

He smiled at self, and, smiling, show'd
his teeth,
And seeing his white teeth, he smiled the
more;

Lifted his eyebrows, spurn'd the path beneath,
Show'd teeth again, and smiled as heretofore,
Until he knock'd at the magician's door;
Where, till the porter answer'd, might be seen,
In the clear panel more he could adore, —
His turban wreathed of gold, and white, and green,
Mustachios, ear-ring, nose-ring, and his sabre keen.

XXXII

'Does not your master give a rout to-night?'
Quoth the dark page; 'Oh, no!' return'd the Swiss,
'Next door but one to us, upon the right,
The *Magazin des Modes* now open is
Against the Emperor's wedding; — and, sir, this
My master finds a monstrous horrid bore;
As he retired, an hour ago iwis,
With his best beard and brimstone, to explore
And cast a quiet figure in his second floor.

XXXIII

'Gad! he's obliged to stick to business!
For chalk, I hear, stands at a pretty price;
And as for aqua vitæ — there's a mess!
The *dentes sapientiæ* of mice
Our barber tells me too are on the rise, —
Tinder's a lighter article, — nitre pure
Goes off like lightning, — grains of Paradise
At an enormous figure! — stars not sure! —
Zodiac will not move without a slight douceur!

XXXIV

'Venus won't stir a peg without a fee,
And master is too partial *entre nous*
To —' 'Hush — hush!' cried Eban, 'sure that is he

Coming down stairs, — by St. Bartholomew!
As backwards as he can, — is't something new?
Or is't his custom, in the name of fun?'
'He always comes down backward, with one shoe' —
Return'd the porter — 'off, and one shoe on,
Like, saving shoe for sock or stocking, my man John!'

XXXV

It was indeed the great Magician,
Feeling, with careful toe, for every stair,
And retrograding careful as he can,
Backwards and downwards from his own two pair:
'Salpietro!' exclaimed Hum, 'is the dog there?
He's always in my way upon the mat!'
'He's in the kitchen, or the Lord knows where,' —
Replied the Swiss, — 'the nasty, yelping brat!'
'Don't beat him!' return'd Hum, and on the floor came pat.

XXXVI

Then facing right about, he saw the Page,
And said: 'Don't tell me what you want, Eban;
The Emperor is now in a huge rage, —
'T is nine to one he'll give you the rattan!
Let us away!' Away together ran
The plain-dress'd sage and spangled blackamoor,
Nor rested till they stood to cool, and fan,
And breathe themselves at th' Emperor's chamber door,
When Eban thought he heard a soft imperial snore.

XXXVII

'I thought you guess'd, foretold, or prophesied,
That's Majesty was in a raving fit?'

'He dreams,' said Hum, ' or I have ever
 lied,
That he is tearing you, sir, bit by bit.'
'He's not asleep, and you have little
 wit,'
Replied the Page, ' that little buzzing
 noise,
Whate'er your palmistry may make of
 it,
Comes from a plaything of the Em-
 peror's choice,
From a Man-Tiger-Organ, prettiest of his
 toys.'

XXXVIII

Eban then usher'd in the learned Seer:
Elfinan's back was turn'd, but, ne'erthe-
 less,
Both, prostrate on the carpet, ear by
 ear,
Crept silently, and waited in distress,
Knowing the Emperor's moody bitter-
 ness;
Eban especially, who on the floor 'gan
Tremble and quake to death, — he feared
 less
A dose of senna-tea, or nightmare Gor-
 gon,
Than the Emperor when he play'd on his
 Man-Tiger-Organ.

XXXIX

They kiss'd nine times the carpet's vel-
 vet face
Of glossy silk, soft, smooth, and meadow-
 green,
Where the close eye in deep rich fur
 might trace
A silver tissue, scantly to be seen,
As daisies lurk'd in June-grass, buds in
 green;
Sudden the music ceased, sudden the
 hand
Of majesty, by dint of passion keen,
Doubled into a common fist, went grand,
And knock'd down three cut glasses, and
 his best ink-stand.

XL

Then turning round, he saw those trem-
 bling two:
'Eban,' said he, ' as slaves should taste
 the fruits
Of diligence, I shall remember you
To-morrow, or next day, as time suits,
In a finger conversation with my mutes, —
Begone ! — for you, Chaldean ! here re-
 main !
Fear not, quake not, and as good wine
 recruits
A conjurer's spirits, what cup will you
 drain ?
Sherry in silver, hock in gold, or glass'd
 champagne ? '

XLI

'Commander of the Faithful ! ' answer'd
 Hum,
In preference to these, I 'll merely taste
A thimble-full of old Jamaica rum.'
'A simple boon ! ' said Elfinan, ' thou
 may'st
Have Nantz, with which my morning-
 coffee 's laced.' [1]
'I 'll have a glass of Nantz, then,' — said
 the Seer, —
'Made racy — (sure my boldness is mis-
 placed !) —
With the third part — (yet that is drink-
 ing dear !) —
Of the least drop of *crème de citron* crystal
 clear.'

XLII

'I pledge you, Hum ! and pledge my
 dearest love,
My Bertha ! ' ' Bertha ! Bertha ! ' cried
 the sage,
'I know a many Berthas ! ' ' Mine 's
 above
All Berthas ! ' sighed the Emperor. ' I
 engage,'
Said Hum, ' in duty, and in vassalage,

[1] ' Mr. Nisby is of opinion that laced coffee is bad for
the head.' — *Spectator.*

To mention all the Berthas in the
earth; —
There 's Bertha Watson, — and Miss
Bertha Page, —
This famed for languid eyes, and that for
mirth, —
There 's Bertha Blount of York, — and
Bertha Knox of Perth.'

XLIII

'You seem to know' — 'I do know,'
answer'd Hum,
'Your Majesty 's in love with some fine
girl
Named Bertha; but her surname will not
come,
Without a little conjuring.' 'T is Pearl,
'T is Bertha Pearl! What makes my
brains so whirl?
And she is softer, fairer than her name !'
'Where does she live?' ask'd Hum.
'Her fair locks curl
So brightly, they put all our fays to
shame ! —
Live? — O ! at Canterbury, with her old
grand dame.'

XLIV

'Good ! good !' cried Hum, 'I 've known
her from a child !
She is a changeling of my management;
She was born at midnight in an Indian
wild;
Her mother's screams with the striped
tiger's blent,
While the torch-bearing slaves a halloo
sent
Into the jungles; and her palanquin,
Rested amid the desert's dreariment,
Shook with her agony, till fair were seen
The little Bertha's eyes ope on the stars
serene.'

XLV

'I can't say,' said the monarch, 'that
may be
Just as it happen'd, true or else a bam !
Drink up your brandy, and sit down by
me,

Feel, feel my pulse, how much in love I
am;
And if your science is not all a sham,
Tell me some means to get the lady
here.'
'Upon my honour !' said the son of
Cham,[1]
'She is my dainty changeling, near and
dear,
Although her story sounds at first a little
queer.'

XLVI

'Convey her to me, Hum, or by my
crown,
My sceptre, and my cross-surmounted
globe,
I 'll knock you — ' 'Does your majesty
mean — *down?*
No, no, you never could my feelings
probe
To such a depth !' The Emperor took
his robe,
And wept upon its purple palatine,
While Hum continued, shamming half
a sob, —
'In Canterbury doth your lady shine?
But let me cool your brandy with a little
wine.'

XLVII

Whereat a narrow Flemish glass he
took,
That since belong'd to Admiral De Witt,
Admired it with a connoisseuring look,
And with the ripest claret crowned it,
And, ere the lively head could burst and
flit,
He turn'd it quickly, nimbly upside
down,
His mouth being held conveniently fit
To catch the treasure: 'Best in all the
town !'
He said, smack'd his moist lips, and gave a
pleasant frown.

[1] Cham is said to have been the inventor of magic.
Lucy learnt this from Bayle's Dictionary, and had
copied a long Latin note from that work.

XLVIII

'Ah ! good my Prince, weep not !' And
 then again
He fill'd a bumper. 'Great Sire, do not
 weep !
Your pulse is shocking, but I 'll ease
 your pain.'
'Fetch me that Ottoman, and prithee
 keep
Your voice low,' said the Emperor, 'and
 steep
Some lady's-fingers nice in Candy wine;
And prithee, Hum, behind the screen do
 peep
For the rose-water vase, magician mine !
And sponge my forehead — so my love doth
 make me pine.'

XLIX

'Ah, cursed Bellanaine !' 'Don't think
 of her,'
Rejoin'd the Mago, 'but on Bertha muse;
For, by my choicest best barometer,
You shall not throttled be in marriage
 noose;
I 've said it, sire; you only have to choose
Bertha or Bellanaine.' So saying, he
 drew
From the left pocket of his threadbare
 hose,
A sampler hoarded slyly, good as new;
Holding it by his thumb and finger full in
 view.

L

'Sire, this is Bertha Pearl's neat handy-
 work,
Her *name*, see here, *Midsummer, ninety-
 one*'—
Elfinan snatch'd it with a sudden jerk,
And wept as if he never would have
 done,
Honouring with royal tears the poor
 homespun;
Whereon were broider'd tigers with black
 eyes,
And long-tailed pheasants, and a rising
 sun,

Plenty of posies, great stags, butterflies
Bigger than stags — a moon — with other
 mysteries.

LI

The monarch handled o'er and o'er again
These day-school hieroglyphics with a
 sigh;
Somewhat in sadness, but pleased in the
 main,
Till this oracular couplet met his eye
Astounded — *Cupid, I do thee defy !*
It was too much. He shrunk back in
 his chair,
Grew pale as death, and fainted — very
 nigh !
'Pho ! nonsense !' exclaim'd Hum, 'now
 don't despair:
She does not mean it really. Cheer up,
 hearty — there !

LII

'And listen to my words. You say you
 won't,
On any terms, marry Miss Bellanaine;
It goes against your conscience — good !
 well, don't.
You say, you love a mortal. I would
 fain
Persuade your honour's highness to re-
 frain
From peccadilloes. But, Sire, as I say,
What good would that do ? And, to be
 more plain,
You would do me a mischief some odd
 day,
Cut off my ears and hands, or head too, by
 my fay !

LIII

'Besides, manners forbid that I should
 pass any
Vile strictures on the conduct of a prince
Who should indulge his genius, if he has
 any,
Not, like a subject, foolish matter mince.
Now I think on't, perhaps I could con-
 vince

Your Majesty there is no crime at all
In loving pretty little Bertha, since
She 's very delicate — not over tall, —
A fairy's hand, and in the waist why —
 very small.'

LIV

'Ring the repeater, gentle Hum !' ''T is
 five,'
Said gentle Hum; 'the nights draw in
 apace;
The little birds I hear are all alive;
I see the dawning touch'd upon your face;
Shall I put out the candles, please your
 Grace ?'
'Do put them out, and, without more
 ado,
Tell me how I may that sweet girl em-
 brace, —
How you can bring her to me.' 'That 's
 for you,
Great Emperor ! to adventure, like a lover
 true.'

LV

'I fetch her !' — 'Yes, an 't like your
 Majesty;
And as she would be frighten'd wide
 awake,
To travel such a distance through the
 sky,
Use of some soft manœuvre you must
 make,
For your convenience, and her dear
 nerves' sake;
Nice way would be to bring her in a
 swoon,
Anon, I 'll tell what course were best to
 take;
You must away this morning.' 'Hum !
 so soon ?'
'Sire, you must be in Kent by twelve
 o'clock at noon.'

LVI

At this great Cæsar started on his feet,
Lifted his wings, and stood attentive-
 wise.

'Those wings to Canterbury you must
 beat,
If you hold Bertha as a worthy prize,
Look in the Almanack — *Moore* never
 lies —
April the twenty-fourth — this coming
 day,
Now breathing its new bloom upon the
 skies,
Will end in St. Mark's Eve; — you must
 away,
For on that eve alone can you the maid
 convey.'

LVII

Then the magician solemnly 'gan to
 frown,
So that his frost-white eye-brows, beet-
 ling low,
Shaded his deep green eyes, and wrinkles
 brown
Plaited upon his furnace-scorched brow:
Forth from his hood that hung his neck
 below
He lifted a bright casket of pure gold,
Touch'd a spring-lock, and there in wool
 or snow,
Charm'd into ever freezing, lay an old
And legend-leaved book, mysterious to
 behold.

LVIII

'Take this same book — it will not bite
 you, Sire;
There, put it underneath your royal
 arm;
Though it 's a pretty weight, it will not
 tire,
But rather on your journey keep you
 warm:
This is the magic, this the potent charm,
That shall drive Bertha to a fainting
 fit !
When the time comes, don't feel the least
 alarm,
But lift her from the ground, and swiftly
 flit
Back to your palace.

LIX

'What shall I do with that same book?'
 'Why merely
Lay it on Bertha's table, close beside
Her work-box, and 't will help your pur-
 pose dearly;
I say no more.' 'Or good or ill betide,
Through the wide air to Kent this morn
 I glide!'
Exclaim'd the Emperor, 'When I return,
Ask what you will, — I 'll give you my
 new bride!
And take some more wine, Hum; — O,
 Heavens! I burn
To be upon the wing! Now, now, that
 minx I spurn!'

LX

'Leave her to me,' rejoin'd the magian:
'But how shall I account, illustrious fay!
For thine imperial absence? Pho! I
 can
Say you are very sick, and bar the way
To your so loving courtiers for one day;
If either of their two Archbishops' graces
Should talk of extreme unction, I shall
 say
You do not like cold pig with Latin
 phrases,
Which never should be used but in alarm-
 ing cases.'

LXI

'Open the window, Hum; I 'm ready
 now!'
'Zooks!' exclaim'd Hum, as up the sash
 he drew,
'Behold, your Majesty, upon the brow
Of yonder hill, what crowds of people!'
 'Whew!
The monster 's always after something
 new,'
Return'd his Highness, 'they are piping
 hot
To see my pigsney Bellanaine. Hum!
 do
Tighten my belt a little, — so, so, — not
Too tight, — the book! — my wand! — so,
 nothing is forgot.'

LXII

'Wounds! how they shout!' said Hum,
 'and there, — see, see,
Th' ambassador 's return'd from Pigmio!
The morning 's very fine, — uncommonly!
See, past the skirts of yon white cloud
 they go,
Tinging it with soft crimsons! Now
 below
The sable-pointed heads of firs and pines
They dip, move on, and with them moves
 a glow
Along the forest side! Now amber lines
Reach the hill top, and now throughout the
 valley shines.'

LXIII

'Why, Hum, you 're getting quite poeti-
 cal!
Those *nows* you managed in a special
 style.'
'If ever you have leisure, Sire, you shall
See scraps of mine will make it worth
 your while,
Tit-bits for Phœbus! — yes, you well
 may smile.
Hark! hark! the bells!' 'A little
 further yet,
Good Hum, and let me view this mighty
 coil.'
Then the great Emperor full graceful set
His elbow for a prop, and snuff'd his
 mignonette.

LXIV

The morn is full of holiday: loud bells
With rival clamors ring from every spire;
Cunningly-station'd music dies and swells
In echoing places; when the winds re-
 spire,
Light flags stream out like gauzy tongues
 of fire;
A metropolitan murmur, lifeful, warm,
Comes from the northern suburbs; rich
 attire
Freckles with red and gold the moving
 swarm;
While here and there clear trumpets blow
 a keen alarm.

LXV

And now the fairy escort was seen clear,
Like the old pageant of Aurora's train,
Above a pearl-built minster, hovering
　near;
First wily Crafticant, the chamberlain,
Balanced upon his gray-grown pinions
　twain,
His slender wand officially reveal'd;
Then black gnomes scattering sixpences
　like rain;
Then pages three and three; and next,
　slave-held,
The Imaian 'scutcheon bright, — one mouse
　in argent field.

LXVI

Gentlemen pensioners next; and after
　them,
A troop of winged Janizaries flew;
Then slaves, as presents bearing many a
　gem;
Then twelve physicians fluttering two
　and two;
And next a chaplain in a cassock new;
Then Lords in waiting; then (what head
　not reels
For pleasure?) — the fair Princess in
　full view,
Borne upon wings, — and very pleased
　she feels
To have such splendour dance attendance
　at her heels.

LXVII

For there was more magnificence behind:
She waved her handkerchief. ' Ah, very
　grand ! '
Cried Elfinan, and closed the window-
　blind;
' And, Hum, we must not shilly-shally
　stand, —
Adieu! adieu! I 'm off for Angle-land !
I say, old Hocus, have you such a thing
About you, — feel your pockets, I com-
　mand, —
I want, this instant, an invisible ring, —
Thank you, old mummy ! — now securely I
　take wing.'

LXVIII

Then Elfinan swift vaulted from the floor,
And lighted graceful on the window-sill;
Under one arm the magic book he bore,
The other he could wave about at will;
Pale was his face, he still look'd very ill:
He bow'd at Bellanaine, and said —
　' Poor Bell !
Farewell ! farewell ! and if for ever ! still
For ever fare thee well !' — and then he
　fell
A laughing ! — snapp'd his fingers ! —
　shame it is to tell !

LXIX

' By 'r Lady ! he is gone !' cries Hum,
　' and I, —
(I own it), — have made too free with
　his wine;
Old Crafticant will smoke me. By-the-
　bye !
This room is full of jewels as a mine, —
Dear valuable creatures, how ye shine !
Some time to-day I must contrive a
　minute,
If Mercury propitiously incline,
To examine his scrutoire, and see what 's
　in it,
For of superfluous diamonds I as well may
　thin it.

LXX

' The Emperor 's horrid bad; yes, that 's
　my cue !'
Some histories say that this was Hum's
　last speech;
That, being fuddled, he went reeling
　through
The corridor, and scarce upright could
　reach
The stair-head; that being glutted as a
　leech,
And used, as we ourselves have just now
　said,
To manage stairs reversely, like a peach
Too ripe, he fell, being puzzled in his
　head
With liquor and the staircase: verdict —
　found stone dead.

LXXI

This, as a falsehood, Crafticanto treats;
And as his style is of strange elegance,
Gentle and tender, full of soft conceits,
(Much like our Boswell's,) we will take a
 glance
At his sweet prose, and, if we can, make
 dance
His woven periods into careless rhyme;
O, little faery Pegasus! rear — prance —
Trot round the quarto — ordinary time!
March, little Pegasus, with pawing hoof
 sublime!

LXXII

' Well, let us see, — *tenth book and chapter
 nine,*' —
Thus Crafticant pursues his diary: —
' 'T was twelve o'clock at night, the wea-
 ther fine,
Latitude thirty-six; our scouts descry
A flight of starlings making rapidly
Towards Thibet. Mem.: — birds fly in
 the night;
From twelve to half-past — wings not fit
 to fly
For a thick fog — the Princess sulky
 quite:
Call'd for an extra shawl, and gave her
 nurse a bite.

LXXIII

' Five minutes before one — brought
 down a moth
With my new double-barrel — stew'd
 the thighs,
And made a very tolerable broth —
Princess turn'd dainty, to our great sur-
 prise,
Alter'd her mind, and thought it very
 nice:
Seeing her pleasant, tried her with a
 pun,
She frown'd; a monstrous owl across us
 flies
About this time, — a sad old figure of
 fun;
Bad omen — this new match can't be a
 happy one.

LXXIV

' From two to half-past, dusky way we
 made,
Above the plains of Gobi, — desert,
 bleak;
Beheld afar off, in the hooded shade
Of darkness, a great mountain (strange
 to speak),
Spitting, from forth its sulphur-baken
 peak,
A fan-shaped burst of blood-red, arrowy
 fire,
Turban'd with smoke, which still away
 did reek,
Solid and black from that eternal pyre,
Upon the laden winds that scantly could
 respire.

LXXV

' Just upon three o'clock, a falling star
Created an alarm among our troop,
Kill'd a man-cook, a page, and broke a
 jar,
A tureen, and three dishes, at one swoop,
Then passing by the Princess, singed her
 hoop:
Could not conceive what Coralline was at,
She clapp'd her hands three times, and
 cried out " Whoop!"
Some strange Imaian custom. A large
 bat
Came sudden 'fore my face, and brush'd
 against my hat.

LXXVI

' Five minutes thirteen seconds after
 three,
Far in the west a mighty fire broke out,
Conjectured, on the instant, it might be
The city of Balk — 't was Balk beyond
 all doubt:
A griffin, wheeling here and there about
Kept reconnoitering us — doubled our
 guard —
Lighted our torches, and kept up a shout,
Till he sheer'd off — the Princess very
 scared —
And many on their marrow-bones for death
 prepared.

LXXVII

'At half-past three arose the cheerful
 moon —
Bivouack'd for four minutes on a cloud —
Where from the earth we heard a lively
 tune
Of tambourines and pipes, severe and
 loud,
While on a flowery lawn a brilliant
 crowd
Cinque-parted danced, some half asleep
 reposed
Beneath the green-faned cedars, some
 did shroud
In silken tents, and 'mid light fragrance
 dozed,
Or on the open turf their soothed eyelids
 closed.

LXXVIII

'Dropp'd my gold watch, and kill'd a
 kettle-drum —
It went for apoplexy — foolish folks ! —
Left it to pay the piper — a good sum —
(I 've got a conscience, maugre people's
 jokes,)
To scrape a little favour; 'gan to coax
Her Highness' pug-dog — got a sharp
 rebuff —
She wish'd a game at whist — made
 three revokes —
Turn'd from myself, her partner, in a
 huff;
His Majesty will know her temper time
 enough.

LXXIX

'She cried for chess — I play'd a game
 with her —
Castled her king with such a vixen
 look,
It bodes ill to his Majesty — (refer
To the second chapter of my fortieth
 book,
And see what hoity-toity airs she took).
At half-past four the morn essay'd to
 beam —
Saluted, as we pass'd, an early rook, —

The Princess fell asleep, and, in her
 dream,
Talk'd of one Master Hubert, deep in her
 esteem.

LXXX

'About this time — making delightful
 way —
Shed a quill-feather from my larboard
 wing —
Wish'd, trusted, hoped 't was no sign of
 decay —
Thank Heaven, I 'm hearty yet ! — 't was
 no such thing: —
At five the golden light began to spring,
With fiery shudder through the bloomed
 east;
At six we heard Panthea's churches
 ring —
The city all his unhived swarms had cast,
To watch our grand approach, and hail us
 as we pass'd.

LXXXI

'As flowers turn their faces to the sun,
So on our flight with hungry eyes they
 gaze,
And, as we shaped our course, this, that
 way run,
With mad-cap pleasure, or hand-clasp'd
 amaze:
Sweet in the air a mild-toned music plays,
And progresses through its own laby-
 rinth;
Buds gather'd from the green spring's
 middle-days,
They scatter'd — daisy, primrose, hya-
 cinth —
Or round white columns wreathed from
 capital to plinth.

LXXXII

'Onward we floated o'er the panting
 streets,
That seem'd throughout with upheld
 faces paved;
Look where we will, our bird's-eye vision
 meets

Legions of holiday; bright standards
 waved,
And fluttering ensigns emulously craved
Our minute's glance; a busy thunderous
 roar,
From square to square, among the build-
 ings raved,
As when the sea, at flow, gluts up once
 more
The craggy hollowness of a wild-reefed
 shore.

LXXXIII

' And " Bellanaine for ever ! " shouted
 they !
While that fair Princess, from her
 winged chair,
Bow'd low with high demeanour, and, to
 pay
Their new-blown loyalty with guerdon
 fair,
Still emptied, at meet distance, here and
 there,
A plenty horn of jewels. And here I
(Who wish to give the devil her due)
 declare
Against that ugly piece of calumny,
Which calls them Highland pebble-stones
 not worth a fly.

LXXXIV

' Still " Bellanaine ! " they shouted, while
 we glide
'Slant to a light Ionic portico,
The city's delicacy, and the pride
Of our Imperial Basilic; a row
Of lords and ladies, on each hand, make
 show
Submissive of knee-bent obeisance,
All down the steps; and, as we enter'd, lo !
The strangest sight — the most unlook'd-
 for chance —
All things turn'd topsy-turvy in a devil's
 dance.

LXXXV

' 'Stead of his anxious Majesty and court
At the open doors, with wide saluting
 eyes,

Congêes and scrape-graces of every sort,
And all the smooth routine of gallan-
 tries,
Was seen, to our immoderate surprise,
A motley crowd thick gather'd in the
 hall,
Lords, scullions, deputy-scullions, with
 wild cries
Stunning the vestibule from wall to wall,
Where the Chief Justice on his knees and
 hands doth crawl.

LXXXVI

' Counts of the palace, and the state pur-
 veyor
Of moth's-down, to make soft the royal
 beds,
The Common Council and my fool Lord
 Mayor
Marching a-row, each other slipshod
 treads;
Powder'd bag-wigs and ruffy-tuffy heads
Of cinder wenches meet and soil each
 other;
Toe crush'd with heel ill-natured fighting
 breeds,
Frill-rumpling elbows brew up many a
 bother,
And fists in the short ribs keep up the yell
 and pother.

LXXXVII

' A Poet, mounted on the Court-Clown's
 back,
Rode to the Princess swift with spurring
 heels,
And close into her face, with rhyming
 clack,
Began a Prothalamion; — she reels,
She falls, she faints ! — while laughter
 peals
Over her woman's weakness. " Where ! "
 cried I,
" Where is his Majesty ? " No person
 feels
Inclined to answer; wherefore instantly
I plunged into the crowd to find him or
 to die.

LXXXVIII

'Jostling my way I gain'd the stairs, and
 ran
To the first landing, where, incredible !
I met, far gone in liquor, that old man,
That vile impostor Hum, ———— '
 So far so well, —
For we have proved the Mago never fell
Down stairs on Crafticanto's evidence;
And therefore duly shall proceed to tell,
Plain in our own original mood and
 tense,
The sequel of this day, though labour 't is
 immense !

.

THE LAST SONNET

On his way to Italy as his last chance of life,
the vessel which bore Keats had been beating
about the English Channel for a fortnight,
when an opportunity was given for landing for
a brief respite on the Dorsetshire coast. 'The
bright beauty of the day,' says Lord Hough-
ton, Keats's biographer, ' and the scene revived
the poet's drooping heart, and the inspiration
remained with him for some time even after
his return to the ship. It was then that he
composed that sonnet of solemn tenderness.'
The date of the poem would thus be Septem-
ber or October, 1820.

BRIGHT star, would I were steadfast as
 thou art !
 Not in lone splendour hung aloft the
 night,
And watching, with eternal lids apart,
 Like Nature's patient sleepless Eremite,
The moving waters at their priestlike task
 Of pure ablution round earth's human
 shores
Or gazing on the new soft fallen mask
 Of snow upon the mountains and the
 moors:
No — yet still steadfast, still unchangeable,
 Pillow'd upon my fair love's ripening
 breast,
To feel for ever its soft fall and swell,
 Awake for ever in a sweet unrest,
Still, still to hear her tender-taken breath,
And so live ever — or else swoon to death.

SUPPLEMENTARY VERSE

The collection which follows is not intended to be taken exactly as containing the leavings of Keats's genius ; there are verses in the previous groups which might be placed here, if the intention was to make a marked division between his well-defined poetry and his experiments and mere scintillations; doubtless, too, on any such principle it would be just to take back into the respectability of larger type some of the lines here included. But it seemed wise to put into a subordinate group the poet's fragmentary and posthumous poems, and those which were plainly the mere playthings of his muse.

I. HYPERION : A VISION

Contributed by Lord Houghton to the third volume of the *Bibliographical and Historical Miscellanies* of the Philobiblion Society, 1856–1857. Lord Houghton afterward included it in a new edition of *The Life and Letters of John Keats*, 1867. He also printed it in the Aldine edition of 1876, and always regarded it as an early version of the poem. But Mr. Colvin quotes from Brown's *MS.* : 'In the evenings [of November and December, 1819] at his own desire, he occupied a separate apartment, and was deeply engaged in remodeling the fragment of *Hyperion* into the form of a Vision.' This attempt may well have added to Keats's reluctance to permit the fragmentary *Hyperion* to appear in the 1820 volume. For a full discussion of the question see the Appendix in *John Keats* by Sidney Colvin.

CANTO I

FANATICS have their dreams, wherewith they weave
A paradise for a sect ; the savage, too,
From forth the loftiest fashion of his sleep
Guesses at heaven ; pity these have not
Trac'd upon vellum or wild Indian leaf
The shadows of melodious utterance,
But bare of laurel they live, dream, and die ;
For Poesy alone can tell her dreams, —
With the fine spell of words alone can save
Imagination from the sable chain 10
And dumb enchantment. Who alive can say,
'Thou art no Poet — may'st not tell thy dreams'?
Since every man whose soul is not a clod

Hath visions and would speak, if he had loved,
And been well nurtured in his mother tongue.
Whether the dream now purpos'd to rehearse
Be poet's or fanatic's will be known
When this warm scribe, my hand, is in the grave.

Methought I stood where trees of every clime,
Palm, myrtle, oak, and sycamore, and beech, 20
With plantane and spice-blossoms, made a screen,
In neighbourhood of fountains (by the noise
Soft-showering in mine ears), and (by the touch
Of scent) not far from roses. Twining round
I saw an arbour with a drooping roof
Of trellis vines, and bells, and larger blooms,
Like floral censers, swinging light in air ;
Before its wreathed doorway, on a mound
Of moss, was spread a feast of summer fruits,
Which, nearer seen, seem'd refuse of a meal 30
By angel tasted or our Mother Eve ;
For empty shells were scatter'd on the grass,
And grapestalks but half-bare, and remnants more
Sweet-smelling, whose pure kinds I could not know.
Still was more plenty than the fabled horn
Thrice emptied could pour forth at banqueting,
For Proserpine return'd to her own fields,
Where the white heifers low. And appetite,
More yearning than on earth I ever felt,
Growing within, I ate deliciously, — 40
And, after not long, thirsted ; for thereby
Stood a cool vessel of transparent juice
Sipp'd by the wander'd bee, the which I took,
And pledging all the mortals of the world,
And all the dead whose names are in our lips,
Drank. That full draught is parent of my theme.

No Asian poppy nor elixir fine
Of the soon-fading, jealous Caliphat,
No poison gender'd in close monkish cell,
To thin the scarlet conclave of old men, 50
Could so have rapt unwilling life away.
Among the fragrant husks and berries crush'd
Upon the grass, I struggled hard against
The domineering potion, but in vain.
The cloudy swoon came on, and down I sank,
Like a Silenus on an antique vase.
How long I slumber'd 't is a chance to guess.
When sense of life return'd, I started up
As if with wings, but the fair trees were gone,
The mossy mound and arbour were no more: 60
I look'd around upon the curved sides
Of an old sanctuary, with roof august,
Builded so high, it seem'd that filmed clouds
Might spread beneath as o'er the stars of hea-
 ven.
So old the place was, I remember'd none
The like upon the earth: what I had seen
Of grey cathedrals, buttress'd walls, rent tow-
 ers,
The superannuations of sunk realms,
Or Nature's rocks toil'd hard in waves and
 winds,
Seem'd but the faulture of decrepit things 70
To that eternal domed monument.
Upon the marble at my feet there lay
Store of strange vessels and large draperies,
Which needs had been of dyed asbestos wove,
Or in that place the moth could not corrupt,
So white the linen, so, in some, distinct
Ran imageries from a sombre loom.
All in a mingled heap confus'd there lay
Robes, golden tongs, censer and chafing-dish,
Girdles, and chains, and holy jewelries. 80

 Turning from these with awe, once more I
 raised
My eyes to fathom the space every way:
The embossed roof, the silent massy range
Of columns north and south, ending in mist
Of nothing; then to eastward, where black
 gates
Were shut against the sunrise evermore;
Then to the west I look'd, and saw far off
An image, huge of feature as a cloud,
At level of whose feet an altar slept,
To be approach'd on either side by steps 90
And marble balustrade, and patient travail
To count with toil the innumerable degrees.
Toward the altar sober-pac'd I went,
Repressing haste as too unholy there;
And, coming nearer, saw beside the shrine
One ministering; and there arose a flame
When in mid-day the sickening east-wind

Shifts sudden to the south, the small warm
 rain
Melts out the frozen incense from all flowers,
And fills the air with so much pleasant health 100
That even the dying man forgets his shroud; —
Even so that lofty sacrificial fire,
Sending forth Maian incense, spread around
Forgetfulness of everything but bliss,
And clouded all the altar with soft smoke;
From whose white fragrant curtains thus I
 heard
Language pronounc'd: 'If thou canst not as-
 cend
These steps, die on that marble where thou
 art.
Thy flesh, near cousin to the common dust,
Will parch for lack of nutriment; thy bones 110
Will wither in few years, and vanish so
That not the quickest eye could find a grain
Of what thou now art on that pavement cold.
The sands of thy short life are spent this
 hour,
And no hand in the universe can turn
Thy hourglass, if these gummed leaves be burnt
Ere thou canst mount up these immortal steps.'
I heard, I look'd: two senses both at once,
So fine, so subtle, felt the tyranny
Of that fierce threat and the hard task pro-
 posed. 120
Prodigious seem'd the toil; the leaves were yet
Burning, when suddenly a palsied chill
Struck from the paved level up my limbs,
And was ascending quick to put cold grasp
Upon those streams that pulse beside the throat.
I shriek'd, and the sharp anguish of my shriek
Stung my own ears; I strove hard to escape
The numbness, strove to gain the lowest step.
Slow, heavy, deadly was my pace: the cold
Grew stifling, suffocating at the heart; 130
And when I clasp'd my hands I felt them not.
One minute before death my ic'd foot touch'd
The lowest stair; and, as it touch'd, life seem'd
To pour in at the toes; I mounted up
As once fair angels on a ladder flew
From the green turf to heaven. 'Holy Power,'
Cried I, approaching near the horned shrine,
'What am I that should so be saved from
 death?
What am I that another death come not
To choke my utterance, sacrilegious, here?' 140
Then said the veiled shadow: 'Thou hast felt
What 't is to die and live again before
Thy fated hour; that thou hadst power to do
 so
Is thine own safety; thou hast dated on
Thy doom.' 'High Prophetess,' said I, 'purge
 off,

Benign, if so it please thee, my mind's film.'
'None can usurp this height,' return'd that
 shade,
'But those to whom the miseries of the world
Are misery, and will not let them rest.
All else who find a haven in the world, 150
Where they may thoughtless sleep away their
 days,
If by a chance into this fane they come,
Rot on the pavement where thou rottedst half.'
'Are there not thousands in the world,' said I,
Encourag'd by the sooth voice of the shade,
'Who love their fellows even to the death,
Who feel the giant agony of the world,
And more, like slaves to poor humanity,
Labour for mortal good? I sure should see
Other men here, but I am here alone.' 160
'Those whom thou spakest of are no visiona-
 ries,'
Rejoin'd that voice; 'they are no dreamers
 weak;
They seek no wonder but the human face,
No music but a happy-noted voice:
They come not here, they have no thought to
 come;
And thou art here, for thou art less than they.
What benefit canst thou do, or all thy tribe,
To the great world? Thou art a dreaming
 thing,
A fever of thyself: think of the earth;
What bliss, even in hope, is there for thee? 170
What haven? every creature hath its home,
Every sole man hath days of joy and pain,
Whether his labours be sublime or low —
The pain alone, the joy alone, distinct:
Only the dreamer venoms all his days,
Bearing more woe than all his sins deserve.
Therefore, that happiness be somewhat shared,
Such things as thou art are admitted oft
Into like gardens thou didst pass erewhile,
And suffer'd in these temples: for that cause 180
Thou standest safe beneath this statue's knees.'
'That I am favour'd for unworthiness,
By such propitious parley medicined
In sickness not ignoble, I rejoice,
Aye, and could weep for love of such award.'
So answer'd I, continuing, 'If it please,
Majestic shadow, tell me where I am,
Whose altar this, for whom this incense curls;
What image this whose face I cannot see
For the broad marble knees; and who thou
 art, 190
Of accent feminine so courteous?'

Then the tall shade, in drooping linen veil'd,
Spoke out, so much more earnest, that her
 breath
Stirr'd the thin folds of gauze that drooping
 hung
About a golden censer from her hand
Pendent; and by her voice I knew she shed
Long-treasured tears. 'This temple, sad and
 lone,
Is all spar'd from the thunder of a war
Foughten long since by giant hierarchy
Against rebellion: this old image here, 200
Whose carved features wrinkled as he fell,
Is Saturn's; I, Moneta, left supreme,
Sole goddess of this desolation.'
I had no words to answer, for my tongue,
Useless, could find about its roofed home
No syllable of a fit majesty
To make rejoinder to Moneta's mourn:
There was a silence, while the altar's blaze
Was fainting for sweet food. I look'd thereon,
And on the paved floor, where nigh were piled
Faggots of cinnamon, and many heaps 211
Of other crisped spicewood: then again
I look'd upon the altar, and its horns
Whiten'd with ashes, and its languorous flame,
And then upon the offerings again;
And so, by turns, till sad Moneta cried:
'The sacrifice is done, but not the less
Will I be kind to thee for thy good will.
My power, which to me is still a curse,
Shall be to thee a wonder; for the scenes 220
Still swooning vivid through my globed brain,
With an electral changing misery,
Thou shalt with these dull mortal eyes behold
Free from all pain, if wonder pain thee not.'
As near as an immortal's sphered words
Could to a mother's soften were these last:
And yet I had a terror of her robes,
And chiefly of the veils that from her brow
Hung pale, and curtain'd her in mysteries,
That made my heart too small to hold its
 blood. 230
This saw that Goddess, and with sacred hand
Parted the veils. Then saw I a wan face,
Not pin'd by human sorrows, but bright-
 blanch'd
By an immortal sickness which kills not;
It works a constant change, which happy death
Can put no end to; deathwards progressing
To no death was that visage; it had past
The lily and the snow; and beyond these
I must not think now, though I saw that face.
But for her eyes I should have fled away; 240
They held me back, with a benignant light,
Soft, mitigated by divinest lids
Half-clos'd, and visionless entire they seem'd
Of all external things; they saw me not,
But in blank splendour beam'd, like the mild
 moon,

Who comforts those she sees not, who knows
 not
What eyes are upward cast. As I had found
A grain of gold upon a mountain's side,
And, twing'd with avarice, strain'd out my
 eyes
To search its sullen entrails rich with ore, 250
So, at the view of sad Moneta's brow,
I ask'd to see what things the hollow brow
Behind environ'd : what high tragedy
In the dark secret chambers of her skull
Was acting, that could give so dread a stress
To her cold lips, and fill with such a light
Her planetary eyes, and touch her voice
With such a sorrow ? 'Shade of Memory !'
Cried I, with act adorant at her feet,
'By all the gloom hung round thy fallen
 house, 260
By this last temple, by the golden age,
By great Apollo, thy dear foster-child,
And by thyself, forlorn divinity,
The pale Omega of a wither'd race,
Let me behold, according as thou saidst,
What in thy brain so ferments to and fro !'
No sooner had this conjuration past
My devout lips, than side by side we stood
(Like a stunt bramble by a solemn pine)
Deep in the shady sadness of a vale 270
Far sunken from the healthy breath of morn,
Far from the fiery noon and eve's one star.
Onward I look'd beneath the gloomy boughs,
And saw what first I thought an image huge,
Like to the image pedestall'd so high
In Saturn's temple ; then Moneta's voice
Came brief upon mine ear. 'So Saturn sat
When he had lost his realms ;' whereon there
 grew
A power within me of enormous ken
To see as a god sees, and take the depth 280
Of things as nimbly as the outward eye
Can size and shape pervade. The lofty theme
Of those few words hung vast before my mind
With half-unravell'd web. I sat myself
Upon an eagle's watch, that I might see,
And seeing ne'er forget. No stir of life
Was in this shrouded vale, — not so much air
As in the zoning of a summer's day
Robs not one light seed from the feather'd grass
But where the dead leaf fell there did it rest.
A stream went noiseless by, still deaden'd more
By reason of the fallen divinity 292
Spreading more shade ; the Naiad 'mid her
 reeds
Prest her cold finger closer to her lips.

Along the margin-sand large foot-marks went
No further than to where old Saturn's feet

Had rested, and there slept how long a sleep !
Degraded, cold, upon the sodden ground
His old right hand lay nerveless, listless, dead,
Unsceptred, and his realmless eyes were closed ;
While his bowed head seem'd listening to the
 Earth, 301
His ancient mother, for some comfort yet.

 It seem'd no force could wake him from his
 place ;
But there came one who, with a kindred hand,
Touch'd his wide shoulders, after bending low
With reverence, though to one who knew it not.
Then came the griev'd voice Mnemosyne,
And griev'd I hearken'd. ' That divinity
Whom thou saw'st step from yon forlornest
 wood, 309
And with slow pace approach our fallen king,
Is Thea, softest-natured of our brood.'
I mark'd the Goddess, in fair statuary
Surpassing wan Moneta by the head,
And in her sorrow nearer woman's tears.
There was a list'ning fear in her regard,
As if calamity had but begun ;
As if the venom'd cloud of evil days
Had spent their malice, and the sullen rear
Was with its stored thunder labouring up,
One hand she press'd upon that aching spot 320
Where beats the human heart, as if just there,
Though an immortal, she felt cruel pain ;
The other upon Saturn's bended neck
She laid, and to the level of his ear
Leaning, with parted lips some words she spoke
In solemn tenour and deep organ-tone ;
Some mourning words, which in our feeble
 tongue
Would come in this like accenting ; how frail
To that large utterance of the early gods !

 'Saturn, look up ! and for what, poor lost
 king ? 330
I have no comfort for thee ; no, not one ;
I cannot say, wherefore thus sleepest thou ?
For Heaven is parted from thee, and the Earth
Knows thee not, so afflicted, for a god.
The Ocean, too, with all its solemn noise,
Has from thy sceptre pass'd ; and all the air
Is emptied of thy hoary majesty.
Thy thunder, captious at the new command,
Rumbles reluctant o'er our fallen house ;
And thy sharp lightning, in unpractis'd hands,
Scourges and burns our once serene domain. 341

 ' With such remorseless speed still come new
 woes,
That unbelief has not a space to breathe.
Saturn ! sleep on : me thoughtless, why should I

Thus violate thy slumbrous solitude?
Why should I ope thy melancholy eyes?
Saturn! sleep on, while at thy feet I weep.'

As when upon a tranced summer-night
Forests, branch-charmed by the earnest stars,
Dream, and so dream all night without a noise,
Save from one gradual solitary gust 351
Swelling upon the silence, dying off,
As if the ebbing air had but one wave,
So came these words and went; the while in tears
She prest her fair large forehead to the earth,
Just where her fallen hair might spread in curls,
A soft and silken net for Saturn's feet.
Long, long these two were postured motionless,
Like sculpture builded-up upon the grave
Of their own power. A long awful time 360
I look'd upon them: still they were the same;
The frozen God still bending to the earth,
And the sad Goddess weeping at his feet;
Moneta silent. Without stay or prop
But my own weak mortality, I bore
The load of this eternal quietude,
The unchanging gloom and the three fixed shapes
Ponderous upon my senses, a whole moon;
For by my burning brain I measured sure
Her silver seasons shedded on the night, 370
And every day by day methought I grew
More gaunt and ghostly. Oftentimes I pray'd
Intense, that death would take me from the vale
And all its burthens; gasping with despair
Of change, hour after hour I curs'd myself,
Until old Saturn rais'd his faded eyes,
And look'd around and saw his kingdom gone,
And all the gloom and sorrow of the place,
And that fair kneeling Goddess at his feet.

As the moist scent of flowers, and grass, and leaves 380
Fills forest-dells with a pervading air,
Known to the woodland nostril, so the words
Of Saturn fill'd the mossy glooms around,
Even to the hollows of time-eaten oaks,
And to the windings of the foxes' hole,
With sad, low tones, while thus he spoke, and sent
Strange moanings to the solitary Pan.
'Moan, brethren, moan, for we are swallow'd up
And buried from all godlike exercise
Of influence benign on planets pale, 390
And peaceful sway upon man's harvesting,
And all those acts which Deity supreme

Doth ease its heart of love in. Moan and wail;
Moan, brethren, moan; for lo, the rebel spheres
Spin round; the stars their ancient courses keep;
Clouds still with shadowy moisture haunt the earth,
Still suck their fill of light from sun and moon;
Still buds the tree, and still the seashores murmur;
There is no death in all the universe,
No smell of death. — There shall be death. 400
Moan, moan;
Moan, Cybele, moan; for thy pernicious babes
Have chang'd a god into an aching palsy.
Moan, brethren, moan, for I have no strength left;
Weak as the reed, weak, feeble as my voice.
Oh! Oh! the pain, the pain of feebleness;
Moan, moan, for still I thaw; or give me help,
Throw down those imps, and give me victory.
Let me hear other groans, and trumpets blown
Of triumph calm, and hymns of festival,
From the gold peaks of heaven's high-piled clouds; 410
Voices of soft proclaim, and silver stir
Of strings in hollow shells; and there shall be
Beautiful things made new, for the surprise
Of the sky-children.' So he feebly ceased,
With such a poor and sickly-sounding pause,
Methought I heard some old man of the earth
Bewailing earthly loss; nor could my eyes
And ears act with that unison of sense
Which marries sweet sound with the grace of form,
And dolorous accent from a tragic harp 420
With large limb'd visions. More I scrutinized.
Still fixt he sat beneath the sable trees,
Whose arms spread straggling in wild serpent forms,
With leaves all hush'd; his awful presence there
(Now all was silent) gave a deadly lie
To what I erewhile heard: only his lips
Trembled amid the white curls of his beard;
They told the truth, though round the snowy locks
Hung nobly, as upon the face of heaven
A mid-day fleece of clouds. Thea arose 430
And stretcht her white arm through the hollow dark,
Pointing somewhither: whereat he too rose,
Like a vast giant, seen by men at sea
To grow pale from the waves at dull midnight.
They melted from my sight into the woods;
Ere I could turn, Moneta cried, 'These twain
Are speeding to the families of grief,

Where, rooft in by black rocks, they waste in
 pain
And darkness, for no hope.' And she spake
 on,
As ye may read who can unwearied pass 440
Onward from the antechamber of this dream,
Where, even at the open doors, awhile
I must delay, and glean my memory
Of her high phrase — perhaps no further dare.

CANTO II

' Mortal, that thou may'st understand aright,
I humanize my sayings to thine ear,
Making comparisons of earthly things ;
Or thou might'st better listen to the wind,
Whose language is to thee a barren noise,
Though it blows legend-laden thro' the trees.
In melancholy realms big tears are shed,
More sorrow like to this, and such like woe,
Too huge for mortal tongue or pen of scribe.
The Titans fierce, self-hid or prison-bound, 10
Groan for the old allegiance once more,
Listening in their doom for Saturn's voice.
But one of the whole eagle-brood still keeps
His sovereignty, and rule, and majesty :
Blazing Hyperion on his orbed fire
Still sits, still snuffs the incense teeming up
From Man to the Sun's God — yet insecure.
For as upon the earth dire prodigies
Fright and perplex, so also shudders he ;
Not at dog's howl or gloom-bird's hated screech,
Or the familiar visiting of one 21
Upon the first toll of his passing bell,
Or prophesyings of the midnight lamp ;
But horrors, portioned to a giant nerve,
Make great Hyperion ache. His palace bright,
Bastion'd with pyramids of shining gold,
And touch'd with shade of bronzed obelisks,
Glares a blood-red thro' all the thousand courts,
Arches, and domes, and fiery galleries ;
And all its curtains of Aurorian clouds 30
Flash angerly ; when he would taste the wreaths
Of incense breath'd aloft from sacred hills,
Instead of sweets, his ample palate takes
Savour of poisonous brass and metals sick ;
Wherefore when harbour'd in the sleepy West,
After the full completion of fair day,
For rest divine upon exalted couch,
And slumber in the arms of melody,
He paces through the pleasant hours of ease,
With strides colossal, on from hall to hall, 40
While far within each aisle and deep recess
His winged minions in close clusters stand
Amaz'd, and full of fear ; like anxious men,
Who on a wide plain gather in sad troops,

When earthquakes jar their battlements and
 towers.
Even now where Saturn, rous'd from icy trance,
Goes step for step with Thea from yon woods,
Hyperion, leaving twilight in the rear,
Is sloping to the threshold of the West.
Thither we tend.' Now in clear light I stood,
Reliev'd from the dusk vale. Mnemosyne 51
Was sitting on a square-edg'd polish'd stone,
That in its lucid depths reflected pure
Her priestess' garments. My quick eyes ran on
From stately nave to nave, from vault to vault,
Through bow'rs of fragrant and enwreathed
 light,
And diamond-paved lustrous long arcades.
Anon rush'd by the bright Hyperion ;
His flaming robes stream'd out beyond his heels,
And gave a roar as if of earthy fire, 60
That scar'd away the meek ethereal hours,
And made their dove-wings tremble. On he
 flared.

II. FRAGMENTS

The three fragments that follow are pub-
lished in *Life, Letters and Literary Remains*,
without date.

I

WHERE 's the Poet ? Show him ! show him,
Muses nine ! that I may know him !
'T is the man who with a man
 Is an equal, be he King,
Or poorest of the beggar-clan, *
 Or any other wondrous thing
A man may be 'twixt ape and Plato :
 'T is the man who with a bird,
Wren, or Eagle, finds his way to
 All its instincts ; he hath heard
The Lion's roaring, and can tell
 What his horny throat expresseth,
And to him the Tiger's yell
 Comes articulate and presseth
On his ear like mother-tongue.

II

MODERN LOVE

AND what is love ? It is a doll dress'd up
For idleness to cosset, nurse, and dandle ;
A thing of soft misnomers, so divine
That silly youth doth think to make itself
Divine by loving, and so goes on
Yawning and doting a whole summer long,
Till Miss's comb is made a pearl tiara,

And common Wellingtons turn Romeo boots ;
Then Cleopatra lives at number seven,
And Antony resides in Brunswick Square.
Fools ! if some passions high have warm'd the
world,
If Queens and Soldiers have play'd deep for
hearts,
It is no reason why such agonies
Should be more common than the growth of
weeds.
Fools ! make me whole again that weighty
pearl
The Queen of Egypt melted, and I 'll say
That ye may love in spite of beaver hats.

III

FRAGMENT OF 'THE CASTLE BUILDER'

To-night I 'll have my friar — let me think
About my room — I 'll have it in the pink ;
It should be rich and sombre, and the moon,
Just in its mid-life in the midst of June,
Should look thro' four large windows and dis-
play
Clear, but for gold-fish vases in the way,
Their glassy diamonding on Turkish floor ;
The tapers keep aside, an hour and more,
To see what else the moon alone can show ;
While the night-breeze doth softly let us know
My terrace is well bower'd with oranges.
Upon the floor the dullest spirit sees
A guitar-ribband and a lady's glove
Beside a crumple-leaved tale of love ;
A tambour-frame, with Venus sleeping there,
All finish'd but some ringlets of her hair ;
A viol, bow-strings torn, cross-wise upon
A glorious folio of Anacreon ;
A skull upon a mat of roses lying,
Ink'd purple with a song concerning dying ;
An hour-glass on the turn, amid the trails
Of passion-flower ; — just in time there sails
A cloud across the moon, — the lights bring
in !
And see what more my phantasy can win.
It is a gorgeous room, but somewhat sad ;
The draperies are so, as tho' they had
Been made for Cleopatra's winding-sheet ;
And opposite the stedfast eye doth meet
A spacious looking-glass, upon whose face,
In letters raven-sombre, you may trace
Old ' Mene, Mene, Tekel Upharsin.'
Greek busts and statuary have ever been
Held, by the finest spirits, fitter far,
Than vase grotesque and Siamesian jar ;
Therefore 't is sure a want of Attic taste

That I should rather love a Gothic waste
Of eyesight on cinque-coloured potter's clay,
Than on the marble fairness of old Greece.
My table-coverlits of Jason's fleece
And black Numidian sheep-wool should be
wrought,
Gold, black, and heavy, from the Lama brought.
My ebon sofas should delicious be
With down from Leda's cygnet progeny.
My pictures all Salvator's, save a few
Of Titian's portraiture, and one, though new,
Of Haydon's in its fresh magnificence.
My wine — O good ! 't is here at my desire,
And I must sit to supper with my friar.

.

IV

EXTRACTS FROM AN OPERA

First given in *Life, Letters and Literary Re-
mains*, and there dated 1818. In that case, it is
most likely that the verses formed a portion of
some experiment going on to the autumn after
Keats's return from his northern journey.

O ! were I one of the Olympian twelve,
Their godships should pass this into a law, —
That when a man doth set himself in toil
After some beauty veiled far away,
Each step he took should make his lady's
hand
More soft, more white, and her fair cheek more
fair ;
And for each briar-berry he might eat,
A kiss should bud upon the tree of love,
And pulp and ripen richer every hour,
To melt away upon the traveller's lips.

.

DAISY'S SONG

The sun, with his great eye,
Sees not so much as I ;
And the moon, all silver-proud,
Might as well be in a cloud.

And O the spring — the spring !
I lead the life of a King !
Couch'd in the teeming grass,
I spy each pretty lass.

I look where no one dares,
And I stare where no one stares,
And when the night is nigh,
Lambs bleat my lullaby.

.

FOLLY'S SONG

WHEN wedding fiddles are a-playing,
　　　　Huzza for folly O!
And when maidens go a-Maying,
　　　　Huzza, etc.
When a milk-pail is upset,
　　　　Huzza, etc.
And the clothes left in the wet,
　　　　Huzza, etc.
When the barrel 's set abroach,
　　　　Huzza, etc.
When Kate Eyebrow keeps a coach,
　　　　Huzza, etc.
When the pig is over-roasted,
　　　　Huzza, etc.
And the cheese is over-toasted.
　　　　Huzza, etc.
When Sir Snap is with his lawyer,
　　　　Huzza, etc.
And Miss Chip has kiss'd the sawyer;
　　　　Huzza, etc.

.　　.　　.　　.　　.　　.　　.　　.　　.

O, I AM frighten'd with most hateful thoughts!
Perhaps her voice is not a nightingale's,
Perhaps her teeth are not the fairest pearl;
Her eye-lashes may be, for aught I know,
Not longer than the May-fly's small fan-
　　horns;
There may not be one dimple on her hand;
And freckles many; ah! a careless nurse,
In haste to teach the little thing to walk,
May have crumpt up a pair of Dian's legs,
And warpt the ivory of a Juno's neck.

.　　.　　.　　.　　.　　.　　.　　.

SONG

THE stranger lighted from his steed,
　　And ere he spake a word,
He seiz'd my lady's lily hand,
　　And kiss'd it all unheard.

The stranger walk'd into the hall,
　　And ere he spake a word,
He kiss'd my lady's cherry lips,
　　And kiss'd 'em all unheard.

The stranger walk'd into the bower, —
　　But my lady first did go, —
Ay hand in hand into the bower,
　　Where my lord's roses blow.

My lady's maid had a silken scarf,
　　And a golden ring had she,
And a kiss from the stranger, as off he went
Again on his palfrey.

.　　.　　.　　.　　.　　.　　.　　.　　.

ASLEEP! O sleep a little while, white pearl!
And let me kneel, and let me pray to thee,
And let me call Heaven's blessing on thine
　　eyes,
And let me breathe into the happy air,
That doth enfold and touch thee all about,
Vows of my slavery, my giving up,
My sudden adoration, my great love!

III. FAMILIAR VERSES

STANZAS TO MISS WYLIE

These verses belong to 1816. It is not im-
possible that like the valentine on p.755, they
were written for the use of George Keats.

O COME, Georgiana! the rose is full blown,
The riches of Flora are lavishly strown,
The air is all softness, and crystal the streams;
The West is resplendently clothed in beams.

O come! let us haste to the freshening shades,
The quaintly carv'd seats, and the opening
　　glades;
Where the faeries are chanting their evening
　　hymns,
And the last sun-beam the sylph lightly swims.

And when thou art weary, I 'll find thee a bed
Of mosses and flowers to pillow thy head:
And there Georgiana I 'll sit at thy feet,
While my story of love I enraptur'd repeat.

So fondly I 'll breathe, and so softly I 'll sigh,
Thou wilt think that some amorous zephyr is
　　nigh;
Yet no — as I breathe I will press thy fair knee,
And then thou wilt know that the sigh comes
　　from me.

Ah! why, dearest girl, should we lose all these
　　blisses?
That mortal 's a fool who such happiness misses:
So smile acquiescence, and give me thy hand,
With love-looking eyes, and with voice sweetly
　　bland.

EPISTLE TO JOHN HAMILTON REYNOLDS

'My dear Reynolds,' writes Keats from
Teignmouth, March 25, 1818, 'In hopes of
cheering you through a minute or two, I was

determined, will he, nill he, to send you some
lines, so you will excuse the unconnected sub-
ject and careless verse. You know, I am sure,
Claude's Enchanted Castle, and I wish you may
be pleased with my remembrance of it.'

DEAR Reynolds! As last night I lay in bed,
There came before my eyes that wonted thread
Of shapes, and shadows, and remembrances,
That every other minute vex and please:
Things all disjointed come from north and
 south, —
Two Witch's eyes above a Cherub's mouth,
Voltaire with casque and shield and habergeon,
And Alexander with his nightcap on;
Old Socrates a-tying his cravat,
And Hazlitt playing with Miss Edgeworth's
 cat; 10
And Junius Brutus, pretty well so so,
Making the best of 's way towards Soho.

Few are there who escape these visitings, —
Perhaps one or two whose lives have patent
 wings,
And thro' whose curtains peeps no hellish nose,
No wild-boar tushes, and no Mermaid's toes;
But flowers bursting out with lusty pride,
And young Æolian harps personify'd;
Some Titian colours touch'd into real life, —
The sacrifice goes on; the pontiff knife 20
Gleams in the Sun, the milk-white heifer lows,
The pipes go shrilly, the libation flows:
A white sail shows above the green-head cliff,
Moves round the point, and throws her anchor
 stiff;
The mariners join hymn with those on land.

You know the Enchanted Castle, — it doth
 stand
Upon a rock, on the border of a Lake,
Nested in trees, which all do seem to shake
From some old magic-like Urganda's sword.
O Phœbus! that I had thy sacred word 30
To show this Castle. in fair dreaming wise,
Unto my friend, while sick and ill he lies!

You know it well enough, where it doth seem
A mossy place, a Merlin's Hall, a dream;
You know the clear Lake, and the little Isles,
The mountains blue, and cold near neighbour
 rills,
All which elsewhere are but half animate;
There do they look alive to love and hate,
To smiles and frowns; they seem a lifted
 mound
Above some giant, pulsing underground. 40

Part of the building was a chosen See,
Built by a banish'd Santon of Chaldee;
The other part, two thousand years from him,
Was built by Cuthbert de Saint Aldebrim;
Then there 's a little wing, far from the Sun,
Built by a Lapland Witch turn'd maudlin Nun;
And many other juts of aged stone
Founded with many a mason-devil's groan.

The doors all look as if they op'd themselves:
The windows as if latch'd by Fays and Elves, 50
And from them comes a silver flash of light,
As from the westward of a Summer's night;
Or like a beauteous woman's large blue eyes
Gone mad through olden songs and poesies.

See! what is coming from the distance dim!
A golden Galley all in silken trim!
Three rows of oars are lightening, moment
 whiles
Into the verd'rous bosoms of those isles;
Towards the shade, under the Castle wall.
It comes in silence, — now 't is hidden all. 60
The Clarion sounds, and from a Postern-gate
An echo of sweet music doth create
A fear in the poor Herdsman who doth bring
His beasts to trouble the enchanted spring, —
He tells of the sweet music, and the spot,
To all his friends, and they believe him not.

O that our dreamings all, of sleep or wake,
Would all their colours from the sunset take:
From something of material sublime, 69
Rather than shadow our own soul's day-time
In the dark void of night. For in the world
We jostle, — but my flag is not unfurl'd
On the Admiral-staff, — and so philosophise
I dare not yet! O, never will the prize,
High reason, and the love of good and ill,
Be my award! Things cannot to the will
Be settled, but they tease us out of thought;
Or is it imagination brought
Beyond its proper bound, yet still confin'd,
Lost in a sort of Purgatory blind, 80
Cannot refer to any standard law
Of either earth or heaven? It is a flaw
In happiness, to see beyond our bourn. —
It forces us in summer skies to mourn,
It spoils the singing of the Nightingale.

Dear Reynolds! I have a mysterious tale,
And cannot speak it: the first page I read
Upon a Lampit rock of green sea-weed
Among the breakers; 't was a quiet eve,
The rocks were silent, the wide sea did weave
An untumultuous fringe of silver foam 91
Along the flat brown sand; I was at home

And should have been most happy, — but I saw
Too far into the sea, where every maw
The greater on the less feeds evermore. —
But I saw too distinct into the core
Of an eternal fierce destruction,
And so from happiness I far was gone.
Still am I sick of it, and tho' to-day,
I 've gather'd young spring-leaves, and flowers
 gay 100
Of periwinkle and wild strawberry,
Still do I that most fierce destruction see, —
The Shark at savage prey, — the Hawk at
 pounce, —
The gentle Robin, like a Pard or Ounce,
Ravening a worm, — Away, ye horrid moods !
Moods of one's mind ! You know I hate them
 well.
You know I 'd sooner be a clapping Bell
To some Kamschatkan Missionary Church,
Than with these horrid moods be left i' the
 lurch.

A DRAUGHT OF SUNSHINE

Sent in a letter to Reynolds, dated January 31, 1818. ' I cannot write in prose,' says Keats ; ' it is a sunshiny day and I cannot, so here goes.'

HENCE Burgundy, Claret, and Port,
 Away with old Hock and Madeira,
Too earthly ye are for my sport ;
 There 's a beverage brighter and clearer.
Instead of a pitiful rummer,
My wine overbrims a whole summer ;
 My bowl is the sky,
 And I drink at my eye,
 Till I feel in the brain
 A Delphian pain —
Then follow, my Caius ! then follow :
 On the green of the hill
 We will drink our fill
 Of golden sunshine,
 Till our brains intertwine
With the glory and grace of Apollo !
God of the Meridian,
 And of the East and West,
To thee my soul is flown,
 And my body is earthward press'd. —
It is an awful mission,
A terrible division ;
And leaves a gulf austere
To be fill'd with worldly fear.
Aye, when the soul is fled
To high above our head,
Affrighted do we gaze
After its airy maze,

As doth a mother wild,
When her young infant child
Is in an eagle's claws —
And is not this the cause
Of madness ? — God of Song,
Thou bearest me along
Through sights I scarce can bear :
O let me, let me share
With the hot lyre and thee,
The staid Philosophy.
Temper my lonely hours,
And let me see thy bowers
More unalarm'd !

AT TEIGNMOUTH

Sent as part of a letter to Haydon, written from Teignmouth, March 21, 1818. ' I have enjoyed the most delightful walks these three fine days beautiful enough to make me content here all the summer could I stay.'

HERE all the summer could I stay,
 For there 's Bishop's teign
 And King's teign
And Coomb at the clear teign head —
 Where close by the stream
 You may have your cream
All spread upon barley bread.

There 's arch Brook
 And there 's larch Brook
Both turning many a mill ;
 And cooling the drouth
 Of the salmon's mouth
And fattening his silver gill.

There is Wild wood,
 A Mild hood
To the sheep on the lea o' the down,
 Where the golden furze
 With its green, thin spurs,
Doth catch at the maiden's gown.

There is Newton marsh
 With its spear grass harsh —
A pleasant summer level
 Where the maidens sweet
 Of the Market Street,
Do meet in the dusk to revel.

There 's the Barton rich
 With dyke and ditch
And hedge for the thrush to live in ;
 And the hollow tree
 For the buzzing bee,
And a bank for the wasp to hive in.

And O, and O
The daisies blow
And the primroses are waken'd,
And the violets white
Sit in silver plight,
And the green bud 's as long as the spike end.

Then who would go
Into dark Soho,
And chatter with dack'd hair'd critics,
When he can stay
For the new-mown hay,
And startle the dappled Prickets?

THE DEVON MAID

Immediately after the preceding, Keats adds: 'I know not if this rhyming fit has done anything — it will be safe with you if worthy to put among my Lyrics. Here 's some doggrel for you,' and these four stanzas follow.

WHERE be ye going, you Devon Maid?
And what have ye there in the Basket?
Ye tight little fairy just fresh from the dairy,
Will ye give me some cream if I ask it?

I love your Meads, and I love your flowers,
And I love your junkets mainly,
But 'hind the door I love kissing more,
O look not so disdainly.

I love your hills, and I love your dales,
And I love your flocks a-bleating —
But O, on the heather to lie together,
With both our hearts a-beating!

I 'll put your Basket all safe in a nook,
Your shawl I hang up on the willow,
And we will sigh in the daisy's eye
And kiss on a grass green pillow.

ACROSTIC:

GEORGIANA AUGUSTA KEATS

This is dated 'Foot of Helvellyn, June 27,' 1818, and was sent, as something overlooked, to his brother and sister. September 18, 1819. 'I wrote it in a great hurry which you will see. Indeed I would not copy it if I thought it would ever be seen by any but yourselves.'

GIVE me your patience, sister, while I frame
Exact in capitals your golden name;
Or sue the fair Apollo and he will
Rouse from his heavy slumber and instill

Great love in me for thee and Poesy.
Imagine not that greatest mastery
And kingdom over all the Realms of verse,
Nears more to heaven in aught, than when we nurse
And surety give to love and Brotherhood.

Anthropophagi in Othello's mood;
Ulysses storm'd and his enchanted belt
Glow with the Muse, but they are never felt
Unbosom'd so and so eternal made,
Such tender incense in their laurel shade
To all the regent sisters of the Nine
As this poor offering to you, sister mine.

Kind sister! ay, this third name says you are;
Enchanted has it been the Lord knows where;
And may it taste to you like good old wine,
Take you to real happiness and give
Sons, daughters and a home like honied hive.

MEG MERRILIES

Sent in a letter to Fanny Keats, written from Auchencairn, July 2, 1818. 'We are in the midst of Meg Merrilies country of whom I suppose you have heard.' Fanny Keats was a girl of fifteen at this time.

OLD Meg she was a Gipsy,
And liv'd upon the Moors:
Her bed it was the brown heath turf,
And her house was out of doors.

Her apples were swart blackberries,
Her currants pods o' broom;
Her wine was dew of the wild white rose,
Her book a churchyard tomb.

Her Brothers were the craggy hills,
Her Sisters larchen trees —
Alone with her great family
She liv'd as she did please.

No breakfast had she many a morn,
No dinner many a noon,
And 'stead of supper she would stare
Full hard against the Moon.

But every morn of woodbine fresh
She made her garlanding,
And every night the dark glen Yew
She wove, and she would sing.

And with her fingers old and brown
She plaited Mats o' Rushes,

And gave them to the Cottagers
She met among the Bushes,

Old Meg was brave as Margaret Queen
And tall as Amazon :
An old red blanket cloak she wore ;
A chip hat had she on.
God rest her aged bones somewhere —
She died full long agone !

A SONG ABOUT MYSELF

'I have so many interruptions,' writes Keats
to his sister Fanny from Kircudbright, July 2,
1818, 'that I cannot manage to fill a Letter
in one day — since I scribbled the song [Meg
Merrilies] we have walked through a beautiful
country to Kircudbright — at which place I
will write you a song about myself.'

THERE was a naughty Boy,
A naughty boy was he,
He would not stop at home,
He could not quiet be —
He took
In his Knapsack
A Book
Full of vowels ;
And a shirt
With some towels —
A slight cap
For night cap —
A hair brush,
Comb ditto,
New Stockings,
For old ones
Would split O !
This Knapsack,
Tight at 's back,
He rivetted close
And follow'd his Nose
To the North,
To the North,
And follow'd his nose
To the North.

There was a naughty boy
And a naughty boy was he,
For nothing would he do
But scribble poetry —
He took
An inkstand
In his hand,
And a Pen
Big as ten
In the other,

And away
In a Pother
He ran
To the mountains,
And fountains
And ghostes,
And Postes,
And witches,
And ditches,
And wrote
In his coat,
When the weather
Was cool,
Fear of gout,
And without
When the weather
Was Warm —
Och the charm
When we choose
To follow one's nose
To the north,
To the north,
To follow one's nose
To the north.

There was a naughty boy
And a naughty boy was he,
He kept little fishes
In washing tubs three
In spite
Of the might
Of the Maid,
Nor afraid
Of his Granny — good —
He often would,
Hurly burly,
Get up early,
And go
By hook or crook
To the brook,
And bring home
Miller's thumb,
Tittlebat
Not over fat,
Minnows small
As the stall
Of a glove,
Not above
The size
Of a nice
Little Baby's
Little fingers —
O, he made,
'T was his trade,
Of Fish a pretty Kettle
A Kettle —
A Kettle

Of Fish, a pretty Kettle,
 A Kettle!

There was a naughty Boy,
 And a naughty Boy was he,
He ran away to Scotland
 The people for to see —
 Then he found
 That the ground
 Was as hard,
 That a yard
 Was as long,
 That a song
 Was as merry,
 That a cherry
 Was as red —
 That lead
 Was as weighty,
 That fourscore
 Was as eighty,
 That a door
 Was as wooden
 As in England —
So he stood in his shoes
 And he wonder'd,
 He wonder'd,
He stood in his shoes
 And he wonder'd.

TO THOMAS KEATS

BELANTREE (for Ballantrae) July 10 [1818.]

AH! ken ye what I met the day
 Out oure the Mountains
A coming down by craggies gray
 An mossie fountains —
Ah goud-hair'd Marie yeve I pray
 Ane minute's guessing —
For that I met upon the way
 Is past expressing.
As I stood where a rocky brig
 A torrent crosses
I spied upon a misty rig
 A troup o' Horses —
And as they trotted down the glen
 I sped to meet them
To see if I might know the Men
 To stop and greet them.
First Willie on his sleek mare came
 At canting gallop
His long hair rustled like a flame
 On board a shallop,
Then came his brother Rab and then
 Young Peggy's Mither
And Peggy too — adown the glen
 They went togither —

I saw her wrappit in her hood
 Frae wind and raining —
Her cheek was flush wi' timid blood
 Twixt growth and waning —
She turn'd her dazed eyes full oft
 For there her Brithers
Came riding with her Bridegroom soft
 And mony ithers.
Young Tam came up and eyed me quick
 With reddened cheek —
Braw Tom was daffed like a chick —
 He couldna speak —
Ah, Marie, they are all gane hame
 Through blustering weather
An' every heart is full on flame
 An' light as feather.
Ah! Marie, they are all gone hame
 Frae happy wadding,
Whilst I — Ah is it not a shame?
 Sad tears am shedding.

THE GADFLY

Inclosed in a letter to Tom Keats, July 17,
1818.

ALL gentle folks who owe a grudge
 To any living thing
Open your ears and stay your t(r)udge
 Whilst I in dudgeon sing.

The Gadfly he hath stung me sore —
 O may he ne'er sting you!
But we have many a horrid bore, —
 He may sting black and blue.

Has any here an old gray Mare
 With three legs all her store,
O put it to her Buttocks bare
 And straight she 'll run on four.

Has any here a Lawyer suit
 Of 1743,
Take Lawyer's nose and put it to 't
 And you the end will see.

Is there a Man in Parliament
 Dum(b)founder'd in his speech,
O let his neighbour make a rent
 And put one in his breech.

O Lowther how much better thou
 Hadst figur'd t' other day
When to the folks thou mad'st a bow
 And hadst no more to say.

If lucky Gadfly had but ta'en
 His seat . . .

And put thee to a little pain
To save thee from a worse.

Better than Southey it had been,
Better than Mr. D———
Better than Wordsworth, too, I ween,
Better than Mr. V———.

Forgive me, pray, good people all,
For deviating so —
In spirit sure I had a call —
And now I on will go.

Has any here a daughter fair
Too fond of reading novels,
Too apt to fall in love with care
And charming Mister Lovels,

O put a Gadfly to that thing
She keeps so white and pert —
I mean the finger for the ring,
And it will breed a wort.

Has any here a pious spouse
Who seven times a day
Scolds as King David pray'd, to chouse
And have her holy way —

O let a Gadfly's little sting
Persuade her sacred tongue
That noises are a common thing,
But that her bell has rung.

And as this is the summum bo-
num of all conquering,
I leave ' withouten wordes mo'
The Gadfly's little sting.

ON HEARING THE BAG-PIPE AND SEEING
'THE STRANGER' PLAYED AT INVERARY

'On entering Inverary,' Keats writes to his
brother Tom, July 18, 1818, ' we saw a Play
Bill. Brown was knocked up from new shoes
— so I went to the Barn alone where I saw the
Stranger accompanied by a Bag-pipe. There
they went on about interesting creaters and
human nater till the Curtain fell and then
came the Bag-pipe. When Mrs. Haller fainted
down went the Curtain and out came the Bag-
pipe — at the heartrending, shoemending recon-
ciliation the Piper blew amain. I never read
or saw this play before ; not the Bag-pipe nor
the wretched players themselves were little in

comparison with it — thank heaven it has been
scoffed at lately almost to a fashion.'

OF late two dainties were before me plac'd
Sweet, holy, pure, sacred and innocent,
From the ninth sphere to me benignly sent
That Gods might know my own particular
 taste :
First the soft Bag-pipe mourn'd with zealous
 haste,
 The Stranger next with head on bosom bent
 Sigh'd ; rueful again the piteous Bag-pipe
 went,
Again the Stranger sighings fresh did waste.
O Bag-pipe, thou didst steal my heart away —
 O Stranger, thou my nerves from Pipe didst
 charm —
O Bag-pipe thou didst re-assert thy sway —
 Again thou, Stranger, gav'st me fresh alarm —
Alas ! I could not choose. Ah ! my poor heart
Mum chance art thou with both oblig'd to part.

LINES WRITTEN IN THE HIGHLANDS AFTER
A VISIT TO BURNS'S COUNTRY

In a letter to Benjamin Bailey from the
Island of Mull, July 22, 1818.

THERE is a charm in footing slow across a silent
 plain,
Where patriot battle has been fought, where
 glory had the gain ;
There is a pleasure on the heath where Druids
 old have been,
Where mantles gray have rustled by and swept
 the nettles green ;
There is Joy in every spot made known by
 times of old,
New to the feet, although each tale a hundred
 times be told ;
There is a deeper Joy than all, more solemn in
 the heart,
More parching to the tongue than all, of more
 divine a smart,
When weary steps forget themselves upon a
 pleasant turf,
Upon hot sand, or flinty road, or sea-shore iron
 scurf,
Toward the Castle or the Cot, where long ago
 was born
One who was great through mortal days, and
 died of fame unshorn.
Light heather-bells may tremble then, but they
 are far away ;
Wood-lark may sing from sandy fern, — the
 Sun may hear his Lay ;

Runnels may kiss the grass on shelves and shallows clear,
But their low voices are not heard, though come on travels drear ;
Blood-red the sun may set behind black mountain peaks ;
Blue tides may sluice and drench their time in Caves and weedy creeks ;
Eagles may seem to sleep wing-wide upon the Air ;
Ring-doves may fly convuls'd across to some high-cedar'd lair ;
But the forgotten eye is still fast lidded to the ground,
As Palmer's, that with weariness, mid-desert shrine hath found.

At such a time the soul's a child, in childhood is the brain ;
Forgotten is the worldly heart — alone, it beats in vain. —
Aye, if a Madman could have leave to pass a healthful day
To tell his forehead's swoon and faint when first began decay,
He might make tremble many a one whose spirit had gone forth
To find a Bard's low cradle-place about the silent North.
Scanty the hour and few the steps beyond the bourn of Care,
Beyond the sweet and bitter world, — beyond it unaware !
Scanty the hour and few the steps, because a longer stay
Would bar return, and make a man forget his mortal way :
O horrible ! to lose the sight of well remember'd face,
Of Brother's eyes, of Sister's brow — constant to every place ;
Filling the Air, as on we move, with Portraiture intense ;
More warm than those heroic tints that pain a Painter's sense,
When shapes of old come striding by, and visages of old,
Locks shining black, hair scanty gray, and passions manifold.
No, no, that horror cannot be, for at the cable's length
Man feels the gentle anchor pull and gladdens in its strength : —
One hour, half-idiot, he stands by mossy waterfall,
But in the very next he reads his soul's Memorial : —

He reads it on the mountain's height, where chance he may sit down
Upon rough marble diadem — that hill's eternal Crown.
Yet be his Anchor e'er so fast, room is there for a prayer
That man may never lose his Mind on Mountains black and bare ;
That he may stray league after league some great birthplace to find
And keep his vision clear from speck, his inward sight unblind.

MRS. CAMERON AND BEN NEVIS

In his letter to Tom Keats, August 3, 1818, which contains the sonnet written on Ben Nevis, Keats concludes a lively account of the ascent they made with this bit of nonsense : —

After all there was one Mrs. Cameron of 50 years of age and the fattest woman in all Inverness-shire who got up this Mountain some few years ago — true she had her servants — but then she had herself. She ought to have hired Sisyphus, — " Up the high hill he heaves a huge round — Mrs. Cameron." 'T is said a little conversation took place between the mountain and the Lady. After taking a glass of Whisky as she was tolerably seated at ease she thus began —

MRS. C.

UPON my life Sir Nevis I am piqued
That I have so far panted tugg'd and reek'd
To do an honor to your old bald pate
And now am sitting on you just to bait,
Without your paying me one compliment.
Alas, 't is so with all, when our intent
Is plain, and in the eye of all Mankind
We fair ones show a preference, too blind !
You Gentle man immediately turn tail —
O let me then my hapless fate bewail !
Ungrateful Baldpate have I not disdain'd
The pleasant Valleys — have I not madbrain'd
Deserted all my Pickles and preserves
My China closet too — with wretched Nerves
To boot — say, wretched ingrate, have I not
Left my soft cushion chair and caudle pot ?
'T is true I had no corns — no ! thank the fates
My Shoemaker was always Mr. Bates.
And if not Mr. Bates why I 'm not old !
Still dumb ungrateful Nevis — still so cold !

Here the Lady took some more whisky and
was putting even more to her lips when she
dashed it to the Ground, for the Mountain be-
gan to grumble — which continued for a few
minutes before he thus began —

BEN NEVIS.

What whining bit of tongue and Mouth thus
 dares
Disturb my slumber of a thousand years?
Even so long my sleep has been secure —
And to be so awak'd I 'll not endure.
Oh pain — for since the Eagle's earliest scream
I 've had a damn'd confounded ugly dream,
A Nightmare sure. What! Madam, was it
 you?
It cannot be! My old eyes are not true!
Red-Crag, my Spectacles! Now let me see!
Good Heavens! Lady, how the gemini
Did you get here? O, I shall split my sides!
I shall earthquake —

MRS. C.

Sweet Nevis do not quake, for though I love
Your honest Countenance all things above,
Truly I should not like to be convey'd
So far into your Bosom — gentle Maid
Loves not too rough a treatment, gentle Sir —
Pray thee be calm and do not quake nor stir
No, not a Stone, or I shall go in fits —

BEN NEVIS.

I must — I shall — I meet not such tit bits —
I meet not such sweet creatures every day —
By my old nightcap night and day
I must have one sweet Buss — I must and shall!
Red Crag! — What! Madam, can you then re-
 pent
Of all the toil and vigour you have spent
To see Ben Nevis and to touch his nose?
Red Crag I say! O I must have them close!
Red Crag, there lies beneath my farthest toe
A vein of Sulphur — go, dear Red Crag, go —
And rub your flinty back against it — budge!
Dear Madam, I must kiss you, faith I must!
I must embrace you with my dearest gust!
Block-head, d' ye hear! — Block-head, I 'll
 make her feel.
There lies beneath my east leg's northern heel
A cave of young earth dragons; — well my
 boy
Go thither quick and so complete my joy.
Take you a bundle of the largest pines,
And when the sun on fiercest Phosphor shines,
Fire them and ram them in the Dragon's nest,
Then will the dragons fry and fizz their best

Until ten thousand now no bigger than
Poor Alligators — poor things of one span —
Will each one swell to twice ten times the
 size
Of northern whale — then for the tender prize —
The moment then — for then will Red Crag rub
His flinty back — and I shall kiss and snub
And press my dainty morsel to my breast.
Block-head make haste!
 O Muses, weep the rest —
The Lady fainted and he thought her dead;
So pulled the clouds again about his head
And went to sleep again; soon she was rous'd
By her affrighted servants — next day, hous'd
Safe on the lowly ground she bless'd her fate
That fainting fit was not delayed too late.

But what surprised me above all is how
the lady got down again. I felt it horribly.
'T was the most vile descent — shook me all
to pieces.

SHARING EVE'S APPLE

Printed by Mr. Forman and assigned to 1818.
Mr. Forman does not give his authority, save
to say that the verses have been handed about
in manuscript.

O blush not so! O blush not so!
 Or I shall think you knowing;
And if you smile the blushing while,
 Then maidenheads are going.

There 's a blush for won't, and a blush for
 shan't,
 And a blush for having done it:
There 's a blush for thought and a blush for
 nought,
 And a blush for just begun it.

O sigh not so! O sigh not so!
 For it sounds of Eve's sweet pippin;
By these loosen'd lips you have tasted the pips
 And fought in an amorous nipping.

Will you play once more at nice-cut-core,
 For it only will last our youth out,
And we have the prime of the kissing time,
 We have not one sweet tooth out.

There 's a sigh for yes, and a sigh for no,
 And a sigh for I can't bear it!
O what can be done, shall we stay or run?
 O cut the sweet apple and share it!

A PROPHECY :

TO GEORGE KEATS IN AMERICA

In a letter to his brother and his wife, October 24, 1818, Keats says : ' If I had a prayer to make for any great good, next to Tom's recovery, it should be that one of your children should be the first American Poet. I have a great mind to make a prophecy, and they say prophecies work on their own fulfilment.'

'T is the witching time of night,
Orbed is the moon and bright,
And the Stars they glisten, glisten,
Seeming with bright eyes to listen.
For what listen they ?
For a song and for a charm,
See they glisten in alarm,
And the Moon is waxing warm
To hear what I shall say.
Moon ! keep wide thy golden ears —
Hearken, Stars ! and hearken, Spheres ! —
Hearken, thou eternal Sky !
I sing an infant's Lullaby,
O pretty lullaby !
Listen, listen, listen, listen,
Glisten, glisten, glisten, glisten,
And hear my Lullaby !
Though the Rushes, that will make
Its cradle, still are in the lake —
Though the linen that will be
Its swathe, is on the cotton tree —
Though the woollen that will keep
It warm, is on the silly sheep —
Listen, Starlight, listen, listen,
Glisten, glisten, glisten, glisten,
And hear my lullaby !
Child, I see thee ! Child, I 've found thee
Midst of the quiet all around thee !
Child, I see thee ! Child, I spy thee !
And thy mother sweet is nigh thee !
Child, I know thee ! Child no more,
But a Poet evermore !
See, see, the Lyre, the Lyre,
In a flame of fire,
Upon the little cradle's top
Flaring, flaring, flaring,
Past the eyesight's bearing.
Awake it from its sleep,
And see if it can keep
Its eyes upon the blaze —
Amaze, amaze !
It stares, it stares, it stares.
It dares what no one dares !
It lifts its little hand into the flame

Unharm'd, and on the strings
Paddles a little tune, and sings,
With dumb endeavour sweetly —
Bard art thou completely !
 Little child
 O' th' western wild,
Bard art thou completely !
Sweetly with dumb endeavour,
A Poet now or never,
 Little child
 O' th' western wild,
A Poet now or never !

A LITTLE EXTEMPORE

Inclosed in a letter to George and Georgiana Keats, written April 15, 1819.

WHEN they were come into the Faery's Court
They rang — no one at home — all gone to sport
And dance and kiss and love as faeries do
For Faries be as humans lovers true.
Amid the woods they were so lone and wild,
Where even the Robin feels himself exil'd,
And where the very brooks, as if afraid,
Hurry along to some less magic shade.
' No one at home ! ' the fretful Princess cry'd ;
' And all for nothing such a dreary ride,
And all for nothing my new diamond cross ;
No one to see my Persian feathers toss,
No one to see my Ape, my Dwarf, my Fool,
Or how I pace my Otaheitan mule.
Ape, Dwarf, and Fool, why stand you gaping
 there,
Burst the door open, quick — or I declare
I 'll switch you soundly and in pieces tear.'
The Dwarf began to tremble, and the Ape
Star'd at the Fool, the Fool was all agape,
The Princess grasp'd her switch, but just in
 time
The dwarf with piteous face began to rhyme.
' O mighty Princess, did you ne'er hear tell
What your poor servants know but too too
 well ?
Know you the three great crimes in Faeryland ?
The first, alas ! poor Dwarf, I understand,
I made a whipstock of a faery's wand ;
The next is snoring in their company ;
The next, the last, the direst of the three,
Is making free when they are not at home.
I was a Prince — a baby prince — my doom,
You see, I made a whipstock of a wand,
My top has henceforth slept in faery land.
He was a Prince, the Fool, a grown-up Prince,
But he has never been a King's son since
He fell a snoring at a faery Ball.

Yon poor Ape was a Prince, and he poor thing
Picklock'd a faery's boudoir — now no king
But ape — so pray your highness stay awhile,
'T is sooth indeed, we know it to our sorrow —
Persist and you may be an ape to-morrow.'
While the Dwarf spake, the Princess, all for spite,
Peel'd the brown hazel twig to lily white,
Clench'd her small teeth, and held her lips apart,
Try'd to look unconcern'd with beating heart.
They saw her highness had made up her mind,
A-quavering like the reeds before the wind —
And they had had it, but O happy chance !
The Ape for very fear began to dance
And grinn'd as all his ugliness did ache —
She staid her vixen fingers for his sake,
He was so very ugly : then she took
Her pocket-mirror and began to look
First at herself and then at him, and then
She smil'd at her own beauteous face again.
Yet for all this — for all her pretty face —
She took it in her head to see the place.
Women gain little from experience
Either in Lovers, husbands, or expense.
The more their beauty the more fortune too —
Beauty before the wide world never knew —
So each fair reasons — tho' it oft miscarries.
She thought *her* pretty face would please the fairies.
' My darling Ape, I wont whip you to-day,
Give me the Picklock sirrah and go play.'
They all three wept but counsel was as vain
As crying cup biddy to drops of rain.
Yet lingering by did the sad Ape forth draw
The Picklock from the Pocket in his Jaw.
The Princess took it, and dismounting straight
Tripp'd in blue silver'd slippers to the gate
And touch'd the wards, the Door full courteous
Opened — she enter'd with her servants three.
Again it clos'd and there was nothing seen
But the Mule grazing on the herbage green.
 End of Canto XII.

CANTO THE XIII

The Mule no sooner saw himself alone
Than he prick'd up his Ears — and said ' well done ;
At least unhappy Prince I may be free —
No more a Princess shall side-saddle me.
O King of Otaheite — tho' a Mule,
" Aye, every inch a King " — tho' " Fortune's Fool,"
Well done — for by what Mr. Dwarfy said
I would not give a sixpence for her head.'
Even as he spake he trotted in high glee
To the knotty side of an old Pollard tree,

And rubb'd his sides against the mossed bark
Till his Girths burst and left him naked stark
Except his Bridle — how get rid of that
Buckled and tied with many a twist and plait.
At last it struck him to pretend to sleep,
And then the thievish Monkeys down would creep
And filch the unpleasant trammels quite away.
No sooner thought of than adown he lay,
Shamm'd a good snore — the Monkey-men descended
And whom they thought to injure they befriended.
They hung his Bridle on a topmost bough
And off he went run, trot, or anyhow —

SPENSERIAN STANZAS ON CHARLES ARMITAGE BROWN

Inclosed in a letter to George and Georgiana Keats, April 16 or 17, 1819 : ' Brown this morning is writing some Spenserian stanzas against Mrs., Miss Brawne and me ; so I shall amuse myself with him a little : in the manner of Spenser.'

HE is to weet a melancholy Carle :
Thin in the waist, with bushy head of hair,
As hath the seeded thistle when in parle
It holds the Zephyr, ere it sendeth fair
Its light balloons into the summer air ;
There to his beard had not begun to bloom,
No brush had touch'd his chin, or razor sheer ;
No care had touched his cheek with mortal doom,
But new he was, and bright, as scarf from Persian loom.

Ne cared he for wine, or half-and-half ;
Ne cared he for fish, or flesh, or fowl ;
And sauces held he worthless as the chaff ;
He 's deigned the swineherd at the wassail bowl ;
Ne with lewd ribbalds sat he cheek by jowl ;
Ne with sly Lemans in the scorner's chair ;
But after water-brooks this Pilgrim's soul
Panted, and all his food was woodland air ;
Though he would oft-times feast on gilliflowers rare.

The slang of cities in no wise he knew ;
Tipping the wink to him was heathen Greek ;
He sipp'd no ' olden Tom,' or ' ruin blue,'
Or Nantz, or cherry-brandy, drunk full meek

By many a Damsel hoarse, and rouge of
 cheek;
Nor did he know each aged Watchman's
 beat,
Nor in obscured purlieus would he seek
For curled Jewesses, with ankles neat,
Who, as they walk abroad, make tinkling with
 their feet.

' TWO OR THREE POSIES '

At the close of a letter, April 17, 1819, to
his sister Fanny, Keats writes : ' Mr. and Mrs.
Dilke are coming to dine with us to-day [at
Wentworth Place]. They will enjoy the
country after Westminster. O there is nothing
like fine weather, and health, and Books, and a
fine country, and a contented Mind, and dili-
gent habit of reading and thinking, and an
amulet against the ennui — and, please hea-
ven, a little claret wine cool out of a cellar a
mile deep — with a few or a good many ratafia
cakes — a rocky basin to bathe in, a strawberry
bed to say your prayers to Flora in, a pad nag
to go you ten miles or so; two or three sensi-
ble people to chat with ; two or three spiteful
folks to spar with ; two or three odd fishes to
laugh at and two or three numskulls to argue
with — instead of using dumb bells on a rainy
day.'

> Two or three Posies
> With two or three simples —
> Two or three Noses
> With two or three pimples —
> Two or three wise men
> And two or three ninny's —
> Two or three purses
> And two or three guineas —
> Two or three raps
> At two or three doors —
> Two or three naps
> Of two or three hours —
> Two or three Cats
> And two or three mice —
> Two or three sprats
> At a very great price —
> Two or three sandies
> And two or three tabbies —
> Two or three dandies
> And two Mrs. mum !
> Two or three Smiles
> And two or three frowns —
> Two or three Miles
> To two or three towns —

> Two or three pegs
> For two or three bonnets —
> Two or three dove eggs
> To hatch into sonnets —

A PARTY OF LOVERS

' Somewhere in the *Spectator* is related an
account of a man inviting a party of stutterers
and squinters to his table. It would please me
more to scrape together a party of lovers —
not to dinner but to tea. There would be no
fighting as among knights of old.' Keats to
George and Georgiana Keats, September 17,
1819. The play on names seems to indicate
some trifling reference to Keats's publishers of
Taylor and Hessey.

PENSIVE they sit, and roll their languid eyes,
Nibble their toast, and cool their tea with sighs,
Or else forget the purpose of the night,
Forget their tea — forget their appetite.
See with cross'd arms they sit — ah ! happy
 crew,
The fire is going out and no one rings
For coals, and therefore no coals Betty brings.
A fly is in the milk-pot — must he die
 By a humane society ?
No, no ; there Mr. Werter takes his spoon,
Inserts it, dips the handle, and lo ! soon
The little straggler, sav'd from perils dark,
Across the teaboard draws a long wet mark.

Arise ! take snuffers by the handle,
There 's a large cauliflower in each candle.
A winding-sheet, ah me ! I must away
To No. 7, just beyond the circus gay.
' Alas, my friend ! your coat sits very well ;
Where may your Taylor live ? ' ' I may not
 tell.
O pardon me — I 'm absent now and then.
Where *might* my Taylor live ? I say again
I cannot tell, let me no more be teaz'd —
He lives in Wapping, *might* live where he
 pleas'd.'

TO GEORGE KEATS

WRITTEN IN SICKNESS

This is from a transcript by George Keats,
and dated 1819 ; but Keats's letters do not dis-
close any sickness during that year which
would be likely to call forth the lines, and the
date is probably 1820, if indeed we are author-

ized to refer this poem to John Keats. It is not impossible that it was written by Tom Keats in 1818.

BROTHER belov'd if health shall smile again,
 Upon this wasted form and fever'd cheek:
If e'er returning vigour bid these weak
And languid limbs their gladsome strength re-
 gain,
Well may thy brow the placid glow retain
 Of sweet content and thy pleas'd eye may
 speak
The conscious self applause, but should I seek
To utter what this heart can feel, — Ah ! vain
Were the attempt ! Yet kindest friends while
 o'er
My couch ye bend, and watch with tenderness
The being whom your cares could e'en restore,
 From the cold grasp of Death, say can you
 guess
 The feelings which these lips can ne'er ex-
 press ?
Feelings, deep fix'd in grateful memory's store.

ON OXFORD

Charles Armitage Brown, writing to Henry Snook from Hampstead 24 March, 1820, says : ' Tom shall have one of his [Keats's] bits of comic verses, — I met with them only yesterday, but they have been written long ago, — it is a song on the City of Oxford.'

THE Gothic looks solemn,
 The plain Doric column
Supports an old Bishop and Crozier ;
 The mouldering arch,
 Shaded o'er by a larch,
Stands next door to Wilson the Hosier.

Vice, — that is, by turns, —
 O'er pale faces mourns
The black tassell'd trencher and common hat ;
 The charity boy sings,
 The Steeple-bell rings
And as for the Chancellor — *dominat.*

There are plenty of trees,
 And plenty of ease,
And plenty of fat deer for Parsons ;
 And when it is venison,
 Short is the benison, —
Then each on a leg or thigh fastens.

TO A CAT

These verses were addressed by Keats to a cat belonging to Mrs. Reynolds of Little Britain, the mother of his friend John Hamilton Reynolds. Mrs. Reynolds gave the verses to her son-in-law, Tom Hood, who published them in his *Comic Annual* for 1830.

CAT ! who has[t] pass'd thy grand clima[c]-
 teric,
 How many mice and rats hast in thy days
 Destroy'd ? — How many tit-bits stolen ?
 Gaze
With those bright languid segments green, and
 prick
Those velvet ears — but pr'ythee do not stick
 Thy latent talons in me — and upraise
 Thy gentle mew — and tell me all thy frays
Of fish and mice, and rats and tender chick :
Nay, look not down, nor lick thy dainty wrists
 For all the wheezy asthma, — and for all
Thy tail's tip is nick'd off — and though the
 fists
Of many a maid has given thee many a maul,
Still is that fur as soft as when the lists
 In youth thou enter'dst on glass-bottled wall.

INDEX OF FIRST LINES

LORD BYRON

PERCY BYSSHE SHELLEY

JOHN KEATS

INDEX OF TITLES

(The titles of major works and of general divisions are set in CAPITALS)

JOHN KEATS